## SPECIAL EDITION

# The Librarian's Guide To Public Records

UNIQUELY ASSEMBLES
OVER 11,500 MAJOR
FEDERAL, STATE
AND COUNTY
PUBLIC RECORD
LOCATIONS

TAKEN DIRECTLY FROM
THE DATABASE OF
**The Public Record Research Library**
PUBLISHED BY BRB PUBLICATIONS, INC.

*The Librarian's Guide to Public Records*

ISBN: 1-879792-23-0
Copyright © 1995 by BRB Publications, Inc.

1st Printing, January 1995
2nd Printing, September 1995 (Revised)

---

All rights reserved. Printed in the United States of America. No part of this book may be used or reproduced in any form or by any means, or stored in a database or retrieval system without the prior written permission of the publisher, except in the case of brief quotations embodied in critical articles or reviews. Making copies of any part of this book for any purpose other than your own personal use is a violation of United States copyright laws. Entering any of the contents into a computer for mailing list or database purposes is strictly prohibited unless written authorization is obtained from BRB Publications, Inc.

This directory is sold as is, without warranty of any kind, either express or implied, respecting the contents of this directory, including but not limited to implied warranties for the directory's quality, performance, merchantability, or fitness for any particular purpose. Neither the publisher nor its dealers or distributors shall be liable to the purchaser or any other person or entity with respect to any liability, loss, or damage caused or alleged to be caused directly or indirectly by this directory.

---

**BRB Publications, Inc.**
**4653 South Lakeshore, Suite 3 • Tempe, Arizona • 85282**
**(602) 838-8909**

Cover Design by Robin Fox & Associates
Photographs by Lynn Beshara Sankey

# Table of Contents

Preface & Acknowledgements — v

Introduction — vii

Before You Start... — ix

## *Section One——County Records*

Summary Information — 1

County Courts and Recording Offices — 3

## *Section Two——State Records*

Summary Information — 255
What You Can Expect to Find in State Public Records

State Agencies — 257

State Restrictions Chart — 284

## *Section Three——Federal Records*

Summary Information — 287

State Cross Reference Chart — 288
Of Federal Record Centers and US Courts of Appeals

US Courts of Appeals — 289

Federal Record Centers — 289

US District and US Bankruptcy Courts — 290

# 1995 Book Titles and Information

*At The State...*

- ☐ **THE SOURCEBOOK OF STATE PUBLIC RECORDS**
  ISBN # 1-879791-22-2    Pub 5/95    Pages 339    Price: 33.00

- ☐ **THE 1995 MVR BOOK** 6th Edition
  ISBN # 1-879792-19-2    Pub 2/95    Pages 272    Price: 18.00

- ☐ **THE 1995 MVR DECODER DIGEST** 5th Edition
  ISBN # 1-879792-20-6    Pub 2/95    Pages 288    Price: 18.00

*At The Court and County Level...*

- ☐ **THE SOURCEBOOK OF FEDERAL COURTS—US DISTRICT & BANKRUPTCY**
  ISBN # 1-879792-10-9    Pub 5/93    Pages 672    Price: 33.00
  Includes insert updating all PACER and VCIS data at all court locations.

- ☐ **THE FEDERAL COURT LOCATOR**
  ISBN # 1-879792-18-4    Pub 2/95    Pages 144    Price: 29.00
  This is a looseleaf and includes one complete update in 1995.

- ☐ **THE SOURCEBOOK OF COUNTY COURT RECORDS** 2nd Edition
  ISBN # 1-879792-16-8    Pub 1/95    Pages 540    Price: 33.00

- ☐ **THE SOURCEBOOK OF COUNTY ASSET/LIEN RECORDS**
  ISBN # 1-879792-17-6    Pub 1/95    Pages 464    Price: 29.00

*Sources, Retrieval and Unique Searching Aids*

- ☐ **THE SOURCEBOOK OF PUBLIC RECORD PROVIDERS** 2nd Edition
  ISBN # 1-879792-13-3    Pub 3/94    Pages 284    Price: 29.00

- ☐ **THE SOURCEBOOK OF LOCAL COURT & COUNTY RECORD RETRIEVERS** 2nd Edition
  ISBN # 1-879792-21-4    Pub 4/95    Pages 480    Price: 45.00

- ☐ **THE COUNTY LOCATOR (LOCUS)**
  ISBN # 1-879792-11-7    Pub 6/93    Pages 928    Price: 25.00
  Includes insert updating new ZIP data at locations.

Published by **BRB Publications, Inc.**
4653 S. Lakeshore Suite #3
Tempe, Arizona 85282
(602) 838-8909

# Preface & Acknowledgements

Quite simply, the objective of this publication is to present a current and comprehensive directory of the county court & real estate offices, state agencies, and federal courts where public records are located. Although specifically designed for public and academic reference libraries, this jurisdictional guide is intended to be useful to any business and/or individual who needs to know where to find public record information.

The over 11,500 addresses herein have been compiled directly from *The Public Record Research Library (PRRL)*—a leading authority on the location, access and retrieval of public records. The PRRL collection of annual sourcebooks and electronic products presents, in great detail, how to find/read public record documents and access the most appropriate public record retrieval firms. Although this book may not contain the individual, in-depth profiles of each jurisdiction, which is the hallmark of the PRRL Sourcebooks, the combination of individual addresses and record location types reflects a one-of-a-kind presentation of facts, uniquely assembled for a quick reference.

We wish to extend a special thank you and appreciation to all the clerks, recorders, administrators, and officials who staff these public agencies. This compendium could not have been realized without their continuous help and on-going support.

We sincerely hope you will find this publication useful in your library, be it large or small. Please feel free to call either of us at 800-929-3811 with your remarks and ideas about how we can make the next edition even more useful.

Carl R. Ernst
Editor-in-Chief

Michael Sankey
Publisher

# Introduction

*Definition*

One of the most useful assets of business owners and administrators, investigators, legal support personnel, risk managers and information providers/brokers is the basic working knowledge of where to find and how to use public records. **Public record information is anything filed at or recorded in government agencies that can be accessed by the general public.** (Or, as defined by Ed Pankau in Check It Out, "...information about people, businesses, or organizations available to anyone without subpoena, subterfuge, or midnight trash runs.")

*Categories*

Many categories of public information are easily recognized as **crucial sources of intelligence** by most businesses, legal firms, insurance companies and other professionals. For example, corporate filings in each state indicate the proper legal name and standing of incorporated companies and real property records list owners of record for land and commercial or residential property. Driving records are the basis for insurance companies setting policy rates. Vital records (birth, death, marriage, and divorce) play a critical role in the record studies of genealogists.

Other kinds of information are less well understood as sources of valuable intelligence about businesses and individuals. For example, UCC financing statements contain information about banking relationships, assets, and persons associated with a business.

*Limitations*

How do you know if the records you are requesting will actually give you the information you seek? Are you legally permitted to access the record? Whether or not the information is available to the public, the degree of authority needed to obtain the record and the data to be found on the record are all subject to **individual state statutes** or to the **interpretation of a regulation** by a County Clerk or Judge and, now, to **federal intervention** with the passage by the US Congress of legislation such as the Driver's Privacy Protection Act.

Therefore, the answers to the questions above can and do vary significantly from jurisdiction to jurisdiction. This issue is raised most obviously at the state level where a multitude of restrictions exist. The chart on page 284 is designed to guide you through this labyrinth of state access restrictions.

*The Librarian's Guide to Public Records*

# Before You Start...

*Basic Information*

Each public record agency is indicated by the specific types of public records available; most listings include the office hours and even the time zone, thus insuring that the Directory goes beyond a standard address listing only book. In almost every instance, the addresses provided in this book are adequate for courier delivery as well as for mail. Phone numbers given are direct to the record office, instead of the general switchboard, when such a number exists. It should be noted that most of these offices will not do public record searches by phone. However, a good number will acknowledge if the record you are seeking does exist and what the search, copy or certification fees will be.

We strongly recommend that those requesters who mail in requests include a self-addressed stamped envelope. This can significantly decrease the turnaround time.

*Section Summaries*

We have divided the book into three sections symbolizing three very distinct public record arenas:

- County Courts and Recorder's Offices
- State Agencies
- Federal Courts

The Section Summaries are important—they tell you how to use the book. Each section begins with a detailed overview of the records to be found within that category. Additional research tools such as helpful charts and searcher hints segments are included to benefit you.

*Section One County Records*

The **County Records** section lists 10,600 locations with addresses, phone numbers and office hours. Possible record types to be found here include—
At the **County Court House**:
- Felony
- Misdemeanor
- Probate
- Civil Judgement Actions
- Small Claims
- Landlord/Tenant Actions

At the **County Recorder's Office**:
- Real Estate Transactions
- UCC Recordings
- Federal and/or State Tax Liens

Note: Also, vital records can be found here, when it is a county function

ix

# Before You Start....

**Section Two
State
Records**

The **State Records** section is printed on yellow paper. The summary section is a re-print of an article taken from the *Sourcebook of State Public Records* and is an excellent overview of "what, how, and where."

Each state segment (there are two states to a page) contains public agency listings with addresses, phone numbers and office hours. Also, we have provided record types at the end of the listing, where needed. The following locations (with number of record types) are covered:

- Archives
- Attorney General
- Secretary of State or similar entity
    (corporate, limited liability, limited partnerships, tradenames trademarks/servicemarks, federal and state tax liens, UCC, etc.)
- Court Administrator (for the State)
- Criminal Records
- DMV (Motor Vehicle) Records
    (driver, vehicle, accident)
- Governor's Office
- Legislation - Passed and Pending
- Uniform Commercial Code
- Vital Records
    (birth, death, marriage, divorce)

The section ends with a **State Public Records Restriction Chart**, also, taken from the *Sourcebook of State Public Records*. We urge you to use this added resource as you go about your record retrieval needs.

**Section Three
Federal
Records**

The **Federal Records** section is printed on blue paper and lists over 600 court locations where retrievable public record documents are maintained. The following locations are listed:

- US District Courts
- US Bankruptcy Courts
- US Courts of Appeals
- Federal Record Centers

On page 288, at the beginning of this section, you will find a **helpful cross reference chart**. Each state is cross referenced to its corresponding Circuit, Appeals Court, and Federal Record Center.

*The Librarian's Guide to Public Records*

# Section One
# County Records

*Organization*

All counties (parishes, towns and cities, where applicable) are headlined in alphabetical order within each state. The first listing is the real estate recording office, followed by the courts of general jurisdiction. Where more than one court of the same type is located in a county, they are listed in the order of the name of the city where they are located.

*Records Types*

As mentioned above, the first listing is the office where real estate is recorded. In most cases this is the same location where UCC filings are recorded and state or federal tax liens (if filed at the county level) can be found.

Do not assume that the structure of the court system in any state near to you is anything like your state's. In one state a "Circuit Court" may be the highest court and in another it may be a court limited jurisdiction. Court structure varies widely from state to state. Each court listing ends with the category of records which are found at that location. These records types include; felony, misdemeanor, civil (judgement actions), small claims, probate, and landlord/tenant actions.

*Time Zones Hours*

The time zone for each county appears in parentheses after the telephone number. The following ares do not convert to daylight savings time: Arizona, Hawaii, and Indiana (EST only). A few counties are split between time zones. Office hours appear after the time zone. Note that many offices close or have reduced staffing during the lunch/noon hour.

*Searching Hints*

You will note that, in many instances, two types of courts are combined. When you phone or write these courts, we recommend that you specifically state in your request the type of record you wish searched and that you want both courts to be included. Also, many courts will not do any searching for the public. If you cannot do the search yourself, you must hire a local retriever to do the search for you. Some of these non-search courts will provide document copies by mail if you have the specific case or docket number. Lastly, remember that a self-addressed, stamped envelope included in a mail request can significantly shorten the turnaround time.

Editor's Note: For more information regarding county courts and recording offices, we suggest you refer to two PRRL Sourcebooks—*County Court Records* and *County Asset/Lien Records*.

# Alabama

## Autauga County

**Real Estate Recording**, Autauga County Judge of Probate, 134 North Court St., Room 104, Prattville, AL 36067. 334-361-3725 (CST) 8:30AM-5PM.

**Circuit & District Court**, PO Box 126, Prattville, AL 36067. 334-361-3737 (CST) 8AM-5PM. Felony, Misdemeanor, Civil, Eviction, Small Claims.

**Probate Court**, PO Drawer 488, Prattville, AL 36067. 334-361-3725 (CST) 8:30AM-5PM. Probate.

## Baldwin County

**Real Estate Recording**, Baldwin County Judge of Probate, Courthouse Square, Bay Minette, AL 36507. 334-937-0230 (CST) 8AM-4:30PM.

**Circuit & District Court**, PO Box 1149, Bay Minette, AL 36507. 334-937-0208 (CST) 8AM-4:30PM. Felony, Misdemeanor, Civil, Eviction, Small Claims.

**Probate Court**, PO Box 1258, Bay Minette, AL 36507. 334-937-9561 (CST) 8AM-4:30PM. Probate.

## Barbour County

**Real Estate Recording**, Barbour County Judge of Probate, Clayton Division, Court Square, Clayton, AL 36016. 334-775-8371 (CST) 8AM-4PM.

**Real Estate Recording**, Barbour County Judge of Probate, Eufaula Division, Broad St., Eufaula, AL 36027. 334-687-7637 (CST) 8AM-4PM.

**Clayton Division-Circuit & District Court**, PO Box 237, Clayton, AL 36016. 334-775-8366 (CST) 8AM-5PM. Felony, Misdemeanor, Civil, Eviction, Small Claims, Probate.

**Eufaula Division-Circuit & District Court**, 303 E Broad St, Rm 201, Eufaula, AL 36027. 334-687-1513 (CST) 8AM-4:30PM. Misdemeanor, Civil, Eviction, Small Claims, Probate.

## Bibb County

**Real Estate Recording**, Bibb County Judge of Probate, Courthouse, 455 Walnut St, Centerville, AL 35042. 205-926-3104 (CST) 8AM-Noon, 1-5PM.

**Circuit & District Court**, Bibb County Courthouse, Centreville, AL 35042. 205-926-3103 (CST) 8AM-5PM. Felony, Misdemeanor, Civil, Eviction, Small Claims, Probate.

## Blount County

**Real Estate Recording**, Blount County Judge of Probate, 220 2nd Avenue East, Oneonta, AL 35121. 205-625-4180 (CST) 8AM-4PM M-W & F; 8AM-12 Th & Sat.

**Circuit & District Court**, PO Box 69, Oneonta, AL 35121. 205-625-4153 (CST) 8AM-5PM. Felony, Misdemeanor, Civil, Eviction, Small Claims.

**Probate Court**, PO Box 549, Oneonta, AL 35121. 205-625-4191 (CST) 8AM-4PM M,W,F 8AM-Noon Th,Sat. Probate.

## Bullock County

**Real Estate Recording**, Bullock County Judge of Probate, 217 North Prairie, Courthouse, Union Springs, AL 36089. 205-738-2250 (CST)

**Circuit & District Court**, PO Box 230, Union Springs, AL 36089. 205-738-2280 (CST) 8AM-4:30PM. Felony, Misdemeanor, Civil, Eviction, Small Claims, Probate.

## Butler County

**Real Estate Recording**, Butler County Judge of Probate, 700 Court Square, Greenville, AL 36037. 334-382-3512 (CST) 8AM-4PM M,T,Th,F; 8AM-Noon W.

**Circuit & District Court**, PO Box 236, Greenville, AL 36037. 334-382-3521 (CST) 8AM-4PM. Felony, Misdemeanor, Civil, Eviction, Small Claims, Probate.

## Calhoun County

**Real Estate Recording**, Calhoun County Judge of Probate, 1702 Noble Street, Suite 102, Anniston, AL 36201. 205-236-8231 (CST) 8AM-4:30PM.

**Circuit Court**, 25 W 11th St, Anniston, AL 36201. 205-231-1750 (CST) Felony, Civil Actions Over $5,000.

**District Court**, 25 W 11th St, Anniston, AL 36201. 205-231-1850 (CST) 8AM-4:30PM. Misdemeanor, Civil Actions Under $5,000, Eviction, Small Claims.

**Probate Court**, 1702 Noble St, #102, Anniston, AL 36201. 205-236-8231 (CST) Probate.

## Chambers County

**Real Estate Recording**, Chambers County Judge of Probate, Courthouse, Lafayette, AL 36862. 334-864-4384 (CST) 8AM-4:30PM.

**Circuit & District Court**, Chambers County Courthouse, Lafayette, AL 36862. 334-864-4348 (CST) 8AM-4:30PM. Felony, Misdemeanor, Civil, Eviction, Small Claims, Probate.

## Cherokee County

**Real Estate Recording**, Cherokee County Judge of Probate, Main Street, Centre, AL 35960. 205-927-3363 (CST) 8AM-4PM M-F, 8AM-Noon Sat.

**Circuit & District Court**, Cherokee County Courthouse, Centre, AL 35960. 205-927-3340 (CST) Felony, Misdemeanor, Civil, Eviction, Small Claims.

**Probate Court**, Cherokee County Courthouse, Centre, AL 35960. 205-927-3363 (CST) 8AM-4PM M-F, 8AM-Noon Sat. Probate.

## Chilton County

**Real Estate Recording**, Chilton County Judge of Probate, 500 2nd Avenue North, Clanton, AL 35045. 205-755-1555 (CST) 8AM-4PM.

**Circuit & District Court**, 500 2nd Ave North, Clanton, AL 35045. 205-755-4275 (CST) 8AM-5PM. Felony, Misdemeanor, Civil, Eviction, Small Claims, Probate.

## Choctaw County

**Real Estate Recording**, Choctaw County Judge of Probate, 117 South Mulberry, Courthouse, Butler, AL 36904. 205-459-2417 (CST) 8AM-4:30PM.

**Circuit & District Court**, Choctaw County Courthouse, Ste 10, Butler, AL 36904. 205-459-2155 (CST) 8AM-4:30PM. Felony, Misdemeanor, Civil, Eviction, Small Claims, Probate.

## Clarke County

**Real Estate Recording**, Clarke County Judge of Probate, 117 Court Street, Courthouse, Grove Hill, AL 36451. 334-275-3251 (CST) 8AM-5PM.

**Circuit & District Court**, PO Box 921, Grove Hill, AL 36451. 334-275-3363 (CST) 8AM-5PM. Felony, Misdemeanor, Civil, Eviction, Small Claims, Probate.

## Clay County

**Real Estate Recording**, Clay County Judge of Probate, Courthouse Square, Ashland, AL 36251. 205-354-2198 (CST) 8AM-4:30PM.

**Circuit & District Court**, PO Box 816, Ashland, AL 36251. 205-354-7926 (CST) 8AM-4:30PM. Felony, Misdemeanor, Civil, Eviction, Small Claims, Probate.

## Cleburne County

**Real Estate Recording**, Cleburne County Judge of Probate, 406 Vickery Street, Heflin, AL 36264. 205-463-5655 (CST) 8AM-5PM.

**Circuit & District Court**, 406 Vickery St, Heflin, AL 36264. 205-463-2651 (CST) 8AM-4:30PM. Felony, Misdemeanor, Civil, Eviction, Small Claims, Probate.

## Coffee County

**Real Estate Recording**, Coffee County Judge of Probate, Elba Division, 230-P North Court Avenue, Elba, AL 36323. 334-897-2211 (CST) 8AM-4:30PM.

**Real Estate Recording**, Coffee County Judge of Probate, Enterprise Division, 99 S. Edwards St., Suite 102, Enterprise, AL 36330. 334-347-2688 (CST) 8AM-4:30PM.

**Elba Division-Circuit & District Court**, PO Box 402, Elba, AL 36323. 334-897-2954 (CST) Felony, Misdemeanor, Civil, Eviction, Small Claims, Probate.

**Enterprise Division-Circuit & District Court**, PO Box 1294, Enterprise, AL 36331. 334-347-2519 (CST) 8AM-4:30PM. Felony, Misdemeanor, Civil, Eviction, Small Claims.

**Enterprise Division-Probate**, PO Box 1256, Enterprise, AL 36331. 334-347-2688 (CST) 8AM-4:30PM. Probate.

## Colbert County

**Real Estate Recording**, Colbert County Judge of Probate, 100 Main Street, Courthouse, Tuscumbia, AL 35674. 205-386-8542 (CST) 8AM-4:30PM.

# Alabama

**Circuit Court**, Colbert County Courthouse, Tuscumbia, AL 35674. 205-386-8512 (CST) 7:30AM-4:30PM. Felony, Civil Actions Over $5,000, Probate.

**District Court**, Colbert County Courthouse, Tuscumbia, AL 35674. 205-386-8518 (CST) Misdemeanor, Civil Actions Under $5,000, Eviction, Small Claims.

## Conecuh County

**Real Estate Recording**, Conecuh County Judge of Probate, Jackson Street, Court Square, Evergreen, AL 36401. 334-578-1221 (CST) 8AM-4PM.

**Circuit & District Court**, PO Box 107, Evergreen, AL 36401. 334-578-2066 (CST) 8AM-4:30PM. Felony, Misdemeanor, Civil, Eviction, Small Claims, Probate.

## Coosa County

**Real Estate Recording**, Coosa County Judge of Probate, Highway 231 and 22, Courthouse, Rockford, AL 35136. 205-377-4919 (CST) 8AM-4PM.

**Circuit & District Court**, PO Box 98, Rockford, AL 35136. 205-377-4988 (CST) Felony, Misdemeanor, Civil, Eviction, Small Claims, Probate.

## Covington County

**Real Estate Recording**, Covington County Judge of Probate, Court Square, Andalusia, AL 36420. 334-222-3189 (CST) 8AM-4:30PM.

**Circuit & District Court**, Covington County Courthouse, Andalusia, AL 36420. 334-222-4213 (CST) 8AM-5PM. Felony, Misdemeanor, Civil, Eviction, Small Claims, Probate.

## Crenshaw County

**Real Estate Recording**, Crenshaw County Judge of Probate, 301 Glenwood Avenue, Luverne, AL 36049. 334-335-6568 (CST) 8AM-4:30PM.

**Circuit & District Court**, PO Box 167, Luverne, AL 36049. 334-335-6575 (CST) 8AM-4:30PM. Felony, Misdemeanor, Civil, Eviction, Small Claims, Probate.

## Cullman County

**Real Estate Recording**, Cullman County Judge of Probate, 500 2nd Avenue SW, Courthouse, Cullman, AL 35055. 205-739-3530 (CST) 8AM-5PM.

**Circuit Court**, Cullman County Courthouse, Rm 303, Cullman, AL 35055. 205-739-3530 (CST) 8AM-5PM. Felony, Civil Actions Over $5,000, Probate.

**District Court**, Cullman County Courthouse, Rm 211, Cullman, AL 35055. 205-739-3530 (CST) 8AM-5PM. Misdemeanor, Civil Actions Under $5,000, Eviction, Small Claims.

## Dale County

**Real Estate Recording**, Dale County Judge of Probate, Courthouse, Ozark, AL 36360. 334-774-2754 (CST) 8AM-5PM.

**Circuit & District Court**, PO Box 1350, Ozark, AL 36361. 334-774-5003 (CST) 8AM-4:30PM. Felony, Misdemeanor, Civil, Eviction, Small Claims, Probate.

## Dallas County

**Real Estate Recording**, Dallas County Judge of Probate, 105 Lauderdale Street, Selma, AL 36701. 334-874-2516 (CST) 8:30AM-4:30PM.

**Circuit Court**, PO Box 1158, Selma, AL 36702. 334-874-2523 (CST) 8AM-5PM. Felony, Civil Actions Over $5,000, Probate.

**District Court**, PO Box 1158, Selma, AL 36702. 334-874-2526 (CST) 8AM-5PM. Misdemeanor, Civil Actions Under $5,000, Eviction, Small Claims.

## De Kalb County

**Real Estate Recording**, De Kalb County Judge of Probate, 300 Grand South, Courthouse, Fort Payne, AL 35967. 205-845-8510 (CST) 7:45AM-4:15PM.

**Circuit & District Court**, Dekalb County Courthouse, Rm 202, Fort Payne, AL 35967. 205-845-8525 (CST) Felony, Misdemeanor, Civil, Eviction, Small Claims, Probate.

## Elmore County

**Real Estate Recording**, Elmore County Judge of Probate, Commerce Street, Wetumpka, AL 36092. 334-567-1143 (CST) 8AM-4:30PM.

**Circuit Court**, PO Box 320, Wetumpka, AL 36092. 334-567-1123 (CST) 8AM-4:30PM. Felony, Civil Actions Over $5,000, Probate.

**District Court**, PO Box 320, Wetumpka, AL 36092. 334-567-1130 (CST) 8AM-4:30PM. Misdemeanor, Civil Actions Under $5,000, Eviction, Small Claims.

## Escambia County

**Real Estate Recording**, Escambia County Judge of Probate, 318 Belleville Avenue, Brewton, AL 36426. 334-867-0206 (CST) 8AM-4PM.

**Circuit & District Court**, PO Box 856, Brewton, AL 36427. 334-867-6261 (CST) Felony, Misdemeanor, Civil, Eviction, Small Claims, Probate.

## Etowah County

**Real Estate Recording**, Etowah County Judge of Probate, 800 Forrest Avenue, Courthouse, Gadsden, AL 35901. 205-549-5341 (CST) 8AM-5PM.

**Circuit & District Court**, PO Box 798, Gadsden, AL 35999. 205-549-5437 (CST) Felony, Misdemeanor, Civil, Eviction, Small Claims, Probate.

## Fayette County

**Real Estate Recording**, Fayette County Judge of Probate, 113 Temple Avenue North, Courthouse, Fayette, AL 35555. 205-932-4519 (CST) 8AM-4PM.

**Circuit & District Court**, PO Box 206, Fayette, AL 35555. 205-932-4617 (CST) 8AM-4:30PM. Felony, Misdemeanor, Civil, Eviction, Small Claims, Probate.

## Franklin County

**Real Estate Recording**, Franklin County Judge of Probate, 410 North Jackson Street, Russellville, AL 35653. 205-332-8801 (CST) 8AM-5PM; 8AM-Noon Sat.

**Circuit & District Court**, PO Box 160, Russellville, AL 35653. 205-332-8861 (CST) 8AM-4:30PM. Felony, Misdemeanor, Civil, Eviction, Small Claims, Probate.

## Geneva County

**Real Estate Recording**, Geneva County Judge of Probate, Commerce Street, Courthouse, Geneva, AL 36340. 205-684-9300 (CST) 8AM-5PM.

**Circuit & District Court**, PO Box 86, Geneva, AL 36340. 205-684-2494 (CST) 8AM-5PM. Felony, Misdemeanor, Civil, Eviction, Small Claims, Probate.

## Greene County

**Real Estate Recording**, Greene County Judge of Probate, 400 Morrow Ave., Greene County Courthouse, Eutaw, AL 35462. 205-372-3340 (CST) 8AM-4PM.

**Circuit & District Court**, PO Box 307, Eutaw, AL 35462. 205-372-3598 (CST) Felony, Misdemeanor, Civil, Eviction, Small Claims, Probate.

## Hale County

**Real Estate Recording**, Hale County Judge of Probate, 1001 Main Street, Courthouse, Greensboro, AL 36744. 334-624-8740 (CST) 8AM-4PM.

**Circuit & District Court**, Hale County Courthouse, Rm 8, Greensboro, AL 36744. 334-624-4334 (CST) 8AM-5PM. Felony, Misdemeanor, Civil, Eviction, Small Claims, Probate.

## Henry County

**Real Estate Recording**, Henry County Judge of Probate, Courthouse Square, Abbeville, AL 36310. 334-585-3257 (CST) 8AM-4:30PM.

**Circuit & District Court**, PO Box 337, Abbeville, AL 36310. 334-585-2753 (CST) 8AM-5PM. Felony, Misdemeanor, Civil, Eviction, Small Claims, Probate.

## Houston County

**Real Estate Recording**, Houston County Judge of Probate, 462 North Oates, 2nd Floor, Dothan, AL 36303. 334-677-4723 (CST) 8AM-4:30PM.

**Circuit & District Court**, PO Drawer 6406, Dothan, AL 36302. 334-677-4800 (CST) 7:30AM-4:30PM. Felony, Misdemeanor, Civil, Eviction, Small Claims, Probate.

## Jackson County

**Real Estate Recording**, Jackson County Judge of Probate, Courthouse Square, Courthouse, Scottsboro, AL 35768. 205-574-9292 (CST) 8AM-4:30PM M,T,W,F; 8AM-Noon Th,Sat.

**Circuit & District Court**, PO Box 397, Scottsboro, AL 35768. 205-574-9324 (CST)

8AM-4:30PM. Felony, Misdemeanor, Civil, Eviction, Small Claims, Probate.

## Jefferson County

**Real Estate Recording**, Jefferson County Judge of Probate, Bessemer Division, 1801 3rd Ave., Bessemer, AL 35020. 205-481-4100 (CST) 8AM-4:45PM.

**Real Estate Recording**, Jefferson County Judge of Probate, Birmingham Division, 716 North 21st Street, Courthouse, Birmingham, AL 35263. 205-325-5112 (CST) 8AM-4:45PM.

**Bessemer Divison-Circuit Court**, Rm 606, Courthouse Annex, Bessemer, AL 35020. 205-481-4165 (CST) 8AM-5PM. Felony, Civil Actions Over $5,000.

**Bessemer Division-District Court**, Rm 506, Courthouse Annex, Bessemer, AL 35020. 205-481-4187 (CST) 8AM-5PM. Misdemeanor, Civil Actions Under $5,000, Eviction, Small Claims.

**Birmingham Division-Civil Circuit Court**, 716 N 21st St, Rm 313, Birmingham, AL 35263. 205-325-5355 (CST) 8AM-5PM. Civil Actions Over $5,000.

**Birmingham Division-Criminal Circuit Court**, 801 N 21st St, Rm 506, Birmingham, AL 35263. 205-325-5285 (CST) 8AM-4:55PM. Felony.

**Birmingham Division-Civil District Court**, 716 N 21st St, Rm 522, Birmingham, AL 35263. 205-325-5331 (CST) 8AM-5PM. Civil Actions Under $5,000, Eviction, Small Claims.

**Birmingham Division-Criminal District Court**, 801 21st St, Rm 207, Birmingham, AL 35263. 205-325-5309 (CST) 8AM-5PM. Misdemeanor.

**Probate Court**, 716 N 21st St, Birmingham, AL 35203. 205-325-5420 (CST) Probate.

## Lamar County

**Real Estate Recording**, Lamar County Judge of Probate, N. Pond St, Vernon, AL 35592. 205-695-9119 (CST) 8AM-5PM M,T,Th,F; 8AM-Noon W,Sat.

**Circuit & District Court**, PO Box 434, Vernon, AL 35592. 205-695-7193 (CST) 8AM-5PM. Felony, Misdemeanor, Civil, Eviction, Small Claims, Probate.

## Lauderdale County

**Real Estate Recording**, Lauderdale County Judge of Probate, 200 South Court Street, Florence, AL 35630. 205-760-5800 (CST) 8AM-5PM.

**Circuit Court**, PO Box 795, Florence, AL 35631. 205-760-5710 (CST) 8AM-5PM. Felony, Civil Actions Over $5,000, Probate.

**District Court**, PO Box 363, Florence, AL 35631. 205-760-5726 (CST) Misdemeanor, Civil Actions Under $5,000, Eviction, Small Claims.

## Lawrence County

**Real Estate Recording**, Lawrence County Judge of Probate, 14330 Court Street, Suite 102, Moulton, AL 35650. 205-974-2439 (CST) 8AM-4PM.

**Circuit & District Court**, PO Box 265, Moulton, AL 35650. 205-974-2432 (CST) 8AM-5PM. Felony, Misdemeanor, Civil, Eviction, Small Claims, Probate.

## Lee County

**Real Estate Recording**, Lee County Judge of Probate, 215 South 9th, Opelika, AL 36803. 334-745-9761 (CST) 8:30AM-4:30PM.

**Circuit & District Court**, 215 S 9th St, Opelika, AL 36801. 334-749-7141 (CST) 8AM-5PM. Felony, Misdemeanor, Civil, Eviction, Small Claims, Probate.

## Limestone County

**Real Estate Recording**, Limestone County Judge of Probate, Courthouse, 2nd Floor, Athens, AL 35611. 205-233-6427 (CST) 8AM-4:30PM.

**Circuit & District Court**, PO Box 964, Athens, AL 35611. 205-233-6406 (CST) 8AM-4:30PM. Felony, Misdemeanor, Civil, Eviction, Small Claims, Probate.

## Lowndes County

**Real Estate Recording**, Lowndes County Judge of Probate, Courthouse, Hayneville, AL 36040. 334-548-2365 (CST) 8AM-4:30PM.

**Circuit & District Court**, PO Box 876, Hayneville, AL 36040. 334-548-2252 (CST) 8AM-4:30PM. Felony, Misdemeanor, Civil, Eviction, Small Claims, Probate.

## Macon County

**Real Estate Recording**, Macon County Judge of Probate, 101 E. Northside St., Suite 101, Tuskegee, AL 36083-1731. 334-724-2611 (CST) 8:30AM-4:30PM.

**Circuit & District Court**, 101 E Northside Ste 300, Tuskegee, AL 36083. 334-724-2614 (CST) 8AM-4:30PM. Felony, Misdemeanor, Civil, Eviction, Small Claims, Probate.

## Madison County

**Real Estate Recording**, Madison County Judge of Probate, Courthouse, Huntsville, AL 35801. 205-532-3341 (CST) 8:30AM-5PM.

**Civil Circuit Court**, 100 N Side Square, Courthouse, Huntsville, AL 35801. 205-532-3381 (CST) 8AM-5PM. Civil Actions Over $5,000, Probate.

**Criminal Circuit Court**, 100 N Side Square, Courthouse, Huntsville, AL 35801-4820. 205-532-3386 (CST) 8AM-5PM. Felony.

**District Court**, 100 N Side Square, Rm 822 Courthouse, Huntsville, AL 35801. 205-532-3622 (CST) 8AM-5PM. Misdemeanor, Civil Actions Under $5,000, Eviction, Small Claims.

## Marengo County

**Real Estate Recording**, Marengo County Judge of Probate, 101 East Coats Avenue, Courthouse, Linden, AL 36748. 334-295-2210 (CST) 8AM-4:30PM.

**Circuit & District Court**, PO Box 566, Linden, AL 36748. 334-295-2223 (CST) 8AM-4:30PM. Felony, Misdemeanor, Civil, Eviction, Small Claims, Probate.

## Marion County

**Real Estate Recording**, Marion County Judge of Probate, Military St, Hamilton, AL 35570. 205-921-2471 (CST) 8AM-Noon, 1-5PM.

**Circuit & District Court**, PO Box 1595, Hamilton, AL 35570. 205-921-7451 (CST) 8AM-5PM. Felony, Misdemeanor, Civil, Eviction, Small Claims, Probate.

## Marshall County

**Real Estate Recording**, Marshall County Judge of Probate, 425 Gunter Avenue, Guntersville, AL 35976. 205-571-7767 (CST) 8AM-4:30PM.

**Albertville Division-Circuit & District Court**, 200 W Main, Albertville, AL 35950. 205-878-4522 (CST) 8AM-4:30PM. Felony, Misdemeanor, Civil, Eviction, Small Claims.

**Guntersville Division-Civil Circuit Court**, 425 Gunter Ave, Guntersville, AL 35976. 205-571-7789 (CST) 8AM-4:30PM. Civil Actions Over $5,000, Small Claims, Probate.

**Guntersville Division-Criminal Circuit Court**, 425 Gunter Ave, Guntersville, AL 35976. 205-571-7791 (CST) 8AM-4:30PM. Felony.

## Mobile County

**Real Estate Recording**, Mobile County Judge of Probate, 101 Government Street, Mobile, AL 36602. 334-690-8490 (CST) 8AM-5PM.

**Circuit Court**, PO Box 298, Mobile, AL 36601. 334-690-8786 (CST) 8AM-5PM. Felony, Civil Actions Over $5,000.

**District Court**, PO Box 829, Mobile, AL 36601. 334-690-8520 (CST) Misdemeanor, Civil Actions Under $5,000, Eviction, Small Claims, Probate.

## Monroe County

**Real Estate Recording**, Monroe County Judge of Probate, South Alabama Avenue, Courthouse Square, Monroeville, AL 36460. 334-743-4107 (CST)

**Circuit & District Court**, County Courthouse, Monroeville, AL 36460. 334-743-2283 (CST) 8AM-5PM. Felony, Misdemeanor, Civil, Eviction, Small Claims, Probate.

## Montgomery County

**Real Estate Recording**, Montgomery County Judge of Probate, 142 Washington Avenue, Montgomery, AL 36104. 205-832-1237 (CST) 8AM-5PM.

**Circuit Court**, PO Box 1667, Montgomery, AL 36102-1667. 205-832-1260 (CST) 8AM-5PM. Felony, Civil Actions Over $5,000, Probate.

**District Court**, PO Box 1667, Montgomery, AL 36102. 205-832-1350 (CST) 8AM-5PM. Misdemeanor, Civil Actions Under $5,000, Eviction, Small Claims.

## Morgan County

**Real Estate Recording**, Morgan County Judge of Probate, 302 Lee Street, Decatur, AL 35601. 205-351-4680 (CST) 8:30AM-4:30PM.

Circuit Court, PO Box 668, Decatur, AL 35602. 205-351-4600 (CST) 8:30AM-4:30PM. Felony, Civil Actions Over $5,000, Probate.

District Court, PO Box 668, Decatur, AL 35602. 205-351-4640 (CST) Misdemeanor, Civil Actions Under $5,000, Eviction, Small Claims.

## Perry County

Real Estate Recording, Perry County Judge of Probate, Washington Street, Courthouse, Marion, AL 36756. 334-683-2210 (CST) 8AM-4:30PM.

Circuit & District Court, PO Box 505, Marion, AL 36756. 334-683-6106 (CST) 8AM-4:30PM. Felony, Misdemeanor, Civil, Eviction, Small Claims, Probate.

## Pickens County

Real Estate Recording, Pickens County Judge of Probate, Court Square, Probate Building, Carrollton, AL 35447. 205-367-2010 (CST) 8AM-4PM.

Circuit & District Court, PO Box 418, Carrollton, AL 35447. 205-367-2050 (CST) 8AM-4:30PM. Felony, Misdemeanor, Civil, Eviction, Small Claims, Probate.

## Pike County

Real Estate Recording, Pike County Judge of Probate, Church Street, Courthouse, Troy, AL 36081. 334-566-1246 (CST) 8AM-5PM.

Circuit & District Court, PO Box 948, Troy, AL 36081. 334-566-4622 (CST) 8AM-5PM. Felony, Misdemeanor, Civil, Eviction, Small Claims, Probate.

## Randolph County

Real Estate Recording, Randolph County Judge of Probate, Main Street, Courthouse, Wedowee, AL 36278. 205-357-4933 (CST) 8AM-5PM.

Circuit & District Court, PO Box 328, Wedowee, AL 36278. 205-357-4551 (CST) 8AM-5PM. Felony, Misdemeanor, Civil, Eviction, Small Claims, Probate.

## Russell County

Real Estate Recording, Russell County Judge of Probate, 501 14th Street, Phenix City, AL 36867. 334-298-7979 (CST) 8:30AM-4:30PM.

Circuit & District Court, PO Box 518, Phenix City, AL 36868. 334-298-0516 (CST) 8:30AM-4:30PM. Felony, Misdemeanor, Civil, Eviction, Small Claims, Probate.

## Shelby County

Real Estate Recording, Shelby County Judge of Probate, Main Street, Columbiana, AL 35051. 205-669-3720 (CST) 8AM-4:30PM.

Circuit & District Court, PO Box 1810, Columbiana, AL 35051. 205-669-3760 (CST) 8AM-4:30PM. Felony, Misdemeanor, Civil, Eviction, Small Claims, Probate.

## St. Clair County

Real Estate Recording, St. Clair County Judge of Probate, Northern Congressional District, 5th Avenue, Ashville, AL 35953. 205-594-2120 (CST) 8AM-5PM.

Real Estate Recording, St. Clair Judge of Probate, Southern Congressional District, Courthouse, Pell City, AL 35125. 205-338-9449 (CST) 8AM-5PM.

Ashville Division-Circuit & District Court, PO Box 476, Ashville, AL 35953. 205-594-7921 (CST) 8AM-5PM. Felony, Misdemeanor, Civil, Eviction, Small Claims, Probate.

Pell City Division-Circuit & District Courts, Cogswell Ave, Pell City, AL 35125. 205-338-2511 (CST) 8AM-5PM. Felony, Misdemeanor, Civil, Eviction, Small Claims, Probate.

## Sumter County

Real Estate Recording, Sumter County Judge of Probate, Courthouse Square, Livingston, AL 35470. 334-652-7281 (CST) 8AM-4PM.

Circuit & District Court, PO Box 936, Livingston, AL 35470. 334-652-2291 (CST) 8AM-5PM. Felony, Misdemeanor, Civil, Eviction, Small Claims, Probate.

## Talladega County

Real Estate Recording, Talladega County Judge of Probate, Courthouse, Talladega, AL 35160. 205-362-4175 (CST) 8AM-5PM.

Circuit & Northern Division District Court, PO Drawer B, Talladega, AL 35160-0755. 205-761-2102 (CST) 8AM-5PM. Felony, Misdemeanor, Civil, Eviction, Small Claims.

Southern Division-District Court, PO Box 183, Sylacauga, AL 35150. 205-245-4352 (CST) 7:30AM-4:30AM. Misdemeanor, Civil Actions Under $5,000, Eviction, Small Claims.

Probate Court, PO Box 755, Talladega, AL 35160. 205-362-4175 (CST) Probate.

## Tallapoosa County

Real Estate Recording, Tallapoosa County Judge of Probate, Broadnax Street, Courthouse, Dadeville, AL 36853. 205-825-4266 (CST) 8AM-5PM.

Western Division-Circuit & District Court, PO Box 189, Alexander City, AL 35010. 205-329-8123 (CST) 8AM-5PM. Felony, Misdemeanor, Civil, Eviction, Small Claims.

Eastern Division-Circuit & District Court, Tallapoosa County Courthouse, Dadeville, AL 36853. 205-825-1098 (CST) 8AM-5PM. Felony, Misdemeanor, Civil, Eviction, Small Claims, Probate.

## Tuscaloosa County

Real Estate Recording, Tuscaloosa County Judge of Probate, 714 Greensboro Avenue, Tuscaloosa, AL 35401. 205-349-3870 (CST) X205 8:30AM-5PM.

Civil Circuit Court, 714 Greensboro Ave, Tuscaloosa, AL 35401. 205-349-3870 (CST) 8:30AM-5PM. Civil Actions Over $5,000, Probate.

Criminal Circuit Court, 714 Greensboro Ave, Tuscaloosa, AL 35401. 205-349-3870 (CST) Felony.

District Court, PO Box 1687, Tuscaloosa, AL 35403. 205-349-3870 (CST) 8:30AM-5PM. Misdemeanor, Civil Actions Under $5,000, Eviction, Small Claims.

## Walker County

Real Estate Recording, Walker County Judge of Probate, 1803 3rd Ave. S.W., Courthouse Room 102, Jasper, AL 35502. 205-384-7282 (CST) 8AM-4PM.

Circuit & District Court, PO Box 749, Jasper, AL 35501. 205-384-7268 (CST) 8AM-4:30PM. Felony, Misdemeanor, Civil, Eviction, Small Claims, Probate.

## Washington County

Real Estate Recording, Washington County Judge of Probate, 1 Court Street, Chatom, AL 36518. 334-847-2201 (CST) 8AM-4:30PM.

Circuit & District Court, PO Box 548, Chatom, AL 36518. 334-847-2239 (CST) 8AM-4:30PM. Felony, Misdemeanor, Civil, Eviction, Small Claims, Probate.

## Wilcox County

Real Estate Recording, Wilcox County Judge of Probate, 100 Broad Street, Courthouse, Camden, AL 36726. 205-682-4883 (CST) 8-11:30AM,Noon-4:30PM.

Circuit & District Court, PO Box 656, Camden, AL 36726. 205-682-4126 (CST) 8AM-4:30PM. Felony, Misdemeanor, Civil, Eviction, Small Claims, Probate.

## Winston County

Real Estate Recording, Winston County Judge of Probate, Main Street, Courthouse, Double Springs, AL 35553. 205-489-5219 (CST) 8AM-4:30PM (8AM-Noon 1st Sat of every month).

Circuit & District Court, PO Box 309, Double Springs, AL 35553. 205-489-5533 (CST) 8AM-4:30PM. Felony, Misdemeanor, Civil, Eviction, Small Claims, Probate.

# Alaska

## Aleutian Islands

**Sand Point Magistrate Court (3rd Dist)**, Box 89, Sand Point, AK 99661-0089. 907-383-3591 (HT) 10AM-3:30PM. Misdemeanor, Civil Actions Under $5,000, Small Claims.

**St Paul Island Magistrate Court (3rd Dist)**, Box 170, St Paul Island, AK 99660-0170. 907-546-2300 (HT) 11AM-2:30PM T/11AM-5PM W-Sat. Misdemeanor, Civil Actions Under $5,000, Small Claims.

**Unalaska Magistrate Court (3rd Dist)**, Box 245, Unalaska, AK 99685-0245. 907-581-1266 (HT) Misdemeanor, Civil Actions Under $5,000, Small Claims.

## Aleutian Islands District

**Real Estate Recording**, Aleutian Islands District Recorder, 3601 C Street, Suite 1140, Anchorage, AK 99503. 907-762-2444 (HT) 7AM-4PM.

## Anchorage Borough

**(3rd Dist) Superior & District Court**, 303 K St, Anchorage, AK 99501-2083. 907-264-0493 (AK) 8AM-4:30PM. Felony, Misdemeanor, Civil, Eviction, Small Claims, Probate.

## Anchorage District

**Real Estate Recording**, Anchorage District Recorder, 3601 C Street, Suite 1140, Anchorage, AK 99503. 907-762-2443 (AK) 7AM-4PM.

## Barrow District

**Real Estate Recording**, Barrow District Recorder, 1648 S. Cushman St. #201, Fairbanks, AK 99701-6206. 907-452-3521 8:30AM-4PM.

## Bethel

**(4th Dist) Superior & District Court**, Box 130, Bethel, AK 99559-0130. 907-543-2298 (AK) 8AM-4:30PM. Felony, Misdemeanor, Civil, Eviction, Small Claims, Probate.

**Aniak Magistrate Court (4th Dist)**, Box 147, Aniak, AK 99557-0147. 907-675-4325 (AK) 8AM-4:30PM. Misdemeanor, Civil Actions Under $5,000, Small Claims.

**Quinhagak Magistrate Court (4th Dist)**, PO Box 109, Quinhagak, AK 99655-0109. 907-556-8015 (AK) Misdemeanor, Civil Actions Under $5,000, Small Claims.

## Bethel District

**Real Estate Recording**, Bethel District Recorder, 204 Chief Eddie Hoffman Highway, City Office Building, Bethel, AK 99559. 907-543-3391 (AK) 8AM-1PM.

## Bristol Bay Borough

**Naknek Magistrate Court (3rd Dist)**, Box 229, Naknek, AK 99633-0229. 907-246-6151 (AK) 8:30AM-4PM. Misdemeanor, Civil Actions Under $5,000, Small Claims.

## Bristol Bay District

**Real Estate Recording**, Bristol Bay District Recorder, 3601 C Street, Suite 1140, Anchorage, AK 99503. 907-762-2444 (AK) 7AM-4PM.

## Cape Nome District

**Real Estate Recording**, Cape Nome District Recorder, Front Street, 3rd Floor, Old Federal Building, Nome, AK 99762. 907-443-5178 8AM-1PM; 8AM-12:30PM Recording Hours.

## Chitina District

**Real Estate Recording**, Chitina District Recorder, Mile 115 Richardson Hwy, Ahtna Bldg., Glennallen, AK 99588. 907-822-3405 8:30AM-4PM.

## Cordova District

**Real Estate Recording**, Cordova District Recorder, 3601 C Street, Suite 1140, Anchorage, AK 99503. 907-762-2443 7AM-4PM.

## Denali

**Healy Magistrate Court (4th Dist)**, Box 298, Healy, AK 99743-0298. 907-683-2589 8AM-4:30PM. Misdemeanor, Civil Actions Under $5,000, Small Claims.

## Dillingham

**Dillingham Magistrate Court (3rd Dist)**, Box 909, Dillingham, AK 99576-0909. 907-842-5215 (AK) 8AM-4:30PM. Misdemeanor, Civil Actions Under $5,000, Small Claims.

## Fairbanks District

**Real Estate Recording**, Fairbanks District Recorder, 1648 S. Cushman St. #201, Fairbanks, AK 99701-6206. 907-452-3521 8:30AM-4PM.

## Fairbanks North Star Borough

**(4th Dist) Superior & District Court**, 604 Barnette St, Fairbanks, AK 99701. 907-452-9265 (AK) 8AM-4:30PM. Felony, Misdemeanor, Civil, Eviction, Small Claims, Probate.

## Fort Gibbon District

**Real Estate Recording**, Fort Gibbon District Recorder, 1648 S. Cushman St. #201, Fairbanks, AK 99701-6206. 907-452-3521 8:30AM-4PM.

## Haines Borough

**(1st Dist) District Court**, Box 169, Haines, AK 99827. 907-766-2801 (AK) 8AM-4:30PM. Misdemeanor, Civil Actions Under $50,000, Small Claims.

## Haines District

**Real Estate Recording**, Haines District Recorder, 400 Willoughby, 3rd Floor, Juneau, AK 99801. 907-465-3449 (AK) 8AM-4PM.

## Homer District

**Real Estate Recording**, Homer District Recorder, 195 E. Bunnell Ave., Suite A, Homer, AK 99603. 907-235-8136

## Iliamna District

**Real Estate Recording**, Iliamna District Recorder, 3601 C Street, Suite 1140, Anchorage, AK 99503. 907-762-2443 7AM-4PM.

## Juneau Borough

**(1st Dist) Superior & District Court**, Box 114100, Juneau, AK 99811-4100. 907-463-4700 (AK) Felony, Misdemeanor, Civil, Eviction, Small Claims, Probate.

## Juneau District

**Real Estate Recording**, Juneau District Recorder, 400 Willoughby, 3rd Floor, Juneau, AK 99801. 907-465-3425 (AK) 8:30AM-4PM.

## Kenai District

**Real Estate Recording**, Kenai District Recorder, 120 Trading Bay Road, Suite 230, Kenai, AK 99611. 907-283-3118 8AM-4:30PM Telephone hours; 8:30AM-4PM Public hours.

## Kenai Peninsula Borough

**(3rd Dist) Superior & District Court**, 125 Trading Bay Dr, Ste 100, Kenai, AK 99611. 907-283-3110 (AK) 8AM-4:30PM. Felony, Misdemeanor, Civil, Eviction, Small Claims, Probate.

**(3rd Dist) District Court**, 3670 Lake St, Ste 400, Homer, AK 99603-7686. 907-235-8171 (AK) 8AM-4:30PM. Misdemeanor, Civil Actions Under $50,000, Small Claims.

**Seward Magistrate Court (3rd Dist)**, Box 1929, Seward, AK 99664-1929. 907-224-3075 (AK) 8AM-4:30PM. Misdemeanor, Civil Actions Under $5,000, Small Claims.

## Ketchikan District

**Real Estate Recording**, Ketchikan District Recorder, 415 Main Street, Room 320, Ketchikan, AK 99901. 907-225-3143

## Ketchikan Gateway Borough

**(1st Dist) Superior & District Court**, 415 Main, Rm 400, Ketchikan, AK 99901-6399. 907-225-3195 (AK) 8AM-4:30PM. Felony, Misdemeanor, Civil, Eviction, Small Claims, Probate.

## Kodiak District

**Real Estate Recording**, Kodiak District Recorder, 204 Mission Road, Room 16, Kodiak, AK 99615. 907-486-9432

## Kodiak Island Borough

**(3rd Dist) Superior & District Court**, 202 Marine Way, Kodiak, AK 99615-9987. 907-486-1600 (AK) 8AM-4:30PM. Felony, Misdemeanor, Civil, Eviction, Small Claims, Probate.

## Kotzebue District

**Real Estate Recording**, Kotzebue District Recorder, 1648 S. Cushman St. #201, Fairbanks, AK 99701-6206. 907-452-3521 8:30AM-4PM.

## Kuskokwim District

**Real Estate Recording**, Kuskokwim District Recorder, 204 Chief Eddie Hoffman High-

# Alaska

way, City Office Building, Bethel, AK 99559. 907-543-3391 8AM-1PM.

## Kvichak District

**Real Estate Recording**, Kvichak District Recorder, 3601 C Street, Suite 1140, Anchorage, AK 99503. 907-762-2444 7AM-4PM.

## Manley Hot Springs District

**Real Estate Recording**, Manley Hot Springs District Recorder, 1648 S. Cushman St. #201, Fairbanks, AK 99701-6206. 907-452-3521 8:30AM-4PM.

## Matanuska-Susitna Borough

**(3rd Dist) Superior & District Court**, 435 S Denali, Palmer, AK 99645-6437. 907-746-8109 (AK) 8AM-4:30PM. Felony, Misdemeanor, Civil, Eviction, Small Claims, Probate.

## Mount McKinley District

**Real Estate Recording**, Mount McKinley District Recorder, 1648 S. Cushman St. #201, Fairbanks, AK 99701-6206. 907-452-3521 8:30AM-4PM.

## Nenana District

**Real Estate Recording**, Nenana District Recorder, 1648 S. Cushman St. #201, Fairbanks, AK 99701-6206. 907-452-3521 8:30AM-4PM.

## Nome

**(2nd Dist) Superior & District Court**, Box 1110, Nome, AK 99762-1110. 907-443-5216 (AK) 8AM-4:30PM. Felony, Misdemeanor, Civil, Eviction, Small Claims, Probate.

**Gambell Magistrate Court (2nd Dist)**, Box 48, Gambell, AK 99742-0048. 907-985-5133 (AK) 9AM-3:30PM, Closed 12-1. Misdemeanor, Civil Actions Under $5,000, Small Claims.

**Unalakleet Magistrate Court (2nd Dist)**, Box 250, Unalakleet, AK 99684-0185. 907-624-3015 (AK) 8AM-1:30PM. Misdemeanor, Civil Actions Under $5,000, Small Claims.

## North Slope Borough

**(2nd Dist) Superior & District Court**, Box 270, Barrow, AK 99723-0270. 907-852-4800 (AK) 8AM-4:30PM. Felony, Misdemeanor, Civil, Eviction, Small Claims, Probate.

## Northwest Arctic Borough

**(2nd Dist) Superior & District Court**, Box 317, Kotzebue, AK 99752-0317. 907-442-3208 (AK) 8AM-4:30PM. Felony, Misdemeanor, Civil, Eviction, Small Claims, Probate.

**Ambler Magistrate Court (2nd Dist)**, Box 86028, Ambler, AK 99786. 907-445-2137 (AK) 9AM-2PM, Closed 12-1. Misdemeanor, Civil Actions Under $5,000, Small Claims.

**Kiana Magistrate Court (2nd Dist)**, Box 170, Kiana, AK 99749-0170. 907-475-2167 (AK) 10AM-3PM M,W,F. Misdemeanor, Civil Actions Under $5,000, Small Claims.

## Nulato District

**Real Estate Recording**, Nulato District Recorder, 1648 S. Cushman St. #201, Fairbanks, AK 99701-6206. 907-452-3521 8:30AM-4PM.

## Palmer District

**Real Estate Recording**, Palmer District Recorder, 836 South Colony Way, Palmer, AK 99645. 907-745-3080

## Petersburg District

**Real Estate Recording**, Petersburg District Recorder, 415 Main Street, Room 320, Ketchikan, AK 99901. 907-225-3142

## Prince of Wales

**Craig Magistrate Court (1st Dist)**, Box 646, Craig, AK 99921. 907-826-3316 8AM-4:30PM. Misdemeanor, Civil Actions Under $5,000, Small Claims.

## Rampart District

**Real Estate Recording**, Rampart District Recorder, 1648 S. Cushman St. #201, Fairbanks, AK 99701-6206. 907-452-3521 8:30AM-4PM.

## Seldovia District

**Real Estate Recording**, Seldovia District Recorder, 195 E. Bunnell Ave., Suite A, Homer, AK 99603. 907-235-8136

## Seward District

**Real Estate Recording**, Seward District Recorder, 5th & Adams, Municipal Building Room 208, Seward, AK 99664. 907-224-3075 8:30AM-4PM.

## Sitka Borough

**(1st Dist) Superior & District Court**, 304 Lake St, Rm 203, Sitka, AK 99835-7759. 907-747-3291 (AK) 8AM-4:30PM. Felony, Misdemeanor, Civil, Eviction, Small Claims, Probate.

## Sitka District

**Real Estate Recording**, Sitka District Recorder, 210C Lake Street, Sitka, AK 99835. 907-747-3275 (AK) 9AM-Noon,1-4PM; Closed Fs.

## Skagway District

**Real Estate Recording**, Skagway District Recorder, 400 Willoughby, 3rd Floor, Juneau, AK 99801. 907-465-3425 8:30AM-4PM.

## Skagway-Yakutat

**Hoonah Magistrate & District Court (1st Dist)**, Box 430, Hoonah, AK 99829-0430. 907-945-3668 8AM-4:30PM, Closed 12-1. Misdemeanor, Civil Actions Under $50,000, Small Claims.

**Angoon Magistrate Court (1st Dist)**, Box 202, Angoon, AK 99820. 907-788-3229 11AM-2PM. Misdemeanor, Civil Actions Under $5,000, Small Claims.

**Pelican Magistrate Court (1st Dist)**, Box 36, Pelican, AK 99832-0036. 907-735-2217 8:305PM M-T, Closed 12-1. Misdemeanor, Civil Actions Under $5,000, Small Claims.

**Skagway Magistrate Court (1st Dist)**, Box 495, Skagway, AK 99840-0495. 907-983-2368 8AM-4:30PM M-Th, Closed 12-1. Misdemeanor, Civil Actions Under $5,000, Small Claims.

**Yakutat Magistrate Court (1st Dist)**, Box 426, Yakutat, AK 99689-0426. 907-784-3274 9AM-4:30PM M,Th/1PM-4:30PM T,W,F. Misdemeanor, Civil Actions Under $5,000, Small Claims.

## Southeast Fairbanks

**Delta Junction Magistrate Court (4th Dist)**, Box 401, Delta Junction, AK 99737-0401. 907-895-4211 (AK) 8AM-4:30PM. Misdemeanor, Civil Actions Under $5,000, Small Claims.

**Tok Magistrate Court (4th Dist)**, Box 187, Tok, AK 99780-0187. 907-883-5171 (AK) 8AM-4:30PM. Misdemeanor, Civil Actions Under $5,000, Small Claims.

## Talkeetna District

**Real Estate Recording**, Talkeetna District Recorder, 836 South Colony Way, Palmer, AK 99645. 907-745-3080

## Valdez District

**Real Estate Recording**, Valdez District Recorder, 213 Meals Avenue, Courthouse, Valdez, AK 99686. 907-835-2266 8:30AM-Noon, 1-4PM.

## Valdez-Cordova

**(3rd Dist) Superior & District Court**, Box 127, Valdez, AK 99686-0127. 907-835-2266 (AK) 8AM-4:30PM. Felony, Misdemeanor, Civil, Eviction, Small Claims, Probate.

**Cordova Magistrate Court (3rd Dist)**, Box 898, Cordova, AK 99574-0898. 907-424-3378 (AK) 8AM-4:30PM. Misdemeanor, Civil Actions Under $5,000, Small Claims.

**Glennallen Magistrate Court (3rd Dist)**, Box 86, Glennallen, AK 99588-0086. 907-822-3405 (AK) 8AM-4:30PM. Misdemeanor, Civil Actions Under $5,000, Small Claims.

**Whittier Magistrate Court (3rd Dist)**, Box 729, Whittier, AK 99693-0729. 907-472-2356 (AK) Misdemeanor, Civil Actions Under $5,000, Small Claims.

## Wade Hampton

**Chevak Magistrate Court (2nd Dist)**, Box 238, Chevak, AK 99563-0238. 907-858-7231 (AK) Misdemeanor, Civil Actions Under $5,000, Small Claims.

**Emmonak Magistrate Court (2nd Dist)**, Box 176, Emmonak, AK 99581-0176. 907-949-1748 (AK) 9AM-3:30PM. Misdemeanor, Civil Actions Under $5,000, Small Claims.

**St Mary's Magistrate Court (2nd Dist)**, Box 183, St Mary's, AK 99658-0183. 907-438-2912 (AK) 8AM-4:30PM. Misdemeanor, Civil Actions Under $5,000, Small Claims.

## Wrangell District

**Real Estate Recording**, Wrangell District Recorder, 415 Main Street, Room 320, Ketchikan, AK 99901. 907-225-3142

## Wrangell-Petersburg

**(1st Dist) Superior & District Court**, Box 1009, Petersburg, AK 99833-1009. 907-772-3824 (AK) 8AM-4:30PM. Felony, Misdemeanor, Civil, Eviction, Small Claims, Probate.

**(1st Dist) Superior & District Court**, Box 869, Wrangell, AK 99929-0869. 907-874-2311 (AK) 8AM-4:30PM. Felony, Misdemeanor, Civil, Eviction, Small Claims, Probate.

**Kake Magistrate Court (1st Dist)**, Box 100, Kake, AK 99830-0100. 907-785-3651 (AK) 8AM-Noon. Misdemeanor, Civil Actions Under $5,000, Small Claims.

## Yukon-Koyukuk

**Fort Yukon Magistrate Court (4th Dist)**, Box 211, Fort Yukon, AK 99740-0211. 907-662-2336 (AK) 10AM-2PM. Misdemeanor, Civil Actions Under $5,000, Small Claims.

**Galena Magistrate Court (4th Dist)**, Box 167, Galena, AK 99741-0167. 907-656-1322 (AK) 8AM-4:30PM. Misdemeanor, Civil Actions Under $5,000, Small Claims.

**McGrath Magistrate Court (4th Dist)**, Box 167, Galena, AK 99741-0167. 907-656-1322 (AK) Misdemeanor, Civil Actions Under $5,000, Small Claims.

**Nenana Magistrate Court (4th Dist)**, Box 449, Nenana, AK 99760-0449. 907-832-5430 (AK) 8:30AM-4PM. Misdemeanor, Civil Actions Under $5,000, Small Claims.

**Tanana Magistrate Court (4th Dist)**, Box 449, Tanana, AK 99777. 907-366-7243 (AK) Th-F 2nd full week ea month. Misdemeanor, Civil Actions Under $5,000, Small Claims.

# Arizona

Note: The new telephone area code, 520, is effective March 19, 1995. Before that, the old area code, 602, should be used.

## Apache County

**Real Estate Recording**, Apache County Recorder, 75 West Cleveland, St. Johns, AZ 85936. 520-337-4364 (MST) X238 8AM-5PM.

**Superior Court**, PO Box 365, St John's, AZ 85936. 520-337-4364 (MST) 8AM-5PM. Felony, Civil Actions Over $5,000, Probate.

**Chinle Justice Court**, PO Box 888, Chinle, AZ 86503. 520-674-3290 (MST) 8AM-5PM. Misdemeanor, Civil Actions Under $5,000, Eviction, Small Claims.

**Puerco Justice Court**, PO Box 336, Sanders, AZ 86512. 520-688-2954 (MST) 8AM-5PM. Misdemeanor, Civil Actions Under $5,000, Eviction, Small Claims.

**Round Valley Justice Court**, PO Box 1356, Springerville, AZ 85938. 520-333-4613 (MST) 8AM-12PM 1PM-5PM. Misdemeanor, Civil Actions Under $5,000, Eviction, Small Claims.

**St John's Justice Court**, PO Box 308, St John's, AZ 85936. 520-337-4364 (MST) 8AM-5PM. Misdemeanor, Civil Actions Under $5,000, Eviction, Small Claims.

## Cochise County

**Real Estate Recording**, Cochise County Recorder, Cochise County Administrative Building, 4 Ledge Ave., Bisbee, AZ 85603. 520-432-9270 (MST) 8AM-5PM.

**Superior Court**, PO Drawer CK, Bisbee, AZ 85620. 520-432-9364 (MST) 8AM-5PM. Felony, Civil Actions Over $5,000, Probate.

**Benson Justice Court**, PO Box 2167, Benson, AZ 85602. 520-586-2247 (MST) 8AM-5PM. Misdemeanor, Civil Actions Under $5,000, Eviction, Small Claims.

**Bisbee Justice Court**, PO Box 1893, Bisbee, AZ 85620. 520-432-9542 (MST) 8AM-5PM. Misdemeanor, Civil Actions Under $5,000, Eviction, Small Claims.

**Bowie Justice Court**, PO Box 317, Bowie, AZ 85605. 520-847-2303 (MST) 8AM-5PM. Misdemeanor, Civil Actions Under $5,000, Eviction, Small Claims.

**Douglas Justice Court**, 661 G Ave, Douglas, AZ 85607. 520-364-3561 (MST) 8AM-5PM. Misdemeanor, Civil Actions Under $5,000, Eviction, Small Claims.

**Sierra Vista Justice Court**, 4001 E Foothills Dr, Sierra Vista, AZ 85635. 520-452-4980 (MST) 8AM-5PM. Misdemeanor, Civil Actions Under $5,000, Eviction, Small Claims.

**Willcox Justice Court**, PO Drawer S, Willcox, AZ 85644. 520-384-2105 (MST) 8AM-5PM. Misdemeanor, Civil Actions Under $5,000, Eviction, Small Claims.

## Coconino County

**Real Estate Recording**, Coconino County Recorder, 100 E. Birch, Flagstaff, AZ 86001. 520-779-6585 (MST) 8AM-5PM.

**Superior Court**, 100 E Birch St, Flagstaff, AZ 86001. 520-779-6535 (MST) 8AM-5PM. Felony, Civil Actions Over $5,000, Probate.

**Flagstaff Justice Court**, 100 E Birch Ave, Flagstaff, AZ 86001. 520-779-6806 (MST) 8AM-5PM. Misdemeanor, Civil Actions Under $5,000, Eviction, Small Claims.

**Fredonia Justice Court**, 100 N Main, Fredonia, AZ 86022. 520-643-7472 (MST) 8AM-5PM. Misdemeanor, Civil Actions Under $5,000, Eviction, Small Claims.

**Page Justice Court**, PO Box 1565, Page, AZ 86040. 520-645-8871 (MST) 8AM-5PM. Misdemeanor, Civil Actions Under $5,000, Eviction, Small Claims.

**Williams Justice Court**, 117 W Bill Williams Ave #180, Williams, AZ 86046. 520-635-2691 (MST) 8AM-5PM. Misdemeanor, Civil Actions Under $5,000, Eviction, Small Claims.

## Gila County

**Real Estate Recording**, Gila County Recorder, 1400 East Ash Street, Globe, AZ 85501. 520-425-3231 (MST) 8AM-5PM.

**Superior Court**, 1400 E Ash, Globe, AZ 85501. 520-425-3231 (MST) 8AM-5PM. Felony, Civil Actions Over $5,000, Probate.

**Globe Justice Court**, 1400 E Ash, Globe, AZ 85501. 520-425-3231 (MST) 8AM-5PM. Misdemeanor, Civil Actions Under $5,000, Eviction, Small Claims.

**Miami Justice Court**, 506 Sullivan St, Miami, AZ 85539. 520-473-4461 (MST) 8AM-5PM. Misdemeanor, Civil Actions Under $5,000, Eviction, Small Claims.

**Payson Justice Court**, 714 S Beeline Hwy #103, Payson, AZ 85541. 520-474-5267 (MST) 8AM-5PM. Misdemeanor, Civil Actions Under $5,000, Eviction, Small Claims.

**Pine Justice Court**, PO Box 2363, Pine, AZ 85544. 520-476-3525 (MST) 8AM-5PM. Misdemeanor, Civil Actions Under $5,000, Eviction, Small Claims.

**Hayden-Winkleman Justice Court**, PO Box 680, Winkelman, AZ 85292. 520-356-7638 (MST) 8AM-5PM. Misdemeanor, Civil Actions Under $5,000, Eviction, Small Claims.

## Graham County

**Real Estate Recording**, Graham County Recorder, 800 Main Street, Safford, AZ 85546. 520-428-3560 (MST) 8AM-5PM.

**Superior Court**, 800 Main St, Safford, AZ 85546. 520-428-3100 (MST) 8AM-5PM. Felony, Civil Actions Over $5,000, Probate.

**Pima Justice Court Precinct #2**, PO Box 159, 136 W Center St, Pima, AZ 85543. 520-485-2771 (MST) 8AM-5PM. Misdemeanor, Civil Actions Under $5,000, Eviction, Small Claims.

**Safford Justice Court**, 523 10th Ave, Safford, AZ 85546. 520-428-1210 (MST) 8AM-5PM. Misdemeanor, Civil Actions Under $5,000, Eviction, Small Claims.

## Greenlee County

**Real Estate Recording**, Greenlee County Recorder, 5th & Webster, Clifton, AZ 85533. 520-865-2632 (MST) 8AM-5PM.

**Superior Court**, PO Box 1027, Clifton, AZ 85513. 520-865-4108 (MST) 8AM-5PM. Felony, Civil Actions Over $5,000, Probate.

**Justice Court, Precinct #1**, PO Box 517, Clifton, AZ 85533. 520-865-4312 (MST) 9AM-5PM. Misdemeanor, Civil Actions Under $5,000, Eviction, Small Claims.

**Justice Court, Precinct #2**, PO Box 208, Duncan, AZ 85534. 520-359-2536 (MST) 9AM-5PM. Misdemeanor, Civil Actions Under $5,000, Eviction, Small Claims.

## La Paz County

**Real Estate Recording**, La Paz County Recorder, 1112 Joshua Ave., Parker, AZ 85344. 520-669-6136 (MST) 8AM-5PM.

**Superior Court**, PO Box 730, Parker, AZ 85344. 520-669-6131 (MST) 8AM-5PM. Felony, Civil Actions Over $5,000, Probate.

**Parker Justice Court**, 1301 Arizona Ave #4, Parker, AZ 85344. 520-669-2504 (MST) 8AM-5PM. Misdemeanor, Civil Actions Under $5,000, Eviction, Small Claims.

**Quartzsite Justice Court**, PO Box 580, Quartzsite, AZ 85346. 520-927-6313 (MST) 8AM-5PM. Misdemeanor, Civil Actions Under $5,000, Eviction, Small Claims.

**Salome Justice Court**, PO Box 661, Salome, AZ 85348. 520-859-3871 (MST) 8AM-5PM. Misdemeanor, Civil Actions Under $5,000, Eviction, Small Claims.

## Maricopa County

**Real Estate Recording**, Maricopa County Recorder, 111 South 3rd Avenue, Phoenix, AZ 85003. 602-506-3535 (MST) 8AM-5PM.

**Superior Court**, 201 W Jefferson, Phoenix, AZ 85003. 602-506-3360 (MST) 8M-5PM. Felony, Civil Actions Over $5,000, Probate.

**Buckeye Justice Court**, 100 N Apache Rd, Buckeye, AZ 85326. 602-386-4289 (MST) 8AM-5PM. Misdemeanor, Civil Actions Under $5,000, Eviction, Small Claims.

**Chandler Justice Court**, 2051 W Warner Rd, Chandler, AZ 85224. 602-963-6691 (MST) 8AM-5PM. Misdemeanor, Civil Actions Under $5,000, Eviction, Small Claims.

**Gila Bend Justice Court**, PO Box 648, Gila Bend, AZ 85337. 602-683-2651 (MST) 8AM-5PM. Misdemeanor, Civil Actions Under $5,000, Eviction, Small Claims.

**Glendale Justice Court**, 6830 N 57th Dr, Glendale, AZ 85301. 602-939-9477 (MST) 8AM-5PM. Misdemeanor, Civil Actions Under $5,000, Eviction, Small Claims.

**West Mesa Justice Court**, 2050 W University Dr, Mesa, AZ 85201. 602-964-2958 (MST) 8AM-5PM. Misdemeanor, Civil Actions Under $5,000, Eviction, Small Claims.

**East Mesa Justice Court**, 4811 E Julep #128, Mesa, AZ 85205. 602-985-0188 (MST) 7AM-5PM. Misdemeanor, Civil Actions Under $5,000, Eviction, Small Claims.

**North Mesa Justice Court**, 1837 S Mesa Dr #A-201, Mesa, AZ 85210. 602-926-9731 (MST) 8AM-5PM. Misdemeanor, Civil Actions Under $5,000, Eviction, Small Claims.

**South Mesa/Gilbert Justice Court**, 1837 S Mesa Dr #B103, Mesa, AZ 85210. 602-926-3051 (MST) 8AM-5PM. Misdemeanor, Civil Actions Under $5,000, Eviction, Small Claims.

**Peoria Justice Court**, 7420 W Cactus Rd, Peoria, AZ 85381. 602-979-3234 (MST) 8AM-5PM. Misdemeanor, Civil Actions Under $5,000, Eviction, Small Claims.

**Central Phoenix Justice Court**, 1 W Madison St, Phoenix, AZ 85003. 602-506-1168 (MST) 8AM-5PM. Misdemeanor, Civil Actions Under $5,000, Eviction, Small Claims.

**East Phoenix Justice Court #1**, 1 W Madison St #1, Phoenix, AZ 85003. 602-506-3577 (MST) 8AM-5PM. Misdemeanor, Civil Actions Under $5,000, Eviction, Small Claims.

**West Phoenix Justice Court**, 527 W McDowell, Phoenix, AZ 85003. 602-256-0292 (MST) 8AM-5PM. Misdemeanor, Civil Actions Under $5,000, Eviction, Small Claims.

**East Phoenix Justice Court #2**, 4109 N 12th St, Phoenix, AZ 85014. 602-266-3741 (MST) 8AM-5PM. Misdemeanor, Civil Actions Under $5,000, Eviction, Small Claims.

**Northeast Phoenix Justice Court**, 10255 N 32nd St, Phoenix, AZ 85028. 602-506-3731 (MST) 8AM-5PM. Misdemeanor, Civil Actions Under $5,000, Eviction, Small Claims.

**Northwest Phoenix Justice Court**, 11601 N 19th Ave, Phoenix, AZ 85029. 602-395-0293 (MST) 8AM-5PM. Misdemeanor, Civil Actions Under $5,000, Eviction, Small Claims.

**Maryvale Justice Court**, 4622 W Indian School Rd Bldg D, Phoenix, AZ 85031. 602-245-0432 (MST) 8AM-5PM. Misdemeanor, Civil Actions Under $5,000, Eviction, Small Claims.

**South Phoenix Justice Court**, 217 E Olympic Dr, Phoenix, AZ 85040. 602-243-0318 (MST) 8AM-5PM. Misdemeanor, Civil Actions Under $5,000, Eviction, Small Claims.

**Scottsdale Justice Court**, 3700 N 75th St, Scottsdale, AZ 85251. 602-947-7569 (MST) 8AM-5PM. Misdemeanor, Civil Actions Under $5,000, Eviction, Small Claims.

**Tempe Justice Court**, 1845 E Broadway #8, Tempe, AZ 85282. 602-967-8856 (MST) 8AM-5PM. Misdemeanor, Civil Actions Under $5,000, Eviction, Small Claims.

**Tolleson Justice Court**, 9550 W Van Buren #6, Tolleson, AZ 85353. 602-936-1449 (MST) 8AM-5PM. Misdemeanor, Civil Actions Under $5,000, Eviction, Small Claims.

**Wickenburg Justice Court**, PO Box Z, Wickenburg, AZ 85358. 602-684-2401 (MST) 8AM-5PM. Misdemeanor, Civil Actions Under $5,000, Eviction, Small Claims.

## Mohave County

**Real Estate Recording**, Mohave County Recorder, 315 Oak Street, Kingman, AZ 86401. 520-753-0701 (MST) 8AM-5PM.

**Superior Court**, PO Box 7000, Kingman, AZ 86402-7000. 520-753-0713 (MST) 8AM-5PM. Felony, Civil Actions Over $5,000, Probate.

**Bullhead City Justice Court**, 1130 Hancock Rd, Bullhead City, AZ 86442. 520-758-0709 (MST) 8AM-5PM. Misdemeanor, Civil Actions Under $5,000, Eviction, Small Claims.

**Kingman Justice Court**, PO Box 29, Kingman, AZ 86402-0029. 520-753-0710 (MST) 8AM-5PM. Misdemeanor, Civil Actions Under $5,000, Eviction, Small Claims.

**Lake Havasu City Justice Court**, 2060 W Acoma, Lake Havasu City, AZ 86403. 520-453-0705 (MST) 8AM-5PM. Misdemeanor, Civil Actions Under $5,000, Eviction, Small Claims.

**Moccasin Justice Court**, HC65 PO 90, Moccasin, AZ 86022. 520-643-7104 (MST) 8AM-4PM. Misdemeanor, Civil Actions Under $5,000, Eviction, Small Claims.

## Navajo County

**Real Estate Recording**, Navajo County Recorder, 100 East Carter Dr, Courthouse, Holbrook, AZ 86025. 520-524-4190 (MST) 8AM-5PM.

**Superior Court**, PO Box 668, Holbrook, AZ 86025. 520-524-6161 (MST) 8AM-5PM. Felony, Civil Actions Over $5,000, Probate.

**Holbrook Justice Court**, PO Box 668, Holbrook, AZ 86025. 520-524-6161 (MST) 8AM-5PM. Misdemeanor, Civil Actions Under $5,000, Eviction, Small Claims.

**Kayenta Justice Court**, Box 38, Kayenta, AZ 86033. 520-697-3522 (MST) 8AM-Noon, 1:30PM-5PM. Misdemeanor, Civil Actions Under $5,000, Eviction, Small Claims.

**Pinetop-Lakeside Justice Court**, Box 2020, Lakeside, AZ 85929. 520-368-6200 (MST) 8AM-5PM. Misdemeanor, Civil Actions Under $5,000, Eviction, Small Claims.

**Show Low Justice Court**, 561 E Deuce of Clubs, Show Low, AZ 85901. 520-537-2213 (MST) 8AM-5PM. Misdemeanor, Civil Actions Under $5,000, Eviction, Small Claims.

**Snowflake Justice Court**, Box 902, Snowflake, AZ 85937. 520-536-4141 (MST) 8AM-5PM. Misdemeanor, Civil Actions Under $5,000, Eviction, Small Claims.

**Winslow Justice Court**, Box 808, Winslow, AZ 86047. 520-289-2942 (MST) 8AM-5PM. Misdemeanor, Civil Actions Under $5,000, Eviction, Small Claims.

## Navajo Nation

**Real Estate Recording**, Business Regulatory Department, State Road 264 West, Window Rock, AZ 86515. 520-871-7365

## Pima County

**Real Estate Recording**, Pima County Recorder, 115 North Church Avenue, Tuscon, AZ 85701. 520-740-8151 (MST) 8AM-5PM.

**Superior Court**, 110 W Congress, Tucson, AZ 85701. 520-740-3200 (MST) 8AM-5PM. Felony, Civil Actions Over $5,000, Probate.

**Ajo Justice Court**, 111 La Mina, Ajo, AZ 85321. 520-387-7684 (MST) 8AM-5PM. Misdemeanor, Civil Actions Under $5,000, Eviction, Small Claims.

**Green Valley Justice Court**, 601 N La-Canada, Green Valley, AZ 85614. 520-648-0658 (MST) 8AM-5PM. Misdemeanor, Civil Actions Under $5,000, Eviction, Small Claims.

**Pima County Consolidated Justice Court**, 115 Church, Tucson, AZ 85701. 520-740-3515 (MST) 8AM-5PM. Misdemeanor, Civil Actions Under $5,000, Eviction, Small Claims.

## Pinal County

**Real Estate Recording**, Pinal County Recorder, 135 North Pinal Street, Courthouse, Florence, AZ 85232. 520-868-6391 (MST) 8AM-5PM.

**Superior Court**, PO Box 889, Florence, AZ 85232-0889. 520-868-6296 (MST) 8AM-5PM. Felony, Civil Actions Over $5,000, Probate.

**Apache Junction Justice Court**, 575 N Idaho, Apache Junction, AZ 85219. 520-982-2921 (MST) 8AM-5PM. Misdemeanor, Civil Actions Under $5,000, Eviction, Small Claims.

**Casa Grande Justice Court**, 820 E Cottonwood Lane, Bldg B, Casa Grande, AZ 85222. 520-836-5471 (MST) 8AM-5PM. Misdemeanor, Civil Actions Under $5,000, Eviction, Small Claims.

**Eloy Justice Court**, PO Box 586, Eloy, AZ 85231. 520-466-9221 (MST) 8AM-5PM. Misdemeanor, Civil Actions Under $5,000, Eviction, Small Claims.

**Florence Justice Court**, PO Box 1818, Florence, AZ 85232. 520-868-6578 (MST) 8AM-5PM. Misdemeanor, Civil Actions Under $5,000, Eviction, Small Claims.

**Mammoth Justice Court**, PO Box 117, Mammoth, AZ 85618. 520-487-2262 (MST) 8AM-5PM. Misdemeanor, Civil Actions Under $5,000, Eviction, Small Claims.

**Maricopa Justice Court**, PO Box 201, Maricopa, AZ 85239. 520-568-2451 (MST) 8AM-4PM. Misdemeanor, Civil Actions Under $5,000, Eviction, Small Claims.

**Oracle Justice Court**, PO Box 3924, Oracle, AZ 85623. 520-896-9250 (MST) 8AM-5PM. Misdemeanor, Civil Actions Under $5,000, Eviction, Small Claims.

**Kearny Justice Court**, 60 E Main St, Superior, AZ 85273. 520-689-5871 (MST) 8AM-5PM. Misdemeanor, Civil Actions Under $5,000, Eviction, Small Claims.

## Santa Cruz County

**Real Estate Recording**, Santa Cruz County Recorder, 2100 West Congress Street, Courthouse, Nogales, AZ 85621. 520-761-7800 (MST) X3037 8AM-5PM.

**Superior Court**, PO Box 1265, Nogales, AZ 85628. 520-761-7808 (MST) 8AM-5PM. Felony, Civil Actions Over $5,000, Probate.

**Santa Cruz Justice Court**, PO Box 1150, Nogales, AZ 85628. 520-761-7853 (MST) 8AM-5PM. Misdemeanor, Civil Actions Under $5,000, Eviction, Small Claims.

**Patagonia Justice Court**, PO Box 100, Patagonia, AZ 85624. 520-394-2251 (MST) 8:30AM-5PM. Misdemeanor, Civil Actions Under $5,000, Eviction, Small Claims.

## Yavapai County

**Real Estate Recording**, Yavapai County Recorder, 255 East Gurley Street, No. 202, Prescott, AZ 86301. 520-771-3244 (MST) 8AM-5PM.

**Superior Court**, Yavapai County Courthouse, Prescott, AZ 86301. 520-771-3313 (MST) 8AM-5PM. Felony, Civil Actions Over $5,000, Probate.

**Bagdad Justice Court**, PO Box 243, Bagdad, AZ 86321. 520-633-2141 (MST) 10AM-3PM M,W,TH,F 9AM-2PM T. Misdemeanor, Civil Actions Under $5,000, Eviction, Small Claims.

**Camp Verde Justice Court**, PO Box 568, Camp Verde, AZ 86322. 520-567-3353 (MST) 8AM-5PM. Misdemeanor, Civil Actions Under $5,000, Eviction, Small Claims.

**Upper Verde Justice Court**, PO Box 188, Cottonwood, AZ 86326. 520-639-8115 (MST) 8AM-5PM M-F, 7AM-7PM T. Misdemeanor, Civil Actions Under $5,000, Eviction, Small Claims.

**Mayer Justice Court**, PO Box 245, Mayer, AZ 86333. 520-771-3355 (MST) 8AM-5PM. Misdemeanor, Civil Actions Under $5,000, Eviction, Small Claims.

**Prescott Justice Court**, Yavapai County Courthouse, Prescott, AZ 86301. 520-771-3300 (MST) 8AM-5PM. Misdemeanor, Civil Actions Under $5,000, Eviction, Small Claims.

**Seligman Justice Court**, PO Box 56, Seligman, AZ 86337. 520-422-3281 (MST) 8AM-5PM. Misdemeanor, Civil Actions Under $5,000, Eviction, Small Claims.

**Yarnell Justice Court**, PO Box 65, Yarnell, AZ 85362. 520-427-3318 (MST) 8AM-5PM. Misdemeanor, Civil Actions Under $5,000, Eviction, Small Claims.

## Yuma County

**Real Estate Recording**, Yuma County Recorder, 198 S. Main St, Yuma, AZ 85364-1424. 520-329-2061 (MST) 8AM-5PM.

**Superior Court**, 168 S 2nd Ave, Yuma, AZ 85364. 520-329-2164 (MST) 8AM-5PM. Felony, Civil Actions Over $5,000, Probate.

**Somerton Justice Court**, PO Box 458, Somerton, AZ 85350. 520-627-2722 (MST) 8AM-5PM. Misdemeanor, Civil Actions Under $5,000, Eviction, Small Claims.

**Wellton Justice Court**, PO Box 384, Wellton, AZ 85356. 520-785-3321 (MST) 8AM-5PM. Misdemeanor, Civil Actions Under $5,000, Eviction, Small Claims.

**Yuma Justice Court**, 168 S 2nd Ave, Yuma, AZ 85364. 520-329-2180 (MST) 8AM-5PM. Misdemeanor, Civil Actions Under $5,000, Eviction, Small Claims.

# Arkansas

## Arkansas County

**Real Estate Recording**, Arkansas County Circuit Clerk, Southern District, 101 Court Square, De Witt, AR 72042. 501-946-4219 (CST) 8AM-Noon,1-5PM.

**Real Estate Recording**, Arkansas County Circuit Clerk, Northern District, 302 South College, Stuttgart, AR 72160. 501-673-2056 (CST) 8AM-Noon,1-5PM.

**Circuit and Chancery Courts**, PO Box 719, Stuttgart, AR 72160. 501-673-2056 (CST) 8:00AM-5:00PM. Felony, Civil Actions Over $3,000, Probate.

**Circuit and County Courts**, 101 Courthouse Sq, De Witt, AR 72042. 501-946-4219 (CST) 8:00AM-5:00PM. Felony, Civil Actions Over $3,000, Probate.

**Municipal Court**, PO Box 819, Stuttgart, AR 72160. 501-673-7951 (CST) 8:00AM-5:00PM. Misdemeanor, Eviction, Small Claims.

## Ashley County

**Real Estate Recording**, Ashley County Circuit Clerk, Jefferson Street, Courthouse, Hamburg, AR 71646. 501-853-2030 (CST) 8AM-4:30PM.

**Circuit and Chancery Courts**, Ashley County Courthouse, Hamburg, AR 71646. 501-853-2005 (CST) 8:00AM-4:30PM. Felony, Civil Actions Over $3,000, Probate.

**Municipal Court**, PO Box 558 City Hall, Hamburg, AR 71646. 501-853-8326 (CST) 7:00AM-4:00PM. Misdemeanor, Eviction, Small Claims.

## Baxter County

**Real Estate Recording**, Baxter County Circuit Clerk, Courthouse Square, 1 East 7th Street, Mountain Home, AR 72653. 501-425-3475 (CST) 8AM-4:30PM.

**Circuit and Chancery Courts**, 1 E 7th St Courthouse Square, Mountain Home, AR 72653. 501-425-3475 (CST) 8:00AM-4:30PM. Felony, Civil Actions Over $3,000, Probate.

**Municipal Court**, 720 S Hickory, Mountain Home, AR 72653. 501-425-3140 (CST) 8:00AM-4:30PM. Misdemeanor, Eviction, Small Claims.

## Benton County

**Real Estate Recording**, Benton County Circuit Clerk, Courthouse on the Square, 102 NE "A" Box 10, Bentonville, AR 72712. 501-271-1015 (CST) 8AM-4:30PM.

**Circuit and Chancery Courts**, 102 NE "A" St, Bentonville, AR 72712. 501-271-1015 (CST) 8:00AM-4:30PM. Felony, Civil Actions Over $3,000, Probate.

**Municipal Court**, 117 W Central, Bentonville, AR 72712. 501-271-3120 (CST) Misdemeanor, Eviction, Small Claims.

## Boone County

**Real Estate Recording**, Boone County Circuit Clerk, Public Square, Courthouse, Harrison, AR 72602. 501-741-5560 (CST) 8:30AM-4PM.

**Circuit and Chancery Courts**, PO Box 957, Harrison, AR 72601. 501-741-5560 (CST) 8:30AM-4:00PM. Felony, Civil Actions Over $3,000, Probate.

**Municipal Court**, PO Box 446, Harrison, AR 72601. 501-741-2788 (CST) Misdemeanor, Eviction, Small Claims.

## Bradley County

**Real Estate Recording**, Bradley County Circuit Clerk, 101 E. Cedar Street, Courthouse, Warren, AR 71671. 501-226-2272 (CST) 8AM-4:30PM.

**Circuit and County Courts**, Bradley Cty Courthouse - Records, Warren, AR 71671. 501-226-2272 (CST) Felony, Civil Actions Over $3,000, Probate.

**Municipal Court**, PO Box 352, Warren, AR 71671. 501-226-2567 (CST) 8:00AM-5:00PM. Misdemeanor, Eviction, Small Claims.

## Calhoun County

**Real Estate Recording**, Calhoun County Circuit Clerk, Main Street, Courthouse, Hampton, AR 71744. 501-798-2517 (CST) 8AM-4:30.

**Circuit and County Courts**, PO Box 626, Hampton, AR 71744. 501-798-2517 (CST) 8:30AM-4:30PM. Felony, Civil Actions Over $3,000, Probate.

**Municipal Court**, PO Box 864, Hampton, AR 71744. 501-798-2165 (CST) 8:00AM-4:30PM. Misdemeanor, Eviction, Small Claims.

## Carroll County

**Real Estate Recording**, Carroll County Circuit Clerk, Eastern District, 210 West Church, Berryville, AR 72616. 501-423-2422 (CST) 8:30AM-4:30PM.

**Real Estate Recording**, Carroll County Circuit Clerk, Western District, 44 South Main, Courthouse, Eureka Springs, AR 72632. 501-253-8646 (CST) 8:30AM-4:30PM.

**Circuit and Chancery Courts**, Berryville Circuit Court, PO Box 71, Berryville, AR 72616. 501-423-2422 (CST) 8:30AM-4:30PM. Felony, Civil Actions Over $3,000, Probate.

**Circuit and County Courts**, 44 S Main, PO Box 109, Eureka Springs, AR 72632. 501-253-8646 (CST) 8:30AM-4:30PM. Felony, Civil Actions Over $3,000, Probate.

**Municipal Court**, 103 S Springs, Berryville, AR 72616. 501-423-6247 (CST) 8:30AM-4:30PM. Misdemeanor, Eviction, Small Claims.

**Municipal Court**, Courthouse, 44 S Main, Eureka Springs, AR 72632. 501-253-8574 (CST) 8:00AM-5:00PM. Misdemeanor, Eviction, Small Claims.

## Chicot County

**Real Estate Recording**, Chicot County Circuit Clerk, Courthouse, Lake Village, AR 71653. 501-265-8000 (CST)

**Circuit and Chancery Courts**, County Courthouse, Lake Village, AR 71653. 501-265-8010 (CST) 8:00AM-4:30PM. Felony, Civil Actions Over $3,000, Probate.

**Municipal Court**, PO Box 832, Lake Village, AR 71653. 501-265-3283 (CST) 9:00AM-5:00PM. Misdemeanor, Eviction, Small Claims.

## Clark County

**Real Estate Recording**, Clark County Circuit Clerk, Courthouse Square, Arkadelphia, AR 71923. 501-246-4281 (CST) 8:30AM-4:30PM.

**Circuit and Chancery Courts**, PO Box 576, Arkadelphia, AR 71923. 501-246-4281 (CST) 8:30AM-4:30PM. Felony, Civil Actions Over $3,000, Probate.

**Municipal Court**, 419 Clay St, Arkadelphia, AR 71923. 501-246-9552 (CST) Misdemeanor, Eviction, Small Claims.

## Clay County

**Real Estate Recording**, Clay County Circuit Clerk, Western District, 800 West Second Street, Corning, AR 72422. 501-857-3271 (CST) 8AM-Noon, 1PM-4:30PM.

**Real Estate Recording**, Clay County Circuit Clerk, Eastern District, Courthouse, Piggott, AR 72454. 501-598-2524 (CST) 8AM-Noon,1-4:30PM.

**Corning Circuit and County Courts**, Courthouse, Corning, AR 72422. 501-857-3271 (CST) Felony, Civil Actions Over $3,000, Probate.

**Piggott Circuit and County Courts**, PO Box 29, Piggott, AR 72454. 501-598-2524 (CST) Felony, Civil Actions Over $3,000, Probate.

**Municipal Court**, 194 W Court, Piggott, AR 72454. 501-598-2265 (CST) 8:00AM-4:30PM. Misdemeanor, Eviction, Small Claims.

## Cleburne County

**Real Estate Recording**, Cleburne County Circuit Clerk, 300 West Main Street, Heber Springs, AR 72543. 501-362-8149 (CST) 8:30AM-4:30PM.

**Circuit and County Courts**, PO Box 543, Heber Springs, AR 72543. 501-362-8149 (CST) 8:30AM-4:30PM. Felony, Civil Actions Over $3,000, Probate.

**Municipal Court**, 102 E Main, Heber Springs, AR 72543. 501-362-6585 (CST) 8:30AM-4:30PM. Misdemeanor, Eviction, Small Claims.

## Cleveland County

**Real Estate Recording**, Cleveland County Circuit Clerk, Courthouse, Corner of Main & Magnolia, Rison, AR 71665. 501-325-6521 (CST)

**Circuit and County Courts**, PO Box 368, Rison, AR 71665. 501-325-6902 (CST) 8:00AM-4:30PM. Felony, Civil Actions Over $3,000, Probate.

**Rison Municipal Court**, PO Box 405, City Hall, Rison, AR 71665. 501-325-7382 (CST) Misdemeanor, Eviction, Small Claims.

# Arkansas

## Columbia County

**Real Estate Recording**, Columbia County Circuit Clerk, Courthouse, Magnolia, AR 71753. 501-235-3700 (CST) 8AM-4:30PM.

**Circuit and County Courts**, PO Box 327, Magnolia, AR 71753. 501-234-4001 (CST) 8:00AM-5:00PM. Felony, Civil Actions Over $3,000, Probate.

**Circuit and County Courts**, 1 Court Square #1, Magnolia, AR 71753-3595. 501-235-3774 (CST) 8AM-4:30PM. Felony, Civil Actions Over $3,000, Probate.

**Magnolia Municipal Court**, PO Box 1126, Magnolia, AR 71753. 501-234-7312 (CST) 8:00AM-5:00PM. Misdemeanor, Eviction, Small Claims.

## Conway County

**Real Estate Recording**, Conway County Circuit Clerk, 115 S. Moose Street, County Courthouse - Room 206, Morrilton, AR 72110. 501-354-9617 (CST) 8AM-5PM.

**Circuit and Chancery Courts**, Conway County Courthouse, Rm 206, Morrilton, AR 72110. 501-354-9617 (CST) 8:00AM-5:00PM. Felony, Civil Actions Over $3,000, Probate.

**Municipal Court**, Conway County Courthouse, Rm 306, Morrilton, AR 72110. 501-354-9615 (CST) 8:00AM-4:30PM. Misdemeanor, Eviction, Small Claims.

## Craighead County

**Real Estate Recording**, Craighead County Circuit Clerk, Western District, Main Street and Washington, Jonesboro, AR 72401. 501-933-4530 (CST) 8AM-5PM.

**Real Estate Recording**, Craighead County Circuit Clerk, Eastern District, 405 Court Street, Lake City, AR 72437. 501-237-4342 (CST) 8AM-Noon,1-5PM.

**Jonesboro Circuit and Chancery Courts**, PO Box 120, Jonesboro, AR 72403. 501-933-4530 (CST) 8:00AM-5:00PM. Felony, Civil Actions Over $3,000, Probate.

**Lake City Circuit and County Courts**, PO Box 537, Lake City, AR 72437. 501-237-4342 (CST) 8:00AM-5:00PM. Felony, Civil Actions Over $3,000, Probate.

**Municipal Court**, 524 S Church St, Jonesboro, AR 72401. 501-933-4580 (CST) 8:00AM-5:00PM. Misdemeanor, Eviction, Small Claims.

## Crawford County

**Real Estate Recording**, Crawford County Circuit Clerk, 300 Main, Courthouse Room 22, Van Buren, AR 72956-5799. 501-474-1821 (CST) 8AM-5PM.

**Circuit and Chancery Courts**, Crawford County Courthouse, 300 Main St,, Van Buren, AR 72956. 501-474-1821 (CST) 8:00AM-5:00PM. Felony, Civil Actions Over $3,000, Probate.

**Municipal Court**, Crawford County Courthouse, 1003 Broadwa, Van Buren, AR 72956. 501-474-1671 (CST) 8:00AM-5:00PM. Misdemeanor, Eviction, Small Claims.

## Crittenden County

**Real Estate Recording**, Crittenden County Circuit Clerk, Jackson Street, Courthouse, Marion, AR 72364. 501-739-3248 (CST) 8AM-4:30PM.

**Circuit and County Courts**, Criminal Records, Marion, AR 72364. 501-739-3248 (CST) Felony, Civil Actions Over $3,000, Probate.

**Municipal Court**, 100 Court St, West Memphis, AR 72301. 501-732-7560 (CST) Misdemeanor, Eviction, Small Claims.

## Cross County

**Real Estate Recording**, Cross County Circuit Clerk, 705 East Union, Room 9, Wynne, AR 72396. 501-238-5720 (CST) 8AM-4PM.

**Circuit and County Courts**, County Courthouse, Wynne, AR 72396. 501-238-5720 (CST) 8:00AM-4:00PM. Felony, Civil Actions Over $3,000, Probate.

**Municipal Court**, 206 S Falls Blvd, Wynne, AR 72396. 501-238-9171 (CST) Misdemeanor, Eviction, Small Claims.

## Dallas County

**Real Estate Recording**, Dallas County Circuit Clerk, 202 Third St. West, Courthouse, Fordyce, AR 71742-3299. 501-352-2307 (CST) 8:30AM-4:30PM.

**Circuit and County Courts**, Dallas County Courthouse, Fordyce, AR 71742. 501-352-2307 (CST) 8:30AM-4:30PM. Felony, Civil Actions Over $3,000, Probate.

**Municipal Court**, Dallas County Courthouse, Fordyce, AR 71742. 501-352-2332 (CST) 8:00AM-4:00PM. Misdemeanor, Eviction, Small Claims.

## Desha County

**Real Estate Recording**, Desha County Circuit Clerk, Robert Moore Drive, Arkansas City Courthouse, Arkansas City, AR 71630. 501-877-2411 (CST)

**Circuit and Chancery Courts**, PO Box 309, Arkansas City, AR 71630. 501-877-2411 (CST) 8:00AM-4:00PM. Felony, Civil Actions Over $3,000, Probate.

**Municipal Court**, PO Box 157, Dumas, AR 71639. 501-382-2121 (CST) 7:00AM-4:00PM. Misdemeanor, Eviction, Small Claims.

## Drew County

**Real Estate Recording**, Drew County Circuit Clerk, 210 South Main, Monticello, AR 71655. 501-460-6250 (CST) 8AM-5PM.

**Circuit and County Courts**, 210 S Main, Monticello, AR 71655. 501-460-6250 (CST) 8:00AM-5:00PM. Felony, Civil Actions Over $3,000, Probate.

**Municipal Court**, PO Box 505, Monticello, AR 71655. 501-367-4420 (CST) 8:30AM-5:00PM. Misdemeanor, Eviction, Small Claims.

## Faulkner County

**Real Estate Recording**, Faulkner County Circuit Clerk, 801 Locust Street, Courthouse, Conway, AR 72032. 501-450-4911 (CST) 8AM-4:30PM.

**Circuit and Chancery Courts**, 801 Locust Rm 15, Conway, AR 72032. 501-450-4911 (CST) 8:00AM-4:30PM. Felony, Civil Actions Over $3,000, Probate.

**Municipal Court**, 1105 Prairie, Conway, AR 72032. 501-450-6112 (CST) Misdemeanor, Eviction, Small Claims.

## Franklin County

**Real Estate Recording**, Franklin County Circuit Clerk, Charleston District, 409 East Main Street, Charleston, AR 72933. 501-965-7332 (CST) 8AM-Noon, 12:30-4:30PM.

**Real Estate Recording**, Franklin County Circuit Clerk, Ozark District, 211 West Commercial, Ozark, AR 72949-3295. 501-667-3818 (CST) 8AM-4:30PM.

**Charleston Circuit and Chancery Courts**, PO Box 387, Charleston, AR 72933. 501-965-7332 (CST) 8:00AM-4:30PM. Felony, Civil Actions Over $3,000, Probate.

**Ozark Circuit and County Courts**, County Courthouse, Ozark, AR 72949. 501-667-3818 (CST) 8:00AM-4:30PM. Felony, Civil Actions Over $3,000, Probate.

**Municipal Court**, PO Box 387, Charleston, AR 72933. 501-965-7455 (CST) 8:00AM-5:00PM. Misdemeanor, Eviction, Small Claims.

## Fulton County

**Real Estate Recording**, Fulton County Circuit Clerk, Court Square Courthouse, Salem, AR 72576. 501-895-3310 (CST) 8AM-4:30PM.

**Circuit and Chancery Courts**, PO Box 485, Salem, AR 72576. 501-895-3310 (CST) 8:00AM-4:30PM. Felony, Civil Actions Over $3,000, Probate.

**Municipal Court**, PO Box 928, Salem, AR 72576. 501-895-4136 (CST) Misdemeanor, Eviction, Small Claims.

## Garland County

**Real Estate Recording**, Garland County Circuit Clerk, Courthouse - Room 207, Quachita and Hawthorn Streets, Hot Springs, AR 71901. 501-622-3630 (CST) 8AM-5PM.

**Circuit and Chancery Courts**, Garland County Courthouse, Hot Springs, AR 71901. 501-622-3630 (CST) 8:00AM-5:00PM. Felony, Civil Actions Over $3,000, Probate.

**Municipal Court**, PO Box 700, Hot Springs, AR 71902. 501-321-6765 (CST) 8:00AM-5:00PM. Misdemeanor, Eviction, Small Claims.

## Grant County

**Real Estate Recording**, Grant County Circuit Clerk, Courthouse, 101 W. Center, Room 106, Sheridan, AR 72150. 501-942-2631 (CST) 8AM-4:30PM.

**Circuit and County Courts**, Grant County Courthouse, Sheridan, AR 72150. 501-942-2631 (CST) 8:00AM-4:30PM. Felony, Civil Actions Over $3,000, Probate.

**Municipal Court**, Courthouse, Sheridan, AR 72150. 501-942-3464 (CST) Misdemeanor, Eviction, Small Claims.

## Greene County

**Real Estate Recording**, Greene County Circuit Clerk, Corner of Court & Third Street, Courthouse, Paragould, AR 72450. 501-239-6330 (CST) 8:30AM-4:30PM.

**Circuit and County Courts**, PO Box 1028, Paragould, AR 72451. 501-239-6330 (CST) 8:30AM-4:30PM. Felony, Civil Actions Over $3,000, Probate.

**Municipal Court**, 221 W Court, Paragould, AR 72450. 501-239-7507 (CST) Misdemeanor, Eviction, Small Claims.

## Hempstead County

**Real Estate Recording**, Hempstead County Circuit Clerk, Fourth & Washington Streets, Courthouse, Hope, AR 71801. 501-777-2384 (CST) 8AM-4PM.

**Circuit and Chancery Courts**, PO Box 1420, Hope, AR 71801. 501-777-2384 (CST) 8:00AM-4:00PM. Felony, Civil Actions Over $3,000, Probate.

**Municipal Court**, PO Box 1420, Hope, AR 71801. 501-777-2525 (CST) Misdemeanor, Eviction, Small Claims.

## Hot Spring County

**Real Estate Recording**, Hot Spring County Circuit Clerk, 200 Locust Street, Courthouse, Malvern, AR 72104. 501-332-2281 (CST) 8AM-4:30PM.

**Circuit and Chancery Courts**, 200 Locust St, PO Box 1200, Malvern, AR 72104. 501-332-2281 (CST) 8:00AM-4:30PM. Felony, Civil Actions Over $3,000, Probate.

**Municipal Court**, 305 Locust, Rm 205, Malvern, AR 72104. 501-332-7604 (CST) 8:00AM-4:30PM. Misdemeanor, Eviction, Small Claims.

## Howard County

**Real Estate Recording**, Howard County Circuit Clerk, 421 North Main Street, Room 7, Nashville, AR 71852. 501-845-7506 (CST) 8AM-4:30PM.

**Circuit and County Courts**, 421 N Main, Rm 7, Nashville, AR 71852. 501-845-7506 (CST) 8:00AM-4:30PM. Felony, Civil Actions Over $3,000, Probate.

**Municipal Court**, 421 N Main, Rm 21, Nashville, AR 71852. 501-845-7522 (CST) 8:00AM-4:30PM. Misdemeanor, Eviction, Small Claims.

## Independence County

**Real Estate Recording**, Independence County Circuit Clerk, 192 Main Street, Batesville, AR 72501. 501-793-8865 (CST) 8AM-4:30PM.

**Circuit and County Courts**, Main and Broad St, Batesville, AR 72501. 501-793-8833 (CST) 8:00AM-4:30PM. Felony, Civil Actions Over $3,000, Probate.

**Municipal Court**, 368 E Main, Batesville, AR 72501. 501-793-8817 (CST) Misdemeanor, Eviction, Small Claims.

## Izard County

**Real Estate Recording**, Izard County Circuit Clerk, Main and Lunen Streets, Courthouse, Melbourne, AR 72556. 501-368-4316 (CST) 8:30AM-4:30PM.

**Circuit and County Courts**, PO Box 95, Melbourne, AR 72556. 501-368-4316 (CST) Felony, Civil Actions Over $3,000, Probate.

**Municipal Court**, PO Box 337, Melbourne, AR 72556. 501-368-4390 (CST) 8:30AM-4:30PM. Misdemeanor, Eviction, Small Claims.

## Jackson County

**Real Estate Recording**, Jackson County Circuit Clerk, Courthouse, Main Street, Newport, AR 72112. 501-523-7423 (CST)

**Circuit and Chancery Courts**, Jackson County Courthouse, Newport, AR 72112. 501-523-7423 (CST) 8:00AM-4:30PM. Felony, Civil Actions Over $3,000, Probate.

**Municipal Court**, PO Box 128, Newport, AR 72112. 501-523-9555 (CST) Misdemeanor, Eviction, Small Claims.

## Jefferson County

**Real Estate Recording**, Jefferson County Circuit Clerk, Main & Barraque, Pine Bluff, AR 71601. 501-541-5309 (CST) 8:30AM-5PM.

**Circuit and Chancery Courts**, PO Box 7433, Pine Bluff, AR 71611. 501-541-5307 (CST) 8:30PM-5:00PM. Felony, Civil Actions Over $3,000, Probate.

**Municipal Court**, 200 E 8th, Pine Bluff, AR 71601. 501-543-1860 (CST) 8:00AM-5:00PM. Misdemeanor, Eviction, Small Claims.

## Johnson County

**Real Estate Recording**, Johnson County Circuit Clerk, Main Street, Courthouse, Clarksville, AR 72830. 501-754-2977 (CST) 8AM-4:30PM.

**Circuit and County Courts**, PO Box 217, Clarksville, AR 72830. 501-754-2977 (CST) 8:00AM-4:30PM. Felony, Civil Actions Over $3,000, Probate.

**Municipal Court**, PO Box 581, Clarksville, AR 72830. 501-754-8533 (CST) 8:00AM-4:30PM. Misdemeanor, Eviction, Small Claims.

## Lafayette County

**Real Estate Recording**, Lafayette County Circuit Clerk, Courthouse Square, Lewisville, AR 71845. 501-921-4878 (CST) 8AM-4:30PM.

**Circuit and Chancery Courts**, PO Box 610, Lewisville, AR 71845. 501-921-4878 (CST) 8:00AM-4:30PM. Felony, Civil Actions Over $3,000, Probate.

**Municipal Court**, PO Box 307, Lewisville, AR 71845. 501-921-5555 (CST) 9:00AM-4:30PM. Misdemeanor, Eviction, Small Claims.

## Lawrence County

**Real Estate Recording**, Lawrence County Circuit Clerk, Main Street, Walnut Ridge, AR 72476. 501-886-1112 (CST) 8AM-4:30PM.

**Circuit and Chancery Courts**, PO Box 581, Walnut Ridge, AR 72476. 501-886-1112 (CST) 8:00AM-4:30PM. Felony, Civil Actions Over $3,000, Probate.

**Municipal Court**, 111 NW 2nd, Walnut Ridge, AR 72476. 501-886-3905 (CST) 8:00AM-4:30PM. Misdemeanor, Eviction, Small Claims.

## Lee County

**Real Estate Recording**, Lee County Circuit Clerk, 15 East Chestnut Street, Courthouse, Marianna, AR 72360. 501-295-7710 (CST) 8:30AM-4:30PM.

**Circuit and Chancery Courts**, Lee County Courthouse, Marianna, AR 72360. 501-295-7710 (CST) 8:30AM-4:30PM. Felony, Civil Actions Over $3,000, Probate.

**Municipal Court**, Police Dept, Marianna, AR 72360. 501-295-3813 (CST) Misdemeanor, Eviction, Small Claims.

## Lincoln County

**Real Estate Recording**, Lincoln County Circuit Clerk, 300 South Drew St, Star City, AR 71667. 501-628-3154 (CST) 8AM-5PM.

**Circuit and County Courts**, Courthouse, 300 S Drew, Star City, AR 71667. 501-628-3154 (CST) 8:00AM-5:00PM. Felony, Civil Actions Over $3,000, Probate.

**Municipal Court**, Lincoln County Courthouse, Star City, AR 71667. 501-628-4904 (CST) 8:00AM-5:00PM. Misdemeanor, Eviction, Small Claims.

## Little River County

**Real Estate Recording**, Little River County Circuit Clerk, 351 North Second, Ashdown, AR 71822. 501-898-7211 (CST) 8:30AM-4:30PM.

**Circuit and County Courts**, PO Box 575, Ashdown, AR 71822. 501-898-7211 (CST) 8:30AM-4:30PM. Felony, Civil Actions Over $3,000, Probate.

**Municipal Court**, Courthouse, Ashdown, AR 71822. 501-898-7230 (CST) 8:30AM-4:30PM. Misdemeanor, Eviction, Small Claims.

## Logan County

**Real Estate Recording**, Logan County Circuit Clerk, Southern District, Courthouse, Booneville, AR 72927. 501-675-2894 (CST) 8AM-Noon, 1-4:30PM.

**Real Estate Recording**, Logan County Circuit Clerk, Northern District, Courthouse, Paris, AR 72855. 501-963-2164 (CST) 8AM-12, 1PM-4:30PM.

**Circuit and County Courts**, Courthouse, Paris, AR 72855. 501-963-2618 (CST) 8:00AM-4:30PM. Felony, Civil Actions Over $3,000, Probate.

**Municipal Court**, Paris Courthouse, Paris, AR 72855. 501-963-3792 (CST) 8:30AM-4:30PM. Misdemeanor, Eviction, Small Claims.

## Lonoke County

**Real Estate Recording**, Lonoke County Circuit Clerk, Courthouse, Lonoke, AR 72086. 501-676-2316 (CST) 8AM-4:30PM.

**Circuit and County Courts**, PO Box 231 Attn: Circuit Clerk, Lonoke, AR 72086. 501-

# Arkansas

676-2316 (CST) 8:00AM-4:30PM. Felony, Civil Actions Over $3,000, Probate.

**Municipal Court**, 203 W Front, Lonoke, AR 72086. 501-676-3585 (CST) 8AM-4:30PM. Misdemeanor, Eviction, Small Claims.

## Madison County

**Real Estate Recording**, Madison County Circuit Clerk, Main Street, Courthouse, Huntsville, AR 72740. 501-738-2215 (CST) 8AM-4:30PM.

**Circuit and County Courts**, PO Box 416, Huntsville, AR 72740. 501-738-2215 (CST) 8:00AM-4:30PM. Felony, Civil Actions Over $3,000, Probate.

**Municipal Court**, PO Box 549, Huntsville, AR 72740. 501-738-2911 (CST) 8:00AM-4:30PM. Misdemeanor, Eviction, Small Claims.

## Marion County

**Real Estate Recording**, Marion County Circuit Clerk, Hwy 62, Courthouse, Yellville, AR 72687. 501-449-6226 (CST) 8AM-4:30PM.

**Circuit and County Courts**, PO Box 385, Yellville, AR 72687. 501-449-6226 (CST) 8:00AM-4:30PM. Felony, Civil Actions Over $3,000, Probate.

**Municipal Court**, Courthouse, Yellville, AR 72687. 501-449-6030 (CST) 8:00AM-4:30PM. Misdemeanor, Eviction, Small Claims.

## Miller County

**Real Estate Recording**, Miller County Circuit Clerk, County Courthouse-Suite 109, 412 Laurel St., Texarkana, AR 75501. 501-774-4501 (CST) 8AM-4:30PM.

**Circuit and County Courts**, 412 Laurel St Rm 109, Texarkana, AR 75502. 501-774-4501 (CST) 8:00AM-4:30PM. Felony, Civil Actions Over $3,000, Probate.

**Municipal Court**, 400 Laurel Suite 101, Texarkana, AR 75501. 501-772-2780 (CST) 8:00AM-4:30PM. Misdemeanor, Eviction, Small Claims.

## Mississippi County

**Real Estate Recording**, Mississippi County Circuit Clerk, Chickasawba District, 2nd & Walnut Street, Blytheville, AR 72315. 501-762-2332 (CST) 9AM-4:30PM.

**Real Estate Recording**, Mississippi County Circuit Clerk, Osceola District, Courthouse, Osceola, AR 72370. 501-563-6471 (CST) 9AM-4:30PM.

**Blytheville Circuit and Chancery Courts**, PO Box 1496, Blytheville, AR 72316. 501-762-2332 (CST) 9:00AM-4:30PM. Felony, Civil Actions Over $3,000, Probate.

**Osceola Circuit and Chancery Courts**, County Courthouse, Osceola, AR 72370. 501-563-2242 (CST) 9:00AM-4:30PM. Felony, Civil Actions Over $3,000, Probate.

**Blytheville Municipal Court**, City Hall, Blytheville, AR 72315. 501-763-7513 (CST) 8:00AM-5:00PM. Misdemeanor, Eviction, Small Claims.

**Osceola Municipal Court**, City Hall, Osceola, AR 72370. 501-563-1303 (CST) Misdemeanor, Eviction, Small Claims.

## Monroe County

**Real Estate Recording**, Monroe County Circuit Clerk, 123 Madison Street, Clarendon, AR 72029. 501-747-3615 (CST) 8AM-4:30PM.

**Circuit and Chancery Courts**, 123 Madison St, Courthouse, Clarendon, AR 72029. 501-747-3615 (CST) 8:00AM-4:30PM. Felony, Civil Actions Over $3,000, Probate.

**Municipal Court**, Courthouse, 270 Madison St, Clarendon, AR 72029. 501-747-5200 (CST) 8:00AM-5:00PM. Misdemeanor, Eviction, Small Claims.

## Montgomery County

**Real Estate Recording**, Montgomery County Circuit Clerk, 101 George Street, Mount Ida, AR 71957. 501-867-3521 (CST) 8AM-4:30PM.

**Circuit and County Courts**, PO Box 377, Courthouse, Mount Ida, AR 71957. 501-867-3521 (CST) Felony, Civil Actions Over $3,000, Probate.

**Municipal Court**, PO Box 558, Mount Ida, AR 71957. 501-867-2221 (CST) 8:00AM-4:30PM M & T, other days hours may vary. Misdemeanor, Eviction, Small Claims.

## Nevada County

**Real Estate Recording**, Nevada County Circuit Clerk, 215 East Second Street, Prescott, AR 71857. 501-887-2511 (CST) 8AM-5PM.

**Circuit and County Courts**, PO Box 552, Prescott, AR 71857. 501-887-2511 (CST) Felony, Civil Actions Over $3,000, Probate.

**Municipal Court**, PO Box 22, Prescott, AR 71857. 501-887-6016 (CST) 8:00AM-5:00PM. Misdemeanor, Eviction, Small Claims.

## Newton County

**Real Estate Recording**, Newton County Circuit Clerk, Courthouse Street, Jasper, AR 72641. 501-446-5125 (CST) 8AM-4:30PM.

**Circuit, Chancery and Probate Courts**, PO Box 410, Jasper, AR 72641. 501-446-5125 (CST) 8:00AM-4:30PM. Felony, Civil Actions Over $3,000, Probate.

**Municipal Court**, PO Box 550, Jasper, AR 72641. 501-446-5335 (CST) 8:00AM-4:30PM M-TH. Misdemeanor, Eviction, Small Claims.

## Ouachita County

**Real Estate Recording**, Ouachita County Circuit Clerk, 145 Jefferson Street, Camden, AR 71701. 501-837-2230 (CST) 8AM-4:30PM.

**Circuit and County Courts**, PO Box 667, Camden, AR 71701. 501-837-2230 (CST) 8:00AM-4:30PM. Felony, Civil Actions Over $3,000, Probate.

**Municipal Court**, 213 Madison St, Camden, AR 71701. 501-836-0331 (CST) 8:00AM-4:30PM. Misdemeanor, Eviction, Small Claims.

## Perry County

**Real Estate Recording**, Perry County Circuit Clerk, Main Street, Courthouse Square, Perryville, AR 72126. 501-889-5126 (CST) 8AM-4:30PM.

**Circuit and Chancery Courts**, PO Box 358, Perryville, AR 72126. 501-889-5126 (CST) 8:00AM-4:30PM. Felony, Civil Actions Over $3,000, Probate.

**Municipal Court**, PO Box 186, Perryville, AR 72126. 501-889-5296 (CST) 8:00AM-4:30PM. Misdemeanor, Eviction, Small Claims.

## Phillips County

**Real Estate Recording**, Phillips County Circuit Clerk, Perry & Cherry Street, Courthouse, Helena, AR 72342. 501-338-5515 (CST) 8AM-4:30PM.

**Circuit and Chancery Court**, Courthouse, 620 Cherry St Suite 206, Helena, AR 72342. 501-338-5515 (CST) 8:00AM-4:30PM. Felony, Civil Actions Over $3,000, Probate.

**Municipal Court**, 226 Perry, Helena, AR 72342. 501-338-6439 (CST) Misdemeanor, Eviction, Small Claims.

## Pike County

**Real Estate Recording**, Pike County Circuit Clerk, Courthouse Square, Murfreesboro, AR 71958. 501-285-2231 (CST) 8AM-4:30PM.

**Circuit and County Courts**, PO Box 219, Murfreesboro, AR 71958. 501-285-2231 (CST) Felony, Civil Actions Over $3,000, Probate.

**Municipal Court**, PO Box 197, Murfreesboro, AR 71958. 501-285-3865 (CST) 9:00AM-4:30PM. Misdemeanor, Eviction, Small Claims.

## Poinsett County

**Real Estate Recording**, Poinsett County Circuit Clerk, 401 Market Street, Courthouse, Harrisburg, AR 72432. 501-578-4420 (CST) 8:30AM-4:30PM.

**Circuit and County Courts**, PO Box 46, Harrisburg, AR 72432. 501-578-2244 (CST) Felony, Civil Actions Over $3,000, Probate.

**Municipal Court**, 202 East St, Harrisburg, AR 72432. 501-578-4110 (CST) 8:00AM-4:30PM. Misdemeanor, Eviction, Small Claims.

## Polk County

**Real Estate Recording**, Polk County Circuit Clerk, 507 Church, Courthouse, Mena, AR 71953. 501-394-8100 (CST) 8AM-4:30PM.

**Circuit and County Courts**, 507 Church St, Mena, AR 71953. 501-394-8100 (CST) 8:00AM-4:30PM. Felony, Civil Actions Over $3,000, Probate.

**Municipal Court**, 507 Church St, Mena, AR 71953. 501-394-3271 (CST) 8:00AM-4:30PM. Misdemeanor, Eviction, Small Claims.

## Pope County

**Real Estate Recording**, Pope County Circuit Clerk, 100 West Main, Room #29, County Courthouse, Russellville, AR 72801. 501-968-7499 (CST) 8:30AM-4:30PM.

**Circuit and Chancery Courts**, 100 W Main, Russellville, AR 72801. 501-968-7499 (CST) 8:30AM-4:30PM. Felony, Civil Actions Over $3,000, Probate.

**Municipal Court**, 205 S Commerce, Russellville, AR 72801. 501-968-1393 (CST)

**County Records**

8:30AM-4:30PM. Misdemeanor, Eviction, Small Claims.

## Prairie County

**Real Estate Recording**, Prairie County Circuit Clerk, Southern District, 200 Court Square, Corner of Prairie & Magnolia, De Valls Bluff, AR 72041. 501-998-2314 (CST) 8AM-Noon, 1-4:30PM.

**Real Estate Recording**, Prairie County Circuit Clerk, Northern District, 200 Court Square, Des Arc, AR 72040. 501-256-4434 (CST) 8AM-4:30PM.

**Circuit and Chancery Court-Southern District**, PO Box 283, De Valls Bluff, AR 72041. 501-998-2314 (CST) 8:00AM-4:30PM. Felony, Civil Actions Over $3,000, Probate.

**Circuit and County Courts-Northern District**, PO Box 1011, Des Arc, AR 72040. 501-256-4434 (CST) Felony, Civil Actions Over $3,000, Probate.

**Municipal Court**, PO Box 389, Des Arc, AR 72040. 501-256-3011 (CST) 8:00AM-5:00PM. Misdemeanor, Eviction, Small Claims.

## Pulaski County

**Real Estate Recording**, Pulaski County Circuit Clerk, Suite 140, 207 West 3rd, Little Rock, AR 72201. 501-340-8433 (CST) 8AM-4:30PM.

**Circuit and County Courts**, Courthouse, Rm 200, Little Rock, AR 72201. 501-340-8431 (CST) 8:30AM-4:30PM. Felony, Civil Actions Over $3,000, Probate.

**Municipal Court**, 3001 W Roosevelt, Little Rock, AR 72204. 501-340-6824 (CST) 8:00AM-4:30PM. Misdemeanor, Eviction, Small Claims.

## Randolph County

**Real Estate Recording**, Randolph County Circuit Clerk, 201 South Marr Street, Courthouse, Pocahontas, AR 72455. 501-892-5522 (CST) 8AM-4:30PM.

**Circuit and Chancery Courts**, County Courthouse 201 S Marr, Pocahontas, AR 72455. 501-892-5522 (CST) 8:00AM-4:30PM. Felony, Civil Actions Over $3,000, Probate.

**Municipal Court**, 410 N Marr, Pocahontas, AR 72455. 501-892-4033 (CST) 7:30AM-4:30PM. Misdemeanor, Eviction, Small Claims.

## Saline County

**Real Estate Recording**, Saline County Circuit Clerk, 200 N. Main St., Courthouse, Benton, AR 72015. 501-776-5615 (CST) 8AM-4:30PM.

**Circuit and County Courts**, PO Box 1560, Benton, AR 72018. 501-776-5615 (CST) 8:00AM-4:30PM. Felony, Civil Actions Over $3,000, Probate.

**Municipal Court**, 1605 Edison Ave, Benton, AR 72015. 501-776-5975 (CST) 8:00AM-4:30PM. Misdemeanor, Eviction, Small Claims.

## Scott County

**Real Estate Recording**, Scott County Circuit Clerk, Main Street, Courthouse, Waldron, AR 72958. 501-637-2642 (CST) 8AM-5PM.

**Circuit and County Courts**, PO Box 464, Waldron, AR 72958. 501-637-2642 (CST) 8:00AM-4:30PM. Felony, Civil Actions Over $3,000, Probate.

**Municipal Court**, PO Box 977, Waldron, AR 72958. 501-637-4694 (CST) 8:00AM-4:30PM. Misdemeanor, Eviction, Small Claims.

## Searcy County

**Real Estate Recording**, Searcy County Circuit Clerk, Courthouse, Town Square, Marshall, AR 72650. 501-448-3807 (CST) 8AM-4:30PM.

**Circuit and Chancery Courts**, PO Box 813, Marshall, AR 72650. 501-448-3807 (CST) 8:00AM-4:30PM. Felony, Civil Actions Over $3,000, Probate.

**Municipal Court**, General Delivery, PO Box 837, Marshall, AR 72650. 501-448-5411 (CST) 9:00AM-5:00AM. Misdemeanor, Eviction, Small Claims.

## Sebastian County

**Real Estate Recording**, Sebastian County Circuit Clerk, Fort Smith District, 35 S. 6th St., Courthouse - 2nd Floor, Fort Smith, AR 72901. 501-782-1046 (CST) 8AM-4:30PM.

**Real Estate Recording**, Sebastian County Circuit Clerk, Southern District, Town Square, Courthouse, Greenwood, AR 72936. 501-996-4175 (CST) 8AM-4:30PM.

**Circuit Court - Greenwood Div**, PO Box 310, County Courthouse, Greenwood, AR 72936. 501-996-4175 (CST) 8:00AM-4:30PM. Felony, Civil Actions Over $3,000.

**Circuit and County Courts**, 35 S 6th St or PO Box 1179, Fort Smith, AR 72902. 501-782-1046 (CST) 8:00AM-4:30PM. Felony, Civil Actions Over $3,000, Probate.

**Municipal Court**, Courthouse, 35 S 6th St, Fort Smith, AR 72901. 501-784-2420 (CST) 8:30AM-5:00PM. Misdemeanor, Eviction, Small Claims.

## Sevier County

**Real Estate Recording**, Sevier County Circuit Clerk, 115 North 3rd Street, De Queen, AR 71832. 501-584-3055 (CST) 8:30AM-4:30PM.

**Circuit and County Court**, 115 N 3rd, Courthouse, De Queen, AR 71832. 501-584-3055 (CST) 8:00AM-4:30PM. Felony, Civil Actions Over $3,000, Probate.

**Municipal Court**, 115 N 3rd, De Queen, AR 71832. 501-584-7311 (CST) 8:00AM-4:30PM. Misdemeanor, Eviction, Small Claims.

## Sharp County

**Real Estate Recording**, Sharp County Circuit Clerk, Highway 167 North, Courthouse, Ash Flat, AR 72513. 501-994-7361 (CST) 8AM-4PM.

**Circuit and County Courts**, PO Box 307, Ash Flat, AR 72513. 501-994-7361 (CST) 8:00AM-4:00PM. Felony, Civil Actions Over $3,000, Probate.

**Municipal Court**, PO Box 2, Ash Flat, AR 72513. 501-994-2745 (CST) 8:00AM-4:00PM. Misdemeanor, Eviction, Small Claims.

## St. Francis County

**Real Estate Recording**, St. Francis County Circuit Clerk, 313 South Izard Street, Forrest City, AR 72335. 501-261-1715 (CST) 8AM-4:30PM.

**Circuit and County Court**, PO Box 1775, Forrest City, AR 72335. 501-261-1715 (CST) 8:00AM-4:30PM. Felony, Civil Actions Over $3,000, Probate.

**Municipal Court**, 313 S Izard, Forrest City, AR 72335. 501-261-1410 (CST) 8:00AM-4:30PM. Misdemeanor, Eviction, Small Claims.

## Stone County

**Real Estate Recording**, Stone County Circuit Clerk, Courthouse, Mountain View, AR 72560. 501-269-3271 (CST) 8AM-4:30PM.

**Circuit and Chancery Courts**, PO Drawer 120, Mountain View, AR 72560. 501-269-3271 (CST) 8:00AM-4:30PM. Felony, Civil Actions Over $3,000, Probate.

**Municipal Court**, PO Box 1284, Mountain View, AR 72560. 501-269-3465 (CST) Misdemeanor, Eviction, Small Claims.

## Union County

**Real Estate Recording**, Union County Circuit Clerk, 101 North Washington, Courthouse - Room 201, El Dorado, AR 71730. 501-864-1940 (CST) 8:30AM-5PM.

**Circuit and Chancery Courts**, PO Box 1626, El Dorado, AR 71730. 501-864-1940 (CST) 8:30AM-5:00PM. Felony, Civil Actions Over $3,000, Probate.

**Municipal Court**, 101 N Washington, Suite 203, El Dorado, AR 71730. 501-864-1950 (CST) 8:30AM-5:00PM. Misdemeanor, Eviction, Small Claims.

## Van Buren County

**Real Estate Recording**, Van Buren County Circuit Clerk, Main Street, Courthouse, Clinton, AR 72031. 501-745-4140 (CST) 8AM-5PM.

**Circuit and County Courts**, PO Box 180, Clinton, AR 72031. 501-745-4140 (CST) 8:00AM-5:00PM. Felony, Civil Actions Over $3,000, Probate.

**Municipal Court**, PO Box 368, Clinton, AR 72031. 501-745-8894 (CST) 9:30AM-4:30PM. Misdemeanor, Eviction, Small Claims.

## Washington County

**Real Estate Recording**, Washington County Circuit Clerk, Courthouse, 280 N. College, Suite 302, Fayetteville, AR 72701. 501-444-1538 (CST) 8AM-4:30PM.

**Circuit and County Courts**, 280 N College, Fayetteville, AR 72701. 501-444-1552 (CST) Felony, Civil Actions Over $3,000, Probate.

**Municipal Court**, 100B W Rock, Fayetteville, AR 72701. 501-587-3596 (CST) Misdemeanor, Eviction, Small Claims.

## White County

**Real Estate Recording**, White County Circuit Clerk, Courthouse, Searcy, AR 72143. 501-279-6203 (CST) 8AM-4:30PM.

# Arkansas

**Circuit and County Courts**, 301 W Arch, Searcy, AR 72143. 501-279-6223 (CST) 8:00AM-4:30PM. Felony, Civil Actions Over $3,000, Probate.

**Municipal Court**, 311 N Gumm, Searcy, AR 72143. 501-268-7622 (CST) 8:30AM-4:30PM. Misdemeanor, Eviction, Small Claims.

## Woodruff County

**Real Estate Recording**, Woodruff County Circuit Clerk, 500 North Third Street, Augusta, AR 72006. 501-347-2391 (CST) 8AM-4PM.

**Circuit and County Courts**, PO Box 492, Augusta, AR 72006. 501-347-2193 (CST) 8:00AM-4:00PM. Felony, Civil Actions Over $3,000, Probate.

**Municipal Court**, PO Box 381, Augusta, AR 72006. 501-347-2790 (CST) 8:30AM-5:00PM. Misdemeanor, Eviction, Small Claims.

## Yell County

**Real Estate Recording**, Yell County Circuit Clerk, Danville District, East 5th & Main, Danville, AR 72833. 501-495-2414 (CST) 8AM-4PM.

**Real Estate Recording**, Yell County Circuit Clerk, Dardanelle District, Union Street, Courthouse, Dardanelle, AR 72834. 501-229-4404 (CST) 8AM-4PM.

**Danville Circuit and County Courts**, PO Box 219, Danville, AR 72833. 501-495-2414 (CST) 8:00AM-4:00PM. Felony, Civil Actions Over $3,000, Probate.

**Dardanelle Circuit and County Courts**, County Courthouse, Dardanelle, AR 72834. 501-229-4404 (CST) 8:00AM-4:00PM. Felony, Civil Actions Over $3,000, Probate.

**Municipal Court**, Courthouse, Dardanelle, AR 72834. 501-229-1389 (CST) 8AM-4PM. Misdemeanor, Eviction, Small Claims.

# California

## Alameda County

**Real Estate Recording**, Alameda County Recorder, 1225 Fallon Street, Courthouse, Room 100, Oakland, CA 94612. 510-272-6363 (PST) 8:30AM-4:30PM.

**Southern Superior Court-Hayward Branch**, 24405 Amador St Rm 108 (PO Box 3038 945, Hayward, CA 94544. 510-670-5060 (PST) 8:30AM-4:30PM. Civil Actions Over $25,000, Probate.

**Northern Superior Court-Civil**, 1225 Fallon St Rm 109, Oakland, CA 94612. 510-272-6799 (PST) 8:30AM-4:30PM. Civil Actions Over $25,000, Probate.

**Eastern Superior Court-Civil**, 5672 Stoneridge Dr 2nd Fl, Pleasanton, CA 94566. 510-551-6886 (PST) 8:30AM-12PM 1PM-4:30PM. Civil Actions Over $25,000, Probate.

**Superior Court-Criminal**, 1225 Fallon St Rm 107, Oakland, CA 94612. 510-272-6777 (PST) 8:30AM-5PM. Felony.

**Alameda Municipal Court**, 2233 Shoreline Dr (PO Box 1470), Alameda, CA 94501. 510-268-7479 (PST) 8AM-4:30PM. Misdemeanor, Civil Actions Under $25,000, Eviction, Small Claims.

**Berkeley-Albany Municipal Court**, 2120 Martin Luther King Jr Way, Berkeley, CA 94704. 510-644-6423 (PST) 8:30AM-4:30PM. Misdemeanor, Civil Actions Under $25,000, Eviction, Small Claims.

**Fremont-Newark-Union City Municipal Court**, 39439 Paseo Padre Pky, Fremont, CA 94538. 510-795-2345 (PST) 8:30AM-5PM. Misdemeanor, Civil Actions Under $25,000, Eviction, Small Claims.

**San Leandro-Hayward Municipal Court**, 24405 Amador St Rm 103 (civil) Rm 104 (, Hayward, CA 94544. 510-670-6432 (PST) 8:30AM-4:30PM. Misdemeanor, Civil Actions Under $25,000, Eviction, Small Claims.

**Oakland Piedmont Municipal Court**, 661 Washington St, Oakland, CA 94607. 510-268-7724 (PST) 8:30AM-4:30PM. Misdemeanor, Civil Actions Under $25,000, Eviction, Small Claims.

**Livermore-Pleasanton-Dublin Municipal Court**, 5672 Stoneridge Dr, Pleasanton, CA 94588-8678. 510-463-7948 (PST) 9AM-4:30PM. Misdemeanor, Civil Actions Under $25,000, Eviction, Small Claims.

## Alpine County

**Real Estate Recording**, Alpine County Treasurer-Tax-Collector-Recorder, Highway 4, Administration Building, Markleeville, CA 96120. 916-694-2286 (PST) 9AM-Noon,1-4PM.

**Superior Court**, Main St (PO Box 158), Markleeville, CA 96120. 916-694-2281 (PST) 8AM-12PM 1PM-5PM. Felony, Civil Actions Over $25,000, Probate.

**Alpine Municipal Court**, Main St Courthouse (Box 515), Markleeville, CA 96120. 916-694-2113 (PST) 8AM-5PM. Misdemeanor, Civil Actions Under $25,000, Eviction, Small Claims.

## Amador County

**Real Estate Recording**, Amador County Recorder, 45 Summit St., Jackson, CA 95642. 209-223-6468 (PST) 8AM-5PM.

**Superior Court**, 108 Court St, Jackson, CA 95642. 209-223-6463 (PST) 8AM-5PM. Felony, Civil Actions Over $25,000, Probate.

**Municipal Court**, 204 Court St, Jackson, CA 95642. 209-223-6358 (PST) 8AM-5PM. Misdemeanor, Civil Actions Under $25,000, Eviction, Small Claims.

## Butte County

**Real Estate Recording**, Butte County Recorder, 25 County Center Drive, Oroville, CA 95965-3375. 916-538-7691 (PST) 9AM-3PM M-Th.

**Superior Court**, 25 County Center Dr, Oroville, CA 95965. 916-538-7551 (PST) 9AM-4PM M-TH (subject to change). Felony, Civil Actions Over $25,000, Probate.

**North Butte County Municipal Court**, 655 Oleander Ave, Chico, CA 95926. 916-891-2702 (PST) 8AM-1PM M-TH. Misdemeanor, Civil Actions Under $25,000, Eviction, Small Claims.

**Gridley Municipal Court**, 239 Sycamore, Gridley, CA 95948. 916-846-5701 (PST) 9AM-12PM 1PM-2PM T-TH. Misdemeanor, Civil Actions Under $25,000, Eviction, Small Claims.

**South Butte County Municipal Court**, 1931 Arlin Rhine Dr, Oroville, CA 95965. 916-538-7727 (PST) 8AM-2PM M-TH (phone hours: 9AM-12PM M-TH). Misdemeanor, Civil Actions Under $25,000, Eviction, Small Claims.

**Paradise Branch-Municipal Court**, 747 Elliot Rd, Paradise, CA 95969. 916-872-6347 (PST) 8AM-1PM M&T, 8AM-12PM W, 8AM-12PM 1PM-5PM TH. Misdemeanor, Civil Actions Under $25,000, Eviction, Small Claims.

## Calaveras County

**Real Estate Recording**, Calaveras County Recorder, Government Center, San Andreas, CA 95249. 209-754-6372 (PST) 8AM-5PM.

**Superior Court**, 891 Mt Ranch Rd, San Andreas, CA 95249. 209-754-6310 (PST) 8AM-5PM. Felony, Civil Actions Over $25,000, Probate.

**Municipal Court**, 891 Mt Ranch Rd, San Andreas, CA 95249. 209-754-6336 (PST) 8AM-4PM. Misdemeanor, Civil Actions Under $25,000, Eviction, Small Claims.

## Colusa County

**Real Estate Recording**, Colusa County Recorder, 546 Jay Street, Colusa, CA 95932. 916-458-0500 (PST) 8:30AM-5PM.

**Superior Court**, 546 Jay St, Colusa, CA 95932. 916-458-0500 (PST) 8:30AM-5PM. Felony, Civil Actions Over $25,000, Probate.

**Colusa Municipal Court**, 532 Oak St, Colusa, CA 95932. 916-458-5149 (PST) 8:30AM-12PM 1PM-5PM. Misdemeanor, Civil Actions Under $25,000, Eviction, Small Claims.

## Contra Costa County

**Real Estate Recording**, Contra Costa County Recorder, 730 Las Juntas, Martinez, CA 94553. 510-646-2360 (PST) 8AM-4PM.

**Superior Court**, 725 Court St Rm 103, Martinez, CA 94553. 510-646-2968 (PST) 8AM-4PM. Felony, Civil Actions Over $25,000, Probate.

**Mt Diablo Municipal Court**, 1950 Parkside Dr, Concord, CA 94519. 510-646-5410 (PST) 9AM-4PM. Misdemeanor, Civil Actions Under $25,000, Eviction, Small Claims.

**Delta Municipal Court**, 45 Civic Ave (PO Box 431), Pittsburg, CA 94565-0431. 510-427-8159 (PST) 8AM-5PM. Misdemeanor, Civil Actions Under $25,000, Eviction, Small Claims.

**Bay Municipal Court**, 100 37th St Rm 185, Richmond, CA 94805. 510-374-3138 (PST) 8AM-4PM. Misdemeanor, Civil Actions Under $25,000, Eviction, Small Claims.

**Walnut Creek-Danville Municipal Court**, 640 Ugnacio Valley Rd (PO Box 5128), Walnut Creek, CA 94596-1128. 510-646-6579 (PST) 8AM-5PM. Misdemeanor, Civil Actions Under $25,000, Eviction, Small Claims.

## Del Norte County

**Real Estate Recording**, Del Norte County Recorder, 457 F Street, Crescent City, CA 95531. 707-464-7216 (PST) 8AM-Noon,1-5PM.

**Superior Court**, 450 "H" St, Crescent City, CA 95531. 707-464-7205 (PST) 8AM-5PM. Felony, Civil Actions Over $25,000, Probate.

**Municipal Court**, 680 5th St, Crescent City, CA 95531. 707-464-7240 (PST) 9AM-12PM 1PM-4:30PM. Misdemeanor, Civil Actions Under $25,000, Eviction, Small Claims.

## El Dorado County

**Real Estate Recording**, El Dorado County Recorder, 360 Fair Lane, Placerville, CA 95667-4197. 916-621-5490 (PST) 8AM-5PM (No recordings after 4PM).

**Placerville Superior Court**, 495 Main St, Placerville, CA 95667. 916-621-6426 (PST) 8AM-4PM. Felony, Civil Actions Over $25,000, Probate.

**South Lake Tahoe Superior Court**, 1354 Johnson Blvd #2, South Lake Tahoe, CA 96151. 916-573-3075 (PST) 8AM-4PM. Felony, Civil Actions Over $25,000, Probate.

**Cameron Park Branch Municipal Court**, 3321 Cameron Park Dr, Cameron Park, CA 95682. 916-621-5867 (PST) 8AM-4PM. Misdemeanor, Civil Actions Under $25,000, Eviction, Small Claims.

**Placerville Municipal Court**, 1319 Broadway, Placerville, CA 95667. 916-621-6453 (PST) 8AM-4PM. Misdemeanor, Civil Actions Under $25,000, Eviction, Small Claims.

**El Dorado Municipal Court**, 1354 Johnson Blvd #1, South Lake Tahoe, CA 96150. 916-573-3045 (PST) 8AM-4PM. Misdemeanor, Civil Actions Under $25,000, Eviction, Small Claims.

**South Lake Tahoe Municipal Court**, 1357 Johnson Blvd, South Lake Tahoe, CA 96151. 916-573-3044 (PST) 8AM-4PM. Misdemeanor, Civil Actions Under $25,000, Eviction, Small Claims.

## Fresno County

**Real Estate Recording**, Fresno County Recorder, 2281 Tulare St., Room 302 / Hall of Records, Fresno, CA 93721. 209-488-3471 (PST) 9AM-4PM.

**Superior Court**, 1100 Van Ness Ave Rm 401 (PO Box 1628-9, Fresno, CA 93721. 209-488-3352 (PST) 8:30AM-4:30PM. Felony, Civil Actions Over $25,000, Probate.

# California

**Clovis Municipal Court**, 1011 5th St, Clovis, CA 93612. 209-299-4964 (PST) 8AM-4PM. Misdemeanor, Civil Actions Under $25,000, Eviction, Small Claims.

**Coalinga Division-Central Valley Municipal Court**, 166 W Elm St, Coalinga, CA 93210. 209-935-2017 (PST) 8AM-12PM 1PM-4PM. Misdemeanor, Civil Actions Under $25,000, Eviction, Small Claims.

**Firebaugh Division-Central Valley Municipal Court**, 1325 "O" St, Firebaugh, CA 93622. 209-659-2011 (PST) 8AM-4:30 M 8AM-4PM T-F. Misdemeanor, Civil Actions Under $25,000, Eviction, Small Claims.

**Fowler/Caruthers Division-Central Valley Municipal Court**, 106 S 6th St (PO Box 400), 2215 W Tahoe, Fowler, Caruthers, CA 93625, 93609. 209-834-3215 (PST) 8AM-4PM. Misdemeanor, Civil Actions Under $25,000, Eviction, Small Claims.

**Consolidated Fresno Municipal Court**, 1100 Van Ness Ave Rm 200, Fresno, CA 93724. 209-488-3453 (PST) 8AM-4PM. Misdemeanor, Civil Actions Under $25,000, Eviction, Small Claims.

**Kerman Division-Central Valley Municipal Court**, 719 S Madera Ave, Kerman, CA 93630. 209-846-7371 (PST) 8AM-4PM M-F (2-4 for phone calls). Misdemeanor, Civil Actions Under $25,000, Eviction, Small Claims.

**Kingsburg Division-Central Valley Municipal Court**, 1380 Draper St, Kingsburg, CA 93631. 209-897-2241 (PST) 8AM-12PM 1PM-4PM M-F (2-4 for phone calls). Misdemeanor, Civil Actions Under $25,000, Eviction, Small Claims.

**Parlier Branch-Central Valley Municipal Court**, 580 Tulare St, Parlier, CA 93648. 209-646-2815 (PST) 8AM-4PM. Misdemeanor, Civil Actions Under $25,000, Eviction, Small Claims.

**Reedley/Dunlap Division-Central Valley Municipal Court**, 815 "G" St, Reedley, CA 93654. 209-638-3114 (PST) 8AM-12PM 1PM-4PM (2-4 for phone calls). Misdemeanor, Civil Actions Under $25,000, Eviction, Small Claims.

**Riverdale Branch-Central Valley Municipal Court**, 3563 Henson (PO Box 595), Riverdale, CA 93656. 209-867-3448 (PST) 8AM-4PM M-F (2-4 phone calls). Misdemeanor, Civil Actions Under $25,000, Eviction, Small Claims.

**Sanger Division-Central Valley Municipal Court**, 619 "N" St, Sanger, CA 93657. 209-875-7158 (PST) 8AM-12PM 1PM-4PM. Misdemeanor, Civil Actions Under $25,000, Eviction, Small Claims.

**Selma Division-Central Valley Municipal Court**, 2117 Selma St, Selma, CA 93662. 209-896-2123 (PST) 8AM-12PM 1 PM-4PM. Misdemeanor, Civil Actions Under $25,000, Eviction, Small Claims.

## Glenn County

**Real Estate Recording**, Glenn County Recorder, 526 West Sycamore Street, Willows, CA 95988. 916-934-6412 (PST) 8AM-5PM.

**Superior Court**, 526 W Sycamore (PO Box 391), Willows, CA 95988. 916-934-6407 (PST) 8AM-5PM. Felony, Civil Actions Over $25,000, Probate.

**Orland Branch-Glenn County Municipal Court**, 821 E South (PO Box 577), Orland, CA 95963. 916-865-1101 (PST) 8AM-12PM 1PM-5PM M-F (window 9AM-12PM 1PM-3PM). Misdemeanor, Civil Actions Under $25,000, Eviction, Small Claims.

**Willows Branch-Glenn County Municipal Court**, 543 W Oak St, Willows, CA 95988. 916-934-6446 (PST) 8AM-12PM 1PM-5PM M-F (phone 9AM-12PM 1PM-3PM). Misdemeanor, Civil Actions Under $25,000, Eviction, Small Claims.

## Humboldt County

**Real Estate Recording**, Humboldt County Recorder, 825 Fifth Street, Room 108, Eureka, CA 95501. 707-445-7593 (PST) 10AM-5PM.

**Superior Court**, 825 5th St Rm 235, Eureka, CA 95501. 707-445-7257 (PST) 8:30AM-12PM 1PM-4PM. Felony, Civil Actions Over $25,000, Probate.

**North Humboldt Division-Municipal Court**, 4605 Valley West Blvd (PO Box 4747), Arcata, CA 95521. 707-822-0342 (PST) 8AM-5PM. Misdemeanor, Civil Actions Under $25,000, Eviction, Small Claims.

**Eureka Division-Municipal Court**, 825 5th St Rm 236, Eureka, CA 95501. 707-445-7431 (PST) 8:30AM-4PM. Misdemeanor, Civil Actions Under $25,000, Eviction, Small Claims.

**Eel River Municipal Court**, 777 9th St, Fortuna, CA 95540. 707-725-5121 (PST) 8AM-5PM. Misdemeanor, Civil Actions Under $25,000, Eviction, Small Claims.

**Gaberville Brancy-Municipal Court**, 483 Conger St, Garberville, CA 95542. 707-923-2141 (PST) 8:30AM-5PM. Misdemeanor, Civil Actions Under $25,000, Eviction, Small Claims.

**Klamath/Trinity Branch-Municipal Court**, PO Box 698, Hoopa, CA 95546. 916-625-4204 (PST) 8:30AM-12PM 1PM-5PM M-TH. Misdemeanor, Civil Actions Under $25,000, Eviction, Small Claims.

## Imperial County

**Real Estate Recording**, Imperial County Recorder, 940 Main Street, Room 206, El Centro, CA 92243. 619-339-4272 (PST) 9AM-4:30PM.

**Superior Court**, 939 W Main St, El Centro, CA 92243. 619-339-4217 (PST) 8AM-4PM. Felony, Civil Actions Over $25,000, Probate.

**Brawley Branch-Municipal Court**, 383 Main St, Brawley, CA 92227. 619-344-0710 (PST) 8AM-4PM. Misdemeanor, Civil Actions Under $25,000, Eviction, Small Claims.

**Calexico Branch-Municipal Court**, 415 4th St, Calexico, CA 92231. 619-357-3726 (PST) 8AM-4PM. Misdemeanor, Civil Actions Under $25,000, Eviction, Small Claims.

**El Centro Branch-Municipal Court**, 939 W Main St, El Centro, CA 92243. 619-339-4256 (PST) 8AM-4PM. Misdemeanor, Civil Actions Under $25,000, Eviction, Small Claims.

**Winterhaven Branch-Municipal Court**, PO Box 1087, Winterhaven, CA 92283. 619-572-0354 (PST) 8AM-4PM. Misdemeanor, Civil Actions Under $25,000, Eviction, Small Claims.

## Inyo County

**Real Estate Recording**, Inyo County Recorder, 168 North Edwards, Independence, CA 93526. 619-878-0222 (PST) 9-Noon,1-5PM.

**Superior Court**, 168 N Edwards St (PO Drawer F), Independence, CA 93526. 619-878-0218 (PST) 9AM-5PM. Felony, Civil Actions Over $25,000, Probate.

**Bishop Branch-Municipal Court**, 301 W Line St, Bishop, CA 93514. 619-872-4971 (PST) 9AM-5PM. Misdemeanor, Civil Actions Under $25,000, Eviction, Small Claims.

**Independence Branch-Municipal Court**, 168 N Edwards St (PO Box 518), Independence, CA 93526. 619-878-0319 (PST) 9AM-12PM 1PM-5PM. Misdemeanor, Civil Actions Under $25,000, Eviction, Small Claims.

## Kern County

**Real Estate Recording**, Kern County Recorder, 1655 Chester Avenue, Hall of Records, Bakersfield, CA 93301. 805-861-2181 (PST) 8AM-4PM; (Recording 8AM-2PM).

**Superior Court**, 1415 Truxtun Ave, Bakersfield, CA 93301. 805-861-2621 (PST) 8AM-5PM. Felony, Civil Actions Over $25,000, Probate.

**Bakersfield Municipal Court**, 1215 Truxtun Ave, Bakersfield, CA 93301. 805-861-2041 (PST) 8AM-5PM. Misdemeanor, Civil Actions Under $25,000, Eviction, Small Claims.

**Delano/McFarland Branch-North Kern Municipal Court**, 1122 Jefferson St, Delano, CA 93215. 805-725-8797 (PST) 8AM-12PM 1PM-4:30PM. Misdemeanor, Civil Actions Under $25,000, Eviction, Small Claims.

**River Branch-East Kern Municipal Court**, 7046 Lake Isabella Blvd, Lake Isabella, CA 93240. 619-379-3636 (PST) 8AM-4PM M-TH 8AM-5PM F. Misdemeanor, Civil Actions Under $25,000, Eviction, Small Claims.

**Arvin/Lamont Branch-South Kern Municipal Court**, 12022 Main St, Lamont, CA 93241. 805-845-3460 (PST) 8AM-5PM. Misdemeanor, Civil Actions Under $25,000, Eviction, Small Claims.

**Mojave Branch-East Kern Municipal Court**, 1773 Hwy 58, Mojave, CA 93501. 805-824-2437 (PST) 8AM-5PM. Misdemeanor, Civil Actions Under $25,000, Eviction, Small Claims.

**East Kern Municipal Court**, 132 E Coso St, Ridgecrest, CA 93555. 619-375-1398 (PST) 8AM-5PM. Misdemeanor, Civil Actions Under $25,000, Eviction, Small Claims.

**Indian Wells Branch-East Kern Municipal Court**, 132 E Coso St, Ridgecrest, CA 93555. 619-375-1397 (PST) 8AM-5PM. Misdemeanor, Civil Actions Under $25,000, Eviction, Small Claims.

**Shafter/Wasco Branch-North Kern Municipal Court**, 325 Central Valley Hwy, Shafter, CA 93263. 805-746-3312 (PST) 8AM-12PM 1PM-4PM. Misdemeanor, Civil Actions Under $25,000, Eviction, Small Claims.

**Maricopa/Taft Branch-Kern Municipal Court**, 311 Lincoln St (PO Bin RB), Taft, CA 93268. 805-763-2401 (PST) 8AM-11AM (Phone). Misdemeanor, Civil Actions Under $25,000, Eviction, Small Claims.

## Kings County

**Real Estate Recording**, Kings County Clerk Recorder, 1400 West Lacey Blvd., Hanford, CA 93230. 209-582-3211 (PST) X2470 8AM-3PM.

**Superior Court**, 1400 W Lacey Blvd, Hanford, CA 93230. 209-582-3211 (PST) 8AM-5PM. Felony, Civil Actions Over $25,000, Probate.

**Avenal Division Municipal Court**, 501 E Kings St, Avenal, CA 93204. 209-386-5225 (PST) 8AM-5PM. Misdemeanor, Civil Actions Under $25,000, Eviction, Small Claims.

**Corcoran Division-Municipal Court**, 1000 Chittenden Ave, Corcoran, CA 93212. 209-992-5193 (PST) 8AM-5PM. Misdemeanor, Civil Actions Under $25,000, Eviction, Small Claims.

**Hanford Division-Municipal Court**, 1400 W Lacey Blvd, Hanford, CA 93230. 209-582-4370 (PST) 8AM-5PM. Misdemeanor, Civil Actions Under $25,000, Eviction, Small Claims.

**Lemoore Division-Municipal Court**, 449 "C" St, PO Box 549, Lemoore, CA 93245. 209-924-7757 (PST) 8AM-5PM. Misdemeanor, Civil Actions Under $25,000, Eviction, Small Claims.

## Lake County

**Real Estate Recording**, Lake County Recorder, 255 North Forbes, Lakeport, CA 95453. 707-263-2293 (PST) 10AM-5PM.

**Superior Court**, 255 N Forbes St, Lakeport, CA 95453. 707-263-2374 (PST) 8AM-5PM. Felony, Civil Actions Over $25,000, Probate.

**South Lake Division-Municipal Court**, PO Box 670, Clearlake, CA 95422. 707-994-8262 (PST) 9AM-12PM 1PM-4PM. Misdemeanor, Civil Actions Under $25,000, Eviction, Small Claims.

**North Lake Division-Municipal Court**, 255 N Forbes St, Lakeport, CA 95453. 707-263-2285 (PST) 8AM-5PM. Misdemeanor, Civil Actions Under $25,000, Eviction, Small Claims.

## Lassen County

**Real Estate Recording**, Lassen County Recorder, Lassen Street, Courthouse, Susanville, CA 96130. 916-251-8234 (PST) Public Hours: 10AM-Noon, 1PM-3PM Phone Hours: 8AM-Noon, 1-5PM.

**Superior Court**, 220 S Lassen St, Susanville, CA 96130. 916-251-8124 (PST) 9AM-12PM 1PM-4PM. Felony, Civil Actions Over $25,000, Probate.

**Lassen Consolidated Municipal Court**, 220 S Lassen St, Susanville, CA 96130. 916-251-8205 (PST) 8AM-5PM M-TH 8AM-12PM F. Misdemeanor, Civil Actions Under $25,000, Eviction, Small Claims.

## Los Angeles County

**Real Estate Recording**, Los Angeles County Recorder, Registrar-Recorder/County Clerk, 12400 E. Imperial Highway, Room 1007, Norwalk, CA 90650. 310-462-2125 (PST) 8AM-5PM.

**Superior Court**, 210 W Temple St Rm M-6 (Certification U, Los Angeles, CA 90012. 213-974-5259 (PST) 9AM-4PM. Felony, Civil Actions Over $25,000, Probate.

**Alhambra Municipal Court**, 150 W Commonwealth Ave, Alhambra, CA 91801. 818-308-5307 (PST) 8AM-4:30PM. Misdemeanor, Civil Actions Under $25,000, Eviction, Small Claims.

**Los Cerritos Municipal Court**, 10025 E Flower St, Bellflower, CA 90706. 310-804-8008 (PST) 8AM-4:30PM. Misdemeanor, Civil Actions Under $25,000, Eviction, Small Claims.

**Beverly Hills Municipal Court**, 9355 Burton Way, Beverly Hills, CA 90210. 310-288-1227 (PST) 8:30AM-4:30PM. Misdemeanor, Civil Actions Under $25,000, Eviction, Small Claims.

**Burbank Municipal Court**, 300 E Olive, Burbank, CA 91502. 818-557-3461 (PST) 8AM-4:30PM. Misdemeanor, Civil Actions Under $25,000, Eviction, Small Claims.

**Calabasas Branch-Malibu Municipal Court**, 5030 N Pkwy Calabasas, Calabasas, CA 91302. 818-222-1896 (PST) 8AM-5PM. Misdemeanor, Civil Actions Under $25,000, Eviction, Small Claims.

**Compton Municipal Court**, 200 W Compton Blvd, Compton, CA 90220. 310-603-7105 (PST) 8AM-4:30PM. Misdemeanor, Civil Actions Under $25,000, Eviction, Small Claims.

**Culver Municipal Court**, 4130 Overland Ave, Culver City, CA 90230. 310-202-3160 (PST) 8:30AM-4:30PM. Misdemeanor, Civil Actions Under $25,000, Eviction, Small Claims.

**Downey Municipal Court**, 7500 E Imperial Hwy, Downey, CA 90242. 310-803-7052 (PST) 8AM-4:30PM T-F 12PM-7:30PM M. Misdemeanor, Civil Actions Under $25,000, Eviction, Small Claims.

**Rio Hondo Municipal Court**, 11234 E Valley Blvd, El Monte, CA 91731. 818-575-4116 (PST) 8:15AM-5:30PM M (Traffic Court Only) 8:15AM-4:30PM T-F. Misdemeanor, Civil Actions Under $25,000, Eviction, Small Claims.

**Glendale Municipal Court**, 600 E Broadway, Glendale, CA 91206. 818-500-3538 (PST) 8:30AM-4:30PM. Misdemeanor, Civil Actions Under $25,000, Eviction, Small Claims.

**Southeast Municipal Court**, 6548 Miles Ave, Huntington Park, CA 90255. 213-586-6365 (PST) 8:30AM-4:30PM. Misdemeanor, Civil Actions Under $25,000, Eviction, Small Claims.

**Inglewood Municipal Court**, 1 Regent St Rm 205, Inglewood, CA 90301. 310-419-5125 (PST) 8AM-4:30PM. Misdemeanor, Civil Actions Under $25,000, Eviction, Small Claims.

**Antelope Municipal Court**, 1040 W Ave J (PO Box 1898 93539), Lancaster, CA 93534. 805-945-6351 (PST) 8AM-4:30PM. Misdemeanor, Civil Actions Under $25,000, Eviction, Small Claims.

**Long Beach Municipal Court**, 415 W Ocean Blvd, Long Beach, CA 90801. 310-491-6234 (PST) 8:30AM-4:30PM. Misdemeanor, Civil Actions Under $25,000, Eviction, Small Claims.

**Metropolitan Branch-Municipal Court**, 1945 S Hill St Rm 101, Los Angeles, CA 90007. 213-744-4001 (PST) 8AM-5PM M-W & F 8AM-7PM TH. Misdemeanor, Eviction.

**Los Angeles Municipal Court-Civil**, 110 N Grand Ave Rm 426, Los Angeles, CA 90012. 213-974-6135 (PST) 8AM-4:30PM. Civil Actions Under $25,000, Eviction, Small Claims.

**Los Angeles Municipal Court-Criminal**, 210 W Temple St Rm 5-111, Los Angeles, CA 90012. 213-974-6151 (PST) 8AM-4:30PM. Misdemeanor.

**East Los Angeles Municipal Court**, 214 S Fetterly Ave, Los Angeles, CA 90022. 213-780-2017 (PST) 8AM-4PM. Misdemeanor, Civil Actions Under $25,000, Eviction, Small Claims.

**West Los Angeles Branch-Municipal Court**, 1633 Purdue Ave, Los Angeles, CA 90025. 310-312-6547 (PST) 8AM-5PM. Misdemeanor, Civil Actions Under $25,000, Eviction, Small Claims.

**Hollywood Branch-Municipal Court**, 5925 Hollywood Blvd Rm 102, Los Angeles, CA 90028. 213-856-5751 (PST) 8:30AM-4:30PM. Misdemeanor, Civil Actions Under $25,000, Eviction, Small Claims.

**Malibu Municipal Court**, 23525 W Civic Center Way, Malibu, CA 90265. 310-317-1312 (PST) 8AM-5PM. Misdemeanor, Civil Actions Under $25,000, Eviction, Small Claims.

**Santa Anita Municipal Court**, 300 W Maple Ave, Monrovia, CA 91016. 818-301-4050 (PST) 8AM-4:30PM. Misdemeanor, Civil Actions Under $25,000, Eviction, Small Claims.

**Pasadena Municipal Court**, 200 N Garfield Ave, Pasadena, CA 91101. 818-356-5449 (PST) 8:30AM-4:30PM. Misdemeanor, Civil Actions Under $25,000, Eviction, Small Claims.

**Pomona Municipal Court**, 350 W Mission Blvd, Pomona, CA 91766. 909-620-3213 (PST) 8AM-12PM 2PM-4PM M-F (civil) 8AM-5PM M-F (criminal). Misdemeanor, Civil Actions Under $25,000, Eviction, Small Claims.

**South Bay Municipal Court-Beach Cities Branch (Redondo Beach Pier**, 117 W Torrance Blvd, Redondo Beach, CA 90277. 310-798-6875 (PST) 8:30AM-4:30PM. Civil Actions Under $25,000, Eviction, Small Claims.

**San Fernando Branch-Municipal Court**, 120 N Maclay, San Fernando, CA 91340. 818-898-2401 (PST) 8:30AM-5PM. Misdemeanor, Civil Actions Under $25,000, Eviction, Small Claims.

**San Pedro Municipal Court**, 505 S Centre St Rm 202, San Pedro, CA 90731. 310-519-6016 (PST) 8AM-4:30PM. Misdemeanor, Civil Actions Under $25,000, Eviction, Small Claims.

**Santa Monica Municipal Court**, 1725 Main St Rm 118, Santa Monica, CA 90401. 310-458-5434 (PST) 8:30AM-4:30PM. Misdemeanor, Civil Actions Under $25,000, Eviction, Small Claims.

**South Gate Branch-Southeast Municipal Court**, 8640 California Ave, South Gate, CA 90280. 213-563-4018 (PST) 8:30AM-4:30PM. Misdemeanor, Civil Actions Under $25,000, Eviction, Small Claims.

**South Bay Municipal Court**, 825 Maple Ave, Torrance, CA 90503-5058. 310-222-6500 (PST) 8:30AM-4:30PM. Misdemeanor, Civil Actions Under $25,000, Eviction, Small Claims.

**Newhall Municipal Court**, 23747 W Valencia Blvd, Valencia, CA 91355. 805-253-7313 (PST) 8:30AM-4:30PM. Misdemeanor, Civil Actions Under $25,000, Eviction, Small Claims.

**Valley Division-Municipal Court**, 14400 Erwin St Mall 2nd Fl, Van Nuys, CA 91401. 818-374-3060 (PST) 8:30AM-4:30PM. Misdemeanor, Civil Actions Under $25,000, Eviction, Small Claims.

**Citrus Municipal Court**, 1427 W Covina Pky, West Covina, CA 91790. 818-813-3236 (PST) 8AM-4:30PM. Misdemeanor, Civil Actions Under $25,000, Eviction, Small Claims.

**Whittier Municipal Court**, 7339 S Painter Ave, Whittier, CA 90602. 310-907-3127 (PST) 12PM-8PM M 8AM-5PM T-F. Misdemeanor, Civil Actions Under $25,000, Eviction, Small Claims.

## Madera County

**Real Estate Recording**, Madera County Recorder, 209 West Yosemite, Madera, CA 93637. 209-675-7724 (PST)

**Superior Court**, 209 W Yosemite Ave, Madera, CA 93637. 209-675-7721 (PST) 8AM-12PM 1PM-4PM. Felony, Civil Actions Over $25,000, Probate.

**Sierra Municipal Court**, 40601 Road 274, Bass Lake, CA 93604. 209-642-3235 (PST) 8AM-5PM. Misdemeanor, Civil Actions Under $25,000, Eviction, Small Claims.

**Madera Municipal Court**, 209 W Yosemite Ave, Madera, CA 93637. 209-675-7734 (PST) 8AM-5PM. Misdemeanor, Civil Actions Under $25,000, Eviction, Small Claims.

**Borden Municipal Court**, 14241 Road 28, Madera, CA 93638. 209-675-7786 (PST) 8AM-5PM. Misdemeanor, Civil Actions Under $25,000, Eviction, Small Claims.

## Marin County

**Real Estate Recording**, Marin County Recorder, Civic Center, Room 290, San Rafael, CA 94903. 415-499-6092 (PST) 8AM-4PM.

**Superior Court**, Civic Center Dr Rm 151 (PO Box E), San Rafael, CA 94913. 415-499-6407 (PST) 8:30AM-4PM. Felony, Civil Actions Over $25,000, Probate.

**Municipal Court**, 3501 Civic Center Dr (PO Box 4988), San Rafael, CA 94903. 415-499-6217 (PST) 8AM-4:30PM. Misdemeanor, Civil Actions Under $25,000, Eviction, Small Claims.

## Mariposa County

**Real Estate Recording**, Mariposa County Recorder, 4982 10th Street, Mariposa, CA 95338. 209-966-5719 (PST) 8AM-5PM (Recording Hours 8AM-3:30PM).

**Superior Court**, 5088 Bullion St (PO Box 28), Mariposa, CA 95338. 209-966-2005 (PST) 8AM-5PM. Felony, Civil Actions Over $25,000, Probate.

**Municipal Court**, 5088 Bullion (PO Box 316), Mariposa, CA 95338. 209-966-5711 (PST) 8AM-5PM. Misdemeanor, Civil Actions Under $25,000, Eviction, Small Claims.

## Mendocino County

**Real Estate Recording**, Mendocino County Recorder, Courthouse Room 6, Ukiah, CA 95482. 707-463-4376 (PST) 8AM-5PM.

**Superior Court**, State & Perkins Sts (PO Box 996), Ukiah, CA 95482. 707-463-4664 (PST) 8AM-5PM M-F 9:15AM-5PM TH. Felony, Civil Actions Over $25,000, Probate.

**Anderson Municipal Court**, 14400 Hwy 128 Veteran Blvd, Boonville, CA 95415. 707-895-3329 (PST) 9AM-1PM 2PM-5PM T-F. Misdemeanor, Civil Actions Under $25,000, Eviction, Small Claims.

**Round Valley Municipal Court**, 76270 Grange St (PO Box 25), Covelo, CA 95428. 707-983-6446 (PST) 8AM-5PM. Misdemeanor, Civil Actions Under $25,000, Eviction, Small Claims.

**Ten Mile Municipal Court**, 700 S Franklin St, Fort Bragg, CA 95437. 707-964-3192 (PST) 8AM-12PM 2PM-4PM. Misdemeanor, Civil Actions Under $25,000, Eviction, Small Claims.

**Long Valley Municipal Court**, PO Box 157, Leggett, CA 95585. 707-925-6460 (PST) 8AM-5PM M-F (closed every 2nd Monday of month). Misdemeanor, Civil Actions Under $25,000, Eviction, Small Claims.

**Arena Municipal Court**, 24000 S Hwy 1 (PO Box 153), Point Arena, CA 95468. 707-882-2116 (PST) 9AM-12PM 1PM-4PM M-TH. Misdemeanor, Civil Actions Under $25,000, Eviction, Small Claims.

**Mt Sanhedrin Municipal Court**, Perkins & State Sts Rm 112 (PO Box 337), Ukiah, CA 95482. 707-463-4486 (PST) 8AM-4PM. Misdemeanor, Civil Actions Under $25,000, Eviction, Small Claims.

**Willits Branch-Municipal Court**, 125 E Commercial St Rm 100, Willits, CA 95490. 707-459-7800 (PST) 8AM-12PM 1PM-4PM. Misdemeanor, Civil Actions Under $25,000, Eviction, Small Claims.

## Merced County

**Real Estate Recording**, Merced County Recorder, 2222 M Street, Merced, CA 95340. 209-385-7627 (PST) 8AM-4:30PM.

**Superior Court**, 2222 "M" St, Merced, CA 95340. 209-385-7531 (PST) 8AM-4PM. Felony, Civil Actions Over $25,000, Probate.

**Dos Palos Branch-Municipal Court**, 1554 Golden Gate Ave, Dos Palos, CA 93620. 209-826-6500 (PST) 8AM-4PM. Misdemeanor, Civil Actions Under $25,000, Eviction, Small Claims.

**Gustine Branch-Municipal Court**, 682 3rd Ave, Gustine, CA 95322. 209-826-6500 (PST) 8AM-4PM. Misdemeanor, Civil Actions Under $25,000, Eviction, Small Claims.

**Los Banos Branch-Municipal Court**, 445 "I" St, Los Banos, CA 93635. 209-826-6500 (PST) 8AM-4PM. Misdemeanor, Civil Actions Under $25,000, Eviction, Small Claims.

**A, B, C & D Divisions-Municipal Court**, 670 W 22nd St, Merced, CA 95340. 209-385-7337 (PST) 8AM-5PM M-F (civil/sc) 12PM-4PM M-F (criminal). Misdemeanor, Civil Actions Under $25,000, Eviction, Small Claims.

## Modoc County

**Real Estate Recording**, Modoc County Recorder, 204 Court Street, Room 107, Alturas, CA 96101. 916-233-6205 (PST) 8:30AM-5PM.

**Superior Court**, 204 Court St (PO Box 131), Alturas, CA 96101. 916-233-6222 (PST) 8:30AM-12PM 1PM-5PM. Felony, Civil Actions Over $25,000, Probate.

**Municipal Court**, 205 S East St, Alturas, CA 96101. 916-233-6516 (PST) 8:30AM-12PM 1PM-5PM. Misdemeanor, Civil Actions Under $25,000, Eviction, Small Claims.

## Mono County

**Real Estate Recording**, Mono County Recorder, Main Street, Courthouse, Bridgeport, CA 93517. 619-932-5240 (PST) 9AM-5PM.

**Superior Court**, PO Box 537, Bridgeport, CA 93517. 619-932-5239 (PST) 8AM-5PM. Felony, Civil Actions Over $25,000, Probate.

**Bridgeport Municipal Court**, PO Box 494 Courthouse Main St, Bridgeport, CA 93517. 619-932-5203 (PST) 9AM-5PM. Misdemeanor, Civil Actions Under $25,000, Eviction, Small Claims.

**Mammoth Municipal Court**, PO Box 1037 Sierra Ctr Old Mammoth Rd, Mammoth Lakes, CA 93546. 619-924-5444 (PST) 9AM-5PM. Misdemeanor, Civil Actions Under $25,000, Eviction, Small Claims.

## Monterey County

**Real Estate Recording**, Monterey County Recorder, 240 Church Street, Room 305, Salinas, CA 93902. 408-755-5041 (PST) 8AM-5PM.

**Monterey Branch-Superior Court**, 1200 Aguajito Rd, Monterey, CA 93940. 408-647-7730 (PST) 8AM-4PM. Felony, Civil Actions Over $25,000, Probate.

**Superior Court**, 240 Church St Rm 318 PO Box 1819, Salinas, CA 93902. 408-755-5030 (PST) 8AM-4PM. Felony, Civil Actions Over $25,000, Probate.

**King City Division-Municipal Court**, 250 Franciscan Way PO Box 467, King City, CA 93930. 408-385-8339 (PST) 7:30AM-4PM. Misdemeanor, Civil Actions Under $25,000, Eviction, Small Claims.

**Monterey Division-Municipal Court**, 1200 Aguajito Rd PO Box 751, Monterey, CA 93940. 408-647-7750 (PST) 8AM-4PM. Misdemeanor, Civil Actions Under $25,000, Eviction, Small Claims.

**Salinas Division-Municipal Court**, 240 Church St PO Box 1051, Salinas, CA 93902. 408-755-5332 (PST) 7:30AM-4PM. Misdemeanor, Civil Actions Under $25,000, Eviction, Small Claims.

## Napa County

**Real Estate Recording**, Napa County Recorder, 900 Coombs Street, Room 116, Napa, CA 94559. 707-253-4247 (PST) 8AM-3PM.

**Superior Court**, 825 Brown St Rm 125, Napa, CA 94559. 707-253-4481 (PST) 8AM-5PM. Civil Actions Over $25,000, Probate.

**Municipal Court**, 825 Brown St (PO Box 880), Napa, CA 94559. 707-253-4481 (PST) 8AM-5PM. Felony, Misdemeanor, Civil Actions Under $25,000, Eviction, Small Claims.

## Nevada County

**Real Estate Recording**, Nevada County Recorder, 950 Maidu Avenue, Nevada City, CA 95959. 916-265-1221 (PST) 9AM-4PM.

**Superior Court**, 201 Church St (PO Box 6126), Nevada City, CA 95959-6126. 916-265-1293 (PST) 9AM-4PM. Felony, Civil Actions Over $25,000, Probate.

**Nevada City Division-Municipal Court**, 201 Church St #7 PO Box 158, Nevada City, CA 95959. 916-265-1318 (PST) 8AM-5PM. Misdemeanor, Civil Actions Under $25,000, Eviction, Small Claims.

**Truckee Division-Municipal Court**, 10075 Levon Ave #301, Truckee, CA 96161. 916-582-7837 (PST) 8AM-5PM. Misdemeanor, Civil Actions Under $25,000, Eviction, Small Claims.

## Orange County

**Real Estate Recording**, Orange County Recorder, 12 Civic Center Plaza, Room 120, Santa Ana, CA 92701. 714-834-2500 (PST) 8AM-4PM.

**South Court Annex**, 23141 Moulton Pkwy 2nd Fl, Laguna Hills, CA 92653-1206. 714-472-6964 (PST) 8AM-4PM. Misdemeanor, Civil Actions Under $25,000, Eviction, Small Claims.

**Superior Court-Civil**, 700 Civic Center Dr W, Santa Ana, CA 92702. 714-834-2208 (PST) 9AM-5PM. Civil Actions Over $25,000.

**Superior Court-Criminal**, 700 Civic Center Dr W (PO Box 838), Santa Ana, CA 92702. 714-834-2266 (PST) 9AM-5PM. Felony.

**North Orange County Municipal Court**, 1275 N Berkeley Ave (PO Box 5000), Fullerton, CA 92635-0500. 714-773-4415 (PST) 7:30AM-5PM. Misdemeanor, Civil Actions Under $25,000, Eviction, Small Claims.

**South Orange Municipal Court**, 30143 Crown Valley Pky, Laguna Niguel, CA 92677. 714-249-5056 (PST) 8AM-4PM. Misdemeanor, Civil Actions Under $25,000, Eviction, Small Claims.

**Harbor Municipal Court**, 4601 Jamboree Road #104, Newport Beach, CA 92660-2595. 714-476-4765 (PST) 8AM-5PM. Misdemeanor, Civil Actions Under $25,000, Eviction, Small Claims.

**Central Orange Municipal Court**, 700 Civic Ctr Dr W (PO Box 1138, 92702), Santa Ana, CA 92701. 714-834-3580 (PST) 8AM-4PM. Misdemeanor, Civil Actions Under $25,000, Eviction, Small Claims.

**Central Orange Municipal Court**, PO Box 1138, Santa Ana, CA 92702. 714-834-3575

(PST) 8AM-4:30PM. Misdemeanor, Civil Actions Under $25,000, Eviction, Small Claims.
**West Orange Municipal Court**, 8141 13th St, Westminster, CA 92683. 714-896-7191 (PST) 8AM-5PM. Misdemeanor, Civil Actions Under $25,000, Eviction, Small Claims.
**Probate Court**, 341 The City Dr, PO Box 14171, Orange, CA 92613. 714-935-6061 (PST) 9AM-5PM. Probate.

## Placer County

**Real Estate Recording**, Placer County Recorder, 11960 Heritage Oaks Place, Suite 15, Auburn, CA 95603. 916-889-7983 (PST) 8AM-5PM (Recording Hours 8AM-4PM).
**Superior Court**, 101 Maple St, Auburn, CA 95603. 916-889-6550 (PST) 8AM-3PM. Felony, Civil Actions Over $25,000, Probate.
**Auburn Municipal Court-Dept 1 (Dept 3 in Auburn - T & TH only)**, 11546 "B" Ave, Auburn, CA 95603. 916-889-7407 (PST) 8AM-4PM. Misdemeanor, Civil Actions Under $25,000, Eviction, Small Claims.
**Colfax Municipal Court-Dept 4**, 10 Culver St (PO Box 735), Colfax, CA 95713. 916-346-8721 (PST) 8AM-4PM. Misdemeanor, Civil Actions Under $25,000, Eviction, Small Claims.
**Foresthill Municipal Court-Dept 4**, 24580 Main St (PO Box 267), Foresthill, CA 95631. 916-367-2302 (PST) 8:30AM-12PM 1PM-4PM Mondays only. Misdemeanor, Civil Actions Under $25,000, Eviction, Small Claims.
**Lincoln Municipal Court-Dept 4**, 453 G St, Lincoln, CA 95648. 916-645-8955 (PST) 8AM-12PM 12:30PM-4PM M & F only. Misdemeanor, Civil Actions Under $25,000, Eviction, Small Claims.
**Loomis Municipal Court-Dept 4**, 3877 Shawn Way (PO Box 44), Loomis, CA 95650. 916-652-7212 (PST) 8AM-4PM. Misdemeanor, Civil Actions Under $25,000, Eviction, Small Claims.
**Roseville Municipal Court-Dept 2 (Dept 3 M, W & F only)**, 300 Taylor St, Roseville, CA 95678. 916-784-6401 (PST) 8AM-4PM. Misdemeanor, Civil Actions Under $25,000, Eviction, Small Claims.
**Tahoe Municipal Court**, PO Box 5669, Tahoe City, CA 96145. 916-581-6337 (PST) 8AM-5PM. Misdemeanor, Civil Actions Under $25,000, Eviction, Small Claims.

## Plumas County

**Real Estate Recording**, Plumas County Recorder, 520 Main Street, Quincy, CA 95971. 916-283-6218 (PST) 8AM-5PM.
**Superior Court**, 520 W Main St (PO Box 10207), Quincy, CA 95971. 916-283-6305 (PST) 8AM-5PM. Felony, Civil Actions Over $25,000, Probate.
**Municipal Court**, 1st & Willow Way (PO Box 722), Chester, CA 96020. 916-258-2646 (PST) 9AM-1PM M-TH. Misdemeanor, Civil Actions Under $25,000, Eviction, Small Claims.
**Municipal Court**, Cresant St (PO Box 706), Greenville, CA 95947. 916-284-7213 (PST) 9AM-1PM M-TH. Misdemeanor, Civil Actions Under $25,000, Eviction, Small Claims.
**Municipal Court**, 161 Nevada St (PO Box 1054), Portola, CA 96122. 916-832-4286 (PST) 9AM-3PM M & W. Misdemeanor, Civil Actions Under $25,000, Eviction, Small Claims.
**Municipal Court**, PO Box 10628, Quincy, CA 95971. 916-283-6232 (PST) 8AM-5PM M-TH 8AM-4PM F. Misdemeanor, Civil Actions Under $25,000, Eviction, Small Claims.

## Riverside County

**Real Estate Recording**, Riverside County Recorder, 4080 Lemon Street, Room 102, Riverside, CA 92501. 909-275-1900 (PST) 8AM-4:30PM (Recording Hours 8AM-2PM) M-Th.
**Superior Court**, 4050 Main St, Riverside, CA 92501. 909-275-1431 (PST) 8AM-5PM. Felony, Civil Actions Over $25,000, Probate.
**Banning Division-Municipal Court**, 155 E Hayes St, Banning, CA 92220. 909-922-7155 (PST) 8AM-4PM. Misdemeanor, Civil Actions Under $25,000, Eviction, Small Claims.
**Blythe Division-Desert Municipal Court**, 260 N Spring St, Blythe, CA 92225. 619-922-8128 (PST) 8AM-5PM. Misdemeanor, Civil Actions Under $25,000, Eviction, Small Claims.
**Corona Branch-Municipal Court**, 505 S Buena Vista Rm 201, Corona, CA 91720. 909-272-5620 (PST) 8AM-5PM. Misdemeanor, Civil Actions Under $25,000, Eviction, Small Claims.
**Hemet Division-Municipal Court**, 880 N State St, Hemet, CA 92543. 909-766-2321 (PST) 7:30AM-4:30PM. Misdemeanor, Civil Actions Under $25,000, Eviction, Small Claims.
**Indio Consolidated Division-Desert Municipal Court**, 46209 Oasis St, Indio, CA 92201. 619-863-8208 (PST) 8AM-5PM. Misdemeanor, Civil Actions Under $25,000, Eviction, Small Claims.
**Lake Elsinore Branch-Three Lakes Division-Municipal Court**, 117 S Langstaff, Lake Elsinore, CA 92530. 909-674-3161 (PST) 7:30AM-4PM. Misdemeanor, Civil Actions Under $25,000, Eviction, Small Claims.
**Moreno Branch-Consolated Municipal Court**, 13800 Heacock Ave Ste D201, Moreno Valley, CA 92553-3338. 909-697-4504 (PST) 7:30AM-5PM T-TH. Misdemeanor, Civil Actions Under $25,000, Eviction, Small Claims.
**Palm Springs Division-Desert Municipal Court**, PO Box 2728, Palm Springs, CA 92262. 619-778-2175 (PST) 8AM-5PM. Misdemeanor, Civil Actions Under $25,000, Eviction, Small Claims.
**Western Riverside-Municipal Court**, 3547 10th St, Riverside, CA 92501. 909-697-4504 (PST) 8AM-5PM. Misdemeanor, Civil Actions Under $25,000, Eviction, Small Claims.

## Sacramento County

**Real Estate Recording**, Sacramento County Clerk and Recorder, 600 8th Street, Sacramento, CA 95814. 916-440-6334 (PST) 8AM-4PM.
**Superior Court**, 720 9th St Rm 611, Sacramento, CA 95814. 916-440-5711 (PST) 8AM-4:30PM. Felony, Civil Actions Over $25,000, Probate.
**Sacramento Municipal Court**, 720 9th St, Sacramento, CA 95814. 916-440-5522 (PST) 8AM-5PM (Superior), 8AM-4:30PM (Municipal). Misdemeanor, Civil Actions Under $25,000, Eviction, Small Claims.

## San Benito County

**Real Estate Recording**, San Benito County Recorder, 440 Fifth Street, Room 206, Hollister, CA 95023. 408-637-3786 (PST) 9AM-4PM Recording hours; 8AM-5PM Office hours.
**Superior Court**, Courthouse, 440 5th St Rm 206, Hollister, CA 95023. 408-637-3786 (PST) 8AM-5PM. Felony, Civil Actions Over $25,000, Probate.
**Municipal Court**, 440 5th St Rm 105 (civil) Rm 103 (traff, Hollister, CA 95023. 408-637-3741 (PST) 8AM-4PM. Misdemeanor, Civil Actions Under $25,000, Eviction, Small Claims.

## San Bernardino County

**Real Estate Recording**, San Bernardino County Recorder, 222 W. Hospitality Ln., 1st Floor, San Bernardino, CA 92415-0022. 909-387-8306 (PST) 8AM-5PM.
**Superior Court**, 351 N Arrowhead, San Bernardino, CA 92415. 909-387-3922 (PST) 8AM-4PM. Felony, Civil Actions Over $25,000, Probate.
**Barstow Division-Municipal Court**, 285 E Mountain View Ave, Barstow, CA 92311. 619-256-4755 (PST) 8AM-4PM. Misdemeanor, Civil Actions Under $25,000, Eviction, Small Claims.
**Bear Valley Municipal Court**, 477 Summit Blvd PO Box 2806, Big Bear Lake, CA 92315. 886-0151 (PST) 8:30AM-4PM. Misdemeanor, Civil Actions Under $25,000, Eviction, Small Claims.
**Chino Division-Municipal Court**, 13260 Central Ave, Chino, CA 91710. 909-590-5266 (PST) 8AM-4PM. Misdemeanor, Civil Actions Under $25,000, Eviction, Small Claims.
**Valley Division-Municipal Court**, 17780 Arrow Blvd, Fontana, CA 92335. 909-884-5766 (PST) 8AM-4PM. Misdemeanor, Civil Actions Under $25,000, Eviction, Small Claims.
**Morongo Basin Division-Municipal Court**, 6527 White Feather Rd PO Box 6602, Joshua Tree, CA 92252. 619-366-4107 (PST) 8AM-4PM. Misdemeanor, Civil Actions Under $25,000, Eviction, Small Claims.
**Needles-Calzona Municipal Court**, 1111 Bailey Ave, Needles, CA 92363. 619-326-9248 (PST) 8AM-4PM. Misdemeanor, Civil Actions Under $25,000, Eviction, Small Claims.
**West Valley Division-Municipal Court**, 8303 Haven Ave, Rancho Cucamonga, CA 91730. 909-885-5532 (PST) 8AM-4PM. Misdemeanor, Civil Actions Under $25,000, Eviction, Small Claims.
**East Division-Municipal Court**, 216 Brookside Ave, Redlands, CA 92374. 909-798-8542 (PST) 8AM-4PM. Misdemeanor, Civil Actions Under $25,000, Eviction, Small Claims.
**Central Division-Municipal Court**, 351 N Arrowhead, San Bernardino, CA 92415. 909-387-3922 (PST) 8AM-4PM. Misdemeanor, Civil Actions Under $25,000, Eviction, Small Claims.
**Trona Municipal Court**, 13207 Market St PO Box 534, Trona, CA 93592. 619-372-5276 (PST) 8AM-5PM. Misdemeanor, Civil Actions Under $25,000, Eviction, Small Claims.
**Crest Forest Municipal Court**, 26010 State Hwy Box 394, Twin Peaks, CA 92391. 909-336-0677 (PST) 8AM-4PM. Misdemeanor, Civil Actions Under $25,000, Eviction, Small Claims.
**Victorville Division-Municipal Court**, 14455 Civic Dr, Victorville, CA 92392. 619-243-8672 (PST) 8AM-4PM. Misdemeanor, Civil Actions Under $25,000, Eviction, Small Claims.

## San Diego County

**Real Estate Recording**, San Diego Recorder/County Clerk, 1600 Pacific Highway, Room 260, San Diego, CA 92101. 619-237-0502 (PST) 8AM-4PM.

**California**

**South Bay Branch-Superior Court**, 500-C 3rd Ave, Chula Vista, CA 91910. 619-691-4439 (PST) 8AM-4:30PM M-F (civil) 7:30AM-4PM M-F (criminal). Felony, Civil Actions Over $25,000, Probate.

**El Cajon Branch-Superior Court**, 250 E Main St, El Cajon, CA 92020. 619-441-4622 (PST) 8AM-4:30PM. Felony, Civil Actions Over $25,000, Probate.

**Superior Court**, PO Box 2724, San Diego, CA 92112-4104. 619-531-3140 (PST) 9AM-4:30PM. Felony, Civil Actions Over $25,000, Probate.

**Superior Court-El Cajon**, PO Box 128, San Diego, CA 92112-4104. 619-531-3151 (PST) 9AM-4:30PM. Felony, Civil Actions Over $25,000, Probate.

**North County Branch-Superior Court**, 325 S Melrose Dr, Vista, CA 92083. 619-940-4442 (PST) 9AM-4:30PM. Felony, Civil Actions Over $25,000, Probate.

**South Bay Municipal Court**, 500C 3rd Ave, Chula Vista, CA 91910. 619-691-4639 (PST) 8AM-5PM. Misdemeanor, Civil Actions Under $25,000, Eviction, Small Claims.

**El Cajon Municipal Court**, 250 E Main St, El Cajon, CA 92020. 619-441-4461 (PST) 8AM-4PM M-F 8AM-6PM W. Misdemeanor, Civil Actions Under $25,000, Eviction, Small Claims.

**Escondido Branch-Municipal Court**, 600 E Valley Pky, Escondido, CA 92025. 619-740-4021 (PST) 8AM-4:30PM. Misdemeanor, Civil Actions Under $25,000, Eviction, Small Claims.

**Ramona Branch-Municipal Court**, 1428 Montecito Rd, Ramona, CA 92065. 619-441-4244 (PST) 8AM-4PM. Misdemeanor, Civil Actions Under $25,000, Eviction, Small Claims.

**San Diego Municipal Court**, 1409 4th Ave (civil) 220 W Broadway Rm, San Diego, CA 92101. 619-687-2180 (PST) 8AM-4:30PM. Misdemeanor, Civil Actions Under $25,000, Eviction, Small Claims.

**San Marcos-Municipal Court**, 338 Via Vera Cruz, San Marcos, CA 92069-2693. 619-940-2888 (PST) 8AM-4PM. Misdemeanor, Civil Actions Under $25,000, Eviction, Small Claims.

**North County Municipal Court**, 325 S Melrose Dr Ste 120, Vista, CA 92083. 619-940-4644 (PST) 8AM-3PM M & F, 8AM-4PM T-TH. Misdemeanor, Civil Actions Under $25,000, Eviction, Small Claims.

**San Marcos/Criminal-North County Municipal Court**, 325 S Melrose Dr #120, Vista, CA 92083. 619-940-2888 (PST) 8AM-3PM M & F 8AM-4PM T-TH. Misdemeanor.

## San Francisco County

**Real Estate Recording**, San Francisco County Recorder, 400 Van Ness Avenue, Room 167, San Francisco, CA 94102-4698. 415-554-4176 (PST) 8AM-4PM.

**Superior Court**, 400 Van Ness Ave-Rm 317 (civil) 850 Brya, San Francisco, CA 94102/94103. 415-554 4171 (PST) 8AM-4PM. Felony, Civil Actions Over $25,000, Probate.

**Municipal Court**, City Hall Rm 300, San Francisco, CA 94102. 415-554-4532 (PST) 8AM-4:30PM. Civil Actions Under $25,000, Eviction, Small Claims.

**Municipal Court**, 850 Bryant St Rm 201, San Francisco, CA 94103. 415-553-9395 (PST) 8AM-4:30PM. Misdemeanor, Civil Actions Under $25,000, Eviction, Small Claims.

## San Joaquin County

**Real Estate Recording**, San Joaquin County Recorder, 24 South Hunter Street, Room 304, Stockton, CA 95202. 209-468-3939 (PST) 7AM-4PM.

**Superior Court**, 222 E Weber St Rm 303, Stockton, CA 95202. 209-468-2355 (PST) 8:15AM-4:30PM. Felony, Civil Actions Over $25,000, Probate.

**Lodi Municipal Court**, 315 W Elm St (civil/sc) 230 W Elm St (cr, Lodi, CA 95240. 209-333-6756 (PST) 8AM-4PM. Misdemeanor, Civil Actions Under $25,000, Eviction, Small Claims.

**Manteca-Ripon-Escalon-Tracy (Eastern Dept) Municipal Court**, 315 E Center St, Manteca, CA 95336. 209-239-9188 (PST) 8AM-4PM. Misdemeanor, Civil Actions Under $25,000, Eviction, Small Claims.

**Stockton Municipal Court**, 222 E Weber Ave, Stockton, CA 95202. 209-468-2933 (PST) 8AM-4PM M-F (office) 8AM-3PM M-F (phones). Misdemeanor, Civil Actions Under $25,000, Eviction, Small Claims.

**Tracy (Western Dept) Municipal Court**, 475 E 10th St, Tracy, CA 95376. 209-831-5902 (PST) 8AM-4PM. Misdemeanor, Civil Actions Under $25,000, Eviction, Small Claims.

## San Luis Obispo County

**Real Estate Recording**, San Luis Obispo County Recorder, 1000 Monterey Street, County Government Center - Room 102, San Luis Obispo, CA 93408. 805-781-5080 (PST) 8AM-5PM.

**Superior Court**, Government Center Rm 385, San Luis Obispo, CA 93408. 805-781-5241 (PST) 8AM-5PM. Felony, Civil Actions Over $25,000, Probate.

**Grover Beach Branch-Municipal Court**, 214 S 16th St, Grover Beach, CA 93433-2299. 805-473-7077 (PST) 9AM-4PM. Misdemeanor, Civil Actions Under $25,000, Eviction, Small Claims.

**Pasp Robles Branch-Municipal Court**, 549 10th St, Paso Robles, CA 93446-2593. 805-237-3079 (PST) 9AM-4PM. Misdemeanor, Civil Actions Under $25,000, Eviction, Small Claims.

**Municipal Court**, County Government Center, 1050 Monterey, San Luis Obispo, CA 93408-2510. 805-781-5678 (PST) 9AM-4PM. Misdemeanor, Civil Actions Under $25,000, Eviction, Small Claims.

## San Mateo County

**Real Estate Recording**, San Mateo County Recorder, 401 Marshall Street, 6th Floor, Redwood City, CA 94063-1636. 415-363-4713 (PST) 8AM-5PM.

**Superior Court**, 401 Marshall St, Redwood City, CA 94063. 415-363-4766 (PST) 8:30AM-4PM. Felony, Civil Actions Over $25,000, Probate.

**Southern Branch-Municipal Court**, 750 Middlefield Rd, Redwood City, CA 94063. 415-363-4302 (PST) 8AM-4PM. Misdemeanor, Civil Actions Under $25,000, Eviction, Small Claims.

**Central Branch-Municipal Court**, 800 N Humboldt St, San Mateo, CA 94401. 415-573-2611 (PST) 8AM-4PM. Civil Actions Under $25,000, Eviction, Small Claims.

**Northern Branch-Municipal Court**, 1050 Mission Rd, South San Francisco, CA 94080. 415-573-2611 (PST) 8AM-4PM. Misdemeanor.

## Santa Barbara County

**Real Estate Recording**, Santa Barbara County Recorder, 1100 Anacapa Street, Santa Barbara, CA 93101. 805-568-2250 (PST) 8AM-4:30PM.

**Superior Court**, Box 21107, Santa Barbara, CA 93121. 805-568-2237 (PST) 8AM-4:45PM. Felony, Civil Actions Over $25,000, Probate.

**Lompoc Municipal Court**, 115 Civic Center Plz, Lompoc, CA 93436. 805-737-7793 (PST) 8:30AM-4:55PM. Misdemeanor, Civil Actions Under $25,000, Eviction, Small Claims.

**Santa Barbara Municipal Court**, 118 E Figueroa St, Santa Barbara, CA 93101. 805-568-2740 (PST) 7:45AM-4PM. Misdemeanor, Civil Actions Under $25,000, Eviction, Small Claims.

**Santa Maria Municipal Court**, 312-M East Cook St, Santa Maria, CA 93454. 805-346-7566 (PST) 7:30AM-4:30PM. Misdemeanor, Civil Actions Under $25,000, Eviction, Small Claims.

**Solvang Municipal Court**, 1745 Mission Dr (PO Box 228), Solvang, CA 93464. 805-686-5040 (PST) 8AM-4PM. Misdemeanor, Civil Actions Under $25,000, Eviction, Small Claims.

## Santa Clara County

**Real Estate Recording**, Santa Clara County Recorder, County Government Center, East Wing, 70 West Hedding St., San Jose, CA 95110. 408-299-2481 (PST) 8AM-4:30PM.

**Superior Court**, 115 Terraine St, San Jose, CA 95113. 408-229-2974 (PST) 8AM-4:30PM. Felony, Civil Actions Over $25,000, Probate.

**Gilroy Facility-Municipal Court**, 7350 Rosanna St, Gilroy, CA 95020. 408-842-6299 (PST) 8:30AM-4PM. Misdemeanor, Civil Actions Under $25,000, Eviction, Small Claims.

**Los Gatos Facility-Municipal Court**, 14205 Capri Dr, Los Gatos, CA 95030. 408-866-8331 (PST) 8:30AM-4PM. Misdemeanor, Civil Actions Under $25,000, Eviction, Small Claims.

**Palo Alto Facility-Municipal Court**, 270 Grant Ave, Palo Alto, CA 94306. 415-324-0391 (PST) 8:30AM-4PM. Misdemeanor, Civil Actions Under $25,000, Eviction, Small Claims.

**San Jose Facility-Municipal Court**, 200 W Hedding St, San Jose, CA 95110. 408-299-2281 (PST) 8AM-5PM. Misdemeanor, Civil Actions Under $25,000, Eviction, Small Claims.

**Santa Clara Facility-Municipal Court**, 1095 Homestead Rd, Santa Clara, CA 95050. 408-244-2027 (PST) 8:30AM-4PM. Misdemeanor, Civil Actions Under $25,000, Eviction, Small Claims.

**Sunnyvale Facility-Municipal Court**, 605 W El Camino Real, Sunnyvale, CA 94087. 408-739-1502 (PST) 8:30AM-4PM. Misdemeanor, Civil Actions Under $25,000, Eviction, Small Claims.

## Santa Cruz County

**Real Estate Recording**, Santa Cruz County Recorder, 701 Ocean Street, Room 230, Santa Cruz, CA 95060. 408-454-2800 (PST) 8AM-4PM.

**Superior Court**, 701 Ocean St Rm 110, Santa Cruz, CA 95060. 408-454-2020 (PST) 8AM-4PM. Felony, Civil Actions Over $25,000, Probate.

**Municipal Court-Dept B, C, D, E, F, G**, 701 Ocean St Rm 120, Santa Cruz, CA 95060. 408-454-2190 (PST) 8AM-3PM. Misdemeanor, Civil Actions Under $25,000, Eviction, Small Claims.

**Municipal Court-Dept A**, 1430 Freedom Blvd, Watsonville, CA 95076. 408-763-8060 (PST)

8AM-4PM. Misdemeanor, Civil Actions Under $25,000, Eviction, Small Claims.

## Shasta County

**Real Estate Recording**, Shasta County Recorder, Courthouse, Room 102, Redding, CA 96001. 916-225-5671 (PST)

**Superior Court**, 1500 Court St Rm 205, Redding, CA 96001. 916-225-5631 (PST) 9AM-4PM. Felony, Civil Actions Over $25,000, Probate.

**Anderson Branch-Municipal Court**, 1925 W Howard St, Anderson, CA 96007. 916-335-3571 (PST) 9AM-4PM. Misdemeanor, Civil Actions Under $25,000, Eviction, Small Claims.

**Burney Branch-Municipal Court**, 20509 Shasta St, Burney, CA 96013. 916-335-3571 (PST) 9AM-4PM. Misdemeanor, Civil Actions Under $25,000, Eviction, Small Claims.

**Redding Branch-Municipal Court**, 1500 Court St, Redding, CA 96001. 916-225-5703 (PST) 9AM-4PM. Misdemeanor, Civil Actions Under $25,000, Eviction, Small Claims.

## Sierra County

**Real Estate Recording**, Sierra County Recorder, Courthouse Square, Downieville, CA 95936. 916-289-3295 (PST) 9-Noon,1-4PM.

**Superior Court**, PO Box 95 Courthouse Square, Downieville, CA 95936. 916-289-3698 (PST) 8AM-5PM. Felony, Civil Actions Over $25,000, Probate.

**Municipal Court**, PO Box 401 Courthouse Square, Downieville, CA 95936. 916-289-3215 (PST) 8AM-5PM. Misdemeanor, Civil Actions Under $25,000, Eviction, Small Claims.

## Siskiyou County

**Real Estate Recording**, Siskiyou County Recorder, 311 Fourth Street, Yreka, CA 96097. 916-842-8065 (PST) 8AM-4PM.

**Superior Court**, 311 4th St PO Box 338, Yreka, CA 96097. 916-842-8084 (PST) 8AM-5PM. Felony, Civil Actions Over $25,000, Probate.

**Dorris-Tulelake Municipal Court**, PO Box 828 (Dorris) PO Box 873 (Tulelake, Dorris/Tulelake, CA 96023/96134. 916-397-3161 (PST) 8AM-5PM. Misdemeanor, Civil Actions Under $25,000, Eviction, Small Claims.

**Western Municipal Court**, 311 4th St Rm 5 PO Box 1034, Yreka, CA 96097. 916-842-8180 (PST) 8AM-4PM. Misdemeanor, Civil Actions Under $25,000, Eviction, Small Claims.

## Solano County

**Real Estate Recording**, Solano County Recorder, 580 Texas Street, Old Courthouse, Fairfield, CA 94533. 707-421-6290 (PST) 8AM-4PM; 8AM-3:30PM Recording hours.

**Superior Court**, 600 Union Ave, Fairfield, CA 94533. 707-421-6479 (PST) 8AM-4PM. Felony, Civil Actions Over $25,000, Probate.

**Northern Solano Municipal Court**, 530 Union Ave #200, Fairfield, CA 94533. 707-421-7435 (PST) 8:15AM-4PM. Misdemeanor, Civil Actions Under $25,000, Eviction, Small Claims.

**Vallejo-Benicia Municipal Court**, 321 Tuolumne St, Vallejo, CA 94590. 707-553-5346 (PST) 8AM-4PM. Misdemeanor, Civil Actions Under $25,000, Eviction, Small Claims.

## Sonoma County

**Real Estate Recording**, Sonoma County Recorder, 585 Fiscal Avenue, Santa Rosa, CA 95403. 707-527-2651 (PST) 8AM-4:30PM.

**Superior Court**, PO Box 11187, Santa Rosa, CA 95406. 707-527-2100 (PST) 8AM-4PM. Felony, Civil Actions Over $25,000, Probate.

**Municipal Court**, 600 Administration Dr Rm 107J (civil), Santa Rosa, CA 95403. 707-527-1100 (PST) 8AM-4PM. Misdemeanor, Civil Actions Under $25,000, Eviction, Small Claims.

## Stanislaus County

**Real Estate Recording**, Stanislaus County Recorder, 912 11th Street, Modesto, CA 95354. 209-558-6310 (PST) 8AM-Noon,1-4PM.

**Superior Court**, 800 11th St Rm 222 PO Box 1098, Modesto, CA 95353. 209-525-6416 (PST) 8AM-3PM. Felony, Civil Actions Over $25,000, Probate.

**Ceres Branch-Municipal Court**, 2744 2nd St, Ceres, CA 95307. 209-525-6511 (PST) 8AM-3PM. Misdemeanor, Civil Actions Under $25,000, Eviction, Small Claims.

**Modesto Division-Municipal Court**, 1100 "I" St PO Box 828, Modesto, CA 95353. 209-558-6000 (PST) 8AM-3PM. Misdemeanor, Civil Actions Under $25,000, Eviction, Small Claims.

**Turlock Division-Municipal Court**, 300 Starr Ave, Turlock, CA 95380. 209-632-3941 (PST) 8AM-3PM M-TH 8AM-12PM F. Misdemeanor, Civil Actions Under $25,000, Eviction, Small Claims.

## Sutter County

**Real Estate Recording**, Sutter County Recorder, 433 Second Street, Yuba City, CA 95991. 916-741-7134 (PST) 8AM-5PM.

**Consolidated Superior and Municipal Court**, 463 2nd St (civil) 446 2nd St (criminal, Yuba City, CA 95991. 916-741-7352 (PST) 8AM-5PM. Felony, Misdemeanor, Civil, Eviction, Small Claims, Probate.

## Tehama County

**Real Estate Recording**, Tehama County Recorder, 633 Washington Street, Red Bluff, CA 96080. 916-527-3350 (PST) 8AM-3PM.

**Superior Court**, PO Box 310, Red Bluff, CA 96080. 916-527-6441 (PST) 9AM-4PM. Felony, Civil Actions Over $25,000, Probate.

**Corning (Southern) Municipal Court**, 720 Hoag St, Corning, CA 96021. 916-824-4601 (PST) 8AM-4PM. Misdemeanor, Civil Actions Under $25,000, Eviction, Small Claims.

**Red Bluff(Northern) Municipal Court**, 445 Pine St PO Box 1170, Red Bluff, CA 96080. 916-527-7364 (PST) 8AM-4PM. Misdemeanor, Civil Actions Under $25,000, Eviction, Small Claims.

## Trinity County

**Real Estate Recording**, Trinity County Recorder, 101 Court Street, Courthouse, Weaverville, CA 96093. 916-623-1215 (PST) 10AM-Noon, 1-4PM.

**Consolidated Superior and Municipal Court**, 101 Court St PO Box 1258, Weaverville, CA 96093. 916-623-1208 (PST) 8AM-4PM. Felony, Misdemeanor, Civil, Eviction, Small Claims, Probate.

## Tulare County

**Real Estate Recording**, Tulare County Recorder, County Civic Center, Room 203, Visalia, CA 93291-4593. 209-733-6377 (PST) 8AM-5PM; (Recording hours 8AM-3PM).

**Superior Court**, Courthouse Rm 201, Visalia, CA 93291. 209-733-6374 (PST) 8AM-5PM. Felony, Civil Actions Over $25,000, Probate.

**Dinuba Municipal Court**, 920 S College, Dinuba, CA 93618. 209-591-5815 (PST) 8AM-4PM. Misdemeanor, Civil Actions Under $25,000, Eviction, Small Claims.

**Central Division (Exeter-Farmersville Branch) Municipal Court**, 125 S "B" St, Exeter, CA 93221. 209-564-3576 (PST) 8:30AM-11:30PM. Misdemeanor, Civil Actions Under $25,000, Eviction, Small Claims.

**Porterville Municipal Court**, 87 E Morton Ave, Porterville, CA 93257. 209-782-4710 (PST) 8AM-4PM. Misdemeanor, Civil Actions Under $25,000, Eviction, Small Claims.

**Tulare/Pixley Division-Municipal Court**, 425 E Kern St PO Box 1136, Tulare, CA 93275. 209-685-2556 (PST) 8AM-4PM. Misdemeanor, Civil Actions Under $25,000, Eviction, Small Claims.

**Visalia Municipal Court**, County Civic Center Rm 124, Visalia, CA 93291. 209-733-6198 (PST) 8AM-4PM. Misdemeanor, Civil Actions Under $25,000, Eviction, Small Claims.

## Tuolumne County

**Real Estate Recording**, Tuolumne County Recorder, 2 South Green Street, County Administration Center, Sonora, CA 95370. 209-533-5531 (PST) 8AM-Noon; 1PM-4PM.

**Superior Court**, 2 S Green St, Sonora, CA 95370. 209-533-5555 (PST) 8AM-4PM. Felony, Civil Actions Over $25,000, Probate.

**West Municipal Court**, 18250 Main St PO Box 535, Jamestown, CA 95327. 209-984-5661 (PST) 8AM-5PM. Misdemeanor, Civil Actions Under $25,000, Eviction, Small Claims.

**Central Municipal Court**, 9 N Washington St, Sonora, CA 95370. 209-533-5671 (PST) 8AM-3PM. Misdemeanor, Civil Actions Under $25,000, Eviction, Small Claims.

## Ventura County

**Real Estate Recording**, Ventura County Recorder, 800 South Victoria Avenue, Ventura, CA 93009. 805-654-2292 (PST) 8AM-5:30PM M-Th.

**Combined Superior and Municipal Court**, 800 S Victoria Ave PO Box 6489, Ventura, CA 93006. 805-654-2965 (PST) 8AM-5PM. Felony, Misdemeanor, Civil, Eviction, Small Claims, Probate.

## Yolo County

**Real Estate Recording**, Yolo County Recorder, 625 Court Street, Room 105, Woodland, CA 95695. 916-666-8130 (PST) 8AM-4PM.

**Combined Superior and Municipal Court**, 725 Court St Rm 103, Woodland, CA 95695. 916-666-8050 (PST) 8AM-3PM. Felony, Misdemeanor, Civil, Eviction, Small Claims, Probate.

## Yuba County

**Real Estate Recording**, Yuba County Recorder, 935 14th Street, Marysville, CA 95901.

916-741-6547 (PST) 8:30AM-4:30PM M-Th; Noon-3PM F (Recordings only).

**Superior Court**, 938 14th St, Marysville, CA 95901. 916-741-6247 (PST) 8:30AM-4:15PM. Felony, Civil Actions Over $25,000, Probate.

**Municipal Court**, 215 5th St, Marysville, CA 95901. 916-741-6351 (PST) 8:30AM-5PM. Misdemeanor, Civil Actions Under $25,000, Eviction, Small Claims.

**County Records**

# Colorado

## Adams County

**Real Estate Recording**, Adams County Clerk and Recorder, 450 South 4th Avenue, Administrative Building, Brighton, CO 80601-3197. 303-654-6020 (MST) 8AM-4:30PM.

**17th District Court**, 1931 E Bridge St, Brighton, CO 80601. 303-659-1161 (MST) 8AM-5PM. Felony, Civil Actions Over $10,000, Probate.

**County Court**, 1931 E Bridge St, Brighton, CO 80601. 303-654-3300 (MST) 8AM-5PM. Misdemeanor, Civil Actions Under $10,000, Eviction, Small Claims.

## Alamosa County

**Real Estate Recording**, Alamosa County Clerk and Recorder, 402 Edison Street, Alamosa, CO 81101. 719-589-6681 (MST) 8AM-4:30PM.

**12th District Court**, 702 4th St, Alamosa, CO 81101. 719-589-4996 (MST) 8AM-4PM. Felony, Civil Actions Over $10,000, Probate.

**County Court**, 4th & San Jaun, Alamosa, CO 81101. 719-589-6213 (MST) 8AM-4PM. Misdemeanor, Civil Actions Under $10,000, Eviction, Small Claims.

## Arapahoe County

**Real Estate Recording**, Arapahoe County Clerk and Recorder, 5334 South Prince Street, Littleton, CO 80166. 303-795-4520 (MST) 8AM-4:30PM.

**18th Judicial District Court**, 7325 S Potomac, Englewood, CO 80112. 303-649-6355 (MST) 8AM-5PM. Felony, Civil Actions Over $10,000, Probate.

**Aurora County Court Division B**, 15400 E 14th Pl, Aurora, CO 80011. 303-363-8004 (MST) 8AM-4:30PM. Misdemeanor, Civil Actions Under $10,000, Eviction, Small Claims.

**Littleton County Court Division A**, 5606 S Court Pl, Littleton, CO 80120. 303-730-0358 (MST) 8AM-4PM. Misdemeanor, Civil Actions Under $10,000, Eviction, Small Claims.

## Archuleta County

**Real Estate Recording**, Archuleta County Clerk and Recorder, 449 San Juan Street, Pagosa Springs, CO 81147. 303-264-5633 (MST) 8AM-4PM.

**6th District & County Court**, PO Box 148, Pagosa Springs, CO 81147. 303-264-2400 (MST) 8AM-5PM. Felony, Misdemeanor, Civil, Eviction, Small Claims, Probate.

## Baca County

**Real Estate Recording**, Baca County Clerk and Recorder, 741 Main Street, Courthouse, Springfield, CO 81073. 719-523-4372 (MST) 8:30AM-4:30PM.

**15th District & County Court**, 741 Main St, Springfield, CO 81073. 719-523-4555 (MST) 8AM-5PM. Felony, Misdemeanor, Civil, Eviction, Small Claims, Probate.

## Bent County

**Real Estate Recording**, Bent County Clerk and Recorder, 725 Carson, Courthouse, Las Animas, CO 81054. 719-456-2009 (MST) 8AM-5PM.

**16th District & County Court**, 7th & Bent, Las Animas, CO 81054. 719-456-1353 (MST) 8AM-5PM. Felony, Misdemeanor, Civil, Eviction, Small Claims, Probate.

## Boulder County

**Real Estate Recording**, Boulder County Clerk and Recorder, 2020 13th Street, Courthouse - 2nd Floor, Boulder, CO 80302. 303-441-3515 (MST) 8AM-4:30PM.

**20th District & County Court**, PO Box 4249, Boulder, CO 80306. 303-441-3750 (MST) 8AM-4:30PM. Felony, Misdemeanor, Civil, Eviction, Small Claims, Probate.

## Chaffee County

**Real Estate Recording**, Chaffee County Clerk and Recorder, 104 Crestone Ave., Salida, CO 81201. 719-539-6913 (MST) 8AM-4PM Recording; 8AM-5PM Researching).

**11th District Court**, PO Box 279, Salida, CO 81201. 719-539-2561 (MST) 8AM-5PM. Felony, Civil Actions Over $10,000, Probate.

**County Court**, PO Box 279, Salida, CO 81201. 719-539-6031 (MST) 8AM-5PM. Misdemeanor, Civil Actions Under $10,000, Eviction, Small Claims.

## Cheyenne County

**Real Estate Recording**, Cheyenne County Clerk and Recorder, 51 South 1st Street, Cheyenne Wells, CO 80810. 719-767-5685 (MST) 8AM-4PM.

**15th District & County Court**, PO Box 696, Cheyenne Wells, CO 80810. 719-767-5649 (MST) 8AM-4:30PM. Felony, Misdemeanor, Civil, Eviction, Small Claims, Probate.

## Clear Creek County

**Real Estate Recording**, Clear Creek County Clerk and Recorder, 405 Argentine, Courthouse, Georgetown, CO 80444. 303-569-3251 (MST) X239 8:30AM-4:30PM.

**5th District & County Court**, PO Box 367, Georgetown, CO 80444. 303-569-3273 (MST) 8AM-5PM. Felony, Misdemeanor, Civil, Eviction, Small Claims, Probate.

## Conejos County

**Real Estate Recording**, Conejos County Clerk and Recorder, 6683 County Road 13, Conejos, CO 81129. 719-376-5422 (MST) 8AM-4:30PM.

**12th District & County Court**, PO Box 128, Conejos, CO 81129. 719-376-5466 (MST) 8AM-5PM. Felony, Misdemeanor, Civil, Eviction, Small Claims, Probate.

## Costilla County

**Real Estate Recording**, Costilla County Clerk and Recorder, 354 Main Street, San Luis, CO 81152. 719-672-3301 (MST)

**12th District & County Court**, PO Box 301, San Luis, CO 81152. 719-672-3681 (MST) 8AM-4PM Closed from 12PM-1PM. Felony, Misdemeanor, Civil, Eviction, Small Claims, Probate.

## Crowley County

**Real Estate Recording**, Crowley County Clerk and Recorder, 6th & Main, Ordway, CO 81063-1092. 719-267-4643 (MST) 8AM-4PM.

**16th District & County Court**, 6th & Main, Ordway, CO 81063. 719-267-4468 (MST) 8AM-4:30PM. Felony, Misdemeanor, Civil, Eviction, Small Claims, Probate.

## Custer County

**Real Estate Recording**, Custer County Clerk and Recorder, 205 South 6th Street, Westcliffe, CO 81252. 719-783-2441 (MST) 8AM-4PM.

**11th District & County Court**, PO Box 60, Westcliffe, CO 81252. 719-783-2274 (MST) 9AM-2PM. Felony, Misdemeanor, Civil, Eviction, Small Claims, Probate.

## Delta County

**Real Estate Recording**, Delta County Clerk and Recorder, 501 Palmer Street, Suite 211, Delta, CO 81416. 303-874-2150 (MST) 8:30AM-4:30PM.

**7th District & County Court**, 501 Palmer St Rm 338, Delta, CO 81416. 303-874-4416 (MST) 8:30AM-4:30PM. Felony, Misdemeanor, Civil, Eviction, Small Claims, Probate.

## Denver County

**Real Estate Recording**, Denver County Clerk and Recorder, 1437 Bannock Street, # 200, Denver, CO 80202. 303-640-7290 (MST) 8AM-4:30PM.

**2nd District Court**, 1437 Bannock Rm 426, Denver, CO 80202. 303-575-2419 (MST) 8AM-5PM. Felony, Civil Actions Over $10,000.

**County Court**, 1515 Cleveland Pl 4th Floor, Denver, CO 80202. 303-640-5161 (MST) 8AM-5PM. Misdemeanor, Civil Actions Under $10,000, Eviction, Small Claims.

**Probate Court**, 1437 Bannock, Rm 230, Denver, CO 80202. 303-640-2327 (MST) 8AM-5PM. Probate.

## Dolores County

**Real Estate Recording**, Dolores County Clerk and Recorder, 409 North Main Street, Dove Creek, CO 81324. 303-677-2381 (MST) 8:30AM-4:30PM.

**22nd District & County Court**, PO Box 511, Dove Creek, CO 81324. 303-677-2258 (MST) 8AM-5PM. Felony, Misdemeanor, Civil, Eviction, Small Claims, Probate.

## Douglas County

**Real Estate Recording**, Douglas County Clerk and Recorder, 301 Wilcox Street, Castle Rock, CO 80104. 303-660-7446 (MST) 8AM-4:30PM.

**18th District & County**, 355 S Wilcox, Castle Rock, CO 80104-1918. 303-660-6804 (MST) 8AM-4PM. Felony, Misdemeanor, Civil, Eviction, Small Claims, Probate.

## Eagle County

**Real Estate Recording**, Eagle County Clerk and Recorder, 500 Broadway, Eagle, CO 81631. 303-328-8710 (MST) 8AM-5PM.

**5th District & County Court**, PO Box 597, Eagle, CO 81631. 303-328-6373 (MST) 8AM-5PM. Felony, Misdemeanor, Civil, Eviction, Small Claims, Probate.

# Colorado

## El Paso County

**Real Estate Recording**, El Paso County Clerk and Recorder, 200 South Cascade, Colorado Springs, CO 80903. 719-520-6200 (MST) 8:30AM-4:30PM.

**4th District Court**, 20 E Vermijo Rm 105, Colorado Springs, CO 80903. 719-630-2837 (MST) 8:30AM-4PM. Felony, Civil Actions Over $10,000, Probate.

**County Court**, 20 E Vermijo, Rm 101, Colorado Springs, CO 80903. 719-630-2813 (MST) 8:30AM-4PM. Misdemeanor, Civil Actions Under $10,000, Eviction, Small Claims.

## Elbert County

**Real Estate Recording**, Elbert County Clerk and Recorder, 215 Comanche Street, Kiowa, CO 80117. 303-621-2341 (MST) 8AM-4:30PM.

**18th District & County Court**, PO Box 232, Kiowa, CO 80117. 303-621-2131 (MST) 8AM-5PM. Felony, Misdemeanor, Civil, Eviction, Small Claims, Probate.

## Fremont County

**Real Estate Recording**, Fremont County Clerk and Recorder, 615 Macon Avenue, Room 100, Canon City, CO 81212-3311. 719-275-1522 (MST) 8:30AM-4:30PM.

**11th District & County Court**, 615 Macon Rm 204, Canon City, CO 81212. 719-275-7522 (MST) 8AM-4PM. Felony, Misdemeanor, Civil, Eviction, Small Claims, Probate.

## Garfield County

**Real Estate Recording**, Garfield County Clerk and Recorder, 109 8th Street, Suite 200, Glenwood Springs, CO 80601. 303-945-2377 (MST) 8:30AM-5PM.

**9th District & County Court**, 109 8th St #104, Glenwood Springs, CO 81601. 303-945-5075 (MST) 8AM-5PM. Felony, Misdemeanor, Civil, Eviction, Small Claims, Probate.

**County Court-Rifle**, 110 E 18th St, Rifle, CO 81650. 303-625-5100 (MST) 8AM-5PM. Misdemeanor, Civil Actions Under $10,000, Eviction, Small Claims.

## Gilpin County

**Real Estate Recording**, Gilpin County Clerk and Recorder, 203 Eureka Street, Central City, CO 80427. 303-582-5321 (MST) 8AM-4:30PM.

**1st District & County Court**, PO Box 426, Central City, CO 80427. 303-582-5323 (MST) 8AM-5PM. Felony, Misdemeanor, Civil, Eviction, Small Claims, Probate.

## Grand County

**Real Estate Recording**, Grand County Clerk and Recorder, 308 Byers Avenue, Hot Sulphur Springs, CO 80451. 303-725-3347 (MST) 8:30AM-5PM.

**14th District & County Court**, PO Box 192, Hot Sulphur Springs, CO 80451. 303-725-3357 (MST) 8AM-5PM. Felony, Misdemeanor, Civil, Eviction, Small Claims, Probate.

## Gunnison County

**Real Estate Recording**, Gunnison County Clerk and Recorder, 200 East Virginia Avenue, Courthouse, Gunnison, CO 81230. 970-641-1516 (MST) 8AM-5PM.

**7th District & County Court**, 200 E Virginia Ave, Gunnison, CO 81230. 970-641-3500 (MST) 8:30AM-4:30PM. Felony, Misdemeanor, Civil, Eviction, Small Claims, Probate.

## Hinsdale County

**Real Estate Recording**, Hinsdale County Clerk and Recorder, 317 Henson Street, Lake City, CO 81235. 303-944-2228 (MST) 8AM-4PM.

**7th District & County Court**, PO Box 245, Lake City, CO 81235. 303-944-2227 (MST) 8:30-12:00PM MWF (Jun-Aug) 8:30-12:00 TF (Sept-May). Felony, Misdemeanor, Civil, Eviction, Small Claims, Probate.

## Huerfano County

**Real Estate Recording**, Huerfano County Clerk and Recorder, 400 Main Street, Courthouse, Walsenburg, CO 81089. 719-738-2380 (MST) 8AM-4PM.

**3rd District & County Court**, 401 Main St, Walsenburg, CO 81089. 719-738-1040 (MST) 8AM-4PM. Felony, Misdemeanor, Civil, Eviction, Small Claims, Probate.

## Jackson County

**Real Estate Recording**, Jackson County Clerk and Recorder, 396 LaFever Street, Walden, CO 80480. 303-723-4334 (MST) 8AM-5PM.

**8th District & County Court**, PO Box 308, Walden, CO 80480. 303-723-4363 (MST) 9AM-1PM. Felony, Misdemeanor, Civil, Eviction, Small Claims, Probate.

## Jefferson County

**Real Estate Recording**, Jefferson County Clerk and Recorder, 100 Jefferson County Parkway, Golden, CO 80419-2530. 303-271-8188 (MST) 7:30AM-5:30PM.

**1st District & County Court**, 1701 Arapahoe, Golden, CO 80401-6199. 303-271-6267 (MST) 8AM-5PM. Felony, Misdemeanor, Civil, Eviction, Small Claims, Probate.

## Kiowa County

**Real Estate Recording**, Kiowa County Clerk and Recorder, 1305 Goff Street, Eads, CO 81036. 719-438-5421 (MST) 8AM-4:30PM.

**15th District & County Court**, PO Box 353, Eads, CO 81036. 719-438-5558 (MST) 8AM-5PM. Felony, Misdemeanor, Civil, Eviction, Small Claims, Probate.

## Kit Carson County

**Real Estate Recording**, Kit Carson County Clerk and Recorder, 251 16th Street, Suite 203, Burlington, CO 80807. 719-346-8638 (MST) 8AM-4PM.

**13th District & County Court**, PO Box 547, Burlington, CO 80807. 719-346-5524 (MST) 8:30AM-5PM. Felony, Misdemeanor, Civil, Eviction, Small Claims, Probate.

## La Plata County

**Real Estate Recording**, La Plata County Clerk and Recorder, Courthouse, Room 134, 1060 E. 2nd Ave., Durango, CO 81301. 303-382-6281 (MST) 8AM-5PM.

**6th District**, PO Box 3340, Durango, CO 81302-3340. 303-247-2304 (MST) 8AM-4PM. Felony, Civil Actions Over $10,000, Probate.

**County Court**, PO Box 759, Durango, CO 81302. 303-247-2004 (MST) 8AM-4PM. Misdemeanor, Civil Actions Under $10,000, Eviction, Small Claims.

## Lake County

**Real Estate Recording**, Lake County Clerk and Recorder, 505 Harrison Avenue, Leadville, CO 80461. 719-486-1413 (MST) 9AM-5PM.

**5th District & County Court**, PO Box 55, Leadville, CO 80461. 719-486-0535 (MST) 8AM-5PM. Felony, Misdemeanor, Civil, Eviction, Small Claims, Probate.

## Larimer County

**Real Estate Recording**, Larimer County Clerk and Recorder, 200 West Oak, Fort Collins, CO 80522. 303-498-7860 (MST) 7:30AM-4:30PM.

**8th District Court**, 200 W Oak, Ft Collins, CO 80521. 303-498-7918 (MST) 8AM-4:15PM. Felony, Civil Actions Over $10,000, Probate.

**County Court**, PO Box 800, Ft Collins, CO 80522. 303-498-7550 (MST) 8AM-4:15PM. Misdemeanor, Civil Actions Under $10,000, Eviction, Small Claims.

## Las Animas County

**Real Estate Recording**, Las Animas County Clerk and Recorder, 200 Maple Street, Trinidad, CO 81082. 719-846-3314 (MST) 8AM-4PM.

**3rd District & County Court**, 200 E 1st St Rm 304, Trinidad, CO 81082. 719-846-3316 (MST) 8AM-5PM. Felony, Misdemeanor, Civil, Eviction, Small Claims, Probate.

## Lincoln County

**Real Estate Recording**, Lincoln County Clerk and Recorder, 103 3rd Avenue, Hugo, CO 80821. 719-743-2444 (MST) 8AM-4PM.

**18th District & County Court**, PO Box 128, Hugo, CO 80821. 719-743-2455 (MST) 8AM-4:30 PM. Felony, Misdemeanor, Civil, Eviction, Small Claims, Probate.

## Logan County

**Real Estate Recording**, Logan County Clerk and Recorder, 315 Main Street, Logan County Courthouse, Sterling, CO 80751-4349. 303-522-1544 (MST) 8AM-5PM.

**13th District Court**, PO Box 71, Sterling, CO 80751. 303-522-6565 (MST) 8AM-4PM. Felony, Civil Actions Over $10,000, Probate.

**County Court**, PO Box 1907, Sterling, CO 80751. 303-522-1572 (MST) 8AM-4PM. Misdemeanor, Civil Actions Under $10,000, Eviction, Small Claims.

## Mesa County

**Real Estate Recording**, Mesa County Clerk and Recorder, 544 Rood Avenue, Grand Junction, CO 81501. 303-244-1679 (MST) 8:30AM-4:30PM.

**21st District Court**, PO Box 20000, Grand Junction, CO 81502-5032. 303-242-4761 (MST) 8AM-5PM. Felony, Civil Actions Over $10,000, Probate.

**County Court**, PO Box 20000, Grand Junction, CO 81502-5032. 303-243-1136 (MST) 8AM-5PM. Misdemeanor, Civil Actions Under $10,000, Eviction, Small Claims.

## Mineral County

**Real Estate Recording**, Mineral County Clerk and Recorder, Second Avenue, Courthouse, Creede, CO 81130. 719-658-2440 (MST) 8AM-4PM.

**12th District & County Court**, PO Box 337, Creede, CO 81130. 719-658-2575 (MST) 10AM-3PM. Felony, Misdemeanor, Civil, Eviction, Small Claims, Probate.

## Moffat County

**Real Estate Recording**, Moffat County Clerk and Recorder, 221 West Victory Way, Craig, CO 81625-2716. 303-824-5484 (MST) 8AM-4PM.

**14th District & County Court**, 221 W Victory Wy, Craig, CO 81625. 303-824-8254 (MST) 8AM-5PM. Felony, Misdemeanor, Civil, Eviction, Small Claims, Probate.

## Montezuma County

**Real Estate Recording**, Montezuma County Clerk and Recorder, 109 West Main Street, Room 108, Cortez, CO 81321. 303-565-3728 (MST) 8:30AM-4:30PM.

**22nd District Court**, 109 W Main St, Cortez, CO 81321. 303-565-1111 (MST) 8AM-5PM. Felony, Civil Actions Over $10,000, Probate.

**County Court**, 601 N Mildred Rd, Cortez, CO 81321. 303-565-7580 (MST) 8AM-4:30PM. Misdemeanor, Civil Actions Under $10,000, Eviction, Small Claims.

## Montrose County

**Real Estate Recording**, Montrose County Clerk and Recorder, 320 South First Street, Courthouse, Montrose, CO 81401. 970-249-3362 (MST) 8:30AM-4:30PM.

**7th District & County Court**, PO Box 368, Montrose, CO 81402. 970-249-9676 (MST) 8:30AM-4:30PM. Felony, Misdemeanor, Civil, Eviction, Small Claims, Probate.

## Morgan County

**Real Estate Recording**, Morgan County Clerk and Recorder, 231 Ensign Street, Administration Building, Fort Morgan, CO 80701. 303-867-5616 (MST) 8AM-4PM.

**13th District Court**, PO Box 130, Ft Morgan, CO 80701. 303-867-8266 (MST) 8AM-4PM. Felony, Civil Actions Over $10,000, Probate.

**County Court**, PO Box 695, Ft Morgan, CO 80701. 303-867-8244 (MST) 8AM-4PM. Misdemeanor, Civil Actions Under $10,000, Eviction, Small Claims.

## Otero County

**Real Estate Recording**, Otero County Clerk and Recorder, 3rd & Colorado, Courthouse, La Junta, CO 81050. 719-384-8701 (MST) 8AM-5PM.

**16th District Court**, Courthouse Rm 207, La Junta, CO 81050. 719-384-4951 (MST) 8AM-5PM. Felony, Civil Actions Over $10,000, Probate.

**County Court**, Courthouse Rm 102, La Junta, CO 81050. 719-384-4721 (MST) 8AM-5PM. Misdemeanor, Civil Actions Under $10,000, Eviction, Small Claims.

## Ouray County

**Real Estate Recording**, Ouray County Clerk and Recorder, 541 Fourth Street, Ouray, CO 81427. 970-325-4961 (MST) 9AM-5PM.

**7th District & County Court**, PO Box 643, Ouray, CO 81427. 970-325-4405 (MST) 8:30AM-4:30PM M-TH, 8AM-11AM F. Felony, Misdemeanor, Civil, Eviction, Small Claims, Probate.

## Park County

**Real Estate Recording**, Park County Clerk and Recorder, 501 Main Street, Fairplay, CO 80440. 719-836-2771 (MST) 8AM-5PM.

**Park County Combined Court**, PO Box 190, Fairplay, CO 80440. 719-836-2940 (MST) 8AM-4PM. Felony, Misdemeanor, Civil, Eviction, Small Claims, Probate.

## Phillips County

**Real Estate Recording**, Phillips County Clerk and Recorder, 221 South Interocean, Holyoke, CO 80734. 303-854-3131 (MST) 8AM-4:30PM.

**13th District & County Court**, 221 S Interocean, Holyoke, CO 80734. 303-854-3279 (MST) 8AM-12:00PM-1:00PM-4:30PM. Felony, Misdemeanor, Civil, Eviction, Small Claims, Probate.

## Pitkin County

**Real Estate Recording**, Pitkin County Clerk and Recorder, 530 East Main St., #101, Aspen, CO 81611. 303-920-5180 (MST) 8:30AM-4:30PM.

**9th District & County Court**, 506 E Main St, Ste E, Aspen, CO 81611. 303-925-7635 (MST) 8AM-5PM. Felony, Misdemeanor, Civil, Eviction, Small Claims, Probate.

## Prowers County

**Real Estate Recording**, Prowers County Clerk and Recorder, 301 South Main Street, Lamar, CO 81052. 719-336-4337 (MST) 8:30AM-4:30PM.

**15th District Court**, PO Box 1178, Lamar, CO 81052. 719-336-7424 (MST) 8AM-5PM. Felony, Civil Actions Over $10,000, Probate.

**County Court**, PO Box 525, Lamar, CO 81052. 719-336-7416 (MST) 8AM-5PM. Misdemeanor, Civil Actions Under $10,000, Eviction, Small Claims.

## Pueblo County

**Real Estate Recording**, Pueblo County Clerk and Recorder, 215 West 10th Street, Pueblo, CO 81003. 719-583-6000 (MST) 8AM-4:30PM.

**10th District & County Court**, 320 West 10th St, Pueblo, CO 81003. 719-546-1791 (MST) 8AM-5PM (District) 8AM-4PM (County). Felony, Misdemeanor, Civil, Eviction, Small Claims, Probate.

## Rio Blanco County

**Real Estate Recording**, Rio Blanco County Clerk and Recorder, 555 Main Street, P.O. Box 1067, Meeker, CO 81641. 970-878-5068 (MST) 8AM-5PM.

**9th District & County Court**, PO Box 1150, Meeker, CO 81641. 970-878-5622 (MST) 8AM-5PM. Felony, Misdemeanor, Civil, Eviction, Small Claims, Probate.

## Rio Grande County

**Real Estate Recording**, Rio Grande County Clerk and Recorder, 6th & Cherry, Del Norte, CO 81132. 719-657-3334 (MST) 8AM-4PM.

**12th District & County Court**, PO Box W, Del Norte, CO 81132. 719-657-3394 (MST) 8AM-4PM. Felony, Misdemeanor, Civil, Eviction, Small Claims, Probate.

## Routt County

**Real Estate Recording**, Routt County Clerk and Recorder, 522 Lincoln Avenue, Steamboat Springs, CO 80477. 303-879-1710 (MST) 8:30AM-4:30PM.

**14th District & County Court**, PO Box 773117, Steamboat Springs, CO 80477. 303-879-5020 (MST) 8AM-5PM. Felony, Misdemeanor, Civil, Eviction, Small Claims, Probate.

## Saguache County

**Real Estate Recording**, Saguache County Clerk and Recorder, Courthouse, Saguache, CO 81149. 719-655-2512 (MST) 8AM-4PM.

**12th District & County Court**, PO Box 164, Saguache, CO 81149. 719-655-2522 (MST) 8AM-4PM. Felony, Misdemeanor, Civil, Eviction, Small Claims, Probate.

## San Juan County

**Real Estate Recording**, San Juan County Clerk and Recorder, 15th & Green Street, Silverton, CO 81433. 303-387-5671 (MST) 9AM-5PM.

**6th District & County Courts**, PO Box 441, Silverton, CO 81433. 303-387-5790 (MST) 8AM-4PM T & TH, 8AM-12AM W. Felony, Misdemeanor, Civil, Eviction, Small Claims, Probate.

## San Miguel County

**Real Estate Recording**, San Miguel County Clerk and Recorder, 305 West Colorado Avenue, Telluride, CO 81435. 303-728-3954 (MST) 9AM-Noon,1-5PM.

**7th District & County Courts**, PO Box 919, Telluride, CO 81435. 303-728-3891 (MST) 9AM-11:30 1:30PM-3:30PM. Felony, Misdemeanor, Civil, Eviction, Small Claims, Probate.

## Sedgwick County

**Real Estate Recording**, Sedgwick County Clerk and Recorder, 3rd & Cedar, Courthouse, Julesburg, CO 80737. 970-474-3346 (MST) 8AM-4PM.

**13th District & County Court**, Courthouse Square, Julesburg, CO 80737. 970-474-3627 (MST) 9AM-1PM. Felony, Misdemeanor, Civil, Eviction, Small Claims, Probate.

## Summit County

**Real Estate Recording**, Summit County Clerk and Recorder, 208 East Lincoln, Breckenridge, CO 80424. 303-453-2561 (MST) X233 8AM-5PM.

**5th District & County Court**, PO Box 269, Breckenridge, CO 80424. 303-453-2241 (MST) 8AM-5PM. Felony, Misdemeanor, Civil, Eviction, Small Claims, Probate.

## Teller County

**Real Estate Recording**, Teller County Clerk and Recorder, 101 West Bennett Avenue, Cripple Creek, CO 80813. 719-689-2951 (MST) 8AM-4:30PM.

**4th District & County Court**, PO Box 997, Cripple Creek, CO 80813. 719-689-2543 (MST) 8:30AM-4PM. Felony, Misdemeanor, Civil, Eviction, Small Claims, Probate.

## Washington County

**Real Estate Recording**, Washington, 150 Ash, Courthouse, Akron, CO 80720. 303-345-6565 (MST) 8AM-4:30PM.

**13th District & County Court**, PO Box 455, Akron, CO 80720. 303-345-2756 (MST) 8AM-4:30PM. Felony, Misdemeanor, Civil, Eviction, Small Claims, Probate.

## Weld County

**Real Estate Recording**, Weld County Clerk and Recorder, 1402 N. 17th Ave., Greeley, CO 80631. 303-353-3840 (MST) X3050 8:30PM-4:30PM.

**19th District & County Court**, PO Box C, Greeley, CO 80632. 303-351-7300 (MST) 8AM-4PM. Felony, Misdemeanor, Civil, Eviction, Small Claims, Probate.

## Yuma County

**Real Estate Recording**, Yuma County Clerk and Recorder, Third & Ash, Wray, CO 80758. 303-332-5809 (MST) 8:30AM-4:30PM.

**13th District & County Court**, PO Box 347, Wray, CO 80758. 303-332-4118 (MST) 8AM-4PM. Felony, Misdemeanor, Civil, Eviction, Small Claims, Probate.

# Connecticut

### Andover Town

**Real Estate Recording**, Andover Town Clerk, Town Office Building, 17 School Road, Andover, CT 06232. 203-742-0188 8:30AM-Noon, 1-4PM M-Th; 8:30AM-12:30PM F; 5-7PM Mon.

### Ansonia City

**Real Estate Recording**, Ansonia City Clerk, 253 Main Street, City Hall, Ansonia, CT 06401. 203-736-5980 8:30AM-4:30PM.

### Ashford Town

**Real Estate Recording**, Ashford Town Clerk, 25 Pompey Hollow Road, Ashford, CT 06278. 203-429-7044 8:30AM-3PM M-W & F; 7-8:30PM Wed.

### Avon Town

**Real Estate Recording**, Avon Town Clerk, 60 West Main Street, Avon, CT 06001. 203-677-2634 8:30AM-4:30PM (Summer hours: 8AM-4:45PM M-Th; 8AM-12:30PM F).

### Barkhamsted Town

**Real Estate Recording**, Barkhamsted Town Clerk, Route 318, 67 Ripley Hill Rd., Town Hall, Pleasant Valley, CT 06063. 203-379-8665 9AM-4PM (F open until 1PM).

### Beacon Falls Town

**Real Estate Recording**, Beacon Falls Town Clerk, 10 Maple Avenue, Beacon Falls, CT 06403. 203-729-8254 9AM-Noon, 1PM-4PM.

### Berlin Town

**Real Estate Recording**, Berlin Town Clerk, 240 Kensington Road, Kensington, CT 06037. 203-828-7075 M-W, 8:30AM-4:30PM; Th 8:30AM-7PM; F 8:30AM-1PM.

### Bethany Town

**Real Estate Recording**, Bethany Town Clerk, 40 Peck Road, Bethany, CT 06524-3338. 203-393-0820 9:30AM-4:30PM (No copying or recording after 4PM).

### Bethel Town

**Real Estate Recording**, Bethel Town Clerk, 5 Library Place, Bethel, CT 06801. 203-794-8505 9AM-5PM.

### Bethlehem Town

**Real Estate Recording**, Bethlehem Town Clerk, 36 Main St. So., Bethlehem, CT 06751. 203-266-7510 9AM-Noon T,W,Th,F,Sat.

### Bloomfield Town

**Real Estate Recording**, Bloomfield Town Clerk, 800 Bloomfield Avenue, Town Hall, Bloomfield, CT 06002. 203-769-3506 9AM-5PM.

### Bolton Town

**Real Estate Recording**, Bolton Town Clerk, 222 Bolton Center Road, Bolton, CT 06043-7698. 203-649-8066 9AM-5PM & 6PM-8PM M; 9AM-4PM T-Th; 9AM-3PM F.

### Bozrah Town

**Real Estate Recording**, Bozrah Town Clerk, 1 River Road, Town Hall, Bozrah, CT 06334. 203-889-2689 9AM-4PM T,W,Th; 9AM-Noon Sat.

### Branford Town

**Real Estate Recording**, Branford Town Clerk, 1019 Main Street, Town Hall, Branford, CT 06405. 203-488-6305 9AM-4:30PM (9AM-4PM Recording hours).

### Bridgeport Town

**Real Estate Recording**, Bridgeport Town Clerk, 45 Lyon Terrace, City Hall, Room 124, Bridgeport, CT 06604. 203-576-7207 9AM-4:30PM; Recording until 4PM.

### Bridgewater Town

**Real Estate Recording**, Bridgewater Town Clerk, Main Street, Town Hall, Bridgewater, CT 06752. 203-354-5102

### Bristol City

**Real Estate Recording**, Bristol City Clerk, 111 North Main Street, City Hall, Bristol, CT 06010. 203-584-7656 8:30AM-5PM.

### Brookfield Town

**Real Estate Recording**, Brookfield Town Clerk, Pocono Road, Town Hall, Brookfield, CT 06804. 203-775-7313 8:30AM-4:30PM.

### Brooklyn Town

**Real Estate Recording**, Brooklyn Town Clerk, 4 Wolf Den Road, Town Hall, Brooklyn, CT 06234. 203-774-9543 M-W 9AM-4:30PM; Th 9AM-6PM; F 9AM-1PM.

### Burlington Town

**Real Estate Recording**, Burlington Town Clerk, 200 Spielman Highway, Burlington, CT 06013. 203-673-2108 8:30AM-4PM.

### Canaan Town

**Real Estate Recording**, Canaan Town Clerk, 107 Main Street, Town Hall, Canaan, CT 06031. 203-824-0707 9AM-3PM.

### Canterbury Town

**Real Estate Recording**, Canterbury Town Clerk, 45 Westminster Road, Town Hall, P.O. Box 27, Canterbury, CT 06331. 203-546-9377 9:30AM-4:30PM M-W; 9:30AM-7PM Th; 9:30AM-2PM F.

### Canton Town

**Real Estate Recording**, Canton Town Clerk, 4 Market Street, Collinsville, CT 06022. 203-693-4112 8:30AM-4:30PM.

### Chaplin Town

**Real Estate Recording**, Chaplin Town Clerk, 495 Phoenixville Road, Town Hall, Chaplin, CT 06235. 203-455-9455 9AM-3PM M,Th,F; 9AM-1PM T; Closed W; (7-9PM T & Th).

### Cheshire Town

**Real Estate Recording**, Cheshire Town Clerk, 84 South Main Street, Town Hall, Cheshire, CT 06410. 203-271-6601 8:30AM-4PM (Recording until 3:30PM).

### Chester Town

**Real Estate Recording**, Chester Town Clerk, 65 Main Street, Chester, CT 06412. 203-526-0006 9AM-Noon, 1-4PM M,W,Th; 9AM-Noon, 1-7PM T; 9AM-Noon F.

### Clinton Town

**Real Estate Recording**, Clinton Town Clerk, 54 East Main Street, Clinton, CT 06413. 203-669-9101 9AM-4PM.

### Colchester Town

**Real Estate Recording**, Colchester Town Clerk, 127 Norwich Avenue, Colchester, CT 06415. 203-537-7215 8:30AM-4:30PM M-W & F; 8:30-7PM Th.

### Colebrook Town

**Real Estate Recording**, Colebrook Town Clerk, 558 Colebrook Road, Town Hall, Colebrook, CT 06021. 203-379-3359

### Columbia Town

**Real Estate Recording**, Columbia Town Clerk, 323 Route 87, Columbia, CT 06237. 203-228-3284 9AM-2PM; 6-8PM M Evening.

### Cornwall Town

**Real Estate Recording**, Cornwall Town Clerk, 26 Pine St., Cornwall, CT 06753. 203-672-2709 9AM-4PM M-Th.

### Coventry Town

**Real Estate Recording**, Coventry Town Clerk, 1712 Main Street, Coventry, CT 06238. 203-742-7966 8:30AM-4:30PM M-Th; 8:30AM-4PM Fri.

### Cromwell Town

**Real Estate Recording**, Cromwell Town Clerk, 41 West Street, Cromwell, CT 06416-2100. 203-632-3440 8:30AM-4PM.

### Danbury City

**Real Estate Recording**, Danbury Town Clerk, 155 Deer Hill Avenue, City Hall, Danbury, CT 06810. 203-797-4531 8:30AM-4:30PM.

### Darien Town

**Real Estate Recording**, Darien Town Clerk, 2 Renshaw Road, Darien, CT 06820-5397. 203-656-7307 8:30AM-4:30PM.

### Deep River Town

**Real Estate Recording**, Deep River Town Clerk, 174 Main Street, Town Hall, Deep River, CT 06417. 203-526-6024 9AM-Noon, 1-4PM.

# Connecticut

## Derby City

**Real Estate Recording**, Derby Town Clerk, 35 Fifth Street, Derby, CT 06418-1897. 203-734-9207 9AM-5PM.

## Durham Town

**Real Estate Recording**, Durham Town Clerk, 30 Town House Road, Town Hall, Durham, CT 06422. 203-349-3452 9AM-4:30PM.

## East Granby Town

**Real Estate Recording**, East Granby Town Clerk, 9 Center Street, Town Hall, East Granby, CT 06026. 203-653-6528 8:30AM-Noon, 1PM-4PM.

## East Haddam Town

**Real Estate Recording**, East Haddam Town Clerk, Goodspeed Plaza, Town Office Building, East Haddam, CT 06423. 203-873-5027 9AM-Noon, 1-4PM M,T,W,Th; 9AM-Noon F (T open until 7PM).

## East Hampton Town

**Real Estate Recording**, East Hampton Town Clerk, 20 East High Street, Town Hall, East Hampton, CT 06424. 203-267-2519 8AM-4PM M,W,Th; 8AM-7:30PM T; 8:30AM-12:30PM F.

## East Hartford Town

**Real Estate Recording**, East Hartford Town Clerk, 740 Main Street, East Hartford, CT 06108-3126. 203-291-7230 8:30AM-4:30PM.

## East Haven Town

**Real Estate Recording**, East Haven Town Clerk, 250 Main Street, East Haven, CT 06512-3034. 203-468-3201 9AM-5PM (9AM-4:15PM Recording hours).

## East Lyme Town

**Real Estate Recording**, East Lyme Town Clerk, 108 Pennsylvania Avenue, Niantic, CT 06357. 203-739-6931 8:30AM-4:30PM.

## East Windsor Town

**Real Estate Recording**, East Windsor Town Clerk, 11 Rye Street, Town Hall, Broad Brook, CT 06016. 203-623-9467 8:30-4:30PM M,T,W; 8:30AM-7:30PM Th; 8:30AM-12:30PM F.

## Eastford Town

**Real Estate Recording**, Eastford Town Clerk, 16 Westford Road, Eastford, CT 06242. 203-974-1885 10AM-Noon, 1PM-4PM T,W.

## Easton Town

**Real Estate Recording**, Easton Town Clerk, 225 Center Road, Easton, CT 06612. 203-268-6291 8:30AM-4:30PM.

## Ellington Town

**Real Estate Recording**, Ellington Town Clerk, 55 Main Street, PO Box 187, Ellington, CT 06029. 203-875-3190 9AM-7PM M; 9AM-4:30PM T-F.

## Enfield Town

**Real Estate Recording**, Enfield Town Clerk, 820 Enfield Street, Enfield, CT 06082-2997. 203-745-0371 9AM-5PM.

## Essex Town

**Real Estate Recording**, Essex Town Clerk, 29 West Avenue, Essex, CT 06426. 203-767-4344 9AM-4PM.

## Fairfield County

**Fairfield Superior Court**, 1061 Main St Attn: criminal or civil, Bridgeport, CT 06604. 203-579-6527 (EST) 9AM-5PM. Felony, Civil Actions Over $2,000.

**Danbury Superior Court**, 146 White St, Danbury, CT 06810. 203-797-4400 (EST) 9AM-5PM. Felony, Civil Actions Over $2,000.

**Stamford-Norwalk Superior Court**, 123 Hoyt St, Stamford, CT 06905. 203-965-5307 (EST) 9AM-5PM. Felony, Civil Actions Over $2,000.

**Geographical Area Court #2**, 172 Golden Hill St, Bridgeport, CT 06604. 203-579-6560 (EST) 9AM-5PM. Misdemeanor, Eviction, Small Claims.

**Geographical Area Court #3**, 146 White St, Danbury, CT 06810. 203-797-4400 (EST) 9AM-5PM. Misdemeanor, Eviction, Small Claims.

**Geographical Area Court #20**, 17 Belden Ave, Norwalk, CT 06850. 203-846-3237 (EST) 9AM-5PM. Misdemeanor, Eviction, Small Claims.

**Bethel Probate Court**, Town Hall, 5 Library Place, Bethel, CT 06801. 203-794-8508 (EST) Probate.

**Bridgeport Probate District**, 202 State St McLevy Hall, Bridgeport, CT 06604. 203-333-4165 (EST) 9AM-4PM. Probate.

**Brookfield Probate Court**, PO Box 5192, Brookfield, CT 06804-5192. 203-775-3700 (EST) 8:30AM-1:30PM M-Thu, (And by appointment). Probate.

**Danbury Probate Court**, 155 Deer Hill Ave, Danbury, CT 06810. 203-797-4521 (EST) 8:30AM-4:30PM. Probate.

**Darien Probate Court**, Town Hall, 2 Renshaw Rd, Darien, CT 06820. 203-656-7342 (EST) 9AM-12:30PM, 1:30PM-4:30PM M-F, 9AM-12:30PM Fri July-Labor Day. Probate.

**Fairfield Probate Court**, Independence Hall, Fairfield, CT 06430. 203-256-3041 (EST) 9AM-5PM M-F, 9AM-4:30PM (July-Aug). Probate.

**Greenwich Probate Court**, PO Box 2540, Greenwich, CT 06836. 203-622-7880 (EST) 9AM-4:30PM M-F, 9AM-12PM Fri (July-Aug). Probate.

**New Canaan Probate Court**, PO Box 326, 77 Main St, New Canaan, CT 06840. 203-972-7500 (EST) 8:30AM-1PM 2PM-4:30PM M-F, 8AM-12PM Fri (July-Aug). Probate.

**New Fairfield Probate Court**, Town Hall, New Fairfield, CT 06810. 203-746-8160 (EST) 9AM-12PM Wed-Thu. Probate.

**Newtown Probate Court**, Edmond Town Hall, 45 Main St, Newtown, CT 06470. 203-270-4280 (EST) 8:30AM-4:30PM. Probate.

**Norwalk Probate Court**, 125 East Ave, PO Box 2009, Norwalk, CT 06859. 203-854-7737 (EST) 9AM-4:30PM M-F (And by appointment). Probate.

**Redding Probate Court**, Po Box 125, Town Hall, Redding, CT 06875. 203-938-2326 (EST) 9AM-1PM. Probate.

**Ridgefield Probate Court**, Town Hall, 400 Main St, Ridgefield, CT 06877. 203-431-2776 (EST) 9AM-5PM M-F, 9AM-12PM (July-Aug). Probate.

**Shelton Probate Court**, PO Box 127, 40 White St, Shelton, CT 06484. 203-924-8462 (EST) 9AM-12PM 1PM-4:30PM. Probate.

**Sherman Probate Court**, Mallory Town Hall, Sherman, CT 06784. 203-355-1821 (EST) 9AM-12PM Tue (And by appointment). Probate.

**Stamford Probate Court**, Stamford Gov't Ct, 8th floor, 888 Washin, Stamford, CT 06904. 203-323-2149 (EST) 9AM-4PM. Probate.

**Stratford Probate Court**, Town Hall, 2725 Main St, Stratford, CT 06497. 203-385-4823 (EST) 8:30AM-4:30PM. Probate.

**Trumbull Probate Court**, Town Hall, Trumbull, CT 06611. 203-452-5068 (EST) 9AM-4:30PM. Probate.

**Westport Probate Court**, Town Hall, 110 Myrtle Ave, Westport, CT 06880. 203-226-8311 (EST) 9AM-4PM. Probate.

## Fairfield Town

**Real Estate Recording**, Fairfield Town Clerk, 611 Old Post Road, Fairfield, CT 06430-6690. 203-256-3090 8:30AM-5PM (8:30AM-4:30PM Third M June-August).

## Farmington Town

**Real Estate Recording**, Farmington Town Clerk, 1 Monteith Drive, Farmington, CT 06032-1053. 203-673-8247 8:30AM-4:30PM.

## Franklin Town

**Real Estate Recording**, Franklin Town Clerk, 7 Meeting House Hill Road, Town Hall, North Franklin, CT 06254. 203-642-7352 9AM-4PM M-Th; 6PM-8PM T.

## Glastonbury Town

**Real Estate Recording**, Glastonbury Town Clerk, 2155 Main Street, Glastonbury, CT 06033. 203-652-7616 8AM-4:30PM.

## Goshen Town

**Real Estate Recording**, Goshen Town Clerk, 42 North Street, Town Office Building, Goshen, CT 06756. 203-491-3647 9AM-Noon,1-4PM.

## Granby Town

**Real Estate Recording**, Granby Town Clerk, 15 North Granby Road, Granby, CT 06035. 203-653-8949 9AM-Noon,1-4PM.

## Greenwich Town

**Real Estate Recording**, Greenwich Town Clerk, 101 Field Point Road, Town Hall, Greenwich, CT 06836. 203-622-7897 8AM-4PM.

## Griswold Town

**Real Estate Recording**, Griswold Town Clerk, 32 School Street, Town Hall, Jewett City, CT 06351-0487. 203-376-7064 8:30AM-4PM M,T,Th,F; 8:30AM-Noon W.

## Groton Town

**Real Estate Recording**, Groton Town Clerk, 45 Fort Hill Road, Groton, CT 06340. 203-441-6642 8:30AM-4:30PM.

## Guilford Town

**Real Estate Recording**, Guilford Town Clerk, 31 Park Street, Town Hall, Guilford, CT 06437. 203-453-8001 8:30AM-4:30PM.

## Haddam Town

**Real Estate Recording**, Haddam Town Clerk, 30 Field Park Drive, Town Hall, Haddam, CT 06438. 203-345-8531 9AM-4PM M,T,W,; 9AM-7PM Th; 9AM-Noon F.

## Hamden Town

**Real Estate Recording**, Hamden Town Clerk, 2372 Whitney Avenue, Memorial Town Hall, Hamden, CT 06518. 203-287-2517 8:30AM-4PM.

## Hampton Town

**Real Estate Recording**, Hampton Town Clerk, Town Office Building, 164 Main St., Hampton, CT 06247. 203-455-9132 9AM-4PM T,Th; 9AM-Noon Sat.

## Hartford City

**Real Estate Recording**, Hartford City Clerk, 550 Main Street, Hartford, CT 06103-2992. 203-543-8580

## Hartford County

**Hartford Superior Court-Civil**, 95 Washington St, Hartford, CT 06106. 203-566-3170 (EST) 9AM-5PM. Civil Actions Over $2,000.
**Hartford Superior Court-Criminal**, 101 LaFayette St, Hartford, CT 06106. 203-566-1634 (EST) 9AM-5PM. Felony.
**New Britain Superior Court**, 177 Columbus Blvd, New Britain, CT 06051. 203-827-7133 (EST) 9AM-5PM. Felony, Civil Actions Over $2,000.
**Geographical Area Court #17**, 131 N Main St, Bristol, CT 06010. 203-582-8111 (EST) 9AM-5PM. Misdemeanor, Eviction, Small Claims.
**Geographical Area Court #13**, 111 Phoenix, Enfield, CT 06082. 203-741-3727 (EST) 9AM-5PM. Misdemeanor, Eviction, Small Claims.
**Geographical Area Court #14**, 101 LaFayette St, Hartford, CT 06106. 203-566-1630 (EST) 9AM-5PM. Misdemeanor, Eviction, Small Claims.
**Geographical Area Court #12**, 410 Center St, Manchester, CT 06040. 203-647-1091 (EST) 9AM-5PM. Misdemeanor, Eviction, Small Claims.
**Geographical Area Court #15**, 125 Columbus Blvd, New Britain, CT 06051. 203-827-7106 (EST) 9AM-5PM. Misdemeanor, Eviction, Small Claims.
**Geographical Area Court #16**, 105 Raymond Rd, West Hartford, CT 06107. 203-236-5166 (EST) 9AM-5PM. Misdemeanor, Eviction, Small Claims.
**Avon Probate Court**, 60 W Main St, Avon, CT 06001-0578. 203-677-2634 (EST) 9AM-12PM. Probate.

**Bloomfield Probate Court**, Town Hall, 800 Bloomfield Ave, Bloomfield, CT 06002. 203-769-3598 (EST) 9AM-1PM, 2AM-4:30PM. Probate.
**Suffield Probate Court**, PO Box 136, 158 Main St, Brendan Heights, CT 06078. 203-668-3835 (EST) 8:30AM-12PM M-F (And by appointment). Probate.
**Bristol Probate Court**, City Hall, 111 N Main St, Bristol, CT 06010. 203-584-7650 (EST) 9AM-5PM. Probate.
**Burlington Probate Court**, Town Hall, Route 4, Burlington, CT 06013. 203-673-2108 (EST) 9AM-1PM Fri. Probate.
**Canton Probate Court**, Town Hall, Main St, Collinsville, CT 06022. 203-693-8684 (EST) 8:30AM-1:30PM Tue-Fri (And by appointment). Probate.
**East Granby Probate Court**, PO Box 542, East Granby, CT 06026. 203-653-3434 (EST) 9AM-12PM Tue-Thu (And by appointment). Probate.
**East Hartford Probate Court**, Town Hall, 740 Main St, East Hartford, CT 06108. 203-291-7278 (EST) 9AM-4:30PM. Probate.
**Enfield Probate Court**, 820 Enfield St, Enfield, CT 06082. 203-745-5065 (EST) 9AM-4:30PM. Probate.
**Farmington Probate Court**, One Monteith, Farmington, CT 06032. 203-673-8250 (EST) 9AM-4PM. Probate.
**Glastonbury Probate Court**, 2155 Main St, PO Box 6523, Glastonbury, CT 06033. 203-633-3723 (EST) 9AM-12:30PM 1:30PM-4:30PM M-Thu, 12AM-4:30PM Fri. Probate.
**Granby Probate Court**, 15 N Granby Rd, Town Hall, Granby, CT 06035. 203-653-8944 (EST) 9AM-12PM Tue, Wed, Fri. Probate.
**Hartford Probate Court**, 10 Prospect St, Hartford, CT 06103. 203-522-1813 (EST) 9AM-4PM. Probate.
**Manchester Probate Court**, 66 Center St, Manchester, CT 06040. 203-647-3227 (EST) 8:30AM-12PM 1AM-4:30PM M-F, 6:30PM-8PM Thu (By appointment). Probate.
**Marlborough Probate Court**, PO Box 29, N Main St, Marlborough, CT 06447. 203-295-9574 (EST) By appointment. Probate.
**Berlin Probate Court**, 67 Ripley Rd, New Britain, CT 06051-2226. 203-826-2696 (EST) 9AM-4PM. Probate.
**Newington Probate Court**, 66 Cedar Street, Newington, CT 06111. 203-665-1285 (EST) 9AM-4PM. Probate.
**Simsbury Probate Court**, PO Box 495, 933 Hopmeadow St, Simsbury, CT 06070. 203-651-3751 (EST) 9AM-1PM 2PM-4:30PM M-F (And by appointment). Probate.
**East Windsor Probate Court**, Twon Hall, 1540 Sullivan Ave, South Windsor, CT 06074. 203-644-2511 (EST) 8AM-1PM M-Thu, 12AM-4:30PM Fri (And by appointment). Probate.
**Southington Probate Court**, PO Box 165, Southington, CT 06489. 203-276-6253 (EST) 8:30AM-12PM 1PM-4:30PM. Probate.
**West Hartford Probate Court**, 50 S Main St, West Hartford, CT 06107. 203-523-3174 (EST) 9AM-4PM. Probate.
**Hartland Probate Court**, PO Box 100, West Hartland, CT 06091. 203-653-9710 (EST) 10AM-1PM Mon-Fri (And by appointment). Probate.
**Windsor Locks Probate Court**, PO Box L, Town Office Bldg, 50 Church St, Windsor Locks,

CT 06096. 203-627-1450 (EST) 9AM-2PM Mon-Thu. Probate.
**Windsor Probate Court**, PO Box 342, 275 Broad St, Windsor, CT 06095. 203-285-1975 (EST) 8:30AM-4:30PM M-F, 8:30AM-12PM Fri (July-Aug). Probate.

## Hartland Town

**Real Estate Recording**, Hartland Town Clerk, Town Office Building, 22 South Road, East Hartland, CT 06027. 203-653-3542 1PM-4PM M,T,W (T open 7-8PM).

## Harwinton Town

**Real Estate Recording**, Harwinton Town Clerk, 100 Bentley Drive, Town Hall, Harwinton, CT 06791. 203-485-9613 8:30AM-4PM.

## Hebron Town

**Real Estate Recording**, Hebron Town Clerk, 15 Gilead Street, Hebron, CT 06248. 203-228-9406 8AM-4PM M-W; 8AM-7PM Th; 8AM-12:30PM F.

## Kent Town

**Real Estate Recording**, Kent Town Clerk, 41 Kent Green Blvd., Town Hall, Kent, CT 06757. 203-927-3433 9AM-Noon, 1PM-4PM.

## Killingly Town

**Real Estate Recording**, Killingly Town Clerk, 172 Main Street, Danielson, CT 06239. 203-774-8601 8:30AM-4:30PM.

## Killingworth Town

**Real Estate Recording**, Killingworth Town Clerk, 323 Route 81, Killingworth, CT 06419-1298. 203-663-1616 9AM-Noon,1-4PM.

## Lebanon Town

**Real Estate Recording**, Lebanon Town Clerk, 579 Exeter Road, Town Hall, Lebanon, CT 06249. 203-642-7319 9AM-4PM M,T,F; 9AM-7PM Th.

## Ledyard Town

**Real Estate Recording**, Ledyard Town Clerk, 741 Col. Ledyard Highway, Ledyard, CT 06339. 203-464-8740 X229 8:30AM-4:30PM.

## Lisbon Town

**Real Estate Recording**, Lisbon Town Clerk, 1 Newent Road, RD 2 Town Hall, Lisbon, CT 06351-9802. 203-376-2708 9AM-4PM M,T,Th; 9AM-8PM W; 9AM-2PM F; 9AM-Noon Sat.

## Litchfield County

**Litchfield Superior Court**, 15 West St (PO Box 247), Litchfield, CT 06759. 203-567-0885 (EST) 9AM-5PM. Felony, Civil Actions Over $2,000.
**Geographical Area Court #18**, 80 Doyle Rd (PO Box 667), Bantam, CT 06750. 203-567-3942 (EST) 9AM-5PM. Misdemeanor, Eviction, Small Claims.
**Canaan Probate Court**, PO Box 905, Town Hall, Canaan, CT 06018-0905. 203-824-7114 (EST) 9AM-1PM M-F (And by appointment). Probate.
**Cornwall Probate Court**, PO Box 157, Town Office Bldg, Cornwall, CT 06753-0157. 203-

# Connecticut

672-2677 (EST) 9AM-12PM Tue-Thu (And by appointment). Probate.

**Harwinton Probate Court**, Town Hall, 100 Bently Dr, Harwinton, CT 06791. 203-485-1403 (EST) 2AM-4PM Tue-Thu, Fri afternoon by appointment. Probate.

**Kent Probate Court**, PO Box 185, Town Hall, Kent, CT 06757. 203-927-3729 (EST) 9AM-12PM Tue & Thu (And by appointment). Probate.

**Litchfield Probate Court**, West St, PO Box 505, Litchfield, CT 06759. 203-567-8065 (EST) 9AM-1PM. Probate.

**New Hartford Probate Court**, PO Box 308, Town Hall, New Hartford, CT 06057. 203-379-3254 (EST) By appointment. Probate.

**New Milford Probate Court**, 10 Main St, New Milford, CT 06776. 203-355-6029 (EST) 9AM-12PM 1PM-5PM M-F, 9AM-12PM Fri (July-Aug). Probate.

**Norfolk Probate Court**, PO Box 648, Marple Ave, Norfolk, CT 06058. 203-542-5134 (EST) 9AM-12PM Tue & Thu (And by appointment). Probate.

**Barkhamsted Probate Court**, 67 Ripley Rd, Pleasant Valley, CT 06063. 203-379-8665 (EST) 9AM-12PM M-W (And by appointment). Probate.

**Roxbury Probate Court**, Town Hall, 29 North St, Roxbury, CT 06783. 203-354-1185 (EST) 9AM-1PM Mon, Wed, Fri. Probate.

**Salisbury Probate Court**, PO Box 266, Town Hall, Salisbury, CT 06068. 203-435-9513 (EST) 9Am-12PM M-F (And by appointment). Probate.

**Sharon Probate Court**, PO Box 1177, Sharon, CT 06069. 203-364-5514 (EST) 3AM-5PM Mon, Tue, Wed, Fri (And by appointment). Probate.

**Plymouth Probate Court**, PO Box 347, 19 E Main St, Terryville, CT 06786. 203-585-4104 (EST) 1:30PM-5:30PM Tue-Thu (And by appointment). Probate.

**Thomaston Probate Court**, PO Box 136, Town Hall Bldg 158 Main St, Thomaston, CT 06787. 203-283-4847 (EST) 9AM-12PM M-F (And by appointment). Probate.

**Torrington Probate Court**, Municipal Bldg, 140 Main St, Torrington, CT 06790. 203-871-3640 (EST) 9AM-12PM 1:30PM-5PM. Probate.

**Washington Probate Court**, PO Box 295, Town Hall, Washington Depot, CT 06794. 203-868-7974 (EST) 9AM-12PM 1PM-3PM Mon, Wed, Fri. Probate.

**Watertown Probate Court**, PO Box 7, 37 DeForest St, Watertown, CT 06795. 203-945-5237 (EST) 9AM-12PM 1AM-3PM. Probate.

**Winchester Probate Court**, PO Box 625, 338 Main St, Winsted, CT 06098. 203-379-5576 (EST) 9AM-12PM 1PM-4PM. Probate.

**Woodbury Probate Court**, PO Box 84, 281 Main St, South, Woodbury, CT 06798. 203-263-2417 (EST) 9AM-12PM 1PM-4PM Tues & Thurs. Probate.

## Litchfield Town

**Real Estate Recording**, Litchfield Town Clerk, 74 West Street, Town Office Building, Litchfield, CT 06759. 203-567-9461 9AM-4:30PM.

## Lyme Town

**Real Estate Recording**, Lyme Town Clerk, 480 Route 156, Town Hall, Lyme, CT 06371. 203-434-7733 9AM-4PM.

## County Records

## Madison Town

**Real Estate Recording**, Madison Town Clerk, 8 Campus Dr., Madison, CT 06443-2538. 203-245-5672 8:30AM-4PM.

## Manchester Town

**Real Estate Recording**, Manchester Town Clerk, 41 Center Street, Manchester, CT 06040. 203-647-3037 8:30AM-5PM.

## Mansfield Town

**Real Estate Recording**, Mansfield Town Clerk, 4 South Eagleville Road, Mansfield, CT 06268. 203-429-3302 8:30AM-4:30PM.

## Marlborough Town

**Real Estate Recording**, Marlborough Town Clerk, 26 North Main Street, Marlborough, CT 06447. 203-295-0713 8AM-4:30PM M-Th; 6-8PM T; 8AM-Noon F.

## Meriden City

**Real Estate Recording**, Meriden City Clerk, 142 East Main Street, Meriden, CT 06450-8022. 203-630-4030 9AM-5PM.

## Middlebury Town

**Real Estate Recording**, Middlebury Town Clerk, 1212 Whittemore Road, Town Hall, Middlebury, CT 06762. 203-758-2557 9AM-Noon,1-5PM.

## Middlefield Town

**Real Estate Recording**, Middlefield Town Clerk, 393 Jackson Hill Road, Middlefield, CT 06455. 203-349-7116 9AM-5PM M; 9AM-4PM T-Th; 9AM-3PM F.

## Middlesex County

**Middlesex Superior Court-Civil**, 1 Court St, 1st Floor, Middletown, CT 06457. 203-343-6400 (EST) 9AM-5PM. Civil Actions Over $2,000.

**Middlesex Superior Court-Criminal**, 1 Court St, 2nd Floor, Middletown, CT 06457. 203-344-3091 (EST) 9AM-5PM. Felony.

**Saybrook Probate Court**, PO Box 628, 65 Main St, Chester, CT 06412. 203-526-0007 (EST) 9:30AM-12:30PM Tue & Thu. Probate.

**Clinton Probate Court**, 54 E Main St, Clinton, CT 06413-0130. 203-669-6447 (EST) 10AM-12PM, 1PM-3PM. Probate.

**Deep River Probate Court**, Town Hall, 174 Main St, Deep River, CT 06417. 203-526-5266 (EST) 10AM-12PM, 2PM-4PM Tue & Thu (And by appointment). Probate.

**East Haddam Probate Court**, Godspeed Plaza, PO Box 217, East Haddam, CT 06423. 203-873-5028 (EST) 10AM-2PM M-F (And by appointment). Probate.

**Essex Probate Court**, Town Hall, 29 West Ave, Essex, CT 06426. 203-767-4347 (EST) 9AM-1PM M-F (And by appointment). Probate.

**Haddam Probate Court**, 30 Field Park Dr, Haddam, CT 06438. 203-345-8531 (EST) 10AM-3PM Tue, Wed, Thu. Probate.

**Killingworth Probate Court**, 323 Routew 81, Killingworth, CT 06419. 203-663-1276 (EST) 9Am-12PM Mon, Wed, Fri (And by appointment). Probate.

**Middletown Probate Court**, 94 Court St, Middletown, CT 06457. 203-347-7424 (EST) 8:30AM-4:30PM M-F, 6PM-7:40PM Tue (Sept-May). Probate.

**Old Saybrook Probate Court**, PO Box 791, 302 Main St, Old Saybrook, CT 06475. 203-395-3128 (EST) 9AM-1PM. Probate.

**Portland Probate Court**, PO Box 71, 265 Main St, Portland, CT 06480. 203-342-2880 (EST) 9AM-12PM Mon-Fri, 7AM-8:40PM Thu. Probate.

**Westbrook Probate Court**, PO Box G, Westbrook, CT 06498. 203-399-5661 (EST) 9AM-12PM 1:30AM-4PM. Probate.

## Middletown City

**Real Estate Recording**, Middletown City Clerk, 245 DeKoven Drive, Middletown, CT 06457. 203-344-3459 8:30AM-4:30PM.

## Milford City

**Real Estate Recording**, Milford City Clerk, 70 West River Street, Milford, CT 06460-3364. 203-783-3210 8:30AM-5PM.

## Monroe Town

**Real Estate Recording**, Monroe Town Clerk, 7 Fan Hill Road, Monroe, CT 06468-1800. 203-452-5417 9AM-5PM.

## Montville Town

**Real Estate Recording**, Montville Town Clerk, 310 Norwich-New London Tpke., Town Hall, Uncasville, CT 06382. 203-848-1349 9AM-5PM.

## Morris Town

**Real Estate Recording**, Morris Town Clerk, 3 East Street, Morris, CT 06763. 203-567-5387 9AM-Noon, 1-4PM.

## Naugatuck Town

**Real Estate Recording**, Naugatuck Town Clerk, 229 Church Street, Town Clerk's Office, Naugatuck, CT 06770. 203-729-4571 8:30AM-4PM.

## New Britain Town

**Real Estate Recording**, New Britain Town Clerk, 27 W. Main Street, New Britain, CT 06051. 203-826-3344 8:15AM-3:45PM M-W & F; 8:15AM-6:45PM Thday.

## New Canaan Town

**Real Estate Recording**, New Canaan Town Clerk, 77 Main Street, Town Hall, New Canaan, CT 06840. 203-972-2323 8AM-4:30PM.

## New Fairfield Town

**Real Estate Recording**, New Fairfield Town Clerk, Route 39, Town Hall, New Fairfield, CT 06812. 203-746-8110 8:30AM-5PM T-F; 8:30AM-Noon Sat.

## New Hartford Town

**Real Estate Recording**, New Hartford, 530 Main Street, Town Hall, New Hartford, CT 06057. 203-379-5037 9AM-Noon, 12:40-4PM M,T,Th; 9AM-Noon, 1PM-6PM W; 9AM-Noon Fri.

## New Haven City

**Real Estate Recording**, New Haven City Clerk, 200 Orange Street, Room 204, New Haven, CT 06510. 203-787-8346 9AM-5PM.

## New Haven County

**Ansonia-Milford Superior Court**, 14 W River St (PO Box 210), Milford, CT 06460. 203-877-4293 (EST) 9AM-5PM. Felony, Civil Actions Over $2,000.

**New Haven Superior Court**, 235 Church St, New Haven, CT 06510. 203-789-7908 (EST) 9AM-5PM. Felony, Civil Actions Over $2,000.

**New Haven Superior Court-Meriden**, 54 W Main St, Meriden, CT 06450. 203-238-6666 (EST) 9AM-5PM. Civil Actions Over $2,000.

**Waterbury Superior Court**, 300 Grand St, Waterbury, CT 06702. 203-596-4023 (EST) 9AM-5PM. Felony, Civil Actions Over $2,000.

**Geographical Area Court #5**, 106 Elizabeth St, Derby, CT 06418. 203-735-7438 (EST) 9AM-5PM. Misdemeanor, Eviction, Small Claims.

**Geographical Area Court #7**, 54 W Main St, Meriden, CT 06450. 203-238-6130 (EST) 9AM-5PM. Misdemeanor, Eviction, Small Claims.

**Geographical Area Court #22**, 14 W River St, Milford, CT 06460. 203-874-1116 (EST) 9AM-5PM. Misdemeanor, Eviction, Small Claims.

**Geographical Area Court #6**, 121 Elm St, New Haven, CT 06510. 203-789-7465 (EST) 9AM-5PM. Misdemeanor, Eviction, Small Claims.

**Geographical Area Court #4**, 7 Kendrick Ave, Waterbury, CT 06702. 203-596-4050 (EST) 9AM-5PM. Misdemeanor, Eviction, Small Claims.

**Derby Probate Court**, PO Box 253, 16 Westford Rd, Ansonia, CT 06401. 203-734-1277 (EST) 9AM-4PM. Probate.

**Bethany Probate Court**, Town Hall, 40 Peck Rd, Bethany, CT 06524. 203-393-3774 (EST) 9:30AM-11:30PM Tue & Thu, Appointments between 9:30AM-8PM. Probate.

**Branford Probate Court**, PO Box 638, 1019 Main St, Branford, CT 06405-0638. 203-488-0318 (EST) 9AM-12PM, 1AM-4:30PM. Probate.

**Cheshire Probate Court**, 84 S Main St, Cheshire, CT 06410-3193. 203-271-608 (EST) 8:30AM-12:30PM, 1:30PM-4PM. Probate.

**East Haven Probate Court**, 250 Main St, East Haven, CT 06512. 203-468-3895 (EST) 9:30AM-1PM 2PM-3:30PM M, 9:30AM-1PM Tu-Wd, 9:30-1PM 2AM-4:30PM. Probate.

**Guilford Probate Court**, Town Hall, Park St, Guilford, CT 06437. 203-453-8007 (EST) 9AM-12PM 1PM-4:30PM. Probate.

**Madison Probate Court**, PO Box 205, Town Hall, Madison, CT 06443. 203-245-5661 (EST) 9AM-3PM M-F (And by appointment). Probate.

**Meriden Probate Court**, City Hall, E Main St, Meriden, CT 06450. 203-235-4325 (EST) 8:30AM-12PM 1PM-4:30PM. Probate.

**Milford Probate Court**, Parsons Office Complex 70 W River St, PO, Milford, CT 06460. 203-783-3205 (EST) 9AM-5PM. Probate.

**Naugatuck Probate Court**, Town Hall, 229 Church St, Naugatuck, CT 06770. 203-729-4571 (EST) 9AM-4PM. Probate.

**New Haven Probate Court**, PO Box 905, 200 Orange St, 4th Floor, New Haven, CT 06504. 203-777-4880 (EST) 9AM-4PM. Probate.

**North Branford Probate Court**, PO Box 214, 1599 Foxon Rd, North Branford, CT 06471. 203-481-0829 (EST) 9AM-12PM. Probate.

**North Haven Probate Court**, PO Box 175, 18 Church St, North Haven, CT 06473. 203-239-5321 (EST) 8:30AM-4:30PM. Probate.

**Orange Probate Court**, 525 Orange Center Rd, Orange, CT 06477. 203-795-0426 (EST) 9AM-12PM. Probate.

**Oxford Probate Court**, Town Hall, Route 67, Oxford, CT 06478. 203-888-2543 (EST) 7AM-9PM Mon, 1PM-5PM Tue & Wed, 9AM-5PM 7PM-9PM Thu. Probate.

**Southbury Probate Court**, PO Box 673, Townhall Annex, 421 S Main S, Southbury, CT 06488. 203-264-0606 (EST) 9AM-4:30PM M-F (And by appointment). Probate.

**Wallingford Probate Court**, 45 S Main St, Wallingford, CT 06492. 203-294-2100 (EST) 9AM-12PM 1PM-3PM. Probate.

**Waterbury Probate Court**, 263 Grand St, Waterbury, CT 06702. 203-755-1127 (EST) 9AM-4:45PM MTWF, 9AM-6PM Thu, 9AM-12PM Sat. Probate.

**West Haven Probate Court**, PO Box 127, 355 Main St, West Haven, CT 06516. 203-937-3552 (EST) 9AM-4PM. Probate.

**Woodbridge Probate Court**, Town Hall, 11 Meetinghouse Ln, Woodbridge, CT 06525. 203-289-3410 (EST) 9AM-12PM Mon, 5PM-7PM Wed. Probate.

## New London City

**Real Estate Recording**, New London City Clerk, 181 State Street, New London, CT 06320. 203-447-5205 8:30AM-4PM.

## New London County

**New London Superior Court**, 70 Huntington St, New London, CT 06320. 203-443-5363 (EST) 9AM-5PM. Felony, Civil Actions Over $2,000.

**Norwich Superior Court**, PO Box 1087, Norwich, CT 06360. 203-887-3515 (EST) 9AM-5PM. Civil Actions Over $2,000.

**Geographical Area Court #10**, 112 Broad St, New London, CT 06320. 203-443-8343 (EST) 9AM-5PM. Misdemeanor, Eviction, Small Claims.

**Geographical Area Court #21**, 1 Courthouse Sq, Norwich, CT 06360. 203-889-7338 (EST) 9AM-5PM. Misdemeanor, Eviction, Small Claims.

**Bozrah Probate Court**, 179 Lake Rd, Bozrah, CT 06334. 203-859-0852 (EST) By appointment only. Probate.

**Colchester Probate Court**, Town Hall, 127 Norwich Ave, Colchester, CT 06415. 203-537-7290 (EST) 12:30AM-4:30PM MTTF, 9AM1PM Wed (And by appointment). Probate.

**Griswold Probate Court**, Town Hall, 32 School St, Jewett City, CT 06351. 203-376-0216 (EST) 9AM-12PM Wed (And by appointment). Probate.

**Lebanon Probate Court**, Town Hall, 579 Exeter Rd, Lebanon, CT 06249. 203-642-7429 (EST) 10AM-12PM Tues & Fri (And by appointment). Probate.

**Ledyard Probate Court**, PO Box 28, Col Ledyard Hwy (Route 117), Ledyard, CT 06339. 203-464-8740 (EST) 9:30AM-12:30PM M-F (And by appointment). Probate.

**Lyme Probate Court**, Town Hall, 480 Hamburg Rd, Lyme, CT 06371. 203-434-7733 (EST) 9AM-1PM M-F (And by appointment). Probate.

**New London Probate Court**, 181 Captain's Walk Municipal Bldg, PO Bo, New London, CT 06320. 203-443-7121 (EST) 9AM-4PM. Probate.

**East Lyme Probate Court**, PO Box 519, 108 Pennsylvania Ave, Niantic, CT 06357. 203-739-6931 (EST) 8:30AM-12:30PM. Probate.

**North Stonington Probate Court**, PO Box 91, Town hall 40 Main St, North Stonington, CT 06359. 203-535-2877 (EST) 8:30AM-4:30PM Mon-Thu (And by appointment). Probate.

**Norwich Probate Court**, PO Box 38, City Hall, Norwich, CT 06360. 203-887-2160 (EST) 9AM-4:30PM. Probate.

**Old Lyme Probate Court**, PO Box 273, 52 Lyme St, Old Lyme, CT 06371. 203-434-1406 (EST) 9AM-12PM. Probate.

**Salem Probate Court**, 270 Hartford Rd, Salem, CT 06415. 203-859-3873 (EST) By appointment. Probate.

**Stonington Probate Court**, PO Box 312, 152 Elm St, Stonington, CT 06378. 203-535-4721 (EST) 9AM-12PM 1PM-4PM. Probate.

**Montville Probate Court**, 310 Norwich-New London Turnpike, Uncasville, CT 06382. 203-848-9847 (EST) 9AM-1PM MTTF, 9AM-6:30PM Wed. Probate.

## New Milford Town

**Real Estate Recording**, New Milford Town Clerk, 18 Church Street, New Milford, CT 06776. 203-355-6020 9AM-5PM.

## Newington Town

**Real Estate Recording**, Newington Town Clerk, 131 Cedar Street, Newington, CT 06111-2696. 203-665-8545 8:30AM-4:30PM.

## Newtown Town

**Real Estate Recording**, Newtown Town Clerk, 45 Main Street, Newtown, CT 06470. 203-270-4210 8AM-4:30PM.

## Norfolk Town

**Real Estate Recording**, Norfolk Town Clerk, 19 Maple Avenue, Norfolk, CT 06058. 203-542-5679 9AM-Noon,1-4PM.

## North Branford Town

**Real Estate Recording**, North Branford Town Clerk, 1599 Foxon Road, North Branford, CT 06471. 203-481-5369 8:30AM-4:30PM.

## North Canaan Town

**Real Estate Recording**, North Canaan Town Clerk, 100 Pease Street, Town Hall, North Canaan, CT 06018. 203-824-7246 9:30AM-Noon, 1-4PM.

## North Haven Town

**Real Estate Recording**, North Haven Town Clerk, 18 Church Street, Town Hall, North Haven, CT 06473. 203-239-5321 X541 8:30AM-4:30PM.

## North Stonington Town

**Real Estate Recording**, North Stonington Town Clerk, 40 Main Street, North Stonington,

# Connecticut

CT 06359. 203-535-2877 9AM-Noon; 12:30PM-4PM.

### Norwalk City
**Real Estate Recording**, Norwalk Town Clerk, 125 East Avenue, City Hall, Norwalk, CT 06851. 203-854-7746 8:30AM-5PM.

### Norwich City
**Real Estate Recording**, Norwich City Clerk, 100 Broadway, City Hall, Norwich, CT 06360. 203-886-2381 8:30AM-4:30PM.

### Old Lyme Town
**Real Estate Recording**, Old Lyme Town Clerk, 52 Lyme Street, Town Hall, Old Lyme, CT 06371. 203-434-1655 9AM-Noon,1-4PM.

### Old Saybrook Town
**Real Estate Recording**, Old Saybrook Town Clerk, 302 Main Street, Old Saybrook, CT 06475. 203-395-3135 8:30AM-4:30PM.

### Orange Town
**Real Estate Recording**, Orange Town Clerk, 617 Orange Center Road, Town Hall, Orange, CT 06477. 203-795-0751 8:30AM-4:30PM.

### Oxford Town
**Real Estate Recording**, Oxford Town Clerk, 486 Oxford Road, Oxford, CT 06478. 203-888-2543 9AM-5PM M-Th; 7-9PM Mon & Th.

### Plainfield Town
**Real Estate Recording**, Plainfield Town Clerk, 8 Community Avenue, Town Hall, Plainfield, CT 06374. 203-564-4075 8:30AM-4:30PM.

### Plainville Town
**Real Estate Recording**, Plainville Town Clerk, 1 Central Square, Municipal Center, Plainville, CT 06062. 203-793-0221 8:30AM-4:30PM.

### Plymouth Town
**Real Estate Recording**, Plymouth Town Clerk, 19 East Main Street, Town Hall, Terryville, CT 06786. 203-585-4039 8:30-4:30PM.

### Pomfret Town
**Real Estate Recording**, Pomfret Town Clerk, 5 Haven Road, Pomfret Center, CT 06259. 203-974-0343 9AM-4PM.

### Portland Town
**Real Estate Recording**, Portland Town Clerk, 265 Main Street, Portland, CT 06480. 203-342-6743 9AM-4:30PM.

### Preston Town
**Real Estate Recording**, Preston Town Clerk, 389 Route 2, Town Hall, Preston, CT 06365-8830. 203-887-9821 9AM-Noon, 12:30PM-4:30PM T-F; Th until 7:30.

### Prospect Town
**Real Estate Recording**, Prospect Town Clerk, 36 Center Street, Prospect, CT 06712-1699. 203-758-4461 9AM-4PM.

### Putnam Town
**Real Estate Recording**, Putnam Town Clerk, 126 Church Street, Putnam, CT 06260. 203-963-6807 8:30AM-4:30PM.

### Redding Town
**Real Estate Recording**, Redding Town Clerk, Route 107, 100 Hill Rd., Town Office Building, Redding, CT 06875. 203-938-2377 9AM-4:30PM.

### Ridgefield Town
**Real Estate Recording**, Ridgefield Town Clerk, 400 Main Street, Ridgefield, CT 06877. 203-431-2783 9AM-5PM.

### Rocky Hill Town
**Real Estate Recording**, Rocky Hill Town Clerk, 699 Old Main Street, Rocky Hill, CT 06067. 203-258-2705 8:30AM-4:30PM.

### Roxbury Town
**Real Estate Recording**, Roxbury Town Clerk, 29 North St., Roxbury, CT 06783-1405. 203-354-3328 9AM-Noon, 1-4PM T & Th; 9AM-Noon F.

### Salem Town
**Real Estate Recording**, Salem Town Clerk, Town Office Building, 270 Hartford Road, Salem, CT 06420. 203-859-3873 X170 8AM-4PM.

### Salisbury Town
**Real Estate Recording**, Salisbury Town Clerk, 27 Main Street, Town Hall, Salisbury, CT 06068. 203-435-9511 9AM-4PM.

### Scotland Town
**Real Estate Recording**, Scotland Town Clerk, 9 Devotion Rd., Town Hall, Scotland, CT 06264. 203-423-9634 9AM-3PM M,T,Th,F; 7-9PM W.

### Seymour Town
**Real Estate Recording**, Seymour Town Clerk, 1 First Street, Town Hall, Seymour, CT 06483-2817. 203-888-0519 9AM-5PM (No Recording after 4PM).

### Sharon Town
**Real Estate Recording**, Sharon Town Clerk, 63 Main Street, Town Hall, Sharon, CT 06069. 203-364-5224 9:00AM-Noon, 1PM-4PM.

### Shelton City
**Real Estate Recording**, Shelton City Clerk, 54 Hill Street, Shelton, CT 06484. 203-924-1555 8AM-5:30PM (Closed M).

### Sherman Town
**Real Estate Recording**, Sherman Town Clerk, 9 Route 39 North, Town Hall, Sherman, CT 06784. 203-354-5281 9AM-Noon, 1-4PM T,W,Th,F; 9AM-Noon Sat.

### Simsbury Town
**Real Estate Recording**, Simsbury Town Clerk, 933 Hopmeadow Street, Simsbury, CT 06070. 203-651-3751 8:30AM-4:30PM.

### Somers Town
**Real Estate Recording**, Somers Town Clerk, 600 Main Street, Somers, CT 06071. 203-763-0841 8:30AM-4:30PM.

### South Windsor Town
**Real Estate Recording**, South Windsor Town Clerk, 1540 Sullivan Avenue, Town Hall, South Windsor, CT 06074-2786. 203-644-2511 X225

### Southbury Town
**Real Estate Recording**, Southbury Town Clerk, 501 Main Street South, Southbury, CT 06488-2295. 203-262-0657 8:30AM-4:30PM.

### Southington Town
**Real Estate Recording**, Southington Town Clerk, 75 Main Street, Town Office Building, Southington, CT 06489. 203-276-6211 8:30AM-4:30PM.

### Sprague Town
**Real Estate Recording**, Sprague Town Clerk, 1 Main Street, Baltic, CT 06330. 203-822-3001 8AM-5PM M-F (Tue Open Until 7:30PM).

### Stafford Town
**Real Estate Recording**, Stafford Town Clerk, Warren Memorial Town Hall, Stafford Springs, CT 06076. 203-684-2532 8:15AM-4PM M-W; 8:15AM-6:30PM Th; 8AM-Noon F.

### Stamford City
**Real Estate Recording**, Stamford City Clerk, 888 Washington Blvd, Stamford, CT 06901. 203-977-4054 8:30AM-4:30PM (July,August 8AM-4PM).

### Sterling Town
**Real Estate Recording**, Sterling Town Clerk, 1114 Plainfield Pike, Oneco, CT 06373. 203-564-2657 8:30AM-3:30PM; June 1-Sept 5th 8AM-3PM.

### Stonington Town
**Real Estate Recording**, Stonington Town Clerk, 152 Elm Street, Stonington, CT 06378. 203-535-5060 8:30AM-4PM.

### Stratford Town
**Real Estate Recording**, Stratford Town Clerk, 2725 Main Street, Room 101, Stratford, CT 06497-5892. 203-385-4020 8AM-4:30PM.

### Suffield Town
**Real Estate Recording**, Suffield Town Clerk, 83 Mountain Road, Town Hall, Suffield, CT 06078. 203-668-7391 8AM-4:30PM M-Th; 8AM-1PM F.

### Thomaston Town
**Real Estate Recording**, Thomaston Town Clerk, 158 Main Street, Thomaston, CT 06787. 203-283-4141 9AM-4PM,7-9PM M; 9AM-4PM T-Th; 9AM-12 F.

## County Records

### Thompson Town

**Real Estate Recording**, Thompson Town Clerk, 815 Riverside Drive, No. Grosvenor Dale, CT 06255. 203-923-9900 9AM-5PM.

### Tolland County

**Tolland Superior Court**, 69 Brooklyn St, Rockville, CT 06066. 203-875-6294 (EST) 9AM-5PM. Felony, Civil Actions Over $2,000.

**Geographical Area Court #19**, 55 W Main St, Rockville, CT 06066. 203-875-2527 (EST) 9AM-5PM. Misdemeanor, Eviction, Small Claims.

**Ashford Probate Court**, 20 Pompey Hollow Rd, Ashford, CT 06278. 203-429-4986 (EST) 1AM-3:00PM Thu (And by appointment). Probate.

**Andover Probate Court**, 222 Bolton Center Rd, Bolton, CT 06043. (EST) Probate.

**Coventry Probate Court**, Town Hall, 1712 Main St, Coventry, CT 06238. 203-742-6791 (EST) 9AM-12PM Wed & Thu, 7:30PM-9PM Tue. Probate.

**Hebron Probate Court**, 15 Gilead Rd, Hebron, CT 06248. 203-228-9406 (EST) 10AM-4PM Mon & Wed, 8AM-12:30PM Fri And by appointment July/Aug. Probate.

**Ellington Probate Court**, PO Box 268, 14 Park Place, Rockville, CT 06066. 203-872-0519 (EST) 9Am-4PM M-F (And by appointment). Probate.

**Somers Probate Court**, PO Box 308, 600 Main St, Somers, CT 06071. 203-749-7012 (EST) 9AM-1PM Tue & Thu (And by appointment). Probate.

**Stafford Probate Court**, PO Box 63, Main St, Stafford Springs, CT 06076. 203-684-3423 (EST) 9AM-12PM 1PM-5PM Mon, 9AM-12PM Tue-Fri. Probate.

**Mansfield Probate Court**, 4 South Eagleville Rd, Storrs, CT 06268. 203-429-3313 (EST) 3AM-4:30PM M, 2:30PM-4:30PM T-W, 2AM-4:30PM Th (By Appointment). Probate.

**Tolland Probate Court**, Po Box 667, Tolland Green, Tolland, CT 06084. 203-871-3640 (EST) 9Am-12PM Tue & Thu, 7PM-9PM Wed (And by appointment). Probate.

### Tolland Town

**Real Estate Recording**, Tolland Town Clerk, Hicks Memorial Municipal Center, 21 Tolland Green, Tolland, CT 06084. 203-871-3630 9AM-4:30PM M,T,W,Th; 9AM-12:30PM F; (Th open 5:30-8:30PM).

### Torrington City

**Real Estate Recording**, Torrington City Clerk, 140 Main Street, City Hall, Torrington, CT 06790. 203-489-2236 9AM-4:30PM.

### Trumbull Town

**Real Estate Recording**, Trumbull Town Clerk, 5866 Main Street, Trumbull, CT 06611. 203-452-5035 9AM-5PM M,T,Th,F; 1PM-5PM W.

### Union Town

**Real Estate Recording**, Union Town Clerk, 1024 Buckley Highway, Route 171, Union, CT 06076-9520. 203-684-3770 9AM-Noon T,Th; 9AM-Noon, 1-3PM W.

### Vernon Town

**Real Estate Recording**, Vernon Town Clerk, 14 Park Place, Rockville, CT 06066. 203-872-8591 9AM-5PM.

### Voluntown Town

**Real Estate Recording**, Voluntown Town Clerk, Main Street, Town Hall, Voluntown, CT 06384. 203-376-4089 9AM-2PM; 6-8PM T Evening.

### Wallingford Town

**Real Estate Recording**, Wallingford Town Clerk, 45 South Main Street, Municipal Building, Wallingford, CT 06492. 203-294-2145 9AM-5PM.

### Warren Town

**Real Estate Recording**, Warren Town Clerk, Sackett Hill Road, Town Hall, Warren, CT 06754. 203-868-0090 10AM-4PM W,Th; 10AM-Noon M,Fday.

### Washington Town

**Real Estate Recording**, Washington Town Clerk, Bryan Memorial Town Hall, Washington Depot, CT 06794. 203-868-2786 9AM-4:45PM M,T,Th,F; 9AM-Noon W.

### Waterbury City

**Real Estate Recording**, Waterbury Town Clerk, 235 Grand Street, City Hall, Waterbury, CT 06702. 203-574-6806 8:30AM-4:50PM.

### Waterford Town

**Real Estate Recording**, Waterford Town Clerk, 15 Rope Ferry Road, Waterford, CT 06385. 203-444-5831 8AM-4PM.

### Watertown Town

**Real Estate Recording**, Watertown Town Clerk, 37 DeForest Street, Watertown, CT 06795. 203-945-5230 9AM-5PM.

### West Hartford Town

**Real Estate Recording**, West Hartford Town Clerk, 50 South Main Street, Room 313 Town Hall Common, West Hartford, CT 06107-2431. 203-523-3148 8:30AM-4:30PM.

### West Haven City

**Real Estate Recording**, West Haven City Clerk, 355 Main Street, West Haven, CT 06516. 203-937-3535 9AM-5PM.

### Westbrook Town

**Real Estate Recording**, Westbrook Town Clerk, 1163 Boston Post Road, Westbrook, CT 06498. 203-399-3044 9AM-4PM M-W & F; 9AM-6:30PM Th.

### Weston Town

**Real Estate Recording**, Weston Town Clerk, 56 Norfield Road, Weston, CT 06883. 203-222-2616 9AM-4:30PM.

### Westport Town

**Real Estate Recording**, Westport Town Clerk, 110 Myrtle Avenue, Westport, CT 06881. 203-226-8311 8:30AM-4:30PM.

### Wethersfield Town

**Real Estate Recording**, Wethersfield Town Clerk, 505 Silas Deane Highway, Wethersfield, CT 06109. 203-721-2880 8AM-4:30PM.

### Willington Town

**Real Estate Recording**, Willington Town Clerk, 40 Old Farms Road, Willington, CT 06279. 203-429-9965 9AM-2PM (M open 6-8PM).

### Wilton Town

**Real Estate Recording**, Wilton Town Clerk, 238 Danbury Road, Wilton, CT 06897. 203-834-9205 8:30AM-4:30PM.

### Winchester Town

**Real Estate Recording**, Winchester Town Clerk, 338 Main Street, Town Hall, Winsted, CT 06098-1640. 203-379-2713 8AM-4PM.

### Windham County

**Windham Superior Court**, 155 Church St, Putnam, CT 06260. 203-928-7749 (EST) 9AM-5PM. Felony, Civil Actions Over $2,000.

**Geographical Area Court #11**, 172 Main St (PO Box 688), Danielson, CT 06239. 203-774-8516 (EST) 9AM-5PM. Misdemeanor, Eviction, Small Claims.

**Brooklyn Probate Court**, Town Hall, Route 6, PO Box 356, Brooklyn, CT 06234-0356. 203-774-5973 (EST) 11:30AM-4:30PM Tues, (And by appointment). Probate.

**Canterbury Probate Court**, 43 Maple Lane, Canterbury, CT 06331. 203-546-9605 (EST) 8AM-4:30PM Wed (And by appointment, evenings). Probate.

**Chaplin Probate Court**, Route 198, Chaplin, CT 06235. 203-455-0027 (EST) 7PM-9PM Tue (And by appointment). Probate.

**Killingly Probate Court**, 172 Main St, Danielson, CT 06239. 203-774-8601 (EST) 1AM-4:30PM. Probate.

**Eastford Probate Court**, PO Box 359, 16 Westford Rd, Eastford, CT 06242. 203-974-1885 (EST) 10AM-12PM Wed (And by appointment). Probate.

**Hampton Probate Court**, Town Hall, 164 Main St, Hampton, CT 06247. 203-455-9132 (EST) 9AM-12PM Thu (And by appointment). Probate.

**Sterling Probate Court**, PO Box 157, Town Hall, Oneco, CT 06373. 203-564-8488 (EST) 9AM-4PM Tue, (And by appointment Sat & evenings). Probate.

**Plainfield Probate Court**, Town Hall, 8 Community Ave, Plainfield, CT 06374. 203-564-0019 (EST) Probate.

**Pomfret Probate Court**, Route 44, 5 Haven Rd, Pomfret Center, CT 06259. 203-974-0186 (EST) 10AM-4PM Tue-Thu (And by appointment). Probate.

**Putnam Probate Court**, 195 Providence Street, Putnam, CT 06260. 203-928-2723 (EST) 9AM-12PM 1PM-4:30PM MTTF, 9AM-12PM Wed. Probate.

# Connecticut

**Thompson Probate Court**, Route 12, Town Hall, Thompson, CT 06277. 203-923-2203 (EST) 9AM-12PM M-F (And by Appointment). Probate.

**Windham Probate Court**, PO Box 34, 979 Main St, Willimantic, CT 06226. 203-456-3593 (EST) 9AM-1PM. Probate.

**Woodstock Probate Court**, PO Box 123, Route 169, Woodstock, CT 06281. 203-928-2223 (EST) 3PM-6PM Wed, 1:30PM-4:30PM Thu (And by appointment). Probate.

## Windham Town

**Real Estate Recording**, Windham Town Clerk, 979 Main Street, Willimantic, CT 06226. 203-456-3593 X215 8:30AM-4:30PM.

## Windsor Locks Town

**Real Estate Recording**, Windsor Locks Town Clerk, 50 Church Street, Town Office Building, Windsor Locks, CT 06096. 203-627-1441 8:30AM-4:30PM.

## Windsor Town

**Real Estate Recording**, Windsor Town Clerk, 275 Broad Street, Windsor, CT 06095. 203-285-1902 8AM-4:45PM.

## Wolcott Town

**Real Estate Recording**, Wolcott Town Clerk, 10 Kenea Avenue, Town Hall, Wolcott, CT 06716. 203-879-8100 9AM-4:30PM.

## Woodbridge Town

**Real Estate Recording**, Woodbridge Town Clerk, 11 Meetinghouse Lane, Woodbridge, CT 06525. 203-389-3422 8:30AM-4PM.

## Woodbury Town

**Real Estate Recording**, Woodbury Town Clerk, 275 Main Street South, Woodbury, CT 06798. 203-263-2144 8:30AM-4:30PM (Summer Hours 8AM-4PM).

## Woodstock Town

**Real Estate Recording**, Woodstock Town Clerk, Town Office Building, 415 Route 169, Woodstock, CT 06281. 203-928-6595 8:30AM-4:30PM M,T,Th; 8:30AM-6PM W; 8:30AM-3PM F.

**County Records**

# Delaware

## Kent County

**Real Estate Recording**, Kent County Recorder of Deeds, County Administration Bldg., 414 Federal St., Dover, DE 19901. 302-736-2060 (EST) 8:30AM-4:30PM.

**Chancery Court**, 45 The Green, Dover, DE 19901. 302-736-2242 (EST) 8:30AM-4:30PM. Civil, Probate.

**Superior Court**, Office of Prothonotary, 38 The Green, Dover, DE 19901. 302-739-3184 (EST) 8AM-5PM. Felony, Misdemeanor, Civil Actions Over $50,000.

**Court of Common Pleas**, 38 The Green, Dover, DE 19901. 302-739-4618 (EST) 8:30AM-4:30PM. Misdemeanor, Civil Actions Under $50,000.

**Dover Justice of the Peace**, 516 W Loockerman, Dover, DE 19901. 302-739-4316 (EST) Civil Actions Under $15,000, Eviction, Small Claims.

**Dover Justice of the Peace**, 516 W Loockerman, Dover, DE 19901. 302-739-4554 (EST) Misdemeanor.

**Harrington Justice of the Peace**, Rte 13 Box 3, Harrington, DE 19952. 302-398-8247 (EST) Misdemeanor, Civil Actions Under $15,000, Eviction, Small Claims.

**Smyrna Justice of the Peace**, 100 Monrovia Ave, Smyrna, DE 19977. 302-653-7083 (EST) Misdemeanor, Civil Actions Under $15,000, Eviction, Small Claims.

## New Castle County

**Real Estate Recording**, New Castle County Recorder of Deeds, 800 French Street, 4th Floor, Wilmington, DE 19801. 302-571-7550 (EST) 9AM-4:45PM.

**Chancery Court**, 1020 N King St, Wilmington, DE 19801. 302-571-7540 (EST) 9AM-5PM. Civil, Probate.

**Superior Court**, County Courthouse, Office of Prothonotar, Wilmington, DE 19801. 302-577-6470 (EST) 8:30AM-5PM. Felony, Misdemeanor, Civil Actions Over $50,000.

**Court of Common Pleas**, 1000 N King St, Wilmington, DE 19801-3348. 302-577-2430 (EST) 8:30AM-4:30PM. Misdemeanor, Civil Actions Under $50,000.

**Wilmington Justice of the Peace**, 820 N French St, 2nd Floor, Wilmington, DE 19801. 302-577-2550 (EST) Civil Actions Under $15,000, Eviction, Small Claims.

**Wilmington Justice of the Peace**, 212 Greenbank Rd, Wilmington, DE 19808. 302-995-8646 (EST) Civil Actions Under $15,000, Eviction, Small Claims.

**New Castle Justice of the Peace**, 61 Christiana Rd, New Castle, DE 19720. 302-323-4450 (EST) Misdemeanor.

**Wilmington Justice of the Peace**, 820 N French St, 2nd Floor, Wilmington, DE 19801. 302-577-2552 (EST) Misdemeanor.

**Wilington Justice of the Peace**, 210 Greenbank Rd, Wilmington, DE 19808. 302-995-8640 (EST) Misdemeanor.

**Wilmington Justice of the Peace**, 716 Philadelphia Pike, Wilmington, DE 19809. 302-764-4142 (EST) Misdemeanor.

**Wilmington Justice of the Peace**, 1301 E 12th St, Wilmington, DE 19809. 302-429-7740 (EST) Misdemeanor.

**Wilmington Municipal Court**, PO Box 8978, Wilmington, DE 19899. 302-571-4530 (EST) 9AM-5PM. Misdemeanor.

## Sussex County

**Real Estate Recording**, Sussex County Recorder of Deeds, Courthouse on the Circle, Second Floor Room 213, Georgetown, DE 19947. 302-855-7785 (EST) 8:30AM-4:30PM.

**Chancery Court**, PO Box 424, Georgetown, DE 19947. 302-855-7842 (EST) 8:30AM-4:30PM. Civil, Probate.

**Superior Court**, PO Box 756 Office of Prothonotary, Georgetown, DE 19947. 302-856-5740 (EST) 8AM-4:30PM. Felony, Misdemeanor, Civil Actions Over $50,000.

**Court of Common Pleas**, PO Box 426, Georgetown, DE 19947. 302-856-5333 (EST) 8:30AM-4:30PM. Misdemeanor, Civil Actions Under $50,000.

**Georgetown Justice of the Peace**, 17 Shortly Rd, Georgetown, DE 19947. 302-856-1447 (EST) Civil Actions Under $15,000, Eviction, Small Claims.

**Seaford Justice of the Peace**, 408 Stein Highway, Seaford, DE 19973. 302-629-5433 (EST) Civil Actions Under $15,000, Eviction, Small Claims.

**Georgetown Justice of the Peace**, 17 Shortly Rd, Georgetown, DE 19947. 302-856-1445 (EST) Misdemeanor.

**Lewes Justice of the Peace**, Rt3 9 Box 175, Lewes, DE 19958. 302-645-6163 (EST) Misdemeanor.

**Milford Justice of the Peace**, 715 S DuPont Highway, Milford, DE 19963. 302-422-5922 (EST) Misdemeanor.

**Millsboro Justice of the Peace**, Pte 113 PO Box 192, Millsboro, DE 19966. 302-934-7268 (EST) Misdemeanor.

**Seaford Justice of the Peace**, 408 Stein Highway, Seaford, DE 19973. 302-628-2036 (EST) Misdemeanor.

# District of Columbia

## District of Columbia

**Real Estate Recording**, District of Columbia Recorder of Deeds, 515 D Street NW, Room 203, Washington, DC 20001. 202-727-5381 (EST)

**Superior Court-Civil Division**, 500 Indiana Ave NW, Washington, DC 20001. 202-879-1135 9AM-4PM. Civil Actions Over $5,000, Eviction, Small Claims.

**Superior Court-Criminal Division**, 500 Indiana Ave NW, Washington, DC 20001. 202-879-1373 9AM-4PM. Felony, Misdemeanor.

**Superior Court-Tax/Probate Division**, 500 Indiana Ave NW, Washington, DC 20001. 202-879-4800 9AM-4PM. Probate.

# Florida

## Alachua County

**Real Estate Recording**, Alachua County Clerk of the Circuit Court, 12 S.E. 1st St., County Administration Bldg.-Room 151, Gainesville, FL 32601. 904-374-3625 (EST) 8:30AM-5PM.

**Circuit and County Court**, PO Box 600, Gainesville, FL 32602. 904-374-3611 (EST) 8AM-5PM. Felony, Misdemeanor, Civil Actions Over $2,500, Eviction, Small Claims, Probate.

## Baker County

**Real Estate Recording**, Baker County Clerk of the Circuit Court, 339 East MacClenny Avenue, MacClenny, FL 32063. 904-259-3121 (EST) 8:30AM-5PM.

**Circuit and County Court-Civil**, 339 E Macclenny Ave, Macclenny, FL 32063. 904-259-3121 (EST) 8:30AM-5PM. Civil Actions Over $2,500, Eviction, Small Claims, Probate.

**Circuit and County Court-Criminal**, 339 E Macclenny Ave, Macclenny, FL 32063. 904-259-3121 (EST) 8:30AM-5PM. Felony, Misdemeanor.

## Bay County

**Real Estate Recording**, Bay County Clerk of the Circuit Court, 300 East 4th Street, Courthouse, Panama City, FL 32401. 904-747-5104 (CST) 8AM-4:30PM.

**Circuit Court-Civil**, PO Box 2269, Panama City, FL 32402. 904-763-9061 (CST) 8AM-4:30PM. Civil Actions Over $15,000, Probate.

**County Court-Civil**, PO Box 2269, Panama City, FL 32402. 904-763-9061 (CST) 8AM-4:30PM. Civil Actions Under $15,000, Eviction, Small Claims.

**Circuit Court-Criminal**, PO Box 2269, Panama City, FL 32402. 904-763-9061 (CST) 8AM-4:30PM. Felony.

**County Court-Misdemeanor**, PO Box 2269, Panama City, FL 32402. 904-747-5144 (CST) 8AM-4:30PM. Misdemeanor.

## Bradford County

**Real Estate Recording**, Bradford County Clerk of the Circuit Court, 945 North Temple Avenue, Starke, FL 32091. 904-964-6280 (EST) 8AM-5PM.

**Circuit Court**, PO Drawer B, Starke, FL 32091. 904-964-6280 (EST) 8AM-5PM. Felony, Civil Actions Over $15,000, Probate.

**County Court**, PO Drawer B, Starke, FL 32091. 904-964-6280 (EST) 8AM-5PM. Misdemeanor, Civil Actions Under $15,000, Eviction, Small Claims.

## Brevard County

**Real Estate Recording**, Brevard County Clerk of the Circuit Court, 700 South Park Ave., Building #2, Titusville, FL 32780. 407-264-5244 (EST) 8AM-5PM.

**Circuit and County Courts-Civil**, 700 Park Ave, Titusville, FL 32780. 407-264-5256 (EST) 8AM-4:30PM. Civil Actions Over $2,500, Eviction, Small Claims, Probate.

**Circuit Court-Felony**, 700 Park Ave, Titusville, FL 32780. 407-264-5259 (EST) 8AM-4:30PM. Felony.

**County Court-Misdemeanor**, 700 Park Ave, Titusville, FL 32780. 407-264-5259 (EST) 8AM-4:30PM. Misdemeanor.

## Broward County

**Real Estate Recording**, Broward County, 115 South Andrews Avenue, Room 114, Fort Lauderdale, FL 33301. 305-357-7273 (EST) 8:30AM-4:30PM M,T,Th,F; 8:30AM-Noon W.

**County and Circuit Court**, 201 SE 6th St, Ft Lauderdale, FL 33301. 305-831-5729 (EST) 9AM-4PM. Felony, Misdemeanor, Civil Actions Over $2,500, Eviction, Small Claims, Probate.

## Calhoun County

**Real Estate Recording**, Calhoun County Clerk of the Circuit Court, 425 East Central Avenue, Blountstown, FL 32424. 904-674-4545 (CST) 8AM-4PM.

**Circuit and County Court**, 425 E Central Ave, Blountstown, FL 32424. 904-674-4545 (CST) 8AM-4PM. Felony, Civil Actions Over $15,000, Probate.

## Charlotte County

**Real Estate Recording**, Charlotte County Clerk of the Circuit Court, Taylor Road & Olympia Avenue, Courthouse Room 141, Punta Gorda, FL 33950. 813-637-2251 (EST) 8AM-5PM.

**Circuit and County Court-Civil Division**, PO Box 1687, Punta Gorda, FL 33951-1687. 813-637-2230 (EST) 8AM-5PM. Civil Actions Over $2,500, Eviction, Small Claims, Probate.

**Circuit and County Court-Criminal Division**, PO Box 1687, Punta Gorda, FL 33951-1687. 813-637-2115 (EST) 8AM-5PM. Felony, Misdemeanor.

## Citrus County

**Real Estate Recording**, Citrus County Clerk of the Circuit Court, 110 North Apopka Avenue, Inverness, FL 34450. 904-637-9478 (EST) 8AM-4:30PM.

**Circuit Court**, 110 N Apopka Rm 101, Inverness, FL 34450. 904-637-9400 (EST) 8AM-4:30PM. Felony, Civil Actions Over $15,000, Probate.

**County Court**, 110 N Apopka, Inverness, FL 34450. 904-637-9400 (EST) 8AM-4:30PM. Misdemeanor, Civil Actions Under $15,000, Eviction, Small Claims.

## Clay County

**Real Estate Recording**, Clay County Clerk of the Circuit Court, 825 North Orange Avenue, Green Cove Springs, FL 32043. 904-284-6300 (EST) 8:30AM-4:30PM.

**Circuit Court**, PO Box 698, Green Cove Springs, FL 32043. 904-284-6316 (EST) 8:30AM-4:30PM. Felony, Civil Actions Over $15,000, Probate.

**County Court**, PO Box 698, Green Cove Springs, FL 32043. 904-284-6316 (EST) 8:30AM-4:30PM. Misdemeanor, Civil Actions Under $15,000, Eviction, Small Claims.

## Collier County

**Real Estate Recording**, Collier County Clerk of the Circuit Court, 3301 Tamiami Trail East, Administration Bldg., 4th floor, Naples, FL 33962. 813-774-8261 (EST) 8AM-5PM (No recording after 4:30PM).

**Circuit Court**, PO Box 413044, Naples, FL 33941. 813-732-2646 (EST) 8AM-5PM. Felony, Civil Actions Over $15,000, Probate.

**County Court**, PO Box 413044, Naples, FL 33941. 813-732-2646 (EST) 8AM-5PM. Misdemeanor, Civil Actions Under $15,000, Eviction, Small Claims.

## Columbia County

**Real Estate Recording**, Columbia County Clerk of the Circuit Court, 145 North Hernando Street, Lake City, FL 32055. 904-758-1342 (EST) 8AM-5PM.

**Circuit and County Court**, PO Drawer 2069, Lake City, FL 32056. 904-758-1353 (EST) 8AM-5PM. Felony, Misdemeanor, Civil Actions Over $2,500, Eviction, Small Claims, Probate.

## Dade County

**Real Estate Recording**, Dade County Clerk of the Circuit Court, 44 West Flager Street, 8th Floor, Miami, FL 33130. 305-372-7777 (EST) 8:30AM-4:30PM.

**Circuit and County Court-Civil**, 73 W Flagler St, Miami, FL 33130. 305-375-5775 (EST) 8AM-5PM. Civil Actions Over $2,500, Eviction, Small Claims, Probate.

**Circuit and County Court-Criminal**, 1351 NW 12th St, Miami, FL 33125. 305-547-4888 (EST) 8:30AM-4:30PM. Felony, Misdemeanor.

## De Soto County

**Real Estate Recording**, De Soto County Clerk of the Circuit Court, 201 East Oak Street, Arcadia, FL 33821. 813-993-4876 (EST) 8:30AM-4:30PM.

**Circuit and County Court**, PO Box 591, Arcadia, FL 33821. 813-993-4876 (EST) 8AM-4:30PM. Felony, Misdemeanor, Civil Actions Over $2,500, Eviction, Small Claims, Probate.

## Dixie County

**Real Estate Recording**, Dixie County Clerk of the Circuit Court, Corner Highway 351 & King Avenue, Courthouse, Cross City, FL 32628. 904-498-1200 (EST) 9AM-Noon,1-5PM.

**Circuit and County Court**, PO Drawer 1206, Cross City, FL 32628-1206. 904-498-1200 (EST) 9AM-5PM. Felony, Misdemeanor, Civil Actions Over $2,500, Eviction, Small Claims, Probate.

## Duval County

**Real Estate Recording**, Duval County Clerk of the Circuit Court, 330 East Bay Street, Courthouse, Jacksonville, FL 32202. 904-630-2043 (EST) 8AM-5PM.

**Circuit and County Court-Civil Division**, 330 E Bay St, Jacksonville, FL 32202. 904-630-2039 (EST) 8AM-5PM. Civil Actions Over $2,500, Eviction, Small Claims, Probate.

**Circuit and County Court-Criminal Division**, 330 E Bay St, Jacksonville, FL 32202. 904-630-2070 (EST) 8AM-5PM. Felony, Misdemeanor.

## Escambia County

**Real Estate Recording**, Escambia County Comptroller, 223 Palafox Place, Old Courthouse, Pensacola, FL 32501. 904-436-5718 (CST) 8AM-5PM.

**Circuit and County Courts-Civil Division**, 190 Governmental Center, Pensacola, FL 32501. 904-436-5260 (CST) 8AM-5PM. Civil Actions Over $2,500, Eviction, Small Claims, Probate.

**Circuit and County Court-Criminal Division**, 190 Governmental Center, Pensacola, FL 32501. 904-436-5200 (CST) 8AM-5PM. Felony, Misdemeanor.

## Flagler County

**Real Estate Recording**, Flagler County Clerk of the Circuit Court, 200 East Moody Blvd., Courthouse 1st floor, Bunnell, FL 32010. 904-437-2224 (EST)

**Circuit and County Courts**, PO Box 787, Bunnell, FL 32110. 904-437-7430 (EST) 8AM-5PM. Felony, Misdemeanor, Civil Actions Over $2,500, Eviction, Small Claims, Probate.

## Franklin County

**Real Estate Recording**, Franklin County Clerk of the Circuit Court, Market Street, Apalachicola, FL 32320. 904-653-8861 (EST) 8:30AM-4:30PM.

**Circuit and County Courts**, PO Box 340, Apalachicola, FL 32321. 904-653-8862 (EST) 8:30AM-4:30PM. Felony, Misdemeanor, Civil Actions Over $2,500, Eviction, Small Claims, Probate.

## Gadsden County

**Real Estate Recording**, Gadsden County Clerk of the Circuit Court, 10 East Jefferson Street, Quincy, FL 32351. 904-875-8603 (EST) 8:30AM-5PM.

**Circuit and County Courts-Civil Division**, PO Box 1649, Quincy, FL 32353. 904-875-8601 (EST) 8:30AM-5PM. Civil Actions Over $2,500, Eviction, Small Claims, Probate.

**Circuit and County Courts-Criminal Division**, 15 Jefferson St, Quincy, FL 32351. 904-875-8609 (EST) 8:30AM-5PM. Felony, Misdemeanor.

## Gilchrist County

**Real Estate Recording**, Gilchrist County Clerk of the Circuit Court, Courthouse, Highway 129 & Highway 26, Trenton, FL 32693. 904-463-3170 (EST) 8:30AM-5PM.

**Circuit and County Courts**, 112 S Main St, Trenton, FL 32693. 904-463-3170 (EST) 8:30AM-5PM. Felony, Misdemeanor, Civil Actions Over $2,500, Eviction, Small Claims, Probate.

## Glades County

**Real Estate Recording**, Glades County Clerk of the Circuit Court, Highway 27 and 5th Street, 500 Ave. J, Moore Haven, FL 33471. 813-946-0113 (EST) 8AM-5PM.

**Circuit and County Courts**, PO Box 10, Moore Haven, FL 33471. 813-946-0113 (EST) 8AM-5PM. Felony, Misdemeanor, Civil Actions Over $2,500, Eviction, Small Claims, Probate.

## Gulf County

**Real Estate Recording**, Gulf County Clerk of the Circuit Court, 1000 5th Street, Port St. Joe, FL 32456-1699. 904-229-6113 (CST) 9AM-5PM.

**Circuit and County Courts**, 1000 5th St, Port St Joe, FL 32456. 904-229-6112 (CST) 9AM-5PM. Felony, Misdemeanor, Civil Actions Over $2,500, Eviction, Small Claims, Probate.

## Hamilton County

**Real Estate Recording**, Hamilton County Clerk of the Circuit Court, 207 NE 1st Street, Room 106, Jasper, FL 32052. 904-792-1288 (EST) 8:30AM-4:30PM.

**Circuit and County Courts**, 202 NE 1st St #106, Jasper, FL 32052. 904-792-1288 (EST) 8:30AM-4:30PM. Felony, Misdemeanor, Civil Actions Over $2,500, Eviction, Small Claims, Probate.

## Hardee County

**Real Estate Recording**, Hardee County Clerk of the Circuit Court, 417 West Main Street, Wauchula, FL 33873. 813-773-4174 (EST) 8:30AM-5PM; 8:30AM-3:15PM Recording hours.

**Circuit and County Courts**, PO Drawer 1749, Wauchula, FL 33873-1749. 813-773-4174 (EST) 8:30AM-5PM. Felony, Misdemeanor, Civil Actions Over $2,500, Eviction, Small Claims, Probate.

## Hendry County

**Real Estate Recording**, Hendry County Clerk of the Circuit Court, Corner of Highway 80 and 29, Courthouse, La Belle, FL 33935. 813-675-5217 (EST) 8:30AM-5PM.

**Circuit and County Courts**, PO Box 1760, LaBelle, FL 33935-1760. 813-675-5217 (EST) 8:30AM-5PM. Felony, Misdemeanor, Civil Actions Over $2,500, Eviction, Small Claims, Probate.

## Hernando County

**Real Estate Recording**, Hernando County Clerk of the Circuit Court, 20 North Main, Room 215, Brooksville, FL 34601. 904-754-4201 (EST) 8:30AM-5PM.

**Circuit and County Courts**, 20 N Main St, Brooksville, FL 34601. 904-754-4201 (EST) 8:30AM-5PM. Felony, Misdemeanor, Civil Actions Over $2,500, Eviction, Small Claims, Probate.

## Highlands County

**Real Estate Recording**, Highlands County Clerk of the Circuit Court, 430 South Commerce Avenue, Sebring, FL 33870. 813-386-6590 (EST) 8:30AM-4:30PM.

**Circuit and County Court**, 430 S Commerce Ave, Sebring, FL 33870. 813-385-2581 (EST) 8AM-4:30PM. Felony, Misdemeanor, Civil Actions Over $2,500, Eviction, Small Claims, Probate.

## Hillsborough County

**Real Estate Recording**, Hillsborough County Clerk of the Circuit Court, 419 Pierce Street, Room 114-K, Tampa, FL 33602. 813-276-8100 (EST) X7507 8AM-5PM.

**Circuit and County Courts**, 419 Pierce St, Tampa, FL 33602. 813-223-7811 (EST) 8AM-5PM. Felony, Misdemeanor, Civil Actions Over $2,500, Eviction, Small Claims, Probate.

## Holmes County

**Real Estate Recording**, Holmes County Clerk of the Circuit Court, 201 North Oklahoma Street, Bonifay, FL 32425. 904-547-1102 (CST) 8AM-4PM.

**Circuit and County Courts**, PO Box 397, Bonifay, FL 32425. 904-547-1100 (CST) 8AM-4PM. Felony, Misdemeanor, Civil Actions Over $2,500, Eviction, Small Claims, Probate.

## Indian River County

**Real Estate Recording**, Indian River County Clerk of the Circuit Court, 2145 14th Avenue, Vero Beach, FL 32960. 407-567-8000 (EST) 8:30AM-5PM.

**Circuit and County Courts**, PO Box 1028, Vero Beach, FL 32961. 407-567-8000 (EST) 8:30AM-5PM. Felony, Misdemeanor, Civil Actions Over $2,500, Eviction, Small Claims, Probate.

## Jackson County

**Real Estate Recording**, Jackson County Clerk of the Circuit Court, 4445 East Lafayette Street, Courthouse, Marianna, FL 32446. 904-482-9552 (CST) 8AM-4:30PM.

**Circuit and County Courts**, PO Box 510, Marianna, FL 32447. 904-482-9552 (CST) 8AM-4:30PM. Felony, Misdemeanor, Civil Actions Over $2,500, Eviction, Small Claims, Probate.

## Jefferson County

**Real Estate Recording**, Jefferson County Clerk of the Circuit Court, Courthouse, Room 10, Monticello, FL 32344. 904-997-3596 (EST) 8AM-5PM.

**Circuit and County Courts**, Jefferson County Courthouse, Rm 10, Monticello, FL 32344. 904-997-3596 (EST) 8AM-5PM. Felony, Misdemeanor, Civil Actions Over $2,500, Eviction, Small Claims, Probate.

## Lafayette County

**Real Estate Recording**, Lafayette County Clerk of the Circuit Court, Main & Fletcher Streets, Courthouse, Mayo, FL 32066. 904-294-1600 (EST) 8AM-5PM.

**Circuit and County Courts**, PO Box 88, Mayo, FL 32066. 904-294-1600 (EST) 8AM-5PM. Felony, Misdemeanor, Civil Actions Over $2,500, Eviction, Small Claims, Probate.

## Lake County

**Real Estate Recording**, Lake County Clerk of the Circuit Court, 550 West Main Street, Tavares, FL 32778. 904-742-4114 (EST) 8:30AM-5PM (Recording hours: 8:30AM-4:30PM).

**Circuit and County Courts**, 550 W Main St or PO Box 7800, Tavares, FL 32778. 904-742-4100 (EST) 8:30AM-5PM. Felony, Misdemeanor, Civil Actions Over $2,500, Eviction, Small Claims, Probate.

## Lee County

**Real Estate Recording**, Lee County Clerk of the Circuit Court, 2115 Second Street, Court-

# Florida

house - 2nd Floor, Fort Myers, FL 33901. 813-335-2291 (EST) 7:45AM-5PM.

**Circuit and County Courts**, PO Box 2469, Ft Myers, FL 33902. 813-335-2283 (EST) 7:45AM-5PM. Felony, Misdemeanor, Civil Actions Over $2,500, Eviction, Small Claims, Probate.

## Leon County

**Real Estate Recording**, Leon County Clerk of the Circuit Court, 301 South Monroe Street, Tallahassee, FL 32301. 904-488-7538 (EST) 8:30AM-5PM.

**Circuit and County Courts**, PO Box 726, Tallahassee, FL 32302. 904-488-7534 (EST) 8:30AM-5PM. Felony, Misdemeanor, Civil Actions Over $2,500, Eviction, Small Claims, Probate.

## Levy County

**Real Estate Recording**, Levy County Clerk of the Circuit Court, Court Street, Courthouse, Bronson, FL 32621. 904-486-5228 (EST) 8AM-5PM.

**Circuit and County Courts**, PO Box 610, Bronson, FL 32621. 904-486-5100 (EST) 8AM-5PM. Felony, Misdemeanor, Civil Actions Over $2,500, Eviction, Small Claims, Probate.

## Liberty County

**Real Estate Recording**, Liberty County Clerk of the Circuit Court, Highway 20, Courthouse, Bristol, FL 32321. 904-643-2215 (EST) 8AM-5PM.

**Circuit and County Courts**, PO Box 399, Bristol, FL 32321. 904-643-2215 (EST) 8AM-5PM. Felony, Misdemeanor, Civil Actions Over $2,500, Eviction, Small Claims, Probate.

## Madison County

**Real Estate Recording**, Madison County Clerk of the Circuit Court, 101 South Range Street, Courthouse, Madison, FL 32340. 904-973-1500 (EST) 8AM-5PM.

**Circuit and County Courts**, PO Box 237, Madison, FL 32341. 904-973-1500 (EST) 8:30AM-5PM. Felony, Misdemeanor, Civil Actions Over $2,500, Eviction, Small Claims, Probate.

## Manatee County

**Real Estate Recording**, Manatee County Clerk of the Circuit Court, 1115 Manatee Avenue West, Bradenton, FL 34205. 813-741-4041 (EST) 8:30AM-5PM.

**Circuit and County Courts**, PO Box 1000, Bradenton, FL 34206. 813-749-1800 (EST) 8:30AM-5PM. Felony, Misdemeanor, Civil Actions Over $2,500, Eviction, Small Claims, Probate.

## Marion County

**Real Estate Recording**, Marion County Clerk of the Circuit Court, 110 N.W. First Avenue, Ocala, FL 34470. 904-620-3925 (EST) 8AM-5PM.

**Circuit and County Courts**, PO Box 1030, Ocala, FL 34478. 904-620-3904 (EST) 8AM-5PM. Felony, Misdemeanor, Civil Actions Over $2,500, Eviction, Small Claims, Probate.

## Martin County

**Real Estate Recording**, Martin County Clerk of the Circuit Court, 1111 S. Federal Hwy., Tower Bldg. 3rd Floor, Stuart, FL 34994. 407-288-5551 (EST) 8AM-5PM.

**Circuit and County Courts**, PO Box 9016, Stuart, FL 34995. 407-288-5576 (EST) 8AM-5PM. Felony, Misdemeanor, Civil Actions Over $2,500, Eviction, Small Claims, Probate.

## Monroe County

**Real Estate Recording**, Monroe County Clerk of the Circuit Court, 500 Whitehead Street, Courthouse, Key West, FL 33040. 305-292-3540 (EST) 8:30AM-5PM.

**Circuit and County Courts**, 500 Whitehead St, Key West, FL 33040. 305-292-3310 (EST) 8:30AM-5PM. Felony, Misdemeanor, Civil Actions Over $2,500, Eviction, Small Claims, Probate.

## Nassau County

**Real Estate Recording**, Nassau County Clerk of the Circuit Court, 416 Centre Street, Fernandina Beach, FL 32034. 904-321-5700 (EST) 9AM-5PM (Recording Hours: 9AM-4PM).

**Circuit and County Courts**, PO Box 456, Fernandina Beach, FL 32035. 904-321-5700 (EST) 9AM-5PM. Felony, Misdemeanor, Civil Actions Over $2,500, Eviction, Small Claims, Probate.

## Okaloosa County

**Real Estate Recording**, Okaloosa County Clerk of the Circuit Court, 101 East James Lee Blvd., Crestview, FL 32536. 904-689-5847 (CST) 8AM-5PM.

**Circuit and County Courts**, 1250 Eglin Pkwy, Shalimar, FL 32579. 904-651-7200 (CST) 8AM-5PM. Felony, Misdemeanor, Civil Actions Over $2,500, Eviction, Small Claims, Probate.

## Okeechobee County

**Real Estate Recording**, Okeechobee County Clerk of the Circuit Court, 304 N.W. 2nd Street, Room 101, Okeechobee, FL 33472. 813-763-2131 (EST) 8:30AM-5PM.

**Circuit and County Courts**, 304 NW 2nd St Rm 101, Okeechobee, FL 34972. 813-763-2131 (EST) 8:30AM-5:30PM. Felony, Misdemeanor, Civil Actions Over $2,500, Eviction, Small Claims, Probate.

## Orange County

**Real Estate Recording**, Orange County Comptroller, 250 N. Orange Ave., Orlando, FL 32801. 407-836-5113 (EST) 8:30AM-4PM.

**Circuit and County Courts**, 37 N Orange Ave #550, Orlando, FL 32802. 407-836-2060 (EST) 8AM-5PM. Felony, Misdemeanor, Civil Actions Over $2,500, Eviction, Small Claims, Probate.

**County Court-Apopka Branch**, 1111 N Rock Springs Rd, Apopka, FL 32712. 407-889-4176 (EST) 8AM-5PM. Misdemeanor, Civil Actions Under $15,000, Eviction, Small Claims.

**County Court #3**, 475 W Story Rd, Ocoee, FL 34761. 407-656-3229 (EST) 8AM-5PM. Misdemeanor, Civil Actions Under $15,000, Eviction, Small Claims.

**County Court, NE Orange Division**, 450 N Lakemont Ave, Winter Park, FL 32792. 407-671-1116 (EST) 8AM-5PM. Misdemeanor, Civil Actions Under $15,000, Eviction, Small Claims.

## Osceola County

**Real Estate Recording**, Osceola County Clerk of the Circuit Court, 12 South Vernon Avenue R, Kissimmee, FL 34741-5491. 407-847-1420 (EST) X1498 8:30AM-5PM; 8:30AM-4PM Recording hours.

**Circuit Court-Civil**, 12 S Vernon Ave, Kissimmee, FL 34741. 407-847-1300 (EST) 8:30AM-5PM. Civil Actions Over $2,500.

**County Court-Civil**, 12 S Vernon Ave, Kissimmee, FL 34741. 407-847-1300 (EST) 8:30AM-5PM. Eviction, Small Claims.

**Circuit Court and County Courts-Criminal Division**, 12 S Vernon Ave, Kissimmee, FL 34741. 407-847-1300 (EST) 8:30AM-5PM. Felony, Misdemeanor.

## Palm Beach County

**Real Estate Recording**, Palm Beach County Clerk of the Circuit Court, 300 North Dixie Highway, Room 201, West Palm Beach, FL 33402. 407-355-2991 (EST) 8AM-5PM.

**Circuit and County Court-Civil Division**, PO Box 2906, West Palm Beach, FL 33402. 407-355-2986 (EST) 8AM-5PM. Civil Actions Over $2,500, Eviction, Small Claims, Probate.

**Circuit and County Courts-Criminal Division**, PO Box 2906, West Palm Beach, FL 33402. 407-355-2519 (EST) 8AM-4:30PM. Felony, Misdemeanor.

## Pasco County

**Real Estate Recording**, Pasco County Clerk of the Circuit Court, 38053 East Live Oak, Dade City, FL 33525-3819. 904-521-4464 (EST) 8:30AM-5PM.

**Circuit and County Courts-Civil Division**, 38053 Live Oak Ave, Dade City, FL 33525. 904-521-4482 (EST) 8:30AM-5PM. Civil Actions Over $2,500, Eviction, Small Claims, Probate.

**Circuit and County Courts-Criminal Division**, 38053 Live Oak Ave, Dade City, FL 33525. 904-521-4482 (EST) 8:30AM-5PM. Felony, Misdemeanor.

## Pinellas County

**Real Estate Recording**, Pinellas County Clerk of the Circuit Court, 315 Court Street, Room 150, Clearwater, FL 34616. 813-464-3204 (EST) 8AM-5PM.

**Circuit and County Court-Civil**, 315 Court St, Clearwater, FL 34616. 813-464-3341 (EST) 8AM-5PM. Civil Actions Over $2,500, Eviction, Small Claims, Probate.

**Circuit Court-Felony**, 5100 144th Ave N, Clearwater, FL 34620. 813-464-6793 (EST) 8AM-5PM. Felony.

**County Court-Criminal Division**, 14255 49th St N, Clearwater, FL 34622-2801. 813-464-6800 (EST) 8AM-5PM. Misdemeanor.

## Polk County

**Real Estate Recording**, Polk County Clerk of the Circuit Court, 240 East Main St., Bartow, FL 33830. 941-534-4516 (EST) 8:30AM-4:30PM.

**Circuit Court-Civil Division**, PO Box 9000, Drawer CC2, Bartow, FL 33830. 941-534-4488

(EST) 8AM-5PM. Civil Actions Over $15,000, Probate.

**Circuit and County Courts-Criminal Division**, PO Box 9000, Drawer CC2, Bartow, FL 33830. 941-534-4000 (EST) 8AM-5PM. Felony, Misdemeanor.

**County Court**, PO Box 9000, Drawer CC12, Bartow, FL 33830. 813-534-4556 (EST) 8:30AM-4:45PM. Misdemeanor, Civil Actions Under $15,000, Eviction, Small Claims.

## Putnam County

**Real Estate Recording**, Putnam County Clerk of the Circuit Court, 518 St. Johns Avenue, Bldg. 1-E, Palatka, FL 32177. 904-329-0256 (EST) 8:30AM-4:40PM.

**Circuit and County Courts-Civil Division**, PO Box 758, Palatka, FL 32178. 904-329-0361 (EST) 8:30AM-5PM. Civil Actions Over $2,500, Eviction, Small Claims, Probate.

**Circuit and County Courts-Criminal Division**, PO Box 758, Palatka, FL 32178. 904-329-0249 (EST) 8:30AM-5PM. Felony, Misdemeanor.

## Santa Rosa County

**Real Estate Recording**, Santa Rosa County Clerk of the Circuit Court, 801 Caroline Street SE, Milton, FL 32570. 904-623-0135 (CST) 8AM-4:30PM.

**Circuit and County Courts-Civil Division**, PO Box 472, Milton, FL 32572. 904-623-0135 (CST) 8AM-4:30PM. Civil Actions Over $2,500, Eviction, Small Claims, Probate.

**Circuit and County Courts-Criminal Division**, PO Box 472, Milton, FL 32572. 904-623-0135 (CST) 8AM-4:30PM. Felony, Misdemeanor.

## Sarasota County

**Real Estate Recording**, Sarasota County Clerk of the Circuit Court, 2000 Main Street, Sarasota, FL 34237. 813-951-5231 (EST) 8:30AM-5PM.

**Circuit and County Courts-Civil Division**, PO Box 3079, Sarasota, FL 34230. 813-951-5206 (EST) 8:30AM-5PM. Civil Actions Over $2,500, Eviction, Small Claims, Probate.

**Circuit and County Courts-Criminal**, PO Box 3079, Sarasota, FL 34230. 813-951-5206 (EST) 8:30AM-5PM. Felony, Misdemeanor.

## Seminole County

**Real Estate Recording**, Seminole County Clerk of the Circuit Court, 301 Park Avenue, Room A-129, Sanford, FL 32771. 407-323-4330 (EST) 8AM-4:30PM.

**Circuit and County Courts-Civil Division**, PO Drawer C, Sanford, FL 32772-0659. 407-323-4330 (EST) 8AM-4:30PM. Civil Actions Over $2,500, Eviction, Small Claims, Probate.

**Circuit and County Courts-Criminal Division**, PO Drawer C, Sanford, FL 32771. 407-323-4330 (EST) 8AM-4:30PM. Felony, Misdemeanor.

## St. Johns County

**Real Estate Recording**, St. Johns County Clerk of the Circuit Court, 4010 Lewis Speedway, St. Augustine, FL 32084. 904-823-2229 (EST) 8AM-5PM (No Recording after 4:15PM).

**Circuit and County Courts-Civil Division**, PO Drawer 300, St Augustine, FL 32085-0300. 904-823-2333 (EST) 8AM-5PM. Civil Actions Over $2,500, Eviction, Small Claims, Probate.

**Circuit and County Courts-Criminal Division**, PO Drawer 300, St Augustine, FL 32085-0300. 904-823-2333 (EST) 8AM-5PM. Felony, Misdemeanor.

## St. Lucie County

**Real Estate Recording**, St. Lucie County Clerk of the Circuit Court, 221 South Indian River Drive, Fort Pierce, FL 34950. 407-489-6930 (EST) 8AM-5PM.

**Circuit and County Court-Civil**, PO Drawer 100, Ft Pierce, FL 34954. 407-467-2758 (EST) 8AM-5PM. Civil Actions Over $2,500, Eviction, Small Claims, Probate.

**Circuit and County Courts-Criminal Division**, PO Drawer 700, Ft Pierce, FL 34954. 407-489-6900 (EST) 8AM-5PM. Felony, Misdemeanor.

## Sumter County

**Real Estate Recording**, Sumter County Clerk of the Circuit Court, 209 North Florida Street, Bushnell, FL 33513. 904-793-0215 (EST) 8:30AM-5PM.

**Circuit and County Courts-Civil Division**, 209 N Florida St, Bushnell, FL 33513. 904-793-0215 (EST) 8:30AM-5PM. Civil Actions Over $2,500, Eviction, Small Claims, Probate.

**Circuit and County Courts-Criminal Division**, 209 N Florida St, Bushnell, FL 33513. 904-793-0215 (EST) 8:30AM-5PM. Felony, Misdemeanor.

## Suwannee County

**Real Estate Recording**, Suwannee County Clerk of the Circuit Court, 200 South Ohio Avenue, Live Oak, FL 32060. 904-364-3498 (EST) 8:30AM-5PM.

**Circuit and County Courts**, 200 S Ohio Ave, Live Oak, FL 32060. 904-362-2827 (EST) 8AM-5PM. Felony, Misdemeanor, Civil Actions Over $2,500, Eviction, Small Claims, Probate.

## Taylor County

**Real Estate Recording**, Taylor County Clerk of the Circuit Court, 108 North Jefferson Street, Perry, FL 32347. 904-838-3506 (EST) 8AM-5PM.

**Circuit and County Courts**, PO Box 620, Perry, FL 32347. 904-584-3531 (EST) 8AM-5PM. Felony, Misdemeanor, Civil Actions Over $2,500, Eviction, Small Claims, Probate.

## Union County

**Real Estate Recording**, Union County Clerk of the Circuit Court, State Road 100, Courthouse Room 103, Lake Butler, FL 32054. 904-496-3711 (EST) 8AM-5PM.

**Circuit and County Courts**, Courthouse Rm 103, Lake Butler, FL 32054. 904-496-3711 (EST) 8AM-5PM. Felony, Misdemeanor, Civil Actions Over $2,500, Eviction, Small Claims, Probate.

## Volusia County

**Real Estate Recording**, Volusia County Clerk of the Circuit Court, 120 West Indiana Avenue, De Land, FL 32720. 904-736-5912 (EST) 8AM-4:30PM.

**Circuit and County Court-Civil Division**, PO Box 43, De Land, FL 32721. 904-736-5915 (EST) 8AM-4:30PM. Civil Actions Over $2,500, Eviction, Small Claims, Probate.

**Circuit and County Courts-Criminal Division**, PO Box 43, De Land, FL 32721-0043. 904-736-5915 (EST) 8AM-4:30PM. Felony, Misdemeanor.

## Wakulla County

**Real Estate Recording**, Wakulla County Clerk of the Circuit Court, Wakulla County Court House, Highway 319, Crawfordville, FL 32327. 904-926-3331 (EST) 8AM-4PM.

**Circuit and County Courts**, PO Box 337, Crawfordville, FL 32326. 904-926-3331 (EST) 8AM-5PM. Felony, Misdemeanor, Civil Actions Over $2,500, Eviction, Small Claims, Probate.

## Walton County

**Real Estate Recording**, Walton County Clerk of the Circuit Court, Highway 90 East, Courthouse, De Funiak Springs, FL 32433. 904-892-8115 (CST) 8AM-4PM.

**Circuit and County Courts**, PO Box 1260, De Funiak Springs, FL 32433. 904-892-8115 (CST) 8AM-4:30PM. Felony, Misdemeanor, Civil Actions Over $2,500, Eviction, Small Claims, Probate.

## Washington County

**Real Estate Recording**, Washington County Clerk of the Circuit Court, 2193 Jackson Avenue, Suite 101, Chipley, FL 32428. 904-638-6285 (CST) 8AM-4PM.

**Circuit and County Courts**, PO Box 647, Chipley, FL 32428-0647. 904-638-6285 (CST) 8AM-4PM. Felony, Misdemeanor, Civil Actions Over $2,500, Eviction, Small Claims, Probate.

# Georgia

## Appling County

**Real Estate Recording**, Appling County Clerk of the Superior Court, Courthouse Square, Baxley, GA 31513. 912-367-8126 (EST) 8AM-5PM.

**Superior & State Court**, PO Box 269, Baxley, GA 31513. 912-367-8126 (EST) 8AM-5PM. Felony, Misdemeanor, Civil Actions Over $5,000.

**Magistrate Court**, Box 366, Baxley, GA 31513. 912-367-8116 (EST) 8:30AM-5PM. Civil Actions Under $5,000, Eviction, Small Claims.

**Probate Court**, Courthouse Square, Baxley, GA 31513. 912-367-8114 (EST) Probate.

## Atkinson County

**Real Estate Recording**, Atkinson County Clerk of the Superior Court, Highway 441 South, Courthouse, Pearson, GA 31642. 912-422-3343 (EST) 8AM-5PM.

**Superior Court**, PO Box 6, Pearson, GA 31642. 912-422-3343 (EST) 8AM-5PM. Felony, Misdemeanor, Civil Actions Over $5,000.

**Magistrate Court**, PO Box 6, Pearson, GA 31642. 912-422-7158 (EST) 9AM-5PM. Civil Actions Under $5,000, Eviction, Small Claims.

**Probate Court**, PO Box 855, Pearson, GA 31642. 912-422-3552 (EST) Probate.

## Bacon County

**Real Estate Recording**, Bacon County Clerk of the Superior Court, 12th Street, Courthouse, Alma, GA 31510. 912-632-4915 (EST) 9AM-5PM.

**Superior Court**, PO Box 376, Alma, GA 31510. 912-632-4915 (EST) 9AM-5PM. Felony, Misdemeanor, Civil Actions Over $5,000.

**Magistrate Court**, Box 389, Alma, GA 31510. 912-632-5961 (EST) 9AM-5PM. Civil Actions Under $5,000, Eviction, Small Claims.

**Probate Court**, PO Box 146, Alma, GA 31510. 912-632-7661 (EST) Probate.

## Baker County

**Real Estate Recording**, Baker County Clerk of the Superior Court, Courthouse Way, Newton, GA 31770. 912-734-3004 (EST) 9AM-5PM.

**Superior Court**, PO Box 10, Newton, GA 31770. 912-734-3004 (EST) 9AM-5PM. Felony, Misdemeanor, Civil Actions Over $5,000.

**Magistrate Court**, Box 535, Newton, GA 31770. 912-734-3009 (EST) 10AM-5PM. Civil Actions Under $5,000, Eviction, Small Claims.

**Probate Court**, PO Box 548, Newton, GA 31770. 912-734-3007 (EST) Probate.

## Baldwin County

**Real Estate Recording**, Baldwin County Clerk of the Superior Court, 201 West Hancock Street, Courthouse Room 7, Milledgeville, GA 31061. 912-453-6327 (EST) 8:30AM-5PM.

**Superior & State Court**, PO Drawer 987, Milledgeville, GA 31061. 912-453-6324 (EST) 8:30AM-5PM. Felony, Misdemeanor, Civil Actions Over $5,000.

**Magistrate Court**, 201 E Hancock, Rm 38, Milledgeville, GA 31061. 912-453-4446 (EST) 8:30AM-5PM. Civil Actions Under $5,000, Eviction, Small Claims.

**Probate Court**, PO Drawer 987, Milledgeville, GA 31061. 912-453-4807 (EST) Probate.

## Banks County

**Real Estate Recording**, Banks County Clerk of the Superior Court, Courthouse, Homer, GA 30547. 706-677-2320 (EST) 8:30AM-5PM.

**Superior Court**, PO Box 337, Homer, GA 30547. 706-677-2320 (EST) 8:30AM-5PM. Felony, Misdemeanor, Civil Actions Over $5,000.

**Magistrate Court**, Box 364, Homer, GA 30547. 404-677-2320 (EST) 8:30AM-5PM. Civil Actions Under $5,000, Eviction, Small Claims.

**Probate Court**, PO Box 7, Homer, GA 30547. 706-677-2320 (EST) Probate.

## Barrow County

**Real Estate Recording**, Barrow County Clerk of the Superior Court, 310 South Broad Street, Winder, GA 30680. 404-867-8965 (EST)

**Superior Court**, PO Box 1280 or PO Box 685, Winder, GA 30680. 404-307-3035 (EST) 8:30AM-5PM. Felony, Misdemeanor, Civil Actions Over $5,000.

**Magistrate Court**, 30 N Broad St, Ste 331, Winder, GA 30680. 404-307-3050 (EST) 8AM-5PM. Civil Actions Under $5,000, Eviction, Small Claims.

**Probate Court**, Barrow County Courthouse, 30 N Broad Str, Winder, GA 30680. 404-307-3045 (EST) Probate.

## Bartow County

**Real Estate Recording**, Bartow County Clerk of the Superior Court, 135 W. Cherokee Ave., Suite 233, Cartersville, GA 30120. 404-387-5025 (EST) 8AM-5PM.

**Superior Court**, 135 W Cherokee #223, Cartersville, GA 30120. 404-387-5025 (EST) 8:30AM-5PM. Felony, Misdemeanor, Civil Actions Over $5,000.

**Magistrate Court**, 135 W Cherokee, PO Box 1203, Cartersville, GA 30120. 404-387-5070 (EST) 8AM-5PM. Civil Actions Under $5,000, Eviction, Small Claims.

**Probate Court**, 135 W Cherokee #243N, Cartersville, GA 30120. 404-387-5075 (EST) Probate.

## Ben Hill County

**Real Estate Recording**, Ben Hill County Clerk of the Superior Court, 401 E. Central Ave., Courthouse, Fitzgerald, GA 31750. 912-423-3736 (EST) 8:30AM-5PM.

**Superior Court**, PO Box 1104, Fitzgerald, GA 31750. 912-423-3736 (EST) 8:30AM-5PM. Felony, Misdemeanor, Civil Actions Over $5,000.

**Magistrate Court**, Box 1163, Fitzgerald, GA 31750. 912-423-5854 (EST) 8:30AM-5:30PM. Civil Actions Under $5,000, Eviction, Small Claims.

**Probate Court**, PO Box 187, Fitzgerald, GA 31750. 912-423-2317 (EST) Probate.

## Berrien County

**Real Estate Recording**, Berrien County Clerk of the Superior Court, 101 E. Marion Ave. #3, Nashville, GA 31639. 912-686-5506 (EST) 8AM-5PM.

**Superior Court**, 101 E Marion Ave, Ste 3, Nashville, GA 31639. 912-686-5506 (EST) 8AM-5PM. Felony, Misdemeanor, Civil Actions Over $5,000.

**Magistrate Court**, 115 S Davis, Box 103, Nashville, GA 31639. 912-686-7019 (EST) 8:30AM-4:30PM. Civil Actions Under $5,000, Eviction, Small Claims.

**Probate Court**, 101 E Marion Ave, Ste 1, Nashville, GA 31639. 912-686-5213 (EST) Probate.

## Bibb County

**Real Estate Recording**, Bibb County Clerk of the Superior Court, 275 Second Street, Macon, GA 31201. 912-749-6527 (EST) 8AM-5PM.

**Superior Court**, PO Box 1015, Macon, GA 31202. 912-749-6527 (EST) 8AM-5PM. Felony, Misdemeanor, Civil Actions Over $5,000.

**State Court**, PO Box 5086, Macon, GA 31213-7199. 912-749-6676 (EST) 8:30AM-5:30PM. Misdemeanor, Civil Actions Over $5,000.

**Civil & Magistrate Court**, 601 Mulberry St, Macon, GA 31201. 912-749-6495 (EST) 8AM-5PM. Civil Actions Under $5,000, Eviction, Small Claims.

**Probate Court**, PO Box 6518, Macon, GA 31202. 912-749-6494 (EST) Probate.

## Bleckley County

**Real Estate Recording**, Bleckley County Clerk of the Superior Court, Courthouse, Cochran, GA 31014. 912-934-3210 (EST)

**Superior Court**, 306 SE 2nd St, Cochran, GA 31014. 912-934-3210 (EST) 8:30AM-5PM. Felony, Misdemeanor, Civil Actions Over $5,000.

**Magistrate Court**, 306 SE 2nd St, Cochran, GA 31014. 912-934-3202 (EST) 8:30AM-5PM. Civil Actions Under $5,000, Eviction, Small Claims.

**Probate Court**, 306 SE Second St, Cochran, GA 31014. 912-934-3204 (EST) Probate.

## Brantley County

**Real Estate Recording**, Brantley County Clerk of the Superior Court, Corner of Brantley & Highway 301, Nahunta, GA 31553. 912-462-5635 (EST) 8AM-5PM.

**Superior Court**, PO Box 1067, Nahunta, GA 31553. 912-462-5635 (EST) 8AM-5PM. Felony, Misdemeanor, Civil Actions Over $5,000.

**Magistrate Court**, PO Box 998, Nahunta, GA 31553. 912-462-6780 (EST) 8AM-4:30PM. Civil Actions Under $5,000, Eviction, Small Claims.

**Probate Court**, PO Box 207, Nahunta, GA 31553. 912-462-5192 (EST) Probate.

## Brooks County

**Real Estate Recording**, Brooks County Clerk of the Superior Court, Screven Street, Courthouse, Quitman, GA 31643. 912-263-4747 (EST) 8:30AM-5PM.

**Superior Court**, PO Box 630, Quitman, GA 31643. 912-263-4747 (EST) 8:30AM-5PM.

# Georgia

Felony, Misdemeanor, Civil Actions Over $5,000.

**Magistrate Court**, Box 387, Quitman, GA 31643. 912-263-9989 (EST) 8:30AM-5PM. Civil Actions Under $5,000, Eviction, Small Claims.

**Probate Court**, PO Box 630, Quitman, GA 31643. 912-263-5567 (EST) Probate.

## Bryan County

**Real Estate Recording**, Bryan County Clerk of the Superior Court, 401 South College Street, Pembroke, GA 31321. 912-653-4681 (EST) 8AM-5PM.

**Superior & State Court**, PO Drawer H, Pembroke, GA 31321. 912-653-4681 (EST) 8AM-5PM. Felony, Misdemeanor, Civil Actions Over $5,000.

**Magistrate Court**, Box 927, Pembroke, GA 31321. 912-653-4681 (EST) 8AM-5PM. Civil Actions Under $5,000, Eviction, Small Claims.

**Probate Court**, PO Drawer H, Pembroke, GA 31321. 912-653-4681 (EST) Probate.

## Bulloch County

**Real Estate Recording**, Bulloch County Clerk of the Superior Court, North Main Street, Courthouse, Room 102, Statesboro, GA 30458. 912-764-9009 (EST) 8:30AM-5PM.

**Superior & State Court**, N Main St, Statesboro, GA 30458. 912-764-9009 (EST) 8:30AM-5PM. Felony, Misdemeanor, Civil Actions Over $5,000.

**Magistrate Court**, Box 1004, Statesboro, GA 30458. 912-764-6458 (EST) 8AM-5PM. Civil Actions Under $5,000, Eviction, Small Claims.

**Probate Court**, PO Box 1005, Statesboro, GA 30459. 912-489-8749 (EST) Probate.

## Burke County

**Real Estate Recording**, Burke County Clerk of the Superior Court, 111 East 6th St., Courthouse, Waynesboro, GA 30830. 706-554-2279 (EST) 9AM-5PM.

**Superior & State Court**, PO Box 803, Waynesboro, GA 30830. 706-554-2279 (EST) 9AM-5PM. Felony, Misdemeanor, Civil Actions Over $5,000.

**Magistrate Court**, Box 401, Waynesboro, GA 30830. 706-554-4281 (EST) 9AM-5PM. Civil Actions Under $5,000, Eviction, Small Claims.

**Probate Court**, PO Box 322, Waynesboro, GA 30830. 706-554-3000 (EST) Probate.

## Butts County

**Real Estate Recording**, Butts County Clerk of the Superior Court, 26 Third Street, Jackson, GA 30233. 404-775-8215 (EST) 8AM-5PM.

**Superior Court**, PO Box 320, Jackson, GA 30233. 404-775-8215 (EST) 8AM-5PM. Felony, Misdemeanor, Civil Actions Over $5,000.

**Magistrate Court**, Box 457, Jackson, GA 30233. 404-775-8220 (EST) 8AM-4PM. Civil Actions Under $5,000, Eviction, Small Claims.

**Probate Court**, PO Box 320, Jackson, GA 30233. 405-775-8204 (EST) Probate.

## Calhoun County

**Real Estate Recording**, Calhoun County Clerk of the Superior Court, Courthouse Square, 111 School Street, Morgan, GA 31766. 912-849-2715 (EST) 8AM-5PM.

**Superior Court**, PO Box 68, Morgan, GA 31766. 912-849-2715 (EST) 8AM-5PM. Felony, Misdemeanor, Civil Actions Over $5,000.

**Magistrate Court**, Box 87, Morgan, GA 31766. 912-849-2115 (EST) 8AM-5PM. Civil Actions Under $5,000, Eviction, Small Claims.

**Probate Court**, PO Box 87, Morgan, GA 31766. 912-849-2115 (EST) Probate.

## Camden County

**Real Estate Recording**, Camden County Clerk of the Superior Court, 200 East 4th St., Courthouse Square, Woodbine, GA 31569. 912-576-5601 (EST) 9AM-5PM.

**Superior Court**, PO Box 578, Woodbine, GA 31569. 912-576-5601 (EST) 9AM-5PM. Felony, Misdemeanor, Civil Actions Over $5,000.

**Magistrate Court**, Box 386, Woodbine, GA 31569. 912-576-5601 (EST) 8AM-5PM. Civil Actions Under $5,000, Eviction, Small Claims.

**Probate Court**, PO Box 578, Woodbine, GA 31569. 912-576-5601 (EST) Probate.

## Candler County

**Real Estate Recording**, Candler County Clerk of the Superior Court, 355 South Broad Street, West, Courthouse, Metter, GA 30439. 912-685-5257 (EST) 8:30AM-5PM.

**Superior & State Court**, PO Box 380, Metter, GA 30439. 912-685-5257 (EST) 8:30AM-5PM. Felony, Misdemeanor, Civil Actions Over $5,000.

**Magistrate Court**, Box 683, Metter, GA 30439. 912-685-2888 (EST) 8AM-5PM. Civil Actions Under $5,000, Eviction, Small Claims.

## Carroll County

**Real Estate Recording**, Carroll County Clerk of the Superior Court, 311 Newnan Street, Room 203, Carrollton, GA 30117. 404-830-5830 (EST) 8AM-5PM.

**Superior & State Court**, PO Box 1620, Carrollton, GA 30117. 404-830-5830 (EST) 8AM-5PM. Felony, Misdemeanor, Civil Actions Over $5,000.

**Magistrate Court**, PO Box 1620, Carrollton, GA 30117. 404-830-5874 (EST) 9AM-5PM. Civil Actions Under $5,000, Eviction, Small Claims.

**Probate Court**, PO Box 338, Rm 204, Carrollton, GA 30117. 404-830-5840 (EST) Probate.

## Catoosa County

**Real Estate Recording**, Catoosa County Clerk of the Superior Court, 206 E. Nashville Street, Courthouse, Ringgold, GA 30736. 706-935-4231 (EST) 8:30AM-5PM.

**Superior & Magistrate Court**, 206 E Nashville St, Ringgold, GA 30736. 706-935-4231 (EST) 8:30AM-5PM. Felony, Misdemeanor, Civil, Eviction, Small Claims.

**Probate Court**, Courthouse, Ringgold, GA 30736. 404-935-3511 (EST) Probate.

## Charlton County

**Real Estate Recording**, Charlton County Clerk of the Superior Court, Courthouse, Folkston, GA 31537. 912-496-2354 (EST) 8AM-5PM.

**Superior Court**, Courthouse, Folkston, GA 31537. 912-496-2354 (EST) 8AM-5PM. Felony, Misdemeanor, Civil Actions Over $5,000.

**Magistrate Court**, 100 A County St, Folkston, GA 31537. 912-496-2617 (EST) 8AM-5PM. Civil Actions Under $5,000, Eviction, Small Claims.

**Probate Court**, Courthouse, Folkston, GA 31537. 912-496-2230 (EST) Probate.

## Chatham County

**Real Estate Recording**, Chatham County Clerk of the Superior Court, 133 Montgomery Street, Courthouse Rm. 304, Savannah, GA 31401. 912-652-7219 (EST) 8AM-5PM.

**Superior Court**, 133 Montgomery St, Savannah, GA 31401. 912-652-7127 (EST) 8AM-5PM. Felony, Misdemeanor, Civil Actions Over $5,000.

**State Court**, Chatam County Courthouse 133 Montgomery, Savannah, GA 31401. 912-652-7224 (EST) 8AM-5PM. Misdemeanor, Civil Actions Over $5,000.

**Magistrate Court**, 133 Montgomery St, Savannah, GA 31401. 912-652-7188 (EST) 8AM-5PM. Civil Actions Under $5,000, Eviction, Small Claims.

**Probate Court**, 133 Montgomery St, Savannah, GA 31401. 912-652-7200 (EST) Probate.

## Chattahoochee County

**Real Estate Recording**, Chattahoochee County Clerk of the Superior Court, Broad Street, Courthouse, Cusseta, GA 31805. 706-989-3424 (EST) 8AM-5PM.

**Superior & Magistrate Court**, PO Box 120, Cusseta, GA 31805. 706-989-3424 (EST) 8AM-5PM. Felony, Misdemeanor, Civil, Eviction, Small Claims.

**Probate Court**, PO Box 119, Cusseta, GA 31805. 706-989-3603 (EST) Probate.

## Chattooga County

**Real Estate Recording**, Chattooga County Clerk of the Superior Court, Commerce Street, Courthouse, Summerville, GA 30747. 706-857-2594 (EST) 8:30AM-5PM.

**Superior, State & Magistrate Court**, PO Box 159, Summerville, GA 30747. 706-857-0706 (EST) 8:30AM-5PM. Felony, Misdemeanor, Civil, Eviction, Small Claims.

**Probate Court**, PO Box 467, Summerville, GA 30747. 706-857-1813 (EST) Probate.

## Cherokee County

**Real Estate Recording**, Cherokee County Clerk of the Superior Court, 90 North Street, Suite G-170, Canton, GA 30114. 404-479-0558 (EST) 8:30AM-5PM.

**Superior & State Court**, 990 North St, Ste G170, Canton, GA 30114. 404-479-0538 (EST) 8:30AM-5PM. Felony, Misdemeanor, Civil Actions Over $5,000.

**Magistrate Court**, PO Box 255, Canton, GA 30114. 404-479-8516 (EST) 8AM-5PM. Civil Actions Under $5,000, Eviction, Small Claims.

**Probate Court**, 90 North St, Rm 340, Canton, GA 30114. 404-479-0541 (EST) Probate.

## Clarke County

**Real Estate Recording**, Clarke County Clerk of the Superior Court, 325 East Washington Street, Room 200, Athens, GA 30601. 706-613-3190 (EST) 8AM-5PM.

**Superior & State Court**, PO Box 1805, Athens, GA 30603. 706-613-3190 (EST) 8AM-5PM. Felony, Misdemeanor, Civil Actions Over $5,000.

**Magistrate Court**, 325 E Washington St, Athens, GA 30601. 706-613-3313 (EST) 8AM-5PM. Civil Actions Under $5,000, Eviction, Small Claims.

**Probate Court**, PO Box 1805, Athens, GA 30603. 706-613-3320 (EST) Probate.

## Clay County

**Real Estate Recording**, Clay County Clerk of the Superior Court, 210 Washington Street, Courthouse, Fort Gaines, GA 31751. 912-768-2631 (EST) 8AM-4:30PM.

**Superior & Magistrate Court**, PO Box 550, Ft Gaines, GA 31751. 912-768-2631 (EST) 8AM-4:30PM. Felony, Misdemeanor, Civil, Eviction, Small Claims.

**Probate Court**, PO Box 448, Ft. Gaines, GA 31751. 912-768-2445 (EST) Probate.

## Clayton County

**Real Estate Recording**, Clayton County Clerk of the Superior Court, 121 South McDonough Street, Room 202, Jonesboro, GA 30236. 404-477-3395 (EST) 8AM-5PM.

**Superior Court**, 121 S McDonaugh St, Jonesboro, GA 30236. 404-477-3405 (EST) 8AM-5PM. Felony, Misdemeanor, Civil Actions Over $5,000.

**State Court**, 121 S McDonaugh St, Jonesboro, GA 30236. 404-477-3389 (EST) 8AM-5PM. Misdemeanor.

**Magistrate Court**, 121 S McDonaugh St, Jonesboro, GA 30236. 404-477-3443 (EST) 8AM-5PM. Civil Actions Under $5,000, Eviction, Small Claims.

**Probate Court**, Courthouse, Jonesboro, GA 30236. 404-477-3299 (EST) Probate.

## Clinch County

**Real Estate Recording**, Clinch County Clerk of the Superior Court, Courthouse, Homerville, GA 31634. 912-487-5854 (EST) 8AM-5PM.

**Superior & State Court**, PO Box 433, Homerville, GA 31634. 912-487-5854 (EST) 8AM-5PM. Felony, Misdemeanor, Civil Actions Over $5,000.

**Magistrate Court**, 100 Court Square, Homerville, GA 31634. 912-487-2514 (EST) 8AM-5PM. Civil Actions Under $5,000, Eviction, Small Claims.

**Probate Court**, PO Box 433, Homerville, GA 31634. 912-487-5523 (EST) Probate.

## Cobb County

**Real Estate Recording**, Cobb County Clerk of the Superior Court, 10 East Park Square, Marietta, GA 30090. 404-528-1363 (EST) 8AM-5PM.

**Superior Court**, 32 Waddell St, Marietta, GA 30090. 404-528-1300 (EST) 8AM-5PM. Misdemeanor.

**State Court-Civil & Criminal Divisions**, 32 Wadell St, Marietta, GA 30090-9630. 404-528-1219 (EST) 8AM-5PM. Felony, Misdemeanor, Civil Actions Over $5,000.

**Magistrate Court**, 32 Waddell St, Marietta, GA 30090-9656. 404-528-8910 (EST) 8AM-5PM. Civil Actions Under $5,000, Eviction, Small Claims.

**Probate Court**, 189 Washington Ave, Marietta, GA 30090. 404-528-1900 (EST) Probate.

## Coffee County

**Real Estate Recording**, Coffee County Clerk of the Superior Court, Courthouse, 109 S. Peterson Ave., Douglas, GA 31533. 912-384-2865 (EST) 8:30AM-5PM.

**Superior & State Court**, 101 S Peterson Ave, Douglas, GA 31533. 912-384-2865 (EST) 8:30AM-5PM. Felony, Misdemeanor, Civil Actions Over $5,000.

**Magistrate Court**, 101 S Peterson Ave, Douglas, GA 31533. 912-384-2983 (EST) 8AM-5PM. Civil Actions Under $5,000, Eviction, Small Claims.

**Probate Court**, 101 S Peterson Ave, Douglas, GA 31533. 912-384-5213 (EST) Probate.

## Colquitt County

**Real Estate Recording**, Colquitt County Clerk of the Superior Court, 9 Main Street, Courthouse, Moultrie, GA 31776. 912-985-1324 (EST) 8AM-5PM.

**Superior & State Court**, PO Box 886, Moultrie, GA 31776. 912-985-1324 (EST) 8AM-5PM. Felony, Misdemeanor, Civil Actions Over $5,000.

**Magistrate Court**, PO Box 70, Moultrie, GA 31776. 912-985-9615 (EST) 8AM-5PM. Civil Actions Under $5,000, Eviction, Small Claims.

**Probate Court**, 1 Main St, Moultrie, GA 31768. 912-985-3088 (EST) Probate.

## Columbia County

**Real Estate Recording**, Columbia County Clerk of the Superior Court, 1954 Appling Harlem Rd., Appling, GA 30802. 706-541-1139 (EST) 8AM-5PM.

**Superior Court**, PO Box 100, Appling, GA 30802. 706-541-1139 (EST) 8AM-5PM. Felony, Misdemeanor, Civil Actions Over $5,000.

**Magistrate Court**, PO Box 777, Evans, GA 30809. 706-868-3316 (EST) 8AM-5PM. Civil Actions Under $5,000, Eviction, Small Claims.

**Probate Court**, Courthouse Annex, Appling, GA 30802. 404-541-1254 (EST) Probate.

## Cook County

**Real Estate Recording**, Cook County Clerk of the Superior Court, 212 North Hutchinson Avenue, Adel, GA 31620. 912-896-7717 (EST) 8:30AM-4:30PM.

**Superior Court**, 212 N Hutchinson Ave, Adel, GA 31620. 912-896-7717 (EST) 8:30AM-4:30PM. Felony, Misdemeanor, Civil Actions Over $5,000.

**Magistrate Court**, 212 N Hutchinson Ave, Adel, GA 31620. 912-896-3151 (EST) 8:30AM-4:30PM. Civil Actions Under $5,000, Eviction, Small Claims.

**Probate Court**, 212 N Hutchinson Ave, Adel, GA 31620. 912-896-3941 (EST) Probate.

## Coweta County

**Real Estate Recording**, Coweta County Clerk of the Superior Court, Courthouse, Court Square, Newnan, GA 30264. 404-254-2690 (EST) 8AM-5PM.

**Superior & State Court**, PO Box 943, Newnan, GA 30264. 404-254-2690 (EST) 8:30AM-5PM. Felony, Misdemeanor, Civil Actions Over $5,000.

**Magistrate Court**, 22-34 E Broad St, Newnan, GA 30263. 404-254-2610 (EST) 8:30AM-5PM. Civil Actions Under $5,000, Eviction, Small Claims.

**Probate Court**, 22 E Broad St, Newnan, GA 30263. 404-254-2640 (EST) Probate.

## Crawford County

**Real Estate Recording**, Crawford County Clerk of the Superior Court, Courthouse, Knoxville, GA 31050. 912-836-3328 (EST) 9AM-5PM.

**Superior & Magistrate Court**, Box 419, Knoxville, GA 31050. 912-836-3328 (EST) 9AM-5PM. Felony, Misdemeanor, Civil, Eviction, Small Claims.

**Probate Court**, PO Box 398, Knoxville, GA 31050. 912-836-3313 (EST) Probate.

## Crisp County

**Real Estate Recording**, Crisp County Clerk of the Superior Court, 210 7th Street South, Courthouse, Cordele, GA 31015. 912-276-2616 (EST) 8:30AM-5PM.

**Superior & Magistrate Court**, PO Box 747, Cordele, GA 31015. 912-276-2616 (EST) 8:30AM-5PM. Felony, Misdemeanor, Civil, Eviction, Small Claims.

**Probate Court**, 201 S 7th St, Cordele, GA 31015. 912-276-2621 (EST) Probate.

## Dade County

**Real Estate Recording**, Dade County Clerk of the Superior Court, Main Street-U.S. Highway 11, Courthouse Sq., Trenton, GA 30752. 404-657-4778 (EST) 8:30AM-5PM.

**Superior & Magistrate Court**, PO Box 417, Trenton, GA 30752. 404-657-4778 (EST) 8:30AM-5PM. Felony, Misdemeanor, Civil, Eviction, Small Claims.

**Probate Court**, PO Box 605, Trenton, GA 30752. 404-657-4414 (EST) Probate.

## Dawson County

**Real Estate Recording**, Dawson County Clerk of the Superior Court, Courthouse, West Third Street, Dawsonville, GA 30534. 706-265-2525 (EST) 8AM-5PM.

**Superior Court**, PO Box 222, Dawsonville, GA 30534. 706-265-2525 (EST) 8AM-5PM. Felony, Misdemeanor, Civil Actions Over $5,000.

**Magistrate Court**, PO Box 254, Dawsonville, GA 30534. 706-265-8000 (EST) 8AM-5PM. Civil Actions Under $5,000, Eviction, Small Claims.

**Probate Court**, PO Box 252, Dawsonville, GA 30534. 706-265-2271 (EST) Probate.

## De Kalb County

**Real Estate Recording**, De Kalb County Clerk of the Superior Court, 556 North

# Georgia

McDonough Street, Courthouse, Room 208, Decatur, GA 30030. 404-371-2032 (EST) 8AM-5PM.

**Superior Court**, 556 N McDonough St, Decatur, GA 30030. 404-371-2028 (EST) 8AM-5PM. Felony, Misdemeanor, Civil Actions Over $5,000.

**State Court**, 556 N McDonough St, Decatur, GA 30030. 404-371-2261 (EST) 8:30AM-5PM. Felony, Misdemeanor, Civil Actions Over $5,000.

**Magistrate Court**, 556 N McDonough St, Decatur, GA 30030. 404-371-2268 (EST) 8:30AM-5PM. Civil Actions Under $5,000, Eviction, Small Claims.

**Probate Court**, 556 N McDonough St, Decatur, GA 30030. 404-371-2601 (EST) Probate.

## Decatur County

**Real Estate Recording**, Decatur County Clerk of the Superior Court, 112 West Water Street, Bainbridge, GA 31717. 912-248-3025 (EST) 9AM-5PM.

**Superior & State Court**, PO Box 336, Bainbridge, GA 31717. 912-248-3025 (EST) 9AM-5PM. Felony, Misdemeanor, Civil Actions Over $5,000.

**Magistrate Court**, 912 Spring Creek Rd Box #3, Bainbridge, GA 31717. 912-248-3014 (EST) 9AM-5PM. Civil Actions Under $5,000, Eviction, Small Claims.

**Probate Court**, 112 W Water, Bainbridge, GA 31717. 912-248-3016 (EST) Probate.

## Dodge County

**Real Estate Recording**, Dodge County Clerk of the Superior Court, Anson Avenue, Courthouse, Eastman, GA 31023. 912-374-2871 (EST) 9AM-Noon,1-5PM.

**Superior Court**, PO Drawer 4276, Eastman, GA 31023. 912-374-2871 (EST) 8AM-5PM. Felony, Misdemeanor, Civil Actions Over $5,000.

**Magistrate Court**, Anson Ave, Courthouse Square, Eastman, GA 31023. 912-374-7243 (EST) 8AM-5PM. Civil Actions Under $5,000, Eviction, Small Claims.

**Probate Court**, PO Box 514, Eastman, GA 31023. 912-374-3775 (EST) Probate.

## Dooly County

**Real Estate Recording**, Dooly County Clerk of the Superior Court, 104 Second Street, Room 12, Vienna, GA 31092. 912-268-4234 (EST) 8:30AM-5PM.

**Superior Court**, PO Box 326, Vienna, GA 31092-0326. 912-268-4234 (EST) 8:30AM-5PM. Felony, Misdemeanor, Civil Actions Over $5,000.

**Magistrate Court**, W Union St, Courthouse Annex, Vienna, GA 31092. 912-268-4324 (EST) 8AM-12PM M,W 1PM-5PM F. Civil Actions Under $5,000, Eviction, Small Claims.

**Probate Court**, 104 2nd St, Vienna, GA 31092. 912-268-4217 (EST) Probate.

## Dougherty County

**Real Estate Recording**, Dougherty County Clerk of the Superior Court, 225 Pine Avenue, Room 126, Albany, GA 31702. 912-431-2198 (EST) 8:30AM-5PM.

**Superior & State Court**, PO Box 1827, Albany, GA 31703. 912-431-2198 (EST) 8:30AM-5PM. Felony, Misdemeanor, Civil Actions Over $5,000.

**Magistrate Court**, 225 Pine Ave, Albany, GA 31703. 912-431-3216 (EST) 8:30AM-5PM. Civil Actions Under $5,000, Eviction, Small Claims.

**Probate Court**, PO Box 1827, Albany, GA 31702. 912-431-2102 (EST) Probate.

## Douglas County

**Real Estate Recording**, Douglas County Clerk of the Superior Court, 6754 Broad Street, Room 210, Douglasville, GA 30134. 404-920-7368 (EST) 8AM-5PM.

**Superior Court**, 6754 Broad St, Douglasville, GA 30134. 404-920-7252 (EST) 8AM-5PM. Felony, Misdemeanor, Civil Actions Over $5,000.

**Magistrate Court**, 6754 Broad St, Rm 202, Douglasville, GA 30134. 404-920-7215 (EST) 8AM-5PM. Civil Actions Under $5,000, Eviction, Small Claims.

**Probate Court**, 6754 Broad St, Douglasville, GA 30134. 404-920-7249 (EST) Probate.

## Early County

**Real Estate Recording**, Early County Clerk of the Superior Court, Courthouse, Court Square, Blakely, GA 31723. 912-723-3033 (EST) 8AM-5PM.

**Superior & State Court**, PO Box 849, Blakely, GA 31723. 912-723-3033 (EST) 8AM-5PM. Felony, Misdemeanor, Civil Actions Over $5,000.

**Magistrate Court**, Courthouse Square, Blakely, GA 31723. 912-723-5492 (EST) 8AM-5PM. Civil Actions Under $5,000, Eviction, Small Claims.

**Probate Court**, Early Courthouse Square, Rm 8, Blakely, GA 31723. 912-723-5492 (EST) Probate.

## Echols County

**Real Estate Recording**, Echols County Clerk of the Superior Court, Courthouse, Highway 94 & Highway 129, Statenville, GA 31648. 912-559-5642 (EST) 8AM-Noon, 1-4:30PM.

**Superior Court**, PO Box 213, Statenville, GA 31648. 912-559-5642 (EST) 8AM-4:30PM. Felony, Misdemeanor, Civil Actions Over $5,000.

**Magistrate Court**, HWY 94 & 129, Statenville, GA 31648. 912-559-7526 (EST) 8AM-4:30PM. Civil Actions Under $5,000, Eviction, Small Claims.

**Probate Court**, Courthouse, HWY 94 & 129, Statenville, GA 31648. 912-559-7526 (EST) Probate.

## Effingham County

**Real Estate Recording**, Effingham County Clerk of the Superior Court, 901 North Pine Street, Courthouse, Springfield, GA 31329. 912-754-6071 (EST) X118 8:30AM-5PM.

**Superior & State Court**, PO Box 387, Springfield, GA 31329. 912-754-6071 (EST) 8:30AM-5PM. Felony, Misdemeanor, Civil Actions Over $5,000.

**Magistrate Court**, PO Box 387, Springfield, GA 31329. 912-754-6071 (EST) 8AM-5PM. Civil Actions Under $5,000, Eviction, Small Claims.

**Probate Court**, PO Box 387, Springfield, GA 31329. 912-754-6071 (EST) Probate.

## Elbert County

**Real Estate Recording**, Elbert County Clerk of the Superior Court, Courthouse, Oliver Street, Elberton, GA 30635. 706-283-2005 (EST) 8AM-5PM.

**Superior & State Court**, PO Box 619, Elberton, GA 30635. 706-283-2005 (EST) 8AM-5PM. Felony, Misdemeanor, Civil Actions Over $5,000.

**Magistrate Court**, PO Box 763, Elberton, GA 30635. 706-283-2027 (EST) 8AM-5PM. Civil Actions Under $5,000, Eviction, Small Claims.

**Probate Court**, Elbert County Courthouse, Elberton, GA 30635. 706-283-2016 (EST) Probate.

## Emanuel County

**Real Estate Recording**, Emanuel County Clerk of the Superior Court, Court Street, Courthouse, Swainsboro, GA 30401. 912-237-8911 (EST) 9AM-5PM.

**Superior & State Court**, PO Box 627, Swainsboro, GA 30401. 912-237-8911 (EST) 9AM-5PM. Felony, Misdemeanor, Civil Actions Over $5,000.

**Magistrate Court**, 107 N Main St, Swainsboro, GA 30401. 912-237-7278 (EST) 8AM-4:30PM. Civil Actions Under $5,000, Eviction, Small Claims.

**Probate Court**, Court St, Swainsboro, GA 30401. 912-237-7091 (EST) Probate.

## Evans County

**Real Estate Recording**, Evans County Clerk of the Superior Court, 123 W. Main Street, Courthouse, Claxton, GA 30417. 912-739-3868 (EST) 8AM-5PM.

**Superior & State Court**, PO Box 845, Claxton, GA 30417. 912-739-3868 (EST) 8AM-5PM. Felony, Misdemeanor, Civil Actions Over $5,000.

**Magistrate Court**, PO Box 773, Claxton, GA 30417. 912-739-3745 (EST) 8AM-5PM. Civil Actions Under $5,000, Eviction, Small Claims.

**Probate Court**, County Courthouse, PO Box 852, Claxton, GA 30417. 912-739-4080 (EST) Probate.

## Fannin County

**Real Estate Recording**, Fannin County Clerk of the Superior Court, 420 West Main St., Courthouse, Blue Ridge, GA 30513. 706-632-2039 (EST) 9AM-5PM.

**Superior Court**, PO Box 1300, Blue Ridge, GA 30513. 706-632-2039 (EST) 9AM-5PM. Felony, Misdemeanor, Civil Actions Over $5,000.

**Magistrate Court**, PO Box 1300, Blue Ridge, GA 30513. 706-632-5558 (EST) 9AM-5PM. Civil Actions Under $5,000, Eviction, Small Claims.

**Probate Court**, PO Box 245, Blue Ridge, GA 30513. 706-632-3011 (EST) Probate.

## Fayette County

**Real Estate Recording**, Fayette County Clerk of the Superior Court, 145 Johnson Avenue, Fayetteville, GA 30214. 404-461-4703 (EST) 8AM-5PM.

**Superior Court**, PO Box 130, Fayetteville, GA 30214. 404-461-4703 (EST) 8AM-5PM. Felony, Misdemeanor, Civil Actions Over $5,000.

**Magistrate Court**, 145 Johnson Ave, Fayetteville, GA 30214. 404-461-2116 (EST) 8AM-5PM. Civil Actions Under $5,000, Eviction, Small Claims.

**Probate Court**, 145 Johnson Ave, Fayetteville, GA 30214. 404-461-9555 (EST) Probate.

## Floyd County

**Real Estate Recording**, Floyd County Clerk of the Superior Court, 3 Government Plaza, Rome, GA 30162. 706-291-5190 (EST) 8AM-5PM.

**Superior Court**, PO Box 1110, Rome, GA 30163. 706-291-5190 (EST) 8AM-5PM. Felony, Misdemeanor, Civil Actions Over $5,000.

**Magistrate Court**, 401 Tribune St 2nd Fl, Rome, GA 30161. 706-291-5250 (EST) 9AM-5PM. Civil Actions Under $5,000, Eviction, Small Claims.

**Probate Court**, 12 E 4th Ave, Rome, GA 30161. 706-291-5136 (EST) Probate.

## Forsyth County

**Real Estate Recording**, Forsyth County Clerk of the Superior Court, 100 Courthouse Square, Room 110, Cumming, GA 30130. 404-781-2120 (EST) 8:30AM-5PM.

**Superior, State, Magistrate Court**, 100 Courthouse Square, Rm 110, Cumming, GA 30130. 404-781-2120 (EST) 8:30AM-5PM. Felony, Misdemeanor, Civil, Eviction, Small Claims.

**Probate Court**, County Courthouse, Cumming, GA 30130. 404-781-2140 (EST) Probate.

## Franklin County

**Real Estate Recording**, Franklin County Clerk of the Superior Court, Courthouse Square, Highway 59, Carnesville, GA 30521. 706-384-2514 (EST) 8AM-4:30PM M,T,Th,F; 8AM-Noon W & Sat.

**Superior Court**, PO Box 70, Carnesville, GA 30521. 706-384-2514 (EST) 8AM-5PM. Felony, Misdemeanor, Civil Actions Over $5,000.

**Magistrate Court**, PO Box 204, Carnesville, GA 30521. 706-384-4611 (EST) 8AM-5PM. Civil Actions Under $5,000, Eviction, Small Claims.

**Probate Court**, PO Box 70, Carnesville, GA 30521. (EST) Probate.

## Fulton County

**Real Estate Recording**, Fulton County Clerk of the Superior Court, 136 Pryor Street, Room 106, Atlanta, GA 30303. 404-730-5276 (EST) 8:30AM-5PM.

**Superior Court**, 136 Pryor St SW, Rm 106, Atlanta, GA 30303. 404-730-5242 (EST) 8:30AM-5PM. Felony.

**State Court**, TG100 Justice Center Tower, 185 Central, Atlanta, GA 30303. 404-730-5000 (EST) 8:30AM-5PM. Misdemeanor, Civil Actions Over $5,000.

**Magistrate Court**, 185 Central Ave SW, Rm TG700, Atlanta, GA 30303. 404-730-5045 (EST) 8:30AM-5PM. Civil Actions to $5,000, Eviction, Small Claims.

**Probate Court**, 136 Pryor St SW #C230, Atlanta, GA 30303. 404-730-4697 (EST) Probate.

## Gilmer County

**Real Estate Recording**, Gilmer County Clerk of the Superior Court, 1 West Side Square, Courthouse, Ellijay, GA 30540. 706-635-4462 (EST) 8:30AM-5PM.

**Superior Court**, #1 Westside Square, Ellijay, GA 30540. 706-635-4462 (EST) 8:30AM-5PM. Felony, Misdemeanor, Civil Actions Over $5,000.

**Magistrate Court**, #1 Westside Square, Ellijay, GA 30540. 706-635-2515 (EST) 8:30AM-5PM. Civil Actions Under $5,000, Eviction, Small Claims.

**Probate Court**, #1 Westside Square, Ellijay, GA 30540. 706-635-4763 (EST) Probate.

## Glascock County

**Real Estate Recording**, Glascock County Clerk of the Superior Court, Main Street, Courthouse, Gibson, GA 30810. 706-598-2084 (EST) 8AM-Noon,1-5PM.

**Superior Court**, PO Box 231, Gibson, GA 30810. 706-598-2084 (EST) 8AM-5PM. Felony, Misdemeanor, Civil Actions Over $5,000.

**Magistrate Court**, PO Box 201, Gibson, GA 30810. 706-598-2013 (EST) 9AM-Noon W,Sat. Civil Actions Under $5,000, Eviction, Small Claims.

**Probate Court**, Courthouse, Main St, Gibson, GA 30810. 706-598-3241 (EST) Probate.

## Glynn County

**Real Estate Recording**, Glynn County Clerk of the Superior Court, 701 H Street, Brunswick, GA 31520. 912-267-5610 (EST) 8:30AM-5PM.

**Superior Court**, PO Box 1355, Brunswick, GA 31521. 912-267-5610 (EST) 9AM-5PM. Felony, Misdemeanor, Civil Actions Over $5,000.

**State Court**, PO Box 879, Brunswick, GA 31521. 912-267-5674 (EST) 9AM-5PM. Misdemeanor, Civil Actions Over $5,000.

**Magistrate Court**, 701 H St, Brunswick, GA 31521. 912-267-5650 (EST) 8:30AM-5PM. Civil Actions Under $5,000, Eviction, Small Claims.

**Probate Court**, 701 H St, Brunswick, GA 31521. 912-267-5626 (EST) Probate.

## Gordon County

**Real Estate Recording**, Gordon County Clerk Court, 100 Wall Street, Courthouse, Calhoun, GA 30701. 706-629-9533 (EST) 9AM-5PM M,T,W,Th; 9AM-5:30PM F.

**Superior Court**, PO Box 367, Calhoun, GA 30703. 706-629-9533 (EST) 8:30AM-5PM. Felony, Misdemeanor, Civil Actions Over $5,000.

**Magistrate Court**, 100 Wall St, Calhoun, GA 30703. 706-629-6818 (EST) 8:30AM-5PM. Civil Actions Under $5,000, Eviction, Small Claims.

**Probate Court**, 100 Wall St, Calhoun, GA 30703. 706-629-7314 (EST) Probate.

## Grady County

**Real Estate Recording**, Grady County Clerk of the Superior Court, 250 North Broad Street, Box 8, Cairo, GA 31728. 912-377-2912 (EST) 8:30AM-5PM.

**Superior Court**, 250 N Broad St, Box 8, Cairo, GA 31728. 912-377-2912 (EST) 8:30AM-5PM. Felony, Misdemeanor, Civil Actions Over $5,000.

**Magistrate Court**, 250 N Broad St, Cairo, GA 31728. 912-377-4132 (EST) 8:30AM-5PM. Civil Actions Under $5,000, Eviction, Small Claims.

**Probate Court**, Courthouse, 250 N Broad St, Cairo, GA 31728. 912-377-4621 (EST) Probate.

## Greene County

**Real Estate Recording**, Greene County Clerk of the Superior Court, Courthouse, 113E North Main St., Greensboro, GA 30642. 706-453-3340 (EST) 7:30AM-5PM.

**Superior & Magistrate Court**, Courthouse, Greensboro, GA 30642. 706-453-3340 (EST) 8AM-5PM. Felony, Misdemeanor, Civil, Eviction, Small Claims.

**Probate Court**, 113C N Main, Greensboro, GA 30642. 706-453-3346 (EST) Probate.

## Gwinnett County

**Real Estate Recording**, Gwinnett County Clerk of the Superior Court, 75 Langley Drive, Lawrenceville, GA 30245. 404-822-8196 (EST) 8AM-5PM.

**Superior, State, Magistrate Court**, PO Box 880, Lawrenceville, GA 30246-0880. 404-822-8100 (EST) 8AM-5PM. Felony, Misdemeanor, Civil, Eviction, Small Claims.

**Probate Court**, 75 Langley Dr, Lawrenceville, GA 30245. 404-822-8250 (EST) Probate.

## Habersham County

**Real Estate Recording**, Habersham County Clerk of the Superior Court, Highway 115, Courthouse, Clarkesville, GA 30523. 706-754-2923 (EST) 8:30AM-5PM.

**Superior & State Court**, PO Box 108, Clarkesville, GA 30523. 706-754-2923 (EST) 8AM-5PM. Felony, Misdemeanor, Civil Actions Over $5,000.

**Magistrate Court**, PO Box 587, Clarkesville, GA 30523. 706-754-4871 (EST) 8AM-5PM. Civil Actions Under $5,000, Eviction, Small Claims.

**Probate Court**, PO Box 615, Clarkesville, GA 30523. 706-754-2013 (EST) Probate.

## Hall County

**Real Estate Recording**, Hall County Clerk of the Superior Court, 116 Spring Street, Courthouse, Gainesville, GA 30501. 404-531-7064 (EST) 8AM-5PM.

**Superior & State Court**, PO Box 1275, Gainesville, GA 30503. 404-531-7025 (EST) 8AM-5PM. Felony, Misdemeanor, Civil Actions Over $5,000.

**Magistrate Court**, PO Box 1435, Gainesville, GA 30503. 404-531-6912 (EST) 8AM-5PM. Civil Actions Under $5,000, Eviction, Small Claims.

**Probate Court**, Hall County Courthouse, Rm 123, Gainesville, GA 30501. 404-531-6921 (EST) Probate.

## Hancock County

**Real Estate Recording**, Hancock County Clerk of the Superior Court, Courthouse Square, Sparta, GA 31087. 404-444-6644 (EST) 8AM-5PM M-W & F; 9AM-12 Th.

**Superior Court**, PO Box 451, Sparta, GA 31087. 706-444-6644 (EST) 8AM-5PM. Felony, Misdemeanor, Civil Actions Over $5,000.

**Magistrate Court**, Courthouse Square, Sparta, GA 31087. 706-444-6234 (EST) 9AM-5PM. Civil Actions Under $5,000, Eviction, Small Claims.

**Probate Court**, PO Box 451, Sparta, GA 31087. 706-444-5343 (EST) Probate.

## Haralson County

**Real Estate Recording**, Haralson County Clerk of the Superior Court, 4485 State Highway 120 East, Buchanan, GA 30113. 706-646-2005 (EST) 8:30AM-5PM.

**Superior Court**, PO Box 373, Buchanan, GA 30113. 404-646-2005 (EST) 8:30AM-5PM. Felony, Misdemeanor, Civil Actions Over $5,000.

**Magistrate Court**, PO Box 1040, Buchanan, GA 30113. 404-646-2015 (EST) 8:30AM-5PM. Civil Actions Under $5,000, Eviction, Small Claims.

**Probate Court**, PO Box 620, Buchanan, GA 30113. 404-646-2008 (EST) Probate.

## Harris County

**Real Estate Recording**, Harris County Clerk of the Superior Court, Courthouse, Highway 27, Hamilton, GA 31811. 706-628-5570 (EST) 8AM-5PM.

**Superior Court**, PO Box 528, Hamilton, GA 31811. 404-628-4944 (EST) 8AM-5PM. Felony, Misdemeanor, Civil Actions Over $5,000.

**Magistrate Court**, PO Box 347, Hamilton, GA 31811. 706-628-4977 (EST) 8AM-5PM. Civil Actions Under $5,000, Eviction, Small Claims.

**Probate Court**, PO Box 569, Hamilton, GA 31811. 706-628-5038 (EST) Probate.

## Hart County

**Real Estate Recording**, Hart County Clerk of the Superior Court, 185 West Franklin Street, Courthouse Annex, Rm 1, Hartwell, GA 30643. 706-376-7189 (EST) 8:30AM-5PM.

**Superior Court**, PO Box 386, Hartwell, GA 30643. 706-376-7189 (EST) 8:30AM-5PM. Felony, Misdemeanor, Civil Actions Over $5,000.

**Magistrate Court**, PO Box 698, Hartwell, GA 30643. 706-376-9872 (EST) 8:30AM-3PM. Civil Actions Under $5,000, Eviction, Small Claims.

**Probate Court**, PO Box 1159, Hartwell, GA 30643. 706-376-2565 (EST) Probate.

## Heard County

**Real Estate Recording**, Heard County Clerk of the Superior Court, Court Square, Courthouse, Franklin, GA 30217. 706-675-3301 (EST)

**Superior Court**, PO Box 240, Franklin, GA 30217. 404-675-3301 (EST) 8AM-5PM. Felony, Misdemeanor, Civil Actions Over $5,000.

**Magistrate Court**, PO Box 395, Franklin, GA 30217. 706-675-3002 (EST) 8:30AM-5PM M,T,TH,F/8:30AM-12PM W. Civil Actions Under $5,000, Eviction, Small Claims.

**Probate Court**, PO Box 478, Franklin, GA 30217. 706-675-3353 (EST) Probate.

## Henry County

**Real Estate Recording**, Henry County Clerk of the Superior Court, Courthouse, #1 Courthouse Square, McDonough, GA 30253. 404-954-2121 (EST) 8AM-5PM.

**Superior Court**, One Courthouse Square, McDonough, GA 30253. 404-954-2121 (EST) 8AM-5PM. Felony, Misdemeanor, Civil Actions Over $5,000.

**Magistrate Court**, 30 Atlanta St, McDonough, GA 30253. 404-954-2111 (EST) 8AM-5PM. Civil Actions Under $5,000, Eviction, Small Claims.

**Probate Court**, 20 Lawrenceville St, McDonough, GA 30253. 404-954-2303 (EST) Probate.

## Houston County

**Real Estate Recording**, Houston County Clerk of the Superior Court, 800 Carroll Street, Perry, GA 31069. 912-987-2170 (EST) 8:30AM-5PM.

**Superior Court**, 800 Carroll St, Perry, GA 31069. 912-987-2170 (EST) 8AM-5PM. Felony, Misdemeanor, Civil Actions Over $5,000.

**State Court**, 202 Carl Vinson Pkwy, Warner Robins, GA 31088. 912-542-2105 (EST) 8AM-5PM. Misdemeanor, Civil Actions Over $5,000.

**Magistrate Court**, 732 Main St, Perry, GA 31069. 912-987-4695 (EST) 8AM-5PM. Civil Actions Under $5,000, Eviction, Small Claims.

**Probate Court**, PO Box 1901, Perry, GA 31069. 912-987-2770 (EST) Probate.

## Irwin County

**Real Estate Recording**, Irwin County Clerk of the Superior Court, Courthouse, Irwin Avenue, Ocilla, GA 31774. 912-468-5356 (EST)

**Superior Court**, PO Box 186, Ocilla, GA 31774. 912-468-5356 (EST) 8:30AM-5PM. Felony, Misdemeanor, Civil Actions Over $5,000.

**Magistrate Court**, PO Box 53, Ocilla, GA 31774. 912-468-7671 (EST) 9AM-5PM M,T,TH 9AM-2PM F. Civil Actions Under $5,000, Eviction, Small Claims.

**Probate Court**, PO Box 186, Ocilla, GA 31774. 912-468-5138 (EST) Probate.

## Jackson County

**Real Estate Recording**, Jackson County Clerk of the Superior Court, Courthouse, 85 Washington Street, Jefferson, GA 30549. 706-367-1199 (EST) 8AM-5PM.

**Superior & State Court**, PO Box 7, Jefferson, GA 30549. 706-367-6360 (EST) 8AM-5PM. Felony, Misdemeanor, Civil Actions Over $5,000.

**Magistrate Court**, PO Box 332, Commerce, GA 30529. 404-335-6545 (EST) 8AM-5PM. Civil Actions Under $5,000, Eviction, Small Claims.

**Probate Court**, 85 Washington St, Jackson, GA 30549. 706-367-1199 (EST) Probate.

## Jasper County

**Real Estate Recording**, Jasper County Clerk of the Superior Court, Courthouse, Monticello, GA 31064. 706-468-4901 (EST) 8:30AM-Noon, 1-5PM.

**Superior Court**, County Courthouse, Monticello, GA 31064. 706-468-4901 (EST) 8:30AM-5PM. Felony, Misdemeanor, Civil Actions Over $5,000.

**Magistrate Court**, County Courthouse, Monticello, GA 31064. 706-468-4909 (EST) 8:30AM-5PM. Civil Actions Under $5,000, Eviction, Small Claims.

**Probate Court**, County Courthouse, Monticello, GA 31064. 706-468-4903 (EST) Probate.

## Jeff Davis County

**Real Estate Recording**, Jeff Davis County Clerk of the Superior Court, Jeff Davis Street, Courthouse Annex, Hazlehurst, GA 31539. 912-375-6615 (EST) 8AM-5PM.

**Superior & State Court**, PO Box 248, Hazlehurst, GA 31539. 912-375-6615 (EST) 8AM-5PM. Felony, Misdemeanor, Civil Actions Over $5,000.

**Magistrate Court**, PO Box 568, Hazlehurst, GA 31539. 912-375-6630 (EST) 8AM-5PM. Civil Actions Under $5,000, Eviction, Small Claims.

**Probate Court**, PO Box 248, Hazlehurst, GA 31539. 912-375-6626 (EST) Probate.

## Jefferson County

**Real Estate Recording**, Jefferson County Clerk of the Superior Court, 202 E. Broad Street, Courthouse, Louisville, GA 30434. 912-625-7922 (EST) 9AM-5PM.

**Superior & State Court**, PO Box 151, Louisville, GA 30434. 912-625-7922 (EST) 9AM-5PM. Felony, Misdemeanor, Civil Actions Over $5,000.

**Magistrate Court**, PO Box 749, Louisville, GA 30434. 912-625-8834 (EST) 8AM-5PM. Civil Actions Under $5,000, Eviction, Small Claims.

**Probate Court**, PO Box 307, Louisville, GA 30434. 912-625-3258 (EST) Probate.

## Jenkins County

**Real Estate Recording**, Jenkins County Clerk of the Superior Court, Harvey Street, Courthouse, Millen, GA 30442. 912-982-4683 (EST) 8:30AM-Noon, 1PM-5PM.

**Superior & State Court**, PO Box 659, Millen, GA 30442. 912-982-4683 (EST) 8:30AM-5PM. Felony, Misdemeanor, Civil Actions Over $5,000.

**Magistrate Court**, PO Box 659, Millen, GA 30442. 912-982-5580 (EST) 8:30AM-5PM. Civil Actions Under $5,000, Eviction, Small Claims.

**Probate Court**, PO Box 904, Millen, GA 30442. 912-982-5581 (EST) Probate.

## Johnson County

**Real Estate Recording**, Johnson County Clerk of the Superior Court, Courthouse Square,

Wrightsville, GA 31096. 912-864-3484 (EST) 9AM-5PM.

**Superior and Magistrate Court**, PO Box 321, Wrightsville, GA 31096. 912-864-3484 (EST) 9AM-5PM. Felony, Misdemeanor, Civil, Eviction, Small Claims.

**Probate Court**, PO Box 264, Wrightsville, GA 31096. 912-864-3316 (EST) Probate.

## Jones County

**Real Estate Recording**, Jones County Clerk of the Superior Court, Jefferson Street, Courthouse, Gray, GA 31032. 912-986-6671 (EST) 8:30AM-4:30PM.

**Superior Court**, PO Drawer 39, Gray, GA 31032. 912-986-6671 (EST) 8:30AM-4:30PM. Felony, Misdemeanor, Civil Actions Over $5,000.

**Magistrate Court**, PO Drawer 159, Gray, GA 31032. 912-986-5113 (EST) 8:30AM-4:30PM. Civil Actions Under $5,000, Eviction, Small Claims.

**Probate Court**, PO Box 1359, Gray, GA 31032. 912-986-6668 (EST) Probate.

## Lamar County

**Real Estate Recording**, Lamar County Clerk of the Superior Court, 326 Thomaston Street, Courthouse, Barnesville, GA 30204. 404-358-5145 (EST) 8AM-5PM.

**Superior Court**, 326 Thomaston St, Barnesville, GA 30204. 404-358-5145 (EST) 8AM-5PM. Felony, Misdemeanor, Civil Actions Over $5,000.

**Magistrate Court**, 121 Roberta Dr, Barnesville, GA 30204. 404-358-5154 (EST) 8AM-5PM. Civil Actions Under $5,000, Eviction, Small Claims.

**Probate Court**, 326 Thomaston St, Barnesville, GA 30204. 404-358-5155 (EST) Probate.

## Lanier County

**Real Estate Recording**, Lanier County Clerk of the Superior Court, County Courthouse, 100 Main Street, Lakeland, GA 31635. 912-482-3594 (EST) 8AM-Noon,1-5PM.

**Superior Court**, County Courthouse, Lakeland, GA 31635. 912-482-3594 (EST) 8AM-5PM. Felony, Misdemeanor, Civil Actions Over $5,000.

**Magistrate Court**, County Courthouse, Lakeland, GA 31635. 912-482-2207 (EST) 8AM-5PM. Civil Actions Under $5,000, Eviction, Small Claims.

**Probate Court**, County Courthouse, 100 Main St, Lakeland, GA 31635. 912-482-3668 (EST) Probate.

## Laurens County

**Real Estate Recording**, Laurens County Clerk of the Superior Court, Courthouse Square, Dublin, GA 31040. 912-272-3210 (EST) 8:30AM-5:30PM.

**Superior and Magistrate Court**, PO Box 2028, Dublin, GA 31040. 912-272-3210 (EST) 8:30AM-5:30PM. Felony, Misdemeanor, Civil, Eviction, Small Claims.

**Probate Court**, PO Box 2098, Dublin, GA 31040. 912-272-2566 (EST) Probate.

## Lee County

**Real Estate Recording**, Lee County Clerk of the Superior Court, 134 Courthouse Avenue, Leesburg, GA 31763. 912-759-6018 (EST) 8AM-5PM.

**Superior Court**, PO Box 597, Leesburg, GA 31763. 912-759-6018 (EST) 8AM-5PM. Felony, Misdemeanor, Civil Actions Over $5,000.

**Magistrate Court**, PO Box 522, Leesburg, GA 31763. 912-759-6016 (EST) 8AM-5PM. Civil Actions Under $5,000, Eviction, Small Claims.

**Probate Court**, PO Box 597, Leesburg, GA 31763. 912-759-6006 (EST) Probate.

## Liberty County

**Real Estate Recording**, Liberty County Clerk of the Superior Court, Courthouse Square, Hinesville, GA 31313. 912-876-3625 (EST)

**Superior and State Court**, PO Box 50, Hinesville, GA 31313-0050. 912-876-3625 (EST) 8AM-5PM. Felony, Misdemeanor, Civil Actions Over $5,000.

**Magistrate Court**, PO Box 50, Hinesville, GA 31313. 912-876-2343 (EST) 8AM-5PM. Civil Actions Under $5,000, Eviction, Small Claims.

**Probate Court**, PO Box 28, Hinesville, GA 31313. 912-876-3589 (EST) Probate.

## Lincoln County

**Real Estate Recording**, Lincoln County Clerk of the Superior Court, 210 Humphrey Street, Courthouse, Lincolnton, GA 30817. 706-359-4444 (EST) 9AM-Noon, 1PM-5PM.

**Superior Court**, PO Box 340, Lincolnton, GA 30817. 706-359-4444 (EST) 9AM-4:30PM. Felony, Misdemeanor, Civil Actions Over $5,000.

**Magistrate Court**, PO Box 205, Lincolnton, GA 30817. 706-359-4444 (EST) 9AM-4PM. Civil Actions Under $5,000, Eviction, Small Claims.

**Probate**, PO Box 340, Lincolnton, GA 30817. 706-359-4444 (EST) Probate.

## Long County

**Real Estate Recording**, Long County Clerk of the Superior Court, Courthouse, MacDonald Street, Ludowici, GA 31316. 912-545-2123 (EST) 8:30AM-4:30PM.

**Superior & State Court**, PO Box 458, Ludowici, GA 31316. 912-545-2123 (EST) 8:30AM-4:30PM. Felony, Misdemeanor, Civil Actions Over $5,000.

**Magistrate Court**, PO Box 87, Ludowici, GA 31316. 912-545-2315 (EST) 8:30AM-4:30PM. Civil Actions Under $5,000, Eviction, Small Claims.

**Probate Court**, PO Box 426, Ludowici, GA 31316. 912-545-2131 (EST) Probate.

## Lowndes County

**Real Estate Recording**, Lowndes County Clerk of the Superior Court, Ashley & Valley Streets, Valdosta, GA 31601. 912-333-5125 (EST) 8:45AM-5PM.

**Superior & State Court**, PO Box 1349, Valdosta, GA 31603. 912-222-5127 (EST) 9AM-5PM. Felony, Misdemeanor, Civil Actions Over $5,000.

**Magistrate Court**, PO Box 1349, Valdosta, GA 31603. 912-333-5110 (EST) 9AM-5PM. Civil Actions Under $5,000, Eviction, Small Claims.

**Probate Court**, PO Box 1349, Valdosta, GA 31603. 912-333-5103 (EST) Probate.

## Lumpkin County

**Real Estate Recording**, Lumpkin County Clerk of the Superior Court, 279 Couthouse Hill, Dahlonega, GA 30533. 706-864-3736 (EST) 8AM-5PM.

**Superior and Magistrate Court**, 279 Courthouse Hill, Dahlonega, GA 30533-1142. 706-864-3736 (EST) 8AM-5PM. Felony, Misdemeanor, Civil, Eviction, Small Claims.

**Probate Court**, 278 Courthouse Hill St, Dahlonega, GA 30533. 706-864-3847 (EST) Probate.

## Macon County

**Real Estate Recording**, Macon County Clerk of the Superior Court, 100 Sumter Street, Courthouse, Oglethorpe, GA 31068. 912-472-7661 (EST) 8:30AM-5PM.

**Superior Court**, PO Box 337, Oglethorpe, GA 31068. 912-472-7661 (EST) 8:30AM-5PM. Felony, Misdemeanor, Civil Actions Over $5,000.

**Magistrate Court**, PO Box 605, Oglethorpe, GA 31068. 912-472-8509 (EST) 8:30AM-5PM. Civil Actions Under $5,000, Eviction, Small Claims.

**Probate Court**, PO Box 216, Oglethorpe, GA 31068. 912-472-7685 (EST) Probate.

## Madison County

**Real Estate Recording**, Madison County Clerk of the Superior Court, Courthouse Square, Hwy 29, Danielsville, GA 30633. 706-795-3351 (EST) 8AM-5PM.

**Superior Court**, PO Box 247, Danielsville, GA 30633. 706-795-3351 (EST) 8AM-5PM. Felony, Misdemeanor, Civil Actions Over $5,000.

**Magistrate Court**, PO Box 6, Danielsville, GA 30633. 706-795-3351 (EST) 8AM-5PM. Civil Actions Under $5,000, Eviction, Small Claims.

**Probate Court**, PO Box 207, Danielsville, GA 30633. 706-795-3354 (EST) Probate.

## Marion County

**Real Estate Recording**, Marion County Clerk of the Superior Court, Courthouse Square, Broad Street, Buena Vista, GA 31803. 912-649-7321 (EST) 9AM-5PM.

**Superior and Magistrate Court**, PO Box 41, Buena Vista, GA 31803. 912-649-7321 (EST) 8:30AM-5PM. Felony, Misdemeanor, Civil, Eviction, Small Claims.

**Probate Court**, PO Box 207, Buena Vista, GA 31803. 912-649-5542 (EST) Probate.

## McDuffie County

**Real Estate Recording**, McDuffie County Clerk of the Superior Court, 337 Main Street, Courthouse, Thomson, GA 30824. 706-595-2134 (EST) 9AM-5PM.

**Superior Court**, PO Box 158, Thomson, GA 30824. 404-595-2134 (EST) 9AM-5PM. Felony, Misdemeanor, Civil Actions Over $5,000.

# Georgia

**Magistrate Court**, PO Box 52, Thomson, GA 30824. 706-595-9453 (EST) 9AM-5PM. Civil Actions Under $5,000, Eviction, Small Claims.

**Probate Court**, PO Box 2028, Thomson, GA 30824. 404-595-2124 (EST) Probate.

## McIntosh County

**Real Estate Recording**, McIntosh County Clerk of the Superior Court, Courthouse, 312 Northway, Darien, GA 31305. 912-437-6641 (EST) 8AM-5PM.

**Superior & State Court**, PO Box 1661, Darien, GA 31305. 912-437-6641 (EST) 8AM-5PM. Felony, Misdemeanor, Civil Actions Over $5,000.

**Magistrate Court**, PO Box 459, Darien, GA 31305. 912-437-4888 (EST) 8AM-5PM. Civil Actions Under $5,000, Eviction, Small Claims.

**Probate Court**, PO Box 453, Darien, GA 31305. 912-437-6636 (EST) Probate.

## Meriwether County

**Real Estate Recording**, Meriwether County Clerk of the Superior Court, 100 Court Square, Meriwether County Courthouse, Greenville, GA 30222. 706-672-4416 (EST) 9AM-5PM.

**Superior Court**, PO Box 160, Greenville, GA 30222. 706-672-4416 (EST) 9AM-5PM. Felony, Misdemeanor, Civil Actions Over $5,000.

**Magistrate Court**, PO Box 702, Greenville, GA 30222. 706-672-1247 (EST) 9AM-4:30PM M,T,TH,F/9AM-11:30PM W. Civil Actions Under $5,000, Eviction, Small Claims.

**Probate Court**, PO Box 608, Greenville, GA 30222. 706-672-4952 (EST) Probate.

## Miller County

**Real Estate Recording**, Miller County Clerk of the Superior Court, 155 First Street, Colquitt, GA 31737. 912-758-4102 (EST) 8AM-Noon,1-5PM.

**Superior & State Court**, PO Box 66, Colquitt, GA 31737. 912-758-4102 (EST) 8AM-5PM. Felony, Misdemeanor, Civil Actions Over $5,000.

**Magistrate & Probate Court**, 155 S 1st St, Rm 1, Colquitt, GA 31737. 912-758-4110 (EST) 8AM-5PM. Civil Actions Under $5,000, Small Claims, Probate.

**Probate Court**, PO Box 66, Colquitt, GA 31737. 912-758-4102 (EST) Probate.

## Mitchell County

**Real Estate Recording**, Mitchell County Clerk of the Superior Court, Broad Street, Courthouse, Camilla, GA 31730. 912-336-2022 (EST) 9AM-5PM.

**Superior & State Court**, PO Box 427, Camilla, GA 31730. 912-336-2022 (EST) 8:30AM-5PM. Felony, Misdemeanor, Civil Actions Over $5,000.

**Magistrate Court**, PO Box 626, Camilla, GA 31730. 912-336-2077 (EST) 8:30AM-5PM. Civil Actions Under $5,000, Eviction, Small Claims.

**Probate Court**, PO Box 229, Camilla, GA 31730. 912-336-2016 (EST) Probate.

## Monroe County

**Real Estate Recording**, Monroe County Clerk of the Superior Court, 2 North Lee St., Courthouse Square, Forsyth, GA 31029. 912-994-7022 (EST) 8:30AM-4:30PM.

**Superior Court**, PO Box 450, Forsyth, GA 31029. 912-994-7022 (EST) 8:30AM-4:30PM. Felony, Misdemeanor, Civil Actions Over $5,000.

**Magistrate Court**, PO Box 974, Forsyth, GA 31029. 912-994-7018 (EST) 8:30AM-4:30PM, Closed 12PM-1:30PM. Civil Actions Under $5,000, Eviction, Small Claims.

**Probate Court**, PO Box 187, Forsyth, GA 31029. 912-994-7036 (EST) Probate.

## Montgomery County

**Real Estate Recording**, Montgomery County Clerk of the Superior Court, Highway 221 & 56, Courthouse, Mount Vernon, GA 30445. 912-583-4401 (EST) 9AM-5PM.

**Superior Court**, PO Box 311, Mt Vernon, GA 30445. 912-583-4401 (EST) 8AM-5PM. Felony, Misdemeanor, Civil Actions Over $5,000.

**Magistrate Court**, PO Box 174, Mt Vernon, GA 30445. 912-583-2170 (EST) 8:30AM-5PM. Civil Actions Under $5,000, Eviction, Small Claims.

**Probate Court**, PO Box 302, Mt Vernon, GA 30445. 912-583-2681 (EST) Probate.

## Morgan County

**Real Estate Recording**, Morgan County Clerk of the Superior Court, 141 East Jefferson Street, Madison, GA 30650. 706-342-3605 (EST)

**Superior Court**, PO Box 130, Madison, GA 30650. 706-342-3605 (EST) 8:30AM-5PM. Felony, Misdemeanor, Civil Actions Over $5,000.

**Magistrate Court**, Courthouse, Rm 105, Madison, GA 30650. 706-342-3088 (EST) 8AM-5PM. Civil Actions Under $5,000, Eviction, Small Claims.

**Probate Court**, Morgan County Courthouse, Madison, GA 30650. 706-342-1373 (EST) Probate.

## Murray County

**Real Estate Recording**, Murray County Clerk of the Superior Court, 3rd Avenue, Courthouse, Chatsworth, GA 30705. 706-695-2932 (EST) 8:30AM-5PM.

**Superior Court**, PO Box 1000, Chatsworth, GA 30705. 706-695-2932 (EST) 8:30AM-5PM. Felony, Misdemeanor, Civil Actions Over $5,000.

**Magistrate Court**, 121 4th Ave, Chatsworth, GA 30705. 706-695-3021 (EST) 8AM-5PM. Civil Actions Under $5,000, Eviction, Small Claims.

**Probate Court**, Courthouse, 3rd Ave, Chatsworth, GA 30705. 706-695-3812 (EST) Probate.

## Muscogee County

**Real Estate Recording**, Muscogee County Clerk of the Superior Court, 100 10th Street, Columbus, GA 31901. 706-571-4919 (EST) 8:30AM-5PM.

**Superior & State Court**, PO Box 2145, Columbus, GA 31994. 706-571-5820 (EST) 8:30AM-5PM. Felony, Misdemeanor, Civil Actions Over $5,000.

**Magistrate Court**, Box 1563, Columbus, GA 31994. 706-571-4870 (EST) 8:30AM-5PM. Civil Actions Under $5,000, Eviction, Small Claims.

**Probate Court**, PO Box 1340, Columbus, GA 31993. 706-571-4847 (EST) Probate.

## Newton County

**Real Estate Recording**, Newton County Clerk of the Superior Court, 1124 Clark Street, Covington, GA 30209. 404-784-2035 (EST)

**Superior Court**, 1124 Clark St, Covington, GA 30209. 404-784-2035 (EST) 8AM-5PM. Felony, Misdemeanor, Civil Actions Over $5,000.

**Magistrate Court**, 1132 Usher St, Covington, GA 30209. 404-784-2050 (EST) 8AM-5PM. Civil Actions Under $5,000, Eviction, Small Claims.

**Probate Court**, 1124 Clark St, Covington, GA 30209. 404-784-2045 (EST) Probate.

## Oconee County

**Real Estate Recording**, Oconee County Clerk of the Superior Court, 23 N. Main Street, Watkinsville, GA 30677. 706-769-3940 (EST) 8:30AM-5PM.

**Superior & Magistrate Courts**, PO Box 113, Watkinsville, GA 30677. 706-769-3940 (EST) 8:30AM-5PM. Felony, Misdemeanor, Civil, Eviction, Small Claims.

**Probate Court**, PO Box 54, Watkinsville, GA 30677. 706-769-3936 (EST) Probate.

## Oglethorpe County

**Real Estate Recording**, Oglethorpe County Clerk of the Superior Court, Main Street, Courthouse, Lexington, GA 30648. 706-743-5731 (EST) 8:30AM-5PM.

**Superior Court**, PO Box 68, Lexington, GA 30648. 706-743-5731 (EST) 8AM-5PM. Felony, Misdemeanor, Civil Actions Over $5,000.

**Magistrate Court**, Box 356, Lexington, GA 30648. 706-743-8321 (EST) 8AM-5PM. Civil Actions Under $5,000, Eviction, Small Claims.

**Probate Court**, PO Box 70, Lexington, GA 30648. 706-743-5350 (EST) Probate.

## Paulding County

**Real Estate Recording**, Paulding County Clerk of the Superior Court, 11 Courthouse Sq., Room G-2, Dallas, GA 30132. 404-443-7527 (EST) 8AM-5PM.

**Superior Court**, 11 Courthouse Square, Rm G2, Dallas, GA 30132. 404-443-7529 (EST) 8AM-5PM. Felony, Misdemeanor, Civil Actions Over $5,000.

**Magistrate Court**, 11 Courthouse Square, Rm G2, Dallas, GA 30132. 404-443-7529 (EST) Civil Actions Under $5,000, Eviction, Small Claims.

**Probate Court**, 11 Courthouse Square, Rm G2, Dallas, GA 30132. 404-443-7529 (EST) Probate.

## Peach County

**Real Estate Recording**, Peach County Clerk of the Superior Court, 205 West Church Street, Courthouse, Fort Valley, GA 31030. 912-825-5331 (EST) 8:30AM-5PM.

**Superior Court**, PO Box 389, Ft Valley, GA 31030. 912-825-5331 (EST) 8:30AM-5PM.

Felony, Misdemeanor, Civil Actions Over $5,000.

**Magistrate Court**, PO Box 853, Ft Valley, GA 31030. 912-825-2060 (EST) 8AM-5PM. Civil Actions Under $5,000, Eviction, Small Claims.

**Probate Court**, PO Box 327, Ft Valley, GA 31030. 912-825-2313 (EST) Probate.

## Pickens County

**Real Estate Recording**, Pickens County Clerk of the Superior Court, 213 North Main Street, Courthouse Annex - Suite 102, Jasper, GA 30143. 706-692-2014 (EST) 8AM-5PM.

**Superior Court**, 213 N Main St, Ste 102, Jasper, GA 30143. 706-692-2014 (EST) 8AM-5PM. Felony, Misdemeanor, Civil Actions Over $5,000.

**Magistrate Court**, 211 N Main St, Jasper, GA 30143. 706-692-3556 (EST) 8AM-5PM. Civil Actions Under $5,000, Eviction, Small Claims.

**Probate Court**, 211 N Main St, Jasper, GA 30143. 706-692-3556 (EST) Probate.

## Pierce County

**Real Estate Recording**, Pierce County Clerk of the Superior Court, Courthouse, Highway 84, Blackshear, GA 31516. 912-449-2020 (EST) 9AM-5PM.

**Superior Court**, PO Box 588, Blackshear, GA 31516. 912-449-2020 (EST) 9AM-5PM. Felony, Misdemeanor, Civil Actions Over $5,000.

**State Court**, PO Box 588, Blackshear, GA 31516. 912-449-2020 (EST) 9AM-5PM. Misdemeanor, Civil Actions Over $5,000.

**Magistrate Court**, 102 Hwy 84 W, Blackshear, GA 31516. 912-449-2027 (EST) 9AM-5PM. Civil Actions Under $5,000, Eviction, Small Claims.

**Probate Court**, PO Box 406, Blackshear, GA 31516. 912-449-2029 (EST) Probate.

## Pike County

**Real Estate Recording**, Pike County Clerk of the Superior Court, Highway 18 & Highway 19, Courthouse Square, Zebulon, GA 30295. 706-567-2000 (EST) 8:30AM-5PM.

**Superior Court**, PO Box 10, Zebulon, GA 30295. 706-567-2000 (EST) 8AM-5PM. Felony, Misdemeanor, Civil Actions Over $5,000.

**Magistrate Court**, PO Box 466, Zebulon, GA 30295. 706-567-2004 (EST) 8AM-5PM. Civil Actions Under $5,000, Eviction, Small Claims.

**Probate Court**, PO Box 324, Zebulon, GA 30295. 702-567-8734 (EST) Probate.

## Polk County

**Real Estate Recording**, Polk County Clerk of the Superior Court, Pryor Street, Courthouse #1, Cedartown, GA 30125. 404-749-2114 (EST) 9AM-5PM.

**Superior Court**, PO Box 948, Cedartown, GA 30125. 404-749-2114 (EST) 9AM-5PM. Felony, Misdemeanor, Civil Actions Over $5,000.

**Magistrate Court**, PO Box 948, Cedartown, GA 30125. 404-749-2130 (EST) 9AM-5PM. Civil Actions Under $5,000, Eviction, Small Claims.

**Probate Court**, PO Box 948, Cedartown, GA 30125. 404-749-2128 (EST) Probate.

## Pulaski County

**Real Estate Recording**, Pulaski County Clerk of the Superior Court, Courthouse, Commerce Street, Hawkinsville, GA 31036. 912-783-1911 (EST)

**Superior Court**, PO Box 60, Hawkinsville, GA 31036. 912-783-1911 (EST) 8AM-5PM. Felony, Misdemeanor, Civil Actions Over $5,000.

**Magistrate Court**, PO Box 667, Hawkinsville, GA 31036. 912-783-1357 (EST) 8AM-5PM. Civil Actions Under $5,000, Eviction, Small Claims.

**Probate Court**, PO Box 156, Hawkinsville, GA 31036. 912-783-2061 (EST) Probate.

## Putnam County

**Real Estate Recording**, Putnam County Clerk of the Superior Court, Courthouse, 100 Jefferson St., Eatonton, GA 31024. 706-485-4501 (EST) 8AM-5PM.

**Superior & State Court**, County Courthouse, Eatonton, GA 31024. 706-485-4501 (EST) 8AM-5PM. Felony, Misdemeanor, Civil Actions Over $5,000.

**Magistrate Court**, 100 N Jefferson Ave, Eatonton, GA 31024. 706-485-4306 (EST) 8AM-5PM. Civil Actions Under $5,000, Eviction, Small Claims.

**Probate Court**, County Courthouse, Eatonton, GA 31024. 404-485-5476 (EST) Probate.

## Quitman County

**Real Estate Recording**, Quitman County Clerk of the Superior Court, Main Street, Courthouse, Georgetown, GA 31754. 912-334-2578 (EST) 9AM-5PM.

**Superior Court**, PO Box 307, Georgetown, GA 31754. 912-334-2578 (EST) 8:30AM-5PM. Felony, Misdemeanor, Civil Actions Over $5,000.

**Magistrate Court**, PO Box 7, Georgetown, GA 31754. 912-334-2224 (EST) 8:30AM-5PM. Civil Actions Under $5,000, Eviction, Small Claims.

**Probate Court**, PO Box 7, Georgetown, GA 31754. 912-334-2224 (EST) Probate.

## Rabun County

**Real Estate Recording**, Rabun County Clerk of the Superior Court, Courthouse, West Savannah Street, Clayton, GA 30525. 706-782-3615 (EST) 8:30AM-5PM.

**Superior Court**, PO Box 893, Clayton, GA 30525. 706-782-3615 (EST) 8:30AM-5PM. Felony, Misdemeanor, Civil Actions Over $5,000.

**Magistrate Court**, PO Box 893, Clayton, GA 30525. 706-782-3615 (EST) 8:30AM-5PM. Civil Actions Under $5,000, Eviction, Small Claims.

**Probate Court**, PO Box 346, Clayton, GA 30525. 706-782-3614 (EST) Probate.

## Randolph County

**Real Estate Recording**, Randolph County Clerk of the Superior Court, 208 Court Street, Cuthbert, GA 31740. 912-732-2216 (EST) 8:30AM-5PM.

**Superior Court**, PO Box 98, Cuthbert, GA 31740. 912-732-2216 (EST) 8:30AM-5PM. Felony, Misdemeanor, Civil Actions Over $5,000.

**Magistrate Court**, PO Box 6, Cuthbert, GA 31740. 912-732-6182 (EST) 9AM-5PM. Civil Actions Under $5,000, Eviction, Small Claims.

**Probate Court**, PO Box 424, Cuthbert, GA 31740. 912-732-2671 (EST) Probate.

## Richmond County

**Real Estate Recording**, Richmond County Clerk of the Superior Court, 530 Green Street, 5th Floor, Room 503, Augusta, GA 30911. 706-821-2568 (EST) 8:30AM-5PM.

**Superior Court**, PO Box 2046, Augusta, GA 30911. 706-821-2460 (EST) 8:30AM-5PM. Felony, Misdemeanor, Civil Actions Over $5,000.

**State Court**, PO Box 2046, Augusta, GA 30911. 706-821-1233 (EST) 8:30AM-5PM. Misdemeanor, Civil Actions Over $5,000.

**Magistrate & Civil Court**, 530 Greene St, Rm 705, Augusta, GA 30911. 706-821-2370 (EST) 8:30AM-5PM. Civil Actions Under $5,000, Eviction, Small Claims.

**Probate Court**, Municipal Bldg Rm 401, 530 Greene St, Augusta, GA 30904. 702-821-2434 (EST) Probate.

## Rockdale County

**Real Estate Recording**, Rockdale County Clerk of the Superior Court, 922 Court Street, Room 203, Conyers, GA 30207. 404-929-4069 (EST) 8AM-5PM.

**Superior Court**, PO Box 937, Conyers, GA 30207. 404-929-4021 (EST) Felony, Misdemeanor, Civil Actions Over $5,000.

**State Court**, PO Box 938, Conyers, GA 30207. 404-929-4019 (EST) 8AM-4:45PM. Misdemeanor, Civil Actions Over $5,000.

**Magistrate Court**, PO Box 289, Conyers, GA 30207. 404-929-4014 (EST) 8:30AM-4:30PM. Civil Actions Under $5,000, Eviction, Small Claims.

**Probate Court**, PO Box 937, Conyers, GA 30207. 404-929-4058 (EST) Probate.

## Schley County

**Real Estate Recording**, Schley County Clerk of the Superior Court, US Highway 19, Courthouse Square, Ellaville, GA 31806. 912-937-5581 (EST) 8AM-Noon,1-5PM.

**Superior Court**, PO Box 7, Ellaville, GA 31806. 912-937-5581 (EST) 8AM-5PM. Felony, Misdemeanor, Civil Actions Over $5,000.

**Magistrate Court**, PO Box 7, Ellaville, GA 31806. 912-937-5581 (EST) 8AM-5PM. Civil Actions Under $5,000, Eviction, Small Claims.

**Probate Court**, PO Box 385, Ellaville, GA 31806. 912-937-2905 (EST) Probate.

## Screven County

**Real Estate Recording**, Screven County Clerk of the Superior Court, 216 Mims Road, Sylvania, GA 30467. 912-564-2614 (EST) 8AM-5PM.

**Superior Court**, PO Box 156, Sylvania, GA 30467. 912-564-2614 (EST) 8AM-5PM. Felony, Misdemeanor, Civil Actions Over $5,000.

**State Court**, PO Box 156, Sylvania, GA 30467. 912-564-2614 (EST) 8AM-5PM. Misdemeanor, Civil Actions Over $5,000.

**Magistrate Court**, PO Box 64, Sylvania, GA 30467. 912-564-7375 (EST) 8:30AM-4:30PM.

Civil Actions Under $5,000, Eviction, Small Claims.

**Probate Court**, 216 Mims Rd, Sylvania, GA 30467. 912-564-2783 (EST) Probate.

## Seminole County

**Real Estate Recording**, Seminole County Clerk of the Superior Court, Second Street, Courthouse, Donalsonville, GA 31745. 912-524-2525 (EST) 9AM-5PM.

**Superior Court**, PO Box 672, Donalsonville, GA 31745. 912-524-2525 (EST) 8AM-5PM. Felony, Misdemeanor, Civil Actions Over $5,000.

**Magistrate Court**, PO Box 672, Donalsonville, GA 31745. 912-524-5256 (EST) 8AM-5PM. Civil Actions Under $5,000, Eviction, Small Claims.

**Probate Court**, Seminole County Courthouse, Donalsonville, GA 31745. 912-524-5256 (EST) Probate.

## Spalding County

**Real Estate Recording**, Spalding County Clerk of the Superior Court, 132 East Solomon Street, Griffin, GA 30223. 404-228-9900 (EST) 8AM-5PM.

**Superior Court**, PO Box 163, Griffin, GA 30224. 404-228-9900 (EST) Felony, Misdemeanor, Civil Actions Over $5,000.

**State Court**, PO Box 163, Griffin, GA 30224. 404-228-9900 (EST) 8AM-5PM. Misdemeanor, Civil Actions Over $5,000.

**Magistrate Court**, 132 E Solomon, Griffin, GA 30224. 404-228-9900 (EST) 8AM-5PM. Civil Actions Under $5,000, Eviction, Small Claims.

**Probate Court**, 132 E Solomon St, Griffin, GA 30223. 404-228-9900 (EST) Probate.

## Stephens County

**Real Estate Recording**, Stephens County Clerk of the Superior Court, Stephens County Courthouse, 150 West Doyle St., Toccoa, GA 30577. 706-886-3598 (EST) 8AM-5PM.

**Superior Court**, PO Box 910, Lumpkin, GA 31815. 912-838-6220 (EST) 8AM-5PM. Felony, Misdemeanor, Civil Actions Over $5,000.

**Superior Court**, 150 W Doyle St, Toccoa, GA 30577. 706-886-3598 (EST) 8AM-5PM. Felony, Misdemeanor, Civil Actions Over $5,000.

**State Court**, 150 W Doyle St, Toccoa, GA 30577. 706-886-3598 (EST) 8AM-5PM. Misdemeanor, Civil Actions Over $5,000.

**Magistrate Court**, PO Box 90, Lumpkin, GA 31815. 912-838-4261 (EST) 8AM-5PM. Civil Actions Under $5,000, Eviction, Small Claims.

**Magistrate Court**, 150 W Doyle St, Toccoa, GA 30577. 404-886-6205 (EST) 8AM-5PM. Civil Actions Under $5,000, Eviction, Small Claims.

**Probate Court**, County Courthouse, Toccoa, GA 30577. 706-886-2828 (EST) Probate.

## Stewart County

**Real Estate Recording**, Stewart County Clerk of the Superior Court, Main Street, Courthouse, Lumpkin, GA 31815. 912-838-6220 (EST) 8AM-4:30PM.

**Superior Court**, PO Box 910, Lumpkin, GA 31815. 912-838-6220 (EST) 8AM-5PM. Felony, Misdemeanor, Civil Actions Over $5,000.

**Magistrate Court**, PO Box 713, Lumpkin, GA 31815. 912-838-4261 (EST) 8AM-5PM. Civil Actions Under $5,000, Eviction, Small Claims.

**Probate Court**, PO Box 876, Lumpkin, GA 31815. 912-838-4394 (EST) Probate.

## Sumter County

**Real Estate Recording**, Sumter County Clerk of the Superior Court, Lamar Street, Courthouse, Americus, GA 31709. 912-924-5626 (EST)

**Superior Court**, PO Box 333, Americus, GA 31709. 912-924-5626 (EST) 9AM-5PM. Felony, Misdemeanor, Civil Actions Over $5,000.

**State Court**, PO Box 333, Americus, GA 31709. 912-924-5626 (EST) 9AM-5PM. Misdemeanor, Civil Actions Over $5,000.

**Magistrate Court**, PO Box 563, Americus, GA 31709. 912-924-6699 (EST) 9AM-5PM. Civil Actions Under $5,000, Eviction, Small Claims.

**Probate Court**, PO Box 246, Americus, GA 31709. 912-924-7693 (EST) Probate.

## Talbot County

**Real Estate Recording**, Talbot County Clerk of the Superior Court, Monroe Street, Courthouse Square #1, Talbotton, GA 31827. 706-665-3239 (EST) 9AM-5PM.

**Superior Court**, PO Box 325, Talbotton, GA 31827. 706-665-3239 (EST) 9AM-5PM. Felony, Misdemeanor, Civil Actions Over $5,000.

**Magistrate Court**, PO Box 325, Talbotton, GA 31827. 706-665-3598 (EST) 8AM-5PM. Civil Actions Under $5,000, Eviction, Small Claims.

**Probate Court**, PO Box 325, Talbotton, GA 31827. 706-665-3598 (EST) Probate.

## Taliaferro County

**Real Estate Recording**, Taliaferro County Clerk of the Superior Court, Monument Street, Courthouse, Crawfordville, GA 30631. 706-456-2123 (EST)

**Superior Court**, PO Box 182, Crawfordville, GA 30631. 706-456-2123 (EST) 9AM-5PM. Felony, Misdemeanor, Civil Actions Over $5,000.

**Magistrate Court**, PO Box 85, Crawfordville, GA 30631. 706-456-2253 (EST) 8AM-5PM. Civil Actions Under $5,000, Eviction, Small Claims.

**Probate Court**, PO Box 85, Crawfordville, GA 30631. 706-456-2253 (EST) Probate.

## Tattnall County

**Real Estate Recording**, Tattnall County Clerk of the Superior Court, 108 Brazell Street, Courthouse, Reidsville, GA 30453. 912-557-6716 (EST) 8AM-4:30PM.

**Superior Court**, PO Box 59, Reidsville, GA 30453. 912-557-6716 (EST) 8AM-4:30PM. Felony, Misdemeanor, Civil Actions Over $5,000.

**State Court**, PO Box 59, Reidsville, GA 30453. 912-557-6716 (EST) 8AM-4:30PM. Misdemeanor, Civil Actions Over $5,000.

**Magistrate Court**, PO Box 513, Reidsville, GA 30453. 912-557-4372 (EST) 8AM-4:30PM. Civil Actions Under $5,000, Eviction, Small Claims.

**Probate Court**, PO Box 710, Reidsville, GA 30453. 912-557-6719 (EST) Probate.

## Taylor County

**Real Estate Recording**, Taylor County Clerk of the Superior Court, Courthouse Square, Butler, GA 31006. 912-862-5594 (EST) 8AM-5PM.

**Superior Court**, PO Box 248, Butler, GA 31006. 912-862-5594 (EST) 8AM-5PM. Felony, Misdemeanor, Civil Actions Over $5,000.

**Magistrate Court**, PO Box 536, Butler, GA 31006. 912-862-3357 (EST) 8AM-5PM. Civil Actions Under $5,000, Eviction, Small Claims.

**Probate Court**, PO Box 536, Butler, GA 31006. 912-862-3357 (EST) Probate.

## Telfair County

**Real Estate Recording**, Telfair County Clerk of the Superior Court, Courthouse, Oak Street, McRae, GA 31055. 912-868-6525 (EST) 8:30AM-Noon, 1-4:30PM.

**Superior Court**, Courthouse, McRae, GA 31055. 912-868-6525 (EST) 8:30AM-4:30PM. Felony, Misdemeanor, Civil Actions Over $5,000.

**Magistrate Court**, County Courthouse, McRae, GA 31055. 912-868-6772 (EST) 8:30AM-4:30PM. Civil Actions Under $5,000, Eviction, Small Claims.

**Probate Court**, Courthouse Square, McRae, GA 31055. 912-868-6038 (EST) Probate.

## Terrell County

**Real Estate Recording**, Terrell County Clerk of the Superior Court, 235 Lee Street, Courthouse, Dawson, GA 31742. 912-995-2631 (EST) 8:30AM-5PM.

**Superior Court**, PO Box 189, Dawson, GA 31742. 912-995-2631 (EST) 8:30AM-5PM. Felony, Misdemeanor, Civil Actions Over $5,000.

**Magistrate Court**, PO Box 793, Dawson, GA 31742. 912-995-3757 (EST) 8AM-5PM. Civil Actions Under $5,000, Eviction, Small Claims.

**Probate Court**, PO Box 67, Dawson, GA 31742. 912-995-5515 (EST) Probate.

## Thomas County

**Real Estate Recording**, Thomas County Clerk of the Superior Court, 225 North Broad Street, Courthouse, Thomasville, GA 31792. 912-225-4108 (EST) 8AM-5PM.

**Superior & State Court**, PO Box 1995, Thomasville, GA 31799. 912-225-4108 (EST) 8AM-5PM. Felony, Misdemeanor, Civil Actions Over $5,000.

**Magistrate Court**, PO Box 879, Thomasville, GA 31799. 912-225-3330 (EST) 8AM-5PM. Civil Actions Under $5,000, Eviction, Small Claims.

**Probate Court**, PO Box 1582, Thomasville, GA 31799. 912-225-4116 (EST) Probate.

## Tift County

**Real Estate Recording**, Tift County Clerk of the Superior Court, Corner of Tift Avenue & 2nd Street, Courthouse, Tifton, GA 31794. 912-386-7810 (EST) 9AM-5PM.

**Superior & State Court**, PO Box 354, Tifton, GA 31793. 912-386-7810 (EST) 8AM-5PM. Felony, Misdemeanor, Civil Actions Over $5,000.

**Magistrate Court**, PO Box 214, Tifton, GA 31793. 912-386-7907 (EST) 8:30AM-5PM. Civil Actions Under $5,000, Eviction, Small Claims.

**Probate Court**, PO Box 792, Tifton, GA 31793. 912-386-7913 (EST) Probate.

## Toombs County

**Real Estate Recording**, Toombs County Clerk of the Superior Court, 100 Courthouse Square, Lyons, GA 30436. 912-526-3501 (EST) 8:30AM-5PM.

**Superior & State Court**, PO Drawer 530, Lyons, GA 30436. 912-526-3501 (EST) 8:30AM-5PM. Felony, Misdemeanor, Civil Actions Over $5,000.

**Magistrate Court**, PO Box 184, Lyons, GA 30436. 912-526-8985 (EST) 8:30AM-5PM. Civil Actions Under $5,000, Eviction, Small Claims.

**Probate Court**, PO Box 1370, Lyons, GA 30436. 912-526-8696 (EST) Probate.

## Towns County

**Real Estate Recording**, Towns County Clerk of the Superior Court, 48 River St., Courthouse, Suite E, Hiawassee, GA 30546. 706-896-2130 (EST) 8:30AM-4:30PM.

**Superior Court**, PO Box 178, Hiawassee, GA 30546. 706-896-2130 (EST) 8:30AM-4:30PM. Felony, Misdemeanor, Civil Actions Over $5,000.

**Magistrate Court**, 48 River St, Hiawassee, GA 30546. 706-896-3467 (EST) 8:30AM-4:30PM. Civil Actions Under $5,000, Eviction, Small Claims, Probate.

## Treutlen County

**Real Estate Recording**, Treutlen County Clerk of the Superior Court, Georgia Ave., Courthouse, Soperton, GA 30457. 912-529-4215 (EST) 8AM-5PM.

**Superior & State Court**, PO Box 356, Soperton, GA 30457. 912-529-4215 (EST) 8AM-5PM. Felony, Misdemeanor, Civil Actions Over $5,000.

**Magistrate Court**, 200 W Georgia Ave, Soperton, GA 30457. 912-529-3342 (EST) Civil Actions Under $5,000, Eviction, Small Claims, Probate.

## Troup County

**Real Estate Recording**, Troup County Clerk of the Superior Court, Courthouse, 118 Ridley Avenue, LaGrange, GA 30241. 706-883-1740 (EST) 8AM-5PM.

**Superior & State Court**, 118 Ridley Ave (PO Box 866, 30241), LaGrange, GA 30240. 706-883-1740 (EST) 8AM-5PM. Felony, Misdemeanor, Civil Actions Over $5,000.

**Magistrate Court**, 900 Dallis St, LaGrange, GA 30240. 706-883-1695 (EST) 8AM-5PM. Civil Actions Under $5,000, Eviction, Small Claims.

**Probate Court**, 900 Dallis St, LaGrange, GA 30240. 706-883-1690 (EST) Probate.

## Turner County

**Real Estate Recording**, Turner County Clerk of the Luperior Court, 219 East College Avenue, Ashburn, GA 31714. 912-567-2011 (EST) 8AM-5PM.

**Superior Court**, PO Box 106, Ashburn, GA 31714. 912-567-2011 (EST) 8AM-5PM. Felony, Misdemeanor, Civil Actions Over $5,000.

**Magistrate Court**, 219 E College Ave, Rm 2, Ashburn, GA 31714. 912-567-3155 (EST) 9AM-6PM M,T,Th/9AM-1PM F. Civil Actions Under $5,000, Eviction, Small Claims.

**Probate Court**, PO Box 2506, Ashburn, GA 31714. 912-567-2151 (EST) Probate.

## Twiggs County

**Real Estate Recording**, Twiggs County Clerk of the Superior Court, Railroad Street, Courthouse Square, Jeffersonville, GA 31044. 912-945-3350 (EST) 8AM-5PM.

**Superior Court**, PO Box 228, Jeffersonville, GA 31044. 912-945-3350 (EST) Felony, Misdemeanor, Civil Actions Over $5,000.

**Magistrate Court**, PO Box 146, Jeffersonville, GA 31044. 912-945-3428 (EST) 8AM-4PM. Civil Actions Under $5,000, Eviction, Small Claims.

**Probate Court**, PO Box 307, Jeffersonville, GA 31044. 912-945-3390 (EST) Probate.

## Union County

**Real Estate Recording**, Union County Clerk of the Superior Court, 114 Courthouse Street, Box 5, Blairsville, GA 30512. 706-745-2611 (EST) 8AM-5PM.

**Superior Court**, 114 Courthouse St, Box 5, Blairsville, GA 30512. 706-745-2611 (EST) 8AM-5PM. Felony, Misdemeanor, Civil Actions Over $5,000.

**Magistrate & Probate Court**, 114 Courthouse St, Box 8, Blairsville, GA 30512. 706-745-2654 (EST) 8AM-4:30PM. Civil Actions Under $5,000, Eviction, Small Claims, Probate.

## Upson County

**Real Estate Recording**, Upson County Clerk of the Superior Court, Main Street, Courthouse Annex, Thomaston, GA 30286. 706-647-7835 (EST) 8AM-5PM.

**Superior Court**, PO Box 469, Thomaston, GA 30286. 404-647-7835 (EST) 8AM-5PM. Felony, Misdemeanor, Civil Actions Over $5,000.

**Magistrate Court**, PO Box 890, Thomaston, GA 30286. 706-647-6891 (EST) 8AM-5PM. Civil Actions Under $5,000, Eviction, Small Claims.

**Probate Court**, PO Box 906, Thomaston, GA 30286. 706-647-7015 (EST) Probate.

## Walker County

**Real Estate Recording**, Walker County Clerk of the Superior Court, South Duke Street, Courthouse, La Fayette, GA 30728. 706-638-1742 (EST) 8AM-5PM.

**Superior & State Court**, PO Box 448, LaFayette, GA 30728. 404-638-1742 (EST) 8AM-5PM. Felony, Misdemeanor, Civil Actions Over $5,000.

**Magistrate Court**, PO Box 854, LaFayette, GA 30728. 706-638-1217 (EST) 8AM-5PM. Civil Actions Under $5,000, Eviction, Small Claims.

**Probate Court**, PO Box 436, LaFayette, GA 30728. 706-638-2852 (EST) Probate.

## Walton County

**Real Estate Recording**, Walton County Clerk of the Superior Court, 111 Spring Street, Courthouse, Monroe, GA 30655. 404-267-1304 (EST) 8:30AM-5PM.

**Superior Court**, PO Box 745, Monroe, GA 30655. 404-267-1305 (EST) 8AM-5PM. Felony, Misdemeanor, Civil Actions Over $5,000.

**Magistrate Court**, PO Box 1188, Monroe, GA 30655. 404-267-1349 (EST) 8:30AM-5PM. Civil Actions Under $5,000, Eviction, Small Claims.

**Probate Court**, PO Box 629, Monroe, GA 30655. 404-267-1345 (EST) Probate.

## Ware County

**Real Estate Recording**, Ware County Clerk of the Superior Court, 800 Church Street, Waycross, GA 31501. 912-287-4340 (EST) 9AM-5PM.

**Superior & State Court**, PO Box 776, Waycross, GA 31502. 912-287-4340 (EST) 9AM-5PM. Felony, Misdemeanor, Civil Actions Over $5,000.

**Magistrate Court**, 201 State St, Rm 102, Waycross, GA 31501. 912-287-4373 (EST) 9AM-5PM. Civil Actions Under $5,000, Eviction, Small Claims.

**Probate Court**, Courthouse, Rm 105, Waycross, GA 31501. 912-287-4315 (EST) Probate.

## Warren County

**Real Estate Recording**, Warren County Clerk of the Superior Court, 100 Main Street, Courthouse, Warrenton, GA 30828. 706-465-2262 (EST)

**Superior Court**, PO Box 346, Warrenton, GA 30828. 706-465-2262 (EST) 8AM-5PM. Felony, Misdemeanor, Civil Actions Over $5,000.

**Magistrate Court**, PO Box 203, Warrenton, GA 30828. 404-465-3123 (EST) 8AM-5PM. Civil Actions Under $5,000, Eviction, Small Claims.

**Probate Court**, PO Box 364, Warrenton, GA 30828. 404-465-2227 (EST) Probate.

## Washington County

**Real Estate Recording**, Washington County Clerk of the Superior Court, Courthouse, Sandersville, GA 31082. 912-552-3186 (EST) 9AM-5PM.

**Superior & State Court**, PO Box 231, Sandersville, GA 31082. 912-552-3186 (EST) Felony, Misdemeanor, Civil Actions Over $5,000.

**Magistrate Court**, PO Box 1053, Sandersville, GA 31082. 912-552-3591 (EST) 9AM-5PM. Civil Actions Under $5,000, Eviction, Small Claims.

**Probate Court**, PO Box 669, Sandersville, GA 31082. 912-552-3304 (EST) Probate.

## Wayne County

**Real Estate Recording**, Wayne County Clerk of the Superior Court, 174 North Brunswick Street, Courthouse, Jesup, GA 31545. 912-427-5930 (EST) 8:30AM-5PM.

**Superior & State Court**, PO Box 918, Jesup, GA 31545. 912-427-5930 (EST) 8:30AM-5PM. Felony, Misdemeanor, Civil Actions Over $5,000.

**Magistrate Court**, PO Box 27, Jesup, GA 31545. 912-427-5960 (EST) 8:30AM-5PM. Civil Actions Under $5,000, Eviction, Small Claims.

**Probate Court**, PO Box 1093, Jesup, GA 31545. 912-427-5940 (EST) Probate.

## Webster County

**Real Estate Recording**, Webster County Clerk of the Superior Court, County Courthouse, U.S. Highway 280, Preston, GA 31824. 912-828-3525 (EST) 8AM-Noon, 12:30PM-4:30PM.

**Superior Court**, PO Box 117, Preston, GA 31824. 912-828-3525 (EST) 8AM-4:30PM. Felony, Misdemeanor, Civil Actions Over $5,000.

**Magistrate Court**, PO Box 18, Preston, GA 31824. 912-828-6030 (EST) 8:30AM-4:30PM. Civil Actions Under $5,000, Eviction, Small Claims.

**Probate Court**, PO Box 135, Preston, GA 31824. 912-828-3615 (EST) Probate.

## Wheeler County

**Real Estate Recording**, Wheeler County Clerk of the Superior Court, 119 West Pearl St., Alamo, GA 30411. 912-568-7137 (EST) 8AM-4PM.

**Superior Court**, PO Box 38, Alamo, GA 30411. 912-568-7137 (EST) Felony, Misdemeanor, Civil Actions Over $5,000.

**Magistrate & Probate Court**, PO Box 477, Alamo, GA 30411. 912-568-7133 (EST) 8AM-4PM. Civil Actions Under $5,000, Eviction, Small Claims, Probate.

## White County

**Real Estate Recording**, White County Clerk of the Superior Court, 59 South Main Street, Courthouse, Suite B, Cleveland, GA 30528. 706-865-2613 (EST) 8:30AM-5PM.

**Superior Court**, 59 S Main St, Ste B, Cleveland, GA 30528. 706-865-2613 (EST) 8:30AM-5PM. Felony, Misdemeanor, Civil Actions Over $5,000.

**Magistrate Court-Civil Division**, 59 S Main St, Ste B, Cleveland, GA 30528. 706-865-2613 (EST) 8:30AM-5PM. Civil Actions Under $5,000, Eviction, Small Claims.

**Magistrate Court-Criminal Division**, 59 S Main St, Ste D, Cleveland, GA 30528. 706-865-6636 (EST) 9AM-5PM. Civil Actions Under $5,000, Eviction, Small Claims.

**Probate Court**, 59 S Main St Ste H, Cleveland, GA 30528. 706-865-4141 (EST) Probate.

## Whitfield County

**Real Estate Recording**, Whitfield County Clerk of the Superior Court, 300 West Crawford Street, Courthouse, Dalton, GA 30722. 706-275-7450 (EST) 8AM-5PM.

**Superior Court**, PO Box 868, Dalton, GA 30722. 706-275-7450 (EST) 8AM-5PM. Felony, Misdemeanor, Civil Actions Over $5,000.

**Magistrate Court**, 210 Thorton Ave, Dalton, GA 30720. 706-278-5052 (EST) 8AM-5PM. Civil Actions Under $5,000, Eviction, Small Claims.

**Probate Court**, 300 Crawford St, Dalton, GA 30720. 706-275-7400 (EST) Probate.

## Wilcox County

**Real Estate Recording**, Wilcox County Clerk of the Superior Court, Courthouse, Abbeville, GA 31001. 912-467-2442 (EST) 9AM-5PM.

**Superior & Magistrate Courts**, Courthouse, Abbeville, GA 31001. 912-467-2442 (EST) 9AM-5PM. Felony, Misdemeanor, Civil, Eviction, Small Claims.

**Probate Court**, 103 N Broad St, Abbeville, GA 31001. 912-467-2220 (EST) Probate.

## Wilkes County

**Real Estate Recording**, Wilkes County Superior Court Clerk, 23 East Court Street, Room 205, Washington, GA 30673. 706-678-2423 (EST) 9AM-5PM.

**Superior Court**, 23 E Court St, Rm 205, Washington, GA 30673. 706-678-2423 (EST) 9AM-5PM. Felony, Misdemeanor, Civil Actions Over $5,000.

**Magistrate Court**, 23 E Court St, Rm 427, Washington, GA 30673. 706-678-1881 (EST) 8:30AM-5PM. Civil Actions Under $5,000, Eviction, Small Claims.

**Probate Court**, 23 E Court St, Rm 422, Washington, GA 30673. 706-678-2523 (EST) Probate.

## Wilkinson County

**Real Estate Recording**, Wilkinson County Clerk of the Superior Court, 100 Main Street, Courthouse, Irwinton, GA 31042. 912-946-2221 (EST) 8AM-5PM.

**Superior Court**, PO Box 250, Irwinton, GA 31042. 912-946-2221 (EST) 8AM-5PM. Felony, Misdemeanor, Civil Actions Over $5,000.

**Magistrate Court**, PO Box 201, Irwinton, GA 31042. 912-946-2222 (EST) 8AM-5PM. Civil Actions Under $5,000, Eviction, Small Claims, Probate.

## Worth County

**Real Estate Recording**, Worth County Clerk of the Superior Court, 201 North Main Street, Courthouse, Room 13, Sylvester, GA 31791. 912-776-8205 (EST) 8AM-5PM.

**Superior, State & Magistrate Court**, 201 N Main St, Rm 13, Sylvester, GA 31791. 912-776-8205 (EST) 8AM-5PM. Felony, Misdemeanor, Civil, Eviction, Small Claims.

**Probate Court**, 201 N Main St, Rm 12, Sylvester, GA 31791. 912-776-8207 (EST) Probate.

# Hawaii

## Secretary of State

**Real Estate Recording**, Bureau of Conveyances, 1151 Punchbowl Street, Dept. of Land and Natural Resources, Honolulu, HI 96813. 808-587-0154 7:45AM-4:30PM.

## Hawaii County

**3rd Circuit Court**, PO Box 1007, Hilo, HI 96721-1007. 808-961-7404 (HT) 7:45AM-4:30PM. Felony, Misdemeanor, Civil Actions Over $5,000, Probate.

**District Court**, PO Box 4879, Hilo, HI 96720. 808-961-7470 (HT) 7:45AM-4:30PM. Misdemeanor, Civil Actions Under $20,000, Eviction, Small Claims.

## Honolulu County

**1st Circuit Court**, PO Box 619, Honolulu, HI 96809. 808-539-4300 (HT) 7:45AM-4:30PM. Felony, Misdemeanor, Civil Actions Over $5,000, Probate.

**District Court**, 1111 Alakea St, 9th Fl Records, Honolulu, HI 96813. 808-538-5300 (HT) 7:45AM-4:30PM. Misdemeanor, Civil Actions Under $20,000, Eviction, Small Claims.

## Kauai County

**5th Circuit Court**, 3059 Umi St, Lihue, HI 96766. 808-246-3300 (HT) Felony, Misdemeanor, Civil Actions Over $5,000, Probate.

**District Court**, 3059 Umi St, Room 111, Lihue, HI 96766. 808-246-3330 (HT) 7:45AM-4:30PM. Misdemeanor, Civil Actions Under $20,000, Eviction, Small Claims.

## Maui County

**2nd Circuit Court**, 2145 Main St, Wailuku, HI 96793. 808-244-2929 (HT) 7:45AM-4:30PM. Felony, Misdemeanor, Civil Actions Over $5,000, Probate.

**Molokai District Court**, PO Box 284, Kaunakakai, HI 96748. 808-533-5451 (HT) 8AM-4:30PM. Misdemeanor, Civil Actions Under $20,000, Eviction, Small Claims.

**Lanai District Court**, PO Box 741, Lanai City, HI 96763. 808-565-6447 (HT) 8AM-4:30PM. Misdemeanor, Civil Actions Under $20,000, Eviction, Small Claims.

**Wailuku District Court**, 2145 Main St, Ste 137, Wailuku, HI 96793. 808-244-2800 (HT) 7:45AM-4:30PM. Misdemeanor, Civil Actions Under $20,000, Eviction, Small Claims.

# Idaho

## Ada County

**Real Estate Recording**, Ada County Clerk and Recorder, 650 Main Street, Boise, ID 83702. 208-364-2223 (MST) 8:30AM-4:30PM.

**District & Magistrate Court I**, 514 W. Jefferson St, Boise, ID 83702-5931. 208-364-2000 (MST) 8AM-5PM. Felony, Misdemeanor, Civil, Eviction, Small Claims, Probate.

**Magistrate Court II-Criminal**, 7180 Barrister, Criminal Cases, Boise, ID 83702. 208-377-0282 (MST) 8AM-5PM. Misdemeanor.

## Adams County

**Real Estate Recording**, Adams County Clerk and Recorder, Michigan St., Council, ID 83612. 208-253-4561 (MST) 8:30AM-Noon, 1-5PM.

**District & Magistrate Courts**, PO Box 48, Council, ID 83612. 208-253-4561 (MST) 8AM-5PM, Closed 12-1. Felony, Misdemeanor, Civil, Eviction, Small Claims, Probate.

## Bannock County

**Real Estate Recording**, Bannock County Clerk and Recorder, 624 East Center, Courthouse, Pocatello, ID 83201. 208-236-7340 (MST) 8AM-5PM.

**District & Magistrate Courts**, PO Box 4777, Pocatello, ID 83205. 208-236-7352 (MST) 8AM-5PM. Felony, Misdemeanor, Civil, Eviction, Small Claims, Probate.

## Bear Lake County

**Real Estate Recording**, Bear Lake County Clerk and Recorder, 7th East Center, Paris, ID 83261. 208-945-2212 (MST) 8:30AM-5PM.

**District & Magistrate Courts**, PO Box 190, Paris, ID 83261. 208-945-2208 (MST) 8:30AM-5PM. Felony, Misdemeanor, Civil, Eviction, Small Claims, Probate.

## Benewah County

**Real Estate Recording**, Benewah County Clerk and Recorder, 701 College, St. Maries, ID 83861. 208-245-3212 (PST) 9AM-5PM.

**District & Magistrate Courts**, Courthouse, St Maries, ID 83861. 208-245-3241 (PST) 9AM-5PM. Felony, Misdemeanor, Civil, Eviction, Small Claims, Probate.

## Bingham County

**Real Estate Recording**, Bingham County Clerk and Recorder, 501 North Maple, Courthouse, Blackfoot, ID 83221. 208-785-5005 (MST) 8AM-5PM.

**District & Magistrate Courts**, PO Box 807 (Mag) PO Box 717 (Dist), Blackfoot, ID 83221. 208-785-5005 (MST) 8AM-5PM. Felony, Misdemeanor, Civil, Eviction, Small Claims, Probate.

## Blaine County

**Real Estate Recording**, Blaine County Clerk and Recorder, 1st & Croy, Courthouse, Hailey, ID 83333. 208-788-5505 (MST) 9AM-5PM.

**District & Magistrate Courts**, PO Box 1006, Hailey, ID 83333. 208-788-5525 (MST) 9AM-5PM. Felony, Misdemeanor, Civil, Eviction, Small Claims, Probate.

## Boise County

**Real Estate Recording**, Boise County Clerk and Recorder, 420 Main, Courthouse, Idaho City, ID 83631. 208-392-4431 (MST) 8AM-5PM.

**District & Magistrate Courts**, PO Box 126, Idaho City, ID 83631. 208-392-4452 (MST) 8AM-5PM. Felony, Misdemeanor, Civil, Eviction, Small Claims, Probate.

## Bonner County

**Real Estate Recording**, Bonner County Clerk and Recorder, 215 South First, Sandpoint, ID 83864. 208-265-1432 (PST) 9AM-5PM.

**District & Magistrate Courts**, 215 S. First St, Sandpoint, ID 83864. 208-265-1432 (PST) 8AM-5PM. Felony, Misdemeanor, Civil, Eviction, Small Claims, Probate.

## Bonneville County

**Real Estate Recording**, Bonneville County Clerk and Recorder, 605 North Capital, Idaho Falls, ID 83402-3582. 208-529-1350 (MST) 8AM-5PM.

**District & Magistrate Courts**, 605 N. Capital, Idaho Falls, ID 83402. 208-529-1342 (MST) 8AM-5PM. Felony, Misdemeanor, Civil, Eviction, Small Claims, Probate.

## Boundary County

**Real Estate Recording**, Boundary County Clerk and Recorder, 315 Kootenai, Courthouse, Bonners Ferry, ID 83805. 208-267-2242 (PST) 9AM-5PM.

**District & Magistrate Courts**, PO Box 419, Bonners Ferry, ID 83805. 208-267-5504 (PST) 9AM-5PM. Felony, Misdemeanor, Civil, Eviction, Small Claims, Probate.

## Butte County

**Real Estate Recording**, Butte County Clerk and Recorder, 248 West Grand, Courthouse, Arco, ID 83213. 208-527-3021 (MST) 9AM-5PM.

**District & Magistrate Courts**, PO Box 171, Arco, ID 83213. 208-527-8259 (MST) 9AM-5PM. Felony, Misdemeanor, Civil, Eviction, Small Claims, Probate.

## Camas County

**Real Estate Recording**, Camas County Clerk and Recorder, Corner of Soldier & Willow, Courthouse, Fairfield, ID 83327. 208-764-2242 (MST) 8:30AM-Noon, 1-5PM.

**District & Magistrate Courts**, PO Box 430, Fairfield, ID 83327. 208-764-2238 (MST) 8:30AM-5PM. Felony, Misdemeanor, Civil, Eviction, Small Claims, Probate.

## Canyon County

**Real Estate Recording**, Canyon County Recorder, 1115 Albany Street, Caldwell, ID 83605. 208-454-7556 (MST) 8:30AM-5PM.

**District & Magistrate Courts**, 1115 Albany, Caldwell, ID 83605. 208-454-7569 (MST) Felony, Misdemeanor, Civil, Eviction, Small Claims, Probate.

## Caribou County

**Real Estate Recording**, Caribou County Clerk and Recorder, 159 South Main, Soda Springs, ID 83276. 208-547-4324 (MST) 9AM-5PM.

**District & Magistrate Courts**, 159 S. Main, Soda Springs, ID 83276. 208-547-4342 (MST) 9AM-5PM. Felony, Misdemeanor, Civil, Eviction, Small Claims, Probate.

## Cassia County

**Real Estate Recording**, Cassia County Clerk and Recorder, 1459 Overland Avenue, Burley, ID 83318. 208-678-5240 (MST) 8:30AM-5PM.

**District & Magistrate Courts**, 1451 Overland, Burley, ID 83318. 208-678-7351 (MST) 8:30AM-5PM. Felony, Misdemeanor, Civil, Eviction, Small Claims, Probate.

## Clark County

**Real Estate Recording**, Clark County Clerk and Recorder, 120 West Main, Courthouse, Dubois, ID 83423. 208-374-5304 (MST) 9AM-5PM.

**District & Magistrate Court**, PO Box 205, DuBois, ID 83423. 208-374-5402 (MST) 9AM-5PM. Felony, Misdemeanor, Civil, Eviction, Small Claims, Probate.

## Clearwater County

**Real Estate Recording**, Clearwater County Clerk and Recorder, 150 Michigan Avenue, Courthouse, Orofino, ID 83544. 208-476-5615 (PST) 8AM-5PM.

**District & Magistrate Courts**, PO Box 586, Orofino, ID 83544. 208-476-5969 (PST) 8AM-5PM. Felony, Misdemeanor, Civil, Eviction, Small Claims, Probate.

## Custer County

**Real Estate Recording**, Custer County Clerk and Recorder, Main Street, Courthouse, Challis, ID 83226. 208-879-2360 (MST) 9AM-5PM.

**District & Magistrate Courts**, PO Box 385, Challis, ID 83226. 208-879-2359 (MST) 8AM-5PM. Felony, Misdemeanor, Civil, Eviction, Small Claims, Probate.

## Elmore County

**Real Estate Recording**, Elmore County Clerk and Recorder, 150 South 4th East, Suite #3, Mountain Home, ID 83647-3097. 208-587-2130 (MST) 9AM-5PM.

**District & Magistrate Courts**, 150 S 4th East, Ste 5, Mountain Home, ID 83647. 208-587-2133 (MST) 9AM-5PM. Felony, Misdemeanor, Civil, Eviction, Small Claims, Probate.

## Franklin County

**Real Estate Recording**, Franklin County Clerk and Recorder, 39 West Oneida, Preston, ID 83263. 208-852-1090 (MST) 9AM-5PM.

**District & Magistrate Courts**, 39 West Oneida, Preston, ID 83263. 208-852-0877 (MST) 9AM-5PM. Felony, Misdemeanor, Civil, Eviction, Small Claims, Probate.

## Fremont County

**Real Estate Recording**, Fremont County Clerk and Recorder, 151 West 1st N. Room 12,

St. Anthony, ID 83445. 208-624-7332 (MST) 9AM-5PM.

**District & Magistrate Courts**, 151 W 1st North, St Anthony, ID 83445. 208-624-7401 (MST) 9AM-5PM. Felony, Misdemeanor, Civil, Eviction, Small Claims, Probate.

## Gem County

**Real Estate Recording**, Gem County Clerk and Recorder, 415 East Main, Emmett, ID 83617. 208-365-4561 (MST) 8AM-5PM.

**District & Magistrate Courts**, 415 East Main St, Emmett, ID 83617. 208-365-4221 (MST) 8AM-5PM. Felony, Misdemeanor, Civil, Eviction, Small Claims, Probate.

## Gooding County

**Real Estate Recording**, Gooding County Clerk and Recorder, 624 Main, Courthouse, Gooding, ID 83330. 208-934-4841 (MST) 9AM-Noon,1-5PM.

**District & Magistrate Courts**, PO Box 477, Gooding, ID 83330. 208-934-4261 (MST) 9AM-5PM. Felony, Misdemeanor, Civil, Eviction, Small Claims, Probate.

## Idaho County

**Real Estate Recording**, Idaho County Clerk and Recorder, 320 W. Main, Room 5, Grangeville, ID 83530. 208-983-2751 (PST) 8:30AM-5PM.

**District & Magistrate Courts**, 320 West Main, Grangeville, ID 83530. 208-983-2776 (PST) 8:30AM-5PM. Felony, Misdemeanor, Civil, Eviction, Small Claims, Probate.

## Jefferson County

**Real Estate Recording**, Jefferson County Clerk and Recorder, 134 North Clark, Courthouse, Rigby, ID 83442. 208-745-7756 (MST) 9AM-5PM.

**District & Magistrate Courts**, PO Box 71, Rigby, ID 83442. 208-745-7736 (MST) Felony, Misdemeanor, Civil, Eviction, Small Claims, Probate.

## Jerome County

**Real Estate Recording**, Jerome County Clerk and Recorder, 300 North Lincoln, Courthouse, Room 301, Jerome, ID 83338. 208-324-8811 (MST) 8:30AM-5PM.

**District & Magistrate Courts**, 300 N Lincoln St (PO Box 407), Jerome, ID 83338. 208-324-8811 (MST) Felony, Misdemeanor, Civil, Eviction, Small Claims, Probate.

## Kootenai County

**Real Estate Recording**, Kootenai County Clerk and Recorder, 501 Government Way, Coeur d'Alene, ID 83814. 208-769-4400 (PST) 9AM-5PM.

**District & Magistrate Courts**, 324 West Garden Ave, Coeur d'Alene, ID 83814. 208-769-4440 (PST) 9AM-5PM. Felony, Misdemeanor, Civil, Eviction, Small Claims, Probate.

## Latah County

**Real Estate Recording**, Latah County Clerk and Recorder, 5th and Adams, Moscow, ID 83843. 208-882-8580 (PST) 8:30AM-5PM.

**District & Magistrate Courts**, PO Box 8068, Moscow, ID 83843. 208-883-2255 (PST) 8:30AM-5PM. Felony, Misdemeanor, Civil, Eviction, Small Claims, Probate.

## Lemhi County

**Real Estate Recording**, Lemhi County Clerk and Recorder, 206 Courthouse Drive, Salmon, ID 83467. 208-756-2815 (MST) 8AM-Noon,1-5PM.

**District & Magistrate Courts**, 206 Courthouse Dr, Salmon, ID 83467. 208-756-2815 (MST) 8AM-5PM. Felony, Misdemeanor, Civil, Eviction, Small Claims, Probate.

## Lewis County

**Real Estate Recording**, Lewis County Clerk and Recorder, 510 Oak, Courthouse, Nezperce, ID 83543. 208-937-2661 (PST) 9AM-5PM.

**District & Magistrate Courts**, 510 Oak St (PO Box 39), Nezperce, ID 83543. 208-937-2251 (PST) 9AM-5PM. Felony, Misdemeanor, Civil, Eviction, Small Claims, Probate.

## Lincoln County

**Real Estate Recording**, Lincoln County Clerk and Recorder, 111 West B Street, Courthouse, Shoshone, ID 83352. 208-886-7641 (MST) 8:30AM-5PM.

**District & Magistrate Courts**, Drawer A, Shoshone, ID 83352. 208-886-2173 (MST) 9AM-5PM. Felony, Misdemeanor, Civil, Eviction, Small Claims, Probate.

## Madison County

**Real Estate Recording**, Madison County Clerk and Recorder, 159 East Main, Courthouse, Rexburg, ID 83440. 208-356-3662 (MST) 9AM-5PM.

**District & Magistrate Courts**, PO Box 389, Rexburg, ID 83440. 208-356-9383 (MST) 9AM-5PM. Felony, Misdemeanor, Civil, Eviction, Small Claims, Probate.

## Minidoka County

**Real Estate Recording**, Minidoka County Clerk and Recorder, 715 G Street, Courthouse, Rupert, ID 83350. 208-436-9511 (MST) 8AM-5PM.

**District & Magistrate Courts**, PO Box 474, Rupert, ID 83350. 208-436-9041 (MST) 8:30AM-5PM. Felony, Misdemeanor, Civil, Eviction, Small Claims, Probate.

## Nez Perce County

**Real Estate Recording**, Nez Perce County Auditor and Recorder, 1230 Main Street, Room 100, Lewiston, ID 83501. 208-799-3020 (PST) 8AM-5PM.

**District & Magistrate Courts**, PO Box 896, Lewiston, ID 83501. 208-799-3040 (PST) 8AM-5PM. Felony, Misdemeanor, Civil, Eviction, Small Claims, Probate.

## Oneida County

**Real Estate Recording**, Oneida County Clerk and Recorder, 10 Court Street, Malad, ID 83252. 208-766-4116 (MST)

**District & Magistrate Courts**, 10 Court St, Malad City, ID 83252. 208-766-4285 (MST) 9AM-5PM. Felony, Misdemeanor, Civil, Eviction, Small Claims, Probate.

## Owyhee County

**Real Estate Recording**, Owyhee County Clerk and Recorder, Highway 78, Courthouse, Murphy, ID 83650. 208-495-2421 (MST) 8:30AM-5PM.

**District & Magistrate Court I**, Courthouse, Murphy, ID 83650. 208-495-2806 (MST) 8:30AM-5PM. Felony, Misdemeanor, Civil, Eviction, Small Claims, Probate.

**Magistrate Court II**, PO Box 896, Homedale, ID 83628. 208-337-4540 (MST) 8:30AM-5PM. Misdemeanor, Civil Actions Under $10,000, Eviction, Small Claims.

## Payette County

**Real Estate Recording**, Payette County Clerk and Recorder, 1130 3rd Avenue North, Courthouse, Payette, ID 83661. 208-642-6000 (MST) 9AM-5PM.

**District & Magistrate Courts**, PO Drawer D, Payette, ID 83661. 208-642-6000 (MST) 9AM-5PM. Felony, Misdemeanor, Civil, Eviction, Small Claims, Probate.

## Power County

**Real Estate Recording**, Power County Clerk and Recorder, 543 Bannock, American Falls, ID 83211. 208-226-7611 (MST) 9AM-5PM.

**District & Magistrate Courts**, 543 Bannock Ave, American Falls, ID 83211. 208-226-7611 (MST) 9AM-5PM. Felony, Misdemeanor, Civil, Eviction, Small Claims, Probate.

## Shoshone County

**Real Estate Recording**, Shoshone County Clerk and Recorder, 700 Bank Street, Courthouse, Wallace, ID 83873-2348. 208-752-1264 (PST) 9AM-5PM.

**District & Magistrate Courts**, 700 Bank St, Wallace, ID 83873. 208-752-1266 (PST) 9AM-5PM. Felony, Misdemeanor, Civil, Eviction, Small Claims, Probate.

## Teton County

**Real Estate Recording**, Teton County Clerk and Recorder, 89 North Main, Courthouse, Driggs, ID 83422. 208-354-2905 (MST) 9AM-5PM.

**District & Magistrate Courts**, PO Box 756, Driggs, ID 83422. 208-354-2905 (MST) 9AM-5PM. Felony, Misdemeanor, Civil, Eviction, Small Claims, Probate.

## Twin Falls County

**Real Estate Recording**, Twin Falls County Clerk and Recorder, 425 Shoshone Street North, Twin Falls, ID 83301. 208-736-4004 (MST) 8:30AM-5PM.

**District & Magistrate Courts**, PO Box 126, Twin Falls, ID 83301. 208-736-4013 (MST) 8:30AM-5PM. Felony, Misdemeanor, Civil, Eviction, Small Claims, Probate.

## Valley County

**Real Estate Recording**, Valley County Clerk and Recorder, 219 North Main, Courthouse, Cascade, ID 83611. 208-382-4297 (MST) 9AM-5PM.

**District & Magistrate Court I**, PO Box 650, Cascade, ID 83611. 208-382-4150 (MST) 9AM-

# Idaho

5PM. Felony, Misdemeanor, Civil, Eviction, Small Claims, Probate.

**Magistrate Court II**, PO Box 1065, McCall, ID 83638. 208-634-7142 (MST) Misdemeanor, Civil Actions Under $10,000, Eviction, Small Claims.

## Washington County

**Real Estate Recording**, Washington County Clerk and Recorder, 256 East Court Street, Weiser, ID 83672. 208-549-2092 (MST) 8:30AM-5PM.

**District & Magistrate Courts**, PO Box 670, Weiser, ID 83672. 208-549-2092 (MST) Felony, Misdemeanor, Civil, Eviction, Small Claims, Probate.

# Illinois

## Adams County

**Real Estate Recording**, Adams County Recorder, 521 Vermont Street, Quincy, IL 62306. 217-223-6300 (CST) 8:30AM-4:30PM.

**Circuit Court**, 521 Vermont St, Quincy, IL 62301. 217-223-6300 (CST) 8AM-4:30PM. Felony, Misdemeanor, Civil, Eviction, Small Claims, Probate.

## Alexander County

**Real Estate Recording**, Alexander County Recorder, 2000 Washington Avenue, Cairo, IL 62914. 618-734-7000 (CST) 8AM-Noon, 1PM-4PM.

**Circuit Court**, 2000 Washington Ave, Cairo, IL 62914. 618-734-0107 (CST) 8AM-4PM. Felony, Misdemeanor, Civil, Eviction, Small Claims, Probate.

## Bond County

**Real Estate Recording**, Bond County Recorder, 203 West College Avenue, Greenville, IL 62246. 618-664-0449 (CST) 8AM-4PM.

**Circuit Court**, 200 W College St, Greenville, IL 62246. 618-664-3208 (CST) 8AM-4PM. Felony, Misdemeanor, Civil, Eviction, Small Claims, Probate.

## Boone County

**Real Estate Recording**, Boone County Recorder, 601 North Main Street, Suite 202, Belvidere, IL 61008. 815-544-3103 (CST) 8:30AM-5PM.

**Circuit Court**, 601 N Main, Belvidere, IL 61008. 815-544-0371 (CST) 8AM-4PM. Felony, Misdemeanor, Civil, Eviction, Small Claims, Probate.

## Brown County

**Real Estate Recording**, Brown County Recorder, Courthouse - Room 4, #1 Court Street, Mount Sterling, IL 62353-1285. 217-773-3421 (CST) 8:30AM-4:30PM.

**Circuit Court**, County Courthouse, Mt Sterling, IL 62353. 217-773-2713 (CST) 8:30AM-4:30PM. Felony, Misdemeanor, Civil, Eviction, Small Claims, Probate.

## Bureau County

**Real Estate Recording**, Bureau County Recorder, 700 South Main St., Courthouse, Princeton, IL 61356. 815-875-2014 (CST) 8AM-4PM.

**Circuit Court**, 700 S Main, Princeton, IL 61356. 815-872-2001 (CST) 8AM-4PM. Felony, Misdemeanor, Civil, Eviction, Small Claims, Probate.

## Calhoun County

**Real Estate Recording**, Calhoun County Clerk and Recorder, County Road, Hardin, IL 62047. 618-576-2351 (CST) 8:30AM-4:30PM.

**Circuit Court**, PO Box 486, Hardin, IL 62047. 618-576-2451 (CST) 8:30AM-4:30PM. Felony, Misdemeanor, Civil, Eviction, Small Claims, Probate.

## Carroll County

**Real Estate Recording**, Carroll County Recorder, 301 North Main, Mount Carroll, IL 61053. 815-244-9171 (CST) X250 8:30AM-4:30AM.

**Circuit Court**, 301 N Main St, Mt Carroll, IL 61053. 815-244-9171 (CST) 8AM-4PM. Felony, Misdemeanor, Civil, Eviction, Small Claims, Probate.

## Cass County

**Real Estate Recording**, Cass County Recorder, Courthouse, Virginia, IL 62691. 217-452-7217 (CST) 8:30AM-4:30PM.

**Circuit Court**, PO Box 203, Virginia, IL 62691. 217-452-7225 (CST) 8:30AM-4:30PM. Felony, Misdemeanor, Civil, Eviction, Small Claims, Probate.

## Champaign County

**Real Estate Recording**, Champaign County Recorder, 101 East Main Street, Courthouse - Room 139, Urbana, IL 61801-2774. 217-384-3774 (CST) 8AM-4:30PM.

**Circuit Court**, 101 E Main, Urbana, IL 61801. 217-384-3725 (CST) 8:30AM-4:30PM. Felony, Misdemeanor, Civil, Eviction, Small Claims, Probate.

## Christian County

**Real Estate Recording**, Christian County Recorder, Courthouse on the Square, Taylorville, IL 62568. 217-824-4960 (CST) 8AM-4PM.

**Circuit Court**, PO Box 160, Taylorville, IL 62568. 217-824-4966 (CST) 8AM-4PM. Felony, Misdemeanor, Civil, Eviction, Small Claims, Probate.

## Clark County

**Real Estate Recording**, Clark County Recorder, Courthouse, Marshall, IL 62441. 217-826-8311 (CST) 8AM-4PM.

## Clay County

**Real Estate Recording**, Clay County Recorder, County Building Room 106, Louisville, IL 62858. 618-665-3626 (CST) 8AM-4PM.

**Circuit Court**, PO Box 100, Louisville, IL 62858. 618-665-3523 (CST) 8AM-4PM. Felony, Misdemeanor, Civil, Eviction, Small Claims, Probate.

## Clinton County

**Real Estate Recording**, Clinton County Recorder, Courthouse, Carlyle, IL 62231. 618-594-2464 (CST) 8AM-4PM.

**Circuit Court**, County Courthouse, Carlyle, IL 62231. 618-594-2415 (CST) 8AM-4PM. Felony, Misdemeanor, Civil, Eviction, Small Claims, Probate.

## Coles County

**Real Estate Recording**, Coles County Recorder, 7th & Monroe Street, Charleston, IL 61920. 217-348-7325 (CST) 8:30AM-4:30PM.

**Circuit Court**, PO Box 48, Charleston, IL 61920. 217-348-0516 (CST) 8:30AM-4:30PM. Felony, Misdemeanor, Civil, Eviction, Small Claims, Probate.

## Cook County

**Circuit Court-Civil**, 50 W Washington Rm 601, Chicago, IL 60602. 312-443-5030 (CST) 9AM-5PM. Civil Actions Over $30,000.

**Circuit Court-Civil**, 50 W Washington, Chicago, IL 60602. 312-443-5030 (CST) 8:30AM-4:30PM. Civil Actions Under $30,000, Eviction, Small Claims, Probate.

**Circuit Court-Criminal**, 50 W Washington Rm 1006, Chicago, IL 60602. 312-443-4641 (CST) 8:30AM-4:30PM (Downtown) 9AM-5PM (Suburban). Misdemeanor.

**Circuit Court-Criminal**, 2650 S California Ave, Chicago, IL 60608. 312-890-3140 (CST) 8:30AM-5:00PM. Felony.

## Cook County Recorder

**Real Estate Recording**, Cook County Recorder, 118 North Clark St., Room 120, Chicago, IL 60602. 312-443-5134 (CST)

## Crawford County

**Real Estate Recording**, Crawford County Recorder, 1 Douglas Street, Courthouse, Robinson, IL 62454. 618-546-1212 (CST) 8AM-4PM.

**Circuit Court**, PO Box 222, Robinson, IL 62454. 618-544-2910 (CST) 8AM-4PM. Felony, Misdemeanor, Civil, Eviction, Small Claims, Probate.

## Cumberland County

**Real Estate Recording**, Cumberland County Recorder, Courthouse Square, Toledo, IL 62468. 217-849-2631 (CST) 8AM-4PM.

**Circuit Court**, PO Box 145, Toledo, IL 62468. 217-849-3601 (CST) 8AM-4PM. Felony, Misdemeanor, Civil, Eviction, Small Claims, Probate.

## De Kalb County

**Real Estate Recording**, De Kalb County Recorder, 110 East Sycamore Street, Sycamore, IL 60178. 815-895-7156 (CST)

**Circuit Court**, 133 W State St, Sycamore, IL 60178. 815-895-7138 (CST) 8:30AM-4:30PM. Felony, Misdemeanor, Civil, Eviction, Small Claims, Probate.

## De Witt County

**Real Estate Recording**, De Witt County Recorder, 201 West Washington Street, Clinton, IL 61727. 217-935-2119 (CST) 8:30AM-4:30PM.

**Circuit Court**, 201 Washington St, Clinton, IL 61727. 217-935-2195 (CST) 8:30AM-4:30PM. Felony, Misdemeanor, Civil, Eviction, Small Claims, Probate.

## Douglas County

**Real Estate Recording**, Douglas County Recorder, 401 South Center, Second Floor, Tuscola, IL 61953. 217-253-4410 (CST) 8:30AM-4:30PM.

**Circuit Clerk**, PO Box 50, Tuscola, IL 61953. 217-253-2352 (CST) 8:30AM-4:30PM. Felony, Misdemeanor, Civil, Eviction, Small Claims, Probate.

## Du Page County

**Real Estate Recording**, Du Page County Recorder, 421 North County Farm Road, Wheaton, IL 60187. 708-682-7200 (CST) 8AM-4:30PM.

**Circuit Court**, PO Box 707, Wheaton, IL 60189-0707. 708-682-7100 (CST) 8:30AM-4:30PM. Felony, Misdemeanor, Civil, Eviction, Small Claims, Probate.

## Edgar County

**Real Estate Recording**, Edgar County Recorder, Courthouse - Room "J", 115 W. Court St., Paris, IL 61944-1785. 217-465-4151 (CST) 8AM-4PM.

**Circuit Court**, County Courthouse, Paris, IL 61944. 217-465-4107 (CST) 8AM-4PM. Felony, Misdemeanor, Civil, Eviction, Small Claims, Probate.

## Edwards County

**Real Estate Recording**, Edwards County Recorder, 50 East Main Street, Courthouse, Albion, IL 62806-1294. 618-445-2115 (CST) 8AM-4PM.

**Circuit Court**, County Courthouse, Albion, IL 62806. 618-445-2016 (CST) 8AM-4PM. Felony, Misdemeanor, Civil, Eviction, Small Claims, Probate.

## Effingham County

**Real Estate Recording**, Effingham County Clerk and Recorder, 101 North 4th Street, Suite 201, Effingham, IL 62401. 217-342-6535 (CST) 8AM-4PM.

**Circuit Court**, PO Box 586, Effingham, IL 62401. 217-342-4065 (CST) 8AM-4PM. Felony, Misdemeanor, Civil, Eviction, Small Claims, Probate.

## Fayette County

**Real Estate Recording**, Fayette County Recorder, 221 South 7th Street, Vandalia, IL 62471. 618-283-5000 (CST) 8AM-4PM.

**Circuit Court**, 221 S 7th St, Vandalia, IL 62471. 618-283-5009 (CST) 8AM-4PM. Felony, Misdemeanor, Civil, Eviction, Small Claims, Probate.

## Ford County

**Real Estate Recording**, Ford County Recorder, 200 West State Street, Room 101, Paxton, IL 60957. 217-379-2721 (CST) 8:30AM-4:30PM.

**Circuit Court**, 200 W State St, Paxton, IL 60957. 217-379-2641 (CST) 8:30AM-4:30PM. Felony, Misdemeanor, Civil, Eviction, Small Claims, Probate.

## Franklin County

**Real Estate Recording**, Franklin County Clerk & Recorder, Courthouse, Benton, IL 62812. 618-438-3221 (CST) 8AM-4PM.

**Circuit Court**, County Courthouse, Benton, IL 62812. 618-439-2011 (CST) 8AM-4PM. Felony, Misdemeanor, Civil, Eviction, Small Claims, Probate.

## Fulton County

**Real Estate Recording**, Fulton County Recorder, 100 North Main, Lewistown, IL 61542. 309-547-3041 (CST) 8AM-4PM.

**Circuit Court**, 100 N Main, Lewistown, IL 61542. 309-547-3041 (CST) 8AM-4PM. Felony, Misdemeanor, Civil, Eviction, Small Claims, Probate.

## Gallatin County

**Real Estate Recording**, Gallatin County Recorder, West Lincoln Blvd, Shawneetown, IL 62984. 618-269-3025 (CST) 8AM-4PM.

**Circuit Court**, County Courthouse, Shawneetown, IL 62984. 618-269-3140 (CST) 8AM-4PM. Felony, Misdemeanor, Civil, Eviction, Small Claims, Probate.

## Greene County

**Real Estate Recording**, Greene County Recorder, 519 North Main Street, Courthouse, Carrollton, IL 62016-1033. 217-942-5443 (CST) 8AM-4PM.

**Circuit Court**, 519 N Main, County Courthouse, Carrollton, IL 62016. 217-942-3421 (CST) 8AM-4PM. Felony, Misdemeanor, Civil, Eviction, Small Claims, Probate.

## Grundy County

**Real Estate Recording**, Grundy County Recorder, 111 East Washington Street, Morris, IL 60450. 815-941-3224 (CST) 8AM-4:30PM.

**Circuit Court**, PO Box 707, Morris, IL 60450. 815-941-3256 (CST) 8AM-4:30PM. Felony, Misdemeanor, Civil, Eviction, Small Claims, Probate.

## Hamilton County

**Real Estate Recording**, Hamilton County Recorder, Courthouse, Room 2, Mcleansboro, IL 62859-1489. 618-643-2721 (CST) 8AM-4:30PM.

**Circuit Court**, County Courthouse, McLeansboro, IL 62859. 618-643-3224 (CST) 8AM-4PM. Felony, Misdemeanor, Civil, Eviction, Small Claims, Probate.

## Hancock County

**Real Estate Recording**, Hancock County Recorder, 500 Blk Main Street, Courthouse, 2nd Floor, Carthage, IL 62321. 217-357-3911 (CST) 8AM-4PM.

**Circuit Court**, PO Box 189, Carthage, IL 62321. 217-357-2616 (CST) 8AM-4PM. Felony, Misdemeanor, Civil, Eviction, Small Claims, Probate.

## Hardin County

**Real Estate Recording**, Hardin County Recorder, Courthouse, Elizabethtown, IL 62931. 618-287-2251 (CST) 8AM-4PM.

**Circuit Court**, County Courthouse, Elizabethtown, IL 62931. 618-287-2735 (CST) 8AM-4PM. Felony, Misdemeanor, Civil, Eviction, Small Claims, Probate.

## Henderson County

**Real Estate Recording**, Henderson County Recorder, 4th & Warren Streets, Oquawka, IL 61469. 309-867-2911 (CST) 8AM-4PM.

**Circuit Court**, County Courthouse, Oquawka, IL 61469. 309-867-3121 (CST) 8AM-4PM. Felony, Misdemeanor, Civil, Eviction, Small Claims, Probate.

## Henry County

**Real Estate Recording**, Henry County Recorder, 100 South Main, Cambridge, IL 61238. 309-937-2426 (CST) 8AM-4PM.

**Circuit Court**, County Courthouse, PO Box 9, Cambridge, IL 61238. 309-937-5192 (CST) 8AM-4PM. Felony, Misdemeanor, Civil, Eviction, Small Claims, Probate.

## Iroquois County

**Real Estate Recording**, Iroquois County Recorder, 1001 East Grant Street, Watseka, IL 60970. 815-432-6962 (CST) 8:30AM-4:30PM.

**Circuit Court**, 550 S 10th St, Watseka, IL 60970. 815-432-6950 (CST) 8AM-4PM. Felony, Misdemeanor, Civil, Eviction, Small Claims, Probate.

## Jackson County

**Real Estate Recording**, Jackson County Recorder, The Courthouse, 10th & Walnut, Murphysboro, IL 62966. 618-687-7360 (CST) 8AM-4PM.

**Circuit Court**, County Courthouse, Murphysboro, IL 62966. 618-687-7300 (CST) 8AM-4PM. Felony, Misdemeanor, Civil, Eviction, Small Claims, Probate.

## Jasper County

**Real Estate Recording**, Jasper County Recorder, 100 West Jourdan, Newton, IL 62448. 618-783-3124 (CST) 8AM-4:30PM.

**Circuit Court**, 100 W Jourdan St, Newton, IL 62448. 618-783-2524 (CST) 8AM-4:30PM. Felony, Misdemeanor, Civil, Eviction, Small Claims, Probate.

## Jefferson County

**Real Estate Recording**, Jefferson County Recorder, Courthouse, Room 105, Mount Vernon, IL 62864. 618-244-8020 (CST) 8AM-5PM.

**Circuit Court**, County Courthouse, Mt Vernon, IL 62864. 618-244-8008 (CST) 8AM-4PM. Felony, Misdemeanor, Civil, Eviction, Small Claims, Probate.

## Jersey County

**Real Estate Recording**, Jersey County Recorder, 201 West Pearl Street, Courthouse, Jerseyville, IL 62052. 618-498-5571 (CST) X117 8:30AM-4:30PM.

**Circuit Court**, 201 W Pearl St, Jerseyville, IL 62052. 618-498-5571 (CST) 8:30AM-4:30PM. Felony, Misdemeanor, Civil, Eviction, Small Claims, Probate.

## Jo Daviess County

**Real Estate Recording**, Jo Daviess County Recorder, 330 North Bench Street, Galena, IL 61036. 815-777-9694 (CST) 8AM-4PM.

**Circuit Court**, 330 N Bench St, Galena, IL 61036. 815-777-2295 (CST) 8AM-4PM. Felony, Misdemeanor, Civil, Eviction, Small Claims, Probate.

## Johnson County

**Real Estate Recording**, Johnson County Recorder, Courthouse Square, Vienna, IL 62995. 618-658-3611 (CST) 8AM-Noon,1-4PM.

**Circuit Court**, PO Box 517, Vienna, IL 62995. 618-658-4751 (CST) 8AM-4PM. Felony, Misdemeanor, Civil, Eviction, Small Claims, Probate.

## Kane County

**Real Estate Recording**, Kane County Recorder, 719 South Batavia Avenue, Geneva, IL 60134. 708-232-5935 (CST) 8:30AM-4:30PM.

**Circuit Court**, 301 W Fabyan Pky, Batavia, IL 60510. 708-232-3413 (CST) 8:30AM-4:30PM. Felony, Misdemeanor, Civil, Eviction, Small Claims, Probate.

## Kankakee County

**Real Estate Recording**, Kankakee County Recorder, 189 East Court Street, Kankakee, IL 60901. 815-937-2980 (CST) 8:30AM-4:30PM.

**Circuit Court**, 450 E Court St, Kankakee County Courthou, Kankakee, IL 60901. 815-937-2905 (CST) 8:30AM-4:30PM. Felony, Misdemeanor, Civil, Eviction, Small Claims, Probate.

## Kendall County

**Real Estate Recording**, Kendall County Recorder, 111 West Fox Street, Yorkville, IL 60560. 708-553-4112 (CST) 8AM-4:30PM.

**Circuit Court**, PO Drawer M, Yorkville, IL 60560. 708-553-4183 (CST) 8AM-4:30PM. Felony, Misdemeanor, Civil, Eviction, Small Claims, Probate.

## Knox County

**Real Estate Recording**, Knox County Recorder, County Court House, Galesburg, IL 61401. 309-345-3818 (CST) 8:30AM-4:30PM.

**Circuit Court**, County Courthouse, Galesburg, IL 61401. 309-345-3817 (CST) 8:30AM-4:30PM. Felony, Misdemeanor, Civil, Eviction, Small Claims, Probate.

## La Salle County

**Real Estate Recording**, La Salle County Recorder, 707 Etna Road, Government Center, Ottawa, IL 61350. 815-434-8226 (CST) 8AM-4:30PM.

**Circuit Court**, County Courthouse, Ottawa, IL 61350-0617. 815-433-1281 (CST) 8AM-4:30PM. Felony, Misdemeanor, Civil, Eviction, Small Claims, Probate.

## Lake County

**Real Estate Recording**, Lake County Recorder, 18 North County Street, Courthouse - Room 507, Waukegan, IL 60085-4358. 708-360-6673 (CST) 8:30AM-5PM.

**Circuit Court**, 18 N County St, Waukegan, IL 60085. 708-360-6794 (CST) 8:30-5PM. Felony, Misdemeanor, Civil, Eviction, Small Claims, Probate.

## Lawrence County

**Real Estate Recording**, Lawrence County Recorder, Courthouse, Lawrenceville, IL 62439. 618-943-5126 (CST) 9AM-5PM.

**Circuit Court**, County Courthouse, Lawrenceville, IL 62439. 618-943-5205 (CST) 9AM-5PM. Felony, Misdemeanor, Civil, Eviction, Small Claims, Probate.

## Lee County

**Real Estate Recording**, Lee County Recorder, 112 E. Second St. Galena Avenue, Dixon, IL 61021. 815-288-3309 (CST) 8:30AM-4:30PM.

**Circuit Court**, PO Box 385, Dixon, IL 61021. 815-284-5234 (CST) 8AM-4:30PM. Felony, Misdemeanor, Civil, Eviction, Small Claims, Probate.

## Livingston County

**Real Estate Recording**, Livingston County Recorder, 112 West Madison, Courthouse, Pontiac, IL 61764-1871. 815-844-5166 (CST) 8AM-4:30PM.

**Circuit Court**, 112 W Madison St, Pontiac, IL 61764. 815-844-5166 (CST) 8AM-4:30PM. Felony, Misdemeanor, Civil, Eviction, Small Claims, Probate.

## Logan County

**Real Estate Recording**, Logan County Recorder, Courthouse, Room 20, Lincoln, IL 62656. 217-732-4148 (CST) 8:30AM-4:30PM.

**Circuit Court**, County Courthouse, Lincoln, IL 62656. 217-735-2376 (CST) 8:30AM-4:30PM. Felony, Misdemeanor, Civil, Eviction, Small Claims, Probate.

## Macon County

**Real Estate Recording**, Macon County Recorder, 253 East Wood Street, Room 101, Decatur, IL 62523. 217-424-1359 (CST) 8:30AM-4:30PM.

**Circuit Court**, 253 E Wood St, Decatur, IL 62523. 217-424-1454 (CST) 8:30AM-4:30PM. Felony, Misdemeanor, Civil, Eviction, Small Claims, Probate.

## Macoupin County

**Real Estate Recording**, Macoupin County Recorder, Courthouse, Carlinville, IL 62626. 217-854-3214 (CST) 8:30AM-4:30PM.

**Circuit Court**, County Courthouse, Carlinville, IL 62626. 217-854-3211 (CST) 8:30AM-4:30PM. Felony, Misdemeanor, Civil, Eviction, Small Claims, Probate.

## Madison County

**Real Estate Recording**, Madison County Recorder, 157 North Main, Suite 221, Madison County Administration Bldg., Edwardsville, IL 62025. 618-692-6200 (CST) 8AM-5PM.

**Circuit Court**, 155 N Main St, Edwardsville, IL 62025. 618-692-6240 (CST) 8AM-4:30PM. Felony, Misdemeanor, Civil, Eviction, Small Claims, Probate.

## Marion County

**Real Estate Recording**, Marion County Recorder, Broadway & Main Street, Courthouse Square, Salem, IL 62881. 618-548-3400 (CST) 8AM-4PM.

**Circuit Court**, PO Box 130, Salem, IL 62881. 618-548-3856 (CST) 8AM-4PM. Felony, Misdemeanor, Civil, Eviction, Small Claims, Probate.

## Marshall County

**Real Estate Recording**, Marshall County Recorder, 122 North Prairie, Lacon, IL 61540. 309-246-6325 (CST) 8:30AM-4:30PM.

**Circuit Court**, 122 N Prairie-Box 98, Lacon, IL 61540. 309-246-6435 (CST) 8:30AM-12PM-1PM-4:30PM. Felony, Misdemeanor, Civil, Eviction, Small Claims, Probate.

## Mason County

**Real Estate Recording**, Mason County Recorder, 100 North Broadway, Havana, IL 62644. 309-543-6661 (CST) 8AM-4PM.

**Circuit Court**, County Courthouse, Havana, IL 62644. 309-543-6619 (CST) 8AM-4PM. Felony, Misdemeanor, Civil, Eviction, Small Claims, Probate.

## Massac County

**Real Estate Recording**, Massac County Recorder, Courthouse, Room 2-A, Superman Square, Metropolis, IL 62960. 618-524-5213 (CST) 8AM-4PM.

**Circuit Court**, PO Box 152, Metropolis, IL 62960. 618-524-9359 (CST) 8AM-12PM-1PM-4PM. Felony, Misdemeanor, Civil, Eviction, Small Claims, Probate.

## McDonough County

**Real Estate Recording**, McDonough County Recorder, Courthouse, Macomb, IL 61455. 309-833-2474 (CST) 8AM-4PM.

**Circuit Court**, County Courthouse, Macomb, IL 61455. 309-837-4889 (CST) 8AM-4PM. Felony, Misdemeanor, Civil, Eviction, Small Claims, Probate.

## McHenry County

**Real Estate Recording**, McHenry County Recorder, 2200 North Seminary Avenue, Room A280, Woodstock, IL 60098. 815-334-4110 (CST) 8AM-4:30PM.

**Circuit Court**, 2200 N Seminary Ave, Woodstock, IL 60098. 815-338-2098 (CST) 8AM-4:30PM. Felony, Misdemeanor, Civil, Eviction, Small Claims, Probate.

## McLean County

**Real Estate Recording**, McLean County Recorder, 104 West Front Street, Room 708, Bloomington, IL 61701. 309-888-5170 (CST) 8AM-4:30PM.

**Circuit Court**, 104 W Front St, Bloomington, IL 61701. 309-888-5320 (CST) 8:30AM-4:30PM. Felony, Misdemeanor, Civil, Eviction, Small Claims, Probate.

## Menard County

**Real Estate Recording**, Menard County Recorder, Seventh Street, Courthouse, Petersburg, IL 62675. 217-632-2415 (CST) 8:30AM-4:30PM.

**Circuit Court**, PO Box 456, Petersburg, IL 62675. 217-632-2615 (CST) 8AM-4:30PM. Felony, Misdemeanor, Civil, Eviction, Small Claims, Probate.

## Mercer County

**Real Estate Recording**, Mercer County Recorder, 100 S.E. 3rd Street, 2nd Floor, Aledo, IL 61231. 309-582-7021 (CST) 8AM-4PM.

**Circuit Court**, PO Box 175, Aledo, IL 61231. 309-582-7122 (CST) 8AM-4PM. Felony, Misdemeanor, Civil, Eviction, Small Claims, Probate.

## Monroe County

**Real Estate Recording**, Monroe County Recorder, 100 South Main, Courthouse, Waterloo, IL 62298-1399. 618-939-8681 (CST) 8AM-4:30PM.

**Circuit Court**, 100 S Main St, Waterloo, IL 62298. 618-939-8681 (CST) 8AM-4:30PM. Felony, Misdemeanor, Civil, Eviction, Small Claims, Probate.

## Montgomery County

**Real Estate Recording**, Montgomery County Recorder, Courthouse, Hillsboro, IL 62049. 217-532-9532 (CST) 8AM-4PM.

**Circuit Court**, County Courthouse, PO Box C, Hillsboro, IL 62049. 217-532-9546 (CST) 8AM-4PM. Felony, Misdemeanor, Civil, Eviction, Small Claims, Probate.

## Morgan County

**Real Estate Recording**, Morgan County Recorder, 300 West State Street, Courthouse, Jacksonville, IL 62650. 217-243-8581 (CST) 8:30AM-4:30PM.

**Circuit Court**, 300 W State St, Jacksonville, IL 62650. 217-243-5419 (CST) 8:30AM-4:30PM. Felony, Misdemeanor, Civil, Eviction, Small Claims, Probate.

## Moultrie County

**Real Estate Recording**, Moultrie County Recorder, Courthouse, Sullivan, IL 61951. 217-728-4389 (CST) 8:30AM-4:30PM.

**Circuit Court**, County Courthouse, Sullivan, IL 61951. 217-728-4622 (CST) 8:30AM-4:30PM. Felony, Misdemeanor, Civil, Eviction, Small Claims, Probate.

## Ogle County

**Real Estate Recording**, Ogle County Recorder, Fourth & Washington Streets, Oregon, IL 61061. 815-732-3201 (CST) X270,1 8:30AM-4:30PM.

**Circuit Court**, PO Box 337, Oregon, IL 61061. 815-732-3201 (CST) 8:30AM-4:30PM. Felony, Misdemeanor, Civil, Eviction, Small Claims, Probate.

## Peoria County

**Real Estate Recording**, Peoria County Recorder, County Courthouse - Room G04, 324 Main Street, Peoria, IL 61602. 309-672-6090 (CST) 9AM-5PM.

**Circuit Court**, 324 Main St, Peoria, IL 61602. 309-672-6953 (CST) 9AM-5PM. Felony, Misdemeanor, Civil, Eviction, Small Claims, Probate.

## Perry County

**Real Estate Recording**, Perry County Recorder, Town Square, Pinckneyville, IL 62274. 618-357-5116 (CST) 8AM-4PM.

**Circuit Court**, PO Box 219, Pinckneyville, IL 62274. 618-357-6726 (CST) 8AM-4PM. Felony, Misdemeanor, Civil, Eviction, Small Claims, Probate.

## Piatt County

**Real Estate Recording**, Piatt County Recorder, 101 West Washington, Courthouse, Monticello, IL 61856. 217-762-9487 (CST) 8:30AM-4:30PM.

**Circuit Court**, PO Box 288, Monticello, IL 61856. 217-762-4966 (CST) 8:30AM-4:30PM. Felony, Misdemeanor, Civil, Eviction, Small Claims, Probate.

## Pike County

**Real Estate Recording**, Pike County Recorder, Courthouse, Pittsfield, IL 62363. 217-285-6812 (CST) 8:30AM-4PM.

**Circuit Court**, County Courthouse, Pittsfield, IL 62363. 217-285-6612 (CST) 8:30AM-4:30PM. Felony, Misdemeanor, Civil, Eviction, Small Claims, Probate.

## Pope County

**Real Estate Recording**, Pope County Recorder, Courthouse, Golconda, IL 62938. 618-683-4466 (CST) 8AM-Noon, 1-4PM.

**Circuit Court**, County Courthouse, Golconda, IL 62938. 618-683-3941 (CST) 8AM-4PM. Felony, Misdemeanor, Civil, Eviction, Small Claims, Probate.

## Pulaski County

**Real Estate Recording**, Pulaski County Recorder, Corner of 2nd & High, Courthouse, Mound City, IL 62963. 618-748-9360 (CST) 8AM-Noon, 1PM-4PM.

**Circuit Court**, PO Box 88, Mound City, IL 62963. 618-748-9300 (CST) 8AM-4PM. Felony, Misdemeanor, Civil, Eviction, Small Claims, Probate.

## Putnam County

**Real Estate Recording**, Putnam County Recorder, Courthouse, 120 North 4th Street, Hennepin, IL 61327. 815-925-7129 (CST) 8AM-Noon, 1-4:30PM.

**Circuit Court**, 120 N 4th St, Hennepin, IL 61327. 815-925-7016 (CST) 8AM-12PM-1PM-4:30PM. Felony, Misdemeanor, Civil, Eviction, Small Claims, Probate.

## Randolph County

**Real Estate Recording**, Randolph County Recorder, 1 Taylor Street, Courthouse, Chester, IL 62233-0309. 618-826-5000 (CST) X1498 8AM-4:30PM.

**Circuit Court**, County Courthouse, Chester, IL 62233. 618-826-5000 (CST) 8AM-4:30PM. Felony, Misdemeanor, Civil, Eviction, Small Claims, Probate.

## Richland County

**Real Estate Recording**, Richland County Recorder, 103 West Main, Courthouse, Olney, IL 62450. 618-392-3111 (CST) 8AM-4PM.

**Circuit Court**, 103 W Main #21, Olney, IL 62450. 618-392-2151 (CST) 8AM-4PM. Felony, Misdemeanor, Civil, Eviction, Small Claims, Probate.

## Rock Island County

**Real Estate Recording**, Rock Island County Recorder, 210 15th Street, Rock Island, IL 61201. 309-786-4451 (CST) X357 8AM-5PM.

**Circuit Court**, County Bldg, 210 15th St, Rock Island, IL 61201. 309-786-4451 (CST) 8AM-4:30PM. Felony, Misdemeanor, Civil, Eviction, Small Claims, Probate.

## Saline County

**Real Estate Recording**, Saline County Recorder, 10 E. Poplar, Harrisburg, IL 62946. 618-253-8197 (CST) 8AM-4PM.

**Circuit Court**, County Courthouse, Harrisburg, IL 62946. 618-253-5096 (CST) 8AM-4PM. Felony, Misdemeanor, Civil, Eviction, Small Claims, Probate.

## Sangamon County

**Real Estate Recording**, Sangamon County Recorder, 200 S. 9th St., Room 211, Springfield, IL 62701. 217-535-3150 (CST) 8:30AM-5PM.

**Circuit Court**, 200 S Ninth St, Springfield, IL 62701. 217-753-6674 (CST) 8:30AM-4:30PM. Felony, Misdemeanor, Civil, Eviction, Small Claims, Probate.

## Schuyler County

**Real Estate Recording**, Schuyler County Recorder, Corner of Congress & Lafayette, Courthouse, Rushville, IL 62681. 217-322-4734 (CST) 8AM-4PM.

**Circuit Court**, PO Box 80, Rushville, IL 62681. 217-322-4633 (CST) 8AM-4PM. Felony, Misdemeanor, Civil, Eviction, Small Claims, Probate.

## Scott County

**Real Estate Recording**, Scott County Recorder, Courthouse, Winchester, IL 62694. 217-742-3178 (CST) 8AM-4PM.

**Circuit Court**, 27 E Market St, Winchester, IL 62694. 217-742-5217 (CST) 8AM-12PM-1PM-4PM. Felony, Misdemeanor, Civil, Eviction, Small Claims, Probate.

## Shelby County

**Real Estate Recording**, Shelby County Recorder, Courthouse, Shelbyville, IL 62565. 217-774-4421 (CST) 8AM-4PM.

**Circuit Court**, County Courthouse, Shelbyville, IL 62565. 217-774-4212 (CST) 8AM-4PM. Felony, Misdemeanor, Civil, Eviction, Small Claims, Probate.

## St. Clair County

**Real Estate Recording**, St. Clair County Recorder, #10 Public Square, County Building, Belleville, IL 62222. 618-277-6600 (CST) 8:30AM-5PM.

Circuit Court, 10 Public Square, Belleville, IL 62220-1623. 618-227-6600 (CST) 9AM-4PM. Felony, Misdemeanor, Civil, Eviction, Small Claims, Probate.

## Stark County

**Real Estate Recording**, Stark County Recorder, 130 West Main, Toulon, IL 61483. 309-286-5911 (CST) 8AM-Noon, 12:30-4:30PM.

Circuit Court, 130 E Main St, Toulon, IL 61483. 309-286-5941 (CST) 8AM-4:30PM. Felony, Misdemeanor, Civil, Eviction, Small Claims, Probate.

## Stephenson County

**Real Estate Recording**, Stephenson County Recorder, 15 North Galena Avenue, Freeport, IL 61032. 815-235-8385 (CST) 8:30AM-4:30PM.

Circuit Court, 15 N Galena Ave, Freeport, IL 61032. 815-235-8266 (CST) 8:30AM-4:30PM. Felony, Misdemeanor, Civil, Eviction, Small Claims, Probate.

## Tazewell County

**Real Estate Recording**, Tazewell County Recorder, 300 Block Court St., Courthouse - Room 206, Pekin, IL 61554. 309-477-2210 (CST) 9AM-5PM.

Circuit Court, Courthouse, 4th & Court Sts, Pekin, IL 61554. 309-477-2214 (CST) 9AM-5PM. Felony, Misdemeanor, Civil, Eviction, Small Claims, Probate.

## Union County

**Real Estate Recording**, Union County Recorder, 311 West Market, Jonesboro, IL 62952. 618-833-5711 (CST) 8AM-4PM.

Circuit Court, PO Box 360, Jonesboro, IL 62952. 618-833-5913 (CST) 8AM-4PM. Felony, Misdemeanor, Civil, Eviction, Small Claims, Probate.

## Vermilion County

**Real Estate Recording**, Vermilion County Recorder, 6 North Vermilion Street, Danville, IL 61832-5877. 217-431-2604 (CST) 8AM-4:30PM.

Circuit Court, 7 N Vermilion, Danville, IL 61832. 217-431-2534 (CST) 8:30AM-4:30PM. Felony, Misdemeanor, Civil, Eviction, Small Claims, Probate.

## Wabash County

**Real Estate Recording**, Wabash County Recorder, 401 Market Street, Mount Carmel, IL 62863. 618-262-4561 (CST) 8AM-5PM.

Circuit Court, 401 Market St, Mt Carmel, IL 62863. 618-262-5362 (CST) 8AM-4PM. Felony, Misdemeanor, Civil, Eviction, Small Claims, Probate.

## Warren County

**Real Estate Recording**, Warren County Recorder, Courthouse, 100 W. Broadway, Monmouth, IL 61462-1797. 309-734-8592 (CST) 8AM-4:30PM.

Circuit Court, 100 W Broadway, Monmouth, IL 61462. 309-734-5179 (CST) 8AM-4:30PM. Felony, Misdemeanor, Civil, Eviction, Small Claims, Probate.

## Washington County

**Real Estate Recording**, Washington County Recorder, County Courthouse, 101 E. St. Louis Street, Nashville, IL 62263-1105. 618-327-8314 (CST) 8AM-4PM.

Circuit Court, 101 E St Louis St, Nashville, IL 62263. 618-327-3383 (CST) 8AM-4PM. Felony, Misdemeanor, Civil, Eviction, Small Claims, Probate.

## Wayne County

**Real Estate Recording**, Wayne County Recorder, 301 East Main, Fairfield, IL 62837. 618-842-5182 (CST) 8AM-4:30PM.

Circuit Court, County Courthouse, Fairfield, IL 62837. 618-842-7684 (CST) 8AM-4:30PM. Felony, Misdemeanor, Civil, Eviction, Small Claims, Probate.

## White County

**Real Estate Recording**, White County Recorder, 301 East Main Street, Courthouse, Carmi, IL 62821. 618-382-7211 (CST) 8AM-4PM.

Circuit Court, County Courthouse, Carmi, IL 62821. 618-382-2321 (CST) 8AM-4PM. Felony, Misdemeanor, Civil, Eviction, Small Claims, Probate.

## Whiteside County

**Real Estate Recording**, Whiteside County Recorder, 200 East Knox, Morrison, IL 61270. 815-772-5192 (CST) 8:30AM-4:30PM.

Circuit Court, 200 E Knox St, Morrison, IL 61270-2698. 815-772-5188 (CST) 8:30AM-4:30PM. Felony, Misdemeanor, Civil, Eviction, Small Claims, Probate.

## Will County

**Real Estate Recording**, Will County Recorder, 302 N. Chicago Street, Joliet, IL 60431. 815-740-4638 (CST) 8:30AM-4:30PM.

Circuit Court, 14 W Jefferson St, Joliet, IL 60432. 815-727-8592 (CST) 8:30AM-4:30PM. Felony, Misdemeanor, Civil, Eviction, Small Claims, Probate.

## Williamson County

**Real Estate Recording**, Williamson County Recorder, 200 West Jefferson, Marion, IL 62959. 618-997-1301 (CST) 8AM-4PM.

Circuit Court, 200 W Jefferson St, Marion, IL 62959. 618-997-1301 (CST) 8AM-4:30PM. Felony, Misdemeanor, Civil, Eviction, Small Claims, Probate.

## Winnebago County

**Real Estate Recording**, Winnebago County Recorder, 404 Elm St., Rockford, IL 61101. 815-987-3100 (CST) 8AM-5PM.

Circuit Court, 400 W State St, Rockford, IL 61101. 815-987-2510 (CST) 8AM-5PM. Felony, Misdemeanor, Civil, Eviction, Small Claims, Probate.

## Woodford County

**Real Estate Recording**, Woodford County Recorder, 115 North Main, Courthouse, Eureka, IL 61530-1273. 309-467-2822 (CST) 8AM-5PM (November-January 8AM-4:30PM).

Circuit Clerk, County Courthouse, Eureka, IL 61530. 309-467-3312 (CST) 8AM-5PM. Felony, Misdemeanor, Civil, Eviction, Small Claims, Probate.

# Indiana

## Adams County

**Real Estate Recording**, Adams County Recorder, 112 South Second Street, Courthouse, Decatur, IN 46733. 219-724-2600 (EST) 8AM-4:30PM.

**Circuit & Superior Court**, 2nd St Courthouse, Decatur, IN 46733. 219-724-2600 (EST) 8AM-4:30PM. Felony, Misdemeanor, Civil, Small Claims, Probate.

## Allen County

**Real Estate Recording**, Allen County Recorder, 1 East Main Street, City County Building Room 206, Fort Wayne, IN 46802-1890. 219-428-7165 (EST) 8AM-4:30PM.

**Circuit & Superior Court**, 715 S. Calhoun St. Rm 200 Courthouse, Ft Wayne, IN 46802. 219-428-7245 (EST) 8AM-4:30PM. Felony, Misdemeanor, Civil, Small Claims, Probate.

## Bartholomew County

**Real Estate Recording**, Bartholomew County Recorder, 440 3rd Street, Suite 203, Columbus, IN 47201. 812-379-1520 (EST) 8AM-5PM.

**Circuit & Superior Court**, Box 924, Columbus, IN 47202-0924. 812-379-1600 (EST) 8AM-5PM. Felony, Misdemeanor, Civil, Small Claims, Probate.

## Benton County

**Real Estate Recording**, Benton County Recorder, 706 East 5th Street, Suite 24, Fowler, IN 47944-1556. 317-884-1630 (EST) 8:30AM-Noon, 1PM-4PM.

**Circuit Court**, 7060 E 5th St, Suite 23, Fowler, IN 47944-1556. 317-884-0930 (EST) 8:30AM-4PM. Felony, Misdemeanor, Civil, Small Claims, Probate.

## Blackford County

**Real Estate Recording**, Blackford County Recorder, 110 West Washington Street, Courthouse, Hartford City, IN 47348. 317-348-2207 (EST) 8AM-4PM.

**Circuit & County Court**, 110 W Washington St, Hartford City, IN 47348. 317-348-1130 (EST) 8AM-4PM. Felony, Misdemeanor, Civil, Eviction, Small Claims, Probate.

## Boone County

**Real Estate Recording**, Boone County Recorder, 202 Courthouse Square, Lebanon, IN 46052. 317-482-3070 (EST) 8AM-4PM.

**Circuit & Superior Court**, Rm 212, Courthouse Sq, Lebanon, IN 46052. 317-482-3510 (EST) Felony, Misdemeanor, Civil, Small Claims, Probate.

## Brown County

**Real Estate Recording**, Brown County Recorder, Corner of Gould St. & Locust Lane, County Office Bldg., Nashville, IN 47448. 812-988-5462 (EST) 8AM-4PM.

**Circuit Court**, Box 85, Nashville, IN 47448. 812-988-5510 (EST) 8AM-4PM. Felony, Misdemeanor, Civil, Small Claims, Probate.

## Carroll County

**Real Estate Recording**, Carroll County Recorder, Court House, 101 West Main St,, Delphi, IN 46923-1522. 317-564-2124 (EST) 8AM-5PM M,T,Th,F; 8AM-Noon W.

**Circuit & Superior Court**, Courthouse, 101 W Main, Delphi, IN 46923. 317-564-4485 (EST) Felony, Misdemeanor, Civil, Small Claims, Probate.

## Cass County

**Real Estate Recording**, Cass County Recorder, 200 Court Park, Logansport, IN 46947. 219-753-7810 (EST) 8AM-4PM; F 8AM-5PM.

**Circuit & Superior Court**, 200 Court Park, Logansport, IN 46947. 219-753-7870 (EST) 8AM-4PM. Felony, Misdemeanor, Civil, Small Claims, Probate.

## Clark County

**Real Estate Recording**, Clark County Recorder, 501 East Court Avenue, Jeffersonville, IN 47130. 812-285-6236 (EST) 8AM-5PM.

**Circuit, Superior, & County Court**, 501 E Court, Jeffersonville, IN 47130. 812-285-6244 (EST) 8:30AM-4:30PM M-F, 8:30-Noon S. Felony, Misdemeanor, Civil, Small Claims, Probate.

## Clay County

**Real Estate Recording**, Clay County Recorder, Courthouse, Brazil, IN 47834. 812-442-1442 (EST) 8AM-4PM.

**Circuit & Superior Court**, Box 33, Brazil, IN 47834. 812-448-8727 (EST) 8AM-4PM. Felony, Misdemeanor, Civil, Small Claims, Probate.

## Clinton County

**Real Estate Recording**, Clinton County Recorder, 270 Courthouse Square, Frankfort, IN 46041-1957. 317-659-6320 (EST) 8AM-4PM M,T,W; 8AM-Noon Th; 8AM-6PM F.

**Circuit & Superior Court**, 265 Courthouse Square, Frankfort, IN 46041. 317-659-6335 (EST) 8AM-4PM M-W, 8AM-Noon Th, 8AM-6PM F. Felony, Misdemeanor, Civil, Small Claims, Probate.

## Crawford County

**Real Estate Recording**, Crawford County Recorder, Courthouse, English, IN 47118-0214. 812-338-2615 (EST)

**Circuit Court**, Box 375, English, IN 47118. 812-338-2565 (EST) Felony, Misdemeanor, Civil, Small Claims, Probate.

## Daviess County

**Real Estate Recording**, Daviess County Recorder, 200 East Walnut Street, Courthouse, Washington, IN 47501-2759. 812-254-8675 (EST) 8AM-4PM.

**Circuit & Superior Court**, Courthouse, Washington, IN 47501. 812-254-8664 (EST) 8AM-4PM. Felony, Misdemeanor, Civil, Small Claims, Probate.

## DeKalb County

**Real Estate Recording**, DeKalb County Recorder, Courthouse, 2nd Floor, Auburn, IN 46706. 219-925-2112 (EST) 8:30AM-4:30PM.

**Circuit & Superior Court**, PO Box 230, Auburn, IN 46706. 219-925-0912 (EST) 8:30AM-4:30PM. Felony, Misdemeanor, Civil, Small Claims, Probate.

## Dearborn County

**Real Estate Recording**, Dearborn County Recorder, 215 B West High Street, Lawrenceburg, IN 47025. 812-537-1040 (EST) 8:30AM-4:30PM.

**Circuit & County Court**, Courthouse, Lawrenceburg, IN 47025. 812-537-8867 (EST) 8:30AM-4:30PM. Felony, Misdemeanor, Civil, Eviction, Small Claims, Probate.

## Decatur County

**Real Estate Recording**, Decatur County Recorder, 150 Courthouse Square, Suite 2, Greensburg, IN 47240. 812-663-4681 (EST) 8AM-4PM (F open until 5PM).

**Circuit & Superior Court**, 150 Courthouse Square, Ste 1, Greensburg, IN 47240. 812-663-8223 (EST) 8AM-4PM. Felony, Misdemeanor, Civil, Small Claims, Probate.

## Delaware County

**Real Estate Recording**, Delaware County Recorder, 100 West Main Street, Room 209, Muncie, IN 47305. 317-747-7804 (EST) 8:30AM-4:30PM.

**Circuit & Superior Court**, Box 1089, Muncie, IN 47308. 317-747-7726 (EST) 8:30AM-4:30PM. Felony, Misdemeanor, Civil, Small Claims, Probate.

## Dubois County

**Real Estate Recording**, Dubois County Recorder, Courthouse - Room 105, Jasper, IN 47546. 812-481-7067 (EST) 8AM-4PM.

**Circuit & Superior Court**, 1 Courthouse Square, Jasper, IN 47546. 812-482-5445 (EST) 8AM-4PM. Felony, Misdemeanor, Civil, Small Claims, Probate.

## Elkhart County

**Real Estate Recording**, Elkhart County Recorder, 117 North 2nd Street, Goshen, IN 46526-3294. 219-535-6754 (EST) 8AM-4PM; F 8AM-5PM.

**Circuit, Superior & County Court**, Courthouse, 101 N. Main St, Goshen, IN 46526. 219-534-3541 (EST) 8AM-4PM M-Th, 8AM-5PM F. Felony, Misdemeanor, Civil, Small Claims, Probate.

## Fayette County

**Real Estate Recording**, Fayette County Recorder, 401 Central Avenue, Connersville, IN 47331. 317-825-3051 (EST) 8:30AM-4PM (8:30AM-5PM F).

**Circuit & Superior Court**, Box 607, Connersville, IN 47331-0607. 317-825-1813 (EST) 8:30AM-4PM M-Th, 8:30AM-5PM F. Felony, Misdemeanor, Civil, Small Claims, Probate.

## Floyd County

**Real Estate Recording**, Floyd County Recorder, 311 West 1st Street, New Albany, IN 47150. 812-948-5430 (EST) 8AM-4PM.

**Circuit, Superior, & County Court**, Box 1056, City County Bldg, New Albany, IN 47150. 812-948-5414 (EST) Felony, Misdemeanor, Civil, Small Claims, Probate.

## Fountain County

**Real Estate Recording**, Fountain County Recorder, 301 4th Street, Covington, IN 47932. 317-793-2431 (EST) 8AM-Noon,1-4PM.

**Circuit Court**, Box 183, Covington, IN 47932. 317-793-2192 (EST) 8AM-4PM. Felony, Misdemeanor, Civil, Small Claims, Probate.

## Franklin County

**Real Estate Recording**, Franklin County Recorder, 459 Main Street, Brookville, IN 47012-1486. 317-647-5131 (EST) 8:30AM-4PM.

**Circuit Court**, 459 Main, Brookville, IN 47012. 317-647-5111 (EST) 8:30AM-4PM. Felony, Misdemeanor, Civil, Small Claims, Probate.

## Fulton County

**Real Estate Recording**, Fulton County Recorder, 815 Main Street, Rochester, IN 46975. 219-223-2914 (EST) 8AM-4PM (F 8AM-5PM).

**Circuit Court**, 815 Main St, PO Box 502, Rochester, IN 46975. 219-223-2911 (EST) 8AM-4PM M-TH, 8AM-5PM F. Felony, Misdemeanor, Civil, Small Claims, Probate.

## Gibson County

**Real Estate Recording**, Gibson County Recorder, 101 North Main, Courthouse, Princeton, IN 47670-1562. 812-385-3332 (CST) 8AM-4PM.

**Circuit & Superior Court**, Courthouse, Princeton, IN 47670. 812-386-8401 (CST) Felony, Misdemeanor, Civil, Small Claims, Probate.

## Grant County

**Real Estate Recording**, Grant County Recorder, 401 South Adams Street, Marion, IN 46953. 317-668-8871 (EST)

**Circuit & Superior Court**, Courthouse, Marion, IN 46952. 317-668-8121 (EST) 8AM-4PM. Felony, Misdemeanor, Civil, Small Claims, Probate.

## Greene County

**Real Estate Recording**, Greene County Recorder, Courthouse, Room 109, Bloomfield, IN 47424-0109. 812-384-2020 (EST) 8AM-4PM.

**Circuit & Superior Court**, PO Box 229, Bloomfield, IN 47424. 812-384-8532 (EST) 8AM-4PM. Felony, Misdemeanor, Civil, Small Claims, Probate.

## Hamilton County

**Real Estate Recording**, Hamilton County Recorder, Courthouse, 1 Hamilton Sq. - Suite 382, Noblesville, IN 46060. 317-776-9618 (EST) 8AM-4:30PM.

**Circuit & Superior Court**, Hamilton Courthouse Square, Suite 106, Noblesville, IN 46060-2233. 317-776-9629 (EST) 8AM-4:30PM. Felony, Misdemeanor, Civil, Small Claims, Probate.

## Hancock County

**Real Estate Recording**, Hancock County Recorder, 9 East Main Street, Courthouse, Room 204, Greenfield, IN 46140. 317-462-1142 (EST) 8AM-4PM.

**Circuit & Superior Court**, 9 E Main St, Rm 201, Greenfield, IN 46140. 317-462-1109 (EST) 8AM-4PM. Felony, Misdemeanor, Civil, Small Claims, Probate.

## Harrison County

**Real Estate Recording**, Harrison County Recorder, 300 Capitol Avenue, Courthouse, Room 204, Corydon, IN 47112. 812-738-3788 (EST) 8AM-4PM.

**Circuit & Superior Court**, 300 N Capitol, Corydon, IN 47112. 812-738-4289 (EST) 8AM-4PM MT,ThF; 8AM-Noon W,S. Felony, Misdemeanor, Civil, Small Claims, Probate.

## Hendricks County

**Real Estate Recording**, Hendricks County Recorder, Courthouse, Danville, IN 46122. 317-745-9224 (EST) 8AM-4PM.

**Circuit & Superior Court**, PO Box 599, Danville, IN 46122. 317-745-9231 (EST) Felony, Misdemeanor, Civil, Small Claims, Probate.

## Henry County

**Real Estate Recording**, Henry County Recorder, Courthouse, New Castle, IN 47362. 317-529-4304 (EST) 8AM-4PM (F 8AM-5PM).

**Circuit & Superior Court**, PO Box B, New Castle, IN 47362. 317-529-6401 (EST) 8AM-4PM. Felony, Misdemeanor, Civil, Small Claims, Probate.

## Howard County

**Real Estate Recording**, Howard County Recorder, Courthouse, Room 202, Kokomo, IN 46901. 317-456-2210 (EST) 8AM-4PM.

**Circuit & Superior Court**, Courthouse, Rm 111, Kokomo, IN 46901. 317-456-2204 (EST) 8AM-4PM. Felony, Misdemeanor, Civil, Small Claims, Probate.

## Huntington County

**Real Estate Recording**, Huntington County Recorder, 201 N. Jefferson St., Room 101, Huntington, IN 46750-2841. 219-358-4848 (EST) 8AM-4:30PM.

**Circuit & Superior Court**, Courthouse, Rm 201, Huntington, IN 46750. 219-358-4817 (EST) 8AM-4:40PM. Felony, Misdemeanor, Civil, Small Claims, Probate.

## Jackson County

**Real Estate Recording**, Jackson County Recorder, 101 S. Main - Main Floor, Brownstown, IN 47220. 812-358-6113 (EST) 8AM-4PM.

**Circuit & Superior Court**, PO Box 122, Brownstown, IN 47220. 812-358-6116 (EST) 8AM-4PM. Felony, Misdemeanor, Civil, Small Claims, Probate.

## Jasper County

**Real Estate Recording**, Jasper County Recorder, 115 W Washington, Rensselaer, IN 47978. 219-866-4923 (CST) 8AM-4PM.

**Circuit & Superior Court**, Courthouse, Rensselaer, IN 47978. 219-866-4926 (CST) 8AM-4PM. Felony, Misdemeanor, Civil, Small Claims, Probate.

## Jay County

**Real Estate Recording**, Jay County Recorder, 120 West Main Street, Portland, IN 47371. 219-726-4572 (EST) 9AM-4PM.

**Circuit & Superior Court**, Courthouse, Portland, IN 47371. 219-726-4951 (EST) 8:30AM-4:30PM. Felony, Misdemeanor, Civil, Small Claims, Probate.

## Jefferson County

**Real Estate Recording**, Jefferson County Recorder, Courthouse - Room 104, 300 E. Main St., Madison, IN 47250. 812-265-8903 (EST) 8AM-4PM.

**Circuit & Superior Court**, Courthouse, Madison, IN 47250. 812-265-8923 (EST) 8AM-4PM. Felony, Misdemeanor, Civil, Small Claims, Probate.

## Jennings County

**Real Estate Recording**, Jennings County Recorder, Courthouse, Vernon, IN 47282. 812-346-3152 (EST) 8AM-4PM.

**Circuit Court**, Courthouse, Vernon, IN 47282. 812-346-5977 (EST) 8AM-4PM. Felony, Misdemeanor, Civil, Small Claims, Probate.

## Johnson County

**Real Estate Recording**, Johnson County Recorder, 86 West Court Street, Franklin, IN 46131. 317-736-3718 (EST) 8AM-4:30PM.

**Circuit & Superior Court**, Courthouse, PO Box 368, Franklin, IN 46131. 317-736-3708 (EST) 8AM-4:30PM. Felony, Misdemeanor, Civil, Small Claims, Probate.

## Knox County

**Real Estate Recording**, Knox County Recorder, Courthouse, Vincennes, IN 47591. 812-885-2508 (EST) 8AM-4PM.

**Circuit & Superior Court**, Courthouse, Vincennes, IN 47591. 812-885-2521 (EST) 8AM-4PM. Felony, Misdemeanor, Civil, Small Claims, Probate.

## Kosciusko County

**Real Estate Recording**, Kosciusko County Recorder, 100 West Center Street, Courthouse Room 14, Warsaw, IN 46580. 219-372-2360 (EST) 8AM-4PM (F open until 6PM).

**Circuit, Superior, & County Court**, 121 N Lake, Warsaw, IN 46580. 219-272-2331 (EST) 8AM-4PM. Felony, Misdemeanor, Civil, Small Claims, Probate.

## La Porte County

**Real Estate Recording**, La Porte County Recorder, Courthouse Square, 2nd Floor, La Porte, IN 46350. 219-326-6808 (CST) 8:30AM-5PM.

# Indiana

**Circuit & Superior Court**, Lincolnway, La Porte, IN 46350. 219-326-6808 (CST) Felony, Misdemeanor, Civil, Small Claims, Probate.

## LaGrange County

**Real Estate Recording**, LaGrange County Recorder, 114 West Michigan Street, County Office Building, LaGrange, IN 46761. 219-463-7807 (EST) 8AM-4PM M-Th; 8AM-5PM F.

**Circuit & Superior Court**, 105 N Detroit St, Courthouse, LaGrange, IN 46761. 219-463-3442 (EST) 8AM-4PM M-TH, 8AM-5PM F. Felony, Misdemeanor, Civil, Small Claims, Probate.

## Lake County

**Real Estate Recording**, Lake County Recorder, 2293 N Main Street, Crown Point, IN 46307. 219-755-3730 (CST) 8:30AM-4:30PM.

**Circuit & Superior Court**, 2293 N Main St, Courthouse, Crown Point, IN 46307. 219-755-3000 (CST) 8:30AM-4:20PM. Felony, Misdemeanor, Civil, Small Claims, Probate.

## Lawrence County

**Real Estate Recording**, Lawrence County Recorder, Courthouse, Room 21, Bedford, IN 47421. 812-275-3245 (EST) 8:30AM-4:30PM.

**Circuit, Superior, & County Court**, 31 Courthouse, Bedford, IN 47421. 812-275-7543 (EST) 8:30AM-4:30PM. Felony, Misdemeanor, Civil, Small Claims, Probate.

## Madison County

**Real Estate Recording**, Madison County Recorder, 16 East 9th Street, Anderson, IN 46016. 317-641-9613 (EST) 8AM-4PM.

**Circuit, Superior, & County Court**, 16 E 9th, Box 5, Anderson, IN 46016. 317-641-9443 (EST) 8AM-4PM. Felony, Misdemeanor, Civil, Small Claims, Probate.

## Marion County

**Real Estate Recording**, Marion County Recorder, 200 E. Washington, Suite 721, Indianapolis, IN 46204. 317-327-4020 (EST) 8AM-4:30PM.

**Circuit & Superior Court**, 200 E Washington St, Indianapolis, IN 46204. 317-327-4724 (EST) 8AM-4:30PM. Felony, Misdemeanor, Civil, Small Claims, Probate.

## Marshall County

**Real Estate Recording**, Marshall County Recorder, 112 West Jefferson Street, Room 201, Plymouth, IN 46563. 219-935-8515 (EST) 8AM-4PM.

**Circuit & Superior Court**, 211 W Madison St, Plymouth, IN 46563. 219-936-8922 (EST) 8AM-4PM M,W-F, 8AM-6PM T. Felony, Misdemeanor, Civil, Small Claims, Probate.

## Martin County

**Real Estate Recording**, Martin County Recorder, Capital Street, Courthouse, Shoals, IN 47581. 812-247-2420 (EST) 8AM-4PM.

**Circuit Court**, PO Box 120, Shoals, IN 47581. 812-247-3651 (EST) 8AM-4PM. Felony, Misdemeanor, Civil, Small Claims, Probate.

## Miami County

**Real Estate Recording**, Miami County Recorder, Courthouse, Peru, IN 46970. 317-472-3901 (EST) 8AM-4PM.

**Circuit & Superior Court**, PO Box 184, Peru, IN 46970. 317-472-3901 (EST) 8AM-4PM. Felony, Misdemeanor, Civil, Small Claims, Probate.

## Monroe County

**Real Estate Recording**, Monroe County Recorder, Courthouse, Bloomington, IN 47404. 812-333-3520 (EST)

**Circuit Court**, PO Box 547, Bloomington, IN 47402. 812-333-3600 (EST) 8AM-4PM. Felony, Misdemeanor, Civil, Small Claims, Probate.

## Montgomery County

**Real Estate Recording**, Montgomery County Recorder, 100 East Main Street, Crawfordsville, IN 47933. 317-364-6415 (EST) 8AM-4PM.

**Circuit, Superior, & County Court**, PO Box 768, Crawfordsville, IN 47933. 317-364-6430 (EST) 8:30AM-4:30PM. Felony, Misdemeanor, Civil, Small Claims, Probate.

## Morgan County

**Real Estate Recording**, Morgan County Recorder, Courthouse, Room 103, Martinsville, IN 46151. 317-342-1078 (EST) 8AM-4PM (8AM-5PM F).

**Circuit, Superior, & County Court**, PO Box 1556, Martinsville, IN 46151. 317-342-1025 (EST) 8AM-4PM M-Th, 8AM-5PM F. Felony, Misdemeanor, Civil, Small Claims, Probate.

## Newton County

**Real Estate Recording**, Newton County Recorder, 201 N. 3rd St., Courthouse - Room 104, Kentland, IN 47951. 219-474-6081 (CST) 8AM-4PM.

**Circuit & Superior Court**, PO Box 49, Kentland, IN 47951. 219-474-6081 (CST) Felony, Misdemeanor, Civil, Small Claims, Probate.

## Noble County

**Real Estate Recording**, Noble County Recorder, 101 North Orange Street, Albion, IN 46701. 219-636-2672 (EST) 8AM-4PM.

**Circuit, Superior, & County Court**, 101 N Orange St, Albion, IN 46701. 219-636-2736 (EST) Felony, Misdemeanor, Civil, Small Claims, Probate.

## Ohio County

**Real Estate Recording**, Ohio County Recorder, Main Street, Courthouse, Rising Sun, IN 47040. 812-438-3369 (EST) 9AM-4PM M,T,Th,F; 9AM-12 Sat; Closed Wed.

**Circuit & Superior Court**, PO Box 185, Rising Sun, IN 47040. 812-438-2610 (EST) 9AM-4PM M,T,Th,F 9AM-Noon S. Felony, Misdemeanor, Civil, Small Claims, Probate.

## Orange County

**Real Estate Recording**, Orange County Recorder, 205 East Main Street, Courthouse, Paoli, IN 47454. 812-723-3600 (EST) 8AM-4PM.

**Circuit & County Court**, Courthouse, Court St, Paoli, IN 47454. 812-723-2649 (EST) Felony, Misdemeanor, Civil, Eviction, Small Claims, Probate.

## Owen County

**Real Estate Recording**, Owen County Recorder, Courthouse, Spencer, IN 47460. 812-829-5014 (EST) 8AM-4PM.

**Circuit Court**, PO Box 146, Courthouse, Spencer, IN 47460. 812-829-5015 (EST) 8AM-4PM. Felony, Misdemeanor, Civil, Small Claims, Probate.

## Parke County

**Real Estate Recording**, Parke County Recorder, 116 W. High St., Room 102, Rockville, IN 47872-1787. 317-569-3419 (EST) 8AM-4PM.

**Circuit Court**, Courthouse, Rockville, IN 47872. 317-569-5132 (EST) 8AM-4PM. Felony, Misdemeanor, Civil, Small Claims, Probate.

## Perry County

**Real Estate Recording**, Perry County Recorder, 2219 Payne St., Room W2, Tell City, IN 47586-2830. 812-547-4261 (EST)

**Circuit Court**, 2219 Payne St, Courthouse, Tell City, IN 47586. 812-547-3741 (EST) 8AM-4PM. Felony, Misdemeanor, Civil, Small Claims, Probate.

## Pike County

**Real Estate Recording**, Pike County Recorder, Main Street, Courthouse, Petersburg, IN 47567-1298. 812-354-6747 (EST) 8AM-4PM.

**Circuit Court**, 801 Main St. Courthouse, Petersburg, IN 47567-1298. 812-354-6025 (EST) 8AM-4PM. Felony, Misdemeanor, Civil, Small Claims, Probate.

## Porter County

**Real Estate Recording**, Porter County Recorder, 155 Indiana Ave, Suite 210, Valparaiso, IN 46383. 219-465-3465 (CST) 8:30AM-4:30PM.

**Circuit & Superior Court**, Adminstration Center #303, Valparaiso, IN 46383. 219-465-3453 (CST) 8:30AM-4:30PM. Felony, Misdemeanor, Civil, Small Claims, Probate.

## Posey County

**Real Estate Recording**, Posey County Recorder, Courthouse, Mount Vernon, IN 47620. 812-838-1314 (CST)

**Circuit & County Court**, 300 Main St, Mount Vernon, IN 47620-1897. 812-838-1306 (CST) Felony, Misdemeanor, Civil, Eviction, Small Claims, Probate.

## Pulaski County

**Real Estate Recording**, Pulaski County Recorder, Courthouse - Room 220, 112 E. Main St., Winamac, IN 46996. 219-946-3844 (EST) 8AM-4PM.

**Circuit & Superior Court**, Courthouse, Winamac, IN 46996. 219-946-3313 (EST) Felony, Misdemeanor, Civil, Small Claims, Probate.

## Putnam County

**Real Estate Recording**, Putnam County Recorder, Courthouse Square, Room 25, Greencastle, IN 46135. 317-653-5613 (EST) 8AM-4PM.

**Circuit & County Court**, PO Box 546, Greencastle, IN 46135. 317-653-2648 (EST) 8AM-4PM. Felony, Misdemeanor, Civil, Eviction, Small Claims, Probate.

## Randolph County

**Real Estate Recording**, Randolph County Recorder, Courthouse, Room 101, Winchester, IN 47394-1899. 317-584-7070 (EST) 8AM-4PM.

**Circuit & Superior Court**, PO Box 230 Courthouse, Winchester, IN 47394-0230. 317-584-7070 (EST) 8AM-4PM. Felony, Misdemeanor, Civil, Small Claims, Probate.

## Ripley County

**Real Estate Recording**, Ripley County Recorder, Courthouse, 115 N. Main St., Versailles, IN 47042. 812-689-5808 (EST) 8AM-4PM.

**Circuit Court**, PO BOX 177, Versailles, IN 47042. 812-689-6115 (EST) 8AM-4PM. Felony, Misdemeanor, Civil, Small Claims, Probate.

## Rush County

**Real Estate Recording**, Rush County Recorder, Courthouse, Room 8, Rushville, IN 46173. 317-932-2388 (EST) 8AM-4PM.

**Circuit & County Court**, PO Box 429, Rushville, IN 46173. 317-932-2086 (EST) 8AM-4PM. Felony, Misdemeanor, Civil, Eviction, Small Claims, Probate.

## Scott County

**Real Estate Recording**, Scott County Recorder, 75 North 1st Street, Scottsburg, IN 47170. 812-752-8442 (EST) 8:30AM-4:30PM.

**Circuit & Superior Court**, 1 E. McClain Ave, Scottsburg, IN 47170. 812-752-4769 (EST) 8:30AM-4PM M-Th, 8:30-5:30 F. Felony, Misdemeanor, Civil, Small Claims, Probate.

## Shelby County

**Real Estate Recording**, Shelby County Recorder, 407 South Harrison, Courthouse, Shelbyville, IN 46176. 317-392-6370 (EST) 8AM-4PM.

**Circuit & Superior Court**, PO Box 198, Shelbyville, IN 46176. 317-392-6320 (EST) 8AM-4PM. Felony, Misdemeanor, Civil, Small Claims, Probate.

## Spencer County

**Real Estate Recording**, Spencer County Recorder, Courthouse, Rockport, IN 47635. 812-649-6013 (CST) 8AM-4PM.

**Circuit Court**, PO Box 12, Rockport, IN 47635. 812-649-6027 (CST) Felony, Misdemeanor, Civil, Small Claims, Probate.

## St. Joseph County

**Real Estate Recording**, St. Joseph County Recorder, 227 West Jefferson, Room 321, South Bend, IN 46601. 219-235-9525 (EST) 8AM-4:30PM.

**Circuit & Superior Court**, 101 South Main St, South Bend, IN 46601. 219-235-9635 (EST) 8AM-4:30PM. Felony, Misdemeanor, Civil, Small Claims, Probate.

## Starke County

**Real Estate Recording**, Starke County Recorder, Courthouse, 53 E. Mound, Knox, IN 46534. 219-772-9110 (CST) 8:30AM-4PM.

**Circuit Court**, Courthouse, Knox, IN 46534. 219-772-9128 (CST) 8:30AM-4PM. Felony, Misdemeanor, Civil, Small Claims, Probate.

## Steuben County

**Real Estate Recording**, Steuben County Recorder, Courthouse, Angola, IN 46703. 219-665-2415 (EST) 8AM-4:30PM.

**Circuit & Superior Court**, Courthouse, 55 S. Public Square, Angola, IN 46703. 219-665-2361 (EST) 8AM-4:30PM. Felony, Misdemeanor, Civil, Small Claims, Probate.

## Sullivan County

**Real Estate Recording**, Sullivan County Recorder, Room 205, 100 Court House Square, Sullivan, IN 47882-1565. 812-268-4844 (EST) 8AM-4PM.

**Circuit & Superior Court**, Courthouse, 3rd Fl, Sullivan, IN 47882. 812-268-4657 (EST) 8AM-4PM. Felony, Misdemeanor, Civil, Small Claims, Probate.

## Switzerland County

**Real Estate Recording**, Switzerland County Recorder, Courthouse, Vevay, IN 47043. 812-427-2544 (EST) 8AM-3:30PM.

**Circuit & Superior Court**, Courthouse, Vevay, IN 47043. 812-427-3175 (EST) 8:30-4PM. Felony, Misdemeanor, Civil, Small Claims, Probate.

## Tippecanoe County

**Real Estate Recording**, Tippecanoe County Recorder, 20 North 3rd Street, Lafayette, IN 47901. 317-423-9353 (EST) 8AM-4:30PM.

**Circuit, Superior, & County Court**, PO Box 1665, Lafayette, IN 47902. 317-423-9326 (EST) Felony, Misdemeanor, Civil, Small Claims, Probate.

## Tipton County

**Real Estate Recording**, Tipton County Recorder, Courthouse, Tipton, IN 46072. 317-675-4614 (EST)

**Circuit Court**, Tipton County Courthouse, Tipton, IN 46072. 317-675-2795 (EST) 8AM-4PM M-Th, 8AM-5PM F. Felony, Misdemeanor, Civil, Small Claims, Probate.

## Union County

**Real Estate Recording**, Union County Recorder, 26 West Union Street, Box 106, Liberty, IN 47353. 317-458-5434 (EST) 8AM-4PM.

**Circuit Court**, 26 W Union St, Liberty, IN 47353. 317-458-6121 (EST) 8AM-4PM. Felony, Misdemeanor, Civil, Small Claims, Probate.

## Vanderburgh County

**Real Estate Recording**, Vanderburgh County Recorder, 231 City-County Admin. Building, 1 NW Martin Luther King, Jr. Blvd., Evansville, IN 47708-1881. 812-435-5215 (CST) 8AM-4:30PM.

**Circuit & Superior Court**, PO Box 3356, Evansville, IN 47732-3356. 812-435-5160 (CST) 8AM-5PM. Felony, Misdemeanor, Civil, Small Claims, Probate.

## Vermillion County

**Real Estate Recording**, Vermillion County Recorder, Courthouse, Room 202, Newport, IN 47966. 317-492-5003 (EST) 8AM-4PM.

**Circuit Court**, PO Box 8, Newport, IN 47966. 317-492-3500 (EST) Felony, Misdemeanor, Civil, Small Claims, Probate.

## Vigo County

**Real Estate Recording**, Vigo County Recorder, 201 Cherry Street, Terre Haute, IN 47807. 812-462-3301 (EST) 8AM-4PM.

**Circuit, Superior, & County Court**, 2nd Fl, Courthouse, Terre Haute, IN 47807. 812-462-3211 (EST) Felony, Misdemeanor, Civil, Small Claims, Probate.

## Wabash County

**Real Estate Recording**, Wabash County Recorder, Courthouse, One West Hill St., Wabash, IN 46992. 219-563-0661 (EST) X24 8AM-4PM.

**Circuit & County Court**, One West Hill St, Wabash, IN 46992. 219-563-0661 (EST) 8AM-4PM. Felony, Misdemeanor, Civil, Eviction, Small Claims, Probate.

## Warren County

**Real Estate Recording**, Warren County Recorder, 125 N. Monroe, Courthouse - Suite 10, Williamsport, IN 47993-1162. 317-762-3174 (EST) 8AM-4PM.

**Circuit Court**, Ste 11, 125 N Monroe, Williamsport, IN 47993. 317-762-3510 (EST) 8AM-4PM. Felony, Misdemeanor, Civil, Small Claims, Probate.

## Warrick County

**Real Estate Recording**, Warrick County Recorder, 1 Courthouse Square, Room 204 Box 28, Boonville, IN 47601. 812-897-6165 (CST) 8AM-4PM.

**Circuit & Superior Court**, 107 W Locust, Rm 201, Boonville, IN 47601. 812-897-6160 (CST) 8AM-4PM. Felony, Misdemeanor, Civil, Small Claims, Probate.

## Washington County

**Real Estate Recording**, Washington County Recorder, Courthouse, Salem, IN 47167. 812-883-4001 (EST) 8:30AM-4PM (F 8:30AM-6PM).

**Circuit & Superior Court**, Courthouse, Salem, IN 47167. 812-883-1634 (EST) 8:30AM-4PM M-Th, 8:30AM-6PM F. Felony, Misdemeanor, Civil, Small Claims, Probate.

## Wayne County

**Real Estate Recording**, Wayne County Recorder, 401 East Main Street, Richmond, IN 47374. 317-973-9235 (EST) 8:30AM-4:30PM (F 8:30AM-5PM).

**Circuit & Superior Court**, PO Box 1172, Richmond, IN 47375. 317-973-9200 (EST) Felony, Misdemeanor, Civil, Small Claims, Probate.

# Indiana

## Wells County

**Real Estate Recording**, Wells County Recorder, Courthouse - Suite 203, 102 W. Market St., Bluffton, IN 46714. 219-824-6507 (EST) 8AM-4:30PM.

**Circuit & Superior Court**, 102 West Market, Rm 201, Bluffton, IN 46714. 219-824-6479 (EST) 8AM-4:30PM. Felony, Misdemeanor, Civil, Small Claims, Probate.

## White County

**Real Estate Recording**, White County Recorder, Corner of Main & Broadway, Courthouse, Monticello, IN 47960. 219-583-5912 (EST) 8AM-4PM.

**Circuit & Superior Court**, PO Box 350, Monticello, IN 47960. 219-583-7032 (EST) 8AM-4PM. Felony, Misdemeanor, Civil, Small Claims, Probate.

## Whitley County

**Real Estate Recording**, Whitley County Recorder, Courthouse, 2nd Floor - Room 18, Columbia City, IN 46725. 219-248-3106 (EST) 8AM-4PM (8AM-6PM F).

**Circuit & Superior Court**, 101 W Van Buren, Rm 10, Columbia City, IN 46725. 219-248-3102 (EST) 8AM-4:30PM. Felony, Misdemeanor, Civil, Small Claims, Probate.

**County Records**

# Iowa

## Adair County

**Real Estate Recording**, Adair County Recorder, Courthouse, Public Square, Greenfield, IA 50849. 515-743-2411 (CST) 8AM-4:30PM.

**5th District Court**, PO Box L, Greenfield, IA 50849. 515-743-2445 (CST) 8AM-4:30PM. Felony, Misdemeanor, Civil, Eviction, Small Claims, Probate.

## Adams County

**Real Estate Recording**, Adams County Recorder, 500 9th St., Corning, IA 50841. 515-322-3744 (CST) 8:30AM-Noon, 1-4:30PM.

**5th District Court**, Courthouse, Corning, IA 50841. 515-322-4711 (CST) 8AM-4:30PM. Felony, Misdemeanor, Civil, Eviction, Small Claims, Probate.

## Allamakee County

**Real Estate Recording**, Allamakee County Recorder, 110 Allamakee Street, Courthouse, Waukon, IA 52172-1794. 319-568-2364 (CST) 8AM-4PM.

**1st District Court**, PO Box 248, Waukon, IA 52172. 319-568-6351 (CST) 8AM-4:30PM. Felony, Misdemeanor, Civil, Eviction, Small Claims, Probate.

## Appanoose County

**Real Estate Recording**, Appanoose County Recorder, Courthouse, Centerville, IA 52544. 515-856-6103 (CST)

**8th District Court**, Courthouse, Centerville, IA 52544. 515-856-6101 (CST) 8AM-4:30PM. Felony, Misdemeanor, Civil, Eviction, Small Claims, Probate.

## Audubon County

**Real Estate Recording**, Audubon County Recorder of Deeds, 318 Leroy St. #7, Audubon, IA 50025-1255. 712-563-2119 (CST) 8AM-4:30PM.

**4th District Court**, Courthouse, Audubon, IA 50025. 712-563-4275 (CST) 8AM-4:30PM. Felony, Misdemeanor, Civil, Eviction, Small Claims, Probate.

## Benton County

**Real Estate Recording**, Benton County Recorder, Courthouse, Vinton, IA 52349. 319-472-3309 (CST) 8AM-4:30PM.

**6th District Court**, PO Box 719, Vinton, IA 52349. 319-472-2766 (CST) 8AM-4:30PM. Felony, Misdemeanor, Civil, Eviction, Small Claims, Probate.

## Black Hawk County

**Real Estate Recording**, Black Hawk County Recorder, 316 East 5th Street, Courthouse, Room 208, Waterloo, IA 50703-4774. 319-291-2472 (CST) 8AM-5PM.

**1st District Court**, 316 E 5th St, Waterloo, IA 50703. 319-291-2612 (CST) 8AM-4:30PM. Felony, Misdemeanor, Civil, Eviction, Small Claims, Probate.

## Boone County

**Real Estate Recording**, Boone County Recorder, 201 State Street, Boone, IA 50036-3987. 515-433-0514 (CST) 8AM-4:30PM.

**2nd District Court**, 201 State St, Boone, IA 50036. 515-433-0561 (CST) 8AM-4:30PM. Felony, Misdemeanor, Civil, Eviction, Small Claims, Probate.

## Bremer County

**Real Estate Recording**, Bremer County Recorder, Courthouse, 415 E. Bremer Ave., Waverly, IA 50677. 319-352-5040 (CST) 8AM-4:30PM.

**2nd District Court**, PO Box 328, Waverly, IA 50677. 319-352-5661 (CST) 8AM-4:30PM. Felony, Misdemeanor, Civil, Eviction, Small Claims, Probate.

## Buchanan County

**Real Estate Recording**, Buchanan County Recorder, 210 5th Avenue NE, Independence, IA 50644. 319-334-4259 (CST) 8AM-4:30PM.

**1st District Court**, PO Box 259, Independence, IA 50644. 319-334-2196 (CST) 8AM-4:30PM. Felony, Misdemeanor, Civil, Eviction, Small Claims, Probate.

## Buena Vista County

**Real Estate Recording**, Buena Vista County Recorder, Courthouse Square, Storm Lake, IA 50588. 712-749-2539 (CST) 8AM-4:30PM.

**3rd District Court**, PO Box 1186, Storm Lake, IA 50588. 712-749-2546 (CST) 8AM-4:30PM. Felony, Misdemeanor, Civil, Eviction, Small Claims, Probate.

## Butler County

**Real Estate Recording**, Butler County Recorder, 428 6th Street, Allison, IA 50602. 319-267-2735 (CST) 8AM-4PM.

**2nd District Court**, PO Box 307, Allison, IA 50602. 319-267-2487 (CST) 8AM-4:30PM. Felony, Misdemeanor, Civil, Eviction, Small Claims, Probate.

## Calhoun County

**Real Estate Recording**, Calhoun County Recorder of Deeds, Courthouse, Rockwell City, IA 50579. 712-297-8121 (CST) 8:30AM-4:30PM.

**2nd District Court**, Box 273, Rockwell City, IA 50579. 712-297-8122 (CST) 8AM-4:30PM. Felony, Misdemeanor, Civil, Eviction, Small Claims, Probate.

## Carroll County

**Real Estate Recording**, Carroll County Recorder of Deeds, 6th & Main, Courthouse, Carroll, IA 51401. 712-792-3328 (CST) 8AM-4:30PM.

**2nd District Court**, Courthouse, Carroll, IA 51401. 712-792-4327 (CST) 8AM-4:30PM. Felony, Misdemeanor, Civil, Eviction, Small Claims, Probate.

## Cass County

**Real Estate Recording**, Cass County Recorder, 5 West 7th, Atlantic, IA 50022. 712-243-1692 (CST) 8AM-4:30PM.

**4th District Court**, 5 W 7th St, Courthouse, Atlantic, IA 50022. 712-243-2105 (CST) 8AM-4:30PM. Felony, Misdemeanor, Civil, Eviction, Small Claims, Probate.

## Cedar County

**Real Estate Recording**, Cedar County Recorder, 400 Cedar Street, Courthouse, Tipton, IA 52772-1752. 319-886-2230 (CST) 8AM-4PM.

**7th District Court**, PO Box 111, Tipton, IA 52772. 319-886-2101 (CST) 8AM-4:30PM. Felony, Misdemeanor, Civil, Eviction, Small Claims, Probate.

## Cerro Gordo County

**Real Estate Recording**, Cerro Gordo County Recorder of Deeds, 220 North Washington, Mason City, IA 50401. 515-421-3056 (CST) 8AM-4:30PM.

**2nd District Court**, 220 W Washington, Mason City, IA 50401. 515-424-6431 (CST) 8AM-4:30PM. Felony, Misdemeanor, Civil, Eviction, Small Claims, Probate.

## Cherokee County

**Real Estate Recording**, Cherokee County Recorder of Deeds, 600 West Main, Cherokee, IA 51012. 712-225-4498 (CST) 8AM-4:30PM.

**3rd District Court**, Courthouse Drawer F, Cherokee, IA 51012. 712-225-2706 (CST) 8AM-4:30PM. Felony, Misdemeanor, Civil, Eviction, Small Claims, Probate.

## Chickasaw County

**Real Estate Recording**, Chickasaw County Recorder, Courthouse, 8 E. Prospect, New Hampton, IA 50659. 515-394-2336 (CST) 8:30AM-4:30PM.

**1st District Court**, County Courthouse, New Hampton, IA 50659. 515-394-2106 (CST) 8AM-4:30PM. Felony, Misdemeanor, Civil, Eviction, Small Claims, Probate.

## Clarke County

**Real Estate Recording**, Clarke County Recorder, Courthouse, Osceola, IA 50213. 515-342-3313 (CST) 8:30AM-4:30PM.

**5th District Court**, Clarke County Courthouse, Osceola, IA 50213. 515-342-6096 (CST) 8AM-4:30PM. Felony, Misdemeanor, Civil, Eviction, Small Claims, Probate.

## Clay County

**Real Estate Recording**, Clay County Recorder of Deeds, Courthouse, Spencer, IA 51301. 712-262-1081 (CST) 8AM-4:30PM.

**3rd District Court**, Courthouse (PO Box 4104), Spencer, IA 51301. 712-262-4335 (CST) 8AM-4:30PM. Felony, Misdemeanor, Civil, Eviction, Small Claims, Probate.

## Clayton County

**Real Estate Recording**, Clayton County Recorder, High Street, Elkader, IA 52043. 319-245-2710 (CST) 8AM-4:30PM.

# Iowa

**1st District Court**, Clayton County Courthouse, Elkader, IA 52043. 319-245-2204 (CST) 8AM-4:30PM. Felony, Misdemeanor, Civil, Eviction, Small Claims, Probate.

## Clinton County

**Real Estate Recording**, Clinton County Recorder of Deeds, Courthouse, 614 N. 2nd St., Clinton, IA 52732. 319-243-6210 (CST) X4252 8AM-4:30PM.

**7th District Court**, Courthouse (PO Box 2957), Clinton, IA 52733. 319-243-6210 (CST) 8AM-3:30PM. Felony, Misdemeanor, Civil, Eviction, Small Claims, Probate.

## Crawford County

**Real Estate Recording**, Crawford County Recorder, 12th & Broadway, Denison, IA 51442. 712-263-3643 (CST) 8AM-4:30PM.

**3rd District Court**, PO Box 546, Denison, IA 51442. 712-263-2242 (CST) 8AM-4:30PM. Felony, Misdemeanor, Civil, Eviction, Small Claims, Probate.

## Dallas County

**Real Estate Recording**, Dallas County Recorder, 801 Court Street, Adel, IA 50003-1484. 515-993-5804 (CST) 8AM-4:30PM.

**5th District Court**, 801 Court St, Adel, IA 50003. 515-993-5816 (CST) 8AM-4:30PM. Felony, Misdemeanor, Civil, Eviction, Small Claims, Probate.

## Davis County

**Real Estate Recording**, Davis County Recorder, Courthouse, Bloomfield, IA 52537. 515-664-2321 (CST) 8AM-4PM.

**8th District Court**, Davis County Courthouse, Bloomfield, IA 52537. 515-664-2011 (CST) 8AM-4:30PM. Felony, Misdemeanor, Civil, Eviction, Small Claims, Probate.

## Decatur County

**Real Estate Recording**, Decatur County Recorder, 207 North Main Street, Leon, IA 50144. 515-446-4322 (CST) 8AM-4:30PM.

**5th District Court**, 297 N Main St, Leon, IA 50144. 515-446-4331 (CST) 8AM-4:30PM. Felony, Misdemeanor, Civil, Eviction, Small Claims, Probate.

## Delaware County

**Real Estate Recording**, Delaware County Recorder, Courthouse, 301 East Main, Manchester, IA 52057. 319-927-4665 (CST)

**1st District Court**, PO Box 527, Manchester, IA 52057. 319-927-4942 (CST) 8AM-4:30PM. Felony, Misdemeanor, Civil, Eviction, Small Claims, Probate.

## Des Moines County

**Real Estate Recording**, Des Moines County Recorder, 513 North Main Street, Burlington, IA 52601. 319-753-8221 (CST) 8AM-4:30PM.

**8th District Court**, PO Box 158, Burlington, IA 52601. 319-753-8262 (CST) 8AM-3:30PM. Felony, Misdemeanor, Civil, Eviction, Small Claims, Probate.

## Dickinson County

**Real Estate Recording**, Dickinson County Recorder, Corner of Hill and 18th Streets, Courthouse, Spirit Lake, IA 51360. 712-336-1495 (CST) 8AM-4:30PM.

**3rd District Court**, PO Drawer O N, Spirit Lake, IA 51360. 712-336-1138 (CST) 8AM-4:30PM. Felony, Misdemeanor, Civil, Eviction, Small Claims, Probate.

## Dubuque County

**Real Estate Recording**, Dubuque County Recorder, 7th & Central, Courthouse, Dubuque, IA 52001. 319-589-4434 (CST) 8:30AM-5PM.

**1st District Court**, 720 Central, Dubuque, IA 52001. 319-589-4418 (CST) 8AM-4:30PM. Felony, Misdemeanor, Civil, Eviction, Small Claims, Probate.

## Emmet County

**Real Estate Recording**, Emmet County Recorder, 609 1st Avenue North, Estherville, IA 51334. 712-362-4115 (CST) 8AM-4:30PM.

**3rd District Court**, Emmet County, Estherville, IA 51334. 712-362-3325 (CST) 8AM-4:30PM. Felony, Misdemeanor, Civil, Eviction, Small Claims, Probate.

## Fayette County

**Real Estate Recording**, Fayette County Recorder, Courthouse, 114 N. Vine St., West Union, IA 52175. 319-422-6061 (CST) X14 8AM-4:30PM.

**1st District Court**, PO Box 458, West Union, IA 52175. 319-422-6061 (CST) 8AM-4:30PM. Felony, Misdemeanor, Civil, Eviction, Small Claims, Probate.

## Floyd County

**Real Estate Recording**, Floyd County Recorder, Courthouse, 101 S. Main, Charles City, IA 50616. 515-257-6154 (CST) 8AM-4:30PM.

**2nd District Court**, 101 S Main St, Charles City, IA 50616. 515-257-6122 (CST) 8AM-4:30PM. Felony, Misdemeanor, Civil, Eviction, Small Claims, Probate.

## Franklin County

**Real Estate Recording**, Franklin County Recorder, Courthouse, Hampton, IA 50441. 515-456-5675 (CST) 8AM-4PM.

**2nd District Court**, PO Box 28, Hampton, IA 50441. 515-456-5626 (CST) 8AM-4:30PM. Felony, Misdemeanor, Civil, Eviction, Small Claims, Probate.

## Fremont County

**Real Estate Recording**, Fremont County Recorder, Courthouse, Sidney, IA 51652. 712-374-2315 (CST) 8AM-4:30PM.

**4th District Court**, PO Box 549, Sidney, IA 51652. 712-374-2232 (CST) 8AM-4PM. Felony, Misdemeanor, Civil, Eviction, Small Claims, Probate.

## Greene County

**Real Estate Recording**, Greene County Recorder, Courthouse, 114 N. Chestnut, Jefferson, IA 50129. 515-386-3716 (CST) 8AM-4:30PM.

**2nd District Court**, Greene County Courthouse, Jefferson, IA 50129. 515-386-2516 (CST) 8AM-4:30PM. Felony, Misdemeanor, Civil, Eviction, Small Claims, Probate.

## Grundy County

**Real Estate Recording**, Grundy County Recorder, 706 G Avenue, Grundy Center, IA 50638-1447. 319-824-3234 (CST) 8AM-4:30PM.

**1st District Court**, Grundy County Courthouse, Grundy Center, IA 50638. 319-824-5229 (CST) 8AM-4:30PM. Felony, Misdemeanor, Civil, Eviction, Small Claims, Probate.

## Guthrie County

**Real Estate Recording**, Guthrie County Recorder, 200 North 5th, Courthouse, Guthrie Center, IA 50115. 515-747-3412 (CST)

**5th District Court**, Courthouse, Guthrie Center, IA 50115. 515-747-3415 (CST) 8AM-4:30PM. Felony, Misdemeanor, Civil, Eviction, Small Claims, Probate.

## Hamilton County

**Real Estate Recording**, Hamilton County Recorder, 2300 Superior Street, Webster City, IA 50595. 515-832-9535 (CST) 8AM-4PM.

**2nd District Court**, Courthouse PO Box 845, Webster City, IA 50595. 515-832-9600 (CST) 8AM-4:30PM. Felony, Misdemeanor, Civil, Eviction, Small Claims, Probate.

## Hancock County

**Real Estate Recording**, Hancock County Recorder, 855 State Street, Garner, IA 50438. 515-923-2464 (CST) 8AM-4PM.

**2nd District Court**, 855 State St, Garner, IA 50438. 515-923-2532 (CST) 8AM-4:30PM. Felony, Misdemeanor, Civil, Eviction, Small Claims, Probate.

## Hardin County

**Real Estate Recording**, Hardin County Recorder, Courthouse, Eldora, IA 50627. 515-858-3461 (CST) 8AM-4:30PM.

**2nd District Court**, Courthouse, Eldora, IA 50627. 515-858-2328 (CST) 8AM-4:30PM. Felony, Misdemeanor, Civil, Eviction, Small Claims, Probate.

## Harrison County

**Real Estate Recording**, Harrison County Recorder, Courthouse, Logan, IA 51546. 712-644-2545 (CST) 8AM-4:30PM.

**4th District Court**, Courthouse, Logan, IA 51546. 712-644-2665 (CST) 8AM-4:30PM. Felony, Misdemeanor, Civil, Eviction, Small Claims, Probate.

## Henry County

**Real Estate Recording**, Henry County Recorder, Washington and Main Streets, Courthouse, Mount Pleasant, IA 52641. 319-385-0765 (CST) 8AM-4:30PM.

**8th District Court**, PO Box 176, Mount Pleasant, IA 52641. 319-385-2632 (CST) 8AM-4:30PM. Felony, Misdemeanor, Civil, Eviction, Small Claims, Probate.

**County Records**

## Howard County

**Real Estate Recording**, Howard County Recorder, Court House, Cresco, IA 52136. 319-547-3621 (CST) 8AM-4:30PM.

**1st District Court**, Courthouse, Cresco, IA 52136. 319-547-2661 (CST) 8AM-4:30PM. Felony, Misdemeanor, Civil, Eviction, Small Claims, Probate.

## Humboldt County

**Real Estate Recording**, Humboldt County Recorder, 203 Main Street, Court House, Dakota City, IA 50529. 515-332-3693 (CST) 8AM-4:30PM.

**2nd District Court**, Courthouse, Dakota City, IA 50529. 515-332-1806 (CST) 8AM-4:30PM. Felony, Misdemeanor, Civil, Eviction, Small Claims, Probate.

## Ida County

**Real Estate Recording**, Ida County Recorder, 401 Moorehead, Courthouse, Ida Grove, IA 51445. 712-364-2220 (CST) 8AM-4:30PM.

**3rd District Court**, Courthouse, Ida Grove, IA 51445. 712-364-2628 (CST) 8AM-4:30PM. Felony, Misdemeanor, Civil, Eviction, Small Claims, Probate.

## Iowa County

**Real Estate Recording**, Iowa County Recorder, Courthouse, Marengo, IA 52301. 319-642-3622 (CST) 8AM-4:30PM.

**6th District Court**, PO Box 266, Marengo, IA 52301. 319-642-3914 (CST) 8AM-4:30PM. Felony, Misdemeanor, Civil, Eviction, Small Claims, Probate.

## Jackson County

**Real Estate Recording**, Jackson County Recorder, 201 West Platt, Maquoketa, IA 52060. 319-652-2504 (CST) 8:30AM-4:30PM.

**7th District Court**, 201 West Platt, Maquoketa, IA 52060. 319-652-4946 (CST) 8AM-4:30PM. Felony, Misdemeanor, Civil, Eviction, Small Claims, Probate.

## Jasper County

**Real Estate Recording**, Jasper County Recorder, Courthouse, Room 205, Newton, IA 50208. 515-792-5442 (CST) 8AM-5PM.

**5th District Court**, PO Box 666, Newton, IA 50208. 515-792-3255 (CST) 8AM-4:30PM. Felony, Misdemeanor, Civil, Eviction, Small Claims, Probate.

## Jefferson County

**Real Estate Recording**, Jefferson County Recorder, 51 West Briggs, Fairfield, IA 52556-2820. 515-472-4331 (CST) 8AM-4:30PM.

**8th District Court**, PO Box 984, Fairfield, IA 52556. 515-472-3454 (CST) 8AM-4:30PM. Felony, Misdemeanor, Civil, Eviction, Small Claims, Probate.

## Johnson County

**Real Estate Recording**, Johnson County Recorder, 913 South Dubuque Street, Iowa City, IA 52240. 319-356-6093 (CST) 8AM-4PM.

**6th District Court**, PO Box 2510, Iowa City, IA 52244. 319-356-6060 (CST) 8AM-4:30PM. Felony, Misdemeanor, Civil, Eviction, Small Claims, Probate.

## Jones County

**Real Estate Recording**, Jones County Recorder, Courthouse, Room 116, 500 W. Main, Anamosa, IA 52205-1632. 319-462-2477 (CST) 8AM-4PM.

**6th District Court**, Courthouse, Anamosa, IA 52205. 319-462-4341 (CST) 8AM-4:30PM. Felony, Misdemeanor, Civil, Eviction, Small Claims, Probate.

## Keokuk County

**Real Estate Recording**, Keokuk County Recorder, Courthouse, Sigourney, IA 52591. 515-622-2540 (CST) 8AM-4:30PM.

**8th District Court**, Courthouse, Sigourney, IA 52591. 515-622-2210 (CST) 8AM-4:30PM. Felony, Misdemeanor, Civil, Eviction, Small Claims, Probate.

## Kossuth County

**Real Estate Recording**, Kossuth County Recorder, 114 West State, Algona, IA 50511. 515-295-5660 (CST) 8AM-4PM.

**3rd District Court**, Courthouse, Algona, IA 50511. 515-295-3240 (CST) 8AM-4PM. Felony, Misdemeanor, Civil, Eviction, Small Claims, Probate.

## Lee County

**Real Estate Recording**, Lee County Recorder, Northern District, 933 Avenue H, Fort Madison, IA 52627. 319-372-4662 (CST) 8:30AM-4:30PM.

**Real Estate Recording**, Lee County Recorder, Southern District, 25 North 7th, Keokuk, IA 52632. 319-524-1126 (CST) 8:30AM-4:30PM.

**8th District Court**, PO Box 1443, Ft Madison, IA 52627. 319-372-3523 (CST) 8AM-4:30PM. Felony, Misdemeanor, Civil, Eviction, Small Claims, Probate.

## Linn County

**Real Estate Recording**, Linn County Recorder, 930 First Street S.W., Cedar Rapids, IA 52404. 319-398-3441 (CST) 8AM-5PM.

**Iowa District Court**, PO Box 1468, Cedar Rapids, IA 52406. 319-398-3411 (CST) 8AM-4:30PM. Felony, Misdemeanor, Civil, Eviction, Small Claims, Probate.

## Louisa County

**Real Estate Recording**, Louisa County Recorder, 117 South Main Street, Wapello, IA 52653. 319-523-5361 (CST) 8AM-4:30PM.

**8th District Court**, PO Box 268, Wapello, IA 52653. 319-523-4541 (CST) 8AM-4:30PM. Felony, Misdemeanor, Civil, Eviction, Small Claims, Probate.

## Lucas County

**Real Estate Recording**, Lucas County Recorder, Courthouse, Chariton, IA 50049. 515-774-2413 (CST)

**5th District Court**, Courthouse Criminal Records, Chariton, IA 50049. 515-774-4421 (CST) 8AM-4:30PM. Felony, Misdemeanor, Civil, Eviction, Small Claims, Probate.

## Lyon County

**Real Estate Recording**, Lyon County Recorder, 206 Second Avenue, Courthouse, Rock Rapids, IA 51246. 712-472-2381 (CST) 8AM-4:30PM.

**3rd District Court**, Courthouse, Rock Rapids, IA 51246. 712-472-2623 (CST) 8AM-4:30PM. Felony, Misdemeanor, Civil, Eviction, Small Claims, Probate.

## Madison County

**Real Estate Recording**, Madison County Recorder, North John Wayne Drive, Courthouse, Winterset, IA 50273. 515-462-3771 (CST) 8AM-4:30PM; 9AM-Noon Last Sat of the month.

**5th District Court**, PO Box 152, Winterset, IA 50273. 515-462-4451 (CST) 8AM-4:30PM. Felony, Misdemeanor, Civil, Eviction, Small Claims, Probate.

## Mahaska County

**Real Estate Recording**, Mahaska County Recorder, Courthouse, Oskaloosa, IA 52577. 515-673-8187 (CST) 8AM-4:30PM.

**8th District Court**, Courthouse, Oskaloosa, IA 52577. 515-673-7786 (CST) 8AM-4:30PM. Felony, Misdemeanor, Civil, Eviction, Small Claims, Probate.

## Marion County

**Real Estate Recording**, Marion County Recorder, Courthouse, Knoxville, IA 50138. 515-828-2211 (CST) 8AM-4:30PM.

**5th District Court**, PO Box 497, Knoxville, IA 50138. 515-828-2207 (CST) 8AM-4:30PM. Felony, Misdemeanor, Civil, Eviction, Small Claims, Probate.

## Marshall County

**Real Estate Recording**, Marshall County Recorder, Courthouse, Third Floor, Marshalltown, IA 50158. 515-754-6355 (CST) 8AM-4:30PM.

**2nd District Court**, Courthouse, Marshalltown, IA 50158. 515-754-6373 (CST) 8AM-4:30PM. Felony, Misdemeanor, Civil, Eviction, Small Claims, Probate.

## Mills County

**Real Estate Recording**, Mills County Recorder, Courthouse, 418 Sharp St., Glenwood, IA 51534. 712-527-9315 (CST) 8AM-4:30PM.

**4th District Court**, 418 Sharp St, Courthouse, Glenwood, IA 51534. 712-527-4880 (CST) 8AM-4:30PM. Felony, Misdemeanor, Civil, Eviction, Small Claims, Probate.

## Mitchell County

**Real Estate Recording**, Mitchell County Recorder, 508 State Street, Osage, IA 50461-1250. 515-732-5861 (CST) 8AM-4:30PM.

**2nd District Court**, 508 State St, Osage, IA 50461. 515-732-3726 (CST) 8AM-4:30PM. Felony, Misdemeanor, Civil, Eviction, Small Claims, Probate.

# Iowa

## Monona County

**Real Estate Recording**, Monona County Recorder, 610 Iowa Avenue, Onawa, IA 51040. 712-423-2575 (CST) 8AM-4:30PM.

**3rd District Court**, 610 Iowa Ave, Onawa, IA 51040. 712-423-2491 (CST) 8AM-4:30PM. Felony, Misdemeanor, Civil, Eviction, Small Claims, Probate.

## Monroe County

**Real Estate Recording**, Monroe County Recorder, Courthouse, Albia, IA 52531. 515-932-5164 (CST) 8AM-4PM.

**8th District Court**, Courthouse, 10 Benton Ave E, Albia, IA 52531. 515-932-5212 (CST) 8AM-4:30PM. Felony, Misdemeanor, Civil, Eviction, Small Claims, Probate.

## Montgomery County

**Real Estate Recording**, Montgomery County Recorder, Courthouse, Red Oak, IA 51566. 712-623-4363 (CST) 8AM-4:30PM.

**4th District Court**, Courthouse, Red Oak, IA 51566. 712-623-4986 (CST) 8AM-4:30PM. Felony, Misdemeanor, Civil, Eviction, Small Claims, Probate.

## Muscatine County

**Real Estate Recording**, Muscatine County Recorder, 401 East 3rd Street, Courthouse, Muscatine, IA 52761-4166. 319-263-7741 (CST) 8AM-4:30PM.

**7th District Court**, PO Box 327, Courthouse, Muscatine, IA 52761. 319-263-6511 (CST) 8AM-4:30PM. Felony, Misdemeanor, Civil, Eviction, Small Claims, Probate.

## O'Brien County

**Real Estate Recording**, O'Brien County Recorder, Courthouse, Primghar, IA 51245. 712-757-3045 (CST) 8AM-4:30PM.

**3rd District Court**, Courthouse Criminal Records, Primghar, IA 51245. 712-757-3255 (CST) 8AM-4:30PM. Felony, Misdemeanor, Civil, Eviction, Small Claims, Probate.

## Osceola County

**Real Estate Recording**, Osceola County Recorder, Courthouse, 300 7th Street, Sibley, IA 51249-1695. 712-754-3345 (CST) 8AM-4:30PM.

**3rd District Court**, Courthouse Criminal Records, Sibley, IA 51249. 712-754-3595 (CST) 8AM-4:30PM. Felony, Misdemeanor, Civil, Eviction, Small Claims, Probate.

## Page County

**Real Estate Recording**, Page County Recorder, 112 S. Main St. St., Courthouse, Clarinda, IA 51632. 712-542-3130 (CST) 8AM-4:30PM.

**4th District Court**, 112 E Main Box 263, Clarinda, IA 51632. 712-542-3214 (CST) 8AM-4:30PM. Felony, Misdemeanor, Civil, Eviction, Small Claims, Probate.

## Palo Alto County

**Real Estate Recording**, Palo Alto County Recorder, 1010 Broadway, Emmetsburg, IA 50536. 712-852-3701 (CST) 8AM-4PM.

**3rd District Court**, PO Box 387, Emmetsburg, IA 50536. 712-852-3603 (CST) 8AM-4:30PM. Felony, Misdemeanor, Civil, Eviction, Small Claims, Probate.

## Plymouth County

**Real Estate Recording**, Plymouth County Recorder, Courthouse, 3rd Ave & 2nd Street SE, Le Mars, IA 51031. 712-546-4020 (CST) 8AM-5PM.

**3rd District Court**, Courthouse, Le Mars, IA 51031. 712-546-4215 (CST) 8AM-4PM. Felony, Misdemeanor, Civil, Eviction, Small Claims, Probate.

## Pocahontas County

**Real Estate Recording**, Pocahontas County Recorder, 99 Court Square, Pocahontas, IA 50574-1621. 712-335-4404 (CST) 8AM-4PM.

**2nd District Court**, Courthouse, Pocahontas, IA 50574. 712-335-4208 (CST) 8AM-4:30PM. Felony, Misdemeanor, Civil, Eviction, Small Claims, Probate.

## Polk County

**Real Estate Recording**, Polk County Recorder, 111 Court Avenue, County Administration Building, Des Moines, IA 50309. 515-286-3160 (CST) 8AM-4:30PM.

**5th District Court**, 5th & Mulberry Rm 210, Des Moines, IA 50309. 515-286-3765 (CST) 8AM-4:30PM. Felony, Misdemeanor, Civil, Eviction, Small Claims, Probate.

## Pottawattamie County

**Real Estate Recording**, Pottawattamie County Recorder, 227 South Sixth Street, Council Bluffs, IA 51501. 712-328-5612 (CST) 8AM-4PM.

**4th District Court**, 227 S 6th St, Council Bluffs, IA 51501. 712-328-5604 (CST) 9AM-4:30PM. Felony, Misdemeanor, Civil, Eviction, Small Claims, Probate.

## Poweshiek County

**Real Estate Recording**, Poweshiek County Recorder, 302 East Main Street, Montezuma, IA 50171. 515-623-5434 (CST) 8AM-4PM.

**8th District Court**, PO Box 218, Montezuma, IA 50171. 515-623-5644 (CST) 8AM-4:30PM. Felony, Misdemeanor, Civil, Eviction, Small Claims, Probate.

## Ringgold County

**Real Estate Recording**, Ringgold County Recorder, Courthouse, Mount Ayr, IA 50854-1641. 515-464-3231 (CST) 8AM-4PM.

**5th District Court**, 109 W Madison (PO Box 523), Mount Ayr, IA 50854. 515-464-3234 (CST) 8AM-4:30PM. Felony, Misdemeanor, Civil, Eviction, Small Claims, Probate.

## Sac County

**Real Estate Recording**, Sac County Recorder, Main & State Streets, Courthouse, Sac City, IA 50583. 712-662-7789 (CST) 8AM-4:30PM.

**2nd District Court**, PO Box 368, SAC City, IA 50583. 712-662-7791 (CST) 8AM-4:30PM. Felony, Misdemeanor, Civil, Eviction, Small Claims, Probate.

## Scott County

**Real Estate Recording**, Scott County Recorder, 416 West 4th Street, Davenport, IA 52801. 319-326-8621 (CST) 8AM-5PM.

**7th District Court**, 416 W 4th St, Davenport, IA 52801. 319-326-8784 (CST) 8AM-4:30PM. Felony, Misdemeanor, Civil, Eviction, Small Claims, Probate.

## Shelby County

**Real Estate Recording**, Shelby County Recorder, 612 Court Street, Harlan, IA 51537. 712-755-5640 (CST) 8AM-4:30PM.

**4th District Court**, PO Box 431, Harlan, IA 51537. 712-755-5543 (CST) 8AM-4:30PM. Felony, Misdemeanor, Civil, Eviction, Small Claims, Probate.

## Sioux County

**Real Estate Recording**, Sioux County Recorder, 210 Central Avenue SW, Courthouse, Orange City, IA 51041. 712-737-2229 (CST) 8AM-4:30PM.

**3rd District Court**, PO Box 40, Courthouse, Orange City, IA 51041. 712-737-2286 (CST) 8AM-4:30PM. Felony, Misdemeanor, Civil, Eviction, Small Claims, Probate.

## Story County

**Real Estate Recording**, Story County Recorder, 900 6th Street, Courthouse, Nevada, IA 50201. 515-382-6581 (CST) X230 8AM-5PM (No recording after 4:30PM).

**2nd District Court**, PO Box 408, Nevada, IA 50201. 515-382-6581 (CST) 8AM-4:30PM. Felony, Misdemeanor, Civil, Eviction, Small Claims, Probate.

## Tama County

**Real Estate Recording**, Tama County Recorder, High Street, Toledo, IA 52342. 515-484-3320 (CST) 8AM-4:30PM.

**6th District Court**, PO Box 306, Toledo, IA 52342. 515-484-3721 (CST) 8AM-4:30PM. Felony, Misdemeanor, Civil, Eviction, Small Claims, Probate.

## Taylor County

**Real Estate Recording**, Taylor County Recorder, Court Street, Courthouse, Bedford, IA 50833. 712-523-2275 (CST)

**5th District Court**, Courthouse, Bedford, IA 50833. 712-523-2095 (CST) 8AM-4:30PM. Felony, Misdemeanor, Civil, Eviction, Small Claims, Probate.

## Union County

**Real Estate Recording**, Union County Recorder, 301 North Pine Street, Creston, IA 50801. 515-782-7616 (CST) 8AM-4:30PM.

**5th District Court**, Courthouse, Creston, IA 50801. 515-782-7315 (CST) 8AM-4:30PM. Felony, Misdemeanor, Civil, Eviction, Small Claims, Probate.

## Van Buren County

**Real Estate Recording**, Van Buren County Recorder, Dodge Street, Keosauqua, IA 52565. 319-293-3240 (CST) 8AM-4:30PM.

**8th District Court**, Courthouse Criminal Records, Keosauqua, IA 52565. 319-293-3108 (CST) 8AM-4:30PM. Felony, Misdemeanor, Civil, Eviction, Small Claims, Probate.

## Wapello County

**Real Estate Recording**, Wapello County Recorder, 101 West 4th Street, Ottumwa, IA 52501. 515-683-0045 (CST) 8AM-4:30PM.

**8th District Court**, Courthouse, Ottumwa, IA 52501. 515-683-0060 (CST) 8AM-3:30PM. Felony, Misdemeanor, Civil, Eviction, Small Claims, Probate.

## Warren County

**Real Estate Recording**, Warren County Recorder, Courthouse, Town Square, Indianola, IA 50125. 515-961-1089 (CST) 8AM-4:30PM.

**5th District Court**, PO Box 379, Indianola, IA 50125. 515-961-1033 (CST) 8AM-4:30PM. Felony, Misdemeanor, Civil, Eviction, Small Claims, Probate.

## Washington County

**Real Estate Recording**, Washington County Recorder, 224 West Main St., Washington, IA 52353. 319-653-7727 (CST) 8AM-4:30PM.

**8th District Court**, PO Box 391, Washington, IA 52353. 319-653-7741 (CST) 8AM-4:30PM. Felony, Misdemeanor, Civil, Eviction, Small Claims, Probate.

## Wayne County

**Real Estate Recording**, Wayne County Recorder, Junction of Highway 2 and 14, Courthouse, Corydon, IA 50060. 515-872-1676 (CST) 8AM-4PM.

**5th District Court**, PO Box 424, Corydon, IA 50060. 515-872-2264 (CST) 8AM-4:30PM. Felony, Misdemeanor, Civil, Eviction, Small Claims, Probate.

## Webster County

**Real Estate Recording**, Webster County Recorder, 701 Central Avenue, Courthouse, Fort Dodge, IA 50501. 515-576-2401 (CST)

**2nd District Court**, 701 Central Ave, Courthouse, Ft Dodge, IA 50501. 515-576-7115 (CST) 8:30AM-3:30PM. Felony, Misdemeanor, Civil, Eviction, Small Claims, Probate.

## Winnebago County

**Real Estate Recording**, Winnebago County Recorder, 126 South Clark Street, Courthouse, Forest City, IA 50436. 515-582-2094 (CST) 8AM-4:30PM.

**2nd District Court**, 126 W Clark, Forest City, IA 50436. 515-582-4520 (CST) 8AM-4:30PM. Felony, Misdemeanor, Civil, Eviction, Small Claims, Probate.

## Winneshiek County

**Real Estate Recording**, Winneshiek County Recorder, 201 West Main Street, Decorah, IA 52101. 319-382-3486 (CST) 8AM-4PM.

**1st District Court**, 201 W Main St, Decorah, IA 52101. 319-382-2469 (CST) 8AM-4:30PM. Felony, Misdemeanor, Civil, Eviction, Small Claims, Probate.

## Woodbury County

**Real Estate Recording**, Woodbury County Recorder, 7th & Douglas Street, Courthouse Room 106, Sioux City, IA 51101. 712-279-6528 (CST) 8AM-4:30PM.

**3rd District Court**, 620 Douglas St, Sioux City, IA 51101. 712-279-6616 (CST) 7:30AM-4:30PM. Felony, Misdemeanor, Civil, Eviction, Small Claims, Probate.

**3rd District Court**, 407 7th St, Sioux City, IA 51101. 712-279-6624 (CST) 8AM-4:30PM. Felony, Misdemeanor, Civil, Eviction, Small Claims, Probate.

## Worth County

**Real Estate Recording**, Worth County Recorder, 1000 Central Avenue, Northwood, IA 50459. 515-324-2734 (CST) 8AM-4PM.

**2nd District Court**, PO Box 172, Courthouse, Northwood, IA 50459. 515-324-2840 (CST) 8AM-4:30PM. Felony, Misdemeanor, Civil, Eviction, Small Claims, Probate.

## Wright County

**Real Estate Recording**, Wright County Recorder, 115 North Main, Courthouse, Clarion, IA 50525. 515-532-3204 (CST) 8AM-4PM.

**2nd District Court**, PO Box 306, Clarion, IA 50525. 515-532-3113 (CST) 8AM-4:30PM. Felony, Misdemeanor, Civil, Eviction, Small Claims, Probate.

# Kansas

## Allen County

**Real Estate Recording**, Allen County Register of Deeds, 1 North Washington, Courthouse, Iola, KS 66749. 316-365-1412 (CST) 8AM-5PM.

**District Court**, PO Box 630, Iola, KS 66749. 316-365-1425 (CST) 8:30AM-4PM. Felony, Misdemeanor, Civil, Eviction, Small Claims, Probate.

## Anderson County

**Real Estate Recording**, Anderson County Register of Deeds, Courthouse, 100 E. 4th Street, Garnett, KS 66032-1503. 913-448-3715 (CST) 8AM-5PM.

**District Court**, PO Box 305, Garnett, KS 66032. 913-448-6886 (CST) 8:30-4PM. Felony, Misdemeanor, Civil, Eviction, Small Claims, Probate.

## Atchison County

**Real Estate Recording**, Atchison County Register of Deeds, 423 North 5th St., Courthouse, Atchison, KS 66002-1861. 913-367-2568 (CST) 8:30AM-5PM.

**District Court**, PO Box 408, Atchison, KS 66002. 913-367-7400 (CST) 8:30AM-5PM. Felony, Misdemeanor, Civil, Eviction, Small Claims, Probate.

## Barber County

**Real Estate Recording**, Barber County Register of Deeds, 120 East Washington Street, Courthouse, Medicine Lodge, KS 67104. 316-886-3981 (CST) 8:30AM-5PM.

**District Court**, PO Box 329, Medicine Lodge, KS 67104. 316-886-5639 (CST) 8:30AM-12PM-1PM-5PM. Felony, Misdemeanor, Civil, Eviction, Small Claims, Probate.

## Barton County

**Real Estate Recording**, Barton County Register of Deeds, 1400 Main Street, Courthouse, Great Bend, KS 67530-4037. 316-793-1849 (CST) 8AM-5PM.

**District Court**, 1400 N Main, Rm 306, Great Bend, KS 67530. 316-793-1856 (CST) 8:30AM-5PM. Felony, Misdemeanor, Civil, Eviction, Small Claims, Probate.

## Bourbon County

**Real Estate Recording**, Bourbon County Register of Deeds, 210 South National, Fort Scott, KS 66701. 316-223-3800 (CST) X24 8:30AM-4:30PM.

**District Court**, PO Box 868, Ft Scott, KS 66701. 316-223-0780 (CST) 8:30AM-4:30PM. Felony, Misdemeanor, Civil, Eviction, Small Claims, Probate.

## Brown County

**Real Estate Recording**, Brown County Register of Deeds, Courthouse, 601 Oregon, Hiawatha, KS 66434. 913-742-3741 (CST) 8AM-5PM.

**District Court**, PO Box 417, Hiawatha, KS 66434. 913-742-7481 (CST) 8:30AM-5PM. Felony, Misdemeanor, Civil, Eviction, Small Claims, Probate.

## Butler County

**Real Estate Recording**, Butler County Register of Deeds, 205 West Central, Courthouse, Suite 104, El Dorado, KS 67042. 316-321-5750 (CST) 8AM-5PM.

**District Court**, PO Box 1367, El Dorado, KS 67042. 316-321-1200 (CST) 8:30AM-5PM. Felony, Misdemeanor, Civil, Eviction, Small Claims, Probate.

## Chase County

**Real Estate Recording**, Chase County Register of Deeds, Courthouse Plaza, Cottonwood Falls, KS 66845. 316-273-6398 (CST) 8AM-5PM.

**District Court**, PO Box 207, Cottonwood Falls, KS 66845. 316-273-6319 (CST) 8:30AM-5PM. Felony, Misdemeanor, Civil, Eviction, Small Claims, Probate.

## Chautauqua County

**Real Estate Recording**, Chautauqua County Register of Deeds, 215 North Chautauqua, Courthouse, Sedan, KS 67361. 316-725-5830 (CST) 8AM-Noon,1-4PM.

**District Court**, 215 N Chautauqua, Sedan, KS 67361. 316-725-5870 (CST) 8AM-4PM. Felony, Misdemeanor, Civil, Eviction, Small Claims, Probate.

## Cherokee County

**Real Estate Recording**, Cherokee County Register of Deeds, 100 West Maple, Courthouse, Columbus, KS 66725. 316-429-3777 (CST) 9AM-5PM.

**District Court**, PO Box 189, Columbus, KS 66725. 316-429-3880 (CST) 8:30AM-5PM. Felony, Misdemeanor, Civil, Eviction, Small Claims, Probate.

## Cheyenne County

**Real Estate Recording**, Cheyenne County Register of Deeds, 212 East Washington, St. Francis, KS 67756. 913-332-8820 (CST) 8AM-Noon,1-5PM.

**District Court**, PO Box 646, St Francis, KS 67756. 913-332-8850 (CST) 8:30AM-12PM-1PM-5PM. Felony, Misdemeanor, Civil, Eviction, Small Claims, Probate.

## Clark County

**Real Estate Recording**, Clark County Register of Deeds, Courthouse, 913 Highland, Ashland, KS 67831. 316-635-2812 (CST) 8:30AM-Noon, 1PM-4:30PM.

**District Court**, PO Box 790, Ashland, KS 67831. 316-635-2753 (CST) 8:30AM-5PM. Felony, Misdemeanor, Civil, Eviction, Small Claims, Probate.

## Clay County

**Real Estate Recording**, Clay County Register of Deeds, Courthouse Square, Clay Center, KS 67432. 913-632-3811 (CST) 8AM-5PM.

**District Court**, PO Box 203, Clay Center, KS 67432. 913-632-3443 (CST) 8:30AM-5PM. Felony, Misdemeanor, Civil, Eviction, Small Claims, Probate.

## Cloud County

**Real Estate Recording**, Cloud County Register of Deeds, 811 Washington Street, Concordia, KS 66901. 913-243-8121 (CST) 8AM-4:30PM.

**District Court**, 811 Washington, Concordia, KS 66901. 913-243-8124 (CST) 8:30AM-5PM. Felony, Misdemeanor, Civil, Eviction, Small Claims, Probate.

## Coffey County

**Real Estate Recording**, Coffey County Register of Deeds, Courthouse, Room 205, 110 S. 6th St., Burlington, KS 66839. 316-364-2423 (CST) 8AM-5PM.

**District Court**, PO Box 330, Burlington, KS 66839. 316-364-8628 (CST) 8:30AM-4PM. Felony, Misdemeanor, Civil, Eviction, Small Claims, Probate.

## Comanche County

**Real Estate Recording**, Comanche County Register of Deeds, 201 South New York, Courthouse, Coldwater, KS 67029. 316-582-2152 (CST) 9AM-Noon,1-5PM.

**District Court**, PO Box 722, Coldwater, KS 67029. 316-582-2182 (CST) 8:30AM-5PM. Felony, Misdemeanor, Civil, Eviction, Small Claims, Probate.

## Cowley County

**Real Estate Recording**, Cowley County Register of Deeds, 311 East 9th, Courthouse, Winfield, KS 67156. 316-221-5461 (CST) 8AM-Noon,1-5PM.

**Arkansas City District Court**, PO Box 1152, Arkansas City, KS 67005. 316-441-4520 (CST) 8:30AM-12PM-1PM-4PM. Felony, Misdemeanor, Civil, Eviction, Small Claims, Probate.

**Winfield District Court**, PO Box 472, Winfield, KS 67156. 316-221-5470 (CST) 8:30AM-12PM-1PM-4PM. Felony, Misdemeanor, Civil, Eviction, Small Claims, Probate.

## Crawford County

**Real Estate Recording**, Crawford County Register of Deeds, Courthouse, Girard, KS 66743. 316-724-8218 (CST) 8:30AM-4:30PM.

**Girard District Court**, PO Box 69, Girard, KS 66743. 316-724-6211 (CST) 8:30AM-12PM-1PM-5PM. Felony, Misdemeanor, Civil, Eviction, Small Claims, Probate.

## Decatur County

**Real Estate Recording**, Decatur County Register of Deeds, 194 South Penn, Courthouse, Oberlin, KS 67749. 913-475-8105 (CST) 8AM-Noon,1-5PM.

**District Court**, PO Box 89, Oberlin, KS 67749. 913-475-8107 (CST) 8:30AM-5PM. Felony, Misdemeanor, Civil, Eviction, Small Claims, Probate.

## Dickinson County

**Real Estate Recording**, Dickinson County Register of Deeds, First & Buckeye, Courthouse, Abilene, KS 67410. 913-263-3073 (CST) 8AM-5PM.

**District Court**, PO Box 127, Abilene, KS 67410. 913-263-3142 (CST) 8:30AM-5PM. Felony, Misdemeanor, Civil, Eviction, Small Claims, Probate.

## Doniphan County

**Real Estate Recording**, Doniphan County Register of Deeds, Courthouse, Troy, KS 66087. 913-985-3932 (CST) 8:30AM-5PM.

**District Court**, PO Box 295, Troy, KS 66087. 913-985-3582 (CST) 8:30AM-5PM. Felony, Misdemeanor, Civil, Eviction, Small Claims, Probate.

## Douglas County

**Real Estate Recording**, Douglas County Register of Deeds, 1100 Massachusetts, Courthouse, Lawrence, KS 66044-3097. 913-841-7700 (CST) 8AM-5PM.

**District Court**, 111 E 11th St Rm 144, Lawrence, KS 66044. 913-841-7700 (CST) 9AM-5PM. Felony, Misdemeanor, Civil, Eviction, Small Claims, Probate.

## Edwards County

**Real Estate Recording**, Edwards County Register of Deeds, 312 Massachusetts, Courthouse, Kinsley, KS 67547. 316-659-3131 (CST) 8AM-5PM.

**District Court**, PO Box 232, Kinsley, KS 67547. 316-659-2442 (CST) 8:30AM-5PM. Felony, Misdemeanor, Civil, Eviction, Small Claims, Probate.

## Elk County

**Real Estate Recording**, Elk County Register of Deeds, Court House, 127 N. Pine, Howard, KS 67349. 316-374-2472 (CST) 8AM-4:30PM.

**District Court**, PO Box 306, Howard, KS 67349. 316-374-2370 (CST) 8:30AM-4:30PM. Felony, Misdemeanor, Civil, Eviction, Small Claims, Probate.

## Ellis County

**Real Estate Recording**, Ellis County Register of Deeds, 1204 Fort Street, Hays, KS 67601. 913-628-9450 (CST) 8AM-5PM.

**District Court**, PO Box 8, Hays, KS 67601. 913-628-9415 (CST) 8:30AM-4:30PM. Felony, Misdemeanor, Civil, Eviction, Small Claims, Probate.

## Ellsworth County

**Real Estate Recording**, Ellsworth County Register of Deeds, 210 N. Kansas, Courthouse, Ellsworth, KS 67439-3118. 913-472-3022 (CST) 8AM-Noon,1-5PM.

**District Court**, 210 N Kansas, Ellsworth, KS 67439-3118. 913-472-3832 (CST) 8:30AM-5PM. Felony, Misdemeanor, Civil, Eviction, Small Claims, Probate.

## Finney County

**Real Estate Recording**, Finney County Register of Deeds, 425 North Eighth Street, Courthouse, Garden City, KS 67846. 316-272-3520 (CST) 9AM-5PM.

**District Court**, PO Box 798, Garden City, KS 67846. 316-272-3534 (CST) 8:30AM-4:30PM. Felony, Misdemeanor, Civil, Eviction, Small Claims, Probate.

## Ford County

**Real Estate Recording**, Ford County Register of Deeds, 100 Gunsmoke, Ford County Government Center, Dodge City, KS 67801. 316-227-4565 (CST) 9AM-5PM.

**District Court**, 101 W Spruce, Dodge City, KS 67801. 316-227-4610 (CST) 9AM-5PM. Felony, Misdemeanor, Civil, Eviction, Small Claims, Probate.

## Franklin County

**Real Estate Recording**, Franklin County Register of Deeds, 315 South Main, Courthouse, Room 103, Ottawa, KS 66067-2335. 913-242-1415 (CST) 8AM-4:30PM.

**District Court**, PO Box 637, Ottawa, KS 66067. 913-242-6000 (CST) 8:30AM-4PM. Felony, Misdemeanor, Civil, Eviction, Small Claims, Probate.

## Geary County

**Real Estate Recording**, Geary County Register of Deeds, 139 East 8th, County Office Building, Junction City, KS 66441-2591. 913-238-5531 (CST) 8:30AM-5PM.

**District Court**, PO Box 1147, Junction City, KS 66441. 913-762-5221 (CST) 8:30AM-4:30PM. Felony, Misdemeanor, Civil, Eviction, Small Claims, Probate.

## Gove County

**Real Estate Recording**, Gove County Register of Deeds, 520 Washington Street, Courthouse, Gove, KS 67736. 913-938-4465 (CST) 8AM-Noon, 1PM-5PM.

**District Court**, PO Box 97, Gove, KS 67736. 913-938-2310 (CST) 8AM-5PM. Felony, Misdemeanor, Civil, Eviction, Small Claims, Probate.

## Graham County

**Real Estate Recording**, Graham County Register of Deeds, 410 North Pomeroy, Hill City, KS 67642. 913-674-2551 (CST) 8:30AM-5PM.

**District Court**, 410 N Pomeroy, Hill City, KS 67642. 913-674-3458 (CST) 8:30AM-5PM. Felony, Misdemeanor, Civil, Eviction, Small Claims, Probate.

## Grant County

**Real Estate Recording**, Grant County Register of Deeds, 108 South Glenn, Courthouse, Ulysses, KS 67880. 316-356-1538 (CST) 9AM-5PM.

**District Court**, 108 S Glenn, Ulysses, KS 67880. 316-356-1526 (CST) 8:30AM-5PM. Felony, Misdemeanor, Civil, Eviction, Small Claims, Probate.

## Gray County

**Real Estate Recording**, Gray County Register of Deeds, 300 South Main, Courthouse, Cimarron, KS 67835. 316-855-3835 (CST) 8AM-5PM.

**District Court**, PO Box 487, Cimarron, KS 67835. 316-855-3812 (CST) 8:30AM-5PM. Felony, Misdemeanor, Civil, Eviction, Small Claims, Probate.

## Greeley County

**Real Estate Recording**, Greeley County Register of Deeds, 616 Second Street, Courthouse, Tribune, KS 67879. 316-376-4275 (MST) 9AM-5PM.

**District Court**, PO Box 516, Tribune, KS 67879. 316-376-4292 (MST) 9AM-12PM-1PM-5PM. Felony, Misdemeanor, Civil, Eviction, Small Claims, Probate.

## Greenwood County

**Real Estate Recording**, Greenwood County Register of Deeds, Courthouse, 311 N. Main, Eureka, KS 67045-1311. 316-583-6021 (CST) 8AM-5PM.

**District Court**, 311 N Main, Eureka, KS 67045. 316-583-8153 (CST) 8:30AM-5PM. Felony, Misdemeanor, Civil, Eviction, Small Claims, Probate.

## Hamilton County

**Real Estate Recording**, Hamilton County Register of Deeds, 219 North Main, Courthouse, Syracuse, KS 67878. 316-384-6925 (MST) 8AM-12, 12:30PM-4:30PM.

**District Court**, PO Box 745, Syracuse, KS 67878. 316-384-5159 (MST) 8:30AM-4:30PM. Felony, Misdemeanor, Civil, Eviction, Small Claims, Probate.

## Harper County

**Real Estate Recording**, Harper County Register of Deeds, Courthouse, 201 North Jennings, Anthony, KS 67003. 316-842-5336 (CST) 8AM-Noon,1-5PM.

**District Court**, PO Box 467, Anthony, KS 67003. 316-842-3721 (CST) 8:30AM-5PM. Felony, Misdemeanor, Civil, Eviction, Small Claims, Probate.

## Harvey County

**Real Estate Recording**, Harvey County Register of Deeds, 8th & Main, Courthouse, Newton, KS 67114. 316-284-6949 (CST) 8AM-5PM.

**District Court**, PO Box 665, Newton, KS 67114-0665. 316-284-6894 (CST) 8:30AM-5PM. Felony, Misdemeanor, Civil, Eviction, Small Claims, Probate.

## Haskell County

**Real Estate Recording**, Haskell County Register of Deeds, 300 S. Inman, Courthouse, Sublette, KS 67877. 316-675-8343 (CST) 9AM-Noon,1-5PM.

**District Court**, PO Box 146, Sublette, KS 67877. 316-675-2671 (CST) 8:30AM-5PM. Felony, Misdemeanor, Civil, Eviction, Small Claims, Probate.

## Hodgeman County

**Real Estate Recording**, Hodgeman County Register of Deeds, Main Street, Courthouse, Jetmore, KS 67854. 316-357-8536 (CST)

**District Court**, PO Box 187, Jetmore, KS 67854. 316-357-6522 (CST) 8:30AM-5PM. Felony, Misdemeanor, Civil, Eviction, Small Claims, Probate.

# Kansas

## Jackson County

**Real Estate Recording**, Jackson County Register of Deeds, Courthouse, Room 203, Holton, KS 66436. 913-364-3591 (CST) 8AM-4:30PM.

**District Court**, PO Box 1026, Holton, KS 66436. 913-364-2191 (CST) 8AM-4:30PM. Felony, Misdemeanor, Civil, Eviction, Small Claims, Probate.

## Jefferson County

**Real Estate Recording**, Jefferson County Register of Deeds, 310 Jefferson Street, Courthouse, Oskaloosa, KS 66066. 913-863-2243 (CST) M 8AM-6:30PM; T-F 8AM-4PM.

**District Court**, PO box 327, Oskaloosa, KS 66066. 913-863-2461 (CST) 8AM-4:30PM. Felony, Misdemeanor, Civil, Eviction, Small Claims, Probate.

## Jewell County

**Real Estate Recording**, Jewell County Register of Deeds, 307 North Commercial Street, Courthouse, Mankato, KS 66956-2093. 913-378-4070 (CST) 8:30AM-Noon, 1-4:30PM.

**District Court**, 307 N Commercial, Mankato, KS 66956. 913-378-3651 (CST) 8:30AM-4:30PM. Felony, Misdemeanor, Civil, Eviction, Small Claims, Probate.

## Johnson County

**Real Estate Recording**, Johnson County Register of Deeds, 111 South Cherry St., Suite 1300, Johnson County Administration Bldg., Olathe, KS 66061. 913-764-8484 (CST) X5375 8AM-5PM.

**District Court**, 100 N Kansas, Olathe, KS 66061. 913-782-5000 (CST) 8:30AM-5PM. Felony, Misdemeanor, Civil, Eviction, Small Claims, Probate.

## Kearny County

**Real Estate Recording**, Kearny County Register of Deeds, 304 North Main, Courthouse, Lakin, KS 67860. 316-355-6241 (MST) 8AM-5PM.

**District Court**, PO Box 64, Lakin, KS 67860. 316-355-6481 (MST) 8:30AM-5PM. Felony, Misdemeanor, Civil, Eviction, Small Claims, Probate.

## Kingman County

**Real Estate Recording**, Kingman County Register of Deeds, 130 North Spruce, Kingman, KS 67068. 316-532-3211 (CST) 8AM-Noon,1-5PM.

**District Court**, PO Box 495, Kingman, KS 67068. 316-532-5151 (CST) 8:30AM-5PM. Felony, Misdemeanor, Civil, Eviction, Small Claims, Probate.

## Kiowa County

**Real Estate Recording**, Kiowa County Register of Deeds, 211 East Florida, Greensburg, KS 67054. 316-723-2441 (CST) 8:30AM-Noon, 1-5PM.

**District Court**, 211 E Florida, Greensburg, KS 67054. 316-723-3317 (CST) 8:30AM-5PM. Felony, Misdemeanor, Civil, Eviction, Small Claims, Probate.

## Labette County

**Real Estate Recording**, Labette County Register of Deeds, Courthouse, 521 Merchant, Oswego, KS 67356. 316-795-4931 (CST) 8:30AM-5PM.

**District Court**, Courthouse, Oswego, KS 67356. 316-795-4533 (CST) 8:30AM-5PM. Felony, Misdemeanor, Civil, Eviction, Small Claims, Probate.

## Lane County

**Real Estate Recording**, Lane County Register of Deeds, 144 South Lane, Courthouse, Dighton, KS 67839. 316-397-2803 (CST) 8AM-Noon,1-5PM.

**District Court**, PO Box 188, Dighton, KS 67839. 316-397-2805 (CST) 8:30AM-5PM. Felony, Misdemeanor, Civil, Eviction, Small Claims, Probate.

## Leavenworth County

**Real Estate Recording**, Leavenworth County Register of Deeds, 4th & Walnut, Courthouse, Leavenworth, KS 66048. 913-684-0424 (CST) 8AM-5PM.

**District Court**, 4th & Walnut, Leavenworth, KS 66048. 913-684-0713 (CST) 8:30AM-5PM. Felony, Misdemeanor, Civil, Eviction, Small Claims, Probate.

## Lincoln County

**Real Estate Recording**, Lincoln County Register of Deeds, 216 East Lincoln, Lincoln, KS 67455-2056. 913-524-4657 (CST) 8AM-Noon,1-5PM.

**District Court**, 216 E Lincoln Ave, Lincoln, KS 67455. 913-524-4057 (CST) 8:30AM-5PM. Felony, Misdemeanor, Civil, Eviction, Small Claims, Probate.

## Linn County

**Real Estate Recording**, Linn County Register of Deeds, Courthouse, 315 Main Street, Mound City, KS 66056. 913-795-2226 (CST) 8AM-Noon, 12:30PM-4:30PM.

**District Court**, PO Box 350, Mound City, KS 66056-0350. 913-795-2660 (CST) 8AM-4:30PM. Felony, Misdemeanor, Civil, Eviction, Small Claims, Probate.

## Logan County

**Real Estate Recording**, Logan County Register of Deeds, 710 West 2nd Street, Courthouse, Oakley, KS 67748. 913-672-4224 (CST) 8AM-Noon,1-5PM.

**District Court**, 710 W 2nd St, Oakley, KS 67748. 913-672-3654 (CST) 8:30AM-12PM-1PM-5PM. Felony, Misdemeanor, Civil, Eviction, Small Claims, Probate.

## Lyon County

**Real Estate Recording**, Lyon County Register of Deeds, 402 Commercial Street, Emporia, KS 66801. 316-341-3241 (CST) 8AM-5PM.

**District Court**, 402 Commercial St, Emporia, KS 66801. 316-342-4950 (CST) 8:30AM-4:30PM. Felony, Misdemeanor, Civil, Eviction, Small Claims, Probate.

## Marion County

**Real Estate Recording**, Marion County Register of Deeds, Courthouse Square, Marion, KS 66861. 316-382-2151 (CST) 8:30AM-5PM.

**District Court**, PO Box 298, Marion, KS 66861. 316-382-2104 (CST) 8:30AM-5PM. Felony, Misdemeanor, Civil, Eviction, Small Claims, Probate.

## Marshall County

**Real Estate Recording**, Marshall County Register of Deeds, 1201 Broadway, Courthouse, Marysville, KS 66508. 913-562-3226 (CST) 8:30AM-5PM.

**District Court**, PO Box 86, Marysville, KS 66508. 913-562-5301 (CST) 8:30AM-5PM. Felony, Misdemeanor, Civil, Eviction, Small Claims, Probate.

## McPherson County

**Real Estate Recording**, McPherson County Register of Deeds, 119 North Maple, Courthouse, McPherson, KS 67460. 316-241-5050 (CST) 8AM-5PM.

**District Court**, PO Box 1106, McPherson, KS 67460. 316-241-3422 (CST) 8:30AM-5PM. Felony, Misdemeanor, Civil, Eviction, Small Claims, Probate.

## Meade County

**Real Estate Recording**, Meade County Register of Deeds, 200 North Fowler, Courthouse, Meade, KS 67864. 316-873-8705 (CST) 8AM-5PM.

**District Court**, PO Box 623, Meade, KS 67864. 316-873-8750 (CST) 8:30AM-5PM. Felony, Misdemeanor, Civil, Eviction, Small Claims, Probate.

## Miami County

**Real Estate Recording**, Miami County Register of Deeds, 120 South Pearl, Courthouse, Paola, KS 66071. 913-294-3716 (CST) 8AM-4:30PM.

**District Court**, PO Box 187, Paola, KS 66071. 913-294-3326 (CST) 8AM-4:30PM. Felony, Misdemeanor, Civil, Eviction, Small Claims, Probate.

## Mitchell County

**Real Estate Recording**, Mitchell County Register of Deeds, 11 South Hersey, Courthouse, Beloit, KS 67420. 913-738-3854 (CST) 8:30AM-5PM.

**District Court**, 115 S Hersey, Beloit, KS 67420. 913-738-3753 (CST) 8:30AM-5PM. Felony, Misdemeanor, Civil, Eviction, Small Claims, Probate.

## Montgomery County

**Real Estate Recording**, Montgomery County Register of Deeds, 5th & Main, Courthouse, Independence, KS 67301. 316-331-2180 (CST) 8:30AM-5PM.

**Coffeyville District Court**, PO Box 409, Coffeyville, KS 67337. 316-251-1060 (CST) 8:30AM-4PM. Felony, Misdemeanor, Civil, Eviction, Small Claims, Probate.

**Independence District Court**, PO Box 768, Independence, KS 67301. 316-331-2550 (CST)

8:30AM-4PM. Felony, Misdemeanor, Civil, Eviction, Small Claims, Probate.

## Morris County

**Real Estate Recording**, Morris County Register of Deeds, Courthouse, Council Grove, KS 66846. 316-767-5614 (CST) 8AM-5PM.

**District Court**, County Courthouse, Council Grove, KS 66846. 316-767-6838 (CST) 8:30AM-5PM. Felony, Misdemeanor, Civil, Eviction, Small Claims, Probate.

## Morton County

**Real Estate Recording**, Morton County Register of Deeds, 1025 Morton, Courthouse, Elkhart, KS 67950. 316-697-2561 (CST) 9AM-5PM.

**District Court**, PO Box 825, Elkhart, KS 67950. 316-697-2563 (CST) 8AM-5PM. Felony, Misdemeanor, Civil, Eviction, Small Claims, Probate.

## Nemaha County

**Real Estate Recording**, Nemaha County Register of Deeds, 607 Nemaha, Courthouse, Seneca, KS 66538. 913-336-2120 (CST) 8AM-4:30PM.

**District Court**, PO Box 213, Seneca, KS 66538. 913-336-2146 (CST) 8:30AM-5PM. Felony, Misdemeanor, Civil, Eviction, Small Claims, Probate.

## Neosho County

**Real Estate Recording**, Neosho County Register of Deeds, 100 Main, Courthouse, Erie, KS 66733. 316-244-3858 (CST) 8AM-4:30PM.

**Chanute District Court**, 102 S Lincoln, Chanute, KS 66720. 316-431-5700 (CST) Felony, Misdemeanor, Civil, Eviction, Small Claims, Probate.

**Erie District Court**, Neosho County Courthouse, Erie, KS 66733. 316-244-3391 (CST) 8AM-4:30PM. Felony, Misdemeanor, Civil, Eviction, Small Claims, Probate.

## Ness County

**Real Estate Recording**, Ness County Register of Deeds, 202 West Sycamore, Courthouse, Ness City, KS 67560. 913-798-3127 (CST) 8AM-Noon, 1PM-5PM.

**District Court**, PO Box 445, Ness City, KS 67560. 913-798-3693 (CST) 8:30AM-12PM-1PM-5PM. Felony, Misdemeanor, Civil, Eviction, Small Claims, Probate.

## Norton County

**Real Estate Recording**, Norton County Register of Deeds, Courthouse, Norton, KS 67654. 913-877-5765 (CST) 8AM-12, 1PM-5PM.

**District Court**, PO Box 70, Norton, KS 67654. 913-877-5720 (CST) 8:30AM-5PM. Felony, Misdemeanor, Civil, Eviction, Small Claims, Probate.

## Osage County

**Real Estate Recording**, Osage County Register of Deeds, Courthouse, Lyndon, KS 66451. 913-828-4523 (CST) 8AM-5PM.

**District Court**, PO Box 549, Lyndon, KS 66451. 913-828-4713 (CST) 8:30AM-12PM-1PM-4PM. Felony, Misdemeanor, Civil, Eviction, Small Claims, Probate.

## Osborne County

**Real Estate Recording**, Osborne County Register of Deeds, Courthouse, 423 W. Main, Osborne, KS 67473. 913-346-2452 (CST) 8:30AM-Noon, 1-5PM.

**District Court**, 423 W Main, Osborne, KS 67473. 913-346-5911 (CST) 8:30AM-5PM. Felony, Misdemeanor, Civil, Eviction, Small Claims, Probate.

## Ottawa County

**Real Estate Recording**, Ottawa County Register of Deeds, Courthouse - Suite 220, 307 N. Concord, Minneapolis, KS 67467-2140. 913-392-2078 (CST) 8AM-Noon, 1-5PM.

**District Court**, 307 N Concord, Minneapolis, KS 67467. 913-392-2917 (CST) 8:30AM-5PM. Felony, Misdemeanor, Civil, Eviction, Small Claims, Probate.

## Pawnee County

**Real Estate Recording**, Pawnee County Register of Deeds, Courthouse, 715 Broadway St., Larned, KS 67550-3097. 316-285-3276 (CST) 8:30AM-5PM.

**District Court**, PO Box 270, Larned, KS 67550. 316-285-6937 (CST) 8:30AM-5PM. Felony, Misdemeanor, Civil, Eviction, Small Claims, Probate.

## Phillips County

**Real Estate Recording**, Phillips County Register of Deeds, Courthouse, 301 State St., Phillipsburg, KS 67661. 913-543-6875 (CST) 8AM-5PM.

**District Court**, PO Box 564, Phillipsburg, KS 67661. 913-543-6830 (CST) 8:30AM-5PM. Felony, Misdemeanor, Civil, Eviction, Small Claims, Probate.

## Pottawatomie County

**Real Estate Recording**, Pottawatomie County Register of Deeds, 106 Main, Courthouse, Westmoreland, KS 66549. 913-457-3471 (CST) 8:30AM-4:40PM.

**District Court**, PO Box 129, Westmoreland, KS 66549. 913-457-3392 (CST) 8:30AM-4:30PM. Felony, Misdemeanor, Civil, Eviction, Small Claims, Probate.

## Pratt County

**Real Estate Recording**, Pratt County Register of Deeds, 3rd & Ninnescah, Courthouse, Pratt, KS 67124. 316-672-4140 (CST) 8AM-Noon, 1-5PM.

**District Court**, PO Box 984, Pratt, KS 67124. 316-672-4100 (CST) 8:30AM-5PM. Felony, Misdemeanor, Civil, Eviction, Small Claims, Probate.

## Rawlins County

**Real Estate Recording**, Rawlins County Register of Deeds, 607 Main, Courthouse, Atwood, KS 67730. 913-626-3172 (CST) 9AM-Noon, 1-5PM.

**District Court**, PO Box 257, Atwood, KS 67730. 913-626-3465 (CST) 9AM-5PM. Felony, Misdemeanor, Civil, Eviction, Small Claims, Probate.

## Reno County

**Real Estate Recording**, Reno County Register of Deeds, 206 West First, Hutchinson, KS 67501. 316-694-2942 (CST) 8AM-5PM.

**District Court**, 206 W 1st, Hutchinson, KS 67501. 316-694-2956 (CST) 8:30AM-12PM-1PM-5PM. Felony, Misdemeanor, Civil, Eviction, Small Claims, Probate.

## Republic County

**Real Estate Recording**, Republic County Register of Deeds, Courthouse, Belleville, KS 66935. 913-527-5691 (CST) X224 8AM-5PM.

**District Court**, PO Box 8, Belleville, KS 66935. 913-527-5691 (CST) 8:30AM-5PM. Felony, Misdemeanor, Civil, Eviction, Small Claims, Probate.

## Rice County

**Real Estate Recording**, Rice County Register of Deeds, 101 West Commercial, Lyons, KS 67554. 316-257-2931 (CST) 8:30AM-5PM.

**District Court**, 101 W Commercial, Lyons, KS 67554. 316-257-2383 (CST) 8:30AM-5PM. Felony, Misdemeanor, Civil, Eviction, Small Claims, Probate.

## Riley County

**Real Estate Recording**, Riley County Register of Deeds, 110 Courthouse Plaza, Manhattan, KS 66502-6018. 913-537-6340 (CST) 8AM-5PM.

**District Court**, PO Box 158, Manhattan, KS 66502. 913-537-6364 (CST) 8:30AM-5PM. Felony, Misdemeanor, Civil, Eviction, Small Claims, Probate.

## Rooks County

**Real Estate Recording**, Rooks County Register of Deeds, 115 North Walnut, Stockton, KS 67669. 913-425-6291 (CST) 8AM-Noon, 1-5PM.

**District Court**, 115 N Walnut, Stockton, KS 67669. 913-425-6718 (CST) 8AM-5PM. Felony, Misdemeanor, Civil, Eviction, Small Claims, Probate.

## Rush County

**Real Estate Recording**, Rush County Register of Deeds, 715 Elm, Courthouse, La Crosse, KS 67548. 913-222-3312 (CST) 8:30AM-Noon, 1-5PM.

**District Court**, PO Box 387, La Crosse, KS 67548. 913-222-2718 (CST) 8:30AM-5PM. Felony, Misdemeanor, Civil, Eviction, Small Claims, Probate.

## Russell County

**Real Estate Recording**, Russell County Register of Deeds, 4th & Main, Courthouse, Russell, KS 67665. 913-483-4612 (CST) 8:30AM-5PM.

**District Court**, PO Box 876, Russell, KS 67665. 913-483-5641 (CST) 8:30AM-5PM. Felony, Misdemeanor, Civil, Eviction, Small Claims, Probate.

## Saline County

**Real Estate Recording**, Saline County Register of Deeds, 300 West Ash, City County Build-

# Kansas

ing, Salina, KS 67401. 913-826-6570 (CST) 8AM-5PM.

**District Court**, PO Box 1756, Salina, KS 67402-1756. 913-826-6617 (CST) 8:30AM-4PM. Felony, Misdemeanor, Civil, Eviction, Small Claims, Probate.

## Scott County

**Real Estate Recording**, Scott County Register of Deeds, Courthouse, 303 Court St., Scott City, KS 67871. 316-872-3155 (CST) 8AM-5PM.

**District Court**, 303 Court, Scott City, KS 67871. 316-872-7208 (CST) 8:30AM-12PM-1PM-5PM. Felony, Misdemeanor, Civil, Eviction, Small Claims, Probate.

## Sedgwick County

**Real Estate Recording**, Sedgwick County Register of Deeds, 525 North Main, 4th Floor/room 415, Wichita, KS 67203-3764. 316-383-7425 (CST) 8AM-5PM.

**District Court**, 525 N Main, Wichita, KS 67203. 316-383-7302 (CST) 8AM-5PM. Felony, Misdemeanor, Civil, Eviction, Small Claims, Probate.

## Seward County

**Real Estate Recording**, Seward County Register of Deeds, 415 North Washington, Courthouse, Liberal, KS 67901. 316-626-3220 (CST) 9AM-5PM.

**District Court**, 415 N Washington, Liberal, KS 67901. 316-626-3238 (CST) 8:30AM-5PM. Felony, Misdemeanor, Civil, Eviction, Small Claims, Probate.

## Shawnee County

**Real Estate Recording**, Shawnee County Register of Deeds, 200 East 7th Street, Suite 108, Topeka, KS 66603-3932. 913-233-8200 (CST) X4021 8AM-4:30PM.

**District Court**, 200 E 7th Rm 209, Topeka, KS 66603. 913-233-8200 (CST) 8:30AM-4PM. Felony, Misdemeanor, Civil, Eviction, Small Claims, Probate.

## Sheridan County

**Real Estate Recording**, Sheridan County Register of Deeds, 925 9th Street, Courthouse, Hoxie, KS 67740. 913-675-3741 (CST) 8AM-Noon,1-5PM.

**District Court**, PO Box 753, Hoxie, KS 67740. 913-675-3451 (CST) 8:30AM-5PM. Felony, Misdemeanor, Civil, Eviction, Small Claims, Probate.

## Sherman County

**Real Estate Recording**, Sherman County Register of Deeds, 813 Broadway, Room 104, Goodland, KS 67735-3097. 913-899-4845 (MST) 8AM-Noon,1-5PM.

**District Court**, 813 Broadway Rm 201, Goodland, KS 67735. 913-899-4850 (MST) 8:30AM-5PM. Felony, Misdemeanor, Civil, Eviction, Small Claims, Probate.

## Smith County

**Real Estate Recording**, Smith County Register of Deeds, 218 South Grant, Smith Center, KS 66967. 913-282-5160 (CST) 8AM-Noon,1-5PM.

**District Court**, PO Box 273, Smith Center, KS 66967. 913-282-5140 (CST) 8:30AM-5PM. Felony, Misdemeanor, Civil, Eviction, Small Claims, Probate.

## Stafford County

**Real Estate Recording**, Stafford County Register of Deeds, 209 North Broadway, St. John, KS 67576. 316-549-3505 (CST) 8AM-Noon,1-5PM.

**District Court**, PO Box 365, St John, KS 67576. 316-549-3295 (CST) 8:30AM-5PM. Felony, Misdemeanor, Civil, Eviction, Small Claims, Probate.

## Stanton County

**Real Estate Recording**, Stanton County Register of Deeds, 201 North Main, Courthouse, Johnson, KS 67855. 316-492-2190 (CST) 8:30AM-Noon, 1-5PM.

**District Court**, PO Box 913, Johnson, KS 67855. 316-492-2180 (CST) 8:30AM-5PM. Felony, Misdemeanor, Civil, Eviction, Small Claims, Probate.

## Stevens County

**Real Estate Recording**, Stevens County Register of Deeds, 200 East 6th, Hugoton, KS 67951. 316-544-2630 (CST) 9AM-5PM.

**District Court**, 200 E 6th, Hugoton, KS 67951. 316-544-2484 (CST) 8:30AM-5PM. Felony, Misdemeanor, Civil, Eviction, Small Claims, Probate.

## Sumner County

**Real Estate Recording**, Sumner County Register of Deeds, 500 Block North Washington, Wellington, KS 67152. 316-326-2041 (CST) 8AM-5PM.

**District Court**, PO Box 399, Wellington, KS 67152. 316-826-5936 (CST) 8:30AM-12PM-1PM-5PM. Felony, Misdemeanor, Civil, Eviction, Small Claims, Probate.

## Thomas County

**Real Estate Recording**, Thomas County Register of Deeds, 300 North Court, Colby, KS 67701. 913-462-4535 (CST) 8AM-Noon, 1PM-5PM.

**District Court**, PO Box 805, Colby, KS 67701. 913-462-4540 (CST) 8:30AM-5PM. Felony, Misdemeanor, Civil, Eviction, Small Claims, Probate.

## Trego County

**Real Estate Recording**, Trego County Register of Deeds, 216 Main, WaKeeney, KS 67672-2189. 913-743-6622 (CST) 8:30AM-5PM.

**District Court**, 216 N Main, Wakeeney, KS 67672. 913-743-2148 (CST) 8:30AM-5PM. Felony, Misdemeanor, Civil, Eviction, Small Claims, Probate.

## Wabaunsee County

**Real Estate Recording**, Wabaunsee County Register of Deeds, 215 Kansas Avenue, Courthouse, Alma, KS 66401. 913-765-3822 (CST) 8AM-4:30PM.

**District Court**, Courthouse, Alma, KS 66401. 913-765-2406 (CST) 8:30AM-5PM. Felony, Misdemeanor, Civil, Eviction, Small Claims, Probate.

## Wallace County

**Real Estate Recording**, Wallace County Register of Deeds, 313 North Main, Courthouse, Sharon Springs, KS 67758. 913-852-4283 (MST) 8AM-12, 1PM-5PM.

**District Court**, PO Box 8, Sharon Springs, KS 67758. 913-852-4289 (MST) 8:30AM-12PM-1PM-5PM. Felony, Misdemeanor, Civil, Eviction, Small Claims, Probate.

## Washington County

**Real Estate Recording**, Washington County Register of Deeds, 214 C Street, Courthouse, Washington, KS 66968-1928. 913-325-2286 (CST) 8AM-5PM.

**District Court**, Courthouse, Washington, KS 66968. 913-325-2381 (CST) 8:30AM-12PM-1PM-5PM. Felony, Misdemeanor, Civil, Eviction, Small Claims, Probate.

## Wichita County

**Real Estate Recording**, Wichita County Register of Deeds, Courthouse, 206 S. 4th, Leoti, KS 67861. 316-375-2733 (CST) 8AM-Noon,1-5PM.

**District Court**, 206 S 4th St, Leoti, KS 67861. 316-375-4454 (CST) 8:30AM-5PM. Felony, Misdemeanor, Civil, Eviction, Small Claims, Probate.

## Wilson County

**Real Estate Recording**, Wilson County Register of Deeds, Courthouse, Room 106, Fredonia, KS 66736-1396. 316-378-3662 (CST) 8:30AM-5PM.

**District Court**, PO Box 246, Fredonia, KS 66736. 316-378-4533 (CST) 8:30AM-5PM. Felony, Misdemeanor, Civil, Eviction, Small Claims, Probate.

## Woodson County

**Real Estate Recording**, Woodson County Register of Deeds, 105 W. Rutledge, Room 101, Yates Center, KS 66783-1499. 316-625-8635 (CST) 8AM-Noon,1-5PM.

**District Court**, PO Box 228, Yates Center, KS 66783. 316-625-2187 (CST) 8:30AM-12PM-1PM-5PM. Felony, Misdemeanor, Civil, Eviction, Small Claims, Probate.

## Wyandotte County

**Real Estate Recording**, Wyandotte County Register of Deeds, Courthouse, 710 N. 7th St., Kansas City, KS 66101-3084. 913-573-2841 (CST) 8:30AM-5PM.

**District Court**, 710 N 7th St, Kansas City, KS 66101. 913-573-2901 (CST) 8:30AM-5PM. Felony, Misdemeanor, Civil, Eviction, Small Claims, Probate.

# Kentucky

## Adair County

**Real Estate Recording**, Adair County Clerk, 424 Public Square, Columbia, KY 42728. 502-384-2801 (CST) 7:30AM-4:15PM.

**Circuit and District Court**, 500 Public Square, Columbia, KY 42728. 502-384-2626 (CST) 7:30AM-4PM. Felony, Misdemeanor, Civil, Eviction, Small Claims, Probate.

## Allen County

**Real Estate Recording**, Allen County Clerk, West Main Street, Scottsville, KY 42164. 502-237-3706 (CST) 8:30AM-4:30PM, 8:30AM-2PM Sat.

**Circuit and District Court**, Box 477, Scottsville, KY 42164. 502-237-3561 (CST) 8AM-4:30PM. Felony, Misdemeanor, Civil, Eviction, Small Claims, Probate.

## Anderson County

**Real Estate Recording**, Anderson County Clerk, 151 South Main, Lawrenceburg, KY 40342. 502-839-3041 (EST) 8:30AM-5PM M-Th; 8:30AM-6PM F.

**Circuit Court**, Courthouse 151 S Main St, Lawrenceburg, KY 40342. 502-839-3508 (EST) 8:30AM-5PM. Felony, Civil Actions Over $4,000, Eviction.

**District Court**, Courthouse, Lawrenceburg, KY 40342. 502-839-5445 (EST) 8:30AM-5PM M-TH, 8:30AM-6PM F. Misdemeanor, Civil Actions Under $4,000, Small Claims, Probate.

## Ballard County

**Real Estate Recording**, Ballard County Clerk, Court Street, Courthouse, Wickliffe, KY 42087. 502-335-5168 (CST) 8AM-4PM; 8AM-5:30PM F.

**Circuit and District Court**, Box 265, Wickliffe, KY 42087. 502-335-5186 (CST) 8AM-4PM. Felony, Misdemeanor, Civil, Eviction, Small Claims, Probate.

## Barren County

**Real Estate Recording**, Barren County Clerk, Courthouse, 103 Courthouse Square, Glasgow, KY 42141-2812. 502-651-5200 (CST) 8AM-4:30AM.

**Circuit Court and District Court**, 102 N Public Square, Glasgow, KY 42141-2812. 502-651-3763 (CST) 8AM-5PM. Felony, Misdemeanor, Civil, Eviction, Small Claims, Probate.

**District Court**, 102 N Public Square, Glasgow, KY 42141-2812. 502-651-9830 (CST) 8AM-4:30PM. Misdemeanor, Civil Actions Under $4,000, Small Claims, Probate.

## Bath County

**Real Estate Recording**, Bath County Clerk, Courthouse, Main St., Owingsville, KY 40360. 606-674-2613 (EST) 8AM-4PM; 8AM-Noon Sat.

**Circuit and District Court**, Box 558, Owingsville, KY 40360. 606-674-2186 (EST) 8AM-4PM. Felony, Misdemeanor, Civil, Eviction, Small Claims, Probate.

## Bell County

**Real Estate Recording**, Bell County Clerk, Courthouse Square, Pineville, KY 40977. 606-337-6143 (EST) 8AM-4PM M-F; 8AM-Noon Sat.

**Circuit and District Court**, Box 306, Pineville, KY 40977. 606-337-2942 (EST) 8:30AM-4PM. Felony, Misdemeanor, Civil, Eviction, Small Claims, Probate.

## Boone County

**Real Estate Recording**, Boone County Clerk, 2950 East Washington Square, Burlington, KY 41005. 606-334-2137 (EST) 8AM-4:30PM.

**Circuit and District Court**, Box 480, Burlington, KY 41005. 606-334-2149 (EST) 8:30AM-5:30PM. Felony, Misdemeanor, Civil, Eviction, Small Claims, Probate.

## Bourbon County

**Real Estate Recording**, Bourbon County Clerk, Main Street, Courthouse, Paris, KY 40361. 606-987-2142 (EST) 8:30AM-4:30PM M-Th; 8:30AM-6PM F.

**Circuit and District Court**, Box 740, Paris, KY 40361. 606-987-2624 (EST) 8:30AM-4PM M-TH, 8:30AM-6PM F. Felony, Misdemeanor, Civil, Eviction, Small Claims, Probate.

## Boyd County

**Real Estate Recording**, Boyd County Clerk, 2800 Louisa Street, Courthouse, Catlettsburg, KY 41129. 606-739-5116 (EST) 8:30AM-4PM Main Office (9AM-4:30PM & 9AM-Noon Sat Branch Office).

**Circuit and District Court**, Box 694, Catlettsburg, KY 41129-0694. 606-739-4131 (EST) 8:30AM-4PM. Felony, Misdemeanor, Civil, Eviction, Small Claims, Probate.

## Boyle County

**Real Estate Recording**, Boyle County Clerk, 321 W. Main St., Room 123, Danville, KY 40422-1837. 606-238-1112 (EST) 8:30AM-4PM M-Th; 8:30AM-5PM F.

**Circuit Court**, Courthouse, Main St, Danville, KY 40422. 606-236-7442 (EST) 8AM-5PM. Felony, Civil Actions Over $4,000, Eviction.

**District Court**, Courthouse 3rd Fl, Danville, KY 40422. 606-236-8362 (EST) 8AM-4:30PM. Misdemeanor, Civil Actions Under $4,000, Small Claims, Probate.

## Bracken County

**Real Estate Recording**, Bracken County Clerk, Courthouse, Brooksville, KY 41004. 606-735-2952 (EST) 9AM-4PM M,T,Th,F; 9AM-Noon W,Sat.

**Circuit and District Court**, Box 132 Courthouse, Brooksville, KY 41004. 606-735-3328 (EST) 9AM-4PM M,T,TH,F, 9AM-12PM W & SAT. Felony, Misdemeanor, Civil, Eviction, Small Claims, Probate.

## Breathitt County

**Real Estate Recording**, Breathitt County Clerk, 1127 Main Street, Jackson, KY 41339. 606-666-3810 (EST) 8AM-4PM M,T,Th,F; 8AM-Noon W,Sat.

**Circuit and District Court**, 1127 Main St, Jackson, KY 41339. 606-666-5768 (EST) 8AM-4PM M,T,TH,F, 8AM-12PM W, 9AM-12PM SAT. Felony, Misdemeanor, Civil, Eviction, Small Claims, Probate.

## Breckinridge County

**Real Estate Recording**, Breckinridge County Clerk, Main St., Hardinsburg, KY 40143. 502-756-6166 (CST) 8AM-4PM, 8AM-12 Sat.

**Circuit and District Court**, Box 111, Hardinsburg, KY 40143. 502-756-2239 (CST) 8AM-4PM. Felony, Misdemeanor, Civil, Eviction, Small Claims, Probate.

## Bullitt County

**Real Estate Recording**, Bullitt County Clerk, Courthouse Annex, Shepherdsville, KY 40165. 502-543-2513 (EST) 8AM-4PM M,T,W,F; 8AM-6PM Th.

**Circuit and District Court**, Box 275, Shephardsville, KY 40165. 502-526-5631 (EST) 8AM-4:30PM. Felony, Misdemeanor, Civil, Eviction, Small Claims, Probate.

## Butler County

**Real Estate Recording**, Butler County Clerk, Courthouse, Morgantown, KY 42261. 502-526-5676 (CST) 8AM-4PM.

**Circuit and District Court**, Box 625, Morgantown, KY 42261. 502-526-5631 (CST) 8AM-4PM M-F, 8AM-12PM SAT. Felony, Misdemeanor, Civil, Eviction, Small Claims, Probate.

## Caldwell County

**Real Estate Recording**, Caldwell County Clerk, 100 East Market Street, Courthouse - Room 3, Princeton, KY 42445. 502-365-6754 (CST) 8AM-4PM.

**Circuit and District Court**, Courthouse Rm 4, Princeton, KY 42445. 502-365-6884 (CST) 8AM-4PM. Felony, Misdemeanor, Civil, Eviction, Small Claims, Probate.

## Calloway County

**Real Estate Recording**, Calloway County Clerk, 101 South 5th Street, Murray, KY 42071-2569. 502-753-3923 (CST) 8:30AM-5PM.

**Circuit and District Court**, 201 S 4th St Miller Annex, Murray, KY 42071. 502-753-2714 (CST) 8AM-4:30PM. Felony, Misdemeanor, Civil, Eviction, Small Claims, Probate.

## Campbell County

**Real Estate Recording**, Campbell County Clerk, 4th and York Streets, Courthouse, Newport, KY 41071. 606-292-3850 (EST) 8:30AM-4PM M-F; Last Mon. of the month 8:30AM-6PM; 9AM-Noon Sat.

**Circuit Court**, 330 York St Rm 8, Newport, KY 41071. 606-292-6314 (EST) 8:30AM-4PM. Felony, Civil Actions Over $4,000, Eviction.

**District Court**, 600 Columbia St, Newport, KY 41071. 602-292-6305 (EST) 8:30AM-4PM. Misdemeanor, Civil Actions Under $4,000, Small Claims, Probate.

# Kentucky

## Carlisle County

**Real Estate Recording**, Carlisle County Clerk, West Court Street, Bardwell, KY 42023. 502-628-3233 (CST) 8:30AM-4PM.

**Circuit and District Court**, Box 337, Bardwell, KY 42023. 502-628-5425 (CST) 8AM-4PM. Felony, Misdemeanor, Civil, Eviction, Small Claims, Probate.

## Carroll County

**Real Estate Recording**, Carroll County Clerk, 440 Main Street, Court House, Carrollton, KY 41008. 502-732-7005 (EST) 8:30AM-4:30PM M,T,Th,F; 8:30AM-Noon W,Sat.

**Circuit and District Court**, 802 Clay St, Carrollton, KY 41008. 502-732-4305 (EST) 8:30AM-4:30PM M-TH, 8:30AM-6PM F. Felony, Misdemeanor, Civil, Eviction, Small Claims, Probate.

## Carter County

**Real Estate Recording**, Carter County Clerk, Main Street, Courthouse, Grayson, KY 41143. 606-474-5188 (EST) 8:30AM-4PM; 8:30AM-Noon Sat.

**Circuit Court**, 308 Courthouse, Grayson, KY 41143. 606-474-5191 (EST) 8:30AM-4PM M-F, 9AM-12PM SAT. Felony, Civil Actions Over $4,000, Eviction.

**District Court**, Courthouse Rm 203, Grayson, KY 41143. 606-474-6572 (EST) 8:30AM-4PM. Misdemeanor, Civil Actions Under $4,000, Small Claims, Probate.

## Casey County

**Real Estate Recording**, Casey County Clerk, Courthouse, Liberty, KY 42539. 606-787-6471 (EST) 8AM-4:30PM; 8AM-Noon Sat.

**Circuit and District Court**, Box 147, Liberty, KY 42539. 606-787-6510 (EST) 8AM-4:30PM M-W, 8AM-4PM TH, 8AM-12PM SAT. Felony, Misdemeanor, Civil, Eviction, Small Claims, Probate.

## Christian County

**Real Estate Recording**, Christian County Clerk, 511 South Main, Hopkinsville, KY 42240. 502-887-4105 (CST) 8AM-4:30PM.

**Circuit and District Court**, Box 635, Hopkinsville, KY 42241. 502-887-2539 (CST) 8AM-4:30PM. Felony, Misdemeanor, Civil, Eviction, Small Claims, Probate.

## Clark County

**Real Estate Recording**, Clark County Clerk, 34 South Main Street, Winchester, KY 40391. 606-745-0280 (EST) 8AM-5PM M; 8AM-5PM T-F.

**Circuit Court**, Box 715, Winchester, KY 40391. 606-744-2264 (EST) 8AM-4:30PM. Felony, Civil Actions Over $4,000, Eviction.

**District Court**, Box 175, Winchester, KY 40392. 606-744-2264 (EST) 8AM-4PM. Misdemeanor, Civil Actions Under $4,000, Small Claims.

## Clay County

**Real Estate Recording**, Clay County Clerk, 316 Main Street, Suite 143, Manchester, KY 40962. 606-598-2544 (EST) 8AM-4PM; 8AM-Noon Sat.

**Circuit and District Court**, Box 463, Manchester, KY 40962. 606-598-3663 (EST) 8AM-4PM. Felony, Misdemeanor, Civil, Eviction, Small Claims, Probate.

## Clinton County

**Real Estate Recording**, Clinton County Clerk, 212 Washington Street, Courthouse, Albany, KY 42602. 606-387-5943 (CST) 8AM-4:30PM; 8AM-Noon Sat.

**Circuit and District Court**, Courthouse 2nd Fl, Albany, KY 42602. 606-387-6424 (CST) 8AM-4PM M-F, 8AM-12PM SAT. Felony, Misdemeanor, Civil, Eviction, Small Claims, Probate.

## Crittenden County

**Real Estate Recording**, Crittenden County Clerk, 107 South Main, Courthouse, Suite 203, Marion, KY 42064. 502-965-3403 (CST) 8AM-4:30PM M,T,Th,F; 8AM-Noon W,Sat.

**Circuit and District Court**, 107 S Main, Marion, KY 42064. 502-965-4200 (CST) 8AM-4:30PM. Felony, Misdemeanor, Civil, Eviction, Small Claims, Probate.

## Cumberland County

**Real Estate Recording**, Cumberland County Clerk, Courthouse - Public Square, Room 6, Burkesville, KY 42717. 502-864-3726 (CST) 8AM-4:30PM; 8AM-Noon Sat.

**Circuit and District Court**, Box 395, Burkesville, KY 42717. 502-864-2611 (CST) 8AM-4PM. Felony, Misdemeanor, Civil, Eviction, Small Claims, Probate.

## Daviess County

**Real Estate Recording**, Daviess County Clerk, 212 St. Ann Street, Owensboro, KY 42303. 502-685-8421 (CST) 8AM-4PM M-Th; 8AM-6PM F.

**Circuit and District Court**, Box 277, Owensboro, KY 42302. 502-686-3222 (CST) 8AM-4PM. Felony, Misdemeanor, Civil, Eviction, Small Claims, Probate.

## Edmonson County

**Real Estate Recording**, Edmonson County Clerk, Main Street, Community Center, Brownsville, KY 42210. 502-597-2624 (CST) 8AM-5PM M,T,W,F; 8AM-Noon Sat.

**Circuit and District Court**, Box 130, Brownsville, KY 42210. 502-597-2584 (CST) 8AM-5PM M,T,W,F, 8AM-12PM SAT. Felony, Misdemeanor, Civil, Eviction, Small Claims, Probate.

## Elliott County

**Real Estate Recording**, Elliott County Clerk, Main Street, Courthouse, Sandy Hook, KY 41171. 606-738-5421 (EST) 8AM-Noon,1-4PM; 9AM-Noon Sat.

**Circuit and District Court**, Box 788, Sandy Hook, KY 41171. 606-738-5238 (EST) 8AM-4PM M-F, 9AM-12PM SAT. Felony, Misdemeanor, Civil, Eviction, Small Claims, Probate.

## Estill County

**Real Estate Recording**, Estill County Clerk, Courthouse, Irvine, KY 40336. 606-723-5156 (EST) 8AM-4PM M,T,Th,F; 8AM-Noon W,Sat.

**Circuit and District Court**, Courthouse 2nd Fl, Irvine, KY 40336. 606-723-3970 (EST) 8AM-5PM. Felony, Misdemeanor, Civil, Eviction, Small Claims, Probate.

## Fayette County

**Real Estate Recording**, Fayette County Clerk, 162 East Main Street, Lexington, KY 40507. 606-253-3344 (EST) 8AM-4:30PM.

**Circuit Court-Criminal and Civil Divisions**, 215 W Main (civil-Rm 200), Lexington, KY 40507. 606-253-1011 (EST) 8:30AM-4:30PM. Felony, Civil Actions Over $4,000, Eviction.

**District Court-Criminal and Civil**, 136 (civil), 140 (criminal) N Martin Lut, Lexington, KY 40507. 606-259-0531 (EST) 8AM-4PM. Misdemeanor, Civil Actions Under $4,000, Small Claims, Probate.

## Fleming County

**Real Estate Recording**, Fleming County Clerk, Court Square, Flemingsburg, KY 41041. 606-845-8461 (EST) 8:30AM-4:30PM M,T,Th,F; 8:30AM-Noon W,Sat.

**Circuit and District Court**, Courthouse 100 Court Square, Flemingsburg, KY 41041. 606-845-7011 (EST) 8AM-4:30PM M-F, 8:30AM-12PM SAT. Felony, Misdemeanor, Civil, Eviction, Small Claims, Probate.

## Floyd County

**Real Estate Recording**, Floyd County Clerk, 3rd Avenue, Courthouse, Prestonsburg, KY 41653. 606-886-3816 (EST) 8AM-4:30PM M,T,W,Th; 8AM-7PM F;9AM-Noon Sat.

**Circuit Court**, Box 109, Prestonsburg, KY 41653. 606-886-3090 (EST) 8AM-4PM. Felony, Civil Actions Over $4,000, Eviction.

**District Court**, Box 109, Prestonsburg, KY 41653. 606-886-9114 (EST) 8AM-4PM. Misdemeanor, Small Claims.

## Franklin County

**Real Estate Recording**, Franklin County Clerk, 315 W. Main Street, Courthouse Annex, Frankfort, KY 40601. 502-875-8703 (EST) 8AM-4:30PM.

**Circuit Court**, Box 678, Frankfort, KY 40602. 502-564-8380 (EST) 8AM-4:30PM. Felony, Civil Actions Over $4,000, Eviction.

**District Court**, Box 678, Frankfort, KY 40602. 502-564-7013 (EST) 8AM-4:30PM. Misdemeanor, Civil Actions Under $4,000, Small Claims, Probate.

## Fulton County

**Real Estate Recording**, Fulton County Clerk, Wellington Street, Johnson Annex, Hickman, KY 42050. 502-236-2061 (CST) 8AM-4PM.

**Circuit and District Court**, Box 198, Hickman, KY 42050. 502-236-3944 (CST) 8:30AM-4PM. Felony, Misdemeanor, Civil, Eviction, Small Claims, Probate.

## Gallatin County

**Real Estate Recording**, Gallatin County Clerk, Franklin & Washington, Warsaw, KY 41095. 606-567-5411 (EST)

**Circuit Court**, Box 256, Warsaw, KY 41095. 606-567-5241 (EST) 8AM-4:30PM. Felony, Civil Actions Over $4,000, Eviction.

**District Court**, Box 256, Warsaw, KY 41095. 606-567-2388 (EST) 8AM-4:30PM M,T,TH,F & SAT. Misdemeanor, Civil Actions Under $4,000, Small Claims, Probate.

## Garrard County

**Real Estate Recording**, Garrard County Clerk, Courthouse Building, Lancaster, KY 40444. 606-792-3071 (EST) 8AM-4PM M,T,Th,F; 8AM-Noon W,Sat.

**Circuit and District Court**, Courthouse Annex, Lancaster, KY 40444. 606-792-6032 (EST) 8AM-4PM M,T,TH,F, 8AM-12PM SAT. Felony, Misdemeanor, Civil, Eviction, Small Claims, Probate.

## Grant County

**Real Estate Recording**, Grant County Clerk, 101 Main Street, Courthouse Basement, Williamstown, KY 41097. 606-824-3321 (EST) 8:30AM-4PM M-F; 8:30AM-Noon Sat.

**Circuit and District Court**, Courthouse 101 N Main, Williamstown, KY 41097. 606-824-4467 (EST) 8:30AM-4PM. Felony, Misdemeanor, Civil, Eviction, Small Claims, Probate.

## Graves County

**Real Estate Recording**, Graves County Clerk, Courthouse, Mayfield, KY 42066. 502-247-1676 (CST) 8AM-4:30PM M-Th; 8AM-6PM F.

**Circuit and District Court**, Courthouse 100 E Broadway, Mayfield, KY 42066. 502-247-1733 (CST) 8AM-4:30PM M-TH, 8AM-6PM F. Felony, Misdemeanor, Civil, Eviction, Small Claims, Probate.

## Grayson County

**Real Estate Recording**, Grayson County Clerk, 10 Public Square, Leitchfield, KY 42754. 502-259-3201 (CST) 8AM-4PM M,T,W,F; 8AM-Noon Th,Sat.

**Circuit and District Court**, 125 E White Oak, Leitchfield, KY 42754. 502-259-3040 (CST) 8AM-4:30PM M-F, 8AM-12PM SAT. Felony, Misdemeanor, Civil, Eviction, Small Claims, Probate.

## Green County

**Real Estate Recording**, Green County Clerk, 203 West Court Street, Greensburg, KY 42743. 502-932-5386 (EST) 8AM-4PM M,T,W,F; 8AM-2PM Sat (Closed Th).

**Circuit and District Court**, 203 W Court St, Greensburg, KY 42743. 502-932-5631 (EST) 8AM-4PM M,T,W,F, 8AM-12:30PM SAT. Felony, Misdemeanor, Civil, Eviction, Small Claims, Probate.

## Greenup County

**Real Estate Recording**, Greenup County Clerk, Main Street, Courthouse, Greenup, KY 41144. 606-473-7396 (EST) 9AM-4:30PM M,T,W,F; 9AM-Noon Th,Sat.

**Circuit and District Court**, Courthouse Annex, Greenup, KY 41144. 606-473-9869 (EST) 8AM-4PM M-F, 9AM-12PM SAT. Felony, Misdemeanor, Civil, Eviction, Small Claims, Probate.

## Hancock County

**Real Estate Recording**, Hancock County Clerk, 225 Main & Cross St., Courthouse, Hawesville, KY 42348. 502-927-6117 (CST) 8AM-4PM M,T,W,F; 8AM-5:30PM Th.

**Circuit and District Court**, Courthouse, Hawesville, KY 42348. 502-927-8144 (CST) 8AM-4PM M,T,W,F, 8AM-5:30PM TH. Felony, Misdemeanor, Civil, Eviction, Small Claims, Probate.

## Hardin County

**Real Estate Recording**, Hardin County Clerk, 14 Public Square, Elizabethtown, KY 42701. 502-765-4116 (EST) 8:30AM-4:30PM.

**Circuit and District Court**, Courthouse 100 Public Square, Elizabethtown, KY 42701. 502-765-5181 (EST) 8AM-4:30PM. Felony, Misdemeanor, Civil, Eviction, Small Claims, Probate.

## Harlan County

**Real Estate Recording**, Harlan County Clerk, Central Street, Harlan, KY 40831. 606-573-3636 (EST) 8:30AM-4:30PM M-W & F; 8:30AM-6PM Th.

**Circuit and District Court**, Box 190, Harlan, KY 40831. 606-573-2680 (EST) 8AM-4:30PM. Felony, Misdemeanor, Civil, Eviction, Small Claims, Probate.

## Harrison County

**Real Estate Recording**, Harrison County Clerk, 190 West Pike Street, Cynthiana, KY 41031-1397. 606-234-7130 (EST) 9AM-4:30PM; 9AM-Noon Sat.

**Circuit and District Court**, Courthouse Box 10, Cynthiana, KY 41031. 606-234-1914 (EST) 8:30AM-4:30PM M-F, 9AM-12PM SAT. Felony, Misdemeanor, Civil, Eviction, Small Claims, Probate.

## Hart County

**Real Estate Recording**, Hart County Clerk, Main Street, Courthouse, Munfordville, KY 42765. 502-524-2751 (CST) 8AM-4PM (8AM-Noon Sat).

**Circuit and District Court**, Box 548, Munfordville, KY 42765. 502-524-5181 (CST) 8AM-4PM. Felony, Misdemeanor, Civil, Eviction, Small Claims, Probate.

## Henderson County

**Real Estate Recording**, Henderson County Clerk, Corner of Main & First, Courthouse, Henderson, KY 42420. 502-826-3906 (CST) 8AM-4:30PM M-Th; 8AM-6PM F.

**Circuit and District Courts**, PO Box 675, Henderson, KY 42420. 502-826-2405 (CST) 8AM-4:30PM T-F 8AM-6PM M. Felony, Civil Actions Over $4,000, Eviction.

## Henry County

**Real Estate Recording**, Henry County Clerk, Courthouse, Court Square, New Castle, KY 40050. 502-845-5705 (EST) 8AM-4PM.

**District and Circuit Court**, PO Box 359, New Castle, KY 40050. 502-845-7551 (EST) 8AM-4:30PM T-F 8AM-6PM M. Felony, Misdemeanor, Civil, Eviction, Small Claims, Probate.

## Hickman County

**Real Estate Recording**, Hickman County Clerk, Courthouse, 110 E. Clay, Clinton, KY 42031-1296. 502-653-2131 (CST) 8:30AM-4PM.

**Circuit and District Court**, Courthouse, Clinton, KY 42031. 502-653-3901 (CST) 8AM-4PM. Felony, Misdemeanor, Civil, Eviction, Small Claims, Probate.

## Hopkins County

**Real Estate Recording**, Hopkins County Clerk, Corner of Main and Center Streets, Courthouse - Room 11, Madisonville, KY 42431. 502-825-5001 (CST) 8AM-4PM.

**Circuit and District Court**, Courthouse 30 S Main St, Madisonville, KY 42431. 502-825-6502 (CST) 8AM-4PM. Felony, Misdemeanor, Civil, Eviction, Small Claims, Probate.

## Jackson County

**Real Estate Recording**, Jackson County Clerk, Main Street, Courthouse, McKee, KY 40447. 606-287-7800 (EST) 8AM-4PM; 8AM-Noon Sat.

**Circuit Court**, PO Box 84, McKee, KY 40447. 606-287-7783 (EST) 8AM-4PM M-F 8AM-12PM SAT. Felony, Civil Actions Over $4,000, Eviction.

**District Court**, PO Box 84, McKee, KY 40447. 606-287-8651 (EST) 8AM-4PM M-F 8AM-12PM SAT. Misdemeanor, Civil Actions Under $4,000, Small Claims, Probate.

## Jefferson County

**Circuit and District Court**, Hall of Justice 600 W Jefferson St, Louisville, KY 40202. 502-595-4629 (EST) 24 HOURS M-SUN. Felony, Misdemeanor, Civil, Eviction, Small Claims, Probate.

## Jefferson County Recorder

**Real Estate Recording**, Jefferson County Recorder, 527 West Jefferson, Louisville, KY 40202. 502-574-5785 (EST)

## Jessamine County

**Real Estate Recording**, Jessamine County Clerk, 101 North Main Street, Nicholasville, KY 40356-1270. 606-885-4161 (EST) 8AM-5PM M; 8AM-4PM T,W,F; 8AM-Noon Th; 9am-Noon Sat.

**Circuit Court**, Courthouse Main St, Nicholasville, KY 40356. 606-885-4531 (EST) 8AM-5PM M 8AM-4:30PM T & W 8AM-12PM TH 8AM-4PM F. Felony, Civil Actions Over $4,000, Eviction.

**District Court**, Courthouse Main St, Nicholasville, KY 40356. 606-887-1005 (EST) 8AM-5PM M 8AM-4:30 T & W 8AM-12PM TH 8AM-4PM F. Misdemeanor, Civil Actions Under $4,000, Small Claims, Probate.

## Johnson County

**Real Estate Recording**, Johnson County Clerk, Courthouse, Court St., Paintsville, KY

41240. 606-789-2557 (EST) 8AM-5PM, 8:30AM-12 Sat.

**Circuit and District Court**, Box 1405, Paintsville, KY 41240. 606-789-5181 (EST) 8AM-4PM. Felony, Misdemeanor, Civil, Eviction, Small Claims, Probate.

## Kenton County

**Real Estate Recording**, Kenton County Clerk, 1st District, 3rd & Court Streets, Room 102, Covington, KY 41012. 606-491-0702 (EST) 9AM-4PM.

**Real Estate Recording**, Kenton County Clerk, 2nd District, 5272 Madison, Independence, KY 41051. 606-356-9272 (EST) 9AM-4PM M,T,Th,F; 9AM-6PM W.

**Circuit Court**, Box 669, Covington, KY 41012. 606-292-6521 (EST) 8AM-4:30PM. Felony, Civil Actions Over $4,000, Eviction.

**District Court**, City Bldg Rm 408, Covington, KY 41011. 606-292-6523 (EST) 8AM-4:30PM. Misdemeanor, Civil Actions Under $4,000, Small Claims, Probate.

## Knott County

**Real Estate Recording**, Knott County Clerk, Main Street, Courthouse, Hindman, KY 41822. 606-785-5651 (EST) 8AM-4PM M,T,W,Th; 8AM-6PM F; 8AM-Noon Sat.

**Circuit and District Court**, Box 515, Hindman, KY 41822. 606-785-5021 (EST) 8AM-4PM. Felony, Misdemeanor, Civil, Eviction, Small Claims, Probate.

## Knox County

**Real Estate Recording**, Knox County Clerk, 401 Court Square, Suite 102, Barbourville, KY 40906. 606-546-3568 (EST) 8:30AM-4PM.

**Circuit and District Court**, PO Box 760, Barbourville, KY 40906. 606-546-3075 (EST) 8AM-4PM. Felony, Misdemeanor, Civil, Eviction, Small Claims, Probate.

## Larue County

**Real Estate Recording**, Larue County Clerk, Courthouse, Hodgenville, KY 42748. 502-358-3544 (EST) 8AM-4:30PM M,T,Th,F; 8AM-Noon W,Sat.

**Circuit and District Court**, Courthouse Annex, Hodgenville, KY 42748. 502-358-9569 (EST) 8AM-4PM. Felony, Misdemeanor, Civil, Eviction, Small Claims, Probate.

## Laurel County

**Real Estate Recording**, Laurel County Clerk, 101 South Main, Courthouse, London, KY 40741. 606-864-5158 (EST) 8AM-4:30PM; 8:30AM-Noon Sat.

**Circuit and District Court**, Box 1798, London, KY 40743-1798. 606-864-2863 (EST) 8AM-4:30PM. Felony, Misdemeanor, Civil, Eviction, Small Claims, Probate.

## Lawrence County

**Real Estate Recording**, Lawrence County Clerk, 122 South Main Cross Street, Louisa, KY 41230. 606-638-4108 (EST) 8:30AM-4PM; 8:30AM-Noon Sat.

**Circuit and District Court**, Courthouse PO Box 212, Louisa, KY 41230. 606-638-4215 (EST) 8:30AM-4:30PM M-F 8:30AM-12PM SAT. Felony, Misdemeanor, Civil, Eviction, Small Claims, Probate.

## Lee County

**Real Estate Recording**, Lee County Clerk, Main Street, Courthouse - Room 11, Beattyville, KY 41311. 606-464-4115 (EST) 8AM-4PM.

**Circuit and District Court**, Box E, Beattyville, KY 41311. 606-464-8400 (EST) 8AM-4PM M-F 8:30AM-11:30 SAT. Felony, Misdemeanor, Civil, Eviction, Small Claims, Probate.

## Leslie County

**Real Estate Recording**, Leslie County Clerk, Main Street, Courthouse, Hyden, KY 41749. 606-672-2193 (EST) 8AM-5PM; 8AM-Noon Sat.

**Circuit and District Court**, Box 114, Hyden, KY 41749. 606-672-2505 (EST) 8AM-4:30PM. Felony, Misdemeanor, Civil, Eviction, Small Claims, Probate.

## Letcher County

**Real Estate Recording**, Letcher County Clerk, Main Street, Courthouse, Whitesburg, KY 41858. 606-633-2432 (EST) 8:30AM-4PM; 8:30AM-Noon Sat.

**Circuit and District Court**, 101 W Main St, Whitesburg, KY 41858. 606-633-7559 (EST) 8AM-4PM M-F 8:30AM-12PM SAT. Felony, Misdemeanor, Civil, Eviction, Small Claims, Probate.

## Lewis County

**Real Estate Recording**, Lewis County Clerk, Second Street, Courthouse, Vanceburg, KY 41179. 606-796-3062 (EST) 8:30AM-4:30PM M,T,Th,F; 8:30AM-2PM Sat.

**Circuit and District Court**, PO Box 70, Vanceburg, KY 41179. 606-796-3053 (EST) 8AM-5PM M,T,TH,F 8:30-12PM SAT. Felony, Misdemeanor, Civil, Eviction, Small Claims, Probate.

## Lincoln County

**Real Estate Recording**, Lincoln County Clerk, 102 East Main, Courthouse, Stanford, KY 40484. 606-365-4570 (EST) 8AM-4PM M,T,W,Th; 8AM-5:30PM F.

**Circuit and District Court**, 102 E Main, Stanford, KY 40484. 606-365-2535 (EST) 8AM-4PM M-TH 8AM-5:30PM F. Felony, Misdemeanor, Civil, Eviction, Small Claims, Probate.

## Livingston County

**Real Estate Recording**, Livingston County Clerk, Court Street, Courthouse, Smithland, KY 42081. 502-928-2162 (CST) 8AM-4PM; 8AM-6PM M.

**Circuit and District Court**, PO Box 160, Smithland, KY 42081. 502-928-2172 (CST) 8AM-6PM M 8AM-4PM T-F. Felony, Misdemeanor, Civil, Eviction, Small Claims, Probate.

## Logan County

**Real Estate Recording**, Logan County Clerk, 229 W. 3rd St., Russellville, KY 42276. 502-726-6061 (CST) 8:30AM-4PM; 9AM-Noon Sat.

**Circuit Court**, Box 420, Russellville, KY 42276-0420. 502-726-2424 (CST) 8AM-4:30PM. Felony, Civil Actions Over $4,000, Eviction.

**District Court**, Box 304, Russellville, KY 42276. 502-726-3107 (CST) 8AM-4:30PM M-TH 8AM-5PM F. Misdemeanor, Civil Actions Under $4,000, Small Claims, Probate.

## Lyon County

**Real Estate Recording**, Lyon County Clerk, Dale Avenue, Courthouse, Eddyville, KY 42038. 502-388-2331 (EST) 8:30AM-4PM; 8:30AM-Noon Sat.

**Circuit and District Court**, Box 565, Eddyville, KY 42038. 502-388-7231 (EST) 8AM-4PM. Felony, Misdemeanor, Civil, Eviction, Small Claims, Probate.

## Madison County

**Real Estate Recording**, Madison County Clerk, 101 W. Main Street, County Court House, Richmond, KY 40475-1415. 606-624-4704 (EST) 8AM-4PM; 8AM-6PM M.

**Circuit Court**, PO Box 813, Richmond, KY 40476-0813. 606-624-4793 (EST) 8AM-4PM. Felony, Civil Actions Over $4,000, Eviction.

**District Court**, Courthouse Annex, Richmond, KY 40475. 606-624-4720 (EST) 8AM-4PM. Misdemeanor, Civil Actions Under $4,000, Small Claims, Probate.

## Magoffin County

**Real Estate Recording**, Magoffin County Clerk, Courthouse, Salyersville, KY 41465. 606-349-2216 (EST) 8:30AM-4PM; 8:30AM-Noon Sat.

**Circuit and District Court**, Box 147, Salyersville, KY 41465. 606-349-2215 (EST) 8AM-4PM. Felony, Misdemeanor, Civil, Eviction, Small Claims, Probate.

## Marion County

**Real Estate Recording**, Marion County Clerk, 120 W. Main Street, Courthouse, Lebanon, KY 40033. 502-692-2651 (EST) 8:30AM-4:30PM; 8:30AM-Noon Sat.

**Circuit and District Court**, 120 W Main St, Lebanon, KY 40033. 502-692-2681 (EST) 8:30AM-4:30PM M-F 8:30AM-12PM SAT. Felony, Misdemeanor, Civil, Eviction, Small Claims, Probate.

## Marshall County

**Real Estate Recording**, Marshall County Clerk, Courthouse, Benton, KY 42025. 502-527-4740 (CST) 8AM-4:30PM T,W,Th,F; 8AM-5PM M.

**Circuit and District Court**, 1101 Main St, Benton, KY 42025. 502-527-3883 (CST) 8AM-4:30PM. Felony, Misdemeanor, Civil, Eviction, Small Claims, Probate.

## Martin County

**Real Estate Recording**, Martin County Clerk, Main Street, Courthouse, Inez, KY 41224. 606-298-2810 (EST) 8AM-5PM; 8AM-Noon Sat.

**Circuit and District Court**, Box 430, Inez, KY 41224. 606-298-3508 (EST) 8AM-4:30PM M-TH, 8AM-5:30PM F, 9AM-12PM SAT. Felony, Misdemeanor, Civil, Eviction, Small Claims, Probate.

## Mason County

**Real Estate Recording**, Mason County Clerk, West Third Street, Courthouse, Maysville, KY 41056. 606-564-3341 (EST) 9AM-5PM; 9AM-Noon Sat.

**Circuit Court**, 27 W 3rd, Maysville, KY 41056. 606-564-4340 (EST) 8:30AM-5PM. Felony, Civil Actions Over $4,000, Eviction.

**District Court**, 221 Court St, Maysville, KY 41056. 606-564-4011 (EST) 8:30AM-4:30PM. Misdemeanor, Civil Actions Under $4,000, Small Claims, Probate.

## McCracken County

**Real Estate Recording**, McCracken County Clerk, 7th Street between Washington & Clark, Courthouse, Paducah, KY 42002. 502-444-4700 (CST) 8:30AM-4:30PM (M open until 5:30PM).

**Circuit Court**, Box 1455, Paducah, KY 42002-1455. 502-444-8280 (CST) 8:30AM-5:30PM M, 8:30AM-4:30PM T-F. Felony, Civil Actions Over $4,000, Eviction.

**District Court**, Box 1436, Paducah, KY 42001. 502-444-8270 (CST) 8:30AM-4:30PM. Misdemeanor, Civil Actions Under $4,000, Small Claims, Probate.

## McCreary County

**Real Estate Recording**, McCreary County Clerk, Main Street, Courthouse, Whitley City, KY 42653. 606-376-2411 (EST) 8:30AM-4:30PM M-F; 9AM-Noon Sat.

**Circuit and District Court**, Box 40, Whitley City, KY 42653. 606-376-5041 (EST) 8AM-4:30PM. Felony, Misdemeanor, Civil, Eviction, Small Claims, Probate.

## McLean County

**Real Estate Recording**, McLean County Clerk, 210 Main Street, Courthouse, Calhoun, KY 42327. 502-273-3082 (CST) 8AM-4:30PM; 9AM-Noon Sat.

**Circuit and District Court**, Box 145, Calhoun, KY 42327. 502-273-3966 (CST) 8AM-4:30PM M-F, 9AM-noon SAT. Felony, Misdemeanor, Civil, Eviction, Small Claims, Probate.

## Meade County

**Real Estate Recording**, Meade County Clerk, Fairway Drive, Brandenburg, KY 40108. 502-422-2152 (EST) 8AM-4:30PM; 9AM-Noon Sat.

**Circuit and District Court**, Courthouse, Brandenburg, KY 40108. 502-422-4961 (EST) 8AM-4:30AM. Felony, Misdemeanor, Civil, Eviction, Small Claims, Probate.

## Menifee County

**Real Estate Recording**, Menifee County Clerk, Main Street, Courthouse, Frenchburg, KY 40322. 606-768-3512 (EST) 8:30AM-4PM M,T,W,F; 8:30-11:30AM Th,Sat.

**Circuit and District Court**, Box 172, Frenchburg, KY 40322. 606-768-2461 (EST) 8:30AM-4PM. Felony, Misdemeanor, Civil, Eviction, Small Claims, Probate.

## Mercer County

**Real Estate Recording**, Mercer County Clerk, Main Street, Courthouse, Harrodsburg, KY 40330. 606-734-6313 (EST) 8AM-4:30PM.

**Circuit and District Court**, Courthouse, 224 Main St S, Harrodsburg, KY 40330-1696. 606-734-6306 (EST) 8AM-4:30PM. Felony, Misdemeanor, Civil, Eviction, Small Claims, Probate.

## Metcalfe County

**Real Estate Recording**, Metcalfe County Clerk, Public Square, Courthouse, Edmonton, KY 42129. 502-432-4821 (CST) 8AM-4PM.

**Circuit and District Court**, Box 485, Edmonton, KY 42129. 502-432-3663 (CST) 8AM-4PM M-F, 8AM-3:30PM TH, 8AM-noon SAT. Felony, Misdemeanor, Civil, Eviction, Small Claims, Probate.

## Monroe County

**Real Estate Recording**, Monroe County Clerk, Main Street, Courthouse, Tompkinsville, KY 42167. 502-487-5471 (CST) 8AM-5PM M,T,W,F; 8AM-4PM Th; 8AM-1PM Sat.

**Circuit and District Court**, Box 245, Tompkinsville, KY 42167. 502-487-5480 (CST) 8AM-5PM-. Felony, Misdemeanor, Civil, Eviction, Small Claims, Probate.

## Montgomery County

**Real Estate Recording**, Montgomery County Clerk, Court Street, Mount Sterling, KY 40353. 606-498-8700 (EST) 8:30AM-4PM; 8:30-6PM F.

**Circuit and District Court**, Courthouse, Mt Sterling, KY 40353. 606-498-5966 (EST) 8AM-4:30PM. Felony, Misdemeanor, Civil, Eviction, Small Claims, Probate.

## Morgan County

**Real Estate Recording**, Morgan County Clerk, 505 Prestonsburg Street, West Liberty, KY 41472. 606-743-3949 (EST) 8AM-4PM; 8AM-Noon Sat.

**Circuit and District Court**, Box 85, West Liberty, KY 41472. 606-743-3763 (EST) 8AM-4PM. Felony, Misdemeanor, Civil, Eviction, Small Claims, Probate.

## Muhlenberg County

**Real Estate Recording**, Muhlenberg County Clerk, Courthouse, Greenville, KY 42345. 502-338-1441 (CST) 8AM-4PM; 8AM-6PM F.

**Circuit Court**, Box 776, Greenville, KY 42345. 502-338-4850 (CST) 8AM-4PM. Felony, Civil Actions Over $4,000, Eviction.

**District Court**, Box 274, Greenville, KY 42345. 502-338-0995 (CST) 8AM-4PM. Misdemeanor, Civil Actions Under $4,000, Small Claims, Probate.

## Nelson County

**Real Estate Recording**, Nelson County Clerk, Courthouse, Bardstown, KY 40004. 502-348-1830 (EST) 8:30AM-4:30PM M-F; 8AM-Noon Sat.

**Circuit and District Court**, Box 845, Bardstown, KY 40004. 502-348-3648 (EST) 8:30AM-4:30PM. Felony, Misdemeanor, Civil, Eviction, Small Claims, Probate.

## Nicholas County

**Real Estate Recording**, Nicholas County Clerk, Main Street, Courthouse, Carlisle, KY 40311. 606-289-3730 (EST) 8AM-4:30PM; 8AM-Noon Sat.

**Circuit and District Court**, Courthouse, Carlisle, KY 40311. 606-289-2336 (EST) 8:30AM-4:30PM M-F, 9AM-noon SAT. Felony, Misdemeanor, Civil, Eviction, Small Claims, Probate.

## Ohio County

**Real Estate Recording**, Ohio County Clerk, Main Street, Courthouse, Hartford, KY 42347. 502-298-4422 (CST) 8AM-4:30PM M-Th; 8AM-6PM F; 8AM-Noon Sat.

**Circuit and District Court**, Community Center, Hartford, KY 42347. 502-298-3671 (CST) 8:30AM-4:30PM. Felony, Misdemeanor, Civil, Eviction, Small Claims, Probate.

## Oldham County

**Real Estate Recording**, Oldham County Clerk, 100 West Jefferson Street, Courthouse, LaGrange, KY 40031. 502-222-9311 (EST) 8:30AM-4PM M,T,W,F; 8:30AM-6PM Th.

**Circuit and District Court**, 105 E Jefferson, La Grange, KY 40031. 502-222-9837 (EST) 8AM-4PM. Felony, Misdemeanor, Civil, Eviction, Small Claims, Probate.

## Owen County

**Real Estate Recording**, Owen County Clerk, Courthouse, Madison St., Owenton, KY 40359. 502-484-2213 (EST) 8AM-Noon, 1-4PM M,T,Th,F; 8AM-3PM Sat.

**Circuit and District Court**, Box 473, Owenton, KY 40359. 502-484-2232 (EST) 8AM-4PM. Felony, Misdemeanor, Civil, Eviction, Small Claims, Probate.

## Owsley County

**Real Estate Recording**, Owsley County Clerk, Courthouse, Main St., Booneville, KY 41314. 606-593-5735 (EST) 8AM-4PM; 8AM-12 Sat.

**Circuit and District Court**, Box 146, Booneville, KY 41314. 606-593-6226 (EST) 8AM-4PM M-F, 8AM-12PM SAT. Felony, Misdemeanor, Civil, Eviction, Small Claims, Probate.

## Pendleton County

**Real Estate Recording**, Pendleton County Clerk, Main Street, Courthouse Square, Falmouth, KY 41040. 606-654-3380 (EST)

**Circuit and District Court**, Courthouse Square, Falmouth, KY 41040. 606-654-3347 (EST) 8AM-4PM. Felony, Misdemeanor, Civil, Eviction, Small Claims, Probate.

## Perry County

**Real Estate Recording**, Perry County Clerk, Main Street, Courthouse, Hazard, KY 41701. 606-436-4614 (EST) 8AM-4PM.

**Circuit Court**, Box 7743, Hazard, KY 41701. 606-436-4042 (EST) 8AM-4PM. Felony, Civil Actions Over $4,000, Eviction.

**District Court**, Box 7743, Hazard, KY 41702. 606-436-3170 (EST) 8AM-4PM. Misdemeanor, Civil Actions Under $4,000, Small Claims, Probate.

## Pike County

**Real Estate Recording**, Pike County Clerk, 320 Main Street, Pikeville, KY 41501. 606-432-6240 (EST) 8:30AM-4:30PM M,T,W.Th; 8:30AM-7PM F; 8:30AM-Noon Sat.

# Kentucky

**Circuit and District Court**, 89 Div St, Hall of Justice, Pikeville, KY 41501. 606-437-5157 (EST) 8AM-4:30PM. Felony, Misdemeanor, Civil, Eviction, Small Claims, Probate.

## Powell County

**Real Estate Recording**, Powell County Clerk, Washington Street, Courthouse, Stanton, KY 40380. 606-663-6444 (EST) 9AM-4PM M-W; 9AM-Noon Th; 9AM-4PM F; 9AM-Noon Sat.

**Circuit and District Court**, Box 578, Stanton, KY 40380. 606-663-4141 (EST) 8AM-4PM M-F, 8AM-noon TH and SAT. Felony, Misdemeanor, Civil, Eviction, Small Claims, Probate.

## Pulaski County

**Real Estate Recording**, Pulaski County Clerk, Main Street, Somerset, KY 42501. 606-679-3652 (EST) 8AM-4:30PM.

**Circuit and District Court**, Box 664, Somerset, KY 42501. 606-678-8981 (EST) 8AM-4:30PM M-F, 8AM-noon SAT. Felony, Misdemeanor, Civil, Eviction, Small Claims, Probate.

## Robertson County

**Real Estate Recording**, Robertson County Clerk, Courthouse, Mount Olivet, KY 41064. 606-724-5212 (EST) 8:30-Noon, 1-4PM M,T,Th,F; 8:30AM-Noon W, Sat.

**Circuit and District Court**, Box 63, Mt Olivet, KY 41064. 606-724-5993 (EST) 8:30AM-4:30PM. Felony, Misdemeanor, Civil, Eviction, Small Claims, Probate.

## Rockcastle County

**Real Estate Recording**, Rockcastle County Clerk, Courthouse, Mount Vernon, KY 40456. 606-256-2831 (EST) 8:30-4PM; 8;30-Noon Sat.

**Circuit and District Court**, Box 750, Mt Vernon, KY 40456. 606-256-2581 (EST) 8AM-4PM M-F 8AM-6PM TH 8:30AM-12PM SAT. Felony, Misdemeanor, Civil, Eviction, Small Claims, Probate.

## Rowan County

**Real Estate Recording**, Rowan County Clerk, Courthouse - 2nd Floor, 627 E. Main Street, Morehead, KY 40351. 606-784-5212 (EST) 8:30-4:30PM; 9AM-Noon Sat.

**Circuit and District Court**, 627 E Main, Morehead, KY 40351-1398. 606-784-4574 (EST) 8:30AM-4:30PM M-F 8:30AM-12PM SAT. Felony, Misdemeanor, Civil, Eviction, Small Claims, Probate.

## Russell County

**Real Estate Recording**, Russell County Clerk, Courthouse, Jamestown, KY 42629. 502-343-2125 (CST) 8AM-4PM; 8AM-Noon Sat.

**Circuit and District Court**, 410 Monument Square, Suite 203, Jamestown, KY 42629. 502-343-2185 (CST) 8AM-4:30PM M-F 8AM-12PM SAT. Felony, Misdemeanor, Civil, Eviction, Small Claims, Probate.

## Scott County

**Real Estate Recording**, Scott County Clerk, Courthouse, Georgetown, KY 40324-1794. 502-863-7875 (EST) 8:30AM-4:30PM.

**Circuit and District Court**, 119 N Hamilton, Georgetown, KY 40324. 502-863-0474 (EST) 8AM-4:30PM. Felony, Misdemeanor, Civil, Eviction, Small Claims, Probate.

## Shelby County

**Real Estate Recording**, Shelby County Clerk, 501 Main Street, Shelbyville, KY 40065. 502-633-4410 (EST) 8:30AM-4:30PM; 8:30AM-Noon Sat.

**Circuit and District Court**, 501 Main St, Shelbyville, KY 40065. 502-633-1289 (EST) 8:30AM-4:30PM. Felony, Misdemeanor, Civil, Eviction, Small Claims, Probate.

## Simpson County

**Real Estate Recording**, Simpson County Clerk, County Annex Building, 103 West Cedar Street, Franklin, KY 42134. 502-586-8161 (CST) 8AM-4PM.

**Circuit and District Court**, Box 261, Franklin, KY 42135-0261. 502-586-8910 (CST) 8AM-4PM. Felony, Misdemeanor, Civil, Eviction, Small Claims, Probate.

## Spencer County

**Real Estate Recording**, Spencer County Clerk, Main Street, Courthouse, Taylorsville, KY 40071. 502-477-3215 (EST) 8AM-4:30PM M,T,Th,F; 8AM-Noon W,Sat.

**Circuit and District Court**, Box 282, Taylorsville, KY 40071. 502-477-3220 (EST) 7:45AM-4PM. Felony, Misdemeanor, Civil, Eviction, Small Claims, Probate.

## Taylor County

**Real Estate Recording**, Taylor County Clerk, 203 North Court Street, Suite # 5, Campbellsville, KY 42718-2298. 502-465-6677 (EST) 8AM-4:30PM M-Th; 8AM-5PM F.

**Circuit and District Court**, 203 N Court Courthouse, Campbellsville, KY 42718. 502-465-6686 (EST) 8AM-4:30PM. Felony, Misdemeanor, Civil, Eviction, Small Claims, Probate.

## Todd County

**Real Estate Recording**, Todd County Clerk, Washington Street, Courthouse, Elkton, KY 42220. 502-265-2363 (CST) 8AM-4:30PM.

**Circuit and District Court**, Box 337, Elkton, KY 42220. 502-265-5631 (CST) 8AM-4:30PM. Felony, Misdemeanor, Civil, Eviction, Small Claims, Probate.

## Trigg County

**Real Estate Recording**, Trigg County Clerk, Main Street, Courthouse, Cadiz, KY 42211. 502-522-6661 (CST) 8AM-4PM M-Th; 8AM-5PM F.

**Circuit and District Court**, Box 673, Cadiz, KY 42211. 502-522-6270 (CST) 8AM-4PM M-F 9AM-11:30AM 1st SAT of each month. Felony, Misdemeanor, Civil, Eviction, Small Claims, Probate.

## Trimble County

**Real Estate Recording**, Trimble County Clerk, Courthouse, Bedford, KY 40006. 502-255-7174 (EST) 8:30AM-4:30PM M,T,Th,F; 8:30AM-Noon Sat.

**Circuit and District Court**, Box 248, Bedford, KY 40006. 502-255-3213 (EST) 8AM-4:30PM M-T TH-F 8AM-12PM SAT. Felony, Misdemeanor, Civil, Eviction, Small Claims, Probate.

## Union County

**Real Estate Recording**, Union County Clerk, Main & Morgan Streets, Courthouse, Morganfield, KY 42437. 502-389-1334 (CST) 8AM-4PM.

**Circuit and District Court**, Box 59, Morganfield, KY 42437. 502-389-1811 (CST) 8AM-4PM. Felony, Misdemeanor, Civil, Eviction, Small Claims, Probate.

## Warren County

**Real Estate Recording**, Warren County Clerk, 429 East 10th Street, Bowling Green, KY 42101. 502-842-9416 (CST) 8:30AM-4:30PM.

**Circuit and District Court**, Box 2170, Bowling Green, KY 42102. 502-843-5400 (CST) 8:30AM-4:30PM. Felony, Misdemeanor, Civil, Eviction, Small Claims, Probate.

## Washington County

**Real Estate Recording**, Washington County Clerk, Cross Main Annex Building, Springfield, KY 40069. 606-336-5425 (EST) 9AM-4:30PM; 9AM-Noon Sat.

**Circuit and District Court**, PO Box 346, Springfield, KY 40069. 606-336-3761 (EST) 8:30AM-4:30PM. Felony, Misdemeanor, Civil, Eviction, Small Claims, Probate.

## Wayne County

**Real Estate Recording**, Wayne County Clerk, Corner of Main Street & Michigan Avenue, Monticello, KY 42633. 606-348-6661 (CST) 8AM-4:30PM; 8AM-Noon Sat.

**Circuit and District Court**, Box 816, Monticello, KY 42633. 606-348-5841 (CST) 8AM-4:30PM M-F 8AM-12PM SAT. Felony, Misdemeanor, Civil, Eviction, Small Claims, Probate.

## Webster County

**Real Estate Recording**, Webster County Clerk, Main Street, Courthouse, Dixon, KY 42409. 502-639-7006 (CST) 8AM-6PM M; 8AM-4PM T-F.

**Circuit and District Court**, Box 217, Dixon, KY 42409. 502-639-9160 (CST) 8AM-4PM. Felony, Misdemeanor, Civil, Eviction, Small Claims, Probate.

## Whitley County

**Real Estate Recording**, Whitley County Clerk, Main Street, Courthouse, Room 2, Williamsburg, KY 40769. 606-549-6002 (EST) 8:30AM-4PM; 8:30AM-Noon Sat.

**Corbin Circuit and District Court**, 805 S Main St, Corbin, KY 40701. 606-523-1085 (EST) 8AM-4PM. Felony, Misdemeanor, Civil, Eviction, Small Claims, Probate.

**Williamsburg Circuit and District Court**, Box 329, Williamsburg, KY 40769. 606-549-5162 (EST) 8AM-4PM. Felony, Misdemeanor, Civil, Eviction, Small Claims, Probate.

## Wolfe County

**Real Estate Recording**, Wolfe County Clerk, Courthouse, Campton, KY 41301. 606-668-3515 (EST) 8AM-4PM M,T,Th,F; 8AM-12 W & Sat.

**Circuit and District Court**, Box 296, Campton, KY 41301. 606-668-3736 (EST) 8AM-4PM.

Felony, Misdemeanor, Civil, Eviction, Small Claims, Probate.

## Woodford County

**Real Estate Recording**, Woodford County Clerk, Courthouse - Room 120, 103 S. Main St., Versailles, KY 40383. 606-873-3421 (EST) 8AM-4PM M,T,W,Th; 8AM-6PM F.

**Circuit and District Court**, 103 S Main St Rm 102, Versailles, KY 40383. 606-873-3711 (EST) 8AM-4PM M-TH 8AM-6PM F. Felony, Misdemeanor, Civil, Eviction, Small Claims, Probate.

# Louisiana

## Acadia Parish

**Real Estate Recording**, Acadia Parish Clerk of Court, Parkerson Avenue, Court Circle, Crowley, LA 70526. 318-788-8881 (CST) 8:30AM-4:30PM.

**15th District Court**, PO Box 922, Crowley, LA 70527. 318-788-8881 (CST) 8:30AM-4:30PM. Felony, Misdemeanor, Civil, Probate.

## Allen Parish

**Real Estate Recording**, Allen Parish Clerk of Court, Main Street, Courthouse Square, Oberlin, LA 70655. 318-639-4351 (CST) 8AM-4:30PM.

**33rd District Court**, PO Box 248, Oberlin, LA 70655. 318-639-4351 (CST) 8AM-4:30PM. Felony, Misdemeanor, Civil, Probate.

## Ascension Parish

**Real Estate Recording**, Ascension Parish Clerk of Court, 300 Houmas Street, Donaldsonville, LA 70346. 504-473-9866 (CST) 8:30AM-4:30PM.

**23rd District Court**, PO Box 192, Donaldsonville, LA 70346. 504-473-9866 (CST) 8:30AM-4:30PM. Felony, Misdemeanor, Civil, Probate.

## Assumption Parish

**Real Estate Recording**, Assumption Parish Clerk of Court, 4809 Highway 1, Courthouse, Napoleonville, LA 70390. 504-369-6653 (CST) 8:30AM-4:30PM.

**23rd District Court**, PO Box 249, Napoleonville, LA 70390. 504-369-6653 (CST) 8:30AM-4:30PM. Felony, Misdemeanor, Civil, Probate.

## Avoyelles Parish

**Real Estate Recording**, Avoyelles Parish Clerk of Court, East Mark Street, Marksville, LA 71351. 318-253-7523 (CST) 8:30AM-4:30PM.

**12th District Court**, PO Box 196, Marksville, LA 71351. 318-253-7523 (CST) 8:15AM-4:30PM. Felony, Misdemeanor, Civil, Probate.

## Beauregard Parish

**Real Estate Recording**, Beauregard Parish Clerk of Court, 201 West First Street, Courthouse, De Ridder, LA 70634. 318-463-8595 (CST) 8AM-4:30PM.

**36th District Court**, PO Box 100, DeRidder, LA 70634. 318-463-8595 (CST) 8:00AM-4:30PM. Felony, Misdemeanor, Civil, Probate.

## Bienville Parish

**Real Estate Recording**, Bienville Parish Clerk of Court, 601 Locust Street, Room 100, Arcadia, LA 71001-3600. 318-263-2123 (CST) 8:30AM-4:30PM.

**2nd District Court**, 601 Locust St., Rm. 100, Arcadia, LA 71001. 318-263-2123 (CST) 8:30AM-4:30PM. Felony, Misdemeanor, Civil, Probate.

## Bossier Parish

**Real Estate Recording**, Bossier Parish Clerk of Court, 200 Burt Blvd, Benton, LA 71006. 318-965-2336 (CST) 8:30AM.

**26th District Court**, PO Box 369, Benton, LA 71006. 318-965-2336 (CST) Felony, Misdemeanor, Civil, Probate.

## Caddo Parish

**Real Estate Recording**, Caddo Parish Clerk of Court, 501 Texas Street, Room 103, Shreveport, LA 71101-5408. 318-226-6783 (CST) 8:30AM-5PM.

**1st District Court**, 50 Texas St, Rm 103, Shreveport, LA 71101-5408. 318-226-6780 (CST) 8:30AM-5:00PM. Felony, Misdemeanor, Civil, Probate.

## Calcasieu Parish

**Real Estate Recording**, Calcasieu Parish Clerk of Court, 1000 Ryan Street, Lake Charles, LA 70601. 318-437-3550 (CST) 8:30AM-4:30PM.

**14th District Court**, PO Box 1030, Lake Charles, LA 70602. 318-437-3550 (CST) 8:30AM-4:30PM. Felony, Misdemeanor, Civil, Probate.

## Caldwell Parish

**Real Estate Recording**, Caldwell Parish Clerk of Court, Main Street, Courthouse, Columbia, LA 71418. 318-649-2272 (CST) 8AM-4:30PM.

**37th District Court**, PO Box 1327, Columbia, LA 71418. 318-649-2272 (CST) 8:00AM-4:30PM. Felony, Misdemeanor, Civil, Probate.

## Cameron Parish

**Real Estate Recording**, Cameron Parish Clerk of Court, Courthouse Square, Cameron, LA 70631. 318-775-5316 (CST) 8:30AM-4:30PM.

**38th District Court**, PO Box 549, Cameron, LA 70631. 318-775-5316 (CST) Felony, Misdemeanor, Civil, Probate.

## Catahoula Parish

**Real Estate Recording**, Catahoula Parish Clerk of Court, Courthouse Square, Harrisonburg, LA 71340. 318-744-5497 (CST) 8:30AM-4:30PM.

**7th District Court**, PO Box 198, Harrisonburg, LA 71340. 318-744-5222 (CST) 8:00AM-4:30PM. Felony, Misdemeanor, Civil, Probate.

## Claiborne Parish

**Real Estate Recording**, Claiborne Parish Clerk of Court, 512 East Main Street, Homer, LA 71040. 318-927-9601 (CST) 8:30AM-4:30PM.

**2nd District Court**, PO Box 330, Homer, LA 71040. 318-927-9601 (CST) 8:30AM-4:30PM. Felony, Misdemeanor, Civil, Probate.

## Concordia Parish

**Real Estate Recording**, Concordia Parish Clerk of Court, Courthouse, P.O. Box 790, Vidalia, LA 71373. 318-336-4204 (CST) 8:30AM-4:30PM.

**7th District Court**, PO Box 790, Vidalia, LA 71373. 318-336-4204 (CST) 8:30AM-5:00PM. Felony, Misdemeanor, Civil, Probate.

## De Soto Parish

**Real Estate Recording**, De Soto Parish Clerk of Court, Texas Street, Courthouse Square, Mansfield, LA 71052. 318-872-3110 (CST) 8AM-4:30PM.

**11th District Court**, PO Box 1206, Mansfield, LA 71052. 318-872-3110 (CST) 8:00AM-4:30PM. Felony, Misdemeanor, Civil, Probate.

## East Baton Rouge Parish

**Real Estate Recording**, East Baton Rouge Parish Clerk of Court, 222 St. Louis Street, Baton Rouge, LA 70821. 504-389-3985 (CST) 7:30AM-5:30PM.

**19th District Court**, PO Box 1991, Baton Rouge, LA 70821. 504-389-3950 (CST) 7:30AM-5:30PM. Felony, Misdemeanor, Civil, Probate.

## East Carroll Parish

**Real Estate Recording**, East Carroll Parish Clerk of Court, 400 First Street, Lake Providence, LA 71254. 318-559-2399 (CST) 8:30AM-4:30PM.

**6th District Court**, 400 1st St, Lake Providence, LA 71254. 318-559-2399 (CST) 8:30AM-4:30PM. Felony, Misdemeanor, Civil, Probate.

## East Feliciana Parish

**Real Estate Recording**, East Feliciana Parish Clerk of Court, 12220 St. Helena Street, Courthouse Square, Clinton, LA 70722. 504-683-5145 (CST) 8AM-4:30PM.

**20th District Court**, PO Box 595, Clinton, LA 70722. 504-683-5145 (CST) 8:00AM-4:30PM. Felony, Misdemeanor, Civil, Probate.

## Evangeline Parish

**Real Estate Recording**, Evangeline Parish Clerk of Court, 200 Court Street, Courthouse Bldg., Ville Platte, LA 70586. 318-363-5671 (CST) 8AM-4:30PM.

**13th District Court**, PO Drawer 347, Ville Platte, LA 70586. 318-363-5671 (CST) 8:00AM-4:30PM. Felony, Misdemeanor, Civil, Probate.

## Franklin Parish

**Real Estate Recording**, Franklin Parish Clerk of Court, 207 Main Street, Courthouse, Winnsboro, LA 71295. 318-435-5133 (CST) 8:30AM-4:30PM.

**5th District Court**, PO Box 431, Winnsboro, LA 71295. 318-435-5133 (CST) 8:30AM-4:30PM. Felony, Misdemeanor, Civil, Probate.

## Grant Parish

**Real Estate Recording**, Grant Parish Clerk of Court, 200 Main Street, Colfax, LA 71417. 318-627-3246 (CST) 8:30AM-4:30PM.

**35th District Court**, PO Box 263, Colfax, LA 71417. 318-627-3246 (CST) 8:30AM-4:30PM. Felony, Misdemeanor, Civil, Probate.

## Iberia Parish

**Real Estate Recording**, Iberia Parish Clerk of Court, 300 Block of Iberia Street, New Iberia, LA 70562. 318-365-7282 (CST) 8:30AM-4:30PM.

**16th District Court**, PO Drawer 12010, New Iberia, LA 70562-2010. 318-365-7282 (CST)

8:30AM-4:30PM. Felony, Misdemeanor, Civil, Probate.

## Iberville Parish

**Real Estate Recording**, Iberville Parish Clerk of Court, 58050 Meriam Street, Plaquemine, LA 70764. 504-687-5160 (CST) 8:30AM-4:30PM.

**18th District Court**, PO Box 423, Plaquemine, LA 70764. 504-687-5160 (CST) 8:30AM-5:00PM. Felony, Misdemeanor, Civil, Probate.

## Jackson Parish

**Real Estate Recording**, Jackson Parish Clerk of Court, 500 East Court Avenue, Jonesboro, LA 71251. 318-259-2424 (CST) 8:30AM-4:30PM.

**2nd District Court**, PO Drawer 730, Jonesboro, LA 71251. 318-259-2424 (CST) 8:30AM-4:30PM. Felony, Misdemeanor, Civil, Probate.

## Jefferson Davis Parish

**Real Estate Recording**, Jefferson Davis Parish Clerk of Court, 300 State Street, Jennings, LA 70546. 318-824-1160 (CST) 8:30AM-4:30PM.

**31st District Court**, PO Box 799, Jennings, LA 70546. 318-824-1160 (CST) 8:30AM-4:30PM. Felony, Misdemeanor, Civil, Probate.

## Jefferson Parish

**Real Estate Recording**, Jefferson Parish Clerk of Court, 848 Second Street, Greenberg Bldg - 2nd Floor, Gretna, LA 70053. 504-364-2881 (CST) 8:30AM-4:30PM.

**24th District Court**, PO Box 10, Gretna, LA 70053. 504-364-2992 (CST) 8:30AM-4:30PM. Felony, Misdemeanor, Civil, Probate.

## La Salle Parish

**Real Estate Recording**, La Salle Parish Clerk of Court, Courthouse Square, Jena, LA 71342. 318-992-2158 (CST) 8:30AM-4:30PM.

**28th District Court**, PO Drawer 1372, Jena, LA 71342. 318-992-2158 (CST) 8:30AM-4:30PM. Felony, Misdemeanor, Civil, Probate.

## Lafayette Parish

**Real Estate Recording**, Lafayette Parish Clerk of Court, 800 South Buchanan Street, Lafayette, LA 70501. 318-233-0150 (CST) 8:30AM-4:30PM.

**15th District Court**, PO Box 2009, Lafayette, LA 70502. 318-233-0150 (CST) 8:30AM-4:30PM. Felony, Misdemeanor, Civil, Probate.

## Lafourche Parish

**Real Estate Recording**, Lafourche Parish Clerk of Court, 309 West Third, Thibodaux, LA 70301. 504-447-4841 (CST) 8:30AM-4:30PM.

**17th District Court**, PO Box 818, Thibodaux, LA 70302. 504-447-4841 (CST) 8:30AM-4:30PM. Felony, Misdemeanor, Civil, Probate.

## Lincoln Parish

**Real Estate Recording**, Lincoln Parish Clerk of Court, 100 Texas Avenue, Courthouse - Room 103, Ruston, LA 71270. 318-251-5130 (CST) 8:30AM-4:30PM.

**3rd District Court**, PO Box 924, Ruston, LA 71273-0924. 318-251-5130 (CST) 8:30AM-4:30PM. Felony, Misdemeanor, Civil, Probate.

## Livingston Parish

**Real Estate Recording**, Livingston Parish Clerk of Court, 20180 Iowa Street, Livingston, LA 70754. 504-686-2216 (CST) 8AM-4:30PM.

**21st District Court**, Courthouse, Livingston, LA 70754. 504-686-2216 (CST) 8:00AM-4:30PM. Felony, Misdemeanor, Civil, Probate.

## Madison Parish

**Real Estate Recording**, Madison Parish Clerk of Court, 100 North Cedar, Courthouse, Tallulah, LA 71282. 318-574-0655 (CST) 8:30AM-4:30PM.

**6th District Court**, 100 N Cedar, Tallulah, LA 71282. 318-574-0655 (CST) 8:30AM-4:30PM. Felony, Misdemeanor, Civil, Probate.

## Morehouse Parish

**Real Estate Recording**, Morehouse Parish Clerk of Court, 100 East Madison Ave., Courthouse Building, Bastrop, LA 71220-3893. 318-281-3343 (CST) 8:30AM-4:30PM.

**4th District Court**, Courthouse, 100 East Madison, Bastrop, LA 71220-3893. 318-281-3343 (CST) 8:30AM-4:30PM. Felony, Misdemeanor, Civil, Probate.

## Natchitoches Parish

**Real Estate Recording**, Natchitoches Parish Clerk of Court, 200 Church Street, New Courthouse Building-Room 104, Natchitoches, LA 71457. 318-352-8152 (CST) 8:30AM-4:30PM.

**10th District Court**, PO Box 476, Natchitoches, LA 71458. 318-352-8152 (CST) 8:15AM-4:30PM. Felony, Misdemeanor, Civil, Probate.

## Orleans Parish

**Real Estate Recording**, Orleans Parish Recorder of Mortgages, 421 Loyola Avenue, B-1, Civil Court Building, New Orleans, LA 70112. 504-592-9189 (CST) 9AM-4PM.

**4th District Court-Civil Division**, 421 Loyola Ave, Rm 402, New Orleans, LA 70112. 504-592-9100 (CST) 8AM-5PM. Civil, Probate.

**New Orleans City Court**, 421 Loyola Ave, Rm 201, New Orleans, LA 70112. 504-592-9155 (CST) 8:30AM-4:30PM M-F. Civil Actions Under $20,000, Small Claims.

**4th District Court-Criminal Division**, 2700 Tulane Ave, Rm 115, New Orleans, LA 70119. 504-827-3520 (CST) 8:15AM-3:30PM. Felony, Misdemeanor.

## Ouachita Parish

**Real Estate Recording**, Ouachita Parish Clerk of Court, 300 St. John, Monroe, LA 71201. 318-327-1444 (CST) 8AM-5PM.

**4th District Court**, PO Box 1862, Monroe, LA 71210-1862. 318-327-1444 (CST) 8:00AM-5:00PM. Felony, Misdemeanor, Civil, Probate.

## Plaquemines Parish

**Real Estate Recording**, Plaquemines Parish Clerk of Court, Highway 39, Courthouse, Pointe a la Hache, LA 70082. 504-333-4377 (CST) 8:30AM-4:30PM.

**25th District Court**, PO Box 129, Pointe A La Hache, LA 70082. 504-333-4377 (CST) 8:30AM-4:30PM. Felony, Misdemeanor, Civil, Probate.

## Pointe Coupee Parish

**Real Estate Recording**, Pointe Coupee Parish Clerk of Court, 201 East Main, New Roads, LA 70760. 504-638-9596 (CST) 8:30AM-4:30PM.

**18th District Court**, PO Box 86, New Roads, LA 70760. 504-638-9596 (CST) 8:30AM-4:30PM. Felony, Misdemeanor, Civil, Probate.

## Rapides Parish

**Real Estate Recording**, Rapides Parish Clerk of Court, Courthouse, Alexandria, LA 71309. 318-473-8153 (CST) 8:30AM-4:30PM.

**9th District Court**, PO Box 952, Alexandria, LA 71309. 318-473-8153 (CST) Felony, Misdemeanor, Civil, Probate.

## Red River Parish

**Real Estate Recording**, Red River Parish Clerk of Court, 615 Carroll Street, Coushatta, LA 71019. 318-932-6741 (CST) 8:30AM-4:30PM.

**39th District Court**, PO Box 485, Coushatta, LA 71019. 318-932-6741 (CST) 8:30AM-4:30PM. Felony, Misdemeanor, Civil, Probate.

## Richland Parish

**Real Estate Recording**, Richland Parish Clerk of Court, 100 Julia Street, Courthouse, Rayville, LA 71269. 318-728-4171 (CST) 8:30AM-4:30PM.

**5th District Court**, PO Box 119, Rayville, LA 71269. 318-728-4171 (CST) 8:30AM-4:30PM. Felony, Misdemeanor, Civil, Probate.

## Sabine Parish

**Real Estate Recording**, Sabine Parish Clerk of Court, Corner of Capitol & Main, Many, LA 71449. 318-256-6223 (CST) 8AM-4:30PM.

**11th District Court**, PO Box 419, Many, LA 71449. 318-256-6223 (CST) Felony, Misdemeanor, Civil, Probate.

## St. Bernard Parish

**Real Estate Recording**, St. Bernard Parish Clerk of Court, 1100 West St. Bernard Highway, Chalmette, LA 70043. 504-271-3434 (CST) 8:30AM-4:30PM.

**34th District Court**, PO Box 1746, Chalmette, LA 70044. 504-271-3434 (CST) 8:30AM-4:30OM. Felony, Misdemeanor, Civil, Probate.

## St. Charles Parish

**Real Estate Recording**, St. Charles Parish Clerk of Court, 15045 River Road, Courthouse, Hahnville, LA 70057. 504-783-6632 (CST) 8:30AM-4:30PM.

**29th District Court**, PO Box 424, Hahnville, LA 70057. 504-783-6632 (CST) Felony, Misdemeanor, Civil, Probate.

## St. Helena Parish

**Real Estate Recording**, St. Helena Parish Clerk of Court, Courthouse Square, Highway 10, P.O. Box 308, Greensburg, LA 70441. 504-222-4514 (CST) 8:30AM-4:30PM.

**21st District Court**, PO Box 308, Greensburg, LA 70441. 504-222-4514 (CST) 8:30AM-4:30PM. Felony, Misdemeanor, Civil, Probate.

## St. James Parish

**Real Estate Recording**, St. James Parish Clerk of Court, 5800 LA Highway 644, Courthouse, Convent, LA 70723. 504-562-2270 (CST) 8AM-4:30PM.

**23rd District Court**, PO Box 63, Convent, LA 70723. 504-562-7496 (CST) 8:00AM-4:30PM. Felony, Misdemeanor, Civil, Probate.

## St. John the Baptist Parish

**Real Estate Recording**, St. John the Baptist Parish Clerk of Court, East 3rd Street & River Road, Edgard, LA 70049. 504-497-3331 (CST) 8:30AM-4:30PM.

**40th District Court**, PO Box 280, Edgard, LA 70049. 504-497-3331 (CST) 8:30AM-4:30PM. Felony, Misdemeanor, Civil, Probate.

## St. Landry Parish

**Real Estate Recording**, St. Landry Parish Clerk of Court, Bellevue & Court Street, Opelousas, LA 70570. 318-942-5606 (CST) 8AM-4:30PM.

**27th District Court**, PO Box 750, Opelousas, LA 70570. 318-942-5606 (CST) 8:00AM-4:30PM. Felony, Misdemeanor, Civil, Probate.

## St. Martin Parish

**Real Estate Recording**, St. Martin Parish Clerk of Court, 415 S. Main Street, Courthouse, St. Martinville, LA 70582. 318-394-2210 (CST) 8:30AM-4:30PM.

**16th District Court**, PO Box 308, St. Martinville, LA 70582. 318-394-2210 (CST) 8:30AM-4:30PM. Felony, Misdemeanor, Civil, Probate.

## St. Mary Parish

**Real Estate Recording**, St. Mary Parish Clerk of Court, 500 Main Street, Courthouse, Franklin, LA 70538. 318-828-4100 (CST) 8:30AM-4:30PM.

**16th District Court**, PO Box 1231, Franklin, LA 70538. 318-828-4100 (CST) 8:30AM-4:30PM. Felony, Misdemeanor, Civil, Probate.

## St. Tammany Parish

**Real Estate Recording**, St. Tammany Parish Clerk of Court, 510 East Boston Street, Covington, LA 70433. 504-898-2430 (CST) 8:30AM-4:30PM.

**22nd District Court**, PO Box 1090, Covington, LA 70434. 504-898-2430 (CST) 8:30AM-4:30PM. Felony, Misdemeanor, Civil, Probate.

## Tangipahoa Parish

**Real Estate Recording**, Tangipahoa Parish Clerk of Court, Mulberry & Bay Street, Amite, LA 70422. 504-549-1611 (CST) 8:30AM-4:30PM.

**21st District Court**, PO Box 667, Amite, LA 70422. 504-748-4146 (CST) 8:30AM-4:30PM. Felony, Misdemeanor, Civil, Probate.

## Tensas Parish

**Real Estate Recording**, Tensas Parish Clerk of Court, Hancock Street, Courthouse, St. Joseph, LA 71366. 318-766-3921 (CST)

**6th District Court**, PO Box 78, St. Joseph, LA 71366. 318-766-3921 (CST) 8:00AM-4:30PM. Felony, Misdemeanor, Civil, Probate.

## Terrebonne Parish

**Real Estate Recording**, Terrebonne Parish Clerk of Court, 400 Main Street, Old Courthouse Building, Houma, LA 70360. 504-868-5660 (CST) 8:30AM-4:30PM.

**32nd District Court**, PO Box 1569, Houma, LA 70361. 504-868-5660 (CST) 8:30AM-4:30PM. Felony, Misdemeanor, Civil, Probate.

## Union Parish

**Real Estate Recording**, Union Parish Clerk of Court, Courthouse, Farmerville, LA 71241. 318-368-3055 (CST) 8:30AM-4:30PM.

**3rd District Court**, Courthouse Bldg, Farmerville, LA 71241. 318-368-3055 (CST) Felony, Misdemeanor, Civil, Probate.

## Vermilion Parish

**Real Estate Recording**, Vermilion Parish Clerk of Court, South State Street, Courthouse, Abbeville, LA 70510. 318-898-1992 (CST) 8:30AM-4:30PM.

**15th District Court**, PO Box 790, Abbeville, LA 70511. 318-898-1992 (CST) 8:30AM-4:30PM. Felony, Misdemeanor, Civil, Probate.

## Vernon Parish

**Real Estate Recording**, Vernon Parish Clerk of Court, 201 South Third Street, Leesville, LA 71446. 318-238-1384 (CST) 8AM-4:30PM.

**30th District Court**, PO Box 40, Leesville, LA 71496. 318-238-1384 (CST) 8:00Am-4:30PM. Felony, Misdemeanor, Civil, Probate.

## Washington Parish

**Real Estate Recording**, Washington Parish Clerk of Court, Corner of Washington & Main, Franklinton, LA 70438. 504-839-4663 (CST) 8AM-4:30PM.

**22nd District Court**, PO Box 607, Franklinton, LA 70438. 504-839-4661 (CST) 8:00AM-4:30PM. Felony, Misdemeanor, Civil, Probate.

## Webster Parish

**Real Estate Recording**, Webster Parish Clerk of Court, 410 Main Street, Courthouse, Minden, LA 71058. 318-371-0366 (CST) 8:30AM-4:30PM.

**26th District Court**, PO Box 370, Minden, LA 71058. 318-371-0366 (CST) 8:30AM-4:30PM. Felony, Misdemeanor, Civil, Probate.

## West Baton Rouge Parish

**Real Estate Recording**, West Baton Rouge Parish Clerk of Court, 850 8th Street, Port Allen, LA 70767. 504-383-0378 (CST) 8:30AM-4:30PM.

**18th District Court**, PO Box 107, Port Allen, LA 70767. 504-383-0378 (CST) 8:30AM-4:30PM. Felony, Misdemeanor, Civil, Probate.

## West Carroll Parish

**Real Estate Recording**, West Carroll Parish Clerk of Court, Main Street, Courthouse, Oak Grove, LA 71263. 318-428-3281 (CST) 8:30AM-4:30PM.

**5th District Court**, PO Box 1078, Livingston, LA 70754. 504-686-2216 (CST) 8:30AM-4:30PM. Felony, Misdemeanor, Civil, Probate.

## West Feliciana Parish

**Real Estate Recording**, West Feliciana Parish Clerk of Court, Corner of Ferdinand & Prosperity, Courthouse, St. Francisville, LA 70775. 504-635-3794 (CST) 8:30AM-4:30PM.

## Winn Parish

**Real Estate Recording**, Winn Parish Clerk of Court, 100 Main Street, Courthouse, Winnfield, LA 71483. 318-628-3515 (CST) 8AM-4:30PM.

**8th District Court**, 100 Main St, Winnfield, LA 71483. 318-628-3515 (CST) 8:00AM-4:30PM. Felony, Misdemeanor, Civil, Probate.

# Maine

## Androscoggin County

**Real Estate Recording**, Androscoggin County Register of Deeds, 2 Turner Street, Courthouse, Auburn, ME 04210-5978. 207-782-0191 (EST) 8AM-5PM.

**Superior Court**, PO Box 3660, Auburn, ME 04210. 207-783-5450 (EST) 8AM-4:30PM. Felony, Misdemeanor, Civil Actions Over $30,000.

**Lewiston District Court-South #8**, PO Box 1345, Lewiston, ME 04243. 207-783-5401 (EST) 8AM-4PM. Misdemeanor, Civil Actions Under $30,000, Eviction, Small Claims.

**Livermore Falls District Court-North #11**, 2 Main St, Livermore Falls, ME 04254. 207-897-3800 (EST) 8AM-4PM T, W, Th. Misdemeanor, Civil Actions Under $30,000, Eviction, Small Claims.

**Probate Court**, PO Box 70, Auburn, ME 04210. 207-782-0281 (EST) Probate.

## Aroostook County

**Real Estate Recording**, Northern Aroostook County Register of Deeds, Northern District, 13 Hall St., Fort Kent, ME 04743. 207-834-3925 (EST) 8AM-4:30PM.

**Real Estate Recording**, Aroostook County Register of Deeds, Southern District, Court Street, Courthouse, Houlton, ME 04730. 207-532-1500 (EST) 8AM-4:30PM.

**Caribou Superior Court**, 240 Sweden St, Caribou, ME 04736. 207-498-8125 (EST) 8AM-4PM. Felony, Misdemeanor, Civil Actions Over $30,000.

**Houlton Superior Court**, PO Box 787, Houlton, ME 04730. 207-532-6563 (EST) 8AM-4PM. Felony, Misdemeanor, Civil Actions Over $30,000.

**Caribou District Court-East #1**, 240 Sweden St, Caribou, ME 04736. 207-493-3144 (EST) 8AM-4PM. Misdemeanor, Civil Actions Under $30,000, Eviction, Small Claims.

**Fort Kent District Court-West #1**, PO Box 473, Fort Kent, ME 04743. 207-834-5003 (EST) 8AM-4PM T-F. Misdemeanor, Civil Actions Under $30,000, Eviction, Small Claims.

**Houlton District Court-South #2**, PO Box 457, Houlton, ME 04730. 207-532-2147 (EST) 8AM-4PM M,TH 9AM-3PM T,W,F. Misdemeanor, Civil Actions Under $30,000, Eviction, Small Claims.

**Madawaska District Court-West**, PO Box 127, Madawaska, ME 04756. 207-728-4700 (EST) 8AM-4PM M,T,F. Misdemeanor, Civil Actions Under $30,000, Eviction, Small Claims.

**Presque Isle District Court-Central #2**, PO Box 794, Presque Isle, ME 04769. 207-764-2055 (EST) 9AM-3PM M,TH 8AM-4PM T,W,F. Misdemeanor, Civil Actions Under $30,000, Eviction, Small Claims.

**Probate Court**, PO Box 787, Houlton, ME 04730. 207-532-1502 (EST) Probate.

## Cumberland County

**Real Estate Recording**, Cumberland County Register of Deeds, 142 Federal Street, Portland, ME 04101. 207-871-8389 (EST) 8:30AM-4:30PM.

**Superior Court-Civil**, PO Box 287-DTS, Portland, ME 04112. 207-822-4105 (EST) 8AM-4:30PM. Civil Actions Over $30,000.

**Superior Court-Criminal**, PO Box 287, Portland, ME 04112. 207-822-4113 (EST) 8AM-4:30PM. Felony, Misdemeanor.

**Portland District Court-South #9-Civil**, PO Box 412, Portland, ME 04112. 207-822-4200 (EST) 8AM-4:30PM. Civil Actions Under $30,000, Eviction, Small Claims.

**Portland District Court-South #9-Criminal**, PO Box 412, Portland, ME 04112. 207-822-4205 (EST) 8AM-4:30PM. Misdemeanor.

**Bath District Court-East #6**, RR 1, Box 310, Bath, ME 04530. 207-442-0200 (EST) 8AM-4:30PM. Misdemeanor, Civil Actions Under $30,000, Eviction, Small Claims.

**Bridgton District Court-North #9**, 2 Chase Common, Bridgton, ME 04009. 207-647-3535 (EST) 8AM-4PM. Misdemeanor, Civil Actions Under $30,000, Eviction, Small Claims.

**Probate Court**, 142 Federal St, Portland, ME 04101-4196. 207-871-8382 (EST) Probate.

## Franklin County

**Real Estate Recording**, Franklin County Register of Deeds, 38 Main Street, Courthouse, Farmington, ME 04938-1818. 207-778-5889 (EST) 8:30AM-4PM.

**Superior Court**, 38 Main St, Farmington, ME 04938. 207-778-3346 (EST) 8AM-4PM. Felony, Misdemeanor, Civil Actions Over $30,000.

**District Court #12**, 25 Main St, Farmington, ME 04938. 207-778-5177 (EST) 8AM-4PM. Misdemeanor, Civil Actions Under $30,000, Eviction, Small Claims.

**Probate Court**, County Courthouse, Farmington, ME 04938. 207-778-5888 (EST) Probate.

## Hancock County

**Real Estate Recording**, Hancock County Register of Deeds, 60 State Street, Ellsworth, ME 04605. 207-667-8353 (EST) 8:30AM-4PM.

**Superior Court**, PO Box 1085, Clerk of Court, Ellsworth, ME 04605. 207-667-7176 (EST) 8AM-4PM. Felony, Misdemeanor, Civil Actions Over $30,000.

**Bar Harbor District Court-South #5**, 93 Cottage St, Bar Harbor, ME 04609. 207-288-3082 (EST) 8AM-4PM. Misdemeanor, Civil Actions Under $30,000, Eviction, Small Claims.

**Ellsworth District Court-Central #5**, 60 State St, Ellsworth, ME 04605. 207-667-7141 (EST) 8AM-4PM. Misdemeanor, Civil Actions Under $30,000, Eviction, Small Claims.

**Probate Court**, 60 State St, Ellsworth, ME 04605. 207-667-8434 (EST) Probate.

## Kennebec County

**Real Estate Recording**, Kennebec County Register of Deeds, 95 State Street, Augusta, ME 04330. 207-622-0431 (EST) 8:30AM-4PM.

**Superior Court**, 95 State St, Clerk of Court, Augusta, ME 04330. 207-622-9357 (EST) 8AM-4PM. Felony, Misdemeanor, Civil Actions Over $30,000.

**Augusta District Court-South #7**, 145 State, Augusta, ME 04330. 207-622-6321 (EST) 8AM-4PM. Misdemeanor, Civil Actions Under $30,000, Eviction, Small Claims.

**Probate Court**, 95 State St, Augusta, ME 04330. 207-622-7558 (EST) Probate.

## Knox County

**Real Estate Recording**, Knox County Register of Deeds, 62 Union Street, Rockland, ME 04841. 207-594-0422 (EST) 8AM-4PM.

**Superior Court**, PO Box 1024, Clerk of Court, Rockland, ME 04841. 207-594-2576 (EST) 8AM-4PM. Felony, Misdemeanor, Civil Actions Over $30,000.

**District Court #6**, PO Box 544, 62 Union St, Rockland, ME 04841. 207-596-2240 (EST) 8AM-4PM. Misdemeanor, Civil Actions Under $30,000, Eviction, Small Claims.

**Probate Court**, 62 Union St, PO Box 885, Rockland, ME 04841. 207-594-0427 (EST) Probate.

## Lincoln County

**Real Estate Recording**, Lincoln County Register of Deeds, High Street, Courthouse, Wiscasset, ME 04578. 207-882-7515 (EST) 8AM-4PM.

**Superior Court**, High St, Wiscasset, ME 04578. 207-882-7517 (EST) 8AM-4PM. Felony, Misdemeanor, Civil Actions Over $30,000.

**District Court #6**, High St, Wiscasset, ME 04578. 207-882-6363 (EST) 8AM-4PM. Misdemeanor, Civil Actions Under $30,000, Eviction, Small Claims.

**Probate Court**, High St, Wiscasset, ME 04578. 207-882-7392 (EST) Probate.

## Oxford County

**Real Estate Recording**, Oxford County Register of Deeds, 126 Western Avenue, South Paris, ME 04281. 207-743-6211 (EST) 8AM-4PM.

**Superior Court**, Courthouse, 26 Western Ave, PO Box 179, South Paris, ME 04281-0179. 207-743-8936 (EST) 8AM-4PM. Felony, Misdemeanor, Civil Actions Over $30,000.

**Rumford District Court-North #11**, Congress St, Rumford, ME 04276. 207-364-7171 (EST) 8AM-4PM. Misdemeanor, Civil Actions Under $30,000, Eviction, Small Claims.

**South Paris District Court-South #11**, 26 Western Ave, South Paris, ME 04281. 207-743-8942 (EST) 8AM-4PM. Misdemeanor, Civil Actions Under $30,000, Eviction, Small Claims.

**Probate Court**, 26 Western Ave, PO Box 179, South Paris, ME 04281. 207-743-6671 (EST) Probate.

## Penobscot County

**Real Estate Recording**, Penobscot County Register of Deeds, 97 Hammond Street, Bangor, ME 04401. 207-942-8797 (EST) 8AM-4:30PM.

**Superior Court**, 97 Hammond St, Bangor, ME 04401. 207-947-0751 (EST) 8AM-4:30 PM. Felony, Misdemeanor, Civil Actions Over $30,000.

**Bangor District Court-South #3**, 73 Hammond St, Bangor, ME 04401. 207-941-3040 (EST) 8AM-4PM. Misdemeanor, Civil Actions Under $30,000, Eviction, Small Claims.

# Maine

**Central District Court-Central #13**, 66 Maine St, Lincoln, ME 04457. 207-794-8512 (EST) 8AM-4PM. Misdemeanor, Civil Actions Under $30,000, Eviction, Small Claims.

**Millinocket District Court-North #13**, 207 Penobscot Ave, Millinocket, ME 04462. 207-723-4786 (EST) 8AM-4PM. Misdemeanor, Civil Actions Under $30,000, Eviction, Small Claims.

**Newport District Court-West #3**, 16 Water St, Newport, ME 04953. 207-368-5778 (EST) 8AM-4PM. Misdemeanor, Civil Actions Under $30,000, Eviction, Small Claims.

**Probate Court**, 97 Hammond St, Bangor, ME 04401-4998. 207-942-8769 (EST) Probate.

## Piscataquis County

**Real Estate Recording**, Piscataquis County Register of Deeds, 51 East Main Street, Dover-Foxcroft, ME 04426. 207-564-2411 (EST) 8:30AM-4PM.

**Superior Court**, 51 E Main St, Dover-Foxcroft, ME 04426. 207-564-8419 (EST) 8AM-4PM. Felony, Misdemeanor, Civil Actions Over $30,000.

**District Court #13**, 59 E Main St, Dover-Foxcroft, ME 04426. 207-564-2240 (EST) 8AM-4PM M-F. Misdemeanor, Civil Actions Under $30,000, Eviction, Small Claims.

**Probate Court**, 51 E Main St, Dover-Foxcroft, ME 04426. 207-564-2431 (EST) Probate.

## Sagadahoc County

**Real Estate Recording**, Sagadahoc County Register of Deeds, 752 High Street, Bath, ME 04530. 207-443-8214 (EST) 9AM-4:30PM.

**Superior Court**, 752 High St, PO Box 246, Bath, ME 04530. 207-443-9733 (EST) 8AM-4:30 PM. Felony, Misdemeanor, Civil Actions Over $30,000.

**District Court #6**, RR 1, Box 310, Bath, ME 04530. 207-442-0200 (EST) 8AM-4PM. Misdemeanor, Civil Actions Under $30,000, Eviction, Small Claims.

**Probate Court**, High St, PO Box 246, Bath, ME 04530. 207-443-8218 (EST) Probate.

## Somerset County

**Real Estate Recording**, Somerset County Register of Deeds, Corner of Court & High Street, Skowhegan, ME 04976. 207-474-3421 (EST) 8:30AM-4:30PM.

**Superior Court**, Clerk of Court, PO Box 725, Skowhegan, ME 04976. 207-474-5161 (EST) 8AM-4PM. Felony, Misdemeanor, Civil Actions Over $30,000.

**District Court #12**, PO Box 525, Skowhegan, ME 04976. 207-474-9518 (EST) 8AM-4PM. Misdemeanor, Civil Actions Under $30,000, Eviction, Small Claims.

**Probate Court**, Court St, Skowhegan, ME 04976. 207-474-3322 (EST) Probate.

## Waldo County

**Real Estate Recording**, Waldo County Register of Deeds, 73 Church Street, Belfast, ME 04915. 207-338-1710 (EST) 8AM-4PM.

**Superior Court**, 73 Church St, PO Box 188, Belfast, ME 04915. 207-338-1940 (EST) 8AM-4PM. Felony, Misdemeanor, Civil Actions Over $30,000.

**District Court #5**, PO Box 382, 37 Church St, Belfast, ME 04915. 207-338-3107 (EST) 8AM-4PM. Misdemeanor, Civil Actions Under $30,000, Eviction, Small Claims.

**Probate Court**, 73 Church St, PO Box 323, Belfast, ME 04915. 207-338-2780 (EST) Probate.

## Washington County

**Real Estate Recording**, Washington County Register of Deeds, 47 Court Street, Machias, ME 04654. 207-255-6512 (EST) 8AM-5PM.

**Superior Court**, Clerk of Court, PO Box 526, Machias, ME 04654. 207-255-3326 (EST) 8AM-4PM. Felony, Misdemeanor, Civil Actions Over $30,000.

**Calais District Court-North #4**, 88 South St, Calais, ME 04619. 207-454-2055 (EST) 8AM-4PM. Misdemeanor, Civil Actions Under $30,000, Eviction, Small Claims.

**Machias District Court-South #4**, PO Box 297, Machias, ME 04654. 207-255-3044 (EST) 8AM-4PM. Misdemeanor, Civil Actions Under $30,000, Eviction, Small Claims.

**Probate Court**, PO Box 297, Machias, ME 04654. 207-255-6591 (EST) Probate.

## York County

**Real Estate Recording**, York County Register of Deeds, Court Street, Courthouse, Alfred, ME 04002. 207-324-1576 (EST) 8:30AM-4:30PM.

**Superior Court**, Clerk of Court, PO Box 160, Alfred, ME 04002. 207-324-5122 (EST) 8AM-4PM. Felony, Misdemeanor, Civil Actions Over $30,000.

**Biddeford District Court-East #10**, 35 Washington St, Biddeford, ME 04005. 207-283-1147 (EST) 8AM-4PM. Misdemeanor, Civil Actions Under $30,000, Eviction, Small Claims.

**Springvale District Court-West #10**, PO Box 95, Springvale, ME 04083. 207-324-6737 (EST) 8AM-4PM M,T,F. Misdemeanor, Civil Actions Under $30,000, Eviction, Small Claims.

**York District Court-South #10**, PO Box 776, York, ME 03909. 207-363-1230 (EST) 8AM-4PM. Misdemeanor, Civil Actions Under $30,000, Eviction, Small Claims.

**Probate Court**, PO Box 399, Alfred, ME 04002. 207-324-1577 (EST) Probate.

# Maryland

## Allegany County

**Real Estate Recording**, Allegany County Clerk of the Circuit Court, 30 Washington Street, Cumberland, MD 21502. 301-777-5922 (EST) 8AM-4:30PM.

**4th Judicial Circuit Court**, Courthouse Washington St, Cumberland, MD 21502. 301-777-5922 (EST) 8:30AM-4:30PM. Felony, Misdemeanor, Civil Actions Over $20,000.

**District Court**, 33 Pershing St, Cumberland, MD 21502. 301-777-2105 (EST) 8:30AM-4:30PM. Misdemeanor, Civil Actions Under $20,000, Eviction, Small Claims.

**Register of Wills**, Courthouse Washington St, Cumberland, MD 21502. 301-724-3760 (EST) 8AM-4:30PM. Probate.

## Anne Arundel County

**Real Estate Recording**, Anne Arundel County Clerk of the Circuit Court, 7 Church Circle Street, Room 101, Annapolis, MD 21404. 410-222-1425 (EST) 8AM-4:30PM.

**5th Judicial Circuit Court**, Box 71, Annapolis, MD 21404. 410-222-1397 (EST) 8:30AM-4:30PM. Felony, Misdemeanor, Civil Actions Over $20,000.

**District Court**, 580 Taylor Ave, Annapolis, MD 21401. 410-974-2678 (EST) 8:30AM-4:30PM. Misdemeanor, Civil Actions Under $20,000, Eviction, Small Claims.

**Register of Wills**, 44 Calvert St (PO Box 2368), Annapolis, MD 21401-2368. 410-222-1430 (EST) 8AM-4:30PM. Probate.

## Baltimore City

**Real Estate Recording**, Circuit Court for Baltimore City, 100 North Calvert Street, Room 610, Baltimore, MD 21202. 410-333-3768 (EST) 8AM-4:30PM.

**8th Judicial Circuit Court-Civil Division**, 111 N Calvert, Rm 462, Baltimore, MD 21202. 410-333-3722 (EST) 8:30AM-4:30PM. Civil Actions Over $20,000.

**8th Judicial Circuit Court-Criminal Division**, 110 N Calvert Rm 200, Baltimore, MD 21202. 410-333-3750 (EST) Felony, Misdemeanor.

**District Court-Civil Division**, 501 E Fayette St, Baltimore, MD 21202. 410-333-4664 (EST) 8:30AM-4:30PM. Civil Actions Under $20,000, Eviction, Small Claims.

**District Court-Criminal Division**, 1400 E North Ave, Baltimore, MD 21213. 410-554-4227 (EST) Misdemeanor.

**Register of Wills**, 111 N Calvert St, Room 352, Baltimore, MD 21202. 410-752-5131 (EST) Probate.

## Baltimore County

**Real Estate Recording**, Baltimore County Clerk of the Circuit Court, 401 Bosley Avenue, County Courts Building, Towson, MD 21285. 410-887-2658 (EST) 8AM-4:30PM.

**3rd Judicial Circuit Court**, 401 Bosley Ave, 2nd Floor, Towson, MD 21204. 410-887-2601 (EST) 8:30AM-4:30PM. Felony, Misdemeanor, Civil Actions Over $20,000.

**District Court**, 120 E Chesapeake Ave, Towson, MD 21286-5307. 410-321-3300 (EST) 8:30AM-4:30PM. Misdemeanor, Civil Actions Under $20,000, Eviction, Small Claims.

**Register of Wills**, 401 Bosley Ave, Towson, MD 21204. 410-887-6685 (EST) 8AM-4:30PM. Probate.

## Calvert County

**Real Estate Recording**, Calvert County Clerk of the Circuit Court, 175 Main Street, Courthouse, Prince Frederick, MD 20678. 410-535-1660 (EST) 8:30AM-4:30PM.

**7th Judicial Circuit Court**, 175 Main St Courthouse, Prince Frederick, MD 20678. 410-535-1600 (EST) 8:30AM-4:30PM. Felony, Misdemeanor, Civil Actions Over $20,000.

**District Court**, 200 Duke St, Prince Frederick, MD 20678. 410-535-8801 (EST) 8:30AM-4:30PM. Misdemeanor, Civil Actions Under $20,000, Eviction, Small Claims.

**Register of Wills**, 175 Main St Courthouse, Prince Frederick, MD 20678. 410-535-1600 (EST) 8:30AM-4:30PM. Probate.

## Caroline County

**Real Estate Recording**, Caroline County Clerk of the Circuit Court, Market Street, Courthouse, Denton, MD 21629. 410-479-1811 (EST) 8:30AM-4:30PM.

**2nd Judicial Circuit Court**, Box 458, Denton, MD 21629. 410-479-1811 (EST) 8:30AM-4:30PM. Felony, Misdemeanor, Civil Actions Over $20,000.

**District Court**, 213 S 3rd St, Denton, MD 21629. 410-479-5800 (EST) 8:30AM-4:30PM. Misdemeanor, Civil Actions Under $20,000, Eviction, Small Claims.

**Register of Wills**, PO Box 416, Denton, MD 21629. 410-479-0717 (EST) 8:30AM-4:30PM. Probate.

## Carroll County

**Real Estate Recording**, Carroll County Clerk of the Circuit Court, 55 North Court Street, Room G8, Westminster, MD 21157. 410-857-2023 (EST) 8:30AM-4:30PM.

**5th Judicial Circuit Court**, Box 190, Westminster, MD 21158-0190. 410-876-1213 (EST) 8:30AM-4:30PM. Felony, Misdemeanor, Civil Actions Over $20,000.

**District Court**, 55 N Court St, Westminster, MD 21157. 410-848-2146 (EST) 8:30AM-4:30PM. Misdemeanor, Civil Actions Under $20,000, Eviction, Small Claims.

**Register of Wills**, 55 N Court St, Rm 104, Westminster, MD 21157. 410-848-2586 (EST) 8:30AM-4:30PM. Probate.

## Cecil County

**Real Estate Recording**, Cecil County Clerk of the Circuit Court, 129 East Main St., Room 108, Elkton, MD 21921-5971. 410-996-5375 (EST) 8:30AM-4:30PM.

**2nd Judicial Circuit Court**, 129 E Main St, Rm 108, Elkton, MD 21921. 410-996-5373 (EST) 8:30AM-4:30PM. Felony, Misdemeanor, Civil Actions Over $20,000.

**District Court**, 170 E Main St, Elkton, MD 21921. 410-996-0700 (EST) Misdemeanor, Civil Actions Under $20,000, Eviction, Small Claims.

**Register of Wills**, County Courthouse, Rm 307, Elkton, MD 21921. 410-996-5330 (EST) 8AM-5PM. Probate.

## Charles County

**Real Estate Recording**, Charles County Clerk of the Circuit Court, Charles Street & Washington Ave., Courthouse, La Plata, MD 20646. 301-932-3235 (EST) 8:30AM-4:30PM.

**7th Judicial Circuit Court**, Box 970, La Plata, MD 20646. 301-932-3220 (EST) Felony, Misdemeanor, Civil Actions Over $20,000.

**District Court**, 200 Charles St, La Plata, MD 20646. 301-932-3290 (EST) 8:30AM-4:30PM. Misdemeanor, Civil Actions Under $20,000, Eviction, Small Claims.

**Register of Wills**, Box 3080, La Plata, MD 20646. 301-932-3345 (EST) 8:30AM-4:30PM. Probate.

## Dorchester County

**Real Estate Recording**, Dorchester County Clerk of the Circuit Court, 206 High Street, Cambridge, MD 21613. 410-228-0481 (EST) 8:30AM-4:30PM.

**1st Judicial Circuit Court**, Box 150, Cambridge, MD 21613. 410-228-0481 (EST) 8:30AM-4:30PM. Felony, Misdemeanor, Civil Actions Over $20,000.

**District Court**, Box 547, Cambridge, MD 21613. 410-221-2580 (EST) 8:30AM-4:30PM. Misdemeanor, Civil Actions Under $20,000, Eviction, Small Claims.

**Register of Wills**, Box 263, Cambridge, MD 21613. 410-228-4181 (EST) 8AM-4:30PM. Probate.

## Frederick County

**Real Estate Recording**, Frederick County Clerk of the Circuit Court, 100 West Patrick Street, Frederick, MD 21701. 301-694-1964 (EST) 8:30AM-4:30PM.

**6th Judicial Circuit Court**, 100 W Patrick St, Frederick, MD 21701. 301-694-1972 (EST) 8AM-4:30PM. Felony, Misdemeanor, Civil Actions Over $20,000.

**District Court**, 100 W Patrick St, Frederick, MD 21701. 301-694-2000 (EST) 8:30AM-4:30PM. Misdemeanor, Civil Actions Under $20,000, Eviction, Small Claims.

**Register of Wills**, 100 W Patrick St, Frederick, MD 21701. 301-663-3722 (EST) 8AM-4:30PM. Probate.

## Garrett County

**Real Estate Recording**, Garrett County Clerk of the Circuit Court, 203 South Fourth Street, Oakland, MD 21550. 301-334-1937 (EST) 8:30AM-4:30PM.

**4th Judicial Circuit Court**, PO Box 447, Oakland, MD 21550. 301-334-1937 (EST) 8:30AM-4:30PM. Felony, Misdemeanor, Civil Actions Over $20,000.

**District Court**, 205 S 3rd St, Oakland, MD 21550. 301-334-8164 (EST) 8:30AM-4:30PM. Misdemeanor, Civil Actions Under $20,000, Eviction, Small Claims.

**Maryland**

Register of Wills, 313 E Alder St, Room 103, Oakland, MD 21550. 301-334-1999 (EST) 8:30AM-4:30PM. Probate.

## Harford County

Real Estate Recording, Harford County Clerk of the Circuit Court, 20 West Courtland Street, Bel Air, MD 21014. 410-638-3474 (EST) 8:30AM-4PM.

3rd Judicial Circuit Court, 20 W Courtland St, Bel Air, MD 21014. 410-638-3426 (EST) 8:30AM-4:30PM. Felony, Misdemeanor, Civil Actions Over $20,000.

District Court, 2 S Bond St, Bel Air, MD 21014. 410-838-2300 (EST) 8:30AM-4:30PM. Misdemeanor, Civil Actions Under $20,000, Eviction, Small Claims.

Register of Wills, 20 W Courtland St, Room 304, Bel Air, MD 21014. 410-638-3275 (EST) 8:30AM-4:30PM. Probate.

## Howard County

Real Estate Recording, Howard County Clerk of the Circuit Court, 8360 Court Avenue, Ellicott City, MD 21043. 410-313-2111 (EST) 8:30AM-4:30PM.

5th Judicial Circuit Court, 8360 Court Ave, Ellicott City, MD 21043. 410-313-2111 (EST) 8:30AM-4:30PM. Felony, Misdemeanor, Civil Actions Over $20,000.

District Court, 3451 Courthouse Dr, Ellicott City, MD 21043. 410-461-0213 (EST) 8:30AM-4:30PM. Misdemeanor, Civil Actions Under $20,000, Eviction, Small Claims.

Register of Wills, 8360 Court Ave, Ellicott City, MD 21043. 410-313-2133 (EST) 8:30AM-4:30PM. Probate.

## Kent County

Real Estate Recording, Kent County Clerk of the Circuit Court, 103 N. Cross Street, Courthouse, Chestertown, MD 21620. 410-778-7400 (EST) 8:30AM-4:30PM.

2nd Judicial Circuit Court, 103 N Cross St Courthouse, Chestertown, MD 21620. 410-778-7460 (EST) Felony, Misdemeanor, Civil Actions Over $20,000.

District Court, 103 N Cross St, Chestertown, MD 21620. 410-778-1830 (EST) 8:30AM-4:30PM. Misdemeanor, Civil Actions Under $20,000, Eviction, Small Claims.

Register of Wills, 103 N Cross St, Chestertown, MD 21620. 410-778-7466 (EST) 8:30AM-4:30PM. Probate.

## Montgomery County

Real Estate Recording, Montgomery County Clerk of the Circuit Court, 50 Courthouse Square, County Courthouse, Rockville, MD 20850. 301-217-7116 (EST) 8:30AM-4:30PM.

6th Judicial Circuit Court, 50 Courthouse Square, Rockville, MD 20850. 301-217-7057 (EST) 8:30AM-4:30PM. Felony, Misdemeanor, Civil Actions Over $20,000.

Rockville District Court, 27 Courthouse Square, Rockville, MD 20850. 301-279-1520 (EST) 8:30AM-4:30PM. Misdemeanor, Civil Actions Under $20,000, Eviction, Small Claims.

Silver Spring District Court, 8665 Georgia Ave, Silver Spring, MD 20901. 301-608-0660 (EST) 8:30AM-4:30PM. Misdemeanor, Civil Actions Under $20,000, Eviction, Small Claims.

Register of Wills, 50 Courthouse, Rockville, MD 20850. 301-217-7150 (EST) 8:30AM-4:30PM. Probate.

## Prince George's County

Real Estate Recording, Prince George's County Clerk of the Circuit Court, 14735 Main Street, Upper Marlboro, MD 20772. 301-952-4895 (EST)

7th Judicial Circuit Court, 14735 Main St, Upper Marlboro, MD 20772. 301-952-3318 (EST) 8:30AM-4:30PM. Felony, Misdemeanor, Civil Actions Over $20,000.

District Court, 14735 Main St, Rm 173B, Upper Marlboro, MD 20772. 301-952-4080 (EST) 8:30AM-4:30PM. Misdemeanor, Civil Actions Under $20,000, Eviction, Small Claims.

Register of Wills, 14735 Main St #306D, Upper Marlboro, MD 20772. 301-952-3250 (EST) 8:30AM-4:30PM. Probate.

## Queen Anne's County

Real Estate Recording, Queen Anne's County Clerk of the Circuit Court, Commerce Street, Courthouse, Centreville, MD 21617. 410-758-1773 (EST) 8:30AM-4:30PM.

2nd Judicial Circuit Court, Courthouse, Centreville, MD 21617. 410-758-1773 (EST) 8:30AM-4:30PM. Felony, Misdemeanor, Civil Actions Over $20,000.

District Court, 120 Broadway, Centreville, MD 21617. 410-758-5200 (EST) 8:30AM-4:30PM. Misdemeanor, Civil Actions Under $20,000, Eviction, Small Claims.

Register of Wills, Liberty Bldg, 107 N Liberty St #220, Centreville, MD 21617. 410-758-0585 (EST) 8:30AM-4:30PM. Probate.

## Somerset County

Real Estate Recording, Somerset County Clerk of the Circuit Court, 30512 Prince William Street, Princess Anne, MD 21853. 410-651-1555 (EST) 8:30AM-4:30PM.

1st Judicial Circuit Court, Box 99, Princess Anne, MD 21853. 410-651-1555 (EST) 8:30AM-4:30PM. Felony, Misdemeanor, Civil Actions Over $20,000.

District Court, 11774 Somerset Ave, Princess Anne, MD 21853. 410-651-0955 (EST) 8:30AM-4:30PM. Misdemeanor, Civil Actions Under $20,000, Eviction, Small Claims.

Register of Wills, 30512 Prince William St, Princess Anne, MD 21853. 410-651-1696 (EST) 8:30AM-4:30PM. Probate.

## St. Mary's County

Real Estate Recording, St. Mary's County Clerk of the Circuit Court, 1 Courthouse Drive, Leonardtown, MD 20650. 301-475-4567 (EST) 8:30AM-4:30PM.

7th Judicial Circuit Court, Box 676, Leonardtown, MD 20650. 301-475-5621 (EST) 8:30AM-4:30PM. Felony, Misdemeanor, Civil Actions Over $20,000.

District Court, 180 Washington St, Leonardtown, MD 20650. 301-475-4530 (EST) 8:30AM-4:30PM. Misdemeanor, Civil Actions Under $20,000, Eviction, Small Claims.

Register of Wills, PO Box 602, Leonardtown, MD 20650. 301-475-5566 (EST) 8:30AM-4:30PM. Probate.

## Talbot County

Real Estate Recording, Talbot County Clerk of the Circuit Court, Washington Street and Federal Street, Courthouse, Easton, MD 21601. 410-822-2611 (EST) 8:30AM-4:30PM.

2nd Judicial Circuit Court, Box 723, Easton, MD 21601. 410-822-2611 (EST) 8:30AM-4:30PM. Felony, Misdemeanor, Civil Actions Over $20,000.

District Court, South Wing, Easton, MD 21601. 410-822-2750 (EST) 8AM-4:30PM. Misdemeanor, Civil Actions Under $20,000, Eviction, Small Claims.

Register of Wills, PO Box 816, Easton, MD 21601. 410-822-2470 (EST) 8:30AM-4:30PM. Probate.

## Washington County

Real Estate Recording, Washington County Clerk of the Circuit Court, 95 West Washington Street, Suite 212, Hagerstown, MD 21740. 301-733-8660 (EST) 8:30AM-4:30PM.

4th Judicial Circuit Court, Box 229, Hagerstown, MD 21741. 301-791-3085 (EST) 8:30AM-4:30PM. Felony, Misdemeanor, Civil Actions Over $20,000.

District Court, 35 W Washington St, Hagerstown, MD 21740. 301-791-4740 (EST) 8:30AM-4:30PM. Misdemeanor, Civil Actions Under $20,000, Eviction, Small Claims.

Register of Wills, 35 W Washington, Hagerstown, MD 21740. 301-739-3612 (EST) 8:30AM-4:30PM. Probate.

## Wicomico County

Real Estate Recording, Wicomico County Clerk of the Circuit Court, 101 North Division St., Courthouse Room 105, Salisbury, MD 21801. 410-543-6551 (EST) 8:30AM-4:30PM.

1st Judicial Circuit Court, PO Box 198, Salisbury, MD 21801. 410-543-6551 (EST) 8:30AM-4:30PM. Felony, Misdemeanor, Civil Actions Over $20,000.

District Court, 201 Baptist St, Salisbury, MD 21801. 410-543-6600 (EST) 8:30AM-4:30PM. Misdemeanor, Civil Actions Under $20,000, Eviction, Small Claims.

Register of Wills, PO Box 787, Salisbury, MD 21803-0787. 410-543-6635 (EST) 8:30AM-4:30PM. Probate.

## Worcester County

Real Estate Recording, Worcester County Clerk of the Circuit Court, Corner of Market & Washington Streets, Courthouse Room 104, Snow Hill, MD 21863. 410-632-1221 (EST) 8:30AM-4:30PM.

1st Judicial Circuit Court, Box 547, Snow Hill, MD 21863. 410-632-1222 (EST) 8:30AM-4:30PM. Felony, Misdemeanor, Civil Actions Over $20,000.

District Court, 301 Commerce St, Snow Hill, MD 21863. 410-632-2525 (EST) Misdemeanor, Civil Actions Under $20,000, Eviction, Small Claims.

Register of Wills, Courthouse, Room 102, Snow Hill, MD 21863-1296. 410-632-1529 (EST) 8:30AM-4:30PM. Probate.

**County Records**

# Massachusetts

## Barnstable County

**Real Estate Recording**, Barnstable County Register of Deeds, Main Street, Route 6A, Barnstable, MA 02630. 508-362-2511 (EST) 8AM-4PM.

**Superior Court**, PO Box 425, Barnstable, MA 02630. 508-362-2511 (EST) 8:00AM-4:30PM. Felony, Civil Actions Over $25,000.

**Barnstable Division District Court**, Route 6A, PO Box 427, Barnstable, MA 02630. 508-362-2511 (EST) 8:30AM-4:30PM. Misdemeanor, Civil Actions Under $25,000, Eviction, Small Claims.

**Orleans Division District Court**, Courthouse, Orleans, MA 02653. 508-255-4700 (EST) 8:30AM-4:30PM. Misdemeanor, Civil Actions Under $25,000, Eviction, Small Claims.

**Probate and Family Court**, PO Box 346, Barnstable, MA 02630. 508-362-2511 (EST) 8:00AM-4:30PM. Probate.

## Berkshire County

**Real Estate Recording**, Berkshire County Register of Deeds, Northern District, 65 Park Street, Adams, MA 01220. 413-743-0035 (EST) 8:30AM-4:30PM.

**Real Estate Recording**, Berkshire County Register of Deeds, Southern District, 334 Main Street, Great Barrington, MA 01230. 413-528-0146 (EST) 8:30AM-4:30PM; Recording hours 8:30AM-4PM.

**Real Estate Recording**, Berkshire County Register of Deeds (Middle District), Middle District, 44 Bank Row, Pittsfield, MA 01201. 413-443-7438 (EST) 8:30AM-4:30PM (No Recording after 3:59PM).

**Superior Court**, 76 East St, Pittsfield, MA 01201. 413-499-7487 (EST) 8:30AM-4:30PM. Felony, Civil Actions Over $25,000.

**North Berkshire (#30) Division District Court**, 65 Park St, Adams, MA 01220. 413-743-0021 (EST) 8:00AM-4:30PM. Misdemeanor, Civil Actions Under $25,000, Eviction, Small Claims.

**South Berkshire Division District Court**, 9 Gilmore Ave, Great Barrington, MA 01230. 413-528-3520 (EST) 8:30AM-4:30PM. Misdemeanor, Civil Actions Under $25,000, Eviction, Small Claims.

**North Berkshire (#28) Division District Court**, City Hall, North Adams, MA 01247. 413-663-5339 (EST) 8:30AM-4:30PM. Misdemeanor, Civil Actions Under $25,000, Eviction, Small Claims.

**Pittsfield Division District Court**, 24 Wendell Ave, PO Box 875, Pittsfield, MA 01201. 413-442-5468 (EST) 8:30AM-4:30PM. Misdemeanor, Civil Actions Under $25,000, Eviction, Small Claims.

**Probate and Family Court**, 44 Bank Row, Pittsfield, MA 01201. 413-442-6941 (EST) 9:00AM-3:00PM. Probate.

## Bristol County

**Real Estate Recording**, Bristol County Register of Deeds (Fall River District), Fall River District, 441 North Main Street, Fall River, MA 02720. 508-673-1651 (EST) 8:30AM-5PM.

**Real Estate Recording**, Bristol County Register of Deeds, Southern District, 25 North 6th Street, New Bedford, MA 02740. 508-993-2605 (EST) 8:30AM-5PM.

**Real Estate Recording**, Bristol County Register of Deeds, Northern District, 11 Court Street, Taunton, MA 02780-0248. 508-822-0502 (EST) 8:30AM-5PM.

**Superior Court-Fall River**, 441 N Main, Fall River, MA 02720. 508-672-4464 (EST) 8:00AM-4:30PM. Felony, Civil Actions Over $25,000.

**Superior Court-Taunton**, 9 Court St, Taunton, MA 02780. 508-823-6588 (EST) 8:00AM-4:30PM. Felony, Civil Actions Over $25,000.

**Attleboro Division District Court**, Courthouse, 88 N Main St, Attleboro, MA 02703. 508-222-5900 (EST) 9:00AM-4:30PM. Misdemeanor, Civil Actions Under $25,000, Eviction, Small Claims.

**Fall River Division District Court**, 45 Rock St, Fall River, MA 02720. 508-679-8161 (EST) Misdemeanor, Civil Actions Under $25,000, Eviction, Small Claims.

**New Bedford Division District Court**, 75 N 6th St, New Bedford, MA 02740. 508-999-9700 (EST) 8:30AM-4:00PM. Misdemeanor, Civil Actions Under $25,000, Eviction, Small Claims.

**Taunton Division District Court**, 15 Court St, Taunton, MA 02780. 508-824-4032 (EST) 8:00AM-4:30PM. Misdemeanor, Civil Actions Under $25,000, Eviction, Small Claims.

**New Bedford Probate and Family Court**, 505 Pleasant St, New Bedford, MA 02740. 508-999-5249 (EST) 8:00AM-4:30PM. Probate.

**Taunton Probate and Family Court**, 11 Court St, Taunton, MA 02780. 508-824-4004 (EST) 8:00AM-4:30PM. Probate.

## Dukes County

**Real Estate Recording**, Dukes County Register of Deeds, Main Street, Courthouse, Edgartown, MA 02539. 508-627-4025 (EST) 8:30AM-4:30PM.

**Superior Court**, PO Box 1267, Edgartown, MA 02539. 508-627-4668 (EST) 8:00AM-4:30PM. Felony, Civil Actions Over $25,000.

**Division District Court**, Courthouse, 81 Main St, Edgartown, MA 02539. 508-627-3751 (EST) 8:30AM-4:30PM. Misdemeanor, Civil Actions Under $25,000, Eviction, Small Claims.

**Probate and Family Court**, PO Box 338, Edgartown, MA 02539. 508-627-4703 (EST) 8:30AM-4:30PM. Probate.

## Essex County

**Real Estate Recording**, Essex County Register of Deeds, Northern District, 381 Common Street, Lawrence, MA 01840. 508-683-2745 (EST) 8AM-4:30PM (recording until 4PM.).

**Real Estate Recording**, Essex County Register of Deeds, Southern District, 36 Federal Street, Salem, MA 01970. 508-741-0201 (EST) 8AM-4PM.

**Superior Court-Lawrence**, 40 Appleton Way, Lawrence, MA 01840. 508-687-7463 (EST) 8:00AM-4:30PM. Civil Actions Over $25,000.

**Superior Court-Newburyport**, 145 High St, Newburyport, MA 01950. 508-462-4474 (EST) 8:00AM-4:30PM. Felony, Civil Actions Over $25,000.

**Superior Court-Salem**, 32 Federal St, Salem, MA 01970. 508-741-0200 (EST) 8:00AM-4:30PM. Felony, Civil Actions Over $25,000.

**Haverhill Division District Court**, PO Box 1389, Haverhill, MA 01831. 508-373-4151 (EST) 8:30AM-4:30PM. Misdemeanor, Civil Actions Under $25,000, Eviction, Small Claims.

**Ipswich Division District Court**, Courthouse, PO Box 246, Ipswich, MA 01938. 508-356-2681 (EST) 8:30AM-4:30PM. Misdemeanor, Civil Actions Under $25,000, Eviction, Small Claims.

**Lawrence Division District Court**, 381 Common St, Lawrence, MA 01840. 508-687-7184 (EST) 8:30AM-4:30PM. Misdemeanor, Civil Actions Under $25,000, Eviction, Small Claims.

**Lynn Division District Court**, 580 Essex St, Lynn, MA 01901. 617-598-5200 (EST) 8:00AM-4:30PM. Misdemeanor, Civil Actions Under $25,000, Eviction, Small Claims.

**Newburyport Division District Court**, 188 State St, Newburyport, MA 01950. 508-462-2652 (EST) 8:30AM-4:30PM. Misdemeanor, Civil Actions Under $25,000, Eviction, Small Claims.

**Peabody Division District Court**, Peabody Square, 1 Lowell St, Peabody, MA 01960. 508-532-3100 (EST) 8:30AM-4:30PM. Misdemeanor, Civil Actions Under $25,000, Eviction, Small Claims.

**Salem Division District Court**, 65 Washington St, Salem, MA 01970. 508-744-1167 (EST) 8:30AM-4:30PM. Misdemeanor, Civil Actions Under $25,000, Eviction, Small Claims.

**Probate and Family Court**, 36 Federal St, Salem, MA 01970. 508-741-0200 (EST) 8:00AM-4:30PM. Probate.

## Franklin County

**Real Estate Recording**, Franklin County Register of Deeds, 425 Main Street, Court House, Greenfield, MA 01301. 413-772-0239 (EST) 8:30AM-4:30PM (Recording until 4PM).

**Superior Court**, PO Box 1573, Greenfield, MA 01302. 413-774-5535 (EST) 8:30AM-4:30PM. Felony, Civil Actions Over $25,000.

**Greenfield Division District Court**, PO Box 1573, Greenfield, MA 01302. 413-774-5533 (EST) 8:30AM-4:30PM. Misdemeanor, Civil Actions Under $25,000, Eviction, Small Claims.

**Orange Division District Court**, One Court Square, Orange, MA 01364. 508-544-8277 (EST) 8:30AM-4:30PM. Misdemeanor, Civil Actions Under $25,000, Eviction, Small Claims.

**Probate and Family Court**, 425 Main St, Greenfield, MA 01301. 413-774-7011 (EST) 9:00AM-4:00PM. Probate.

## Hampden County

**Real Estate Recording**, Hampden County Register of Deeds, 50 State Street, Hall of Justice, Springfield, MA 01103. 413-748-8622 (EST) 9AM-4PM.

**Superior Court**, 50 State St, Springfield, MA 01103. 413-748-8600 (EST) 8:00AM-4:30PM. Felony, Civil Actions Over $25,000.

**Chicopee Division District Court**, 30 Church St, Chicopee, MA 01020. 413-598-0099

(EST) 8:00AM-4:00PM. Misdemeanor, Civil Actions Under $25,000, Eviction, Small Claims.

**Holyoke Division District Court**, 20 Court Plaza (PO Box 965), Holyoke, MA 01041. 413-538-9710 (EST) 8:30AM-4:30PM. Misdemeanor, Civil Actions Under $25,000, Eviction, Small Claims.

**Palmer Division District Court**, 234 Sykes St, Palmer, MA 01069. 413-283-8916 (EST) 8:30AM-4:30PM. Misdemeanor, Civil Actions Under $25,000, Eviction, Small Claims.

**Springfield Division District Court**, 50 State St, Springfield, MA 01103. 413-781-8100 (EST) 8:00AM-4:30PM. Misdemeanor, Civil Actions Under $25,000, Eviction, Small Claims.

**Westfield Division District Court**, Courthouse, Westfield, MA 01085. 413-568-8946 (EST) 8:00AM-4:00PM. Misdemeanor, Civil Actions Under $25,000, Eviction, Small Claims.

**Probate and Family Court**, 50 State St, Springfield, MA 01103. 413-748-8600 (EST) 8:00AM-4:30PM. Probate.

## Hampshire County

**Real Estate Recording**, Hampshire County Register of Deeds, 33 King Street, Hall of Records, Northampton, MA 01060. 413-584-3637 (EST) 8:30AM-4:30PM (Recording ends at 4PM).

**Superior Court**, PO Box 1119, Northampton, MA 01061. 413-584-5810 (EST) 9:00AM-4:00PM. Felony, Civil Actions Over $25,000.

**Northampton Division District Court**, Courthouse, 15 Gothic St, Northampton, MA 01060. 413-584-7400 (EST) 8:30AM-4:30PM. Misdemeanor, Civil Actions Under $25,000, Eviction, Small Claims.

**Ware Division District Court**, 71 South St (PO Box 300), Ware, MA 01082. 413-967-3301 (EST) 8:00AM-4:30PM. Misdemeanor, Civil Actions Under $25,000, Eviction, Small Claims.

**Probate and Family Court**, 33 King St, Northampton, MA 01060. 413-586-8500 (EST) 9:00AM-4:30PM. Probate.

## Middlesex County

**Real Estate Recording**, Middlesex County Register of Deeds, Southern District, 208 Cambridge Street, East Cambridge, MA 02141. 617-494-4500 (EST) 8AM-4PM.

**Real Estate Recording**, Middlesex County Register of Deeds, Northern District, 360 Gorham Street, Lowell, MA 01852. 508-458-8474 (EST) 8:30AM-4:30PM.

**Superior Court-East Cambridge**, 40 Thorndike St, East Cambridge, MA 02141. 617-494-4010 (EST) 8:30AM-4:30PM. Felony, Civil Actions Over $25,000.

**Superior Court-Lowell**, 360 Gorham St, Lowell, MA 01852. 508-453-0201 (EST) 8:30AM-4:30PM. Felony, Civil Actions Over $25,000.

**Ayer Division District Court**, 25 E Main St, Ayer, MA 01432. 508-772-2100 (EST) 8:30AM-4:30PM. Misdemeanor, Civil Actions Under $25,000, Eviction, Small Claims.

**Concord Division District Court**, 305 Walden St, Concord, MA 01742. 508-369-0500 (EST) 8:30AM-4:30PM. Misdemeanor, Civil Actions Under $25,000, Eviction, Small Claims.

**Cambridge Division District Court**, PO Box 338, East Cambridge, MA 02141. 617-494-4310 (EST) 8:30AM-4:30PM. Misdemeanor, Civil Actions Under $25,000, Eviction, Small Claims.

**Framingham Division District Court**, 600 Concord St, Framingham, MA 01701. 508-875-7461 (EST) 8:30AM-4:30PM. Misdemeanor, Civil Actions Under $25,000, Eviction, Small Claims.

**Lowell Division District Court**, 41 Hurd St, Lowell, MA 01852. 508-459-4101 (EST) 8:30AM-4:30PM. Misdemeanor, Civil Actions Under $25,000, Eviction, Small Claims.

**Malden Division District Court**, 89 Summer, Malden, MA 02148. 617-322-7500 (EST) 8:30AM-4:30PM. Misdemeanor, Civil Actions Under $25,000, Eviction, Small Claims.

**Marlborough Division District Court**, Williams St (PO Box 64), Marlborough, MA 01752. 508-485-3700 (EST) 8:30AM-4:30PM. Misdemeanor, Civil Actions Under $25,000, Eviction, Small Claims.

**Natick Division District Court**, 117 E Central, Natick, MA 01760. 508-653-4332 (EST) 8:30AM-4:30PM. Misdemeanor, Civil Actions Under $25,000, Eviction, Small Claims.

**Somerville Division District Court**, 175 Fellsway, Somerville, MA 02145. 617-666-8000 (EST) Misdemeanor, Civil Actions Under $25,000, Eviction, Small Claims.

**Waltham Division District Court**, 38 Linden St, Waltham, MA 02154. 617-894-4500 (EST) 8:30AM-4:30PM. Misdemeanor, Civil Actions Under $25,000, Eviction, Small Claims.

**Newton Division District Court**, 1309 Washington, West Newton, MA 02165. 617-244-3600 (EST) 8:30AM-4:30PM. Misdemeanor, Civil Actions Under $25,000, Eviction, Small Claims.

**Woburn Division District Court**, 30 Pleasant St, Woburn, MA 01801. 617-935-4000 (EST) 8:30AM-4:30PM. Misdemeanor, Civil Actions Under $25,000, Eviction, Small Claims.

**Probate and Family Court**, 208 Cambridge St. PO Box 410480, East Cambridge, MA 02141-0005. 617-494-4530 (EST) 8:00AM-4:00PM. Probate.

## Nantucket County

**Real Estate Recording**, Nantucket County Register of Deeds, 16 Broad Street, Nantucket, MA 02554. 508-228-7250 (EST) 8AM-4PM; Recording Hours: 8AM-Noon, 1PM-3:45PM.

**Superior Court**, PO Box 967, Nantucket, MA 02554. 508-228-2559 (EST) 8:30AM-4:00PM. Felony, Civil Actions Over $25,000.

**Nantucket Division District Court**, Broad Street, Nantucket, MA 02554. 508-228-0460 (EST) Misdemeanor, Civil Actions Under $25,000, Eviction, Small Claims.

**Probate and Family Court**, PO Box 1116, Nantucket, MA 02554. 508-228-2669 (EST) 8:30AM-4:00PM. Probate.

## Norfolk County

**Real Estate Recording**, Norfolk County Register of Deeds, 649 High Street, Dedham, MA 02026. 617-461-6122 (EST) 8:30AM-5PM.

**Superior Court**, 650 High St, Dedham, MA 02026. 617-326-1600 (EST) 8:30AM-4:30PM. Felony, Civil Actions Over $25,000.

**Brookline Division District Court**, 360 Washington St, Brookline, MA 02146. 617-232-4660 (EST) 8:30AM-4:30PM. Misdemeanor, Civil Actions Under $25,000, Eviction, Small Claims.

**Dedham Division District Court**, 631 High St, Dedham, MA 02026. 617-329-4777 (EST) 8:15AM-4:30PM. Misdemeanor, Civil Actions Under $25,000, Eviction, Small Claims.

**Quincy Division District Court**, One Dennis Ryan Parkway, Quincy, MA 02169. 617-471-1650 (EST) 8:30AM-4:30PM. Misdemeanor, Civil Actions Under $25,000, Eviction, Small Claims.

**Stoughton Division District Court**, 1288 Central St, Stoughton, MA 02072. 617-344-2131 (EST) 8:30AM-4:30PM. Misdemeanor, Civil Actions Under $25,000, Eviction, Small Claims.

**Wrentham Division District Court**, 60 East St (PO Box 248), Wrentham, MA 02093. 508-384-3106 (EST) 8:30AM-4:30PM. Misdemeanor, Civil Actions Under $25,000, Eviction, Small Claims.

**Probate and Family Court**, PO Box 269, Dedham, MA 02026. 617-326-7200 (EST) 8:30AM-4:30PM. Probate.

## Plymouth County

**Real Estate Recording**, Plymouth County Register of Deeds, 11 Russell Street, Plymouth, MA 02360. 508-830-9200 (EST) 8:30AM-4:30PM (Recording ends at 4PM.).

**Superior Court-Brockton**, 72 Belmont St, Brockton, MA 02401. 508-583-8250 (EST) 8:30AM-4:30PM. Felony, Civil Actions Over $25,000.

**Superior Court-Plymouth**, Court St, Plymouth, MA 02360. 508-747-6911 (EST) 8:30AM-4:30PM. Felony, Civil Actions Over $25,000.

**Brockton Division District Court**, 155 West Elm, Brockton, MA 02401. 508-587-8000 (EST) 8:30AM-4:30PM. Misdemeanor, Civil Actions Under $25,000, Eviction, Small Claims.

**Hingham Division District Court**, 28 Washington Blvd, Hingham, MA 02043. 617-749-7000 (EST) 8:30AM-4:30PM. Misdemeanor, Civil Actions Under $25,000, Eviction, Small Claims.

**Plymouth Division District Court**, Courthouse, South Russell St, Plymouth, MA 02360. 508-747-0500 (EST) 8:30AM-4:30PM. Misdemeanor, Civil Actions Under $25,000, Eviction, Small Claims.

**Wareham Division District Court**, Junction Routes 28 & 58, Wareham, MA 02571. 508-295-8300 (EST) Misdemeanor, Civil Actions Under $25,000, Eviction, Small Claims.

**Probate and Family Court**, PO Box 3640, Plymouth, MA 02361. 508-747-0500 (EST) 8:30AM-4:30PM. Probate.

## Suffolk County

**Real Estate Recording**, Suffolk County Register of Deeds, 1 Pemberton Square, The Old Courthouse, Boston, MA 02108-1772. 617-725-8575 (EST) 9AM-4:30PM.

**Superior Court-Civil**, Old Courthouse Bldg, Boston, MA 02108. 617-725-8235 (EST) 8:30AM-5:00PM. Civil Actions Over $25,000.

**Superior Court-Criminal**, New Courthouse, 712 Pemberton, Boston, MA 02108. 617-725-8160 (EST) 8:30AM-4:30PM. Felony.

**Boston Municipal Court**, Government Center, Boston, MA 02108. 617-725-8000 (EST)

# Massachusetts

8:30AM-4:30PM. Misdemeanor, Civil, Small Claims.

**Brighton Division District Court**, 52 Academy Hill Rd, Brighton, MA 02135. 617-782-6521 (EST) 8:30AM-4:30PM. Misdemeanor, Civil Actions Under $25,000, Eviction, Small Claims.

**Charleston Division District Court**, Courthouse, City Square, Charleston, MA 02129. 617-242-5400 (EST) 8:30AM-4:30PM. Misdemeanor, Civil Actions Under $25,000, Eviction, Small Claims.

**Chelsea Division District Court**, 19 Park St, Chelsea, MA 02150. 617-252-0960 (EST) 8:30AM-4:30PM. Misdemeanor, Civil Actions Under $25,000, Eviction, Small Claims.

**Dorchester Division District Court**, 510 Washington St, Dorchester, MA 02124. 617-288-9500 (EST) 8:30AM-4:30PM. Misdemeanor, Civil Actions Under $25,000, Eviction, Small Claims.

**East Boston Division District Court**, 37 Meridian St, East Boston, MA 02128. 617-569-7550 (EST) 8:30AM-4:30PM. Misdemeanor, Civil Actions Under $25,000, Eviction, Small Claims.

**West Roxbury Division District Court**, Courthouse, 445 Arborway, Jamaica Plain, MA 02130. 617-522-4710 (EST) 8:30AM-4:30PM. Misdemeanor, Civil Actions Under $25,000, Eviction, Small Claims.

**Roxbury Division District Court**, 85 Warren St, Roxbury, MA 02119. 617-427-7000 (EST) 8:30AM-5:30PM. Misdemeanor, Civil Actions Under $25,000, Eviction, Small Claims.

**South Boston Division District Court**, 535 East Broadway, South Boston, MA 02127. 617-268-9292 (EST) 8:30AM-4:30PM. Misdemeanor, Civil Actions Under $25,000, Eviction, Small Claims.

**Probate and Family Court**, Old Courthouse Bldg, Rm 120, Boston, MA 02108-1706. 617-725-8300 (EST) 8:30AM-4:30PM. Probate.

## Worcester County

**Real Estate Recording**, Worcester County Register of Deeds, Northern District, Courthouse, 84 Elm St., Fitchburg, MA 01420. 508-342-2637 (EST) 8:30AM-4:30; PMRecording Hours 8:30AM-4PM.

**Real Estate Recording**, Worcester County Register of Deeds (Worcester District), Worcester District, 2 Main Street, Courthouse, Worcester, MA 01608. 508-798-7713 (EST) 8:15AM-4:30PM (Recording Hours: 9AM-Noon, 1-4PM).

**Superior Court**, 2 Main St, Worcester, MA 01608. 508-756-2441 (EST) 8:30AM-4:30PM. Felony, Civil Actions Over $25,000.

**Clinton Division District Court**, Routes 62 & 70, Boylston St, PO Box 30, Clinton, MA 01510-0030. 508-368-7811 (EST) 8:30AM-4:00PM. Misdemeanor, Civil Actions Under $25,000, Eviction, Small Claims.

**Dudley Division District Court**, PO Box 100, Dudley, MA 01571. 508-943-7123 (EST) 8:00AM-4:30PM. Misdemeanor, Civil Actions Under $25,000, Eviction, Small Claims.

**Fitchburg Division District Court**, 100 Elm St, Fitchburg, MA 01420. 508-345-2111 (EST) 8:30AM-4:30PM. Misdemeanor, Civil Actions Under $25,000, Eviction, Small Claims.

**Gardner Division District Court**, 108 Matthews St, Gardner, MA 01440. 508-632-2373 (EST) 8:30AM-4:30PM. Misdemeanor, Civil Actions Under $25,000, Eviction, Small Claims.

**Leominster Division District Court**, 29 Church St, Leominster, MA 01453. 508-537-3722 (EST) 8:30AM-4:30PM. Misdemeanor, Civil Actions Under $25,000, Eviction, Small Claims.

**Milford Division District Court**, 161 West St, Rte 140 (PO Box 370), Milford, MA 01757. 508-473-1260 (EST) 8:00AM-4:30PM. Misdemeanor, Civil Actions Under $25,000, Eviction, Small Claims.

**Spencer Division District Court**, 501 Main, Spencer, MA 01562. 508-885-6305 (EST) 8:30AM-4:30PM. Misdemeanor, Civil Actions Under $25,000, Eviction, Small Claims.

**Uxbridge Division District Court**, PO Box 580, Uxbridge, MA 01569. 508-278-2454 (EST) 8:30AM-4:30PM. Misdemeanor, Civil Actions Under $25,000, Eviction, Small Claims.

**Westborough Division District Court**, 175 Milk St, (PO Box 1449), Westborough, MA 01581. 508-366-8266 (EST) 8:00AM-4:30PM. Misdemeanor, Civil Actions Under $25,000, Eviction, Small Claims.

**Winchendon Division District Court**, 80 Central, (PO Box 309), Winchendon, MA 01475. 508-297-0156 (EST) 8:30AM-4:30PM. Misdemeanor, Civil Actions Under $25,000, Eviction, Small Claims.

**Worcester Division District Court**, 50 Harvard St., Worcester, MA 01608. 508-757-8352 (EST) 8:00AM-4:30PM. Misdemeanor, Civil Actions Under $25,000, Eviction, Small Claims.

**Probate and Family Court**, 2 Main St, Worcester, MA 01608. 508-756-2441 (EST) Probate.

## County Records

# Michigan

## Alcona County

**Real Estate Recording**, Alcona County Register of Deeds, 5th Street, Courthouse, Harrisville, MI 48740. 517-724-6802 (EST) 9AM-5PM.

**26th Circuit Court**, PO Box 308, Harrisville, MI 48740. 517-724-5374 (EST) 9:00AM-12:00PM, 1:00PM-5:00PM. Felony, Civil Actions Over $10,000.

**82nd District Court**, PO Box 385, Harrisville, MI 48740. 517-724-5313 (EST) 8:30AM-4:30PM. Misdemeanor, Civil Actions Under $10,000, Eviction, Small Claims.

**Probate Court**, PO Box 328, Harrisville, MI 48740. 517-724-6880 (EST) Probate.

## Alger County

**Real Estate Recording**, Alger County Register of Deeds, 101 Court Street, Munising, MI 49862. 906-387-2076 (EST) 8AM-4PM.

**11th Circuit Court**, 101 Court St, PO Box 538, Munising, MI 49862. 906-387-2076 (EST) 8:00AM-4:00PM. Felony, Civil Actions Over $10,000.

**93rd District Court**, PO Box 186, Munising, MI 49862. 906-387-3879 (EST) 8:00AM-4:00PM. Misdemeanor, Civil Actions Under $10,000, Eviction, Small Claims.

**Probate Court**, PO Box 646, Munising, MI 49862. 906-387-2080 (EST) Probate.

## Allegan County

**Real Estate Recording**, Allegan County Register of Deeds, 113 Chestnut Street, County Court House, Allegan, MI 49010. 616-673-0390 (EST) X3280 8AM-5PM.

**48th Circuit Court**, 113 Chesnut St, Allegan, MI 49010. 616-673-8471 (EST) 8:00AM-5:00PM. Felony, Civil Actions Over $10,000.

**57th District Court**, 113 Chesnut St, Allegan, MI 49010. 616-673-0400 (EST) 8:00AM-5:00PM. Misdemeanor, Civil Actions Under $10,000, Eviction, Small Claims.

**Probate Court**, 113 Chesnut St, Allegan, MI 49010. 616-673-0250 (EST) Probate.

## Alpena County

**Real Estate Recording**, Alpena County Register of Deeds, 720 West Chisholm Street, Courthouse, Alpena, MI 49707. 517-356-3887 (EST) 8:30AM-4:30PM.

**26th Circuit Court**, 720 West Chisholm, Alpena, MI 49707. 517-354-4513 (EST) 8:30AM-4:30PM. Felony, Civil Actions Over $10,000.

**88th District Court**, 719 West Chisholm, Alpena, MI 49707. 517-354-3330 (EST) 8:30AM-4:30PM. Misdemeanor, Civil Actions Under $10,000, Eviction, Small Claims.

**Probate Court**, 719 West Chisholm, Alpena, MI 49707. 517-354-8785 (EST) Probate.

## Antrim County

**Real Estate Recording**, Antrim County Register of Deeds, 205 East Cayuga Street, Bellaire, MI 49615. 616-533-6683 (EST) 8:30AM-5PM.

**13th Circuit Court**, PO Box 520, Bellaire, MI 49615. 616-533-8607 (EST) 8:30AM-5:00PM. Felony, Civil Actions Over $10,000.

**87th District Court**, PO Box 1218, Gaylord, MI 49735. 517-732-6486 (EST) 8:00AM-4:30PM. Misdemeanor, Civil Actions Under $10,000, Eviction, Small Claims.

**Probate Court**, PO Box 130, Bellaire, MI 49615. 616-533-6681 (EST) Probate.

## Arenac County

**Real Estate Recording**, Arenac County Register of Deeds, 120 Grove Street, Standish, MI 48658. 517-846-9201 (EST) 8:30AM-5PM.

**34th Circuit Court**, 120 N Grove St, Standish, MI 48658. 517-846-6200 (EST) 9:00AM-5:00PM. Felony, Civil Actions Over $10,000.

**81st District Court**, PO Box 129, Standish, MI 48658. 517-846-9538 (EST) 8:30AM-5:00PM M,T,W,F Thurs 8:30AM-6:30PM. Misdemeanor, Civil Actions Under $10,000, Eviction, Small Claims.

**Probate Court**, PO Box 666, Standish, MI 48658. 517-846-6941 (EST) Probate.

## Baraga County

**Real Estate Recording**, Baraga County Register of Deeds, Courthouse, 16 N. 3rd St., L'Anse, MI 49946. 906-524-6183 (EST) 8:30AM-Noon, 1-4:30PM.

**12th Circuit Court**, 16 North 3rd St, L'Anse, MI 49946. 906-524-6183 (EST) 8:30AM-4:30PM. Felony, Civil Actions Over $10,000.

**97th District Court**, 96 North 3rd St, L'Anse, MI 49946. 906-524-6109 (EST) Misdemeanor, Civil Actions Under $10,000, Eviction, Small Claims.

**Probate Court**, County Courthouse, L'Anse, MI 49946. 906-524-6390 (EST) Probate.

## Barry County

**Real Estate Recording**, Barry County Register of Deeds, 220 West State Street, Courthouse, Hastings, MI 49058. 616-948-4824 (EST) 8AM-5PM.

**5th Circuit Court**, 220 West State St, Hastings, MI 49058. 616-948-4810 (EST) 8:00AM-5:00PM. Felony, Civil Actions Over $10,000.

**56th & 1st District Court**, 220 West Court St, Suite 202, Hastings, MI 49058. 616-948-4835 (EST) 8:00AM-5:00PM. Misdemeanor, Civil Actions Under $10,000, Eviction, Small Claims.

**Probate Court**, 220 West Court St., Ste. 302, Hastings, MI 49058. 616-948-4842 (EST) Probate.

## Bay County

**Real Estate Recording**, Bay County Register of Deeds, 515 Center Avenue, Bay City, MI 48708. 517-895-4228 (EST) 8AM-5PM (June-September 7:30AM-4PM).

**18th Circuit Court**, 515 Center Ave, Bay City, MI 48708. 517-895-4280 (EST) Felony, Civil Actions Over $10,000.

**74th District Court**, 515 Center Ave., Bay City, MI 48708. 517-895-4203 (EST) Misdemeanor, Civil Actions Under $10,000, Eviction, Small Claims.

**Probate Court**, 515 Center Ave., Bay City, MI 48708. 517-895-4205 (EST) Probate.

## Benzie County

**Real Estate Recording**, Benzie County Register of Deeds, 448 Court Place, Beulah, MI 49617. 616-882-0016 (EST) 8AM-5PM.

**19th Circuit Court**, PO Box 398, Beulah, MI 49617. 616-882-9671 (EST) 8:00AM-5:00PM. Felony, Civil Actions Over $10,000.

**85th District Court**, PO Box 398, Beulah, MI 49617. 800-759-5175 (EST) 9:00AM-5:00PM. Misdemeanor, Civil Actions Under $10,000, Eviction, Small Claims.

**Probate Court**, PO Box 398, Beulah, MI 49617. 616-882-9675 (EST) Probate.

## Berrien County

**Real Estate Recording**, Berrien County Register of Deeds, 811 Port Street, Courthouse Room 106, St. Joseph, MI 49085. 616-983-7111 (EST) 8:30AM-5PM.

**2nd Circuit Court**, 811 Port St, St Joseph, MI 49085. 616-983-7111 (EST) 8:30AM-4:00PM. Felony, Civil Actions Over $10,000.

**5th District Court**, 811 Port St., St Joseph, MI 49085. 616-983-7111 (EST) 8:30AM-4:00PM. Misdemeanor, Civil Actions Under $10,000, Eviction, Small Claims.

**Probate Court**, 811 Port St., St Joseph, MI 49085. 616-983-7111 (EST) Probate.

## Branch County

**Real Estate Recording**, Branch County Register of Deeds, 31 Division Street, Coldwater, MI 49036. 517-279-8411 (EST) 9AM-12, 1-5PM.

**15th Circuit Court**, 31 Division St, Coldwater, MI 49036. 517-279-8411 (EST) 9:00AM-5:00PM. Felony, Civil Actions Over $10,000.

**3A District Court**, 31 Division St., Coldwater, MI 49036. 517-279-8411 (EST) 8:00AM-5:00PM. Misdemeanor, Civil Actions Under $10,000, Eviction, Small Claims.

**Probate Court**, 31 Division St., Coldwater, MI 49036. 517-279-8411 (EST) Probate.

## Calhoun County

**Real Estate Recording**, Calhoun County Register of Deeds, 315 West Green Street, Marshall, MI 49068. 616-781-0730 (EST) 8AM-5PM.

**37th Circuit Court**, 315 West Green, Marshall, MI 49068. 616-781-0713 (EST) 8:30AM-4:00PM. Felony, Civil Actions Over $10,000.

**10th District Court-Marshall Branch**, 315 West Green, Marshall, MI 49068. 616-781-0714 (EST) 8:30AM-4:00PM. Misdemeanor, Civil Actions Under $10,000, Eviction, Small Claims.

**10th District Court-Civil Division**, 161 E Michigan Ave, Battle Creek, MI 49017. 616-966-1634 (EST) 8:30AM-4:00PM. Civil Actions Under $10,000, Eviction, Small Claims.

**10th District Court-Criminal Division**, 161 E Michigan Ave, Battle Creek, MI 49017. 616-969-6666 (EST) 8:30AM-4:00PM. Misdemeanor.

**Probate Court**, Justice Center, 161 E Michigan Ave, Battle Creek, MI 49017-4005. 616-969-6795 (EST) Probate.

## Cass County

**Real Estate Recording**, Cass County Register of Deeds, 120 North Broadway, Suite 123, Cas-

# Michigan

sopolis, MI 49031. 616-445-4464 (EST) 8AM-5PM.

**43rd Circuit Court**, 120 North Broadway, Cassopolis, MI 49031-1398. 616-445-4416 (EST) 8:00AM-5:00PM. Felony, Civil Actions Over $10,000.

**4th District Court**, 110 North Broadway, Cassopolis, MI 49031. 616-445-4424 (EST) 8:00AM-5:00PM. Misdemeanor, Civil Actions Under $10,000, Eviction, Small Claims.

**Probate Court**, 110 North Broadway, Rm 202, Cassopolis, MI 49031. 616-445-4454 (EST) Probate.

## Charlevoix County

**Real Estate Recording**, Charlevoix County Register of Deeds, 301 State Street, County Building, Charlevoix, MI 49720. 616-547-7204 (EST) 9AM-5PM.

**33rd Circuit Court**, 203 Antrim St, Charlevoix, MI 49720. 616-547-7200 (EST) Felony, Civil Actions Over $10,000.

**90th District Court**, 301 State St, Court Bldg, Charlevoix, MI 49720. 616-547-7227 (EST) Misdemeanor, Civil Actions Under $10,000, Eviction, Small Claims.

**Probate Court**, 301 State St, County Bldg, Charlevoix, MI 49720. 616-547-7214 (EST) 9AM-5PM. Probate.

## Cheboygan County

**Real Estate Recording**, Cheboygan County Register of Deeds, 870 South Main Street, Cheboygan, MI 49721. 616-627-8866 (EST) 9AM-5PM.

**53rd District**, PO Box 70, Cheboygan, MI 49721. 616-627-8899 (EST) Felony, Civil Actions Over $10,000.

**89th District Court**, PO Box 70, Cheboygan, MI 49721. 616-627-8853 (EST) 8:30AM-4:00PM. Misdemeanor, Civil Actions Under $10,000, Eviction, Small Claims.

**Probate Court**, PO Box 70, Cheboygan, MI 49721. 616-627-8823 (EST) Probate.

## Chippewa County

**Real Estate Recording**, Chippewa County Register of Deeds, Courthouse, 319 Court St., Sault Ste. Marie, MI 49783. 906-635-6312 (EST) 9AM-5PM.

**50th Circuit Court**, 319 Court St, Sault Ste Marie, MI 49783. 906-635-6300 (EST) 8:30AM-5:00PM. Felony, Civil Actions Over $10,000.

**91st District Court**, 325 Court St, Sault Ste Marie, MI 49783. 906-635-6320 (EST) Misdemeanor, Civil Actions Under $10,000, Eviction, Small Claims.

**Probate Court**, 319 Court St., Sault Ste Marie, MI 49783. 906-635-6314 (EST) 8:30AM-5:00PM. Probate.

## Clare County

**Real Estate Recording**, Clare County Register of Deeds, 225 West Main, Harrison, MI 48625. 517-539-7131 (EST) 8AM-4:30PM.

**55th Circuit Court**, 225 West Main St, PO Box 438, Harrison, MI 48625. 517-539-7131 (EST) 8:00AM-4:30PM. Felony, Civil Actions Over $10,000.

**80th District Court**, 225 W. Main St, Harrison, MI 48625. 517-539-7173 (EST) 8:00AM-4:30PM. Misdemeanor, Civil Actions Under $10,000, Eviction, Small Claims.

**Probate Court**, 225 W. Main St., Harrison, MI 48625. 517-539-7109 (EST) 8:00AM-4:30PM. Probate.

## Clinton County

**Real Estate Recording**, Clinton County Register of Deeds, 100 East State Street, St. Johns, MI 48879. 517-224-5270 (EST) 8AM-5PM.

**29th Circuit Court**, PO Box 69, St Johns, MI 48879-0069. 517-224-5140 (EST) 8:00AM-5:00PM. Felony, Civil Actions Over $10,000.

**65th District Court**, 409 South Whittemore St., St Johns, MI 48879. 517-224-5150 (EST) 8:00AM-5:00PM. Misdemeanor, Civil Actions Under $10,000, Eviction, Small Claims.

**Probate Court**, 100 E. State St., St Johns, MI 48879. 517-224-5190 (EST) Probate.

## Crawford County

**Real Estate Recording**, Crawford County Register of Deeds, 200 West Michigan, Grayling, MI 49738. 517-348-2841 (EST)

**46th Circuit Court**, 200 West Michigan Ave, Grayling, MI 49738. 517-348-2841 (EST) 8:30AM-4:30PM. Felony, Civil Actions Over $10,000.

**83rd District Court**, 200 West Michigan Ave., Grayling, MI 49738. 517-348-2841 (EST) 8:30AM-4:30PM. Misdemeanor, Civil Actions Under $10,000, Eviction, Small Claims.

**Probate Court**, 200 West Michigan Ave., Grayling, MI 49738. 517-348-2841 (EST) 8:30AM-4:30PM. Probate.

## Delta County

**Real Estate Recording**, Delta County Register of Deeds, 310 Ludington Street, Escanaba, MI 49829. 906-789-5116 (EST) 8AM-4PM.

**47th Circuit Court**, 310 Ludington St, Escanaba, MI 49829. 906-789-5105 (EST) 8:00AM-4:00PM. Felony, Civil Actions Over $10,000.

**94th District Court**, 310 Ludington St., Escanaba, MI 49829. 906-789-5106 (EST) 8:00AM-4:00PM. Misdemeanor, Civil Actions Under $10,000, Eviction, Small Claims.

**Probate Court**, 310 Ludington St., Escanaba, MI 49829. 906-786-5112 (EST) 8:00AM-4:00PM. Probate.

## Dickinson County

**Real Estate Recording**, Dickinson County Register of Deeds, 700 Stephenson Avenue, Courthouse, Iron Mountain, MI 49801. 906-774-0955 (CST) 8AM-Noon, 1-4:30PM.

**41st Circuit Court**, PO Box 609, Iron Mountain, MI 49801. 906-774-0988 (CST) 8:00AM-4:30PM. Felony, Civil Actions Over $10,000.

**95 B District Court**, County Courthouse, Iron Mountain, MI 49801. 906-774-0506 (CST) 8:00AM-4:30PM. Misdemeanor, Civil Actions Under $10,000, Eviction, Small Claims.

**Probate Court**, PO Box 609, Iron Mountain, MI 49801. 906-774-1555 (CST) 8:00AM-4:30PM. Probate.

## Eaton County

**Real Estate Recording**, Eaton County Register of Deeds, 1045 Independence Blvd., Charlotte, MI 48813. 517-543-7500 (EST) X232 8AM-5PM.

**56th Circuit Court**, 1045 Independence Blvd, Charlotte, MI 48813. 517-543-7500 (EST) 8:00AM-5:00PM. Felony, Civil Actions Over $10,000.

**56th District Court-Civil Division**, 1045 Independence Blvd, Cheboygan, MI 49721. 616-627-8808 (EST) Civil Actions Under $10,000, Eviction, Small Claims.

**56th District Court-Criminal**, 1045 Independence Blvd, Charlotte, MI 48813. 517-543-7500 (EST) 8:00AM-5:00PM. Misdemeanor.

## Emmet County

**Real Estate Recording**, Emmet County Register of Deeds, 200 Division, Petoskey, MI 49770. 616-348-1761 (EST) 8:30AM-5PM.

**57th Circuit Court**, 200 Division St, Petoskey, MI 49770. 616-348-1744 (EST) 8:00AM-5:00PM. Felony, Civil Actions Over $10,000.

**90th District Court**, 200 Division St., Petoskey, MI 49770. 616-348-1750 (EST) 8:30AM-5:00PM. Misdemeanor, Civil Actions Under $10,000, Eviction, Small Claims.

**Probate Court**, 200 Division St., Petoskey, MI 49770. 616-348-1707 (EST) 8:00AM-5:00PM. Probate.

## Genesee County

**Real Estate Recording**, Genesee County Register of Deeds, 1101 Beach Street, Administration Building, Flint, MI 48502. 313-257-3060 (EST) 8AM-5PM.

**7th Circuit Court**, 900 South Saginaw, Flint, MI 48502. 810-257-3220 (EST) 8:00AM-5:00PM. Felony, Civil Actions Over $10,000.

**67th and 68th District Courts**, 630 South Saginaw, Flint, MI 48502. 810-257-3170 (EST) 8:00AM-4:45PM M-F. Misdemeanor, Civil Actions Under $10,000, Eviction, Small Claims.

**Probate Court**, 919 Beach St, Flint, MI 48502. 810-257-3528 (EST) Probate.

## Gladwin County

**Real Estate Recording**, Gladwin County Register of Deeds, 401 West Cedar Ave., Gladwin, MI 48624. 517-426-7551 (EST) 8:30AM-4:30PM.

**55th Circuit Court**, 401 West Cedar, Gladwin, MI 48624. 517-426-7351 (EST) 8:30AM-4:30PM. Felony, Civil Actions Over $10,000.

**80th District Court**, 401 West Cedar, Gladwin, MI 48624. 517-426-9207 (EST) 8:30AM-4:30PM. Misdemeanor, Civil Actions Under $10,000, Eviction, Small Claims.

**Probate Court**, 401 West Cedar, Gladwin, MI 48624. 517-426-7451 (EST) 8:30AM-4:30PM. Probate.

## Gogebic County

**Real Estate Recording**, Gogebic County Register of Deeds, Courthouse, 200 N. Moore St., Bessemer, MI 49911. 906-667-0381 (CST) 8:30AM-4:30PM.

**32nd Circuit Court**, 200 North Moore St, Bessemer, MI 49911. 906-663-4518 (CST) 8:30AM-4:30PM. Felony, Civil Actions Over $10,000.

**98th District Court**, 200 North Moore St, Bessemer, MI 49911. 906-663-4611 (CST)

8:30AM-4:30PM. Misdemeanor, Civil Actions Under $10,000, Eviction, Small Claims.

**Probate Court**, 200 North Moore St., Bessemer, MI 49911. 906-667-0421 (CST) 8:30AM-4:30PM. Probate.

## Grand Traverse County

**Real Estate Recording**, Grand Traverse County Register of Deeds, 400 Boardman Avenue, Traverse City, MI 49684. 616-922-4753 (EST) 8AM-5PM (Vault closes at 4PM).

**13th Circuit Court**, 328 Washington St, Traverse City, MI 49684. 616-922-4710 (EST) 8:00AM-5:00PM. Felony, Civil Actions Over $10,000.

**86th District Court**, 328 Washington St., Traverse City, MI 49684. 616-922-4580 (EST) 8:00AM-5:00PM. Misdemeanor, Civil Actions Under $10,000, Eviction, Small Claims.

**Probate Court**, 400 Boardmen, Traverse City, MI 49684. 616-922-4640 (EST) 8:00AM-5:00PM. Probate.

## Gratiot County

**Real Estate Recording**, Gratiot County Register of Deeds, 214 East Center Street, Ithaca, MI 48847. 517-875-5217 (EST) 8:30AM-5PM.

**29th Circuit Court**, 214 East Center St, Ithaca, MI 48847. 517-875-5215 (EST) 8:30AM-5:00PM. Felony, Civil Actions Over $10,000.

**65-1 District Court**, 245 East Newark St, Ithaca, MI 48847. 517-875-5240 (EST) 8:30AM-5:00PM. Misdemeanor, Civil Actions Under $10,000, Eviction, Small Claims.

**Probate Court**, 214 East Center St., Ithaca, MI 48847. 517-875-5231 (EST) 8:30AM-5PM. Probate.

## Hillsdale County

**Real Estate Recording**, Hillsdale County Register of Deeds, Courthouse, Hillsdale, MI 49242. 517-437-2231 (EST) 8:30AM-Noon, 1-5PM.

**1st Circuit Court**, 29 North Howell, Hillsdale, MI 49242. 517-437-3391 (EST) 8:30AM-5:00PM. Felony, Civil Actions Over $10,000.

**2nd District Court**, 49 North Howell, Hillsdale, MI 49242. 517-437-7329 (EST) 8:00AM-4:30PM. Misdemeanor, Civil Actions Under $10,000, Eviction, Small Claims.

**Probate Court**, 29 North Howell, Hillsdale, MI 49242. 517-437-4643 (EST) Probate.

## Houghton County

**Real Estate Recording**, Houghton County Register of Deeds, 401 East Houghton Avenue, Houghton, MI 49931. 906-482-1311 (EST) 8AM-4:30PM.

**12th Circuit Court**, 401 East Houghton Ave, Houghton, MI 49931. 906-482-5420 (EST) 8:00AM-4:30PM. Felony, Civil Actions Over $10,000.

**97th District Court**, 401 East Houghton Ave., Houghton, MI 49931. 906-482-4980 (EST) Misdemeanor, Civil Actions Under $10,000, Eviction, Small Claims.

**Probate Court**, 401 East Houghton Ave., Houghton, MI 49931. 906-482-3120 (EST) Probate.

## Huron County

**Real Estate Recording**, Huron County Register of Deeds, 250 East Huron Avenue, Bad Axe, MI 48413. 517-269-9941 (EST) 8:30AM-5PM.

**52nd Circuit Court**, 250 East Huron Ave, Bad Axe, MI 48413. 517-269-9942 (EST) 8:30AM-5:00PM. Felony, Civil Actions Over $10,000.

**73rd District Court**, 250 East Huron Ave., Bad Axe, MI 48413. 517-269-9987 (EST) 8:30AM-5:00PM. Misdemeanor, Civil Actions Under $10,000, Eviction, Small Claims.

**Probate Court**, 250 East Huron Ave., Bad Axe, MI 48413. 517-269-9944 (EST) 8:30AM-5PM. Probate.

## Ingham County

**Real Estate Recording**, Ingham County Register of Deeds, Jefferson St., Courthouse Square, Mason, MI 48854. 517-676-7223 (EST) 8AM-5PM.

**30th Circuit Court**, 333 South Capital Ave, Ste C, Lansing, MI 48933. 517-483-6500 (EST) 9:AM-5:PM MT-THF, 8AM-5PM W. Felony, Civil Actions Over $10,000.

**54 B District Court**, 101 Linden, East Lansing, MI 48823. 517-351-1730 (EST) 8:00AM-4:30PM. Misdemeanor, Civil Actions Under $10,000, Eviction, Small Claims.

**54 A District Court**, 124 West Michigan Ave, Lansing, MI 48933. 517-483-4333 (EST) 8:00AM-5:00PM. Misdemeanor, Civil Actions Under $10,000, Eviction, Small Claims.

**55th District Court**, 700 Buhl, Mason, MI 48854. 517-676-8400 (EST) 8:30AM-4:30PM. Misdemeanor, Civil Actions Under $10,000, Eviction, Small Claims.

**Lansing Probate Court**, 303 West Kalamazoo, Lansing, MI 48933. 517-483-6105 (EST) Probate.

**Mason Probate Court**, PO Box 176, Mason, MI 48854. 517-676-7276 (EST) Probate.

## Ionia County

**Real Estate Recording**, Ionia County Register of Deeds, Main Street, Courthouse, Ionia, MI 48846. 616-527-5320 (EST) 8:30AM-Noon, 1-5PM.

**8th Circuit Court**, 100 Main, Ionia, MI 48846. 616-527-5322 (EST) 8:30AM-5:00PM. Felony, Civil Actions Over $10,000.

**64 A District Court**, 101 West Main, Ionia, MI 48846. 616-527-5346 (EST) Misdemeanor, Civil Actions Under $10,000, Eviction, Small Claims.

**Probate Court**, 100 West Main, Ionia, MI 48846. 616-527-5326 (EST) 8:30AM-5PM. Probate.

## Iosco County

**Real Estate Recording**, Iosco County Register of Deeds, 422 West Lake Street, Tawas City, MI 48763. 517-362-2021 (EST) 9AM-5PM.

**23rd Circuit Court**, PO Box 838, Tawas City, MI 48764. 517-362-3497 (EST) 9:00AM-5:00PM. Felony, Civil Actions Over $10,000.

**81st District Court**, PO Box 388, Tawas City, MI 48764. 517-362-4441 (EST) 8:30AM-5:00PM. Misdemeanor, Civil Actions Under $10,000, Eviction, Small Claims.

**Probate Court**, PO Box 421, Tawas City, MI 48764. 517-362-3991 (EST) Probate.

## Iron County

**Real Estate Recording**, Iron County Register of Deeds, 2 South Sixth Street, Courthouse Annex, Suite 11, Crystal Falls, MI 49920. 906-875-3321 (CST) 8AM-Noon, 12:30-4PM.

**41st Circuit Court**, 2 South 6th St, Crystal Falls, MI 49920. 906-875-3221 (CST) 8:00AM-4:00PM. Felony, Civil Actions Over $10,000.

**95 B District Court**, 2 South 6th St., Crystal Falls, MI 49920. 906-875-6659 (CST) 8:00AM-4:00PM. Misdemeanor, Civil Actions Under $10,000, Eviction, Small Claims.

**Probate Court**, 2 South 6th St., Crystal Falls, MI 49920. 906-875-3121 (CST) Probate.

## Isabella County

**Real Estate Recording**, Isabella County Register of Deeds, 200 North Main Street, Mt. Pleasant, MI 48858. 517-772-0911 (EST) X251 8AM-4:30PM.

**21st Circuit Court**, 200 North Main St, Mount Pleasant, MI 48858. 517-772-0911 (EST) 8:00AM-4:30PM. Felony, Civil Actions Over $10,000.

**76th District Court**, 200 North Main St., Mount Pleasant, MI 48858. 517-772-0911 (EST) 8:00AM-4:30PM. Misdemeanor, Civil Actions Under $10,000, Eviction, Small Claims.

**Probate Court**, 200 N Main St, Mount Pleasant, MI 48858. 517-772-0911 (EST) Probate.

## Jackson County

**Real Estate Recording**, Jackson County Register of Deeds, 120 West Michigan Avenue, 11th Floor, Jackson, MI 49201. 517-788-4350 (EST) 8:30AM-4:30PM.

**4th Circuit Court**, 312 South Jackson St, Jackson, MI 49201. 517-788-4268 (EST) 8:00AM-5:00PM. Felony, Civil Actions Over $10,000.

**12th District Court**, 312 South Jackson St., Jackson, MI 49201. 517-788-4260 (EST) Misdemeanor, Civil Actions Under $10,000, Eviction, Small Claims.

**Probate Court**, 120 West Michigan Ave, Jackson, MI 49201. 517-788-4388 (EST) Probate.

## Kalamazoo County

**Real Estate Recording**, Kalamazoo County Register of Deeds, 201 West Kalamazoo Avenue, Kalamazoo, MI 49007. 616-383-8970 (EST) 8AM-4:30PM.

**9th Circuit Court**, 227 West Michigan St, Kalamazoo, MI 49007. 616-384-8250 (EST) 9:00AM-4:00PM. Felony, Civil Actions Over $10,000.

**8th District Court**, 227 West Michigan St., Kalamazoo, MI 49007. 616-384-8171 (EST) 8:30AM-4:30PM. Misdemeanor, Civil Actions Under $10,000, Eviction, Small Claims.

**9th District Court Division 1**, 416 S. Rose, Kalamazoo, MI 49007. 616-337-8379 (EST) 8:00AM-4:15PM. Misdemeanor, Civil Actions Under $10,000, Eviction, Small Claims.

**9th District Court Division 2**, 7810 Shaver Rd., Portage, MI 49002. 616-329-4590 (EST) 8:00AM-4:30PM. Misdemeanor, Civil Actions Under $10,000, Eviction, Small Claims.

**Probate Court**, 227 West Michigan Ave., Kalamazoo, MI 49007. 616-384-3666 (EST) Probate.

# Michigan

## Kalkaska County

**Real Estate Recording**, Kalkaska County Register of Deeds, 605 North Birch Street, Kalkaska, MI 49646. 616-258-3315 (EST) 9AM-5PM.

**46th Circuit Court**, PO Box 10, Kalkaska, MI 49646. 616-258-3300 (EST) 9:00AM-5:00PM. Felony, Civil Actions Over $10,000.

**87th District Court**, PO Box 1218, Gaylord, MI 49735. 517-732-6486 (EST) 8:00AM-4:30PM. Misdemeanor, Civil Actions Under $10,000, Eviction, Small Claims.

**Probate Court**, 605 North Birch, PO Box 780, Kalkaska, MI 49646. 616-258-3330 (EST) Probate.

## Kent County

**Real Estate Recording**, Kent County Register of Deeds, 300 Monroe Avenue NW, Grand Rapids, MI 49503. 616-336-3558 (EST) 8AM-5PM.

**17th Circuit Court**, 333 Monroe Ave NW, Grand Rapids, MI 49503. 616-336-3679 (EST) 8:00AM-5:00PM. Felony, Civil Actions Over $10,000.

**61st District Court (Grand Rapids)**, 333 Monroe Ave NW, Grand Rapids, MI 49503. 616-456-3370 (EST) 8:00AM-5:00PM. Misdemeanor, Civil Actions Under $10,000, Eviction, Small Claims.

**59th District Court (Grandville & Walker)**, 3181 Wilson Ave SW, Grandville, MI 49418. 616-538-9660 (EST) Misdemeanor, Civil Actions Under $10,000, Eviction, Small Claims.

**62 B District Court (Kentwood)**, PO Box 8848, Kentwood, MI 49518. 616-698-9310 (EST) 8:00AM-5:00PM. Misdemeanor, Civil Actions Under $10,000, Eviction, Small Claims.

**63rd District Court-1st Division (rest of county)**, 105 Maple St, Rockford, MI 49341. 616-866-1576 (EST) 8:00AM-5:00PM. Misdemeanor, Civil Actions Under $10,000, Eviction, Small Claims.

**62 A District Court (Wyoming)**, 2650 De Hoop Ave SW, Wyoming, MI 49509. 616-530-7385 (EST) 8:00AM-5:00PM. Misdemeanor, Civil Actions Under $10,000, Eviction, Small Claims.

**Probate Court**, 320 Ottawa NW, Grand Rapids, MI 49503. 616-336-3630 (EST) Probate.

## Keweenaw County

**Real Estate Recording**, Keweenaw County Register of Deeds, 4th Street, Courthouse, Eagle River, MI 49924. 906-337-2229 (EST) 9AM-4PM.

**12th Circuit Court**, Unit 1, Box 7, Eagle River, MI 49924. 906-337-2229 (EST) 9:00AM-4:00PM. Felony, Civil Actions Over $10,000.

**97th District Court**, Unit 1, Box 7, Eagle River, MI 49924. 906-337-2229 (EST) 9:00AM-4:00PM. Misdemeanor, Civil Actions Under $10,000, Eviction, Small Claims.

**Probate Court**, PO Box 3, Eagle River, MI 49924. 906-337-1927 (EST) Probate.

## Lake County

**Real Estate Recording**, Lake County Register of Deeds, 800 Tenth Street, Courthouse, Baldwin, MI 49304. 616-745-4641 (EST) 8:30AM-Noon, 1-5PM.

**51st Circuit Court**, PO Drawer B, Baldwin, MI 49304. 616-745-4641 (EST) 8:30AM-5:00PM. Felony, Civil Actions Over $10,000.

**78th District Court**, PO Box 73, Baldwin, MI 49304. 616-745-2738 (EST) Misdemeanor, Civil Actions Under $10,000, Eviction, Small Claims.

**Probate Court**, PO Box 308, Baldwin, MI 49304. 616-745-4614 (EST) Probate.

## Lapeer County

**Real Estate Recording**, Lapeer County Register of Deeds, 279 North Court Street, Lapeer, MI 48446. 810-667-0211 (EST) 8AM-5PM.

**40th Circuit Court**, 255 Clay St, Lapeer, MI 48446. 313-667-0358 (EST) 8:00AM-5:00PM. Felony, Civil Actions Over $10,000.

**71 A District Court**, 255 Clay St., Lapeer, MI 48446. 810-667-0300 (EST) 8:00AM-5:00PM. Misdemeanor, Civil Actions Under $10,000, Eviction, Small Claims.

**Probate Court**, 255 Clay St., Lapeer, MI 48446. 313-667-0261 (EST) Probate.

## Leelanau County

**Real Estate Recording**, Leelanau County Register of Deeds, 301 S. Cedar, Leland, MI 49654. 616-256-9682 (EST) 9AM-5PM.

**13th Circuit Court**, PO Box 467, Leland, MI 49654. 616-256-9824 (EST) 9:00AM-5:00PM. Felony, Civil Actions Over $10,000.

**86th District Court**, PO Box 486, Leland, MI 49654. 616-256-9931 (EST) 8:00AM-4:00PM. Misdemeanor, Civil Actions Under $10,000, Eviction, Small Claims.

**Probate Court**, PO Box 595, Leland, MI 49654. 616-256-9803 (EST) Probate.

## Lenawee County

**Real Estate Recording**, Lenawee County Register of Deeds, Courthouse, Adrian, MI 49221. 517-263-8831 (EST) 8AM-4:30PM.

**39th Circuit Court**, 425 North Main St, Adrian, MI 49221. 517-264-4597 (EST) 8:00AM-4:30PM. Felony, Civil Actions Over $10,000.

**2nd District Court**, 425 North Main St., Adrian, MI 49221. 517-263-8831 (EST) 8:00AM-4:30PM. Misdemeanor, Civil Actions Under $10,000, Eviction, Small Claims.

**Probate Court**, 425 North Main St., Adrian, MI 49221. 517-263-8831 (EST) Probate.

## Livingston County

**Real Estate Recording**, Livingston County Register of Deeds, Courthouse, Howell, MI 48843. 517-546-0270 (EST) 8AM-5PM.

**44th Circuit Court**, 210 South Highlander Way, Howell, MI 48843. 517-546-9816 (EST) 8:00AM-5:00PM. Felony, Civil Actions Over $10,000.

**53 B District Court**, 224 North First, Brighton, MI 48116. 313-229-6615 (EST) 8:00AM-4:45PM. Misdemeanor, Civil Actions Under $10,000, Eviction, Small Claims.

**53 A District Court**, 300 South Highlander Way, Howell, MI 48843. 517-548-1000 (EST) 8:00AM-4:45PM. Misdemeanor, Civil Actions Under $10,000, Eviction, Small Claims.

**Probate Court**, 200 East Grand River, Howell, MI 48843. 517-546-3750 (EST) Probate.

## Luce County

**Real Estate Recording**, Luce County Register of Deeds, County Government Building, Newberry, MI 49868. 906-293-5521 (EST) 8AM-4PM.

**11th Circuit Court**, East Court St, Newberry, MI 49868. 906-293-5521 (EST) 9:00AM-5:00PM. Felony, Civil Actions Over $10,000.

**92nd District Court**, 407 W Harrie, Newberry, MI 49868. 906-293-5531 (EST) 8:00AM-4:00PM. Misdemeanor, Civil Actions Under $10,000, Eviction, Small Claims.

**Probate Court**, 407 W. Harrie, Newberry, MI 49868. 906-293-5601 (EST) Probate.

## Mackinac County

**Real Estate Recording**, Mackinac County Register of Deeds, 100 Marley Street, Saint Ignace, MI 49781. 906-643-7306 (EST) 8:30AM-4:30PM.

**50th Circuit Court**, 100 Marley, St Ignace, MI 49781. 906-643-7300 (EST) 8:30AM-4:30PM. Felony, Civil Actions Over $10,000.

**92nd District Court**, 100 Marley, St Ignace, MI 49781. 906-643-7321 (EST) 8:30AM-4:30PM. Misdemeanor, Civil Actions Under $10,000, Eviction, Small Claims.

**Probate Court**, 100 Marley, St Ignace, MI 49781. 906-643-7303 (EST) Probate.

## Macomb County

**Real Estate Recording**, Macomb County Register of Deeds, 10 North Main, Chesterfield, MI 48043. 810-469-5342 (EST) 8:30AM-5PM.

**16th Circuit Court**, 40 N Main St, Mount Clemens, MI 48043. 810-469-5208 (EST) 8:00AM-4:30PM. Felony, Civil Actions Over $10,000.

**41 B District Court (Clinton, Harrison)**, 40700 Romeo Plank Rd, Clinton Township, MI 48038. 810-286-8010 (EST) 8:30AM-4:30PM. Misdemeanor, Civil Actions Under $10,000, Eviction, Small Claims.

**42nd District Court Division 2 (Lenox, Chesterfield)**, 36540 Green St, New Baltimore, MI 48047. 810-725-9520 (EST) 8:30AM-5:00PM. Misdemeanor, Civil Actions Under $10,000, Eviction, Small Claims.

**42nd District Court Division 1**, 14713 Thirty-three Mile Rd., Romeo, MI 48065. 313-752-9679 (EST) 8:30AM-5:00PM. Misdemeanor, Civil Actions Under $10,000, Eviction, Small Claims.

**39th District Court (Roseville and Frasier)**, 29733 Gratiot, Roseville, MI 48066. 810-773-2010 (EST) 8:00AM-4:30PM. Misdemeanor, Civil Actions Under $10,000, Eviction, Small Claims.

**41 A District Court (Shelby)**, 51660 Van Dyke, Shelby Township, MI 48316. 810-739-7325 (EST) 8:00AM-4:00PM. Misdemeanor, Civil Actions Under $10,000, Eviction, Small Claims.

**40th District Court (St. Clair Shores only)**, 27701 Jefferson, St. Clair Shores, MI 48081. 810-445-5288 (EST) 8:30AM-5:00PM. Misdemeanor, Civil Actions Under $10,000, Eviction, Small Claims.

**41 A District Court (Sterling Heights)**, 40555 Utica Rd, Sterling Heights, MI 48311. 313-977-6123 (EST) 8:00AM-4:30PM. Misdemeanor, Civil Actions Under $10,000, Eviction, Small Claims.

**37th District Court (Warren and Center Line)**, 8300 Common Rd., Warren, MI 48093. 810-574-4928 (EST) 8:30AM-4:30PM. Misdemeanor, Civil Actions Under $10,000, Eviction, Small Claims.

**41 B District Court (Mt Clemens)**, 1 Crocker Blvd, Mount Clemens, MI 48043. 810-469-6870 (EST) 8:30AM-4:30PM. Civil Actions Under $10,000, Eviction, Small Claims.

**Probate Court**, 21850 Dumham, Mount Clemens, MI 48043. 313-469-5290 (EST) Probate.

## Manistee County

**Real Estate Recording**, Manistee County Register of Deeds, 415 Third Street, Courthouse, Manistee, MI 49660. 616-723-2146 (EST) 8:30AM-12, 1PM-5PM M; 8:30AM-12, 1-3:30PM T-F.

**19th Circuit Court**, 415 3rd St, Manistee, MI 49660. 616-723-3331 (EST) 8:00AM-4:30PM. Felony, Civil Actions Over $10,000.

**85th District Court**, 415 3rd St, Manistee, MI 49660. 616-723-5010 (EST) 8:30AM-5:00PM. Misdemeanor, Civil Actions Under $10,000, Eviction, Small Claims.

**Probate Court**, 415 3rd St, Manistee, MI 49660. 616-723-3261 (EST) Probate.

## Marquette County

**Real Estate Recording**, Marquette County Register of Deeds, 234 West Baraga Avenue, Courthouse, Marquette, MI 49855. 906-228-1528 (EST)

**25th Circuit Court**, 234 W Baraga, Marquette, MI 49855. 906-228-1525 (EST) 8:00AM-5:00PM. Felony, Civil Actions Over $10,000.

**96th District Court**, County Courthouse, Marquette, MI 49855. 906-228-1550 (EST) 8:30AM-5:00PM. Misdemeanor, Civil Actions Under $10,000, Eviction, Small Claims.

**Probate Court**, 234 W Baraga, Marquette, MI 49855. 906-228-1514 (EST) Probate.

## Mason County

**Real Estate Recording**, Mason County Register of Deeds, West Ludington Avenue, Courthouse, Ludington, MI 49431. 616-843-4466 (EST) 9AM-5PM.

**51st Circuit Court**, 304 E Ludington Ave, Ludington, MI 49431. 616-845-1445 (EST) 9:00AM-5:00PM. Felony, Civil Actions Over $10,000.

**79th District Court**, County Court, Ludington, MI 49431. 616-843-4130 (EST) 8:00AM-5:00PM. Misdemeanor, Civil Actions Under $10,000, Eviction, Small Claims.

**Probate Court**, PO Box 186, Ludington, MI 49431. 616-843-8666 (EST) Probate.

## Mecosta County

**Real Estate Recording**, Mecosta County Register of Deeds, 400 Elm Street, Big Rapids, MI 49307. 616-592-0148 (EST) 8:30AM-5PM.

**49th Circuit Court**, 400 Elm, Big Rapids, MI 49307. 616-592-0783 (EST) Felony, Civil Actions Over $10,000.

**77th District Court**, 400 Elm, Big Rapids, MI 49307. 616-592-0799 (EST) 8:30AM-4:30PM. Misdemeanor, Civil Actions Under $10,000, Eviction, Small Claims.

**Probate Court**, PO Box 820, Big Rapids, MI 49307. 616-592-0135 (EST) Probate.

## Menominee County

**Real Estate Recording**, Menominee County Register of Deeds, Courthouse, 839 10th Ave., Menominee, MI 49858. 906-863-2822 (CST) 8AM-4PM.

**41st Circuit Court**, 839 10th Ave, Menominee, MI 49858. 906-863-9968 (CST) 8:00AM-4:00PM. Felony, Civil Actions Over $10,000.

**95th District Court**, 837 10th Ave, Menominee, MI 49858. 906-863-8532 (CST) 8:00AM-4:00PM. Misdemeanor, Civil Actions Under $10,000, Eviction, Small Claims.

**Probate Court**, 837 10th Ave., Menominee, MI 49858. 906-863-2634 (CST) Probate.

## Midland County

**Real Estate Recording**, Midland County Register of Deeds, 220 West Ellsworth Street, County Services Building, Midland, MI 48640. 517-832-6820 (EST) 8AM-5PM.

**42nd Circuit Court**, Courthouse, 301 W Main St, Midland, MI 48640. 517-832-6735 (EST) 8:00AM-5:00PM. Felony, Civil Actions Over $10,000.

**75th District Court-Civil Division**, 301 W Main St, Midland, MI 48640. 517-832-6701 (EST) 8:00AM-5:00PM. Civil Actions Under $10,000, Eviction, Small Claims.

**75th District Court-Criminal Division**, 301 W Main St, Midland, MI 48640. 517-832-6702 (EST) 8:00AM-5:00PM. Misdemeanor.

**Probate Court**, 301 W Main St, Midland, MI 48640. 517-832-6880 (EST) Probate.

## Missaukee County

**Real Estate Recording**, Missaukee County Register of Deeds, 111 S. Canal St., Lake City, MI 49651. 616-839-4967 (EST) 9AM-5PM.

**28th Circuit Court**, PO Box 800, Lake City, MI 49651. 616-839-4867 (EST) 9:00AM-5:00PM. Felony, Civil Actions Over $10,000.

**84th District Court**, PO Box 800, Lake City, MI 49651. 616-839-4590 (EST) Misdemeanor, Civil Actions Under $10,000, Eviction, Small Claims.

**Probate Court**, PO Box 800, Lake City, MI 49651. 616-839-2266 (EST) Probate.

## Monroe County

**Real Estate Recording**, Monroe County Register of Deeds, 106 East First Street, Monroe, MI 48161. 313-243-7046 (EST) 8:30AM-5PM.

**38th Circuit Court**, 106 E 1st St, Monroe, MI 48161. 313-243-7081 (EST) 8:30AM-5:00PM. Felony, Civil Actions Over $10,000.

**1st District Court**, 106 E 1st St, Monroe, MI 48161. 313-243-7030 (EST) Misdemeanor, Civil Actions Under $10,000, Eviction, Small Claims.

**Probate Court**, 106 E 1st St, Monroe, MI 48161. 313-243-7018 (EST) Probate.

## Montcalm County

**Real Estate Recording**, Montcalm County Register of Deeds, 211 West Main Street, Courthouse, Stanton, MI 48888. 517-831-5226 (EST) 8AM-5PM.

**8th Circuit Court**, PO Box 368, Stanton, MI 48888. 517-831-5226 (EST) 8:00AM-5:00PM. Felony, Civil Actions Over $10,000.

**64 B District Court**, PO Box 608, Stanton, MI 48888. 517-831-5226 (EST) 8:00AM-5:00PM. Misdemeanor, Civil Actions Under $10,000, Eviction, Small Claims.

**Probate Court**, PO Box 368, Stanton, MI 48888. 517-831-5226 (EST) Probate.

## Montmorency County

**Real Estate Recording**, Montmorency County Register of Deeds, State Street, Courthouse, Atlanta, MI 49709. 517-785-3374 (EST) 8:30AM-Noon, 1-4:30PM.

**26th Circuit Court**, PO Box 415, Atlanta, MI 49709. 517-785-4794 (EST) 8:30AM-4:30PM. Felony, Civil Actions Over $10,000.

**88th District Court**, PO Box 415, Atlanta, MI 49709. 517-785-3122 (EST) 8:30AM-4:30PM. Misdemeanor, Civil Actions Under $10,000, Eviction, Small Claims.

**Probate Court**, PO Box 415, Atlanta, MI 49709. 517-785-4403 (EST) Probate.

## Muskegon County

**Real Estate Recording**, Muskegon County Register of Deeds, County Building, Muskegon, MI 49442. 616-724-6271 (EST) 8AM-5PM.

**14th Circuit Court**, 990 Terrace, 6th Floor, Muskegon, MI 49442. 616-724-6447 (EST) 8:00AM-5:00PM. Felony, Civil Actions Over $10,000.

**60th District Court**, 990 Terrace, 1st Floor, Muskegon, MI 49442. 616-724-6250 (EST) 8:30AM-4:45PM. Misdemeanor, Civil Actions Under $10,000, Eviction, Small Claims.

**Probate Court**, 990 Terrace St, 5th Floor, Muskegon, MI 49442. 616-724-6241 (EST) Probate.

## Newaygo County

**Real Estate Recording**, Newaygo County Register of Deeds, 1087 Newell Street, County Administration Building, White Cloud, MI 49349. 616-689-7246 (EST) 8AM-5PM.

**27th Circuit Court**, PO Box 885, White Cloud, MI 49349. 616-689-7269 (EST) 8:00AM-5:00PM. Felony, Civil Actions Over $10,000.

**78th District Court**, 1092 Newell St, White Cloud, MI 49349. 616-689-7257 (EST) 8:00AM-5:00PM. Misdemeanor, Civil Actions Under $10,000, Eviction, Small Claims.

**Probate Court**, 1084 Wilcox, White Cloud, MI 49349. 616-689-7270 (EST) Probate.

## Oakland County

**Real Estate Recording**, Oakland County Register of Deeds, 1200 North Telegraph Road, Dept 480, Pontiac, MI 48341. 810-858-0599 (EST) 8:30AM-5PM.

**6th Circuit Court**, 1200 N Telegraph Rd, Pontiac, MI 48341. 313-858-0581 (EST) 8:30AM-4:30PM. Felony, Civil Actions Over $10,000.

**45 A District Court (Berkley)**, 3338 Coolidge, Berkley, MI 48072. 810-544-3300 (EST) 8:30AM-4:30PM. Misdemeanor, Civil Actions Under $10,000, Eviction, Small Claims.

# Michigan

**48th District Court**, 4280 Telegraph Rd, Bloomfield Hills, MI 48302. 810-647-1141 (EST) 8:30AM-4:30PM. Misdemeanor, Civil Actions Under $10,000, Eviction, Small Claims.

**52nd District Court-Division 2 (Springfield, Holly, Groveland, Br**, 5850 Lorac, PO Box 169, Clarkston, MI 48347-0169. Criminal 313 (EST) 8:30AM-4:30PM. Misdemeanor, Civil Actions Under $10,000, Eviction, Small Claims.

**47th District Court (Farmington, Farmington Hills)**, 32795 W Ten Mile Rd, Farmington, MI 48336. 810-477-5630 (EST) 8:30AM-4:30PM. Misdemeanor, Civil Actions Under $10,000, Eviction, Small Claims.

**43rd District Court**, 43 E Nine Mile Rd, Hazel Park, MI 48030. 810-547-3034 (EST) 8:30AM-5:00PM. Misdemeanor, Civil Actions Under $10,000, Eviction, Small Claims.

**45 B District Court (Huntington Woods, Oak Park, Pleasant Ridge,**, 13600 Oak Park Blvd, Oak Park, MI 48237. 313-542-7042 (EST) 9:00AM-4:45PM. Misdemeanor, Civil Actions Under $10,000, Eviction, Small Claims.

**52nd District Court-Division 3**, 135 Barclay Circle, Rochester Hills, MI 48307. 313-863-5553 (EST) 8:30AM-4:45PM. Misdemeanor, Civil Actions Under $10,000, Eviction, Small Claims.

**44th District Court (Royal Oak)**, 3rd Fl City Hall, 211 Williams St, Royal Oak, MI 48068. 810-546-7780 (EST) 8:00AM-4:30PM. Misdemeanor, Civil Actions Under $10,000, Eviction, Small Claims.

**46th District Court (Southfield & Lathrup)**, 26000 Evergreen Rd, Southfield, MI 48076. 810-354-9506 (EST) 8:00AM-5:00PM. Misdemeanor, Civil Actions Under $10,000, Eviction, Small Claims.

**52nd District Court-Division 4 (Troy, Clawson)**, 500 W Big Beaver Rd, Troy, MI 48084. 810-528-0400 (EST) 8:30AM-4:45PM. Misdemeanor, Civil Actions Under $10,000, Eviction, Small Claims.

**52nd District Court-Division 1**, 1010 E West Maple Rd, Walled Lake, MI 48390. 810-624-0260 (EST) Misdemeanor, Civil Actions Under $10,000, Eviction, Small Claims.

**51st District Court (Waterford)**, 5100 Civic Center Dr, Waterford, MI 48329. 810-674-4655 (EST) Misdemeanor, Civil Actions Under $10,000, Eviction, Small Claims.

**50th District Court-Pontiac Civil Division**, 70 N Saganaw, Pontiac, MI 48342. 810-857-8090 (EST) 8:30AM-5:00PM. Civil Actions Under $10,000, Eviction, Small Claims.

**50th District Court-Pontiac Criminal Division**, 70 N Saganaw, Pontiac, MI 48342. 810-857-8027 (EST) 8:30AM-5:00PM. Misdemeanor.

**Probate Court**, 1200 N Telegraph Rd, Pontiac, MI 48343. 313-858-0260 (EST) Probate.

## Oceana County

**Real Estate Recording**, Oceana County Register of Deeds, 100 State Street, Courthouse, Hart, MI 49420. 616-873-4158 (EST) 9AM-5PM.

**27th Circuit Court**, PO Box 189, Hart, MI 49420. 616-873-3977 (EST) 9:00AM-5:00PM. Felony, Civil Actions Over $10,000.

**79th District Court**, PO Box 167, Hart, MI 49420. 616-873-4530 (EST) 8:00AM-5:00PM. Misdemeanor, Civil Actions Under $10,000, Eviction, Small Claims.

**Probate Court**, PO Box 129, Hart, MI 49420. 616-873-3666 (EST) Probate.

## Ogemaw County

**Real Estate Recording**, Ogemaw County Register of Deeds, 806 West Houghton Ave, Room 104, West Branch, MI 48661. 517-345-0728 (EST) 8:30AM-4:30PM.

**34th Circuit Court**, 806 W Houghton, West Branch, MI 48661. 517-345-0215 (EST) 9:00AM-5:00PM. Felony, Civil Actions Over $10,000.

**82nd District Court**, PO Box 365, West Branch, MI 48661. 517-345-5040 (EST) 8:30AM-4:30PM. Misdemeanor, Civil Actions Under $10,000, Eviction, Small Claims.

**Probate Court**, County Courthouse, Rm 203, West Branch, MI 48661. 517-345-0145 (EST) Probate.

## Ontonagon County

**Real Estate Recording**, Ontonagon County Register of Deeds, 725 Greenland Road, Ontonagon, MI 49953. 906-884-4255 (EST) 8:30AM-4:30PM.

**32nd Circuit Court**, 725 Greenland Rd, Ontonagon, MI 49953. 906-884-4255 (EST) 8:30AM-4:30PM. Felony, Civil Actions Over $10,000.

**98th District Court**, 725 Greenland Rd, Ontonagon, MI 49953. 906-884-2865 (EST) 8:30AM-4:30PM. Misdemeanor, Civil Actions Under $10,000, Eviction, Small Claims.

**Probate Court**, 725 Greenland Rd, Ontonagon, MI 49953. 906-884-4117 (EST) Probate.

## Osceola County

**Real Estate Recording**, Osceola County Register of Deeds, 301 West Upton Ave., Reed City, MI 49677. 616-832-6113 (EST) 9AM-5PM.

**49th Circuit Court**, 301 W Upton, Osceola, MI 49677. 616-832-6102 (EST) 9:00AM-5:00PM. Felony, Civil Actions Over $10,000.

**77th District Court**, 410 W Upton, Osceola, MI 49677. 616-832-6155 (EST) 8:30AM-4:30PM. Misdemeanor, Civil Actions Under $10,000, Eviction, Small Claims.

**Probate Court**, 301 W Upton, Osceola, MI 49677. 616-832-6124 (EST) Probate.

## Oscoda County

**Real Estate Recording**, Oscoda County Register of Deeds, 310 Morenci Street, Courthouse, Mio, MI 48647. 517-826-3241 (EST) 8:30AM-4:30PM.

**23rd Circuit Court**, PO Box 399, Mio, MI 48647. 517-826-3241 (EST) 8:30AM-4:30PM. Felony, Civil Actions Over $10,000.

**82nd District Court**, PO Box 399, Mio, MI 48647. 517-826-3241 (EST) 8:30AM-4:30PM. Misdemeanor, Civil Actions Under $10,000, Eviction, Small Claims.

**Probate Court**, PO Box 399, Mio, MI 48647. 517-826-3241 (EST) Probate.

## Otsego County

**Real Estate Recording**, Otsego County Register of Deeds, 225 West Main St., Room 108, Gaylord, MI 49735. 517-732-6484 (EST) X201-2 8AM-Noon, 1-4:30PM.

**46th Circuit Court**, 225 Main St, Gaylord, MI 49735. 517-732-6484 (EST) 8:00AM-4:30PM. Felony, Civil Actions Over $10,000.

**87th District Court**, PO Box 1218, Gaylord, MI 49735. 517-732-6486 (EST) 8:00AM-4:30PM. Misdemeanor, Civil Actions Under $10,000, Eviction, Small Claims.

**Probate Court**, 225 Main St, Gaylord, MI 49735. 517-732-6484 (EST) Probate.

## Ottawa County

**Real Estate Recording**, Ottawa County Register of Deeds, 414 Washington Avenue, Room 305, Grand Haven, MI 49417. 616-846-8240 (EST) 8AM-5PM.

**20th Circuit Court**, 414 Washington Ave, Grand Haven, MI 49417. 616-846-8310 (EST) 8:00AM-5:00PM. Felony, Civil Actions Over $10,000.

**58th District Court-Grand Haven**, 414 Washington Ave, Grand Haven, MI 49417. 616-846-8280 (EST) 8:00AM-5:00PM. Misdemeanor, Civil Actions Under $10,000, Eviction, Small Claims.

**58th District Court-Holland**, 57 W 8th St, Holland, MI 49423. 616-392-6991 (EST) 8:00AM-5:00PM. Misdemeanor, Civil Actions Under $10,000, Eviction, Small Claims.

**58th District Court-Hudsonville**, 3100 Port Sheldon, Hudsonville, MI 49426. 616-669-1570 (EST) 8:00AM-5:00PM. Misdemeanor, Civil Actions Under $10,000, Eviction, Small Claims.

**Probate Court**, 12120 Fillmore St, West Olive, MI 49460. 616-786-4110 (EST) Probate.

## Presque Isle County

**Real Estate Recording**, Presque Isle County Register of Deeds, 151 East Huron Street, Rogers City, MI 49779. 517-734-2676 (EST) 9AM-5PM.

**26th Circuit Court**, PO Box 110, Rogers City, MI 49779. 517-734-3288 (EST) 9:00AM-5:00PM. Felony, Civil Actions Over $10,000.

**89th District Court**, PO Box 110, Rogers City, MI 49779. 517-734-2411 (EST) 8:30AM-4:30PM. Misdemeanor, Civil Actions Under $10,000, Eviction, Small Claims.

**Probate Court**, PO Box 110, Rogers City, MI 49779. 517-734-3268 (EST) Probate.

## Roscommon County

**Real Estate Recording**, Roscommon County Register of Deeds, 500 Lake Street, Roscommon, MI 48653. 517-275-5931 (EST) 8:30AM-4:30PM.

**34th Circuit Court**, PO Box 98, Roscommon, MI 48653. 517-275-5923 (EST) 8:30AM-4:30PM. Felony, Civil Actions Over $10,000.

**83rd District Court**, PO Box 189, Roscommon, MI 48653. 517-275-5312 (EST) 8:30AM-4:30PM. Misdemeanor, Civil Actions Under $10,000, Eviction, Small Claims.

**Probate Court**, PO Box 607, Roscommon, MI 48653. 517-275-4620 (EST) Probate.

## Saginaw County

**Real Estate Recording**, Saginaw County Register of Deeds, 111 South Michigan Avenue,

Saginaw, MI 48602. 517-790-5270 (EST) 8AM-5PM.

**10th Circuit Court**, 111 S Michigan Ave, Saginaw, MI 48602. 517-790-5247 (EST) 8:00AM-5:00PM. Felony, Civil Actions Over $10,000.

**70th District Court-Civil Division**, 111 S Michigan Ave, Saginaw, MI 48602. 517-790-5380 (EST) 8:00AM-4:45PM. Civil Actions Under $10,000, Eviction, Small Claims.

**70th District Court-Criminal Division**, 111 S Michigan Ave, Saginaw, MI 48602. 517-790-5385 (EST) 8:00AM-4:45PM. Misdemeanor.

**Probate Court**, 111 S Michigan St, Saginaw, MI 48602. 517-790-5320 (EST) Probate.

## Sanilac County

**Real Estate Recording**, Sanilac County Register of Deeds, 60 West Sanilac, Sandusky, MI 48471. 313-648-2313 (EST) 8AM-Noon, 1-4:30PM.

**24th Circuit Court**, 60 W Sanilac, Sandusky, MI 48471. 810-648-3212 (EST) 8:00AM-4:30PM. Felony, Civil Actions Over $10,000.

**73rd District Court**, 60 W Sanilac, Sandusky, MI 48471. 810-648-3250 (EST) 8:00AM-4:30PM. Misdemeanor, Civil Actions Under $10,000, Eviction, Small Claims.

**Probate Court**, 60 W Sanilac, Sandusky, MI 48471. 810-648-3221 (EST) Probate.

## Schoolcraft County

**Real Estate Recording**, Schoolcraft County Register of Deeds, 300 Walnut Street, Room 164, Manistique, MI 49854. 906-341-5532 (EST) 8AM-4PM.

**11th Circuit Court**, 300 Walnut St, Rm 164, Manistique, MI 49854. 906-341-3618 (EST) 8:00AM-4:00AM. Felony, Civil Actions Over $10,000.

**93rd District Court**, 300 Walnut St, Rm 135, Manistique, MI 49854. 906-341-5650 (EST) 8:00AM-4:00PM. Misdemeanor, Civil Actions Under $10,000, Eviction, Small Claims.

**Probate Court**, 300 Walnut St, Manistique, MI 49854. 906-341-2633 (EST) Probate.

## Shiawassee County

**Real Estate Recording**, Shiawassee County Register of Deeds, 208 North Shiawassee, Courthouse, Corunna, MI 48817. 517-743-2316 (EST) 8AM-5PM.

**35th Circuit Court**, 200 N Shiawassee St, Corunna, MI 48817. 517-743-2302 (EST) 8:00AM-5:00PM. Felony, Civil Actions Over $10,000.

**66th District Court**, 110 E Mack St, Corunna, MI 48817. 517-743-2244 (EST) 8:00AM-5:00PM. Misdemeanor, Civil Actions Under $10,000, Eviction, Small Claims.

**Probate Court**, 110 E Mack St, Corunna, MI 48817. 517-743-2211 (EST) Probate.

## St. Clair County

**Real Estate Recording**, St. Clair County Register of Deeds, 201 McMorran Blvd., Room 116, Port Huron, MI 48060. 810-985-2275 (EST) 8AM-4:30PM.

**31st Circuit Court**, 201 McMorran Blvd, Port Huron, MI 48060. 810-985-2200 (EST) 8:00AM-4:30PM. Felony, Civil Actions Over $10,000.

**72nd District Court**, 201 McMorran Rd, Port Huron, MI 48060. 313-985-2072 (EST) 8:00AM-4:30PM. Misdemeanor, Civil Actions Under $10,000, Eviction, Small Claims.

**Probate Court**, 201 McMorran Rd, Port Huron, MI 48060. 313-985-2066 (EST) Probate.

## St. Joseph County

**Real Estate Recording**, St. Joseph County Register of Deeds, 125 W. Main Street, Centreville, MI 49032. 616-467-5553 (EST) X553 9AM-5PM.

**45th Circuit Court**, PO Box 189, Centreville, MI 49032. 616-467-5602 (EST) 9:00AM-5:00PM. Felony, Civil Actions Over $10,000.

**3-B District Court**, PO Box 67, Centreville, MI 49032. 616-467-5513 (EST) Misdemeanor, Civil Actions Under $10,000, Eviction, Small Claims.

**Probate Court**, PO Box 190, Centreville, MI 49032. 616-467-6361 (EST) Probate.

## Tuscola County

**Real Estate Recording**, Tuscola County Register of Deeds, 440 North State Street, Caro, MI 48723. 517-673-5999 (EST) 8AM-Noon, 1-4:30PM.

**54th Circuit Court**, 440 N State St, Caro, MI 48723. 517-673-5999 (EST) 8:00AM-3:30PM. Felony, Civil Actions Over $10,000.

**71 B District Court**, 440 N State St., Caro, MI 48723. 517-673-5999 (EST) 8:00AM-4:30PM. Misdemeanor, Civil Actions Under $10,000, Eviction, Small Claims.

**Probate Court**, 440 N State St, Caro, MI 48723. 517-673-5999 (EST) Probate.

## Van Buren County

**Real Estate Recording**, Van Buren County Register of Deeds, 212 Paw Paw Street, Paw Paw, MI 49079. 616-657-8242 (EST) 8:30AM-5PM.

**36th Circuit Court**, 212 Paw Paw St, Paw Paw, MI 49079. 616-657-8218 (EST) 8:30AM-5:00PM. Felony, Civil Actions Over $10,000.

**7th District Court**, 212 Paw Paw St, Paw Paw, MI 49079. 616-657-8222 (EST) 9:00AM-4:30PM. Misdemeanor, Civil Actions Under $10,000, Eviction, Small Claims.

**7th District Court-West Division**, 1007 E Wells, South Haven, MI 49090. 616-637-5258 (EST) 8:30AM-4:30PM. Misdemeanor, Civil Actions Under $10,000, Eviction, Small Claims.

**Probate Court**, 212 Paw Paw St, Paw Paw, MI 49079. 616-657-8225 (EST) Probate.

## Washtenaw County

**Real Estate Recording**, Washtenaw County Register of Deeds, 101 East Huron, Courthouse, Ann Arbor, MI 48107. 313-994-2517 (EST) 8:30AM-5PM.

**22nd Circuit Court**, PO Box 8645, Ann Arbor, MI 48107-8645. 313-994-2507 (EST) 8:30AM-4:30PM. Felony, Civil Actions Over $10,000.

**14th District Court A-1**, 4133 Washtenaw, Ann Arbor, MI 48107-8645. 313-971-6050 (EST) 8:00AM-4:30PM. Misdemeanor, Civil Actions Under $10,000, Eviction, Small Claims.

**14th District Court A-3**, 122 S Main St, Chelsea, MI 48118. 313-475-8606 (EST) 8:00AM-4:30PM. Misdemeanor, Civil Actions Under $10,000, Eviction, Small Claims.

**14th District Court A-4**, 7605 N Maple St, Saline, MI 48176. 313-475-8606 (EST) 8:00AM-4:30PM M-F (Office), 8:00AM-3:30PM M-F (Phone). Misdemeanor, Civil Actions Under $10,000, Eviction, Small Claims.

**14th District Court A-2**, 415 W Michigan Ave, Ypsilanti, MI 48197. 313-484-6690 (EST) 8:00AM-4:30PM. Misdemeanor, Civil Actions Under $10,000, Eviction, Small Claims.

**14th District Court-B-Civil Division**, 7200 S Huron River Dr, Ypsilanti, MI 48197. 313-483-5300 (EST) 8:00AM-5:00PM. Civil Actions Under $10,000, Eviction, Small Claims.

**14th District Court-B-Criminal Division**, 7200 S Huron River Dr, Ypsilanti, MI 48197. 313-483-1333 (EST) 8:00AM-5:00PM. Misdemeanor.

**15th District Court-Civil Division**, 101 E Huron, Box 8650, Ann Arbor, MI 48107. 313-994-2749 (EST) 8:00AM-4:30PM. Civil Actions Under $10,000, Eviction, Small Claims.

**15th District Court-Criminal Division**, 101 E Huron, Box 8650, Ann Arbor, MI 48107-8650. 313-994-2745 (EST) 8:00AM-4:30PM. Misdemeanor.

**Probate Court**, PO Box 8645, Ann Arbor, MI 48107. 313-994-2474 (EST) Probate.

## Wayne County

**Real Estate Recording**, Wayne County Register of Deeds, 400 Monroe, Room 620, Detroit, MI 48226. 313-224-5860 (EST) 8AM-4:30PM.

**3rd Circuit Court**, 201 County Building, 2 Woodward, Detroit, MI 48226. 313-224-5509 (EST) 8:00AM-4:30PM. Civil Actions Over $10,000.

**Recorders Court of Detroit**, Hall of Justice, 1441 St Antoine, Detroit, MI 48226. 313-224-2500 (EST) 8:00AM-4:30PM. Felony.

**36th District Court-Civil (Detroit)**, 421 Madison Ave, Detroit, MI 48226. 313-965-5972 (EST) 8:00AM-4:30PM. Civil Actions Under $10,000, Eviction, Small Claims.

**24th District Court (Allen Park & Melvindale)**, 6515 Roosevelt, Allen Park, MI 48101-2524. 313-928-0535 (EST) 8:30AM-4:30PM. Misdemeanor, Civil Actions Under $10,000, Eviction, Small Claims.

**20th District Court**, 6045 Fenton, Dearborn Heights, MI 48127. 313-277-7480 (EST) 9:00AM-5:00PM. Misdemeanor, Civil Actions Under $10,000, Eviction, Small Claims.

**19th District Court**, 16077 Michigan Ave, Dearborn, MI 48126. 313-943-2065 (EST) 8:30AM-4:30PM. Misdemeanor, Civil Actions Under $10,000, Eviction, Small Claims.

**26-2 District Court**, 3869 W Jefferson, Ecorse, MI 48229. 313-386-7900 (EST) 9:00AM-4:00PM. Misdemeanor, Civil Actions Under $10,000, Eviction, Small Claims.

**21st District Court**, 6000 North Middlebelt Rd, Garden City, MI 48135. 313-525-8805 (EST) 8:30AM-5:00PM. Misdemeanor, Civil Actions Under $10,000, Eviction, Small Claims.

**31st District Court**, 3401 Evaline Ave, Hamtramck, MI 48212. 313-876-7710 (EST) 8:00AM-4:00PM. Misdemeanor, Civil Actions Under $10,000, Eviction, Small Claims.

**32A District Court**, 19617 Harper Ave, Harper Woods, MI 48225. 313-343-2590 (EST) 8:30AM-4:30PM. Misdemeanor, Civil Actions Under $10,000, Eviction, Small Claims.

**30th District Court**, 28 Gerard Ave, Highland Park, MI 48203. 313-252-0300 (EST) 8:00AM-4:30PM. Misdemeanor, Civil Actions Under $10,000, Eviction, Small Claims.

**22nd District Court**, 27331 S River Park Dr, Inkster, MI 48141. 313-277-8200 (EST) 8:30AM-4:30PM. Misdemeanor, Civil Actions Under $10,000, Eviction, Small Claims.

**25th District Court**, 1475 Cleophus, Lincoln Park, MI 48146. 313-382-9317 (EST) 9:00AM-4:30PM. Misdemeanor, Civil Actions Under $10,000, Eviction, Small Claims.

**16th District Court**, 15140 Farmington Rd, Livonia, MI 48154. 313-522-5900 (EST) 8:30AM-4:30PM. Misdemeanor, Civil Actions Under $10,000, Eviction, Small Claims.

**35th District Court**, 660 Plymouth Rd, Plymouth, MI 48170. 313-459-4740 (EST) 8:30AM-4:30PM. Misdemeanor, Civil Actions Under $10,000, Eviction, Small Claims.

**17th District Court**, 15111 Beech-Daly Rd, Redford, MI 48239. 313-531-3110 (EST) 8:30AM-4:15PM. Misdemeanor, Civil Actions Under $10,000, Eviction, Small Claims.

**26-1 District Court**, 10600 W Jefferson, River Rouge, MI 48218. 313-842-7819 (EST) 8:30AM-4:30PM. Misdemeanor, Civil Actions Under $10,000, Eviction, Small Claims.

**27-2 District Court**, 14100 Civic Park Dr, Riverview, MI 48192. 313-281-4204 (EST) 8:30AM-4:30PM. Misdemeanor, Civil Actions Under $10,000, Eviction, Small Claims.

**34th District Court**, 11131 S Wayne Rd, Romulus, MI 48174. 313-941-4462 (EST) 8:30AM-4:30PM. Misdemeanor, Civil Actions Under $10,000, Eviction, Small Claims.

**28th District Court**, 14720 Reaume Parkway, Southgate, MI 48195. 313-246-1360 (EST) 8:30AM-4:30PM. Misdemeanor, Civil Actions Under $10,000, Eviction, Small Claims.

**23rd District Court**, 23511 Goddard Rd, Taylor, MI 48180. 313-374-1328 (EST) 8:30AM-4:45PM. Misdemeanor, Civil Actions Under $10,000, Eviction, Small Claims.

**29th District Court**, 34808 Sims Ave, Wayne, MI 48184. 313-722-5220 (EST) 8:00AM-4:30PM. Misdemeanor, Civil Actions Under $10,000, Eviction, Small Claims.

**18th District Court**, 36675 Ford Rd, Westland, MI 48185. 313-595-8720 (EST) 8:30AM-4:00PM M&F, 8:30AM-5:30PM Tue-Wed., 8:30AM-6:00 Th. Misdemeanor, Civil Actions Under $10,000, Eviction, Small Claims.

**33rd District Court**, 19000 Van Horn Rd, Woodhaven, MI 48183. 313-671-0201 (EST) 8:45AM-4:30PM. Misdemeanor, Civil Actions Under $10,000, Eviction, Small Claims.

**27-1 District Court**, 2015 Biddle Ave, Wyandotte, MI 48192. 313-246-4475 (EST) 8:30AM-4:30PM. Misdemeanor, Civil Actions Under $10,000, Eviction, Small Claims.

## Wexford County

**Real Estate Recording**, Wexford County Register of Deeds, 437 East Division Street, Cadillac, MI 49601. 616-779-9455 (EST) 8:30AM-5PM.

**28th Circuit Court**, PO Box 490, Cadillac, MI 49601. 616-779-9450 (EST) 8:30AM-5:00PM. Felony, Civil Actions Over $10,000.

**84th District Court**, 501 S Garfield, Cadillac, MI 49601. 616-779-9515 (EST) 8:30AM-5:00PM. Misdemeanor, Civil Actions Under $10,000, Eviction, Small Claims.

**Probate Court**, 503 S Garfield, Cadillac, MI 49601. 616-779-9501 (EST) Probate.

# Minnesota

## Aitkin County

**Real Estate Recording**, Aitkin County Recorder, 209 Second Street NW, Aitkin, MN 56431. 218-927-7336 (CST) 8AM-4PM.

**9th Judicial District Court**, 209 Second St NW, Aitkin, MN 56431. 218-927-7350 (CST) 8AM-4PM. Felony, Misdemeanor, Civil, Eviction, Small Claims, Probate.

## Anoka County

**Real Estate Recording**, Anoka County Recorder, 2100 3rd Ave., Anoka, MN 55303. 612-323-5416 (CST) 8AM-4:30PM.

**10th Judicial District Court**, 325 E Main St, Anoka, MN 55303. 612-442-7350 (CST) 8AM-4:30PM. Felony, Misdemeanor, Civil, Eviction, Small Claims, Probate.

## Becker County

**Real Estate Recording**, Becker County Recorder, 915 Lake Avenue, Detroit Lakes, MN 56501. 218-846-7304 (CST) 8:30AM-4:30PM.

**7th Judicial District Court**, PO Box 787, Detroit Lakes, MN 56502. 218-846-7305 (CST) Felony, Misdemeanor, Civil, Eviction, Small Claims, Probate.

## Beltrami County

**Real Estate Recording**, Beltrami County Recorder, 619 Beltrami Ave. NW, Courthouse, Bemidji, MN 56601. 218-759-4170 (CST) 8AM-4:30PM.

**9th Judicial District Court**, PO Box 108, Bemidji, MN 56601. 218-759-4120 (CST) 8AM-4:30PM. Felony, Misdemeanor, Civil, Eviction, Small Claims, Probate.

## Benton County

**Real Estate Recording**, Benton County Recorder's Office, 531 Dewey Street, Foley, MN 56329. 612-968-6254 (CST) 8AM-4:30PM.

**7th Judicial District Court**, 531 Dewey St, Foley, MN 56329. 612-968-6254 (CST) 8AM-4:30PM. Felony, Misdemeanor, Civil, Eviction, Small Claims, Probate.

## Big Stone County

**Real Estate Recording**, Big Stone County Recorder, Courthouse, 20 SE 2nd St., Ortonville, MN 56278. 612-839-2308 (CST)

**8th Judicial District Court**, 20 SE 2nd St, Ortonville, MN 56278. 612-839-2536 (CST) 8AM-4:30PM. Felony, Misdemeanor, Civil, Eviction, Small Claims, Probate.

## Blue Earth County

**Real Estate Recording**, Blue Earth County Recorder, 204 South 5th Street, Mankato, MN 56001. 507-389-8222 (CST) 8AM-5PM.

**5th Judicial District Court**, 204 S 5th St (PO Box 0347), Mankato, MN 56002-0347. 507-389-8310 (CST) 8AM-5PM. Felony, Misdemeanor, Civil, Eviction, Small Claims, Probate.

## Brown County

**Real Estate Recording**, Brown County Recorder, Center & State Streets, Courthouse, New Ulm, MN 56073. 507-359-7900 (CST) 8AM-5PM.

**5th Judicial District Court**, PO Box 248, New Ulm, MN 56073-0248. 507-359-7900 (CST) 8AM-5PM. Felony, Misdemeanor, Civil, Eviction, Small Claims, Probate.

## Carlton County

**Real Estate Recording**, Carlton County Recorder, Courthouse, Carlton, MN 55718. 218-384-9122 (CST) 8AM-4PM.

**6th Judicial District Court**, PO Box 190, Carlton, MN 55718. 218-384-4281 (CST) 8AM-4PM. Felony, Misdemeanor, Civil, Eviction, Small Claims, Probate.

## Carver County

**Real Estate Recording**, Carver County Recorder, 600 East Fourth Street, Room 140, Chaska, MN 55318. 612-361-1938 (CST) 8AM-4:30PM.

**1st Judicial District Court**, 600 E 4th St, Chaska, MN 55318. 612-361-1420 (CST) 8AM-4:30PM. Felony, Misdemeanor, Civil, Eviction, Small Claims, Probate.

## Cass County

**Real Estate Recording**, Cass County Recorder, Courthouse, Highway 371, Walker, MN 56484. 218-547-3300 (CST) 8AM-4:30PM.

**9th Judicial District Court**, 300 Minnesota Ave, Walker, MN 56484. 218-547-3300 (CST) 8AM-4:30PM. Felony, Misdemeanor, Civil, Eviction, Small Claims, Probate.

## Chippewa County

**Real Estate Recording**, Chippewa County Recorder, 629 No. 11th St., Montevideo, MN 56265. 612-269-9431 (CST) 8AM-4:30PM.

**8th Judicial District Court**, 11th St and Hwy 7, Montevideo, MN 56265. 612-269-7774 (CST) 8AM-4:30PM. Felony, Misdemeanor, Civil, Eviction, Small Claims, Probate.

## Chisago County

**Real Estate Recording**, Chisago County Recorder, Government Center, Room/Box 277, 313 N. Main St., Center City, MN 55012. 612-257-1300 (CST) 8AM-4:30PM.

**10th Judicial District Court**, 313 N Main St, Rm 359, Center City, MN 55012. 612-257-1300 (CST) 8AM-4:30PM. Felony, Misdemeanor, Civil, Eviction, Small Claims, Probate.

## Clay County

**Real Estate Recording**, Clay County Recorder, 807 North 11th Street, Courthouse, Moorhead, MN 56560. 218-299-5031 (CST) 8AM-4:30PM.

**7th Judicial District Court**, PO Box 280, Moorhead, MN 56561. 218-299-5043 (CST) 8AM-4:30PM. Felony, Misdemeanor, Civil, Eviction, Small Claims, Probate.

## Clearwater County

**Real Estate Recording**, Clearwater County Recorder, 213 Main Avenue North, Bagley, MN 56621. 218-694-6129 (CST) 8AM-4:30PM.

**9th Judicial District Court**, 213 Main Ave North, Bagley, MN 56621. 218-694-6177 (CST) 8AM-4:30PM. Felony, Misdemeanor, Civil, Eviction, Small Claims, Probate.

## Cook County

**Real Estate Recording**, Cook County Recorder, Courthouse, 411 W. 2nd St., Grand Marais, MN 55604. 218-387-2282 (CST) 8AM-4PM.

**6th Judicial District Court**, 441 2nd St (PO Box E), Grand Marais, MN 55604. 218-387-2282 (CST) 8AM-4PM. Felony, Misdemeanor, Civil, Eviction, Small Claims, Probate.

## Cottonwood County

**Real Estate Recording**, Cottonwood County Recorder, 900 Third Avenue, Courthouse Room 6, Windom, MN 56101. 507-831-1458 (CST) 8AM-4:30PM.

**5th Judicial District Court**, PO Box 97, Windom, MN 56101. 507-831-1356 (CST) 8AM-4:30PM. Felony, Misdemeanor, Civil, Eviction, Small Claims, Probate.

## Crow Wing County

**Real Estate Recording**, Crow Wing County Recorder, 326 Laurel Street, Courthouse, Brainerd, MN 56401. 218-828-3965 (CST) 8AM-5PM.

**9th Judicial District Court**, 326 Laurel St, Brainerd, MN 56401. 218-828-3959 (CST) 8AM-5PM. Felony, Misdemeanor, Civil, Eviction, Small Claims, Probate.

## Dakota County

**Real Estate Recording**, Dakota County Recorder, 1590 West Highway 55, Government Center, Hastings, MN 55033. 612-438-4355 (CST) 8AM-4:30PM.

**1st Judicial District Court #5**, 14955 Galaxie Ave, Apple Valley, MN 55124. 612-891-7256 612-438-8104 (CST) 8AM-4:30PM. Felony, Misdemeanor, Civil, Eviction, Small Claims, Probate.

**1st Judicial District Court-Hastings**, 1560 Hwy 55, Hastings, MN 55033. (CST) Felony, Misdemeanor, Civil, Eviction, Small Claims, Probate.

**1st Judicial District Court-South St Paul**, 125 3rd Ave North, South St Paul, MN 55075. 612-451-1791 (CST) 8AM-4:30PM. Felony, Misdemeanor, Civil, Eviction, Small Claims, Probate.

## Dodge County

**Real Estate Recording**, Dodge County Recorder, Courthouse, 22 6th St. East, Mantorville, MN 55955. 507-635-6250 (CST) 8:30AM-4:30PM.

**3rd Judicial District Court**, PO Box 96, Mantorville, MN 55955. 507-635-6260 (CST) 8AM-4:30PM. Felony, Misdemeanor, Civil, Eviction, Small Claims, Probate.

## Douglas County

**Real Estate Recording**, Douglas County Recorder, 305 8th Avenue West, Courthouse, Alexandria, MN 56308. 612-762-2381 (CST) 8AM-4:30PM.

**7th Judicial District Court**, 305 8th Ave West, Alexandria, MN 56308. 612-762-2381 (CST) 8AM-4:30PM. Felony, Misdemeanor, Civil, Eviction, Small Claims, Probate.

## Faribault County

**Real Estate Recording**, Faribault County Recorder, 415 North Main Street, Blue Earth, MN 56013. 507-526-6252 (CST) 8:30AM-5PM.

**5th Judicial District Court**, PO Box 130, Blue Earth, MN 56013. 507-526-6273 (CST) 8:30AM-5PM. Felony, Misdemeanor, Civil, Eviction, Small Claims, Probate.

## Fillmore County

**Real Estate Recording**, Fillmore County Recorder, Courthouse, Preston, MN 55965. 507-765-3852 (CST) 8AM-4:30PM.

**3rd Judicial District Court**, 101 Fillmore St, Preston, MN 55965. 507-765-4483 (CST) 8AM-4:30PM. Felony, Misdemeanor, Civil, Eviction, Small Claims, Probate.

## Freeborn County

**Real Estate Recording**, Freeborn County Recorder, 411 South Broadway, Court House, Albert Lea, MN 56007. 507-377-5130 (CST) 8AM-5PM.

**3rd Judicial District Court**, 411 S Broadway, Albert Lea, MN 56007. 507-377-5153 (CST) 8AM-5PM. Felony, Misdemeanor, Civil, Eviction, Small Claims, Probate.

## Goodhue County

**Real Estate Recording**, Goodhue County Recorder, 5th & West Avenue, Courthouse, Red Wing, MN 55066. 612-385-3149 (CST) 8AM-4:30PM.

**1st Judicial District Court**, PO Box 408, Rm 310, Red Wing, MN 55066. 612-385-3051 (CST) 8AM-4:30PM. Felony, Misdemeanor, Civil, Eviction, Small Claims, Probate.

## Grant County

**Real Estate Recording**, Grant County Recorder, 10th Second Street NE, Courthouse, Elbow Lake, MN 56531. 218-685-4133 (CST)

**8th Judicial District Court**, 10 2nd St NE, Elbow Lake, MN 56531. 218-685-4825 (CST) 8AM-4PM. Felony, Misdemeanor, Civil, Eviction, Small Claims, Probate.

## Hennepin County

**Real Estate Recording**, Hennepin County Recorder, 300 South 6th Street, 8-A Government Center, Minneapolis, MN 55487. 612-348-3049 (CST) 8AM-4:30PM (UCC); 8AM-5PM (Real Estate).

**4th Judicial District Court-Division 2 Brookdale Area**, 6125 Shingle Creek Pkwy, Brooklyn Center, MN 55430. 612-569-3700 (CST) 7:45AM-4:30PM. Misdemeanor, Eviction, Small Claims.

**4th Judicial District Court-Division 4 Southdale Area**, 7009 York Ave South, Edina, MN 55435. 612-830-4905 (CST) 8AM-4:30PM. Misdemeanor, Eviction, Small Claims.

**4th Judicial District Court-Division 1**, 1153 C Government Center, 300 S 6th St, Minneapolis, MN 55487. 612-348-2611 (CST) 8AM-4:30PM. Felony, Misdemeanor, Civil, Probate.

**4th Judicial District Court-Division 3 Ridgedale Area**, 12601 Ridgedale Dr, Minnetonka, MN 55305. 612-541-8500 (CST) 8AM-4:30PM. Misdemeanor, Eviction, Small Claims.

## Houston County

**Real Estate Recording**, Houston County Recorder, 304 South Marshall Street, Caledonia, MN 55921. 507-724-5813 (CST) 8:30AM-5PM.

**3rd Judicial District Court**, 304 S Marshall, Caledonia, MN 55921. 507-724-5806 (CST) 8:30AM-5PM. Felony, Misdemeanor, Civil, Eviction, Small Claims, Probate.

## Hubbard County

**Real Estate Recording**, Hubbard County Recorder, Courthouse, Park Rapids, MN 56470. 218-732-3552 (CST) 8AM-4:30PM.

**9th Judicial District Court**, 301 Court St, Park Rapids, MN 56470. 218-732-3573 (CST) 8AM-4:30PM. Felony, Misdemeanor, Civil, Eviction, Small Claims, Probate.

## Isanti County

**Real Estate Recording**, Isanti County Recorder, Courthouse, Cambridge, MN 55008. 612-689-1191 (CST) 8AM-4:30PM.

**10th Judicial District Court**, 237 SW 2nd Ave, Cambridge, MN 55008. 612-689-2292 (CST) 8AM-4:30PM. Felony, Misdemeanor, Civil, Eviction, Small Claims, Probate.

## Itasca County

**Real Estate Recording**, Itasca County Recorder, 123 NE 4th Street, Grand Rapids, MN 55744. 218-327-2856 (CST) 8AM-4:30PM.

**9th Judicial District Court**, 123 4th St NE, Grand Rapids, MN 55744-2600. 218-327-2870 (CST) 8AM-4PM. Felony, Misdemeanor, Civil, Eviction, Small Claims, Probate.

## Jackson County

**Real Estate Recording**, Jackson County Recorder, Courthouse, Jackson, MN 56143. 507-847-2580 (CST) 8:30AM-4:30PM.

**5th Judicial District Court**, PO Box G, Jackson, MN 56143. 507-847-4400 (CST) 8:30AM-4:30PM. Felony, Misdemeanor, Civil, Eviction, Small Claims, Probate.

## Kanabec County

**Real Estate Recording**, Kanabec County Recorder, 18 North Vine Street, Mora, MN 55051. 612-679-1441 (CST)

**10th Judicial District Court**, 18 North Vine, Mora, MN 55051. 612-679-1022 (CST) 8AM-4PM. Felony, Misdemeanor, Civil, Eviction, Small Claims, Probate.

## Kandiyohi County

**Real Estate Recording**, Kandiyohi County Recorder, 505 West Becker, Willmar, MN 56201. 612-231-6223 (CST) 8AM-4:30PM.

**8th Judicial District Court**, PO Box 1337, Willmar, MN 56201. 612-231-6206 (CST) 8AM-4:30PM. Felony, Misdemeanor, Civil, Eviction, Small Claims, Probate.

## Kittson County

**Real Estate Recording**, Kittson County Recorder, Courthouse, Hallock, MN 56728. 218-843-2842 (CST) 8:30AM-4:30PM.

**9th Judicial District Court**, PO Box 39, Hallock, MN 56728. 218-843-3632 (CST) 8:30AM-4:30PM. Felony, Misdemeanor, Civil, Eviction, Small Claims, Probate.

## Koochiching County

**Real Estate Recording**, Koochiching County Recorder, Courthouse, International Falls, MN 56649. 218-283-6290 (CST) 8AM-5PM.

**9th Judicial District Court**, Court House, International Falls, MN 56649. 218-283-6261 (CST) 8AM-5PM. Felony, Misdemeanor, Civil, Eviction, Small Claims, Probate.

## Lac qui Parle County

**Real Estate Recording**, Lac qui Parle County Recorder, 600 6th Street, Courthouse, Madison, MN 56256. 612-598-3724 (CST) 8:30AM-4:30PM.

**8th Judicial District Court**, PO Box 36, Madison, MN 56256. 612-598-3536 (CST) 8:30AM-4:30PM. Felony, Misdemeanor, Civil, Eviction, Small Claims, Probate.

## Lake County

**Real Estate Recording**, Lake County Recorder, 601 Third Avenue, Two Harbors, MN 55616. 218-834-8347 (CST) 8AM-4:30PM.

**6th Judicial District Court**, 601 3rd Ave, Two Harbors, MN 55616. 218-834-8330 (CST) 8AM-4:30PM. Felony, Misdemeanor, Civil, Eviction, Small Claims, Probate.

## Lake of the Woods County

**Real Estate Recording**, Lake of the Woods County Recorder, 206 Southeast Eighth Avenue, Baudette, MN 56623. 218-634-1902 (CST) 7:30AM-4PM.

**9th Judicial District Court**, PO Box 808, Baudette, MN 56623. 218-634-1451 (CST) 7:30AM-4PM. Felony, Misdemeanor, Civil, Eviction, Small Claims, Probate.

## Le Sueur County

**Real Estate Recording**, Le Sueur County Recorder, 88 South Park Avenue, Courthouse, Le Center, MN 56057. 612-357-2251 (CST) 8AM-4:30PM.

**1st Judicial District Court**, Box 10, Le Center, MN 56057. 612-357-2251 (CST) 8AM-4:30PM. Felony, Misdemeanor, Civil, Eviction, Small Claims, Probate.

## Lincoln County

**Real Estate Recording**, Lincoln County Recorder, 319 North Rebecca, Ivanhoe, MN 56142. 507-694-1360 (CST) 8:30AM-4:30PM.

**5th Judicial District Court**, PO Box 15, Ivanhoe, MN 56142-0015. 507-694-1505 (CST) Felony, Misdemeanor, Civil, Eviction, Small Claims, Probate.

## Lyon County

**Real Estate Recording**, Lyon County Recorder, 607 West Main Street, Marshall, MN 56258. 507-537-6722 (CST) 8:30AM-4:30PM.

**5th Judicial District Court**, 607 W Main, Marshall, MN 56258. 507-537-6734 (CST) 8:30AM-4:30PM. Felony, Misdemeanor, Civil, Eviction, Small Claims, Probate.

## Mahnomen County

**Real Estate Recording**, Mahnomen County Recorder, Courthouse, Mahnomen, MN 56557. 218-935-5528 (CST) 8AM-4:30PM M-T.

**9th Judicial District Court**, PO Box 459, Mahnomen, MN 56557. 218-935-2251 (CST) 8AM-4:30PM. Felony, Misdemeanor, Civil, Eviction, Small Claims, Probate.

## Marshall County

**Real Estate Recording**, Marshall County Recorder, 208 East Colvin, Warren, MN 56762. 218-745-4801 (CST) 8AM-4:30PM.

**9th Judicial District Court**, 208 E Colvin, Warren, MN 56762. 218-745-4921 (CST) 8AM-4:30PM. Felony, Misdemeanor, Civil, Eviction, Small Claims, Probate.

## Martin County

**Real Estate Recording**, Martin County Recorder, 201 Lake Avenue, Courthouse, Fairmont, MN 56031. 507-238-3213 (CST) 8:30AM-4:30PM.

**5th Judicial District Court**, 201 Lake Ave, Rm 304, Fairmont, MN 56031. 507-238-3214 (CST) 8:30AM-4:30PM. Felony, Misdemeanor, Civil, Eviction, Small Claims, Probate.

## McLeod County

**Real Estate Recording**, McLeod County Recorder, 830 East 11th Street, Courthouse, Glencoe, MN 55336. 612-864-5551 (CST) 8AM-4:30PM.

**1st Judicial District Court**, 830 E 11th, Glencoe, MN 55336. 612-864-5551 (CST) 8AM-4:30PM. Felony, Misdemeanor, Civil, Eviction, Small Claims, Probate.

## Meeker County

**Real Estate Recording**, Meeker County Recorder, 325 North Sibley Avenue, Courthouse, Litchfield, MN 55355. 612-693-6112 (CST) 8AM-4:30PM.

**8th Judicial District Court**, 325 N Sibley, Litchfield, MN 55355. 612-693-2458 (CST) 8AM-4:30PM. Felony, Misdemeanor, Civil, Eviction, Small Claims, Probate.

## Mille Lacs County

**Real Estate Recording**, Mille Lacs County Recorder, 635 2nd Street S.E., Milaca, MN 56353. 612-983-8309 (CST) 8AM-4:30PM.

**7th Judicial District Court**, Courthouse, Milaca, MN 56353. 612-983-8313 (CST) Felony, Misdemeanor, Civil, Eviction, Small Claims, Probate.

## Morrison County

**Real Estate Recording**, Morrison County Recorder, Administration Building, 213 SE 1st Ave., Little Falls, MN 56345. 612-632-0145 (CST) 8AM-4:30PM.

**7th Judicial District Court**, 213 SE 1st Ave, Little Falls, MN 56345. 612-632-2035 (CST) 8AM-4:30PM. Felony, Misdemeanor, Civil, Eviction, Small Claims, Probate.

## Mower County

**Real Estate Recording**, Mower County Recorder, 201 First Street NE, Austin, MN 55912. 507-437-9446 (CST) 8AM-5PM.

**3rd Judicial District Court**, 201 1st St NE, Austin, MN 55912. 507-437-9465 (CST) 8AM-5PM. Felony, Misdemeanor, Civil, Eviction, Small Claims, Probate.

## Murray County

**Real Estate Recording**, Murray County Recorder, 28th & Broadway Avenue, Slayton, MN 56172. 507-836-6148 (CST) X144 8:30AM-Noon, 1-5PM.

**5th Judicial District Court**, PO Box 57, Slayton, MN 56172-0057. 507-836-6163 (CST) 8:30AM-5PM. Felony, Misdemeanor, Civil, Eviction, Small Claims, Probate.

## Nicollet County

**Real Estate Recording**, Nicollet County Recorder, 501 South Minnesota Avenue, St. Peter, MN 56082. 507-931-6800 (CST) 8AM-5PM.

**5th Judicial District Court (Branch)**, PO Box 2055, North Mankato, MN 56002-2055. 507-625-4141 (CST) 8AM-5PM. Felony, Misdemeanor, Civil, Eviction, Small Claims, Probate.

**5th Judicial District Court**, PO Box 496, St Peter, MN 56082. 507-931-6800 (CST) 8AM-5PM. Felony, Misdemeanor, Civil, Eviction, Small Claims, Probate.

## Nobles County

**Real Estate Recording**, Nobles County Recorder, 315 10th Street, Nobles County Government Center, Worthington, MN 56187. 507-372-8236 (CST)

**5th Judicial District Court**, PO Box 547, Worthington, MN 56187. 507-372-8263 (CST) 8AM-5PM. Felony, Misdemeanor, Civil, Eviction, Small Claims, Probate.

## Norman County

**Real Estate Recording**, Norman County Recorder, 16 East 3rd Avenue, Ada, MN 56510. 218-784-4422 (CST) 8:30AM-4:30PM.

**9th Judicial District Court**, PO Box 272, Ada, MN 56510-0146. 218-784-7131 (CST) 8:30AM-4:30PM. Felony, Misdemeanor, Civil, Eviction, Small Claims, Probate.

## Olmsted County

**Real Estate Recording**, Olmsted County Recorder, 151 4th St. SE, Rochester, MN 55904. 507-285-8194 (CST) 8AM-5PM.

**3rd Judicial District Court**, 515 SW 2nd St, Rochester, MN 55902. 507-285-8210 (CST) 8AM-5PM. Felony, Misdemeanor, Civil, Eviction, Small Claims, Probate.

## Otter Tail County

**Real Estate Recording**, Otter Tail County Recorder, Junius Avenue, Courthouse, Fergus Falls, MN 56537. 218-739-2271 (CST) 8AM-5PM.

**7th Judicial District Court**, PO Box 417, Fergus Falls, MN 56538. 218-739-2271 (CST) 8AM-5PM. Felony, Misdemeanor, Civil, Eviction, Small Claims, Probate.

## Pennington County

**Real Estate Recording**, Pennington County Recorder, 1st & Main Street, Courthouse, Thief River Falls, MN 56701. 218-681-2522 (CST) 8AM-4:30PM.

**9th Judicial District Court**, PO Box 619, Thief River Falls, MN 56701. 218-681-2407 (CST) 8AM-4:30PM. Felony, Misdemeanor, Civil, Eviction, Small Claims, Probate.

## Pine County

**Real Estate Recording**, Pine County Recorder, Courthouse, 315 Sixth St., Suite 3, Pine City, MN 55063. 612-629-6781 (CST) 8AM-4:30PM.

**10th Judicial District Court**, 315 6th St, Pine City, MN 55063. 612-629-6781 (CST) 8AM-4:30PM. Felony, Misdemeanor, Civil, Eviction, Small Claims, Probate.

## Pipestone County

**Real Estate Recording**, Pipestone County Recorder, 4165 Hiawatha, Pipestone, MN 56164. 507-825-4646 (CST) 8:30AM-4:30PM.

**5th Judicial District Court**, 416 S Hiawatha Ave (PO Box 337), Pipestone, MN 56164. 507-825-4550 (CST) 8:30AM-4:30PM. Felony, Misdemeanor, Civil, Eviction, Small Claims, Probate.

## Polk County

**Real Estate Recording**, Polk County Recorder, 612 Broadway, Courthouse, Suite 213, Crookston, MN 56716. 218-281-3464 (CST) 8AM-4:30PM.

**9th Judicial District Court**, PO Box 438, Crookston, MN 56716. 218-281-2332 (CST) 8AM-4:30PM. Felony, Misdemeanor, Civil, Eviction, Small Claims, Probate.

## Pope County

**Real Estate Recording**, Pope County Recorder, 130 East Minnesota, Glenwood, MN 56334. 612-634-5723 (CST) 8AM-4:30PM.

**8th Judicial District Court**, 130 E Minnesota Ave (PO Box 195), Glenwood, MN 56334. 612-634-5222 (CST) 8AM-4:30PM. Felony, Misdemeanor, Civil, Eviction, Small Claims, Probate.

## Ramsey County

**Real Estate Recording**, Ramsey County Recorder, 50 West Kellogg Blvd., Suite 812 RCGC-W, St. Paul, MN 55102. 612-266-2070 (CST) 8AM-4:30PM.

**2nd Judicial District Court-Maplewood Area**, 2785 White Bear Ave, Maplewood, MN 55109. 612-777-9111 (CST) 8AM-4:30PM. Misdemeanor, Eviction, Small Claims.

**2nd Judicial District Court-New Brighton Area**, 803 5th Ave NW, New Brighton, MN

# Minnesota

55112. 612-636-7101 (CST) 8AM-4:30PM. Misdemeanor, Eviction, Small Claims.

**2nd Judicial District Court**, 15 E Kellogg, St Paul, MN 55101. 612-266-8266 (CST) 8AM-4:30PM. Felony, Misdemeanor, Civil, Probate.

## Red Lake County

**Real Estate Recording**, Red Lake County Recorder, 124 Main Avenue North, Red Lake Falls, MN 56750. 218-253-2997 (CST) 9AM-5PM.

**9th Judicial District Court**, PO Box 339, Red Lake Falls, MN 56750. 218-253-4281 (CST) 9AM-5PM. Felony, Misdemeanor, Civil, Eviction, Small Claims, Probate.

## Redwood County

**Real Estate Recording**, Redwood County Recorder, Courthouse Square, Main Floor, Redwood Falls, MN 56283. 507-637-8330 (CST) 8AM-4:30PM.

**5th Judicial District Court**, PO Box 130, Redwood Falls, MN 56283. 507-637-8327 (CST) 8AM-4:30PM. Felony, Misdemeanor, Civil, Eviction, Small Claims, Probate.

## Renville County

**Real Estate Recording**, Renville County Recorder, 500 East DePue, Olivia, MN 56277. 612-523-1000 (CST) 8AM-4:30PM.

**8th Judicial District Court**, 500 E DePue Ave, Olivia, MN 56277. 612-523-2080 (CST) 8AM-4:30PM. Felony, Misdemeanor, Civil, Eviction, Small Claims, Probate.

## Rice County

**Real Estate Recording**, Rice County Recorder, 218 NW 3rd Street, Courthouse, Faribault, MN 55021. 507-332-6114 (CST) 8AM-4:30PM.

**3rd Judicial District Court**, 218 NW 3rd St, Faribault, MN 55021. 507-332-6107 (CST) 8AM-4:30PM. Felony, Misdemeanor, Civil, Eviction, Small Claims, Probate.

## Rock County

**Real Estate Recording**, Rock County Recorder, 204 East Brown, Luverne, MN 56156. 507-283-9177 (CST) 8AM-5PM.

**5th Judicial District Court**, PO Box 745, Luverne, MN 56156. 507-283-9501 (CST) 8AM-5PM. Felony, Misdemeanor, Civil, Eviction, Small Claims, Probate.

## Roseau County

**Real Estate Recording**, Roseau County Recorder, 216 Center Street West, Roseau, MN 56751. 218-463-2061 (CST) 8AM-4:30PM.

**9th Judicial District Court**, 216 Center St West, Roseau, MN 56751. 218-463-2541 (CST) 8AM-4:30PM. Felony, Misdemeanor, Civil, Eviction, Small Claims, Probate.

## Scott County

**Real Estate Recording**, Scott County Recorder, 428 South Holmes Street, Shakopee, MN 55379. 612-496-8143 (CST) 8AM-4:30PM.

**1st Judicial District Court**, 428 S Holmes, Rm 212, Shakopee, MN 55379. 612-445-7750 (CST) 8AM-4:30PM. Felony, Misdemeanor, Civil, Eviction, Small Claims, Probate.

## Sherburne County

**Real Estate Recording**, Sherburne County Recorder, 13880 Highway 10, Elk River, MN 55330. 612-241-2860 (CST) 8AM-5PM.

**10th Judicial District Court**, PO Box 318, Elk River, MN 55330. 612-241-2800 (CST) 8AM-5PM. Felony, Misdemeanor, Civil, Eviction, Small Claims, Probate.

## Sibley County

**Real Estate Recording**, Sibley County Recorder, 400 Court Street, Room 26, Gaylord, MN 55334. 612-237-5526 (CST) 8AM-5PM.

**1st Judicial District Court**, PO Box 867, Gaylord, MN 55334. 612-237-2427 (CST) 8AM-5PM. Felony, Misdemeanor, Civil, Eviction, Small Claims, Probate.

## St. Louis County

**Real Estate Recording**, St. Louis County Recorder, 100 North 5th Avenue West, Room 101, Duluth, MN 55802. 218-726-2677 (CST) 8AM-4:30PM.

**6th Judicial District Court**, 100 N 5th Ave W, Rm 320, Duluth, MN 55802-1294. 218-726-2442 (CST) 8AM-4:30PM. Felony, Misdemeanor, Civil, Eviction, Small Claims, Probate.

**6th Judicial District Court-Hibbing Branch**, 1810 12th Ave East, Hibbing, MN 55746. 218-262-0100 (CST) 8AM-4:30PM. Felony, Misdemeanor, Civil, Eviction, Small Claims, Probate.

**6th Judicial District Court-Virginia Branch**, 300 S 5th Ave, Virginia, MN 55792. 218-749-7106 (CST) 8AM-4:30PM, closed at lunch. Felony, Misdemeanor, Civil, Eviction, Small Claims, Probate.

## Stearns County

**Real Estate Recording**, Stearns County Recorder, 705 Courthouse Square, Administration Center, Room 131, St. Cloud, MN 56303. 612-656-3855 (CST) 8AM-4:30PM.

**7th Judicial District Court**, PO Box 1168, St Cloud, MN 56302. 612-656-3620 (CST) 8AM-4:30PM. Felony, Misdemeanor, Civil, Eviction, Small Claims, Probate.

## Steele County

**Real Estate Recording**, Steele County Recorder, 111 East Main, Courthouse, Owatonna, MN 55060. 507-451-8040 (CST) 8AM-5PM.

**3rd Judicial District Court**, PO Box 487, Owatonna, MN 55060. 507-451-8040 (CST) 8AM-5PM. Felony, Misdemeanor, Civil, Eviction, Small Claims, Probate.

## Stevens County

**Real Estate Recording**, Stevens County Recorder, 5th & Colorado, Morris, MN 56267. 612-589-7414 (CST) 8:30AM-4:30PM (Summer Hours 8AM-4PM).

**8th Judicial District Court**, PO Box 530, Morris, MN 56267. 612-589-1033 (CST) Felony, Misdemeanor, Civil, Eviction, Small Claims, Probate.

## Swift County

**Real Estate Recording**, Swift County Recorder, 301 14th Street North, Benson, MN 56215. 612-843-3377 (CST) 8AM-4:30PM.

**8th Judicial District Court**, PO Box 110, Benson, MN 56215. 612-843-2744 (CST) 8AM-4:30PM. Felony, Misdemeanor, Civil, Eviction, Small Claims, Probate.

## Todd County

**Real Estate Recording**, Todd County Recorder, 215 First Avenue South, Long Prairie, MN 56347. 612-732-4428 (CST) 8AM-4:30PM.

**7th Judicial District Court**, 215 1st Ave South, Long Prairie, MN 56347. 612-732-4460 (CST) 8AM-4:30PM. Felony, Misdemeanor, Civil, Eviction, Small Claims, Probate.

## Traverse County

**Real Estate Recording**, Traverse County Recorder, Courthouse, 702 2nd Ave. North, Wheaton, MN 56296. 612-563-4622 (CST) 8AM-4:30PM.

**8th Judicial District Court**, 702 2nd Ave N (PO Box 867), Wheaton, MN 56296. 612-563-4343 (CST) 8AM-4:30PM, Closed 12-12:30. Felony, Misdemeanor, Civil, Eviction, Small Claims, Probate.

## Wabasha County

**Real Estate Recording**, Wabasha County Recorder, 625 Jefferson Avenue, Wabasha, MN 55981. 612-565-3623 (CST) 8AM-4PM.

**3rd Judicial District Court**, 625 Jefferson Ave, Wabasha, MN 55981. 612-565-3579 (CST) 8AM-4PM. Felony, Misdemeanor, Civil, Eviction, Small Claims, Probate.

## Wadena County

**Real Estate Recording**, Wadena County Recorder, 415 South Jefferson, Courthouse, Wadena, MN 56482. 218-631-2362 (CST) 8:30AM-4:30PM.

**7th Judicial District Court**, County Courthouse, Wadena, MN 56482. 218-631-2895 (CST) 8AM-4:30PM. Felony, Misdemeanor, Civil, Eviction, Small Claims, Probate.

## Waseca County

**Real Estate Recording**, Waseca County Recorder, 307 North State Street, Waseca, MN 56093. 507-835-0670 (CST) 8AM-4:30PM.

**3rd Judicial District Court**, 307 N State St, Waseca, MN 56093. 507-835-0540 (CST) 8AM-4:30PM. Felony, Misdemeanor, Civil, Eviction, Small Claims, Probate.

## Washington County

**Real Estate Recording**, Washington County Recorder, 14900 North 61st Street, P.O. Box 6, Stillwater, MN 55082. 612-430-6755 (CST) 8AM-4:30PM.

**10th Judicial District Court**, 14900 61st St North, Stillwater, MN 55082-0006. 612-439-3220 (CST) 8AM-4:30PM. Felony, Misdemeanor, Civil, Eviction, Small Claims, Probate.

## Watonwan County

**Real Estate Recording**, Watonwan County Recorder, Courthouse, St. James, MN 56081. 507-375-1216 (CST) 8:30AM-Noon, 1-5PM.

**5th Judicial District Court**, PO Box 518, St James, MN 56081. 507-375-3341 (CST) 8:30AM-5PM. Felony, Misdemeanor, Civil, Eviction, Small Claims, Probate.

## Wilkin County

**Real Estate Recording**, Wilkin County Recorder, 300 South 5th Street, Courthouse, Breckenridge, MN 56520. 218-643-4012 (CST) 8AM-4:30PM.

**8th Judicial District Court**, PO Box 219, Breckenridge, MN 56520. 218-643-4972 (CST) 8AM-4:30PM. Felony, Misdemeanor, Civil, Eviction, Small Claims, Probate.

## Winona County

**Real Estate Recording**, Winona County Recorder, 171 West 3rd Street, Winona, MN 55987. 507-457-6340 (CST) 8AM-5PM.

**3rd Judicial District Court**, 171 West 3rd St, Winona, MN 55987. 507-457-6375 (CST) 8AM-5PM. Felony, Misdemeanor, Civil, Eviction, Small Claims, Probate.

## Wright County

**Real Estate Recording**, Wright County Recorder, 10 NW 2nd Street, Buffalo, MN 55313. 612-682-7360 (CST) 8AM-4:30PM.

**10th Judicial District Court**, 10 NW 2nd St, Buffalo, MN 55313. 612-682-7539 (CST) 8AM-4:30PM. Felony, Misdemeanor, Civil, Eviction, Small Claims, Probate.

## Yellow Medicine County

**Real Estate Recording**, Yellow Medicine County Recorder, 415 9th Avenue, Courthouse, Granite Falls, MN 56241. 612-564-2529 (CST) 8AM-4PM.

**8th Judicial District Court**, 415 9th Ave, Granite Falls, MN 56241. 612-564-3325 (CST) Felony, Misdemeanor, Civil, Eviction, Small Claims, Probate.

# Mississippi

## Adams County

**Real Estate Recording**, Adams County Clerk of the Chancery Court, 1 Courthouse Square, Natchez, MS 39120. 601-446-6684 (CST) 8AM-5PM.

**Circuit and County Court**, PO Box 1224, Natchez, MS 39121. 601-446-6326 (CST) 8:00AM-5:00PM. Felony, Misdemeanor, Civil.

**Justice Court**, PO Box 1048, Natchez, MS 39121. 601-442-0199 (CST) 8:00AM-5:00PM. Misdemeanor, Civil Actions Under $1,000, Eviction, Small Claims.

**Chancery Court**, PO Box 1006, Natchez, MS 39121. 601-446-6684 (CST) Probate.

## Alcorn County

**Real Estate Recording**, Alcorn County Clerk of the Chancery Court, 501 Waldron Street, Corinth, MS 38834. 601-286-7700 (CST) 8AM-5PM.

**Circuit Court**, PO Box 430 Attn: Circuit Clerk, Corinth, MS 38834. 601-286-7740 (CST) 8:00AM-5:00PM. Felony, Civil Actions Over $1,000.

**Justice Court**, PO Box 226, Corinth, MS 38834. 601-286-7776 (CST) 8:00AM-5:00PM. Misdemeanor, Civil Actions Under $1,000, Eviction, Small Claims.

**Chancery Court**, 3135 Kendrick Rd, Corinth, MS 38834. 601-286-6265 (CST) Probate.

## Amite County

**Real Estate Recording**, Amite County Clerk of the Chancery Court, 143 West Main Street, Liberty, MS 39645. 601-657-8022 (CST) 8AM-5PM.

**Circuit Court**, PO Box 312, Liberty, MS 39645. 601-657-8932 (CST) 8:00AM-5:00PM. Felony, Civil Actions Over $1,000.

**Justice Court**, PO Box 362, Liberty, MS 39645. 601-657-4527 (CST) Misdemeanor, Civil Actions Under $1,000, Eviction, Small Claims.

**Chancery Court**, PO Box 680, Liberty, MS 39645. 601-657-8022 (CST) Probate.

## Attala County

**Real Estate Recording**, Attala County Clerk of the Chancery Court, West Washington Street, Chancery Court Building, Kosciusko, MS 39090. 601-289-2921 (CST) 8AM-5PM.

**Circuit Court**, Courthouse, Kosciusko, MS 39090. 601-289-1471 (CST) 8:00AM-5:00PM. Felony, Civil Actions Over $1,000.

**Justice Court**, Courthouse, Kosciusko, MS 39090. 601-289-7272 (CST) 8:00AM-5:00PM. Misdemeanor, Civil Actions Under $1,000, Eviction, Small Claims.

**Chancery Court**, 230 W. Washington, Kosciusko, MS 39090. 601-289-2921 (CST) Probate.

## Benton County

**Real Estate Recording**, Benton County Clerk of the Chancery Court, Main Street, Courthouse, Ashland, MS 38603. 601-224-6300 (CST) 8AM-5PM.

**Circuit Court**, PO Box 262, Ashland, MS 38603. 601-224-6310 (CST) 8:00AM-5:00PM. Felony, Civil Actions Over $1,000.

**Justice Court**, PO Box 152, Ashland, MS 38603. 601-224-6320 (CST) 8:00AM-5:00PM. Misdemeanor, Civil Actions Under $1,000, Eviction, Small Claims.

**Chancery Court**, PO Box 218, Ashland, MS 38603. 601-224-6300 (CST) Probate.

## Bolivar County

**Real Estate Recording**, Bolivar County Clerk of the Chancery Court, 2nd District, Court Street, Courthouse, Cleveland, MS 38732. 601-843-2071 (CST) 8AM-5PM.

**Real Estate Recording**, Bolivar County Clerk of the Chancery Court, 1st District, 801 Main Street, Courthouse, Rosedale, MS 38769. 601-759-3762 (CST) 8AM-Noon,1-5PM.

**Circuit and County Court - 2nd District**, PO Box 670, Cleveland, MS 38732. 601-843-2061 (CST) 8:00AM-5:00PM. Felony, Misdemeanor, Civil.

**Circuit and County Court - 1st District**, PO Box 205, Rosedale, MS 38769. 601-759-6521 (CST) 8:00AM-5:00PM. Felony, Misdemeanor, Civil.

**Justice Court**, PO Box 1507, Cleveland, MS 38732. 601-843-4008 (CST) 8:00AM-5:00PM. Misdemeanor, Civil Actions Under $1,000, Eviction, Small Claims.

**Cleveland Chancery Court**, PO Box 789, Cleveland, MS 38732. 601-843-2071 (CST) Probate.

**Rosedale Chancery Court**, PO Box 238, Rosedale, MS 38769. 601-759-3762 (CST) Probate.

## Calhoun County

**Real Estate Recording**, Calhoun County Clerk of the Chancery Court, Courthouse Square, Pittsboro, MS 38951. 601-983-3117 (CST) 8AM-5PM.

**Circuit Court**, PO Box 25, Pittsboro, MS 38951. 601-983-3101 (CST) 8:00AM-5:00PM. Felony, Civil Actions Over $1,000.

**Justice Court**, PO Box 7, Pittsboro, MS 38951. 601-983-3134 (CST) 9:00AM-5:00PM. Misdemeanor, Civil Actions Under $1,000, Eviction, Small Claims.

**Chancery Court**, PO Box 8, Pittsboro, MS 38951. 601-983-3117 (CST) Probate.

## Carroll County

**Real Estate Recording**, Carroll County Clerk of the Chancery Court, 1st District, Courthouse, Carrollton, MS 38917. 601-237-9274 (CST)

**Real Estate Recording**, Carroll County Clerk of the Chancery Court, 2nd District, 101 Highway 51, Courthouse, Vaiden, MS 39176. 601-464-5476 (CST) 8AM-5PM.

**Circuit Court**, PO Box 6, Vaiden, MS 39176. 601-464-5476 (CST) 8:00AM-5:00PM. Felony, Civil Actions Over $1,000.

**Justice Court**, PO Box 10, Carrollton, MS 38917. 601-237-9285 (CST) 8:00AM-4:00PM. Misdemeanor, Civil Actions Under $1,000, Eviction, Small Claims.

**Chancery Court**, PO Box 60, Carrollton, MS 38917. 601-237-9274 (CST) Probate.

## Chickasaw County

**Real Estate Recording**, Chickasaw County Clerk of the Chancery Court, 1st District, Courthouse, Houston, MS 38851. 601-456-2513 (CST) 8AM-5PM.

**Real Estate Recording**, Chickasaw County Clerk of the Chancery Court, 2nd District, 234 Main Street, Room 201, Okolona, MS 38860-1438. 601-447-2092 (CST) 8AM-Noon,1-5PM.

**Circuit Court - 1st District**, Courthouse, Houston, MS 38851. 601-456-2331 (CST) 8:00AM-5:00PM. Felony, Civil Actions Over $1,000.

**Circuit Court - 2nd District**, Courthouse, Okolona, MS 38860. 601-447-2838 (CST) 8:00AM-5:00PM. Felony, Civil Actions Over $1,000.

**Justice Court**, Courthouse, Houston, MS 38851. 601-456-3941 (CST) 8:00AM-5:00PM. Misdemeanor, Civil Actions Under $1,000, Eviction, Small Claims.

**Chancery Court**, Courthouse Bldg, Houston, MS 38851. 601-456-2513 (CST) Probate.

**Chancery Court**, Courthouse, Okolona, MS 38860. 601-447-2090 (CST) Probate.

## Choctaw County

**Real Estate Recording**, Choctaw County Clerk of the Chancery Court, Quinn Street, Ackerman, MS 39735. 601-285-6329 (CST) 8AM-Noon,1-5PM.

**Circuit Court**, PO Box 34, Ackerman, MS 39735. 601-285-6245 (CST) 8:00AM-5:00PM. Felony, Civil Actions Over $1,000.

**Justice Court**, PO Box 357, Ackerman, MS 39735. 601-285-3599 (CST) 8:00AM-5:00PM. Misdemeanor, Civil Actions Under $1,000, Eviction, Small Claims.

**Chancery Court**, PO Box 250, Ackerman, MS 39735. 601-285-6329 (CST) Probate.

## Claiborne County

**Real Estate Recording**, Claiborne County Clerk of the Chancery Court, 410 Main Street, Port Gibson, MS 39150. 601-437-4992 (CST) 8AM-5PM.

**Circuit Court**, PO Box 549, Port Gibson, MS 39150. 601-437-5841 (CST) 8:00AM-5:00PM. Felony, Civil Actions Over $1,000.

**Justice Court**, PO Box 497, Port Gibson, MS 39150. 601-437-4478 (CST) 8:00AM-5:00PM. Misdemeanor, Civil Actions Under $1,000, Eviction, Small Claims.

**Chancery Court**, PO Box 449, Port Gibson, MS 39150. 601-437-4992 (CST) Probate.

## Clarke County

**Real Estate Recording**, Clarke County Clerk of the Chancery Court, Archusa Street, Courthouse, Quitman, MS 39355. 601-776-2126 (CST) 8AM-5PM.

**Circuit Court**, PO Box 216, Quitman, MS 39355. 601-776-3111 (CST) 8:00AM-5:00PM. Felony, Civil Actions Over $1,000.

**Justice Court**, PO Box 4, Quitman, MS 39355. 601-776-5371 (CST) Misdemeanor, Civil Actions Under $1,000, Eviction, Small Claims.

**Chancery Court**, PO Drawer M, Quitman, MS 39355. 601-776-2126 (CST) Probate.

## Clay County

**Real Estate Recording**, Clay County Clerk of the Chancery Court, 205 Court Street, West Point, MS 39773. 601-494-3124 (CST) 8AM-5PM.

**Circuit Court**, PO Box 364, West Point, MS 39773. 601-494-3384 (CST) 8:00AM-5:00PM. Felony, Civil Actions Over $1,000.

**Justice Court**, PO Box 674, West Point, MS 39773. 601-494-6141 (CST) Misdemeanor, Civil Actions Under $1,000, Eviction, Small Claims.

**Chancery Court**, PO Box 815, West Point, MS 39773. 601-494-3124 (CST) Probate.

## Coahoma County

**Real Estate Recording**, Coahoma County Clerk of the Chancery Court, 115 First Street, Clarksdale, MS 38614. 601-624-3000 (CST) 8AM-5PM.

**Circuit and County Court**, PO Box 849, Clarksdale, MS 38614. 601-624-3014 (CST) 8:00AM-5:00PM. Felony, Misdemeanor, Civil.

**Justice Court**, 144 Ritch, Clarksdale, MS 38614. 601-624-3060 (CST) 8:00AM-5:00PM. Misdemeanor, Civil Actions Under $1,000, Eviction, Small Claims.

**Chancery Court**, PO Box 98, Clarksdale, MS 38614. 601-624-3000 (CST) Probate.

## Copiah County

**Real Estate Recording**, Copiah County Clerk of the Chancery Court, 100 Caldwell Drive, Courthouse Square, Hazlehurst, MS 39083. 601-894-3021 (CST) 8AM-5PM.

**Circuit Court**, PO Box 467, Hazlehurst, MS 39083. 601-894-1241 (CST) 8:00AM-5:00PM. Felony, Civil Actions Over $1,000.

**Justice Court**, PO Box 798, Hazlehurst, MS 39083. 601-894-3218 (CST) 8:00AM-5:00PM. Misdemeanor, Civil Actions Under $1,000, Eviction, Small Claims.

**Chancery Court**, PO Box 507, Hazlehurst, MS 39083. 601-894-3021 (CST) Probate.

## Covington County

**Real Estate Recording**, Covington County Clerk of the Chancery Court, Courthouse Square & Main Street, Collins, MS 39428. 601-765-4242 (CST) 8AM-5PM.

**Circuit Court**, PO Box 667, Collins, MS 39428. 601-765-6506 (CST) 8:00AM-5:00PM. Felony, Civil Actions Over $1,000.

**Justice Court**, PO Box 665, Collins, MS 39428. 601-765-6581 (CST) 8:00AM-5:00PM. Misdemeanor, Civil Actions Under $1,000, Eviction, Small Claims.

**Chancery Court**, PO Box 1679, Collins, MS 39428. 601-765-4242 (CST) Probate.

## De Soto County

**Real Estate Recording**, De Soto County Clerk of the Chancery Court, 2535 Highway 51 South, Courthouse, Hernando, MS 38632. 601-429-1361 (CST) 8AM-5PM.

**Circuit and County Court**, 2535 Hwy 51 South, Hernando, MS 38632. 601-429-1325 (CST) 8:00AM-5:00PM. Felony, Misdemeanor, Civil.

**Justice Court**, 891 E. Rasco, Southaven, MS 38671. 601-393-5810 (CST) 8:00AM-5:00PM. Misdemeanor, Civil Actions Under $1,000, Eviction, Small Claims.

**Chancery Court**, 2535 Hwy 51 South, Hernando, MS 38632. 601-429-1318 (CST) Probate.

## Forrest County

**Real Estate Recording**, Forrest County Clerk of the Chancery Court, 641 Main Street, Chancery Court Building, Hattiesburg, MS 39401. 601-545-6014 (CST) 8AM-5PM.

**Circuit and County Court**, PO Box 992, Hattiesburg, MS 39403. 601-582-3213 (CST) 8:00AM-5:00PM. Felony, Misdemeanor, Civil.

**Justice Court**, 316 Forrest St, Hattiesburg, MS 39401. 601-544-3136 (CST) 8:00AM-5:00PM. Misdemeanor, Civil Actions Under $1,000, Eviction, Small Claims.

**Chancery Court**, PO Box 951, Hattiesburg, MS 39403. 601-545-6014 (CST) Probate.

## Franklin County

**Real Estate Recording**, Franklin County Clerk of the Chancery Court, 101 Main Street, Courthouse, Meadville, MS 39653. 601-384-2330 (CST) 8AM-5PM.

**Circuit Court**, PO Box 267, Meadville, MS 39653. 601-384-2320 (CST) 8:00AM-5:00PM. Felony, Civil Actions Over $1,000.

**Justice Court**, PO Box 365, Meadville, MS 39653. 601-384-2002 (CST) 8:00AM-5:00PM. Misdemeanor, Civil Actions Under $1,000, Eviction, Small Claims.

**Chancery Court**, PO Box 297, Meadville, MS 39653. 601-384-2330 (CST) Probate.

## George County

**Real Estate Recording**, George County Clerk of the Chancery Court, Court House Square, Lucedale, MS 39452. 601-947-4801 (CST) 8AM-5PM; 9AM-Noon Sat.

**Circuit Court**, 200 Courthouse Square, Lucedale, MS 39452. 601-947-4881 (CST) 8:00AM-5:00PM M-F, 9:00AM-12:00PM Sat. Felony, Civil Actions Over $1,000.

**Justice Court**, 200 Cox St, Lucedale, MS 39452. 601-947-4834 (CST) Misdemeanor, Civil Actions Under $1,000, Eviction, Small Claims.

**Chancery Court**, 200 Courthouse Square, Lucedale, MS 39452. 601-947-4801 (CST) Probate.

## Greene County

**Real Estate Recording**, Greene County Clerk of the Chancery Court, Courthouse, Main St., Leakesville, MS 39451. 601-394-2377 (CST)

**Circuit Court**, PO Box 310, Leakesville, MS 39451. 601-394-2379 (CST) 8:00AM-5:00PM M-F, 8:00AM-12:00PM Sat. Felony, Civil Actions Over $1,000.

**Justice Court**, PO Box 547, Leakesville, MS 39451. 601-394-2347 (CST) 8:00AM-5:00PM. Misdemeanor, Civil Actions Under $1,000, Eviction, Small Claims.

**Chancery Court**, PO Box 610, Leakesville, MS 39451. 601-394-2377 (CST) Probate.

## Grenada County

**Real Estate Recording**, Grenada County Clerk of the Chancery Court, 59 Green Street, Courthouse, Grenada, MS 38901. 601-226-1821 (CST) 8AM-5PM.

**Circuit Court**, 59 Green St, Ste #8, Grenada, MS 38901. 601-226-1941 (CST) 8:00AM-5:00PM. Felony, Civil Actions Over $1,000.

**Justice Court**, 16 First St, Grenada, MS 38901. 601-226-3331 (CST) 8:00AM-5:00PM. Misdemeanor, Civil Actions Under $1,000, Eviction, Small Claims.

**Chancery Court**, PO Box 1208, Grenada, MS 38901. 601-226-1821 (CST) Probate.

## Hancock County

**Real Estate Recording**, Hancock County Clerk of the Chancery Court, Courthouse, Bay Saint Louis, MS 39520. 601-467-5404 (CST) 8AM-5PM.

**Circuit Court**, PO Box 249 Bay St., Bay St. Louis, MS 39520. 601-467-5265 (CST) 8:00AM-5:00PM. Felony, Civil Actions Over $1,000.

**Justice Court**, PO Box 147, Bay St, Bay St. Louis, MS 39520. 601-467-5573 (CST) 8:00AM-5:00PM. Misdemeanor, Civil Actions Under $1,000, Eviction, Small Claims.

**Chancery Court**, PO Box 429 Bay St., Bay St. Louis, MS 39520. 601-467-5404 (CST) Probate.

## Harrison County

**Real Estate Recording**, Harrison County Chancery Clerk, 2nd District, 730 Washington Loop, Biloxi, MS 39530. 601-435-8220 (CST) 8AM-5PM.

**Real Estate Recording**, Harrison County Clerk of the Chancery Court, 1st District, 1801 23rd Avenue, Gulfport, MS 39501. 601-865-4036 (CST) 8AM-5PM.

**Circuit Court - 2nd District**, PO Box 235, Biloxi, MS 39533. 601-435-8258 (CST) 8:00AM-5:00PM. Felony, Civil Actions Over $1,000.

**Circuit Court - 1st District**, PO Box 998, Gulfport, MS 39502. 601-865-4187 (CST) 8:00AM-5:00PM. Felony, Civil Actions Over $1,000.

**County Court - 2nd District**, PO Box 235, Biloxi, MS 39533. 601-435-8231 (CST) 8:00AM-5:00PM. Misdemeanor, Civil Actions Under $50,000.

**County Court - 1st District**, PO Box 998, Gulfport, MS 39502. 601-865-4097 (CST) 8:00AM-5:00PM. Misdemeanor, Civil Actions Under $50,000.

**Justice Court**, PO Box 1754, Gulfport, MS 39502. 601-865-4193 (CST) 8:00AM-5:00PM. Misdemeanor, Civil Actions Under $1,000, Eviction, Small Claims.

**Biloxi Chancery Court**, PO Box 544, Biloxi, MS 39533. 601-435-8224 (CST) Probate.

**Gulfport Chancery Court**, PO Drawer CC, Gulfport, MS 39502. 601-865-4036 (CST) Probate.

## Hinds County

**Real Estate Recording**, Hinds County Clerk of the Chancery Court, 1st District, 316 South President Street, Jackson, MS 39201. 601-968-6516 (CST) 8AM-5PM.

# Mississippi

**Real Estate Recording**, Hinds County Clerk of the Chancery Court, 2nd District, Main Street, Courthouse Annex, Raymond, MS 39154. 601-857-8055 (CST) 8AM-5PM.

**Circuit and County Court - 1st District**, PO Box 327, Jackson, MS 39205. 601-968-6628 (CST) Felony, Misdemeanor, Civil.

**Circuit and County Court - 2nd District**, PO Box 33, Raymond, MS 39154. 601-968-6653 (CST) 8:00AM-5:00PM. Felony, Misdemeanor, Civil.

**Justice Court**, 407 E Pascagoula, 3rd floor, Jackson, MS 39207. 601-968-6781 (CST) Misdemeanor, Civil Actions Under $1,000, Eviction, Small Claims.

**Jackson Chancery Court**, PO Box 686, Jackson, MS 39205. 601-968-6540 (CST) Probate.

**Raymond Chancery Court**, PO Box 88, Raymond, MS 39154. 601-857-8055 (CST) Probate.

## Holmes County

**Real Estate Recording**, Holmes County Clerk of the Chancery Court, Courthouse, Lexington, MS 39095. 601-834-2508 (CST) 8AM-Noon,1-5PM.

**Circuit Court**, PO Box 265, Lexington, MS 39095. 601-834-2476 (CST) 8:00AM-5:00PM. Felony, Civil Actions Over $1,000.

**Justice Court**, PO Drawer D, Lexington, MS 39095. 601-834-4565 (CST) 8:00AM-5:00PM. Misdemeanor, Civil Actions Under $1,000, Eviction, Small Claims.

**Chancery Court**, PO Box 239, Lexington, MS 39095. 601-834-2508 (CST) Probate.

## Humphreys County

**Real Estate Recording**, Humphreys County Clerk of the Chancery Court, 102 Castleman, Courthouse, Belzoni, MS 39038. 601-247-1740 (CST) 8AM-Noon, 1-5PM.

**Circuit Court**, PO Box 696, Belzoni, MS 39038. 601-247-3065 (CST) 8:00AM-5:00PM. Felony, Civil Actions Over $1,000.

**Justice Court**, 102 Castleman St, Belzoni, MS 39038. 601-247-4337 (CST) 8:00AM-5:00PM. Misdemeanor, Civil Actions Under $1,000, Eviction, Small Claims.

**Chancery Court**, PO Box 547, Belzoni, MS 39038. 601-247-1740 (CST) Probate.

## Issaquena County

**Real Estate Recording**, Issaquena County Clerk of the Chancery Court, 129 Court Street, Mayersville, MS 39113. 601-873-2761 (CST) 8AM-Noon,1-5PM.

**Circuit Court**, PO Box 27, Mayersville, MS 39113. 601-873-2761 (CST) 8:00AM-5:00PM. Felony, Civil Actions Over $1,000.

**Justice Court**, PO Box 27, Mayersville, MS 39113. 601-873-2761 (CST) 8:00AM-5:00PM. Misdemeanor, Civil Actions Under $1,000, Eviction, Small Claims.

**Chancery Court**, PO Box 27, Mayersville, MS 39113. 601-873-2761 (CST) Probate.

## Itawamba County

**Real Estate Recording**, Itawamba County Clerk of the Chancery Court, 201 West Main Street, Fulton, MS 38843. 601-862-3421 (CST) 8AM-5PM; 8AM-Noon Sat.

**Circuit Court**, 201 W Main, Fulton, MS 38843. 601-862-3511 (CST) 8:00AM-5:00PM. Felony, Civil Actions Over $1,000.

**Justice Court**, 201 W Main, Fulton, MS 38843. 601-862-4315 (CST) Misdemeanor, Civil Actions Under $1,000, Eviction, Small Claims.

**Chancery Court**, 201 W Main, Fulton, MS 38843. 601-862-3421 (CST) Probate.

## Jackson County

**Real Estate Recording**, Jackson County Chancery Clerk, 3109 Canty Street, Pascagoula, MS 39567. 601-769-3131 (CST) 8AM-5PM.

**Circuit Court**, PO Box 998, Pascagoula, MS 39568-0998. 601-769-3025 (CST) 8:00AM-5:00PM. Felony, Civil Actions Over $1,000.

**County Court**, PO Box 998, Pascagoula, MS 39568. 601-769-3181 (CST) Misdemeanor, Civil Actions Under $50,000.

**Justice Court**, 5343 Jefferson St, Moss Point, MS 39563. 601-769-3080 (CST) Misdemeanor, Civil Actions Under $1,000, Eviction, Small Claims.

**Chancery Court**, PO Box 998, Pascagoula, MS 39568. 601-769-3131 (CST) Probate.

## Jasper County

**Real Estate Recording**, Jasper County Clerk of the Chancery Court, 2nd District, Court Street, Bay Springs, MS 39422. 601-764-3026 (CST) 8AM-5PM.

**Real Estate Recording**, Jasper County Clerk of the Chancery Court, 1st District, Courthouse, Paulding, MS 39348. 601-727-4941 (CST) 8AM-5PM.

**Circuit Court - 2nd District**, PO Box 447, Bay Springs, MS 39422. 601-764-2245 (CST) 8:00AM-5:00PM. Felony, Civil Actions Over $1,000.

**Circuit Court - 1st District**, PO Box 485, Paulding, MS 39348. 601-727-4941 (CST) Felony, Civil Actions Over $1,000.

**Justice Court**, PO Box 1054, Bay Springs, MS 39422. 601-764-2065 (CST) 8:00AM-5:00PM. Misdemeanor, Civil Actions Under $1,000, Eviction, Small Claims.

**Bay Springs Chancery Court**, PO Box 447, Bay Springs, MS 39422. 601-764-3368 (CST) Probate.

**Paulding Chancery Court**, PO Box 494, Paulding, MS 39348. 601-727-4941 (CST) Probate.

## Jefferson County

**Real Estate Recording**, Jefferson County Clerk of the Chancery Court, 307 Main, Fayette, MS 39069. 601-786-3021 (CST) 8AM-5PM.

**Circuit Court**, PO Box 305, Fayette, MS 39069. 601-786-3422 (CST) 8:00AM-5:00PM. Felony, Civil Actions Over $1,000.

**Justice Court**, PO Box 1047, Fayette, MS 39069. 601-786-8594 (CST) 8:00AM-5:00PM. Misdemeanor, Civil Actions Under $1,000, Eviction, Small Claims.

**Chancery Court**, PO Box 145, Fayette, MS 39069. 601-786-3021 (CST) Probate.

## Jefferson Davis County

**Real Estate Recording**, Jefferson Davis County Clerk of the Chancery Court, 1025 3rd St., Prentiss, MS 39474. 601-792-4204 (CST) 8AM-5PM.

**Circuit Court**, PO Box 1082, Prentiss, MS 39474. 601-792-4231 (CST) 8:00AM-5:00PM. Felony, Civil Actions Over $1,000.

**Justice Court**, PO Drawer 1407, Prentiss, MS 39474. 601-792-5129 (CST) 8:00AM-5:00PM. Misdemeanor, Civil Actions Under $1,000, Eviction, Small Claims.

**Chancery Court**, PO Box 1137, Prentiss, MS 39474. 601-792-4231 (CST) Probate.

## Jones County

**Real Estate Recording**, Jones County Clerk of the Chancery Court, 1st District, Court Street, Jones County Courthouse, Ellisville, MS 39437. 601-477-3307 (CST)

**Real Estate Recording**, Jones County Clerk of the Chancery Court, 2nd District, 415 North 5th Avenue, Laurel, MS 39441. 601-428-0527 (CST) 8AM-5PM.

**Circuit and County Court - 1st District**, 101 N. Court St, Ellisville, MS 39437. 601-477-8538 (CST) 8:00AM-5:00PM. Felony, Misdemeanor, Civil.

**Circuit and County Court - 2nd District**, PO Box 1336, Laurel, MS 39441. 601-425-2556 (CST) 8:00AM-5:00PM. Felony, Misdemeanor, Civil.

**Justice Court**, PO Box 1997, Laurel, MS 39441. 601-428-3137 (CST) 8:00AM-5:00PM. Misdemeanor, Civil Actions Under $1,000, Eviction, Small Claims.

**Ellisville Chancery Court**, 101 N. Court St., Ellisville, MS 39437. 601-477-3307 (CST) Probate.

**Laurel Chancery Court**, PO Box 1468, Laurel, MS 39441. 601-428-0527 (CST) Probate.

## Kemper County

**Real Estate Recording**, Kemper County Clerk of the Chancery Court, Courthouse Square, De Kalb, MS 39328. 601-743-2460 (CST) 8AM-5PM.

**Circuit Court**, PO Box 130, De Kalb, MS 39328. 601-743-2224 (CST) 8:00AM-5:00PM. Felony, Civil Actions Over $1,000.

**Justice Court**, PO Box 661, De Kalb, MS 39328. 601-743-2793 (CST) 8:00AM-5:00PM. Misdemeanor, Civil Actions Under $1,000, Eviction, Small Claims.

**Chancery Court**, PO Box 130, De Kalb, MS 39328. 601-743-2460 (CST) Probate.

## Lafayette County

**Real Estate Recording**, Lafayette County Clerk of the Chancery Court, Courthouse, Oxford, MS 38655. 601-234-2131 (CST)

**Circuit Court**, LaFayette County Courthouse, Oxford, MS 38655. 601-234-4951 (CST) 8:00AM-5:00PM. Felony, Civil Actions Over $1,000.

**Justice Court**, 1219 Monroe, Oxford, MS 38655. 601-234-1545 (CST) 8:00AM-5:00PM. Misdemeanor, Civil Actions Under $1,000, Eviction, Small Claims.

**Chancery Court**, PO Box 1240, Oxford, MS 38655. 601-234-2131 (CST) Probate.

## Lamar County

**Real Estate Recording**, Lamar County Clerk of the Chancery Court, 203 Main Street, Purvis, MS 39475. 601-794-8504 (CST) 8AM-5PM.

**Circuit Court**, PO Box 369, Purvis, MS 39475. 601-794-8504 (CST) 8:00AM-5:00PM. Felony, Civil Actions Over $1,000.

**Justice Court**, PO Box 1010, Purvis, MS 39475. 601-794-2950 (CST) 8:00AM-5:00PM. Misdemeanor, Civil Actions Under $1,000, Eviction, Small Claims.

**Chancery Court**, PO Box 247, Purvis, MS 39475. 601-794-8504 (CST) Probate.

## Lauderdale County

**Real Estate Recording**, Lauderdale County Clerk of the Chancery Court, 500 Constitution Avenue, Room 105, Meridian, MS 39301. 601-482-9701 (CST) 8AM-5PM.

**Circuit and County Court**, PO Box 1005, Meridian, MS 39302. 601-482-9738 (CST) 8:00AM-5:00PM. Felony, Civil.

**Justice Court**, PO Box 5126, Meridian, MS 39302. 601-482-9879 (CST) Misdemeanor, Civil Actions Under $1,000, Eviction, Small Claims.

**Chancery Court**, PO Box 1587, Meridian, MS 39302. 601-489-9701 (CST) Probate.

## Lawrence County

**Real Estate Recording**, Lawrence County Clerk of the Chancery Court, Courthouse Square, Monticello, MS 39654. 601-587-7162 (CST)

**Circuit Court**, PO Box 1249, Monticello, MS 39654. 601-587-4791 (CST) 8:00AM-5:00PM. Felony, Civil Actions Over $1,000.

**Justice Court**, PO Box 903, Monticello, MS 39654. 601-587-7183 (CST) 8:00AM-5:00PM. Misdemeanor, Civil Actions Under $1,000, Eviction, Small Claims.

**Chancery Court**, PO Box 40, Monticello, MS 39654. 601-587-7162 (CST) Probate.

## Leake County

**Real Estate Recording**, Leake County Clerk of the Chancery Court, Courthouse, Court Square, Carthage, MS 39051. 601-267-7371 (CST) 8AM-5PM.

**Circuit Court**, PO Box 67, Carthage, MS 39051. 601-267-8357 (CST) 8:00AM-5:00PM. Felony, Civil Actions Over $1,000.

**Justice Court**, PO Box 69, Carthage, MS 39051. 601-267-5677 (CST) 8:00AM-5:00PM. Misdemeanor, Civil Actions Under $1,000, Eviction, Small Claims.

**Chancery Court**, PO Box 72, Carthage, MS 39051. 601-267-7371 (CST) Probate.

## Lee County

**Real Estate Recording**, Lee County Clerk of the Chancery Court, 200 Jefferson Street, Tupelo, MS 38801. 601-841-9100 (CST) 8AM-5PM.

**Circuit and County Court**, Circuit Court-PO Box 762, County Court-P, Tupelo, MS 38802. 601-841-9024 (CST) 8:00AM-5:00PM. Felony, Civil.

**Justice Court**, PO Box 108, Tupelo, MS 38802. 601-841-9014 (CST) 8:00AM-5:00PM. Misdemeanor, Civil Actions Under $1,000, Eviction, Small Claims.

**Chancery Court**, PO Box 1785, Tupelo, MS 38801. 601-841-9024 (CST) Probate.

## Leflore County

**Real Estate Recording**, Leflore County Clerk of the Chancery Court, 310 West Market, Courthouse, Greenwood, MS 38930. 601-455-7913 (CST) 8AM-5PM.

**Circuit and County Court**, PO Box 1953, Greenwood, MS 38930. 601-453-1041 (CST) Felony, Civil.

**Justice Court**, PO Box 8056, Greenwood, MS 38930. 601-453-1605 (CST) 8:00AM-5:00PM. Misdemeanor, Civil Actions Under $1,000, Eviction, Small Claims.

**Chancery Court**, PO Box 1468, Greenwood, MS 38930. 601-453-1041 (CST) Probate.

## Lincoln County

**Real Estate Recording**, Lincoln County Clerk of the Chancery Court, 231 South First Street, Brookhaven, MS 39601. 601-835-3416 (CST) 8AM-5PM.

**Circuit Court**, PO Box 357, Brookhaven, MS 39601. 601-835-3435 (CST) 8:00AM-5:00PM. Felony, Civil Actions Over $1,000.

**Justice Court**, PO Box 767, Brookhaven, MS 39601. 601-835-3474 (CST) 8:00AM-5:00PM. Misdemeanor, Civil Actions Under $1,000, Eviction, Small Claims.

**Chancery Court**, PO Box 555, Brookhaven, MS 39601. 601-835-3412 (CST) Probate.

## Lowndes County

**Real Estate Recording**, Lowndes County Clerk of the Chancery Court, 515 2nd Avenue North, Courthouse, Columbus, MS 39703. 601-329-5807 (CST) 8AM-5PM.

**Circuit and County Court**, PO Box 31, Columbus, MS 39703. 601-329-5900 (CST) 8:30AM-4:30PM. Felony, Civil.

**Justice Court**, 11 Airline Rd, Columbus, MS 39702. 601-329-5929 (CST) 8:00AM-5:00PM. Misdemeanor, Civil Actions Under $1,000, Eviction, Small Claims.

**Chancery Court**, PO Box 684, Columbus, MS 39703. 601-329-5800 (CST) Probate.

## Madison County

**Real Estate Recording**, Madison County Clerk, 146 W. Center St.eet, Courtyard Square, Canton, MS 39046. 601-859-1177 (CST) 8AM-5PM.

**Circuit and County Court**, PO Box 1626, Canton, MS 39046. 601-859-4365 (CST) 8:00AM-5:00PM. Felony, Civil.

**Justice Court**, 175 N Union, Canton, MS 39046. 601-859-6337 (CST) Misdemeanor, Civil Actions Under $1,000, Eviction, Small Claims.

**Chancery Court**, PO Box 404, Canton, MS 39046. 601-859-1177 (CST) Probate.

## Marion County

**Real Estate Recording**, Marion County Clerk of the Chancery Court, 250 Broad Street, Suite 2, Columbia, MS 39429. 601-736-2691 (CST) 8AM-5PM.

**Circuit Court**, 250 Broad St, Suite 1, Columbia, MS 39429. 601-736-8246 (CST) 8:00AM-5:00PM. Felony, Civil Actions Over $1,000.

**Justice Court**, 500 Courthouse Square, Columbia, MS 39429. 601-736-7572 (CST) Misdemeanor, Civil Actions Under $1,000, Eviction, Small Claims.

**Chancery Court**, 250 Broad St, Suite 2, Columbia, MS 39429. 601-736-2691 (CST) Probate.

## Marshall County

**Real Estate Recording**, Marshall County Clerk of the Chancery Court, Court Square, Holly Springs, MS 38635. 601-252-4431 (CST) 8AM-5PM.

**Circuit Court**, PO Box 459, Holly Springs, MS 38635. 601-252-3434 (CST) 8:00AM-5:00PM. Felony, Civil Actions Over $1,000.

**Justice Court-North and South Districts**, PO Box 867, Holly Springs, MS 38635. 601-252-2585 (CST) Misdemeanor, Civil Actions Under $1,000, Eviction, Small Claims.

**Chancery Court**, PO Box 219, Holly Springs, MS 38635. 601-252-4431 (CST) Probate.

## Monroe County

**Real Estate Recording**, Monroe County Clerk of the Chancery Court, 201 West Commerce Street, Aberdeen, MS 39730. 601-369-8143 (CST) 8AM-5PM.

**Circuit Court**, PO Box 843, Aberdeen, MS 39730. 601-369-8695 (CST) 8:00AM-5:00PM. Felony, Civil Actions Over $1,000.

**Justice Court-District 2**, PO Box F, Aberdeen, MS 39730. 601-369-4971 (CST) Misdemeanor, Civil Actions Under $1,000, Eviction, Small Claims.

**Justice Court-District 1 & 3**, 101 9th St, Amory, MS 38821. 601-256-8493 (CST) Misdemeanor, Civil Actions Under $1,000, Eviction, Small Claims.

**Chancery Court**, PO Box 578, Aberdeen, MS 39730. 601-369-8143 (CST) Probate.

## Montgomery County

**Real Estate Recording**, Montgomery County Clerk of the Chancery Court, 614 Summit Street, Courthouse, Winona, MS 38967. 601-283-2333 (CST) 8AM-5PM.

**Circuit Court**, PO Box 765, Winona, MS 38967. 601-283-4161 (CST) 8:00AM-5:00PM. Felony, Civil Actions Over $1,000.

**Justice Court**, PO Box 229, Winona, MS 38967. 601-283-2290 (CST) Misdemeanor, Civil Actions Under $1,000, Eviction, Small Claims.

**Chancery Court**, PO Box 71, Winona, MS 38967. 601-283-2333 (CST) Probate.

## Neshoba County

**Real Estate Recording**, Neshoba County Clerk of the Chancery Court, 401 Beacon Street, Suite 107, Philadelphia, MS 39350. 601-656-3581 (CST) 8AM-5PM.

**Circuit Court**, 401 E Beacon St, Philadelphia, MS 39350. 601-656-4781 (CST) 8:00AM-5:00PM. Felony, Civil Actions Over $1,000.

**Justice Court**, 401 E Beacon St, Philadelphia, MS 39350. 601-656-5361 (CST) Misdemeanor, Civil Actions Under $1,000, Eviction, Small Claims.

**Chancery Court**, PO Box 67, Philadelphia, MS 39350. 601-656-3581 (CST) Probate.

## Newton County

**Real Estate Recording**, Newton County Clerk of the Chancery Court, 92 West Broad St., Courthouse, Decatur, MS 39327. 601-635-2367 (CST) 8AM-5PM.

**Circuit Court**, PO Box 447, Decatur, MS 39327. 601-635-2368 (CST) 8:00AM-5:00PM. Felony, Civil Actions Over $1,000.

**Justice Court**, PO Box 69, Decatur, MS 39327. 601-635-2740 (CST) Misdemeanor, Civil Actions Under $1,000, Eviction, Small Claims.

**Chancery Court**, PO Box 68, Decatur, MS 39327. 601-635-2367 (CST) Probate.

## Noxubee County

**Real Estate Recording**, Noxubee County Clerk of the Chancery Court, 505 South Jefferson, Macon, MS 39341. 601-726-4243 (CST) 8AM-5PM.

**Circuit Court**, PO Box 431, Macon, MS 39341. 601-726-5737 (CST) 8:00AM-5:00PM. Felony, Civil Actions Over $1,000.

**Justice Court-North & South Districts**, 507 S Jefferson, Macon, MS 39341. 601-726-5834 (CST) Misdemeanor, Civil Actions Under $1,000, Eviction, Small Claims.

**Chancery Court**, 505 S. Jefferson St, Macon, MS 39341. 601-726-4243 (CST) Probate.

## Oktibbeha County

**Real Estate Recording**, Oktibbeha County Clerk of the Chancery Court, 101 East Main, Courthouse, Starkville, MS 39759. 601-323-5834 (CST) 8AM-5PM.

**Circuit Court**, Courthouse, Starkville, MS 39759. 601-323-1356 (CST) 8:00AM-5:00PM. Felony, Civil Actions Over $1,000.

**Justice Court-Districts 1-3**, 104 Felix Long Dr, Starkville, MS 39759. 601-324-3032 (CST) Misdemeanor, Civil Actions Under $1,000, Eviction, Small Claims.

**Chancery Court**, Courthouse, Starkville, MS 39759. 601-323-5834 (CST) Probate.

## Panola County

**Real Estate Recording**, Panola County Clerk of the Chancery Court, 2nd District, 151 Public Square, Batesville, MS 38606. 601-563-6205 (CST) 8AM-5PM.

**Real Estate Recording**, Panola County Clerk of the Chancery Court, 1st District, 215 Pocohontas Street, Sardis, MS 38666. 601-487-2070 (CST) 8AM-5PM.

**Circuit Court - 2nd District**, PO Box 346, Batesville, MS 38606. 601-487-2073 (CST) 8:00AM-5:00PM. Felony, Civil Actions Over $1,000.

**Circuit Court - 1st District**, PO Box 130, Sardis, MS 38666. 601-487-2073 (CST) 8:00AM-5:00PM. Felony, Civil Actions Over $1,000.

**Justice Court**, PO Box 249, Sardis, MS 38666. 601-487-2080 (CST) Misdemeanor, Civil Actions Under $1,000, Eviction, Small Claims.

**Batesville Chancery Court**, 151 Public Square, Batesville, MS 38606. 601-563-6205 (CST) Probate.

**Sardis Chancery Court**, PO Box 130, Sardis, MS 38666. 601-487-2070 (CST) Probate.

## Pearl River County

**Real Estate Recording**, Pearl River County Clerk of the Chancery Court, 200 Main Street, Poplarville, MS 39470. 601-795-2237 (CST) 8AM-5PM.

**Circuit Court**, Courthouse, Poplarville, MS 39470. 601-795-4911 (CST) 8:00AM-5:00PM. Felony, Civil Actions Over $1,000.

**Justice Court-Northern, Southeastern, and Southwestern Distircts**, 204 Julia St, Poplarville, MS 39470. 601-795-8018 (CST) Misdemeanor, Civil Actions Under $1,000, Eviction, Small Claims.

**Chancery Court**, PO Box 431, Poplarville, MS 39470. 601-795-4911 (CST) Probate.

## Perry County

**Real Estate Recording**, Perry County Clerk of the Chancery Court, Main Street, New Augusta, MS 39462. 601-964-8398 (CST)

**Circuit Court**, PO Box 198, New Augusta, MS 39462. 601-964-8663 (CST) 8:00AM-5:00PM. Felony, Civil Actions Over $1,000.

**Justice Court-District 2**, PO Box 455, New Augusta, MS 39462. 601-964-8291 (CST) Misdemeanor, Civil Actions Under $1,000, Eviction, Small Claims.

**Justice Court-District 1**, 5091 Hwy 29, Petal, MS 39465. 601-584-7860 (CST) Misdemeanor, Civil Actions Under $1,000, Eviction, Small Claims.

**Chancery Court**, PO Box 198, New Augusta, MS 39462. 601-964-8398 (CST) Probate.

## Pike County

**Real Estate Recording**, Pike County Clerk of the Chancery Court, East Bay, Magnolia, MS 39652. 601-783-3362 (CST) 8AM-5PM.

**Circuit and County Court**, PO Drawer 31, Magnolia, MS 39652. 601-783-2581 (CST) 8:00AM-5:00PM. Felony, Misdemeanor, Civil.

**Justice Court-Divisions 1-3**, PO Box 509, Magnolia, MS 39652. 601-783-5333 (CST) Misdemeanor, Civil Actions Under $1,000, Eviction, Small Claims.

**Chancery Court**, PO Box 309, Magnolia, MS 39652. 601-783-3362 (CST) Probate.

## Pontotoc County

**Real Estate Recording**, Pontotoc County Clerk of the Chancery Court, Corner of Washington & Main Streets, Courthouse, Pontotoc, MS 38863. 601-489-3900 (CST) 8AM-5PM.

**Circuit Court**, PO Box 428, Pontotoc, MS 38863. 601-489-3908 (CST) 8AM-5PM. Felony, Civil Actions Over $1,000.

**Justice Court-East & West Districts**, PO Box 582, Pontotoc, MS 38863. 601-489-3920 (CST) Misdemeanor, Civil Actions Under $1,000, Eviction, Small Claims.

**Chancery Court**, 12 Washington, Pontotoc, MS 38863. 601-489-3900 (CST) Probate.

## Prentiss County

**Real Estate Recording**, Prentiss County Clerk of the Chancery Court, 100 North Main Street, Booneville, MS 38829. 601-728-8151 (CST) 8AM-5PM.

**Circuit Court**, 101 N Main St, Booneville, MS 38829. 601-728-4611 (CST) 8:00AM-5:00PM. Felony, Civil Actions Over $1,000.

**Justice Court-Northern & Southern Districts**, 101-C N Main St, Booneville, MS 38829. 601-728-2001 (CST) Misdemeanor, Civil Actions Under $1,000, Eviction, Small Claims.

**Chancery Court**, PO Box 477, Booneville, MS 38829. 601-728-4611 (CST) Probate.

## Quitman County

**Real Estate Recording**, Quitman County Clerk of the Chancery Court, Chestnut Street, Courthouse, Marks, MS 38646. 601-326-2661 (CST) 8AM-5PM.

**Circuit Court**, Courthouse, Marks, MS 38646. 601-326-8003 (CST) 8:00AM-5:00PM. Felony, Civil Actions Over $1,000.

**Justice Court-Districts 1 & 2**, PO Box 100, Marks, MS 38646. 601-326-2104 (CST) Misdemeanor, Civil Actions Under $1,000, Eviction, Small Claims.

**Chancery Court**, Courthouse, Marks, MS 38646. 601-326-2661 (CST) Probate.

## Rankin County

**Real Estate Recording**, Rankin County Chancery Clerk, 305 West Government Street, Brandon, MS 39042. 601-825-1469 (CST) 8AM-5PM.

**Circuit and County Court**, PO Drawer 1599, Brandon, MS 39043. 601-825-1466 (CST) 8:00AM-5:00PM. Felony, Misdemeanor, Civil.

**Justice Court-Districts 1-4**, 110 Paul Truitt Lane, Pearl, MS 39208. 601-939-1885 (CST) Misdemeanor, Civil Actions Under $1,000, Eviction, Small Claims.

**Chancery Court**, PO Box 190, Brandon, MS 39043. 601-825-1469 (CST) Probate.

## Scott County

**Real Estate Recording**, Scott County Clerk of the Chancery Court, 100 Main Street, Forest, MS 39074. 601-469-1922 (CST) 8AM-5PM.

**Circuit Court**, PO Box 371, Forest, MS 39074. 601-469-3601 (CST) 8:00AM-5:00PM. Felony, Civil Actions Over $1,000.

**Justice Court**, PO Box 371, Forest, MS 39074. 601-469-4555 (CST) Misdemeanor, Civil Actions Under $1,000, Eviction, Small Claims.

**Chancery Court**, PO Box 630, Forest, MS 39074. 601-469-1922 (CST) Probate.

## Sharkey County

**Real Estate Recording**, Sharkey County Clerk of the Chancery Court, 400 Locust St.are, Rolling Fork, MS 39159. 601-873-2755 (CST) 8AM-Noon,1-5PM.

**Circuit Court**, PO Box 218, Rolling Fork, MS 39159. 601-873-2766 (CST) 8AM-5PM, closed 12-1. Felony, Civil Actions Over $1,000.

**Justice Court**, PO Box 218, Rolling Fork, MS 39159. 601-873-2755 (CST) Misdemeanor, Civil Actions Under $1,000, Eviction, Small Claims.

**Chancery Court**, PO Box 218, Rolling Fork, MS 39159. 601-873-2755 (CST) Probate.

## Simpson County

**Real Estate Recording**, Simpson County Clerk of the Chancery Court, 109 Pine Avenue,

Mendenhall, MS 39114. 601-847-2626 (CST) 8AM-5PM.

**Circuit Court**, PO Box 307, Mendenhall, MS 39114. 601-847-2474 (CST) 8:00AM-5:00PM. Felony, Civil Actions Over $1,000.

**Justice Court**, 159 Court Ave, Mendenhall, MS 39114. 601-847-5848 (CST) Misdemeanor, Civil Actions Under $1,000, Eviction, Small Claims.

**Chancery Court**, Chancery Building, Mendenhall, MS 39114. 601-847-2626 (CST) Probate.

## Smith County

**Real Estate Recording**, Smith County Clerk of the Chancery Court, Courthouse, Raleigh, MS 39153. 601-782-9811 (CST)

**Circuit Court**, PO Box 517, Raleigh, MS 39153. 601-782-4751 (CST) 8:00AM-5:00PM. Felony, Civil Actions Over $1,000.

**Justice Court**, PO Box 171, Raleigh, MS 39153. 601-782-4334 (CST) Misdemeanor, Civil Actions Under $1,000, Eviction, Small Claims.

**Chancery Court**, PO Box 39, Raleigh, MS 39153. 601-782-9811 (CST) Probate.

## Stone County

**Real Estate Recording**, Stone County Clerk of the Chancery Court, 323 Cavers Avenue, Wiggins, MS 39577. 601-928-5266 (CST) 8AM-5PM.

**Circuit Court**, Courthouse, 323 Cavers Ave, Wiggins, MS 39577. 601-928-5246 (CST) Felony, Civil Actions Over $1,000.

**Justice Court-West District**, 720 Project Road, Perkinston, MS 39573. 601-928-7535 (CST) Misdemeanor, Civil Actions Under $1,000, Eviction, Small Claims.

**Justice Court-East District**, 1108 E Central Ave, Wiggins, MS 39577. 601-928-3996 (CST) Misdemeanor, Civil Actions Under $1,000, Eviction, Small Claims.

**Chancery Court**, PO Drawer 7, Wiggins, MS 39577. 601-928-5266 (CST) Probate.

## Sunflower County

**Real Estate Recording**, Sunflower County Clerk of the Chancery Court, 100 Court Street, Indianola, MS 38751. 601-887-4703 (CST) 8AM-5PM.

**Circuit Court**, PO Box 576, Indianola, MS 38751. 601-887-1252 (CST) 8:00AM-5:00PM. Felony, Civil Actions Over $1,000.

**Justice Court-Southern District**, PO Box 487, Indianola, MS 38751. 601-887-6921 (CST) Misdemeanor, Civil Actions Under $1,000, Eviction, Small Claims.

**Justice Court-Northern District**, PO Box 52, Ruleville, MS 38771. 601-756-2775 (CST) Misdemeanor, Civil Actions Under $1,000, Eviction, Small Claims.

**Chancery Court**, PO Box 988, Indianola, MS 38751. 601-887-4703 (CST) Probate.

## Tallahatchie County

**Real Estate Recording**, Tallahatchie County Clerk of the Chancery Court, 1st District, Courthouse, Charleston, MS 38921. 601-647-5551 (CST) 8AM-Noon,1-5PM.

**Real Estate Recording**, Tallahatchie County Clerk of the Chancery Court, 2nd District, Main Street, Courthouse, Sumner, MS 38957. 601-375-8731 (CST)

**Charleston Circuit Court**, PO Box 86, Charleston, MS 38921. 601-647-8758 (CST) Felony, Civil Actions Over $1,000.

**Sumner Circuit Court**, PO Box 96, Sumner, MS 38957. 601-375-8515 (CST) 8:00AM-5:00PM. Misdemeanor, Civil Actions Under $1,000, Eviction, Small Claims.

**Chancery Court**, PO Drawer H, Charleston, MS 38921. 601-647-5551 (CST) Probate.

**Chancery Court**, PO Box 180, Sumner, MS 38957. 601-375-8731 (CST) Probate.

## Tate County

**Real Estate Recording**, Tate County Clerk of the Chancery Court, 201 Ward Street, Senatobia, MS 38668. 601-562-5661 (CST) 8AM-5PM.

**Circuit Court**, 201 Ward St, Senatobia, MS 38668. 601-562-5211 (CST) Felony, Civil Actions Over $1,000.

**Justice Court**, Justice Court, 201 Ward, Senatobia, MS 38668. 601-562-7626 (CST) Misdemeanor, Civil Actions Under $1,000, Eviction, Small Claims.

**Chancery Court**, 201 Ward St, Senatobia, MS 38668. 601-562-5661 (CST) Probate.

## Tippah County

**Real Estate Recording**, Tippah County Clerk of the Chancery Court, Courthouse, Ripley, MS 38663. 601-837-7374 (CST) 8AM-5PM.

**Circuit Court**, Courthouse, Ripley, MS 38663. 601-837-7370 (CST) 8:00AM-5:00PM. Felony, Civil Actions Over $1,000.

**Justice Court**, Justice Court, 205-B Spring Ave, Ripley, MS 38663. 601-837-8842 (CST) Misdemeanor, Civil Actions Under $1,000, Eviction, Small Claims.

**Chancery Court**, PO Box 99, Ripley, MS 38663. 601-837-7374 (CST) Probate.

## Tishomingo County

**Real Estate Recording**, Tishomingo County Clerk of the Chancery Court, 1008 Battleground Dr., Courthouse, Iuka, MS 38852. 601-423-7010 (CST) 8AM-5PM.

**Circuit Court**, 1008 Battleground Dr, Iuka, MS 38852. 601-423-7026 (CST) 8:00AM-5:00PM. Felony, Civil Actions Over $1,000.

**Justice Court-Northern & Southern Districts**, 1008 Battleground Drive, Iuka, MS 38852. 601-423-7033 (CST) Misdemeanor, Civil Actions Under $1,000, Eviction, Small Claims.

**Chancery Court**, 1008 Hwy 25 S, Iuka, MS 38852. 601-423-7010 (CST) Probate.

## Tunica County

**Real Estate Recording**, Tunica County Clerk of the Chancery Court, Courthouse, Tunica, MS 38676. 601-363-2451 (CST) 8AM-Noon, 1-5PM.

**Circuit Court**, PO Box 184, Tunica, MS 38676. 601-363-2842 (CST) 8AM-5PM. Felony, Civil Actions Over $1,000.

**Justice Court-Southern District**, Rt 2, Box 1950, Dundee, MS 38626. 601-363-2178 (CST) Misdemeanor, Civil Actions Under $1,000, Eviction, Small Claims.

**Justice Court-Northern District**, PO Box 876, Tunica, MS 38676. 601-363-2178 (CST) Misdemeanor, Civil Actions Under $1,000, Eviction, Small Claims.

**Chancery Court**, PO Box 217, Tunica, MS 38676. 601-363-2451 (CST) Probate.

## Union County

**Real Estate Recording**, Union County Clerk of the Chancery Court, Courthouse, New Albany, MS 38652. 601-534-1900 (CST)

**Circuit Court**, PO Box 298, New Albany, MS 38652. 601-534-1910 (CST) Felony, Civil Actions Over $1,000.

**Justice Court-East & West Posts**, PO Box 27, New Albany, MS 38652. 601-534-1951 (CST) Misdemeanor, Civil Actions Under $1,000, Eviction, Small Claims.

**Chancery Court**, PO Box 847, New Albany, MS 38652. 601-534-1900 (CST) Probate.

## Walthall County

**Real Estate Recording**, Walthall County Clerk of the Chancery Court, 200 Ball Avenue, Tylertown, MS 39667. 601-876-3553 (CST) 8AM-5PM.

**Circuit Court**, 200 Ball Ave, Tylertown, MS 39667. 601-876-5677 (CST) 8:00AM-5:00PM. Felony, Civil Actions Over $1,000.

**Justice Court-Districts 1 & 2**, PO Box 507, Tylertown, MS 39667. 601-876-2311 (CST) Misdemeanor, Civil Actions Under $1,000, Eviction, Small Claims.

**Chancery Court**, 200 Ball Ave, Tylertown, MS 39667. 601-876-3553 (CST) Probate.

## Warren County

**Real Estate Recording**, Warren County Clerk of the Chancery Court, 1009 Cherry Street, Vicksburg, MS 39180. 601-636-4415 (CST) 8AM-5PM.

**Circuit and County Court**, PO Box 351, Vicksburg, MS 39181. 601-636-3961 (CST) 8:00AM-5:00PM. Felony, Misdemeanor, Civil.

**Justice Court-Northern, Central, and Southern Districts**, PO Box 1598, Vicksburg, MS 39181. 601-634-6402 (CST) Misdemeanor, Civil Actions Under $1,000, Eviction, Small Claims.

**Chancery Court**, PO Box 351, Vicksburg, MS 39181. 601-636-4451 (CST) Probate.

## Washington County

**Real Estate Recording**, Washington County Clerk of the Chancery Court, 900 Washington Avenue, Greenville, MS 38701. 601-332-1595 (CST) 8AM-5PM.

**Circuit and County Court**, PO Box 1276, Greenville, MS 38702. 601-378-2747 (CST) Felony, Misdemeanor, Civil.

**Justice Court-Districts 1-3**, 905 W Alexander, Greenville, MS 38701. 601-332-0633 (CST) Misdemeanor, Civil Actions Under $1,000, Eviction, Small Claims.

**Chancery Court**, PO Box 309, Greenville, MS 38702. 601-332-1595 (CST) Probate.

## Wayne County

**Real Estate Recording**, Wayne County Chancery Clerk, Wayne Co. Courthouse, 609 Azalea Dr., Waynesboro, MS 39367. 601-735-2873 (CST) 8AM-5PM.

**Circuit Court**, PO Box 428, Waynesboro, MS 39367. 601-735-1171 (CST) 8:00AM-5:00PM. Felony, Civil Actions Over $1,000.

**Justice Court-Posts 1 & 2**, Courthouse, Waynesboro, MS 39367. 601-735-3118 (CST) Misdemeanor, Civil Actions Under $1,000, Eviction, Small Claims.

**Chancery Court**, Courthouse, Waynesboro, MS 39367. 601-735-2873 (CST) Probate.

## Webster County

**Real Estate Recording**, Webster County Clerk of the Chancery Court, Highway 9 North, Courthouse, Walthall, MS 39771. 601-258-4131 (CST) 8AM-5PM.

**Circuit Court**, PO Box 308, Walthall, MS 39771. 601-258-6287 (CST) 8:00AM-5:00PM. Felony, Civil Actions Over $1,000.

**Justice Court-Districts 1 & 2**, 114 Hwy 9 N, Eupora, MS 39744. 601-258-2590 (CST) Misdemeanor, Civil Actions Under $1,000, Eviction, Small Claims.

**Chancery Court**, PO Box 398, Walthall, MS 39771. 601-258-4131 (CST) Probate.

## Wilkinson County

**Real Estate Recording**, Wilkinson County Clerk of the Chancery Court, 525 Main Street, Woodville, MS 39669. 601-888-4381 (CST) 8AM-5PM.

**Circuit Court**, PO Box 327, Woodville, MS 39669. 601-888-6697 (CST) 8:00AM-5:00PM. Felony, Civil Actions Over $1,000.

**Justice Court-East & West Districts**, PO Box 40, Woodville, MS 39669. 601-888-3538 (CST) Misdemeanor, Civil Actions Under $1,000, Eviction, Small Claims.

**Chancery Court**, Box 1310, Rt 2, Woodville, MS 39669. 601-888-4381 (CST) Probate.

## Winston County

**Real Estate Recording**, Winston County Clerk of the Chancery Court, South Court Street, Louisville, MS 39339. 601-773-3631 (CST) 8AM-5PM.

**Circuit Court**, PO Drawer 785, Louisville, MS 39339. 601-773-3581 (CST) 8:00AM-5:00PM. Felony, Civil Actions Over $1,000.

**Justice Court**, PO Box 337, Louisville, MS 39339. 601-773-6016 (CST) Misdemeanor, Civil Actions Under $1,000, Eviction, Small Claims.

**Chancery Court**, PO Drawer 69, Louisville, MS 39339. 601-773-3631 (CST) Probate.

## Yalobusha County

**Real Estate Recording**, Yalobusha County Clerk of the Chancery Court, 1st District, Courthouse, Coffeeville, MS 38922. 601-675-2716 (CST) 8AM-12, 1-5PM.

**Real Estate Recording**, Yalobusha County Clerk of the Chancery Court, 2nd District, Blackmur Drive, Courthouse, Water Valley, MS 38965. 601-473-2091 (CST) 8AM-Noon,1-5PM.

**Coffeeville Circuit Court**, PO Box 260, Coffeeville, MS 38922. 601-675-8187 (CST) 8:00AM-5:00PM. Felony, Civil Actions Over $1,000.

**Water Valley Circuit Court**, PO Box 431, Water Valley, MS 38965. 601-473-1341 (CST) 8:00AM-5:00PM. Felony, Civil Actions Over $1,000.

**Justice Court-District 1**, Rt. 3, Box 237, Coffeeville, MS 38922. 601-675-8115 (CST) Misdemeanor, Civil Actions Under $1,000, Eviction, Small Claims.

**Justice Court-Division 2**, PO Box 33, Water Valley, MS 38965. 601-473-4502 (CST) Misdemeanor, Civil Actions Under $1,000, Eviction, Small Claims.

**Chancery Court**, PO Box 260, Coffeeville, MS 38922. 601-675-2716 (CST) Probate.

**Chancery Court**, PO Box 664, Water Valley, MS 38965. 601-473-2091 (CST) Probate.

## Yazoo County

**Real Estate Recording**, Yazoo County Clerk of the Chancery Court, 211 East Broadway, Yazoo City, MS 39194. 601-746-2661 (CST) 8AM-5PM.

**Circuit and County Court**, PO Box 108, Yazoo City, MS 39194. 601-746-1872 (CST) 8:00AM-5:00PM. Felony, Misdemeanor, Civil.

**Justice Court-Northern & Southern Districts**, PO Box 108, Yazoo City, MS 39194. 601-746-8181 (CST) Misdemeanor, Civil Actions Under $1,000, Eviction, Small Claims.

**Chancery Court**, PO Box 68, Yazoo City, MS 39194. 601-746-2661 (CST) Probate.

**County Records**

# Missouri

## Adair County

**Real Estate Recording**, Adair County Recorder of Deeds, Courthouse, 2nd Floor, Kirksville, MO 63501. 816-665-3890 (CST) 8:30AM-Noon, 1-4:30PM.

**Circuit Court**, PO Box 690, Kirksville, MO 63501. 816-665-2552 (CST) 8:00AM-5:00PM. Felony, Misdemeanor, Civil Actions Over $25,000, Eviction.

**Associate Circuit Court**, Courthouse, Kirksville, MO 63501. 816-665-3420 (CST) 8:00AM-5:00PM. Misdemeanor, Civil Actions Under $25,000, Eviction, Small Claims, Probate.

## Andrew County

**Real Estate Recording**, Andrew County Recorder of Deeds, Courthouse, Savannah, MO 64485. 816-324-4221 (CST) 8AM-5PM.

**Circuit Court**, PO Box 208, Savannah, MO 64485. 816-324-4221 (CST) 8:00AM-5:00PM. Felony, Misdemeanor, Civil Actions Over $25,000, Eviction.

**Associate Circuit Court**, PO Box 49, Savannah, MO 64485. 816-324-3921 (CST) 8:00AM-5:00PM. Misdemeanor, Civil Actions Under $25,000, Eviction, Small Claims, Probate.

## Atchison County

**Real Estate Recording**, Atchison County Recorder of Deeds, Courthouse, 400 Washington St., Rockport, MO 64482. 816-744-2707 (CST) 8AM-Noon, 1-4:30PM.

**Circuit Court**, Box J, Rock Port, MO 64482. 816-744-2707 (CST) 8:30AM-4:30PM. Felony, Misdemeanor, Civil Actions Over $25,000, Eviction.

**Associate Circuit Court**, PO Box 187, Rock Port, MO 64482. 816-744-2700 (CST) 8:00AM-4:30PM. Misdemeanor, Civil Actions Under $25,000, Eviction, Small Claims, Probate.

## Audrain County

**Real Estate Recording**, Audrain County Recorder of Deeds, Audrain County Courthouse, 101 N. Jefferson, Room 105, Mexico, MO 65265-2969. 314-473-5830 (CST) 8AM-5PM.

**Circuit Court**, Courthouse, 101 N Jefferson, Mexico, MO 65265. 341-473-5840 (CST) 8:00AM-5:00PM. Felony, Misdemeanor, Civil Actions Over $25,000, Eviction.

**Associate Circuit Court**, Courthouse, 101 N Jefferson, Rm 205, Mexico, MO 65265. 314-473-5850 (CST) 8:00AM-5:00PM. Misdemeanor, Civil Actions Under $25,000, Eviction, Small Claims, Probate.

## Barry County

**Real Estate Recording**, Barry County Recorder of Deeds, Courthouse, Cassville, MO 65625. 417-847-2914 (CST) 8AM-Noon,1-4PM.

**Circuit Court**, Barry County Courthouse, 700 Main, Ste1, Cassville, MO 65625. 417-847-2361 (CST) 8:00AM-4:00PM. Felony, Misdemeanor, Civil Actions Over $25,000, Eviction.

**Associate Circuit Court**, Barry County Courthouse, Cassville, MO 65625. 417-847-2127 (CST) 7:30AM-4:00PM. Misdemeanor, Civil Actions Under $25,000, Eviction, Small Claims, Probate.

## Barton County

**Real Estate Recording**, Barton County Recorder of Deeds, Courthouse, 1004 Gulf Street, Lamar, MO 64759. 417-682-2110 (CST) 8:30AM-Noon, 12:30-4:30PM.

**Circuit Court**, Courthouse, Lamar, MO 64759. 417-682-2444 (CST) 8:00AM-4:30PM. Felony, Misdemeanor, Civil Actions Over $25,000, Eviction.

**Associate Circuit Court**, Courthouse, 1004 Gulf, Lamar, MO 64759. 417-682-5754 (CST) 8:00AM-4:30PM. Misdemeanor, Civil Actions Under $25,000, Eviction, Small Claims, Probate.

## Bates County

**Real Estate Recording**, Bates County Recorder of Deeds, Courthouse, Butler, MO 64730. 816-679-3611 (CST) 8:30AM-4:30PM.

**Circuit Court**, PO Box 288, Butler, MO 64730. 816-679-5171 (CST) 8:00AM-4:30PM. Felony, Misdemeanor, Civil Actions Over $25,000, Eviction.

**Associate Circuit Court**, Courthouse, Butler, MO 64730. 816-679-3311 (CST) 8:30AM-4:00PM. Misdemeanor, Civil Actions Under $25,000, Eviction, Small Claims, Probate.

## Benton County

**Real Estate Recording**, Benton County Recorder of Deeds, Van Buren Street, Courthouse, Warsaw, MO 65355. 816-438-5732 (CST) 8:30AM-Noon, 1-4:30PM.

**Circuit Court**, PO Box 37, Warsaw, MO 65355. 816-438-7712 (CST) 8:00AM-5:00PM. Felony, Misdemeanor, Civil Actions Over $25,000, Eviction.

**Associate Circuit Court**, PO Box 666, Warsaw, MO 65355. 816-438-6231 (CST) 8:00AM-4:30PM. Misdemeanor, Civil Actions Under $25,000, Eviction, Small Claims, Probate.

## Bollinger County

**Real Estate Recording**, Bollinger County Recorder of Deeds, Courthouse, Marble Hill, MO 63764. 314-238-2710 (CST) 8AM-Noon, 1-4PM.

**Circuit Court**, PO Box 12, Marble Hill, MO 63764. 314-238-2710 (CST) 8:00AM-4:00PM. Felony, Misdemeanor, Civil Actions Over $25,000, Eviction.

**Associate Circuit Court**, PO Box 34, Marble Hill, MO 63764-0034. 314-238-2730 (CST) 8:00AM-4:00PM. Misdemeanor, Civil Actions Under $25,000, Eviction, Small Claims, Probate.

## Boone County

**Real Estate Recording**, Boone County Recorder of Deeds, 701 East Broadway, Columbia, MO 65201. 314-886-4355 (CST) 8AM-5PM.

**Circuit and Associate Circuit Courts**, 701 E Walnut, Columbia, MO 65201. 314-886-4000 (CST) 8:00AM-5:00AM. Felony, Misdemeanor, Civil, Eviction, Small Claims, Probate.

## Buchanan County

**Real Estate Recording**, Buchanan County Recorder of Deeds, 411 Jules Streets, Courthouse, St. Joseph, MO 64501-1789. 816-271-1437 (CST) 8AM-4:30PM.

**Circuit Court**, 411 Jules St, St Joseph, MO 64501. 816-271-1462 (CST) 8:00AM-5:00PM. Felony, Misdemeanor, Civil Actions Over $25,000, Eviction.

**Associate Circuit Court**, 411 Jules St, Rm 331, St Joseph, MO 64501. 816-271-1456 (CST) 8:00AM-5:00PM. Misdemeanor, Civil Actions Under $25,000, Eviction, Small Claims.

**Probate Court**, 411 Jules St, St Joseph, MO 64501. 816-271-1478 (CST) Probate.

## Butler County

**Real Estate Recording**, Butler County Recorder of Deeds, 100 N. Main Street, Courthouse, Poplar Bluff, MO 63901. 314-686-8086 (CST) 8AM-Noon,1-4PM.

**Circuit Court**, Courthouse, Poplar Bluff, MO 63901. 314-686-8082 (CST) 7:30AM-4:00PM. Felony, Misdemeanor, Civil Actions Over $25,000, Eviction.

**Associate Circuit Court**, Courthouse, Poplar Bluff, MO 63901. 314-686-8087 (CST) 7:30AM-4:00PM. Misdemeanor, Civil Actions Under $25,000, Eviction, Small Claims, Probate.

## Caldwell County

**Real Estate Recording**, Caldwell County Recorder of Deeds, Main Street, Courthouse, Kingston, MO 64650. 816-586-2581 (CST) X29 8:30AM-4:30PM.

**Circuit Court**, PO Box 86, Kingston, MO 64650. 816-586-2581 (CST) Felony, Misdemeanor, Civil Actions Over $25,000, Eviction.

**Associate Circuit Court**, PO Box 8, Kingston, MO 64650. 816-586-2771 (CST) 8:00AM-4:30MM. Misdemeanor, Civil Actions Under $25,000, Eviction, Small Claims, Probate.

## Callaway County

**Real Estate Recording**, Callaway County Recorder of Deeds, 10 East 5th Street, Fulton, MO 65251. 314-642-0787 (CST) 7:30AM-4:30PM.

**Circuit Court**, Courthouse, Fulton, MO 65251. 314-642-0780 (CST) 8:00AM-5:00PM. Felony, Misdemeanor, Civil Actions Over $25,000, Eviction.

**Associate Circuit Court**, Courthouse, Fulton, MO 65251. 314-642-0777 (CST) Misdemeanor, Civil Actions Under $25,000, Eviction, Small Claims, Probate.

## Camden County

**Real Estate Recording**, Camden County Recorder of Deeds, 1 Court Circle, Camdenton, MO 65020. 314-346-4440 (CST) 8:30AM-4:30PM.

**Circuit Court**, PO Box 930, Camdenton, MO 65020. 314-346-4440 (CST) 8:30AM-4:30PM. Felony, Misdemeanor, Civil Actions Over $25,000, Eviction.

**Associate Circuit Court-Civil Division**, PO Box 19, Camdenton, MO 65020. 314-346-4440 (CST) 8:00AM-5:00PM. Civil Actions Under $25,000, Eviction, Small Claims, Probate.

# Missouri

**Associate Circuit Court-Criminal Division**, PO Box 19, Camdenton, MO 65020. 314-346-4440 (CST) 8:00AM-5:00PM. Misdemeanor.

## Cape Girardeau County

**Real Estate Recording**, Cape Girardeau County Recorder of Deeds, #1 Barton Square, Jackson, MO 63755. 314-243-8123 (CST) 8AM-4:30PM.

**Circuit Court-Civil Division**, 44 N Lorimier, Cape Girardeau, MO 63701. 314-335-8253 (CST) 8:00AM-5:00PM. Civil Actions Over $25,000, Eviction.

**Circuit Court-Criminal Division**, Courthouse, Jackson, MO 63755. 314-243-8446 (CST) 8:00AM-4:30PM. Felony, Misdemeanor.

## Carroll County

**Real Estate Recording**, Carroll County Recorder of Deeds, 1 Main Street, Courthouse, Carrollton, MO 64633. 816-542-1466 (CST) 8:30AM-Noon, 1-4:30PM.

**Circuit Court**, PO Box 245, Carrollton, MO 64633. 816-542-1466 (CST) 8:30AM-4:30PM. Felony, Misdemeanor, Civil Actions Over $25,000, Eviction.

**Associate Circuit Court**, Courthouse, Carrollton, MO 64633. 816-542-1818 (CST) 8:30AM-4:30PM. Misdemeanor, Civil Actions Under $25,000, Eviction, Small Claims, Probate.

## Carter County

**Real Estate Recording**, Carter County Recorder of Deeds, Main Street, Van Buren, MO 63965. 314-323-4513 (CST) 8AM-4PM.

**Circuit Court**, PO Box 578, Van Buren, MO 63965. 314-323-4513 (CST) 8:00AM-4:00PM. Felony, Misdemeanor, Civil Actions Over $25,000, Eviction.

**Associate Circuit Court**, PO Box 328, Van Buren, MO 63965. 314-323-4344 (CST) 8:00AM-4:00PM. Misdemeanor, Civil Actions Under $25,000, Eviction, Small Claims, Probate.

## Cass County

**Real Estate Recording**, Cass County Recorder of Deeds, 102 East Wall Street, County Court House, Harrisonville, MO 64701. 816-380-1510 (CST) 8AM-4:30PM.

**Circuit Court**, 100 E Wall, Harrisonville, MO 64701. 816-380-5100 (CST) 8:00AM-4:30PM. Felony, Misdemeanor, Civil Actions Over $25,000, Eviction.

**Associate Circuit Court**, PO Box 384, Harrisonville, MO 64701. 816-380-1494 (CST) 8:00AM-4:30PM. Misdemeanor, Civil Actions Under $25,000, Eviction, Small Claims, Probate.

## Cedar County

**Real Estate Recording**, Cedar County Recorder of Deeds, Courthouse, Stockton, MO 65785. 417-276-3213 (CST) 8AM-Noon, 1-4PM.

**Circuit Court**, PO Box 665, Stockton, MO 65785. 417-276-3213 (CST) 8:00AM-4:00PM. Felony, Misdemeanor, Civil Actions Over $25,000, Eviction.

**Associate Circuit Court**, PO Box 156, Stockton, MO 65785. 417-276-4213 (CST) 8:00AM-4:00PM. Misdemeanor, Civil Actions Under $25,000, Eviction, Small Claims, Probate.

## Chariton County

**Real Estate Recording**, Chariton County Recorder of Deeds, Highway 24 West, Courthouse, Keytesville, MO 65261. 816-288-3602 (CST) 8:30AM-Noon, 1-4:30PM.

**Circuit Court**, PO Box 112, Keytesville, MO 65261. 816-288-3602 (CST) 8:30AM-4:30PM. Felony, Misdemeanor, Civil Actions Over $25,000, Eviction.

**Associate Circuit Court**, 306 South Cherry, Keytesville, MO 65261. 816-288-3271 (CST) 8:00AM-4:30PM. Misdemeanor, Civil Actions Under $25,000, Eviction, Small Claims, Probate.

## Christian County

**Real Estate Recording**, Christian County Recorder of Deeds, Church Street, North Side Square, Ozark, MO 65721. 417-581-6372 (CST)

**Circuit Court**, PO Box 278, Ozark, MO 65721. 417-581-6372 (CST) 8:00AM-4:00PM. Felony, Misdemeanor, Civil Actions Over $25,000, Eviction.

**Associate Circuit Court**, PO Box 175 (criminal), PO Box 296 (cvil), Ozark, MO 65721. 417-581-4524 (CST) 8:00AM-4:00PM. Misdemeanor, Civil Actions Under $25,000, Eviction, Small Claims, Probate.

## Clark County

**Real Estate Recording**, Clark County Recorder of Deeds, 111 East Court, Courthouse, Kahoka, MO 63445. 816-727-3292 (CST) 8AM-Noon, 1-4PM.

**Circuit Court**, 111 E Court, Kahoka, MO 63445. 816-727-3292 (CST) 8:00AM-4:00PM. Felony, Misdemeanor, Civil Actions Over $25,000, Eviction.

**Associate Circuit Court**, 113 W Court, Kahoka, MO 63445. 816-727-3628 (CST) 8:00AM-4:00PM. Misdemeanor, Civil Actions Under $25,000, Eviction, Small Claims, Probate.

## Clay County

**Real Estate Recording**, Clay County Recorder of Deeds, Courthouse Square, Liberty, MO 64068. 816-792-7641 (CST) 8AM-4PM.

**Circuit Court**, PO Box 218, Liberty, MO 64068. 816-792-7707 (CST) 8:00AM-5:00PM. Felony, Misdemeanor, Civil Actions Over $25,000, Eviction.

**Associate Circuit Court**, 11 S Water, Liberty, MO 64068. 816-792-7706 (CST) 8:00AM-5:00PM. Misdemeanor, Civil Actions Under $25,000, Eviction, Small Claims, Probate.

## Clinton County

**Real Estate Recording**, Clinton County Recorder of Deeds, 211 North Street, Plattsburg, MO 64477. 816-539-3893 (CST) 8:30AM-4:30PM.

**Circuit Court**, PO Box 275, Plattsburg, MO 64477. 816-539-3731 (CST) 8:30AM-4:30PM. Felony, Misdemeanor, Civil Actions Over $25,000, Eviction.

**Associate Circuit Court**, PO Box 383, Plattsburg, MO 64477. 816-539-3755 (CST) 8:00AM-4:30PM. Misdemeanor, Civil Actions Under $25,000, Eviction, Small Claims, Probate.

## Cole County

**Real Estate Recording**, Cole County Recorder of Deeds, 301 East High, Jefferson City, MO 65101. 314-634-9115 (CST) 8AM-4:30PM.

**Circuit Court**, PO Box 1156, Jefferson City, MO 65102-1156. 314-634-9151 (CST) 7:00AM-4:30PM. Felony, Misdemeanor, Civil Actions Over $25,000, Eviction.

**Associate Circuit Court**, PO Box 503, Jefferson City, MO 65102. 314-634-9171 (CST) 8:00AM-4:30PM. Misdemeanor, Civil Actions Under $25,000, Eviction, Small Claims, Probate.

## Cooper County

**Real Estate Recording**, Cooper County Recorder of Deeds, 200 Main Street, Courthouse - Room 26, Boonville, MO 65233-1276. 816-882-2232 (CST) 8:30AM-5PM.

**Circuit Court**, 200 Main St, Rm 26, Boonville, MO 65233. 816-882-2232 (CST) 8:30AM-5:00PM. Felony, Misdemeanor, Civil Actions Over $25,000, Eviction.

**Associate Circuit Court**, 200 Main, Rm 31, Boonville, MO 65233. 816-882-5604 (CST) 8:30AM-5:00PM. Misdemeanor, Civil Actions Under $25,000, Eviction, Small Claims, Probate.

## Crawford County

**Real Estate Recording**, Crawford County Recorder of Deeds, Main Street, Steelville, MO 65565. 314-775-5048 (CST) 8AM-4:30PM.

**Circuit Court**, PO Box 177, Steelville, MO 65565. 314-775-2866 (CST) 8:00AM-5:00PM. Felony, Misdemeanor, Civil Actions Over $25,000, Eviction.

**Associate Circuit Court**, Courthouse, Steelville, MO 65565. 314-775-2149 (CST) 8:00AM-5:00PM. Misdemeanor, Civil Actions Under $25,000, Eviction, Small Claims, Probate.

## Dade County

**Real Estate Recording**, Dade County Recorder of Deeds, Courthouse, Greenfield, MO 65661. 417-637-2271 (CST) 8AM-4PM.

**Circuit Court**, Courthouse, Greenfield, MO 65661. 417-637-2271 (CST) 8:00AM-4:00PM. Felony, Misdemeanor, Civil Actions Over $25,000, Eviction.

**Associate Circuit Court**, Courthouse, Greenfield, MO 65661. 417-637-2741 (CST) 8:00AM-4:00PM. Misdemeanor, Civil Actions Under $25,000, Eviction, Small Claims, Probate.

## Dallas County

**Real Estate Recording**, Dallas County Recorder of Deeds, Courthouse, Buffalo, MO 65622. 417-345-2243 (CST) 8AM-Noon, 1-4PM.

**Circuit Court**, PO Box 373, Buffalo, MO 65622. 417-345-2243 (CST) 8:00AM-4:00PM. Felony, Misdemeanor, Civil Actions Over $25,000, Eviction.

**Associate Circuit Court**, PO Box 1150, Buffalo, MO 65622. 417-345-7641 (CST) 8:00AM-4:00PM. Misdemeanor, Civil Actions Under $25,000, Eviction, Small Claims, Probate.

## Daviess County

**Real Estate Recording**, Daviess County Recorder of Deeds, Courthouse, 2nd Floor, Gallatin,

MO 64640. 816-663-2932 (CST) 8AM-Noon, 1-4:30PM.

**Circuit Court**, PO Box 337, Gallatin, MO 64640. 816-663-2932 (CST) 8:00AM-4:30PM. Felony, Misdemeanor, Civil Actions Over $25,000, Eviction.

**Associate Circuit Court**, Courthouse, Gallatin, MO 64640. 816-663-2532 (CST) 8:00AM-4:30PM. Misdemeanor, Civil Actions Under $25,000, Eviction, Small Claims, Probate.

## De Kalb County

**Real Estate Recording**, De Kalb County Recorder of Deeds, Main Street & Highway 33, Courthouse, Maysville, MO 64469. 816-449-2602 (CST) 8:30AM-Noon, 1-4:30PM.

**Circuit Court**, Courthouse, Maysville, MO 64469. 816-449-2602 (CST) 8:30AM-4:30PM. Felony, Misdemeanor, Civil Actions Over $25,000, Eviction.

**Associate Circuit Court**, PO Box 512, Maysville, MO 64469. 816-449-5400 (CST) 8:30AM-4:30PM. Misdemeanor, Civil Actions Under $25,000, Eviction, Small Claims, Probate.

## Dent County

**Real Estate Recording**, Dent County Recorder of Deeds, 112 East 5th Street, Salem, MO 65560-1444. 314-729-3931 (CST) 8AM-4:30PM.

**Circuit Court**, 112 E 5th St, Salem, MO 65560. 314-729-3931 (CST) 8:00AM-4:30PM. Felony, Misdemeanor, Civil Actions Over $25,000, Eviction.

**Associate Circuit Court**, 112 E 5th St, Salem, MO 65560. 314-729-3134 (CST) 8:00AM-4:30PM. Misdemeanor, Civil Actions Under $25,000, Eviction, Small Claims, Probate.

## Douglas County

**Real Estate Recording**, Douglas County Recorder of Deeds, 203 Southeast 2nd Street, Ava, MO 65608. 417-683-4713 (CST) 8AM-12, 1-5PM.

**Circuit Court**, PO Box 655, Ava, MO 65608. 417-683-4713 (CST) 8:00AM-5:00PM. Felony, Misdemeanor, Civil Actions Over $25,000, Eviction.

**Associate Circuit Court**, PO Box 276, Ava, MO 65608. 417-683-2114 (CST) Misdemeanor, Civil Actions Under $25,000, Eviction, Small Claims, Probate.

## Dunklin County

**Real Estate Recording**, Dunklin County Recorder of Deeds, Courthouse Square, Room 204, Kennett, MO 63857. 314-888-3468 (CST) 8:30AM-Noon, 1-4:30PM.

**Circuit Court**, PO Box 567, Kennett, MO 63857. 314-888-2456 (CST) 8:30AM-4:30PM. Felony, Misdemeanor, Civil Actions Over $25,000, Eviction.

**Associate Circuit Court**, Courthouse Rm 103, Kennett, MO 63857. 314-888-3378 (CST) 8:30AM-4:30PM. Misdemeanor, Civil Actions Under $25,000, Eviction, Small Claims, Probate.

## Franklin County

**Real Estate Recording**, Franklin County Recorder of Deeds, 300 East Main St., Room 101, Union, MO 63084. 314-583-6367 (CST) 8AM-4:30PM.

**Circuit Court**, PO Box 272, Union, MO 63084. 314-583-6300 (CST) 8:00AM-4:30PM. Felony, Misdemeanor, Civil Actions Over $25,000, Eviction.

**Associate Circuit Court**, PO Box 526, Union, MO 63084. 314-583-6326 (CST) 8:00AM-4:30PM. Misdemeanor, Civil Actions Under $25,000, Eviction, Small Claims, Probate.

## Gasconade County

**Real Estate Recording**, Gasconade County Recorder of Deeds, 119 E.1st St., Room 6, Hermann, MO 65041-1182. 314-486-2632 (CST) 8AM-4:30PM.

**Circuit Court**, 119 E 1st St, Rm 6, Hermann, MO 65041. 314-486-2632 (CST) 8:00AM-4:30PM. Felony, Misdemeanor, Civil Actions Over $25,000, Eviction.

**Associate Circuit Court**, PO Box 228, Hermann, MO 65041. 314-486-2321 (CST) 8:00AM-4:30PM. Misdemeanor, Civil Actions Under $25,000, Eviction, Small Claims, Probate.

## Gentry County

**Real Estate Recording**, Gentry County Recorder of Deeds, Courthouse, Albany, MO 64402. 816-726-3618 (CST) 9AM-4:30PM.

**Circuit Court**, PO Box 27, Albany, MO 64402. 816-726-3618 (CST) 9:00AM-4:30PM. Felony, Misdemeanor, Civil Actions Over $25,000, Eviction.

**Associate Circuit Court**, Courthouse, Albany, MO 64402. 816-726-3411 (CST) 8:00AM-4:30PM. Misdemeanor, Civil Actions Under $25,000, Eviction, Small Claims, Probate.

## Greene County

**Real Estate Recording**, Greene County Recorder of Deeds, 940 Boonville, Springfield, MO 65802. 417-868-4068 (CST) 8AM-4:30PM.

**Circuit Court**, 940 Boonville, Springfield, MO 65802. 417-868-4674 (CST) 7:30AM-5:30AM. Felony, Misdemeanor, Civil Actions Over $25,000, Eviction.

**Associate Circuit Court**, 940 Boonville, Springfield, MO 65802. 417-868-4110 (CST) 7:30AM-5:30PM. Misdemeanor, Civil Actions Under $25,000, Eviction, Small Claims, Probate.

## Grundy County

**Real Estate Recording**, Grundy County Recorder of Deeds, Courthouse, Trenton, MO 64683. 816-359-6605 (CST) 8:30AM-Noon, 1-4:30PM.

**Circuit Court**, Courthouse, Trenton, MO 64683. 816-359-6605 (CST) 8:30AM-4:30PM. Felony, Misdemeanor, Civil Actions Over $25,000, Eviction.

**Associate Circuit Court**, Courthouse, Trenton, MO 64683. 816-359-6606 (CST) 8:30AM-4:30PM. Misdemeanor, Civil Actions Under $25,000, Eviction, Small Claims, Probate.

## Harrison County

**Real Estate Recording**, Harrison County Recorder of Deeds, 1515 Main Street, Courthouse, Bethany, MO 64424. 816-425-6425 (CST) 8AM-Noon, 1-4:30PM.

**Circuit Court**, PO Box 525, Bethany, MO 64424. 816-425-6425 (CST) 8:00AM-4:30PM. Felony, Misdemeanor, Civil Actions Over $25,000, Eviction.

**Associate Circuit Court**, Box 525, Bethany, MO 64424. 816-425-6432 (CST) 9:00AM-4:00PM. Misdemeanor, Civil Actions Under $25,000, Eviction, Small Claims, Probate.

## Henry County

**Real Estate Recording**, Henry County Recorder of Deeds, 100 W. Franklin #4, Courthouse, Clinton, MO 64735. 816-885-6963 (CST) 8:30AM-4:30PM.

**Circuit Court**, 100 W Franklin, Rm 12, Clinton, MO 64735. 816-885-6963 (CST) 8:00AM-4:30PM. Felony, Misdemeanor, Civil Actions Over $25,000, Eviction.

**Associate Circuit Court**, Courthouse, Clinton, MO 64735. 816-885-6963 (CST) 8:00AM-4:30PM. Misdemeanor, Civil Actions Under $25,000, Eviction, Small Claims, Probate.

## Hickory County

**Real Estate Recording**, Hickory County Recorder of Deeds, Courthouse, On the Square, Hermitage, MO 65668. 417-745-6421 (CST) 8AM-Noon, 12:30-4:30PM.

**Circuit Court**, PO Box 101, Hermitage, MO 65668. 417-745-6421 (CST) 8:00AM-4:30PM. Felony, Misdemeanor, Civil Actions Over $25,000, Eviction.

**Associate Circuit Court**, PO Box 75, Hermitage, MO 65668. 417-745-6822 (CST) 8:00AM-4:30PM. Misdemeanor, Civil Actions Under $25,000, Eviction, Small Claims, Probate.

## Holt County

**Real Estate Recording**, Holt County Recorder of Deeds, 100 West Nodaway, Courthouse, Oregon, MO 64473. 816-446-3301 (CST) 8:30AM-Noon, 1-4:30PM.

**Circuit Court**, Courthouse, Oregon, MO 64473. 816-446-3301 (CST) 8:30AM-4:30PM. Felony, Misdemeanor, Civil Actions Over $25,000, Eviction.

**Associate Circuit Court**, PO Box 173, Oregon, MO 64473. 816-446-3380 (CST) 8:30AM-4:30PM. Misdemeanor, Civil Actions Under $25,000, Eviction, Small Claims, Probate.

## Howard County

**Real Estate Recording**, Howard County Recorder of Deeds, 1 Courthouse Square, Fayette, MO 65248. 816-248-2194 (CST) 8:30AM-4:30PM.

**Circuit Court**, Courthouse, Fayette, MO 65248. 816-248-2194 (CST) 8:30AM-4:30PM. Felony, Misdemeanor, Civil Actions Over $25,000, Eviction.

**Associate Circuit Court**, PO Box 370, Fayette, MO 65248. 816-248-3326 (CST) 8:30AM-4:30PM. Misdemeanor, Civil Actions Under $25,000, Eviction, Small Claims, Probate.

## Howell County

**Real Estate Recording**, Howell County Recorder of Deeds, Courthouse, West Plains, MO 65775. 417-256-3750 (CST) 8AM-5PM.

**Circuit Court**, PO Box 1011, West Plains, MO 65775. 417-256-3741 (CST) 8:00AM-5:00PM.

# Missouri

Felony, Misdemeanor, Civil Actions Over $25,000, Eviction.

**Associate Circuit Court**, Courthouse, Rm 222, West Plains, MO 65775. 417-256-4050 (CST) 8:00AM-4:30PM. Misdemeanor, Civil Actions Under $25,000, Eviction, Small Claims, Probate.

## Iron County

**Real Estate Recording**, Iron County Recorder of Deeds, 250 South Main, Ironton, MO 63650. 314-546-2811 (CST) 8AM-12:30PM, 1PM-4PM M-Th; 8AM-Noon, 1-4PM F.

**Circuit Court**, PO Box 24, Ironton, MO 63650. 314-546-2811 (CST) 8:00AM-4:00PM. Felony, Misdemeanor, Civil Actions Over $25,000, Eviction.

**Associate Circuit Court**, PO Box 325, Ironton, MO 63650. 314-546-2511 (CST) 9:00AM-4:00PM. Misdemeanor, Civil Actions Under $25,000, Eviction, Small Claims, Probate.

## Jackson County

**Real Estate Recording**, Jackson County Recorder of Deeds, 415 East 12th Street, Room 104, Kansas City, MO 64106. 816-881-3197 (CST) 8AM-5PM.

**Independence Circuit Court-Civil Annex**, 308 W Kansas, Independence, MO 64050. 816-881-4497 (CST) Civil, Eviction, Small Claims, Probate.

**Circuit Court-Civil Division**, 415 E 12th, Kansas City, MO 64106. 816-881-3926 (CST) 8:00AM-4:30PM. Civil, Eviction, Small Claims, Probate.

**Circuit Court-Criminal Division**, 1315 Locust, Kansas City, MO 64106. 816-881-4350 (CST) 8:00AM-5:00PM. Felony, Misdemeanor.

## Jasper County

**Real Estate Recording**, Jasper County Recorder of Deeds, 3rd & Main, Room 207, Carthage, MO 64836. 417-358-0432 (CST) 8:30AM-4:30PM.

**Circuit Court**, Courthouse, Rm 303, Carthage, MO 64836. 417-358-0441 (CST) 8:00AM-5:00PM. Felony, Misdemeanor, Civil Actions Over $25,000, Eviction.

**Associate Circuit Court**, Courthouse, Carthage, MO 64836. 417-358-0450 (CST) 8:30AM-4:30PM. Misdemeanor, Civil Actions Under $25,000, Eviction, Small Claims, Probate.

## Jefferson County

**Real Estate Recording**, Jefferson County Recorder of Deeds, 2nd & Maple, Courthouse, Hillsboro, MO 63050. 314-789-5499 (CST) 8:30AM-4:30PM.

**Circuit Court**, PO Box 100, Hillsboro, MO 63050. 314-789-5370 (CST) 8AM-4:30PM. Felony, Misdemeanor.

**Associate Circuit Court**, PO Box 100, Hillsboro, MO 63050. 314-789-5443 (CST) 8:00AM-4:30PM. Civil Actions Under $25,000, Eviction, Small Claims, Probate.

**Associate Circuit Court**, PO Box 100, Hillsboro, MO 63050. 314-789-5365 (CST) 8:00AM-4:30PM. Eviction, Small Claims, Probate.

## Johnson County

**Real Estate Recording**, Johnson County Recorder of Deeds, North Holden Street, Courthouse, Warrensburg, MO 64093. 816-747-6811 (CST) 8:30AM-4:30PM.

**Circuit Court**, Courthouse, PO Box 436, Warrensburg, MO 64093. 316-747-6331 (CST) Felony, Misdemeanor, Civil Actions Over $25,000, Eviction.

**Associate Circuit Court**, Courthouse, Warrensburg, MO 64093. 816-747-2227 (CST) 8:00AM-4:30PM. Misdemeanor, Civil Actions Under $25,000, Eviction, Small Claims, Probate.

## Knox County

**Real Estate Recording**, Knox County Recorder of Deeds, Courthouse, Edina, MO 63537. 816-397-2305 (CST) 8:30AM-4PM.

**Circuit Court**, PO Box 116, Edina, MO 63537. 816-397-2305 (CST) Felony, Misdemeanor, Civil Actions Over $25,000, Eviction.

**Associate Circuit Court**, PO Box 126, Edina, MO 63537. 816-397-3146 (CST) 8:30AM-4:00PM. Misdemeanor, Civil Actions Under $25,000, Eviction, Small Claims, Probate.

## Laclede County

**Real Estate Recording**, Laclede County Recorder of Deeds, 204 North Adams, Room 105, Courthouse, Lebanon, MO 65536-3046. 417-532-4011 (CST) 8AM-4PM.

**Circuit Court**, 204 N Adams St, Lebanon, MO 65536. 417-532-2471 (CST) 8:00AM-4:00PM. Felony, Misdemeanor, Civil Actions Over $25,000, Eviction.

**Associate Circuit Court**, 250 N Adams St, Lebanon, MO 65536. 417-532-9196 (CST) Misdemeanor, Civil Actions Under $25,000, Eviction, Small Claims, Probate.

## Lafayette County

**Real Estate Recording**, Lafayette County Recorder of Deeds, 11th & Main, Lexington, MO 64067. 816-259-6178 (CST) 8:30AM-4:30PM.

**Circuit Court**, PO Box 340, Lexington, MO 64067. 816-259-6101 (CST) 8:00AM-5:00PM. Felony, Misdemeanor, Civil Actions Over $25,000, Eviction.

**Associate Circuit Court**, PO Box 236, Lexington, MO 64067. 816-259-6151 (CST) 8:00AM-4:30PM. Misdemeanor, Civil Actions Under $25,000, Eviction, Small Claims, Probate.

## Lawrence County

**Real Estate Recording**, Lawrence County Recorder of Deeds, Courthouse on the Square, Mount Vernon, MO 65712. 417-466-2670 (CST) 9AM-Noon, 1-5PM.

**Circuit Court**, PO Box 488, Mt Vernon, MO 65712. 417-466-2471 (CST) 8:00AM-5:00PM. Felony, Misdemeanor, Civil Actions Over $25,000, Eviction.

**Associate Circuit Court**, PO Box 390, Mt Vernon, MO 65712. 417-466-2463 (CST) 8:30AM-5:00PM. Misdemeanor, Civil Actions Under $25,000, Eviction, Small Claims, Probate.

## Lewis County

**Real Estate Recording**, Lewis County Recorder of Deeds, Courthouse, Monticello, MO 63457. 314-767-5440 (CST) 8AM-Noon, 1-4PM.

**Circuit Court**, PO Box 97, Monticello, MO 63457. 314-767-5440 (CST) Felony, Misdemeanor, Civil Actions Over $25,000, Eviction.

**Associate Circuit Court**, PO Box 36, Monticello, MO 63457. 314-767-5352 (CST) 8:00AM-4:30PM. Misdemeanor, Civil Actions Under $25,000, Eviction, Small Claims, Probate.

## Lincoln County

**Real Estate Recording**, Lincoln County Recorder of Deeds, 201 Main Street, Troy, MO 63379. 314-528-7122 (CST) 8AM-4:30PM.

**Circuit Court**, 201 Main St, Troy, MO 63379. 314-528-4418 (CST) 8:00AM-4:30PM. Felony, Misdemeanor, Civil Actions Over $25,000, Eviction.

**Associate Circuit Court**, 201 Main St, Troy, MO 63379. 314-528-4521 (CST) 8:00AM-4:30PM. Misdemeanor, Civil Actions Under $25,000, Eviction, Small Claims, Probate.

## Linn County

**Real Estate Recording**, Linn County Recorder of Deeds, Courthouse, Linneus, MO 64653. 816-895-5216 (CST) 9AM-Noon, 1-4:30PM.

**Brookfield Circuit Court**, 309 1/2 N Main, Brookfield, MO 64628. 816-258-7062 (CST) 8:00AM-4:30PM. Felony, Misdemeanor, Civil Actions Over $25,000, Eviction.

**Linneus Circuit Court**, PO Box 142, Linneus, MO 64653. 816-895-5212 (CST) 9:00AM-1:00PM. Felony, Misdemeanor, Civil Actions Over $25,000, Eviction.

**Associate Circuit Court**, Box 93, Linneus, MO 64653. 816-895-5419 (CST) 8:30AM-4:00PM. Misdemeanor, Civil Actions Under $25,000, Eviction, Small Claims, Probate.

## Livingston County

**Real Estate Recording**, Livingston County Recorder of Deeds, Courthouse, Suite 6, 700 Webster St., Chillicothe, MO 64601. 816-646-0166 (CST) 8:30AM-Noon, 1-4:30PM.

**Circuit Court**, 700 Webster St, Chillicothe, MO 64601. 816-646-1718 (CST) 8:30AM-4:30PM. Felony, Misdemeanor, Civil Actions Over $25,000, Eviction.

**Associate Circuit Court**, Courthouse, Chillicothe, MO 64601. 816-646-3103 (CST) 8:30AM-4:30PM. Misdemeanor, Civil Actions Under $25,000, Eviction, Small Claims, Probate.

## Macon County

**Real Estate Recording**, Macon County Recorder of Deeds, Washington & Rollins Streets, Macon, MO 63552. 816-385-2732 (CST) 8:30AM-4PM.

**Circuit Court**, PO Box 382, Macon, MO 63552. 816-385-4631 (CST) 8:30AM-4:00PM. Felony, Misdemeanor, Civil Actions Over $25,000, Eviction.

**Associate Circuit Court**, PO Box 491, Macon, MO 63552. 816-385-3531 (CST) 8:00AM-4:30PM. Misdemeanor, Civil Actions Under $25,000, Eviction, Small Claims, Probate.

## Madison County

**Real Estate Recording**, Madison County Recorder of Deeds, Courthouse, Courtsquare, Fredericktown, MO 63645. 314-783-2102 (CST) 8AM-5PM.

**Circuit Court**, PO Box 5, Fredericktown, MO 63645. 314-783-2102 (CST) 8:00AM-5:00PM. Felony, Misdemeanor, Civil Actions Over $25,000, Eviction.

**Associate Circuit Court**, PO Box 521, Fredericktown, MO 63645. 314-783-3105 (CST) 8:00AM-5:00PM. Misdemeanor, Civil Actions Under $25,000, Eviction, Small Claims, Probate.

## Maries County

**Real Estate Recording**, Maries County Recorder of Deeds, 4th & Main, Courthouse, Vienna, MO 65582. 314-422-3338 (CST) 8AM-4PM.

**Circuit Court**, PO Box 213, Vienna, MO 65582. 314-422-3338 (CST) 8:00AM-4:00PM. Felony, Misdemeanor, Civil Actions Over $25,000, Eviction.

**Associate Circuit Court**, PO Box 140, Vienna, MO 65582. 314-422-3303 (CST) 8:00AM-4:00PM. Misdemeanor, Civil Actions Under $25,000, Eviction, Small Claims, Probate.

## Marion County

**Real Estate Recording**, Marion County Recorder of Deeds, 100 South Main, Palmyra, MO 63461. 314-769-2550 (CST) 8AM-5PM.

**Circuit Court (Twps of Miller and Mason only)**, 906 Broadway, Rm 6, Hannibal, MO 63401. 314-221-0198 (CST) 8:00AM-5:00PM. Felony, Misdemeanor, Civil Actions Over $25,000, Eviction.

**Circuit Court**, 100 S Main, Palmyra, MO 63461. 314-769-2550 (CST) 8:00AM-5:00PM. Felony, Misdemeanor, Civil Actions Over $25,000, Eviction.

**Hannibal Associate Circuit Court**, 906 Broadway, Hannibal, MO 63401. 314-221-0288 (CST) 8:00AM-5:00PM. Misdemeanor, Civil Actions Under $25,000, Eviction, Small Claims, Probate.

**Palmyra Associate Circuit Court**, 100 S Main, Palmyra, MO 63461. 314-769-2318 (CST) 8:00AM-5:00PM. Misdemeanor, Civil Actions Under $25,000, Eviction, Small Claims, Probate.

## McDonald County

**Real Estate Recording**, McDonald County Recorder of Deeds, Highway W, Courthouse, Pineville, MO 64856. 417-223-4123 (CST) 8AM-4PM.

**Circuit Court**, PO Box 157, Pineville, MO 64856. 417-223-4729 (CST) 8:00AM-4:30PM. Felony, Misdemeanor, Civil Actions Over $25,000, Eviction.

**Associate Circuit Court**, PO Box 674, Pineville, MO 64856. 417-223-4467 (CST) 8:00AM-4:30PM. Misdemeanor, Civil Actions Under $25,000, Eviction, Small Claims, Probate.

## Mercer County

**Real Estate Recording**, Mercer County Recorder of Deeds, Courthouse, Princeton, MO 64673. 816-748-4335 (CST) 8:30AM-Noon, 1-4:30PM.

**Circuit Court**, Courthouse, Princeton, MO 64673. 816-748-4335 (CST) 8:30AM-4:30PM. Felony, Misdemeanor, Civil Actions Over $25,000, Eviction.

**Associate Circuit Court**, Courthouse, Princeton, MO 64673. 816-748-4232 (CST) 8:30AM-4:30PM. Misdemeanor, Civil Actions Under $25,000, Eviction, Small Claims, Probate.

## Miller County

**Real Estate Recording**, Miller County Recorder of Deeds, Main Street, Courthouse, Tuscumbia, MO 65082. 314-369-2911 (CST) 8AM-4:30PM.

**Circuit Court**, PO Box 11, Tuscumbia, MO 65082. 314-369-2303 (CST) 8:0AM-4:30PM. Felony, Misdemeanor, Civil Actions Over $25,000, Eviction.

**Charleston Associate Circuit Court**, PO Box 369, Charleston, MO 63834. 314-683-6228 (CST) 8:00AM-5:00PM. Misdemeanor, Civil Actions Under $25,000, Eviction, Small Claims, Probate.

**Tuscumbia Associate Circuit Court**, Miller County Courthouse Annex, Tuscumbia, MO 65082. 314-369-2330 (CST) 8:00AM-4:00PM. Misdemeanor, Civil Actions Under $25,000, Eviction, Small Claims, Probate.

## Mississippi County

**Real Estate Recording**, Mississippi County Recorder of Deeds, North Main Street, Courthouse, Charleston, MO 63834. 314-683-2104 (CST) 8:30AM-4:30PM.

**Circuit Court**, PO Box 369, Charleston, MO 63834. 314-683-2104 (CST) 8:30AM-4:30PM. Felony, Misdemeanor, Civil Actions Over $25,000, Eviction.

**Associate Circuit Court**, PO Box 369, Charleston, MO 63834. 314-683-6228 (CST) 8:00AM-4:30PM. Misdemeanor, Civil Actions Under $25,000, Eviction, Small Claims, Probate.

## Moniteau County

**Real Estate Recording**, Moniteau County Recorder of Deeds, 200 East Main Street, California, MO 65018. 314-796-2071 (CST) 8AM-4:30PM.

**Circuit Court**, 200 E Main, California, MO 65018. 314-796-2071 (CST) 8:00AM-4:30PM. Felony, Misdemeanor, Civil Actions Over $25,000, Eviction.

**Associate Circuit Court**, 200 E Main, California, MO 65018. 314-796-2814 (CST) 8AM-4:30PM. Misdemeanor, Civil Actions Under $25,000, Eviction, Small Claims, Probate.

## Monroe County

**Real Estate Recording**, Monroe County Recorder of Deeds, 300 Main Street, Courthouse, Paris, MO 65275. 816-327-5204 (CST) 8AM-4:30PM.

**Circuit Court**, PO Box 227, Paris, MO 65275. 816-327-5204 (CST) 8:00AM-4:30PM. Felony, Misdemeanor, Civil Actions Over $25,000, Eviction.

**Associate Circuit Court**, County Courthouse, 300 N Main, Paris, MO 65275. 816-327-5220 (CST) 8:00AM-4:30PM. Misdemeanor, Civil Actions Under $25,000, Eviction, Small Claims, Probate.

## Montgomery County

**Real Estate Recording**, Montgomery County Recorder of Deeds, 211 East 3rd Street, Montgomery City, MO 63361. 314-564-3157 (CST) 8AM-4:30PM.

**Circuit Court**, 211 E 3rd, Montgomery City, MO 63361. 314-564-3341 (CST) 8:00AM-4:30PM. Felony, Misdemeanor, Civil Actions Over $25,000, Eviction.

**Associate Circuit Court**, County Courthouse, Montgomery City, MO 63361. 314-564-3348 (CST) 8:00AM-4:30PM. Misdemeanor, Civil Actions Under $25,000, Eviction, Small Claims, Probate.

## Morgan County

**Real Estate Recording**, Morgan County Recorder of Deeds, 100 Newton Street, Courthouse, Versailles, MO 65084. 314-378-4029 (CST) 8:30AM-Noon, 1-4:30PM.

**Circuit Court**, 100 E Newton, Versailles, MO 65084. 314-378-4413 (CST) 8:30AM-4:30PM. Felony, Misdemeanor, Civil Actions Over $25,000, Eviction.

**Associate Circuit Court**, 102 N Monroe, Versailles, MO 65084. 314-378-4235 (CST) 8:30AM-5:00PM. Misdemeanor, Civil Actions Under $25,000, Eviction, Small Claims, Probate.

## New Madrid County

**Real Estate Recording**, New Madrid County Recorder of Deeds, 450 Main Street, New Madrid, MO 63869. 314-748-5146 (CST) 8AM-12, 1-4:30PM.

**Circuit Court**, County Courthouse, New Madrid, MO 63869. 314-748-2228 (CST) 8:00AM-5:00PM. Felony, Misdemeanor, Civil Actions Over $25,000, Eviction.

**Associate Circuit Court**, County Courthouse, New Madrid, MO 63869. 314-748-5556 (CST) 8AM-5PM. Misdemeanor, Civil Actions Under $25,000, Eviction, Small Claims, Probate.

## Newton County

**Real Estate Recording**, Newton County Recorder of Deeds, Wood & Main Streets, Neosho, MO 64850. 417-451-8224 (CST) 8:30AM-5PM.

**Circuit Court**, PO Box 130, Neosho, MO 64850. 417-451-8257 (CST) 8:30AM-5:00PM. Felony, Misdemeanor, Civil Actions Over $25,000, Eviction.

**Associate Circuit Court**, PO Box 170, Neosho, MO 64850. 417-451-8212 (CST) 8:00AM-5:00PM. Misdemeanor, Civil Actions Under $25,000, Eviction, Small Claims, Probate.

## Nodaway County

**Real Estate Recording**, Nodaway County Recorder of Deeds, Courthouse Square, Maryville, MO 64468. 816-582-5711 (CST) 8:30AM-Noon, 1-4:30PM.

**Circuit Court**, PO Box 218, Maryville, MO 64468. 816-582-5431 (CST) 8:00AM-4:30PM. Felony, Misdemeanor, Civil Actions Over $25,000, Eviction.

**Associate Circuit Court**, Courthouse Annex, 303 N Market, Maryville, MO 64468. 816-582-2531 (CST) 8:00AM-4:30PM. Misdemeanor, Civil Actions Under $25,000, Eviction, Small Claims, Probate.

## Oregon County

**Real Estate Recording**, Oregon County Recorder of Deeds, Courthouse, Alton, MO 65606. 417-778-7460 (CST) 8AM-4PM.

**Circuit Court**, PO Box 406, Alton, MO 65606. 417-778-7460 (CST) 8:00AM-5:00PM. Felony, Misdemeanor, Civil Actions Over $25,000, Eviction.

**Associate Circuit Court**, PO Box 211, Alton, MO 65606. 417-778-7461 (CST) 8:00AM-4:00PM. Misdemeanor, Civil Actions Under $25,000, Eviction, Small Claims, Probate.

## Osage County

**Real Estate Recording**, Osage County Recorder of Deeds, Main Street, Courthouse, Linn, MO 65051. 314-897-3114 (CST) 8AM-4:30PM.

**Circuit Court**, PO Box 825, Linn, MO 65051. 314-897-3114 (CST) 8:00AM-4:30PM. Felony, Misdemeanor, Civil Actions Over $25,000, Eviction.

**Associate Circuit Court**, PO Box 470, Linn, MO 65051. 314-897-2136 (CST) 8AM-4:30PM. Misdemeanor, Civil Actions Under $25,000, Eviction, Small Claims, Probate.

## Ozark County

**Real Estate Recording**, Ozark County Recorder of Deeds, Courthouse, Gainesville, MO 65655. 417-679-4232 (CST) 8AM-Noon,1-5PM.

**Circuit Court**, PO Box 36, Gainesville, MO 65655. 417-679-4232 (CST) 8AM-4:30PM. Felony, Misdemeanor, Civil Actions Over $25,000, Eviction.

**Associate Circuit Court**, PO Box 278, Gainesville, MO 65655. 417-679-4611 (CST) 8AM-4:30PM. Misdemeanor, Civil Actions Under $25,000, Eviction, Small Claims, Probate.

## Pemiscot County

**Real Estate Recording**, Pemiscot County Recorder of Deeds, Courthouse, Caruthersville, MO 63830. 314-333-2204 (CST) 8:30AM-4:30PM.

**Circuit Court**, County Courthouse, Caruthersville, MO 63830. 314-333-0182 (CST) 7:30AM-4:30PM. Felony, Misdemeanor, Civil Actions Over $25,000, Eviction.

**Associate Circuit Court**, County Courthouse, Caruthersville, MO 63830. 314-333-2784 (CST) 7:30AM-4:30PM. Misdemeanor, Civil Actions Under $25,000, Eviction, Small Claims, Probate.

## Perry County

**Real Estate Recording**, Perry County Recorder of Deeds, 15 West Ste. Marie Street, Suite 1, Perryville, MO 63775. 314-547-1611 (CST)

**Circuit Court**, 15 W Saint Maries St, Suite 6, Perryville, MO 63775-1399. 314-547-6581 (CST) 8:00AM-5:00PM. Felony, Misdemeanor, Civil Actions Over $25,000, Eviction.

**Associate Circuit Court**, 15 W Saint Maries, Suite 3, Perryville, MO 63775-1399. 314-547-7861 (CST) 8:00AM-5:00PM. Misdemeanor, Civil Actions Under $25,000, Eviction, Small Claims, Probate.

## Pettis County

**Real Estate Recording**, Pettis County Recorder of Deeds, 415 South Ohio, Sedalia, MO 65301. 816-826-1136 (CST) 9AM-4:30PM.

**Circuit Court**, PO Box 804, Sedalia, MO 65302-0804. 816-826-0617 (CST) 8:00AM-5:00PM. Felony, Misdemeanor, Civil Actions Over $25,000, Eviction.

**Associate Circuit Court**, 415 S Ohio, Sedalia, MO 65301. 816-826-4699 (CST) 8:30AM-5:00PM. Misdemeanor, Civil Actions Under $25,000, Eviction, Small Claims.

**Probate Court**, 415 S. Ohio, Sedalia, MO 65301. 816-826-0368 (CST) Probate.

## Phelps County

**Real Estate Recording**, Phelps County Recorder of Deeds, Courthouse, 200 N. Main, Rolla, MO 65401. 314-364-1891 (CST) 7:30AM-5PM.

**Circuit Court**, 3rd and Roll Sts, Rolla, MO 65401. 314-364-1891 (CST) 8AM-4:30PM. Felony, Misdemeanor, Civil Actions Over $25,000, Eviction.

**Associate Circuit Court**, 200 N Main, Rolla, MO 65401. 314-364-1891 (CST) 8AM-4:30PM. Misdemeanor, Civil Actions Under $25,000, Eviction, Small Claims.

**Probate Court**, PO Box 1550, Rolla, MO 65401. 314-364-1891 (CST) Probate.

## Pike County

**Real Estate Recording**, Pike County Recorder of Deeds, 115 West Main Street, Bowling Green, MO 63334. 314-324-5567 (CST) 9AM-12:30, 1-4:30PM.

**Circuit Court**, 115 W Main, Bowling Green, MO 63334. 314-324-3112 (CST) 8:00AM-4:30PM. Felony, Misdemeanor, Civil Actions Over $25,000, Eviction.

**Associate Circuit Court**, 115 W Main, Bowling Green, MO 63334. 314-324-5582 (CST) 8:00AM-4:30PM. Misdemeanor, Civil Actions Under $25,000, Eviction, Small Claims, Probate.

## Platte County

**Real Estate Recording**, Platte County Recorder of Deeds, 409 Third Street, Platte City, MO 64079. 816-858-3323 (CST) 8AM-5PM.

**Circuit Court**, 328 Main St, Box 5CH, Platte City, MO 64079. 816-848-2232 (CST) 8:00AM-5:00PM. Felony, Misdemeanor, Civil Actions Over $25,000, Eviction.

**Associate Circuit Court**, 328 Main St, Box 5CH, Platte City, MO 64079. 816-858-2232 (CST) 8:00AM-5:00PM. Misdemeanor, Civil Actions Under $25,000, Eviction, Small Claims.

**Probate Court**, 328 Main St, Box 95CH, Platte City, MO 64079. 816-431-2232 (CST) Probate.

## Polk County

**Real Estate Recording**, Polk County Recorder of Deeds, 102 E. Broadway, Courthouse, Bolivar, MO 65613-1502. 417-326-4924 (CST) 8AM-5PM.

**Circuit Court**, 102 E Broadway, Rm 14, Bolivar, MO 65613. 417-326-4912 (CST) Felony, Misdemeanor, Civil Actions Over $25,000, Eviction.

**Associate Circuit Court**, Courthouse, Rm 7, Bolivar, MO 65613. 417-326-4921 (CST) 8:00AM-5:00PM. Misdemeanor, Civil Actions Under $25,000, Eviction, Small Claims, Probate.

## Pulaski County

**Real Estate Recording**, Pulaski County Recorder of Deeds, 301 US Highway 44E, Courthouse Suite 202, Waynesville, MO 65583. 314-774-6609 (CST) 8AM-4:30PM.

**Circuit & Associate Circuit Court**, 301 US Hwy 44, Suite 202, Waynesville, MO 65583. 314-774-6609 (CST) 8:00AM-4:30PM. Felony, Misdemeanor, Civil, Eviction, Small Claims.

**Probate Court**, 301 US Hwy 44, Suite 202, Waynesville, MO 65583. 314-774-6609 (CST) Probate.

## Putnam County

**Real Estate Recording**, Putnam County Recorder of Deeds, Courthouse - Room 202, Unionville, MO 63565-1659. 816-947-2071 (CST) 9AM-Noon,1-5PM.

**Circuit Court**, Courthouse Rm 202, Unionville, MO 63565. 816-947-2071 (CST) 9:00AM-5:00PM. Felony, Misdemeanor, Civil Actions Over $25,000, Eviction.

**Associate Circuit Court**, Courthouse Rm 101, Unionville, MO 63565. 816-947-2117 (CST) 9:00AM-5:00PM. Misdemeanor, Civil Actions Under $25,000, Eviction, Small Claims, Probate.

## Ralls County

**Real Estate Recording**, Ralls County Recorder of Deeds, Main Street, Courthouse, New London, MO 63459. 314-985-5631 (CST) 8:30AM-Noon, 1-4:30PM.

**Circuit Court**, PO Box 444, New London, MO 63459. 314-985-5631 (CST) 8:30AM-4:30PM. Felony, Misdemeanor, Civil Actions Over $25,000, Eviction.

**Associate Circuit Court**, PO Box 466, New London, MO 63459. 314-985-5641 (CST) 8:30AM-4:30PM. Misdemeanor, Civil Actions Under $25,000, Eviction, Small Claims, Probate.

## Randolph County

**Real Estate Recording**, Randolph County Recorder of Deeds, 110 S. Main St., Courthouse, Huntsville, MO 65259. 816-277-4718 (CST) 8AM-4PM.

**Circuit Court**, 223 N Williams, Moberly, MO 65270. 816-263-4474 (CST) 8:00AM-4:30PM. Felony, Misdemeanor, Civil Actions Over $25,000, Eviction.

**Associate Circuit Court**, 223 N Williams, Moberly, MO 65270. 816-263-4450 (CST) 8:00AM-4:30PM. Misdemeanor, Civil Actions Under $25,000, Eviction, Small Claims, Probate.

## Ray County

**Real Estate Recording**, Ray County Recorder of Deeds, Main Street, Courthouse, Richmond, MO 64085. 816-776-2400 (CST)

**Circuit Court**, PO Box 594, Richmond, MO 64085. 816-776-3377 (CST) 8:00AM-4:00PM. Felony, Misdemeanor, Civil Actions Over $25,000, Eviction.

**Associate Circuit Court**, Courthouse, Richmond, MO 64085. 816-776-2335 (CST)

8:00AM-4:00PM. Misdemeanor, Civil Actions Under $25,000, Eviction, Small Claims, Probate.

## Reynolds County

**Real Estate Recording**, Reynolds County Recorder of Deeds, Courthouse, Centerville, MO 63633. 314-648-2494 (CST) 8AM-4PM.

**Circuit Court**, PO Box 76, Centerville, MO 63633. 314-648-2494 (CST) Felony, Misdemeanor, Civil Actions Over $25,000, Eviction.

**Associate Circuit Court**, PO Box 39, Centerville, MO 63633. 314-648-2494 (CST) Misdemeanor, Civil Actions Under $25,000, Eviction, Small Claims, Probate.

## Ripley County

**Real Estate Recording**, Ripley County Recorder of Deeds, 100 Courthouse Square, Suite 3, Doniphan, MO 63935. 314-996-2818 (CST) 8AM-4PM.

**Circuit Court**, Courthouse, Doniphan, MO 63935. 314-996-2818 (CST) 8:00AM-4:00PM. Felony, Misdemeanor, Civil Actions Over $25,000, Eviction.

**Associate Circuit Court**, 100 Court Sq, Courthouse, Doniphan, MO 63935. 314-996-2013 (CST) 8:00AM-4:00PM. Misdemeanor, Civil Actions Under $25,000, Eviction, Small Claims, Probate.

## Saline County

**Real Estate Recording**, Saline County Recorder of Deeds, Courthouse, Room 206, Marshall, MO 65340. 816-886-2677 (CST) 8:30AM-Noon, 1-5PM.

**Circuit Court**, PO Box 597, Marshall, MO 65340. 816-886-2300 (CST) 8:00AM-5:00PM. Felony, Misdemeanor, Civil Actions Over $25,000, Eviction.

**Associate Circuit Court**, PO Box 751, Marshall, MO 65340. 816-886-6988 (CST) 8:00AM-5:00PM. Misdemeanor, Civil Actions Under $25,000, Eviction, Small Claims, Probate.

## Schuyler County

**Real Estate Recording**, Schuyler County Recorder of Deeds, Courthouse, Highway 136 East, Lancaster, MO 63548. 816-457-3784 (CST) 9AM-Noon,1-4PM.

**Circuit Court**, PO Box 186, Lancaster, MO 63548. 816-457-3784 (CST) 9:00AM-4:00PM. Felony, Misdemeanor, Civil Actions Over $25,000, Eviction.

**Associate Circuit Court**, Box 158, Lancaster, MO 63548. 816-457-3755 (CST) Misdemeanor, Civil Actions Under $25,000, Eviction, Small Claims, Probate.

## Scotland County

**Real Estate Recording**, Scotland County Recorder of Deeds, Courthouse, Memphis, MO 63555. 816-465-8605 (CST) 9AM-Noon,1-4PM.

**Circuit Court**, Courthouse, Rm 106, Memphis, MO 63555. 816-465-8605 (CST) 9:00AM-4:00PM. Felony, Misdemeanor, Civil Actions Over $25,000, Eviction.

**Associate Circuit Court**, Courthouse, Rm 102, Memphis, MO 63555. 816-465-2404 (CST) Misdemeanor, Civil Actions Under $25,000, Eviction, Small Claims, Probate.

## Scott County

**Real Estate Recording**, Scott County Recorder of Deeds, Courthouse, Benton, MO 63736. 314-545-3551 (CST) 8:30AM-5PM.

**Circuit Court**, PO Box 277, Benton, MO 63736. 314-545-3596 (CST) 8:30AM-5:00PM. Felony, Misdemeanor, Civil Actions Over $25,000, Eviction.

**Associate Circuit Court**, PO Box 249, Benton, MO 63736. 314-545-3576 (CST) 8:30AM-5:00PM. Misdemeanor, Civil Actions Under $25,000, Eviction, Small Claims, Probate.

## Shannon County

**Real Estate Recording**, Shannon County Recorder of Deeds, Courthouse, Eminence, MO 65466. 314-226-3315 (CST) 8AM-Noon, 12:30-4:30PM.

**Circuit Court**, PO Box 148, Eminence, MO 65466. 314-226-3315 (CST) 8:00AM-4:30PM. Felony, Misdemeanor, Civil Actions Over $25,000, Eviction.

**Associate Circuit Court**, PO Box AB, Eminence, MO 65466. 314-226-5515 (CST) 8:00AM-4:30PM. Misdemeanor, Civil Actions Under $25,000, Eviction, Small Claims, Probate.

## Shelby County

**Real Estate Recording**, Shelby County Recorder of Deeds, Courthouse, Shelbyville, MO 63469. 314-633-2151 (CST) 8AM-4:30PM.

**Circuit Court**, PO Box 176, Shelbyville, MO 63469. 314-633-2151 (CST) 8:00AM-4:30PM. Felony, Misdemeanor, Civil Actions Over $25,000, Eviction.

**Associate Circuit Court**, PO Box 206, Shelbyville, MO 63469. 314-633-2251 (CST) 8:00AM-4:00PM. Misdemeanor, Civil Actions Under $25,000, Eviction, Small Claims, Probate.

## St. Charles County

**Real Estate Recording**, St. Charles County Recorder of Deeds, 201 North 2nd, Room 338, St. Charles, MO 63301. 314-949-7505 (CST) 8:30AM-5PM.

**Circuit Court**, 300 N 2nd St, St. Charles, MO 63301. 314-949-3080 (CST) 8:30AM-5:00PM. Felony, Misdemeanor, Civil Actions Over $25,000, Eviction.

**Associate Circuit Court**, 100 N 3rd, St Charles, MO 63301. 314-949-3080 (CST) 8:30AM-5:00PM. Misdemeanor, Civil Actions Under $25,000, Eviction, Small Claims, Probate.

## St. Clair County

**Real Estate Recording**, St. Clair County Recorder of Deeds, Courthouse, Osceola, MO 64776. 417-646-2226 (CST) 8AM-4:30PM.

**Circuit & Associate Circuit Court**, PO Box 334, Osceola, MO 64776. 417-646-2226 (CST) 8:00AM-4:30PM. Felony, Misdemeanor, Civil, Eviction, Small Claims, Probate.

## St. Francois County

**Real Estate Recording**, St. Francois County Recorder of Deeds, Courthouse, Farmington, MO 63640. 314-756-2323 (CST) 8AM-4PM.

**Circuit Court**, County Courthouse, 3rd Fl, Farmington, MO 63640. 314-756-4551 (CST) Felony, Misdemeanor, Civil Actions Over $25,000, Eviction.

**Associate Circuit Court**, County Courthouse, 2nd Fl, Farmington, MO 63640. 314-756-5755 (CST) 8:00AM-5:00PM. Misdemeanor, Civil Actions Under $25,000, Eviction, Small Claims, Probate.

## St. Louis City

**Real Estate Recording**, St. Louis City Recorder, Tucker & Market Streets, City Hall Room 126, St. Louis, MO 63103. 314-622-4328 (CST) 9AM-5PM.

**Circuit & Associate Circuit Courts**, 10 N Tucker, Civil Courts Bldg, St Louis, MO 63101. 314-622-4367 (CST) 8:00AM-5:00PM. Civil, Eviction, Small Claims, Probate.

**City of St Louis Circuit Court**, 1320 Market, St Louis, MO 63103. 314-622-4582 (CST) 8:00AM-5:00PM. Felony, Misdemeanor.

## St. Louis County

**Real Estate Recording**, St. Louis County Recorder of Deeds, 41 S. Central Avenue, Clayton, MO 63105. 314-889-2185 (CST) 8AM-5PM.

**Circuit Court**, 7900 Carondolet, Clayton, MO 63105. 314-889-3029 (CST) 8AM-5PM. Felony, Misdemeanor, Civil Actions Over $25,000, Eviction.

**Associate Circuit Court-Civil Division**, 7900 Carondolet, Clayton, MO 63105. 314-889-3090 (CST) 8:00AM-5:00PM. Civil Actions Under $25,000, Eviction, Small Claims, Probate.

**Associate Circuit Court-Criminal Division**, 7900 Carondolet, Clayton, MO 63105. 314-889-2675 (CST) Misdemeanor.

## Ste. Genevieve County

**Real Estate Recording**, Ste. Genevieve County Recorder of Deeds, 3rd Street, Court House, Ste. Genevieve, MO 63670. 314-883-2706 (CST) 8AM-4:30PM.

**Circuit Court**, 55 S 3rd, Rm 23, Ste Genevieve, MO 63670. 317-883-2705 (CST) 8:00AM-5:00PM. Felony, Misdemeanor, Civil Actions Over $25,000, Eviction.

**Associate Circuit Court**, 3rd and Market, Ste Genevieve, MO 63670. 314-883-2265 (CST) 8AM-5PM. Misdemeanor, Civil Actions Under $25,000, Eviction, Small Claims, Probate.

## Stoddard County

**Real Estate Recording**, Stoddard County Recorder of Deeds, Courthouse Square, Prairie St., Bloomfield, MO 63825. 314-568-3444 (CST) 8:30AM-4:30PM.

**Circuit Court**, PO Box 30, Bloomfield, MO 63825. 314-568-4640 (CST) 8:30AM-4:30PM. Felony, Misdemeanor, Civil Actions Over $25,000, Eviction.

**Associate Circuit Court**, PO Box 218, Bloomfield, MO 63825. 314-568-4671 (CST) 8:30AM-4:30PM. Misdemeanor, Civil Actions Under $25,000, Eviction, Small Claims, Probate.

## Stone County

**Real Estate Recording**, Stone County Recorder of Deeds, Courthouse Square, Galena, MO 65656. 417-357-6362 (CST) 8AM-4PM.

# Missouri

Circuit Court, PO Box 18, Galena, MO 65656. 417-357-6114 (CST) Felony, Misdemeanor, Civil Actions Over $25,000, Eviction.

Associate Circuit Court, PO Box 186, Galena, MO 65656. 417-357-6511 (CST) 7:30AM-4:00PM. Misdemeanor, Civil Actions Under $25,000, Eviction, Small Claims, Probate.

## Sullivan County

Real Estate Recording, Sullivan County Recorder of Deeds, Courthouse, Milan, MO 63556. 816-265-3630 (CST) 9AM-Noon, 1-4:30PM.

Circuit Court, Courthouse, Milan, MO 63556-1358. 816-265-4717 (CST) 9:00AM-4:30PM. Felony, Misdemeanor, Civil Actions Over $25,000, Eviction.

Associate Circuit Court, Courthouse, Milan, MO 63556. 816-265-3303 (CST) 9:00AM-4:30PM. Misdemeanor, Civil Actions Under $25,000, Eviction, Small Claims, Probate.

## Taney County

Real Estate Recording, Taney County Recorder of Deeds, Main & David, Courthouse, Forsyth, MO 65653. 417-546-6131 (CST) 8AM-5PM.

Circuit Court, PO Box 335, Forsyth, MO 65653. 417-546-6132 (CST) 8:00AM-5:00PM. Felony, Misdemeanor, Civil Actions Over $25,000, Eviction.

Associate Circuit Court, PO Box 129, Forsyth, MO 65653. 417-546-4716 (CST) 8:00AM-5:00PM. Misdemeanor, Civil Actions Under $25,000, Eviction, Small Claims, Probate.

## Texas County

Real Estate Recording, Texas County Recorder of Deeds, 210 North Grand, Houston, MO 65483. 417-967-3742 (CST) 8AM-5PM.

Circuit Court, 210 N Grand, Houston, MO 65483. 417-967-3742 (CST) 8:00AM-5:00PM. Felony, Misdemeanor, Civil Actions Over $25,000, Eviction.

Associate Circuit Court, County Courthouse, Houston, MO 65483. 417-967-3663 (CST) 8:00AM-5:00PM. Misdemeanor, Civil Actions Under $25,000, Eviction, Small Claims, Probate.

## Vernon County

Real Estate Recording, Vernon County Recorder of Deeds, Courthouse, Nevada, MO 64772. 417-448-2520 (CST) 8:30AM-Noon, 1-4:30PM.

Circuit Court, Courthouse, 3rd Fl, Nevada, MO 64772. 417-448-2525 (CST) 8:30AM-4:30PM. Felony, Misdemeanor, Civil Actions Over $25,000, Eviction.

Associate Circuit Court, County Courthouse, Rm 9, Nevada, MO 64772. 417-448-2550 (CST) Misdemeanor, Civil Actions Under $25,000, Eviction, Small Claims, Probate.

## Warren County

Real Estate Recording, Warren County Recorder of Deeds, 104 West Boone's Lick Rd., Warrenton, MO 63383. 314-456-3363 (CST) 8AM-4:30PM.

Circuit Court, 104 W Main, Warrenton, MO 63383. 314-456-3363 (CST) 8:00AM-4:30PM. Felony, Misdemeanor, Civil Actions Over $25,000, Eviction.

Associate Circuit Court, County Courthouse, Rm 102, Warrenton, MO 63383. 314-456-3375 (CST) 8:30AM-4:30PM. Misdemeanor, Civil Actions Under $25,000, Eviction, Small Claims, Probate.

## Washington County

Real Estate Recording, Washington County Recorder of Deeds, 102 North Missouri Street, Potosi, MO 63664. 314-438-4171 (CST) 8AM-5PM.

Circuit Court, PO Box 216, Potosi, MO 63664. 314-438-4171 (CST) 8:00AM-5:00PM. Felony, Misdemeanor, Civil Actions Over $25,000, Eviction.

Associate Circuit Court, 102 N Missouri St, Potosi, MO 63664. 314-438-3691 (CST) 8:00AM-5:00PM. Misdemeanor, Civil Actions Under $25,000, Eviction, Small Claims, Probate.

## Wayne County

Real Estate Recording, Wayne County Recorder of Deeds, Main Street, Courthouse, Greenville, MO 63944. 314-224-3221 (CST) 8:30AM-Noon, 1-4:30PM.

Circuit Court, PO Box 187A, Greenville, MO 63944. 314-224-3221 (CST) 8:30AM-4:30PM. Felony, Misdemeanor, Civil Actions Over $25,000, Eviction.

Associate Circuit Court, PO Box 188, Greenville, MO 63944. 314-224-3221 (CST) 8:30AM-4:30PM. Misdemeanor, Civil Actions Under $25,000, Eviction, Small Claims, Probate.

## Webster County

Real Estate Recording, Webster County Recorder of Deeds, Courthouse, Marshfield, MO 65706. 417-468-2173 (CST) 8AM-4PM.

Circuit Court, PO Box 529, Marshfield, MO 65706. 417-859-2006 (CST) 8:00AM-4:00PM. Felony, Misdemeanor, Civil Actions Over $25,000, Eviction.

Associate Circuit Court, Courthouse, Marshfield, MO 65706. 417-859-2041 (CST) 8:00AM-4:30PM. Misdemeanor, Civil Actions Under $25,000, Eviction, Small Claims, Probate.

## Worth County

Real Estate Recording, Worth County Recorder of Deeds, Courthouse on the Square, Grant City, MO 64456. 816-564-2210 (CST) 8:30AM-Noon, 1-4:30PM.

Circuit Court, PO Box H, Grant City, MO 64456. 816-564-2210 (CST) 8:30AM-4:30PM. Felony, Misdemeanor, Civil Actions Over $25,000, Eviction.

Associate Circuit Court, PO Box 428, Grant City, MO 64456. 816-564-2152 (CST) 9:00AM-4:30PM. Misdemeanor, Civil Actions Under $25,000, Eviction, Small Claims, Probate.

## Wright County

Real Estate Recording, Wright County Recorder of Deeds, Courthouse, Hartville, MO 65667. 417-741-7322 (CST) 8AM-4:30PM.

Circuit Court, PO Box 39, Hartville, MO 65667. 417-741-7121 (CST) Felony, Misdemeanor, Civil Actions Over $25,000, Eviction.

Associate Circuit Court, PO Box 58, Hartville, MO 65667. 417-741-6450 (CST) 8:00AM-4:30PM. Misdemeanor, Civil Actions Under $25,000, Eviction, Small Claims, Probate.

# Montana

## Beaverhead County

**Real Estate Recording**, Beaverhead County Clerk and Recorder, 2 South Pacific, Dillon, MT 59725-2799. 406-683-2642 (MST) 8AM-5PM.

**District Court**, 2 S Pacific St, Dillon, MT 59725. 406-683-5831 (MST) 8AM-5PM. Felony, Civil Actions Over $5,000, Eviction, Probate.

**Dillon Justice Court**, 2 S Pacific, Cluster #16, Dillon, MT 59725. 406-683-2383 (MST) Misdemeanor, Civil Actions Under $5,000, Eviction, Small Claims.

**Lima Justice Court**, PO Box 107, Lima, MT 59739. 406-276-3205 (MST) 4PM-6PM. Misdemeanor, Civil Actions Under $5,000, Eviction, Small Claims.

## Big Horn County

**Real Estate Recording**, Big Horn County Clerk and Recorder, 121 West 3rd Street, Hardin, MT 59034. 406-665-1506 (MST) 8AM-5PM.

**District Court**, PO Box Drawer H, Hardin, MT 59034. 406-665-1504 (MST) Felony, Civil Actions Over $5,000, Eviction, Probate.

**Justice Court**, PO Box Drawer H, Hardin, MT 59034. 406-665-2275 (MST) 8AM-5PM. Misdemeanor, Civil Actions Under $5,000, Eviction, Small Claims.

## Blaine County

**Real Estate Recording**, Blaine County Clerk and Recorder, 400 Ohio Street, Chinook, MT 59523. 406-357-3240 (MST) 8AM-5PM.

**District Court**, PO Box 969, Chinook, MT 59523. 406-357-3230 (MST) 8AM-5PM. Felony, Civil Actions Over $5,000, Eviction, Probate.

**Chinook Justice Court**, PO Box 1266, Chinook, MT 59523. 406-357-2335 (MST) 8AM-Noon. Misdemeanor, Civil Actions Under $5,000, Eviction, Small Claims.

**Harlem Justice Court**, PO Box 354, Harlem, MT 59526. 406-353-4971 (MST) 8AM-Noon. Misdemeanor, Civil Actions Under $5,000, Eviction, Small Claims.

## Broadwater County

**Real Estate Recording**, Broadwater County Clerk and Recorder, 515 Broadway, Townsend, MT 59644. 406-266-3443 (MST) 8AM-5PM.

**District Court**, 515 Broadway, Townsend, MT 59644. 406-266-3418 (MST) 8AM-5PM, Closed 12-1. Felony, Civil Actions Over $5,000, Eviction, Probate.

**Justice Court**, 515 Broadway, Townsend, MT 59644. 406-266-3145 (MST) 8AM-5PM. Misdemeanor, Civil Actions Under $5,000, Eviction, Small Claims.

## Carbon County

**Real Estate Recording**, Carbon County Clerk and Recorder, Courthouse, Red Lodge, MT 59068. 406-446-1220 (MST) 8AM-5PM.

**District Court**, PO Box 948, Red Lodge, MT 59068. 406-446-1225 (MST) 8AM-5PM. Felony, Civil Actions Over $5,000, Eviction, Probate.

**Boyd Justice Court**, PO Box 102, Boyd, MT 59013. 406-962-3567 (MST) 9AM-2PM M-W. Misdemeanor, Civil Actions Under $5,000, Eviction, Small Claims.

**Red Lodge Justice Court**, Box 2, Red Lodge, MT 59068. 406-446-1440 (MST) 8AM-5PM. Misdemeanor, Civil Actions Under $5,000, Eviction, Small Claims.

## Carter County

**Real Estate Recording**, Carter County Clerk and Recorder, Courthouse, 101 Park Street, Ekalaka, MT 59324. 406-775-8749 (MST) 8AM-5PM.

**District Court**, PO Box 322, Ekalaka Route, Ekalaka, MT 59324. 406-775-8714 (MST) 8AM-5PM. Felony, Civil Actions Over $5,000, Eviction, Probate.

**Justice Court**, HC 50 Box 10, Alzada, MT 59311. 406-775-8749 (MST) 1PM-5PM 1&3rd Th. Misdemeanor, Civil Actions Under $5,000, Eviction, Small Claims.

## Cascade County

**Real Estate Recording**, Cascade County Clerk and Recorder, 415 2nd Ave North, Great Falls, MT 59401. 406-454-6800 (MST) 8AM-5PM.

**District Court**, County Courthouse, Great Falls, MT 59403. 406-454-6780 (MST) 8AM-5PM. Felony, Civil Actions Over $5,000, Eviction, Probate.

**Justice Court**, County Courthouse, Great Falls, MT 59401. 406-454-6780 (MST) Misdemeanor, Civil Actions Under $5,000, Eviction, Small Claims.

## Chouteau County

**Real Estate Recording**, Chouteau County Clerk and Recorder, 1308 Franklin, Fort Benton, MT 59442. 406-622-5151 (MST) 8AM-5PM.

**District Court**, PO Box 459, Ft Benton, MT 59442. 406-622-5024 (MST) 8AM-5PM. Felony, Civil Actions Over $5,000, Eviction, Probate.

**Big Sandy Justice Court**, PO Box 234, Big Sandy, MT 59520. 406-378-2297 (MST) 1PM-5PM Th. Misdemeanor, Civil Actions Under $5,000, Eviction, Small Claims.

**Ft Benton Justice Court**, PO Box 459, Ft Benton, MT 59442. 406-622-5502 (MST) 8AM-5PM M,W; 8AM-4PM, 7:30PM-9PM T. Misdemeanor, Civil Actions Under $5,000, Eviction, Small Claims.

## Custer County

**Real Estate Recording**, Custer County Clerk and Recorder, 1010 Main Street, Miles City, MT 59301-1010. 406-232-7800 (MST) 8AM-5PM.

**District Court**, 1010 Main, Miles City, MT 59301-3418. 406-232-7800 (MST) 8AM-5PM. Felony, Civil Actions Over $5,000, Eviction, Probate.

**Justice Court**, 1010 Main St, Miles City, MT 59301-3418. 406-232-7800 (MST) 8AM-5PM, Closed 12-1. Misdemeanor, Civil Actions Under $5,000, Eviction, Small Claims.

## Daniels County

**Real Estate Recording**, Daniels County Clerk and Recorder, 213 Main Street, Scobey, MT 59263. 406-487-5561 (MST) 8AM-5PM.

**District Court**, PO Box 67, Scobey, MT 59263. 406-487-2651 (MST) 8AM-5PM. Felony, Civil Actions Over $5,000, Eviction, Probate.

**Justice Court**, PO Box 838, Scobey, MT 59263. 406-487-5432 (MST) 8AM-5PM. Misdemeanor, Civil Actions Under $5,000, Eviction, Small Claims.

## Dawson County

**Real Estate Recording**, Dawson County Clerk and Recorder, 207 West Bell, Glendive, MT 59330. 406-365-3058 (MST) 8AM-5PM.

**District Court**, 207 W Bell, Glendive, MT 59330. 406-365-3967 (MST) 8AM-5PM. Felony, Civil Actions Over $5,000, Eviction, Probate.

**Justice Court**, 207 W Bell, Glendive, MT 59330. 406-365-5425 (MST) 8AM-5PM. Misdemeanor, Civil Actions Under $5,000, Eviction, Small Claims.

## Deer Lodge County

**Real Estate Recording**, Deer Lodge County Clerk and Recorder, 800 South Main St., Courthouse, Anaconda, MT 59711-2999. 406-563-8421 (MST) 8AM-5PM.

**District Court**, 800 S Main, Anaconda, MT 59711. 406-563-8421 (MST) 8AM-5PM. Felony, Civil Actions Over $5,000, Eviction, Probate.

**Justice Court**, 800 S Main, Anaconda, MT 59711. 406-563-8421 (MST) 8AM-5PM. Misdemeanor, Civil Actions Under $5,000, Eviction, Small Claims.

## Fallon County

**Real Estate Recording**, Fallon County Clerk and Recorder, 10 West Fallon Avenue, Baker, MT 59313. 406-778-2883 (MST) X42 8AM-5PM.

**District Court**, PO Box 1521, Baker, MT 59313. 406-778-2883 (MST) 8AM-5PM. Felony, Civil Actions Over $5,000, Eviction, Probate.

**Justice Court**, Box 846, Baker, MT 59313. 406-778-2883 (MST) 11:30AM-4:30PM M-W. Misdemeanor, Civil Actions Under $5,000, Eviction, Small Claims.

## Fergus County

**Real Estate Recording**, Fergus County Clerk and Recorder, 712 West Main, Lewistown, MT 59457. 406-538-5242 (MST) 8AM-5PM.

**District Court**, PO Box 1074, Lewistown, MT 59457. 406-538-5026 (MST) 8AM-5PM. Felony, Civil Actions Over $5,000, Eviction, Probate.

**Justice Court**, 121 8th Ave S, Lewistown, MT 59457. 406-538-5418 (MST) 9AM-5PM. Misdemeanor, Civil Actions Under $5,000, Eviction, Small Claims.

## Flathead County

**Real Estate Recording**, Flathead County Clerk and Recorder, 800 South Main, Courthouse, Kalispell, MT 59901-5400. 406-758-5532 (MST) 8AM-5PM.

**District Court**, 800 S Main, Kalispell, MT 59901. 406-758-5660 (MST) 8AM-5PM. Felony, Civil Actions Over $5,000, Eviction, Probate.

**Justice Court**, 800 S Main St, Kalispell, MT 59901. 406-758-5660 (MST) 8AM-5PM. Misdemeanor, Civil Actions Under $5,000, Eviction, Small Claims.

# Montana

## Gallatin County

**Real Estate Recording**, Gallatin County Clerk and Recorder, 311 West Main, Room 204, Bozeman, MT 59715. 406-585-1430 (MST) 8AM-5PM.

**District Court**, 615 S 16th, Rm 200, Bozeman, MT 59715. 406-585-1360 (MST) Felony, Civil Actions Over $5,000, Eviction, Probate.

**Belgrade Justice and City Court**, 88 N Broadway, Belgrade, MT 59714. 406-388-4262 (MST) 8AM-5PM. Misdemeanor, Civil Actions Under $5,000, Eviction, Small Claims.

**Bozeman Justice Court**, 615 S 16th St, Bozeman, MT 59715. 406-585-1370 (MST) Misdemeanor, Civil Actions Under $5,000, Eviction, Small Claims.

## Garfield County

**Real Estate Recording**, Garfield County Clerk and Recorder, Courthouse, Jordan, MT 59337. 406-557-2760 (MST) 8AM-5PM.

**District Court**, PO Box 8, Jordan, MT 59337. 406-557-6254 (MST) 8AM-5PM. Felony, Civil Actions Over $5,000, Eviction, Probate.

**Justice Court**, PO Box 317, Jordan, MT 59337. 406-557-2733 (MST) 8AM-5PM W. Misdemeanor, Civil Actions Under $5,000, Eviction, Small Claims.

## Glacier County

**Real Estate Recording**, Glacier County Clerk and Recorder, 512 East Main, Cut Bank, MT 59427. 406-873-5063 (MST) 8AM-5PM.

**District Court**, 512 E Main St, Cut Bank, MT 59427. 406-873-5063 (MST) 8AM-5PM. Felony, Civil Actions Over $5,000, Eviction, Probate.

**Justice Court**, 512 E Main St, Cut Bank, MT 59427. 406-873-5063 (MST) 8AM-5PM, Closed 12-1. Misdemeanor, Civil Actions Under $5,000, Eviction, Small Claims.

## Golden Valley County

**Real Estate Recording**, Golden Valley County Clerk and Recorder, 107 Kemp, Ryegate, MT 59074. 406-568-2231 (MST) 8AM-5PM.

**District Court**, PO Box 10, Ryegate, MT 59074. 406-568-2231 (MST) 8AM-5PM. Felony, Civil Actions Over $5,000, Eviction, Probate.

**Justice Court**, PO Box 10, Ryegate, MT 59074. 406-568-2231 (MST) 8AM-5PM. Misdemeanor, Civil Actions Under $5,000, Eviction, Small Claims.

## Granite County

**Real Estate Recording**, Granite County Clerk and Recorder, 220 North Sansome, Philipsburg, MT 59858. 406-859-3771 (MST) 8AM-Noon,1-5PM.

**District Court**, PO Box J, Philipsburg, MT 59858. 406-859-3712 (MST) 8AM-5PM, Closed 12-1. Felony, Civil Actions Over $5,000, Eviction, Probate.

**Drummond Justice Court**, PO Box 159, Drummond, MT 59832. 406-288-3446 (MST) 10AM-4PM. Misdemeanor, Civil Actions Under $5,000, Eviction, Small Claims.

**Philipsburg Justice Court**, PO Box 356, Philipsburg, MT 59858. 406-859-3712 (MST) 11AM-5PM MWF, Closed 12-1. Misdemeanor, Civil Actions Under $5,000, Eviction, Small Claims.

## Hill County

**Real Estate Recording**, Hill County Clerk and Recorder, 315 4th Street, Courthouse, Havre, MT 59501. 406-265-5481 (MST) 8AM-5PM.

**District Court**, County Courthouse, Havre, MT 59501. 406-265-5481 (MST) 8AM-5PM. Felony, Civil Actions Over $5,000, Eviction, Probate.

**Justice Court**, County Courthouse, Havre, MT 59501. 406-265-5481 (MST) 8AM-5PM. Misdemeanor, Civil Actions Under $5,000, Eviction, Small Claims.

## Jefferson County

**Real Estate Recording**, Jefferson County Clerk and Recorder, Corner Centennial & Washington, Boulder, MT 59632. 406-225-4251 (MST) 8AM-5PM.

**District Court**, PO Box H, Boulder, MT 59632. 406-225-4251 (MST) 8AM-5PM, Closed 12-1. Felony, Civil Actions Over $5,000, Eviction, Probate.

**Justice Court**, PO Box H, Boulder, MT 59632. 406-225-4251 (MST) 8AM-5PM. Misdemeanor, Civil Actions Under $5,000, Eviction, Small Claims.

## Judith Basin County

**Real Estate Recording**, Judith Basin County Clerk and Recorder, Courthouse, Stanford, MT 59479. 406-566-2301 (MST) 8AM-5PM.

**District Court**, PO Box 307, Stanford, MT 59479. 406-566-2491 (MST) 8AM-5PM. Felony, Civil Actions Over $5,000, Eviction, Probate.

**Hobson Justice Court**, PO Box 276, Hobson, MT 59452. 406-423-5503 (MST) 4PM-9PM. Misdemeanor, Civil Actions Under $5,000, Eviction, Small Claims.

**Stanford Justice Court**, PO Box 339, Stanford, MT 59479. 406-566-2711 (MST) 9AM-Noon MWF. Misdemeanor, Civil Actions Under $5,000, Eviction, Small Claims.

## Lake County

**Real Estate Recording**, Lake County Clerk and Recorder, 106 4th Avenue East, Polson, MT 59860. 406-883-7208 (MST) 8AM-5PM.

**District Court**, 106 4th Ave E, Polson, MT 59860. 406-883-7254 (MST) 8AM-5PM. Felony, Civil Actions Over $5,000, Eviction, Probate.

**Justice Court**, 106 4th Ave E, Polson, MT 59860. 406-883-7258 (MST) 8AM-5PM. Misdemeanor, Civil Actions Under $5,000, Eviction, Small Claims.

## Lewis and Clark County

**Real Estate Recording**, Lewis and Clark County Clerk and Recorder, 316 North Park Avenue, Helena, MT 59601. 406-447-8337 (MST) 8AM-5PM.

**District Court**, 228 Broadway, Helena, MT 59601. 406-443-1010 (MST) Felony, Civil Actions Over $5,000, Eviction, Probate.

**Justice Court**, 228 Broadway, Helena, MT 59601. 406-447-8202 (MST) 8AM-4PM, Closed 12-1. Misdemeanor, Civil Actions Under $5,000, Eviction, Small Claims.

## Liberty County

**Real Estate Recording**, Liberty County Clerk and Recorder, 101 First Street East, Chester, MT 59522. 406-759-5365 (MST) 8AM-5PM.

**District Court**, PO Box 549, Chester, MT 59522. 406-759-5615 (MST) 8AM-5PM. Felony, Civil Actions Over $5,000, Eviction, Probate.

**Justice Court**, PO Box 170, Chester, MT 59522. 406-759-5172 (MST) 9AM-5PM T. Misdemeanor, Civil Actions Under $5,000, Eviction, Small Claims.

## Lincoln County

**Real Estate Recording**, Lincoln County Clerk and Recorder, 512 California Avenue, Libby, MT 59923. 406-293-7781 (MST) 8AM-5PM.

**District Court**, 512 California Ave, Libby, MT 59923. 406-293-7781 (MST) 8AM-5PM. Felony, Civil Actions Over $5,000, Eviction, Probate.

**Eureka Justice Court #2**, PO Box 403, Eureka, MT 59917. 406-296-2622 (MST) 8AM-5PM, Closed 12-1. Misdemeanor, Civil Actions Under $5,000, Eviction, Small Claims.

**Libby Justice Court #1**, 418 Mineral Ave, Libby, MT 59923. 406-293-7781 (MST) 8AM-5PM. Misdemeanor, Civil Actions Under $5,000, Eviction, Small Claims.

## Madison County

**Real Estate Recording**, Madison County Clerk and Recorder, 110 West Wallace, Virginia City, MT 59755. 406-843-5392 (MST) 8AM-Noon,1-5PM.

**District Court**, PO Box 185, Virginia City, MT 59755. 406-843-5392 (MST) 8AM-5PM. Felony, Civil Actions Over $5,000, Eviction, Probate.

**Justice Court**, PO Box 277, Virginia City, MT 59755. 406-843-5392 (MST) 8AM-5PM. Misdemeanor, Civil Actions Under $5,000, Eviction, Small Claims.

## McCone County

**Real Estate Recording**, McCone County Clerk and Recorder, 206 Second Avenue, Circle, MT 59215. 406-485-3505 (MST) 8AM-5PM.

**District Court**, PO Box 199, Circle, MT 59215. 406-485-3410 (MST) 8AM-5PM. Felony, Civil Actions Over $5,000, Eviction, Probate.

**Justice Court**, PO Box 192, Circle, MT 59215. 406-485-3548 (MST) Misdemeanor, Civil Actions Under $5,000, Eviction, Small Claims.

## Meagher County

**Real Estate Recording**, Meagher County Clerk and Recorder, 15 West Main, White Sulphur Springs, MT 59645. 406-547-3612 (MST) 8AM-Noon,1-5PM.

**District Court**, PO Box 443, White Sulphur Springs, MT 59645. 406-547-3941 (MST) 8AM-5PM. Felony, Civil Actions Over $5,000, Eviction, Probate.

**Justice Court**, PO Box 698, White Sulphur Springs, MT 59645. 406-547-3954 (MST) 8AM-5PM M-Th. Misdemeanor, Civil Actions Under $5,000, Eviction, Small Claims.

## Mineral County

**Real Estate Recording**, Mineral County Clerk and Recorder, 300 River Street, Superior, MT 59872. 406-822-4541 (MST) 8AM-5PM.

**District Court**, PO Box 96, Superior, MT 59872. 406-822-4612 (MST) 8AM-5PM, Closed 12-1. Felony, Civil Actions Over $5,000, Eviction, Probate.

**Justice Court**, PO Box 658, Superior, MT 59872. 406-822-4516 (MST) 8AM-5PM. Misdemeanor, Civil Actions Under $5,000, Eviction, Small Claims.

## Missoula County

**Real Estate Recording**, Missoula County Clerk and Recorder, 200 West Broadway, Missoula, MT 59802-4292. 406-721-5700 (MST) 8AM-5PM.

**District Court**, 200 W Broadway, Missoula, MT 59802. 406-523-4780 (MST) Felony, Civil Actions Over $5,000, Eviction, Probate.

**Justice Court**, 200 W Broadway, Missoula, MT 59802. 406-721-5700 (MST) 8AM-5PM. Misdemeanor, Civil Actions Under $5,000, Eviction, Small Claims.

## Musselshell County

**Real Estate Recording**, Musselshell County Clerk and Recorder, 506 Main Street, Courthouse, Roundup, MT 59072. 406-323-1104 (MST) 8AM-5PM.

**District Court**, PO Box 357, Roundup, MT 59072. 406-323-1413 (MST) 8AM-5PM. Felony, Civil Actions Over $5,000, Eviction, Probate.

**Justice Court**, PO Box 656, Roundup, MT 59072. 406-323-1078 (MST) 9AM-Noon. Misdemeanor, Civil Actions Under $5,000, Eviction, Small Claims.

## Park County

**Real Estate Recording**, Park County Clerk and Recorder, 414 East Callendar, Livingston, MT 59047. 406-222-6120 (MST) 8AM-5PM.

**District Court**, PO Box 437, Livingston, MT 59047. 406-222-6120 (MST) Felony, Civil Actions Over $5,000, Eviction, Probate.

**Justice Court**, 414 E Callendar, Livingston, MT 59047. 406-222-6120 (MST) Misdemeanor, Civil Actions Under $5,000, Eviction, Small Claims.

## Petroleum County

**Real Estate Recording**, Petroleum County Clerk and Recorder, 201 East Main, Winnett, MT 59087. 406-429-5311 (MST) 8AM-5PM.

**District Court**, PO Box 226, Winnett, MT 59087. 406-429-5311 (MST) 8AM-5PM. Felony, Civil Actions Over $5,000, Eviction, Probate.

**Justice Court**, PO Box 223, Winnett, MT 59087. 406-429-5311 (MST) 9AM-Noon Th. Misdemeanor, Civil Actions Under $5,000, Eviction, Small Claims.

## Phillips County

**Real Estate Recording**, Phillips County Clerk and Recorder, 314 Second Avenue West, Malta, MT 59538. 406-654-2423 (MST) 8AM-5PM.

**District Court**, PO Box I, Malta, MT 59538. 406-654-1023 (MST) 8AM-5PM. Felony, Civil Actions Over $5,000, Eviction, Probate.

**Justice Court**, PO Box 909, Malta, MT 59538. 406-654-1118 (MST) 10AM-4PM. Misdemeanor, Civil Actions Under $5,000, Eviction, Small Claims.

## Pondera County

**Real Estate Recording**, Pondera County Clerk and Recorder, 20 4th Avenue S.W., Conrad, MT 59425. 406-278-7681 (MST) X15 8AM-5PM.

**District Court**, 20 Fourth Ave SW, Conrad, MT 59425. 406-278-7681 (MST) Felony, Civil Actions Over $5,000, Eviction, Probate.

**Justice Court**, 20 Fourth Ave SW, Conrad, MT 59425. 406-278-3565 (MST) 9AM-4PM. Misdemeanor, Civil Actions Under $5,000, Eviction, Small Claims.

## Powder River County

**Real Estate Recording**, Powder River County Clerk and Recorder, Courthouse Square, Broadus, MT 59317. 406-436-2361 (MST) 8AM-5PM.

**District Court**, PO Box G, Broadus, MT 59317. 406-436-2320 (MST) Felony, Civil Actions Over $5,000, Eviction, Probate.

**Justice Court**, PO Box 488, Broadus, MT 59317. 406-436-2503 (MST) 9AM-3:30PM M-Th. Misdemeanor, Civil Actions Under $5,000, Eviction, Small Claims.

## Powell County

**Real Estate Recording**, Powell County Clerk and Recorder, 409 Missouri Avenue, Deer Lodge, MT 59722. 406-846-3680 (MST) 8AM-5PM.

**District Court**, 409 Missouri Ave, Deer Lodge, MT 59722. 406-846-3680 (MST) 8AM-5PM. Felony, Civil Actions Over $5,000, Eviction, Probate.

**Justice Court**, 313 4th St, Deer Lodge, MT 59722. 406-846-3680 (MST) Misdemeanor, Civil Actions Under $5,000, Eviction, Small Claims.

## Prairie County

**Real Estate Recording**, Prairie County Clerk and Recorder, Courthouse, Terry, MT 59349. 406-637-5575 (MST) 8AM-5PM.

**District Court**, PO Box 125, Terry, MT 59349. 406-637-5575 (MST) 8AM-5PM. Felony, Civil Actions Over $5,000, Eviction, Probate.

**Justice Court**, PO Box 446, Terry, MT 59349. 406-637-2124 (MST) Misdemeanor, Civil Actions Under $5,000, Eviction, Small Claims.

## Ravalli County

**Real Estate Recording**, Ravalli County Clerk and Recorder, 205 Bedford, Courthouse, Hamilton, MT 59840. 406-363-1833 (MST) 8AM-5PM.

**District Court**, PO Box 5014, Hamilton, MT 59840. 406-363-1900 (MST) 8AM-5PM. Felony, Civil Actions Over $5,000, Eviction, Probate.

**Justice Court**, PO Box 5023, Hamilton, MT 59840. 406-363-1381 (MST) 8AM-5PM. Misdemeanor, Civil Actions Under $5,000, Eviction, Small Claims.

## Richland County

**Real Estate Recording**, Richland County Clerk and Recorder, 201 West Main Street, Sidney, MT 59270. 406-482-1708 (MST) 8AM-5PM.

**District Court**, 201 W Main, Sidney, MT 59270. 406-482-1709 (MST) Felony, Civil Actions Over $5,000, Eviction, Probate.

**Justice Court**, 123 W Main, Sidney, MT 59270. 406-482-2815 (MST) 8AM-5PM. Misdemeanor, Civil Actions Under $5,000, Eviction, Small Claims.

## Roosevelt County

**Real Estate Recording**, Roosevelt County Clerk and Recorder, 400 Second Avenue South, Wolf Point, MT 59201. 406-653-1590 (MST) X52 8AM-5PM.

**District Court**, County Courthouse, Wolf Point, MT 59201. 406-653-1590 (MST) 8AM-5PM. Felony, Civil Actions Over $5,000, Eviction, Probate.

**Culbertson Justice Court Post #2**, PO Box 392, Culbertson, MT 59218. 406-787-6607 (MST) 9AM-3PM M-Th. Misdemeanor, Civil Actions Under $5,000, Eviction, Small Claims.

**Wolf Point Justice Court Post #1**, County Courthouse, Wolf Point, MT 59201. 406-653-1590 (MST) 8AM-5PM, Closed 11:30-12:30. Misdemeanor, Civil Actions Under $5,000, Eviction, Small Claims.

## Rosebud County

**Real Estate Recording**, Rosebud County Clerk and Recorder, 1200 Main Street, Forsyth, MT 59327. 406-356-7318 (MST) 8AM-5PM.

**District Court**, PO Box 48, Forsyth, MT 59327. 406-356-7322 (MST) 8AM-5PM. Felony, Civil Actions Over $5,000, Eviction, Probate.

**Colstrip Justice Court #2**, PO Box 511, Colstrip, MT 59323. 406-748-2934 (MST) 8AM-5PM. Misdemeanor, Civil Actions Under $5,000, Eviction, Small Claims.

**Forsyth Justice Court #1**, PO Box 504, Forsyth, MT 59327. 406-356-2638 (MST) 9AM-5PM. Misdemeanor, Civil Actions Under $5,000, Eviction, Small Claims.

## Sanders County

**Real Estate Recording**, Sanders County Clerk and Recorder, Courthouse, 1111 Main St., Thompson Falls, MT 59873. 406-827-4392 (MST) 8AM-5PM.

**District Court**, PO Box 519, Thompson Falls, MT 59873. 406-827-4316 (MST) 8AM-5PM. Felony, Civil Actions Over $5,000, Eviction, Probate.

**Justice Court**, PO Box 519, Thompson Falls, MT 59873. 406-827-4318 (MST) 8AM-5PM. Misdemeanor, Civil Actions Under $5,000, Eviction, Small Claims.

## Sheridan County

**Real Estate Recording**, Sheridan County Clerk and Recorder, 100 West Laurel Avenue, Plentywood, MT 59254. 406-765-2310 (MST) 8AM-5PM.

**District Court**, 100 W Laurel, Plentywood, MT 59254. 406-765-2310 (MST) 8AM-5PM, Closed 12-1. Felony, Civil Actions Over $5,000, Eviction, Probate.

**Justice Court**, 100 W Laurel, Plentywood, MT 59254. 406-765-2310 (MST) 8AM-5PM. Misdemeanor, Civil Actions Under $5,000, Eviction, Small Claims.

## Silver Bow County

**Real Estate Recording**, Silver Bow County Clerk and Recorder, 155 West Granite, Butte, MT 59701. 406-723-8262 (MST) 8AM-5PM.

**District Court**, 155 W Granite St, Butte, MT 59701. 406-723-8262 (MST) Felony, Civil Actions Over $5,000, Eviction, Probate.

**Justice Court #1 & #2**, 155 W Granite St, Butte, MT 59701. 406-723-8262 (MST) 8AM-5PM. Misdemeanor, Civil Actions Under $5,000, Eviction, Small Claims.

## Stillwater County

**Real Estate Recording**, Stillwater County Clerk and Recorder, 400 Third Avenue North, Columbus, MT 59019. 406-322-4546 (MST) 8AM-5PM.

**District Court**, PO Box 367, Columbus, MT 59019. 406-322-5332 (MST) 8AM-5PM. Felony, Civil Actions Over $5,000, Eviction, Probate.

**Justice Court**, PO Box 77, Columbus, MT 59019. 406-322-4577 (MST) 8AM-5PM. Misdemeanor, Civil Actions Under $5,000, Eviction, Small Claims.

## Sweet Grass County

**Real Estate Recording**, Sweet Grass County Clerk and Recorder, Courthouse, 200 W. 1st Ave., Big Timber, MT 59011. 406-932-5152 (MST) 8AM-5PM.

**District Court**, PO Box 698, Big Timber, MT 59011. 406-932-5154 (MST) 8AM-5PM, Closed 12-1. Felony, Civil Actions Over $5,000, Eviction, Probate.

**Justice Court**, Box 1206, Big Timber, MT 59011. 406-932-5150 (MST) 8AM-5PM. Misdemeanor, Civil Actions Under $5,000, Eviction, Small Claims.

## Teton County

**Real Estate Recording**, Teton County Clerk and Recorder, Courthouse, Choteau, MT 59422. 406-466-2693 (MST) 8AM-5PM.

**District Court**, PO Box 487, Choteau, MT 59422. 406-466-2909 (MST) 8AM-5PM. Felony, Civil Actions Over $5,000, Eviction, Probate.

**Justice Court**, PO Box 337, Choteau, MT 59422. 406-466-5611 (MST) Misdemeanor, Civil Actions Under $5,000, Eviction, Small Claims.

## Toole County

**Real Estate Recording**, Toole County Clerk and Recorder, 226 1st Street South, Shelby, MT 59474. 406-434-2232 (MST) 8AM-5PM.

**District Court**, PO Box 850, Shelby, MT 59474. 406-434-2271 (MST) Felony, Civil Actions Over $5,000, Eviction, Probate.

**Justice Court**, PO Box 738, Shelby, MT 59474. 406-434-2651 (MST) 10AM-5PM. Misdemeanor, Civil Actions Under $5,000, Eviction, Small Claims.

## Treasure County

**Real Estate Recording**, Treasure County Clerk and Recorder, 307 Rapelje Ave., Hysham, MT 59038. 406-342-5547 (MST) 8AM-Noon,1-5PM.

**District Court**, PO Box 392, Hysham, MT 59038. 406-342-5547 (MST) 8AM-5PM. Felony, Civil Actions Over $5,000, Eviction, Probate.

**Justice Court**, PO Box 267, Hysham, MT 59038. 406-342-5532 (MST) 9AM-Noon. Misdemeanor, Civil Actions Under $5,000, Eviction, Small Claims.

## Valley County

**Real Estate Recording**, Valley County Clerk and Recorder, 501 Court Square, Box 2, Glasgow, MT 59230. 406-228-8221 (MST) 8AM-5PM.

**District Court**, 501 Court Sq #6, Glasgow, MT 59230. 406-228-8221 (MST) 8AM-5PM. Felony, Civil Actions Over $5,000, Eviction, Probate.

**Justice Court**, 501 Court Sq #10, Glasgow, MT 59230. 406-228-8221 (MST) 8AM-5PM. Misdemeanor, Civil Actions Under $5,000, Eviction, Small Claims.

## Wheatland County

**Real Estate Recording**, Wheatland County Clerk and Recorder, Courthouse, Harlowton, MT 59036. 406-632-4891 (MST) 8AM-5PM.

**District Court**, Box 227, Harlowton, MT 59036. 406-632-4893 (MST) 8AM-5PM. Felony, Civil Actions Over $5,000, Eviction, Probate.

**Justice Court**, PO Box 524, Harlowton, MT 59036. 406-632-4893 (MST) 10AM-1PM T,Th. Misdemeanor, Civil Actions Under $5,000, Eviction, Small Claims.

## Wibaux County

**Real Estate Recording**, Wibaux County Clerk and Recorder, 200 South Wibaux Street, Wibaux, MT 59353. 406-795-2481 (MST) 8AM-5PM.

**District Court**, PO Box 292, Wibaux, MT 59353. 406-795-2484 (MST) 8AM-5PM, Closed 12-1. Felony, Civil Actions Over $5,000, Eviction, Probate.

**Justice Court**, PO Box 445, Wibaux, MT 59353. 406-795-2484 (MST) 8AM-Noon M,F; 1PM-5PM W. Misdemeanor, Civil Actions Under $5,000, Eviction, Small Claims.

## Yellowstone County

**Real Estate Recording**, Yellowstone County Clerk and Recorder, 217 North 27th, Room 402, Billings, MT 59101. 406-256-2785 (MST) 8AM-5PM.

**District Court**, PO Box 35030, Billings, MT 59107. 406-256-2860 (MST) 8AM-5PM. Felony, Civil Actions Over $5,000, Eviction, Probate.

**Justice Court**, PO Box 35032, Billings, MT 59107. 406-256-2895 (MST) 8AM-5PM. Misdemeanor, Civil Actions Under $5,000, Eviction, Small Claims.

# Nebraska

## Adams County

**Real Estate Recording**, Adams County Register of Deeds, 500 W. 4th, Room 100, Hastings, NE 68901. 402-461-7148 (CST) 9AM-5PM.

**District Court**, PO Box 9, Hastings, NE 68902. 402-461-7264 (CST) 8:30AM-5PM. Felony, Civil Actions Over $15,000.

**Adams County Court**, PO Box 95, Hastings, NE 68902-0095. 402-461-7143 (CST) 8AM-5PM. Misdemeanor, Civil Actions Under $15,000, Eviction, Small Claims, Probate.

## Antelope County

**Real Estate Recording**, Antelope County Clerk, 501 Main, Courthouse, Neligh, NE 68756. 402-887-4410 (CST) 8:30AM-Noon, 1-5PM.

**District Court**, PO Box 45, Neligh, NE 68756. 402-887-4508 (CST) 8:30AM-5PM. Felony, Civil Actions Over $15,000.

**Antelope County Court**, 501 Main, Neligh, NE 68756. 402-887-4650 (CST) 8:30AM-5PM. Misdemeanor, Civil Actions Under $15,000, Eviction, Small Claims, Probate.

## Arthur County

**Real Estate Recording**, Arthur County Clerk, Main Street, Courthouse, Arthur, NE 69121. 308-764-2203 (MST) 8AM-4PM.

**District and County Court**, PO Box 126, Arthur, NE 69121. 308-764-2203 (MST) 8AM-4PM. Felony, Misdemeanor, Civil, Eviction, Small Claims aims, Probate.

## Banner County

**Real Estate Recording**, Banner County Clerk, State Street, Courthouse, Harrisburg, NE 69345. 308-436-5265 (MST) 8AM-12, 1-5PM.

**District Court**, PO Box 67, Harrisburg, NE 69345. 308-436-5265 (MST) 8AM-5PM. Felony, Civil Actions Over $15,000.

**Banner County Court**, PO Box 67, Harrisburg, NE 69345. 308-436-5268 (MST) 8AM-5PM. Misdemeanor, Civil Actions Under $15,000, Eviction, Small Claims, Probate.

## Blaine County

**Real Estate Recording**, Blaine County Clerk, Lincoln Avenue, Courthouse, Brewster, NE 68821. 308-547-2222 (CST) 8AM-Noon, 1-4PM.

**District Court**, Lincoln Ave, Box 136, Brewster, NE 68821. 308-547-2222 (CST) 8AM-4PM. Felony, Civil Actions Over $15,000.

**Blaine County Court**, Lincoln Ave, Box 136, Brewster, NE 68821. 308-547-2225 (CST) 8AM-4PM. Misdemeanor, Civil Actions Under $15,000, Eviction, Small Claims, Probate.

## Boone County

**Real Estate Recording**, Boone County Clerk, 222 South 4th Street, Albion, NE 68620-1247. 402-395-2055 (CST) 8:30AM-5PM.

**District Court**, 222 Fourth St, Albion, NE 68620. 402-395-2057 (CST) 8:30AM-5PM. Felony, Civil Actions Over $15,000.

**Boone County Court**, 222 Fourth St, Albion, NE 68620. 402-395-2057 (CST) 8:30AM-5PM. Misdemeanor, Civil Actions Under $15,000, Eviction, Small Claims, Probate.

## Box Butte County

**Real Estate Recording**, Box Butte County Clerk, 5th Box Butte, Courthouse, Alliance, NE 69301. 308-762-6565 (MST) 9AM-5PM.

**District Court**, PO Box 613, Alliance, NE 69301. 308-762-6293 (MST) 8AM-4:30PM. Felony, Civil Actions Over $15,000.

**Box Butte County Court**, PO Box 613, Alliance, NE 69301. 308-762-6800 (MST) 8AM-4:30PM. Misdemeanor, Civil Actions Under $15,000, Eviction, Small Claims, Probate.

## Boyd County

**Real Estate Recording**, Boyd County Clerk, Thayer Street, Courthouse, Butte, NE 68722. 402-775-2391 (CST) 8:15AM-12, 1-5PM.

**District Court**, PO Box 26, Butte, NE 68722. 402-775-2391 (CST) 8:45AM-5PM. Felony, Civil Actions Over $15,000.

**Boyd County Court**, PO Box 396, Butte, NE 68722. 402-775-2211 (CST) 8AM-5PM. Misdemeanor, Civil Actions Under $15,000, Eviction, Small Claims, Probate.

## Brown County

**Real Estate Recording**, Brown County Clerk, Courthouse, 148 W. 4th St., Ainsworth, NE 69210. 402-387-2705 (CST) 9AM-5PM.

**District Court**, 148 W Fourth St, Ainsworth, NE 69210. 402-387-2705 (CST) 9AM-5PM. Felony, Civil Actions Over $15,000.

**Brown County Court**, 148 W Fourth St, Ainsworth, NE 69210. 402-387-2864 (CST) 9AM-5PM. Misdemeanor, Civil Actions Under $15,000, Eviction, Small Claims, Probate.

## Buffalo County

**Real Estate Recording**, Buffalo County Clerk, 16th & Central Avenue, Kearney, NE 68847. 308-236-1226 (CST) 8AM-5PM.

**District Court**, PO Box 520, Kearney, NE 68848. 308-236-1246 (CST) 8AM-5PM. Felony, Civil Actions Over $15,000.

**Buffalo County Court**, PO Box 520, Kearney, NE 68848. 308-236-1228 (CST) 8AM-5PM. Misdemeanor, Civil Actions Under $15,000, Eviction, Small Claims, Probate.

## Burt County

**Real Estate Recording**, Burt County Clerk, Courthouse, Tekamah, NE 68061. 402-374-1955 (CST) 8AM-4:30PM.

**District Court**, 111 N 13th St, Tekamah, NE 68061. 402-374-2605 (CST) 8AM-4:30PM. Felony, Civil Actions Over $15,000.

**Burt County Court**, 111 N 13th St, Tekamah, NE 68061. 402-374-2000 (CST) 8AM-4:30PM. Misdemeanor, Civil Actions Under $15,000, Eviction, Small Claims, Probate.

## Butler County

**Real Estate Recording**, Butler County Clerk, 451 5th Street, David City, NE 68632. 402-367-7430 (CST) 8:30AM-5PM.

**District Court**, 451 5th St, David City, NE 68632-1666. 402-367-7460 (CST) 8:30AM-5PM. Felony, Civil Actions Over $15,000.

**Butler County Court**, 451 5th St, David City, NE 68632-1666. 402-367-7480 (CST) 8AM-5PM, Closed 12-1. Misdemeanor, Civil Actions Under $15,000, Eviction, Small Claims, Probate.

## Cass County

**Real Estate Recording**, Cass County Register od Deeds, County Courthouse, 346 Main St., Plattsmouth, NE 68048-1964. 402-296-3159 (CST) 8AM-5PM.

**District Court**, Cass County Courthouse, Plattsmouth, NE 68048. 402-296-3278 (CST) 8AM-5PM. Felony, Civil Actions Over $15,000.

**Cass County Court**, Cass County Courthouse, Plattsmouth, NE 68048. 402-296-3343 (CST) 8AM-5PM. Misdemeanor, Civil Actions Under $15,000, Eviction, Small Claims, Probate.

## Cedar County

**Real Estate Recording**, Cedar County Clerk, Courthouse, Hartington, NE 68739. 402-254-7411 (CST) 8AM-5PM.

**District Court**, 101 S Broadway Ave, Hartington, NE 68739. 402-254-6957 (CST) 8AM-5PM. Felony, Civil Actions Over $15,000.

**Cedar County Court**, 101 S Broadway Ave, Hartington, NE 68739. 402-254-7441 (CST) 8AM-5PM. Misdemeanor, Civil Actions Under $15,000, Eviction, Small Claims, Probate.

## Chase County

**Real Estate Recording**, Chase County Clerk, 921 Broadway, Courthouse, Imperial, NE 69033. 308-882-5266 (MST) 8AM-4PM.

**District Court**, PO Box 1299, Imperial, NE 69033. 308-882-5266 (MST) Felony, Civil Actions Over $15,000.

**Chase County Court**, PO Box 310, Imperial, NE 69033. 308-882-4690 (MST) 7:30AM-4:30PM. Misdemeanor, Civil Actions Under $15,000, Eviction, Small Claims, Probate.

## Cherry County

**Real Estate Recording**, Cherry County Clerk, 365 North Main, Valentine, NE 69201. 402-376-2771 (MST) 8:30AM-4:30PM.

**District Court**, 365 N Main St, Valentine, NE 69201. 402-376-1840 (MST) 8:30AM-4:30PM. Felony, Civil Actions Over $15,000.

**Cherry County Court**, 365 N Main St, Valentine, NE 69201. 402-376-2590 (MST) 8AM-5PM. Misdemeanor, Civil Actions Under $15,000, Eviction, Small Claims, Probate.

## Cheyenne County

**Real Estate Recording**, Cheyenne County Clerk, 1000 10th Avenue, Sidney, NE 69162. 308-254-2141 (MST) 8AM-5PM.

**District Court**, PO Box 217, Sidney, NE 69162. 308-254-2814 (MST) 8AM-5PM, Closed 12-1. Felony, Civil Actions Over $15,000.

**Cheyenne County Court**, 1000 10th Ave, Sidney, NE 69162. 308-254-2929 (MST) 8AM-5PM. Misdemeanor, Civil Actions Under $15,000, Eviction, Small Claims, Probate.

# Nebraska

## Clay County

**Real Estate Recording**, Clay County Clerk, 111 West Fairfield Street, Clay Center, NE 68933-1499. 402-762-3463 (CST) 8:30AM-5PM.

**District Court**, 111 W Fairfield St, Clay Center, NE 68933. 402-762-3595 (CST) 8:30AM-5PM. Felony, Civil Actions Over $15,000.

**Clay County Court**, 111 W Fairfield St, Clay Center, NE 68933. 402-762-3651 (CST) 8:30AM-5PM. Misdemeanor, Civil Actions Under $15,000, Eviction, Small Claims, Probate.

## Colfax County

**Real Estate Recording**, Colfax County Clerk, 411 East 11th Street, Schuyler, NE 68661. 402-352-3434 (CST) 8:30AM-Noon, 1-5PM.

**District Court**, 411 E 11th St, Schuyler, NE 68661. 402-352-2205 (CST) 8:30AM-5PM. Felony, Civil Actions Over $15,000.

**Colfax County Court**, 411 E 11th St, Schuyler, NE 68661. 402-352-3322 (CST) 8AM-5PM. Misdemeanor, Civil Actions Under $15,000, Eviction, Small Claims, Probate.

## Cuming County

**Real Estate Recording**, Cuming County Clerk, Courthouse, West Point, NE 68788. 402-372-6002 (CST)

**District Court**, 200 S Lincoln, Rm 200, West Point, NE 68788. 402-372-6004 (CST) 8:30AM-4:30PM. Felony, Civil Actions Over $15,000.

**Cuming County Court**, 200 S Lincoln, West Point, NE 68788. 402-372-6004 (CST) 8:30AM-4:30PM. Misdemeanor, Civil Actions Under $15,000, Eviction, Small Claims, Probate.

## Custer County

**Real Estate Recording**, Custer County Clerk, 431 South 10th, Broken Bow, NE 68822. 308-872-5701 (CST) 9AM-5PM.

**District Court**, 431 S 10th Ave, Broken Bow, NE 68822. 308-872-2121 (CST) 9AM-5PM. Felony, Civil Actions Over $15,000.

**Custer County Court**, 431 S 10th Ave, Broken Bow, NE 68822. 308-872-5761 (CST) 8AM-5PM. Misdemeanor, Civil Actions Under $15,000, Eviction, Small Claims, Probate.

## Dakota County

**Real Estate Recording**, Dakota County Register of Deeds, 1601 Broadway, Courthouse Square, Dakota City, NE 68731. 402-987-2166 (CST) 8AM-4:30PM.

**District Court**, PO Box 66, Dakota City, NE 68731. 402-987-2114 (CST) 8AM-4:30PM. Felony, Civil Actions Over $15,000.

**Dakota County Court**, PO Box 385, Dakota City, NE 68731. 402-987-2145 (CST) 8AM-4:30PM. Misdemeanor, Civil Actions Under $15,000, Eviction, Small Claims, Probate.

## Dawes County

**Real Estate Recording**, Dawes County Clerk, 451 Main Street, Courthouse, Chadron, NE 69337-2698. 308-432-0100 (MST) 8:30AM-4:30PM.

**District Court**, PO Box 630, Chadron, NE 69337. 308-432-0109 (MST) 8:30AM-4:30PM. Felony, Civil Actions Over $15,000.

**Dawes County Court**, PO Box 806, Chadron, NE 69337. 308-432-0116 (MST) 7:30AM-4:30PM. Misdemeanor, Civil Actions Under $15,000, Eviction, Small Claims, Probate.

## Dawson County

**Real Estate Recording**, Register of Deeds, County Courthouse, Lexington, NE 68850. 308-324-4271 (CST) 8AM-Noon, 1PM-5PM.

**District Court**, PO Box 429, Lexington, NE 68850. 308-324-4261 (CST) 8AM-5PM. Felony, Civil Actions Over $15,000.

**Dawson County Court**, 700 N Washington St, Lexington, NE 68850. 308-324-5606 (CST) 8AM-5PM. Misdemeanor, Civil Actions Under $15,000, Eviction, Small Claims, Probate.

## Deuel County

**Real Estate Recording**, Deuel County Clerk, 3rd & Vincent, Chappell, NE 69129. 308-874-3308 (MST)

**District Court**, PO Box 327, Chappell, NE 69129. 308-874-3308 (MST) 8AM-4PM. Felony, Civil Actions Over $15,000.

**Deuel County Court**, PO Box 327, Chappell, NE 69129. 308-874-2909 (MST) 8AM-4PM. Misdemeanor, Civil Actions Under $15,000, Eviction, Small Claims, Probate.

## Dixon County

**Real Estate Recording**, Dixon County Clerk, Courthouse, 302 Third St., Ponca, NE 68770. 402-755-2208 (CST) 8AM-4:30PM.

**District Court**, PO Box 395, Ponca, NE 68770. 402-755-2881 (CST) 8AM-5PM, Closed 12-1. Felony, Civil Actions Over $15,000.

**Dixon County Court**, PO Box 497, Ponca, NE 68770. 402-755-2355 (CST) 8AM-4:30PM. Misdemeanor, Civil Actions Under $15,000, Eviction, Small Claims, Probate.

## Dodge County

**Real Estate Recording**, Dodge County Register of Deeds, 435 North Park, Courthouse, Fremont, NE 68025. 402-727-2735 (CST) 8:30AM-4:30PM.

**District Court**, PO Box 1237, Fremont, NE 68025. 402-727-2780 (CST) 8:30AM-4:30PM. Felony, Civil Actions Over $15,000.

**Dodge County Court**, 428 N Broad St, Fremont, NE 68025. 402-727-2755 (CST) 8AM-5PM. Misdemeanor, Civil Actions Under $15,000, Eviction, Small Claims, Probate.

## Douglas County

**Real Estate Recording**, Douglas County Register of Deeds, 1819 Farnam, Room H09, Omaha, NE 68183. 402-444-7162 (CST) 8:30AM-4:30PM.

**District Court**, 1819 Farnam, Omaha, NE 68183. 402-444-7018 (CST) 8:30AM-4:30PM. Felony, Civil Actions Over $15,000.

**Douglas County Court**, 1819 Farnam, 2nd Fl, Omaha, NE 68183. 402-444-5425 (CST) 8AM-4:30PM. Misdemeanor, Civil Actions Under $15,000, Eviction, Small Claims, Probate.

## Dundy County

**Real Estate Recording**, Dundy County Clerk, Courthouse, Benkelman, NE 69021. 308-423-2058 (MST) 8AM-5PM.

**District Court**, PO Box 506, Benkelman, NE 69021. 308-423-2058 (MST) 8AM-5PM. Felony, Civil Actions Over $15,000.

**Dundy County Court**, PO Box 377, Benkelman, NE 69021. 308-423-2374 (MST) Misdemeanor, Civil Actions Under $15,000, Eviction, Small Claims, Probate.

## Fillmore County

**Real Estate Recording**, Fillmore County Clerk, Courthouse, 900 G st., Geneva, NE 68361. 402-759-4931 (CST) 8AM-5PM.

**District Court**, PO Box 147, Geneva, NE 68361. 402-759-3811 (CST) 8AM-5PM, Closed 12-1. Felony, Civil Actions Over $15,000.

**Fillmore County Court**, PO Box 66, Geneva, NE 68361. 402-759-3514 (CST) 8AM-5PM. Misdemeanor, Civil Actions Under $15,000, Eviction, Small Claims, Probate.

## Franklin County

**Real Estate Recording**, Franklin County Clerk, 405 15th Avenue, Franklin, NE 68939. 308-425-6202 (CST) 8:30AM-4:30PM.

**District Court**, PO Box 146, Franklin, NE 68939. 308-425-6202 (CST) 8:30AM-4:30PM. Felony, Civil Actions Over $15,000.

**Franklin County Court**, PO Box 174, Franklin, NE 68939. 308-425-6288 (CST) 8:30AM-4:30PM M-F. Misdemeanor, Civil Actions Under $15,000, Eviction, Small Claims, Probate.

## Frontier County

**Real Estate Recording**, Frontier County Clerk, 1 Wellington Street, Stockville, NE 69042. 308-367-8641 (CST) 8:30AM-Noon, 1-5PM.

**District Court**, PO Box 40, Stockville, NE 69042. 308-367-8641 (CST) Felony, Civil Actions Over $15,000.

**Frontier County Court**, PO Box 38, Stockville, NE 69042. 308-367-8629 (CST) Misdemeanor, Civil Actions Under $15,000, Eviction, Small Claims, Probate.

## Furnas County

**Real Estate Recording**, Furnas County Clerk, Courthouse, 912 R Street, Beaver City, NE 68926. 308-268-4145 (CST)

**District Court**, PO Box 413, Beaver City, NE 68926. 308-268-4015 (CST) 10AM-3PM, Closed 12-1. Felony, Civil Actions Over $15,000.

**Furnas County Court**, 912 R St (PO Box 373), Beaver City, NE 68926. 308-268-4025 (CST) 8AM-4PM. Misdemeanor, Civil Actions Under $15,000, Eviction, Small Claims, Probate.

## Gage County

**Real Estate Recording**, Gage County Register of Deeds, 6th & Lincoln, Courthouse, Beatrice, NE 68310. 402-223-1361 (CST) 8AM-4:30PM.

**District Court**, PO Box 845, Beatrice, NE 68310. 402-223-1332 (CST) 8AM-5PM. Felony, Civil Actions Over $15,000.

**Gage County Court**, PO Box 219, Beatrice, NE 68310. 402-223-1323 (CST) Misdemeanor, Civil Actions Under $15,000, Eviction, Small Claims, Probate.

**County Records**

## Garden County

**Real Estate Recording**, Garden County Clerk, 611 Main Street, Courthouse, Oshkosh, NE 69154. 308-772-3924 (MST) 8AM-4PM.

**District Court**, PO Box 486, Oshkosh, NE 69154. 308-772-3924 (MST) 8AM-4PM. Felony, Civil Actions Over $15,000.

**Garden County Court**, PO Box 486, Oshkosh, NE 69154. 308-772-3696 (MST) Misdemeanor, Civil Actions Under $15,000, Eviction, Small Claims, Probate.

## Garfield County

**Real Estate Recording**, Garfield County Clerk, 250 South 8th Street, Burwell, NE 68823. 308-346-4161 (CST) 9AM-Noon, 1-5PM.

**District Court**, PO Box 218, Burwell, NE 68823. 308-346-4161 (CST) 9AM-5PM. Felony, Civil Actions Over $15,000.

**Garfield County Court**, PO Box 431, Burwell, NE 68823. 308-346-4123 (CST) Misdemeanor, Civil Actions Under $15,000, Eviction, Small Claims, Probate.

## Gosper County

**Real Estate Recording**, Gosper County Clerk, Courthouse, 500 Smith, Elwood, NE 68937. 308-785-2611 (CST) 8:30AM-4:30PM.

**District Court**, PO Box 136, Elwood, NE 68937. 308-785-2611 (CST) 8:30AM-4:30PM. Felony, Civil Actions Over $15,000.

**Gosper County Court**, PO Box 55, Elwood, NE 68937. 308-785-2531 (CST) 8:30AM-4:30PM. Misdemeanor, Civil Actions Under $15,000, Eviction, Small Claims, Probate.

## Grant County

**Real Estate Recording**, Grant County Clerk, Harrison Avenue, Courthouse, Hyannis, NE 69350. 308-458-2488 (MST) 8AM-Noon,1-4PM.

**District Court**, PO Box 139, Hyannis, NE 69350. 308-458-2488 (MST) 8AM-4PM. Felony, Civil Actions Over $15,000.

**Grant County Court**, PO Box 97, Hyannis, NE 69350. 308-458-2433 (MST) 8AM-4PM. Misdemeanor, Civil Actions Under $15,000, Eviction, Small Claims, Probate.

## Greeley County

**Real Estate Recording**, Greeley County Clerk, Courthouse, Greeley, NE 68842. 308-428-3625 (CST)

**District Court**, PO Box 287, Greeley, NE 68842. 308-428-3625 (CST) 8AM-5PM. Felony, Civil Actions Over $15,000.

**Greeley County Court**, PO Box 287, Greeley, NE 68842. 308-428-2705 (CST) 8AM-5PM. Misdemeanor, Civil Actions Under $15,000, Eviction, Small Claims, Probate.

## Hall County

**Real Estate Recording**, Hall County Register of Deeds, 121 South Pine, Grand Island, NE 68801. 308-385-5040 (CST)

**District Court**, PO Box 1926, Grand Island, NE 68802. 308-385-5144 (CST) 8AM-5PM. Felony, Civil Actions Over $15,000.

**Hall County Court**, PO Box 1985, Grand Island, NE 68802. 308-385-5135 (CST) 8:30AM-5PM. Misdemeanor, Civil Actions Under $15,000, Eviction, Small Claims, Probate.

## Hamilton County

**Real Estate Recording**, Hamilton County Clerk, Courthouse, 1111 13th St. - Suite 1, Aurora, NE 68818-2017. 402-694-3443 (CST) 8AM-5PM.

**District Court**, Courthouse, Aurora, NE 68818. 402-694-3533 (CST) 8AM-5PM. Felony, Civil Actions Over $15,000.

**Hamilton County Court**, PO Box 323, Aurora, NE 68818. 402-694-6188 (CST) Misdemeanor, Civil Actions Under $15,000, Eviction, Small Claims, Probate.

## Harlan County

**Real Estate Recording**, Harlan County Clerk, 706 West 2nd Street, Alma, NE 68920. 308-928-2173 (CST) 8:30AM-4:30PM.

**District Court**, PO Box 379, Alma, NE 68920. 308-928-2173 (CST) 8:30AM-4:30PM. Felony, Civil Actions Over $15,000.

**Harlan County Court**, PO Box 379, Alma, NE 68920. 308-928-2179 (CST) 8AM-4PM. Misdemeanor, Civil Actions Under $15,000, Eviction, Small Claims, Probate.

## Hayes County

**Real Estate Recording**, Hayes County Clerk, Troth Street, Courthouse, Hayes Center, NE 69032. 308-286-3413 (CST)

**District Court**, PO Box 370, Hayes Center, NE 69032. 308-286-3413 (CST) 8AM-5PM. Felony, Civil Actions Over $15,000.

**Hayes County Court**, PO Box 370, Hayes Center, NE 69032. 308-286-3315 (CST) 1PM-5PM M,W,F (Clerk's hours). Misdemeanor, Civil Actions Under $15,000, Eviction, Small Claims, Probate.

## Hitchcock County

**Real Estate Recording**, Hitchcock County Clerk, 229 East D, Trenton, NE 69044. 308-334-5646 (CST) 8:30AM-4PM.

**District Court**, PO Box 248, Trenton, NE 69044. 308-334-5646 (CST) 8:30AM-4PM. Felony, Civil Actions Over $15,000.

**Hitchcock County Court**, PO Box 366, Trenton, NE 69044. 308-334-5383 (CST) 8:30AM-4PM. Misdemeanor, Civil Actions Under $15,000, Eviction, Small Claims, Probate.

## Holt County

**Real Estate Recording**, Holt County Clerk, 204 North 4th, O'Neill, NE 68763. 402-336-1762 (CST) 8AM-Noon,1-5PM.

**District Court**, PO Box 755, O'Neill, NE 68763. 402-336-2840 (CST) 8AM-5PM. Felony, Civil Actions Over $15,000.

**Holt County Court**, 204 N 4th St, O'Neill, NE 68763. 402-336-1662 (CST) 8AM-5PM. Misdemeanor, Civil Actions Under $15,000, Eviction, Small Claims, Probate.

## Hooker County

**Real Estate Recording**, Hooker County Clerk, 303 NW 1st, Courthouse, Mullen, NE 69152. 308-546-2244 (MST) 8:30AM-Noon, 1-4:30PM.

**District Court**, PO Box 184, Mullen, NE 69152. 308-546-2244 (MST) 8:30AM-4:30PM. Felony, Civil Actions Over $15,000.

**Hooker County Court**, PO Box 263, Mullen, NE 69152. 308-546-2249 (MST) 8:30AM-4:30PM. Misdemeanor, Civil Actions Under $15,000, Eviction, Small Claims, Probate.

## Howard County

**Real Estate Recording**, Howard County Clerk, 612 Indian Street, St. Paul, NE 68873. 308-754-4343 (CST) 8AM-5PM.

**District Court**, PO Box 25, St Paul, NE 68873. 308-754-4343 (CST) 8AM-5PM. Felony, Civil Actions Over $15,000.

**Howard County Court**, PO Box 94, St Paul, NE 68873. 308-754-4192 (CST) 8AM-5PM. Misdemeanor, Civil Actions Under $15,000, Eviction, Small Claims, Probate.

## Jefferson County

**Real Estate Recording**, Jefferson County Clerk, 411 4th, Courthouse, Fairbury, NE 68352-1619. 402-729-2323 (CST) 9AM-5PM UCC; 9AM-Noon, 1-5PM Real Property.

**District Court**, 411 Fourth St, Fairbury, NE 68352. 402-729-2019 (CST) 9AM-5PM. Felony, Civil Actions Over $15,000.

**Jefferson County Court**, 411 Fourth St, Fairbury, NE 68352. 402-729-2312 (CST) 8AM-5PM. Misdemeanor, Civil Actions Under $15,000, Eviction, Small Claims, Probate.

## Johnson County

**Real Estate Recording**, Johnson County Clerk, Courthouse, Tecumseh, NE 68450. 402-335-3246 (CST) 8AM-12:30PM, 1-4:30PM.

**District Court**, PO Box 416, Tecumseh, NE 68450. 402-335-2871 (CST) 8AM-4:30PM, Closed 12:30-1. Felony, Civil Actions Over $15,000.

**Johnson County Court**, PO Box 285, Tecumseh, NE 68450. 402-335-3050 (CST) 8AM-4:30PM. Misdemeanor, Civil Actions Under $15,000, Eviction, Small Claims, Probate.

## Kearney County

**Real Estate Recording**, Kearney County Clerk, 424 North Colorado, Minden, NE 68959. 308-832-2723 (CST) 8:30AM-5PM.

**District Court**, PO Box 208, Minden, NE 68959. 308-832-1742 (CST) 8:30AM-5PM. Felony, Civil Actions Over $15,000.

**Kearney County Court**, PO Box 377, Minden, NE 68959. 308-832-2723 (CST) 8:30AM-5PM. Misdemeanor, Civil Actions Under $15,000, Eviction, Small Claims, Probate.

## Keith County

**Real Estate Recording**, Keith County Clerk, 511 North Spruce, Ogallala, NE 69153. 308-284-4726 (MST)

**District Court**, PO Box 686, Ogallala, NE 69153. 308-284-3849 (MST) Felony, Civil Actions Over $15,000.

**Keith County Court**, PO Box 358, Ogallala, NE 69153. 308-284-3693 (MST) Misdemeanor, Civil Actions Under $15,000, Eviction, Small Claims, Probate.

# Nebraska

## Keya Paha County

**Real Estate Recording**, Keya Paha County Clerk, Courthouse, Springview, NE 68778. 402-497-3791 (CST) 8AM-Noon,1-5PM.

**District Court**, PO Box 349, Springview, NE 68778. 402-497-3791 (CST) 8AM-5PM. Felony, Civil Actions Over $15,000.

**Keya Paha County Court**, PO Box 311, Springview, NE 68778. 402-497-3021 (CST) 8AM-5PM Th,F. Misdemeanor, Civil Actions Under $15,000, Eviction, Small Claims, Probate.

## Kimball County

**Real Estate Recording**, Kimball County Clerk, 114 East Third Street, Kimball, NE 69145-1296. 308-235-2241 (MST) 8AM-5PM M,T,W,Th; 8AM-4PM F.

**District Court**, 114 E 3rd St, Kimball, NE 69145. 308-235-3591 (MST) 8AM-5PM M-Th, 8AM-4PM F. Felony, Civil Actions Over $15,000.

**Kimball County Court**, 114 E 3rd St, Kimball, NE 69145. 308-235-2831 (MST) 8AM-5PM. Misdemeanor, Civil Actions Under $15,000, Eviction, Small Claims, Probate.

## Knox County

**Real Estate Recording**, Knox County Clerk (ex-officio Register of Deeds), Main Street, Courthouse, Center, NE 68724. 402-288-4282 (CST) 8:30AM-4:30PM.

**District Court**, PO Box 126, Center, NE 68724. 402-288-4484 (CST) 8:30AM-4:30PM. Felony, Civil Actions Over $15,000.

**Knox County Court**, PO Box 125, Center, NE 68724. 402-288-4277 (CST) 8:30AM-4:30PM. Misdemeanor, Civil Actions Under $15,000, Eviction, Small Claims, Probate.

## Lancaster County

**Real Estate Recording**, Lancaster County Register of Deeds, 555 South 10th Street, Lincoln, NE 68500. 402-441-7577 (CST) 8AM-4:30PM.

**District Court**, 555 S Tenth St, Lincoln, NE 68508. 402-441-7328 (CST) 8:30AM-4:30PM. Felony, Civil Actions Over $15,000.

**Lancaster County Court**, 555 S Tenth St, Lincoln, NE 68508. 402-441-7270 (CST) 8AM-4:30PM. Misdemeanor, Civil Actions Under $15,000, Eviction, Small Claims, Probate.

## Lincoln County

**Real Estate Recording**, Lincoln County Reister of Deeds, 301 N. Jeffers, Room 103, North Platte, NE 69101-3931. 308-534-4350 (CST) 9AM-5PM.

**District Court**, 301 N Jeffers (PO Box 1616), North Platte, NE 69101. 308-534-4350 (CST) 8AM-5PM. Felony, Civil Actions Over $15,000.

**Lincoln County Court**, 301 N Jeffers, North Platte, NE 69101. 308-534-4350 (CST) 8AM-5PM. Misdemeanor, Civil Actions Under $15,000, Eviction, Small Claims, Probate.

## Logan County

**Real Estate Recording**, Logan County Clerk, Courthouse, Stapleton, NE 69163. 308-636-2311 (CST) 8:30AM-4:30PM M,T,W,Th; 8:30AM-4PM F.

**District Court**, PO Box 8, Stapleton, NE 69163. 308-636-2311 (CST) 8:30AM-4:30PM M-Thurs. 8:30AM-4:00PM Fri. Felony, Civil Actions Over $15,000.

**Logan County Court**, PO Box 205, Stapleton, NE 69163. 308-636-2677 (CST) 8AM-4:30PM M-Th, 8AM-4PM F. Misdemeanor, Civil Actions Under $15,000, Eviction, Small Claims, Probate.

## Loup County

**Real Estate Recording**, Loup County Clerk, Courthouse, Taylor, NE 68879. 308-942-3135 (CST) 8:30AM-Noon, 1-5PM M,T,W,Th; 8:30AM-Noon F.

**District Court**, PO Box 187, Taylor, NE 68879. 308-942-6035 (CST) 8:30AM-5PM M-Th, 8:30AM-Noon F. Felony, Civil Actions Over $15,000.

**Loup County Court**, PO Box 187, Taylor, NE 68879. 308-942-3135 (CST) 8:30AM-5PM M-Th, 8:30AM-Noon F. Misdemeanor, Civil Actions Under $15,000, Eviction, Small Claims, Probate.

## Madison County

**Real Estate Recording**, Madison County Register of Deeds, Clara Davis Drive, Courthouse, Madison, NE 68748. 402-454-3311 (CST) 8:30AM-5PM.

**District Court**, PO Box 249, Madison, NE 68748. 402-454-3311 (CST) Felony, Civil Actions Over $15,000.

**Madison County Court**, PO Box 230, Madison, NE 68748. 402-454-3311 (CST) Misdemeanor, Civil Actions Under $15,000, Eviction, Small Claims, Probate.

## McPherson County

**Real Estate Recording**, McPherson County Clerk, 5th & Anderson, Courthouse, Tryon, NE 69167. 308-587-2363 (CST) 8:30AM-Noon, 1-4:30PM.

**District Court**, PO Box 122, Tryon, NE 69167. 308-587-2363 (CST) 8:30AM-4:30PM. Felony, Civil Actions Over $15,000.

**McPherson County Court**, PO Box 122, Tryon, NE 69167. 308-587-2363 (CST) 8:30AM-4:30PM. Misdemeanor, Civil Actions Under $15,000, Eviction, Small Claims, Probate.

## Merrick County

**Real Estate Recording**, Merrick County Clerk, Courthouse, Central City, NE 68826. 308-946-2881 (CST) 8AM-5PM.

**District Court**, PO Box 27, Central City, NE 68826. 308-946-2461 (CST) 8AM-5PM. Felony, Civil Actions Over $15,000.

**Merrick County Court**, County Courthouse, Central City, NE 68826. 308-946-2812 (CST) Misdemeanor, Civil Actions Under $15,000, Eviction, Small Claims, Probate.

## Morrill County

**Real Estate Recording**, Morrill County Clerk, 6th & Main Street, Courthouse, Bridgeport, NE 69336. 308-262-0860 (MST) 8AM-4:30PM.

**District Court**, PO Box 824, Bridgeport, NE 69336. 308-262-1261 (MST) 8AM-4:30PM, Closed 12-1. Felony, Civil Actions Over $15,000.

**Morrill County Court**, PO Box 418, Bridgeport, NE 69336. 308-262-0860 (MST) 8AM-4:30PM. Misdemeanor, Civil Actions Under $15,000, Eviction, Small Claims, Probate.

## Nance County

**Real Estate Recording**, Nance County Clerk, 209 Esther Street, Fullerton, NE 68638. 308-536-2331 (CST)

**District Court**, PO Box 338, Fullerton, NE 68638. 308-536-2365 (CST) 8AM-5PM. Felony, Civil Actions Over $15,000.

**Nance County Court**, PO Box 837, Fullerton, NE 68638. 308-536-2675 (CST) 8AM-5PM. Misdemeanor, Civil Actions Under $15,000, Eviction, Small Claims, Probate.

## Nemaha County

**Real Estate Recording**, Nemaha County Clerk, 1824 N Street, Courthouse, Auburn, NE 68305-2399. 402-274-4213 (CST) 8AM-5PM.

**District Court**, 1824 N St, Auburn, NE 68305. 402-274-3616 (CST) 8AM-5PM. Felony, Civil Actions Over $15,000.

**Nemaha County Court**, 1824 N St, Auburn, NE 68305. 402-274-3008 (CST) 8AM-5PM, Closed 12-1. Misdemeanor, Civil Actions Under $15,000, Eviction, Small Claims, Probate.

## Nuckolls County

**Real Estate Recording**, Nuckolls County Clerk, 150 South Main, Courthouse, Nelson, NE 68961. 402-225-4361 (CST) 8:30AM-Noon, 1-5PM.

**District Court**, PO Box 366, Nelson, NE 68961. 402-225-4341 (CST) 8:30AM-5PM. Felony, Civil Actions Over $15,000.

**Nuckolls County Court**, PO Box 372, Nelson, NE 68961. 402-225-2371 (CST) 8AM-5PM. Misdemeanor, Civil Actions Under $15,000, Eviction, Small Claims, Probate.

## Otoe County

**Real Estate Recording**, Otoe County Register of Deeds, 1021 Central Ave., Room 203, Nebraska City, NE 68410. 402-873-6439 (CST) 8AM-Noon, 1PM-5PM.

**District Court**, 1021 Central Ave, Rm 201, Nebraska City, NE 68410. 402-873-6440 (CST) 8AM-5PM. Felony, Civil Actions Over $15,000.

**Otoe County Court**, 1021 Central Ave, Rm 201, Nebraska City, NE 68410. 402-873-5588 (CST) 8AM-5PM. Misdemeanor, Civil Actions Under $15,000, Eviction, Small Claims, Probate.

## Pawnee County

**Real Estate Recording**, Pawnee County Clerk, 625 6th Street, Pawnee City, NE 68420. 402-852-2962 (CST) 8AM-4PM.

**District Court**, PO Box 431, Pawnee City, NE 68420. 402-852-2963 (CST) Felony, Civil Actions Over $15,000.

**Pawnee County Court**, PO Box 471, Pawnee City, NE 68420. 402-852-2388 (CST) 8AM-4:30PM. Misdemeanor, Civil Actions Under $15,000, Eviction, Small Claims, Probate.

## Perkins County

**Real Estate Recording**, Perkins County Clerk, 200 Lincoln Avenue, Grant, NE 69140. 308-352-4643 (MST) 8AM-4PM.

**District Court**, PO Box 156, Grant, NE 69140. 308-352-4643 (MST) 8AM-4PM. Felony, Civil Actions Over $15,000.

**Perkins County Court**, PO Box 222, Grant, NE 69140. 308-352-4415 (MST) 8AM-4PM. Misdemeanor, Civil Actions Under $15,000, Eviction, Small Claims, Probate.

## Phelps County

**Real Estate Recording**, Phelps County Clerk, Courthouse, Holdrege, NE 68949. 308-995-4469 (CST) 9AM-5PM.

**District Court**, PO Box 462, Holdrege, NE 68949. 308-995-2281 (CST) 9AM-5PM. Felony, Civil Actions Over $15,000.

**Phelps County Court**, PO Box 324, Holdrege, NE 68949. 308-995-6561 (CST) 8AM-5PM. Misdemeanor, Civil Actions Under $15,000, Eviction, Small Claims, Probate.

## Pierce County

**Real Estate Recording**, Pierce County Clerk, 111 West Court, Courthouse - Room 1, Pierce, NE 68767-1224. 402-329-4225 (CST) 9AM-5PM.

**District Court**, 111 W Court St, Rm 12, Pierce, NE 68767. 402-329-4335 (CST) 9AM-5PM. Felony, Civil Actions Over $15,000.

**Pierce County Court**, 111 W Court St, Rm 11, Pierce, NE 68767. 402-329-6245 (CST) 8:30AM-5PM. Misdemeanor, Civil Actions Under $15,000, Eviction, Small Claims, Probate.

## Platte County

**Real Estate Recording**, Platte County Register of Deeds, 2610 14th Street, Columbus, NE 68601. 402-563-4911 (CST) 8AM-5PM.

**District Court**, PO Box 1188, Columbus, NE 68602-1188. 402-563-4906 (CST) 8:30AM-5:00PM. Felony, Civil Actions Over $15,000.

**Platte County Court**, PO Box 426, Columbus, NE 68602-1188. 402-563-4937 (CST) 8AM-5PM. Misdemeanor, Civil Actions Under $15,000, Eviction, Small Claims, Probate.

## Polk County

**Real Estate Recording**, Polk County Clerk, Courthouse Square, Osceola, NE 68651. 402-747-5431 (CST) 8AM-5PM.

**District Court**, PO Box 447, Osceola, NE 68651. 402-747-3487 (CST) 8AM-5PM. Felony, Civil Actions Over $15,000.

**Polk County Court**, PO Box 506, Osceola, NE 68651. 402-747-5371 (CST) 8AM-5PM M-Th, 8AM-4PM F. Misdemeanor, Civil Actions Under $15,000, Eviction, Small Claims, Probate.

## Red Willow County

**Real Estate Recording**, Red Willow County Clerk, 502 Norris Avenue, McCook, NE 69001. 308-345-1552 (CST)

**District Court**, 520 Norris Ave (PO Box 847), McCook, NE 69001. 308-345-4583 (CST) 8AM-4PM. Felony, Civil Actions Over $15,000.

**Red Willow County Court**, 520 Norris Ave, McCook, NE 69001. 308-345-1904 (CST) 8AM-4PM. Misdemeanor, Civil Actions Under $15,000, Eviction, Small Claims, Probate.

## Richardson County

**Real Estate Recording**, Richardson County Clerk, Courthouse, 1700 Stone, Falls City, NE 68355. 402-245-2911 (CST) 8:30AM-5PM.

**District Court**, 1700 Stone St, Falls City, NE 68355. 402-245-2023 (CST) 8:30AM-5PM. Felony, Civil Actions Over $15,000.

**Richardson County Court**, 1700 Stone St, Falls City, NE 68355. 402-245-2812 (CST) 8AM-5PM. Misdemeanor, Civil Actions Under $15,000, Eviction, Small Claims, Probate.

## Rock County

**Real Estate Recording**, Rock County Clerk, 400 State Street, Bassett, NE 68714. 402-684-3933 (CST)

**District Court**, 400 State St, Bassett, NE 68714. 402-684-3933 (CST) 9AM-5PM. Felony, Civil Actions Over $15,000.

**Rock County Court**, 400 State St, Bassett, NE 68714. 402-684-3601 (CST) 8AM-4:30PM. Misdemeanor, Civil Actions Under $15,000, Eviction, Small Claims, Probate.

## Saline County

**Real Estate Recording**, Saline County Clerk, 215 South Court, Wilber, NE 68465. 402-821-2374 (CST) 8AM-5PM.

**District Court**, 215 S Court St, Wilber, NE 68465. 402-821-2823 (CST) 8AM-5PM. Felony, Civil Actions Over $15,000.

**Saline County Court**, 215 S Court St, Wilber, NE 68465. 402-821-2131 (CST) 8AM-5PM. Misdemeanor, Civil Actions Under $15,000, Eviction, Small Claims, Probate.

## Sarpy County

**Real Estate Recording**, Sarpy County Register of Deeds, 1210 Golden Gate Drive #1109, Papillion, NE 68046. 402-593-2186 (CST) 8AM-4:45PM.

**District Court**, 1210 Golden Gate Dr, Ste 3131, Papillion, NE 68046. 402-593-2267 (CST) 8AM-4:45PM. Felony, Civil Actions Over $15,000.

**Sarpy County Court**, 1210 Golden Gate Dr, Ste 3142, Papillion, NE 68046. 402-593-2248 (CST) 8AM-4:45PM. Misdemeanor, Civil Actions Under $15,000, Eviction, Small Claims, Probate.

## Saunders County

**Real Estate Recording**, Saunders County Register of Deeds, 5th & Chestnut, Courthouse, Wahoo, NE 68066. 402-443-8111 (CST) 8AM-5PM.

**District Court**, County Courthouse, Wahoo, NE 68066. 402-443-8113 (CST) 8AM-5PM. Felony, Civil Actions Over $15,000.

**Saunders County Court**, County Courthouse, Wahoo, NE 68066. 402-443-8119 (CST) 8AM-5PM. Misdemeanor, Civil Actions Under $15,000, Eviction, Small Claims, Probate.

## Scotts Bluff County

**Real Estate Recording**, Scotts Bluff County Register of Deeds, 1825 10th Street, Administration Office Building, Gering, NE 69341. 308-436-6607 (MST) 8AM-4:30PM.

**District Court**, 1825 10th St, Gering, NE 69341. 308-436-6641 (MST) 8AM-4:30PM. Felony, Civil Actions Over $15,000.

**Scotts Bluff County Court**, 1825 10th St, Gering, NE 69341. 308-436-6648 (MST) 8AM-5PM. Misdemeanor, Civil Actions Under $15,000, Eviction, Small Claims, Probate.

## Seward County

**Real Estate Recording**, Seward County Clerk, 529 Seward Street, Seward, NE 68434. 402-643-2883 (CST) 8AM-5PM.

**District Court**, PO Box 36, Seward, NE 68434. 402-643-4895 (CST) 8AM-5PM. Felony, Civil Actions Over $15,000.

**Seward County Court**, PO Box 37, Seward, NE 68434. 402-643-3341 (CST) 8AM-5PM. Misdemeanor, Civil Actions Under $15,000, Eviction, Small Claims, Probate.

## Sheridan County

**Real Estate Recording**, Sheridan County Clerk, 301 East 2nd Street, Rushville, NE 69360. 308-327-2633 (MST) 8:30AM-4:30PM.

**District Court**, PO Box 581, Rushville, NE 69360. 308-327-2123 (MST) 8:30AM-4:30PM. Felony, Civil Actions Over $15,000.

**Sheridan County Court**, PO Box 430, Rushville, NE 69360. 308-327-2692 (MST) 8AM-4:30PM. Misdemeanor, Civil Actions Under $15,000, Eviction, Small Claims, Probate.

## Sherman County

**Real Estate Recording**, Sherman County Clerk, Courthouse, 630 "O" Street, Loup City, NE 68853. 308-745-1513 (CST) 8:30AM-4:30PM.

**District Court**, 630 O St, Loup City, NE 68853. 308-745-1841 (CST) 8:30AM-4:30PM. Felony, Civil Actions Over $15,000.

**Sherman County Court**, 630 O St, Loup City, NE 68853. 308-745-1510 (CST) 8:30AM-4:30PM. Misdemeanor, Civil Actions Under $15,000, Eviction, Small Claims, Probate.

## Sioux County

**Real Estate Recording**, Sioux County Clerk, Courthouse, Harrison, NE 69346. 308-668-2443 (MST) 8AM-5PM.

**District Court**, PO Box 158, Harrison, NE 69346. 308-668-2443 (MST) 8AM-5PM. Felony, Civil Actions Over $15,000.

**Sioux County Court**, PO Box 477, Harrison, NE 69346. 308-668-2475 (MST) 8AM-5PM. Misdemeanor, Civil Actions Under $15,000, Eviction, Small Claims, Probate.

## Stanton County

**Real Estate Recording**, Stanton County Clerk, 804 Ivy Street, Stanton, NE 68779. 402-439-2222 (CST) 8:30AM-4:30PM.

**District Court**, PO Box 347, Stanton, NE 68779. 402-439-2222 (CST) 8:30AM-4:30PM. Felony, Civil Actions Over $15,000.

**Stanton County Court**, 804 Ivey St, Stanton, NE 68779. 402-439-2221 (CST) Misdemeanor, Civil Actions Under $15,000, Eviction, Small Claims, Probate.

## Thayer County

**Real Estate Recording**, Thayer County Clerk, 225 N. 4th, Hebron, NE 68370. 402-768-6126 (CST) 8AM-Noon,1-5PM.

**District Court**, PO Box 297, Hebron, NE 68370. 402-768-6116 (CST) 8AM-5PM, Closed 12-1. Felony, Civil Actions Over $15,000.

**Thayer County Court**, PO Box 94, Hebron, NE 68370. 402-768-6325 (CST) 8AM-5PM. Misdemeanor, Civil Actions Under $15,000, Eviction, Small Claims, Probate.

## Thomas County

**Real Estate Recording**, Thomas County Clerk, 503 Main Street, Thedford, NE 69166. 308-645-2261 (CST) 8:30AM-Noon, 1-4:30PM.

**District Court**, PO Box 226, Thedford, NE 69166. 308-645-2261 (CST) 8:30AM-4:30PM, Closed 12-1. Felony, Civil Actions Over $15,000.

**Thomas County Court**, PO Box 131, Thedford, NE 69166. 308-645-2266 (CST) 8AM-4:30PM. Misdemeanor, Civil Actions Under $15,000, Eviction, Small Claims, Probate.

## Thurston County

**Real Estate Recording**, Thurston County Clerk, 106 South 5th Street, Pender, NE 68047. 402-385-2343 (CST) 8:30AM-5PM.

**District Court**, PO Box 216, Pender, NE 68047. 402-385-3318 (CST) 8:30AM-5PM. Felony, Civil Actions Over $15,000.

**Thurston County Court**, County Courthouse, Pender, NE 68047. 402-385-3136 (CST) Misdemeanor, Civil Actions Under $15,000, Eviction, Small Claims, Probate.

## Valley County

**Real Estate Recording**, Valley County Clerk, 125 South 15th, Ord, NE 68862-1499. 308-728-3700 (CST) 8AM-5PM.

**District Court**, 125 S 5th St, Ord, NE 68862. 308-728-3700 (CST) 8AM-5PM. Felony, Civil Actions Over $15,000.

**Valley County Court**, 125 S 5th St, Ord, NE 68862. 308-728-3831 (CST) Misdemeanor, Civil Actions Under $15,000, Eviction, Small Claims, Probate.

## Washington County

**Real Estate Recording**, Washington County Clerk, 1555 Colfax Street, Blair, NE 68008. 402-426-6822 (CST) 8AM-4:30PM.

**District Court**, PO Box 431, Blair, NE 68008. 402-426-6899 (CST) 8AM-4:30PM. Felony, Civil Actions Over $15,000.

**Washington County Court**, PO Box 615, Blair, NE 68008. 402-426-6833 (CST) 8AM-4:30PM. Misdemeanor, Civil Actions Under $15,000, Eviction, Small Claims, Probate.

## Wayne County

**Real Estate Recording**, Wayne County Clerk, 510 Pearl Street, Wayne, NE 68787. 402-375-2288 (CST) 8:30AM-5PM.

**District Court**, 510 Pearl St, Wayne, NE 68787. 402-375-2260 (CST) 8:30AM-5PM. Felony, Civil Actions Over $15,000.

**Wayne County Court**, 510 Pearl St, Wayne, NE 68787. 402-375-1622 (CST) 8AM-5:15PM. Misdemeanor, Civil Actions Under $15,000, Eviction, Small Claims, Probate.

## Webster County

**Real Estate Recording**, Webster County Clerk, 621 North Cedar, Court House, Red Cloud, NE 68970. 402-746-2716 (CST) 8AM-4:30PM.

**District Court**, 621 N Cedar, Red Cloud, NE 68970. 402-746-2716 (CST) 8:30AM-4:30PM. Felony, Civil Actions Over $15,000.

**Webster County Court**, 621 N Cedar, Red Cloud, NE 68970. 402-746-2777 (CST) 8:30AM-4:30PM. Misdemeanor, Civil Actions Under $15,000, Eviction, Small Claims, Probate.

## Wheeler County

**Real Estate Recording**, Wheeler County Clerk, Courthouse, Bartlett, NE 68622. 308-654-3235 (CST)

**District Court**, PO Box 127, Bartlett, NE 68622. 308-654-3235 (CST) 9AM-5PM. Felony, Civil Actions Over $15,000.

**Wheeler County Court**, PO Box 127, Bartlett, NE 68622. 308-654-3376 (CST) 9AM-5PM. Misdemeanor, Civil Actions Under $15,000, Eviction, Small Claims, Probate.

## York County

**Real Estate Recording**, York County Clerk, Courthouse, York, NE 68467. 402-362-7759 (CST) 8:30AM-5PM.

**District Court**, 510 Lincoln Ave, York, NE 68467. 402-362-4038 (CST) 8:30AM-5PM. Felony, Civil Actions Over $15,000.

**York County Court**, 510 Lincoln Ave, York, NE 68467. 402-362-4925 (CST) 8AM-5PM. Misdemeanor, Civil Actions Under $15,000, Eviction, Small Claims, Probate.

# Nevada

## Carson City

**Real Estate Recording**, Carson City Recorder, 198 North Carson Street, Carson City, NV 89701. 702-887-2260 (PST) 8AM-5PM.

**1st Judicial District Court**, 198 N Carson St, Carson City, NV 89701. 702-887-2082 (PST) 9AM-5PM. Felony, Misdemeanor, Civil Actions Over $7,500, Probate.

**Justice Court**, 320 N Carson St, Carson City, NV 89701. 702-887-2275 (PST) 9AM-4PM M-W/9AM-5:30PM Th/9AM-3:30PM F (crim)/8:30AM-4PM (civ). Misdemeanor, Civil Actions Under $7,500, Eviction, Small Claims.

## Churchill County

**Real Estate Recording**, Churchill County Recorder, 10 West Williams Avenue, Fallon, NV 89406-2989. 702-423-6001 (PST) 8AM-5PM.

**3rd Judicial District Court**, 73 N Maine St, Fallon, NV 89406. 702-423-6080 (PST) 8AM-5PM, Closed 12-1. Felony, Misdemeanor, Civil Actions Over $7,500, Probate.

**Justice Court**, 73 N Maine St, Fallon, NV 89406. 702-423-2845 (PST) 8AM-5PM, Closed 12-1. Misdemeanor, Civil Actions Under $7,500, Eviction, Small Claims.

## Clark County

**Real Estate Recording**, Clark County Recorder, 309 South 3rd Street, Las Vegas, NV 89101. 702-455-4336 (PST) 9AM-5PM.

**8th Judicial District Court**, 200 S 3rd (PO Box 551601), Las Vegas, NV 89155. 702-455-3156 (PST) 8AM-4PM. Felony, Misdemeanor, Civil Actions Over $7,500, Probate.

**Boulder Township Justice Court**, 401 California Ave, Boulder City, NV 89005. 702-455-8000 (PST) 8AM-5:30PM. Misdemeanor, Civil Actions Under $7,500, Eviction, Small Claims.

**Bunkerville Township Justice**, 1st West & 1st North (PO Box 7185), Bunkerville, NV 89007. 702-346-5711 (PST) 8AM-5PM M-Th. Misdemeanor, Civil Actions Under $7,500, Eviction, Small Claims.

**Henderson Township Justice**, 241 Water St, Henderson, NV 89015. 702-455-7951 (PST) 7AM-6PM M-Th. Misdemeanor, Civil Actions Under $7,500, Eviction, Small Claims.

**Goodsprings Township Justice**, 1 Main St (PO Box 19155), Jean, NV 89019. 702-874-1405 (PST) 8AM-4PM. Misdemeanor, Civil Actions Under $7,500, Eviction, Small Claims.

**Las Vegas Township Justice**, 200 S 3rd, 2nd Fl, Las Vegas, NV 89155. 702-455-4435 (PST) 8AM-5PM. Misdemeanor, Civil Actions Under $7,500, Eviction, Small Claims.

**Laughlin Township Justice Court**, PO Box 2305, Laughlin, NV 89029. 702-298-4622 (PST) 8AM-5PM. Misdemeanor, Civil Actions Under $7,500, Eviction, Small Claims.

**Moapa Valley Township Justice**, PO Box 359, Logandale, NV 89021. 702-398-3213 (PST) 7AM-Noon M-Th. Misdemeanor, Civil Actions Under $7,500, Eviction, Small Claims.

**Mesquite Township Justice Court**, PO Box 1209, Mesquite, NV 89024. 702-346-5298 (PST) 8AM-12:30PM. Misdemeanor, Civil Actions Under $7,500, Eviction, Small Claims.

**Moapa Township Justice Court**, PO Box 280, Moapa, NV 89025. 702-864-2333 (PST) 8AM-5PM M-Th. Misdemeanor, Civil Actions Under $7,500, Eviction, Small Claims.

**North Las Vegas Township Justice**, 1916 N Bruce, N Las Vegas, NV 89030. 702-455-7801 (PST) 8AM-5PM. Misdemeanor, Civil Actions Under $7,500, Eviction, Small Claims.

**Searchlight Township Justice**, PO Box 815, Searchlight, NV 89046. 702-297-1252 (PST) 7:30AM-6:30PM M-Th. Misdemeanor, Civil Actions Under $7,500, Eviction, Small Claims.

## Douglas County

**Real Estate Recording**, Douglas County Recorder, 1616 8th Street, Minden, NV 89423. 702-782-9026 (PST) 9AM-5PM.

**9th District Court**, Box 218, Minden, NV 89423. 702-782-9820 (PST) 8AM-5PM. Felony, Misdemeanor, Civil Actions Over $7,500, Probate.

**E Fork Justice Court**, PO Box 218, Minden, NV 89423. 702-782-9955 (PST) 8AM-5PM. Misdemeanor, Civil Actions Under $7,500, Eviction, Small Claims.

**Tahoe Justice Court**, PO Box 7169, Stateline, NV 89449. 702-588-8100 (PST) 9AM-5PM. Misdemeanor, Civil Actions Under $7,500, Eviction, Small Claims.

## Elko County

**Real Estate Recording**, Elko County Recorder, 571 Idaho St., Room 103, Elko, NV 89801-3770. 702-738-6526 (PST) 9AM-5PM.

**4th District Court**, 571 Idaho St, Elko, NV 89801. 702-738-3044 (PST) 9AM-5PM. Felony, Misdemeanor, Civil Actions Over $7,500, Probate.

**Carlin Justice Court**, PO Box 789, Carlin, NV 89822. 702-754-6321 (PST) 8AM-5PM. Misdemeanor, Civil Actions Under $7,500, Eviction, Small Claims.

**Elko Justice Court**, PO Box 176, Elko, NV 89803. 702-738-8403 (PST) Misdemeanor, Civil Actions Under $7,500, Eviction, Small Claims.

**Jackpot Justice Court**, PO Box 229, Jackpot, NV 89825. 702-755-2456 (PST) Misdemeanor, Civil Actions Under $7,500, Eviction, Small Claims.

**Jarbidge Justice Court**, PO Box 26001, Jarbidge, NV 89826-2001. 702-488-2331 (PST) Misdemeanor, Civil Actions Under $7,500, Eviction, Small Claims.

**Mountain City Justice Court**, Courthouse, Mountain City, NV 89831. 702-763-6686 (PST) Misdemeanor, Civil Actions Under $7,500, Eviction, Small Claims.

**Wells Justice Municipal Court**, PO Box 297, Wells, NV 89835. 702-752-3726 (PST) 9AM-5PM. Misdemeanor, Civil Actions Under $7,500, Eviction, Small Claims.

**Eastline Justice Court**, PO Box 2300, Wendover, NV 89883. 702-664-2305 (PST) 9AM-4PM. Misdemeanor, Civil Actions Under $7,500, Eviction, Small Claims.

## Esmeralda County

**Real Estate Recording**, Esmeralda County Recorder, 491 Crook Street, Courthouse, Goldfield, NV 89013. 702-485-6337 (PST) 8AM-Noon,1-5PM.

**5th Judicial District Court**, PO Box 547, Goldfield, NV 89013. 702-485-6367 (PST) 8AM-5PM. Felony, Misdemeanor, Civil Actions Over $7,500, Probate.

**Esmeralda Justice Court**, PO Box 370, Goldfield, NV 89013. 702-485-6359 (PST) 8AM-5PM. Misdemeanor, Civil Actions Under $7,500, Eviction, Small Claims.

## Eureka County

**Real Estate Recording**, Eureka County Recorder, 10204 Main Street, Eureka, NV 89316. 702-237-5263 (PST) 8AM-Noon, 1-5PM.

**7th Judicial District Court**, PO Box 677, Eureka, NV 89316. 702-237-5262 (PST) 8AM-5PM, Closed 12-1. Felony, Misdemeanor, Civil Actions Over $7,500, Probate.

**Crescent Valley Justice Court**, PO Box 211065A, Crescent Valley, NV 89821. 702-468-0244 (PST) Misdemeanor, Civil Actions Under $7,500, Eviction, Small Claims.

**Eureka Justice Court**, PO Box 496, Eureka, NV 89316. 702-237-5540 (PST) 8AM-4PM. Misdemeanor, Civil Actions Under $7,500, Eviction, Small Claims.

## Humboldt County

**Real Estate Recording**, Humboldt County Recorder, 25 West 4th Street, Winnemucca, NV 89445. 702-623-6414 (PST) 8AM-5PM.

**6th District Court**, 50 W Fifth St, Winnemucca, NV 89445. 702-623-6343 (PST) 8AM-5PM. Felony, Misdemeanor, Civil Actions Over $7,500, Probate.

**Union Justice Court**, PO Box 1218, Winnemucca, NV 89446. 702-623-6377 (PST) 7AM-5PM. Misdemeanor, Civil Actions Under $7,500, Eviction, Small Claims.

## Lander County

**Real Estate Recording**, Lander County Recorder, 315 South Humboldt, Battle Mountain, NV 89820. 702-635-5173 (PST) 8AM-5PM.

**6th District Court**, 315 S Humboldt, Battle Mountain, NV 89820. 702-635-5738 (PST) 8AM-5PM. Felony, Misdemeanor, Civil Actions Over $7,500, Probate.

**Austin Justice Court**, PO Box 100, Austin, NV 89310. 702-964-2380 (PST) 8AM-5PM M, 8AM-Noon T-Th. Misdemeanor, Civil Actions Under $7,500, Eviction, Small Claims.

**Argenta Justice Court**, 315 S Humboldt, Battle Mountain, NV 89820. 702-635-5151 (PST) 8AM-5PM. Misdemeanor, Civil Actions Under $7,500, Eviction, Small Claims.

## Lincoln County

**Real Estate Recording**, Lincoln County Recorder, 1 Main Street, Courthouse, Pioche, NV 89043. 702-962-5495 (PST) 9AM-5PM.

**7th District Court**, PO Box 90, Pioche, NV 89043. 702-962-5390 (PST) 9AM-5PM. Felony, Misdemeanor, Civil Actions Over $7,500, Probate.

**Pahranagat Valley Justice Court**, PO Box 449, Alamo, NV 89001. 702-725-3357 (PST) 9AM-5PM. Misdemeanor, Civil Actions Under $7,500, Eviction, Small Claims.

**Meadow Valley Justice Court**, PO Box 36, Pioche, NV 89043. 702-962-5140 (PST) 9AM-5PM. Misdemeanor, Civil Actions Under $7,500, Eviction, Small Claims.

## Lyon County

**Real Estate Recording**, Lyon County Recorder, 31 South Main Street, Yerington, NV 89447. 702-463-3341 (PST) 8AM-5PM.

**3rd District Court**, PO Box 816, Yerington, NV 89447. 702-463-3341 (PST) 8AM-5PM. Felony, Misdemeanor, Civil Actions Over $7,500, Probate.

**Dayton Township Justice Court**, PO Box 490, Dayton, NV 89403. 702-246-0329 (PST) 8AM-5PM. Misdemeanor, Civil Actions Under $7,500, Eviction, Small Claims.

**Canal Justice Court**, PO Box 497, Fernley, NV 89408. 702-575-4492 (PST) 8AM-5PM. Misdemeanor, Civil Actions Under $7,500, Eviction, Small Claims.

**Smith Valley Justice Court**, PO Box 141, Smith, NV 89430. 702-465-2313 (PST) Misdemeanor, Civil Actions Under $7,500, Eviction, Small Claims.

**Mason Valley Justice Court**, 30 Nevin Way, Yerington, NV 89447. 702-463-3341 (PST) 8AM-5PM. Misdemeanor, Civil Actions Under $7,500, Eviction, Small Claims.

## Mineral County

**Real Estate Recording**, Mineral County Recorder, 105 South A Street, P.O. Box 1447, Hawthorne, NV 89415. 702-945-3676 (PST) 8AM-5PM.

**5th Judicial District Court**, PO Box 1450, Hawthorne, NV 89415. 702-945-2446 (PST) 8AM-5PM. Felony, Misdemeanor, Civil Actions Over $7,500, Probate.

**Hawthorne Justice Court**, PO Box 1660, Hawthorne, NV 89415. 702-945-3859 (PST) 8AM-5PM. Misdemeanor, Civil Actions Under $7,500, Eviction, Small Claims.

**Mina Justice Court**, PO Box 415, Mina, NV 89422. 702-573-2547 (PST) 9AM-4PM. Misdemeanor, Civil Actions Under $7,500, Eviction, Small Claims.

**Schurz Justice Court**, PO Box 220, Schurz, NV 89427. 702-773-2241 (PST) Misdemeanor, Civil Actions Under $7,500, Eviction, Small Claims.

## Nye County

**Real Estate Recording**, Nye County Recorder, 1 Courthouse Rd., Tonopah, NV 89049. 702-482-8116 (PST) 8AM-Noon, 1-5PM.

**5th Judicial District Court**, PO Box 1031, Tonopah, NV 89049. 702-482-8131 (PST) Felony, Misdemeanor, Civil Actions Over $7,500, Probate.

**Beatty Justice Court**, PO Box 805, Beatty, NV 89003. 702-553-2951 (PST) 8AM-5PM. Misdemeanor, Civil Actions Under $7,500, Eviction, Small Claims.

**Gabbs Justice Court**, PO Box 533, Gabbs, NV 89409. 702-285-2379 (PST) 9AM-4PM M-Th. Misdemeanor, Civil Actions Under $7,500, Eviction, Small Claims.

**Tonopah Justice Court**, PO Box 1151, Tonopah, NV 89049. 702-482-8153 (PST) 8AM-5PM. Misdemeanor, Civil Actions Under $7,500, Eviction, Small Claims.

## Pershing County

**Real Estate Recording**, Pershing County Recorder, Courthouse, 400 Main Street, Lovelock, NV 89419. 702-273-2408 (PST) 8AM-5PM.

**6th Judicial District Court**, PO Box 820, Lovelock, NV 89419. 702-273-2208 (PST) 9AM-5PM. Felony, Misdemeanor, Civil Actions Over $7,500, Probate.

**Lake Justice Court**, PO Box 8, Lovelock, NV 89419. 702-273-2753 (PST) 8AM-5PM. Misdemeanor, Civil Actions Under $7,500, Eviction, Small Claims.

## Storey County

**Real Estate Recording**, Storey County Recorder, B Street, Courthouse, Virginia City, NV 89440. 702-847-0967 (PST) 9AM-5PM.

**1st Judicial District Court**, PO Drawer D, Virginia City, NV 89440. 702-847-0969 (PST) 9AM-5PM. Felony, Misdemeanor, Civil Actions Over $7,500, Probate.

**Virginia City Justice Court**, PO Box 674, Virginia City, NV 89440. 702-847-0962 (PST) 9AM-5PM. Misdemeanor, Civil Actions Under $7,500, Eviction, Small Claims.

## Washoe County

**Real Estate Recording**, Washoe County Recorder, 1001 East 9th Street, Reno, NV 89512. 702-328-3661 (PST) 8AM-5PM.

**2nd Judicial District Court**, PO Box 11130, Reno, NV 89520. 702-328-3110 (PST) 8AM-5PM. Felony, Misdemeanor, Civil Actions Over $7,500, Probate.

**Reno Justice Court**, PO Box 11130, Reno, NV 89520. 702-785-4230 (PST) 8AM-5PM. Misdemeanor, Civil Actions Under $7,500, Eviction, Small Claims.

**Sparks Justice Court**, 630 Greenbrae Dr, Sparks, NV 89431. 702-352-3000 (PST) 8AM-4PM for service. Misdemeanor, Civil Actions Under $7,500, Eviction, Small Claims.

## White Pine County

**Real Estate Recording**, White Pine County Recorder, Courthouse Plaza, Ely, NV 89301. 702-289-4567 (PST) 9AM-5PM.

**7th Judicial District Court**, PO Box 659, Ely, NV 89301. 702-289-2341 (PST) 9AM-5PM. Felony, Misdemeanor, Civil Actions Over $7,500, Probate.

**Baker Justice Court**, PO Box 2, Baker, NV 89311. 702-234-7304 (PST) Misdemeanor, Civil Actions Under $7,500, Eviction, Small Claims.

**Ely Justice Court**, PO Box 396, Ely, NV 89301. 702-289-2678 (PST) 9AM-5PM. Misdemeanor, Civil Actions Under $7,500, Eviction, Small Claims.

**Lund Justice Court**, PO Box 86, Lund, NV 89317. 702-238-5400 (PST) 10AM-2:30PM, Closed 11:30-1 M,T,Th,F. Misdemeanor, Civil Actions Under $7,500, Eviction, Small Claims.

# New Hampshire

## Belknap County

**Real Estate Recording**, Belknap County Register of Deeds, 64 Court St., Laconia, NH 03246. 603-524-0618 (EST) 8:30AM-4PM.

**Superior Court**, 64 Court St, Laconia, NH 03247. 603-524-3570 (EST) 8AM-4:30PM. Felony, Civil Actions Over $10,000.

**Laconia District Court**, 26 Academy St, Laconia, NH 03246. 603-524-4128 (EST) 8AM-4:30PM. Misdemeanor, Civil Actions Under $25,000, Eviction, Small Claims.

**Probate Court**, 64 Court St, Laconia, NH 03246. 603-524-3570 (EST) 8AM-4:30PM. Probate.

## Carroll County

**Real Estate Recording**, Carroll County Register of Deeds, Route 171, Ossipee, NH 03864. 603-539-4872 (EST) 9AM-5PM.

**Superior Court**, PO Box 157, Ossipee, NH 03864. 603-539-2201 (EST) 8AM-4:30PM. Felony, Civil Actions Over $10,000.

**Northern Carroll County District Court**, PO Box 940, Conway, NH 03818. 603-356-7710 (EST) 8:30AM-4:30PM. Misdemeanor, Civil Actions Under $25,000, Eviction, Small Claims.

**Ossipee District Court**, PO Box 127 Route 171, Ossipee, NH 03864. 603-539-4561 (EST) 9AM-4PM. Misdemeanor, Civil Actions Under $25,000, Eviction, Small Claims.

**Wolfeboro District Court**, PO Box 90, Wolfeboro, NH 03894. 603-569-2427 (EST) 9AM-4PM. Misdemeanor, Civil Actions Under $25,000, Eviction, Small Claims.

**Probate Court**, PO Box 157, Ossipee, NH 03864. 603-539-4123 (EST) 8:30AM-4:30PM (phone is answered from 11:30 AM-4:30 PM. Probate.

## Cheshire County

**Real Estate Recording**, Cheshire County Register of Deeds, 33 West Street, Keene, NH 03431. 603-352-0403 (EST) 8:30-4:30PM.

**Superior Court**, PO Box 444, Keene, NH 03431. 603-352-6902 (EST) 9AM-4:30PM. Felony, Civil Actions Over $10,000.

**Jaffrey-Peterborough District Court**, 173 E Main St (PO Box 39), Jaffrey, NH 03452. 603-532-8698 (EST) 8AM-4PM M-Th. Misdemeanor, Civil Actions Under $25,000, Eviction, Small Claims.

**Keene District Court**, PO Box 364, Keene, NH 03431. 603-352-2559 (EST) Misdemeanor, Civil Actions Under $25,000, Eviction, Small Claims.

**Probate Court**, 12 Court St, Keene, NH 03431. 603-357-7786 (EST) 8:30AM-4:30PM M-W, 8:30AM-3:30PM Th-F. Probate.

## Coos County

**Real Estate Recording**, Coos County Register of Deeds, 148 Main Street, Courthouse, Lancaster, NH 03584. 603-788-2392 (EST) 8AM-4PM.

**Superior Court**, PO Box 309, Lancaster, NH 03584. 603-788-4900 (EST) 8AM-4:15PM. Felony, Civil Actions Over $10,000.

**Berlin District Court**, 220 Main St, Berlin, NH 03570. 603-752-3160 (EST) 8AM-4PM M-W,F. Misdemeanor, Civil Actions Under $25,000, Eviction, Small Claims.

**Colebrook District Court**, PO Box 5, Colebrook, NH 03576. 603-237-4229 (EST) 8AM-4PM. Misdemeanor, Civil Actions Under $25,000, Eviction, Small Claims.

**Gorham District Court**, PO Box 176, Gorham, NH 03581. 603-466-2454 (EST) 8AM-4PM. Misdemeanor, Civil Actions Under $25,000, Eviction, Small Claims.

**Lancaster District Court**, PO Box 485, Lancaster, NH 03584. 603-788-4485 (EST) 8:30 AM-4:00PM. Misdemeanor, Civil Actions Under $25,000, Eviction, Small Claims.

**Probate Court**, Box 306, Lancaster, NH 03584. 603-788-2001 (EST) Probate.

## Grafton County

**Real Estate Recording**, Grafton County Register of Deeds, Route 10, North Haverhill, NH 03785. 603-787-6921 (EST) 7:30AM-4:30PM.

**Superior Court**, RR1 Box 65, Haverhill, NH 03774-9708. 603-787-6961 (EST) 8AM-4:30PM. Felony, Civil Actions Over $10,000.

**Hanover District Court**, PO Box 631, Hanover, NH 03755. 603-643-5681 (EST) 8AM-4:30PM. Misdemeanor, Civil Actions Under $25,000, Eviction, Small Claims.

**Littleton District Court**, 165 Main St, Littleton, NH 03561. 603-444-7750 (EST) 8:30AM-4PM M,W-F. Misdemeanor, Civil Actions Under $25,000, Eviction, Small Claims.

**Plymouth District Court**, PO Box 159, Plymouth, NH 03264. 603-536-3326 (EST) 8AM-4:30PM. Misdemeanor, Civil Actions Under $25,000, Eviction, Small Claims.

**Haverhill District Court**, Municipal Bldg, Court St, Woodsville, NH 03785. 603-747-3063 (EST) 8:30AM-4:30PM. Misdemeanor, Civil Actions Under $25,000, Eviction, Small Claims.

**Probate Court**, RR1 Box 65C, North Haverhill, NH 03774-9700. 603-787-6931 (EST) 8AM-4:30PM. Probate.

## Hillsborough County

**Real Estate Recording**, Hillsborough County Treasurer, 19 Temple Street, Nashua, NH 03060. 603-882-6933 (EST) 8AM-3:45PM.

**Superior Court-North District**, 300 Chestnut St, Rm 127, Manchester, NH 03101. 603-424-9951 (EST) 8:30AM-4PM. Felony, Civil Actions Over $10,000.

**Superior Court-South District**, 30 Spring St, Nashua, NH 03061. 603-883-6461 (EST) 8:30AM-4:30PM. Felony, Civil Actions Over $10,000.

**Milford District Court**, PO Box 148, Amherst, NH 03031. 603-673-2900 (EST) 8AM-3PM. Misdemeanor, Civil Actions Under $25,000, Eviction, Small Claims.

**Goffstown District Court**, 16 Main St, Goffstown, NH 03045. 603-497-2597 (EST) 8AM-4PM. Misdemeanor, Civil Actions Under $25,000, Eviction, Small Claims.

**Hillsborough District Court**, PO Box 763, Hillsborough, NH 03244. 603-464-5811 (EST) 8AM-3:30PM. Misdemeanor, Civil Actions Under $25,000, Eviction, Small Claims.

**Manchester District Court**, PO Box 456, Manchester, NH 03105. 603-624-6510 (EST) 8AM-4PM. Misdemeanor, Civil Actions Under $25,000, Eviction, Small Claims.

**Merrimack District Court**, PO Box 324, Merrimack, NH 03054-0324. 603-424-9916 (EST) 8:30AM-3PM. Misdemeanor, Civil Actions Under $25,000, Eviction, Small Claims.

**Nashua District Court**, Walnut St Oval, Nashua, NH 03060. 603-880-3333 (EST) 8AM-4:15PM. Misdemeanor, Civil Actions Under $25,000, Eviction, Small Claims.

**Probate Court**, PO Box P, Nashua, NH 03061. 603-882-1231 (EST) 8AM-4PM. Probate.

## Merrimack County

**Real Estate Recording**, Merrimack County Register of Deeds, 163 North Main, Concord, NH 03301. 603-228-0101 (EST) 8AM-4:15PM.

**Superior Court**, PO Box 2880, Concord, NH 03302-2880. 603-225-5501 (EST) 8:30AM-4PM. Felony, Civil Actions Over $10,000.

**Concord District Court**, PO Box 1512, Concord, NH 03302-1512. 603-271-6400 (EST) 8AM-4PM. Misdemeanor, Civil Actions Under $25,000, Eviction, Small Claims.

**Franklin District Court**, PO Box 172, Franklin, NH 03235. 603-934-3290 (EST) 8:30AM-3:30PM. Misdemeanor, Civil Actions Under $25,000, Eviction, Small Claims.

**Henniker District Court**, 2 Depot St, Henniker, NH 03242. 603-428-3214 (EST) 8AM-4PM. Misdemeanor, Civil Actions Under $25,000, Eviction, Small Claims.

**Hooksett District Court**, 101 Merrimack, Hooksett, NH 03106. 603-485-9901 (EST) 8:30AM-4PM. Misdemeanor, Civil Actions Under $25,000, Eviction, Small Claims.

**New London District Court**, PO Box 1966, New London, NH 03257. 603-526-6519 (EST) 8:30AM-4:30PM. Misdemeanor, Civil Actions Under $25,000, Eviction, Small Claims.

**Pittsfield District Court**, PO Box 86, Pittsfield, NH 03263. 603-435-7192 (EST) 9AM-4PM M-Th. Misdemeanor, Civil Actions Under $25,000, Eviction, Small Claims.

**Probate Court**, 163 N Main St, Concord, NH 03301. 603-224-9589 (EST) 8AM-4:30PM. Probate.

## Rockingham County

**Real Estate Recording**, Rockingham County Register of Deeds, Hampton Road, Exeter, NH 03833-4823. 603-772-4712 (EST) 7AM-4PM.

**Superior Court**, 1 Hampton Rd, Exeter, NH 03833. 603-772-3714 (EST) 8:30AM-4PM. Felony, Civil Actions Over $10,000.

**Auburn District Court**, 284 Route 28 Bypass, Auburn, NH 03032. 603-624-2084 (EST) 8AM-4:30PM. Misdemeanor, Civil Actions Under $25,000, Eviction, Small Claims.

**Derry District Court**, 29 W Broadway, Derry, NH 03038. 603-434-4676 (EST) 8AM-4PM. Misdemeanor, Civil Actions Under $25,000, Eviction, Small Claims.

**Hampton District Court**, 132 Winnacunnet Rd, Hampton, NH 03842. 603-926-8117 (EST) 8AM-4PM. Misdemeanor, Civil Actions Under $25,000, Eviction, Small Claims.

**Plaistow District Court**, PO Box 129, Plaistow, NH 03865. 603-382-4651 (EST) 8AM-4PM. Misdemeanor, Civil Actions Under $25,000, Eviction, Small Claims.

**Portsmouth District Court**, 111 Parrott Ave, Portsmouth, NH 03801. 603-431-2192 (EST) 8AM-3PM. Misdemeanor, Civil Actions Under $25,000, Eviction, Small Claims.

**Salem District Court**, 35 Geremonty Dr, Salem, NH 03079. 603-893-4483 (EST) 8AM-4PM. Misdemeanor, Civil Actions Under $25,000, Eviction, Small Claims.

**Probate Court**, 1 Hampton Rd, Exeter, NH 03833. 603-772-9347 (EST) 8AM-4PM. Probate.

## Strafford County

**Real Estate Recording**, Strafford County Register of Deeds, County Farm Road, Dover, NH 03820. 603-742-1741 (EST) 8:30AM-4:30PM.

**Superior Court**, PO Box 799, Dover, NH 03820. 603-742-3065 (EST) 8:30AM-4:30PM. Felony, Civil Actions Over $10,000.

**Dover District Court**, 25 St Thomas St, Dover, NH 03820. 603-742-7202 (EST) 8AM-4PM. Misdemeanor, Civil Actions Under $25,000, Eviction, Small Claims.

**Durham District Court**, 1 New Market Rd, Durham, NH 03824-2897. 603-868-2323 (EST) 8AM-4:30PM. Misdemeanor, Civil Actions Under $25,000, Eviction, Small Claims.

**Rochester District Court**, PO Box 68, Rochester, NH 03866. 603-332-3516 (EST) 8AM-4:30PM. Misdemeanor, Civil Actions Under $25,000, Eviction, Small Claims.

**Somersworth District Court**, 2 Pleasant St, Somersworth, NH 03878-2543. 603-692-5967 (EST) 8AM-3PM. Misdemeanor, Civil Actions Under $25,000, Eviction, Small Claims.

**Probate Court**, PO Box 799, Dover, NH 03821-0799. 603-742-2550 (EST) 8AM-4:30PM. Probate.

## Sullivan County

**Real Estate Recording**, Sullivan County Register of Deeds, 20 Main Street, Newport, NH 03773. 603-863-2110 (EST) 8AM-4PM.

**Superior Court**, 22 Main St, Newport, NH 03773. 603-863-3450 (EST) 8AM-4:30PM. Felony, Civil Actions Over $10,000.

**Claremont District Court**, PO Box 313, Claremont, NH 03743. 603-542-6064 (EST) 8AM-3PM. Misdemeanor, Civil Actions Under $25,000, Eviction, Small Claims.

**Newport District Court**, PO Box 581, Newport, NH 03773. 603-863-1832 (EST) 8AM-3PM MWF, 8AM-4PM T,Th. Misdemeanor, Civil Actions Under $25,000, Eviction, Small Claims.

**Probate Court**, PO Box 417, Newport, NH 03773. 603-863-3150 (EST) 8AM-4:30PM. Probate.

# New Jersey

## Atlantic County

**Real Estate Recording**, Atlantic County Clerk, 5901 E. Main Street, Courthouse, Mays Landing, NJ 08330-1797. 609-625-4011 (EST) 8:30AM-4:30PM.

**Superior Court**, Criminal Courthouse, 5909 Main St, Mays Landing, NJ 08330. 609-625-7000 (EST) 8:30AM-4:30PM. Felony, Civil Actions Over $10,000, Probate.

**Special Civil Part**, 1201 Bacharach Blvd., Atlantic City, NJ 08401. 609-345-6700 (EST) 8:30AM-4:30PM. Civil Actions Under $10,000, Eviction, Small Claims.

## Bergen County

**Real Estate Recording**, Bergen County Clerk, Justice Center Room 214, 10 Main St., Hackensack, NJ 07601-7000. 201-646-2291 (EST) 9AM-4PM.

**Superior Court**, 10 Main St. Rm 119, Justice Center, Hackensack, NJ 07601. 201-646-2105 (EST) 8:30AM-5PM. Felony, Civil Actions Over $10,000, Probate.

**Special Civil Part**, 10 Main St. Rm 430, Justice Center, Hackensack, NJ 07601. 201-646-2289 (EST) 8:30AM-4:30PM. Civil Actions Under $10,000, Eviction, Small Claims.

## Burlington County

**Real Estate Recording**, Burlington County Clerk, 49 Rancocas Road, Mount Holly, NJ 08060. 609-265-5180 (EST)

**Superior Court**, 49 Rancocas Rd, Mount Holly, NJ 08060. 609-265-5075 (EST) 8AM-5PM. Felony, Civil Actions Over $10,000, Probate.

**Special Civil Part**, 49 Racocas Rd., Mount Holly, NJ 08060. 609-265-5075 (EST) 8AM-5PM. Civil Actions Under $10,000, Eviction, Small Claims.

## Camden County

**Real Estate Recording**, Camden County Register of Deeds, Courthouse Room 102, 520 Market Street, Camden, NJ 08102-1375. 609-225-5320 (EST) 9AM-4PM.

**Superior Court**, Hall of Justice Complex, 101 S 5th St, Camden, NJ 08103-4002. 609-225-7433 (EST) 8:30AM-4:30 PM. Felony, Civil Actions Over $10,000, Probate.

**Special Civil Part**, Hall of Justice Complex, 101 S. 5th St., Camden, NJ 08103. 609-225-7433 (EST) 8:30AM-4:30PM. Civil Actions Under $10,000, Eviction, Small Claims.

## Cape May County

**Real Estate Recording**, Cape May County Clerk, 7 North Main Street, DN 109, Cape May Court House, NJ 08210. 609-465-1010 (EST) 8:30AM-4:30PM.

**Superior Court**, 7 North Main St (Civil); DN-209-B 4 More, Cape May Courthouse, NJ 08210. 609-463-6550 (EST) 8:30AM-4:30PM. Felony, Civil Actions Over $10,000, Probate.

**Special Civil Part**, 9 N Main St, Dept #203, Cape May Court House, NJ 08210. 609-463-6446 (EST) 8:30AM-4:30PM. Civil Actions Under $10,000, Eviction, Small Claims.

## Cumberland County

**Real Estate Recording**, Cumberland County Clerk, 60 W. Broad St., Courthouse, Bridgeton, NJ 08302. 609-451-8000 (EST) X209 8:30AM-4PM.

**Superior Court**, PO Box 757, Bridgeton, NJ 08302. 609-451-8000 (EST) 8:30AM-4:30PM. Felony, Civil Actions Over $10,000, Probate.

**Special Civil Part**, Box 615, Bridgeton, NJ 08302. 609-451-8000 (EST) 8:30AM-4:30PM. Civil Actions Under $10,000, Eviction, Small Claims.

## Essex County

**Real Estate Recording**, Essex County Register of Deeds, 465 Martin Luther King Boulevard, Hall of Records, Newark, NJ 07102. 201-621-4962 (EST) 9AM-4PM.

**Superior Court**, Rm 610, Essex County Court Bld, Newark, NJ 07102-1681. 201-621-4862 (EST) 8:30AM-4:30PM. Felony, Civil Actions Over $10,000, Probate.

**Special Civil Part**, 470 Martin Luther King Blvd, Newark, NJ 07102. 201-621-5368 (EST) 8:30AM-4:30PM. Civil Actions Under $10,000, Eviction, Small Claims.

## Gloucester County

**Real Estate Recording**, Gloucester County Clerk, 1 North Broad Street, Corner of Broad & Delaware, Woodbury, NJ 08096. 609-853-3230 (EST)

**Superior Court**, PO Box 187, Woodbury, NJ 08096. 609-853-3531 (EST) 8:30AM-4:30 PM. Felony, Civil Actions Over $10,000, Probate.

**Special Civil Part**, Old Courthouse, 1 N Broad St., Woodbury, NJ 08096. 609-853-3365 (EST) 8:30AM-4:30PM. Civil Actions Under $10,000, Eviction, Small Claims.

## Hudson County

**Real Estate Recording**, Hudson County Register of Deeds, 595 Newark Ave, Room 105, Jersey City, NJ 07306. 201-795-6571 (EST) 9AM-4PM.

**Superior Court**, 583 Newark Ave (Civil); 595 Newark Ave (, Jersey City, NJ 07306. 201-795-6723 (EST) 8:30AM-4:30PM. Felony, Civil Actions Over $10,000, Probate.

**Special Civil Part**, 595 Newark Ave, Jersey City, NJ 07306. 201-795-6680 (EST) 8:30AM-4:30PM. Civil Actions Under $10,000, Eviction, Small Claims.

## Hunterdon County

**Real Estate Recording**, Hunterdon County Clerk, 71 Main Street, Hall of Records, Flemington, NJ 08822. 908-788-1221 (EST) 8:30AM-4PM.

**Superior Court**, 71 Main St. ATTN:Law Division-Civil or C, Flemington, NJ 08822. 908-788-1239 (EST) 8:30AM-4:30PM. Felony, Civil Actions Over $10,000, Probate.

**Special Civil Part**, 71 Main St, Hall of Records, Flemington, NJ 08822. 908-788-1214 (EST) 8:30AM-4:30PM. Civil Actions Under $10,000, Eviction, Small Claims.

## Mercer County

**Real Estate Recording**, Mercer County Clerk, 209 South Broad Street, Courthouse, Room 100, Trenton, NJ 08650. 609-989-6466 (EST) 8:30AM-4PM.

**Superior Court**, 209 S. Broad (PO Box 8068), Trenton, NJ 08650-0068. 609-989-6454 (EST) 8:30AM-4:40PM. Felony, Civil Actions Over $10,000, Probate.

**Special Civil Part**, Box 8068, Trenton, NJ 08650. 609-989-6206 (EST) 8:30AM-4:30PM. Civil Actions Under $10,000, Eviction, Small Claims.

## Middlesex County

**Real Estate Recording**, Middlesex County Clerk, 1 JFK Square between Patterson & Bayard, Main Lobby in East Wing of Courthouse, New Brunswick, NJ 08903. 908-745-3204 (EST) 8:30AM-4PM.

**Superior Court**, PO Box 1110 (Civil); 2673 (Criminal), New Brunswick, NJ 08903. 908-745-3422 (EST) 8:30AM-4:30PM. Felony, Civil Actions Over $10,000, Probate.

**Special Civil Part**, PO Box 1146, New Brunswick, NJ 08903. 908-745-3380 (EST) 8:30AM-4:30PM. Civil Actions Under $10,000, Eviction, Small Claims.

## Monmouth County

**Real Estate Recording**, Monmouth County Clerk, Hall of Records, Main Street, Room 101, Freehold, NJ 07728. 908-431-7318 (EST) 8:30AM-4:30PM.

**Superior Court**, PO Box 1255, Freehold, NJ 07728-1255. 908-431-7069 (EST) 8:30AM-4:30PM. Felony, Civil Actions Over $10,000, Probate.

**Special Civil Part**, Courthouse, Courthouse and Monument St., Freehold, NJ 07728. 908-577-6749 (EST) 8:30AM-4:30PM. Civil Actions Under $10,000, Eviction, Small Claims.

## Morris County

**Real Estate Recording**, Morris County Clerk, Administration & Records Bldg., Court Street, Morristown, NJ 07960. 201-285-6135 (EST) 8:30AM-4PM.

**Superior Court**, PO Box 910, Morristown, NJ 079630-0910. 201-285-6165 (EST) 8:30AM-4:30PM. Felony, Civil Actions Over $10,000, Probate.

**Special Civil Part**, Washington and Court St, Morristown, NJ 07963. 201-285-6150 (EST) 8:30AM-4:30PM. Civil Actions Under $10,000, Eviction, Small Claims.

## Ocean County

**Real Estate Recording**, Ocean County Clerk, 118 Washington Street, 1st Floor Room 108, Toms River, NJ 08753. 908-929-2110 (EST) 8:30AM-4PM.

**Superior Court**, 118 Washington(Civil); PO Box 2192(Crimi, Toms River, NJ 08754. 908-929-2035 (EST) 8:30AM-4:30PM. Felony, Civil Actions Over $10,000, Probate.

**Special Civil Part**, Box 2191, Toms River, NJ 08754. 908-929-2016 (EST) 8:30AM-4:40PM.

Civil Actions Under $10,000, Eviction, Small Claims.

## Passaic County

**Real Estate Recording**, Passaic County Register of Deeds, 77 Hamilton Street, Courthouse, Paterson, NJ 07505. 201-881-4777 (EST) 8:30AM-4:30PM.

**Superior Court**, 77 Hamilton St., Paterson, NJ 07505-2108. 201-881-4125 (EST) 8:30AM-4:30PM. Felony, Civil Actions Over $10,000, Probate.

**Special Civil Part**, 71 Hamilton St., Paterson, NJ 07505. 201-881-4107 (EST) 8:30AM-4:30PM. Civil Actions Under $10,000, Eviction, Small Claims.

## Salem County

**Real Estate Recording**, Salem County Clerk, 92 Market Street, Salem, NJ 08079-1911. 609-935-7510 (EST) X219 8:30AM-4:30PM.

**Superior Court**, PO Box 78, Salem, NJ 08079-1913. 609-935-7510 (EST) 8:30AM-4:30PM. Felony, Civil Actions Over $10,000, Probate.

**Special Civil Part**, 92 Market St., Salem, NJ 08079. 609-935-7510 (EST) 8:30AM-4:30PM. Civil Actions Under $10,000, Eviction, Small Claims.

## Somerset County

**Real Estate Recording**, Somerset County Clerk, 20 Grove St., Administration Building, Somerville, NJ 08876. 908-231-7006 (EST) 9AM-4PM.

**Superior Court**, PO Box 3000-3d Floor(Civil); PO Box 3000, Somerville, NJ 08876-1262. 908-231-7010 (EST) 8:30AM-4:30PM. Felony, Civil Actions Over $10,000, Probate.

**Special Civil Part**, Courthouse, Bridge and Main St. (PO Box, Somerville, NJ 08876. 908-231-7014 (EST) 8:30AM-4:30PM. Civil Actions Under $10,000, Eviction, Small Claims.

## Sussex County

**Real Estate Recording**, Sussex County Clerk, 4 Park Place, Hall of Records, Newton, NJ 07860-1795. 201-579-0900 (EST) 8:30AM-4:30PM.

**Superior Court**, 43-47 High St, Sussex Judicial Center, Newton, NJ 07860. 201-579-0914 (EST) 8:30AM-4:30PM. Felony, Civil Actions Over $10,000, Probate.

**Special Civil Part**, 43-47 High St., Newton, NJ 07860. 201-579-0918 (EST) 8:30AM-4:30PM. Civil Actions Under $10,000, Eviction, Small Claims.

## Union County

**Real Estate Recording**, Union County Register of Deeds, 2 Broad Street, Courthouse, Elizabeth, NJ 07207. 908-527-4787 (EST) 8:30AM-4:30PM.

**Superior Court**, 2 Broad St.(Civil); Union County Courtho, Elizabeth, NJ 07207. 908-527-4000 (EST) 8:30AM-4:30PM. Felony, Civil Actions Over $10,000, Probate.

**Special Civil Part**, 2 Broad St, Elizabeth, NJ 07207. 908-527-4319 (EST) 8:30AM-4:30PM. Civil Actions Under $10,000, Eviction, Small Claims.

## Warren County

**Real Estate Recording**, Warren County Clerk, 413 Second Street, Courthouse, Belvidere, NJ 07823-1500. 908-475-6211 (EST) 8:30AM-4PM.

**Superior Court**, 2nd St, Belvidere, NJ 07823. 908-475-5361 (EST) 8:30AM-4:30PM. Felony, Civil Actions Over $10,000, Probate.

**Special Civil Part**, 314 2nd St, Belvidere, NJ 07823. 908-475-6227 (EST) 8:30AM-4:30PM. Civil Actions Under $10,000, Eviction, Small Claims.

# New Mexico

## Bernalillo County

**Real Estate Recording**, Bernalillo County Clerk, 1 Civic Plaza NW, Room 6009, Albuquerque, NM 87102. 505-768-4130 (MST) 8AM-4:30PM.

**2nd Judicial District Court**, PO Box 488, Albuquerque, NM 87103. 505-841-7437 (MST) 8AM-5PM. Felony, Civil, Probate.

**Metropolitan Court**, 401 Roma NW, Albuquerque, NM 87102. 505-841-8164 (MST) 8AM-5PM. Misdemeanor, Civil Actions Under $5,000, Small Claims.

**County Clerk**, #1 Civic Plaza NW, Albuquerque, NM 87102. 505-768-4247 (MST) 8AM-4:30PM. Probate.

## Catron County

**Real Estate Recording**, Catron County Clerk, Main Street, Reserve, NM 87830. 505-533-6400 (MST) 8AM-4:30PM.

**7th Judicial District Court**, PO Drawer 1129, Socorro, NM 87801. 505-835-0050 (MST) 8AM-4PM. Felony, Civil, Probate.

**Quemado Magistrate Court**, PO Box 283, Quemado, NM 87829. 505-773-4604 (MST) Misdemeanor, Civil Actions Under $5,000, Eviction, Small Claims.

**Reserve Magistrate Court**, PO Box 447, Reserve, NM 87830. 505-533-6474 (MST) Misdemeanor, Civil Actions Under $5,000, Eviction, Small Claims.

**County Clerk**, PO Box I, Socorro, NM 87801. 505-835-0423 (MST) 8AM-5PM. Probate.

## Chaves County

**Real Estate Recording**, Chaves County Clerk, 401 North Main, Courthouse, Roswell, NM 88201. 505-624-6614 (MST) 7AM-5PM.

**5th Judicial District Court**, Box 1776, Roswell, NM 88202. 505-622-2212 (MST) 8AM-4PM. Felony, Civil, Probate.

**Magistrate Court**, 200 E 4th, Roswell, NM 88202. 505-624-6088 (MST) Misdemeanor, Civil Actions Under $5,000, Eviction, Small Claims.

**County Clerk**, Box 580, Roswell, NM 88202. 505-624-6614 (MST) 7AM-5PM. Probate.

## Cibola County

**Real Estate Recording**, Cibola County Clerk, 515 West High Street, Grants, NM 87020. 505-287-9431 (MST) 8AM-5PM.

**13th Judicial District Court**, Box 758, Grants, NM 87020. 505-287-8831 (MST) 8AM-4PM. Felony, Civil, Probate.

**Magistrate Court**, 600 W Santa Fe, Grants, NM 87020. 505-285-4605 (MST) Misdemeanor, Civil Actions Under $5,000, Eviction, Small Claims.

**County Clerk**, 515 W. High, Grants, NM 87020. 505-287-8107 (MST) 8AM-5PM. Probate.

## Colfax County

**Real Estate Recording**, Colfax County Clerk, Third Street & Savage Avenue, Courthouse, Raton, NM 87740. 505-445-5551 (MST) 8AM-Noon, 1-5PM.

**8th Judicial District Court**, Box 160, Raton, NM 87740. 505-445-5585 (MST) 8AM-5PM, closed 12-1. Felony, Civil, Probate.

**Cimarron Magistrate Court**, PO Drawer 367, Highway 21, Cimarron, NM 87714. 505-376-2634 (MST) Misdemeanor, Civil Actions Under $5,000, Eviction, Small Claims.

**Raton Magistrate Court**, 122 S Third, Raton, NM 87740. 505-445-2220 (MST) Misdemeanor, Civil Actions Under $5,000, Eviction, Small Claims.

**Springer Magistrate Court**, 612 Colvert, Springer, NM 87747. 505-483-2417 (MST) Misdemeanor, Civil Actions Under $5,000, Eviction, Small Claims.

**County Clerk**, PO Box 159, Raton, NM 87740. 505-445-5551 (MST) 8AM-5PM. Probate.

## Curry County

**Real Estate Recording**, Curry County Clerk, 700 Main Street, Clovis, NM 88101. 505-763-5591 (MST) 8AM-Noon, 1-5PM.

**9th Judicial District Court**, Curry County Courthouse, Clovis, NM 88101. 505-762-9148 (MST) 8AM-4PM. Felony, Civil, Probate.

**Magistrate Court**, 900 Main St, Clovis, NM 88101. 505-762-3766 (MST) Misdemeanor, Civil Actions Under $5,000, Eviction, Small Claims.

**County Clerk**, Curry County Courthouse, Clovis, NM 88101. 505-762-9148 (MST) 8AM-4PM. Probate.

## De Baca County

**Real Estate Recording**, De Baca County Clerk, 514 Ave. C, Courthouse Square, Fort Sumner, NM 88119. 505-355-2601 (MST) 8AM-Noon, 1-4:30PM.

**10th Judicial District Court**, Box 910, Ft. Sumner, NM 88119. 505-355-2896 (MST) Felony, Civil, Probate.

**Magistrate Court**, Box 24, Ft Sumner, NM 88119. 505-355-7371 (MST) Misdemeanor, Civil Actions Under $5,000, Eviction, Small Claims.

**County Clerk**, Box 347, Ft. Sumner, NM 88119. 505-355-2601 (MST) 8AM-4:30PM. Probate.

## Dona Ana County

**Real Estate Recording**, Dona Ana County Clerk, 251 West Amador, Room 103, Las Cruces, NM 88005-2893. 505-525-6663 (MST) 8AM-5PM.

**3rd Judicial District Court**, 151 N. Church St., Las Cruces, NM 88001. 505-523-8200 (MST) 8AM-5PM. Felony, Civil, Probate.

**Anthony Magistrate Court**, 880 N Main, Anthony, NM 88021. 505-233-3147 (MST) Misdemeanor, Civil Actions Under $5,000, Eviction, Small Claims.

**Las Cruces Magistrate Court**, 125 S Downtown Mall, Las Cruces, NM 88005. 505-524-2814 (MST) Misdemeanor, Civil Actions Under $5,000, Eviction, Small Claims.

## Eddy County

**Real Estate Recording**, Eddy County Clerk, 202 West Mermod, Carlsbad, NM 88220. 505-885-3383 (MST) 8AM-5PM.

**5th Judicial District Court**, Box 1838, Carlsbad, NM 88221. 505-885-4740 (MST) 8AM-5PM, closed 12-1. Felony, Civil, Probate.

**Artesia Magistrate Court**, 611 Mahone Dr, Artesia, NM 88210. 505-746-2481 (MST) Misdemeanor, Civil Actions Under $5,000, Eviction, Small Claims.

**Carlsbad Magistrate Court**, 302 N Main St, Carlsbad, NM 88221. 505-887-7119 (MST) Misdemeanor, Civil Actions Under $5,000, Eviction, Small Claims.

**County Clerk**, Eddy County Courthouse, Room 100, Carlsbad, NM 88220. 505-885-4008 (MST) 9AM-4PM. Probate.

## Grant County

**Real Estate Recording**, Grant County Clerk, 201 North Cooper, Silver City, NM 88061. 505-538-2979 (MST) 8:30AM-5PM.

**6th Judicial District Court**, Box 2339, Silver City, NM 88062. 505-538-3250 (MST) 8AM-5PM. Felony, Civil, Probate.

**Bayard Magistrate Court**, PO Box 125, Bayard, NM 88023. 505-537-3402 (MST) Misdemeanor, Civil Actions Under $5,000, Eviction, Small Claims.

**Silver City Magistrate Court**, Box 1089, Silver City, NM 88062. 505-538-3811 (MST) Misdemeanor, Civil Actions Under $5,000, Eviction, Small Claims.

**County Clerk**, Box 898, Silver City, NM 88062. 505-538-2979 (MST) Probate.

## Guadalupe County

**Real Estate Recording**, Guadalupe County Clerk, 420 Parker Avenue, Courthouse-Suite 1, Santa Rosa, NM 88435. 505-472-3791 (MST) 8AM-5PM.

**4th Judicial District Court**, Guadalupe County Courthouse, Santa Rosa, NM 88435. 505-472-3888 (MST) 8AM-5PM. Felony, Civil, Probate.

**Santa Rosa Magistrate Court**, 421 Corona Ave, Santa Rosa, NM 88435. 505-472-3237 (MST) Misdemeanor, Civil Actions Under $5,000, Eviction, Small Claims.

**Vaughn Magistrate Court**, PO Box 246, Vaughn, NM 88353. 505-584-2345 (MST) Misdemeanor, Civil Actions Under $5,000, Eviction, Small Claims.

**County Clerk**, 4200 Parker Ave Courthouse, Santa Rosa, NM 88435. 505-472-3791 (MST) 8AM-5PM. Probate.

## Harding County

**Real Estate Recording**, Harding County Clerk, Third & Pine, Mosquero, NM 87733. 505-673-2301 (MST) 8AM-4PM.

**10th Judicial District Court**, Box 1002, Mosquero, NM 87733. 505-673-2252 (MST) 9AM-3PM M,T,W,F. Felony, Civil, Probate.

**Magistrate Court**, Box 9, Roy, NM 87743. 505-485-2549 (MST) Misdemeanor, Civil Actions Under $5,000, Eviction, Small Claims.

County Clerk, County Clerk, Box 1002, Mosquero, NM 87733. 505-673-2301 (MST) 8AM-4PM. Probate.

## Hidalgo County

Real Estate Recording, Hidalgo County Clerk, 300 Shakespeare Street, Lordsburg, NM 88045. 505-542-9213 (MST) 9AM-5PM.

6th Judicial District Court, PO Drawer E, Lordsburg, NM 88045. 505-542-3411 (MST) 8AM-5PM, Closed 12-1. Felony, Civil, Probate.

Magistrate Court, 205 E 2nd St, Lordsburg, NM 88045. 505-542-3582 (MST) Misdemeanor, Civil Actions Under $5,000, Eviction, Small Claims.

County Clerk, 300 Shakespeare, Lordsburg, NM 88045. 505-542-9512 (MST) 9AM-Noon. Probate.

## Lea County

Real Estate Recording, Lea County Clerk, 100 Main Street, Courthouse, Lovington, NM 88260. 505-396-8531 (MST) 8AM-5PM.

5th Judicial District Court, 100 N. Main, Box 6C, Lovington, NM 88260. 505-396-8571 (MST) 8AM-5PM. Felony, Civil, Probate.

Eunice Magistrate Court, PO Box 240, Eunice, NM 88231. 505-394-3368 (MST) Misdemeanor, Civil Actions Under $5,000, Eviction, Small Claims.

Hobbs Magistrate Court, 114 E Taylor St, Hobbs, NM 88240. 505-397-3621 (MST) Misdemeanor, Civil Actions Under $5,000, Eviction, Small Claims.

Lovington Magistrate Court, 100 W Central, Suite D, Lovington, NM 88260. 505-396-6677 (MST) Misdemeanor, Civil Actions Under $5,000, Eviction, Small Claims.

Tatum Magistrate Court, 10 N Ave A, Tatum, NM 88267. 505-398-5300 (MST) Misdemeanor, Civil Actions Under $5,000, Eviction, Small Claims.

County Clerk, Box 1507, Lovington, NM 88260. 505-396-8531 (MST) Probate.

## Lincoln County

Real Estate Recording, Lincoln County Clerk, 300 Central Avenue, Carrizozo, NM 88301. 505-648-2394 (MST) 8AM-5PM.

12th Judicial District Court, Box 725, Carrizozo, NM 88301. 505-648-2432 (MST) 8AM-5PM. Felony, Civil, Probate.

Ruidoso Magistrate court, PO Box 2426, Ruidoso, NM 88345. 505-257-7022 (MST) Misdemeanor, Civil Actions Under $5,000, Eviction, Small Claims.

County Clerk, Box 338, Carrizozo, NM 88301. 505-648-2394 (MST) 8AM-5PM. Probate.

## Los Alamos County

Real Estate Recording, Los Alamos County Clerk, 2300 Trinity Drive, Los Alamos, NM 87544. 505-662-8010 (MST) 8AM-5PM.

1st Judicial District Court, , NM. (MST) Felony, Misdemeanor, Civil, Eviction, Small Claims, Probate.

Magistrate Court, 1319 Trinity Dr, Los Alamos, NM 87544. 505-662-2727 (MST) Misdemeanor, Civil Actions Under $5,000, Eviction, Small Claims.

County Clerk, Box 30, Los Alamos, NM 87544. 505-662-8010 (MST) 8AM-5PM. Probate.

## Luna County

Real Estate Recording, Luna County Clerk, 700 South Silver, Courthouse, Deming, NM 88030. 505-546-0491 (MST) 8AM-5PM.

6th Judicial District Court, Luna County Courthouse Room 40, Deming, NM 88030. 505-546-9611 (MST) 8AM-5PM, Closed 12-1. Felony, Civil, Probate.

Magistrate Court, 121 W Spruce St, Deming, NM 88030. 505-546-9321 (MST) Misdemeanor, Civil Actions Under $5,000, Eviction, Small Claims.

County Clerk, PO Box 1838, Deming, NM 88030. 505-546-0491 (MST) 8AM-5PM. Probate.

## McKinley County

Real Estate Recording, McKinley County Clerk, 201 West Hill Avenue, Courthouse, Gallup, NM 87301. 505-863-6866 (MST) 8AM-5PM.

11th Judicial District Court, 201 W. Hill, Room 21, Gallup, NM 87301. 505-863-6816 (MST) 8AM-5PM. Felony, Civil, Probate.

Magistrate Court, 451 State Rd 564, Gallup, NM 87301. 505-722-6636 (MST) Misdemeanor, Civil Actions Under $5,000, Eviction, Small Claims.

County Clerk, 201 W. Hill, Room 21, Gallup, NM 87301. 505-863-6866 (MST) 8AM-5PM. Probate.

## Mora County

Real Estate Recording, Mora County Clerk, Main Street, Mora, NM 87732. 505-387-2448 (MST) 8AM-4:30PM.

4th Judicial District Court, PO Bin N, Las Vegas, NM 87701. 505-425-7281 (MST) 8AM-5PM. Felony, Civil, Probate.

Magistrate Court, 1900 Hot Springs Blvd, Mora, NM 87732. 505-425-5204 (MST) Misdemeanor, Civil Actions Under $5,000, Eviction, Small Claims.

County Clerk, Box 360, Mora, NM 87732. 505-387-2448 (MST) 8AM-4:30PM. Probate.

## Otero County

Real Estate Recording, Otero County Clerk, 1000 New York Avenue, Room 108, Alamogordo, NM 88310-6932. 505-437-4942 (MST) 7:30AM-6PM.

12th Judicial District Court, 1000 New York Ave, Rm 209, Alamogordo, NM 88310-6940. 505-437-7310 (MST) 8AM-4PM. Felony, Civil, Probate.

Magistrate Court, 1106 New York Ave, Alamogordo, NM 88310. 505-437-9000 (MST) Misdemeanor, Civil Actions Under $5,000, Eviction, Small Claims.

County Clerk, 1000 New York Ave, Rm 108, Alamogordo, NM 88310. 505-437-4942 (MST) 7:30AM-6PM. Probate.

## Quay County

Real Estate Recording, Quay County Clerk, 301 South Third Street, Tucumcari, NM 88401. 505-461-0510 (MST) 8AM-Noon,1-5PM.

10th Judicial District Court, Box 1067, Tucumcari, NM 88401. 505-461-2764 (MST) 8AM-5PM. Felony, Civil, Probate.

San Jon Magistrate Court, PO Box 35, San Jon, NM 88434. 505-576-2591 (MST) Misdemeanor, Civil Actions Under $5,000, Eviction, Small Claims.

Tucumcari Magistrate Court, PO Box 1301, Tucumcari, NM 88401. 505-461-1700 (MST) Misdemeanor, Civil Actions Under $5,000, Eviction, Small Claims.

County Clerk, Box 1225, Tucumcari, NM 88401. 505-461-0510 (MST) 8AM-5PM. Probate.

## Rio Arriba County

Real Estate Recording, Rio Arriba County Clerk, Courthouse, Tierra Amarilla, NM 87575. 505-588-7724 (MST) 8AM-4:30PM.

1st Judicial District Court, All cases are handled by Santa Fe District Court, Felony, Civil, Probate.

Chama Magistrate Court, PO Box 538, Chama, NM 87520. 505-756-2278 (MST) Misdemeanor, Civil Actions Under $5,000, Eviction, Small Claims.

Espanola Magistrate Court, 935 Paseo de Onate, Espanola, NM 87532. 505-753-2532 (MST) Misdemeanor, Civil Actions Under $5,000, Eviction, Small Claims.

## Roosevelt County

Real Estate Recording, Roosevelt County Clerk, 101 West First, Portales, NM 88130. 505-356-8562 (MST) 8AM-5PM.

9th Judicial District Court, Roosevelt County Courthouse, Portales, NM 88130. 505-356-4463 (MST) 8AM-4PM. Felony, Civil, Probate.

Magistrate Court, 1700 N Boston, Portales, NM 88130. 505-356-8560 (MST) Misdemeanor, Civil Actions Under $5,000, Eviction, Small Claims.

County Clerk, Roosevelt County Courthouse, Portales, NM 88130. 505-356-8562 (MST) 8AM-5PM. Probate.

## San Juan County

Real Estate Recording, San Juan County Clerk, 112 South Mesa Verde, Aztec, NM 87410. 505-334-9471 (MST) 7:30AM-5:30PM.

11th Judicial District Court, 103 S. Oliver, Aztec, NM 87410. 505-334-6151 (MST) 8AM-5PM, Closed 12-1. Felony, Civil, Probate.

Aztec Magistrate Court, 101 S Oliver Dr, Aztec, NM 87410. 505-334-9479 (MST) Misdemeanor, Civil Actions Under $5,000, Eviction, Small Claims.

Farmington Magistrate Court, 920 Municipal Dr, Suite 1, Farmington, NM 87401. 505-326-4338 (MST) Misdemeanor, Civil Actions Under $5,000, Eviction, Small Claims.

County Clerk, Box 550, Aztec, NM 87410. 505-334-9471 (MST) 7:30AM-5:30PM. Probate.

## San Miguel County

Real Estate Recording, San Miguel County Clerk, Courthouse, Las Vegas, NM 87701. 505-425-9331 (MST) 8AM-Noon, 1-5PM.

4th Judicial District Court, PO Bin N, Las Vegas, NM 87701. 505-425-7281 (MST) 8AM-5PM. Felony, Civil, Probate.

**Magistrate Court**, 1900 Hot Springs Blvd, Las Vegas, NM 87701. 505-425-5204 (MST) Misdemeanor, Civil Actions Under $5,000, Eviction, Small Claims.

**County Clerk**, San Miguel County Clerk, Las Vegas, NM 87701. 505-425-9331 (MST) 8AM-5PM. Probate.

## Sandoval County

**Real Estate Recording**, Sandoval County Clerk, 711 Camino Del Pueblo, Courthouse, 2nd Floor, Bernalillo, NM 87004. 505-867-2209 (MST) 8AM-5PM.

**13th Judicial District Court**, PO Box 130, Bernalillo, NM 87004. 505-867-2376 (MST) Felony, Civil, Probate.

**Bernalillo Magistrate Court**, PO Box 818, Bernalillo, NM 87004. 505-867-5202 (MST) Misdemeanor, Civil Actions Under $5,000, Eviction, Small Claims.

**Cuba Magistrate Court**, 16B Cordova St, Cuba, NM 87013. 505-289-3519 (MST) Misdemeanor, Civil Actions Under $5,000, Eviction, Small Claims.

**County Clerk**, Box 40, Bernalillo, NM 87004. 505-867-2209 (MST) 8AM-5PM. Probate.

## Santa Fe County

**Real Estate Recording**, Santa Fe County Clerk, 102 Grant Avenue, Santa Fe, NM 87504. 505-986-6280 (MST) 8AM-5PM.

**1st Judicial District Court**, Box 2268, Santa Fe, NM 87504. 505-827-5035 (MST) 8AM-4PM. Felony, Civil, Probate.

**Magistrate Court**, Rte 11, Box 2111, Pojoaque, NM 87501. 505-455-7938 (MST) Misdemeanor, Civil Actions Under $5,000, Eviction, Small Claims.

**County Clerk**, Box 276, Santa Fe, NM 87501. 505-986-6279 (MST) 8AM-5PM. Probate.

## Sierra County

**Real Estate Recording**, Sierra County Clerk, 311 Date Street, Truth or Consequences, NM 87901. 505-894-2840 (MST) 8AM-5PM.

**7th Judicial District Court**, 311 N Date, Truth or Consequences, NM 87901. 505-894-7167 (MST) 8AM-4PM. Felony, Civil, Probate.

**Magistrate Court**, 100 Date St, Truth or Consequences, NM 87901. 505-894-3051 (MST) Misdemeanor, Civil Actions Under $5,000, Eviction, Small Claims.

**County Clerk**, 311 Date St., Truth or Consequences, NM 87901. 505-894-2840 (MST) 8AM-5PM. Probate.

## Socorro County

**Real Estate Recording**, Socorro County Clerk, 200 Church Street, Socorro, NM 87801. 505-835-3263 (MST) 8AM-5PM.

**7th Judicial District Court**, All cases are handled by Catron District Court. Felony, Civil, Probate.

**Magistrate Court**, 404 Park St, Socorro, NM 87801. 505-835-2500 (MST) Misdemeanor, Civil Actions Under $5,000, Eviction, Small Claims.

## Taos County

**Real Estate Recording**, Taos County Clerk, 105 Albright Street, Taos, NM 87571. 505-758-8836 (MST) 8AM-Noon, 1-5PM.

**8th Judicial District Court**, Box 1885, Taos, NM 87571. 505-758-3173 (MST) 8AM-5PM. Felony, Civil, Probate.

**Questa Magistrate Court**, PO Box 586, Questa, NM 87556. 505-586-0761 (MST) Misdemeanor, Civil Actions Under $5,000, Eviction, Small Claims.

**Taos Magistrate Court**, 205 Cruz Alta Rd, Taos, NM 87571. 505-758-4030 (MST) Misdemeanor, Civil Actions Under $5,000, Eviction, Small Claims.

**County Clerk**, Box 676, Taos, NM 87571. 505-758-8836 (MST) 8AM-5PM. Probate.

## Torrance County

**Real Estate Recording**, Torrance County Clerk, 9th & Allen Streets, Estancia, NM 87016. 505-384-2221 (MST) 8AM-5PM.

**7th Judicial District Court**, County Courthouse, Box 78, Estancia, NM 87016. 505-384-2974 (MST) 8AM-5PM. Felony, Civil, Probate.

**Moriarty Magistrate Court**, PO Box 1968, Moriarty, NM 87035. 505-832-4476 (MST) Misdemeanor, Civil Actions Under $5,000, Eviction, Small Claims.

**County Clerk**, Box 48, Estancia, NM 87016. 505-384-2221 (MST) 10AM-Noon, Thur only. Probate.

## Union County

**Real Estate Recording**, Union County Clerk, 200 Court Street, Courthouse, Clayton, NM 88415. 505-374-9491 (MST) 9AM-5PM.

**8th Judicial District Court**, Box 310, Clayton, NM 88415. 505-374-9577 (MST) 8AM-5PM. Felony, Civil, Probate.

**Magistrate Court**, 118 Walnut St, Clayton, NM 88415. 505-374-9472 (MST) Misdemeanor, Civil Actions Under $5,000, Eviction, Small Claims.

**County Clerk**, PO Box 397, Clayton, NM 88415. 505-374-8137 (MST) Probate.

## Valencia County

**Real Estate Recording**, Valencia County Clerk, 444 Luna Avenue, Los Lunas, NM 87031. 505-866-2073 (MST) 8AM-4:30PM.

**13th Judicial District Court**, Box 1089, Los Lunas, NM 87031. 505-865-4291 (MST) 8AM-5PM. Felony, Civil, Probate.

**Belen Magistrate Court**, 237 N Main St, Belen, NM 87002. 505-864-7509 (MST) Misdemeanor, Civil Actions Under $5,000, Eviction, Small Claims.

**Los Lunas Magistrate Court**, 121 Don Diego, Los Lunas, NM 87031. 505-865-4637 (MST) Misdemeanor, Civil Actions Under $5,000, Eviction, Small Claims.

**County Clerk**, Box 969, Los Lunas, NM 87031. 505-865-9681 (MST) Probate.

# New York

## Albany County

**Real Estate Recording**, Albany County Clerk, Courthouse Bldg Room 128, Albany, NY 12207. 518-487-5120 (EST) 9AM-5PM.

**Supreme and County Court**, Courthouse, Albany, NY 12207. 518-487-5118 (EST) 9AM-5PM. Felony, Civil Actions Over $15,000.

**Albany City Court-Civil Part**, 209 City Hall, Eagle & Maiden Ln, Albany, NY 12207. 518-434-5113 (EST) 8:30AM-4:30PM. Civil Actions Under $15,000, Eviction, Small Claims.

**Albany City Court-Misdemeanors**, Morton & Broad St, ALbany, NY 12202. 518-449-7109 (EST) 8AM-4PM. Misdemeanor.

**Cohoes City Court**, PO Box 678, Cohoes, NY 12047-0678. 518-237-7646 (EST) 9AM-4PM. Misdemeanor, Civil Actions Under $15,000, Eviction, Small Claims.

**Watervliet City Court**, 15th & Broadway, Watervliet, NY 12189. 518-270-3803 (EST) 8AM-3PM. Misdemeanor, Civil Actions Under $15,000, Eviction, Small Claims.

**Surrogate Court**, Courthouse, Albany, NY 12207. 518-487-5393 (EST) Probate.

## Allegany County

**Real Estate Recording**, Allegany County Clerk, Court Street, Courthouse, Belmont, NY 14813-0087. 716-268-9270 (EST) 9AM-5PM (June-August 8:30AM-4PM).

**Supreme and County Court**, Courthouse, Belmont, NY 14813. 716-268-5813 (EST) 9AM-5PM. Felony, Civil Actions Over $15,000.

**Surrogate Court**, Courthouse, Belmont, NY 14813. 716-268-5815 (EST) Probate.

## Bronx County

**Real Estate Recording**, Bronx City Register, 1932 Arthur Avenue, Bronx, NY 10457. 718-579-6820 (EST)

**Civil Court of the City of New York-Bronx Branch**, 851 Grand Concourse, Bronx, NY 10451. 718-590-3601 (EST) 9AM-5PM. Civil Actions Under $25,000, Eviction, Small Claims.

**Supreme Court-Civil Division**, 851 Grand Concourse, Bronx, NY 10451. 718-590-3641 (EST) 9AM-5PM. Civil Actions Over $25,000.

**Supreme Court-Criminal Division**, 80 Centre St, Rm 544, New York, NY 10013. 212-417-5853 (EST) 9:30AM-4:30PM, Closed 12-2. Felony.

**Surrogate Court**, 851 Grand Concourse, Bronx, NY 10451. 718-590-3611 (EST) Probate.

## Broome County

**Real Estate Recording**, Broome County Clerk, 44 Hawley Street, Binghamton, NY 13901. 607-778-2451 (EST) 9AM-5PM.

**Supreme and County Court**, PO Box 2062, Binghamton, NY 13902. 607-778-2448 (EST) 9AM-5PM. Felony, Civil Actions Over $15,000.

**Binghampton City Court**, Governmental Plaza, Binghamton, NY 13901. 607-772-7006 (EST) 9AM-5PM. Misdemeanor, Civil Actions Under $15,000, Eviction, Small Claims.

**Surrogate Court**, Courthouse Rm 109, Binghamton, NY 13901. 607-778-2111 (EST) Probate.

## Cattaraugus County

**Real Estate Recording**, Cattaraugus County Clerk, 303 Court Street, Little Valley, NY 14755. 716-938-9111 (EST) X297 9AM-5PM.

**Supreme and County Court**, 303 Court St, Little Valley, NY 14755. 716-938-9111 (EST) 9AM-5PM. Felony, Civil Actions Over $15,000.

**Olean City Court**, PO Box 631, Olean, NY 14760. 716-375-5620 (EST) 8:30AM-4:30PM. Misdemeanor, Civil Actions Under $15,000, Eviction, Small Claims.

**Salamanca City Court**, Municipal Center, Salamanca, NY 14779. 716-945-4153 (EST) 8AM-4PM. Misdemeanor, Civil Actions Under $15,000, Eviction, Small Claims.

**Surrogate Court**, 303 Court St, Little Valley, NY 14755. 716-938-9111 (EST) Probate.

## Cayuga County

**Real Estate Recording**, Cayuga County Clerk, 160 Genesee Street, Auburn, NY 13021. 315-253-1271 (EST) 9AM-5PM (July-Aug 8AM-4PM).

**Supreme and County Court**, 160 Genesee St, Auburn, NY 13021-3424. 315-253-1271 (EST) 9AM-5PM. Felony, Civil Actions Over $15,000.

**Auburn City Court**, 153 Genesee St, Auburn, NY 13021-3434. 315-253-1570 (EST) 8AM-4PM. Misdemeanor, Civil Actions Under $15,000, Eviction, Small Claims.

**Surrogate Court**, 160 Genesee St, Auburn, NY 13021-3471. 315-255-4316 (EST) Probate.

## Chautauqua County

**Real Estate Recording**, Chautauqua County Clerk, Corner of North Erie and W. Chautauqua, Courthouse, Mayville, NY 14757. 716-753-4331 (EST) 9AM-5PM.

**Supreme and County Court**, Courthouse, Mayville, NY 14757. 716-753-4266 (EST) 9AM-5PM/Summer 8:30AM-4:30PM. Felony, Civil Actions Over $15,000.

**Dunkirk City Court**, City Hall, Dunkirk, NY 14048. 716-366-2055 (EST) 9AM-5PM. Misdemeanor, Civil Actions Under $15,000, Eviction, Small Claims.

**Jamestown City Court**, City Hall, Jamestown, NY 14701. 716-483-7561 (EST) 9AM-5PM. Misdemeanor, Civil Actions Under $15,000, Eviction, Small Claims.

**Surrogate Court**, Gerace Office Bldg, Rm 231 (PO Box C), Mayville, NY 14757-0299. 716-753-4339 (EST) Probate.

## Chemung County

**Real Estate Recording**, Chemung County Clerk, 210 Lake Street, Elmira, NY 14902. 607-737-2920 (EST) 8:30AM-4:30PM.

**Supreme and County Court**, 203 Lake St, Elmira, NY 14901-0588. 607-737-2920 (EST) 8:30AM-4:30PM. Felony, Civil Actions Over $15,000.

**Elmira City Court**, 317 E Church St, Elmira, NY 14901. 607-737-5681 (EST) 8AM-4PM. Misdemeanor, Civil Actions Under $15,000, Eviction, Small Claims.

**Surrogate Court**, 224 Laice St (PO Box 588), Elmira, NY 14902. 607-737-2946 (EST) Probate.

## Chenango County

**Real Estate Recording**, Chenango County Clerk, 5 Court Street, Norwich, NY 13815. 607-337-1452 (EST) 8:30AM-5PM.

**Supreme and County Court**, County Office Bldg, Norwich, NY 13815-1676. 607-337-1450 (EST) Felony, Civil Actions Over $15,000.

**Norwich City Court**, 45 Broad St, Norwich, NY 13815-0430. 607-334-1224 (EST) 8:30AM-4:30PM. Misdemeanor, Civil Actions Under $15,000, Eviction, Small Claims.

**Surrogate Court**, County Office Bldg, Norwich, NY 13815-1676. 607-337-1822 (EST) Probate.

## Clinton County

**Real Estate Recording**, Clinton County Clerk, 137 Margaret Street, Government Center, Plattsburgh, NY 12901-2974. 518-565-4700 (EST) 8AM-5PM.

**Supreme and County Court**, County Government Center, Plattsburgh, NY 12901-2933. 518-565-4700 (EST) 9AM-5PM. Felony, Civil Actions Over $15,000.

**Plattsburg City Court**, 41 City Hall Pl, Plattsburgh, NY 12901. 518-563-7870 (EST) 8AM-4PM. Misdemeanor, Civil Actions Under $15,000, Eviction, Small Claims.

**Surrogate Court**, 137 Margaret St, Plattsburgh, NY 12901-2933. 518-565-4630 (EST) Probate.

## Columbia County

**Real Estate Recording**, Columbia County Clerk, Courthouse, Hudson, NY 12534. 518-828-3339 (EST) 9AM-5PM.

**Supreme and County Court**, Courthouse, Hudson, NY 12534. 518-828-3339 (EST) 9AM-5PM. Felony, Civil Actions Over $15,000.

**Hudson City Court**, 427 Warren St, Hudson, NY 12534. 518-828-3100 (EST) 8:30AM-4:30PM. Misdemeanor, Civil Actions Under $15,000, Eviction, Small Claims.

**Surrogate Court**, Courthouse, Hudson, NY 12534. 518-828-0414 (EST) Probate.

## Cortland County

**Real Estate Recording**, Cortland County Clerk, Greenbush Street, Courthouse, Cortland, NY 13045. 607-753-5021 (EST) 9AM-5PM.

**Supreme and County Court**, 46 Greenbush St, Ste 301, Cortland, NY 13045. 607-753-5021 (EST) 9AM-5PM. Felony, Civil Actions Over $15,000.

**Cortland City Court**, 25 Court St, Cortland, NY 13045. 607-753-1811 (EST) 8:30AM-4:30PM. Misdemeanor, Civil Actions Under $15,000, Eviction, Small Claims.

**Surrogate Court**, 46 Greenbush St, Ste 301, Cortland, NY 13045. 607-753-5355 (EST) Probate.

# New York

## Delaware County

**Real Estate Recording**, Delaware County Clerk, Court House Square, Delhi, NY 13753. 607-746-2123 (EST) 9AM-5PM.

**Supreme and County Court**, 3 Court St, Delhi, NY 13753. 607-746-2123 (EST) 9AM-5PM. Felony, Civil Actions Over $15,000.

**Surrogate Court**, 3 Court St, Delhi, NY 13753. 607-746-2126 (EST) Probate.

## Dutchess County

**Real Estate Recording**, Dutchess County Clerk, 22 Market Street, Poughkeepsie, NY 12601. 914-431-2120 (EST) 9AM-4:45PM.

**Supreme and County Court**, 10 Market St, Poughkeepsie, NY 12601-3203. 914-431-2125 (EST) 9AM-5PM. Felony, Civil Actions Over $15,000.

**Beacon City Court**, 463 Main St, Beacon, NY 12508. 914-831-7480 (EST) 9AM-5PM. Misdemeanor, Civil Actions Under $15,000, Eviction, Small Claims.

**Poughkeepsie City Court**, Civic Center Plaza, Poughkeepsie, NY 12601. 914-451-4091 (EST) 8AM-4PM. Misdemeanor, Civil Actions Under $15,000, Eviction, Small Claims.

**Surrogate Court**, 10 Market St, Poughkeepsie, NY 12601-3203. 914-431-1935 (EST) Probate.

## Erie County

**Real Estate Recording**, Erie County Clerk, 25 Delaware Avenue, County Hall, Buffalo, NY 14202. 716-858-6425 (EST) 9AM-5PM.

**Supreme and County Court**, 25 Delaware Ave, Buffalo, NY 14202. 716-858-6481 (EST) 9AM-5PM. Felony, Civil Actions Over $15,000.

**Buffalo City Court**, 50 Delaware Ave, Buffalo, NY 14202. 716-847-8200 (EST) 9AM-5PM. Misdemeanor, Civil Actions Under $15,000, Eviction, Small Claims.

**Lackawanna City Court**, 714 Ridge Rd, Rm 225, Lackawanna, NY 14218. 716-827-6486 (EST) 8:30AM-5PM. Misdemeanor, Civil Actions Under $15,000, Eviction, Small Claims.

**Tonawanda City Court**, 200 Niagara St, Tonawanda, NY 14150. 716-693-3484 (EST) 9AM-5PM. Misdemeanor, Civil Actions Under $15,000, Eviction, Small Claims.

**Surrogate Court**, 92 Franklin St, Buffalo, NY 14202. 716-854-7867 (EST) Probate.

## Essex County

**Real Estate Recording**, Essex County Clerk, Court Street, Elizabethtown, NY 12932. 518-873-3600 (EST) 8AM-5PM.

**Supreme and County Court**, County Government Center, Court St, Elizabethtown, NY 12932. 518-873-3600 (EST) 8:30AM-5PM. Felony, Civil Actions Over $15,000.

**Surrogate Court**, County Government Center, Court St, Elizabethtown, NY 12932. 518-873-3384 (EST) Probate.

## Franklin County

**Real Estate Recording**, Franklin County Clerk, 63 West Main Street, Malone, NY 12953. 518-483-6767 (EST) 9AM-5PM Jan-May 31; 8AM-5PM June; 8AM-4PM July-Aug; 9AM-5PM Sept-Dec.

**Supreme and County Court**, 63 W Main St, Malone, NY 12953-1817. 518-483-6767 (EST) 9AM-5PM. Felony, Civil Actions Over $15,000.

**Surrogate Court**, Courthouse, Malone, NY 12953-1817. 518-483-6767 (EST) Probate.

## Fulton County

**Real Estate Recording**, Fulton County Clerk, 223 West Main Street, Johnstown, NY 12095. 518-762-0555 (EST) 9AM-5PM (July-August 9AM-4PM).

**Supreme and County Court**, County Bldg, West Main St, Johnstown, NY 12095. 518-762-0539 (EST) 9AM-5PM. Felony, Civil Actions Over $15,000.

**Gloversville City Court**, City Hall, Frontage Rd, Gloversville, NY 12078. 518-773-4527 (EST) 9AM-5PM. Misdemeanor, Civil Actions Under $15,000, Eviction, Small Claims.

**Johnstown City Court**, City Hall, Johnstown, NY 12095. 518-762-0007 (EST) 9AM-5PM. Misdemeanor, Civil Actions Under $15,000, Eviction, Small Claims.

**Surrogate Court**, County Bldg, West Main St, Johnstown, NY 12095. 518-762-0685 (EST) Probate.

## Genesee County

**Real Estate Recording**, Genesee County Clerk, Main & Court Streets, Batavia, NY 14020. 716-344-2550 (EST) X245 8:30AM-5PM.

**Supreme and County Court**, Courthouse, Batavia, NY 14021-0462. 716-344-2550 (EST) 9AM-5PM. Felony, Civil Actions Over $15,000.

**Batavia City Court**, PO Box 385, Batavia, NY 14021-0385. 716-343-8180 (EST) 8:30AM-4:30PM. Misdemeanor, Civil Actions Under $15,000, Eviction, Small Claims.

**Surrogate Court**, Courthouse, Batavia, NY 14021-0462. 716-344-2550 (EST) Probate.

## Greene County

**Real Estate Recording**, Greene County Clerk, 320 Main Street, Catskill, NY 12414. 518-943-2050 (EST) 9AM-5PM (July-August 9AM-4PM).

**Supreme and County Court**, Courthouse, Catskill, NY 12414. 518-943-2050 (EST) 9AM-5PM. Felony, Civil Actions Over $15,000.

**Surrogate Court**, Courthouse, Catskill, NY 12414. 518-943-2484 (EST) Probate.

## Hamilton County

**Real Estate Recording**, Hamilton County Clerk, County Clerk's Office Bldg., Rte. 8, Lake Pleasant, NY 12108. 518-548-7111 (EST) 9AM-5PM (9AM-4PM July-Aug).

**Supreme and County Court**, Courthouse, Lake Pleasant, NY 12108. 518-548-7111 (EST) 9AM-5PM. Felony, Civil Actions Over $15,000.

**Surrogate Court**, PO Box 780, Indian Lake, NY 12842-0780. 518-648-5411 (EST) Probate.

## Herkimer County

**Real Estate Recording**, Herkimer County Clerk, 109-111 Mary Street, County Office Building, Herkimer, NY 13350. 315-867-1137 (EST) 9AM-5PM (June-August 8:30AM-4PM).

**Supreme and County Court**, Courthouse, PO Box 111, Herkimer, NY 13350. 315-867-1137 (EST) 9AM-5PM. Felony, Civil Actions Over $15,000.

**Little Falls City Court**, 659 E Main St, Little Falls, NY 13365. 315-823-1690 (EST) 8:30AM-4:30PM. Misdemeanor, Civil Actions Under $15,000, Eviction, Small Claims.

**Surrogate Court**, 320 N Main St (PO Box 550), Herkimer, NY 13350-0749. 315-867-1170 (EST) Probate.

## Jefferson County

**Real Estate Recording**, Jefferson County Clerk, 175 Arsenal Street, Watertown, NY 13601-2555. 315-785-3081 (EST) 9AM-5PM (8:30AM-4PM July-Aug).

**Supreme and County Court**, State Office Bldg, Watertown, NY 13601-3783. 315-785-3200 (EST) 9AM-5PM. Felony, Civil Actions Over $15,000.

**Watertown City Court**, Municipal Bldg, 245 Washington St, Watertown, NY 13601. 315-785-7785 (EST) 9AM-5PM. Misdemeanor, Civil Actions Under $15,000, Eviction, Small Claims.

**Surrogate Court**, 175 Arsenal St, Watertown, NY 13601-2562. 315-785-3019 (EST) Probate.

## Kings County

**Real Estate Recording**, Kings City Register, 210 Joralemon Street, Municipal Building, Brooklyn, NY 11201. 718-802-3590 (EST)

**Supreme Court-Civil Division**, 360 Adams St, Brooklyn, NY 11201. 718-643-5894 (EST) 9AM-5PM. Civil Actions Over $25,000.

**Court of the City of New York-Criminal Division**, 80 Centre St, Rm 544, New York, NY 10013. 212-417-5853 (EST) 9:30AM-4:30PM. Felony, Misdemeanor.

**Civil Court of the City of New York-Kings Branch**, 141 Livingston St, Brooklyn, NY 11201. 718-643-5069 (EST) 9AM-5PM. Civil Actions Under $25,000, Eviction, Small Claims.

**Surrogate Court**, 2 Johnson St, Brooklyn, NY 11201. 718-643-5262 (EST) Probate.

## Lewis County

**Real Estate Recording**, Lewis County Clerk, 7660 State Street, Courthouse Building, Lowville, NY 13367-1396. 315-376-5333 (EST) 8:30AM-4:30PM.

**Supreme and County Court**, Courthouse, Lowville, NY 13367-1396. 315-376-5333 (EST) 8:30AM-4:30PM. Felony, Civil Actions Over $15,000.

**Surrogate Court**, Courthouse, Lowville, NY 13367-1396. 315-376-5344 (EST) Probate.

## Livingston County

**Real Estate Recording**, Livingston County Clerk, Government Center, 6 Court St., Room 201, Geneseo, NY 14454-1043. 716-243-7010 (EST) 9AM-5PM.

**Supreme and County Court**, 6 Court St, Rm 201, Geneseo, NY 14454. 716-243-7010 (EST) 9AM-5PM. Felony, Civil Actions Over $15,000.

**Surrogate Court**, 1150 E River Rd, Avon, NY 14414. 716-226-7070 (EST) Probate.

## Madison County

**Real Estate Recording**, Madison County Clerk, North Court Street, County Office Building, Wampsville, NY 13163. 315-366-2262 (EST) 9AM-5PM.

**Supreme and County Court**, County Office Bldg, Wampsville, NY 13163. 315-366-2261 (EST) 9AM-5PM. Felony, Civil Actions Over $15,000.

**Oneida City Court**, 109 N Main St, Oneida, NY 13421. 315-363-1310 (EST) 8:30AM-4:30PM. Misdemeanor, Civil Actions Under $15,000, Eviction, Small Claims.

**Surrogate Court**, Courthouse, Wampsville, NY 13163. 315-366-2392 (EST) Probate.

## Monroe County

**Real Estate Recording**, Monroe County Clerk, 39 West Main Street, Rochester, NY 14614. 716-428-5157 (EST) 9AM-5PM.

**Supreme and County Court**, 39 W Main Stice, Rochester, NY 14614. 716-428-5888 (EST) 9AM-5PM. Felony, Civil Actions Over $15,000.

**Rochester City Court**, Hall of Justice, Rochester, NY 14614. 716-428-2444 (EST) 9AM-5PM. Misdemeanor, Civil Actions Under $15,000, Eviction, Small Claims.

**Surrogate Court**, Hall of Justice, Rm 304, Rochester, NY 14614-2185. 716-428-5200 (EST) Probate.

## Montgomery County

**Real Estate Recording**, Montgomery County Clerk, County Office Building, Fonda, NY 12068. 518-853-8115 (EST) 8:30AM-4PM.

**Supreme and County Court**, Courthouse, Fonda, NY 12068. 518-853-8113 (EST) 9AM-5PM. Felony, Civil Actions Over $15,000.

**Amsterdam City Court**, Public Safety Bldg, Rm 208, Amsterdam, NY 12210. 518-842-9510 (EST) 8AM-4PM. Misdemeanor, Civil Actions Under $15,000, Eviction, Small Claims.

**Surrogate Court**, PO Box 1500, Fonda, NY 12068-1500. 518-853-8108 (EST) Probate.

## Nassau County

**Real Estate Recording**, Nassau County Clerk, 240 Old Country Road, Mineola, NY 11501. 516-571-2667 (EST) 9AM-4:45PM.

**Supreme Court**, Supreme Court Bldg, Mineola, NY 11501. 516-571-3250 (EST) 9AM-5PM. Felony, Civil Actions Over $25,000.

**County Court**, 262 Old County Rd, Mineola, NY 11501. 516-571-2720 (EST) 9AM-5PM. Felony, Civil Actions Under $25,000.

**Glen Cove City Court**, 146 Glen St, Glen Cove, NY 11542. 516-676-0109 (EST) 9AM-5PM. Misdemeanor, Civil Actions Under $15,000, Eviction, Small Claims.

**3rd District Court**, 435 Middle Neck, Great Neck, NY 11023. 516-571-8400 (EST) 9AM-5PM. Misdemeanor, Civil Actions Under $15,000, Eviction, Small Claims.

**1st District Court**, 99 Main St, Hempstead, NY 11550. 516-572-2200 (EST) 9AM-5PM. Felony, Misdemeanor, Civil Actions Under $15,000, Eviction, Small Claims.

**2nd District Court**, 99 Mina St, Hempstead, NY 11550. 516-572-2264 (EST) 9AM-5PM. Felony, Misdemeanor, Civil Actions Under $15,000, Eviction, Small Claims.

**4th District Court**, 87 Bethpage Rd, Hicksville, NY 11801. 516-571-7090 (EST) 9AM-5PM.

Civil Actions Under $15,000, Eviction, Small Claims.

**Long Beach City Court**, 1 West Chester St, Long Beach, NY 11561. 516-431-1000 (EST) 9AM-5PM. Misdemeanor, Civil Actions Under $15,000, Eviction, Small Claims.

**Surrogate Court**, 262 Old County Rd, Mineola, NY 11501. 516-535-2082 (EST) Probate.

## New York County

**Real Estate Recording**, New York City Register, 31 Chambers Street, Room 202, New York, NY 10007. 212-788-8529 (EST) 9AM-4PM.

**Supreme Court-Civil Division**, County Clerk, 60 Centre St, New York City, NY 10007. 212-374-8591 (EST) 9AM-5PM. Civil Actions Over $25,000.

**Supreme Court-Criminal Division**, 80 Center St, Rm 544, New York, NY 10013. 212-417-5853 (EST) 9:30AM-12:30PM 2-4:30PM. Felony, Misdemeanor.

**Civil Court of the City of New York**, 111 Centre St, New York, NY 10013. 212-374-7915 (EST) 9AM-5PM. Civil Actions Under $25,000, Eviction, Small Claims.

**Surrogate Court**, 31 Chambers St, New York City, NY 10007. 212-374-8233 (EST) Probate.

## Niagara County

**Real Estate Recording**, Niagara County Clerk, 175 Hawley Street, Lockport, NY 14094. 716-439-7029 (EST) 9AM-5PM (Summer 8:30AM-4:30PM).

**Supreme Court**, 775 3rd St, Niagara Falls, NY 14302. 716-278-1800 (EST) 9AM-5PM. Felony, Civil Actions Over $25,000.

**County Court**, Courthouse, Lockport, NY 14094. 716-434-3272 (EST) 9AM-5PM. Felony, Civil Actions Under $25,000.

**Lockport City Court**, Municipal Bldg, One Locks Plaza, Lockport, NY 14094. 716-439-6660 (EST) 8:00AM-4:30PM. Misdemeanor, Civil Actions Under $15,000, Eviction, Small Claims.

**Niagara Falls City Court**, 520 Hyde Park Blvd, Niagara Falls, NY 14301-2725. 716-286-4505 (EST) 8:30AM-4:30PM. Misdemeanor, Civil Actions Under $15,000, Eviction, Small Claims.

**North Tonawanda City Court**, City Hall, North Tonawanda, NY 14120-5446. 716-693-1010 (EST) 8AM-5PM. Misdemeanor, Civil Actions Under $15,000, Eviction, Small Claims.

**Surrogate Court**, 175 Hawley St, Lockport, NY 14094. 716-434-8575 (EST) Probate.

## Oneida County

**Real Estate Recording**, Oneida County Clerk, 800 Park Avenue, Utica, NY 13501. 315-798-5792 (EST) 9AM-5PM.

**Supreme and County Court**, 800 Park Ave, Utica, NY 13501. 315-798-5790 (EST) 9AM-5PM. Felony, Civil Actions Over $15,000.

**Rome City Court**, 301 James St, Rome, NY 13440. 315-339-7693 (EST) Misdemeanor, Civil Actions Under $15,000, Eviction, Small Claims.

**Sherrill City Court**, 601 Sherrill Rd, Sherrill, NY 13461. 315-363-0996 (EST) 8AM-4PM. Misdemeanor, Civil Actions Under $15,000, Eviction, Small Claims.

**Utica City Court**, 413 Oriskany St West, Utica, NY 13502. 315-724-8157 (EST) Misdemeanor, Civil Actions Under $15,000, Eviction, Small Claims.

**Surrogate Court**, Courthouse, Utica, NY 13501. 315-798-5866 (EST) Probate.

## Onondaga County

**Real Estate Recording**, Onondaga County Clerk, 401 Montgomery Street, Syracuse, NY 13202. 315-435-2238 (EST) 9AM-5PM.

**Supreme and County Court**, 401 Montgomery St, Syracuse, NY 13202. 315-435-2226 (EST) 8AM-5PM. Felony, Civil Actions Over $15,000.

**Syracuse City Court**, 511 State St, Syracuse, NY 13202-2179. 815-477-2782 (EST) 9AM-5PM. Misdemeanor, Civil Actions Under $15,000, Eviction, Small Claims.

**Surrogate Court**, 401 Montgomery St, Syracuse, NY 13202. 315-435-2101 (EST) Probate.

## Ontario County

**Real Estate Recording**, Ontario County Clerk, 25 Pleasant Street, Canandaigua, NY 14424. 716-396-4052 (EST) 8:30AM-5PM.

**Supreme and County Court**, 27 N Main St, Rm 130, Canandaigua, NY 14424-1447. 716-396-4239 (EST) 9AM-5PM. Felony, Civil Actions Over $15,000.

**Canandaigua City Court**, 2 N Main St, Canandaigua, NY 14424-1448. 716-396-5011 (EST) 8AM-4PM. Misdemeanor, Civil Actions Under $15,000, Eviction, Small Claims.

**Geneva City Court**, Castle St, City Hall, Geneva, NY 14456. 315-789-6560 (EST) 8AM-4PM. Misdemeanor, Civil Actions Under $15,000, Eviction, Small Claims.

**Surrogate Court**, 27 N Main St, Canandaigua, NY 14424-1447. 716-396-4055 (EST) Probate.

## Orange County

**Real Estate Recording**, Orange County Clerk, 255-275 Main Street, Goshen, NY 10924. 914-294-5151 (EST) X1254 9AM-5PM.

**Supreme and County Court**, 255 Main St, Goshen, NY 10924. 914-294-5151 (EST) 9AM-5PM. Felony, Civil Actions Over $15,000.

**Middletown City Court**, 2 James St, Middletown, NY 10940. 914-346-4050 (EST) 9AM-5PM. Misdemeanor, Civil Actions Under $15,000, Eviction, Small Claims.

**Newburgh City Court**, 57 Broadway, Newburgh, NY 12550. 914-565-3208 (EST) 8:30AM-4:30PM. Misdemeanor, Civil Actions Under $15,000, Eviction, Small Claims.

**Port Jervis City Court**, 14-18 Hammond St, Port Jervis, NY 12771-2495. 914-858-4034 (EST) 9AM-5PM. Misdemeanor, Civil Actions Under $15,000, Eviction, Small Claims.

**Surrogate Court**, Park Place, Goshen, NY 10924. 914-294-3277 (EST) Probate.

## Orleans County

**Real Estate Recording**, Orleans County Clerk, 3 South Main Street, Courthouse Square, Albion, NY 14411-1498. 716-589-5334 (EST) 9AM-5PM (July-August 8:30AM-4PM).

**Supreme and County Court**, Courthouse, Albion, NY 14411-9998. 716-589-5334 (EST) 9AM-5PM. Felony, Civil Actions Over $15,000.

Surrogate Court, Courthouse, Albion, NY 14411-9998. 716-589-4457 (EST) Probate.

## Oswego County

**Real Estate Recording**, Oswego County Clerk, 46 East Bridge Street, Oswego, NY 13126. 315-349-8385 (EST) 9AM-5PM.

**Supreme and County Court**, 46 E Bridge St, Oswego, NY 13126. 315-349-8385 (EST) 9AM-5PM. Felony, Civil Actions Over $15,000.

**Fulton City Court**, 141 S 1st St, Fulton, NY 13069. 315-593-8400 (EST) 8:30AM-4:30PM/Summer 8:30AM-4PM. Misdemeanor, Civil Actions Under $15,000, Eviction, Small Claims.

**Oswego City Court**, City Hall, Oswego, NY 13126. 315-343-0415 (EST) 9AM-5PM. Misdemeanor, Civil Actions Under $15,000, Eviction, Small Claims.

**Surrogate Court**, Courthouse, East Oneida St, Oswego, NY 13126-2693. 315-349-3295 (EST) Probate.

## Otsego County

**Real Estate Recording**, Otsego County Clerk, 197 Main Street, Cooperstown, NY 13326. 607-547-4278 (EST) 9AM-5PM (July-August 9AM-4PM).

**Supreme and County Court**, 197 Main St, Cooperstown, NY 13326. 607-547-4276 (EST) Felony, Civil Actions Over $15,000.

**Otsego City Court**, City Hall, Otsego, NY 13137. 607-432-4480 (EST) 8:30AM-4:30PM. Misdemeanor, Civil Actions Under $15,000, Eviction, Small Claims.

**Surrogate Court**, 197 Main St, Cooperstown, NY 13326. 607-547-4338 (EST) Probate.

## Putnam County

**Real Estate Recording**, Putnam County Clerk, 40 Gleneida Ave., Carmel, NY 10512. 914-225-3641 (EST) 9AM-5PM (Summer 8AM-4PM).

**Supreme and County Court**, 40 Gleneida Ave, Carmel, NY 10512. 914-225-3641 (EST) 9AM-5PM. Felony, Civil Actions Over $15,000.

**Surrogate Court**, 1 County Center, Carmel, NY 10512. 914-225-3641 (EST) Probate.

## Queens County

**Real Estate Recording**, Queens City Register, 90-27 Sutphin Blvd., Jamaica, NY 11435. 718-658-4600 (EST) 9AM-4PM.

**Supreme Court-Civil Division**, 88-11 Sutphin Blvd, Jamaica, NY 11435. 718-520-3136 (EST) 9AM-5PM. Civil Actions Over $25,000.

**Supreme Court-Criminal Division**, 80 Center St, Rm 544, New York, NY 10013. 212-417-5853 (EST) 8:30AM-4:30PM. Felony, Misdemeanor.

**Civil Court of the City of New York-Queens Branch**, 120-55 Queens Blvd, Kew Gardens, NY 11415. 718-520-3610 (EST) 9AM-5PM. Civil Actions Under $25,000, Eviction, Small Claims.

**Surrogate Court**, 88-11 Sutphin Blvd, Jamaica, NY 11435. 718-520-3132 (EST) Probate.

## Rensselaer County

**Real Estate Recording**, Rensselaer County Clerk, Courthouse, Troy, NY 12180. 518-270-4080 (EST) 8AM-4:45PM.

**Supreme and County Court**, Congress & 2nd Sts, Troy, NY 12180. 518-270-4080 (EST) 9AM-5PM. Felony, Civil Actions Over $15,000.

**Rensselaer City Court**, City Hall, Rensselaer, NY 12144. 518-462-6751 (EST) 7:30AM-3:00PM. Misdemeanor, Civil Actions Under $15,000, Eviction, Small Claims.

**Troy City Court**, 51 State St, Troy, NY 12180. 518-271-1602 (EST) 9AM-3:30PM. Misdemeanor, Civil Actions Under $15,000, Eviction, Small Claims.

**Surrogate Court**, Courthouse, Troy, NY 12180. 518-270-3724 (EST) Probate.

## Richmond County

**Real Estate Recording**, Richmond County Clerk, 18 Richmond Terrace, County Courthouse, Staten Island, NY 10301-1990. 718-390-5386 (EST) 9AM-5PM.

**Supreme Court-Civil Division**, 18 Richmond Terrace, Staten Island, NY 10301. 718-390-5389 (EST) 9AM-5PM. Civil Actions Over $25,000.

**Supreme Court-Criminal Division**, 80 Center St, Rm 544, New York, NY 10013. 212-417-5853 (EST) 9:30AM-4:30PM, Closed 12-2. Felony, Misdemeanor.

**Civil Court of the City of New York-Richmond Branch**, 927 Castleton Ave, Staten Island, NY 10310. 718-390-5352 (EST) 8AM-4:30PM. Civil Actions Under $25,000, Eviction, Small Claims.

**Surrogate Court**, 18 Richmond Terrace, Staten Island, NY 10301. 718-390-5400 (EST) Probate.

## Rockland County

**Real Estate Recording**, Rockland County Clerk, 27 New Hempstead Road, New City, NY 10956. 914-638-5354 (EST) 9AM-5PM.

**Supreme and County Court**, 27 New Hempstead Rd, New City, NY 10956. 914-638-5070 (EST) 8AM-5PM. Felony, Civil Actions Over $15,000.

**Surrogate Court**, 27 New Hemstead Rd, New City, NY 10956. 914-638-5330 (EST) Probate.

## Saratoga County

**Real Estate Recording**, Saratoga County Clerk, 40 McMaster Street, Ballston Spa, NY 12020. 518-885-5381 (EST) 9AM-5PM.

**Supreme and County Court**, 40 McMaster St, Ballston Spa, NY 12020. 518-885-2213 (EST) 9AM-5PM. Felony, Civil Actions Over $15,000.

**Mechanicville City Court**, 36 N Main St, Mechanicville, NY 12118. 518-664-9876 (EST) 8AM-4PM. Misdemeanor, Civil Actions Under $15,000, Eviction, Small Claims.

**Saratoga Springs City Court**, City Hall, Saratoga Springs, NY 12866. 518-587-3550 (EST) Misdemeanor, Civil Actions Under $15,000, Eviction, Small Claims.

**Surrogate Court**, 30 McMaster St, Ballston Spa, NY 12020. 518-884-4722 (EST) Probate.

## Schenectady County

**Real Estate Recording**, Schenectady County Clerk, 620 State Street, Schenectady, NY 12305-2114. 518-388-4220 (EST) 9AM-5PM.

**Supreme and County Court**, 612 State St, Schenectady, NY 12305. 518-388-4220 (EST) 9AM-5PM. Felony, Civil Actions Over $15,000.

**Schenectady City Court**, Jay St, City Hall, Schenectady, NY 12305. 518-382-5077 (EST) 8AM-4PM. Misdemeanor, Civil Actions Under $15,000, Eviction, Small Claims.

**Surrogate Court**, 612 State St, Schenectady, NY 12305. 518-388-4293 (EST) Probate.

## Schoharie County

**Real Estate Recording**, Schoharie County Clerk, 300 Main Street, County Office Building, Schoharie, NY 12157. 518-295-8316 (EST) 8:30AM-5PM.

**Supreme and County Court**, PO Box 549, Schoharie, NY 12157. 518-295-8316 (EST) 8:30AM-5PM. Felony, Civil Actions Over $15,000.

**Surrogate Court**, Courthouse, Schoharie, NY 12157-0669. 518-395-8383 (EST) Probate.

## Schuyler County

**Real Estate Recording**, Schuyler County Clerk, 105 Ninth Street Box 8, County Office Building, Watkins Glen, NY 14891. 607-535-8133 (EST) 9AM-5PM.

**Supreme and County Court**, Courthouse, Watkins Glen, NY 14891. 607-535-7760 (EST) 9AM-5PM. Felony, Civil Actions Over $15,000.

**Surrogate Court**, Courthouse, Watkins Glen, NY 14891. 607-535-7144 (EST) Probate.

## Seneca County

**Real Estate Recording**, Seneca County Clerk, 1 DiPronio Drive, Waterloo, NY 13165. 315-539-5655 (EST) 8:30AM-5PM.

**Supreme and County Court**, 48 W Williams St, Waterloo, NY 13165-1396. 315-539-5655 (EST) 8AM-4:30PM. Felony, Civil Actions Over $15,000.

**Surrogate Court**, 48 W Williams St, Waterloo, NY 13165-1396. 315-539-7531 (EST) Probate.

## St. Lawrence County

**Real Estate Recording**, St. Lawrence County Clerk, 48 Court Street, Canton, NY 13617-1198. 315-379-2237 (EST) 8:30AM-4:30PM.

**Supreme and County Court**, 48 Court St, Canton, NY 13617-1199. 315-379-2237 (EST) 8:30AM-4:30PM. Felony, Civil Actions Over $15,000.

**Ogdensburg City Court**, 330 Ford St, Ogdensburg, NY 13669. 315-393-3941 (EST) 8AM-4PM. Misdemeanor, Civil Actions Under $15,000, Eviction, Small Claims.

**Surrogate Court**, 48 Court St, Canton, NY 13617. 315-379-2217 (EST) Probate.

## Steuben County

**Real Estate Recording**, Steuben County Clerk, 3 East Pulteney Square, County Office Building, Bath, NY 14810. 607-776-9631 (EST) X3207 8:30AM-5PM (July-August 8:30AM-4PM).

**Supreme and County Court**, Pulteney Square, Bath, NY 14810-1575. 607-776-9631 (EST) Felony, Civil Actions Over $15,000.

**Corning City Court**, 12 Civic Center Plaza, Corning, NY 14830-2884. 607-936-4111 (EST) 8AM-4PM. Misdemeanor, Civil Actions Under $15,000, Eviction, Small Claims.

**Hornell City Court**, 108 Broadway, Hornell, NY 14843-0627. 607-324-7531 (EST) 8AM-4PM. Misdemeanor, Civil Actions Under $15,000, Eviction, Small Claims.

**Surrogate Court**, Pulteney Square #13, Bath, NY 14810-1575. 607-776-9631 (EST) Probate.

## Suffolk County

**Real Estate Recording**, Suffolk County Clerk, 310 Center Drive, Riverhead, NY 11901-3392. 516-852-2038 (EST) 9AM-5PM.

**Supreme and County Court**, 310 Centre Dr, Riverhead, NY 11901. 516-852-2016 (EST) 9AM-5PM. Felony, Civil Actions Over $15,000.

**2nd District Court**, 72 E Main St, Babylon, NY 11702. 516-669-6100 (EST) 9AM-5PM. Misdemeanor, Civil Actions Under $15,000, Eviction, Small Claims.

**5th District Court**, 400 Carlton Ave, Central Islip, NY 11722. 516-853-7626 (EST) 9AM-5PM. Misdemeanor, Civil Actions Under $15,000, Eviction, Small Claims.

**Suffolk District Court**, 400 Carleton Ave, Central Islip, NY 11722. 516-853-5400 (EST) 9AM-5PM. Misdemeanor, Civil Actions Under $15,000, Eviction, Small Claims.

**4th District Court**, North County Complex Bldg C158, Hauppauge, NY 11787. 516-853-5357 (EST) 9AM-5PM. Misdemeanor, Civil Actions Under $15,000, Eviction, Small Claims.

**3rd District Court**, 1850 New York Ave, Huntington Station, NY 11746. 516-854-4545 (EST) 9AM-4:30PM. Misdemeanor, Civil Actions Under $15,000, Eviction, Small Claims.

**6th District Court**, 150 W Main St, Patchogue, NY 11772. 516-854-1440 (EST) 9AM-5PM. Misdemeanor, Civil Actions Under $15,000, Eviction, Small Claims.

**Surrogate Court**, 320 Centre Dr, Riverhead, NY 11901. 516-852-1745 (EST) Probate.

## Sullivan County

**Real Estate Recording**, Sullivan County Clerk, 100 North Street, Government Center, Monticello, NY 12701. 914-794-3000 (EST) X3161 9AM-5PM.

**Supreme and County Court**, Courthouse, Monticello, NY 12701. 914-794-4066 (EST) 9AM-5PM. Felony, Civil Actions Over $15,000.

**Surrogate Court**, PO Box 5012, Monticello, NY 12701. 914-794-3000 (EST) Probate.

## Tioga County

**Real Estate Recording**, Tioga County Clerk, 16 Court Street, Owego, NY 13827. 607-687-3133 (EST) 9AM-5PM.

**Supreme and County Court**, Courthouse, Owego, NY 13827. 607-687-0544 (EST) Felony, Civil Actions Over $15,000.

**Surrogate Court**, Courthouse, Owego, NY 13827. 607-687-1303 (EST) Probate.

## Tompkins County

**Real Estate Recording**, Tompkins County Clerk, 320 North Tioga Street, Ithaca, NY 14850-4284. 607-274-5432 (EST) 9AM-5PM.

**Supreme and County Court**, 320 N Tioga St (PO Box 70), Ithaca, NY 14851-0070. 607-272-0466 (EST) 9AM-5PM. Felony, Civil Actions Over $15,000.

**Ithaca City Court**, 120 E Clinton St, Ithaca, NY 14850. 607-274-6594 (EST) 9AM-5PM. Misdemeanor, Civil Actions Under $15,000, Eviction, Small Claims.

**Surrogate Court**, PO Box 70, Ithaca, NY 14851. 607-277-0622 (EST) Probate.

## Ulster County

**Real Estate Recording**, Ulster County Clerk, 240-244 Fair Street, County Office Building, Kingston, NY 12401. 914-331-9300 (EST) 9AM-5PM.

**Supreme and County Court**, PO Box 1800, Kingston, NY 12401. 914-331-9300 (EST) 9AM-5PM. Felony, Civil Actions Over $15,000.

**Kingston City Court**, 1 Garraghan Dr, Kingston, NY 12401. 914-338-2974 (EST) 8AM-4PM. Misdemeanor, Civil Actions Under $15,000, Eviction, Small Claims.

**Surrogate Court**, PO Box 1800, Kingston, NY 12401-1800. 914-331-9300 (EST) Probate.

## Warren County

**Real Estate Recording**, Warren County Clerk, Municipal Center, Route 9, Lake George, NY 12845. 518-761-6429 (EST) 9AM-5PM.

**Supreme and County Court**, Rt US 9, Lake George, NY 12845. 518-761-6430 (EST) 9AM-5PM. Felony, Civil Actions Over $15,000.

**Glens Falls City Court**, 42 Ridge St, Glens Falls, NY 12801. 518-798-4714 (EST) 8:30AM-4:30PM. Misdemeanor, Civil Actions Under $15,000, Eviction, Small Claims.

**Surrogate Court**, Rt US 9, Lake George, NY 12845. 518-761-6514 (EST) Probate.

## Washington County

**Real Estate Recording**, Washington County Clerk, 383 Broadway, Fort Edward, NY 12828. 518-747-3374 (EST) 8:30AM-4:30PM.

**Supreme and County Court**, 383 Broadway, Fort Edward, NY 12828. 518-746-2520 (EST) 8:30AM-4:30PM. Felony, Civil Actions Over $15,000.

**Surrogate Court**, 383 Boradway, Fort Edward, NY 12828. 518-746-2545 (EST) Probate.

## Wayne County

**Real Estate Recording**, Wayne County Clerk, 9 Pearl Street, Lyons, NY 14489. 315-946-5971 (EST) 9AM-5PM.

**Supreme and County Court**, 26 Church St, Lyons, NY 14489-1134. 315-946-5870 (EST) 9AM-5PM. Felony, Civil Actions Over $15,000.

**Surrogate Court**, 26 Church St, Lyons, NY 14489-1134. 315-946-5430 (EST) Probate.

## Westchester County

**Real Estate Recording**, Westchester County Clerk, Room 330, 110 Grove Street, White Plains, NY 10601. 914-285-3098 (EST) 9AM-5PM.

**Supreme and County Court**, 111 Grove St, White Plains, NY 10601. 914-285-3070 (EST) 9AM-5PM. Felony, Civil Actions Over $15,000.

**Mt Vernon City Court**, Municipal Bldg, Mt Vernon, NY 10550-2019. 914-665-2400 (EST) 8:30AM-4:30PM. Misdemeanor, Civil Actions Under $15,000, Eviction, Small Claims.

**Peekskill City Court**, 2 Nelson Ave, Peekskill, NY 10566. 914-737-3405 (EST) 9AM-5PM. Misdemeanor, Civil Actions Under $15,000, Eviction, Small Claims.

**Rye City Court**, 21 Third St, Rye, NY 10580. 914-967-1599 (EST) 8:30AM-5PM. Misdemeanor, Civil Actions Under $15,000, Eviction, Small Claims.

**White Plains City Court**, 77 S Lexington Ave, White Plains, NY 10601. 914-422-6050 (EST) 9AM-5PM. Misdemeanor, Civil Actions Under $15,000, Eviction, Small Claims.

**Yonkers City Court**, 100 S Broadway, Yonkers, NY 10701. 914-377-6352 (EST) 8:45AM-6PM. Misdemeanor, Civil Actions Under $15,000, Eviction, Small Claims.

**Surrogate Court**, 140 Grand St, White Plains, NY 10601. 914-285-3712 (EST) Probate.

## Wyoming County

**Real Estate Recording**, Wyoming County Clerk, 143 North Main Street, Warsaw, NY 14569. 716-786-8810 (EST) 9AM-5PM.

**Supreme and County Court**, 143 N Main St, Warsaw, NY 14569. 716-786-3148 (EST) 9AM-5PM. Felony, Civil Actions Over $15,000.

**Surrogate Court**, 143 N Main St, Warsaw, NY 14569-1193. 716-786-3148 (EST) Probate.

## Yates County

**Real Estate Recording**, Yates County Clerk, 110 Court Street, Penn Yan, NY 14527. 315-536-5120 (EST) 9AM-5PM.

**Supreme and County Court**, 226 N Main St, Penn Yan, NY 14527-1191. 315-536-5120 (EST) 8:30AM-5PM. Felony, Civil Actions Over $15,000.

**Surrogate Court**, 108 Court St, Penn Yan, NY 14527. 315-536-5190 (EST) Probate.

# North Carolina

## Alamance County

**Real Estate Recording**, Alamance County Register of Deeds, 118 West Harden Street, Graham, NC 27253. 910-570-6565 (EST) 8AM-5PM.

**Superior-District Court**, Courthouse, Graham, NC 27253. 919-570-6865 (EST) Felony, Misdemeanor, Civil, Eviction, Small Claims, Probate.

## Alexander County

**Real Estate Recording**, Alexander County Register of Deeds, 201 First Street SW, Suite 1, Taylorsville, NC 28681-2504. 704-632-3400 (EST) 8AM-5PM.

**Superior-District Court**, PO Box 100, Taylorsville, NC 28681. 704-632-2215 (EST) 8AM-5PM. Felony, Misdemeanor, Civil, Eviction, Small Claims, Probate.

## Alleghany County

**Real Estate Recording**, Alleghany County Register of Deeds, Main Street, Sparta, NC 28675. 919-372-4342 (EST) 8AM-5PM.

**Superior-District Court**, PO Box 61, Sparta, NC 28675. 910-372-8949 (EST) 8AM-5PM. Felony, Misdemeanor, Civil, Eviction, Small Claims, Probate.

## Anson County

**Real Estate Recording**, Anson County Register of Deeds, Green Street Courthouse, Wadesboro, NC 28170. 704-694-3212 (EST) 8:30AM-5PM.

**Superior-District Court**, PO Box 1064, Wadesboro, NC 28170. 704-694-2314 (EST) 8AM-5PM. Felony, Misdemeanor, Civil, Eviction, Small Claims, Probate.

## Ashe County

**Real Estate Recording**, Ashe County Register of Deeds, East Main Street, Courthouse, Jefferson, NC 28640. 910-246-9338 (EST) 8AM-5PM.

**Superior-District Court**, PO Box 95, Jefferson, NC 28640. 910-246-5641 (EST) 8AM-5PM. Felony, Misdemeanor, Civil, Eviction, Small Claims, Probate.

## Avery County

**Real Estate Recording**, Avery County Register of Deeds, Avery Square, Courthouse - Room 101, Newland, NC 28657. 704-733-8260 (EST) 8AM-4:30PM.

**Superior-District Court**, PO Box 115, Newland, NC 28657. 704-733-2900 (EST) 8:00AM-4:30PM. Felony, Misdemeanor, Civil, Eviction, Small Claims, Probate.

## Beaufort County

**Real Estate Recording**, Beaufort County Register of Deeds, 112 West Second Street, Courthouse, Washington, NC 27889. 919-946-2323 (EST) 8:30AM-5PM.

**Superior-District Court**, PO Box 1403, Washington, NC 27889. 919-946-5184 (EST) 8:00AM-5:30PM. Felony, Misdemeanor, Civil, Eviction, Small Claims, Probate.

## Bertie County

**Real Estate Recording**, Bertie County Register of Deeds, Corner of King & Dundee, Windsor, NC 27983. 919-794-5309 (EST) 8:30AM-5PM.

**Superior-District Court**, PO Box 370, Windsor, NC 27983. 919-794-3039 (EST) 8:00AM-5:00PM. Felony, Misdemeanor, Civil, Eviction, Small Claims, Probate.

## Bladen County

**Real Estate Recording**, Bladen County Register of Deeds, Courthouse Drive, Elizabethtown, NC 28337. 919-862-6710 (EST) 8:30AM-5PM.

**Superior-District Court**, PO Box 547, Elizabethtown, NC 28337. 910-862-2143 (EST) 8:30AM-5:00PM. Felony, Misdemeanor, Civil, Eviction, Small Claims, Probate.

## Brunswick County

**Real Estate Recording**, Brunswick County Register of Deeds, Government Complex, Highway 17-Business, Bolivia, NC 28422. 910-253-4371 (EST) 8:30AM-5PM.

**Superior-District Court**, PO Box 127, Bolivia, NC 28422. 910-253-4446 (EST) 8:30AM-5:00PM. Felony, Misdemeanor, Civil, Eviction, Small Claims, Probate.

## Buncombe County

**Real Estate Recording**, Buncombe County Register of Deeds, 60 Court Plaza, Asheville, NC 28801-3563. 704-255-5541 (EST) 8:30AM-5PM.

**Superior-District Court**, 60 Court Plaza, Asheville, NC 28801-3519. 704-255-4702 (EST) 8:30AM-5:00PM. Felony, Misdemeanor, Civil, Eviction, Small Claims, Probate.

## Burke County

**Real Estate Recording**, Burke County Register of Deeds, 201 South Green Street, Courthouse, Morganton, NC 28655. 704-438-5450 (EST) 8AM-5PM.

**Superior-District Court**, PO Box 796, Morganton, NC 28655. 704-438-5540 (EST) 8:00AM-5:00PM. Felony, Misdemeanor, Civil, Eviction, Small Claims, Probate.

## Cabarrus County

**Real Estate Recording**, Cabarrus County Register of Deeds, 65 Church Street S.E., Concord, NC 28025. 704-788-8112 (EST) 8AM-5PM.

**Superior-District Court**, PO Box 70, Concord, NC 28026-0070. 704-786-4137 (EST) 8:30AM-5:00PM. Felony, Misdemeanor, Civil, Eviction, Small Claims, Probate.

## Caldwell County

**Real Estate Recording**, Caldwell County Register of Deeds, 905 West Avenue N.W., County Office Building, Lenoir, NC 28645. 704-757-1310 (EST) 8AM-5PM.

**Superior-District Court**, PO Box 1376, Lenoir, NC 28645. 704-757-1375 (EST) 8:00AM-5:00PM. Felony, Misdemeanor, Civil, Eviction, Small Claims, Probate.

## Camden County

**Real Estate Recording**, Camden County Register of Deeds, County Courthouse, 117 North 343, Camden, NC 27921. 919-335-4077 (EST) 8AM-5PM.

**Superior-District Court**, PO Box 219, Camden, NC 27921. 919-335-7942 (EST) 8:00AM-5:00PM. Felony, Misdemeanor, Civil, Eviction, Small Claims, Probate.

## Carteret County

**Real Estate Recording**, Carteret County Register of Deeds, Courthouse Square, Beaufort, NC 28516-1898. 919-728-8474 (EST) 8AM-5PM.

**Superior-District Court**, Courthouse Square, Beaufort, NC 28516. 919-728-8500 (EST) 8:00AM-5:00PM. Felony, Misdemeanor, Civil, Eviction, Small Claims, Probate.

## Caswell County

**Real Estate Recording**, Caswell County Register of Deeds, 139 E. Church St., Courthouse, Yanceyville, NC 27379. 910-694-4193 (EST) 8AM-5PM.

**Superior-District Court**, PO Drawer 790, Yanceyville, NC 27379. 910-694-4171 (EST) 8:00AM-5:00PM. Felony, Misdemeanor, Civil, Eviction, Small Claims, Probate.

## Catawba County

**Real Estate Recording**, Catawba County Register of Deeds, Catawba County Justice Center, Highway 321, Newton, NC 28658. 704-465-1573 (EST) 8AM-5PM.

**Superior-District Court**, PO Box 723, Newton, NC 28658. 704-464-5216 (EST) 8:00AM-5:00PM. Felony, Misdemeanor, Civil, Eviction, Small Claims, Probate.

## Chatham County

**Real Estate Recording**, Chatham County Register of Deeds, Courthouse Circle, Pittsboro, NC 27312. 919-542-8235 (EST) 8AM-5PM.

**Superior-District Court**, PO Box 368, Pittsboro, NC 27312. 919-542-3240 (EST) 8:00AM-5:00PM. Felony, Misdemeanor, Civil, Eviction, Small Claims, Probate.

## Cherokee County

**Real Estate Recording**, Cherokee County Register of Deeds, Courthouse, Murphy, NC 28906. 704-837-2613 (EST) 8AM-5PM.

**Superior-District Court**, 201 Peachtree St, Murphy, NC 28906. 704-837-2522 (EST) 9:00AM-5:00PM. Felony, Misdemeanor, Civil, Eviction, Small Claims, Probate.

## Chowan County

**Real Estate Recording**, Chowan County Register of Deeds, South Broad Street, Courthouse, Edenton, NC 27932. 919-482-2619 (EST) 8AM-5PM.

**Superior-District Court**, PO Box 588, Edenton, NC 27932. 919-482-4150 (EST) 8:00AM-5:00PM. Felony, Misdemeanor, Civil, Eviction, Small Claims, Probate.

## Clay County

**Real Estate Recording**, Clay County Register of Deeds, Main Street, Hayesville, NC 28904. 704-389-6301 (EST) 8AM-5PM.

**Superior-District Court**, PO Box 506, Hayesville, NC 28904. 704-389-8334 (EST) 8:00AM-5:00PM. Felony, Misdemeanor, Civil, Eviction, Small Claims, Probate.

## Cleveland County

**Real Estate Recording**, Cleveland County Register of Deeds, 311 East Marion St., Shelby, NC 28150. 704-484-4834 (EST) 8AM-5PM.

**Superior-District Court**, 100 Justice Place, Shelby, NC 28150. 704-484-4851 (EST) 8:00AM-5:00PM. Felony, Misdemeanor, Civil, Eviction, Small Claims, Probate.

## Columbus County

**Real Estate Recording**, Columbus County Register of Deeds, Courthouse, Whiteville, NC 28472. 919-640-6625 (EST) 8:30AM-5PM.

**Superior-District Court**, PO Box 1587, Whiteville, NC 28472. 910-642-3119 (EST) 8:30AM-5:00PM. Felony, Misdemeanor, Civil, Eviction, Small Claims, Probate.

## Craven County

**Real Estate Recording**, Craven County Register of Deeds, 406 Craven Street, New Bern, NC 28560. 919-636-6617 (EST) 8AM-5PM.

**Superior-District Court**, PO Box 1187, New Bern, NC 28563. 919-514-4774 (EST) 8AM-5PM. Felony, Misdemeanor, Civil, Eviction, Small Claims, Probate.

## Cumberland County

**Real Estate Recording**, Cumberland County Register of Deeds, 117 Dick Street, Room 114, Fayetteville, NC 28302. 910-678-7718 (EST) 8AM-5PM.

**Superior-District Court**, PO Box 363, Fayetteville, NC 28302. 910-678-2909 (EST) 8:30AM-5:00PM. Felony, Misdemeanor, Civil, Eviction, Small Claims, Probate.

## Currituck County

**Real Estate Recording**, Currituck County Register of Deeds, 101 Courthouse Road, Currituck, NC 27929. 919-232-3297 (EST) 8AM-5PM.

**Superior-District Court**, PO Box 175, Currituck, NC 27929. 919-232-2010 (EST) 8:00AM-5:00PM. Felony, Misdemeanor, Civil, Eviction, Small Claims, Probate.

## Dare County

**Real Estate Recording**, Dare County Register of Deeds, Queen Elizabeth Avenue, Courthouse, PO Box 70, Manteo, NC 27954. 919-473-3438 (EST) 8:30AM-5PM.

**Superior-District Court**, PO Box 1849, Manteo, NC 27954. 919-473-2143 (EST) Felony, Misdemeanor, Civil, Eviction, Small Claims, Probate.

## Davidson County

**Real Estate Recording**, Davidson County Register of Deeds, 110 West Center Street, Court House, Lexington, NC 27292. 704-242-2150 (EST) 8AM-5PM.

**Superior-District Court**, PO Box 1064, Lexington, NC 27293-1064. 704-249-0351 (EST) 8:00AM-5:00PM. Felony, Misdemeanor, Civil, Eviction, Small Claims, Probate.

## Davie County

**Real Estate Recording**, Davie County Register of Deeds, 123 South Main Street, Courthouse, Mocksville, NC 27028. 704-634-2513 (EST) 8:30AM-5PM.

**Superior-District Court**, 140 S Main St, Mocksville, NC 27028. 704-634-3507 (EST) 8:30AM-5:00PM. Felony, Misdemeanor, Civil, Eviction, Small Claims, Probate.

## Duplin County

**Real Estate Recording**, Duplin County Register of Deeds, Courthouse, Kenansville, NC 28349. 919-296-2108 (EST) 8AM-5PM.

**Superior-District Court**, PO Box 189, Kenansville, NC 28349. 910-296-1686 (EST) 8:00AM-5:00PM. Felony, Misdemeanor, Civil, Eviction, Small Claims, Probate.

## Durham County

**Real Estate Recording**, Durham County Register of Deeds, 200 East Main Street, Ground Floor, Durham, NC 27701. 919-560-0480 (EST) 8:30-5PM.

**Superior-District Court**, PO Box 1772, Durham, NC 27702. 919-560-6833 (EST) 8:30AM-5:00PM. Felony, Misdemeanor, Civil, Eviction, Small Claims, Probate.

## Edgecombe County

**Real Estate Recording**, Edgecombe County Register of Deeds, 301 St. Andrews Street, Courthouse, Tarboro, NC 27886. 919-641-7924 (EST) 8AM-5PM.

**Superior-District Court**, PO Drawer 9, Tarboro, NC 27886. 919-823-6161 (EST) 8:00AM-5:00PM. Felony, Misdemeanor, Civil, Eviction, Small Claims, Probate.

## Forsyth County

**Real Estate Recording**, Forsyth County Register of Deeds, 200 North Main, Winston-Salem, NC 27101. 910-727-2903 (EST) 8AM-5PM.

**Superior-District Court**, PO Box 20099, Winston Salem, NC 27120-0099. 910-761-2340 (EST) 8:00AM-5:00PM. Felony, Misdemeanor, Civil, Eviction, Small Claims, Probate.

## Franklin County

**Real Estate Recording**, Franklin County Register of Deeds, 102 South Main Street, Courthouse, Louisburg, NC 27549. 919-496-3500 (EST) 8AM-5PM.

**Superior-District Court**, 102 S Main St, Louisburg, NC 27549. 919-496-5104 (EST) 8:30AM-5:00PM. Felony, Misdemeanor, Civil, Eviction, Small Claims, Probate.

## Gaston County

**Real Estate Recording**, Gaston County Register of Deeds, 151 South Street, Gastonia, NC 28052. 704-866-3083 (EST) 8:30AM-5PM.

**Superior-District Court**, PO Box 340, Gastonia, NC 28053. 704-868-5801 (EST) 8:00AM-5:00PM. Felony, Misdemeanor, Civil, Eviction, Small Claims, Probate.

## Gates County

**Real Estate Recording**, Gates County Register of Deeds, Court Street, Gatesville, NC 27938. 919-357-0850 (EST) 9AM-5PM.

**Superior-District Court**, PO Box 31, Gatesville, NC 27938. 919-357-1365 (EST) 8:00AM-5:00PM. Felony, Misdemeanor, Civil, Eviction, Small Claims, Probate.

## Graham County

**Real Estate Recording**, Graham County Register of Deeds, Main Street, Courthouse, Robbinsville, NC 28771. 704-479-7971 (EST) 8:30AM-4:30PM.

**Superior-District Court**, PO Box 1179, Robbinsville, NC 28771. 704-479-7986 (EST) 8:00AM-4:30PM. Felony, Misdemeanor, Civil, Eviction, Small Claims, Probate.

## Granville County

**Real Estate Recording**, Granville County Register of Deeds, 101 Main Street, Courthouse, Oxford, NC 27565. 919-693-6314 (EST) 8:30AM-5PM.

**Superior-District Court**, Courthouse, 101 Main Street, Oxford, NC 27565. 919-693-2649 (EST) Felony, Misdemeanor, Civil, Eviction, Small Claims, Probate.

## Greene County

**Real Estate Recording**, Greene County Register of Deeds, Greene Street, Courthouse, Snow Hill, NC 28580. 919-747-3620 (EST) 8AM-5PM.

**Superior-District Court**, PO Box 675, Snow Hill, NC 28580. 919-747-3505 (EST) 8:00AM-5:00PM. Felony, Misdemeanor, Civil, Eviction, Small Claims, Probate.

## Guilford County

**Real Estate Recording**, Guilford County Register of Deeds, 505 East Green Drive, Room 132, High Point, NC 27260. 910-884-7931 (EST) 8AM-5PM.

**Superior-District Court**, 201 S Eugene, PO Box 3008, Greensboro, NC 27402. 910-574-4305 (EST) 8:00AM-5:00PM. Felony, Misdemeanor, Civil, Eviction, Small Claims, Probate.

## Halifax County

**Real Estate Recording**, Halifax County Register of Deeds, Ferrell Lane, Halifax, NC 27839. 919-583-2101 (EST) 8:30AM-5PM.

**Superior-District Court**, PO Box 66, Halifax, NC 27839. 919-583-5061 (EST) 8:15AM-5:15PM. Felony, Misdemeanor, Civil, Eviction, Small Claims, Probate.

## Harnett County

**Real Estate Recording**, Harnett County Register of Deeds, Courthouse, 729 Main Street, Lillington, NC 27546. 919-893-7540 (EST) 8AM-5PM.

**Superior-District Court**, PO Box 849, Lillington, NC 27546. 910-893-5164 (EST) 8:15AM-

5:15PM. Felony, Misdemeanor, Civil, Eviction, Small Claims, Probate.

### Haywood County

**Real Estate Recording**, Haywood County Register of Deeds, Courthouse, 420 N. Main St., Waynesville, NC 28786. 704-452-6635 (EST) 8AM-5PM.

**Superior-District Court**, 420 N. Main, Waynesville, NC 28786. 704-456-3540 (EST) 8:30AM-5:30PM. Felony, Misdemeanor, Civil, Eviction, Small Claims, Probate.

### Henderson County

**Real Estate Recording**, Henderson County Register of Deeds, 113 North Main Street, Courthouse, Hendersonville, NC 28739. 704-697-4901 (EST) 8:30AM-5PM.

**Superior-District Court**, PO Box 965, Hendersonville, NC 28793. 704-697-4851 (EST) 8:00AM-5:00PM. Felony, Misdemeanor, Civil, Eviction, Small Claims, Probate.

### Hertford County

**Real Estate Recording**, Hertford County Register of Deeds, Courthouse, Winton, NC 27986. 919-358-7850 (EST) 8:30AM-5PM.

**Superior-District Court**, PO Box 86, Winton, NC 27986. 919-358-7845 (EST) 8:00AM-5:00PM. Felony, Misdemeanor, Civil, Eviction, Small Claims, Probate.

### Hoke County

**Real Estate Recording**, Hoke County Register of Deeds, 036103, 304 N. Main St., Raeford, NC 28376. 910-875-2035 (EST) 8AM-5PM.

**Superior-District Court**, PO Drawer 410, Raeford, NC 28376. 910-875-3728 (EST) 8:30AM-5:00PM. Felony, Misdemeanor, Civil, Eviction, Small Claims, Probate.

### Hyde County

**Real Estate Recording**, Hyde County Register of Deeds, Courthouse Square, Swanquarter, NC 27885. 910-926-3011 (EST) 8AM-5PM.

**Superior-District Court**, PO Box 337, Swanquarter, NC 27885. 919-926-4101 (EST) 8:30AM-5:30PM. Felony, Misdemeanor, Civil, Eviction, Small Claims, Probate.

### Iredell County

**Real Estate Recording**, Iredell County Register of Deeds, 201 Water Street, Statesville, NC 28677. 704-872-7468 (EST) 8AM-5PM.

**Superior-District Court**, PO Box 186, Statesville, NC 28677. 704-878-4204 (EST) 8:00AM-5:00PM. Felony, Misdemeanor, Civil, Eviction, Small Claims, Probate.

### Jackson County

**Real Estate Recording**, Jackson County Register of Deeds, 401 Grindstaff Cove Rd., Sylva, NC 28779. 704-586-4055 (EST) 8:30AM-5PM.

**Superior-District Court**, 401 Grind Staff Cove Rd, Sylva, NC 28779. 704-586-4312 (EST) 8:30AM-5:00PM. Felony, Misdemeanor, Civil, Eviction, Small Claims, Probate.

### Johnston County

**Real Estate Recording**, Johnston County Register of Deeds, Market Street, Courthouse Square, Smithfield, NC 27577. 919-989-5164 (EST) 8AM-5PM.

**Superior-District Court**, PO Box 297, Smithfield, NC 27577. 919-934-3192 (EST) 8:00AM-5:00PM. Felony, Misdemeanor, Civil, Eviction, Small Claims, Probate.

### Jones County

**Real Estate Recording**, Jones County Register of Deeds, 101 Market St., Trenton, NC 28585. 919-448-2551 (EST) 8AM-5PM.

**Superior-District Court**, PO Box 280, Trenton, NC 28585. 919-448-7351 (EST) 8:00AM-5:00PM. Felony, Misdemeanor, Civil, Eviction, Small Claims, Probate.

### Lee County

**Real Estate Recording**, Lee County Register of Deeds, 1408 South Horner Blvd., Sanford, NC 27331. 919-774-4821 (EST) 8AM-5PM.

**Superior-District Court**, PO Box 4209, Sanford, NC 27331. 919-708-4401 (EST) 8:00AM-5:00PM. Felony, Misdemeanor, Civil, Eviction, Small Claims, Probate.

### Lenoir County

**Real Estate Recording**, Lenoir County Register of Deeds, County Courthouse, 130 S. Queen St., Kinston, NC 28501. 919-523-2390 (EST)

**Superior-District Court**, PO Box 68, Kinston, NC 28502-0068. 919-527-6231 (EST) 8:00AM-5:00PM. Felony, Misdemeanor, Civil, Eviction, Small Claims, Probate.

### Lincoln County

**Real Estate Recording**, Lincoln County Register of Deeds, Courthouse, Lincolnton, NC 28092. 704-736-8530 (EST) 8AM-5PM.

**Superior-District Court**, PO Box 8, Lincolnton, NC 28093. 704-732-9000 (EST) 8:00AM-5:00PM. Felony, Misdemeanor, Civil, Eviction, Small Claims, Probate.

### Macon County

**Real Estate Recording**, Macon County Register of Deeds, 5 West Main Street, Franklin, NC 28734. 704-524-6421 (EST) 8AM-5PM.

**Superior-District Court**, PO Box 288, Franklin, NC 28734. 704-524-6421 (EST) 8:00AM-5:00PM. Felony, Misdemeanor, Civil, Eviction, Small Claims, Probate.

### Madison County

**Real Estate Recording**, Madison County Register of Deeds, Courthouse, Marshall, NC 28753. 704-649-3131 (EST) 8:30AM-4:30PM.

**Superior-District Court**, PO Box 217, Marshall, NC 28753. 704-649-2531 (EST) Felony, Misdemeanor, Civil, Eviction, Small Claims, Probate.

### Martin County

**Real Estate Recording**, Martin County Register of Deeds, 305 East Main Street, Williamston, NC 27892. 919-792-1683 (EST) 8AM-5PM.

**Superior-District Court**, PO Box 807, Williamston, NC 27892. 919-792-2515 (EST) Felony, Misdemeanor, Civil, Eviction, Small Claims, Probate.

### McDowell County

**Real Estate Recording**, McDowell County Register of Deeds, 1 South Main Street, Courthouse, Marion, NC 28752-3992. 704-652-4727 (EST) 8:30AM-5PM.

**Superior-District Court**, PO Drawer 729, Marion, NC 28752. 704-652-7717 (EST) 8:30AM-5:00PM. Felony, Misdemeanor, Civil, Eviction, Small Claims, Probate.

### Mecklenburg County

**Real Estate Recording**, Mecklenburg County Register of Deeds, 720 East 4th Street, UCC Department, Charlotte, NC 28202. 704-336-2443 (EST)

**Superior-District Court**, 800 E 4th St, Charlotte, NC 28202. 704-347-7814 (EST) 8:00AM-5:00PM. Felony, Misdemeanor, Civil, Eviction, Small Claims, Probate.

### Mitchell County

**Real Estate Recording**, Mitchell County Register of Deeds, Crimson Laurel Way, Administrative Building, Bakersville, NC 28705. 704-688-2139 (EST) 8AM-5PM.

**Superior-District Court**, PO Box 402, Bakersville, NC 28705. 704-688-2161 (EST) Felony, Misdemeanor, Civil, Eviction, Small Claims, Probate.

### Montgomery County

**Real Estate Recording**, Montgomery County Register of Deeds, 102 East Spring St., Troy, NC 27371. 910-576-4271 (EST) 8AM-5PM.

**Superior-District Court**, PO Box 182, Troy, NC 27371. 910-576-4211 (EST) 8:00AM-5:00PM. Felony, Misdemeanor, Civil, Eviction, Small Claims, Probate.

### Moore County

**Real Estate Recording**, Moore County Register of Deeds, Courthouse Circle, Carthage, NC 28327. 910-947-6370 (EST) 8AM-5PM.

**Superior-District Court**, PO Box 936, Carthage, NC 28327. 910-947-2396 (EST) 8:00AM-5;00PM. Felony, Misdemeanor, Civil, Eviction, Small Claims, Probate.

### Nash County

**Real Estate Recording**, Nash County Register of Deeds, Washington Street, Nashville, NC 27856. 919-459-9832 (EST) 8AM-5PM.

**Superior-District Court**, PO Box 759, Nashville, NC 27856. 919-459-4081 (EST) 8:00AM-5:00PM. Felony, Misdemeanor, Civil, Eviction, Small Claims, Probate.

### New Hanover County

**Real Estate Recording**, New Hanover County Register of Deeds, 316 Princess Street, Room 216, Wilmington, NC 28401. 910-341-4091 (EST) 8:30AM-4:45PM.

**Superior-District Court**, PO Box 2023, Wilmington, NC 28402. 910-341-4430 (EST) 8:00AM-5:00PM. Felony, Misdemeanor, Civil, Eviction, Small Claims, Probate.

## Northampton County

**Real Estate Recording**, Northampton County Register of Deeds, Courthouse, Jackson, NC 27845. 919-534-2511 (EST)

**Superior-District Court**, PO Box 217, Jackson, NC 27845. 919-534-1631 (EST) 8:30AM-5:00PM. Felony, Misdemeanor, Civil, Eviction, Small Claims, Probate.

## Onslow County

**Real Estate Recording**, Onslow County Register of Deeds, 109 Old Bridge Street, Jacksonville, NC 28540. 919-347-3451 (EST) 8AM-5PM.

**Superior-District Court**, 625 Court St, Jacksonville, NC 28540. 910-455-4458 (EST) 8:00AM-5:00PM. Felony, Misdemeanor, Civil, Eviction, Small Claims, Probate.

## Orange County

**Real Estate Recording**, Orange County Register of Deeds, 200 South Cameron Street, Hillsborough, NC 27278. 919-732-8181 (EST) 8AM-5PM.

**Superior-District Court**, 106 E Margaret Lane, Hillsborough, NC 27278. 919-732-8181 (EST) 8:00AM-5:00PM. Felony, Misdemeanor, Civil, Eviction, Small Claims, Probate.

## Pamlico County

**Real Estate Recording**, Pamlico County Register of Deeds, Courthouse, Bayboro, NC 28515. 919-745-4421 (EST) 8AM-5PM.

**Superior-District Court**, PO Box 38, Bayboro, NC 28515. 919-745-3881 (EST) 8:00AM-5:00PM. Felony, Misdemeanor, Civil, Eviction, Small Claims, Probate.

## Pasquotank County

**Real Estate Recording**, Pasquotank County Register of Deeds, 206 East Main Street, Elizabeth City, NC 27909. 919-335-4367 (EST) 8AM-5PM.

**Superior-District Court**, PO Box 449, Elizabeth City, NC 27909. 919-331-4751 (EST) 8:00AM-5:00PM. Felony, Misdemeanor, Civil, Eviction, Small Claims, Probate.

## Pender County

**Real Estate Recording**, Pender County Register of Deeds, 102 Wright Street, Courthouse, Burgaw, NC 28425. 910-259-1225 (EST) 8AM-5PM.

**Superior-District Court**, PO Box 308, Burgaw, NC 28425. 910-259-1229 (EST) 8:00AM-5:00PM. Felony, Misdemeanor, Civil, Eviction, Small Claims, Probate.

## Perquimans County

**Real Estate Recording**, Perquimans County Register of Deeds, 128 North Church Street, Hertford, NC 27944. 919-426-5660 (EST) 8:30AM-5PM.

**Superior-District Court**, PO Box 33, Hertford, NC 27944. 919-426-5676 (EST) 8:00AM-5:00PM. Felony, Misdemeanor, Civil, Eviction, Small Claims, Probate.

## Person County

**Real Estate Recording**, Person County Register of Deeds, Courthouse Square, Roxboro, NC 27573. 910-597-1733 (EST) 8:30AM-5PM.

**Superior-District Court**, Main St, Roxboro, NC 27573. 910-597-7231 (EST) 9:00AM-5:00PM. Felony, Misdemeanor, Civil, Eviction, Small Claims, Probate.

## Pitt County

**Real Estate Recording**, Pitt County Register of Deeds, 3rd & Evans Streets, Courthouse, Greenville, NC 27834. 919-830-4128 (EST) 8AM-5PM.

**Superior-District Court**, PO Box 6067, Greenville, NC 27834. 919-830-6420 (EST) 8:00AM-5:00PM. Felony, Misdemeanor, Civil, Eviction, Small Claims, Probate.

## Polk County

**Real Estate Recording**, Polk County Register of Deeds, 102 Courthouse Street, Columbus, NC 28722. 704-894-8450 (EST) 8:30AM-5PM.

**Superior-District Court**, PO Box 38, Columbus, NC 28722. 704-894-8231 (EST) Felony, Misdemeanor, Civil, Eviction, Small Claims, Probate.

## Randolph County

**Real Estate Recording**, Randolph County Register of Deeds, 145 Worth Street, Courthouse, Asheboro, NC 27203. 910-318-6960 (EST) 8AM-5PM.

**Superior-District Court**, PO Box 1925, Asheboro, NC 27204-1925. 910-629-2131 (EST) 8:00AM-5:00PM. Felony, Misdemeanor, Civil, Eviction, Small Claims, Probate.

## Richmond County

**Real Estate Recording**, Richmond County Register of Deeds, Franklin & South Hancock, Rockingham, NC 28379. 910-997-8250 (EST) 8AM-5PM.

**Superior-District Court**, PO Box 724, Rockingham, NC 28379. 910-997-9100 (EST) 8:00AM-5:00PM. Felony, Misdemeanor, Civil, Eviction, Small Claims, Probate.

## Robeson County

**Real Estate Recording**, Robeson County Register of Deeds, 500 North Elm Street, Courthouse - Room 102, Lumberton, NC 28358. 910-671-3046 (EST) 8:15AM-5:15PM.

**Superior-District Court**, PO Box 1084, Lumberton, NC 28358. 910-671-3372 (EST) 8:15AM-5:15AM. Felony, Misdemeanor, Civil, Eviction, Small Claims, Probate.

## Rockingham County

**Real Estate Recording**, Rockingham County Register of Deeds, County Courthouse, Suite 99, 1086 NC 65, Wentworth, NC 27375. 910-342-8820 (EST) 8AM-5PM.

**Superior-District Court**, PO Box 26, Wentworth, NC 27375. 910-342-8700 (EST) 8:00AM-5:00PM. Felony, Misdemeanor, Civil, Eviction, Small Claims, Probate.

## Rowan County

**Real Estate Recording**, Rowan County Register of Deeds, 402 North Main Street, County Office Building, Salisbury, NC 28144. 704-638-3102 (EST) 8AM-5PM.

**Superior-District Court**, PO Box 4599, 210 N Main St, Salisbury, NC 28144. 704-639-7505 (EST) 8:00AM-5:00PM. Felony, Misdemeanor, Civil, Eviction, Small Claims, Probate.

## Rutherford County

**Real Estate Recording**, Rutherford County Register of Deeds, Main Street, Rutherfordton, NC 28139. 704-287-6155 (EST) 8:30AM-5PM.

**Superior-District Court**, PO Box 630, Rutherfordton, NC 28139. 704-286-9136 (EST) 8:30AM-5:00PM. Felony, Misdemeanor, Civil, Eviction, Small Claims, Probate.

## Sampson County

**Real Estate Recording**, Sampson County Register of Deeds, Main Street, Courthouse, Clinton, NC 28328. 919-592-8026 (EST) 8AM-5:15PM.

**Superior-District Court**, Courthouse, Clinton, NC 28328. 910-592-5192 (EST) 8:00AM-5:00PM. Felony, Misdemeanor, Civil, Eviction, Small Claims, Probate.

## Scotland County

**Real Estate Recording**, Scotland County Register of Deeds, 212 Biggs Street, Courthouse, Laurinburg, NC 28352. 919-277-2575 (EST) 8AM-5PM.

**Superior-District Court**, PO Box 769, Laurinburg, NC 28352. 919-276-1951 (EST) Felony, Misdemeanor, Civil, Eviction, Small Claims, Probate.

## Stanly County

**Real Estate Recording**, Stanly County Register of Deeds, 201 South Second Street, Albemarle, NC 28001. 704-983-7235 (EST) 8:30AM-5PM.

**Superior-District Court**, PO Box 668, Albemarle, NC 28002-0668. 704-982-2161 (EST) 8:30AM-5:00PM. Felony, Misdemeanor, Civil, Eviction, Small Claims, Probate.

## Stokes County

**Real Estate Recording**, Stokes County Register of Deeds, Main Street, Government Center, Danbury, NC 27016. 910-593-2811 (EST) 8:30AM-5PM.

**Superior-District Court**, PO Box 56, Danbury, NC 27016. 910-593-2416 (EST) 8:00AM-5:00PM. Felony, Misdemeanor, Civil, Eviction, Small Claims, Probate.

## Surry County

**Real Estate Recording**, Surry County Register of Deeds, 114 W. Atkins St., Courthouse, Dobson, NC 27017. 910-386-9235 (EST) 8:15AM-5PM.

**Superior-District Court**, PO Box 345, Dobson, NC 27017. 910-386-8131 (EST) 8:00AM-5:00PM. Felony, Misdemeanor, Civil, Eviction, Small Claims, Probate.

### Swain County

**Real Estate Recording**, Swain County Register of Deeds, 101 Mitchell Street, Bryson City, NC 28713. 704-488-9273 (EST) 8:30AM-4:30PM.

**Superior-District Court**, PO Box 1397, Bryson City, NC 28713. 704-488-2288 (EST) 8:30AM-5:00PM. Felony, Misdemeanor, Civil, Eviction, Small Claims, Probate.

### Transylvania County

**Real Estate Recording**, Transylvania County Register of Deeds, 12 East Main Street, Courthouse, Brevard, NC 28712. 704-884-3162 (EST) 8:30AM-5PM.

**Superior-District Court**, 12 E Main St, Brevard, NC 28712. 704-884-3120 (EST) Felony, Misdemeanor, Civil, Eviction, Small Claims, Probate.

### Tyrrell County

**Real Estate Recording**, Tyrrell County Register of Deeds, 403 Main Street, Columbia, NC 27925. 919-796-2901 (EST) 9AM-5PM.

**Superior-District Court**, PO Box 406, Columbia, NC 27925. 919-796-6281 (EST) 8:30AM-5:00PM. Felony, Misdemeanor, Civil, Eviction, Small Claims, Probate.

### Union County

**Real Estate Recording**, Union County Register of Deeds, 500 North Main Street, Monroe, NC 28112. 704-283-3610 (EST) 9AM-5PM.

**Superior-District Court**, PO Box 5038, Monroe, NC 28111. 704-283-4313 (EST) 8:00AM-5:00PM. Felony, Misdemeanor, Civil, Eviction, Small Claims, Probate.

### Vance County

**Real Estate Recording**, Vance County Register of Deeds, 122 Young Street, Courthouse, Henderson, NC 27536. 919-438-4155 (EST) 8:30AM-5PM.

**Superior-District Court**, 122 Young St, Henderson, NC 27536. 919-492-0031 (EST) 8:00AM-5:00PM. Felony, Misdemeanor, Civil, Eviction, Small Claims, Probate.

### Wake County

**Real Estate Recording**, Wake County Register of Deeds, 316 Fayetteville Street, Courthouse, 8th Floor, Room 823, Raleigh, NC 27602. 919-856-5460 (EST) 8:30AM-5:15PM.

**Superior-District Court**, PO Box 351, Raleigh, NC 27602. 919-755-4108 (EST) 8:30AM-5:00PM. Felony, Misdemeanor, Civil, Eviction, Small Claims, Probate.

### Warren County

**Real Estate Recording**, Warren County Register of Deeds, Main Street, Courthouse, Warrenton, NC 27589. 919-257-3265 (EST) 8:30AM-5PM.

**Superior-District Court**, PO Box 709, Warrenton, NC 27589. 919-257-3261 (EST) 8:30AM-5:00PM. Felony, Misdemeanor, Civil, Eviction, Small Claims, Probate.

### Washington County

**Real Estate Recording**, Washington County Register of Deeds, 122 Adams Street, Courthouse, Plymouth, NC 27962. 919-793-2325 (EST) 8:30AM-5PM.

**Superior-District Court**, PO Box 901, Plymouth, NC 27962. 919-793-3013 (EST) 8:00AM-5:00PM. Felony, Misdemeanor, Civil, Eviction, Small Claims, Probate.

### Watauga County

**Real Estate Recording**, Watauga County Register of Deeds, Courthouse, Box 9, Boone, NC 28607-3585. 704-265-8052 (EST) 8AM-5PM.

**Superior-District Court**, 403 W King St, Boone, NC 28607-3525. 704-265-5364 (EST) 8:00AM-5:00PM. Felony, Misdemeanor, Civil, Eviction, Small Claims, Probate.

### Wayne County

**Real Estate Recording**, Wayne County Register of Deeds, Corner of Walnut & William Street, Courthouse, Goldsboro, NC 27530. 919-731-1449 (EST) 8AM-5PM.

**Superior-District Court**, PO Box 267, Goldsboro, NC 27530. 919-731-7910 (EST) 8:00AM-5:00PM. Felony, Misdemeanor, Civil, Eviction, Small Claims, Probate.

### Wilkes County

**Real Estate Recording**, Wilkes County Register of Deeds, Main Street, Courthouse, Wilkesboro, NC 28697. 910-838-2052 (EST) 8:30AM-5PM.

**Superior-District Court**, Main St., PO Box 58, Wilkesboro, NC 28697. 910-667-1201 (EST) 8:00AM-5:00PM. Felony, Misdemeanor, Civil, Eviction, Small Claims, Probate.

### Wilson County

**Real Estate Recording**, Wilson County Register of Deeds, 125 East Nash Street, Wilson, NC 27893. 919-399-2935 (EST) 8AM-5PM.

**Superior-District Court**, PO Box 1608, Wilson, NC 27893. 919-291-8635 (EST) Felony, Misdemeanor, Civil, Eviction, Small Claims, Probate.

### Yadkin County

**Real Estate Recording**, Yadkin County Register of Deeds, Courthouse, Yadkinville, NC 27055. 919-679-4225 (EST) 8AM-5PM.

**Superior-District Court**, PO Box 95, Yadkinville, NC 27055. 910-679-8838 (EST) 8:00AM-5:00PM. Felony, Misdemeanor, Civil, Eviction, Small Claims, Probate.

### Yancey County

**Real Estate Recording**, Yancey County Register of Deeds, Courthouse, Room #4, Burnsville, NC 28714. 704-682-2174 (EST) 9AM-5PM.

**Superior-District Court**, 110 Town Square, Burnsville, NC 28714. 704-682-2122 (EST) 8:30AM-5:00PM. Felony, Misdemeanor, Civil, Eviction, Small Claims, Probate.

# North Dakota

### Adams County

**Real Estate Recording**, Adams County Register of Deeds, 602 Adams Avenue, Courthouse, Hettinger, ND 58639. 701-567-2460 (MST) 8:30AM-Noon, 1-5PM.

**Southwest Judicial District Court**, 602 Adams Ave, Hettinger, ND 58639. 701-567-2460 (MST) 8:30AM-5PM. Felony, Misdemeanor, Civil, Eviction, Probate.

### Barnes County

**Real Estate Recording**, Barnes County Register of Deeds, 231 NE Third Street, Valley City, ND 58072. 701-845-8506 (CST) 8AM-Noon, 1-5PM.

**Southeast Judicial District Court**, PO Box 774, Valley City, ND 58072. 701-845-8512 (CST) 8AM-5PM. Felony, Misdemeanor, Civil, Eviction, Probate.

### Benson County

**Real Estate Recording**, Benson County Register of Deeds, Courthouse, Minnewaukan, ND 58351. 701-473-5332 (CST) 8:30AM-Noon, 12:30-4:30PM.

**Northeast Judicial District Court**, PO Box 213, Minnewaukan, ND 58351. 701-473-5345 (CST) 8:30AM-4:30PM. Felony, Misdemeanor, Civil, Eviction, Probate.

### Billings County

**Real Estate Recording**, Billings County Register of Deeds, Courthouse, Medora, ND 58645. 701-623-4491 (MST) 8AM-Noon, 1-5PM.

**Southwest Judicial District Court**, PO Box 138, Medora, ND 58645. 701-623-4492 (MST) 9AM-5PM, Closed 12-1. Felony, Misdemeanor, Civil, Eviction, Probate.

### Bottineau County

**Real Estate Recording**, Bottineau County Register of Deeds, 314 West 5th Street, Bottineau, ND 58318-1265. 701-228-2786 (CST) 8:30AM-5PM.

**Northeast Judicial District Court**, 314 W 5th St, Bottineau, ND 58318. 701-228-3983 (CST) Felony, Misdemeanor, Civil, Eviction, Probate.

### Bowman County

**Real Estate Recording**, Bowman County Register of Deeds, 104 West 1st Street, Courthouse, Bowman, ND 58623. 701-523-3450 (MST) 8:30AM-5PM.

**Southwest Judicial District Court**, PO Box 379, Bowman, ND 58623. 701-523-3450 (MST) 8:30AM-5PM, Closed 12-1. Felony, Misdemeanor, Civil, Eviction, Probate.

### Burke County

**Real Estate Recording**, Burke County Register of Deeds, Main Street, Courthouse, Bowbells, ND 58721. 701-377-2718 (CST) 8:30AM-Noon, 1-5PM.

**Northwest Judicial District Court**, PO Box 219, Bowbells, ND 58721. 701-377-2718 (CST) 8:30AM-5PM, Closed 12-1. Felony, Misdemeanor, Civil, Eviction, Probate.

### Burleigh County

**Real Estate Recording**, Burleigh County Register of Deeds, 221 North 5th Street, Bismarck, ND 58501. 701-222-6749 (CST) 8AM-5PM.

**South Central Judicial District Court**, PO Box 1055, Bismarck, ND 58502. 701-222-6690 (CST) 8AM-5PM. Felony, Misdemeanor, Civil, Eviction, Probate.

### Cass County

**Real Estate Recording**, Cass County Register of Deeds, 201 Ninth Street South, Fargo, ND 58103. 701-241-5620 (CST) 8AM-5PM.

**Southeast Central Judicial District Court**, 211 South 9th St, Fargo, ND 58108. 701-241-5645 (CST) 8AM-5PM. Felony, Misdemeanor, Civil, Eviction, Probate.

### Cavalier County

**Real Estate Recording**, Cavalier County Register of Deeds, 901 3rd Street, Langdon, ND 58249. 701-256-2136 (CST) 8:30AM-4:30PM.

**Northeast Judicial District Court**, 901 Third St, Langdon, ND 58249. 701-256-2124 (CST) Felony, Misdemeanor, Civil, Eviction, Probate.

### Dickey County

**Real Estate Recording**, Dickey County Register of Deeds, 309 North 2nd, Courthouse, Ellendale, ND 58436. 701-349-3029 (CST) 8:30AM-5PM.

**Southeast Judicial District Court**, PO Box 336, Ellendale, ND 58436. 701-349-3560 (CST) 9AM-5PM, Closed 12-1. Felony, Misdemeanor, Civil, Eviction, Probate.

### Divide County

**Real Estate Recording**, Divide County Register of Deeds, Courthouse, Crosby, ND 58730. 701-965-6661 (CST)

**Northwest Judicial District Court**, PO Box 68, Crosby, ND 58730. 701-965-6831 (CST) 8:30AM-5PM. Felony, Misdemeanor, Civil, Eviction, Probate.

### Dunn County

**Real Estate Recording**, Dunn County Register of Deeds, Courthouse, Manning, ND 58642. 701-573-4443 (MST) 8AM-Noon, 12:30-4:30PM.

**Southwest Judicial Judicial District Court**, PO Box 136, Manning, ND 58642-0136. 701-573-4447 (MST) 8AM-4:30PM, Closed 12-12:30. Felony, Misdemeanor, Civil, Eviction, Probate.

### Eddy County

**Real Estate Recording**, Eddy County Register of Deeds, 524 Central Avenue, Rockford, ND 58356-1698. 701-947-2813 (CST) 8AM-Noon, 12:30-4PM.

**Southeast Judicial District Court**, 524 Central Ave, New Rockford, ND 58356. 701-947-2813 (CST) 8AM-4PM. Felony, Misdemeanor, Civil, Eviction, Probate.

### Emmons County

**Real Estate Recording**, Emmons County Register of Deeds, Courthouse, Linton, ND 58552. 701-254-4812 (CST) 8:30AM-Noon, 1-5PM.

**South Central Judicial District Court**, PO Box 905, Linton, ND 58552. 701-254-4812 (CST) 8:30AM-5PM. Felony, Misdemeanor, Civil, Eviction, Probate.

### Foster County

**Real Estate Recording**, Foster County Register of Deeds, 1000 Central Avenue, Carrington, ND 58421. 701-652-2491 (CST) 9AM-5PM (8AM-4PM Summer Hours).

**Southeast Judicial District Court**, PO Box 257, Carrington, ND 58421. 701-652-2491 (CST) 8AM-4PM in summer, 9AM-5PM in winter. Felony, Misdemeanor, Civil, Eviction, Probate.

### Golden Valley County

**Real Estate Recording**, Golden Valley County Register of Deeds, 150 1st Avenue S.E., Courthouse, Beach, ND 58621. 701-872-4352 (MST) 8AM-Noon, 1-4PM.

**Southwest Judicial District Court**, PO Box 596, Beach, ND 58621. 701-872-4352 (MST) 8AM-5PM. Felony, Misdemeanor, Civil, Eviction, Probate.

### Grand Forks County

**Real Estate Recording**, Grand Forks County Register of Deeds, 124 South 4th Street, Courthouse Box 5066, Grand Forks, ND 58201. 701-780-8261 (CST) 8AM-5PM.

**Northeast Central Judicial District Court**, PO Box 5939, Grand Forks, ND 58206-5939. 701-780-8214 (CST) 8AM-5PM. Felony, Misdemeanor, Civil, Eviction, Probate.

### Grant County

**Real Estate Recording**, Grant County Register of Deeds, Courthouse, Carson, ND 58529. 701-622-3544 (MST) 8AM-4PM.

**South Central Judicial District Court**, PO Box 258, Hettinger, ND 58639. 701-622-3615 (MST) 8AM-4PM, Closed 12-12:30. Felony, Misdemeanor, Civil, Eviction, Probate.

### Griggs County

**Real Estate Recording**, Griggs County Register of Deeds, Courthouse, 45th & Rollins, Cooperstown, ND 58425. 701-797-2771 (CST) 8AM-12, 1-4:30PM.

**Northeast Central Judicial District Court**, PO Box 326, Cooperstown, ND 58425. 701-797-2772 (CST) 8AM-4:30PM. Felony, Misdemeanor, Civil, Eviction, Probate.

### Hettinger County

**Real Estate Recording**, Hettinger County Register of Deeds, Courthouse, 336 Pacific Ave., Mott, ND 58646. 701-824-2545 (MST) 8AM-4:30PM.

**Southwest Judicial District Court**, PO Box 668, Mott, ND 58646. 701-824-2645 (MST) 8AM-4:30PM. Felony, Misdemeanor, Civil, Eviction, Probate.

## Kidder County

**Real Estate Recording**, Kidder County Register of Deeds, Courthouse on Broadway, Steele, ND 58482. 701-475-2651 (CST) 9AM-5PM.

**South Central Judicial District Court**, PO Box 66, Steele, ND 58482. 701-475-2663 (CST) 9AM-5PM. Felony, Misdemeanor, Civil, Eviction, Probate.

## La Moure County

**Real Estate Recording**, La Moure County Register of Deeds, Courthouse, 202 4th Ave. N.E., La Moure, ND 58458. 701-883-5304 (CST) 9AM-5PM.

**Southeast Judicial District Court**, PO Box 5, LaMoure, ND 58458. 701-883-5193 (CST) 9AM-5PM, Closed 12-1. Felony, Misdemeanor, Civil, Eviction, Probate.

## Logan County

**Real Estate Recording**, Logan County Register of Deeds, Highway 3, Courthouse, Napoleon, ND 58561. 701-754-2751 (CST) 8:30AM-Noon, 1-5PM.

**South Central Judicial District Court**, PO Box 6, Napoleon, ND 58561. 701-754-2751 (CST) 8:30AM-5PM. Felony, Misdemeanor, Civil, Eviction, Probate.

## McHenry County

**Real Estate Recording**, McHenry County Register of Deeds, South Main, Courthouse, Towner, ND 58788. 701-537-5634 (CST) 8AM-Noon, 1-4:30PM.

**Northeast Judicial District Court**, PO Box 117, Towner, ND 58788. 701-537-5729 (CST) 8AM-4:30PM. Felony, Misdemeanor, Civil, Eviction, Probate.

## McIntosh County

**Real Estate Recording**, McIntosh County Register of Deeds, 112 North East 1st, Ashley, ND 58413. 701-288-3589 (CST) 8AM-4:30PM.

**South Central Judicial District Court**, PO Box 179, Ashley, ND 58413. 701-288-3450 (CST) Felony, Misdemeanor, Civil, Eviction, Probate.

## McKenzie County

**Real Estate Recording**, McKenzie County Register of Deeds, 201 West 5th Street, Watford City, ND 58854. 701-842-3453 (CST) 8:30AM-Noon, 1-5PM.

**Northwest Judicial District Court**, PO Box 524, Watford City, ND 58854. 701-842-3452 (CST) 8:30AM-5PM, Closed 12-1. Felony, Misdemeanor, Civil, Eviction, Probate.

## McLean County

**Real Estate Recording**, McLean County Register of Deeds, 712 5th Avenue, Courthouse, Washburn, ND 58577. 701-462-8541 (CST) X225-6 8AM-Noon, 12:30-4:30PM.

**South Central Judicial District Court**, PO Box 1108, Washburn, ND 58577. 701-462-8541 (CST) 8AM-4:30PM, Closed 12-12:30. Felony, Misdemeanor, Civil, Eviction, Probate.

## Mercer County

**Real Estate Recording**, Mercer County Register of Deeds, 1021 Arthur Street, Stanton, ND 58571. 701-745-3272 (MST) 8AM-4PM.

**South Central Judicial District Court**, PO Box 39, Stanton, ND 58571. 701-745-3262 (MST) 8AM-4PM. Felony, Misdemeanor, Civil, Eviction, Probate.

## Morton County

**Real Estate Recording**, Morton County Register of Deeds, 210 2nd Avenue, Mandan, ND 58554. 701-667-3305 (MST) 8AM-Noon, 1-5PM.

**South Central Judicial District Court**, 210 2nd Ave NW, Mandan, ND 58554. 701-667-3358 (MST) 8AM-5PM. Felony, Misdemeanor, Civil, Eviction, Probate.

## Mountrail County

**Real Estate Recording**, Mountrail County Register of Deeds, North Main, Courthouse, Stanley, ND 58784. 701-628-2945 (CST) 8:30AM-Noon, 1-4:30PM.

**Northwest Judicial District Court**, PO Box 69, Stanley, ND 58784. 701-628-2915 (CST) 8:30AM-4:30PM. Felony, Misdemeanor, Civil, Eviction, Probate.

## Nelson County

**Real Estate Recording**, Nelson County Register of Deeds, Courthouse, Lakota, ND 58344. 701-247-2433 (CST) 8:30AM-Noon, 1-5PM.

**Northeast Central Judicial District Court**, PO Box 565, Lakota, ND 58344. 701-247-2462 (CST) 8:30AM-5PM. Felony, Misdemeanor, Civil, Eviction, Probate.

## Oliver County

**Real Estate Recording**, Oliver County Register of Deeds, Courthouse, Center, ND 58530. 701-794-8777 (MST) 8AM-Noon, 1-4PM.

**South Central Judicial District Court**, Box 125, Center, ND 58530. 701-794-8777 (MST) 8AM-4PM. Felony, Misdemeanor, Civil, Eviction, Probate.

## Pembina County

**Real Estate Recording**, Pembina County Register of Deeds, 306 Dakota Street, Cavalier, ND 58220. 701-265-4373 (CST) 8:30AM-5PM.

**Northeast Judicial District Court**, PO Box 357, Cavalier, ND 58220. 701-265-4275 (CST) 8:30AM-5PM. Felony, Misdemeanor, Civil, Eviction, Probate.

## Pierce County

**Real Estate Recording**, Pierce County Register of Deeds, 240 S.E. 2nd Street, Rugby, ND 58368. 701-776-5206 (CST) 9AM-Noon, 1PM-5PM.

**Northeast Judicial District Court**, 240 SE 2nd St, Rugby, ND 58368. 701-776-6161 (CST) 9AM-5PM. Felony, Misdemeanor, Civil, Eviction, Probate.

## Ramsey County

**Real Estate Recording**, Ramsey County Register of Deeds, 524 4th Avenue #30, Devils Lake, ND 58301. 701-662-7018 (CST) 8AM-Noon, 1-5PM.

**Northeast Judicial District Court**, 524 4th Ave #4, Devils Lake, ND 58301. 701-662-7066 (CST) 8AM-5PM. Felony, Misdemeanor, Civil, Eviction, Probate.

## Ransom County

**Real Estate Recording**, Ransom County Register of Deeds, Courthouse, Lisbon, ND 58054. 701-683-5823 (CST) 8:30AM-Noon, 1-4:30PM.

**Southeast Judicial District Court**, PO Box 626, Lisbon, ND 58054. 701-683-5823 (CST) 8:30AM-4:30PM. Felony, Misdemeanor, Civil, Eviction, Probate.

## Renville County

**Real Estate Recording**, Renville County Register of Deeds, 217 Main Street East, Mohall, ND 58761. 701-756-6398 (CST) 9AM-4:30PM.

**Northeast Judicial District Court**, PO Box 68, Mohall, ND 58761. 701-756-6398 (CST) 9AM-4:30PM. Felony, Misdemeanor, Civil, Eviction, Probate.

## Richland County

**Real Estate Recording**, Richland County Register of Deeds, 418 2nd Avenue North, Courthouse, Wahpeton, ND 58075-4400. 701-642-7800 (CST) 8AM-5PM.

**Southeast Judicial District Court**, 418 2nd Ave North, Wahpeton, ND 58074. 701-642-7818 (CST) Felony, Misdemeanor, Civil, Eviction, Probate.

## Rolette County

**Real Estate Recording**, Rolette County Register of Deeds, 102 NE 2nd, Rolla, ND 58367. 701-477-3166 (CST) 8:30AM-12:30PM, 1-4:30PM.

**Northeast Judicial District Court**, PO Box 460, Rolla, ND 58367. 701-477-3816 (CST) 8:30AM-4:30PM. Felony, Misdemeanor, Civil, Eviction, Probate.

## Sargent County

**Real Estate Recording**, Sargent County Register of Deeds, 645 Main Street, Forman, ND 58032. 701-724-6241 (CST) 9AM-Noon, 12:30-4:30PM.

**Southeast Judicial District Court**, 645 Main St (PO Box 176), Forman, ND 58032. 701-724-6241 (CST) Felony, Misdemeanor, Civil, Eviction, Probate.

## Sheridan County

**Real Estate Recording**, Sheridan County Register of Deeds, 215 2nd Street, Courthouse, McClusky, ND 58463. 701-363-2207 (CST) 9AM-Noon, 1-5PM.

**South Central Judicial District Court**, PO Box 668, McClusky, ND 58463. 701-363-2207 (CST) 9AM-5PM, Closed 12-1. Felony, Misdemeanor, Civil, Eviction, Probate.

## Sioux County

**Real Estate Recording**, Sioux County Register of Deeds, Courthouse, Fort Yates, ND 58538. 701-854-3853 (MST)

**South Central Judicial District Court**, Box L, Fort Yates, ND 58538. 701-854-3853 (MST) 9AM-5PM. Felony, Misdemeanor, Civil, Eviction, Probate.

## Slope County

**Real Estate Recording**, Slope County Register of Deeds, Courthouse, Amidon, ND 58620. 701-879-6275 (MST) 9AM-Noon, 1-5PM.

**Southwest Judicial District Court**, PO Box JJ, Amidon, ND 58620. 701-879-6275 (MST) 9AM-5PM. Felony, Misdemeanor, Civil, Eviction, Probate.

## Stark County

**Real Estate Recording**, Stark County Register of Deeds, Sims & 3rd Avenue, Courthouse, Dickinson, ND 58601. 701-264-7645 (MST) 8AM-5PM.

## Steele County

**Real Estate Recording**, Steele County Register of Deeds, Washington Street, Courthouse, Finley, ND 58230. 701-524-2152 (CST)

**East Central Judicial District Court**, PO Box 296, Finley, ND 58230. 701-524-2790 (CST) 8AM-4:30PM. Felony, Misdemeanor, Civil, Eviction, Probate.

## Stutsman County

**Real Estate Recording**, Stutsman County Register of Deeds, 511 2nd Avenue S.E., Courthouse, Jamestown, ND 58401. 701-252-9034 (CST) 8AM-5PM.

**Southeast Judicial District Court**, 511 2nd Ave SE, Jamestown, ND 58401. 701-252-9042 (CST) 8AM-5PM. Felony, Misdemeanor, Civil, Eviction, Probate.

## Towner County

**Real Estate Recording**, Towner County Register of Deeds, Courthouse, 315 2nd Street, Cando, ND 58324. 701-968-4343 (CST) 8:30AM-Noon, 1-5PM.

**Northeast Judicial District Court**, Box 517, Cando, ND 58324. 701-968-4345 (CST) 8:30AM-5PM. Felony, Misdemeanor, Civil, Eviction, Probate.

## Traill County

**Real Estate Recording**, Traill County Register of Deeds, 13 1st Street N.W., Courthouse, Hillsboro, ND 58045. 701-436-4457 (CST) 8AM-Noon, 12:30PM-4:30PM.

**East Central Judicial District Court**, PO Box 805, Hillsboro, ND 58045. 701-436-4454 (CST) 8AM-4:30PM. Felony, Misdemeanor, Civil, Eviction, Probate.

## Walsh County

**Real Estate Recording**, Walsh County Register of Deeds, 600 Cooper Avenue, Courthouse, Grafton, ND 58237. 701-352-2380 (CST) 8:30-Noon, 12:30-5PM.

**Northeast Judicial District Court**, 600 Cooper Ave, Grafton, ND 58237. 701-352-0350 (CST) 8:30AM-5PM. Felony, Misdemeanor, Civil, Eviction, Probate.

## Ward County

**Real Estate Recording**, Ward County Register of Deeds, 315 S.E. Third Street, Courthouse, Minot, ND 58702-5005. 701-857-6410 (CST) 8AM-4:30PM.

**Northwest Judicial District Court**, PO Box 5005, Minot, ND 58702-5005. 701-857-6460 (CST) 8AM-4:30PM. Felony, Misdemeanor, Civil, Eviction, Probate.

## Wells County

**Real Estate Recording**, Wells County Register of Deeds, Court Street, Courthouse, P.O. Box 125, Fessenden, ND 58438. 701-547-3141 (CST) 8AM-Noon, 1-4:30PM.

**South Central Judicial District Court**, PO Box 596, Fessenden, ND 58438. 701-547-3122 (CST) 8AM-4:30PM. Felony, Misdemeanor, Civil, Eviction, Probate.

## Williams County

**Real Estate Recording**, Williams County Treasurer/Recorder, 205 East Broadway, Williston, ND 58801. 701-572-1740 (CST) 9AM-5PM.

**Northwest Judicial District Court**, PO Box 2047, Williston, ND 58802. 701-572-1720 (CST) 9AM-5PM. Felony, Misdemeanor, Civil, Eviction, Probate.

# Ohio

## Adams County

**Real Estate Recording**, Adams County Recorder, 110 West Main, Courthouse, West Union, OH 45693. 513-544-5051 (EST) 8AM-4PM.

**Common Pleas Court**, 110 W Main, West Union, OH 45693. 513-544-2344 (EST) 8:30AM-4PM. Felony, Civil Actions Over $3,000, Probate.

**County Court**, 110 W Main, Rm 202, West Union, OH 45693. 513-544-2011 (EST) 8AM-4PM. Misdemeanor, Civil Actions Under $3,000, Small Claims.

## Allen County

**Real Estate Recording**, Allen County Recorder, 301 North Main Street, Lima, OH 45801. 419-228-3700 (EST) X371 8AM-4:30PM.

**Common Pleas Court**, PO Box 1243, Lima, OH 45802. 419-228-3700 (EST) 8AM-4:30PM. Felony, Civil Actions Over $10,000, Probate.

**Lima Municipal Court**, 109 N Union St (PO Box 1529), Lima, OH 45802. 419-221-5275 (EST) 8AM-5PM. Misdemeanor, Civil Actions Under $10,000, Eviction, Small Claims.

## Ashland County

**Real Estate Recording**, Ashland County Recorder, 2nd Street, Courthouse, Ashland, OH 44805-2193. 419-282-4238 (EST) 8AM-4PM.

**Common Pleas Court**, PO Box 365, Ashland, OH 44805. 419-289-0000 (EST) 8AM-4PM. Felony, Civil Actions Over $10,000, Probate.

**Ashland Municipal Court**, PO Box 354, Ashland, OH 44805. 419-289-8137 (EST) 8AM-5PM. Misdemeanor, Civil Actions Under $10,000, Eviction, Small Claims.

## Ashtabula County

**Real Estate Recording**, Ashtabula County Recorder, 25 West Jefferson Street, Jefferson, OH 44047. 216-576-3762 (EST) 8AM-4:30PM.

**Common Pleas Court**, 25 W Jefferson St, Jefferson, OH 44047. 216-576-3637 (EST) 8AM-4:30PM. Felony, Civil Actions Over $10,000, Probate.

**County Court Western Division**, 185 Water St, Geneva, OH 44041. 216-466-1184 (EST) 8AM-4:30PM. Misdemeanor, Civil Actions Under $3,000, Small Claims.

**County Court Eastern Division**, 25 W Jefferson St, Jefferson, OH 44047. 216-576-3617 (EST) 8AM-4:30PM. Misdemeanor, Civil Actions Under $3,000, Small Claims.

**Ashtabula Municipal Court**, 4400 Main Ave, Ashtabula, OH 44004. 216-992-7110 (EST) 8AM-4:30PM. Misdemeanor, Civil Actions Under $10,000, Eviction, Small Claims.

## Athens County

**Real Estate Recording**, Athens County Recorder, Room 236, 15 South Court, Athens, OH 45701. 614-592-3228 (EST) 8AM-4PM.

**Common Pleas Court**, PO Box 290, Athens, OH 45701-0290. 614-592-3236 (EST) 8AM-4PM. Felony, Civil Actions Over $10,000, Probate.

**Athens Municipal Court**, 8 Washington St, Athens, OH 45701. 614-592-3328 (EST) 8AM-4PM. Misdemeanor, Civil Actions Under $10,000, Eviction, Small Claims.

## Auglaize County

**Real Estate Recording**, Auglaize County Recorder, Courthouse, Wapakoneta, OH 45895-1972. 419-738-4318 (EST) 8AM-4:30PM.

**Common Pleas Court**, PO Box 1958, Wapakoneta, OH 45895. 419-738-4219 (EST) 8AM-4:30PM. Felony, Civil Actions Over $10,000, Probate.

**Auglaize County Municipal Court**, PO Box 1958, Wapakoneta, OH 45895. 419-738-2923 (EST) 8AM-4:30PM. Misdemeanor, Civil Actions Under $10,000, Eviction, Small Claims.

## Belmont County

**Real Estate Recording**, Belmont County Recorder, 101 West Main Street, Courthouse, Room 105, St. Clairsville, OH 43950. 614-695-2121 (EST)

**Common Pleas Court**, Main St, Courthouse, St Clairsville, OH 43950. 614-695-2121 (EST) 8:30AM-4:30PM. Felony, Civil Actions Over $3,000, Probate.

**County Court Eastern Division**, 400 W 26th St, Bellaire, OH 43906. 614-676-4490 (EST) 8AM-4:30PM. Misdemeanor, Civil Actions Under $3,000, Small Claims.

**County Court Northern Division**, 101 4th St, Martins Ferry, OH 43935. 614-633-3147 (EST) 8AM-4PM. Misdemeanor, Civil Actions Under $3,000, Small Claims.

**County Court Western Division**, 147 W Main St, St Clairsville, OH 43950. 614-695-2875 (EST) 8AM-4PM. Misdemeanor, Civil Actions Under $3,000, Small Claims.

## Brown County

**Real Estate Recording**, Brown County Recorder, Administration Building, 800 Mt. Orab Pike, Georgetown, OH 45121. 513-378-6478 (EST) 8AM-4PM.

**Common Pleas Court**, Courthouse, Georgetown, OH 45121. 513-378-3100 (EST) 8AM-4PM. Felony, Civil Actions Over $3,000, Probate.

**County Court**, 770 Mount Orab Pike, Georgetown, OH 45121. 513-378-6358 (EST) 8AM-4PM. Misdemeanor, Civil Actions Under $3,000, Small Claims.

## Butler County

**Real Estate Recording**, Butler County Recorder, 130 High Street, Hamilton, OH 45011. 513-887-3191 (EST) 8:30AM-4:30PM.

**Common Pleas Court**, 130 High St, Hamilton, OH 45011. 513-887-3996 (EST) 8:30AM-4:30PM. Felony, Civil Actions Over $3,000, Probate.

**County Court Area #2**, 130 High St, Hamilton, OH 45011. 513-887-3462 (EST) 8:30AM-4:30PM. Misdemeanor, Civil Actions Under $3,000, Small Claims.

**County Court Area #1**, City Building, Oxford, OH 45056. 513-523-4748 (EST) 8:30AM-4:30PM. Misdemeanor, Civil Actions Under $3,000, Small Claims.

**County Court Area #3**, 9113 Cincinnati, Dayton Rd, West Chester, OH 45069. 513-867-5070 (EST) 8:30AM-4:30PM. Misdemeanor, Civil Actions Under $3,000, Small Claims.

## Carroll County

**Real Estate Recording**, Carroll County Recorder, Courthouse, 119 Public Square, Carrollton, OH 44615-1494. 216-627-4545 (EST) 8AM-4PM.

**Common Pleas Court**, PO Box 367, Carrollton, OH 44615. 216-627-4886 (EST) 8AM-4PM. Felony, Civil Actions Over $3,000, Probate.

**County Court**, Courthouse, 3rd Fl, Carrollton, OH 44615. 216-627-5049 (EST) 8AM-4PM. Misdemeanor, Civil Actions Under $3,000, Small Claims.

## Champaign County

**Real Estate Recording**, Champaign County Recorder, 200 North Main Street, Urbana, OH 43078-1679. 513-652-2263 (EST) 8AM-4PM.

**Common Pleas Court**, 200 N Main St, Urbana, OH 43078. 513-653-4152 (EST) 8AM-4PM. Felony, Civil Actions Over $10,000, Probate.

**Champaign County Municipal Court**, PO Box 85, Urbana, OH 43078. 513-653-7376 (EST) 8AM-4PM. Misdemeanor, Civil Actions Under $10,000, Eviction, Small Claims.

## Clark County

**Real Estate Recording**, Clark County Recorder, 31 North Limestone Street, Springfield, OH 45503. 513-328-2445 (EST) 8AM-4:30PM.

**Common Pleas Court**, 101 N Limestone St, Springfield, OH 45502. 513-328-2458 (EST) 8AM-4:30PM. Felony, Civil Actions Over $10,000, Probate.

**Clark County Municipal Court**, 50 E Columbia St, Springfield, OH 45502. 513-328-3700 (EST) 8AM-5PM. Misdemeanor, Civil Actions Under $10,000, Eviction, Small Claims.

## Clermont County

**Real Estate Recording**, Clermont County Recorder, 270 Main Street, Batavia, OH 45103. 513-732-7237 (EST) 8:30AM-7PM; 9AM-Noon Sat.

**Common Pleas Court**, 270 Main St, Batavia, OH 45103. 513-732-7130 (EST) 8:30AM-4:30PM. Felony, Civil Actions Over $10,000, Probate.

**Clermont County Municipal Court**, 289 Main St, Batavia, OH 45103. 513-732-7290 (EST) 8:30AM-4:30PM. Misdemeanor, Civil Actions Under $10,000, Eviction, Small Claims.

## Clinton County

**Real Estate Recording**, Clinton County Recorder, 46 S. South Street, Courthouse, Wilmington, OH 45177. 513-382-2067 (EST) 8AM-4PM.

**Common Pleas Court**, 46 S South St, Wilmington, OH 45177. 513-382-2316 (EST) 8AM-3:30PM. Felony, Civil Actions Over $3,000, Probate.

**Clinton County Municipal Court**, 69 N South St, Wilmington, OH 45177. 513-382-8985 (EST) 8AM-3:30PM. Misdemeanor, Civil Actions Under $10,000, Eviction, Small Claims.

# Columbiana County

**Real Estate Recording**, Columbiana County Recorder, County Courthouse, 105 South Market St., Lisbon, OH 44432. 216-424-9511 (EST) X233 8AM-4PM.

**Common Pleas Court**, 105 S Market St, Lisbon, OH 44432. 216-424-9511 (EST) 8AM-4PM. Felony, Civil Actions Over $10,000, Probate.

**County Court East Area**, 31 Market St, East Palestine, OH 44413. 216-426-3774 (EST) 8AM-4PM. Misdemeanor, Civil Actions Under $3,000, Small Claims.

**County Court Southwest Area**, 41 N Park Ave, Lisbon, OH 44432. 216-424-5326 (EST) 8AM-4PM. Misdemeanor, Civil Actions Under $3,000, Small Claims.

**County Court Northwest Area**, 130 Penn Ave, Salem, OH 44460. 216-332-0297 (EST) 8AM-4PM. Misdemeanor, Civil Actions Under $3,000, Small Claims.

**East Liverpool Municipal Court**, 126 W 6th St, East Liverpool, OH 43920. 216-385-5151 (EST) 8AM-4PM. Misdemeanor, Civil Actions Under $10,000, Eviction, Small Claims.

# Coshocton County

**Real Estate Recording**, Coshocton County Recorder, 349 Main Street, Courthouse Annex, P.O. Box 806, Coshocton, OH 43812. 614-622-2817 (EST) 8AM-4PM.

**Common Pleas Court**, 318 Main St, Coshocton, OH 43812. 614-622-1456 (EST) 8AM-4PM. Felony, Civil Actions Over $10,000, Probate.

**Coshocton Municipal Court**, 760 Chesnut St, Coshocton, OH 43812. 614-622-2871 (EST) 8AM-4:30PM M-W,F 8AM-12PM TH. Misdemeanor, Civil Actions Under $10,000, Eviction, Small Claims.

# Crawford County

**Real Estate Recording**, Crawford County Recorder, 112 East Mansfield Street, Bucyrus, OH 44820. 419-562-6961 (EST) 8:30AM-4:30PM.

**Common Pleas Court**, PO Box 470, Bucyrus, OH 44820. 419-562-2766 (EST) 8:30AM-4:30PM. Felony, Civil Actions Over $3,000, Probate.

**Crawford County Municipal Court**, PO Box 550, Bucyrus, OH 44820. 419-562-2731 (EST) 8:30AM-4:30PM. Misdemeanor, Civil Actions Under $10,000, Eviction, Small Claims.

**Galion Municipal Court Branch Office**, 301 Harding Way East, Galion, OH 44833. 419-468-6819 (EST) 8:30AM-4:30PM. Misdemeanor, Civil Actions Under $10,000, Eviction, Small Claims.

# Cuyahoga County

**Real Estate Recording**, Cuyahoga County Recorder, 1219 Ontario Street, Room 220, Cleveland, OH 44113. 216-443-7314 (EST) 8:30AM-4:30PM.

**Common Pleas Court**, 1200 Ontario St, Cleveland, OH 44113. 216-443-8560 (EST) 8:30AM-4:30PM. Felony, Civil Actions Over $10,000, Probate.

**Cleveland Municipal Court-Civil Division**, 1200 Ontario St, Cleveland, OH 44113. 216-664-4870 (EST) 8AM-3:50PM. Civil Actions Under $10,000, Eviction, Small Claims.

**Cleveland Municipal Court-Criminal Division**, 1200 Ontario St, Cleveland, OH 44113. 216-664-4790 (EST) 8AM-3:50PM. Misdemeanor.

**Bedford Municipal Court**, 65 Columbus Rd, Bedford, OH 44146. 216-232-3420 (EST) 8:30AM-4:30PM. Misdemeanor, Civil Actions Under $10,000, Eviction, Small Claims.

**Berea Municipal Court**, 11 Berea Commons, Berea, OH 44017. 216-826-5860 (EST) Misdemeanor, Civil Actions Under $10,000, Eviction, Small Claims.

**Cleveland Heights Municipal Court**, 40 Severence Circle, Cleveland Heights, OH 44118. 216-291-4901 (EST) 8AM-5PM. Misdemeanor, Civil Actions Under $10,000, Eviction, Small Claims.

**East Cleveland Municipal Court**, 14340 Euclid Ave, East Cleveland, OH 44112. 216-681-5020 (EST) 8AM-4:30PM. Misdemeanor, Civil Actions Under $10,000, Eviction, Small Claims.

**Euclid Municipal Court**, 555 E 222 St, Euclid, OH 44123. 216-289-2888 (EST) 8:30AM-4:30PM. Misdemeanor, Civil Actions Under $10,000, Eviction, Small Claims.

**Garfield Heights Municipal Court**, 5555 Turney Rd, Garfield Heights, OH 44125. 216-475-1900 (EST) 8:30AM-4:30PM. Misdemeanor, Civil Actions Under $10,000, Eviction, Small Claims.

**Lakewood Municipal Court**, 12650 Detroit Ave, Lakewood, OH 44107. 216-226-2460 (EST) 8AM-5PM. Misdemeanor, Civil Actions Under $10,000, Eviction, Small Claims.

**Lyndhurst Municipal Court**, 5301 Mayfield Rd, Lyndhurst, OH 44124. 216-461-6500 (EST) 8:30AM-5PM. Misdemeanor, Civil Actions Under $10,000, Eviction, Small Claims.

**Parma Municipal Court**, 5750 W 54th St, Parma, OH 44129. 216-884-4000 (EST) 8:30AM-4:30PM. Misdemeanor, Civil Actions Under $10,000, Eviction, Small Claims.

**Rocky River Municipal Court**, 21012 Hilliard Blvd, Rocky River, OH 44116. 216-333-0066 (EST) 8:30AM-4:30PM. Misdemeanor, Civil Actions Under $10,000, Eviction, Small Claims.

**Shaker Heights Municipal Court**, 3355 Lee Rd, Shaker Heights, OH 44120. 216-491-1304 (EST) 8:30AM-5PM. Misdemeanor, Civil Actions Under $10,000, Eviction, Small Claims.

**South Euclid Municipal Court**, 1349 S Green Rd, South Euclid, OH 44121. 216-381-0400 (EST) 8:30AM-5PM. Misdemeanor, Civil Actions Under $10,000, Eviction, Small Claims.

# Darke County

**Real Estate Recording**, Darke County Recorder, 504 Broadway, Courthouse, Greenville, OH 45331. 513-547-7390 (EST) 8:30AM-4:30PM.

**Common Pleas Court**, Courthouse, Greenville, OH 45331. 513-547-7335 (EST) 8:30AM-4:30PM. Felony, Civil Actions Over $3,000, Probate.

**County Court**, Courthouse, Greenville, OH 45331. 513-547-7340 (EST) 8:30AM-4:30PM. Misdemeanor, Civil Actions Under $3,000, Small Claims.

# Defiance County

**Real Estate Recording**, Defiance County Recorder, 221 Clinton Street, Courthouse, Defiance, OH 43512. 419-782-4741 (EST) 8:30AM-4:30PM.

**Common Pleas Court**, PO Box 716, Defiance, OH 43512. 419-782-1936 (EST) 8AM-4:30PM. Felony, Civil Actions Over $10,000, Probate.

**Defiance Municipal Court**, 324 Perry St, Defiance, OH 43512. 419-782-5756 (EST) 8AM-5PM. Misdemeanor, Civil Actions Under $10,000, Eviction, Small Claims.

# Delaware County

**Real Estate Recording**, Delaware County Recorder, 91 North Sandusky Street, Courthouse, Delaware, OH 43015. 614-368-1835 (EST) 8:30AM-4:30PM.

**Common Pleas Court**, 91 N Sandusky, Delaware, OH 43015. 614-368-1850 (EST) 8:30AM-4:30PM. Felony, Civil Actions Over $10,000, Probate.

**Delaware Municipal Court**, 70 N Union St, Delaware, OH 43015. 614-363-1296 (EST) 8AM-5PM. Misdemeanor, Civil Actions Under $10,000, Eviction, Small Claims.

# Erie County

**Real Estate Recording**, Erie County Recorder, 323 Columbus Avenue, Courthouse, Sandusky, OH 44870-2696. 419-627-7686 (EST) 8AM-4PM; 8AM-5PM F.

**Common Pleas Court**, 323 Columbus Ave, Sandusky, OH 44870. 419-627-7705 (EST) 8AM-4PM M-Th/8AM-5PM F. Felony, Civil Actions Over $10,000, Probate.

**County Court**, 150 W Mason Rd, Milan, OH 44846. 419-499-4689 (EST) 8AM-4PM. Misdemeanor, Civil Actions Under $3,000, Small Claims.

**Sandusky Municipal Court**, 222 Meigs St, Sandusky, OH 44870. 419-627-5917 (EST) Misdemeanor, Civil Actions Under $10,000, Eviction, Small Claims.

**Vermilion Municipal Court**, PO Box 258, Vermilion, OH 44089. 216-967-6543 (EST) Misdemeanor, Civil Actions Under $10,000, Eviction, Small Claims.

# Fairfield County

**Real Estate Recording**, Fairfield County Recorder, 210 East Main Street, Courthouse, Lancaster, OH 43130. 614-687-7100 (EST) 8AM-4PM.

**Common Pleas Court**, 224 E Main (PO Box 370), Lancaster, OH 43130-0370. 614-687-7030 (EST) 8AM-4PM. Felony, Civil Actions Over $10,000, Probate.

**Lancaster Municipal Court**, PO Box 2390, Lancaster, OH 43130. 614-687-6621 (EST) 8AM-4PM. Misdemeanor, Civil Actions Under $10,000, Eviction, Small Claims.

# Fayette County

**Real Estate Recording**, Fayette County Recorder, 110 East Court Street, Courthouse Building, Washington Court House, OH 43160-1393. 614-335-1770 (EST) 9AM-4PM.

**Common Pleas Court**, 110 E Court St, Washington Court House, OH 43160. 614-335-

6371 (EST) 9AM-4PM. Felony, Civil Actions Over $10,000, Probate.

**Washington Courthouse Municipal Court**, 130 N Fayette St, Washington Court House, OH 43160. 614-335-2901 (EST) 8AM-4PM. Misdemeanor, Civil Actions Under $10,000, Eviction, Small Claims.

## Franklin County

**Real Estate Recording**, Franklin County Recorder, 373 S. High Street, 18th Floor, Columbus, OH 43215-6307. 614-462-3937 (EST) 8AM-5PM.

**Common Pleas Court**, 369 S High St, Columbus, OH 43215. 614-462-3650 (EST) 8AM-5PM. Felony, Civil Actions Over $10,000, Probate.

**Franklin County Municipal Court**, 375 S High St, Columbus, OH 43215. 614-645-7220 (EST) 8AM-5PM. Misdemeanor, Civil Actions Under $10,000, Eviction, Small Claims.

## Fulton County

**Real Estate Recording**, Fulton County Recorder, Courthouse, 210 S. Fulton St., Wauseon, OH 43567. 419-337-9232 (EST) 8:30AM-4:30PM.

**Common Pleas Court**, 210 S Fulton, Wauseon, OH 43567. 419-337-9230 (EST) 8:30AM-4:30PM. Felony, Civil Actions Over $3,000, Probate.

**County Court-Eastern District**, 128 N Main St, Swanton, OH 43558. 419-826-5636 (EST) Misdemeanor, Civil Actions Under $3,000, Small Claims.

**County Court-Western District**, 224 S Fulton St, Wauseon, OH 43567. 419-337-9212 (EST) 8:30AM-4:30PM. Misdemeanor, Civil Actions Under $3,000, Small Claims.

## Gallia County

**Real Estate Recording**, Gallia County Recorder, 18 Locust Street, Room 1265, Gallipolis, OH 45631-1265. 614-446-4612 (EST) X248 8AM-4PM.

**Common Pleas Court**, 18 Locust St, Gallipolis, OH 45631-1290. 614-446-4612 (EST) 8AM-4PM. Felony, Civil Actions Over $10,000, Probate.

**Gallipolis Municipal Court**, 518 2nd Ave, Gallipolis, OH 45631. 614-446-9400 (EST) 8:30AM-4:30PM. Misdemeanor, Civil Actions Under $10,000, Eviction, Small Claims.

## Geauga County

**Real Estate Recording**, Geauga County Recorder, 231 Main Street, Courthouse Annex, Chardon, OH 44024-1299. 216-285-2222 (EST) X368 8AM-4:30PM.

**Common Pleas Court**, 100 Short Court, Chardon, OH 44024. 216-285-2222 (EST) 8AM-4:30PM. Felony, Civil Actions Over $10,000, Probate.

**Chardon Municipal Court**, 108 S Hambden (PO Box 339), Chardon, OH 44024-0339. 216-285-3113 (EST) 8AM-4:30PM. Misdemeanor, Civil Actions Under $10,000, Eviction, Small Claims.

## Greene County

**Real Estate Recording**, Greene County Recorder, 69 Greene Street, Courthouse, Xenia, OH 45385. 513-376-5270 (EST) 8AM-4:30PM.

**Common Pleas Court**, 45 N Detroit St (PO Box 156), Xenia, OH 45385. 513-376-5290 (EST) 8AM-4:30PM. Felony, Civil Actions Over $10,000, Probate.

**Fairborn Municipal Court**, 44 W Hebble Ave, Fairborn, OH 45324. 513-879-1735 (EST) 7:30AM-4:30PM. Misdemeanor, Civil Actions Under $10,000, Eviction, Small Claims.

**Xenia Municipal Court**, 101 N Detroit, Xenia, OH 45385. 513-376-7292 (EST) 8AM-4:30PM. Misdemeanor, Civil Actions Under $10,000, Eviction, Small Claims.

## Guernsey County

**Real Estate Recording**, Guernsey County Recorder, Courthouse D-202, Wheeling Avenue, Cambridge, OH 43725. 614-432-9275 (EST) 8:30AM-4PM.

**Common Pleas Court**, 801 E Wheeling Ave, Cambridge, OH 43725. 614-432-9230 (EST) 8:30AM-4PM. Felony, Civil Actions Over $10,000, Probate.

**Cambridge Municipal Court**, 134 Southgate Parkway (Civil is 2nd fl), Cambridge, OH 43725. 614-439-5585 (EST) 8:30AM-4:30PM. Misdemeanor, Civil Actions Under $10,000, Eviction, Small Claims.

## Hamilton County

**Real Estate Recording**, Hamilton County Recorder, 138 East Court Street, Room 205-A, Cincinnati, OH 45202. 513-632-8343 (EST) 8AM-4PM.

**Common Pleas Court**, 1000 Main St, Cincinnati, OH 45202. 513-632-8247 (EST) 8AM-4PM. Felony, Civil Actions Over $10,000, Probate.

**Hamilton County Municipal Court**, 1000 Main St, Cincinnati, OH 45202. 513-632-8891 (EST) Misdemeanor, Civil Actions Under $10,000, Eviction, Small Claims.

## Hancock County

**Real Estate Recording**, Hancock County Recorder, 300 South Main Street, Courthouse, Findlay, OH 45840. 419-424-7091 (EST) 8:30AM-4:30PM.

**Common Pleas Court**, 300 S Main St, Findlay, OH 45840. 419-424-7037 (EST) 8:30AM-4:30PM. Felony, Civil Actions Over $10,000, Probate.

**Findlay Municipal Court**, PO Box 826, Findlay, OH 45839. 419-424-7141 (EST) 8AM-5PM. Misdemeanor, Civil Actions Under $10,000, Eviction, Small Claims.

## Hardin County

**Real Estate Recording**, Hardin County Recorder, One Courthouse Square, Suite 220, Kenton, OH 43326. 419-674-2250 (EST) 8:30AM-4PM; 8:30AM-6PM F.

**Common Pleas Court**, Courthouse, Ste 310, Kenton, OH 43326. 419-674-2278 (EST) 8:30AM-4PM M-Th/8:30AM-6PM F. Felony, Civil Actions Over $10,000, Probate.

**Hardin County Municipal Court**, PO Box 250, Kenton, OH 43326. 419-674-4362 (EST) Misdemeanor, Civil Actions Under $10,000, Eviction, Small Claims.

## Harrison County

**Real Estate Recording**, Harrison County Recorder, 100 West Market Street, Courthouse, Cadiz, OH 43907. 614-942-8869 (EST) 8:30AM-4:30PM.

**Common Pleas Court**, County Courthouse, Cadiz, OH 43907. 614-942-8863 (EST) 8:30AM-4:30PM. Felony, Civil Actions Over $3,000, Probate.

**County Court**, 100 W Market St, Cadiz, OH 43907. 614-942-8861 (EST) 8:30AM-4:30PM. Misdemeanor, Civil Actions Under $3,000, Small Claims.

## Henry County

**Real Estate Recording**, Henry County Recorder, 660 North Perry Street, Courthouse, Napoleon, OH 43545-1747. 419-592-1766 (EST) 8:30AM-4:30PM.

**Common Pleas Court**, PO Box 71, Napoleon, OH 43545. 419-592-5886 (EST) 8:30AM-4:30PM. Felony, Civil Actions Over $10,000, Probate.

**Napoleon Municipal Court**, PO Box 502, Napoleon, OH 43545. 419-592-2851 (EST) 8AM-5PM. Misdemeanor, Civil Actions Under $10,000, Eviction, Small Claims.

## Highland County

**Real Estate Recording**, Highland County Recorder, 119 Governor Foraker, County Administration Building, Hillsboro, OH 45133. 513-393-9954 (EST) 8:30AM-4PM.

**Common Pleas Court**, PO Box 821, Hillsboro, OH 45133. 513-393-9957 (EST) 8AM-4PM. Felony, Civil Actions Over $10,000, Probate.

**Highland County Municipal Court**, 108 Governor Trimble Pl, Hillsboro, OH 45133. 513-393-3022 (EST) 7AM-3:30PM M,T,Th,F/7AM-Noon W. Misdemeanor, Civil Actions Under $10,000, Eviction, Small Claims.

## Hocking County

**Real Estate Recording**, Hocking County Recorder, 1 East Main Street, Courthouse, Logan, OH 43138-1277. 614-385-2031 (EST) 8:30AM-4PM.

**Common Pleas Court**, PO Box 108, Logan, OH 43138. 614-385-2616 (EST) 8:30AM-4:30PM. Felony, Civil Actions Over $10,000, Probate.

**Hocking County Municipal Court**, 1 E Main St (PO Box 950), Logan, OH 43138-1278. 614-385-2250 (EST) 8:30AM-4:30PM. Misdemeanor, Civil Actions Under $10,000, Eviction, Small Claims.

## Holmes County

**Real Estate Recording**, Holmes County Recorder, Courthouse - Suite 202, 1 East Jackson St., Millersburg, OH 44654. 216-674-5916 (EST) 8:30AM-4:30PM.

**Common Pleas Court**, County Courthouse, Millersburg, OH 44654. 216-674-1876 (EST) 8:30AM-4:30PM. Felony, Civil Actions Over $10,000, Probate.

# Ohio

**County Court**, 1 E Jackson St, Ste 101, Millersburg, OH 44654. 216-674-4901 (EST) 8:30AM-4:30PM. Misdemeanor, Civil Actions Under $3,000, Small Claims.

## Huron County

**Real Estate Recording**, Huron County Recorder, 2 East Main Street, Norwalk, OH 44857. 419-668-1916 (EST) 8AM-4:30PM.

**Common Pleas Court**, 2 E Main St, Norwalk, OH 44857. 419-668-5113 (EST) 8AM-4:30PM. Felony, Civil Actions Over $10,000, Probate.

**Bellevue Municipal Court**, 117 N Sandusky, Bellevue, OH 44811. 419-483-5880 (EST) 8:30AM-4PM. Misdemeanor, Civil Actions Under $10,000, Eviction, Small Claims.

**Norwalk Municipal Court**, 45 N Linwood, Norwalk, OH 44857. 419-663-6750 (EST) Misdemeanor, Civil Actions Under $10,000, Eviction, Small Claims.

## Jackson County

**Real Estate Recording**, Jackson County Recorder, 226 E. Main St., Courthouse, Suite 1, Jackson, OH 45640. 614-286-1919 (EST) 8AM-4PM.

**Common Pleas Court**, 226 Main St, Jackson, OH 45640. 614-286-2006 (EST) 8AM-4PM. Felony, Civil Actions Over $10,000, Probate.

**Jackson County Municipal Court**, 226 Main St, Jackson, OH 45640-2006. 614-286-2718 (EST) 8AM-4PM. Misdemeanor, Civil Actions Under $10,000, Eviction, Small Claims.

## Jefferson County

**Real Estate Recording**, Jefferson County Recorder, 3rd & Market Street, Courthouse, Steubenville, OH 43952. 614-283-8566 (EST) 8:30AM-4:30PM.

**Common Pleas Court**, 301 Market St, 4th Fl (PO Box 1326), Steubenville, OH 43952. 614-283-8583 (EST) 8:30AM-4:30PM. Felony, Civil Actions Over $10,000, Probate.

**County Court #3**, PO Box 495, Dillonvale, OH 43917. 614-769-2903 (EST) Misdemeanor, Civil Actions Under $3,000, Small Claims.

**County Court #1**, Unibank, 4th & Main, Toronto, OH 43964. 614-537-2020 (EST) 9AM-4PM. Misdemeanor, Civil Actions Under $3,000, Small Claims.

**County Court #2**, PO Box 2207, Wintersville, OH 43952. 614-264-7644 (EST) 8:30AM-4PM. Misdemeanor, Civil Actions Under $3,000, Small Claims.

**Steubenville Municipal Court**, 123 S 3rd St, Steubenville, OH 43952. 614-283-6020 (EST) 8:30AM-4PM. Misdemeanor, Civil Actions Under $10,000, Eviction, Small Claims.

## Knox County

**Real Estate Recording**, Knox County Recorder, 106 East High Street, Mount Vernon, OH 43050. 614-393-6755 (EST) 8AM-4PM.

**Common Pleas Court**, 114 E Chestnut St, Mt Vernon, OH 43050. 614-393-6788 (EST) 8AM-4PM, til 6PM on Wed. Felony, Civil Actions Over $10,000, Probate.

**Mount Vernon Municipal Court**, 5 North Gay St, Mount Vernon, OH 43050. 614-393-9510 (EST) 8AM-4PM. Misdemeanor, Civil Actions Under $10,000, Eviction, Small Claims.

## Lake County

**Real Estate Recording**, Lake County Recorder, 105 Main Street, Painesville, OH 44077. 216-350-2510 (EST) 8AM-4:30PM.

**Common Pleas Court**, PO Box 490, Painesville, OH 44077. 216-350-2720 (EST) 8AM-4:30 PM. Felony, Civil Actions Over $10,000, Probate.

**Painesville Municipal Court**, 7 Richmond St (PO Box 601), Painesville, OH 44077. 216-352-6281 (EST) 8AM-4:30PM. Misdemeanor, Civil Actions Under $10,000, Eviction, Small Claims.

## Lawrence County

**Real Estate Recording**, Lawrence County Recorder, 111 South 4th Street, Courthouse, Ironton, OH 45638. 614-533-4314 (EST) 8AM-4PM.

**Common Pleas Court**, PO Box 208, Ironton, OH 45638. 614-533-4355 (EST) 8:30AM-4PM. Felony, Civil Actions Over $10,000, Probate.

**Lawrence County Municipal Court**, PO Box 126, Chesapeake, OH 45619. 614-867-3128 (EST) 8:30AM-4PM. Misdemeanor, Civil Actions Under $10,000, Eviction, Small Claims.

**Ironton Municipal Court**, PO Box 237, Ironton, OH 45638. 614-532-3062 (EST) 8:30AM-4PM. Misdemeanor, Civil Actions Under $10,000, Eviction, Small Claims.

## Licking County

**Real Estate Recording**, Licking County Recorder, 20 South Second Street, Third Floor, Newark, OH 43055. 614-349-6061 (EST) 8:30AM-4:30PM.

**Common Pleas Court**, PO Box 4370, Newark, OH 43058-4370. 614-349-6171 (EST) 8AM-4:30PM. Felony, Civil Actions Over $10,000, Probate.

**Licking County Municipal Court**, 40 W Main St, Newark, OH 43055. 614-349-6627 (EST) 8:30AM-4:30PM. Misdemeanor, Civil Actions Under $10,000, Eviction, Small Claims.

## Logan County

**Real Estate Recording**, Logan County Recorder, 100 South Madriver, Suite A, Bellefontaine, OH 43311-2075. 513-599-7201 (EST) 8:30AM-4:30PM; 8:30AM-5PM F.

**Common Pleas Court**, PO Box 429, Bellefontaine, OH 43311. 513-599-7275 (EST) 8AM-4:30PM. Felony, Civil Actions Over $10,000, Probate.

**Bellefontaine Municipal Court**, 226 W Columbus Ave, Bellefontaine, OH 43311. 513-599-6127 (EST) 8:30AM-4:30PM. Misdemeanor, Civil Actions Under $10,000, Eviction, Small Claims.

## Lorain County

**Real Estate Recording**, Lorain County Recorder, 226 Middle Avenue, Elyria, OH 44035-5643. 216-329-5148 (EST) 8AM-4:30PM.

**Common Pleas Court**, 226 Middle Ave, Elyria, OH 44035. 216-329-5536 (EST) 8AM-4:30PM. Felony, Civil Actions Over $10,000, Probate.

**Avon Lake Municipal Court**, 150 Avon Beldon Rd, Avon Lake, OH 44012. 216-933-5289 (EST) 8:30AM-4:30PM. Misdemeanor, Civil Actions Under $10,000, Eviction, Small Claims.

**Elyria Municipal Court**, 328 Broad St (PO Box 1498), Elyria, OH 44036. 216-323-5743 (EST) 8AM-4:25PM. Misdemeanor, Civil Actions Under $10,000, Eviction, Small Claims.

**Lorain Municipal Court**, 100 W Erie Ave, Lorain, OH 44052. 216-244-2286 (EST) 8:30AM-4:30PM. Misdemeanor, Civil Actions Under $10,000, Eviction, Small Claims.

**Oberlin Municipal Court**, 85 S Main St, Oberlin, OH 44074. 216-775-1751 (EST) 8AM-4PM. Misdemeanor, Civil Actions Under $10,000, Eviction, Small Claims.

**Vermilion Municipal Court**, PO Box 258, Vermilion, OH 44089. 216-967-6543 (EST) 8AM-4PM. Misdemeanor, Civil Actions Under $10,000, Eviction, Small Claims.

## Lucas County

**Real Estate Recording**, Lucas County Recorder, 1 Government Center, Jackson Street, Toledo, OH 43604. 419-245-4400 (EST) 8AM-5PM.

**Common Pleas Court**, 700 Adams, Courthouse, Toledo, OH 43624. 419-245-4483 (EST) 8:15AM-4:30PM. Felony, Civil Actions Over $10,000, Probate.

**Toledo Municipal Court**, 555 N Erie St, Toledo, OH 43624. 419-245-1776 (EST) 8AM-4:45PM. Misdemeanor, Civil Actions Under $10,000, Eviction, Small Claims.

## Madison County

**Real Estate Recording**, Madison County Recorder, High & Main Streets, Courthouse, London, OH 43140. 614-852-1854 (EST) 8AM-4PM.

**Common Pleas Court**, PO Box 227, London, OH 43140. 614-852-9776 (EST) 8AM-4PM. Felony, Civil Actions Over $10,000, Probate.

**Madison County Municipal Court**, Main & High St, London, OH 43140. 614-852-1669 (EST) 8AM-4PM. Misdemeanor, Civil Actions Under $10,000, Eviction, Small Claims.

## Mahoning County

**Real Estate Recording**, Mahoning County Recorder, 120 Market Street, Youngstown, OH 44503. 216-740-2345 (EST) 8AM-4:30PM.

**Common Pleas Court**, 120 Market St, Youngstown, OH 44503. 216-740-2104 (EST) 8AM-4PM. Felony, Civil Actions Over $10,000, Probate.

**County Court #2**, 127 Boardman Canfield Rd, Boardman, OH 44512. 216-726-5546 (EST) 8:30AM-4PM. Misdemeanor, Civil Actions Under $3,000, Small Claims.

**County Court #5**, 72 N Broad St, Canfield, OH 44406. 216-533-3643 (EST) 8:30AM-4PM. Misdemeanor, Civil Actions Under $3,000, Small Claims.

**County Court #3**, 605 E Ohio Ave, Sebring, OH 44672. 216-938-9873 (EST) 8:30AM-4PM. Misdemeanor, Civil Actions Under $3,000, Small Claims.

**County Court #4**, 6000 Mahoning Ave, Youngstown, OH 44515. 216-740-2001 (EST) 8:30AM-4PM. Misdemeanor, Civil Actions Under $3,000, Small Claims.

**Youngstown Municipal Court-Civil Records**, PO Box 6047, Youngstown, OH 44501. 216-742-8863 (EST) 8AM-4PM. Civil Actions Under $10,000, Eviction, Small Claims.

**Youngstown Municipal Court-Criminal Records**, 116 W Boardman, Youngstown, OH 44503. 216-742-8900 (EST) 8AM-4PM. Misdemeanor.

**Campbell Municipal Court**, 351 Tenney Ave, Campbell, OH 44405. 216-755-2165 (EST) 8AM-4PM. Misdemeanor, Civil Actions Under $10,000, Eviction, Small Claims.

**Struthers Municipal Court**, 6 Elm St, Struthers, OH 44471. 216-755-1800 (EST) 8AM-4PM. Misdemeanor, Civil Actions Under $10,000, Eviction, Small Claims.

## Marion County

**Real Estate Recording**, Marion County Recorder, 100 North Main Street, Courthouse Square, Marion, OH 43302-3089. 614-387-5871 (EST) X206 8:30AM-4:30PM.

**Common Pleas Court**, 100 N Main St, Marion, OH 43302. 614-387-5871 (EST) 8:30AM-4:30PM. Felony, Civil Actions Over $10,000, Probate.

**Marion Municipal Court**, 233 W Center St, Marion, OH 43302-0326. 614-387-2020 (EST) 8:30AM-4:30PM. Misdemeanor, Civil Actions Under $10,000, Eviction, Small Claims.

## Medina County

**Real Estate Recording**, Medina County Recorder, County Administration Bldg, 144 N. Broadway, Medina, OH 44256-2295. 216-725-9782 (EST) 8AM-4:30PM.

**Common Pleas Court**, 93 Public Square, Medina, OH 44256. 216-723-3641 (EST) 8AM-4:30PM. Felony, Civil Actions Over $10,000, Probate.

**Medina Municipal Court**, 135 N Elmwood, Medina, OH 44256. 216-723-3287 (EST) Misdemeanor, Civil Actions Under $10,000, Eviction, Small Claims.

**Wadsworth Municipal Court**, 145 High St, Wadsworth, OH 44281. 216-335-1596 (EST) 8AM-4PM. Misdemeanor, Civil Actions Under $10,000, Eviction, Small Claims.

## Meigs County

**Real Estate Recording**, Meigs County Recorder, 100 East Second Street, Courthouse, Pomeroy, OH 45769. 614-992-3806 (EST) 8:30AM-4:30PM.

**Common Pleas Court**, PO Box 151, Pomeroy, OH 45769. 614-992-5290 (EST) 8:30AM-4:30PM. Felony, Civil Actions Over $3,000, Probate.

**County Court**, County Courthouse, Pomeroy, OH 45769. 614-992-2279 (EST) 8:30AM-4:30PM. Misdemeanor, Civil Actions Under $3,000, Small Claims.

## Mercer County

**Real Estate Recording**, Mercer County Recorder, 101 North Main Street, Courthouse Square-Room 203, Celina, OH 45822. 419-586-4232 (EST) 8:30AM-4PM (M-open until 5PM).

**Common Pleas Court**, PO Box 28, Celina, OH 45822. 419-586-6461 (EST) 8:30AM-4PM. Felony, Civil Actions Over $10,000, Probate.

**Celina Municipal Court**, PO Box 362, Celina, OH 45822. 419-586-6491 (EST) 8AM-5PM. Misdemeanor, Civil Actions Under $10,000, Eviction, Small Claims.

## Miami County

**Real Estate Recording**, Miami County Recorder, 201 West Main Street, Troy, OH 45373. 513-332-6890 (EST) 8AM-4PM.

**Common Pleas Court**, Safety Bldg, West Main St, Troy, OH 45373. 513-332-6855 (EST) Felony, Civil Actions Over $10,000, Probate.

**Miami County Municipal Court**, 201 West Main St, Troy, OH 45373. 513-332-6920 (EST) 8AM-4PM. Misdemeanor, Civil Actions Under $10,000, Eviction, Small Claims.

## Monroe County

**Real Estate Recording**, Monroe County Recorder, 101 North Main Street, Courthouse, Room 20, Woodsfield, OH 43793. 614-472-5264 (EST) 8AM-4PM.

**Common Pleas Court**, 101 N Main St, Woodsfield, OH 43793. 614-472-0761 (EST) 8:30AM-4:30PM. Felony, Civil Actions Over $3,000, Probate.

**County Court**, 101 N Main St, Woodsfield, OH 43793. 614-472-5181 (EST) 9AM-4:30PM. Misdemeanor, Civil Actions Under $3,000, Small Claims.

## Montgomery County

**Real Estate Recording**, Montgomery County Recorder, 451 West Third Street, 5th Floor, County Administration Building, Dayton, OH 45422. 513-225-4282 (EST) 8AM-4PM.

**Common Pleas Court**, 41 N Perry St, Dayton, OH 45422. 513-225-4512 (EST) 8AM-4:30PM. Felony, Civil Actions Over $10,000, Probate.

**County Court-District #2**, 7525 Brandt Pk, Huber Heights, OH 45424. 513-496-7231 (EST) 8AM-4PM. Misdemeanor, Civil Actions Under $3,000, Small Claims.

**County Court-District #1**, 3100 Shiloh Springs Rd, Trotwood, OH 45426. 513-837-3351 (EST) 8:30AM-4:30PM. Misdemeanor, Civil Actions Under $3,000, Small Claims.

**Dayton Municipal Court-Civil Division**, PO Box 968, Dayton, OH 45402-0968. 513-443-4480 (EST) 8AM-4:30PM. Civil Actions Under $10,000, Eviction, Small Claims.

**Dayton Municipal Court-Criminal Division**, 301 W 3rd St, Rm 331, Dayton, OH 45402. 513-443-4315 (EST) 8AM-4:30PM. Misdemeanor.

**Dayton Municipal Court-Traffic Division**, 301 W 3rd St (PO Box 968), Dayton, OH 45402. 513-443-4313 (EST) 8AM-4:30PM. Misdemeanor, Civil Actions Under $10,000, Eviction, Small Claims.

**Kettering Municipal Court**, 3600 Shroyer Rd, Dayton, OH 45429. 513-296-2461 (EST) 8:30AM-4:30PM. Misdemeanor, Civil Actions Under $10,000, Eviction, Small Claims.

**Oakwood Municipal Court**, 30 Park Ave, Dayton, OH 45429. 513-293-3058 (EST) 8AM-5PM. Misdemeanor, Civil Actions Under $10,000, Eviction, Small Claims.

**Miamisburg Municipal Court**, 10 N First St, Miamisburg, OH 45342. 513-866-2203 (EST) 8AM-4PM. Misdemeanor, Civil Actions Under $10,000, Eviction, Small Claims.

**Vandalia Municipal Court**, 333 James Bohanan, Vandalia, OH 45377. 513-898-3996 (EST) 8AM-4PM. Misdemeanor, Civil Actions Under $10,000, Eviction, Small Claims.

## Morgan County

**Real Estate Recording**, Morgan County Recorder, 19 East Main Street, McConnelsville, OH 43756. 614-962-4051 (EST) 8AM-4PM.

**Common Pleas Court**, 19 E Main St, McConnelsville, OH 43756. 614-962-4752 (EST) 8AM-4PM. Felony, Civil Actions Over $3,000, Probate.

**County Court**, 37 E Main St, McConnelsville, OH 43756. 614-962-4031 (EST) 8AM-4PM. Misdemeanor, Civil Actions Under $3,000, Small Claims.

## Morrow County

**Real Estate Recording**, Morrow County Recorder, 48 East High Street, Mount Gilead, OH 43338. 419-947-3060 (EST) 8:30AM-4PM.

**Common Pleas Court**, 48 E High St, Mount Gilead, OH 43338. 419-947-2085 (EST) 7AM-5PM. Felony, Civil Actions Over $3,000, Probate.

**County Court**, 48 E High St, Mount Gilead, OH 43338. 419-947-5045 (EST) 8:30AM-4PM. Misdemeanor, Civil Actions Under $3,000, Small Claims.

## Muskingum County

**Real Estate Recording**, Muskingum County Recorder, Corner 4th & Main, Courthouse, Zanesville, OH 43701. 614-455-7107 (EST) 8:30AM-4:30PM.

**Common Pleas Court**, PO Box 268, Zanesville, OH 43702-0268. 614-455-7104 (EST) 8:30AM-4:30PM. Felony, Civil Actions Over $10,000, Probate.

**County Court**, 27 N 5th St, Zanesville, OH 43701. 614-455-7138 (EST) 8:30AM-4PM. Misdemeanor, Civil Actions Under $3,000, Small Claims.

**Zanesville Municipal Court**, PO Box 566, Zanesville, OH 43702. 614-454-3269 (EST) 9AM-4:30PM. Misdemeanor, Civil Actions Under $10,000, Eviction, Small Claims.

## Noble County

**Real Estate Recording**, Noble County Recorder, 260 Courthouse, Caldwell, OH 43724. 614-732-4319 (EST) 8AM-4PM M-W; 8AM-11:30AM Th; 8am-7PM F.

**Common Pleas Court**, 350 Courthouse, Caldwell, OH 43724. 614-732-4408 (EST) 8AM-4PM M-W/8AM-11:30AM Th/8AM-7PM F. Felony, Civil Actions Over $3,000, Probate.

**County Court**, 100 Courthouse, Caldwell, OH 43724. 614-732-5795 (EST) 8:30AM-4PM M-W,F/8:30AM-11:30AM Th. Misdemeanor, Civil Actions Under $3,000, Small Claims.

## Ottawa County

**Real Estate Recording**, Ottawa County Recorder, 315 Madison Street, Room 204, Port Clinton, OH 43452. 419-734-6730 (EST) 8:30AM-4:30PM.

**Common Pleas Court**, 315 Madison St, Port Clinton, OH 43452. 419-734-6755 (EST) 8:30AM-4:30PM. Felony, Civil Actions Over $10,000, Probate.

**Port Clinton Municipal Court**, PO Box Q, Port Clinton, OH 43452. 419-734-4143 (EST) 8:30AM-4:30PM. Misdemeanor, Civil Actions Under $10,000, Eviction, Small Claims.

## Paulding County

**Real Estate Recording**, Paulding County Recorder, Courthouse, 115 N. Williams St., Paulding, OH 45879. 419-399-8275 (EST) 8AM-4PM.

**Common Pleas Court**, 115 N Williams St, Paulding, OH 45879. 419-399-8210 (EST) 8AM-4PM. Felony, Civil Actions Over $3,000, Probate.

**County Court**, 103B East Perry, Paulding, OH 45879. 419-399-8235 (EST) 8AM-4PM. Misdemeanor, Civil Actions Under $3,000, Small Claims.

## Perry County

**Real Estate Recording**, Perry County Recorder, 105 Main Street, Courthouse, New Lexington, OH 43764. 614-342-2494 (EST) 8:30AM-4:30PM.

**Common Pleas Court**, PO Box 67, New Lexington, OH 43764. 614-342-1022 (EST) Felony, Civil Actions Over $3,000, Probate.

**County Court**, PO Box 207, New Lexington, OH 43764-0207. 614-342-3156 (EST) 8:30AM-4:30PM. Misdemeanor, Civil Actions Under $3,000, Small Claims.

## Pickaway County

**Real Estate Recording**, Pickaway County Recorder, 207 South Court Street, Circleville, OH 43113. 614-474-5826 (EST) 8AM-4PM.

**Common Pleas Court**, County Courthouse, Circleville, OH 43113. 614-474-5231 (EST) 8AM-4PM. Felony, Civil Actions Over $10,000, Probate.

**Circleville Municipal Court**, PO Box 128, Circleville, OH 43113. 614-474-3171 (EST) 8AM-4PM. Misdemeanor, Civil Actions Under $10,000, Eviction, Small Claims.

## Pike County

**Real Estate Recording**, Pike County Recorder, Courthouse, 100 E. 2nd St., Waverly, OH 45690. 614-947-2622 (EST) 8:30AM-4PM.

**Common Pleas Court**, 100 East 2nd St, Waverly, OH 45690. 614-947-2715 (EST) 8:30AM-4PM. Felony, Civil Actions Over $3,000, Probate.

**County Court**, 106 N Market St, Waverly, OH 45690. 614-947-4003 (EST) 8:30AM-4:30PM. Misdemeanor, Civil Actions Under $3,000, Small Claims.

## Portage County

**Real Estate Recording**, Portage County Recorder, 449 South Meridian Street, Ravenna, OH 44266. 216-297-3553 (EST) 8AM-4:30PM.

**Common Pleas Court**, PO Box 1035, Ravenna, OH 44266. 216-297-3644 (EST) 8AM-4PM. Felony, Civil Actions Over $10,000, Probate.

**Kent Municipal Court**, 214 S Water, Kent, OH 44240. 216-678-9170 (EST) 8AM-4PM. Misdemeanor, Civil Actions Under $10,000, Eviction, Small Claims.

**Ravenna Municipal Court**, PO Box 958, Ravenna, OH 44266. 216-297-3636 (EST) 8AM-4PM. Misdemeanor, Civil Actions Under $10,000, Eviction, Small Claims.

## Preble County

**Real Estate Recording**, Preble County Recorder, Courthouse, 101 East Main St., Eaton, OH 45320-1744. 513-456-8173 (EST) 8AM-4:30PM.

**Common Pleas Court**, 100 E Main, 3rd Fl, Eaton, OH 45320. 513-456-8160 (EST) 8AM-4:30PM. Felony, Civil Actions Over $10,000, Probate.

**Eaton Municipal Court**, PO Box 65, Eaton, OH 45320. 513-456-4941 (EST) 8AM-5PM, Closed 12-1PM. Misdemeanor, Civil Actions Under $10,000, Eviction, Small Claims.

## Putnam County

**Real Estate Recording**, Putnam County Recorder, 245 East Main Street, Courthouse - Suite 202, Ottawa, OH 45875-1959. 419-523-6490 (EST) 8:30AM-4:30PM.

**Common Pleas Court**, 245 E Main, Rm 303, Ottawa, OH 45875. 419-523-3110 (EST) 8:30AM-4:30PM. Felony, Civil Actions Over $3,000, Probate.

**County Court**, 245 E Main, Rm 301, Ottawa, OH 45875. 419-523-3110 (EST) 8:30AM-4:30PM. Misdemeanor, Civil Actions Under $3,000, Small Claims.

## Richland County

**Real Estate Recording**, Richland County Recorder, 50 Park Avenue East, Mansfield, OH 44902. 419-774-5599 (EST) 8AM-4PM.

**Common Pleas Court**, PO Box 127, Mansfield, OH 44901. 419-774-5690 (EST) 8AM-4PM. Felony, Civil Actions Over $10,000, Probate.

**Mansfield Municipal Court**, PO Box 1228, Mansfield, OH 44901. 419-755-9600 (EST) 8AM-4PM. Misdemeanor, Civil Actions Under $10,000, Eviction, Small Claims.

## Ross County

**Real Estate Recording**, Ross County Recorder, 2 North Paint Street, Courthouse, Chillicothe, OH 45601. 614-774-1213 (EST) 8:30AM-4:30PM.

**Common Pleas Court**, County Courthouse, Chillicothe, OH 45601. 614-773-2330 (EST) 8AM-4PM. Felony, Civil Actions Over $10,000, Probate.

**Chillicothe Municipal Court**, 26 S Paint St, Chillicothe, OH 45601. 614-773-3515 (EST) 7:30AM-4:30PM. Misdemeanor, Civil Actions Under $10,000, Eviction, Small Claims.

## Sandusky County

**Real Estate Recording**, Sandusky County Recorder, 100 N. Park Ave., Courthouse, Fremont, OH 43420-2477. 419-334-6226 (EST) 8AM-4:30PM.

**Common Pleas Court**, 100 N Park Ave, Fremont, OH 43420. 419-334-6161 (EST) 8AM-4:30PM. Felony, Civil Actions Over $3,000, Probate.

**County Court #1**, 123 W Buckeye St, Clyde, OH 43410. 419-547-0915 (EST) 8AM-4:30PM. Misdemeanor, Civil Actions Under $3,000, Small Claims.

**County Court #2**, 128 E Main St, Woodville, OH 43469. 419-849-3961 (EST) 8AM-4:30PM. Misdemeanor, Civil Actions Under $3,000, Small Claims.

## Scioto County

**Real Estate Recording**, Scioto County Recorder, 602 7th Street, Room 110, Portsmouth, OH 45662-3950. 614-355-8304 (EST) 8AM-4:30PM.

**Common Pleas Court**, 602 7th St, Portsmouth, OH 45662. 614-355-8226 (EST) 8AM-4:30PM. Felony, Civil Actions Over $10,000, Probate.

**Portsmouth Municipal Court**, 728 2nd St, Portsmouth, OH 45662. 614-354-3283 (EST) 8AM-4PM. Misdemeanor, Civil Actions Under $10,000, Eviction, Small Claims.

## Seneca County

**Real Estate Recording**, Seneca County Recorder, 103 South Washington Street, Tiffin, OH 44883-2352. 419-447-4434 (EST) 8:30AM-4:30PM.

**Common Pleas Court**, 103 S Washington St, Tiffin, OH 44883. 419-447-0671 (EST) 8:30AM-4:30PM. Felony, Civil Actions Over $10,000, Probate.

**Tiffin Municipal Court**, PO Box 694, Tiffin, OH 44883. 419-448-5411 (EST) 8:30AM-4:30PM. Misdemeanor, Civil Actions Under $10,000, Eviction, Small Claims.

## Shelby County

**Real Estate Recording**, Shelby County Recorder, 129 East Court Street, Shelby County Annex, Sidney, OH 45365. 513-498-7270 (EST) 7:30AM-4PM (F open until 6PM).

**Common Pleas Court**, PO Box 809, Sidney, OH 45365. 513-498-7221 (EST) 8:30AM-4:30PM M-Th/8:30AM-6PM F. Felony, Civil Actions Over $10,000, Probate.

**Sidney Municipal Court**, 201 W Poplar, Sidney, OH 45365. 513-498-8109 (EST) 8AM-4:30PM. Misdemeanor, Civil Actions Under $10,000, Eviction, Small Claims.

## Stark County

**Real Estate Recording**, Stark County Recorder, 110 Central Plaza South, Suite 170, Canton, OH 44702-1409. 216-438-0441 (EST) 8:30AM-4:30PM (Recording: 8:30AM-4PM).

**Common Pleas Court-Civil Division**, PO Box 21160, Canton, OH 44701. 216-438-0795 (EST) 8:30AM-4:30PM. Civil Actions Over $10,000, Probate.

**Common Pleas Court-Criminal Division**, PO Box 21160, Canton, OH 44701. 216-438-0929 (EST) 8:30AM-4:15PM. Felony.

**Canton Municipal Court**, 218 Cleveland Ave S (PO Box 24218), Canton, OH 44702-4218. 216-489-3203 (EST) 8:30AM-4:30PM. Misdemeanor, Civil Actions Under $10,000, Eviction, Small Claims.

## Summit County

**Real Estate Recording**, Summit County Recorder, 175 South Main Street, Akron, OH 44308-1355. 216-643-2717 (EST) 7:30AM-4PM.

**Common Pleas Court**, 53 University Ave, Co Safety Bldg, 2nd F, Akron, OH 44308. 216-643-2217 (EST) 7:30AM-4:15PM. Felony, Civil Actions Over $10,000, Probate.

**Akron Municipal Court**, 217 S High St, Rm 837, Akron, OH 44308. 216-375-2570 (EST) 8AM-4:30PM. Misdemeanor, Civil Actions Under $10,000, Eviction, Small Claims.

## Trumbull County

**Real Estate Recording**, Trumbull County Recorder, 160 High Street N.W., Warren, OH 44481. 216-675-2401 (EST) 8:30AM-4:30PM.

**Common Pleas Court**, 160 High St, Warren, OH 44481. 216-675-2557 (EST) 8AM-4:30PM. Felony, Civil Actions Over $10,000, Probate.

**Warren Municipal Court**, 141 South St SE (PO Box 1550), Warren, OH 44482. 216-841-2527 (EST) 8AM-4:30PM. Misdemeanor, Civil Actions Under $10,000, Eviction, Small Claims.

## Tuscarawas County

**Real Estate Recording**, Tuscarawas County Recorder, 125 East High Avenue, New Philadelphia, OH 44663. 216-364-8811 (EST) 8AM-4:30PM.

**Common Pleas Court**, 125 E High (PO Box 628), New Philadelphia, OH 44663. 216-364-8811 (EST) 8AM-4:30PM. Felony, Civil Actions Over $10,000, Probate.

**County Court**, 220 E 3rd, Uhrichsville, OH 44683. 614-922-4795 (EST) 8AM-4:30PM. Misdemeanor, Civil Actions Under $3,000, Small Claims.

**New Philadelphia Municipal Court**, 166 E High Ave, New Philadelphia, OH 44663. 216-364-4491 (EST) 8AM-4PM. Misdemeanor, Civil Actions Under $10,000, Eviction, Small Claims.

## Union County

**Real Estate Recording**, Union County Recorder, 233 West Sixth St., Marysville, OH 43040. 513-645-3032 (EST) 8:30AM-4PM.

**Common Pleas Court**, County Courthouse, Marysville, OH 43040. 513-645-3006 (EST) Felony, Civil Actions Over $10,000, Probate.

**Marysville Municipal Court**, PO Box 322, Marysville, OH 43040. 513-644-9102 (EST) 8AM-4PM. Misdemeanor, Civil Actions Under $10,000, Eviction, Small Claims.

## Van Wert County

**Real Estate Recording**, Van Wert County Recorder, 121 East Main Street, Courthouse - Room 206, Van Wert, OH 45891-1729. 419-238-2558 (EST) 8:30AM-4PM (M-open until 5PM).

**Common Pleas Court**, PO Box 366, Van Wert, OH 45891. 419-238-1022 (EST) 8AM-4PM. Felony, Civil Actions Over $10,000, Probate.

**Van Wert Municipal Court**, 124 S Market, Van Wert, OH 45891. 419-238-5767 (EST) 8AM-4PM. Misdemeanor, Civil Actions Under $10,000, Eviction, Small Claims.

## Vinton County

**Real Estate Recording**, Vinton County Recorder, East Main Street, Courthouse, McArthur, OH 45651. 614-596-4314 (EST) 8:30-11:30AM, 12:30-3:30PM M,T,W,F; 8:30AM-11:30AM Th.

**Common Pleas Court**, County Courthouse, McArthur, OH 45651. 614-596-3001 (EST) 8:30AM-4PM M-F/8:30AM-Noon S. Felony, Civil Actions Over $3,000, Probate.

**County Court**, County Courthouse, McArthur, OH 45651. 614-596-5000 (EST) Misdemeanor, Civil Actions Under $3,000, Small Claims.

## Warren County

**Real Estate Recording**, Warren County Recorder, 320 East Silver Street, Lebanon, OH 45036-1887. 513-933-1382 (EST) 8:30AM-4:30PM.

**Common Pleas Court**, PO Box 238, Lebanon, OH 45036. 513-933-1120 (EST) 8:30AM-4:30PM. Felony, Civil Actions Over $3,000, Probate.

**County Court**, 550 Justice Dr, Lebanon, OH 45036. 513-933-1370 (EST) 8:30AM-4:30PM. Misdemeanor, Civil Actions Under $3,000, Small Claims.

## Washington County

**Real Estate Recording**, Washington County Recorder, 205 Putnam Street, Courthouse, Marietta, OH 45750. 614-373-6623 (EST) 8AM-5PM.

**Common Pleas Court**, 205 Putname St, Marietta, OH 45750. 614-373-6623 (EST) 8AM-4:15PM. Felony, Civil Actions Over $10,000, Probate.

**Marietta Municipal Court**, PO Box 615, Marietta, OH 45750. 614-373-4474 (EST) 8AM-5PM. Misdemeanor, Civil Actions Under $10,000, Eviction, Small Claims.

## Wayne County

**Real Estate Recording**, Wayne County Recorder, 428 West Liberty Street, Wooster, OH 44691-5097. 216-287-5460 (EST) 8AM-4:30PM.

**Common Pleas Court**, PO Box 507, Wooster, OH 44691. 216-287-5590 (EST) Felony, Civil Actions Over $10,000, Probate.

**Wooster County Municipal Court**, 538 N Market St, Wooster, OH 44691. 216-287-5650 (EST) 8AM-4:30PM. Misdemeanor, Civil Actions Under $10,000, Eviction, Small Claims.

## Williams County

**Real Estate Recording**, Williams County Recorder, 1 Courthouse Square, Bryan, OH 43506. 419-636-3259 (EST) 8:30AM-4:30PM.

**Common Pleas Court**, 1 Courthouse Square, Bryan, OH 43506. 419-636-1551 (EST) 8:30AM-4:30PM. Felony, Civil Actions Over $10,000, Probate.

**Bryan Municipal Court**, 516 E High, Bryan, OH 43506. 419-636-6939 (EST) 8:30AM-4:30PM. Misdemeanor, Civil Actions Under $10,000, Eviction, Small Claims.

## Wood County

**Real Estate Recording**, Wood County Recorder, 1 Courthouse Square, Bowling Green, OH 43402-2427. 419-354-9140 (EST) 8:30AM-4:30PM.

**Common Pleas Court**, County Courthouse, Bowling Green, OH 43402. 419-354-9280 (EST) 8:30AM-4:30PM. Felony, Civil Actions Over $10,000, Probate.

**Bowling Green Municipal Court**, PO Box 326, Bowling Green, OH 43402. 419-352-5263 (EST) 8:30AM-4:30PM. Misdemeanor, Civil Actions Under $10,000, Eviction, Small Claims.

**Perrysburg Municipal Court**, 300 Walnut, Perrysburg, OH 43551. 419-872-7900 (EST) 8AM-4:30PM. Misdemeanor, Civil Actions Under $10,000, Eviction, Small Claims.

## Wyandot County

**Real Estate Recording**, Wyandot County Recorder, Courthouse, 109 S. Sandusky Ave., Upper Sandusky, OH 43351. 419-294-1442 (EST) 8:30AM-4:30PM.

**Common Pleas Court**, 109 S Sandusky Ave, Upper Sandusky, OH 43351. 419-294-1432 (EST) 8:30AM-4:30PM. Felony, Civil Actions Over $10,000, Probate.

**Upper Sandusky Municipal Court**, 119 N 7th St, Upper Sandusky, OH 43351. 419-294-3354 (EST) 8AM-4:30PM. Misdemeanor, Civil Actions Under $10,000, Eviction, Small Claims.

# Oklahoma

## Adair County

**Real Estate Recording**, Adair County Clerk, Division Street & Highway 59, Stilwell, OK 74960. 918-696-7198 (CST) 8AM-4PM.

**15th Judicial District Court**, 210 W Division, Stilwell, OK 74960. 918-696-7633 (CST) 8:00AM-4:00PM. Felony, Misdemeanor, Civil, Eviction, Small Claims, Probate.

## Alfalfa County

**Real Estate Recording**, Alfalfa County Clerk, 300 South Grand, Cherokee, OK 73728. 405-596-3158 (CST) 8:30AM-4:30PM.

**4th Judicial District Court**, County Courthouse, Cherokee, OK 73728. 405-596-3523 (CST) 8:30AM-4:30PM. Felony, Misdemeanor, Civil, Eviction, Small Claims, Probate.

## Atoka County

**Real Estate Recording**, Atoka County Clerk, 200 East Court Street, Atoka, OK 74525. 405-889-5157 (CST) 8:30AM-4:30PM.

**25th Judicial District Court**, 200 E. Court St, Atoka, OK 74525. 405-889-3565 (CST) 8:30AM-4:30PM. Felony, Misdemeanor, Civil, Eviction, Small Claims, Probate.

## Beaver County

**Real Estate Recording**, Beaver County Clerk, 111 West Second Street, Beaver, OK 73932. 405-625-3141 (CST) 9AM-5PM.

**1st Judicial District Court**, PO Box 237, Beaver, OK 73932. 405-625-3191 (CST) Felony, Misdemeanor, Civil, Eviction, Small Claims, Probate.

## Beckham County

**Real Estate Recording**, Beckham County Clerk, Courthouse, 302 E. Main St., Sayre, OK 73662. 405-928-3383 (CST) 9AM-5PM.

**2nd Judicial District Court**, PO Box 520, Sayre, OK 73662. 405-928-3330 (CST) 9:00AM-5:00PM. Felony, Misdemeanor, Civil, Eviction, Small Claims, Probate.

## Blaine County

**Real Estate Recording**, Blaine County Clerk, 212 North Weigel, Watonga, OK 73772. 405-623-5890 (CST) 8AM-4PM.

**4th Judicial District Court**, PO Box 399, Watonga, OK 73772. 405-623-5970 (CST) 8:00AM-4:00PM. Felony, Misdemeanor, Civil, Eviction, Small Claims, Probate.

## Bryan County

**Real Estate Recording**, Bryan County Clerk, 402 West Evergreen, Durant, OK 74701. 405-924-2202 (CST) 8AM-Noon,1-5PM.

**19th Judicial District Court**, Courthouse 3rd Fl, Durant, OK 74701. 405-924-1446 (CST) 8:00AM-12:00PM,1:00PM-5:00PM. Felony, Misdemeanor, Civil, Eviction, Small Claims, Probate.

## Caddo County

**Real Estate Recording**, Caddo County Clerk, Southwest Second & Oklahoma, Anadarko, OK 73005. 405-247-6609 (CST) 8:30AM-4PM.

**6th Judicial District Court**, PO Box 10, Anadarko, OK 73005. 405-247-3393 (CST) 8:30AM-4:00PM. Felony, Misdemeanor, Civil, Eviction, Small Claims, Probate.

## Canadian County

**Real Estate Recording**, Canadian County Clerk, 201 North Choctaw, El Reno, OK 73036. 405-262-1070 (CST) 8AM-4:30PM.

**26th Judicial District Court**, PO Box 730, El Reno, OK 73036. 405-262-1070 (CST) 8:00AM-4:30PM. Felony, Misdemeanor, Civil, Eviction, Small Claims, Probate.

## Carter County

**Real Estate Recording**, Carter County Clerk, 1st & B SW, Ardmore, OK 73401. 405-223-8162 (CST) 8AM-5PM.

**20th Judicial District Court**, PO Box 37, Ardmore, OK 73402. 405-223-5253 (CST) 1:00PM-5:00PM. Felony, Misdemeanor, Civil, Eviction, Small Claims, Probate.

## Cherokee County

**Real Estate Recording**, Cherokee County Clerk, 213 West Delaware, Room 200, Tahlequah, OK 74464. 918-456-3171 (CST) 8AM-4:30PM (Recording hours 8AM-4PM).

**15th Judicial District Court**, 213 W. Delaware, Tahlequah, OK 74464. 918-456-0691 (CST) 8:00AM-4:30PM. Felony, Misdemeanor, Civil, Eviction, Small Claims, Probate.

## Choctaw County

**Real Estate Recording**, Choctaw County Clerk, Courthouse, 300 E. Duke, Hugo, OK 74743. 405-326-3778 (CST) 8:30AM-4:30PM.

**17th Judicial District Court**, 300 E. Duke, Hugo, OK 74743. 405-326-3241 (CST) 8:00AM-4:00PM. Felony, Misdemeanor, Civil, Eviction, Small Claims, Probate.

## Cimarron County

**Real Estate Recording**, Cimarron County Clerk, Courthouse Square, Boise City, OK 73933. 405-544-2251 (CST) 8AM-Noon,1-5PM.

**1st Judicial District Court**, PO Box 788, Boise City, OK 73933. 405-544-2221 (CST) 9:00Am-5:00PM. Felony, Misdemeanor, Civil, Eviction, Small Claims, Probate.

## Cleveland County

**Real Estate Recording**, Cleveland County Clerk, 201 South Jones, Room 204, Norman, OK 73069-6099. 405-366-0253 (CST) 8:30AM-4:30PM.

**21st Judicial District Court-Civil Branch**, 200 S. Peters, Norman, OK 73069. 405-544-6402 (CST) 8:00AM-5:00PM. Civil, Eviction, Small Claims, Probate.

**21st Judicial District Court-Criminal**, 200 S. Peters, Norman, OK 73069. (CST) 8:00AM-5:00PM. Felony, Misdemeanor.

## Coal County

**Real Estate Recording**, Coal County Clerk, 4 North Main, Suite 1, Coalgate, OK 74538. 405-927-2103 (CST) 8AM-5PM.

**25th Judicial District Court**, Courthouse, Coalgate, OK 74538. 405-927-2281 (CST) Felony, Misdemeanor, Civil, Eviction, Small Claims, Probate.

## Comanche County

**Real Estate Recording**, Comanche County Clerk, 315 SW 5th, Room 304, Lawton, OK 73501-4347. 405-355-5214 (CST) 8:30AM-5PM.

**5th Judicial District Court**, 315 SW 5th Street, Rm 504, Lawton, OK 73501-4390. 405-355-4017 (CST) 8:00AM-5:00PM. Felony, Misdemeanor, Civil, Eviction, Small Claims, Probate.

## Cotton County

**Real Estate Recording**, Cotton County Clerk, 301 North Broadway, Walters, OK 73572. 405-875-3026 (CST) 8AM-4:30PM.

**5th Judicial District Court**, 301 N. Broadway, Walters, OK 73572. 405-875-3029 (CST) 8:00AM-4:30PM. Felony, Misdemeanor, Civil, Eviction, Small Claims, Probate.

## Craig County

**Real Estate Recording**, Craig County Clerk, Courthouse, Vinita, OK 74301. 918-256-2507 (CST) 8:30AM-4:30PM.

**12th Judicial District Court**, 301 W. Canadian, Vinita, OK 74301. 918-256-6451 (CST) 8:30AM-4:30PM. Felony, Misdemeanor, Civil, Eviction, Small Claims, Probate.

## Creek County

**Real Estate Recording**, Creek County Clerk, 222 East Dewey, Courthouse 2nd Floor, Sapulpa, OK 74066-4208. 918-227-6306 (CST) 8AM-5PM.

**24th Judicial District Court**, PO Box 1410, Sapulpa, OK 74067. 918-227-2525 (CST) 8:00AM-5:00PM. Felony, Misdemeanor, Civil, Eviction, Small Claims, Probate.

## Custer County

**Real Estate Recording**, Custer County Clerk, 675 West "B" Street, Arapaho, OK 73620. 405-323-1221 (CST) 8AM-4PM.

**2nd Judicial District Court**, Box D, Arapaho, OK 73620. 405-323-3233 (CST) 8:00AM-4:00PM. Felony, Misdemeanor, Civil, Eviction, Small Claims, Probate.

## Delaware County

**Real Estate Recording**, Delaware County Clerk, 327 5th Street, Jay, OK 74346. 918-253-4520 (CST) 8AM-4:30PM.

**13th Judicial District Court**, Box 407, Jay, OK 74346. 918-253-4420 (CST) 8:30AM-4:30PM. Felony, Misdemeanor, Civil, Eviction, Small Claims, Probate.

## Dewey County

**Real Estate Recording**, Dewey County Clerk, Corner of Broadway & Ruble, Taloga, OK 73667. 405-328-5361 (CST) 8AM-4PM.

**4th Judicial District Court**, Box 278, Taloga, OK 73667. 405-328-5521 (CST) Felony, Misdemeanor, Civil, Eviction, Small Claims, Probate.

## Ellis County

**Real Estate Recording**, Ellis County Clerk, 100 Courthouse Square, Arnett, OK 73832. 405-885-7301 (CST) 8AM-Noon,1-5PM.

**2nd Judicial District Court**, Box 217, Arnett, OK 73832. 405-885-7255 (CST) 8:00AM-12:00PM, 1:00PM-5:00PM. Felony, Misdemeanor, Civil, Eviction, Small Claims, Probate.

## Garfield County

**Real Estate Recording**, Garfield County Clerk, 114 West Broadway, Enid, OK 73701. 405-237-0226 (CST) 8AM-4PM.

**4th Judicial District Court**, Box 3340, Enid, OK 73702. 405-237-0232 (CST) 8:00AM-4:30PM. Felony, Misdemeanor, Civil, Eviction, Small Claims, Probate.

## Garvin County

**Real Estate Recording**, Garvin County Clerk, 201 West Grant, Pauls Valley, OK 73075. 405-238-2772 (CST) 8:30AM-4:30PM.

**21st Judicial District Court**, PO Box 239, Pauls Valley, OK 73075. 405-238-5596 (CST) 8:30AM-4:30PM. Felony, Misdemeanor, Civil, Eviction, Small Claims, Probate.

## Grady County

**Real Estate Recording**, Grady County Clerk, 4th & Choctaw, Chickasha, OK 73018. 405-224-7388 (CST) 8AM-4:30PM.

**6th Judicial District Court**, PO Box 605, Chickasha, OK 73023. 405-224-7446 (CST) 8:00AM-4:30PM. Felony, Misdemeanor, Civil, Eviction, Small Claims, Probate.

## Grant County

**Real Estate Recording**, Grant County Clerk, 112 East Guthrie, Medford, OK 73759. 405-395-2274 (CST) 8AM-4:30PM.

**4th Judicial District Court**, 100 E Guthrie, Medford, OK 73759. 405-395-2828 (CST) 8AM-4:30PM. Felony, Misdemeanor, Civil, Eviction, Small Claims, Probate.

## Greer County

**Real Estate Recording**, Greer County Clerk, Courthouse Square, Mangum, OK 73554. 405-782-3664 (CST) 9AM-Noon,1-5PM.

**2nd Judicial District Court**, Courthouse, Mangum, OK 73554. 405-782-3665 (CST) 9:00AM-5:00PM. Felony, Misdemeanor, Civil, Eviction, Small Claims, Probate.

## Harmon County

**Real Estate Recording**, Harmon County Clerk, Courthouse, Hollis, OK 73550. 405-688-3658 (CST)

**2nd Judicial District Court**, 114 W. Hollis, Hollis, OK 73550. 405-688-3617 (CST) 8:00AM-5:00PM. Felony, Misdemeanor, Civil, Eviction, Small Claims, Probate.

## Harper County

**Real Estate Recording**, Harper County Clerk, 311 SE First Street, Buffalo, OK 73834. 405-735-2012 (CST) 9AM-5PM.

**1st Judicial District Court**, Box 347, Buffalo, OK 73834. 405-735-2010 (CST) 9:00AM-5:00PM. Felony, Misdemeanor, Civil, Eviction, Small Claims, Probate.

## Haskell County

**Real Estate Recording**, Haskell County Clerk, 202 East Main, Courthouse, Stigler, OK 74462. 918-967-2884 (CST) 8AM-4:30PM.

**16th Judicial District Court**, 202 E. Main, Stigler, OK 74462. 918-967-3323 (CST) 8:00AM-4:30PM. Felony, Misdemeanor, Civil, Eviction, Small Claims, Probate.

## Hughes County

**Real Estate Recording**, Hughes County Clerk, 200 North Broadway ST. #5, Holdenville, OK 74848-3417. 405-379-5487 (CST) 8AM-4:30PM.

**22nd Judicial District Court**, Box 32, Holdenville, OK 74848. 405-379-3384 (CST) 8:00AM-4:30PM. Felony, Misdemeanor, Civil, Eviction, Small Claims, Probate.

## Jackson County

**Real Estate Recording**, Jackson County Clerk, Main & Broadway, Courthouse-Room 203, Altus, OK 73522. 405-482-4070 (CST) 9AM-5PM.

**3rd Judicial District Court**, 101 N. Main, Rm. 303, Altus, OK 73521. 405-482-0448 (CST) 9:00AM-5:00PM. Felony, Misdemeanor, Civil, Eviction, Small Claims, Probate.

## Jefferson County

**Real Estate Recording**, Jefferson County Clerk, 220 North Main, Courthouse - Room 103, Waurika, OK 73573. 405-228-2029 (CST) 8AM-4PM.

**5th Judicial District Court**, 220 N. Main, Waurika, OK 73573. 405-228-2961 (CST) 8:00AM-4:00PM. Felony, Misdemeanor, Civil, Eviction, Small Claims, Probate.

## Johnston County

**Real Estate Recording**, Johnston County Clerk, 414 West Main, Room 101, Tishomingo, OK 73460. 405-371-3184 (CST) 8:30AM-4:30PM.

**20th Judicial District Court**, 414 W. 9th Suite 201, Tishomingo, OK 73460. 405-371-3281 (CST) 8:30AM-4:30PM. Felony, Misdemeanor, Civil, Eviction, Small Claims, Probate.

## Kay County

**Real Estate Recording**, Kay County Clerk, Courthouse, Newkirk, OK 74647. 405-362-2537 (CST) 8AM-4:30PM.

**8th Judicial District Court**, Box 428, Newkirk, OK 74647. 405-362-3350 (CST) 8:00AM-4:30PM. Felony, Misdemeanor, Civil, Eviction, Small Claims, Probate.

## Kingfisher County

**Real Estate Recording**, Kingfisher County Clerk, 101 South Main, Room #3, Courthouse, Kingfisher, OK 73750. 405-375-3887 (CST) 8AM-4:30PM.

**4th Judicial District Court**, Box 328, Kingfisher, OK 73750. 405-375-3813 (CST) 8:30AM-4:30PM. Felony, Misdemeanor, Civil, Eviction, Small Claims, Probate.

## Kiowa County

**Real Estate Recording**, Kiowa County Clerk, 316 South Main, Hobart, OK 73651. 405-726-5286 (CST) 9AM-5PM.

**3rd Judicial District Court**, Box 854, Hobart, OK 73651. 405-726-5125 (CST) 9:00AM-5:00PM. Felony, Misdemeanor, Civil, Eviction, Small Claims, Probate.

## Latimer County

**Real Estate Recording**, Latimer County Clerk, 109 North Central, Room 103, Wilburton, OK 74578. 918-465-3543 (CST) 8AM-4:30PM.

**16th Judicial District Court**, 109 N. Central, Rm 200, Wilburton, OK 74578. 918-465-2011 (CST) Felony, Misdemeanor, Civil, Eviction, Small Claims, Probate.

## Le Flore County

**Real Estate Recording**, Le Flore County Clerk, 100 South Broadway, Poteau, OK 74953. 918-647-9151 (CST) 8AM-5PM.

**16th Judicial District Court**, 100 S. Broadway, Rm 14, Poteau, OK 74953. 918-647-3181 (CST) 8:00AM-5:00PM. Felony, Misdemeanor, Civil, Eviction, Small Claims, Probate.

## Lincoln County

**Real Estate Recording**, Lincoln County Clerk, Courthouse, 800 Manvel Ave., Chandler, OK 74834. 405-258-1264 (CST) 8:30AM-4:30PM.

**23rd Judicial District Court**, PO Box 307, Chandler, OK 74834. 405-258-1309 (CST) 8:00AM-4:30PM. Felony, Misdemeanor, Civil, Eviction, Small Claims, Probate.

## Logan County

**Real Estate Recording**, Logan County Clerk, 301 East Harrison, Suite 102, Guthrie, OK 73044-4999. 405-282-0266 (CST) 8:30AM-4:30PM.

**9th Judicial District Court**, 301 E. Harrison, Guthrie, OK 73044. 405-282-0123 (CST) 8:30AM-4:30PM. Felony, Misdemeanor, Civil, Eviction, Small Claims, Probate.

## Love County

**Real Estate Recording**, Love County Clerk, 405 West Main, Room 203, Marietta, OK 73448. 405-276-3059 (CST) 8AM-Noon, 12:30-4:30PM.

**20th Judicial District Court**, 405 W. Main, Marietta, OK 73448. 405-276-2235 (CST) 8:00AM-4:30PM. Felony, Misdemeanor, Civil, Eviction, Small Claims, Probate.

## Major County

**Real Estate Recording**, Major County Clerk, 9th & Broadway, Fairview, OK 73737. 405-227-4732 (CST) 8:30AM-4:30PM.

**4th Judicial District Court**, 500 E Broadway, Fairview, OK 73737. 405-227-4690 (CST)

8:30AM-4:30PM. Felony, Misdemeanor, Civil, Eviction, Small Claims, Probate.

## Marshall County

**Real Estate Recording**, Marshall County Clerk, Marshall County Courthouse, Room 101, Madill, OK 73446. 405-795-3220 (CST) 8:30AM-Noon, 12:30-5PM.

**20th Judicial District Court**, Box 58, Madill, OK 73446. 405-795-3278 (CST) 8:30AM-5:00PM. Felony, Misdemeanor, Civil, Eviction, Small Claims, Probate.

## Mayes County

**Real Estate Recording**, Mayes County Clerk, Northeast 1st Street, Pryor, OK 74361. 918-825-2426 (CST) 9AM-5PM.

**12th Judicial District Court**, Box 867, Pryor, OK 74362. 918-825-2185 (CST) 8:30AM-4:30PM. Felony, Misdemeanor, Civil, Eviction, Small Claims, Probate.

## McClain County

**Real Estate Recording**, McClain County Clerk, 2nd & Washington, Purcell, OK 73080. 405-527-3360 (CST) 8AM-4:30PM.

**21st Judicial District Court**, Box 631, Purcell, OK 73080. 405-527-3221 (CST) 8:00AM-4:30PM. Felony, Misdemeanor, Civil, Eviction, Small Claims, Probate.

## McCurtain County

**Real Estate Recording**, McCurtain County Clerk, 108 North Central, Idabel, OK 74745. 405-286-2370 (CST) 8AM-4PM.

**17th Judicial District Court**, Box 1378, Idabel, OK 74745. 405-286-3693 (CST) 8:00AM-4:00PM. Felony, Misdemeanor, Civil, Eviction, Small Claims, Probate.

## McIntosh County

**Real Estate Recording**, McIntosh County Clerk, 110 North 1st Street, Eufaula, OK 74432. 918-689-2741 (CST) 8AM-4PM.

**18th Judicial District Court**, Box 426, Eufaula, OK 74432. 918-689-2282 (CST) 8:00AM-4:00PM. Felony, Misdemeanor, Civil, Eviction, Small Claims, Probate.

## Murray County

**Real Estate Recording**, Murray County Clerk, 10th & Wyandotte, Sulphur, OK 73086. 405-622-3920 (CST) 7:30AM-Noon, 1-4:30PM.

**20th Judicial District Court**, Box 578, Sulphur, OK 73086. 405-622-3223 (CST) 8AM-4:30PM, closed for lunch. Felony, Misdemeanor, Civil, Eviction, Small Claims, Probate.

## Muskogee County

**Real Estate Recording**, Muskogee County Clerk, Corner of State & Court Streets, Muskogee, OK 74401. 918-682-7781 (CST) 8AM-4:30PM.

**15th Judicial District Court**, Box 1350, Muskogee, OK 74402. 918-682-7873 (CST) 8:00AM-4:30PM. Felony, Misdemeanor, Civil, Eviction, Small Claims, Probate.

## Noble County

**Real Estate Recording**, Noble County Clerk, 300 Courthouse Dr., Courthouse, Box 11, Perry, OK 73077. 405-336-2141 (CST) 8AM-4PM.

**8th Judicial District Court**, 300 Courthouse Dr, Box 14, Perry, OK 73077. 405-336-5187 (CST) 8:00AM-4:30PM. Felony, Misdemeanor, Civil, Eviction, Small Claims, Probate.

## Nowata County

**Real Estate Recording**, Nowata County Clerk, 229 North Maple, Nowata, OK 74048. 918-273-2480 (CST) 8AM-4:30PM.

**11th Judicial District Court**, 229 N. Maple, Nowata, OK 74048. 918-273-0127 (CST) 8:00AM-4:30PM. Felony, Misdemeanor, Civil, Eviction, Small Claims, Probate.

## Okfuskee County

**Real Estate Recording**, Okfuskee County Clerk, 3rd & Atlanta, Courthouse, Okemah, OK 74859. 918-623-1724 (CST) 8AM-4PM.

**24th Judicial District Court**, Box 30, Okemah, OK 74859. 918-623-0525 (CST) 8:30AM-4:30PM. Felony, Misdemeanor, Civil, Eviction, Small Claims, Probate.

## Oklahoma County

**Real Estate Recording**, Oklahoma County Clerk, 320 Robert S. Kerr Avenue, Courthouse - Room 107, Oklahoma City, OK 73102. 405-278-1521 (CST) 8AM-5PM.

**7th Judicial District Court**, 320 Robert S. Kerr St, Oklahoma City, OK 73102. 405-236-2727 (CST) 8:30AM-4:30PM. Felony, Misdemeanor, Civil, Eviction, Small Claims, Probate.

## Okmulgee County

**Real Estate Recording**, Okmulgee County Clerk, 7th & Seminole, Courthouse, Okmulgee, OK 74447. 918-756-0788 (CST) 8AM-4:30PM.

**24th Judicial District Court-Henryetta Branch**, 114 S 4th, Henryetta, OK 74437. 918-652-7142 (CST) 8:30AM-4:30PM. Felony, Misdemeanor, Civil, Eviction, Small Claims, Probate.

**24th Judicial District Court-Okmulgee Branch**, Courthouse, Okmulgee, OK 74447. 918-756-3042 (CST) 8AM-4:30PM. Felony, Misdemeanor, Civil, Eviction, Small Claims, Probate.

## Osage County

**Real Estate Recording**, Osage County Clerk, 6th & Grandview, Courthouse, Pawhuska, OK 74056. 918-287-3136 (CST) 8:30AM-5PM.

**10th Judicial District Court**, County Courthouse, Pawhuska, OK 74056. 918-287-4104 (CST) 9:00AM-5:00PM. Felony, Misdemeanor, Civil, Eviction, Small Claims, Probate.

## Ottawa County

**Real Estate Recording**, Ottawa County Clerk, 102 E. Central, Suite 203, Miami, OK 74354-7043. 918-542-3332 (CST) 9AM-Noon,1-5PM.

**13th Judicial District Court**, 102 E Central Ave, Suite 300, Miami, OK 74354. 918-542-2801 (CST) 9:00AM-5:00PM. Felony, Misdemeanor, Civil, Eviction, Small Claims, Probate.

## Pawnee County

**Real Estate Recording**, Pawnee County Clerk, Courthouse, Room 202, 500 Harrison St., Pawnee, OK 74058. 918-762-2732 (CST) 8AM-4:30PM.

**14th Judicial District Court**, Courthouse, 500 Harrison St, Pawnee, OK 74058. 918-762-2547 (CST) Felony, Misdemeanor, Civil, Eviction, Small Claims, Probate.

## Payne County

**Real Estate Recording**, Payne County Clerk, 606 South Husband Street, Room 209, Stillwater, OK 74074. 405-747-8310 (CST) 8AM-5PM.

**9th Judicial District Court**, County Courthouse, Stillwater, OK 74074. 405-372-4774 (CST) 8:00AM-5:00PM. Felony, Misdemeanor, Civil, Eviction, Small Claims, Probate.

## Pittsburg County

**Real Estate Recording**, Pittsburg County Clerk, 115 East Carl Albert Parkway, McAlester, OK 74501. 918-423-6865 (CST) 8AM-5PM.

**18th Judicial District Court**, Box 460, McAlester, OK 74502. 918-423-4859 (CST) Felony, Misdemeanor, Civil, Eviction, Small Claims, Probate.

## Pontotoc County

**Real Estate Recording**, Pontotoc County Clerk, 13th & Broadway, Ada, OK 74820. 405-332-1425 (CST) 8AM-5PM.

**22nd Judicial District Court**, Box 427, Ada, OK 74820. 405-332-5763 (CST) 8:00AM-5:00PM. Felony, Misdemeanor, Civil, Eviction, Small Claims, Probate.

## Pottawatomie County

**Real Estate Recording**, Pottawatomie County Clerk, 325 North Broadway, Shawnee, OK 74801. 405-273-8222 (CST) 8:30AM-5PM.

**23rd Judicial District Court**, 325 N. Broadway, Shawnee, OK 74801. 405-273-3624 (CST) 8:30AM-Noon. Felony, Misdemeanor, Civil, Eviction, Small Claims, Probate.

## Pushmataha County

**Real Estate Recording**, Pushmataha County Clerk, 203 Southwest Third, Antlers, OK 74523. 405-298-3626 (CST)

**17th Judicial District Court**, Courthouse, Antlers, OK 74523. 405-298-2274 (CST) 8:00AM-4:30PM. Felony, Misdemeanor, Civil, Eviction, Small Claims, Probate.

## Roger Mills County

**Real Estate Recording**, Roger Mills County Clerk, Broadway & L.L. Males Avenue, Cheyenne, OK 73628. 405-497-3395 (CST) 9AM-4:30PM.

**2nd Judicial District Court**, Box 409, Cheyenne, OK 73628. 405-497-3361 (CST) 8:00AM-12:00PM, 1:00AM-4:30PM. Felony, Misdemeanor, Civil, Eviction, Small Claims, Probate.

## Rogers County

**Real Estate Recording**, Rogers County Clerk, 219 South Missouri, Claremore, OK 74017. 918-341-1860 (CST) 8AM-5PM.

**12th Judicial District Court**, Box 839, Claremore, OK 74018. 918-341-5711 (CST) 8:00AM-4:30PM. Felony, Misdemeanor, Civil, Eviction, Small Claims, Probate.

## Seminole County

**Real Estate Recording**, Seminole County Clerk, 100 South Wewoka, Courthouse, Wewoka, OK 74884. 405-257-2501 (CST) 8AM-4PM.

**22nd Judicial District Court-Seminole Branch**, Box 1320, Seminole, OK 74868. 405-382-3424 (CST) 8:00AM-12:00PM, 1:00PM-4:00PM. Felony, Misdemeanor, Civil, Eviction, Small Claims, Probate.

**22nd Judicial District Court-Wewoka Branch**, Box 130, Wewoka, OK 74884. 405-257-6236 (CST) 8:00AM-4:00PM. Felony, Misdemeanor, Civil, Eviction, Small Claims, Probate.

## Sequoyah County

**Real Estate Recording**, Sequoyah County Clerk, 120 East Chickasaw, Sallisaw, OK 74955. 918-775-4516 (CST) 8AM-4PM.

**15th Judicial District Court**, Courthouse Room 10, Sallisaw, OK 74955. 918-775-4411 (CST) 8AM-4PM. Felony, Misdemeanor, Civil, Eviction, Small Claims, Probate.

## Stephens County

**Real Estate Recording**, Stephens County Clerk, 11th & Willow, Courthouse, Duncan, OK 73533. 405-255-0977 (CST) 8:30AM-4:30PM.

**5th Judicial District Court**, County Courthouse, Duncan, OK 73533. 405-255-8460 (CST) 8:30AM-4:30PM. Felony, Misdemeanor, Civil, Eviction, Small Claims, Probate.

## Texas County

**Real Estate Recording**, Texas County Clerk, 319 North Main, Guymon, OK 73942. 405-338-3141 (CST) 8AM-5PM.

**1st Judicial District Court**, Box 1081, Guymon, OK 73942. 405-338-3003 (CST) 9:00AM-5:00PM. Felony, Misdemeanor, Civil, Eviction, Small Claims, Probate.

## Tillman County

**Real Estate Recording**, Tillman County Clerk, 10th & Gladstone, Courthouse, Frederick, OK 73542. 405-335-3421 (CST) 8:30AM-Noon, 1PM-5PM.

**3rd Judicial District Court**, Box 116, Frederick, OK 73542. 405-335-3023 (CST) 9:00AM-5:00PM. Felony, Misdemeanor, Civil, Eviction, Small Claims, Probate.

## Tulsa County

**Real Estate Recording**, Tulsa County Clerk, 500 South Denver Avenue, County Admin. Bldg.-Room 112, Tulsa, OK 74103-3832. 918-596-5801 (CST) 8:30AM-5PM.

**14th Judicial District Court**, 500 S. Denver, Tulsa, OK 74103-3832. 918-596-5000 (CST) 8:30AM-5:00PM. Felony, Misdemeanor, Civil, Eviction, Small Claims, Probate.

## Wagoner County

**Real Estate Recording**, Wagoner County Clerk, 307 East Cherokee, Wagoner, OK 74467. 918-485-2216 (CST) 8AM-4:45PM.

**15th Judicial District Court**, Box 249, Wagoner, OK 74477. 918-485-4508 (CST) 8:00AM-4:30PM. Felony, Misdemeanor, Civil, Eviction, Small Claims, Probate.

## Washington County

**Real Estate Recording**, Washington County Clerk, 420 South Johnstone, Room 102, Bartlesville, OK 74003. 918-337-2840 (CST) 8AM-5PM.

**11th Judicial District Court**, Courthouse, Rm 212, Bartlesville, OK 74003. 918-337-2870 (CST) 8:00AM-5:00PM. Felony, Misdemeanor, Civil, Eviction, Small Claims, Probate.

## Washita County

**Real Estate Recording**, Washita County Clerk, 100 East Main, Cordell, OK 73632. 405-832-3548 (CST) 8AM-4PM.

**3rd Judicial District Court**, Box 397, Cordell, OK 73632,. 405-832-3836 (CST) 8:00AM-4:00PM. Felony, Misdemeanor, Civil, Eviction, Small Claims, Probate.

## Woods County

**Real Estate Recording**, Woods County Clerk, Courthouse, 407 Government Street, Alva, OK 73717. 405-327-0998 (CST) 9AM-5PM.

**4th Judicial District Court**, Box 924, Alva, OK 73717. 405-327-3119 (CST) 9:00AM-5:00PM. Felony, Misdemeanor, Civil, Eviction, Small Claims, Probate.

## Woodward County

**Real Estate Recording**, Woodward County Clerk, 1600 Main Street, Woodward, OK 73801-3051. 405-254-6800 (CST) 9AM-5PM.

**4th Judicial District Court**, 1600 Main, Woodward, OK 73801. 405-256-3413 (CST) 9AM-5PM. Felony, Misdemeanor, Civil, Eviction, Small Claims, Probate.

# Oregon

## Baker County

**Real Estate Recording**, Baker County Clerk, 1995 Third Street, Baker, OR 97814-3398. 503-523-8207 (PST) 8AM-Noon,1-5PM.

**Circuit Court**, 1995 3rd St., Baker City, OR 97814. 503-523-6305 (PST) 8AM-5PM, Closed 12-1. Felony, Civil Actions Over $2,500, Probate.

## Benton County

**Real Estate Recording**, Benton County Recorder, 120 NW 4th Street, Corvallis, OR 97330. 503-757-6831 (PST) 8AM-Noon, 1PM-5PM (Recording Hours: 9AM-Noon, 1-4PM).

**Circuit & District Court**, Box 1870, Corvallis, OR 97339. 503-757-6828 (PST) Felony, Misdemeanor, Civil Actions Over $2,500, Eviction, Small Claims, Probate.

## Clackamas County

**Real Estate Recording**, Clackamas County Clerk, 807 Main Street, Room 104, Oregon City, OR 97045. 503-655-8551 (PST) 8:30AM-5PM M,W,Th,F; 9:30AM-5PM T.

**Circuit & District Court**, 807 Main St., Oregon City, OR 97045. 503-655-8447 (PST) 8:30AM-5PM. Felony, Misdemeanor, Civil Actions Over $2,500, Eviction, Small Claims, Probate.

## Clatsop County

**Real Estate Recording**, Clatsop County Clerk, 749 Commercial, Astoria, OR 97103. 503-325-8511 (PST) 8:30AM-5PM.

**Circuit Court**, Box 835, Astoria, OR 97103. 503-325-8583 (PST) 8AM-5PM. Felony, Civil Actions Over $10,000, Probate.

**District Court**, Box 659, Astoria, OR 97103. 503-325-8536 (PST) 8AM-5PM. Misdemeanor, Civil Actions Under $10,000, Eviction, Small Claims.

## Columbia County

**Real Estate Recording**, Columbia County Clerk, Courthouse, St. Helens, OR 97051-2041. 503-397-3796 (PST) 8:30AM-5PM.

**Circuit & District Court**, Columbia County Courthouse, St. Helens, OR 97051. 503-397-2327 (PST) 8AM-5PM. Felony, Civil Actions Over $2,500, Eviction, Small Claims, Probate.

## Coos County

**Real Estate Recording**, Coos County Clerk, Courthouse, 2nd and Baxter, Coquille, OR 97423-1899. 503-396-3121 (PST) 8AM-5PM (Closed to public: 8AM-10AM & Noon-1PM).

**Circuit & District Court**, Courthouse, Coquille, OR 97423. 503-396-3121 (PST) 8AM-5PM, Closed 12-1. Felony, Misdemeanor, Civil Actions Over $2,500, Eviction, Small Claims, Probate.

## Crook County

**Real Estate Recording**, Crook County Clerk, 300 East Third, Prineville, OR 97754. 503-447-6553 (PST) 8:30AM-5PM.

**Circuit & District Court**, Courthouse, Prineville, OR 97754. 503-447-6541 (PST) 8AM-5PM. Felony, Misdemeanor, Civil Actions Over $2,500, Eviction, Small Claims, Probate.

## Curry County

**Real Estate Recording**, Curry County Clerk, 450 North Ellensburg, Gold Beach, OR 97444. 503-247-7011 (PST) X209 8:30AM-Noon, 1-5PM.

**Circuit & District Court**, Box H, Gold Beach, OR 97444. 503-247-4511 (PST) 8AM-5PM. Felony, Misdemeanor, Civil Actions Over $2,500, Eviction, Small Claims, Probate.

## Deschutes County

**Real Estate Recording**, Deschutes County Clerk, 1130 N.W. Harriman, Bend, OR 97701. 503-388-6549 (PST) 8AM-5PM.

**Circuit & District Court**, 1164 NW Bond, Bend, OR 97701. 503-388-5300 (PST) 8AM-5PM. Felony, Misdemeanor, Civil Actions Over $2,500, Eviction, Small Claims, Probate.

## Douglas County

**Real Estate Recording**, Douglas County Clerk, 1036 SE Douglas, Room 221, Roseburg, OR 97470. 503-440-4322 (PST) 8AM-4PM.

**Circuit & District Court**, Rm. 202, Roseburg, OR 97470. 503-440-4363 (PST) 8AM-5PM. Felony, Misdemeanor, Civil Actions Over $2,500, Eviction, Small Claims, Probate.

## Gilliam County

**Real Estate Recording**, Gilliam County Clerk, 221 South Oregon Street, Condon, OR 97823. 503-384-2311 (PST) 8:30AM-Noon, 1-5PM.

**Circuit Court**, Box 622, Condon, OR 97823. 503-384-3572 (PST) 1PM-5PM. Felony, Misdemeanor, Civil Actions Over $2,500.

**County Court**, 221 S Oregon, Condon, OR 97823. 503-384-2311 (PST) Probate.

## Grant County

**Real Estate Recording**, Grant County Clerk, 200 South Humbolt, Canyon City, OR 97820. 503-575-1675 (PST) 8AM-5PM.

**Circuit Court**, Box 159, Canyon City, OR 97820. 503-575-1438 (PST) 8AM-5PM, Closed 12-1. Felony, Civil Actions Over $2,500.

**County Court**, PO Box 39, Canyon City, OR 97820. 503-575-1675 (PST) Probate.

## Harney County

**Real Estate Recording**, Harney County Clerk, 450 North Buena Vista, Burns, OR 97720. 503-573-6641 (PST) 8:30AM-Noon, 1-5PM.

**Circuit Court**, 450 N. Buena Vista, Burns, OR 97720. 503-573-5207 (PST) 8AM-5PM. Felony, Misdemeanor, Civil Actions Over $2,500.

**County Court**, 450 N Buena Vista, Burns, OR 97720. 503-573-6641 (PST) Probate.

## Hood River County

**Real Estate Recording**, Hood River County Recorder, 309 State Street, Hood River, OR 97031-2093. 503-386-1442 (PST) 8AM-5PM (Recording 9AM-4PM).

**Circuit & District Court**, 309 State St., Hood River, OR 97031. 503-386-1862 (PST) 8AM-5PM, Closed 12-1. Felony, Misdemeanor, Civil Actions Over $2,500, Eviction, Small Claims, Probate.

## Jackson County

**Real Estate Recording**, Jackson County Clerk, 10 South Oakdale, Medford, OR 97501. 503-776-7258 (PST) 8AM-5PM.

**Circuit & District Court**, 100 S. Oakdale, Medford, OR 97501. 503-776-7243 (PST) 8AM-5PM. Felony, Misdemeanor, Civil Actions Over $2,500, Eviction, Small Claims, Probate.

## Jefferson County

**Real Estate Recording**, Jefferson County Clerk, 75 S.E. C Street, Madras, OR 97741. 503-475-4451 (PST) 8:30AM-5PM.

**Circuit & District Court**, 75 SE C St., Madras, OR 97741-1794. 503-475-3317 (PST) 8AM-5PM. Felony, Misdemeanor, Civil Actions Over $2,500, Eviction, Small Claims, Probate.

## Josephine County

**Real Estate Recording**, Josephine County Clerk, Courthouse, 6 & C Streets, Grants Pass, OR 97526. 503-474-5240 (PST) 9AM-5PM.

**Circuit & District Court**, Josephine County Courthouse, Rm 254, Grants Pass, OR 97526. 503-476-2309 (PST) 8AM-5PM. Felony, Misdemeanor, Civil Actions Over $2,500, Eviction, Small Claims, Probate.

## Klamath County

**Real Estate Recording**, Klamath County Clerk, 830 Klamath Ave., Klamath Falls, OR 97601. 503-883-5134 (PST) 8:30AM-5PM; Recording Hours 9AM-Noon, 1-4PM.

**Circuit & District Court**, 317 S 7th St, 2nd Fl, Klamath Falls, OR 97601. 503-883-5504 (PST) 8:30AM-5PM. Felony, Misdemeanor, Civil Actions Over $2,500, Eviction, Small Claims, Probate.

## Lake County

**Real Estate Recording**, Lake County Clerk, 513 Center Street, Lakeview, OR 97630-1539. 503-947-6006 (PST) 8AM-5PM.

**Circuit & District Court**, 513 Center St., Lakeview, OR 97630. 503-947-6051 (PST) 8AM-5PM. Felony, Misdemeanor, Civil Actions Over $2,500, Eviction, Small Claims, Probate.

## Lane County

**Real Estate Recording**, Deeds & Records, 125 East 8th Avenue, Eugene, OR 97401. 503-687-3654 (PST) 8AM-5PM; Recording 9AM-4PM.

**Circuit & District Court**, 125 E. 8th Ave., Eugene, OR 97401. 503-687-4020 (PST) 8AM-5PM. Felony, Misdemeanor, Civil Actions Over $2,500, Eviction, Small Claims, Probate.

## Lincoln County

**Real Estate Recording**, Lincoln County Clerk, 225 West Olive Street, Room 201, Newport, OR 97365-3869. 503-265-4121 (PST) 8:30AM-5PM.

**Circuit & District Court**, PO Box 100, Newport, OR 97365. 503-265-4236 (PST) 8AM-5PM. Felony, Misdemeanor, Civil Actions Over $2,500, Eviction, Small Claims, Probate.

## Linn County

**Real Estate Recording**, Linn County Recorder, 300 SW 4th St., Courthouse Room 207, Albany, OR 97321. 503-967-3829 (PST) 8:30AM-5PM (Recording ends at 4PM).

**Circuit & District Court**, PO Box 1749, Albany, OR 97321. 503-967-3845 (PST) 8AM-5PM. Felony, Misdemeanor, Civil Actions Over $2,500, Eviction, Small Claims, Probate.

## Malheur County

**Real Estate Recording**, Malheur County Clerk, 251 B Street West, Vale, OR 97918. 503-473-5151 (MST) 8:30AM-5PM.

**Circuit & District Court**, 251 B St West, Vale, OR 97918. 503-473-5171 (MST) 8AM-5PM. Felony, Misdemeanor, Civil Actions Over $2,500, Eviction, Small Claims.

**County Court**, 251 B St W, Courthouse Box 4, Vale, OR 97918. 503-473-5151 (MST) Probate.

## Marion County

**Real Estate Recording**, Marion County Clerk, 100 High Street NE, Room 110, Salem, OR 97301. 503-588-5225 (PST) 8:30AM-5PM.

**Circuit & District Court**, 100 High St NE, 1st Floor, Salem, OR 97301. 503-588-5101 (PST) 8AM-5PM. Felony, Misdemeanor, Civil Actions Over $2,500, Eviction, Small Claims, Probate.

## Morrow County

**Real Estate Recording**, Morrow County Clerk, 100 Court Street, Heppner, OR 97836. 503-676-9061 (PST) 8AM-5PM.

**Circuit & District Court**, PO Box 609, Heppner, OR 97836. 503-676-5264 (PST) 8AM-4:45PM, Closed 12-1. Felony, Misdemeanor, Civil Actions Over $2,500, Eviction, Small Claims, Probate.

## Multnomah County

**Real Estate Recording**, Multnomah County Recorder, 610 S.W. Alder, Room 300, Portland, OR 97205-3603. 503-248-3034 (PST) 8AM-5PM; Phone hours: 9AM-4:30PM.

**Circuit Court**, 1021 SW 4th Ave, Rm 131, Portland, OR 97204. 503-248-3003 (PST) 8AM-5PM. Felony, Misdemeanor, Civil Actions Over $10,000, Probate.

**District Court**, 1021 SW 4th Ave, Rm 210, Portland, OR 97204. 503-248-3022 (PST) 8:30AM-5PM. Misdemeanor, Civil Actions Under $10,000, Eviction, Small Claims.

## Polk County

**Real Estate Recording**, Polk County Clerk, Courthouse, Room 201, Dallas, OR 97338-3179. 503-623-9217 (PST) 8AM-5PM.

**Circuit & District Court**, Polk County Courthouse, Rm 301, Dallas, OR 97338. 503-623-3154 (PST) 8AM-5PM, Closed 12-1. Felony, Misdemeanor, Civil Actions Over $2,500, Eviction, Small Claims, Probate.

## Sherman County

**Real Estate Recording**, Sherman County Clerk, 500 Court Street, Moro, OR 97039. 503-565-3606 (PST) 8AM-5PM.

**Circuit Court**, PO Box 402, Moro, OR 97039. 503-565-3650 (PST) 8AM-5PM. Felony, Misdemeanor, Civil Actions Over $2,500.

**County Court**, PO Box 365, Moro, OR 97039. 503-565-3606 (PST) 8AM-5PM. Probate.

## Tillamook County

**Real Estate Recording**, Tillamook County Clerk, 201 Laurel Avenue, Tillamook, OR 97141. 503-842-3402 (PST) 8AM-5PM.

**Circuit & District Court**, 201 Laurel Ave, Tillamook, OR 97141. 503-842-8014 (PST) 8AM-5PM. Felony, Misdemeanor, Civil Actions Over $2,500, Eviction, Small Claims, Probate.

## Umatilla County

**Real Estate Recording**, Umatilla County Clerk, 216 SE 4th Street, Room 106, Pendleton, OR 97801. 503-276-7111 (PST) 8AM-5PM; Recording Hours 9AM-4PM.

**Circuit & District Court**, PO Box 1307, Pendleton, OR 97801. 503-278-0341 (PST) 8AM-5PM. Felony, Misdemeanor, Civil Actions Over $2,500, Eviction, Small Claims, Probate.

## Union County

**Real Estate Recording**, Union County Clerk, 1100 L Avenue, La Grande, OR 97850. 503-963-1006 (PST) 8:30AM-5PM (Recording ends at 4:30PM).

**Circuit & District Court**, PO Box 2950, La Grande, OR 97850. 503-963-2816 (PST) 8AM-5PM. Felony, Misdemeanor, Civil Actions Over $2,500, Eviction, Small Claims, Probate.

## Wallowa County

**Real Estate Recording**, Wallowa County Clerk, 101 South River, Room 100 Door16, Enterprise, OR 97828. 503-426-4543 (PST) X16 8:30AM-5PM.

**Circuit & District Court**, 101 S River St, Rm 204, Enterprise, OR 97828. 503-426-4991 (PST) 8AM-5PM. Felony, Misdemeanor, Civil Actions Over $2,500, Eviction, Small Claims, Probate.

## Wasco County

**Real Estate Recording**, Wasco County Clerk, 511 Washington St., Courthouse, The Dalles, OR 97058-2237. 503-296-6159 (PST) 8:30AM-5PM.

**Circuit & District Court**, PO Box 821, The Dalles, OR 97058. 503-296-3196 (PST) 8AM-5PM. Felony, Misdemeanor, Civil Actions Over $2,500, Eviction, Small Claims, Probate.

## Washington County

**Real Estate Recording**, Washington County Clerk, Public Services Building, 155 North First Avenue Suite 130, Hillsboro, OR 97124. 503-648-8752 (PST) 8:30AM-4:30PM.

**Circuit & District Court**, 145 NE 2nd, Hillsboro, OR 97124. 503-648-8888 (PST) 8AM-5PM. Felony, Misdemeanor, Civil Actions Over $2,500, Eviction, Small Claims, Probate.

## Wheeler County

**Real Estate Recording**, Wheeler County Clerk, 701 Adams Street, Room204, Fossil, OR 97830. 503-763-2400 (PST) 8:30AM-Noon, 1-5PM.

**Circuit Court**, Courthouse, Fossil, OR 97830. 503-763-2541 (PST) 8:30AM-11:30AM. Felony, Misdemeanor, Civil Actions Over $2,500.

**County Court**, PO Box 327, Fossil, OR 97830. 503-763-2400 (PST) Probate.

## Yamhill County

**Real Estate Recording**, Yamhill County Clerk, 535 East 5th Street, McMinnville, OR 97128-4593. 503-434-7518 (PST) 9AM-5PM.

**Circuit & District Court**, 5th & Evans St, McMinnville, OR 97128. 503-472-9371 (PST) Felony, Misdemeanor, Civil Actions Over $2,500, Eviction, Small Claims, Probate.

# Pennsylvania

## Adams County

**Court of Common Pleas-Civil**, 111-117 Baltimore St Rm 103, Gettysburg, PA 17325. 717-334-6781 (EST) 8AM-4:30PM. Civil, Eviction, Small Claims.

**Court of Common Pleas-Criminal**, 111-117 Baltimore St, Gettysburg, PA 17325. 717-334-6781 (EST) 8AM-4:30PM. Felony, Misdemeanor.

**Register in Wills**, 111-117 Baltimore St Rm 102, Gettysburg, PA 17325. 717-334-6781 (EST) 8AM-4:30PM. Probate.

## Adams County Recorder

**Real Estate Recording**, Adams County Recorder of Deeds, 111-117 Baltimore Street, County Courthouse Room 102, Gettysburg, PA 17325. 717-334-6781 (EST) 8AM-4:30PM.

## Allegheny County

**Court of Common Pleas-Civil**, City County Bldg, 414 Grant St, Pittsburgh, PA 15219. 412-355-4213 (EST) 8:30AM-4:30PM. Civil, Eviction, Small Claims.

**Court of Common Pleas-Criminal**, Grant St, Rm 114 Courthouse, Pittsburgh, PA 15219. 412-355-5378 (EST) 8:30AM-4:30PM. Felony, Misdemeanor.

**Register in Wills**, 414 Grant St, City County Bldg, PIttsburgh, PA 15219. 412-355-4183 (EST) 8:30AM-4:30PM. Probate.

## Allegheny County Recorder

**Real Estate Recording**, Allegheny County Recorder of Deeds, 101 County Office Building, 542 Forbes Avenue, Pittsburgh, PA 15219-2947. 412-355-4226 (EST) 8:30AM-4:30PM.

## Armstrong County

**Court of Common Pleas-Civil**, Market Street, Room 103, Kittanning, PA 16201. 412-548-3251 (EST) 8:30AM-4PM. Civil, Eviction, Small Claims.

**Court of Common Pleas-Criminal**, Armstrong County Courthouse, Kittanning, PA 16201. 412-548-3252 (EST) 8:30AM-4:00PM. Felony, Misdemeanor.

## Armstrong County Recorder

**Real Estate Recording**, Armstrong County Recorder of Deeds, County Courthouse, Kittanning, PA 16201-1495. 412-548-3256 (EST) 8:30AM-4PM.

## Beaver County

**Court of Common Pleas-Civil**, Beaver County Courthouse, 3rd St, Beaver, PA 15009. 412-728-5700 (EST) 8:30AM-4:30PM. Civil, Eviction, Small Claims.

**Court of Common Pleas-Criminal**, Beaver County Courthouse, 3rd St, Beaver, PA 15009. 412-728-5700 (EST) 8:30AM-4:30PM. Felony, Misdemeanor.

**Register in Wills**, Beaver County Courthouse, 3rd St, Beaver, PA 15009. 412-728-5700 (EST) 8:30AM-4:30PM. Probate.

## Beaver County Recorder

**Real Estate Recording**, Beaver County Recorder of Deeds, 3rd Street, County Courthouse, Beaver, PA 15009. 412-728-5700 (EST) 8:30AM-4:30PM.

## Bedford County

**Court of Common Pleas-Criminal and Civil**, Bedford County Courthouse, Bedford, PA 15522. 814-623-4833 (EST) 8:30AM-4:30PM. Felony, Misdemeanor, Civil, Eviction, Small Claims.

## Bedford County Recorder

**Real Estate Recording**, Bedford County Recorder of Deeds, 200 South Juliana Street, County Courthouse, Bedford, PA 15522. 814-623-4836 (EST) 8:30AM-4:30PM.

## Berks County

**Court of Common Pleas-Civil**, 2nd Floor, 633 Court St, Reading, PA 19601. 610-478-6970 (EST) 8AM-5PM. Civil, Eviction, Small Claims.

**Court of Common Pleas-Criminal**, 4th Floor, 633 Court St, Reading, PA 19601. 610-378-8119 (EST) 8AM-5PM. Felony, Misdemeanor.

**Register in Wills**, 633 Court St 2nd Floor Berks Co Service, Reading, PA 19601. 610-478-6600 (EST) 8AM-5PM. Probate.

## Berks County Recorder

**Real Estate Recording**, Berks County Recorder of Deeds, 633 Court St., 3rd Floor, Reading, PA 19601. 610-478-3380 (EST) 8AM-5PM.

## Blair County

**Court of Common Pleas-Criminal/Civil**, PO Box 719, Hollidaysburg, PA 16648. 814-695-5541 (EST) 8AM-4PM. Felony, Misdemeanor, Civil, Eviction, Small Claims.

## Blair County Recorder

**Real Estate Recording**, Blair County Recorder of Deeds, 423 Allegheny Street, Hollidaysburg, PA 16648-2022. 814-695-5541 (EST) 8AM-4PM.

## Bradford County

**Court of Common Pleas-Criminal/Civil**, Courthouse, Main St, Towanda, PA 18848. 717-265-1705 (EST) 9AM-5PM. Felony, Misdemeanor, Civil, Eviction, Small Claims.

**Register in Wills**, Courthouse, Main St., Towanda, PA 18848. 717-265-1702 (EST) 9AM-5PM. Probate.

## Bradford County Recorder

**Real Estate Recording**, Bradford County Recorder of Deeds, 301 Main Street, Courthouse, Towanda, PA 18848. 717-265-1702 (EST) 8AM-5PM.

## Bucks County

**Court of Common Pleas-Civil**, Main and Court St, Doylestown, PA 18901. 215-348-6191 (EST) 8:15AM-4:15PM. Civil, Eviction, Small Claims.

**Court of Common Pleas-Criminal**, Bucks County Courthouse, Doylestown, PA 18901. 215-348-6389 (EST) 8AM-4:30PM. Felony, Misdemeanor.

**Register in Wills**, Bucks County Courthouse, Doylestown, PA 18901. 215-348-6285 (EST) 8:15AM-4:15PM M-F, 8:15AM-7:30PM 2nd and 4th Wed of month. Probate.

## Bucks County Recorder

**Real Estate Recording**, Bucks County Recorder of Deeds, Court & Main, Courthouse, Doylestown, PA 18901-4367. 215-348-6209 (EST) 8:15AM-4:15PM (Recording Hours 8:15AM-4PM).

## Butler County

**Court of Common Pleas-Civil**, Butler County Courthouse, PO Box 1208, Butler, PA 16001-1208. 412-284-5214 (EST) 8:30AM-4:30PM. Civil, Eviction, Small Claims.

**Court of Common Pleas-Criminal**, Butler County Courthouse, PO Box 1208, Butler, PA 16001-1208. 412-284-5233 (EST) 8:30AM-4:30PM. Felony, Misdemeanor.

**Register in Wills**, Butler County Coutrhouse, PO Box 1208, Butler, PA 16003-1208. 412-284-5348 (EST) 8:30AM-4:30PM. Probate.

## Butler County Recorder

**Real Estate Recording**, Butler County Recorder of Deeds, 124 West Diamond St., County Government Bldg., Butler, PA 16001. 412-284-5340 (EST) 8:30AM-4:30PM.

## Cambria County

**Court of Common Pleas-Civil**, PO Box 208, Ebensburg, PA 15931. 814-472-5440 (EST) 9AM-4PM. Civil, Eviction, Small Claims.

**Court of Common Pleas-Criminal**, Cambria County Courthouse S Center St, Ebensburg, PA 15931. 814-472-5440 (EST) 9AM-4PM. Felony, Misdemeanor.

**Register in Wills**, PO Box 298, Ebensburg, PA 15931. 814-472-5440 (EST) 9AM-4PM. Probate.

## Cambria County Recorder

**Real Estate Recording**, Cambria County Recorder of Deeds, S. Center Street, Courthouse, Ebensburg, PA 15931. 814-472-5440 (EST) 9AM-4PM.

## Cameron County

**Court of Common Pleas-Civil**, Cameron County Courthouse, East 5th St, Emporium, PA 15834. 814-486-3355 (EST) 8:30AM-4:30PM. Civil, Eviction, Small Claims.

**Court of Common Pleas-Criminal**, Cameron County Courthouse, East 5th St, Emporium, PA 15834. 814-486-3349 (EST) 8:30AM-4:30PM. Felony, Misdemeanor.

**Register in Wills**, Cameron County Coutrhouse, East 5th St., Emporium, PA 15834. 814-486-3355 (EST) 8:30AM-4PM. Probate.

## Cameron County Recorder

**Real Estate Recording**, Cameron County Recorder of Deeds, 5th Street, County Courthhouse, Emporium, PA 15834. 814-486-3349 (EST) 8:30AM-4Pm.

### Carbon County

**Court of Common Pleas-Civil**, PO Box 127, Courthouse, Jim Thorpe, PA 18229. 717-325-2481 (EST) 8:30AM-4:30PM. Civil, Eviction, Small Claims.

**Court of Common Pleas-Criminal**, County Courthouse, Jim Thorpe, PA 18229. 717-325-3637 (EST) 8:30AM-4:30PM. Felony, Misdemeanor.

### Carbon County Recorder

**Real Estate Recording**, Carbon County Recorder of Deeds, Courthouse Annexe, Rte. 209 & Hazard Square, Jim Thorpe, PA 18229. 717-325-2651 (EST) 8:30AM-4:30PM.

### Centre County

**Court of Common Pleas-Criminal and Civil**, Centre County Courthouse, Bellefonte, PA 16823. 814-355-6796 (EST) 8:30AM-5PM. Felony, Misdemeanor, Civil, Eviction, Small Claims.

**Register in Wills**, Centre County Courthouse, Bellefonte, PA 16823. 814-355-6760 (EST) 8:30AM-5PM. Probate.

### Centre County Recorder

**Real Estate Recording**, Centre County Recorder of Deeds, County Courthouse, Bellefonte, PA 16823. 814-355-6801 (EST) 8:30AM-5PM.

### Chester County

**Court of Common Pleas-Civil**, 2 North High St, Ste 1, West Chester, PA 19380. 610-344-6300 (EST) 8:30AM-4:30PM. Civil, Eviction, Small Claims.

**Court of Common Pleas-Criminal**, 2 North High St, West Chester, PA 19380. 215-344-6135 (EST) 8:30AM-4:30PM. Felony, Misdemeanor.

**Register in Wills**, 2 North High St, Suite 109, West Chester, PA 19380-3073. 610-344-6335 (EST) 8:30AM-4:30PM. Probate.

### Chester County Recorder

**Real Estate Recording**, Chester County Recorder of Deeds, 2 N High St. Suite 3, Courthouse, West Chester, PA 19380-3079. 610-344-6330 (EST) 8:30AM-4:30PM.

### Clarion County

**Court of Common Pleas-Civil**, Clarion County Courthouse, Main St, Clarion, PA 16214. 814-226-1119 (EST) 8AM-4:30PM. Civil, Eviction, Small Claims.

**Court of Common Pleas-Criminal**, Clarion County Courthouse, Main St, Clarion, PA 16214. 814-226-4000 (EST) 8AM-4:30PM. Felony, Misdemeanor.

**Register in Wills**, Clarion County Courthouse, Main St, Clarion, PA 16214. 814-226-4000 (EST) 8:30AM-4:30PM. Probate.

### Clarion County Recorder

**Real Estate Recording**, Clarion County Recorder of Deeds, Main Street, Courthouse, Clarion, PA 16214. 814-226-4000 (EST) X2500 8:30AM-4:30PM.

### Clearfield County

**Court of Common Pleas-Criminal/Civil**, 1 N 2nd St, Clearfield, PA 16830. 814-765-2641 (EST) 8:30AM-4PM. Felony, Misdemeanor, Civil, Eviction, Small Claims.

**Register in Wills**, PO Box 361, Clearfield, PA 16830. 814-765-2641 (EST) 8:30AM-4PM. Probate.

### Clearfield County Recorder

**Real Estate Recording**, Clearfield County Recorder of Deeds, Corner of 2nd & Market Streets, Clearfield, PA 16830. 814-765-2641 (EST) 8:30AM-4PM.

### Clinton County

**Court of Common Pleas-Criminal/Civil**, PO Box 630, Lock Haven, PA 17745. 717-893-4007 (EST) 8:30AM-5PM. Felony, Misdemeanor, Civil, Eviction, Small Claims.

**Register in Wills**, PO Box 943, Lock Haven, PA 17745. 717-893-4010 (EST) 8:30AM-5PM. Probate.

### Clinton County Recorder

**Real Estate Recording**, Clinton County Recorder of Deeds, Corner of Water & Jay Streets, Courthouse, Lock Haven, PA 17745. 717-893-4010 (EST) 8:30AM-5PM.

### Columbia County

**Court of Common Pleas-Criminal/Civil**, PO Box 380, Bloomsburg, PA 17815. 717-389-5600 (EST) 8AM-4:30PM. Felony, Misdemeanor, Civil, Eviction, Small Claims.

**Register in Wills**, Columbia County Courthouse, PO Box 380, Bloomsburg, PA 17815. 717-389-5632 (EST) 8AM-4:30PM. Probate.

### Columbia County Recorder

**Real Estate Recording**, Columbia County Recorder of Deeds, Main Street, Court House, Bloomsburg, PA 17815. 717-389-5632 (EST) 8AM-4:30PM.

### Crawford County

**Court of Common Pleas-Civil**, Crawford County Courthouse, Meadville, PA 16335. 814-425-2541 (EST) 8:30AM-4:30PM. Civil, Eviction, Small Claims.

**Court of Common Pleas-Criminal**, Crawford County Courthouse, Meadville, PA 16335. 814-336-1151 (EST) 8:30AM-4:30PM. Felony, Misdemeanor.

**Register in Wills**, 903 Diamond Park, Meadville, PA 16335. 814-336-1151 (EST) 8:30AM-4:30PM. Probate.

### Crawford County Recorder

**Real Estate Recording**, Crawford County Recorder of Deeds, Courthouse, Meadville, PA 16335. 814-333-7300 (EST) 8:30AM-4:30PM.

### Cumberland County

**Court of Common Pleas-Civil**, Cumberland County Courthouse, Rm 203, Carlisle, PA 17013. 717-240-6195 (EST) 8AM-4:30PM. Civil, Eviction, Small Claims.

**Court of Common Pleas-Criminal**, Cumberland County Courthouse, Rm 203, Carlisle, PA 17013. 717-240-6250 (EST) 8AM-4:30PM. Felony, Misdemeanor.

**Register in Wills**, Cumberland County Courthouse, Rm 203, Carlisle, PA 17013. 717-240-6345 (EST) 8AM-4:30PM. Probate.

### Cumberland County Recorder

**Real Estate Recording**, Cumberland County Recorder of Deeds, County Courthouse, 1 Courthouse Square, Carlisle, PA 17013. 717-240-6370 (EST) 8AM-4:30PM.

### Dauphin County

**Court of Common Pleas-Civil**, PO Box 945, Harrisburg, PA 17101. 717-255-2698 (EST) 8:30AM-4:40PM M-Th, 8:30AM-4PM F. Civil, Eviction, Small Claims.

**Court of Common Pleas-Criminal**, Front & Market St, Harrisburg, PA 17101. 717-255-2692 (EST) 8AM-4:30PM. Felony, Misdemeanor.

**Register in Wills**, PO Box 1295, Harrisburg, PA 17101. 717-255-2656 (EST) 8:30AM-4:30PM M-Th, 8:30AM-4PM F. Probate.

### Dauphin County Recorder

**Real Estate Recording**, Dauphin County Recorder of Deeds, Front & Market Streets, Courthouse, Harrisburg, PA 17101. 717-255-2802 (EST) 8:30AM-4:30PM (F 8:30AM-4PM).

### Delaware County

**Court of Common Pleas-Criminal/Civil**, Veteran's Square Courthouse, PO Box 1057, Media, PA 19063. 215-891-4370 (EST) 8:30AM-4:30PM. Felony, Misdemeanor, Civil, Eviction, Small Claims.

**Register in Wills**, 2nd & Orange St, Fronefield Bldg, Media, PA 19063. 215-891-4400 (EST) 8:30AM-4:30PM. Probate.

### Delaware County Recorder

**Real Estate Recording**, Delaware County Recorder of Deeds, Front Street, Room 107, Government Center Building, Media, PA 19063. 610-891-4156 (EST) 8:30AM-4:30PM.

### Elk County

**Court of Common Pleas-Criminal/Civil**, PO Box 237, Ridgway, PA 15853. 814-776-5344 (EST) 8:30AM-4PM. Felony, Misdemeanor, Civil, Eviction, Small Claims.

**Register in Wills**, PO Box 314, Ridgway, PA 15853. 814-776-5349 (EST) 8:30AM-4PM. Probate.

### Elk County Recorder

**Real Estate Recording**, Elk County Recorder of Deeds, Main Street, Courthouse, Ridgway, PA 15853. 814-776-5349 (EST) 8:30AM-4PM.

### Erie County

**Court of Common Pleas-Civil**, Erie County Courthouse, 140 West 6th St., Erie, PA 16501. 814-451-6250 (EST) 8:30AM-4:30PM. Civil, Eviction, Small Claims.

**Court of Common Pleas-Criminal**, Erie County Courthouse, 140 West 6th St, Erie, PA

16501. 814-451-6229 (EST) 8:30AM-4:30PM. Felony, Misdemeanor.

**Register in Wills**, Erie County Courthouse 140 W 6th St, Erie, PA 16501. 814-451-6260 (EST) 8:30AM-4:30PM. Probate.

### Erie County Recorder

**Real Estate Recording**, Erie County Recorder of Deeds, 140 West 6th Street, Erie, PA 16501. 814-451-6246 (EST)

### Fayette County

**Court of Common Pleas-Civil**, 61 East Main St, Uniontown, PA 15401. 412-430-1272 (EST) 8AM-4:30PM. Civil, Eviction, Small Claims.

**Court of Common Pleas-Criminal**, 61 East Main St, Uniontown, PA 15401. 412-430-1253 (EST) 8AM-4:30PM. Felony, Misdemeanor.

**Register in Wills**, 61 East Main St, Uniontown, PA 15401. 412-430-1206 (EST) 8AM-4:30PM. Probate.

### Fayette County Recorder

**Real Estate Recording**, Fayette County Recorder of Deeds, 61 East Main Street, Courthouse, Uniontown, PA 15401-3389. 412-430-1238 (EST) 8AM-4:30PM.

### Forest County

**Court of Common Pleas-Criminal/Civil**, Forest County Courthouse, PO Box 423, Tionesta, PA 16353. 814-755-3526 (EST) 9AM-4PM. Felony, Misdemeanor, Civil, Eviction, Small Claims.

### Forest County Recorder

**Real Estate Recording**, Forest County Recorder of Deeds, 526 Elm Street, Courthouse, Tionesta, PA 16353. 814-755-3526 (EST) 9AM-4PM.

### Franklin County

**Court of Common Pleas-Civil**, 157 Lincoln Way East, Chambersburg, PA 17201. 717-261-3858 (EST) 8:30AM-4:30PM. Civil, Eviction, Small Claims.

**Court of Common Pleas-Criminal**, 157 Lincoln Way East, Chambersburg, PA 17201. 717-261-3805 (EST) 8:30AM-4:30PM. Felony, Misdemeanor.

**Register in Wills**, 157 Lincoln Way East, Chambersburg, PA 17201. 717-261-3872 (EST) 8:30AM-4:30PM. Probate.

### Franklin County Recorder

**Real Estate Recording**, Franklin County Recorder of Deeds, 157 Lincoln Way East, Chambersburg, PA 17201. 717-264-4125 (EST) 8:30AM-4:30PM.

### Fulton County

**Court of Common Pleas-Criminal/Civil**, Fulton County Courthouse, McConnellsburg, PA 17233. 717-485-4212 (EST) 8:30AM-4:30PM. Felony, Misdemeanor, Civil, Eviction, Small Claims.

### Fulton County Recorder

**Real Estate Recording**, Fulton County Recorder of Deeds, 201 North Second Street, Fulton County Courthouse, McConnellsburg, PA 17233-1198. 717-485-4212 (EST) 8:30AM-4:30PM.

### Greene County

**Court of Common Pleas-Civil**, Greene County Courthouse, Waynesburg, PA 15370. 412-852-5289 (EST) 8:30AM-4:30PM. Civil, Eviction, Small Claims.

**Court of Common Pleas-Criminal**, Greene County Courthouse, Waynesburg, PA 15370. 412-852-5282 (EST) 8:30AM-4:30PM. Felony, Misdemeanor.

**Register in Wills**, 2 E High St, Waynesburg, PA 15370. 412-852-5283 (EST) 8:30AM-4:30PM. Probate.

### Greene County Recorder

**Real Estate Recording**, Greene County Recorder of Deeds, High Street, Courthouse, Waynesburg, PA 15370. 412-852-5283 (EST) 8:30AM-4:30PM.

### Huntingdon County

**Court of Common Pleas-Criminal/Civil**, PO Box 39, Courthouse, Huntingdon, PA 16652. 814-643-1610 (EST) 8:30AM-4:30PM. Felony, Misdemeanor, Civil, Eviction, Small Claims.

**Register in Wills**, 223 Penn St, Huntingdon, PA 16652. 814-643-2740 (EST) 8:30AM-4:30PM. Probate.

### Huntingdon County Recorder

**Real Estate Recording**, Huntingdon County Recorder of Deeds, 223 Penn Street, Courthouse, Huntingdon, PA 16652. 814-643-2740 (EST) 8:30AM-4:30PM.

### Indiana County

**Court of Common Pleas-Criminal/Civil**, Indiana County Courthouse, 825 Philadelp, Indiana, PA 15701. 412-465-3855 (EST) 9AM-4:30PM. Felony, Misdemeanor, Civil, Eviction, Small Claims.

**Register in Wills**, Indiana County Courthouse, 825 Philadelp, Indiana, PA 15701. 412-465-3860 (EST) Probate.

### Indiana County Recorder

**Real Estate Recording**, Indiana County Recorder of Deeds, 825 Philadelphia Street, Courthouse, Indiana, PA 15701. 412-465-3860 (EST) 9AM-4:30PM.

### Jefferson County

**Court of Common Pleas-Criminal/Civil**, Courthouse, 200 Main St, Brookville, PA 15825. 814-849-8031 (EST) 8:30AM-4:30PM. Felony, Misdemeanor, Civil, Eviction, Small Claims.

**Register in Wills**, Jefferson County Courthouse, 200 Main St, Brookville, PA 15825. 814-849-1610 (EST) 8:30AM-4:30PM. Probate.

### Jefferson County Recorder

**Real Estate Recording**, Jefferson County Recorder of Deeds, 200 Main Street, Courthouse, Brookville, PA 15825. 814-849-1610 (EST) 8:30AM-4:30PM.

### Juniata County

**Court of Common Pleas-Criminal/Civil**, Juniata County Courthouse, Mifflintown, PA 17059. 717-436-8991 (EST) 8AM-4:30PM. Felony, Misdemeanor, Civil, Eviction, Small Claims.

**Register in Wills**, Juniata County Courthouse, Mifflintown, PA 17059. 717-436-8991 (EST) 8AM-4:30PM M-F, 8AM-12PM Wed (June-Sept). Probate.

### Juniata County Recorder

**Real Estate Recording**, Juniata County Recorder of Deeds, Courthouse, Mifflintown, PA 17059. 717-436-8991 (EST) 8AM-4:30PM.

### Lackawanna County

**Court of Common Pleas-Civil**, Clerk of Judicial Records, PO Box 133, Scranton, PA 18503. 717-963-6724 (EST) 9AM-4PM. Civil, Eviction, Small Claims.

**Court of Common Pleas-Criminal**, Lackawanna County Courthouse, Scranton, PA 18503. 717-963-6759 (EST) 9AM-4PM. Felony, Misdemeanor.

**Register in Wills**, Registrar of Wills, Lackawanna Co Courth, Scranton, PA 18503. 717-963-6708 (EST) 9AM-4PM. Probate.

### Lackawanna County Recorder

**Real Estate Recording**, Lackawanna County Recorder of Deeds, 200 North Washington, Courthouse, Scranton, PA 18503. 717-963-6775 (EST) 9AM-4PM.

### Lancaster County

**Court of Common Pleas-Civil**, 50 N Duke St, PO Box 83480, Lancaster, PA 17608-3480. 717-299-8282 (EST) 8:30AM-5PM. Civil, Eviction, Small Claims.

**Court of Common Pleas-Criminal**, 50 North Duke St, Lancaster, PA 17602. 717-299-8275 (EST) 8:30AM-5PM. Felony, Misdemeanor.

**Register in Wills**, 50 N. Duke St., Lancaster, PA 17602. 717-299-8243 (EST) 8:30AM-5PM. Probate.

### Lancaster County Recorder

**Real Estate Recording**, Lancaster County Recorder of Deeds, 50 North Duke Street, Lancaster, PA 17602. 717-299-8238 (EST) 8:30AM-4:30PM (for recording); 8:30AM-5PM (for the public).

### Lawrence County

**Court of Common Pleas-Criminal/Civil**, 430 Court St, New Castle, PA 16101-3593. 412-656-2143 (EST) 8AM-4PM. Felony, Misdemeanor, Civil, Eviction, Small Claims.

**Register in Wills**, 430 Court St., New Castle, PA 16101-3593. 412-656-2143 (EST) 8AM-4PM. Probate.

### Lawrence County Recorder

**Real Estate Recording**, Lawrence County Recorder of Deeds, 430 Court Street, Government Center, New Castle, PA 16101. 412-656-2127 (EST) 8AM-4PM.

## Lebanon County

**Court of Common Pleas-Civil**, Municipal Bldg, Rm 104, 400 S 8th St, Lebanon, PA 17042. 717-274 2801 (EST) 8:30AM-4:30PM. Civil, Eviction, Small Claims.

**Court of Common Pleas-Criminal**, Municipal Bldg, Rm 106, 400 S 8th St, Lebanon, PA 17042. 717-274-2801 (EST) 8:30AM-4:30PM. Felony, Misdemeanor.

**Register in Wills**, Municipal Bldg, Rm 106, 400 S 8th St, Lebanon, PA 17042. 717-274-2801 (EST) 8:30AM-4:30PM. Probate.

## Lebanon County Recorder

**Real Estate Recording**, Lebanon County Recorder of Deeds, 400 South 8th Street, Room 107, Lebanon, PA 17042. 717-274-2801 (EST) Recording Hours 8:30AM-4PM.

## Lehigh County

**Court of Common Pleas-Civil**, Civil Division, PO Box 1548, Allentown, PA 18105. 610-820-3148 (EST) 8AM-4PM. Civil, Eviction, Small Claims.

**Court of Common Pleas-Criminal**, PO Box 1548, Allentown, PA 18105-1548. 215-820-3077 (EST) 8:30AM-4:30PM. Felony, Misdemeanor.

**Register in Wills**, Registrar of Wills, Box 1548, Allentown, PA 18105. 215-820-3170 (EST) 7:30AM-4PM. Probate.

## Lehigh County Recorder

**Real Estate Recording**, Lehigh County Recorder of Deeds, 455 Hamilton Street, Allentown, PA 18101. 610-820-3162 (EST) 8AM-4PM.

## Luzerne County

**Court of Common Pleas-Civil**, 200 N River St, Wilkes Barre, PA 18711. 717-825-1745 (EST) 9AM-4:30PM. Civil, Eviction, Small Claims.

**Court of Common Pleas-Criminal**, 200 N River St, Wilkes Barre, PA 18711. 717-825-1585 (EST) 9AM-4:30PM. Felony, Misdemeanor.

**Register in Wills**, 200 N River St, Wilkes Barre, PA 18711. 717-825-1672 (EST) 9AM-4:30PM. Probate.

## Luzerne County Recorder

**Real Estate Recording**, Luzerne County Recorder of Deeds, 200 North River Street, Courthouse, Wilkes-Barre, PA 18711. 717-825-1641 (EST) 9AM-4:30PM.

## Lycoming County

**Court of Common Pleas-Criminal/Civil**, 48 W 3rd St, Williamsport, PA 17701. 717-327-2200 (EST) 8:30AM-5PM. Felony, Misdemeanor, Civil, Eviction, Small Claims.

**Register in Wills**, Lycoming Co Courthouse, 48 W 3rd St, Williamsport, PA 17701. 717-327-2258 (EST) 8:30AM-5PM. Probate.

## Lycoming County Recorder

**Real Estate Recording**, Lycoming County Recorder of Deeds, 48 West Third Street, Williamsport, PA 17701. 717-327-2263 (EST) 8:30AM-5PM.

## McKean County

**Court of Common Pleas-Criminal and Civil**, PO Box 273, Smethport, PA 16749. 814-887-5571 (EST) 8:30AM-4:30PM. Felony, Misdemeanor, Civil, Eviction, Small Claims.

**Register in Wills**, PO Box 202, Smethport, PA 16749-0202. 814-887-5571 (EST) 8:30AM-4:30PM. Probate.

## McKean County Recorder

**Real Estate Recording**, McKean County Recorder of Deeds, Main Street, Courthouse, Smethport, PA 16749. 814-887-5571 (EST) 8:30AM-4:30PM.

## Mercer County

**Court of Common Pleas-Civil**, 105 Mercer County Courthouse, Mercer, PA 16137. 412-662-3800 (EST) 8:30AM-4:30PM. Civil, Eviction, Small Claims.

**Court of Common Pleas-Criminal**, 112 Mercer County Courthouse, Mercer, PA 16137. 412-662-3800 (EST) 8:30AM-4:30PM. Felony, Misdemeanor.

**Register in Wills**, 112 Mercer County Courthouse, Mercer, PA 16137. 412-662-3800 (EST) 8:30AM-4:30PM. Probate.

## Mercer County Recorder

**Real Estate Recording**, Mercer County Recorder of Deeds, North Diamond Street, Courthouse Room 109, Mercer, PA 16137. 412-662-3800 (EST) X274 8:30AM-4:30PM.

## Mifflin County

**Court of Common Pleas-Criminal and Civil**, 20 N Wayne St, Lewistown, PA 17044. 717-248-8146 (EST) 8AM-4:30PM M-F, 8:30-12PM Wed (June-Sept). Felony, Misdemeanor, Civil, Eviction, Small Claims.

**Register in Wills**, 20 N. Wayne St., Lewistown, PA 17044. 717-242-1449 (EST) 8:30AM-4:30PM M-F, 8:30AM-4:30PM Wed (June-Sept). Probate.

## Mifflin County Recorder

**Real Estate Recording**, Mifflin County Recorder of Deeds, 20 North Wayne Street, Lewistown, PA 17044. 717-242-1449 (EST) 8AM-4:30PM.

## Monroe County

**Court of Common Pleas-Civil**, Monroe County Courthouse, Stroudsburg, PA 18360. 717-420-3570 (EST) 8:30AM-4:30PM. Civil, Eviction, Small Claims.

**Court of Common Pleas-Criminal**, Monroe County Courthouse, Stroudsburg, PA 18360. 717-420-3710 (EST) 8:30AM-4:30PM. Felony, Misdemeanor.

**Register in Wills**, Monroe County Courthouse, Stroudsburg, PA 18360. 717-420-3540 (EST) 8:30AM-4:30PM. Probate.

## Monroe County Recorder

**Real Estate Recording**, Monroe County Recorder of Deeds, 7th & Monroe Street, Courthouse, Stroudsburg, PA 18360-2185. 717-420-3530 (EST) X277 8:30AM-4:30PM.

## Montgomery County

**Court of Common Pleas-Civil**, Airy & Swede St, Norristown, PA 19404. 215-278-3360 (EST) 8:30AM-4:15PM. Civil, Eviction, Small Claims.

**Court of Common Pleas-Criminal**, Airy & Swede St, Norristown, PA 19404. 610-278-3346 (EST) 8:30AM-4:15PM. Felony, Misdemeanor.

**Register in Wills**, Airy & Swede St, Norristown, PA 19404. 215-278-3400 (EST) 8:30AM-4:15PM. Probate.

## Montgomery County Recorder

**Real Estate Recording**, Montgomery County Recorder of Deeds, One Montgomery Plaza, Suite 303, County Courthouse, Norristown, PA 19404. 610-278-3289 (EST) 8:30AM-4:15PM.

## Montour County

**Court of Common Pleas-Criminal and Civil**, Montour County Courthouse, 29 Mill St, Danville, PA 17821. 717-271-3010 (EST) Felony, Misdemeanor, Civil, Eviction, Small Claims.

**Register in Wills**, 29 Mill St, Danville, PA 17821. 717-271-3012 (EST) 9AM-4PM. Probate.

## Montour County Recorder

**Real Estate Recording**, Montour County Recorder of Deeds, 29 Mill Street, Courthouse, Danville, PA 17821. 717-271-3012 (EST) 9AM-4PM.

## Northampton County

**Court of Common Pleas-Civil**, Gov't Center, 669 Washington St, Easton, PA 18042. 610-559-3060 (EST) 8:30AM-4:30PM. Civil, Eviction, Small Claims.

**Court of Common Pleas-Criminal**, Govt Center, 7th & Washington St, Easton, PA 18042. 215-559-3000 (EST) 8:30AM-4:30PM. Felony, Misdemeanor.

**Register in Wills**, Gov't Center, 7th & Washington St, Easton, PA 18042. 610-559-3092 (EST) 8:30AM-4:30PM. Probate.

## Northampton County Recorder

**Real Estate Recording**, Northampton County Recorder of Deeds, 669 Washington Streets, Government Center, Easton, PA 18042. 610-559-3077 (EST) 8:30AM-4:30PM.

## Northumberland County

**Court of Common Pleas-Civil**, County Courthouse, 2nd & Market St, Sunbury, PA 17801. 717-988-4151 (EST) 9AM-5PM Mon, 9AM-4:30PM Tue-Fri. Civil, Eviction, Small Claims.

**Court of Common Pleas-Criminal**, County Courthouse, 2nd & Market St, Sunbury, PA 17801. 717-988-4148 (EST) 9AM-4:30PM. Felony, Misdemeanor.

**Register in Wills**, County Courthouse, 201 Market St, Sunbury, PA 17801. 717-988-4143 (EST) 9AM-4:30PM. Probate.

## Northumberland County Recorder

**Real Estate Recording**, Northumberland County Recorder of Deeds, 2nd & Market Streets, Court House, Sunbury, PA 17801. 717-988-4141 (EST) 9AM-4:30PM.

## Perry County

**Court of Common Pleas-Criminal and Civil**, PO Box 325, New Bloomfield, PA 17068. 717-582-2131 (EST) 8AM-4PM. Felony, Misdemeanor, Civil, Eviction, Small Claims.

**Register in Wills**, PO Box 223, New Bloomfield, PA 17068. 717-582-2131 (EST) 8AM-4PM. Probate.

## Perry County Recorder

**Real Estate Recording**, Perry County Recorder of Deeds, Courthouse, New Bloomfield, PA 17068. 717-582-2131 (EST) 8AM-4PM.

## Philadelphia County

**Prothonotary Court**, Common Pleas, Rm 280, City Hall, Philadelphia, PA 19107. 215-686-8859 (EST) 9AM-5PM. Civil, Eviction, Small Claims.

**Clerk of Quarter Session**, Rm 673, City Hall, Philadelphia, PA 19107. 215-686-4280 (EST) 8AM-5PM. Felony, Misdemeanor, Small Claims.

**Municipal Court**, 34 S 11th St, 5th floor, Philadelphia, PA 19107. 215-686-7997 (EST) 9AM-5PM. Civil Actions Under $5,000, Eviction, Small Claims.

**Register in Wills**, City Hall Rm 180, Philadelphia, PA 19107. 215-686-6250 (EST) 8:30AM-4:30PM. Probate.

## Philadelphia County Recorder

**Real Estate Recording**, Philadelphia County Recorder of Deeds, Broad & Market Streets, City Hall Room 156, Philadelphia, PA 19107. 215-686-2260 (EST)

## Pike County

**Court of Common Pleas-Criminal and Civil**, 412 Broad St, Milford, PA 18337. 717-296-7231 (EST) 8:30AM-4:30PM. Felony, Misdemeanor, Civil, Eviction, Small Claims.

## Pike County Recorder

**Real Estate Recording**, Pike County Recorder of Deeds, 412 Broad Street, Milford, PA 18337. 717-296-7231 (EST) 8:30AM-4:30PM.

## Potter County

**Court of Common Pleas-Criminal and Civil**, 1 E 2nd St, Coudersport, PA 16915. 814-274-9740 (EST) 8:30AM-4:30PM. Felony, Misdemeanor, Civil, Eviction, Small Claims.

**Register in Wills**, 1 E 2nd St, Coudersport, PA 16915. 814-274-8370 (EST) 8:30AM-4:30PM. Probate.

## Potter County Recorder

**Real Estate Recording**, Potter County Recorder of Deeds, Courthouse, Coudersport, PA 16915. 814-274-8370 (EST) 8:30AM-4:30PM.

## Schuylkill County

**Court of Common Pleas-Civil**, 401 N 2nd St, Pottsville, PA 17901-2528. 717-628-1270 (EST) 9AM-4PM. Civil, Eviction, Small Claims.

**Court of Common Pleas-Criminal**, County Courthouse, 2nd and Laurel Blvd, Pottsville, PA 17901. 717-622-5570 (EST) 9AM-4PM. Felony, Misdemeanor.

**Register in Wills**, 401 N 2nd St, Pottsville, PA 17901-2528. 717-628-1377 (EST) 9AM-4PM. Probate.

## Schuylkill County Recorder

**Real Estate Recording**, Schuylkill County Recorder of Deeds, 401 N. Second St.., Pottsville, PA 17901. 717-628-1480 (EST) 9AM-4PM.

## Snyder County

**Court of Common Pleas-Criminal and Civil**, Snyder County Courthouse, PO Box 217, Middleburg, PA 17842. 717-837-4202 (EST) 8:30AM-4PM. Felony, Misdemeanor, Civil, Eviction, Small Claims.

**Register in Wills**, County Courthouse, PO Box 217, Middleburg, PA 17842. 717-837-4224 (EST) 8:30AM-4PM. Probate.

## Snyder County Recorder

**Real Estate Recording**, Snyder County Recorder of Deeds, 9 West Market Street, Courthouse, Middleburg, PA 17842. 717-837-4225 (EST) 8:30AM-4PM.

## Somerset County

**Court of Common Pleas-Civil**, 111 E Union St Suite 190, Somerset, PA 15501-0586. 814-445-2186 (EST) 8:30AM-4PM. Civil, Eviction, Small Claims.

**Court of Common Pleas-Criminal**, 111 E Union St Suite 180, Somerset, PA 15501. 814-445-5154 (EST) 8:30AM-4PM. Felony, Misdemeanor.

**Register in Wills**, 111 E Union St Suite 170, Somerset, PA 15501-0586. 814-445-2096 (EST) 8:30AM-4PM. Probate.

## Somerset County Recorder

**Real Estate Recording**, Somerset County Recorder of Deeds, Corner of Union & North Center Avenue, Somerset, PA 15501. 814-445-2160 (EST) 8:30AM-4PM.

## Sullivan County

**Court of Common Pleas-Criminal and Civil**, Main Street, Laporte, PA 18626. 717-946-7351 (EST) 8:30AM-4PM. Felony, Misdemeanor, Civil, Eviction, Small Claims.

## Sullivan County Recorder

**Real Estate Recording**, Sullivan County Recorder of Deeds, Main Street, Courthouse, Laporte, PA 18626. 717-946-7351 (EST) 8:30AM-4:30PM.

## Susquehanna County

**Court of Common Pleas-Civil**, Susquehanna Courthouse, Montrose, PA 18801. 717-278-4600 (EST) 8:30AM-4:30PM. Civil, Eviction, Small Claims.

**Court of Common Pleas-Criminal**, Susquehanna Courthouse, Montrose, PA 18801. 717-278-4600 (EST) 8:30AM-4:30PM. Felony, Misdemeanor.

**Register in Wills**, Susquehanna Courthouse, PO Box 218, Montrose, PA 18801. 717-278-4600 (EST) 8:30AM-4:30PM. Probate.

## Susquehanna County Recorder

**Real Estate Recording**, Susquehanna County Recorder of Deeds, Courthouse, Montrose, PA 18801. 717-278-4600 (EST) X112 9AM-4:30PM.

## Tioga County

**Court of Common Pleas-Criminal and Civil**, Main St, Wellsboro, PA 16901. 717-724-9281 (EST) 9AM-4:30PM. Felony, Misdemeanor, Civil, Eviction, Small Claims.

**Register in Wills**, 118 Main St, Wellsboro, PA 16901. 717-724-9260 (EST) 9AM-4:30PM. Probate.

## Tioga County Recorder

**Real Estate Recording**, Tioga County Recorder of Deeds, 116 Main Street, Courthouse, Wellsboro, PA 16901. 717-724-9260 (EST) 9AM-4:30PM.

## Union County

**Court of Common Pleas-Criminal and Civil**, Union County Courthouse, Lewisburg, PA 17837. 717-524-8751 (EST) 8:30AM-4:30PM. Felony, Misdemeanor, Civil, Eviction, Small Claims.

**Register in Wills**, 103 S 2nd St, Lewisburg, PA 17837. 717-524-8761 (EST) 8:30AM-4:30PM. Probate.

## Union County Recorder

**Real Estate Recording**, Union County Recorder of Deeds, 103 South 2nd Street, Courthouse, Lewisburg, PA 17837. 717-524-8761 (EST) 8:30AM-4:30PM.

## Venango County

**Court of Common Pleas-Criminal and Civil**, Venango County Courthouse, Franklin, PA 16323. 814-432-9577 (EST) 8:30AM-4:30PM. Felony, Misdemeanor, Civil, Eviction, Small Claims.

**Register in Wills**, Liberty St, Franklin, PA 16323. 814-432-9539 (EST) 8:30AM-4:30PM. Probate.

## Venango County Recorder

**Real Estate Recording**, Venango County Recorder of Deeds, Courthouse, Franklin, PA 16323. 814-432-9539 (EST) 8:30AM-4:30PM.

## Warren County

**Court of Common Pleas-Criminal and Civil**, 4th & Market St, Warren, PA 16365. 814-723-7550 (EST) 8:30AM-4:30PM. Felony, Misdemeanor, Civil, Eviction, Small Claims.

**Register in Wills**, Courthouse, 204 4th Ave, Warren, PA 16365. 814-723-7550 (EST) 8:30AM-4:30PM. Probate.

## Warren County Recorder

**Real Estate Recording**, Warren County Recorder of Deeds, 4th & Market Streets, Courthouse, Warren, PA 16365. 814-723-7550 (EST) 8:30AM-3:30PM.

## Washington County

**Court of Common Pleas-Civil**, Courthouse Main St, Washington, PA 15301. 412-228-6770 (EST) 9AM-4:30PM. Civil, Eviction, Small Claims.

**Court of Common Pleas-Criminal**, Courthouse, Washington, PA 15301. 412-228-6787 (EST) 9AM-4:30PM. Felony, Misdemeanor.

**Register in Wills**, Courthouse, Washington, PA 15301. 412-228-6775 (EST) 9AM-4:30PM. Probate.

## Washington County Recorder

**Real Estate Recording**, Washington County Recorder of Deeds, Main and Beau Streets, Washington County Courthouse, Washington, PA 15301. 412-228-6806 (EST) 9AM-4:30PM.

## Wayne County

**Court of Common Pleas-Criminal and Civil**, 925 Court St, Honesdale, PA 18431. 717-253-5970 (EST) 8:30AM-4:30PM. Felony, Misdemeanor, Civil, Eviction, Small Claims.

**Register in Wills**, 925 Court St, Honesdale, PA 18431. 717-253-5970 (EST) 8:30AM-4:30PM. Probate.

## Wayne County Recorder

**Real Estate Recording**, Wayne County Recorder of Deeds, 925 Court Street, Honesdale, PA 18431-1996. 717-253-5970 (EST) X212 8:30AM-4:30PM.

## Westmoreland County

**Court of Common Pleas-Civil**, Criminal Division, 203 Courthouse Square, Greensburg, PA 15601-1168. 412-830-3500 (EST) 8:30AM-4PM. Civil, Eviction, Small Claims.

**Court of Common Pleas-Criminal**, Criminal Division, 203 Courthouse Square, Greensburg, PA 15601-1168. 412-830-3734 (EST) 8:30AM-4PM. Felony, Misdemeanor.

**Register in Wills**, Registrars of Wills, Courthouse Sq, Main, Greensburg, PA 15601-1168. 412-830-3177 (EST) 8:30AM-4PM. Probate.

## Westmoreland County Recorder

**Real Estate Recording**, Westmoreland County Recorder of Deeds, Main Street, Courthouse Square Room 503, Greensburg, PA 15601. 412-830-3520 (EST) 8:30AM-4PM.

## Wyoming County

**Court of Common Pleas-Criminal and Civil**, Wyoming County Courthouse, Tunkhannock, PA 18657. 717-836-3200 (EST) 8:30AM-4PM. Felony, Misdemeanor, Civil, Eviction, Small Claims.

**Register in Wills**, Wyoming County Courthouse, 1 Courthouse, Tunkhannock, PA 18657. 717-836-3200 (EST) 8:30AM-4PM. Probate.

## Wyoming County Recorder

**Real Estate Recording**, Wyoming County Recorder of Deeds, 1 Courthouse Square, Tunkhannock, PA 18657. 717-836-3200 (EST) X235-6 8:30AM-4PM.

## York County

**Court of Common Pleas-Civil**, York County Courthouse, 28 Market St, York, PA 17401. 717-771-9611 (EST) 8:30AM-4:30PM. Civil, Eviction, Small Claims.

**Court of Common Pleas-Criminal**, York County Courthouse 28 E Market St, York, PA 17401. 717-771-9612 (EST) 8:30AM-4:30PM. Felony, Misdemeanor.

**Register in Wills**, York County Courthouse 28 E Market St, York, PA 17401. 717-771-9607 (EST) 8:30AM-4:30PM. Probate.

## York County Recorder

**Real Estate Recording**, York County Recorder of Deeds, 28 East Market Street, York, PA 17401. 717-771-9608 (EST) 8:30AM-4:30PM.

# Rhode Island

## Barrington Town

**Real Estate Recording**, Barrington Town Clerk, 283 County Road, Town Hall, Barrington, RI 02806. 401-247-1900 8:30AM-4:30PM.

## Bristol County

**Superior and District Court**, All cases are handled by the Providence Courts. Felony, Civil Actions Over $10,000.

**Barrington Town Hall**, 283 County Road, Barrington, RI 02806. 401-247-1900 (EST) Probate.

**Bristol Town Hall**, 10 Court Street, Bristol, RI 02809. 401-253-7000 (EST) Probate.

**Warren Town Hall**, 514 Main Street, Warren, RI 02885. 401-245-7340 (EST) Probate.

## Bristol Town

**Real Estate Recording**, Bristol Town Clerk, 10 Court Street, Town Hall, Bristol, RI 02809. 401-253-7000 8:30AM-4:30PM.

## Burrillville Town

**Real Estate Recording**, Burrillville Town Clerk, 105 Harrisville Main Street, Town Hall, Harrisville, RI 02830-1499. 401-568-4300 8:30AM-4:30PM (Recording until 4PM).

## Central Falls City

**Real Estate Recording**, Central Falls City Clerk, 580 Broad Street, City Hall, Central Falls, RI 02863. 401-727-7400 8:30AM-4:30PM.

## Charlestown Town

**Real Estate Recording**, Charlestown Town Clerk, 4540 South County Trail, Town Hall, Charlestown, RI 02813. 401-364-1200 8:30AM-4:30PM (Recording until 4PM).

## Coventry Town

**Real Estate Recording**, Coventry Town Clerk, 1670 Flat River Road, Town Hall, Coventry, RI 02816-8911. 401-822-9174 8:30AM-4:30PM.

## Cranston City

**Real Estate Recording**, Cranston City Clerk, 869 Park Avenue, City Hall, Cranston, RI 02910. 401-461-1000 8AM-5PM (June-September 8AM-4PM).

## Cumberland Town

**Real Estate Recording**, Cumberland Town Clerk, 45 Broad Street, Town Hall, Cumberland, RI 02864. 401-728-2400 8:30AM-4:30PM.

## East Greenwich Town

**Real Estate Recording**, East Greenwich Town Clerk, 111 Peirce Street, Town Hall, East Greenwich, RI 02818. 401-886-8603 8:30AM-4:30PM (June-August 8:30AM-4PM).

## East Providence City

**Real Estate Recording**, East Providence City Clerk, 145 Taunton Avenue, City Hall, East Providence, RI 02914. 401-435-7500 8AM-4PM.

## Exeter Town

**Real Estate Recording**, Exeter Town Clerk, 675 Ten Rod Road, Town Hall, Exeter, RI 02822. 401-294-3891 9AM-4PM.

## Foster Town

**Real Estate Recording**, Foster Town Clerk, 181 Howard Hill Road, Town Hall, Foster, RI 02825-1227. 401-392-9200 9AM-3:30PM.

## Glocester Town

**Real Estate Recording**, Glocester Town Clerk, 1145 Putnam Pike, Town Hall, Glocester/Chepachet, RI 02814. 401-568-6206 8AM-4:30PM.

## Hopkinton Town

**Real Estate Recording**, Hopkinton Town Clerk, 1 Town House Road, Town Hall, Hopkinton, RI 02833. 401-377-7777 8:30AM-4:30PM.

## Jamestown Town

**Real Estate Recording**, Jamestown Town Clerk, 93 Narragansett Avenue, Town Hall, Jamestown, RI 02835. 401-423-7200 8AM-4:30PM.

## Johnston Town

**Real Estate Recording**, Johnston Town Clerk, 1385 Hartford Avenue, Town Hall, Johnston, RI 02919. 401-351-6618 9AM-4:30PM.

## Kent County

**Superior Court**, 222 Quaker Lane, Warwick, RI 02886-0107. 401-822-1311 (EST) 8:30AM-4:30PM. Felony, Civil Actions Over $10,000.

**3rd Division District Court**, 222 Quaker Lane, Warwick, RI 02886-0107. 401-822-1771 (EST) 8:30AM-4:30PM. Misdemeanor, Civil Actions Under $10,000, Eviction, Small Claims.

**Coventry Town Hall**, 1670 Flat River Road, Coventry, RI 02816. 401-822-9174 (EST) Probate.

**East Greenwich Town Hall**, 111 Peirce Street, East Greenwich, RI 02818. 401-886-8603 (EST) Probate.

**Warwick City Hall**, 3275 Post Road, Warwick, RI 02886. 401-738-2000 (EST) Probate.

**West Greenwich Town Hall**, 280 Victory Highway, West Greenwich, RI 02817. 401-397-5016 (EST) Probate.

**West Warwick Town Hall**, 1170 Main Street, West Warwick, RI 02893. 401-822-9200 (EST) Probate.

## Lincoln Town

**Real Estate Recording**, Lincoln Town Clerk, 100 Old River Road, Town Hall, Lincoln, RI 02865. 401-333-1100 9AM-4:30PM.

## Little Compton Town

**Real Estate Recording**, Little Compton Town Clerk, 40 Commons, Town Hall, Little Compton, RI 02837. 401-635-4400 8AM-4PM.

## Middletown Town

**Real Estate Recording**, Middletown Town Clerk, 350 East Main Road, Town Hall, Middletown, RI 02842. 401-847-0009 9AM-5PM.

## Narragansett Town

**Real Estate Recording**, Narragansett Town Clerk, 25 Fifth Avenue, Town Hall, Narragansett, RI 02882. 401-789-1044 8:30AM-4:30PM.

## New Shoreham Town

**Real Estate Recording**, New Shoreham Town Clerk, Old Town Road, Town Hall, Block Island, RI 02807. 401-466-3200 9AM-3PM; 9AM-1PM Sat.

## Newport City

**Real Estate Recording**, 43 Broadway, Town Hall, Newport, RI 02840-2798. 401-846-9600 9AM-5PM (Recording Hours 9AM-4PM).

## Newport County

**Superior Court**, 45 Washington Square, Newport, RI 02840. 401-841-8330 (EST) 8:30AM-4:30PM (July and August till 4PM). Felony, Civil Actions Over $10,000.

**2nd Division District Court**, Isenhower Square, Newport, RI 02840. 401-841-8350 (EST) 8:30AM-4:30PM (4PM-summer months). Civil Actions Under $10,000, Eviction, Small Claims.

**Jamestown Town Hall**, 93 Narragansett Avenue, Jamestown, RI 02835. 401-423-7200 (EST) Probate.

**Little Compton Town Hall**, 40 Commons, Little Compton, RI 02837. 401-635-4400 (EST) Probate.

**Middletown Town Hall**, 350 East Main Road, Middletown, RI 02842. 401-847-0009 (EST) Probate.

**Newport Town Hall**, 43 Broadway, Newport, RI 02840. 401-846-9600 (EST) Probate.

**Portsmouth Town Hall**, 2200 East Main Road, Portsmouth, RI 02871. 401-683-2101 (EST) Probate.

**Tiverton Town Hall**, 343 Highland Road, Tiverton, RI 02878. 401-625-6700 (EST) Probate.

## North Kingstown Town

**Real Estate Recording**, North Kingstown Town Clerk, 80 Boston Neck Road, Town Hall, North Kingstown, RI 02852. 401-294-3331 8:30AM-4:30PM.

## North Providence Town

**Real Estate Recording**, North Providence Town Clerk, 2000 Smith Street, Town Hall, North Providence, RI 02911. 401-232-0900 8:30AM-4:30PM.

## North Smithfield Town

**Real Estate Recording**, North Smithfield Town Clerk, 1 Main Street, Town Hall,

Slatersville, RI 02876. 401-767-2200 8AM-4PM (Recording until 3:30PM).

## Pawtucket City

**Real Estate Recording**, Pawtucket City Clerk, 137 Roosevelt Avenue, City Hall, Pawtucket, RI 02860. 401-728-0500 8:30AM-4:30PM; Recording until 3:30PM.

## Portsmouth Town

**Real Estate Recording**, Portsmouth Town Clerk, 2200 East Main Road, Town Hall, Portsmouth, RI 02871. 401-683-2101 Recording Hours 9AM-3:45PM.

## Providence City

**Real Estate Recording**, Providence City Recorder of Deeds, 25 Dorrance Street, City Hall, Providence, RI 02903. 401-421-7740 X312 8:30AM-4:30PM (Recording Hours 8:30AM-4PM).

## Providence County

**Providence/Bristol Superior Court**, 250 Benefit St, Providence, RI 02903. 401 277 3250 (EST) 8:30AM-4:30PM. Felony, Civil Actions Over $10,000.

**6th Division District Court**, 1 Darrance Plaza 2nd Floor, Providence, RI 02903. 401-277-6710 (EST) 8:30AM-4:30PM. Misdemeanor, Civil Actions Under $10,000, Eviction, Small Claims.

**Central Falls City Hall**, 580 Broad Street, Central Falls, RI 02863. 401-727-7400 (EST) Probate.

**Cranston City Hall**, 869 Park Avenue, Cranston, RI 02910. 401-461-1000 (EST) Probate.

**Cumberland Town Hall**, 45 Broad Street, Cumberland, RI 02864. 401-728-2400 (EST) Probate.

**East Providence City Hall**, 145 Taunton Avenue, East Providence, RI 02914. 401-435-7500 (EST) Probate.

**Smithfield Town Hall**, 64 Farnum Pike, Esmond, RI 02917. 401-233-1000 (EST) Probate.

**Foster Town Hall**, 181 Howard Hill Road, Foster, RI 02825. 401-392-9200 (EST) Probate.

**Glocester Town Hall**, 1145 Putnam Pike, Glocester/ Chepachet, RI 02814. 401-568-6206 (EST) Probate.

**Burrillville Town Hall**, 105 Harrisville Main Street, Harrisville, RI 02830. 401-568-4300 (EST) Probate.

**Johnston Town Hall**, 1385 Hartford Avenue, Johnston, RI 02919. 401-351-6618 (EST) Probate.

**Lincoln Town Hall**, 100 Old River Road, Lincoln, RI 02865. 401-333-1100 (EST) Probate.

**North Providence Town Hall**, 2000 Smith Street, North Providence, RI 02911. 401-232-0900 (EST) Probate.

**Scituate Town Hall**, 195 Danielson Pike, North Scituate, RI 02857. 401-647-7466 (EST) Probate.

**Pawtucket City Hall**, 137 Roosevelt Avenue, Pawtucket, RI 02860. 401-728-0500 (EST) Probate.

**Providence City Hall**, 25 Dorrance Street, Providence, RI 02903. 401-421-7740 (EST) Probate.

**North Smithfield Town Hall**, 1 Main Street, Slatersville, RI 02876. 401-767-2200 (EST) Probate.

**Woonsocket City Hall**, 169 Main Street, Woonsocket, RI 02895. 401-762-6400 (EST) Probate.

## Richmond Town

**Real Estate Recording**, Richmond Town Clerk, 5 Richmond Townhouse Rd., Town Hall, Wyoming, RI 02898. 401-539-2497 9AM-4PM (6-7:30PM M).

## Scituate Town

**Real Estate Recording**, Scituate Town Clerk, 195 Danielson Pike, Town Hall, North Scituate, RI 02857. 401-647-7466 9AM-4PM.

## Smithfield Town

**Real Estate Recording**, Smithfield Town Clerk, 64 Farnum Pike, Town Hall, Esmond, RI 02917. 401-233-1000 9AM-4PM.

## South Kingstown Town

**Real Estate Recording**, South Kingstown Town Clerk, 180 High Street, Town Hall, Wakefield, RI 02879. 401-789-9331

## Tiverton Town

**Real Estate Recording**, Tiverton Town Clerk, 343 Highland Road, Town Hall, Tiverton, RI 02878. 401-625-6700 8:30AM-4PM.

## Warren Town

**Real Estate Recording**, Warren Town Clerk, 514 Main Street, Town Hall, Warren, RI 02885. 401-245-7340 9AM-4PM.

## Warwick City

**Real Estate Recording**, Warwick City Clerk, 3275 Post Road, City Hall, Warwick, RI 02886. 401-738-2000 8:30AM-4:30PM.

## Washington County

**Superior Court**, J Howard McGrath Judicial Complex 4800, Wakefield, RI 02879. 401-782-4121 (EST) 8:30AM-4:30PM (Sept-June) 8:30AM-4PM (July & Aug). Felony, Civil Actions Over $10,000.

**4th District Court**, 4800 Power Hill Rd, Wakefield, RI 02879. 401-782-4131 (EST) 8:30AM-4:30PM. Misdemeanor, Civil Actions Under $10,000, Eviction, Small Claims.

**New Shoreham Town Hall**, Old Town Road, Block Island, RI 02807. 401-466-3200 (EST) Probate.

**Charlestown Town Hall**, 4540 South County Trail, Charlestown, RI 02813. 401-364-1200 (EST) Probate.

**Exeter Town Hall**, 675 Ten Rod Road, Exeter, RI 02822. 401-294-3891 (EST) Probate.

**Hopkinton Town Hall**, 1 Town House Road, Hopkinton, RI 02833. 401-377-7777 (EST) Probate.

**Narragansett Town Hall**, 25 Fifth Avenue, Narragansett, RI 02882. 401-789-1044 (EST) Probate.

**North Kingstown Town Hall**, 80 Boston Neck Road, North Kingstown, RI 02852. 401-294-3331 (EST) Probate.

**South Kingstown Town Hall**, 180 High Street, Wakefield, RI 02879. 401-789-9331 (EST) Probate.

**Westerly Town Hall**, 45 Broad Street, Westerly, RI 02891. 401-348-2500 (EST) Probate.

**Richmond Town Hall**, 5 Richmond Townhouse Rd., Wyoming, RI 02898. 401-539-2497 (EST) Probate.

## West Greenwich Town

**Real Estate Recording**, West Greenwich Town Clerk, 280 Victory Highway, Town Hall, West Greenwich, RI 02817. 401-397-5016

## West Warwick Town

**Real Estate Recording**, West Warwick Town Clerk, 1170 Main Street, Town Hall, West Warwick, RI 02893-4829. 401-822-9200 8:30AM-4:30PM (June-August 8:30AM-4PM).

## Westerly Town

**Real Estate Recording**, Westerly Town Clerk, 45 Broad Street, Town Hall, Westerly, RI 02891. 401-348-2500 8:30AM-4:30PM.

## Woonsocket City

**Real Estate Recording**, Woonsocket City Clerk, 169 Main Street, City Hall, Woonsocket, RI 02895. 401-762-6400 8:30-4PM.

# South Carolina

## Abbeville County

**Real Estate Recording**, Abbeville Clerk of Court, Court Square, Abbeville, SC 29620. 803-459-5074 (EST) 9AM-5PM.

**Circuit Court**, PO Box 99, Abbeville, SC 29620. 803-459-5074 (EST) 9AM-5PM. Felony, Misdemeanor, Civil Actions Over $2,500.

**Abbeville Magistrate Court**, 111 Pinckney St (PO Box 1156), Abbeville, SC 29620. 803-459-2080 (EST) 9AM-5PM. Civil Actions Under $2,500, Eviction, Small Claims.

**Calhoun Falls Magistrate Court**, PO Box 414, Calhoun Falls, SC 29628. 803-447-8214 (EST) Civil Actions Under $2,500, Eviction, Small Claims.

**Probate Court**, PO Box 70, Abbeville, SC 29620. 803-459-4626 (EST) 9AM-5PM. Probate.

## Aiken County

**Real Estate Recording**, Aiken County Register of Mesne Conveyances, 828 Richland Avenue West, Aiken, SC 29801. 803-642-2072 (EST) 8:30AM-5PM.

**Circuit Court**, PO Box 583, Aiken, SC 29802. 803-642-2099 (EST) 8:30AM-5PM. Felony, Misdemeanor, Civil Actions Over $2,500.

**Aiken Magistrate Court**, 1680 Richland Ave W, Ste 70, Aiken, SC 29802. 803-642-1744 (EST) Civil Actions Under $2,500, Eviction, Small Claims.

**Aiken Magistrate Court**, PO Box 1977, Aiken, SC 29802. 803-652-7227 (EST) Civil Actions Under $2,500, Eviction, Small Claims.

**Graniteville Magistrate Court**, 14 Masonic Shopping Ctr, Graniteville, SC 29829. 803-663-6634 (EST) Civil Actions Under $2,500, Eviction, Small Claims.

**Langley Magistrate Court**, PO Box 769, Langley, SC 29834. 803-593-5171 (EST) Civil Actions Under $2,500, Eviction, Small Claims.

**Langley Magistrate Court**, PO Box 26, Langley, SC 29834-0026. 803-642-7552 (EST) Civil Actions Under $2,500, Eviction, Small Claims.

**Monetta Magistrate Court**, 5697 Columbia Hwy N (PO Box 190), Monetta, SC 29105. 803-685-7125 (EST) Civil Actions Under $2,500, Eviction, Small Claims.

**New Ellenton Magistrate Court**, PO Box 40, New Ellenton, SC 29809. 803-652-3609 (EST) 9AM-4:30PM, Closed 1-2. Civil Actions Under $2,500, Eviction, Small Claims.

**North Augusta Magistrate Court**, PO Box 6493, North Augusta, SC 29841. 803-279-1909 (EST) Civil Actions Under $2,500, Eviction, Small Claims.

**Salley Magistrate Court**, PO Box 422, Salley, SC 29137. 803-258-3118 (EST) Civil Actions Under $2,500, Eviction, Small Claims.

**Probate Court**, PO Box 583, Aiken, SC 29802. 803-642-2099 (EST) 8:30AM-5PM. Probate.

## Allendale County

**Real Estate Recording**, Allendale Clerk of Court, Pine Street, Courthouse, Allendale, SC 29810. 803-584-2737 (EST)

**Circuit Court**, PO Box 126, Allendale, SC 29810. 803-584-2737 (EST) 9AM-5PM. Felony, Misdemeanor, Civil Actions Over $2,500.

**Allendale Magistrate Court**, 205 N Main St, Allendale, SC 29810. 803-584-3755 (EST) 9AM-5PM. Civil Actions Under $2,500, Eviction, Small Claims.

**Fairfax Magistrate Court**, 115 N Hampton Ave (PO Box 421), Fairfax, SC 29827. 803-632-3871 (EST) Civil Actions Under $2,500, Eviction, Small Claims.

**Probate Court**, PO Box 737, Allendale, SC 29810. 803-584-3157 (EST) Probate.

## Anderson County

**Real Estate Recording**, Anderson County Register of Mesne Conveyances, 100 South Main Street, Courthouse, Anderson, SC 29624. 803-260-4054 (EST)

**Circuit Court**, 100 S Main, Anderson, SC 29624. 803-260-4053 (EST) 8:30AM-5PM. Felony, Misdemeanor, Civil Actions Over $2,500.

**Anderson Magistrate Court**, 100 S Main St (PO Box 4046), Anderson, SC 29624. 803-260-4156 (EST) Civil Actions Under $2,500, Eviction, Small Claims.

**Anderson Magistrate Court**, 209 Lee St, Anderson, SC 29625. 803-260-9361 (EST) Civil Actions Under $2,500, Eviction, Small Claims.

**Honea Path Magistrate Court**, PO Box 214, Honea Path, SC 29654. 803-369-0015 (EST) Civil Actions Under $2,500, Eviction, Small Claims.

**Honea Path Magistrate Court**, 310 W Oak Dr Extension, Honea Path, SC 29654. 803-260-4362 (EST) Civil Actions Under $2,500, Eviction, Small Claims.

**Iva Magistrate Court**, 626 E Front St (PO Box 1163), Iva, SC 29655. 803-348-3456 (EST) Civil Actions Under $2,500, Eviction, Small Claims.

**Pelzer Magistrate Court**, PO Box 731, Pelzer, SC 29669. 803-947-1700 (EST) Civil Actions Under $2,500, Eviction, Small Claims.

**Pendleton Magistrate Court**, 100 E Queen St (PO Box 181), Pendleton, SC 29670. 803-646-6701 (EST) Civil Actions Under $2,500, Eviction, Small Claims.

**Piedmont Magistrate Court**, 1903 Hwy 86, Piedmont, SC 29673. 803-845-7620 (EST) Civil Actions Under $2,500, Eviction, Small Claims.

**Starr Magistrate Court**, 7626 Hwy 81, Starr, SC 29684. 803-352-3157 (EST) Civil Actions Under $2,500, Eviction, Small Claims.

**Townville Magistrate Court**, 105 Conneross Rd (PO Box 99), Townville, SC 29689. 803-287-0550 (EST) Civil Actions Under $2,500, Eviction, Small Claims.

**Williamston Magistrate Court**, 12 W Main St (PO Box 175), Williamston, SC 29697. 803-847-7280 (EST) Civil Actions Under $2,500, Eviction, Small Claims.

**Probate Court**, PO Box 4046, Anderson, SC 29622. 803-260-4049 (EST) 8:30AM-5PM. Probate.

## Bamberg County

**Real Estate Recording**, Bamberg Clerk of Court, 110 North Main Street, Bamberg, SC 29003. 803-245-3025 (EST) 9AM-5PM.

**Circuit Court**, PO Box 150, Bamberg, SC 29003. 803-245-3025 (EST) 9AM-5PM. Felony, Misdemeanor, Civil Actions Over $2,500.

**Bamberg Magistrate Court**, PO Box 187, Bamberg, SC 29003. 803-245-3016 (EST) Civil Actions Under $2,500, Eviction, Small Claims.

**Olar Magistrate Court**, PO Box 108, Olar, SC 29843. 803-368-2162 (EST) Civil Actions Under $2,500, Eviction, Small Claims.

**Probate Court**, PO Box 180, Bamberg, SC 29003. 803-245-3008 (EST) Probate.

## Barnwell County

**Real Estate Recording**, Barnwell Clerk of Court, Courthouse Building, Room 114, Barnwell, SC 29812. 803-541-1020 (EST) 9AM-5PM.

**Circuit Court**, PO Box 723, Barnwell, SC 29812. 803-541-1020 (EST) 9AM-5PM. Felony, Misdemeanor, Civil Actions Over $2,500.

**Barnwell Magistrate Court**, PO Box 929, Barnwell, SC 29812. 803-541-1035 (EST) Civil Actions Under $2,500, Eviction, Small Claims.

**Blackville Magistrate Court**, 213 Lartique St, Blackville, SC 29817. 803-284-2765 (EST) Civil Actions Under $2,500, Eviction, Small Claims.

**Williston Magistrate Court**, PO Box 485, Williston, SC 29853. 803-266-3700 (EST) Civil Actions Under $2,500, Eviction, Small Claims.

**Probate Court**, Room 112, County Courthouse, Barnwell, SC 29812. 803-259-5145 (EST) Probate.

## Beaufort County

**Real Estate Recording**, Beaufort County Register of Mesne Conveyances, 1000 Ribaut Rd., Administration Bldg. Rm 205, Beaufort, SC 29902. 803-525-7525 (EST) 8AM-5PM.

**Circuit Court**, PO Drawer 1128, Beaufort, SC 29901. 803-525-7306 (EST) 8AM-5PM. Felony, Misdemeanor, Civil Actions Over $2,500.

**Beaufort Magistrate Court**, PO Box 2207, Beaufort, SC 29901-2207. 803-525-7402 (EST) Civil Actions Under $2,500, Eviction, Small Claims.

**Bluffton Magistrate Court**, PO Box 840, Bluffton, SC 29910. 803-757-2270 (EST) Civil Actions Under $2,500, Eviction, Small Claims.

**Hilton Head Magistrate Court**, PO Box 22895, Hilton Head, SC 29925. 803-681-4690 (EST) Civil Actions Under $2,500, Eviction, Small Claims.

**Hilton Head Magistrate Court**, PO Box 24054, Hilton Head, SC 29925. 803-842-4266 (EST) Civil Actions Under $2,500, Eviction, Small Claims.

**Lobeco Magistrate Court**, PO Box 845, Lobeco, SC 29931-0845. 803-846-3902 (EST) Civil Actions Under $2,500, Eviction, Small Claims.

**St Helena Island Magistrate Court**, PO Box 126, St Helena Island, SC 29920. 803-838-3212 (EST) Civil Actions Under $2,500, Eviction, Small Claims.

**Probate Court**, PO Box 1083, Beaufort, SC 29901-1083. 803-525-7440 (EST) Probate.

# South Carolina

## Berkeley County

**Real Estate Recording**, Berkeley County Register of Mesne Conveyances, 223 North Live Oak Drive, Moncks Corner, SC 29461. 803-761-6900 (EST) 9AM-5PM.

**Circuit Court**, PO Box 219, Moncks Corner, SC 29461. 803-761-6900 (EST) 9AM-5PM. Felony, Misdemeanor, Civil Actions Over $2,500.

**Alvin Magistrate Court**, Rt 2 Box 735, Alvin, SC 29479. 803-257-2122 (EST) Civil Actions Under $2,500, Eviction, Small Claims.

**Cross Magistrate Court**, Rt 1 Box 2565, Cross, SC 29436. 803-753-2334 (EST) Civil Actions Under $2,500, Eviction, Small Claims.

**Goose Creek Magistrate Court**, 225 Red Bank Rd (PO Box 98), Goose Creek, SC 29445. 803-553-7080 (EST) 11AM-7PM M-TH, 11AM-5PM F. Civil Actions Under $2,500, Eviction, Small Claims.

**Goose Creek Magistrate Court**, 632 Alexander Cir (PO Box 1548), Goose Creek, SC 29445. 803-761-5999 (EST) Civil Actions Under $2,500, Eviction, Small Claims.

**Hanahan Magistrate Court**, 1255 Yeamens Hall Rd, Hanahan, SC 29406. 803-747-6864 (EST) Civil Actions Under $2,500, Eviction, Small Claims.

**Moncks Corner Magistrate Court**, 300 California Ave (PO Box 685), Moncks Corner, SC 29461. 803-761-8180 (EST) Civil Actions Under $2,500, Eviction, Small Claims.

**Moncks Corner Magistrate Court**, HC 69 Box 1570, Moncks Corner, SC 29461. 803-336-3463 (EST) Civil Actions Under $2,500, Eviction, Small Claims.

**St Stephen Magistrate Court**, PO Box 1433, St Stephen, SC 29479. 803-567-7400 (EST) Civil Actions Under $2,500, Eviction, Small Claims.

**Summerville Magistrate Court**, Rt 2 Box 484, Summerville, SC 29483. (EST) Civil Actions Under $2,500, Eviction, Small Claims.

**Wando Magistrate Court**, Rt 1 Box 21-E, Wando, SC 29492. 803-884-0957 (EST) Civil Actions Under $2,500, Eviction, Small Claims.

**Probate Court**, 300 B California Ave, Moncks Corner, SC 29461. 803-761-6900 (EST) Probate.

## Calhoun County

**Real Estate Recording**, Calhoun Clerk of Court, 302 F.R. Huff Drive, Courthouse, St. Matthews, SC 29135. 803-874-3524 (EST) 9AM-5PM.

**Circuit Court**, 302 S Huff Dr, St Matthews, SC 29135. 803-874-3524 (EST) 9AM-5PM. Felony, Misdemeanor, Civil Actions Over $2,500.

**Cameron Magistrate Court**, Rt 1 Box 541, Cameron, SC 29030. 803-826-6000 (EST) Civil Actions Under $2,500, Eviction, Small Claims.

**Cameron Magistrate Court**, PO Box 623, Cameron, SC 29030. 803-823-2277 (EST) Civil Actions Under $2,500, Eviction, Small Claims.

**Cameron Magistrate Court**, Main St, Town Hall (PO Box 643), Cameron, SC 29030. 803-823-2612 (EST) Civil Actions Under $2,500, Eviction, Small Claims.

**Gaston Magistrate Court**, Rd 31 & Hwy 21, Sandy Run Fire Station, Gaston, SC 29053. 803-794-4706 (EST) Civil Actions Under $2,500, Eviction, Small Claims.

**St Matthews Magistrate Court**, 112 W Bridge St (PO Box 191), St Matthews, SC 29135. 803-874-1112 (EST) Civil Actions Under $2,500, Eviction, Small Claims.

**Probate Court**, 302 S Railroad Ave, St Matthews, SC 29135. 803-874-3514 (EST) Probate.

## Charleston County

**Real Estate Recording**, Charleston County Register of Mesne Conveyances, 2 Courthouse Square, Meeting Street, Charleston, SC 29401. 803-723-6780 (EST) 8AM-5PM.

**Circuit Court**, PO Box 70219, Charleston, SC 29415. 803-740-5700 (EST) Felony, Misdemeanor, Civil Actions Over $2,500.

**Charleston Magistrate Court**, PO Box 941, Charleston, SC 29401. 803-724-6719 (EST) Civil Actions Under $2,500, Eviction, Small Claims.

**Charleston Magistrate Court**, Old Citadel Bldg, Rm 110, Hutson St, Charleston, SC 29401. 803-724-6720 (EST) Civil Actions Under $2,500, Eviction, Small Claims.

**Charleston Magistrate Court**, PO Box 31861, Charleston, SC 29407. 803-766-6531 (EST) Civil Actions Under $2,500, Eviction, Small Claims.

**Charleston Magistrate Court**, PO Box 12226, Charleston, SC 29412. 803-795-1140 (EST) Civil Actions Under $2,500, Eviction, Small Claims.

**Charleston Magistrate Court**, PO Box 20190, Charleston, SC 29413-0190. 803-724-6766 (EST) Civil Actions Under $2,500, Eviction, Small Claims.

**Charleston Magistrate Court**, PO Box 21830, Charleston, SC 29413-1830. 803-724-6719 (EST) Civil Actions Under $2,500, Eviction, Small Claims.

**Charleston Magistrate Court**, PO Box 32412, Charleston, SC 29417. 803-745-2223 (EST) 9AM-5PM. Civil Actions Under $2,500, Eviction, Small Claims.

**Charleston Magistrate Court**, 2156 Leeds Ave (PO Box 60037), Charleston, SC 29419-0037. 803-745-2217 (EST) Civil Actions Under $2,500, Eviction, Small Claims.

**Esidto Island Magistrate Court**, 8070 Indigo Hill Rd (PO Box 216), Edisto Island, SC 29438. 803-869-2909 (EST) Civil Actions Under $2,500, Eviction, Small Claims.

**Johns Island Magistrate Court**, 1527 Main Rd, Johns Island, SC 29455. 803-559-1218 (EST) Civil Actions Under $2,500, Eviction, Small Claims.

**McClellanville Magistrate Court**, 9888 Randall Rd (PO Box 7), McClellanville, SC 29458. 803-887-3334 (EST) Civil Actions Under $2,500, Eviction, Small Claims.

**Mt Pleasant Magistrate Court**, 1189 Iron Bridge Rd, Ste 300 (PO Box 584, Mt Pleasant, SC 29464. 803-856-1206 (EST) 8:30AM-5PM. Civil Actions Under $2,500, Eviction, Small Claims.

**North Charleston Magistrate Court**, 2144 Melbourne St, North Charleston, SC 29405. 803-740-5873 (EST) Civil Actions Under $2,500, Eviction, Small Claims.

**North Charleston Magistrate Court**, 3505 Pinehaven Dr (PO Box 71316, 29415), North Charleston, SC 29406. 803-745-2216 (EST) Civil Actions Under $2,500, Eviction, Small Claims.

**North Charleston Magistrate Court**, 7272 Cross County Rd (PO Box 61870), North Charleston, SC 29419. 803-767-2743 (EST) Civil Actions Under $2,500, Eviction, Small Claims.

**Ravenel Magistrate Court**, PO Box 61, Ravenel, SC 29470. 803-889-8332 (EST) Civil Actions Under $2,500, Eviction, Small Claims.

**Probate Court**, PO Box 70398, Charleston, SC 29415-0398. 803-740-5889 (EST) Probate.

## Cherokee County

**Real Estate Recording**, Cherokee Clerk of Court, Floyd Baker Blvd, Gaffney, SC 29340. 803-487-2571 (EST) 9AM-5PM.

**Circuit Court**, PO Drawer 2289, Gaffney, SC 29342. 803-487-2571 (EST) 9AM-5PM. Felony, Misdemeanor, Civil Actions Over $2,500.

**Blacksburg Magistrate Court**, 104 Colonial Heights Dr, Blacksburg, SC 29702. 803-839-2492 (EST) Civil Actions Under $2,500, Eviction, Small Claims.

**Gaffney Magistrate Court**, PO Box 336, Gaffney, SC 29342. 803-487-2533 (EST) Civil Actions Under $2,500, Eviction, Small Claims.

**Probate Court**, PO Box 22, Gaffney, SC 29340. 803-487-2583 (EST) Probate.

## Chester County

**Real Estate Recording**, Chester Clerk of Court, 140 Main Street, Chester, SC 29706. 803-385-2605 (EST) 8:30AM-5PM.

**Circuit Court**, PO Drawer 580, Chester, SC 29706. 803-385-2605 (EST) 8:30AM-5PM. Felony, Misdemeanor, Civil Actions Over $2,500.

**Chester Magistrate Court**, 123 Dawson Dr (PO Box 723), Chester, SC 29706. 803-581-5136 (EST) Civil Actions Under $2,500, Eviction, Small Claims.

**Chester Magistrate Court**, Rt 3 Box 516, Chester, SC 29706. 803-789-5010 (EST) Civil Actions Under $2,500, Eviction, Small Claims.

**Richburg Magistrate Court**, PO Box 148, Richburg, SC 29729. 803-789-5010 (EST) Civil Actions Under $2,500, Eviction, Small Claims.

**Probate Court**, PO Drawer 580, Chester, SC 29706. 803-385-2604 (EST) Probate.

## Chesterfield County

**Real Estate Recording**, Chesterfield Clerk of Court, 200 West Main Street, Chesterfield, SC 29709. 803-623-2574 (EST) 8:30AM-5PM.

**Circuit Court**, PO Box 529, Chesterfield, SC 29709. 803-623-2574 (EST) 8:30AM-5PM. Felony, Misdemeanor, Civil Actions Over $2,500.

**Cheraw Magistrate Court**, Rt 2 Box 727, Cheraw, SC 29520. 803-537-7139 (EST) Civil Actions Under $2,500, Eviction, Small Claims.

**Cheraw Magistrate Court**, Rt 1 Box 366-A, Hinson Hill Rd, Cheraw, SC 29520. 803-623-2955 (EST) Civil Actions Under $2,500, Eviction, Small Claims.

**Cheraw Magistrate Court**, 309 Clyde Ave (PO Box 749), Cheraw, SC 29520. 803-537-7292 (EST) Civil Actions Under $2,500, Eviction, Small Claims.

**Chesterfield Magistrate Court**, Rt 1 Box 40, Chesterfield, SC 29709. 803-623-7929 (EST)

Civil Actions Under $2,500, Eviction, Small Claims.

**Chesterfield Magistrate Court**, PO Box 306, Chesterfield, SC 29709. (EST) Civil Actions Under $2,500, Eviction, Small Claims.

**Jefferson Magistrate Court**, 167 S Main St (PO Box 396), Jefferson, SC 29718. 803-658-7180 (EST) Civil Actions Under $2,500, Eviction, Small Claims.

**McBee Magistrate Court**, Rt 1 Box 455, McBee, SC 29101. 803-335-8467 (EST) Civil Actions Under $2,500, Eviction, Small Claims.

**Pageland Magistrate Court**, 126 N Pearl St, Pageland, SC 29728. 803-672-6914 (EST) Civil Actions Under $2,500, Eviction, Small Claims.

**Patrick Magistrate Court**, McLain St (PO Box 116), Patrick, SC 29584. 803-498-6701 (EST) Civil Actions Under $2,500, Eviction, Small Claims.

**Patrick Magistrate Court**, Rt 1 Box 105, Patrick, SC 29584. 803-498-6640 (EST) Civil Actions Under $2,500, Eviction, Small Claims.

**Ruby Magistrate Court**, PO Box 131, Ruby, SC 29741. 803-634-6597 (EST) Civil Actions Under $2,500, Eviction, Small Claims.

**Probate Court**, County Courthouse, Chesterfield, SC 29709. 803-623-2376 (EST) Probate.

## Clarendon County

**Real Estate Recording**, Clarendon Clerk of Court, Boyce Street, Courthouse, Manning, SC 29102. 803-435-4443 (EST) 8:30AM-5PM.

**Circuit Court**, Drawer E, Manning, SC 29102. 803-435-4444 (EST) 8:30AM-5PM. Felony, Misdemeanor, Civil Actions Over $2,500.

**Gable Magistrate Court**, PO Box 93, Gable, SC 29051. 803-435-4414 (EST) Civil Actions Under $2,500, Eviction, Small Claims.

**Lake City Magistrate Court**, Rt 1 Box 617, Lake City, SC 29560. 803-389-2484 (EST) Civil Actions Under $2,500, Eviction, Small Claims.

**Manning Magistrate Court**, PO Box 371, Manning, SC 29102. 803-435-2670 (EST) Civil Actions Under $2,500, Eviction, Small Claims.

**Manning Magistrate Court**, Rt 5 Box 636-A, Manning, SC 29102. 803-435-8925 (EST) Civil Actions Under $2,500, Eviction, Small Claims.

**New Zion Magistrate Court**, Rt 1 Box 286-B, New Zion, SC 29111. 803-659-2149 (EST) Civil Actions Under $2,500, Eviction, Small Claims.

**Summerton Magistrate Court**, 102 Main St (PO Box 277), Summerton, SC 29148. 803-435-2855 (EST) Civil Actions Under $2,500, Eviction, Small Claims.

**Probate Court**, PO Box 307, Manning, SC 29102. 803-435-8774 (EST) 8:30AM-5PM. Probate.

## Colleton County

**Real Estate Recording**, Colleton Clerk of Court, No. 1 Washington Street, Courthouse, Walterboro, SC 29488. 803-549-5791 (EST) 8:30AM-5PM.

**Circuit Court**, PO Box 620, Walterboro, SC 29488. 803-549-5791 (EST) 8:30AM-5PM. Felony, Misdemeanor, Civil Actions Over $2,500.

**Green Pond Magistrate Court**, Rt 2 Box 131, Green Pond, SC 29446. 803-844-2594 (EST) Civil Actions Under $2,500, Eviction, Small Claims.

**Walterboro Magistrate Court**, PO Box 1732, Walterboro, SC 29488. 803-549-1122 (EST) 8:30AM-5PM. Civil Actions Under $2,500, Eviction, Small Claims.

**Walterboro Magistrate Court**, Rt 7 Box 239-C, Walterboro, SC 29488. 803-538-3637 (EST) Civil Actions Under $2,500, Eviction, Small Claims.

**Walterboro Magistrate Court**, 1201 Green Pond Hwy, Walterboro, SC 29488. 803-549-1522 (EST) Civil Actions Under $2,500, Eviction, Small Claims.

**Walterboro Magistrate Court**, 1201 Green Pond Highway, Walterboro, SC 29488. 803-549-1522 (EST) Civil Actions Under $2,500, Eviction, Small Claims.

**Probate Court**, PO Box 1036, Walterboro, SC 29488. 803-549-7216 (EST) 8:30AM-5PM. Probate.

## Darlington County

**Real Estate Recording**, Darlington Clerk of Court, Courthouse, Darlington, SC 29532. 803-398-4330 (EST) 8:30AM-5PM.

**Circuit Court**, PO Box 498, Darlington, SC 29532. 803-398-4339 (EST) 8:30AM-5PM. Felony, Misdemeanor, Civil Actions Over $2,500.

**Darlington Magistrate Court**, PO Box 782, Darlington, SC 29532. 803-398-4341 (EST) Civil Actions Under $2,500, Eviction, Small Claims.

**Florence Magistrate Court**, 4522 Blitzgel Dr, Florence, SC 29501. (EST) Civil Actions Under $2,500, Eviction, Small Claims.

**Hartsville Magistrate Court**, 202 East Richardson Circle, Hartsville, SC 29550. (EST) Civil Actions Under $2,500, Eviction, Small Claims.

**Lamar Magistrate Court**, 1317 Cartersville Hwy, Lamar, SC 29069. 803-326-5441 (EST) Civil Actions Under $2,500, Eviction, Small Claims.

**Society Hill Magistrate Court**, Rt 2 Box 297, Society Hill, SC 29593. 803-378-4601 (EST) Civil Actions Under $2,500, Eviction, Small Claims.

**Probate Court**, PO Box 498, Darlington, SC 29532. 803-398-4339 (EST) Probate.

## Dillon County

**Real Estate Recording**, Dillon Clerk of Court, 401 West Main Street, City-County Complex, Suite 201, Dillon, SC 29536. 803-774-1425 (EST) 8:30AM-5PM.

**Circuit Court**, PO Drawer 1220, Dillon, SC 29536. 803-774-1425 (EST) 8:30AM-5PM. Felony, Misdemeanor, Civil Actions Over $2,500.

**Dillon Magistrate Court**, 200 S 5th Ave (PO Box 1016), Dillon, SC 29536. 803-774-1407 (EST) Civil Actions Under $2,500, Eviction, Small Claims.

**Dillon Magistrate Court**, PO Box 1281, Dillon, SC 29536. 803-774-5330 (EST) Civil Actions Under $2,500, Eviction, Small Claims.

**Hamer Magistrate Court**, 101 Lee Blvd (PO Box 1), Hamer, SC 29547. 803-774-2041 (EST) Civil Actions Under $2,500, Eviction, Small Claims.

**Lake View Magistrate Court**, PO Box 272, Lake View, SC 29563. (EST) Civil Actions Under $2,500, Eviction, Small Claims.

**Probate Court**, PO Box 189, Dillon, SC 29536. 803-774-1423 (EST) Probate.

## Dorchester County

**Real Estate Recording**, Dorchester County Register of Mesne Conveyances, 101 Ridge Street, St. George, SC 29477. 803-563-0182 (EST)

**Circuit Court**, PO Box 158, St George, SC 29477. 803-563-0160 (EST) 8:30AM-5PM. Felony, Misdemeanor, Civil Actions Over $2,500.

**Ridgeville Magistrate Court**, 339 S Railroad Ave, Ridgeville, SC 29472. 803-871-4854 (EST) Civil Actions Under $2,500, Eviction, Small Claims.

**St George Magistrate Court**, 102 Sears St, St George, SC 29477. 803-563-4854 (EST) Civil Actions Under $2,500, Eviction, Small Claims.

**Summerville Magistrate Court**, 133 E 1st North St, Summerville, SC 29483. 803-873-0781 (EST) Civil Actions Under $2,500, Eviction, Small Claims.

**Summerville Magistrate Court**, 212 Deming Way Box 10, Summerville, SC 29483. 803-873-0781 (EST) Civil Actions Under $2,500, Eviction, Small Claims.

**Summerville Magistrate Court**, PO Box 1372, Summerville, SC 29485. 803-871-1000 (EST) ?. Civil Actions Under $2,500, Eviction, Small Claims.

**Probate Court**, 101 Ridge St, St George, SC 29477. 803-563-0105 (EST) Probate.

## Edgefield County

**Real Estate Recording**, Edgefield Clerk of Court, 129 Courthouse Square, Edgefield, SC 29824. 803-637-4080 (EST) 8:30AM-5PM.

**Circuit Court**, PO Box 34, Edgefield, SC 29824. 803-637-4082 (EST) 8:30AM-5PM. Felony, Misdemeanor, Civil Actions Over $2,500.

**Edgefield Magistrate Court**, PO Box 664, Edgefield, SC 29824. 803-637-4090 (EST) Civil Actions Under $2,500, Eviction, Small Claims.

**Probate Court**, 127 Courthouse Square, Edgefield, SC 29824. 803-637-4076 (EST) Probate.

## Fairfield County

**Real Estate Recording**, Fairfield Clerk of Court, Congress Street, Courthouse, Winnsboro, SC 29180. 803-635-1411 (EST) 9AM-5PM.

**Circuit Court**, PO Drawer 299, Winnsboro, SC 29180. 803-635-1411 (EST) 9AM-5PM. Felony, Misdemeanor, Civil Actions Over $2,500.

**Great Falls Magistrate Court**, Rt 1 Box 1064, Great Falls, SC 29055. 803-482-2283 (EST) Civil Actions Under $2,500, Eviction, Small Claims.

**Jenkinsville Magistrate Court**, Rt 1 Box 148, Jenkinsville, SC 29065. 803-345-4635 (EST) Civil Actions Under $2,500, Eviction, Small Claims.

**Winnsboro Magistrate Court**, PO Box 423, Winnsboro, SC 29180. 803-635-4525 (EST) Civil Actions Under $2,500, Eviction, Small Claims.

**Probate Court**, PO Box 385, Winnsboro, SC 29180. 803-635-1411 (EST) 9AM-5PM. Probate.

## Florence County

**Real Estate Recording**, Florence Clerk of Court, 180 North Irby, Courthouse, Florence, SC 29501. 803-665-3031 (EST) 8:30AM-5PM.

**Circuit Court**, Drawer E, City County Complex, Florence, SC 29501. 803-665-3031 (EST) 8:30AM-5PM. Felony, Misdemeanor, Civil Actions Over $2,500.

**Florence Magistrate Court**, Drawer W, City-County Complex, Rm 401, Florence, SC 29501. 803-665-3001 (EST) Civil Actions Under $2,500, Eviction, Small Claims.

**Johnsonville Magistrate Court**, 119 Broadway St (PO Box 186), Johnsonville, SC 29555. 803-386-3422 (EST) Civil Actions Under $2,500, Eviction, Small Claims.

**Lake City Magistrate Court**, 345 S Ron McNair Blvd (PO Box 1463), Lake City, SC 29560. 803-394-5461 (EST) Civil Actions Under $2,500, Eviction, Small Claims.

**Olanta Magistrate Court**, PO Box 277, Olanta, SC 29114. 803-396-4798 (EST) Civil Actions Under $2,500, Eviction, Small Claims.

**Pamplico Magistrate Court**, 136 Third St (PO Box 367), Pamplico, SC 29583. 803-493-0072 (EST) Civil Actions Under $2,500, Eviction, Small Claims.

**Timmonsville Magistrate Court**, 500 Smith St (PO Box 190), Timmonsville, SC 29161. 803-346-7472 (EST) Civil Actions Under $2,500, Eviction, Small Claims.

**Probate Court**, 180 N Irby, MSC-L, Florence, SC 29501. 803-665-3085 (EST) 8:30AM-5PM. Probate.

## Georgetown County

**Real Estate Recording**, Georgetown Clerk of Court, 715 Prince Street, Georgetown, SC 29440. 803-527-6315 (EST) 8:30AM-5PM.

**Circuit Court**, PO Box 1270, Georgetown, SC 29442. 803-546-5011 (EST) 8:30AM-5PM. Felony, Misdemeanor, Civil Actions Over $2,500.

**Andrews Magistrate Court**, PO Box 44, Andrews, SC 29510. 803-264-8811 (EST) Civil Actions Under $2,500, Eviction, Small Claims.

**Georgetown Magistrate Court**, 2226 Beck St, Georgetown, SC 29440. 803-546-4075 (EST) Civil Actions Under $2,500, Eviction, Small Claims.

**Georgetown Magistrate Court**, PO Box 807, Georgetown, SC 29442. 803-546-4650 (EST) Civil Actions Under $2,500, Eviction, Small Claims.

**Georgetown Magistrate Court**, PO Box 1838, Georgetown, SC 29442. 803-527-8980 (EST) Civil Actions Under $2,500, Eviction, Small Claims.

**Hemingway Magistrate Court**, Rt 3 Box 46, Hemingway, SC 29564. 803-558-2837 (EST) Civil Actions Under $2,500, Eviction, Small Claims.

**Murrells Inlet Magistrate Court**, PO Box 859, Murrells Inlet, SC 29576. 803-651-6292 (EST) Civil Actions Under $2,500, Eviction, Small Claims.

**Pawleys Island Magistrate Court**, PO Box 1830, Pawleys Island, SC 29585. 803-237-8995 (EST) Civil Actions Under $2,500, Eviction, Small Claims.

**Probate Court**, PO Box 1270, Georgetown, SC 29442. 803-527-6325 (EST) 8:30AM-5PM. Probate.

## Greenville County

**Real Estate Recording**, Greenville County Register of Mesne Conveyances, 301 University Ridge, County Square Suite 1300, Greenville, SC 29601-3655. 803-467-7240 (EST) 8:30AM-5PM.

**Circuit Court**, 305 E. North St, Greenville, SC 29601. 803-467-8551 (EST) 8:30AM-5PM. Felony, Misdemeanor, Civil Actions Over $2,500.

**Greenville Magistrate Court**, Law Enforcement Ctr-116A, 4 McGee St, Greenville, SC 29601. 803-467-5312 (EST) Civil Actions Under $2,500, Eviction, Small Claims.

**Greenville Magistrate Court**, 12 Howe St, Greenville, SC 29601. 803-467-5295 (EST) Civil Actions Under $2,500, Eviction, Small Claims.

**Greenville Magistrate Court**, 720 S Washington Ave, Greenville, SC 29611. 803-269-0991 (EST) Civil Actions Under $2,500, Eviction, Small Claims.

**Greenville Magistrate Court**, 6247 White Horse Rd, Greenville, SC 29611. 803-294-4810 (EST) Civil Actions Under $2,500, Eviction, Small Claims.

**Greer Magistrate Court**, 117 S Main St, Greer, SC 29650. 803-877-7464 (EST) Civil Actions Under $2,500, Eviction, Small Claims.

**Landrum Magistrate Court**, 2015 Hwy 11, Landrum, SC 29356. 803-895-0478 (EST) Civil Actions Under $2,500, Eviction, Small Claims.

**Marietta Magistrate Court**, #3208 Geer Hwy (PO Box 506), Marietta, SC 29661. 803-836-3671 (EST) Civil Actions Under $2,500, Eviction, Small Claims.

**Mauldin Magistrate Court**, 206 Owens Ln #2, Mauldin, SC 29662. (EST) Civil Actions Under $2,500, Eviction, Small Claims.

**Piedmont Magistrate Court**, 8150 August Rd, Piedmont, SC 29673. 803-277-9555 (EST) Civil Actions Under $2,500, Eviction, Small Claims.

**Simpsonville Magistrate Court**, 116 S Main St, Simpsonville, SC 29681. 803-963-3457 (EST) Civil Actions Under $2,500, Eviction, Small Claims.

**Taylors Magistrate Court**, 2801 Wade Hampton Blvd, Taylors, SC 29687. 803-244-2922 (EST) 8:30AM-5PM. Civil Actions Under $2,500, Eviction, Small Claims.

**Travelers Rest Magistrate Court**, 114 N Poinsett Hwy, Travelers Rest, SC 29690. 803-834-6910 (EST) 9AM-4PM M,T,Th,F/9AM-1PM W. Civil Actions Under $2,500, Eviction, Small Claims.

**Probate Court**, 301 University Ridge, Ste 1200, Greenville, SC 29601. 803-467-7170 (EST) 8:30AM-5PM. Probate.

## Greenwood County

**Real Estate Recording**, Greenwood Clerk of Court, Courthouse, 528 Monument St., Greenwood, SC 29646. 803-942-8551 (EST) 8:30AM-5PM.

**Circuit Court**, Courthouse, Rm 114, Greenwood, SC 29646. 803-942-8612 (EST) 8:30AM-5PM. Felony, Misdemeanor, Civil Actions Over $2,500.

**Greenwood Magistrate Court**, Greenood County Courthouse, Rm 106, Greenwood, SC 29646. 803-942-8655 (EST) Civil Actions Under $2,500, Eviction, Small Claims.

**Greenwood Magistrate Court**, 300 Hwy 246 South, Greenwood, SC 29646. (EST) Civil Actions Under $2,500, Eviction, Small Claims.

**Greenwood Magistrate Court**, 107 St Andrews Ln, Greenwood, SC 29646. (EST) Civil Actions Under $2,500, Eviction, Small Claims.

**Greenwood Magistrate Court**, PO Box 752, Greenwood, SC 29648. 803-942-8655 (EST) Civil Actions Under $2,500, Eviction, Small Claims.

**Probate Court**, PO Box 1210, Greenwood, SC 29648. 803-942-8625 (EST) 8:30AM-5PM. Probate.

## Hampton County

**Real Estate Recording**, Hampton Clerk of Court, Courthouse Square, Elm Street, Hampton, SC 29924. 803-943-7510 (EST) 8AM-5PM.

**Circuit Court**, PO Box 7, Hampton, SC 29924. 803-943-7500 (EST) 8AM-5PM. Felony, Misdemeanor, Civil Actions Over $2,500.

**Estill Magistrate Court**, Rt 2 Box 15, Estill, SC 29918. 803-943-3272 (EST) Civil Actions Under $2,500, Eviction, Small Claims.

**Estill Magistrate Court**, PO Box 969, Estill, SC 29918. 803-625-3232 (EST) Civil Actions Under $2,500, Eviction, Small Claims.

**Hampton Magistrate Court**, PO Box 314, Hampton, SC 29924. 803-943-7511 (EST) Civil Actions Under $2,500, Eviction, Small Claims.

**Probate Court**, PO Box 601, Hampton, SC 29924. 803-943-7512 (EST) 8AM-5PM. Probate.

## Horry County

**Real Estate Recording**, Horry County Register of Mesne Conveyances, 101-A Beaty Street, Conway, SC 29526. 803-248-1252 (EST) 8AM-5PM.

**Circuit Court**, PO Box 677, Conway, SC 29526. 803-248-1270 (EST) 8AM-5PM. Felony, Misdemeanor, Civil Actions Over $2,500.

**Aynor Magistrate Court**, 601 Eight Ave.(PO Box 115), Aynor, SC 29511. 803-358-6320 (EST) 8AM-5PM. Civil Actions Under $2,500, Eviction, Small Claims.

**Conway Magistrate Court**, 944 Hwy 90, Conway, SC 29526. 803-365-9222 (EST) Civil Actions Under $2,500, Eviction, Small Claims.

**Conway Magistrate Court**, 1316 1st Ave (PO Box 544), Conway, SC 29526. 803-248-6356 (EST) Civil Actions Under $2,500, Eviction, Small Claims.

**Conway Magistrate Court**, 4152 J Reuben Long Ave (PO Box 2115), Conway, SC 29526. 803-365-7715 (EST) Civil Actions Under $2,500, Eviction, Small Claims.

**Conway Magistrate Court**, 3880 Tillmond Rd (PO Box 1071), Conway, SC 29526. 803-248-1373 (EST) Civil Actions Under $2,500, Eviction, Small Claims.

**Green Sea Magistrate Court**, 5527 Hwy #9 (PO Box 153), Green Sea, SC 29545. 803-756-5250 (EST) Civil Actions Under $2,500, Eviction, Small Claims.

**Loris Magistrate Court**, 3817 Walnut St, Loris, SC 29569. 803-756-7918 (EST) Civil Actions Under $2,500, Eviction, Small Claims.

**Myrtle Beach Magistrate Court**, 1201 21st North Ave, Myrtle Beach, SC 29575. 803-448-7810 (EST) Civil Actions Under $2,500, Eviction, Small Claims.

**N Myrtle Beach Magistrate Court**, PO Box 33, N Myrtle Beach, SC 29597-0033. 803-249-2411 (EST) 8AM-5PM. Civil Actions Under $2,500, Eviction, Small Claims.

**Surfside Beach Magistrate Court**, 1106 Glenns Bay Rd, Surfside Beach, SC 29575. 803-238-3277 (EST) 8AM-5PM. Civil Actions Under $2,500, Eviction, Small Claims.

**Probate Court**, PO Box 288, Conway, SC 29526. 803-248-1294 (EST) 8AM-5PM. Probate.

## Jasper County

**Real Estate Recording**, Jasper Clerk of Court, 305 Russell Street, Ridgeland, SC 29936. 803-726-7710 (EST) 9AM-5PM.

**Circuit Court**, PO Box 248, Ridgeland, SC 29936. 803-726-7710 (EST) 8:30AM-5PM. Felony, Misdemeanor, Civil Actions Over $2,500.

**Hardeeville Magistrate Court**, Rt 1 Box 184-A, Hardeeville, SC 29927. (EST) Civil Actions Under $2,500, Eviction, Small Claims.

**Ridgeland Magistrate Court**, PO Box 1281, Ridgeland, SC 29936. 803-726-6831 (EST) Civil Actions Under $2,500, Eviction, Small Claims.

**Ridgeland Magistrate Court**, Rt 2 Box 529, Ridgeland, SC 29936. 803-726-5053 (EST) Civil Actions Under $2,500, Eviction, Small Claims.

**Ridgeland Magistrate Court**, 111 W Adams St (PO Box 665), Ridgeland, SC 29936. 803-726-7737 (EST) Civil Actions Under $2,500, Eviction, Small Claims.

**Probate Court**, PO Box 1739, Ridgeland, SC 29936. 803-726-7719 (EST) 9AM-5PM. Probate.

## Kershaw County

**Real Estate Recording**, Kershaw Clerk of Court, Courthouse - Room 313, 1121 Broad St., Camden, SC 29020. 803-425-1527 (EST) 9AM-5PM.

**Circuit Court**, County Courthouse, Rm 313 (PO Box 1557), Camden, SC 29020. 803-425-1527 (EST) 9AM-5PM. Felony, Misdemeanor, Civil Actions Over $2,500.

**Bethune Magistrate Court**, 202 N Main St (PO Box 215), Bethune, SC 29009. 803-334-8450 (EST) Civil Actions Under $2,500, Eviction, Small Claims.

**Camden Magistrate Court**, Kershaw County Courthouse, Rm 118, Camden, SC 29020. 803-425-1529 (EST) Civil Actions Under $2,500, Eviction, Small Claims.

**Camden Magistrate Court**, 217 Welsh St, Camden, SC 29020. 803-425-1516 (EST) Civil Actions Under $2,500, Eviction, Small Claims.

**Camden Magistrate Court**, 1121 Broad St (PO Drawer 1528), Camden, SC 29020. 803-425-1520 (EST) Civil Actions Under $2,500, Eviction, Small Claims.

**Probate Court**, 1121 Broad St, Rm 302, Camden, SC 29020. 803-425-1525 (EST) 9AM-5PM. Probate.

## Lancaster County

**Real Estate Recording**, Lancaster Clerk of Court, Corner of Cawtaba & Dunlap Streets, Lancaster, SC 29720. 803-285-1581 (EST) 8:30AM-5PM.

**Circuit Court**, PO Box 1809, Lancaster, SC 29720. 803-285-1581 (EST) 8:30AM-5PM. Felony, Misdemeanor, Civil Actions Over $2,500.

**Fort Mill Magistrate Court**, 8097 Charlotte Hwy, Fort Mill, SC 29715. 803-547-5332 (EST) Civil Actions Under $2,500, Eviction, Small Claims.

**Kershaw Magistrate Court**, Rt 2 Box 174, Kershaw, SC 29067. 803-475-6643 (EST) Civil Actions Under $2,500, Eviction, Small Claims.

**Lancaster Magistrate Court**, 4141 Bessie Hudson Rd, Lancaster, SC 29720. 803-285-1048 (EST) Civil Actions Under $2,500, Eviction, Small Claims.

**Lancaster Magistrate Court**, PO Box 1809, Lancaster, SC 29720. 803-283-3983 (EST) Civil Actions Under $2,500, Eviction, Small Claims.

**Lancaster Magistrate Court**, 2055 Lynwood Dr, Lancaster, SC 29720. 803-285-1587 (EST) Civil Actions Under $2,500, Eviction, Small Claims.

**Probate Court**, PO Box 1028, Lancaster, SC 29721. 803-283-3379 (EST) 8:30AM-5PM. Probate.

## Laurens County

**Real Estate Recording**, Laurens Clerk of Court, Public Square, Laurens, SC 29360. 803-984-3538 (EST) 9AM-5PM.

**Circuit Court**, PO Box 287, Laurens, SC 29360. 803-984-3538 (EST) 9AM-5PM. Felony, Misdemeanor, Civil Actions Over $2,500.

**Clinton Magistrate Court**, 102 N Broad St, Clinton, SC 29325. 803-833-5879 (EST) Civil Actions Under $2,500, Eviction, Small Claims.

**Gray Court Magistrate Court**, Rt 3 Box 152, Gray Court, SC 29645. 803-876-3533 (EST) Civil Actions Under $2,500, Eviction, Small Claims.

**Laurens Magistrate Court**, PO Box 925, Laurens, SC 29360. 803-984-4022 (EST) Civil Actions Under $2,500, Eviction, Small Claims.

**Laurens Magistrate Court**, Rt 4 Box 2069, Laurens, SC 29360. 803-984-4022 (EST) Civil Actions Under $2,500, Eviction, Small Claims.

**Probate Court**, PO Box 194, Laurens, SC 29360. 803-984-7315 (EST) 9AM-5PM. Probate.

## Lee County

**Real Estate Recording**, Lee Clerk of Court, 123 South Main Street, Courthouse, Bishopville, SC 29010. 803-484-5341 (EST) 9AM-5PM.

**Circuit Court**, PO Box 281, Bishopville, SC 29010. 803-484-5341 (EST) 9AM-5PM. Felony, Misdemeanor, Civil Actions Over $2,500.

**Bishopville Magistrate Court**, Main St, Courthouse (PO Box 2), Bishopville, SC 29010. 803-484-9442 (EST) Civil Actions Under $2,500, Eviction, Small Claims.

**Dalzell Magistrate Court**, Rt 1 Box 108-A, Dalzell, SC 29040. 803-484-5341 (EST) Civil Actions Under $2,500, Eviction, Small Claims.

**Mayesville Magistrate Court**, Rt 1 Box 191, Mayesville, SC 29104. 803-428-6762 (EST) Civil Actions Under $2,500, Eviction, Small Claims.

**Probate Court**, PO Box 24, Bishopville, SC 29010. 803-484-5341 (EST) 9AM-5PM. Probate.

## Lexington County

**Real Estate Recording**, Lexington County Register Mesne Conveyance, 212 South Lake Drive, Lexington, SC 29072. 803-359-8491 (EST) 8AM-5PM.

**Circuit Court**, County Courthouse, Rm 107, Lexington, SC 29072. 803-359-8212 (EST) 8AM-5PM. Felony, Misdemeanor, Civil Actions Over $2,500.

**Batesburg Magistrate Court**, 231 W Church St, Batesburg, SC 29006. 803-359-8330 (EST) Civil Actions Under $2,500, Eviction, Small Claims.

**Cayce Magistrate Court**, 650 Knox Abbott Dr, Cayce, SC 29033. 803-796-7100 (EST) Civil Actions Under $2,500, Eviction, Small Claims.

**Columbia Magistrate Court**, 108 Harbison Blvd, Columbia, SC 29212. 803-781-7584 (EST) Civil Actions Under $2,500, Eviction, Small Claims.

**Lexington Magistrate Court**, County Courthouse, Rm 6, Lexington, SC 29072. 803-359-8221 (EST) Civil Actions Under $2,500, Eviction, Small Claims.

**Lexington Magistrate Court**, 521 Gibson Rd, Lexington, SC 29072. 803-951-8522 (EST) Civil Actions Under $2,500, Eviction, Small Claims.

**Swansea Magistrate Court**, 500 Charlie Rast Rd (PO Box 457), Swansea, SC 29160. 803-568-3616 (EST) Civil Actions Under $2,500, Eviction, Small Claims.

**Probate Court**, County Courthouse, Rm 110, Lexington, SC 29072. 803-359-8324 (EST) 8:30AM-4:30PM. Probate.

## Marion County

**Real Estate Recording**, Marion Clerk of Court, West Court Street, Marion, SC 29571. 803-423-8240 (EST) 8:30AM-5PM.

**Circuit Court**, PO Box 295, Marion, SC 29571. 803-423-8240 (EST) 8:30AM-5PM. Felony, Misdemeanor, Civil Actions Over $2,500.

**Gresham Magistrate Court**, PO Box 35, Gresham, SC 29546. 803-362-0180 (EST) Civil Actions Under $2,500, Eviction, Small Claims.

**Marion Magistrate Court**, PO Box 847, Marion, SC 29571. 803-423-8208 (EST) Civil Actions Under $2,500, Eviction, Small Claims.

**Mullins Magistrate Court**, 151 N East Front St (PO Box 612), Mullins, SC 29574. 803-464-6027 (EST) Civil Actions Under $2,500, Eviction, Small Claims.

**Probate Court**, PO Box 583, Marion, SC 29571. 803-423-8244 (EST) 8:30AM-5PM. Probate.

## Marlboro County

**Real Estate Recording**, Marlboro Clerk of Court, Main Street, Courthouse, Bennettsville, SC 29512. 803-479-5613 (EST) 8:30AM-5PM.

**Circuit Court**, PO Drawer 996, Bennettsville, SC 29512. 803-479-5613 (EST) 8:30AM-5PM. Felony, Misdemeanor, Civil Actions Over $2,500.

**Bennettsville Magistrate Court**, PO Box 418, Bennettsville, SC 29512. 803-479-5620 (EST) Civil Actions Under $2,500, Eviction, Small Claims.

**Blenheim Magistrate Court**, 5646 Allen Ridge Rd, Blenheim, SC 29516. 803-528-9148

(EST) Civil Actions Under $2,500, Eviction, Small Claims.

**Clio Magistrate Court**, 114 Church St (PO Box 387), Clio, SC 29525. 803-586-2211 (EST) Civil Actions Under $2,500, Eviction, Small Claims.

**McColl Magistrate Court**, 210 E Gibson Ave (PO Box 502), McColl, SC 29570. 803-523-5695 (EST) Civil Actions Under $2,500, Eviction, Small Claims.

**Probate Court**, PO Box 455, Bennettsville, SC 29512. 803-479-5610 (EST) 8:30AM-5PM. Probate.

## McCormick County

**Real Estate Recording**, McCormick Clerk of Court, 133 South Mine Street, Courthouse, Room 102, McCormick, SC 29835. 803-465-2195 (EST) 9AM-5PM.

**Circuit Court**, 133 Mine St, McCormick, SC 29835. 803-465-2195 (EST) 9AM-5PM. Felony, Misdemeanor, Civil Actions Over $2,500.

**McCormick Magistrate Court**, County Courthouse Hwy 28 (PO Box 1116), McCormick, SC 29835. 803-465-2316 (EST) Civil Actions Under $2,500, Eviction, Small Claims.

**Probate Court**, PO Box 225, McCormick, SC 29835. 803-465-2630 (EST) Probate.

## Newberry County

**Real Estate Recording**, Newberry Clerk of Court, College Street, Courthouse Room 5, Newberry, SC 29108. 803-321-2110 (EST) 8:30AM-5PM.

**Circuit Court**, PO Box 278, Newberry, SC 29108. 803-321-2110 (EST) 8:30AM-5PM. Felony, Misdemeanor, Civil Actions Over $2,500.

**Chappells Magistrate Court**, Rt 1 Box 79-A, Chappells, SC 29037. 803-995-3671 (EST) Civil Actions Under $2,500, Eviction, Small Claims.

**Little Mountain Magistrate Court**, Rt 1 Box 11, Little Mountain, SC 29075. 803-345-1562 (EST) Civil Actions Under $2,500, Eviction, Small Claims.

**Newberry Magistrate Court**, 3239 Louis Rich Rd, Newberry, SC 29108. 803-321-2144 (EST) Civil Actions Under $2,500, Eviction, Small Claims.

**Peak Magistrate Court**, 6 River St (PO Box 198), Peak, SC 29122. 803-945-7455 (EST) Civil Actions Under $2,500, Eviction, Small Claims.

**Whitmire Magistrate Court**, PO Box 62, Whitmire, SC 29178. 803-694-4927 (EST) Civil Actions Under $2,500, Eviction, Small Claims.

**Probate Court**, PO Box 442, Newberry, SC 29108. 803-321-2118 (EST) 8:30AM-5PM. Probate.

## Oconee County

**Real Estate Recording**, Oconee Clerk of Court, Main Street, Walhalla, SC 29691. 803-638-4280 (EST) 8:30AM-5PM.

**Circuit Court**, PO Box 678, Walhalla, SC 29691. 803-638-4280 (EST) 8:30AM-5PM. Felony, Misdemeanor, Civil Actions Over $2,500.

**Seneca Magistrate Court**, 312 W North 1st St, Seneca, SC 29678. 803-882-7321 (EST) Civil Actions Under $2,500, Eviction, Small Claims.

**Walhalla Magistrate Court**, 300 S Church St, Walhalla, SC 29691. 803-638-4125 (EST) Civil Actions Under $2,500, Eviction, Small Claims.

**Probate Court**, PO Box 471, Walhalla, SC 29691. 803-638-4275 (EST) 8:30AM-5PM. Probate.

## Orangeburg County

**Real Estate Recording**, Orangeburg County Register Mesne Conveyance, 190 Sunnyside Street N.E., Room 108, Orangeburg, SC 29115. 803-533-6237 (EST) 8:30AM-5PM.

**Circuit Court**, PO Box 9000, Orangeburg, SC 29116. 803-533-6243 (EST) 8:30AM-5PM. Felony, Misdemeanor, Civil Actions Over $2,500.

**Bowman Magistrate Court**, Main St (PO Box 365), Bowman, SC 29018. 803-829-2831 (EST) Civil Actions Under $2,500, Eviction, Small Claims.

**Branchville Magistrate Court**, Rt 1 Box 71-AA, Branchville, SC 29432. 803-274-8820 (EST) Civil Actions Under $2,500, Eviction, Small Claims.

**Elloree Magistrate Court**, PO Box 646, Elloree, SC 29047. 803-897-1064 (EST) Civil Actions Under $2,500, Eviction, Small Claims.

**Eutawville Magistrate Court**, Hwy #6, Rt 1 Box 467 (PO Box 188), Eutawville, SC 29048. 803-492-3697 (EST) Civil Actions Under $2,500, Eviction, Small Claims.

**Holly Hill Magistrate Court**, PO Box 957, Holly Hill, SC 29059. 803-496-9533 (EST) Civil Actions Under $2,500, Eviction, Small Claims.

**North Magistrate Court**, PO Box 321, North, SC 29112. 803-642-1530 (EST) Civil Actions Under $2,500, Eviction, Small Claims.

**Norway Magistrate Court**, Pinehurst St (PO Box 437), Norway, SC 29113. 803-263-4433 (EST) Civil Actions Under $2,500, Eviction, Small Claims.

**Orangeburg Magistrate Court**, Rt 3 Box 1633, Orangeburg, SC 29115. 803-534-8933 (EST) Civil Actions Under $2,500, Eviction, Small Claims.

**Orangeburg Magistrate Court**, PO Box 854, Orangeburg, SC 29115. 803-533-5847 (EST) Civil Actions Under $2,500, Eviction, Small Claims.

**Orangeburg Magistrate Court**, PO Box 9000, Orangeburg, SC 29116-9000. 803-533-5852 (EST) Civil Actions Under $2,500, Eviction, Small Claims.

**Springfield Magistrate Court**, 705 Railroad Ave (PO Box 355), Springfield, SC 29146. 803-258-3315 (EST) Civil Actions Under $2,500, Eviction, Small Claims.

**Probate Court**, PO Drawer 9000, Orangeburg, SC 29116-9000. 803-533-6280 (EST) 8:30AM-5PM. Probate.

## Pickens County

**Real Estate Recording**, Pickens Register of Mesne Conveyance, 222 McDaniel Ave. B-5, Pickens, SC 29671. 803-898-5868 (EST) 8:30AM-5PM.

**Circuit Court**, PO Box 215, Pickens, SC 29671. 803-898-5866 (EST) 8:30AM-5PM. Felony, Misdemeanor, Civil Actions Over $2,500.

**Clemson Magistrate Court**, 170 Clemson Ctr, Hwy 176, Clemson, SC 29631. 803-654-3338 (EST) Civil Actions Under $2,500, Eviction, Small Claims.

**Easley Magistrate Court**, 135 Folger Ave, West End Hall, Easley, SC 29640. 803-850-7076 (EST) Civil Actions Under $2,500, Eviction, Small Claims.

**Liberty Magistrate Court**, 431 E Main St, Liberty, SC 29657. 803-850-3500 (EST) Civil Actions Under $2,500, Eviction, Small Claims.

**Pickens Magistrate Court**, 216-Ste A, LEC Rd, Pickens, SC 29671. 803-898-5551 (EST) 8:30AM-5PM. Civil Actions Under $2,500, Eviction, Small Claims.

**Probate Court**, 222 McDaniel Ave B-16, Pickens, SC 29671. 803-898-5903 (EST) 8:30AM-5PM. Probate.

## Richland County

**Real Estate Recording**, Richland County Register of Mesne Conveyances, 1701 Main Street, Columbia, SC 29201. 803-748-4797 (EST) 8:45AM-5PM.

**Circuit Court**, PO Box 1781, Columbia, SC 29202. 803-748-4684 (EST) 8:45AM-5PM. Felony, Misdemeanor, Civil Actions Over $2,500.

**Columbia Magistrate Court**, 1328 Huger St, Columbia, SC 29201. 803-748-4928 (EST) Civil Actions Under $2,500, Eviction, Small Claims.

**Columbia Magistrate Court**, 1215 1/2 Rosewood Dr, Columbia, SC 29201. 803-799-1779 (EST) Civil Actions Under $2,500, Eviction, Small Claims.

**Columbia Magistrate Court**, PO Box 192, Columbia, SC 29202. 803-748-4741 (EST) Civil Actions Under $2,500, Eviction, Small Claims.

**Columbia Magistrate Court**, 4919 Rhett St, Columbia, SC 29203. 803-754-2250 (EST) Civil Actions Under $2,500, Eviction, Small Claims.

**Columbia Magistrate Court**, 6941 A North Trenholm Rd, Columbia, SC 29206. 803-782-2807 (EST) Civil Actions Under $2,500, Eviction, Small Claims.

**Columbia Magistrate Court**, 5205 Trenholm Rd #201, Columbia, SC 29206. 803-738-9019 (EST) Civil Actions Under $2,500, Eviction, Small Claims.

**Columbia Magistrate Court**, 1223 St Andrews Rd, Columbia, SC 29210. 803-772-6464 (EST) Civil Actions Under $2,500, Eviction, Small Claims.

**Columbia Magistrate Court**, PO Box 9523, Columbia, SC 29290. 803-776-0454 (EST) Civil Actions Under $2,500, Eviction, Small Claims.

**Columbia Magistrate Court**, PO Box 9246, Columbia, SC 29290. 803-776-3962 (EST) Civil Actions Under $2,500, Eviction, Small Claims.

**Elgin Magistrate Court**, 10535 Two Notch Rd, Elgin, SC 29045. 803-788-8232 (EST) Civil Actions Under $2,500, Eviction, Small Claims.

**Hopkins Magistrate Court**, 135 American Ave, Hopkins, SC 29209. 803-783-2424 (EST) Civil Actions Under $2,500, Eviction, Small Claims.

**Probate Court**, PO Box 192, Columbia, SC 29202. 803-748-4705 (EST) 8:45AM-5PM. Probate.

## Saluda County

**Real Estate Recording**, Saluda Clerk of Court, Courthouse, Saluda, SC 29138. 803-445-3303 (EST) 8:30AM-5PM.

**Circuit Court**, County Courthouse, Saluda, SC 29138. 803-445-3303 (EST) 8:30AM-5PM. Felony, Misdemeanor, Civil Actions Over $2,500.

**Saluda Magistrate Court**, 120 S Main St, Saluda, SC 29138. 803-445-2846 (EST) Civil Actions Under $2,500, Eviction, Small Claims.

**Probate Court**, County Courthouse, Saluda, SC 29138. 803-445-7110 (EST) 8:30AM-5PM. Probate.

## Spartanburg County

**Real Estate Recording**, Spartanburg County Register of Mesne Conveyances, 366 North Church Street, County Administrative Offices, Spartanburg, SC 29303. 803-596-2514 (EST) 8:30AM-5PM.

**Circuit Court**, County Courthouse, Spartanburg, SC 29301. 803-596-2591 (EST) 8:30AM-5PM. Felony, Misdemeanor, Civil Actions Over $2,500.

**Inman Magistrate Court**, 7 Mill St, Inman, SC 29349. 803-472-4447 (EST) Civil Actions Under $2,500, Eviction, Small Claims.

**Landrum Magistrate Court**, 100 N Bomar Ave, Landrum, SC 29356. 803-457-7245 (EST) Civil Actions Under $2,500, Eviction, Small Claims.

**Landrum Magistrate Court**, PO Box 128, Landrum, SC 29356. 803-596-2564 (EST) Civil Actions Under $2,500, Eviction, Small Claims.

**Lyman Magistrate Court**, #7 Brookdale Acres Dr, Lyman, SC 29365. 803-877-2581 (EST) Civil Actions Under $2,500, Eviction, Small Claims.

**Pacolet Magistrate Court**, 651 Hillbrook Cir, Pacolet, SC 29372. 803-474-9504 (EST) Civil Actions Under $2,500, Eviction, Small Claims.

**Reidville Magistrate Court**, PO Box 37, Reidville, SC 29375. 803-949-5023 (EST) Civil Actions Under $2,500, Eviction, Small Claims.

**Spartanburg Magistrate Court**, County Courthouse, Rm 134, Spartanburg, SC 29301. 803-596-2564 (EST) Civil Actions Under $2,500, Eviction, Small Claims.

**Spartanburg Magistrate Court**, 180 Magnolia St, Spartanburg, SC 29301. 803-596-2228 (EST) Civil Actions Under $2,500, Eviction, Small Claims.

**Spartanburg Magistrate Court**, 767 California Ave, Spartanburg, SC 29303. 803-461-3402 (EST) Civil Actions Under $2,500, Eviction, Small Claims.

**Spartanburg Magistrate Court**, PO Box 5221, Spartanburg, SC 29304. 803-594-4452 (EST) Civil Actions Under $2,500, Eviction, Small Claims.

**Spartanburg Magistrate Court**, PO Box 16243, Spartanburg, SC 29316. 803-578-6319 (EST) Civil Actions Under $2,500, Eviction, Small Claims.

**Probate Court**, 180 Magnolia St, Spartanburg, SC 29301. 803-596-2556 (EST) 8:30AM-5PM. Probate.

## Sumter County

**Real Estate Recording**, Sumter County Register of Mesne Conveyance, Courthouse, Room 202, 141 N. Main St., Sumter, SC 29150. 803-436-2177 (EST) 8:30AM-5PM.

**Circuit Court**, 141 N Main, Sumter, SC 29150. 803-436-2227 (EST) 8:30AM-5PM. Felony, Misdemeanor, Civil Actions Over $2,500.

**Mayesville Magistrate Court**, PO Box 236, Mayesville, SC 29104. 803-499-3366 (EST) Civil Actions Under $2,500, Eviction, Small Claims.

**Pinewood Magistrate Court**, PO Box 371, Pinewood, SC 29125. 803-452-5878 (EST) Civil Actions Under $2,500, Eviction, Small Claims.

**Rembert Magistrate Court**, 5070 John W Sanders Rd, Rembert, SC 29128. 803-436-2347 (EST) Civil Actions Under $2,500, Eviction, Small Claims.

**Sumter Magistrate Court**, 115 N Harvin St (PO Box 1394, 29151), Sumter, SC 29150. 803-436-2280 (EST) Civil Actions Under $2,500, Eviction, Small Claims.

**Sumter Magistrate Court**, PO Box 1394, Sumter, SC 29151. 803-436-2280 (EST) Civil Actions Under $2,500, Eviction, Small Claims.

**Sumter Magistrate Court**, 3310 Nazarene Church Rd, Sumter, SC 29154. 803-481-2739 (EST) Civil Actions Under $2,500, Eviction, Small Claims.

**Probate Court**, 141 N Main, Rm 206, Sumter, SC 29150. 803-436-2166 (EST) 8:30AM-5PM. Probate.

## Union County

**Real Estate Recording**, Union Clerk of Court, 210 West Main Street, Union, SC 29379. 803-429-1630 (EST) 9AM-5PM.

**Circuit Court**, PO Box 200, Union, SC 29379. 803-429-1630 (EST) 9AM-5PM. Felony, Misdemeanor, Civil Actions Over $2,500.

**Carlisle Magistrate Court**, PO Box 35, Carlisle, SC 29031. 803-427-6987 (EST) Civil Actions Under $2,500, Eviction, Small Claims.

**Jonesville Magistrate Court**, PO Box 484, Jonesville, SC 29353. 803-674-5102 (EST) Civil Actions Under $2,500, Eviction, Small Claims.

**Lockhart Magistrate Court**, PO Box 357, Lockhart, SC 29364. 803-545-6636 (EST) Civil Actions Under $2,500, Eviction, Small Claims.

**Union Magistrate Court**, Union County Courthouse, Union, SC 29379. 803-429-1648 (EST) Civil Actions Under $2,500, Eviction, Small Claims.

**Probate Court**, PO Box 447, Union, SC 29379. 803-429-1625 (EST) 9AM-5PM. Probate.

## Williamsburg County

**Real Estate Recording**, Williamsburg Clerk of Court, 125 West Main Street, Courthouse Square, Kingstree, SC 29556. 803-354-6855 (EST) 9AM-5PM.

**Circuit Court**, PO Box 86, Kingstree, SC 29556. 803-354-6855 (EST) 9AM-5PM. Felony, Misdemeanor, Civil Actions Over $2,500.

**Andrews Magistrate Court**, Rt 4 Box 87, Andrews, SC 29510. 803-221-5438 (EST) Civil Actions Under $2,500, Eviction, Small Claims.

**Cades Magistrate Court**, Rt 1 Box 146, Cades, SC 29568. 803-389-4494 (EST) Civil Actions Under $2,500, Eviction, Small Claims.

**Greeleyville Magistrate Court**, Rt 2 Box 19-A, Greeleyville, SC 29056. 803-426-2945 (EST) Civil Actions Under $2,500, Eviction, Small Claims.

**Hemingway Magistrate Court**, PO Box 416, Hemingway, SC 29554. 803-558-2116 (EST) Civil Actions Under $2,500, Eviction, Small Claims.

**Kingstree Magistrate Court**, Rt 4 Box 200, Kingstree, SC 29556. 803-382-9723 (EST) Civil Actions Under $2,500, Eviction, Small Claims.

**Kingstree Magistrate Court**, Rt 1 Box 216-A (PO Box 956), Kingstree, SC 29556. 803-382-2181 (EST) Civil Actions Under $2,500, Eviction, Small Claims.

**Kingstree Magistrate Court**, 10 Courthouse Sq (PO Box 673), Kingstree, SC 29556. 803-354-9602 (EST) Civil Actions Under $2,500, Eviction, Small Claims.

**Lake city Magistrate Court**, Rt 2 Box 253-D, Lake city, SC 29560. 803-389-4787 (EST) Civil Actions Under $2,500, Eviction, Small Claims.

**Lane Magistrate Court**, Rt 2 Box 94-A, Lane, SC 29564. 803-387-5726 (EST) Civil Actions Under $2,500, Eviction, Small Claims.

**Nesmith Magistrate Court**, Rt 1 Box 297, Nesmith, SC 29580. 803-382-2249 (EST) Civil Actions Under $2,500, Eviction, Small Claims.

**Probate Court**, PO Box 1005, Kingstree, SC 29556. 803-354-6655 (EST) 9AM-5PM. Probate.

## York County

**Real Estate Recording**, York Clerk of Court, 2 South Congress, York, SC 29745. 803-684-8510 (EST) 8AM-5PM.

**Circuit Court**, PO Box 649, York, SC 29745. 803-648-8507 (EST) Felony, Misdemeanor, Civil Actions Over $2,500.

**Clover Magistrate Court**, 201 S Main St (PO Box 165), Clover, SC 29710. 803-222-9404 (EST) Civil Actions Under $2,500, Eviction, Small Claims.

**Fort Mill Magistrate Court**, 114 Springs St, Fort Mill, SC 29715. 803-547-5572 (EST) Civil Actions Under $2,500, Eviction, Small Claims.

**Hickoy Grove Magistrate Court**, PO Box 37, Hickory Grove, SC 29717. 803-925-2815 (EST) Civil Actions Under $2,500, Eviction, Small Claims.

**Rock Hill Magistrate Court**, 529 S Cherry Rd (PO Box 11166), Rock Hill, SC 29730. 803-328-1866 (EST) Civil Actions Under $2,500, Eviction, Small Claims.

**Rock Hill Magistrate Court**, 2211 Zinker Rd, Rock Hill, SC 29732. 803-328-1866 (EST) Civil Actions Under $2,500, Eviction, Small Claims.

**York Magistrate Court**, 1675-1D York Hwy, York, SC 29745. 803-628-3029 (EST) Civil Actions Under $2,500, Eviction, Small Claims.

**Probate Court**, PO Box 219, York, SC 29745. 803-684-8513 (EST) 8AM-5PM. Probate.

# South Dakota

## Aurora County

**Real Estate Recording**, Aurora County Register of Deeds, Main Street, Courthouse, Plankinton, SD 57368. 605-942-7161 (CST) 8AM-Noon,1-5PM.

**Circuit Court**, PO Box 366, Plankinton, SD 57368. 605-942-7165 (CST) 8AM-12PM 1PM-5PM. Felony, Misdemeanor, Civil, Eviction, Small Claims, Probate.

## Beadle County

**Real Estate Recording**, Beadle County Register of Deeds, 400 Block of 3rd Street S.W., Huron, SD 57350. 605-352-3168 (CST) 8AM-5PM.

**Circuit Court**, PO Box 1358, Huron, SD 57350. 605-353-7165 (CST) 8AM-5PM. Felony, Misdemeanor, Civil, Eviction, Small Claims, Probate.

## Bennett County

**Real Estate Recording**, Bennett County Register of Deeds, 202 Main Street, Courthouse, Martin, SD 57551. 605-685-6054 (MST) 8AM-Noon, 12:30-4:30PM.

**Circuit Court**, PO Box 281, Martin, SD 57551. 605-685-6969 (MST) 8AM-4:30PM. Felony, Misdemeanor, Civil, Eviction, Small Claims, Probate.

## Bon Homme County

**Real Estate Recording**, Bon Homme County Register of Deeds, Cherry Street, Courthouse, Tyndall, SD 57066. 605-589-4217 (CST)

**Circuit Court**, PO Box 6, Tyndall, SD 57066. 605-589-4215 (CST) 8AM-4:30PM. Felony, Misdemeanor, Civil, Eviction, Small Claims, Probate.

## Brookings County

**Real Estate Recording**, Brookings County Register of Deeds, 314 6th Avenue, Courthouse, Brookings, SD 57006-2084. 605-692-2724 (CST) 8AM-5PM.

**Circuit Court**, 314 6th Ave, Brookings, SD 57006. 605-688-4200 (CST) 8AM-5PM. Felony, Misdemeanor, Civil, Eviction, Small Claims, Probate.

## Brown County

**Real Estate Recording**, Brown County Register of Deeds, 25 Market Street, Aberdeen, SD 57402. 605-622-7140 (CST) 8AM-5PM.

**Circuit Court**, 101 1st Ave SE, Aberdeen, SD 57401. 605-626-2451 (CST) 8AM-5PM. Felony, Misdemeanor, Civil, Eviction, Small Claims, Probate.

## Brule County

**Real Estate Recording**, Brule County Register of Deeds, 300 South Courtland, Suite 110, Chamberlain, SD 57325. 605-734-5310 (CST) 8AM-Noon,1-5PM.

**Circuit Court**, 300 S Courtland, Chamberlain, SD 57325. 605-734-5443 (CST) 8AM-12PM 1PM-5PM. Felony, Misdemeanor, Civil, Eviction, Small Claims, Probate.

## Buffalo County

**Real Estate Recording**, Buffalo County Register of Deeds, Main Street, Courthouse, Gannvalley, SD 57341. 605-293-3239 (CST) 9AM-5PM.

**Circuit Court**, PO Box 148, Gann Valley, SD 57341. 605-293-3234 (CST) 9AM-12PM. Felony, Misdemeanor, Civil, Eviction, Small Claims, Probate.

## Butte County

**Real Estate Recording**, Butte County Register of Deeds, 839 Fifth Avenue, Belle Fourche, SD 57717. 605-892-2912 (MST) 8AM-5PM.

**8th Circuit Court**, PO Box 237, Belle Fourche, SD 57717. 605-892-2516 (MST) 8AM-12PM 1PM-5PM. Felony, Misdemeanor, Civil, Eviction, Small Claims, Probate.

## Campbell County

**Real Estate Recording**, Campbell County Register of Deeds, 2nd and Main Street, Courthouse, Mound City, SD 57646. 605-955-3505 (CST) 8AM-Noon,1-5PM.

**Circuit Court**, PO Box 146, Mound City, SD 57646. 605-955-3536 (CST) 8AM-12PM. Felony, Misdemeanor, Civil, Eviction, Small Claims, Probate.

## Charles Mix County

**Real Estate Recording**, Charles Mix County Register of Deeds, Courthouse, Main Street, Lake Andes, SD 57356. 605-487-7141 (CST) 8AM-4:30PM.

**Circuit Court**, PO Box 640, Lake Andes, SD 57356. 605-487-7511 (CST) 8AM-4:30PM. Felony, Misdemeanor, Civil, Eviction, Small Claims, Probate.

## Clark County

**Real Estate Recording**, Clark County Register of Deeds, 202 N. Commercial St., Clark, SD 57225. 605-532-5363 (CST) 8AM-5PM.

**Circuit Court**, PO Box 294, Clark, SD 57225. 605-532-5851 (CST) 8AM-5PM. Felony, Misdemeanor, Civil, Eviction, Small Claims, Probate.

## Clay County

**Real Estate Recording**, Clay County Register of Deeds, 211 West Main Street, Courthouse, Vermillion, SD 57069. 605-624-2871 (CST) 8AM-5PM.

**Circuit Court**, PO Box 377, Vermillion, SD 57069. 605-677-6482 (CST) 8AM-5PM. Felony, Misdemeanor, Civil, Eviction, Small Claims, Probate.

## Codington County

**Real Estate Recording**, Codington County Register of Deeds, 14 1st Avenue S.E., Watertown, SD 57201-3695. 605-886-4719 (CST) 8AM-5PM.

**Circuit Court**, PO Box 1054, Watertown, SD 57201. 605-882-5095 (CST) 8AM-5PM. Felony, Misdemeanor, Civil, Eviction, Small Claims, Probate.

## Corson County

**Real Estate Recording**, Corson County Register of Deeds, Courthouse, McIntosh, SD 57641. 605-273-4395 (MST) 8AM-Noon,1-5PM.

**Circuit Court**, PO Box 175, McIntosh, SD 57641. 605-273-4201 (MST) 8AM-12PM 1PM-3PM. Felony, Misdemeanor, Civil, Eviction, Small Claims, Probate.

## Custer County

**Real Estate Recording**, Custer County Register of Deeds, 420 Mount Rushmore Road, Custer, SD 57730-1934. 605-673-2784 (MST) 8AM-5PM.

**Circuit Court**, 420 Mt Rushmore Rd, Custer, SD 57730. 605-673-4816 (MST) 8AM-5PM. Felony, Misdemeanor, Civil, Eviction, Small Claims, Probate.

## Davison County

**Real Estate Recording**, Davison County Register of Deeds, 200 East 4th, Courthouse, Mitchell, SD 57301-2692. 605-996-2209 (CST) 8AM-5PM.

**Circuit Court**, PO Box 927, Mitchell, SD 57301. 605-996-2450 (CST) 8AM-12PM. Felony, Misdemeanor, Civil, Eviction, Small Claims, Probate.

## Day County

**Real Estate Recording**, Day County Register of Deeds, 710 West First Street, Webster, SD 57274-1396. 605-345-4162 (CST) 8AM-5PM.

**Circuit Court**, 710 W 1st St, Webster, SD 57274. 605-345-3771 (CST) 8AM-5PM. Felony, Misdemeanor, Civil, Eviction, Small Claims, Probate.

## Deuel County

**Real Estate Recording**, Deuel County Register of Deeds, Courthouse, Clear Lake, SD 57226. 605-874-2268 (CST) 8AM-Noon,1-5PM.

**Circuit Court**, PO Box 308, Clear Lake, SD 57226. 605-874-2120 (CST) 8AM-5PM. Felony, Misdemeanor, Civil, Eviction, Small Claims, Probate.

## Dewey County

**Real Estate Recording**, Dewey County Register of Deeds, C Street, Courthouse, Timber Lake, SD 57656. 605-865-3661 (MST) 8AM-Noon,1-5PM.

**Circuit Court**, PO Box 96, Timber Lake, SD 57656. 605-865-3566 (MST) 9:30AM-12PM 1PM-2:30PM. Felony, Misdemeanor, Civil, Eviction, Small Claims, Probate.

## Douglas County

**Real Estate Recording**, Douglas County Register of Deeds, Courthouse, Armour, SD 57313. 605-724-2204 (CST) 8AM-Noon,1-5PM.

**Circuit Court**, PO Box 36, Armour, SD 57313. 605-724-2585 (CST) 8AM-12PM 1PM-5PM. Felony, Misdemeanor, Civil, Eviction, Small Claims, Probate.

## Edmunds County

**Real Estate Recording**, Edmunds County Register of Deeds, Courthouse, Ipswich, SD 57451. 605-426-6431 (CST) 8AM-Noon,1-5PM.

**Circuit Court**, PO Box 384, Ipswich, SD 57451. 605-426-6671 (CST) 8AM-12PM 1PM-5PM. Felony, Misdemeanor, Civil, Eviction, Small Claims, Probate.

## Fall River County

**Real Estate Recording**, Fall River County Register of Deeds, 906 North River Street, Hot Springs, SD 57747. 605-745-5139 (MST) 8AM-5PM.

**Circuit Court**, 906 N River St, Hot Springs, SD 57747. 605-745-5131 (MST) 8AM-5PM. Felony, Misdemeanor, Civil, Eviction, Small Claims, Probate.

## Faulk County

**Real Estate Recording**, Faulk County Register of Deeds, Courthouse, Faulkton, SD 57438. 605-598-6228 (CST) 8AM-Noon,1-5PM.

**Circuit Court**, PO Box 357, Faulkton, SD 57438. 605-598-6223 (CST) 9AM-3PM. Felony, Misdemeanor, Civil, Eviction, Small Claims, Probate.

## Grant County

**Real Estate Recording**, Grant County Register of Deeds, 210 East Fifth Avenue, Milbank, SD 57252. 605-432-4752 (CST) 8AM-5PM.

**Circuit Court**, PO Box 509, Sioux Falls, SD 57102. 605-339-6418 (CST) 8AM-12PM 1PM-5PM. Felony, Misdemeanor, Civil, Eviction, Small Claims, Probate.

## Gregory County

**Real Estate Recording**, Gregory County Register of Deeds, Courthouse, Burke, SD 57523. 605-775-2624 (CST) 8AM-Noon,1-5PM.

**Circuit Court**, PO Box 430, Burke, SD 57523. 605-775-2665 (CST) 8AM-12PM 1PM-5PM. Felony, Misdemeanor, Civil, Eviction, Small Claims, Probate.

## Haakon County

**Real Estate Recording**, Haakon County Register of Deeds, 130 South Howard, Courthouse, Philip, SD 57567. 605-859-2785 (MST) 8AM-Noon,1-5PM.

**Circuit Court**, PO Box 70, Philip, SD 57567. 605-859-2627 (MST) 1PM-5PM. Felony, Misdemeanor, Civil, Eviction, Small Claims, Probate.

## Hamlin County

**Real Estate Recording**, Hamlin County Register of Deeds, Main Street, Courthouse, Hayti, SD 57241. 605-783-3206 (CST) 8AM-12, 1PM-5PM.

**Circuit Court**, PO Box 256, Hayti, SD 57241. 605-783-3751 (CST) 8AM-12PM 1PM 5PM. Felony, Misdemeanor, Civil, Eviction, Small Claims, Probate.

## Hand County

**Real Estate Recording**, Hand County Register of Deeds, 415 West 1st Avenue, Miller, SD 57362-1346. 605-853-3512 (CST) 8AM-5PM.

**Circuit Court**, PO Box 122, Miller, SD 57362. 605-853-3337 (CST) 8AM-5PM. Felony, Misdemeanor, Civil, Eviction, Small Claims, Probate.

## Hanson County

**Real Estate Recording**, Hanson County Register of Deeds, Courthouse, 720 5th Street, Alexandria, SD 57311. 605-239-4512 (CST) 8AM-Noon,1-5PM.

**Circuit Court**, PO Box 127, Alexandria, SD 57311. 605-239-4446 (CST) 8AM-5PM. Felony, Misdemeanor, Civil, Eviction, Small Claims, Probate.

## Harding County

**Real Estate Recording**, Harding County Register of Deeds, Courthouse, Buffalo, SD 57720. 605-375-3321 (MST) 8AM-12, 1PM-5PM.

**Circuit Court**, PO Box 534, Buffalo, SD 57720. 605-375-3351 (MST) 9:30AM-12PM 1PM-2:30PM. Felony, Misdemeanor, Civil, Eviction, Small Claims, Probate.

## Hughes County

**Real Estate Recording**, Hughes County Register of Deeds, 104 East Capital, Pierre, SD 57501. 605-224-7891 (CST) 8AM-5PM.

**Circuit Court**, 104 E Capital, Pierre, SD 57501. 605-773-3713 (CST) 8AM-5PM. Felony, Misdemeanor, Civil, Eviction, Small Claims, Probate.

## Hutchinson County

**Real Estate Recording**, Hutchinson County Register of Deeds, 140 Euclid Street, Room 37, Olivet, SD 57052-2103. 605-387-4217 (CST) 8AM-5PM.

**Circuit Court**, PO Box 7, Olivet, SD 57052. 605-387-5335 (CST) 8AM-12PM 1PM-5PM. Felony, Misdemeanor, Civil, Eviction, Small Claims, Probate.

## Hyde County

**Real Estate Recording**, Hyde County Register of Deeds, 412 Commercial S.E., Courthouse, Highmore, SD 57345. 605-852-2517 (CST)

**Circuit Court**, PO Box 306, Highmore, SD 57345. (CST) 8AM-5PM. Felony, Misdemeanor, Civil, Eviction, Small Claims, Probate.

## Jackson County

**Real Estate Recording**, Jackson County Register of Deeds, Main Street, Courthouse, Kadoka, SD 57453. 605-837-2420 (MST) 8AM-5PM.

**Circuit Court**, PO Box 128, Kadoka, SD 57543. 605-837-2121 (MST) 8AM-5PM. Felony, Misdemeanor, Civil, Eviction, Small Claims, Probate.

## Jerauld County

**Real Estate Recording**, Jerauld County Register of Deeds, Courthouse, 205 So. Wallace, Wessington Springs, SD 57382. 605-539-1221 (CST) 8AM-12, 1PM-5PM.

**Circuit Court**, PO Box 435, Wessington Springs, SD 57382. 605-539-1202 (CST) 8AM-5PM. Felony, Misdemeanor, Civil, Eviction, Small Claims, Probate.

## Jones County

**Real Estate Recording**, Jones County Register of Deeds, 310 Main Street, Courthouse, Murdo, SD 57559. 605-669-2132 (CST) 8AM-5PM.

**Circuit Court**, PO Box 448, Murdo, SD 57559. 605-669-2361 (CST) 8AM-5PM. Felony, Misdemeanor, Civil, Eviction, Small Claims, Probate.

## Kingsbury County

**Real Estate Recording**, Kingsbury County Register of Deeds, Courthouse, 101 2nd St. SE, De Smet, SD 57231. 605-854-3591 (CST) 8AM-Noon,1-5PM.

**Circuit Court**, PO Box 176, De Smet, SD 57231-0176. 605-854-3811 (CST) 8AM-12PM 1PM-5-PM. Felony, Misdemeanor, Civil, Eviction, Small Claims, Probate.

## Lake County

**Real Estate Recording**, Lake County Register of Deeds, 200 East Center, Courthouse, Madison, SD 57042. 605-256-7614 (CST) 8AM-12, 1PM-5PM.

**Circuit Court**, 200 E Center st, Madison, SD 57042. 605-256-5644 (CST) 8AM-5PM. Felony, Misdemeanor, Civil, Eviction, Small Claims, Probate.

## Lawrence County

**Real Estate Recording**, Lawrence County Register of Deeds, 90 Sherman Street, Deadwood, SD 57732. 605-578-3930 (MST) 8AM-5PM.

**Circuit Court**, PO Box 626, Deadwood, SD 57732. 605-578-2040 (MST) 8AM-5PM. Felony, Misdemeanor, Civil, Eviction, Small Claims, Probate.

## Lincoln County

**Real Estate Recording**, Lincoln County Register of Deeds, 100 East 5th, Canton, SD 57013-1789. 605-987-5661 (CST) 8AM-5PM.

**Circuit Court**, 100 E 5th St, Canton, SD 57013. 605-987-5891 (CST) 8AM-5PM. Felony, Misdemeanor, Civil, Eviction, Small Claims, Probate.

## Lyman County

**Real Estate Recording**, Lyman County Register of Deeds, 100 Main Street, Courthouse, Kennebec, SD 57544. 605-869-2297 (CST) 8AM-Noon,1-5PM.

**Circuit Court**, PO Box 235, Kennebec, SD 57544. 605-869-2277 (CST) 8AM-5PM. Felony, Misdemeanor, Civil, Eviction, Small Claims, Probate.

## Marshall County

**Real Estate Recording**, Marshall County Register of Deeds, Vander Horck Avenue, Courthouse, Britton, SD 57430. 605-448-2352 (CST) 8AM-Noon,1-5PM.

**Circuit Court**, PO Box 130, Britton, SD 57430. 605-448-5213 (CST) 8AM-5PM. Felony, Misdemeanor, Civil, Eviction, Small Claims, Probate.

## McCook County

**Real Estate Recording**, McCook County Register of Deeds, 130 West Essex Street, Salem, SD 57058. 605-425-2701 (CST) 8:30AM-4:30PM.

**Circuit Court**, PO Box 504, Salem, SD 57058. 605-425-2781 (CST) 8AM-5PM. Felony, Misdemeanor, Civil, Eviction, Small Claims, Probate.

## McPherson County

**Real Estate Recording**, McPherson County Register of Deeds, Main Street, Courthouse, Leola, SD 57456. 605-439-3151 (CST) 8AM-12, 1PM-5PM.

**Circuit Court**, PO Box 248, Leola, SD 57456. 605-439-3361 (CST) 8AM-12PM. Felony, Misdemeanor, Civil, Eviction, Small Claims, Probate.

## Meade County

**Real Estate Recording**, Meade County Register of Deeds, 1425 Sherman Street, Sturgis, SD 57785. 605-347-2356 (MST) 8AM-5PM.

**Circuit Court**, PO Box 939, Sturgis, SD 57785. 605-347-4411 (MST) 8AM-5PM. Felony, Misdemeanor, Civil, Eviction, Small Claims, Probate.

## Mellette County

**Real Estate Recording**, Mellette County Register of Deeds, Courthouse, White River, SD 57579. 605-259-3371 (MST) 8AM-Noon,1-5PM.

**Circuit Court**, PO Box 257, White River, SD 57579. 605-259-3230 (MST) 8AM-12PM. Felony, Misdemeanor, Civil, Eviction, Small Claims, Probate.

## Miner County

**Real Estate Recording**, Miner County Register of Deeds, Main Street, Courthouse, Howard, SD 57349. 605-772-5621 (CST) 8AM-Noon,1-5PM.

**Circuit Court**, PO Box 265, Howard, SD 57349. 605-772-4612 (CST) 8AM-5PM. Felony, Misdemeanor, Civil, Eviction, Small Claims, Probate.

## Minnehaha County

**Real Estate Recording**, Minnehaha County Register of Deeds, 415 North Dakota Avenue, Sioux Falls, SD 57102. 605-335-4223 (CST) 8AM-5PM.

**Circuit Court**, 415 N Dakota Ave, Sioux Falls, SD 57102. 605-339-6418 (CST) 8AM-5PM. Felony, Misdemeanor, Civil, Eviction, Small Claims, Probate.

## Moody County

**Real Estate Recording**, Moody County Register of Deeds, Pipestone Avenue, Courthouse, Flandreau, SD 57028. 605-997-3151 (CST) 8AM-5PM.

**Circuit Court**, 101 E Pipestone, Flandreau, SD 57028. 605-997-3181 (CST) 8AM-5PM. Felony, Misdemeanor, Civil, Eviction, Small Claims, Probate.

## Pennington County

**Real Estate Recording**, Pennington County Register of Deeds, 315 St. Joe Street, Rapid City, SD 57701. 605-394-2177 (MST) 8AM-5PM.

**Circuit Court**, PO Box 230, Rapid City, SD 57709. 605-394-2575 (MST) 8AM-5PM. Felony, Misdemeanor, Civil, Eviction, Small Claims, Probate.

## Perkins County

**Real Estate Recording**, Perkins County Register of Deeds, Main Street, Courthouse, Bison, SD 57620. 605-244-5620 (MST) 8AM-Noon,1-5PM.

**8th Circuit Court**, PO Box 426, Bison, SD 57620-0426. 605-244-5626 (MST) 8AM-12PM 1PM-5PM. Felony, Misdemeanor, Civil, Eviction, Small Claims, Probate.

## Potter County

**Real Estate Recording**, Potter County Register of Deeds, 201 South Exene, Gettysburg, SD 57442. 605-765-9467 (CST) 8AM-Noon, 1PM-5PM.

**Circuit Court**, 201 S Exene, Gettysburg, SD 57442. 605-765-9472 (CST) 8AM-5PM. Felony, Misdemeanor, Civil, Eviction, Small Claims, Probate.

## Roberts County

**Real Estate Recording**, Roberts County Register of Deeds, 411 East 2nd Avenue, Sisseton, SD 57262. 605-698-7152 (CST) 8AM-5PM.

**Circuit Court**, 411 2nd Ave E, Sisseton, SD 57262. 605-698-3395 (CST) 8AM-5PM. Felony, Misdemeanor, Civil, Eviction, Small Claims, Probate.

## Sanborn County

**Real Estate Recording**, Sanborn County Register of Deeds, Courthouse, Woonsocket, SD 57385. 605-796-4516 (CST)

**Circuit Court**, PO Box 56, Woonsocket, SD 57385. 605-796-4515 (CST) 8AM-5PM. Felony, Misdemeanor, Civil, Eviction, Small Claims, Probate.

## Shannon County

**Real Estate Recording**, Shannon County Register of Deeds, 906 North River Street, Hot Springs, SD 57747. 605-745-5139 (MST) 8AM-5PM.

**Circuit Court**, 906 N River St, Hot Springs, SD 57747. 605-745-5131 (MST) 8AM-5PM. Felony, Misdemeanor, Civil, Eviction, Small Claims, Probate.

## Spink County

**Real Estate Recording**, Spink County Register of Deeds, 210 East 7th Avenue, Redfield, SD 57469. 605-472-0150 (CST) 8AM-5PM.

**Circuit Court**, 210 E 7th Ave, Redfield, SD 57469. 605-472-1922 (CST) 8AM-5PM. Felony, Misdemeanor, Civil, Eviction, Small Claims, Probate.

## Stanley County

**Real Estate Recording**, Stanley County Register of Deeds, 8 East 2nd Avenue, Courthouse, Fort Pierre, SD 57532. 605-223-2610 (MST) 8AM-Noon,1-5PM.

**Circuit Court**, PO Box 758, Fort Pierre, SD 57532. 605-773-3992 (MST) 8AM-5PM. Felony, Misdemeanor, Civil, Eviction, Small Claims, Probate.

## Sully County

**Real Estate Recording**, Sully County Register of Deeds, 700 Ash Avenue, Courthouse, Onida, SD 57564. 605-258-2331 (CST) 8AM-Noon,1-5PM.

**Circuit Court**, PO Box 188, Onida, SD 57564. 605-258-2535 (CST) 8AM-12PM. Felony, Misdemeanor, Civil, Eviction, Small Claims, Probate.

## Todd County

**Real Estate Recording**, Todd County Register of Deeds, Courthouse, 200 E. 3rd St., Winner, SD 57580-1806. 605-842-2208 (MST) 8AM-5PM.

**Circuit Court**, 200 E 3rd St, Winner, SD 57580. 605-842-2266 (MST) 8AM-5PM. Felony, Misdemeanor, Civil, Eviction, Small Claims, Probate.

## Tripp County

**Real Estate Recording**, Tripp County Register of Deeds, Courthouse, 200 E. 3rd St., Winner, SD 57580-1806. 605-842-2208 (CST) 8AM-5PM.

**Circuit Court**, 200 E 3rd St, Winner, SD 57580. 605-842-2266 (CST) 8AM-5PM. Felony, Misdemeanor, Civil, Eviction, Small Claims, Probate.

## Turner County

**Real Estate Recording**, Turner County Register of Deeds, South Main Street, Courthouse, Parker, SD 57053. 605-297-3443 (CST) 8:30AM-5PM.

**Circuit Court**, PO Box 446, Parker, SD 57053. 605-297-3115 (CST) 8AM-5PM. Felony, Misdemeanor, Civil, Eviction, Small Claims, Probate.

## Union County

**Real Estate Recording**, Union County Register of Deeds, Courthouse, 200 E. Main, Elk Point, SD 57025. 605-356-2191 (CST) 8:30AM-5PM.

**Circuit Court**, PO Box 757, Elk Point, SD 57025. 605-356-2132 (CST) 8:30AM-5PM. Felony, Misdemeanor, Civil, Eviction, Small Claims, Probate.

## Walworth County

**Real Estate Recording**, Walworth County Register of Deeds, Courthouse, Selby, SD 57472. 605-649-7057 (CST) 8AM-Noon,1-5PM.

**Circuit Court**, PO Box 328, Selby, SD 57472. 605-649-7311 (CST) 8AM-5PM. Felony, Misdemeanor, Civil, Eviction, Small Claims, Probate.

## Yankton County

**Real Estate Recording**, Yankton County Register of Deeds, 3rd & Broadway, Courthouse, Yankton, SD 57078. 605-665-2422 (CST) 9AM-5PM.

**Circuit Court**, PO Box 155, Yankton, SD 57078. 605-668-3438 (CST) 8AM-5PM. Felony, Misdemeanor, Civil, Eviction, Small Claims, Probate.

## Ziebach County

**Real Estate Recording**, Ziebach County Register of Deeds, Courthouse, Dupree, SD 57623. 605-365-5165 (MST) 8AM-5PM.

**Circuit Court**, PO Box 306, Dupree, SD 57623. 605-365-5159 (MST) 9:30AM-2:30PM. Felony, Misdemeanor, Civil, Eviction, Small Claims, Probate.

# Tennessee

## Anderson County

**Real Estate Recording**, Anderson County Register of Deeds, 100 North Main Street, Courthouse, Room 205, Clinton, TN 37716-3688. 615-457-5400 (EST) 8:30AM-4:30PM.

**7th District Circuit Court and General Sessions**, 100 Main St, Rm 301, Clinton, TN 37716. 615-457-5400 (EST) 8AM-4:30PM. Felony, Misdemeanor, Civil, Eviction, Small Claims.

**Chancery Court**, PO Box 501, Clinton, TN 37716. 615-457-5400 (EST) 8:30AM-4:30PM. Civil, Probate.

## Bedford County

**Real Estate Recording**, Bedford County Register of Deeds, One Public Square, Suite 104, Shelbyville, TN 37160-3961. 615-684-5719 (CST) 8AM-4PM M,T,Th,F; 8AM-4PM W; 8AM-Noon Sat.

**17th District Circuit Court and General Sessions**, 1 Public Sq, Suite 200, Shelbyville, TN 37160. 615-684-3223 (CST) 8AM-4PM M-Th, 8AM-5PM Fri. Felony, Misdemeanor, Civil, Eviction, Small Claims.

**Chancery Court**, Chancery Court, 1 Public Sq, Suite 302, Shelbyville, TN 37160. 615-684-1672 (CST) 8AM-4PM M-Th, 8AM-5PM Fri. Civil, Probate.

## Benton County

**Real Estate Recording**, Benton County Register of Deeds, Main Street, Courthouse, Camden, TN 38320. 901-584-6661 (CST) 8AM-4PM; 8AM-5PM F.

**24th District Circuit Court, General Sessions and Juvenile**, PO Box 466, Camden, TN 38320. 901-584-6711 (CST) 8AM-4PM. Felony, Misdemeanor, Civil, Eviction, Small Claims.

**Chancery Court**, Chancery Court, PO Box 531, Camden, TN 38320. 901-584-4435 (CST) Civil, Probate.

## Bledsoe County

**Real Estate Recording**, Bledsoe County Register of Deeds, Main Street, Courthouse, Pikeville, TN 37367. 615-447-2020 (CST) 8AM-4PM M,T,W,F; 8AM-Noon Sat.

**12th District Circuit Court and General Sessions**, PO Box 455, Pikeville, TN 37367. 615-447-6488 (CST) 8AM-4PM. Felony, Misdemeanor, Civil, Eviction, Small Claims.

**Chancery Court**, Chancery Court, Clerk & Master, PO Box 4, Pikeville, TN 37367. 615-447-2484 (CST) 8AM-4PM. Civil, Probate.

## Blount County

**Real Estate Recording**, Blount County Register of Deeds, 349 Court Street, Maryville, TN 37804-5906. 615-982-5741 (EST) 8AM-4:30PM.

**5th District Circuit Court and General Sessions**, 301 Court St, Maryville, TN 37801. 615-982-3762 (EST) 8AM-4:30PM. Felony, Misdemeanor, Civil, Eviction, Small Claims.

**County Court**, 301 Court St, Maryville, TN 37801. 615-982-4391 (EST) 8AM-4:30PM. Civil, Probate.

## Bradley County

**Real Estate Recording**, Bradley County Register of Deeds, 155 North Ocoee, Courthouse, Cleveland, TN 37364. 615-476-0513 (EST) 8:30AM-4PM M-Th; 8:30AM-5PM F.

**10th District Criminal, Circuit, and General Sessions Court**, PO Box 1167, Cleveland, TN 37311. 615-476-0544 (EST) 8:30AM-4PM M-Th, 8:30AM-5PM Fri. Felony, Misdemeanor, Civil, Eviction, Small Claims.

**Chancery Court**, Chancery Court, Clerk & Master, 155 N., Cleveland, TN 37311. 615-476-0526 (EST) 8:30AM-4PM M-Th, 8:30AM-5PM Fri. Civil, Probate.

## Campbell County

**Real Estate Recording**, Campbell County Register of Deeds, Main Street, Courthouse, Jacksboro, TN 37757. 615-562-3864 (EST) 8AM-4:30PM.

**8th District Criminal, Circuit, and General Sessions Court**, PO Box 26, Jacksboro, TN 37757. 615-562-2624 (EST) 8AM-4:30PM. Felony, Misdemeanor, Civil, Eviction, Small Claims.

**Chancery Court**, PO Box 182, Jacksboro, TN 37757. 615-562-3496 (EST) 8AM-4:30PM. Civil, Probate.

## Cannon County

**Real Estate Recording**, Cannon County Register of Deeds, Courthouse, Woodbury, TN 37190. 615-563-2041 (CST) 8AM-4PM M,T,Th,F; 8AM-Noon Sat.

**16th District Circuit Court and General Sessions**, County Courthouse Public Sq, Woodbury, TN 37190. 615-563-4461 (CST) 8AM-4PM MTTF, 8AM-12PM Sat, closed Wed. Felony, Misdemeanor, Civil, Eviction, Small Claims.

**County Court**, Public Sq, Woodbury, TN 37190. 615-563-4278 (CST) 8AM-4PM MTTF, closed Wed. Civil, Probate.

## Carroll County

**Real Estate Recording**, Carroll County Register of Deeds, Court Square, Courthouse, Huntingdon, TN 38344. 901-986-1952 (CST) 8AM-4PM; 8AM-Noon Sat.

**24th District Circuit Court and General Sessions**, PO Box 487, Huntingdon, TN 38344. 901-986-1931 (CST) 8AM-4PM. Felony, Misdemeanor, Civil, Eviction, Small Claims.

**Chancery Court**, PO Box 186, Huntingdon, TN 38344. 901-986-1920 (CST) 8AM-4PM. Civil, Probate.

## Carter County

**Real Estate Recording**, Carter County Register of Deeds, 801 East Elk Avenue, Elizabethton, TN 37643. 615-542-1830 (EST) 8:30AM-5PM.

**1st District Criminal, Circuit, and General Sessions Court**, Courthouse Annex, Elizabethton, TN 37643. 615-542-1835 (EST) 8AM-5PM. Felony, Misdemeanor, Civil, Eviction, Small Claims.

**County Court**, Old Courthouse, Main St, Elizabethton, TN 37643. 615-542-1812 (EST) 8AM-5PM. Civil, Probate.

## Cheatham County

**Real Estate Recording**, Cheatham County Register of Deeds, 100 Public Square, Suite 117, Ashland City, TN 37015. 615-792-4317 (CST) 8AM-4PM.

**23rd District Circuit Court and General Sessions**, 100 Public Sq, Ashland City, TN 37015. 615-792-3272 (CST) 8AM-4PM. Felony, Misdemeanor, Civil, Eviction, Small Claims.

**Chancery Court**, Clerk & Master, Suite 106, Ashland City, TN 37015. 615-792-4620 (CST) 8AM-4PM. Civil, Probate.

## Chester County

**Real Estate Recording**, Chester County Register of Deeds, Main Street, Courthouse, Henderson, TN 38340. 901-989-4991 (CST) 8AM-4PM.

**26th District Circuit Court and General Sessions**, PO Box 133, Henderson, TN 38340. 901-989-2454 (CST) 8AM-4PM. Felony, Misdemeanor, Civil, Eviction, Small Claims.

**Chancery Court**, Clerk & Master, PO Box 262, Henderson, TN 38340. 901-989-7171 (CST) 8AM-4PM. Civil, Probate.

## Claiborne County

**Real Estate Recording**, Claiborne County Register of Deeds, Main Street, Courthouse, Tazewell, TN 37879. 615-626-3325 (EST) 8:30AM-4PM.

**8th District Criminal, Circuit, and General Sessions Court**, Box 34, Tazewell, TN 37879. 615-626-3334 (EST) 8:30AM-4PM M-F, 8AM-noon SAT. Felony, Misdemeanor, Civil, Eviction, Small Claims.

**Chancery Court**, PO Drawer G, Tazewell, TN 37879. 615-626-3284 (EST) 8:30AM-4PM. Civil, Probate.

## Clay County

**Real Estate Recording**, Clay County Register of Deeds, East Lake Avenue, Celina, TN 38551. 615-243-3298 (CST) 8AM-4PM M,T,Th,F; 8AM-Noon Sat.

**13th District Criminal, Circuit, and General Sessions Court**, PO Box 749, Celina, TN 38551. 615-243-2557 (CST) 8AM-4PM. Felony, Misdemeanor, Civil, Eviction, Small Claims.

**Chancery Court**, PO Box 332, Celina, TN 38551. 615-243-3145 (CST) 8AM-4PM. Civil, Probate.

## Cocke County

**Real Estate Recording**, Cocke County Register of Deeds, 111 Court Ave., Room 102, Courthouse, Newport, TN 37821. 615-623-7540 (EST) 8AM-4PM M,T,Th,F; 8AM-Noon W,Sat.

**4th District Circuit Court**, 111 Court Ave Rm 201, Newport, TN 37821. 615-623-6124 (EST) 8AM-4PM. Felony, Misdemeanor, Civil Actions Over $10,000.

**General Sessions**, 111 Court Ave, Newport, TN 37821. 615-623-8619 (EST) 8AM-4PM. Misdemeanor, Civil Actions Under $10,000, Eviction, Small Claims.

**Chancery Court**, Chancery Court, Clerk & Master, Newport, TN 37821. 615-623-3321 (EST) 8AM-4PM. Civil, Probate.

## Coffee County

**Real Estate Recording**, Coffee County Register of Deeds, Spring Street, Manchester, TN 37355. 615-723-5130 (CST) 8AM-4:30PM.

**14th District Circuit Court and General Sessions**, PO Box 629, Manchester, TN 37355. 615-723-5110 (CST) 8AM-4:30PM. Felony, Misdemeanor, Civil, Eviction, Small Claims.

**Chancery Court**, 101 W. Fort St, Box 5, Manchester, TN 37355. 615-723-5132 (CST) 8AM-4:30PM. Civil, Probate.

## Crockett County

**Real Estate Recording**, Crockett County Register of Deeds, Courthouse, Alamo, TN 38001. 901-696-5455 (CST) 8AM-4PM.

**28th District Circuit Court and General Sessions**, Courthouse, Alamo, TN 38001. 901-696-5462 (CST) 8AM-4PM. Felony, Misdemeanor, Civil, Eviction, Small Claims.

**Chancery Court**, Clerk & Master, Alamo, TN 38001. 901-696-5458 (CST) 8AM-4PM. Civil, Probate.

## Cumberland County

**Real Estate Recording**, Cumberland County Register of Deeds, Highway 127 Main Street, Courthouse Box 3, Crossville, TN 38555. 615-484-5559 (CST) 8AM-4PM.

**13th District Criminal, Circuit, and General Sessions Court**, Box 7, Crossville, TN 38555. 615-484-6647 (CST) 8AM-4PM. Felony, Misdemeanor, Civil, Eviction, Small Claims.

**Chancery Court**, Box 6, Crossville, TN 38555. 615-484-4731 (CST) 8AM-4PM. Civil, Probate.

## Davidson County

**Real Estate Recording**, Davidson County Register of Deeds, 103 Courthouse, Nashville, TN 37201. 615-862-6790 (CST) 8AM-4:25PM.

**General Sessions**, 100 James Robinson Parkway, Ben West Bui, Nashville, TN 37201. 615-862-5195 (CST) 8AM-4:30PM. Misdemeanor, Civil Actions Under $10,000, Eviction, Small Claims.

**Circuit Court**, 303 Metro Courthouse, Nashville, TN 37201. 615-862-5181 (CST) 8AM-4:30PM. Civil Actions Over $10,000.

**20th District Criminal Court**, 506 Metro Courthouse, Nashville, TN 37201. 615-862-5656 (CST) 8AM-4:30PM. Felony, Misdemeanor.

## De Kalb County

**Real Estate Recording**, De Kalb County Register of Deeds, 201 Courthouse, Smithville, TN 37166. 615-597-4153 (CST) 8AM-4:30PM M-Th; 8AM-5PM F.

**13th District Criminal, Circuit, and General Sessions Court**, Public Sq, Smithville, TN 37166. 615-497-5711 (CST) 8AM-4:30PM MTWTh, 8AM-5PM Fri. Felony, Misdemeanor, Civil, Eviction, Small Claims.

**Chancery Court**, Dekalb County Courthouse Rm 302, Smithville, TN 37166. 615-597-4360 (CST) Civil, Probate.

## Decatur County

**Real Estate Recording**, Decatur County Register of Deeds, Main Street, Courthouse, Decaturville, TN 38329. 901-852-3712 (CST) 8AM-4PM M,T,Th,F; 8AM-Noon W,Sat.

**24th District Circuit Court and General Sessions**, PO Box 488, Decaturville, TN 38329. 901-852-3125 (CST) 8AM-4PM. Felony, Misdemeanor, Civil, Eviction, Small Claims.

**Chancery Court**, Chancery Court, Clerk & Master, Decaturville, TN 38329. 901-852-3422 (CST) Civil, Probate.

## Dickson County

**Real Estate Recording**, Dickson County Register of Deeds, Court Square, Courthouse, Charlotte, TN 37036. 615-789-4171 (CST) 8AM-4PM M,T,W,F; 8AM-Noon Th,Sat.

**23rd District Circuit Court**, Court Square, PO Box 220, Charlotte, TN 37036. 615-789-7010 (CST) Felony, Misdemeanor, Civil Actions Over $10,000.

**General Sessions**, PO Box 217, Charlotte, TN 37036. 615-789-5414 (CST) Civil Actions Under $10,000, Eviction, Small Claims.

**County Court**, Court Square, PO Box 220, Charlotte, TN 37036. 615-789-5093 (CST) 8AM-4PM MTWF, 8AM-12PM Th and Sat. Probate.

## Dyer County

**Real Estate Recording**, Dyer County Register of Deeds, Main Street, Courthouse - Veteran's Square, Dyersburg, TN 38024. 901-286-7806 (CST) 8:30AM-4:30PM; 8:30AM-5PM F.

**29th District Circuit Court and General Sessions**, PO Box 1360, Dyersburg, TN 38024. 901-286-7809 (CST) 8:30AM-5PM. Felony, Misdemeanor, Civil, Eviction, Small Claims.

**Chancery Court**, PO Box 1360, Dyersburg, TN 38024. 901-286-7818 (CST) 8:30AM-4:30PM MTWT, 8AM-5PM Fri. Civil, Probate.

## Fayette County

**Real Estate Recording**, Fayette County Register of Deeds, 1 Court Square, Courthouse, Somerville, TN 38068. 901-465-5251 (CST) 9AM-5PM.

**25th District Circuit Court and General Sessions**, PO Box 177, Somerville, TN 38068. 901-465-5205 (CST) 9AM-5PM. Misdemeanor, Civil, Eviction, Small Claims.

**Chancery Court**, PO Box 220, Somerville, TN 38068. 901-465-5220 (CST) 9AM-5PM. Civil, Probate.

## Fentress County

**Real Estate Recording**, Fentress County Register of Deeds, Courthouse, Jamestown, TN 38556. 615-879-7818 (CST) 8AM-4PM.

**8th District Criminal, Circuit and General Sessions Court**, PO Box 699, Jamestown, TN 38556. 615-879-7919 (CST) Felony, Misdemeanor, Civil, Eviction, Small Claims.

**Chancery Court**, PO Box 151, Jamestown, TN 38556. 615-879-8615 (CST) 9AM-5PM MTTF, 9AM-12PM Wed. Civil, Probate.

## Franklin County

**Real Estate Recording**, Franklin County Register of Deeds, Public Square, Winchester, TN 37398. 615-967-2840 (CST) 8AM-4:30PM; 8AM-Noon Sat.

**12th District Circuit Court and General Sessions**, 1 South Jefferson St, Winchester, TN 37398. 615-967-2923 (CST) 8AM-4:30PM. Felony, Misdemeanor, Civil, Eviction, Small Claims.

**County Court**, 1 South Jefferson St, Winchester, TN 37398. 615-967-2541 (CST) 8AM-4:30PM M-F, 8AM-12PM Sat. Probate.

## Gibson County

**Real Estate Recording**, Gibson County Register of Deeds, Courthouse, Trenton, TN 38382. 901-855-7628 (CST) 8AM-4:30PM; 8AM-Noon Sat.

**28th District Circuit Court and General Sessions**, Courthouse, Trenton, TN 38382. 901-855-7615 (CST) 8AM-4:30PM. Felony, Misdemeanor, Civil, Eviction, Small Claims.

**Chancery Court**, Chancery Court, Clerk & Master, Trenton, TN 38382. 901-855-7639 (CST) 8AM-4:30PM. Civil, Probate.

## Giles County

**Real Estate Recording**, Giles County Register of Deeds, Courthouse, Pulaski, TN 38478. 615-363-5137 (CST) 8AM-4PM; 8AM-5PM M.

**22nd District Circuit Court and General Sessions**, PO Box 678, Pulaski, TN 38478. 615-363-5495 (CST) 8AM-4:30PM. Felony, Misdemeanor, Civil, Eviction, Small Claims.

**County Court**, PO Box 678, Pulaski, TN 38478. 615-363-1509 (CST) 8AM-4PM M-F, 8AM-12PM Wed. Probate.

## Grainger County

**Real Estate Recording**, Grainger County Register of Deeds, Main Street, Highway 11W, Rutledge, TN 37861. 615-828-3523 (EST) 8:30AM-4:30PM M,T,Th,F; 8:30AM-Noon W,Sat.

**4th District Circuit Court and General Sessions**, PO Box 157, Rutledge, TN 37861. 615-828-3605 (EST) 8:30AM-4:30PM. Felony, Misdemeanor, Civil, Eviction, Small Claims.

**Chancery Court**, Chancery Court, Clerk & Master, Rutledge, TN 37861. 615-828-4436 (EST) 8:30AM-4:30PM MTTF, 8:30AM-12PM Wed. Civil, Probate.

## Greene County

**Real Estate Recording**, Greene County Register of Deeds, Courthouse, 101 S. Main St. Suite 201, Greeneville, TN 37743. 615-639-0196 (EST) 8AM-4:30PM.

**3rd District Criminal, Circuit and General Sessions Court**, 101 S Main, Geene County Courthouse, Greeneville, TN 37743. 615-638-4332 (EST) 8AM-4:30PM. Felony, Misdemeanor, Civil, Eviction, Small Claims.

**County Court**, Main St., Greeneville, TN 37743. 615-638-4841 (EST) 8AM-4:30PM. Probate.

## Grundy County

**Real Estate Recording**, Grundy County Register of Deeds, Highway 56 & 108, City Hall, Altamont, TN 37301. 615-692-3621 (CST) 8AM-4PM M,T,Th,F; 8AM-Noon W,Sat.

**12th District Circuit Court and General Sessions**, PO Box 161, Altamont, TN 37301. 615-692-3368 (CST) 8AM-4:30PM. Felony, Misdemeanor, Civil, Eviction, Small Claims.

**Chancery Court**, PO Box 174, Altamont, TN 37301. 615-692-3455 (CST) 8AM-4PM MTTF, 8AM-12PM Wed & Sat. Civil, Probate.

## Hamblen County

**Real Estate Recording**, Hamblen County Register of Deeds, 511 West 2nd North Street, Morristown, TN 37814. 615-586-6551 (CST)

**3rd District, Criminal, Circuit and General Sessions Court**, 510 Allison St, Morristown, TN 37814. 615-586-5640 (CST) 8AM-4PM M-Th, 8AM-5PM Fri, 9AM-11:30AM Sat. Felony, Misdemeanor, Civil, Eviction, Small Claims.

**County Court**, 511 West 2nd North St, Morristown, TN 37814. 615-586-9112 (CST) Civil, Probate.

## Hamilton County

**Real Estate Recording**, Hamilton County Register of Deeds, 615 Walnut Street, Court House, Room 204, Chattanooga, TN 37402. 615-209-6560 (EST) 8AM-4PM.

**11th District Circuit Court**, 6th & Walnut St. Room 500, Chattanooga, TN 37402. 615-209-6700 (EST) Civil Actions Over $10,000.

**11th District General Sessions**, Civil Division, 600 Market St, Room 111, Chattanooga, TN 37402. 615-209-7603 (EST) Civil Actions Under $10,000, Eviction, Small Claims.

**11th District Criminal Court**, 600 Market St, Room 102, Chattanooga, TN 37402. 615-209-7500 (EST) 8AM-4PM. Felony, Misdemeanor.

**Chancery Court**, Chancery Court, Clerk & Master, Room 300, Chattanooga, TN 37402. 615-209-6615 (EST) 8AM-4PM. Civil, Probate.

## Hancock County

**Real Estate Recording**, Hancock County Register of Deeds, Courthouse, Sneedville, TN 37869. 615-733-4545 (EST) 9AM-4PM; 9AM-Noon W,Sat.

**3rd District, Criminal, Circuit and General Sessions Court**, PO Box 347, Sneedville, TN 37869. 615-733-2954 (EST) 8AM-4PM. Felony, Misdemeanor, Civil, Eviction, Small Claims.

**Chancery Court**, PO Box 277, Sneedville, TN 37869. 615-733-4524 (EST) 9AM-4PM. Civil, Probate.

## Hardeman County

**Real Estate Recording**, Hardeman County Register of Deeds, Courthouse, Bolivar, TN 38008. 901-658-3476 (CST) 8:30AM-4:30PM; 8:30AM-5PM F.

**25th District Circuit Court and General Sessions**, Courthouse, 100 N Main, Bolivar, TN 38008. 901-658-6524 (CST) 8:30AM-4:30PM M-Th, 8AM-5PM Fri. Felony, Misdemeanor, Civil, Eviction, Small Claims.

**Chancery Court**, PO Box 45, Bolivar, TN 38008. 901-658-3142 (CST) 8:30AM-4:30PM M-Th, 8:30AM-5PM Fri. Civil, Probate.

## Hardin County

**Real Estate Recording**, Hardin County Register of Deeds, Courthouse, Savannah, TN 38372. 901-925-4936 (CST) 8AM-5PM M,T,Th,F; 8AM-Noon W.

**24th District Circuit Court and General Sessions**, 601 Main St, Savannah, TN 38372. 901-925-3583 (CST) 8AM-5PM MTTF, 8AM-12PM Fri. Felony, Misdemeanor, Civil, Eviction, Small Claims.

**County Court**, 601 Main St, Savannah, TN 38372. 901-925-3921 (CST) 8AM-4:30PM MTTF, 8AM-12PM Wed & Sat. Civil, Probate.

## Hawkins County

**Real Estate Recording**, Hawkins County Register of Deeds, Main Street, Courthouse - Room 101, Rogersville, TN 37857. 615-272-8304 (EST) 8AM-4PM; 8AM-Noon W,Sat.

**3rd District Criminal, Circuit and General Sessions Court**, PO Box 9, Rogersville, TN 37857. 615-272-3397 (EST) 8AM-4PM. Felony, Misdemeanor, Civil, Eviction, Small Claims.

**Chancery Court**, Chancery Court, Clerk & Master, Rogersville, TN 37857. 615-272-8150 (EST) 8AM-4PM. Civil, Probate.

## Haywood County

**Real Estate Recording**, Haywood County Register of Deeds, 1 North Washington, Courthouse, Brownsville, TN 38012. 901-772-0332 (CST) 8:30AM-5PM.

**28th District Circuit Court and General Sessions**, 1 N Washington, Brownsville, TN 38012. 901-772-1112 (CST) 8:30AM-5PM. Felony, Misdemeanor, Civil, Eviction, Small Claims.

**Chancery Court**, Chancery Court, Clerk & Master, 1 N Wash, Brownsville, TN 38012. 901-772-0122 (CST) 8:30AM-5PM. Civil, Probate.

## Henderson County

**Real Estate Recording**, Henderson County Register of Deeds, Courthouse, Lexington, TN 38351. 901-968-2941 (CST) 8AM-4:30PM M,T,Th,F; 8AM-Noon Sat.

**26th District Circuit Court and General Sessions**, Henderson County Courthouse, Lexington, TN 38351. 901-968-2031 (CST) Felony, Misdemeanor, Civil, Eviction, Small Claims.

**Chancery Court**, PO Box 67, Lexington, TN 38351. 901-968-2801 (CST) 8AM-4:30PM. Civil, Probate.

## Henry County

**Real Estate Recording**, Henry County Register of Deeds, Court Square, Paris, TN 38242. 901-642-4081 (CST) 8:30AM-4:30PM.

**24th District Circuit Court and General Sessions**, PO Box 429, Paris, TN 38242. 901-642-0461 (CST) Felony, Misdemeanor, Civil, Eviction, Small Claims.

**County Court**, PO Box 24, Paris, TN 38242. 901-642-2412 (CST) 8AM-4:30PM. Probate.

## Hickman County

**Real Estate Recording**, Hickman County Register of Deeds, #1 Courthouse, Centerville, TN 37033-1639. 615-729-4882 (CST) 7:30AM-4PM; 8AM-Noon Sat.

**21st District Circuit Court and General Sessions**, #9 Courthouse, Centerville, TN 37033. 615-729-2211 (CST) 7:30AM-5PM. Felony, Misdemeanor, Civil, Eviction, Small Claims.

**Chancery Court**, Chancery Court, #10, Centerville, TN 37033. 615-729-2522 (CST) 8AM-4PM. Civil, Probate.

## Houston County

**Real Estate Recording**, Houston County Register of Deeds, Main Street, Court Square, Erin, TN 37061. 615-289-3510 (CST) 8AM-4:30PM; 8AM-Noon Sat.

**23rd District Circuit Court and General Sessions**, PO Box 403, Erin, TN 37061. 615-289-4673 (CST) 8AM-4:30PM. Felony, Misdemeanor, Civil, Eviction, Small Claims.

**Chancery Court**, PO Box 332, Erin, TN 37061. 615-289-3870 (CST) 8AM-4:30PM. Civil, Probate.

## Humphreys County

**Real Estate Recording**, Humphreys County Register of Deeds, 102 Thompson Street, Courthouse Annex, Room 3, Waverly, TN 37185. 615-296-7681 (CST) 8AM-4:30PM.

**23rd District Circuit Court and General Sessions**, Room 106, Waverly, TN 37185. 615-296-2461 (CST) Felony, Misdemeanor, Civil, Eviction, Small Claims.

**County Court**, Taylor Hall Clerk, Room 2 Courthouse Ann, Waverly, TN 37185. 615-296-7671 (CST) 8AM-4:30PM. Probate.

## Jackson County

**Real Estate Recording**, Jackson County Register of Deeds, Main Street, Courthouse, Gainesboro, TN 38562. 615-268-9012 (CST) 8AM-4PM; 8AM-12 Sat.

**15th District Criminal, Circuit and General Sessions Court**, PO Box 205, Gainesboro, TN 38562. 615-268-9314 (CST) 8AM-4:00PM. Felony, Misdemeanor, Civil, Eviction, Small Claims.

**County Court**, PO Box 346, Gainesboro, TN 38562. 615-268-9212 (CST) 8AM-4PM. Probate.

## Jefferson County

**Real Estate Recording**, Jefferson County Register of Deeds, 202 Main Street, Courthouse, Dandridge, TN 37725. 615-397-2918 (EST) 8AM-4PM; 8-11AM Sat.

**4th District Circuit Court and General Sessions**, PO Box 671, Dandridge, TN 37725. 615-397-2786 (EST) 8AM-4PM. Felony, Misdemeanor, Civil, Eviction, Small Claims.

**County Court**, PO Box 710, Dandridge, TN 37725. 615-397-2935 (EST) 8AM-4PM M-F, 8AM-11PM Sat. Probate.

## Johnson County

**Real Estate Recording**, Johnson County Register of Deeds, 222 Main Street, Mountain City, TN 37683. 615-727-7841 (EST) 8:30AM-5PM M,T,Th,F; 8:30AM-Noon W,Sat.

**1st District Criminal, Circuit and General Sessions Court**, PO Box 73, Mountain City, TN 37683. 615-727-9012 (EST) 8:30AM-5PM. Felony, Misdemeanor, Civil, Eviction, Small Claims.

**Chancery Court**, PO Box 196, Mountain City, TN 37683. 615-727-7853 (EST) 8:30AM-5PM. Civil, Probate.

## Knox County

**Real Estate Recording**, Knox County Register of Deeds, 400 W. Main Avenue, Room 224, Knoxville, TN 37902. 615-521-2330 (EST) X3891 8AM-4:30PM.

**Circuit Court**, 400 Main Ave, Room M-30 or PO Box 379, Knoxville, TN 37901. 615-521-2400 (EST) 8AM-7:30PM. Civil Actions Over $10,000.

**General Sessions**, 400 Main Ave, Knoxville, TN 37902. 615-521-2375 (EST) 8AM-4:30PM. Civil Actions Under $10,000, Eviction, Small Claims.

**6th District Criminal Court**, 400 Main Ave, Room 149, Knoxville, TN 37902. 615-521-2492 (EST) 8AM-5PM. Felony, Misdemeanor.

**Chancery Court**, 400 Main Ave, Suite 352, Knoxville, TN 37902. 615-521-2555 (EST) 8AM-4:30PM. Civil, Probate.

## Lake County

**Real Estate Recording**, Lake County Register of Deeds, 229 Church St., Courthouse, Tiptonville, TN 38079. 901-253-7462 (CST) 9AM-4PM; 9AM-1PM Th.

**29th District Circuit Court and General Sessions**, 227 Church St, PO Box 11, Tiptonville, TN 38079. 901-253-7137 (CST) 8AM-4PM. Felony, Misdemeanor, Civil, Eviction, Small Claims.

**Chancery Court**, PO Box 12, Tiptonville, TN 38079. 901-253-8926 (CST) 9AM-4PM MTWF, 8AM-12PM Th. Civil, Probate.

## Lauderdale County

**Real Estate Recording**, Lauderdale County Register of Deeds, Courthouse, Ripley, TN 38063. 901-635-2171 (CST) 8AM-4:30PM M,T,Th,F; 8AM-Noon W,Sat.

**25th District Circuit Court**, Courthouse, Ripley, TN 38063. 901-635-0101 (CST) Felony, Misdemeanor, Civil Actions Over $10,000.

**General Sessions**, Courthouse, Ripley, TN 38063. 901-635-2572 (CST) Civil Actions Under $10,000, Eviction, Small Claims.

**County Court**, Courthouse, Ripley, TN 38063. 901-635-2561 (CST) 8AM-4:30PM. Probate.

## Lawrence County

**Real Estate Recording**, Lawrence County Register of Deeds, 240 West Gaines Street, N.B.U. #18, Lawrenceburg, TN 38464. 615-766-4100 (CST) 8AM-4:30PM.

**22nd District Circuit Court and General Sessions**, NBU #12, Lawrenceburg, TN 38464. 615-762-4398 (CST) 8AM-4:30PM. Felony, Misdemeanor, Civil, Eviction, Small Claims.

**County Court**, 240 Gaines St, NBU #2, Lawrenceburg, TN 38464. 615-762-7700 (CST) 8AM-4:30PM. Civil, Probate.

## Lewis County

**Real Estate Recording**, Lewis County Register of Deeds, Courthouse, Hohenwald, TN 38462. 615-796-2255 (CST) 8AM-4:30PM.

**21st District Circuit Court and General Sessions**, Courthouse, Hohenwald, TN 38462. 615-796-3724 (CST) 8AM-4:30PM. Felony, Misdemeanor, Civil, Eviction, Small Claims.

**Chancery Court**, Chancery Court, Clerk & Master, Hohenwald, TN 38462. 615-796-3734 (CST) 8AM-4:30PM. Civil, Probate.

## Lincoln County

**Real Estate Recording**, Lincoln County Register of Deeds, Courthouse, Room 104, Fayetteville, TN 37334. 615-433-5366 (CST) 8AM-4PM.

**17th District Circuit Court and General Sessions**, PO Box 78, Fayetteville, TN 37334. 615-433-2334 (CST) 8AM-4PM. Felony, Misdemeanor, Civil, Eviction, Small Claims.

**Chancery Court**, PO Box 57, Fayetteville, TN 37334. 615-433-1482 (CST) 8AM-4PM. Civil, Probate.

## Loudon County

**Real Estate Recording**, Loudon County Register of Deeds, 601 Grove Street, Courthouse, Room 102, Loudon, TN 37774. 615-458-2605 (EST) 8AM-4:30PM (M-open until 5:30PM).

**9th District Criminal, Circuit, and General Sessions Court**, PO Box 160, Loudon, TN 37774. 615-458-2042 (EST) 8AM-5:30PM Mon, 8AM-4:30PM T-F. Felony, Misdemeanor, Civil, Eviction, Small Claims.

**County Court**, PO Box 303, Loudon, TN 37774. 615-458-2726 (EST) 8AM-5:30PM Mon, 8AM-4:30PM T-F. Probate.

## Macon County

**Real Estate Recording**, Macon County Register of Deeds, Courthouse, Room 102, Lafayette, TN 37083. 615-666-2353 (CST)

**15th District Criminal, Circuit, and General Sessions Court**, Room 202, Lafayette, TN 37083. 615-666-2354 (CST) Felony, Misdemeanor, Civil, Eviction, Small Claims.

**County Court**, County Court Clerk, Lafayette, TN 37083. 615-666-2333 (CST) 8AM-4:30PM M-W, Closed Thu, 8AM-5PM Fri, 8AM-1:30PM Sat. Probate.

## Madison County

**Real Estate Recording**, Madison County Register of Deeds, Courthouse, Room 109, 100 Main St., Jackson, TN 38301. 901-423-6028 (CST) 9AM-5PM.

**26th District Circuit Court**, Room 203, Jackson, TN 38301. 901-423-6035 (CST) 9AM-5PM. Felony, Misdemeanor, Civil Actions Over $10,000.

**General Sessions**, 100 E. Main St, Jackson, TN 38301. 901-423-6041 (CST) 9AM-5PM. Civil Actions Under $10,000, Eviction, Small Claims.

**General Sessions Division II, Probate Division**, 100 Main St, Room 204, Jackson, TN 38301. 901-423-6023 (CST) 9AM-4:30PM. Probate.

## Marion County

**Real Estate Recording**, Marion County Register of Deeds, Highway 41, Courthouse, Jasper, TN 37347. 615-942-2573 (CST) 8AM-4PM.

**12th District Circuit Court and General Sessions**, PO Box 789, Courthouse Sq, Jasper, TN 37347. 615-942-2134 (CST) 8AM-4PM. Felony, Misdemeanor, Civil, Eviction, Small Claims.

**Chancery Court**, PO Box 789, Jasper, TN 37347. 615-942-2601 (CST) 8AM-4PM. Civil, Probate.

## Marshall County

**Real Estate Recording**, Marshall County Register of Deeds, 205 Marshall County Courthouse, Lewisburg, TN 37091. 615-359-4933 (CST)

**17th District Circuit Court and General Sessions**, Courthouse, Lewisburg, TN 37091. 615-359-1312 (CST) Felony, Misdemeanor, Civil, Eviction, Small Claims.

**County Court**, 207 Marshall County Courthouse, Lewisburg, TN 37091. 615-359-1072 (CST) Probate.

## Maury County

**Real Estate Recording**, Maury County Register of Deeds, #1 Public Square, Columbia, TN 38401. 615-381-3690 (CST) X358 8AM-4PM.

**22nd Circuit Court and General Sessions**, Public Square, Room 202, Columbia, TN 38401. 615-745-1923 (CST) 8:00AM-5:00PM. Felony, Misdemeanor, Civil, Eviction, Small Claims.

## McMinn County

**Real Estate Recording**, McMinn County Register of Deeds, Washington Avenue, Courthouse, Athens, TN 37303. 615-745-1232 (EST) 8:30AM-4PM.

**10th District Criminal, Circuit and General Sessions Court**, PO Box 506, Athens, TN 37303. 615-745-1923 (EST) 8:30AM-4PM. Felony, Misdemeanor, Civil, Eviction, Small Claims.

## McNairy County

**Real Estate Recording**, McNairy County Register of Deeds, Court Avenue, Courthouse, Selmer, TN 38375. 901-645-3656 (CST) 8AM-4:30PM M,T,Th,F; 8AM-Noon Sat.

**25th District Circuit Court and General Sessions**, 300 Industrial Park, Selmer, TN 38375. 901-645-1015 (CST) 8AM-4:30PM M-F, closed Wed. Felony, Misdemeanor, Civil, Eviction, Small Claims.

**Chancery Court**, Chancery Court, Clerk & Master, Selmer, TN 38375. 901-645-5446 (CST) 8AM-4:30PM. Civil, Probate.

## Meigs County

**Real Estate Recording**, Meigs County Register of Deeds, Courthouse, Decatur, TN 37322. 615-334-5228 (EST)

**9th District Criminal, Circuit and General Sessions Court**, PO Box 205, Decatur, TN 37322. 615-334-5821 (EST) 8AM-5PM MTTF, Closed Wed, 8AM-12PM Sat. Felony, Misdemeanor, Civil, Eviction, Small Claims.

**Chancery Court**, PO Box 5, Decatur, TN 37322. 615-334-5243 (EST) 8AM-5PM MTTF, 8:30AM-12:00PM Wed. Civil, Probate.

## Monroe County

**Real Estate Recording**, Monroe County Register of Deeds, 103 College Street - Suite 4, Courthouse Annex Building, Madisonville, TN 37354. 615-442-2440 (EST) 8:30AM-4:30PM M,T,Th,F; 8:30AM-Noon W,Sat.

**10th District Criminal, Circuit and General Sessions Court**, Courthouse, Madisonville, TN 37354. 615-442-2396 (EST) 8:30AM-4:30PM. Felony, Misdemeanor, Civil, Eviction, Small Claims.

**Chancery Court**, PO Box 56, Madisonville, TN 37354. 615-442-2644 (EST) 8:30AM-4:30PM. Civil, Probate.

## Montgomery County

**Real Estate Recording**, Montgomery County Register of Deeds, 214 Franklin St., 2nd Floor, # 202, Clarksville, TN 37040. 615-648-5713 (CST)

**19th District Circuit Court**, PO Box 384, Clarksville, TN 37041-0384. 615-648-5700 (CST) 8AM-4:30PM. Felony, Civil Actions Over $10,000.

**General Sessions**, 120 Commerce St, Clarksville, TN 37040. 615-648-5769 (CST) 8AM-4:30PM. Misdemeanor, Civil Actions Under $10,000, Eviction, Small Claims.

**Chancery Court**, Chancery Court, Clerk & Master, Clarksville, TN 37040. 615-648-5703 (CST) 8AM-4:30PM. Civil, Probate.

## Moore County

**Real Estate Recording**, Moore County Register of Deeds, Courthouse, Lynchburg, TN 37352. 615-759-7913 (CST) 8AM-4:30PM; Closed Th; 8AM-Noon Sat.

**17th District Circuit Court and General Sessions**, Courthouse, Lynchburg, TN 37352. 615-759-7208 (CST) 8AM-4:30PM MTWF, Closed Th, 8AM-12PM Sat. Felony, Misdemeanor, Civil, Eviction, Small Claims.

**Chancery Court**, PO Box 206, Lynchburg, TN 37352. 615-759-7044 (CST) 8AM-4:30PM. Civil, Probate.

## Morgan County

**Real Estate Recording**, Morgan County Register of Deeds, Courthouse Square, Room 102, Wartburg, TN 37887. 615-346-3105 (EST) 8AM-4PM M,T,Th,F; 8AM-Noon W,Sat.

**9th District Criminal, Circuit and General Sessions Court**, PO Box 163, Wartburg, TN 37887. 615-346-3503 (EST) 8AM-4PM. Felony, Misdemeanor, Civil, Eviction, Small Claims.

**Chancery Court**, PO Box 789, Wartburg, TN 37887. 615-346-3881 (EST) 8AM-4PM. Civil, Probate.

## Obion County

**Real Estate Recording**, Obion County Register of Deeds, 5 Bill Burnch Circle, Union City, TN 38261. 901-885-9351 (CST) 8AM-4:30PM.

**27th District Circuit Court**, Courthouse, 7 Bill Burnett Circle, Union City, TN 38261. 901-885-1372 (CST) 8:30AM-4:30PM. Felony, Misdemeanor, Civil Actions Over $10,000.

**General Sessions**, Courthouse, Union City, TN 38261. 901-885-1811 (CST) 9AM-4PM. Civil Actions Under $10,000, Eviction, Small Claims.

**Chancery Court**, PO Box 187, Union City, TN 38281. 901-885-2562 (CST) 8:30AM-4:30PM. Civil, Probate.

## Overton County

**Real Estate Recording**, Overton County Register of Deeds, University Street, Courthouse Annex, Livingston, TN 38570. 615-823-4011 (CST) 8AM-4:30PM M,T,Th,F; 8AM-12 W, Sat.

**13th District Criminal, Circuit and General Sessions Court**, Overton County Courthouse, Livingston, TN 38570. 615-823-2312 (CST) 8:30AM-4:30PM MTTF, 8AM-12PM Wed and Sat. Felony, Misdemeanor, Civil, Eviction, Small Claims.

**County Court**, Courthouse Annex, University St, Livingston, TN 38570. 615-823-2631 (CST) 8AM-4:30PM. Probate.

## Perry County

**Real Estate Recording**, Perry County Register of Deeds, Main Street, Courthouse, Linden, TN 37096. 615-589-2210 (CST) 8AM-4PM M,T,Th,F; Closed Wed; 8-11AM Sat.

**21st District Circuit Court and General Sessions**, PO Box 91, Linden, TN 37096. 615-589-2218 (CST) 8AM-4PM. Felony, Misdemeanor, Civil, Eviction, Small Claims.

**Chancery Court**, PO Box 251, Linden, TN 37096. 615-589-2217 (CST) 8AM-4PM. Civil, Probate.

## Pickett County

**Real Estate Recording**, Pickett County Register of Deeds, Main Street, Courthouse, Byrdstown, TN 38549. 615-864-3316 (CST) 8AM-4PM.

**13th District, Criminal, Circuit and General Sessions Court**, PO Box 5, Byrdstown, TN 38549. 615-864-3958 (CST) 8AM-4PM. Felony, Misdemeanor, Civil, Eviction, Small Claims.

**County Court**, PO Box 5 Courthoue Square, Byrdstown, TN 38549. 615-864-3879 (CST) 8Am-4PM MTTF, 8AM-12PM Wed and Sat. Probate.

## Polk County

**Real Estate Recording**, Polk County Register of Deeds, 411 Highway, Courthouse, Benton, TN 37307. 615-338-4537 (EST) 9AM-4:30PM; Closed Th; 9AM-Noon Sat.

**10th District Criminal, Circuit and General Sessions Court**, PO Box 256, Benton, TN 37307. 615-338-4524 (EST) Felony, Misdemeanor, Civil, Eviction, Small Claims.

**Chancery Court**, PO Drawer L, Benton, TN 37307. 615-338-4522 (EST) 8:30AM-4:30PM M-F, 8AM-12 PM Sat. Civil, Probate.

## Putnam County

**Real Estate Recording**, Putnam County Register of Deeds, 300 East Spring Street, Courthouse - Room 3, Cookeville, TN 38501. 615-526-7101 (CST) 8AM-4PM.

**13th District Criminal, Circuit and General Sessions Court**, 429 E Spring St, 1C-49A, Cookeville, TN 38501. 615-528-1508 (CST) 8Am-4PM. Felony, Misdemeanor, Civil, Eviction, Small Claims.

**County Court**, 300 E Spring St, Room 11, Cookeville, TN 38501. 615-526-7106 (CST) 8AM-4:30PM. Probate.

## Rhea County

**Real Estate Recording**, Rhea County Register of Deeds, 1475 Market Street, Dayton, TN 37321. 615-775-7841 (EST) 8AM-4PM.

**12th District Circuit Court and General Sessions**, Room 200, Dayton, TN 37321. 615-775-7805 (EST) 8AM-4PM. Felony, Misdemeanor, Civil, Eviction, Small Claims.

**County Court**, 1475 Market St, Rm 105, Dayton, TN 37321. 615-775-7808 (EST) 8AM-4PM. Probate.

## Roane County

**Real Estate Recording**, Roane County Register of Deeds, 200 Race Street, Courthouse, Kingston, TN 37763. 615-376-4673 (EST) 8:30AM-6PM M; 8:30AM-4:30PM T-F.

**9th District Criminal, Circuit, and General Sessions Court**, PO Box 73, Kingston, TN 37763. 615-376-2390 (EST) 8:30AM-6PM Mon, 8:30AM-4:40PM T-F. Felony, Misdemeanor, Civil, Eviction, Small Claims.

**Chancery Court**, PO Box 402, Kingston, TN 37763. 615-376-2487 (EST) 8:30AM-6PM Mon, 8:30AM-4:30PM T-F. Civil, Probate.

## Robertson County

**Real Estate Recording**, Robertson County Register of Deeds, Court Square, 124 6th Ave. West, Springfield, TN 37172. 615-384-3772 (CST) 8AM-4:30PM.

**19th District Circuit Court and General Sessions**, Room 200, Springfield, TN 37172. 615-384-7864 (CST) 8:30AM-4:30PM. Felony, Misdemeanor, Civil, Eviction, Small Claims.

**Chancery Court**, Room 207, Springfield, TN 37172. 615-384-5650 (CST) 8:30AM-4:30PM. Civil, Probate.

## Rutherford County

**Real Estate Recording**, Rutherford County Register of Deeds, Judicial Building Room 501, Public Square, Murfreesboro, TN 37133. 615-898-7870 (CST) 8AM-4PM.

**16th District Circuit Court**, Room 201, Murfreesboro, TN 37130. 615-898-7812 (CST) 8AM-4PM. Felony, Misdemeanor, Civil Actions Over $10,000.

**General Sessions**, Room 101, Murfreesboro, TN 37130. 615-898-7831 (CST) 8AM-4PM. Civil Actions Under $10,000, Eviction, Small Claims.

**County Court**, 26 Public Sq, Murfreesboro, TN 37130. 615-898-7798 (CST) 8AM-4PM. Probate.

## Scott County

**Real Estate Recording**, Scott County Register of Deeds, 3 Courthouse Square, Huntsville, TN 37756. 615-663-2417 (EST) 8AM-4:30PM.

**8th District Criminal, Circuit, and General Sessions Court**, PO Box 73, Huntsville, TN 37756. 615-663-2440 (EST) 8AM-4:30PM. Felony, Misdemeanor, Civil, Eviction, Small Claims.

## Sequatchie County

**Real Estate Recording**, Sequatchie County Register of Deeds, Cherry Street, Courthouse - 307E, Dunlap, TN 37327. 615-949-2512 (CST) 8AM-4:30PM; Closed Th; 8AM-Noon Sat.

**12th District Circuit Court and General Sessions**, PO Box 551, Dunlap, TN 37327. 615-949-2618 (CST) 8AM-4PM MTWF, Closed Thu. Felony, Misdemeanor, Civil, Eviction, Small Claims.

**Chancery Court**, PO Box 1651, Dunlap, TN 37327. 615-949-3670 (CST) 8AM-4PM MTWF, Closed Thu, 8AM-12PM Sat. Civil, Probate.

## Sevier County

**Real Estate Recording**, Sevier County Register of Deeds, 125 Court Avenue, Courthouse Suite 209W, Sevierville, TN 37862. 615-453-2758 (EST) 8AM-4:30PM M-Th; 8AM-6PM F.

**4th District Circuit Court and General Sessions**, Room 207, 125 Court Ave, Sevierville, TN 37862. 615-453-5536 (EST) 8AM-4:30PM M-T, 8AM-6PM Fri. Felony, Misdemeanor, Civil, Eviction, Small Claims.

**County Court**, 125 Court Ave, Suite 202, Sevierville, TN 37862. 615-453-5502 (EST) 8:30AM-4:30PM. Probate.

## Shelby County

**Real Estate Recording**, Shelby County Register of Deeds, 160 North Mid America Mall, Room 519, Memphis, TN 38103. 901-576-4366 (CST) 8AM-4:30PM.

**Circuit Court**, 140 Adams, Memphis, TN 38103. 901-576-4006 (CST) 8AM-4:30PM. Civil Actions Over $10,000.

**30th District Criminal Court**, 201 Poplar, Room 401, Memphis, TN 38103. 901-576-5001 (CST) 8AM-4:30PM. Felony.

**General Sessions-Civil**, 140 Adams, Room 106, Memphis, TN 38103. 901-576-4031 (CST) 8:15AM-4:15PM. Civil Actions Under $10,000, Eviction, Small Claims.

**General Sessions-Criminal**, 201 Poplar, Room 81, Memphis, TN 38103. 901-576-5098 (CST) Misdemeanor.

**Probate Court**, 140 Adams, Room 124, Memphis, TN 38103. 901-576-4040 (CST) 8AM-4:30PM. Probate.

## Smith County

**Real Estate Recording**, Smith County Register of Deeds, 211 N. Main St., Carthage, TN 37030. 615-735-1760 (CST) 8AM-4PM; 8AM-12 Sat.

**15th District Criminal, Circuit, and General Sessions Court**, 211 Main St, Carthage, TN 37030. 615-735-0500 (CST) 8AM-4PM. Felony, Misdemeanor, Civil, Eviction, Small Claims.

**Chancery Court**, 211 N Main St, Carthage, TN 37030. 615-735-2092 (CST) 8AM-4PM. Civil, Probate.

## Stewart County

**Real Estate Recording**, Stewart County Register of Deeds, Courthouse, Dover, TN 37058. 615-232-5990 (CST) 8AM-4:30PM.

**23rd District Circuit Court and General Sessions**, PO Box 193, Dover, TN 37058. 615-232-7042 (CST) 8AM-4:30PM. Felony, Misdemeanor, Civil, Eviction, Small Claims.

**Chancery Court**, PO Box 102, Dover, TN 37058. 615-232-5665 (CST) 8AM-4:30PM. Civil, Probate.

## Sullivan County

**Real Estate Recording**, Sullivan County Register of Deeds, Blountville Office, 3411 Highway 126, Courthouse, Blountville, TN 37617. 615-323-6420 (EST) 8:30AM-5PM.

**Real Estate Recording**, Sullivan County Register of Deeds, Bristol Office, 801 Broad St., Bristol, TN 37620. 615-989-4370 (EST) 8:30AM-5PM.

**Bristol Circuit Court-Civil Division**, Room 211 Courthouse, Bristol, TN 37620. 615-989-4354 (EST) 8AM-5PM. Civil Actions Over $10,000.

**Kingsport Circuit Court-Civil Division**, 225 W Center St, Kingsport, TN 37660. 615-245-1311 (EST) 8AM-5PM. Civil Actions Over $10,000.

**2nd District Circuit Court**, 140 Blockville ByPass, PO Box 585, Blountville, TN 37617. 615-323-5158 (EST) 8AM-5PM. Felony, Misdemeanor.

**Bristol General Sessions**, Room 211 Courthouse, Bristol, TN 37620. 615-989-4352 (EST) 8AM-5PM. Misdemeanor, Civil Actions Under $10,000, Eviction, Small Claims.

**Kingsport General Sessions**, 200 Shelby St, Kingsport, TN 37660. 615-378-0710 (EST) 8AM-5PM. Misdemeanor, Civil Actions Under $10,000, Eviction, Small Claims.

**Chancery Court**, PO Box 327, Blountville, TN 37617. 615-323-6483 (EST) 8:30AM-5PM. Civil, Probate.

## Sumner County

**Real Estate Recording**, Sumner County Register of Deeds, 355 N. Belvedere Dr., S.C. Admin. Bldg, Rm 201, Gallatin, TN 37066. 615-452-3892 (CST) 8AM-4:30PM.

**18th District Criminal, Circuit, and General Sessions Court**, Public Sq, PO Box 549, Gallatin, TN 37066. 615-452-4367 (CST) 8AM-4:30PM. Felony, Misdemeanor, Civil, Eviction, Small Claims.

**Chancery Court**, Room 300, Sumner County Courthouse, Gallatin, TN 37066. 615-452-4282 (CST) 8AM-4:30PM. Civil, Probate.

## Tipton County

**Real Estate Recording**, Tipton County Register of Deeds, Court Square, Courthouse, Room 105, Covington, TN 38019. 901-476-0204 (CST) 8AM-5PM.

**25th District Circuit Court and General Sessions**, PO Box 1008, Covington, TN 38019. 901-476-0216 (CST) 8:30AM-4:30PM. Felony, Misdemeanor, Civil, Eviction, Small Claims.

**Chancery Court**, Tipton County Courthouse, Court Sq, Covington, TN 38019. 901-476-0209 (CST) 8AM-5PM. Civil, Probate.

## Trousdale County

**Real Estate Recording**, Trousdale County Register of Deeds, Court Street, Room #8, Hartsville, TN 37074. 615-374-2921 (CST) 8AM-4:30PM.

**15th District Criminal, Circuit, and General Sessions Court**, PO Box 119, Room 5, Hartsville, TN 37074. 615-374-3411 (CST) 8AM-4:30PM. Felony, Misdemeanor, Civil, Eviction, Small Claims.

**Chancery Court**, PO Box 74, Hartsville, TN 37074. 615-374-2996 (CST) 8AM-4:30PM. Civil, Probate.

## Unicoi County

**Real Estate Recording**, Unicoi County Register of Deeds, Main Street, Courthouse, Erwin, TN 37650. 615-743-6104 (EST) 9AM-5PM; 9AM-Noon Sat.

**1st District Criminal, Circuit, and General Sessions Court**, PO Box 376, Erwin, TN 37650. 615-743-3541 (EST) 8AM-5PM. Felony, Misdemeanor, Civil, Eviction, Small Claims.

**Probate Court**, PO Box 340, Erwin, TN 37650. 615-743-3381 (EST) 9AM-5PM M-F, 9AM-12PM Sat. Probate.

## Union County

**Real Estate Recording**, Union County Register of Deeds, Main Street, Maynardville, TN 37807. 615-992-8024 (EST) 8AM-4PMM,T,Th.F; 8AM-Noon W,Sat.

**8th District Criminal, Circuit, and General Sessions Court**, PO Box 306, Maynardville, TN 37807. 615-992-5493 (EST) 8AM-4PM MTTF, 8AM-12PM Wed & Sat. Felony, Misdemeanor, Civil, Eviction, Small Claims.

**Chancery Court**, Chancery Court, Clerk & Master, Maynardville, TN 37807. 615-992-5942 (EST) 8AM-4PM MTTF, 8AM-12PM Wed & Sat. Civil, Probate.

## Van Buren County

**Real Estate Recording**, Van Buren County Register of Deeds, Courthouse Square, Spencer, TN 38585. 615-946-2263 (CST) 8AM-4PM M,T,Th,F; Closed Wed; 8AM-Noon Sat.

**31st District Circuit Court and General Sessions**, PO Box 126, Spencer, TN 38585. 615-946-2153 (CST) 8AM-4PM MTTF, 8AM-12PM Wed & Sat. Felony, Misdemeanor, Civil, Eviction, Small Claims.

**County Court**, PO Box 126, Spencer, TN 38585. 615-946-2121 (CST) 8AM-4PM MTTF, 8AM-12PM Wed & Sat. Probate.

## Warren County

**Real Estate Recording**, Warren County Register of Deeds, 111 S. Court Square, McMinnville, TN 37110. 615-473-2926 (CST)

**31st District Circuit Court and General Sessions**, Main St, PO Box 639, McMinnville, TN 37110. 615-473-2373 (CST) 8AM-4PM. Felony, Misdemeanor, Civil, Eviction, Small Claims.

**Chancery Court**, PO Box 639, McMinnville, TN 37110. 615-473-2364 (CST) 8AM-4PM MTWF, 8AM-12PM Th & Sat. Civil, Probate.

## Washington County

**Real Estate Recording**, Washington County Register of Deeds, Main Street, Courthouse, Jonesboro, TN 37659. 615-753-1644 (EST) 8AM-5PM.

**1st District Circuit Court and General Sessions**, PO Box 356, Jonesborough, TN 37659. 615-753-1611 (EST) 8AM-5PM. Felony, Misdemeanor, Civil, Eviction, Small Claims.

**General Sessions**, 101 E Market St, Johnson City, TN 37604. 615-461-1412 (EST) 8AM-5PM. Civil Actions Under $10,000, Eviction, Small Claims.

**Johnson City Circuit Court-Civil**, 101 E Market St, Johnson City, TN 37604. 615-461-1418 (EST) 8AM-5PM. Civil Actions Over $10,000.

**County Court**, PO Box 218, Jonesborough, TN 37659. 615-753-1623 (EST) 8AM-5PM. Probate.

## Wayne County

**Real Estate Recording**, Wayne County Register of Deeds, Court Square, Waynesboro, TN 38485. 615-722-5518 (CST) 8AM-4PM M,T,Th,F; 8AM-Noon W,Sat.

**22nd District Circuit Court and General Sessions**, PO Box 869, Waynesboro, TN 38485. 615-722-5519 (CST) 8AM-4PM MTTF, 8AM-12PM Wed & Sat. Felony, Misdemeanor, Civil, Eviction, Small Claims.

**Chancery Court**, PO Box 101, Waynesboro, TN 38485. 615-722-5517 (CST) 8AM-4PM M-F, 8AM-12PM Sat. Civil, Probate.

## Weakley County

**Real Estate Recording**, Weakley County Register of Deeds, Courthouse, Room 102, Dresden, TN 38225. 901-364-3646 (CST) 8AM-4:30PM.

**27th District Circuit Court and General Sessions**, PO Box 28, Dresden, TN 38225. 901-364-3455 (CST) 8AM-4:30PM. Felony, Misdemeanor, Civil, Eviction, Small Claims.

**Chancery Court**, PO Box 197, Dresden, TN 38225. 901-364-3454 (CST) 8AM-4:30PM. Civil, Probate.

## White County

**Real Estate Recording**, White County Register of Deeds, Courthouse Rm 118, 1 East Bockman Way, Sparta, TN 38583-1414. 615-836-2817 (CST) 8AM-5PM.

**13th District Criminal, Circuit, and General Sessions Court**, Room 304, Sparta, TN 38583. 615-836-3205 (CST) 8AM-5PM MTTF, 8AM-12PM Wed & Sat. Felony, Misdemeanor, Civil, Eviction, Small Claims.

**Chancery Court**, Chancery Court, Clerk & Master, Sparta, TN 38583. 615-836-3787 (CST) 8AM-4:30PM. Civil, Probate.

## Williamson County

**Real Estate Recording**, Williamson County Register of Deeds, 1320 West Main Street, Room 201, Franklin, TN 37064. 615-790-5706 (CST) 8AM-4:30PM.

**21st District Circuit Court and General Sessions**, Room 107, Franklin, TN 37064. 615-790-5454 (CST) 8AM-4:30PM. Felony, Misdemeanor, Civil, Eviction, Small Claims.

**Chancery Court**, Chancery Court, Clerk & Master, Franklin, TN 37064. 615-790-5428 (CST) 8AM-4:30PM. Civil, Probate.

## Wilson County

**Real Estate Recording**, Wilson County Register of Deeds, East Main, Courthouse, Lebanon, TN 37087. 615-443-2611 (CST) 8AM-4PM; 8AM-5PM F.

**15th District Criminal, Circuit, and General Sessions Court**, PO Box 518, Lebanon, TN 37088-1366. 615-444-2042 (CST) 8AM-4PM M-Th, 8AM-5PM Fri. Felony, Misdemeanor, Civil, Eviction, Small Claims.

**County Court**, PO Box 918, Lebanon, TN 37088-0918. 615-443-2627 (CST) 8AM-4:30PM M-Th, 8AM-5PM Fri. Probate.

# Texas

## Anderson County

**Real Estate Recording**, Anderson County Clerk, 500 North Church Street, Palestine, TX 75801. 903-723-7402 (CST) 8AM-Noon,1-5PM.

**District Court**, PO Box 1159, Palestine, TX 75802-1159. 903-723-7412 (CST) 8AM-12PM 1PM-5PM. Felony, Civil.

**County Court**, 500 N Church, Palestine, TX 75801. 903-723-7432 (CST) 8AM-5PM. Misdemeanor, Civil, Probate.

## Andrews County

**Real Estate Recording**, Andrews County Clerk, 215 N.W. 1st Street, Annex Building Room 121A, Andrews, TX 79714. 915-524-1426 (CST) 8AM-5PM.

**District Court**, PO Box 328, Andrews, TX 79714. 915-524-1417 (CST) 8AM-5PM. Felony, Civil.

**County Court**, PO Box 727, Andrews, TX 79714. 915-524-1426 (CST) 8AM-5PM. Misdemeanor, Civil, Probate.

## Angelina County

**Real Estate Recording**, Angelina County Clerk, 215 East Lufkin Avenue, Lufkin, TX 75901. 409-634-8339 (CST) 8AM-5PM.

**District Court**, PO Box 908, Lufkin, TX 75902. 409-634-4312 (CST) 8AM-5PM. Felony, Civil.

**County Court**, PO Box 908, Lufkin, TX 75902. 409-634-8339 (CST) 8AM-5PM. Misdemeanor, Civil, Probate.

## Aransas County

**Real Estate Recording**, Aransas County Clerk, 301 North Live Oak, Rockport, TX 78382. 512-790-0122 (CST) 8AM-5PM.

**District Court**, 301 North Live Oak, Rockport, TX 78382. 512-790-0128 (CST) 8AM-5PM. Felony, Civil.

**County Court**, 301 N Live Oak, Rockport, TX 78382. 512-790-0122 (CST) 8AM-5PM. Misdemeanor, Civil, Probate.

## Archer County

**Real Estate Recording**, Archer County Clerk, Center & Main, Archer City, TX 76351. 817-574-4615 (CST) 8:30AM-5PM.

**District and County Court**, PO Box 815, Archer City, TX 76351. 817-574-4615 (CST) 8:30AM-5PM. Felony, Misdemeanor, Civil, Eviction, Probate.

## Armstrong County

**Real Estate Recording**, Armstrong County Clerk, Trice Street, Courthouse, Claude, TX 79019. 806-226-2081 (CST) 8AM-12, 1-5PM.

**District and County Court**, PO Box 309, Claude, TX 79019. 806-226-2081 (CST) 8AM-12PM 1PM-5PM. Felony, Misdemeanor, Civil, Eviction, Probate.

## Atascosa County

**Real Estate Recording**, Atascosa County Clerk, Circle Drive, Room 6-1, Jourdanton, TX 78026. 210-769-2511 (CST) 8AM-5PM.

**81st & 218th Judicial District Court**, #52 Courthouse Circle, Jourdanton, TX 78026. 512-769-3011 (CST) 8AM-12PM 1PM-5PM. Felony, Civil.

**County Court**, Circle Dr Rm 6-1, Jourdanton, TX 78026. 210-769-2511 (CST) 8AM-5PM. Misdemeanor, Civil, Probate.

## Austin County

**Real Estate Recording**, Austin County Clerk, 1 East Main, Bellville, TX 77418-1551. 409-865-5911 (CST) 8AM-5PM.

**District Court**, 1 East Main, Bellville, TX 77418. 409-865-5911 (CST) 8AM-5PM. Felony, Civil.

**County Court**, 1 E Main, Bellville, TX 77418. 409-865-5911 (CST) 8AM-5PM. Misdemeanor, Civil, Probate.

## Bailey County

**Real Estate Recording**, Bailey County Clerk, 300 South First, Muleshoe, TX 79347. 806-272-3044 (CST) 8AM-4PM.

**District Court**, 300 S 1st St, Muleshoe, TX 79347. 806-272-3165 (CST) 8AM-5PM. Felony, Civil.

**County Court**, 300 S 1st St, Muleshoe, TX 79347. 806-272-3044 (CST) 8AM-4PM. Misdemeanor, Civil, Probate.

## Bandera County

**Real Estate Recording**, Bandera County Clerk, 500 Main Street, Bandera, TX 78003. 210-796-3332 (CST) 8AM-5PM.

**District and County Court**, PO Box 823, Bandera, TX 78003. 210-796-3332 (CST) 8AM-5PM. Felony, Misdemeanor, Civil, Eviction, Probate.

## Bastrop County

**Real Estate Recording**, Bastrop County Clerk, 803 Pine Street, Courthouse, Bastrop, TX 78602. 512-321-4443 (CST) 8AM-12, 1-5PM.

**District Court**, PO Box 770, Bastrop, TX 78602. 512-321-2114 (CST) 8AM-5PM. Felony, Civil.

**County Court**, PO Box 577, Bastrop, TX 78602. 512-321-4443 (CST) 8AM-5PM. Misdemeanor, Civil, Probate.

## Baylor County

**Real Estate Recording**, Baylor County Clerk, 101 South Washington, Seymour, TX 76380. 817-888-3322 (CST) 8:30AM-5PM.

**District and County Court**, PO Box 689, Seymour, TX 76380. 817-888-3322 (CST) 8:30AM-5PM. Felony, Misdemeanor, Civil, Eviction, Probate.

## Bee County

**Real Estate Recording**, Bee County Clerk, 105 West Corpus Christi Street, Beeville, TX 78102. 512-362-3245 (CST) 8AM-Noon, 1-5PM.

**District Court**, PO Box 666, Beeville, TX 78102-0666. 512-362-3242 (CST) 8AM-5PM. Felony, Civil.

**County Court**, 105 W Corpus Christi St Rm 103, Beeville, TX 78102. 512-362-3245 (CST) 8AM-5PM. Misdemeanor, Civil, Probate.

## Bell County

**Real Estate Recording**, Bell County Clerk, Corner of Central and Main, Courthouse, Belton, TX 76513. 817-933-5171 (CST) 8AM-5PM.

**District Court**, 104 S Main, Belton, TX 76513. 817-939-3521 (CST) 8AM-5PM. Felony, Civil.

**County Court**, PO Box 480, Belton, TX 76513. 817-939-5174 (CST) 8AM-5PM. Misdemeanor, Civil, Probate.

## Bexar County

**Real Estate Recording**, Bexar County Clerk, Courthouse, 100 Dolorosa, San Antonio, TX 78205-3083. 210-220-2581 (CST) 8AM-5PM.

**District Court**, 100 Dolorosa, County Courthouse, San Antonio, TX 78205. 210-220-2083 (CST) 8AM-5PM. Felony, Civil.

**County Court-Civil**, 300 Dolorosa, Suite 4101, San Antonio, TX 78205-3029. 210-220-2216 (CST) 8AM-5PM. Civil.

**County Court-Criminal**, 100 Dolorosa, San Antonio, TX 78205. 210-220-2113 (CST) 8AM-5PM. Misdemeanor.

**Probate Court**, 100 Dolorosa St, San Antonio, TX 78205. 210-220-2546 (CST) Probate.

## Blanco County

**Real Estate Recording**, Blanco County Clerk, 7th Street, Courthouse, Johnson City, TX 78636. 210-868-7357 (CST) 8AM-5PM.

**District and County Court**, PO Box 65, Johnson City, TX 78636. 210-868-7357 (CST) 8AM-5PM. Felony, Misdemeanor, Civil, Eviction, Probate.

## Borden County

**Real Estate Recording**, Borden County Clerk, 101 Main, Gail, TX 79738. 806-756-4312 (CST) 8AM-12, 1-5PM.

**District and County Court**, PO Box 124, Gail, TX 79738. 806-756-4312 (CST) 8AM-5PM. Felony, Misdemeanor, Civil, Eviction, Probate.

## Bosque County

**Real Estate Recording**, Bosque County Clerk, 103 River Street, Meridian, TX 76665. 817-435-2201 (CST) 8AM-Noon, 1-5PM.

**District Court**, PO Box 647, Meridian, TX 76665. 817-435-2334 (CST) 8AM-12PM 1PM-5PM. Felony, Civil.

**County Court**, PO Box 617, Meridian, TX 76665. 817-435-2382 (CST) 8AM-5PM. Misdemeanor, Civil, Probate.

## Bowie County

**Real Estate Recording**, Bowie County Clerk, 1000 James Bowie Drive, New Boston, TX 75570. 903-628-2571 (CST) 8AM-5PM.

**District Court**, PO Box 248, New Boston, TX 75570. 903-628-2571 (CST) 8AM-5PM. Felony, Civil.

County Court, PO Box 248, New Boston, TX 75570. 903-628-2571 (CST) 8AM-5PM. Misdemeanor, Civil, Probate.

## Brazoria County

Real Estate Recording, Brazoria County Clerk, 111 East Locust, Suite 200, Angleton, TX 77515-4654. 409-849-5711 (CST) 8AM-5PM.

District Court, 111 E Locus #400, Angleton, TX 77515. 409-849-5711 (CST) 8AM-5PM. Felony, Civil.

County Court, 111 E Locust #200, Angleton, TX 77515. 409-849-5711 (CST) 8AM-5PM. Misdemeanor, Civil.

Probate Court, County Courthouse, Angleton, TX 77515. 409-849-5711 (CST) Probate.

## Brazos County

Real Estate Recording, Brazos County Clerk, 300 East 26th Street, Suite 120, Bryan, TX 77803. 409-361-4132 (CST) 8AM-5PM.

District Court, 300 E 26th St #216 (PO Box 2208), Bryan, TX 77806. 409-361-4233 (CST) 8AM-5PM. Felony, Civil.

County Court, 300 E 26th St #120, Bryan, TX 77803. 409-361-4128 (CST) 8AM-5PM. Misdemeanor, Civil, Probate.

## Brewster County

Real Estate Recording, Brewster County Clerk, 201 West Avenue E, Alpine, TX 79830. 915-837-3366 (CST) 9AM-12, 1-5PM.

District and County Court, PO Box 119, Alpine, TX 79831. 915-837-3366 (CST) 9AM-5PM. Felony, Misdemeanor, Civil, Eviction, Probate.

## Briscoe County

Real Estate Recording, Briscoe County Clerk, 415 Main Street, Silverton, TX 79257. 806-823-2134 (CST) 8AM-5PM.

District and County Court, PO Box 375, Silverton, TX 79257. 806-823-2134 (CST) 8AM-5PM. Felony, Misdemeanor, Civil, Eviction, Probate.

## Brooks County

Real Estate Recording, Brooks County Clerk, 110 East Miller, Falfurrias, TX 78355. 512-325-5604 (CST) 8AM-5PM.

District Court, PO Box 534, Falfurrias, TX 78355. 512-325-5604 (CST) 8AM-5PM. Felony, Civil.

County Court, PO Box 427, Falfurrias, TX 78355. 512-325-5604 (CST) 8AM-5PM. Misdemeanor, Civil, Probate.

## Brown County

Real Estate Recording, Brown County Clerk, 200 South Broadway, Courthouse, Brownwood, TX 76801. 915-643-2594 (CST) 8:30AM-5PM.

District Court, 200 S Broadway, Brownwood, TX 76801. 915-646-5514 (CST) 8:30AM-5PM. Felony, Civil.

County Court, 200 S Broadway, Brownwood, TX 76801. 915-643-2594 (CST) 8:30AM-5PM. Misdemeanor, Civil, Probate.

## Burleson County

Real Estate Recording, Burleson County Clerk, Buck & Main Street, Courthouse, 2nd Floor, Caldwell, TX 77836. 409-567-4326 (CST) 9AM-5PM.

District Court, PO Box 179, Caldwell, TX 77836. 409-567-4237 (CST) 8AM-5PM. Felony, Civil.

County Court, PO Box 57, Caldwell, TX 77836. 409-567-4326 (CST) 9AM-5PM. Misdemeanor, Civil, Probate.

## Burnet County

Real Estate Recording, Burnet County Clerk, 220 South Pierce Street, Burnet, TX 78611. 512-756-5406 (CST) 8AM-5PM.

District Court, 220 S Pierce, Burnet, TX 78611. 512-756-5450 (CST) 8AM-5PM. Felony, Civil.

County Court, 220 S Pierce, Burnet, TX 78611. 512-756-5403 (CST) 8AM-5PM. Misdemeanor, Civil, Probate.

## Caldwell County

Real Estate Recording, Caldwell County Clerk, Main & Market, Courthouse, Lockhart, TX 78644. 512-398-1804 (CST) 8:30-12, 1-4:30.

District Court, PO Box 749, Lockhart, TX 78644. 512-398-1806 (CST) 8:30 AM-5PM. Felony, Civil.

County Court, PO Box 906, Lockhart, TX 78644. 512-398-1804 (CST) 8:30AM-4:30PM. Misdemeanor, Civil, Probate.

## Calhoun County

Real Estate Recording, Calhoun County Clerk, 211 South Ann, Port Lavaca, TX 77979. 512-553-4411 (CST) 8AM-5PM.

District Court, 211 S Ann, Port Lavaca, TX 77979. 512-553-4630 (CST) 8AM-5PM. Felony, Civil.

County Court, 211 S Ann, Port Lavaca, TX 77979. 512-553-4411 (CST) 8AM-5PM. Misdemeanor, Civil, Probate.

## Callahan County

Real Estate Recording, Callahan County Clerk, 400 Market, Ste. 104, Courthouse, Baird, TX 79504. 915-854-1217 (CST) 8AM-5PM.

District Court, 400 Market St #300, Baird, TX 79504. 915-854-1800 (CST) 8AM-5PM. Felony, Civil.

County Court, 400 Market St #104, Baird, TX 79504. 915-854-1217 (CST) 8AM-5PM. Misdemeanor, Civil, Probate.

## Cameron County

Real Estate Recording, Cameron County Clerk, 964 East Harrison, Brownsville, TX 78520. 210-544-0815 (CST) 8AM-5PM.

District Court, 974 E Harrison St, Brownsville, TX 78520. 210-544-0839 (CST) 8AM-12PM 1PM-5PM. Felony, Civil.

County Court, PO Box 2178, Brownsville, TX 78522-2178. 210-544-0848 (CST) 8AM-5PM. Misdemeanor, Civil, Probate.

## Camp County

Real Estate Recording, Camp County Clerk, 126 Church Street, Room 102, Pittsburg, TX 75686. 903-856-2731 (CST) 8AM-12, 1-5PM.

District Court, 126 Church St Rm 203, Pittsburg, TX 75686. 903-856-3221 (CST) 8AM-5PM. Felony, Civil.

County Court, 126 Church St Rm 102, Pittsburg, TX 75686. 903-856-2731 (CST) 8AM-12PM 1PM-5PM. Misdemeanor, Civil, Probate.

## Carson County

Real Estate Recording, Carson County Clerk, 5th & Main Street, Courthouse, Panhandle, TX 79068. 806-537-3873 (CST) 8AM-12, 1-5PM.

District and County Court, PO Box 487, Panhandle, TX 79068. 806-537-3873 (CST) 8AM-5PM. Felony, Misdemeanor, Civil, Eviction, Probate.

## Cass County

Real Estate Recording, Cass County Clerk, Main & Houston, Courthouse, Linden, TX 75563. 903-756-5071 (CST) 8AM-5PM.

5th Judicial District Court, PO Box 510, Linden, TX 75563. 903-756-7514 (CST) 8AM-5PM. Felony, Civil.

County Court, PO Box 468, Linden, TX 75563. 903-756-5071 (CST) 8AM-5PM. Misdemeanor, Civil, Probate.

## Castro County

Real Estate Recording, Castro County Clerk, 100 East Bedford, Dimmitt, TX 79027-2643. 806-647-3338 (CST) 8AM-12, 1-5PM.

District and County Court, 100 E Bedford, Dimmitt, TX 79027. 806-647-3338 (CST) 8AM-5PM. Felony, Misdemeanor, Civil, Eviction, Probate.

## Chambers County

Real Estate Recording, Chambers County Clerk, 404 Washington Street, Anahuac, TX 77514. 409-267-8309 (CST) 8AM-5PM.

District Court, Drawer NN, Anahuac, TX 77514. 409-267-8276 (CST) 8AM-12PM 1PM-5PM. Felony, Civil.

County Court, PO Box 728, Anahuac, TX 77514. 409-267-8301 (CST) 8AM-5PM. Misdemeanor, Civil, Probate.

## Cherokee County

Real Estate Recording, Cherokee County Clerk, 402 N. Main, Courthouse, Rusk, TX 75785. 903-683-2350 (CST) 8AM-5PM.

District Court, Drawer C, Rusk, TX 75785. 903-683-4533 (CST) 8AM-12PM 1PM-5PM. Felony, Civil.

County Court, Cherokee County Clerk, PO Box 420, Rusk, TX 75785. 903-683-2350 (CST) 8AM-5PM. Misdemeanor, Civil, Probate.

## Childress County

Real Estate Recording, Childress County Clerk, 100 Avenue E NW, Childress, TX 79201. 817-937-6143 (CST) 8:30AM-Noon, 1-5PM.

District and County Court, Courthouse Box 4, Childress, TX 79201. 817-937-6143 (CST)

8:30AM-12PM 1PM-5PM. Felony, Misdemeanor, Civil, Eviction, Probate.

## Clay County

**Real Estate Recording**, Clay County Clerk, 100 North Bridge, Henrietta, TX 76365. 817-538-4631 (CST) 8AM-5PM.

**District Court**, PO Box 554, Henrietta, TX 76365. 817-538-4561 (CST) 8AM-5PM. Felony, Civil.

**County Court**, PO Box 548, Henrietta, TX 76365. 817-538-4631 (CST) 8AM-5PM. Misdemeanor, Civil, Probate.

## Cochran County

**Real Estate Recording**, Cochran County Clerk, 100 North Main, Courthouse, Morton, TX 79346-2598. 806-266-5450 (CST) 8AM-5PM.

**District and County Court**, County Courthouse Rm 102, Morton, TX 79346. 806-266-5450 (CST) 8AM-5PM. Felony, Misdemeanor, Civil, Eviction, Probate.

## Coke County

**Real Estate Recording**, Coke County Clerk, 13 East 7th Street, Courthouse, Robert Lee, TX 76945. 915-453-2631 (CST) 8AM-5PM.

**District and County Court**, PO Box 150, Robert Lee, TX 76945. 915-453-2631 (CST) 8AM-5PM. Felony, Misdemeanor, Civil, Eviction, Probate.

## Coleman County

**Real Estate Recording**, Coleman County Clerk, Courthouse, Coleman, TX 76834. 915-625-2889 (CST)

**District Court**, PO Box 957, Coleman, TX 76834. 915-625-2568 (CST) 8AM-5PM. Felony, Civil.

**County Court**, PO Box 591, Coleman, TX 76834. 915-625-2889 (CST) 8AM-5PM. Misdemeanor, Civil, Probate.

## Collin County

**Real Estate Recording**, Collin County Clerk, 210 South McDonald #124, County Courthouse, McKinney, TX 75069. 214-548-4134 (CST) 8AM-5PM (8AM-4PM Land Recording).

**District Court**, PO Box 578, McKinney, TX 75069. 214-548-4365 (CST) 8AM-5PM. Felony, Civil.

**County Court**, 210 S McDonald St Rm 542, McKinney, TX 75069. 214-548-4529 (CST) 8AM-5PM. Misdemeanor, Civil, Probate.

## Collingsworth County

**Real Estate Recording**, Collingsworth County Clerk, Courthouse, Room 3, Wellington, TX 79095. 806-447-2408 (CST) 9AM-5PM.

**District and County Court**, County Courthouse, Rm 3, Wellington, TX 79095. 806-447-2408 (CST) 8AM-5PM. Felony, Misdemeanor, Civil, Eviction, Probate.

## Colorado County

**Real Estate Recording**, Colorado County Clerk, 400 Spring Street, Courthouse, Columbus, TX 78934. 409-732-2155 (CST) 8AM-5PM.

**District Court**, 400 Spring, County Courthouse, Columbus, TX 78934. 409-732-2536 (CST) 8AM-5PM. Felony, Civil.

**County Court**, County Courthouse, Columbus, TX 78934. 409-732-2155 (CST) 8AM-5PM. Misdemeanor, Civil, Probate.

## Comal County

**Real Estate Recording**, Comal County Clerk, 100 Main Plaza, Suite 104, New Braunfels, TX 78130. 210-620-5513 (CST) 8AM-4:30PM.

**District Court**, 150 N Sequin Ste 304, New Braunfels, TX 78130-5161. 210-620-5562 (CST) 8AM-5PM. Felony, Civil.

**County Court**, 100 Main Plaza, Ste 203, New Braunfels, TX 78130. 210-620-5513 (CST) 8:30AM-5:00PM. Misdemeanor, Civil, Probate.

## Comanche County

**Real Estate Recording**, Comanche County Clerk, Courthouse, Comanche, TX 76442. 915-356-2655 (CST) 8:30-5PM.

**District Court**, County Courthouse, Comanche, TX 76442. 915-356-2342 (CST) 8:30AM-5PM. Felony, Civil.

**County Court**, County Courthouse, Comanche, TX 76442. 915-356-2655 (CST) 8:30AM-5PM. Misdemeanor, Civil, Probate.

## Concho County

**Real Estate Recording**, Concho County Clerk, Highway 83, Courthouse, Paint Rock, TX 76866. 915-732-4322 (CST) 8:30AM-5PM.

**District and County Court**, PO Box 98, Paint Rock, TX 76866. 915-732-4322 (CST) 8:30AM-5PM. Felony, Misdemeanor, Civil, Eviction, Probate.

## Cooke County

**Real Estate Recording**, Cooke County Clerk, Courthouse, Gainesville, TX 76240. 817-668-5420 (CST) 8AM-5PM.

**District Court**, County Courthouse, Gainesville, TX 76240. 817-668-5450 (CST) 8AM-5PM. Felony, Civil.

**County Court**, County Courthouse, Gainesville, TX 76240. 817-668-5422 (CST) 8AM-5PM. Misdemeanor, Civil, Probate.

## Coryell County

**Real Estate Recording**, Coryell County Clerk, Courthouse, Gatesville, TX 76528. 817-865-5016 (CST) 8AM-5PM.

**District Court**, PO Box 4, Gatesville, TX 76528. 817-865-6115 (CST) 8AM-5PM. Felony, Civil.

**County Court**, PO Box 237, Gatesville, TX 76528. 817-865-5016 (CST) 8AM-5PM. Misdemeanor, Civil, Probate.

## Cottle County

**Real Estate Recording**, Cottle County Clerk, Courthouse, 9th & Richards, Paducah, TX 79248. 806-492-3823 (CST)

**50th Judicial District and County Court**, PO Box 717, Paducah, TX 79248. 806-492-3823 (CST) 9AM-12PM 1PM-5PM. Felony, Misdemeanor, Civil, Eviction, Probate.

## Crane County

**Real Estate Recording**, Crane County Clerk, 6th East Alford Street, Courthouse, Crane, TX 79731. 915-558-3581 (CST) 9AM-12, 1-5PM.

**District and County Court**, PO Box 578, Crane, TX 79731. 915-558-3581 (CST) 9AM-5PM. Felony, Misdemeanor, Civil, Eviction, Probate.

## Crockett County

**Real Estate Recording**, Crockett County Clerk, 907 Avenue D, Ozona, TX 76943. 915-392-2022 (CST) 8AM-5PM.

**District and County Court**, PO Drawer C, Ozona, TX 76943. 915-392-2022 (CST) 8AM-5PM. Felony, Misdemeanor, Civil, Eviction, Probate.

## Crosby County

**Real Estate Recording**, Crosby County Clerk, Aspen & Berkshire Streets, Courthouse, Crosbyton, TX 79322. 806-675-2334 (CST) 8AM-12, 1-5PM.

**District Court**, PO Box 495, Crosbyton, TX 79322. 806-675-2071 (CST) 8AM-5PM. Felony, Civil.

**County Court**, PO Box 218, Crosbyton, TX 79322. 806-675-2334 (CST) 8AM-5PM. Misdemeanor, Civil, Probate.

## Culberson County

**Real Estate Recording**, Culberson County Clerk, 301 La Caverna, Courthouse, Van Horn, TX 79855. 915-283-2058 (CST) 8AM-Noon,1-5PM.

**District and County Court**, PO Box 158, Van Horn, TX 79855. 915-283-2058 (CST) 8AM-5PM. Felony, Misdemeanor, Civil, Eviction, Probate.

## Dallam County

**Real Estate Recording**, Dallam County Clerk, 101 East 5th, Dalhart, TX 79022. 806-249-4751 (CST) 9AM-5PM.

**District and County Court**, PO Box 1352, Dalhart, TX 79022. 806-249-4751 (CST) 8AM-5PM. Felony, Misdemeanor, Civil, Eviction, Probate.

## Dallas County

**Real Estate Recording**, Dallas County Clerk, 509 Main Street, Records Building, Dallas, TX 75202-3502. 214-653-7131 (CST) 8AM-4:30PM.

**County Court-Civil**, 509 W Main, Dallas, TX 75202. 214-653-7441 (CST) 8AM-4:30PM. Civil.

**District Court-Civil**, 600 Commerce, Dallas, TX 75202-4606. 214-653-7421 (CST) 8AM-5PM. Civil.

**District Court-Criminal**, 133 N Industrial, Dallas, TX 75202. 214-653-5950 (CST) 8AM-5PM. Felony.

**Criminal District Courts 1-5**, 133 N Industrial Blvd, Dallas, TX 75207. 214-653-7421 (CST) 8:00AM-4:30PM M-F. Felony.

**District Court-Misdemeanor**, 133 N Industrial, Dallas, TX 75207-4313. 214-653-5740 (CST) 8AM-4:30PM. Misdemeanor.

**County Court-Civil**, 509 W Main 3rd Floor, Dallas, TX 75202. 214-653-7131 (CST) 8AM-4:30PM. Civil.

**Probate Court**, Records Bldg, 2nd Floor, Dallas, TX 75202. 214-653-6166 (CST) Probate.

## Dawson County

**Real Estate Recording**, Dawson County Clerk, North 1st & Main Street, Courthouse, Lamesa, TX 79331. 806-872-3778 (CST) 8:30AM-5PM.

**District Court**, Drawer 1268, Lamesa, TX 79331. 806-872-7373 (CST) 8:30AM-5PM. Felony, Civil.

**County Court**, Drawer 1268, Lamesa, TX 79331. 806-872-3778 (CST) 8:30AM-5PM. Misdemeanor, Civil, Probate.

## De Witt County

**Real Estate Recording**, De Witt County Clerk, 307 North Gonzales, Courthouse, Cuero, TX 77954. 512-275-3724 (CST) 8AM-12, 1-5PM.

**District and County Court**, 100 Main Plaza Ste 203, New Braunfels, TX 78130. 512-620-5582 (CST) 8AM-5PM. Felony, Misdemeanor, Civil, Probate.

## Deaf Smith County

**Real Estate Recording**, Deaf Smith County Clerk, 235 East 3rd, Room 203, Hereford, TX 79045-5593. 806-364-1746 (CST) 8AM-5PM.

**District Court**, Deaf Smith Courthouse, Hereford, TX 79045. 806-364-3901 (CST) 8AM-5PM. Felony, Civil.

**County Court**, Deaf Smith Courthouse, Hereford, TX 79045. 806-364-1746 (CST) 8AM-5PM. Misdemeanor, Civil, Probate.

## Delta County

**Real Estate Recording**, Delta County Clerk, 200 West Dallas Avenue, Cooper, TX 75432. 903-395-4110 (CST) 8AM-5PM.

**District and County Court**, PO Box 455, Cooper, TX 75432. 903-395-4110 (CST) 8AM-5PM. Felony, Misdemeanor, Civil, Eviction, Probate.

## Denton County

**Real Estate Recording**, Denton County Clerk, 401 West Hickory, Denton, TX 76201. 817-565-8510 (CST) 8AM-4:30PM.

**District Court**, PO Box 2146, Denton, TX 76202. 817-565-8528 (CST) 8AM-4:30PM. Felony, Civil.

**County Court**, PO Box 2187, Denton, TX 76202. 817-565-8500 (CST) 8AM-4:30PM. Misdemeanor, Civil, Probate.

## Dickens County

**Real Estate Recording**, Dickens County Clerk, Montgomery Street, Courthouse, Dickens, TX 79229. 806-623-5531 (CST) 8AM-12, 1-5PM.

**District and County Court**, PO Box 120, Dickens, TX 79229. 806-623-5319 (CST) 8AM-5PM. Felony, Misdemeanor, Civil, Eviction, Probate.

## Dimmit County

**Real Estate Recording**, Dimmit County Clerk, 103 North 5th Street, Carrizo Springs, TX 78834. 210-876-3569 (CST) 8AM-12, 1-5PM.

**District Court**, 103 N 5th, Carrizo Springs, TX 78834. 210-876-2321 (CST) 8AM-5PM. Felony, Civil.

**County Court**, 103 N 5th, Carrizo Springs, TX 78834. 210-876-3569 (CST) 8AM-5PM. Misdemeanor, Civil, Probate.

## Donley County

**Real Estate Recording**, Donley County Clerk, 300 South Sully, Clarendon, TX 79226. 806-874-3436 (CST) 8AM-Noon,1-5PM.

**District and County Court**, PO Drawer U, Clarendon, TX 79226. 806-874-3436 (CST) 8AM-12PM 1PM-5PM. Felony, Misdemeanor, Civil, Eviction, Probate.

## Duval County

**Real Estate Recording**, Duval County Clerk, 400 East Gravis on Highway 44, San Diego, TX 78384. 512-279-3322 (CST) X271,2 8AM-12, 1-5PM.

**District Court**, PO Box 487, San Diego, TX 78384. 512-279-3322 (CST) 8AM-5PM. Felony, Civil.

**County Court**, PO Box 248, San Diego, TX 78384. 512-279-3322 (CST) 8AM-5PM. Misdemeanor, Civil, Probate.

## Eastland County

**Real Estate Recording**, Eastland County Clerk, 100 West Main, Courthouse, Eastland, TX 76448. 817-629-1583 (CST) 8:30AM-5PM.

**District Court**, PO Box 670, Eastland, TX 76448. 817-629-2664 (CST) 8AM-4:30PM. Felony, Civil.

**County Court**, PO Box 110, Eastland, TX 76448. 817-629-1583 (CST) 8:30AM-5PM. Misdemeanor, Civil, Probate.

## Ector County

**Real Estate Recording**, Ector County Clerk, 300 Grant Avenue, Courthouse, Room 111, Odessa, TX 79761. 915-335-3045 (CST) 8AM-5PM.

**District Court**, County Courthouse Rm 301, Odessa, TX 79761. 915-335-3144 (CST) 8AM-5PM. Felony, Civil.

**County Court**, PO Box 707, Odessa, TX 79760. 915-335-3045 (CST) 8AM-5PM. Misdemeanor, Civil, Probate.

## Edwards County

**Real Estate Recording**, Edwards County Clerk, 400 Main, Rocksprings, TX 78880. 210-683-2235 (CST) 8AM-5PM.

**District and County Court**, PO Box 184, Rocksprings, TX 78880. 512-683-2235 (CST) 8AM-12PM 1PM-5PM. Felony, Misdemeanor, Civil, Eviction, Probate.

## El Paso County

**Real Estate Recording**, El Paso County Clerk, 501 East Overland Street, Room 105, El Paso, TX 79901-2496. 915-546-2074 (MST) 8AM-4:45PM.

**District Court**, #103 County Court Bldg, El Paso, TX 79901. 915-546-2021 (MST) 8AM-4:45PM. Felony, Civil.

**County Court**, 500 E San Antonio St Rm 105, El Paso, TX 79901. 915-546-2071 (MST) 8AM-4:45PM. Misdemeanor, Civil.

**Probate Court**, 500 E San Antonio, Rm 1003, El Paso, TX 79901. 915-546-2161 (MST) Probate.

## Ellis County

**Real Estate Recording**, Ellis County Clerk, Corner of Franklin & Rogers, Courthouse, Waxahachie, TX 75165. 214-923-5070 (CST) 8AM-5PM.

**40th Judicial District Court**, 101 W Main St County Courthouse, Waxahachie, TX 75165. 214-923-5000 (CST) 8AM-5PM. Felony, Civil.

**County Court**, PO Box 250, Waxahachie, TX 75165. 214-923-5070 (CST) 8AM-4:30PM. Misdemeanor, Civil, Probate.

## Erath County

**Real Estate Recording**, Erath County Clerk, Courthouse, Stephenville, TX 76401. 817-965-1482 (CST) 8AM-12, 1-5PM.

**District Court**, 112 W College, County Courthouse, Stephenville, TX 76401. 817-965-1431 (CST) 8AM-5PM. Felony, Civil.

**County Court**, County Courthouse, Stephenville, TX 76401. 817-965-1482 (CST) 8AM-5PM. Misdemeanor, Civil, Probate.

## Falls County

**Real Estate Recording**, Falls County Clerk, Corner of Business Hwy 6 and Hwy 7, Courthouse, Marlin, TX 76661. 817-883-2061 (CST) 8AM-12, 1-5PM.

**District Court**, PO Box 229, Marlin, TX 76661. 817-883-3181 (CST) 8AM-12PM 1PM-5PM. Felony, Civil.

**County Court**, PO Box 458, Marlin, TX 76661. 817-883-2061 (CST) 8AM-5PM. Misdemeanor, Civil, Probate.

## Fannin County

**Real Estate Recording**, Fannin County Clerk, Courthouse, Bonham, TX 75418. 903-583-7486 (CST) 8AM-5PM.

**District Court**, County Courthouse, Bonham, TX 75418. 903-583-7459 (CST) 8AM-5PM. Felony, Civil.

**County Court**, County Courthouse, Bonham, TX 75418. 903-583-7486 (CST) 8AM-5PM. Misdemeanor, Civil, Probate.

## Fayette County

**Real Estate Recording**, Fayette County Clerk, 151 North Washington, Courthouse, La Grange, TX 78945. 409-968-3251 (CST) 8AM-12, 1-5PM.

**District Court**, County Courthouse, La Grange, TX 78945. 409-968-3548 (CST) 8AM-5PM. Felony, Civil.

**County Court**, PO Box 296, La Grange, TX 78945. 409-968-3251 (CST) 8AM-5PM. Misdemeanor, Civil, Probate.

## Fisher County

**Real Estate Recording**, Fisher County Clerk, Corner of US Highway 180 & 70, Courthouse, Roby, TX 79543. 915-776-2401 (CST) 8AM-12, 1-5PM.

**District Court**, PO Box 88, Roby, TX 79543. 915-776-2279 (CST) 8AM-5PM. Felony, Civil.

**County Court**, County Courthouse Box 368, Roby, TX 79543. 915-776-2401 (CST) 8AM-5PM. Misdemeanor, Civil, Probate.

## Floyd County

**Real Estate Recording**, Floyd County Clerk, 100 Main Street, Courthouse, Floydada, TX 79235. 806-983-3236 (CST) 8:30AM-12, 1-5PM.

**District Court**, PO Box 67, Floydada, TX 79235. 806-983-2232 (CST) 8:30AM-12PM 1PM-5PM. Felony, Civil.

**County Court**, PO Box 476, Floydada, TX 79235. 806-983-3236 (CST) 8:30AM-12PM 1PM-5PM. Misdemeanor, Civil, Probate.

## Foard County

**Real Estate Recording**, Foard County Clerk, 100 North Main and Commerce, Crowell, TX 79227. 817-684-1365 (CST) 9AM-11:45AM, 1-4:30PM.

**District and County Court**, PO Box 539, Crowell, TX 79227. 817-684-1365 (CST) 8AM-5PM. Felony, Misdemeanor, Civil, Eviction, Probate.

## Fort Bend County

**Real Estate Recording**, Fort Bend County Clerk, 301 Jackson, Richmond, TX 77469. 713-341-8650 (CST) 8AM-4:30PM.

**District Court**, PO Drawer E, Richmond, TX 77469. 713-342-3411 (CST) 8AM-5PM. Felony, Civil.

**County Court**, PO Box 520, Richmond, TX 77469. 713-342-3411 (CST) 8AM-4PM. Misdemeanor, Civil, Probate.

## Franklin County

**Real Estate Recording**, Franklin County Clerk, Corner of Dallas & Kaufman Streets, Courthouse, Mount Vernon, TX 75457. 903-537-4252 (CST) 8AM-5PM.

**District Court**, PO Box 68, Mount Vernon, TX 75457. 903-537-4786 (CST) 8AM-5PM. Felony, Civil.

**County Court**, PO Box 68, Mount Vernon, TX 75457. 903-537-4252 (CST) 8AM-5PM. Misdemeanor, Civil, Probate.

## Freestone County

**Real Estate Recording**, Freestone County Clerk, Corner of Main & Mount Streets, Courthouse Annex, Fairfield, TX 75840. 903-389-2635 (CST) 8AM-5PM.

**District Court**, PO Box 722, Fairfield, TX 75840. 903-389-2534 (CST) 8AM-5PM. Felony, Civil.

**County Court**, PO Box 1017, Fairfield, TX 75840. 903-389-2635 (CST) 8AM-5PM. Misdemeanor, Civil, Probate.

## Frio County

**Real Estate Recording**, Frio County Clerk, 528 East San Antonio Street, Pearsall, TX 78061. 210-334-2214 (CST) 8AM-12, 1-5PM.

**District Court**, PO Box 242, Pearsall, TX 78061. 512-334-8073 (CST) 8AM-5PM. Felony, Civil.

**County Court**, PO Box X, Pearsall, TX 78061. 210-334-3200 (CST) 8AM-5PM. Misdemeanor, Civil, Probate.

## Gaines County

**Real Estate Recording**, Gaines County Clerk, 100 Main Street, Courthouse, Seminole, TX 79360. 915-758-4003 (CST) 8AM-5PM.

**District Court**, County Courthouse, Seminole, TX 79360. 915-758-4013 (CST) 8AM-5PM. Felony, Civil.

**County Court**, County Courthouse, Seminole, TX 79360. 915-758-4003 (CST) 8AM-5PM. Misdemeanor, Civil, Probate.

## Galveston County

**Real Estate Recording**, Galveston County Clerk, 722 Moody Avenue, Galveston, TX 77550. 409-766-2208 (CST) 8:30AM-5PM.

**District Court**, 722 Moody Rm 404, Galveston, TX 77550. 409-766-2424 (CST) 8AM-5PM. Felony, Civil.

**County Court**, PO Box 2450, Galveston, TX 77553-2450. 409-766-2203 (CST) 8:30AM-5PM. Misdemeanor, Civil.

**Probate Court**, County Courthouse, No 305, Galveston, TX 77550. 409-766-2251 (CST) Probate.

## Garza County

**Real Estate Recording**, Garza County Clerk, Courthouse, Post, TX 79356. 806-495-3535 (CST) 8AM-12, 1-5PM.

**District and County Court**, PO Box 366, Post, TX 79356. 806-495-3535 (CST) 8AM-12, 1-5PM. Felony, Misdemeanor, Civil, Eviction, Probate.

## Gillespie County

**Real Estate Recording**, Gillespie County Clerk, 101 West Main, Room 109, Unit #13, Fredericksburg, TX 78624. 210-997-6515 (CST) 8AM-4:30PM.

**District Court**, 101 W Main Rm 204, Fredericksburg, TX 78624. 210-997-6517 (CST) 8AM-12 1-5PM. Felony, Civil.

**County Court**, 101 W Main Unit #13, Fredericksburg, TX 78624. 210-997-6515 (CST) 8AM-4:30PM. Misdemeanor, Civil, Probate.

## Glasscock County

**Real Estate Recording**, Glasscock County Clerk, Courthouse, Highway 158, Garden City, TX 79739. 915-354-2371 (CST) 8AM-12, 1-5PM.

**District and County Court**, County Courthouse, Garden City, TX 79739. 915-354-2371 (CST) 8AM-5PM. Felony, Misdemeanor, Civil, Eviction, Probate.

## Goliad County

**Real Estate Recording**, Goliad County Clerk, 127 N. Courthouse Square, Goliad, TX 77963. 512-645-3294 (CST) 8AM-5PM.

**District and County Court**, PO Box 5, Goliad, TX 77963. 512-645-2443 (CST) 8AM-5PM. Felony, Misdemeanor, Civil, Eviction, Probate.

## Gonzales County

**Real Estate Recording**, Gonzales County Clerk, 1709 Sarah DeWitt Dr., Courthouse, Gonzales, TX 78629. 210-672-2801 (CST) 8AM-5PM.

**District Court**, PO Box 34, Gonzales, TX 78629-0034. 512-672-2326 (CST) 8AM-12PM 1PM-5PM. Felony, Civil.

**County Court**, PO Box 77, Gonzales, TX 78629. 210-672-2801 (CST) 8AM-5PM. Misdemeanor, Civil, Probate.

## Gray County

**Real Estate Recording**, Gray County Clerk, 205 North Russell, Courthouse, Pampa, TX 79065. 806-669-8004 (CST) 8:30AM-12, 1-5PM.

**District Court**, PO Box 1139, Pampa, TX 79066-1139. 806-669-8010 (CST) 8:30AM-5PM. Felony, Civil.

**County Court**, PO Box 1902, Pampa, TX 79066-1902. 806-669-8004 (CST) 8AM-5PM. Misdemeanor, Civil, Probate.

## Grayson County

**Real Estate Recording**, Grayson County Clerk, 100 West Houston #17, Sherman, TX 75090. 903-813-4238 (CST) 8AM-5PM.

**District Court**, 200 S Crockett Rm 120-A, Sherman, TX 75090-7167. 903-868-9515 (CST) 8AM-5PM. Felony, Civil.

**County Court**, 200 S Crockett, Sherman, TX 75090. 903-868-4200 (CST) 8AM-5PM. Misdemeanor, Civil, Probate.

## Gregg County

**Real Estate Recording**, Gregg County Clerk, 100 East Methvin, Suite 200, Longview, TX 75601. 903-236-8430 (CST) 8AM-5PM.

**District Court**, PO Box 711, Longview, TX 75606. 903-758-6181 (CST) 8AM-5PM. Felony, Civil.

**County Court**, PO Box 3049, Longview, TX 75606. 903-236-8430 (CST) 8AM-5PM. Misdemeanor, Civil, Probate.

## Grimes County

**Real Estate Recording**, Grimes County Clerk, Courthouse, Anderson, TX 77830. 409-873-2111 (CST) 8AM-Noon, 1-4:45PM.

**12th & 278th Judicial District Court**, PO Box 234, Anderson, TX 77830. 409-873-2111 (CST) 8AM-4:45PM. Felony, Civil.

**County Court**, PO Box 209, Anderson, TX 77830. 409-873-2662 (CST) 8AM-4:45PM. Misdemeanor, Civil, Probate.

## Guadalupe County

**Real Estate Recording**, Guadalupe County Clerk, 101 East Court Street, Rm 209, Seguin,

TX 78155. 210-379-4188 (CST) X236 8AM-4:30PM.

**District Court**, 101 E Court St, Seguin, TX 78155. 210-379-4188 (CST) 8AM-5PM. Felony, Civil.

**County Court**, 101 E Court St, Seguin, TX 78155. 210-379-4188 (CST) 8AM-4:30PM. Misdemeanor, Civil, Probate.

## Hale County

**Real Estate Recording**, Hale County Clerk, 500 Broadway #140, Plainview, TX 79072-8030. 806-293-8482 (CST) 8AM-Noon,1-5PM.

**District Court**, 500 Broadway #200, Plainview, TX 79072. 806-293-0327 (CST) 8AM-5PM. Felony, Civil.

**County Court**, 500 Broadway #140, Plainview, TX 79072-8030. 806-293-8482 (CST) 8AM-5PM. Misdemeanor, Civil, Probate.

## Hall County

**Real Estate Recording**, Hall County Clerk, Courthouse, Box 8, Memphis, TX 79245. 806-259-2627 (CST) 8:30AM-5PM.

**District and County Court**, County Courthouse, Memphis, TX 79245. 806-259-2627 (CST) 8:30AM-5PM. Felony, Misdemeanor, Civil, Eviction, Probate.

## Hamilton County

**Real Estate Recording**, Hamilton County Clerk, Main Street, Courthouse, Hamilton, TX 76531. 817-386-3518 (CST) 8AM-5PM.

**District Court**, County Courthouse, Hamilton, TX 76531. 817-386-3417 (CST) 8AM-5PM. Felony, Civil.

**County Court**, County Courthouse, Hamilton, TX 76531. 817-386-3518 (CST) 8AM-5PM. Misdemeanor, Civil, Probate.

## Hansford County

**Real Estate Recording**, Hansford County Clerk, Courthouse, Spearman, TX 79081. 806-659-2666 (CST) 8:30AM-5PM.

**District and County Court**, PO Box 397, Spearman, TX 79081. 806-659-2666 (CST) 8AM-5PM. Felony, Misdemeanor, Civil, Eviction, Probate.

## Hardeman County

**Real Estate Recording**, Hardeman County Clerk, 300 Main Street, Quanah, TX 79252. 817-663-2901 (CST) 8:30AM-5PM.

**District and County Court**, PO Box 30, Quanah, TX 79252. 817-663-2901 (CST) 8:30AM-5PM. Felony, Misdemeanor, Civil, Eviction, Probate.

## Hardin County

**Real Estate Recording**, Hardin County Clerk, Courthouse Square, Highway 326, Kountze, TX 77625. 409-246-5185 (CST)

**District Court**, PO Box 2997, Kountze, TX 77625. 409-246-5150 (CST) 8AM-4PM. Felony, Civil.

**County Court**, PO Box 38, Kountze, TX 77625. 409-246-5185 (CST) 8AM-5PM. Misdemeanor, Civil, Probate.

## Harris County

**Real Estate Recording**, Harris County Clerk, 1001 Preston, 4th Floor, Houston, TX 77002. 713-755-6405 (CST) 8AM-4:30PM.

**District Court**, PO Box 4651, Houston, TX 77210. 713-755-5711 (CST) 8AM-5PM. Felony, Civil.

**County Court**, PO Box 1525, Houston, TX 77251. 713-755-6421 (CST) 8AM-4:30PM. Misdemeanor, Civil.

**Probate Court**, 1115 Congress, 6th Floor, Houston, TX 77002. 713-755-6084 (CST) Probate.

## Harrison County

**Real Estate Recording**, Harrison County Clerk, Corner of W. Houston & S. Wellington, Courthouse, Marshall, TX 75670. 903-935-4858 (CST) 8AM-5PM.

**District Court**, County Courthouse, Marshall, TX 75670. 903-935-4845 (CST) 8AM-12PM 1PM-5PM. Felony, Civil.

**County Court**, PO Box 1365, Marshall, TX 75671. 903-935-4858 (CST) 8AM-5PM. Misdemeanor, Civil, Probate.

## Hartley County

**Real Estate Recording**, Hartley County Clerk, 9th & Railroad, Channing, TX 79018. 806-235-3582 (CST) 8:30AM-12, 1-5PM.

**District and County Court**, PO Box 22, Channing, TX 79018. 806-235-3582 (CST) 8:30AM-12PM 1PM-5PM. Felony, Misdemeanor, Civil, Eviction, Probate.

## Haskell County

**Real Estate Recording**, Haskell County Clerk, Courthouse, 1 Ave. D, Haskell, TX 79521. 817-864-2451 (CST) 8AM-5PM.

**39th Judicial District Court**, PO Box 27, Haskell, TX 79521. 817-864-2030 (CST) 8AM-12PM 1PM-5PM. Felony, Civil.

**County Court**, PO Box 725, Haskell, TX 79521. 817-864-2451 (CST) 8AM-5PM. Misdemeanor, Civil, Probate.

## Hays County

**Real Estate Recording**, Hays County Clerk, 137 N. Guadalupe, Hays County Records Building, San Marcos, TX 78666. 512-396-2601 (CST) 8AM-5PM.

**District Court**, County Courthouse Rm 304, San Marcos, TX 78666. 512-353-4346 (CST) 9AM-5PM. Felony, Civil.

**County Court**, County Courthouse, San Marcos, TX 78666. 512-396-2601 (CST) 8AM-5PM. Misdemeanor, Civil, Probate.

## Hemphill County

**Real Estate Recording**, Hemphill County Clerk, 400 Main Street, Courthouse, Canadian, TX 79014. 806-323-6212 (CST) 8AM-5PM.

**District and County Court**, PO Box 867, Canadian, TX 79014. 806-323-6212 (CST) 8AM-5PM. Felony, Misdemeanor, Civil, Eviction, Probate.

## Henderson County

**Real Estate Recording**, Henderson County Clerk, Courthouse Square, South Side, First Floor, Athens, TX 75751. 903-675-6140 (CST) 8AM-5PM.

**District Court**, Henderson County Courthouse, Athens, TX 75751. 903-675-6115 (CST) 8AM-5PM. Felony, Civil.

**County Court**, PO Box 632, Athens, TX 75751. 903-675-6140 (CST) 8AM-5PM. Misdemeanor, Civil, Probate.

## Hidalgo County

**Real Estate Recording**, Hidalgo County Clerk, 100 North Closner, Courthouse, Edinburg, TX 78539. 210-318-2100 (CST) 8AM-5PM.

**District Court**, 100 S Closner, Box 87, Edinburg, TX 78540. 210-318-2200 (CST) 8AM-5PM. Felony, Civil.

**County Court**, PO Box 58, Edinburg, TX 78539. 210-318-2100 (CST) 8AM-5PM. Misdemeanor, Civil, Probate.

## Hill County

**Real Estate Recording**, Hill County Clerk, Courthouse, 126 S. Covington, Hillsboro, TX 76645. 817-582-2161 (CST) 8AM-5PM.

**District Court**, PO Box 634, Hillsboro, TX 76645. 817-582-3512 (CST) 8AM-5PM. Felony, Civil.

**County Court**, PO Box 398, Hillsboro, TX 76645. 817-582-2161 (CST) 8AM-5PM. Misdemeanor, Civil, Probate.

## Hockley County

**Real Estate Recording**, Hockley County Clerk, 800 Houston St., Courthouse, Box 13, Levelland, TX 79336. 806-894-3185 (CST) 9AM-5PM.

**District Court**, County Courthouse #16, Levelland, TX 79336. 806-894-8527 (CST) 9AM-5PM. Felony, Civil.

**County Court**, County Courthouse, Levelland, TX 79336. 806-894-3185 (CST) 9AM-5PM. Misdemeanor, Civil, Probate.

## Hood County

**Real Estate Recording**, Hood County Clerk, 101 East Pearl, Courthouse, Granbury, TX 76048. 817-579-3222 (CST) 8AM-5PM.

**District Court**, County Courthouse, Granbury, TX 76048. 817-579-3236 (CST) 8AM-5PM. Felony, Civil.

**County Court**, PO Box 339, Granbury, TX 76048. 817-579-3222 (CST) 8AM-5PM. Misdemeanor, Civil, Probate.

## Hopkins County

**Real Estate Recording**, Hopkins County Clerk, 118 Church Street, Courthouse, Sulphur Springs, TX 75482. 903-885-3929 (CST) 8AM-5PM.

**District Court**, PO Box 391, Sulphur Springs, TX 75482. 903-885-2656 (CST) 8AM-5PM. Felony, Civil.

**County Court**, PO Box 288, Sulphur Springs, TX 75482. 903-885-3929 (CST) 8AM-5PM. Misdemeanor, Civil, Probate.

## Houston County

**Real Estate Recording**, Houston County Clerk, Courthouse Square, 401 E. Houston, Crockett, TX 75835. 409-544-3255 (CST) 8AM-4:30PM.

**District Court**, County Courthouse, Crockett, TX 75835. 409-544-3255 (CST) 8AM-4:30PM. Felony, Civil.

**County Court**, PO Box 370, Crockett, TX 75835. 409-544-3255 (CST) 8AM-5PM. Misdemeanor, Civil, Probate.

## Howard County

**Real Estate Recording**, Howard County Clerk, 300 Main, Courthouse, Big Spring, TX 79720. 915-264-2213 (CST) 8AM-5PM.

**District Court**, PO Box 2138, Big Spring, TX 79721. 915-264-2223 (CST) 8AM-5PM. Felony, Civil.

**County Court**, PO Box 1468, Big Spring, TX 79721. 915-264-2213 (CST) 8AM-5PM. Misdemeanor, Civil, Probate.

## Hudspeth County

**Real Estate Recording**, Hudspeth County Clerk, Courthouse, Sierra Blanca, TX 79851. 915-369-2301 (MST) 8AM-5PM.

**District and County Court**, PO Drawer A, Sierra Blanca, TX 79851. 915-369-2301 (MST) 8AM-5PM. Felony, Misdemeanor, Civil, Eviction, Probate.

## Hunt County

**Real Estate Recording**, Hunt County Clerk, 2500 Lee Street, Courthouse, 2nd Fl., East End, Greenville, TX 75401. 903-408-4130 (CST) 8AM-5PM.

**District Court**, PO Box 1627, Greenville, TX 75401. 903-455-4525 (CST) 8AM-5PM. Felony, Civil.

**County Court**, PO Box 1316, Greenville, TX 75401. 903-455-6460 (CST) 8AM-5PM. Misdemeanor, Civil, Probate.

## Hutchinson County

**Real Estate Recording**, Hutchinson County Clerk, 6th & Main, Courthouse, Stinnett, TX 79083. 806-878-4002 (CST) 9AM-5PM.

**84th & 316th Judicial District Court**, PO Box 580, Stinnett, TX 79083. 806-878-4017 (CST) 9AM-5PM. Felony, Civil.

**County Court**, PO Drawer 1186, Stinnett, TX 79083. 806-878-2829 (CST) 9AM-5PM. Misdemeanor, Civil, Probate.

## Irion County

**Real Estate Recording**, Irion County Clerk, 209 N. Parkview, Mertzon, TX 76941. 915-835-2421 (CST) 8AM-4PM.

**District and County Court**, PO Box 736, Mertzon, TX 76941. 915-835-2421 (CST) 8AM-4PM. Felony, Misdemeanor, Civil, Eviction, Probate.

## Jack County

**Real Estate Recording**, Jack County Clerk, 100 Main Street, Jacksboro, TX 76458. 817-567-2111 (CST) 8AM-12, 1-5PM.

**District Court**, 100 Main, County Courthouse, Jacksboro, TX 76458. 817-567-2141 (CST) 8AM-5PM. Felony, Civil.

**County Court**, 100 Main, Jacksboro, TX 76458. 817-567-2111 (CST) 8AM-12PM 1PM-5PM. Misdemeanor, Civil, Probate.

## Jackson County

**Real Estate Recording**, Jackson County Clerk, 115 West Main, Edna, TX 77957. 512-782-3563 (CST) 8AM-5PM.

**District Court**, 115 W Main, Edna, TX 77957. 512-782-3812 (CST) 8AM-5PM. Felony, Civil.

**County Court**, 115 W Main, Edna, TX 77957. 512-782-3563 (CST) 8AM-5PM. Misdemeanor, Civil, Probate.

## Jasper County

**Real Estate Recording**, Jasper County Clerk, Courthouse, Room 103, Main at Lamar St., Jasper, TX 75951. 409-384-2632 (CST) 8AM-5PM.

**1st Judicial District Court**, County Courthouse #202, Jasper, TX 75951. 409-384-2721 (CST) 8AM-12PM 1PM-5PM. Felony, Civil.

**County Court**, PO Box 2070 (Rm 103, Courthouse, Main at, Jasper, TX 75951. 409-384-9481 (CST) 8AM-5PM. Misdemeanor, Civil, Probate.

## Jeff Davis County

**Real Estate Recording**, Jeff Davis County Clerk, Main Street, Fort Davis, TX 79734. 915-426-3251 (CST) 9AM-Noon, 1-5PM.

**District and County Court**, PO Box 398, Fort Davis, TX 79734. 915-426-3251 (CST) 8AM-5PM. Felony, Misdemeanor, Civil, Eviction, Probate.

## Jefferson County

**Real Estate Recording**, Jefferson County Clerk, 1001 Pearl Street, Beaumont, TX 77701. 409-835-8475 (CST) 8AM-5PM.

**District Court**, PO Box 3707, Beaumont, TX 77704. 409-835-8580 (CST) 8AM-5PM. Felony, Civil.

**County Court**, PO Box 1151, Beaumont, TX 77704. 409-835-8479 (CST) 8AM-5PM. Misdemeanor, Civil, Probate.

**Criminal District Court**, Jefferson County Courthouse, 1001 Pearl, Beaumont, TX 77701. 409-835-8580 (CST) 8:00AM-4:30PM M-F. Felony.

## Jim Hogg County

**Real Estate Recording**, Jim Hogg County Clerk, 102 East Tilley, Hebbronville, TX 78361. 512-527-4031 (CST) 9AM-5PM.

**District and County Court**, PO Box 870, Hebbronville, TX 78361. 512-527-4031 (CST) 9AM-5PM. Felony, Misdemeanor, Civil, Eviction, Probate.

## Jim Wells County

**Real Estate Recording**, Jim Wells County Clerk, 200 North Almond Street, Alice, TX 78332. 512-668-5702 (CST) 8:30AM-12, 1-5PM.

**District Court**, PO Drawer 2219, Alice, TX 78333. 512-668-5717 (CST) 8AM-5PM. Felony, Civil.

**County Court**, County Courthouse, Alice, TX 78333. 512-668-5702 (CST) 8:30AM-5PM. Misdemeanor, Civil, Probate.

## Johnson County

**Real Estate Recording**, Johnson County Clerk, 2 North Main, Room 101, Cleburne, TX 76031. 817-556-6300 (CST) 8AM-4:30PM.

**District Court**, PO Box 495, Cleburne, TX 76033-0495. 817-556-6300 (CST) 8AM-5PM. Felony, Civil.

**County Court**, PO Box 662, Cleburne, TX 76033-0662. 817-556-6300 (CST) 8AM-4:30PM. Misdemeanor, Civil, Probate.

## Jones County

**Real Estate Recording**, Jones County Clerk, 12th & Commercial, Courthouse, Anson, TX 79501. 915-823-3762 (CST) 8AM-5PM.

**District Court**, PO Box 308, Anson, TX 79501. 915-823-3731 (CST) 8AM-5PM. Felony, Civil.

## Karnes County

**Real Estate Recording**, Karnes County Clerk, 101 North Panna Maria Ave., Courthouse - Suite 9, Karnes City, TX 78118-2929. 210-780-3938 (CST) 8AM-5PM.

**District Court**, County Courthouse, Karnes City, TX 78118. 512-780-2562 (CST) 8AM-5PM. Felony, Civil.

**County Court**, 101 N Panna Maria Ave #9 Courthouse, Karnes City, TX 78118-2929. 512-780-3938 (CST) 8AM-5PM. Misdemeanor, Civil, Probate.

## Kaufman County

**Real Estate Recording**, Kaufman County Clerk, Courthouse, Kaufman, TX 75142. 214-932-4331 (CST) 8AM-5PM.

**District Court**, County Courthouse, Kaufman, TX 75142. 214-932-4331 (CST) 8AM-5PM. Felony, Civil.

**County Court**, County Courthouse, Kaufman, TX 75142. 214-932-4331 (CST) 8AM-5PM. Misdemeanor, Civil, Probate.

## Kendall County

**Real Estate Recording**, Kendall County Clerk, 204 East San Antonio, Suite 2, Boerne, TX 78006. 210-249-9343 (CST) 8:30AM-Noon, 1-5PM.

**District Court**, 204 E San Antonio #3, Boerne, TX 78006. 210-249-9343 (CST) 8:30AM-5PM. Felony, Civil.

**County Court**, 204 E San Antonio #2, Boerne, TX 78006. 210-249-9343 (CST) 8:30AM-5PM. Misdemeanor, Civil, Probate.

## Kenedy County

**Real Estate Recording**, Kenedy County Clerk, 101 Mallory Street, Sarita, TX 78385. 512-294-5220 (CST) 8:30AM-11:30AM, 1:30-4:30PM.

**District and County Court**, PO Box 1519, Sarita, TX 78385. 512-294-5220 (CST) 8:30AM-11:30AM 1:30PM-4:30PM. Felony, Misdemeanor, Civil, Eviction, Probate.

## Kent County

**Real Estate Recording**, Kent County Clerk, Courthouse, Jayton, TX 79528. 806-237-3881 (CST) 8:30AM-12, 1-5PM.

**District and County Court**, PO Box 9, Jayton, TX 79528. 806-237-3881 (CST) 8:30AM-12PM 1PM-5PM. Felony, Misdemeanor, Civil, Eviction, Probate.

## Kerr County

**Real Estate Recording**, Kerr County Clerk, 700 Main, Courthouse, Kerrville, TX 78028-5389. 210-257-6181 (CST) 9AM-5PM.

**District Court**, 700 Main, County Courthouse, Kerrville, TX 78028. 210-257-4396 (CST) 8AM-5PM. Felony, Civil.

**County Court**, 700 Main St, County Courthouse, Kerrville, TX 78028-5389. 210-896-2844 (CST) 8AM-5PM. Misdemeanor, Civil, Probate.

## Kimble County

**Real Estate Recording**, Kimble County Clerk, 501 Main Street, Junction, TX 76849. 915-446-3353 (CST) 8AM-12, 1-5PM.

**District and County Court**, 501 Main St, Junction, TX 76849. 915-446-3353 (CST) 8AM-12PM 1PM-5PM. Felony, Misdemeanor, Civil, Eviction, Probate.

## King County

**Real Estate Recording**, King County Clerk, Courthouse, Highway 82, Guthrie, TX 79236. 806-596-4412 (CST) 9AM-Noon, 1-5PM.

**District and County Court**, PO Box 135, Guthrie, TX 79236. 806-596-4412 (CST) 9AM-5PM. Felony, Misdemeanor, Civil, Eviction, Probate.

## Kinney County

**Real Estate Recording**, Kinney County Clerk, 501 Ann Street, Brackettville, TX 78832. 210-563-2521 (CST) 8AM-12, 1-5PM.

**District and County Court**, PO Drawer 9, Brackettville, TX 78832. 512-563-2521 (CST) 8AM-5PM. Felony, Misdemeanor, Civil, Eviction, Probate.

## Kleberg County

**Real Estate Recording**, Kleberg County Clerk, 700 East Kleberg Street, First Floor, East Wing, Kingsville, TX 78363. 512-595-8548 (CST) 8AM-12, 1-5PM.

**105th Judicial District & County Court**, PO Box 312, Kingsville, TX 78364-0312. 512-595-8561 (CST) 8AM-5PM. Felony, Misdemeanor, Civil, Eviction, Probate.

**County Court-Criminal**, PO Box 1327, Kingsville, TX 78364. 512-595-8548 (CST) 8AM-5PM. Misdemeanor.

## Knox County

**Real Estate Recording**, Knox County Clerk, Corner of Highway 6 & 82, Benjamin, TX 79505. 817-454-2441 (CST) 8AM-12, 1-5PM.

**District and County Court**, PO Box 196, Benjamin, TX 79505. 817-454-2441 (CST) 8AM-5PM. Felony, Misdemeanor, Civil, Eviction, Probate.

## La Salle County

**Real Estate Recording**, La Salle County Clerk, Courthouse Square, Cotulla, TX 78014. 210-879-2117 (CST) 8AM-12, 1-5PM.

**District Court**, PO Box 340, Cotulla, TX 78014. 210-879-2421 (CST) 8AM-5PM. Felony, Civil.

**County Court**, PO Box 340, Cotulla, TX 78014. 210-879-2117 (CST) 8AM-5PM. Misdemeanor, Civil, Probate.

## Lamar County

**Real Estate Recording**, Lamar County Clerk, Courthouse, 119 N. Main #109, Paris, TX 75460. 903-737-2420 (CST) 8AM-5PM.

**District Court**, 119 N Main Rm 306, Paris, TX 75460. 903-737-2427 (CST) 8AM-5PM. Felony, Civil.

**County Court**, 119 N Main, Paris, TX 75460. 903-737-2420 (CST) 8AM-5PM. Misdemeanor, Civil, Probate.

## Lamb County

**Real Estate Recording**, Lamb County Clerk, 100 6th Street, Room 103 Box 3, Littlefield, TX 79339-3366. 806-385-5173 (CST) 8:30AM-5PM.

**154th Judicial District Court**, 100 6th Rm 212, Courthouse, Littlefield, TX 79339. 806-385-3840 (CST) 9AM-12PM 1PM-5PM. Felony, Civil.

**County Court**, County Courthouse Rm 103, Littlefield, TX 79339-3366. 806-385-5173 (CST) 8AM-5PM. Misdemeanor, Civil, Probate.

## Lampasas County

**Real Estate Recording**, Lampasas County Clerk, 400 Live Oak Street, Lampasas, TX 76550. 512-556-8271 (CST) 8AM-5PM.

**District Court**, PO Box 327, Lampasas, TX 76550. 512-556-8271 (CST) 8AM-5PM. Felony, Civil.

**County Court**, PO Box 347, Lampasas, TX 76550. 512-556-8271 (CST) 8AM-5PM. Misdemeanor, Civil, Probate.

## Lavaca County

**Real Estate Recording**, Lavaca County Clerk, 201 North LaGrange Street, Courthouse, Hallettsville, TX 77964. 512-798-3612 (CST) 8AM-5PM.

**District Court**, PO Box 306, Hallettsville, TX 77964. 512-798-2351 (CST) 8AM-12PM 1PM-5PM. Felony, Civil.

**County Court**, PO Box 326, Hallettsville, TX 77964. 512-798-3612 (CST) 8AM-5PM. Misdemeanor, Civil, Probate.

## Lee County

**Real Estate Recording**, Lee County Clerk, Hempstead & Main, Courthouse, Giddings, TX 78942. 409-542-3684 (CST) 8AM-5PM.

**District Court**, PO Box 176, Giddings, TX 78942. 409-542-2947 (CST) 8AM-5PM. Felony, Civil.

**County Court**, PO Box 419, Giddings, TX 78942. 409-542-3684 (CST) 8AM-5PM. Misdemeanor, Civil, Probate.

## Leon County

**Real Estate Recording**, Leon County Clerk, Corner Cass and St. Mary Street, Courthouse Square, Centerville, TX 75833. 903-536-2352 (CST) 8AM-5PM.

**District Court**, PO Box 39, Centerville, TX 75833. 903-536-2227 (CST) 8AM-5PM. Felony, Civil.

**County Court**, PO Box 98, Centerville, TX 75833. 903-536-2352 (CST) 8AM-5PM. Misdemeanor, Civil, Probate.

## Liberty County

**Real Estate Recording**, Liberty County Clerk, 1923 Sam Houston, Liberty, TX 77575. 409-336-4673 (CST) 8AM-5PM.

**District Court**, 1923 Sam Houston Rm 303, Liberty, TX 77575. 409-336-8071 (CST) 8AM-5PM. Felony, Civil.

**County Court**, PO Box 369, Liberty, TX 77575. 409-336-4670 (CST) 8AM-5PM. Misdemeanor, Civil, Probate.

## Limestone County

**Real Estate Recording**, Limestone County Clerk, 200 West State Street, Groesbeck, TX 76642. 817-729-5504 (CST) 8AM-5PM.

**District Court**, PO Box 230, Groesbeck, TX 76642. 817-729-3206 (CST) 8AM-12PM 1PM-5PM. Felony, Civil.

**County Court**, PO Box 350, Groesbeck, TX 76642. 817-729-5504 (CST) 8AM-5PM. Misdemeanor, Civil, Probate.

## Lipscomb County

**Real Estate Recording**, Lipscomb County Clerk, Main Street, Courthouse, Lipscomb, TX 79056. 806-862-3091 (CST) 8:30AM-5PM.

**District and County Court**, PO Box 70, Lipscomb, TX 79056. 806-862-3091 (CST) 8:30AM-5PM. Felony, Misdemeanor, Civil, Eviction, Probate.

## Live Oak County

**Real Estate Recording**, Live Oak County Clerk, 301 Houston, George West, TX 78022. 512-449-2733 (CST) X3

**District Court**, PO Drawer O, George West, TX 78022. 512-449-2733 (CST) 8AM-5PM. Felony, Civil.

**County Court**, PO Box 280, George West, TX 78022. 512-449-2733 (CST) 8AM-5PM. Misdemeanor, Civil, Probate.

## Llano County

**Real Estate Recording**, Llano County Clerk, 107 W. Sandstone, Llano, TX 78643-2318. 915-247-4455 (CST) 8AM-5PM.

**District Court**, 801 Ford Rm 209, Llano, TX 78643. 915-247-5036 (CST) 8AM-12PM 1PM-5PM. Felony, Civil.

**County Court**, 107 W Sandstone, Llano, TX 78643. 915-247-4455 (CST) 8AM-5PM. Misdemeanor, Civil, Probate.

## Loving County

**Real Estate Recording**, Loving County Clerk, Courthouse, 100 Bell St., Mentone, TX 79754. 915-377-2441 (CST) 9AM-12, 1-5PM.

**Texas**

**District and County Court**, PO Box 194, Mentone, TX 79754. 915-377-2441 (CST) 8AM-5PM. Felony, Misdemeanor, Civil, Eviction, Probate.

## Lubbock County

**Real Estate Recording**, Lubbock County Clerk, 904 Broadway, 2nd Floor Rm.207, Lubbock, TX 79401. 806-767-1056 (CST) 8:30-5PM.

**District Court**, PO Box 10536, Lubbock, TX 79408-3536. 806-767-1311 (CST) 8:30AM-5PM. Felony, Civil.

**County Court**, PO Box 10536, Lubbock, TX 79408. 806-767-1051 (CST) 8:30AM-5PM. Misdemeanor, Civil, Probate.

## Lynn County

**Real Estate Recording**, Lynn County Clerk, Courthouse, Tahoka, TX 79373. 806-998-4750 (CST) 8:30AM-5PM.

**District Court**, PO Box 939, Tahoka, TX 79373. 806-998-4274 (CST) 8:30AM-5PM. Felony, Civil.

**County Court**, PO Box 937, Tahoka, TX 79373. 806-998-4750 (CST) 8:30AM-5PM. Misdemeanor, Civil, Probate.

## Madison County

**Real Estate Recording**, Madison County Clerk, 101 West Main, Room 102, Madisonville, TX 77864. 409-348-2638 (CST) 8AM-5PM.

**District Court**, County Courthouse Rm 226, Madisonville, TX 77864. 409-348-9203 (CST) 8AM-5PM. Felony, Civil.

**County Court**, 101 W Main Rm 102, Madisonville, TX 77864. 409-348-2638 (CST) 8AM-5PM. Misdemeanor, Civil, Probate.

## Marion County

**Real Estate Recording**, Marion County Clerk, 102 West Austin, Room 206, Jefferson, TX 75657. 903-665-3971 (CST) 8AM-12, 1-5PM.

**District Court**, PO Box 628, Jefferson, TX 75657. 903-665-2441 (CST) 8AM-5PM. Felony, Civil.

**County Court**, PO Drawer F, Jefferson, TX 75657. 903-665-3971 (CST) 8AM-5PM. Misdemeanor, Civil, Probate.

## Martin County

**Real Estate Recording**, Martin County Clerk, 301 North St. Peter Street, Stanton, TX 79782. 915-756-3412 (CST) 8AM-5PM.

**District and County Court**, PO Box 906, Stanton, TX 79782. 915-756-3412 (CST) 8AM-5PM. Felony, Misdemeanor, Civil, Eviction, Probate.

## Mason County

**Real Estate Recording**, Mason County Clerk, Corner of Post Hill & Westmoreland, Mason, TX 76856. 915-347-5253 (CST) 8AM-Noon,1-5PM.

**District and County Court**, PO Box 707, Mason, TX 76856. 915-347-5253 (CST) 8AM-12PM 1PM-5PM. Felony, Misdemeanor, Civil, Eviction, Probate.

## Matagorda County

**Real Estate Recording**, Matagorda County Clerk, 1700 7th Street, Bay City, TX 77404. 409-244-7680 (CST) 8AM-5PM.

**District Court**, PO Drawer 188, Bay City, TX 77414. 409-244-7621 (CST) 8AM-5PM. Felony, Civil.

**County Court**, PO Box 69, Bay City, TX 77404-0069. 409-244-7680 (CST) 8AM-5PM. Misdemeanor, Civil, Probate.

## Maverick County

**Real Estate Recording**, Maverick County Clerk, 500 Quarry Street, Eagle Pass, TX 78852. 210-773-2829 (CST) 8AM-12, 1-5PM.

**District Court**, PO Box 3659, Eagle Pass, TX 78853. 210-773-2629 (CST) 8AM-5PM. Felony, Civil.

**County Court**, PO Box 4050, Liberty, TX 77575. 409-336-8071 (CST) 8AM-12PM 1PM-5PM. Misdemeanor, Civil, Probate.

## McCulloch County

**Real Estate Recording**, McCulloch County Clerk, Courthouse, Brady, TX 76825. 915-597-0733 (CST) 8AM-5PM.

**District Court**, County Courthouse Rm 205, Brady, TX 76825. 915-597-0733 (CST) 8AM-5PM. Felony, Civil.

**County Court**, County Courthouse, Brady, TX 76825. 915-597-0733 (CST) 8AM-5PM. Misdemeanor, Civil, Probate.

## McLennan County

**Real Estate Recording**, McLennan County Clerk, 215 North 5th, Waco, TX 76701. 817-757-5078 (CST) 8AM-5PM.

**District Court**, PO Box 2451, Waco, TX 76703. 817-757-5054 (CST) 8AM-5PM. Felony, Civil.

**County Court**, PO Box 1727, Waco, TX 76703. 817-757-5078 (CST) 8AM-5PM. Misdemeanor, Civil, Probate.

## McMullen County

**Real Estate Recording**, McMullen County Clerk, River Street & Elm, Courthouse, Tilden, TX 78072. 512-274-3215 (CST) 8AM-4PM.

**District and County Court**, PO Box 235, Tilden, TX 78072. 512-274-3215 (CST) 8AM-4PM. Felony, Misdemeanor, Civil, Eviction, Probate.

## Medina County

**Real Estate Recording**, Medina County Clerk, Courthouse, Room 109, Hondo, TX 78861. 210-426-5381 (CST) 8AM-12, 1-5PM.

**38th Judicial District Court**, County Courthouse, Hondo, TX 78861. 210-741-6000 (CST) 8AM-12PM 1PM-5PM. Felony, Civil.

**County Court**, County Courthouse Rm 109, Hondo, TX 78861. 210 741 6000 (CST) 8AM-5PM. Misdemeanor, Civil, Probate.

## Menard County

**Real Estate Recording**, Menard County Clerk, 210 East San Saba, Menard, TX 76859. 915-396-4682 (CST) 8AM-12, 1PM-5PM.

**District and County Court**, PO Box 1028, Menard, TX 76859. 915-396-4682 (CST) 8AM-5PM. Felony, Misdemeanor, Civil, Eviction, Probate.

## Midland County

**Real Estate Recording**, Midland County Clerk, 200 West Wall Street, Midland, TX 79701. 915-688-1075 (CST) 8AM-5PM.

**District Court**, 200 W Wall #301, Midland, TX 79701. 915-688-1107 (CST) 8AM-5PM. Felony, Civil.

**County Court**, PO Box 211, Midland, TX 79702. 915-688-1070 (CST) 8AM-5PM. Misdemeanor, Civil, Probate.

## Milam County

**Real Estate Recording**, Milam County Clerk, 103 South Fannin, Cameron, TX 76520. 817-697-6596 (CST) 8AM-5PM.

**District Court**, PO Box 999, Cameron, TX 76520. 817-697-3952 (CST) 8AM-5PM. Felony, Civil.

**County Court**, PO Box 191, Cameron, TX 76520. 817-697-6596 (CST) 8AM-5PM. Misdemeanor, Civil, Probate.

## Mills County

**Real Estate Recording**, Mills County Clerk, 1011 4th Street, Goldthwaite, TX 76844. 915-648-2711 (CST) 8AM-Noon, 1-5PM.

**District and County Court**, PO Box 646, Goldthwaite, TX 76844. 915-648-2711 (CST) 8AM-12PM 1PM-5PM. Felony, Misdemeanor, Civil, Eviction, Probate.

## Mitchell County

**Real Estate Recording**, Mitchell County Clerk, 349 Oak St., Courthouse, Colorado City, TX 79512. 915-728-3481 (CST) 8AM-12, 1-5PM.

**District Court**, County Courthouse, Colorado City, TX 79512. 915-728-5918 (CST) 8AM-5PM. Felony, Civil.

**County Court**, PO Box 1166, Colorado City, TX 79512. 915-728-3481 (CST) 8AM-5PM. Misdemeanor, Civil, Probate.

## Montague County

**Real Estate Recording**, Montague County Clerk, Rush & Washington, Courthouse, Montague, TX 76251. 817-894-2461 (CST) 8AM-5PM.

**District Court**, PO Box 155, Montague, TX 76251. 817-894-2571 (CST) 8AM-5PM. Felony, Civil.

**County Court**, PO Box 77, Montague, TX 76251. 817-894-2461 (CST) 8AM-5PM. Misdemeanor, Civil, Probate.

## Montgomery County

**Real Estate Recording**, Montgomery County Clerk, 300 North Main, Conroe, TX 77301. 409-539-7885 (CST) 8AM-5PM (Filing Hours until 4:30PM).

**District Court**, PO Box 2985, Conroe, TX 77305. 409-539-7949 (CST) 8AM-5PM. Felony, Civil.

County Court, PO Box 959, Conroe, TX 77305. 409-539-7885 (CST) 8AM-5PM. Misdemeanor, Civil, Probate.

## Moore County

**Real Estate Recording**, Moore County Clerk, 715 Dumas Ave., Rm. 105, Dumas, TX 79029. 806-935-2009 (CST) 8:30AM-5PM.

**District Court**, 715 Dumas Ave #109, Dumas, TX 79029. 806-935-4218 (CST) 8:30AM-5PM. Felony, Civil.

**County Court**, 715 Dumas Ave Rm 105, Dumas, TX 79029. 806-935-6164 (CST) 8:30AM-5PM. Misdemeanor, Civil, Probate.

## Morris County

**Real Estate Recording**, Morris County Clerk, 500 Broadnax Street, Daingerfield, TX 75638. 903-645-3911 (CST) 8AM-5PM.

**District Court**, 500 Brodnax, Daingerfield, TX 75638. 903-645-2321 (CST) 8AM-5PM. Felony, Civil.

**County Court**, 500 Brodnax, Daingerfield, TX 75638. 903-645-3911 (CST) 8AM-5PM. Misdemeanor, Civil, Probate.

## Motley County

**Real Estate Recording**, Motley County Clerk, Main & Dundee, Courthouse, Matador, TX 79244. 806-347-2621 (CST) 9AM-5PM.

**District and County Court**, PO Box 66, Matador, TX 79244. 806-347-2621 (CST) 9AM-5PM. Felony, Misdemeanor, Civil, Eviction, Probate.

## Nacogdoches County

**Real Estate Recording**, Nacogdoches County Clerk, 101 West Main, Nacogdoches, TX 75961. 409-560-7733 (CST) 8AM-5PM.

**District Court**, 101 W Main, Nacogdoches, TX 75961. 409-560-7730 (CST) 8AM-5PM. Felony, Civil.

**County Court**, 101 W Main, Nacogdoches, TX 75961. 409-560-7730 (CST) 8AM-5PM. Misdemeanor, Civil, Probate.

## Navarro County

**Real Estate Recording**, Navarro County Clerk, 300 West Third Avenue, Courthouse - Suite 101, Corsicana, TX 75110. 903-654-3035 (CST) 8AM-5PM.

**District Court**, PO Box 1439, Corsicana, TX 75151. 903-654-3040 (CST) 8AM-5PM. Felony, Civil.

**County Court**, PO Box 423, Corsicana, TX 75151. 903-654-3035 (CST) 8AM-5PM. Misdemeanor, Civil, Probate.

## Newton County

**Real Estate Recording**, Newton County Clerk, Courthouse Square, Newton, TX 75966. 409-379-5341 (CST) 8AM-4:30PM.

**District Court**, PO Box 535, Newton, TX 75966. 409-379-3951 (CST) 8AM-4:30PM. Felony, Civil.

**County Court**, PO Box 484, Newton, TX 75966. 409-379-5341 (CST) 8AM-4:30PM. Misdemeanor, Civil, Probate.

## Nolan County

**Real Estate Recording**, Nolan County Clerk, 100 East 3rd, East Wing - Room 100-A, Sweetwater, TX 79556. 915-235-2462 (CST) 8:30AM-Noon, 1-5PM.

**District Court**, PO Box 1236, Sweetwater, TX 79556. 915-235-2111 (CST) 8:30AM-12PM 1PM-5PM. Felony, Civil.

**County Court**, PO Drawer 98, Sweetwater, TX 79556. 915-235-2462 (CST) 8:30AM-5PM. Misdemeanor, Civil, Probate.

## Nueces County

**Real Estate Recording**, Recording Section, 901 Leopard St., Rm.201, Courthouse, Corpus Christi, TX 78401. 512-888-0611 (CST) 8AM-5PM.

**District Court**, PO Box 2987, Corpus Christi, TX 78403. 512-888-0719 (CST) 8AM-5PM. Felony, Civil.

**County Court**, PO Box 2627, Corpus Christi, TX 78403. 512-888-0757 (CST) 8AM-5PM. Misdemeanor, Civil, Probate.

## Ochiltree County

**Real Estate Recording**, Ochiltree County Clerk, 511 South Main, Perryton, TX 79070. 806-435-8105 (CST) 8:30AM-12, 1-5PM.

**District Court**, 511 S Main, Perryton, TX 79070. 806-435-8160 (CST) 8:30AM-5PM. Felony, Civil.

**County Court**, 511 Main St, Perryton, TX 79070. 806-435-8105 (CST) 8:30AM-5PM. Misdemeanor, Civil, Probate.

## Oldham County

**Real Estate Recording**, Oldham County Clerk, Highway 385 & Main Street, Courthouse, Vega, TX 79092. 806-267-2667 (CST) 8:30AM-5PM.

**District and County Court**, PO Box 360, Vega, TX 79092. 806-267-2667 (CST) 8:30AM-5PM. Felony, Misdemeanor, Civil, Eviction, Probate.

## Orange County

**Real Estate Recording**, Orange County Clerk, 801 Division, Courthouse, Orange, TX 77630. 409-883-7740 (CST) 8AM-5PM.

**District Court**, PO Box 427, Orange, TX 77630. 409-883-7740 (CST) 8AM-5PM. Felony, Civil.

**County Court**, PO Box 1536, Orange, TX 77630. 409-883-7740 (CST) 8AM-5PM. Misdemeanor, Civil, Probate.

## Palo Pinto County

**Real Estate Recording**, Palo Pinto County Clerk, 520 Oak St., Courthouse, Palo Pinto, TX 76484. 817-659-1219 (CST) 8:30AM-4:30PM.

**District Court**, PO Box 188, Palo Pinto, TX 76484. 817-659-3651 (CST) 8AM-4:30PM. Felony, Civil.

**County Court**, PO Box 219, Palo Pinto, TX 76484. 817-659-3651 (CST) 8:30AM-4:30PM. Misdemeanor, Civil, Probate.

## Panola County

**Real Estate Recording**, Panola County Clerk, Sabine & Sycamore, Courthouse Bldg., Room 201, Carthage, TX 75633. 903-693-0302 (CST) 8AM-5PM.

**District Court**, County Courthouse, Carthage, TX 75633. 903-693-0306 (CST) 8AM-5PM. Felony, Civil.

**County Court**, County Courthouse Rm 201, Carthage, TX 75633. 903-693-0302 (CST) 8AM-5PM. Misdemeanor, Civil, Probate.

## Parker County

**Real Estate Recording**, Parker County Clerk, 1112 Sante Fe Drive, Weatherford, TX 76086. 817-599-6591 (CST) 8AM-5PM.

**District Court**, PO Box 340, Weatherford, TX 76086-0340. 817-599-6591 (CST) 8AM-5PM. Felony, Civil.

**County Court**, PO Box 819, Weatherford, TX 76086-0819. 817-599-6591 (CST) 8AM-5PM. Misdemeanor, Civil, Probate.

## Parmer County

**Real Estate Recording**, Parmer County Clerk, 400 Third Street, Farwell, TX 79325. 806-481-3691 (CST) 8:30AM-5PM.

**District Court**, PO Box 888, Farwell, TX 79325. 806-481-3419 (CST) 8:30AM-12PM 1PM-5PM. Felony, Civil.

**County Court**, PO Box 356, Farwell, TX 79325. 806-481-3691 (CST) 8:30AM-5PM. Misdemeanor, Civil, Probate.

## Pecos County

**Real Estate Recording**, Pecos County Clerk, 103 West Callaghan Street, Fort Stockton, TX 79735. 915-336-7555 (CST) 8AM-5PM.

**District Court**, 400 S Nelson, Fort Stockton, TX 79735. 915-336-3503 (CST) 8AM-5PM. Felony, Civil.

**County Court**, 103 W Callaghan, Fort Stockton, TX 79735. 915-336-7555 (CST) 8AM-5PM. Misdemeanor, Civil, Probate.

## Polk County

**Real Estate Recording**, Polk County Clerk, 101 West Church Street, Livingston, TX 77351. 409-327-6804 (CST) 8AM-5PM.

**District Court**, 101 W Church, Livingston, TX 77351. 409-327-6814 (CST) 8AM-5PM. Felony, Civil.

**County Court**, PO Drawer 2119, Livingston, TX 77351. 409-327-6804 (CST) 8AM-5PM. Misdemeanor, Civil, Probate.

## Potter County

**Real Estate Recording**, Potter County Clerk, 500 S. Fillmore, Room 205, Amarillo, TX 79101. 806-379-2275 (CST) 8AM-5PM.

**District Court**, PO Box 9570, Amarillo, TX 79105-9570. 806-379-2300 (CST) 8AM-5PM. Felony, Civil.

**County Court & County Courts at Law NO. 1 & NO. 2**, PO Box 9638, Amarillo, TX 79105. 806-379-2275 (CST) 8AM-5PM. Misdemeanor, Civil, Probate.

## Presidio County

**Real Estate Recording**, Presidio County Clerk, Courthouse, 320 N. Highland, Marfa, TX 79843. 915-729-4812 (CST) 8AM-12, 1-5PM.

**District and County Court**, PO Box 789, Marfa, TX 79843. 915-729-4812 (CST) 8AM-5PM. Felony, Misdemeanor, Civil, Eviction, Probate.

## Rains County

**Real Estate Recording**, Rains County Clerk, 100 Quitman Street, Emory, TX 75440. 903-473-2461 (CST) 8AM-5PM.

**District and County Court**, PO Box 187, Emory, TX 75440. 903-473-2461 (CST) 8AM-5PM. Felony, Misdemeanor, Civil, Eviction, Probate.

## Randall County

**Real Estate Recording**, Randall County Clerk, 401 15th Street, Canyon, TX 79015. 806-655-6330 (CST) 8AM-5PM (On Weekends by Appointment).

**District Court**, PO Box 1096, Canyon, TX 79015. 806-655-6200 (CST) 8AM-5PM. Felony, Civil.

**County Court**, PO Box 660, Canyon, TX 79015. 806-655-6330 (CST) 8AM-5PM. Misdemeanor, Civil, Probate.

## Reagan County

**Real Estate Recording**, Reagan County Clerk, 3rd at Plaza, Courthouse, Big Lake, TX 76932. 915-884-2442 (CST) 8:30AM-5PM.

**District and County Court**, PO Box 100, Big Lake, TX 76932. 915-884-2442 (CST) 8:30AM-5PM. Felony, Misdemeanor, Civil, Eviction, Probate.

## Real County

**Real Estate Recording**, Real County Clerk, Courthouse Square, Leakey, TX 78873. 210-232-5202 (CST) 8AM-5PM.

**District and County Court**, PO Box 656, Leakey, TX 78873. 210-232-5202 (CST) 8AM-5PM. Felony, Misdemeanor, Civil, Eviction, Probate.

## Red River County

**Real Estate Recording**, Red River County Clerk, 200 North Walnut, Courthouse Annex, Clarksville, TX 75426-3075. 903-427-2401 (CST) 8:30AM-5PM.

**District Court**, 400 N Walnut, Clarksville, TX 75426. 903-427-3761 (CST) 8AM-5PM. Felony, Civil.

**County Court**, 200 N Walnut, Clarksville, TX 75426. 903-427-2401 (CST) 8:30AM-5PM. Misdemeanor, Civil, Probate.

## Reeves County

**Real Estate Recording**, Reeves County Clerk, 100 East 4th Street, Room 101, Pecos, TX 79772. 915-445-5467 (CST) 8AM-5PM.

**District Court**, PO Box 848, Pecos, TX 79772. 915-445-2714 (CST) 8AM-5PM. Felony, Civil.

**County Court**, PO Box 867, Pecos, TX 79772. 915-445-5467 (CST) 8AM-5PM. Misdemeanor, Civil, Probate.

## Refugio County

**Real Estate Recording**, Refugio County Clerk, 808 Commerce, Rm.112, Courthouse, Refugio, TX 78377. 512-526-2233 (CST) 8AM-5PM.

**District Court**, PO Box 736, Refugio, TX 78377. 512-526-2721 (CST) 8AM-5PM. Felony, Civil.

**County Court**, PO Box 704, Refugio, TX 78377. 512-526-2233 (CST) 8AM-5PM. Misdemeanor, Civil, Probate.

## Roberts County

**Real Estate Recording**, Roberts County Clerk, Highway 60 & Kiowa Street, Courthouse, Miami, TX 79059. 806-868-2341 (CST) 8AM-4PM.

**District and County Court**, PO Box 477, Miami, TX 79059. 806-868-2341 (CST) 8AM-4PM. Felony, Misdemeanor, Civil, Eviction, Probate.

## Robertson County

**Real Estate Recording**, Robertson County Clerk, Courthouse Square on Center Street, Room 104, Franklin, TX 77856. 409-828-4130 (CST) 8AM-5PM.

**District Court**, PO Box 250, Franklin, TX 77856. 409-828-3636 (CST) 8AM-5PM. Felony, Civil.

**County Court**, PO Box 1029, Franklin, TX 77856. 409-828-4130 (CST) 8AM-5PM. Misdemeanor, Civil, Probate.

## Rockwall County

**Real Estate Recording**, Rockwall County Clerk, 1101 Ridge Rd., Courthouse Annex, Rockwall, TX 75087. 214-771-5141 (CST) 8AM-5PM.

**District Court**, County Courthouse, Rockwall, TX 75087. 214-722-3382 (CST) 8AM-4PM. Felony, Civil.

**County Court**, 101 E Rusk, Rockwall, TX 75087. 214-771-5141 (CST) 8AM-5PM. Misdemeanor, Civil, Probate.

## Runnels County

**Real Estate Recording**, County Clerk, Runnels County, Broadway & Hutchings, Courthouse, Ballinger, TX 76821. 915-365-2720 (CST) 8:30AM-12, 1-5PM.

**District Court**, PO Box 166, Ballinger, TX 76821. 915-365-2638 (CST) 8:30AM-5PM. Felony, Civil.

**County Court**, PO Box 189, Ballinger, TX 76821. 915-365-2720 (CST) 8:30AM-12PM 1PM-5PM. Misdemeanor, Civil, Probate.

## Rusk County

**Real Estate Recording**, Rusk County Clerk, 115 North Main, Courthouse, Henderson, TX 75652. 903-657-0330 (CST) 8AM-5PM.

**District Court**, County Courthouse, 115 N Main, Henderson, TX 75652. 903-657-0353 (CST) 8AM-5PM. Felony, Civil.

**County Court**, PO Box 1687, Henderson, TX 75653. 903-657-0353 (CST) 8AM-5PM. Misdemeanor, Civil, Probate.

## Sabine County

**Real Estate Recording**, Sabine County Clerk, Corner of Oak & Main, Courthouse, Hemphill, TX 75948. 409-787-3786 (CST) 8AM-4PM.

**District Court**, PO Box 850, Hemphill, TX 75948. 409-787-2912 (CST) 8AM-4PM. Felony, Civil.

**County Court**, PO Drawer 580, Hemphill, TX 75948-0580. 409-787-3786 (CST) 8AM-4PM. Misdemeanor, Civil, Probate.

## San Augustine County

**Real Estate Recording**, San Augustine County Clerk, Courthouse, Room 106, San Augustine, TX 75972-1335. 409-275-2452 (CST) 8AM-11:45AM, 1-4:45PM.

**District Court**, County Courthouse Rm 202, San Augustine, TX 75972. 409-275-2231 (CST) 8AM-4:30PM. Felony, Civil.

**County Court**, County Courthouse Rm 106, San Augustine, TX 75972. 409-275-2452 (CST) 8AM-4:30PM. Misdemeanor, Civil, Probate.

## San Jacinto County

**Real Estate Recording**, San Jacinto County Clerk, Corner of Church & Byrd, Courthouse, Coldspring, TX 77331. 409-653-2324 (CST) 8AM-4:30PM.

**District Court**, PO Box 369, Coldspring, TX 77331. 409-653-2909 (CST) 8AM-5PM. Felony, Civil.

**County Court**, PO Box 669, Coldspring, TX 77331. 409-653-2324 (CST) 8AM-4:30PM. Misdemeanor, Civil, Probate.

## San Patricio County

**Real Estate Recording**, San Patricio County Clerk, 400 West Sinton Street, Sinton, TX 78387. 512-364-6290 (CST) 8AM-5PM.

**District Court**, PO Box 1084, Sinton, TX 78387. 512-364-6225 (CST) 8AM-5PM. Felony, Civil.

**County Court**, PO Box 578, Sinton, TX 78387. 512-364-6290 (CST) 8AM-5PM. Misdemeanor, Civil, Probate.

## San Saba County

**Real Estate Recording**, San Saba County Clerk, 500 East Wallace, San Saba, TX 76877. 915-372-3614 (CST) 8AM-12, 1-5PM.

**District and County Court**, County Courthouse, San Saba, TX 76877. 915-372-3375 (CST) 8AM-5PM. Felony, Misdemeanor, Civil, Eviction, Probate.

## Schleicher County

**Real Estate Recording**, Schleicher County Clerk, Highway 277, Courthouse, Eldorado, TX 76936. 915-853-2833 (CST) 9AM-5PM.

**District and County Court**, PO Drawer 580, Eldorado, TX 76936. 915-853-2833 (CST) 9AM-5PM. Felony, Misdemeanor, Civil, Eviction, Probate.

## Scurry County

**Real Estate Recording**, Scurry County Clerk, 1806 25th Street, Suite 300, Snyder, TX 79549-2530. 915-573-5332 (CST) 8:30AM-5PM.

**District Court**, 1806 25th St #402, Snyder, TX 79549. 915-573-5641 (CST) 8:30AM-5PM. Felony, Civil.

**County Court**, County Courthouse, Snyder, TX 79549. 915-573-5332 (CST) 8:30AM-5PM. Misdemeanor, Civil, Probate.

## Shackelford County

**Real Estate Recording**, Shackelford County Clerk, 200 Main, Albany, TX 76430. 915-762-2232 (CST) 8:30AM-Noon, 1-5PM.

**259th Judicial District and County Court**, PO Box 247, Albany, TX 76430. 915-762-2232 (CST) 8:30AM-12PM 1PM-5PM. Felony, Misdemeanor, Civil, Eviction, Probate.

## Shelby County

**Real Estate Recording**, Shelby County Clerk, 200 San Augustine St., Suite A, Center, TX 75935. 409-598-6361 (CST) 8AM-4:30PM.

**District Court**, PO Box 1546, Center, TX 75935. 409-598-4164 (CST) 8AM-4:30PM. Felony, Civil.

**County Court**, PO Box 592, Center, TX 75935. 409-598-6361 (CST) 8AM-5PM. Misdemeanor, Civil, Probate.

## Sherman County

**Real Estate Recording**, Sherman County Clerk, 701 North 3rd Street, Stratford, TX 79084. 806-396-2371 (CST) 8AM-Noon,1-5PM.

**District and County Court**, PO Box 270, Stratford, TX 79084. 806-396-2371 (CST) 8AM-5PM. Felony, Misdemeanor, Civil, Eviction, Probate.

## Smith County

**Real Estate Recording**, Smith County Clerk, Courthouse, 100 Broadway, Rm.104, Tyler, TX 75702. 903-535-0650 (CST) 8AM-5PM.

**District Court**, PO Box 1077, Tyler, TX 75706. 903-535-0666 (CST) 8AM-5PM. Felony, Civil.

**County Court**, PO Box 1018, Tyler, TX 75710. 903-535-0634 (CST) 8AM-5PM. Misdemeanor, Civil, Probate.

## Somervell County

**Real Estate Recording**, Somervell County Clerk, 107 N.E. Vernon St., Glen Rose, TX 76043. 817-897-4427 (CST) 9AM-5PM.

**District and County Court**, PO Box 1098, Glen Rose, TX 76043. 817-897-4427 (CST) 8AM-5PM. Felony, Misdemeanor, Civil, Eviction, Probate.

## Starr County

**Real Estate Recording**, Starr County Clerk, Courthouse, Rio Grande City, TX 78582. 210-487-2954 (CST) 8AM-5PM.

**District and County Court**, Starr County Courthouse, Room 304, Rio Grande City, TX 78582. 210-487-2610 (CST) 8AM-5PM. Felony, Misdemeanor, Civil, Eviction, Probate.

**District and County Court**, Starr County Courthouse, Room 304, Rio Grande City, TX 78582. 210-487-2610 (CST) 8AM-5PM. Felony, Misdemeanor, Civil, Eviction, Probate.

## Stephens County

**Real Estate Recording**, Stephens County Clerk, Courthouse, Breckenridge, TX 76424. 817-559-3700 (CST) 8AM-5PM.

**District and County Court**, 200 W Walker, Breckenridge, TX 76424. 817-559-3151 (CST) 8AM-5PM. Felony, Civil.

## Sterling County

**Real Estate Recording**, Sterling County Clerk, 609 4th Street, Courthouse, Sterling City, TX 76951. 915-378-5191 (CST) 8:30AM-12, 1-5PM.

**District and County Court**, PO Box 55, Sterling City, TX 76951. 915-378-5191 (CST) 8:30AM-12PM 1PM-5PM. Felony, Misdemeanor, Civil, Eviction, Probate.

## Stonewall County

**Real Estate Recording**, Stonewall County Clerk, 510 South Broadway, Aspermont, TX 79502. 817-989-2272 (CST) 8AM-4:30PM.

**District and County Court**, PO Drawer P, Aspermont, TX 79502. 817-989-2272 (CST) 8AM-4:30PM. Felony, Misdemeanor, Civil, Eviction, Probate.

## Sutton County

**Real Estate Recording**, Sutton County Clerk, Sutton County Annex, 300 E. Oak, Suite 3, Sonora, TX 76950. 915-387-3815 (CST) 8:30AM-4:30PM.

**District and County Court**, 300 E Oak, Ste 3, Sonora, TX 76950. 915-387-3815 (CST) 8:30AM-4:30PM. Felony, Misdemeanor, Civil, Eviction, Probate.

## Swisher County

**Real Estate Recording**, Swisher County Clerk, Courthouse, Tulia, TX 79088. 806-995-3294 (CST) 8AM-12, 1-5PM.

**District and County Court**, County Courthouse, Tulia, TX 79088. 806-995-4396 (CST) 8AM-5PM. Felony, Misdemeanor, Civil, Eviction, Probate.

## Tarrant County

**Real Estate Recording**, Tarrant County Clerk, 100 West Weatherford, Courthouse, Fort Worth, TX 76196-0401. 817-884-1550 (CST) 8AM-4:30PM.

**District Court**, 401 W Belknap, Fort Worth, TX 76196-0402. 817-884-1240 (CST) 8AM-5PM. Felony, Civil.

**County Court**, 100 W Weatherford, Fort Worth, TX 76196. 817-884-1076 (CST) 7:30AM-4:30PM. Misdemeanor, Civil.

**Criminal District Courts 1-4**, 401 W Belknap, Fort Worth, TX 76196-0402. 817-884-1574 (CST) 8:00AM-4:30PM M-F. Felony.

**Probate Court**, County Courthouse, Fort Worth, TX 76196-0241. 817-884-1200 (CST) Probate.

## Taylor County

**Real Estate Recording**, Taylor County Clerk, 300 Oak, Courthouse, Abilene, TX 79602. 915-674-1202 (CST) 8:30AM-5PM.

**District Court**, 300 Oak St, Abilene, TX 79602. 915-674-1316 (CST) 8AM-5PM. Felony, Civil.

**County Court**, PO Box 5497, Abilene, TX 79608. 915-674-1202 (CST) 8AM-5PM. Misdemeanor, Civil, Probate.

## Terrell County

**Real Estate Recording**, Terrell County Clerk, Courthouse Square, 108 Hackberry, Sanderson, TX 79848. 915-345-2391 (CST) 9AM-5PM.

**District and County Court**, PO Drawer 410, Sanderson, TX 79848. 915-345-2391 (CST) 9AM-5PM. Felony, Misdemeanor, Civil, Eviction, Probate.

## Terry County

**Real Estate Recording**, Terry County Clerk, 500 West Main, Room 105, Brownfield, TX 79316-4398. 806-637-8551 (CST) 8:30AM-5PM.

**District Court**, 500 W Main Rm 209E, Brownfield, TX 79316. 806-637-4202 (CST) 8:30AM-5PM. Felony, Civil.

**County Court**, 500 W Main Rm 105, Brownfield, TX 79316-4398. 806-637-8551 (CST) 8:30AM-5PM. Misdemeanor, Civil, Probate.

## Throckmorton County

**Real Estate Recording**, Throckmorton County Clerk, 105 Minter Street, Courthouse, Throckmorton, TX 76483. 817-849-2501 (CST) 8AM-5PM.

**District and County Court**, PO Box 309, Throckmorton, TX 76483. 817-849-2501 (CST) 8AM-5PM. Felony, Misdemeanor, Civil, Eviction, Probate.

## Titus County

**Real Estate Recording**, Titus County Clerk, Courthouse, 2nd Floor, Suite 204, Mount Pleasant, TX 75455. 903-577-6796 (CST) 8AM-5PM.

**District Court**, 105 W 1st St, Mount Pleasant, TX 75455. 903-577-6721 (CST) 8AM-5PM. Felony, Civil.

**County Court**, 100 W 1st St #204, Mount Pleasant, TX 75455. 903-577-6796 (CST) 8AM-5PM. Misdemeanor, Civil, Probate.

## Tom Green County

**Real Estate Recording**, Tom Green County Clerk, 124 West Beauregard, San Angelo, TX 76903-5850. 915-659-3262 (CST) 8AM-12, 1-4:30PM.

**District Court**, County Courthouse, San Angelo, TX 76903. 915-659-6579 (CST) 8AM-5PM. Felony, Civil.

**County Court**, 124 W Beaureguard, San Angelo, TX 76903. 915-659-6555 (CST) 8AM-5PM. Misdemeanor, Civil, Probate.

## Travis County

**Real Estate Recording**, Travis County Clerk, 1000 Guadalupe, Austin, TX 78701. 512-473-9188 (CST) 8AM-5PM.

**District Court**, PO Box 1748, Austin, TX 78767. 512-473-9420 (CST) 8AM-5PM. Felony, Civil.

**County Court**, PO Box 1748, Austin, TX 78767-1748. 512-473-9440 (CST) 8AM-5PM. Misdemeanor, Civil.

Probate Court, PO Box 1748, Austin, TX 78767. 512-473-9258 (CST) Probate.

### Trinity County

Real Estate Recording, Trinity County Clerk, First Street, Courthouse, Groveton, TX 75845. 409-642-1208 (CST) 8AM-5PM.

District Court, PO Box 548, Groveton, TX 75845. 409-642-1118 (CST) 8AM-5PM. Felony, Civil.

County Court, PO Box 456, Groveton, TX 75845. 409-642-1208 (CST) 8AM-5PM. Misdemeanor, Civil, Probate.

### Tyler County

Real Estate Recording, Tyler County Clerk, 110 Courthouse, Woodville, TX 75979. 409-283-2281 (CST) 8AM-4:30PM.

District Court, 203 Courthouse, Woodville, TX 75979. 409-283-2162 (CST) 8AM-4:30PM. Felony, Civil.

County Court, County Courthouse Rm 110, Woodville, TX 75979. 409-283-2281 (CST) 8AM-4:30PM. Misdemeanor, Civil, Probate.

### Upshur County

Real Estate Recording, Upshur County Clerk, Highway 154, Courthouse, Gilmer, TX 75644. 903-843-3083 (CST) 8AM-5PM.

District and County Court, PO Box 730, Gilmer, TX 75644. 903-843-4015 (CST) 8AM-5PM. Felony, Misdemeanor, Civil, Probate.

### Upton County

Real Estate Recording, Upton County Clerk, 205 East 10th Street, Rankin, TX 79778. 915-693-2861 (CST) 8AM-5PM.

District and County Court, PO Box 465, Rankin, TX 79778. 915-693-2861 (CST) 8AM-5PM. Felony, Misdemeanor, Civil, Eviction, Probate.

### Uvalde County

Real Estate Recording, Uvalde County Clerk, Main & Getty, Courthouse, Uvalde, TX 78801. 210-278-6614 (CST) 8AM-5PM.

District Court, County Courthouse #15, Uvalde, TX 78801. 210-278-3918 (CST) 8AM-5PM. Felony, Civil.

County Court, PO Box 284, Uvalde, TX 78802. 512-278-6614 (CST) 8AM-5PM. Misdemeanor, Civil, Probate.

### Val Verde County

Real Estate Recording, Val Verde County Clerk, 400 Pecan Street, Del Rio, TX 78840. 210-774-7564 (CST) 8AM-4:30PM.

District Court, PO Box 1544, Del Rio, TX 78841. 210-774-7538 (CST) 8AM-4:30PM. Felony, Civil.

County Court, PO Box 1267, Del Rio, TX 78841-1267. 512-774-7564 (CST) 8AM-4:30PM. Misdemeanor, Civil, Probate.

### Van Zandt County

Real Estate Recording, Van Zandt County Clerk, 121 East Dallas St, Courthouse - Room 202, Canton, TX 75103. 903-567-6503 (CST) 8AM-5PM.

294th Judicial District Court, 121 E Dallas St Rm 302, Canton, TX 75103. 903-567-6576 (CST) 8AM-5PM. Felony, Civil.

County Court, 121 E Dallas St #202, Canton, TX 75103. 903-567-6503 (CST) 8AM-5PM. Misdemeanor, Civil, Probate.

### Victoria County

Real Estate Recording, Victoria County Clerk, 115 North Bridge Street #103, Victoria, TX 77901. 512-575-1478 (CST) 8AM-5PM.

District Court, PO Box 2238, Victoria, TX 77902. 512-575-0581 (CST) 8AM-5PM. Felony, Civil.

County Court, PO Box 2410, Victoria, TX 77902. 512-575-1478 (CST) 8AM-5PM. Misdemeanor, Civil, Probate.

### Walker County

Real Estate Recording, Walker County Clerk, 1100 University Avenue, Huntsville, TX 77340. 409-291-9500 (CST) 8AM-5PM.

District Court, 1100 University Ave Rm 301, Huntsville, TX 77340. 409-291-9500 (CST) 8AM-4:30PM. Felony, Civil.

County Court, PO Box 210, Huntsville, TX 77342-0210. 409-291-9500 (CST) 8AM-4:30PM. Misdemeanor, Civil, Probate.

### Waller County

Real Estate Recording, Waller County Clerk, 836 Austin Street, Room 217, Hempstead, TX 77445. 409-826-3357 (CST) 8AM-5PM.

District Court, 836 Austin St Rm 318, Hempstead, TX 77445. 409-826-3357 (CST) 8AM-12PM 1PM-5PM. Felony, Civil.

County Court, 836 Austin St, Hempstead, TX 77445. 409-826-3357 (CST) 8AM-5PM. Misdemeanor, Civil, Probate.

### Ward County

Real Estate Recording, Ward County Clerk, Courthouse, 400 S. Allen St., Monahans, TX 79756-4602. 915-943-3294 (CST) 8AM-5PM.

District Court, PO Box 440, Monahans, TX 79756. 915-943-2751 (CST) 8AM-5PM. Felony, Civil.

County Court, County Courthouse, Monahans, TX 79756. 915-943-3294 (CST) 8AM-5PM. Misdemeanor, Civil, Probate.

### Washington County

Real Estate Recording, Washington County Clerk, 100 East Main, Suite 102, Brenham, TX 77833. 409-277-6200 (CST) 8AM-5PM.

District Court, 100 E Main #304, Brenham, TX 77833-3753. 409-277-6200 (CST) 8AM-5PM. Felony, Civil.

County Court, 100 E Main #102, Brenham, TX 77833. 409-277-6200 (CST) 8AM-5PM. Misdemeanor, Civil, Probate.

### Webb County

Real Estate Recording, Webb County Clerk, 1110 Victoria Street, Suite 201, Laredo, TX 78040. 210-721-2645 (CST)

District Court, PO Box 667, Laredo, TX 78042-0667. 210-721-2455 (CST) 8AM-5PM. Felony, Civil.

County Court, 1110 Victoria #210, Laredo, TX 78042. 210-721-2640 (CST) 8AM-5PM. Misdemeanor, Civil, Probate.

### Wharton County

Real Estate Recording, Wharton County Clerk, 100 East Milam, Wharton, TX 77488. 409-532-2381 (CST) 8AM-5PM.

District Court, PO Drawer 391, Wharton, TX 77488. 409-532-5542 (CST) 8AM-5PM. Felony, Civil.

County Court, PO Box 69, Wharton, TX 77488. 409-532-2381 (CST) 8AM-5PM. Misdemeanor, Civil, Probate.

### Wheeler County

Real Estate Recording, Wheeler County Clerk, 400 Main Street, Courthouse, Wheeler, TX 79096. 806-826-5544 (CST) 8AM-5PM.

District Court, PO Box 528, Wheeler, TX 79096. 806-826-5931 (CST) 8AM-5PM. Felony, Civil.

County Court, PO Box 465, Wheeler, TX 79096. 806-826-5544 (CST) 8AM-5PM. Misdemeanor, Civil, Probate.

### Wichita County

Real Estate Recording, Wichita County Clerk, 900 7th Street, Room 250, Wichita Falls, TX 76301. 817-766-8160 (CST) 8AM-5PM.

District Court, PO Box 718, Wichita Falls, TX 76307. 817-766-8100 (CST) 8AM-5PM. Felony, Civil.

County Court, PO Box 1679, Wichita Falls, TX 76307. 817-766-8100 (CST) 8AM-5PM. Misdemeanor, Civil, Probate.

### Wilbarger County

Real Estate Recording, Wilbarger County Clerk, 1700 Main Street #15, Vernon, TX 76384. 817-552-5486 (CST) 8AM-5PM.

District Court, 1700 Wilbarger Rm 33, Vernon, TX 76384. 817-553-3411 (CST) 8AM-5PM. Felony, Civil.

County Court, 1700 Wilbarger Rm 15, Vernon, TX 76384. 817-552-5486 (CST) 8AM-5PM. Misdemeanor, Civil, Probate.

### Willacy County

Real Estate Recording, Willacy County Clerk, 540 West Hidalgo Avenue, Courthouse Building, Raymondville, TX 78580. 210-689-2710 (CST) 8AM-12, 1-5PM.

District Court, County Courthouse, Raymondville, TX 78580. 210-689-2532 (CST) 8AM-5PM. Felony, Civil.

County Court, 540 W Hidalgo, Raymondville, TX 78580. 210-689-2710 (CST) 8AM-5PM. Misdemeanor, Civil, Probate.

### Williamson County

Real Estate Recording, Williamson County Clerk, 8th & Austin Avenue, Courthouse, Georgetown, TX 78626. 512-930-4315 (CST) 8AM-5PM.

District Court, PO Box 24, Georgetown, TX 78627. 512-930-4426 (CST) 8AM-5PM. Felony, Civil.

County Court, PO Box 18, Georgetown, TX 78627. 512-930-4315 (CST) 8AM-5PM. Misdemeanor, Civil, Probate.

## Wilson County

Real Estate Recording, Wilson County Clerk, 1420 3rd Street, Floresville, TX 78114. 210-393-7308 (CST) 8AM-5PM.

District Court, PO Box 812, Floresville, TX 78114. 210-393-7322 (CST) 8AM-5PM. Felony, Civil.

County Court, PO Box 27, Floresville, TX 78114. 512-393-7308 (CST) 8AM-5PM. Misdemeanor, Civil, Probate.

## Winkler County

Real Estate Recording, Winkler County Clerk, 100 East Winkler Street, Courthouse, Kermit, TX 79745. 915-586-3401 (CST) 8AM-5PM.

District Court, PO Box 1065, Kermit, TX 79745. 915-586-3359 (CST) 8:30AM-5PM. Felony, Civil.

County Court, PO Box 1007, Kermit, TX 79745. 915-586-3401 (CST) 8AM-5PM. Misdemeanor, Civil, Probate.

## Wise County

Real Estate Recording, Wise County Clerk, 200 North Trinity, Records Bldg., Decatur, TX 76234. 817-627-3351 (CST) 8AM-5PM.

District Court, PO Box 308, Decatur, TX 76234. 817-627-5535 (CST) 8AM-5PM. Felony, Civil.

County Court, PO Box 359, Decatur, TX 76234. 817-627-3351 (CST) 8AM-5PM. Misdemeanor, Civil, Probate.

## Wood County

Real Estate Recording, Wood County Clerk, 1 Main Street, Courthouse, Quitman, TX 75783. 903-763-2711 (CST) 8AM-5PM.

District Court, PO Box 488, Quitman, TX 75783. 903-763-2361 (CST) 8AM-12PM 1PM-5PM. Felony, Civil.

County Court, PO Box 338, Quitman, TX 75783. 903-763-2711 (CST) 8AM-5PM. Misdemeanor, Civil, Probate.

## Yoakum County

Real Estate Recording, Yoakum County Clerk, Courthouse, 10th & Avenue G, Plains, TX 79335. 806-456-2721 (CST) 8AM-5PM.

District Court, PO Box 899, Plains, TX 79355. 806-456-7453 (CST) 8AM-5PM. Felony, Civil.

County Court, PO Box 309, Plains, TX 79355. 806-456-2721 (CST) 8AM-5PM. Misdemeanor, Civil, Probate.

## Young County

Real Estate Recording, Young County Clerk, Young County Courthouse, 516 Fourth St., Room 104, Graham, TX 76450. 817-549-8432 (CST) 8:30AM-5PM.

District Court, 516 4th St Rm 201, Courthouse, Graham, TX 76450. 817-549-0029 (CST) 8:30AM-5PM. Felony, Civil.

County Court, 516 4th St Rm 104, Graham, TX 76450. 817-549-8432 (CST) 8:30AM-12PM 1PM-5PM. Misdemeanor, Civil, Probate.

## Zapata County

Real Estate Recording, Zapata County Clerk, 7th Avenue & Hidalgo Street, Zapata, TX 78076. 210-765-9915 (CST) 8AM-5PM.

District Court, PO Box 788, Zapata, TX 78076. 210-765-9930 (CST) 8AM-5PM. Felony, Civil.

County Court, PO Box 789, Zapata, TX 78076. 210-765-9915 (CST) 8AM-12PM 1PM-5PM. Misdemeanor, Civil, Probate.

## Zavala County

Real Estate Recording, Zavala County Clerk, Zavala Courthouse, Crystal City, TX 78839. 210-374-2331 (CST) 8AM-5PM.

District Court, PO Box 704, Crystal City, TX 78839. 210-374-3456 (CST) 8AM-12PM 1PM-5PM. Felony, Civil.

County Court, County Courthouse, Crystal City, TX 78839. 210-374-2331 (CST) 8AM-5PM. Misdemeanor, Civil, Probate.

# Utah

## Beaver County

**Real Estate Recording**, Beaver County Recorder, 105 East Center, Beaver, UT 84713. 801-438-5881 (MST) 9AM-5PM.

**5th District Court**, PO Box 392, Beaver, UT 84713. 801-438-2352 (MST) 9AM-5PM, closed 12-1. Felony, Misdemeanor, Civil, Eviction, Small Claims, Probate.

## Box Elder County

**Real Estate Recording**, Box Elder County Recorder, 1 South Main, Courthouse, Brigham City, UT 84302-2599. 801-734-2031 (MST) 8AM-5PM.

**1st District Court**, 43 N Main, Brigham City, UT 84302. 801-734-2433 (MST) Felony, Civil Actions Over $20,000, Probate.

**1st Circuit Court**, 43 N Main, Brigham City, UT 84302. 801-723-2862 (MST) 8AM-5PM. Misdemeanor, Civil Actions Under $20,000, Eviction, Small Claims.

## Cache County

**Real Estate Recording**, Cache County Recorder, 179 North Main Street, Logan, UT 84321. 801-752-5561 (MST) 8AM-5PM.

**1st District and Circuit Court**, 140 N. 100 W., Logan, UT 84321. 801-752-6893 (MST) 8AM-5PM. Felony, Misdemeanor, Civil, Eviction, Small Claims, Probate.

## Carbon County

**Real Estate Recording**, Carbon County Recorder, Courthouse Building, 120 East Main, Price, UT 84501. 801-637-4700 (MST) 9AM-5PM.

**7th District Court**, 149 E. 100 South, Price, UT 84501. 801-637-0180 (MST) Felony, Misdemeanor, Civil, Eviction, Small Claims, Probate.

## Daggett County

**Real Estate Recording**, Daggett County Recorder, 91 North 1st West, Manila, UT 84046. 801-784-3154 (MST) 9AM-Noon, 1-5PM.

**8th District Court**, PO Box 219, Manila, UT 84046. 801-784-3154 (MST) 9AM-5PM. Felony, Misdemeanor, Civil, Eviction, Small Claims, Probate.

## Davis County

**Real Estate Recording**, Davis County Recorder, 28 East State, Farmington, UT 84025. 801-451-3224 (MST) 8:30AM-5PM.

**2nd District Court**, PO Box 769, Farmington, UT 84025. 801-451-4400 (MST) 8AM-5PM. Felony, Civil Actions Over $20,000, Probate.

**2nd Circuit Court-Bountiful**, 745 South Main, Bountiful, UT 84010. 801-298-6152 (MST) 8AM-5PM. Misdemeanor, Civil Actions Under $20,000, Eviction, Small Claims.

**2nd Circuit Court-Layton**, 425 Wasatch Dr, Layton, UT 84041. 801-546-2484 (MST) 8AM-5PM. Misdemeanor, Civil Actions Under $20,000, Eviction, Small Claims.

## Duchesne County

**Real Estate Recording**, Duchesne County Recorder, 100 South 50 East, Duchesne, UT 84021. 801-738-2435 (MST) 8:30AM-5PM.

**8th District Court**, PO Box 990, Duchesne, UT 84021. 801-738-2753 (MST) 8AM-5PM. Felony, Misdemeanor, Civil, Eviction, Small Claims, Probate.

## Emery County

**Real Estate Recording**, Emery County Recorder, 95 East Main, Castle Dale, UT 84513. 801-381-2414 (MST) 8AM-5PM.

**7th District Court**, PO Box 907, Castle Dale, UT 84513. 801-381-2465 (MST) 8:30AM-5PM. Felony, Misdemeanor, Civil, Eviction, Small Claims, Probate.

## Garfield County

**Real Estate Recording**, Garfield County Recorder, 55 South Main, Panguitch, UT 84759. 801-676-8826 (MST) X112 9AM-Noon, 1-5PM.

**6th District Court**, PO Box 77, Panguitch, UT 84759. 801-676-8826 (MST) Felony, Misdemeanor, Civil, Eviction, Small Claims, Probate.

## Grand County

**Real Estate Recording**, Grand County Recorder, 125 East Center St., Moab, UT 84532. 801-259-1331 (MST) 8AM-5PM.

**7th District Court**, 125 E. Center, Moab, UT 84532. 801-259-1349 (MST) 8AM-5PM. Felony, Misdemeanor, Civil, Eviction, Small Claims, Probate.

## Iron County

**Real Estate Recording**, Iron County Recorder, 68 South 100 East, Parowan, UT 84761. 801-477-3375 (MST) X15 8:30AM-5PM.

**5th District Court**, 40 North 100 East, Cedar City, UT 84720. 801-586-7440 (MST) 8AM-5PM. Felony, Misdemeanor, Civil, Eviction, Small Claims, Probate.

## Juab County

**Real Estate Recording**, Juab County Recorder, 160 North Main, Nephi, UT 84648. 801-623-1480 (MST) 8:30AM-5PM.

**4th District and Circuit Court**, 160 N. Main, Nephi, UT 84648. 801-623-0271 (MST) 8:30AM-5PM. Felony, Misdemeanor, Civil, Eviction, Small Claims, Probate.

## Kane County

**Real Estate Recording**, Kane County Recorder, 76 North Main #14, Kanab, UT 84741. 801-644-2360 (MST) 8AM-Noon, 1-5PM.

**6th Circuit and District Court**, PO Box 50, Kanab, UT 84741. 801-644-2458 (MST) 8AM-5PM. Felony, Misdemeanor, Civil, Eviction, Small Claims, Probate.

## Millard County

**Real Estate Recording**, Millard County Recorder, 60 South Main, Fillmore, UT 84631. 801-743-6210 (MST) 8AM-5PM.

**4th District and Circuit Court**, PO Box 226, Fillmore, UT 84631. 801-743-6223 (MST) 8AM-5PM. Felony, Misdemeanor, Civil, Eviction, Small Claims, Probate.

## Morgan County

**Real Estate Recording**, Morgan County Recorder, 48 West Young Street, Morgan, UT 84050. 801-829-3277 (MST) 9AM-5PM.

**2nd District and Circuit Court**, PO Box 886, Morgan, UT 84050. 801-829-6811 (MST) 8AM-5PM. Felony, Misdemeanor, Civil, Eviction, Small Claims, Probate.

## Piute County

**Real Estate Recording**, Piute County Recorder, Courthouse, Junction, UT 84740. 801-577-2505 (MST) 9AM-5PM.

**6th District Court**, PO Box 99, Junction, UT 84740. 801-577-2840 (MST) 8:30AM-5PM. Felony, Misdemeanor, Civil, Eviction, Small Claims, Probate.

## Rich County

**Real Estate Recording**, Rich County Recorder, 20 South Main, Randolph, UT 84064. 801-793-2005 (MST) 9AM-Noon, 1-5PM.

**1st District and Circuit Court**, PO Box 218, Randolph, UT 84064. 801-793-2415 (MST) 9AM-5PM. Felony, Misdemeanor, Civil, Eviction, Small Claims, Probate.

## Salt Lake County

**Real Estate Recording**, Salt Lake County Recorder, 2001 South State Street, Room N-1600, Salt Lake City, UT 84190-1150. 801-468-3391 (MST) 8AM-5PM.

**3rd District Court**, 240 East 400 South, Salt Lake City, UT 84111. 801-535-5581 (MST) 8AM-5PM. Felony, Civil Actions Over $20,000, Probate.

**3rd Circuit Court-Murray**, 5022 S. State St, Murray, UT 84107. 801-261-0562 (MST) 8AM-5PM. Misdemeanor, Civil Actions Under $20,000, Eviction, Small Claims.

**3rd Circuit Court-Salt Lake City**, 451 South 2nd East, Salt Lake City, UT 84111. 801-533-3900 (MST) 8AM-5PM. Misdemeanor, Civil Actions Under $20,000, Eviction, Small Claims.

**3rd Circuit Court-Sandy**, 210 West 10,000 South, Sandy, UT 84070-3282. 801-565-5700 (MST) 8AM-5PM. Misdemeanor, Civil Actions Under $20,000, Eviction, Small Claims.

**3rd Circuit Court-West Valley**, 3636 S. Constitution Bldg, West Valley, UT 84119. 801-963-8181 (MST) 8AM-5PM. Misdemeanor, Civil Actions Under $20,000, Eviction, Small Claims.

## San Juan County

**Real Estate Recording**, San Juan County Recorder, 117 South Main, Room 103, Monticello, UT 84535. 801-587-3228 (MST) 8:30AM-5PM.

**7th District Court**, PO Box 68, Monticello, UT 84535. 801-587-2122 (MST) 8AM-5PM. Felony, Misdemeanor, Civil, Eviction, Small Claims, Probate.

## Sanpete County

**Real Estate Recording**, Sanpete County Recorder, 160 North Main, Manti, UT 84642. 801-835-2181 (MST) 8:30AM-5PM.

**6th District Court**, 160 N. Main, Manti, UT 84642. 801-835-2131 (MST) Felony, Misdemeanor, Civil, Eviction, Small Claims, Probate.

## Sevier County

**Real Estate Recording**, Sevier County Recorder, 250 North Main, Richfield, UT 84701. 801-896-9262 (MST) 8:30AM-5PM.

**6th District Court**, 250 N. Main, Richfield, UT 84701. 801-896-9256 (MST) Felony, Misdemeanor, Civil, Eviction, Small Claims, Probate.

## Summit County

**Real Estate Recording**, Summit County Recorder, 54 North Main, Coalville, UT 84017. 801-336-4451 (MST) X5 8AM-5PM.

**3rd District and Circuit Court**, PO Box 128, Coalville, UT 84017. 801-336-4451 (MST) 8AM-5PM. Felony, Misdemeanor, Civil, Eviction, Small Claims, Probate.

## Tooele County

**Real Estate Recording**, Tooele County Recorder, 47 South Main Street, Courthouse, Tooele, UT 84074-2194. 801-882-9181 (MST) 8:30AM-5PM.

**3rd District Court**, 47 S. Main, Tooele, UT 84074. 801-882-9210 (MST) 8AM-5PM. Felony, Civil Actions Over $20,000, Probate.

**3rd Circuit Court**, 47 S. Main, Tooele, UT 84074. 801-882-9211 (MST) Misdemeanor, Civil Actions Under $20,000, Eviction, Small Claims.

## Uintah County

**Real Estate Recording**, Uintah County Recorder, 147 East Main St., County Building, Vernal, UT 84078. 801-781-5461 (MST) 8AM-5PM.

**8th District Court**, 147 E. Main, Vernal, UT 84078. 801-789-7534 (MST) Felony, Misdemeanor, Civil, Eviction, Small Claims, Probate.

## Utah County

**Real Estate Recording**, Utah County Recorder, County Administration Bldg.-Room 1300, 100 East Center, Provo, UT 84606. 801-370-8179 (MST) 8:30AM-5PM.

**4th District Court**, PO Box 1847, Provo, UT 84603. 801-429-1039 (MST) 8AM-5PM. Felony, Civil Actions Over $20,000, Probate.

**Circuit Court**, PO Box 1847, Provo, UT 84603. 801-429-1001 (MST) 8AM-5PM. Misdemeanor, Civil Actions Under $20,000, Eviction, Small Claims.

## Wasatch County

**Real Estate Recording**, Wasatch County Recorder, 25 North Main, Heber, UT 84032. 801-654-3211 (MST) 8AM-5PM.

**4th District and Circuit Court**, 25 N. Main, Heber City, UT 84032. 801-654-3211 (MST) 8AM-5PM. Felony, Misdemeanor, Civil, Eviction, Small Claims, Probate.

## Washington County

**Real Estate Recording**, Washington County Recorder, 197 East Tabernacle, St. George, UT 84770. 801-634-5709 (MST) 8AM-5PM.

**5th District Court**, 220 North 200 East, St. George, UT 84770. 801-673-7225 (MST) 8AM-5PM. Felony, Misdemeanor, Civil, Eviction, Small Claims, Probate.

## Wayne County

**Real Estate Recording**, Wayne County Recorder, 88 South Main, Loa, UT 84747. 801-836-2765 (MST) 8:30AM-5PM.

**6th District Court**, 18 S. Main, Loa, UT 84747. 801-836-2731 (MST) 9AM-5PM. Felony, Misdemeanor, Civil, Eviction, Small Claims, Probate.

## Weber County

**Real Estate Recording**, Weber County Recorder, 2549 Washington Blvd, Ogden, UT 84401. 801-399-8441 (MST) 8AM-5PM.

**2nd District Court**, 2549 Washington Blvd., Ogden, UT 84401. 801-399-8019 (MST) 8AM-5PM. Felony, Civil Actions Over $20,000, Probate.

**2nd Circuit Court**, 2549 Washington Blvd, Ogden, UT 84401. 801-629-8019 (MST) 8AM-5PM. Misdemeanor, Civil Actions Under $20,000, Eviction, Small Claims.

# Vermont

## Addison County

**Superior Court**, Court St, Middlebury, VT 05753. 802-388-7741 (EST) 8:30AM-4:30PM. Civil, Eviction.

**District Court**, Court St, Middlebury, VT 05753. 802-388-4237 (EST) 8AM-4:30PM. Felony, Misdemeanor, Small Claims.

**Probate Court**, PO Box 270, Middlebury, VT 05753. 802-388-2612 (EST) 8AM-4:30PM. Probate.

## Addison Town

**Real Estate Recording**, Addison Town Clerk, RD 1, Vergennes, VT 05491. 802-759-2020 8:30AM-4:30PM (Summer hours 12:30PM-4:30PM).

## Albany Town

**Real Estate Recording**, Albany Town Clerk, Rt 14, Albany, VT 05820. 802-755-6100 9AM-4PM T,Th; 9AM-7PM W.

## Alburg Town

**Real Estate Recording**, Alburg Town Clerk, Main Street, Alburg, VT 05440. 802-796-3468 9AM-Noon,1-5PM.

## Andover Town

**Real Estate Recording**, Andover Town Clerk, Route 1, Box 179, Chester, VT 05143. 802-875-2765 9AM-1PM.

## Arlington Town

**Real Estate Recording**, Arlington Town Clerk, Main Street, Town Hall, Arlington, VT 05250. 802-375-2332 9AM-2PM.

## Athens Town

**Real Estate Recording**, Athens Town Clerk, RD 3, Box 195C, Athens, VT 05143. 802-869-3370 By Appointment.

## Bakersfield Town

**Real Estate Recording**, Bakersfield Town Clerk, Town Road 3, Bakersfield, VT 05441. 802-827-4495 9AM-Noon.

## Baltimore Town

**Real Estate Recording**, Baltimore Town Clerk, RD 4, Box 365, Chester, VT 05143. 802-263-5419 By Appointmment Evenings M-F; 10AM-Noon Sat.

## Barnard Town

**Real Estate Recording**, Barnard Town Clerk, North Rd., Barnard, VT 05031. 802-234-9211 8:30AM-4:30PM M,T.

## Barnet Town

**Real Estate Recording**, Barnet Town Clerk, US Route 5, Main Street, Barnet, VT 05821. 802-633-2256 9AM-Noon, 1-4:30PM.

## Barre City

**Real Estate Recording**, Barre City Clerk, 12 North Main Street, Barre, VT 05641. 802-476-0242 8:30AM-5PM.

## Barre Town

**Real Estate Recording**, Barre Town Clerk, Municipal Building, 149 Websterville Road, Websterville, VT 05678. 802-479-9391 8AM-Noon, 1-4:30PM.

## Barton Town

**Real Estate Recording**, Barton Town Clerk, Main Street, Howard Bank Building, Barton, VT 05822. 802-525-6222 8:30AM-5PM.

## Belvidere Town

**Real Estate Recording**, Belvidere Town Clerk, RR 1, Box 1062, Belvidere Center, VT 05492. 802-644-2498

## Bennington County

**Superior Court**, 207 South St, Bennington, VT 05201. 802-447-2700 (EST) 8AM-4:30PM. Civil, Eviction.

**District Court**, 1 Veterans Memorial Dr, Bennington, VT 05201. 802-447-2727 (EST) 7:45AM-4:30PM. Felony, Misdemeanor, Small Claims.

**Probate Court-Bennington District**, 207 South St.(PO BOX 607), Bennington, VT 05201. 802-447-2705 (EST) 9AM-4PM. Probate.

**Probate Court-Manchester District**, PO Box 446, Manchester, VT 05254. 802-362-1410 (EST) Probate.

## Bennington Town

**Real Estate Recording**, Bennington Town Clerk, 205 South Street, Bennington, VT 05201. 802-442-1043 9AM-5PM.

## Benson Town

**Real Estate Recording**, Benson Town Clerk, Main Street, Benson, VT 05731. 802-537-2611 9AM-4:30PM M-W & F.

## Berkshire Town

**Real Estate Recording**, Berkshire Town Clerk, RFD 1, Box 2560, Enosburg Falls, VT 05450. 802-933-2335

## Berlin Town

**Real Estate Recording**, Berlin Town Clerk, Shed Road, Berlin Municipal Building, Berlin, VT 05602. 802-229-9298 8:30AM-Noon,1-4:30PM (July-August 8:30AM-Noon, 1PM-3:30PM).

## Bethel Town

**Real Estate Recording**, Bethel Town Clerk, South Main Street, Town Office, Bethel, VT 05032. 802-234-9722 8AM-Noon T,F; 8AM-12:30, 1-4PM M,Th.

## Bloomfield Town

**Real Estate Recording**, Bloomfield Town Clerk, RFD 1 Box 900 Rte 102, Guildhall, VT 05905. 802-962-5191 9AM-3PM T or by appointment.

## Bolton Town

**Real Estate Recording**, Bolton Town Clerk, Route 2 Town Hall, Waterbury, VT 05676. 802-434-3064 7AM-3PM M, T, Th; 8AM-5PM W; 7AM-Noon F.

## Bradford Town

**Real Estate Recording**, Bradford Town Clerk, Main Street, Bradford, VT 05033. 802-222-4727 8:30AM-4:30PM.

## Braintree Town

**Real Estate Recording**, Braintree Town Clerk, Route 12A, Braintree, VT 05060. 802-728-9787 M 9AM-4:30PM; W 1:30PM-4:30PM; F 9AM-Noon.

## Brandon Town

**Real Estate Recording**, Brandon Town Clerk, 49 Center Street, Brandon, VT 05733. 802-247-5721 8:30AM-4PM.

## Brattleboro Town

**Real Estate Recording**, Brattleboro Town Clerk, 230 Main Street, Brattleboro, VT 05301. 802-254-4541 8:30AM-5PM.

## Bridgewater Town

**Real Estate Recording**, Bridgewater Town Clerk, Route 4, Clerk's Office, Bridgewater, VT 05034. 802-672-3334 10AM-4PM (Closed F).

## Bridport Town

**Real Estate Recording**, Bridport Town Clerk, Town Hall, Bridport, VT 05734. 802-758-2483

## Brighton Town

**Real Estate Recording**, Brighton Town Clerk, Main Street, Town Hall, Island Pond, VT 05846. 802-723-4405

## Bristol Town

**Real Estate Recording**, Bristol Town Clerk, 1 South Street, Bristol, VT 05443. 802-453-2486 8:30AM-4PM.

## Brookfield Town

**Real Estate Recording**, Brookfield Town Clerk, Ralph Rd., Brookfield, VT 05036. 802-276-3352 9AM-4PM M,T,F.

## Brookline Town

**Real Estate Recording**, Brookline Town Clerk, PO Box 403, Brookline, VT 05345. 802-365-4648 9AM-Noon Th.

## Brownington Town

**Real Estate Recording**, Brownington Town Clerk, RFD 2, Box 158, Orleans, VT 05860. 802-754-8401 1PM-3:30PM W; 9AM-Noon Th.

## Brunswick Town

**Real Estate Recording**, Brunswick Town Clerk, Route 102, RFD 1, Box 470, Guildhall, VT 05905. 802-962-5283 M-Sat by appointment.

## Burke Town

**Real Estate Recording**, Burke Town Clerk, RR 2, Box 24, Town Hall, West Burke, VT 05871.

802-467-3717 8AM-4PM M,T,W,F; 7AM-5PM Th.

## Burlington City

**Real Estate Recording**, Burlington City Clerk, City Hall, Room 20, Burlington, VT 05401. 802-865-7135 8AM-7:30PM M; 8AM-4:30PM T-F.

## Cabot Town

**Real Estate Recording**, Cabot Town Clerk, Main Street, Town Hall, Cabot, VT 05647. 802-563-2279 M 9-6; Tu 9-3; W 12-5; Th 9-3; F 9-1; S 10-1.

## Calais Town

**Real Estate Recording**, Calais Town Clerk, RR 1, Box 35, W. County Rd., Calais, VT 05648. 802-223-5952 8AM-5PM M,T,Th; 8AM-Noon Sat.

## Caledonia County

**Superior Court**, Box 4129, St Johnsbury, VT 05819. 802-748-6600 (EST) 8AM-4:30PM. Civil, Eviction.

**District Court**, 27 Main St, St Johnsbury, VT 05819. 802-748-6610 (EST) 8AM-4:30PM. Felony, Misdemeanor, Small Claims.

**Probate Court**, 27 Main St, St Johnsbury, VT 05819. 802-748-6605 (EST) 8AM-4:30PM. Probate.

## Cambridge Town

**Real Estate Recording**, Cambridge Town Clerk, Clerk's Office, Jeffersonville, VT 05464. 802-644-2251 8AM-Noon,1-4PM.

## Canaan Town

**Real Estate Recording**, Canaan Town Clerk, Route 253, Town Hall, Canaan, VT 05903. 802-266-3370 9AM-3PM.

## Castleton Town

**Real Estate Recording**, Castleton Town Clerk, Main Street, Town Hall, Castleton, VT 05735. 802-468-2212 8:30AM-Noon, 1-4PM.

## Cavendish Town

**Real Estate Recording**, Cavendish Town Clerk, High Street, Town Hall, Cavendish, VT 05142. 802-226-7292 9AM-Noon, 1-4:30PM.

## Charleston Town

**Real Estate Recording**, Charleston Town Clerk, Route 105, Town Hall, West Charleston, VT 05872. 802-895-2814 8AM-3PM M,T,Th,F.

## Charlotte Town

**Real Estate Recording**, Charlotte Town Clerk, Ferry Road, Charlotte, VT 05445. 802-425-3071 8AM-4PM.

## Chelsea Town

**Real Estate Recording**, Chelsea Town Clerk, Main Street, Town Hall, Chelsea, VT 05038. 802-685-4460

## Chester Town

**Real Estate Recording**, Chester Town Clerk, Depot Street, Town Hall, Chester, VT 05143. 802-875-2173 8AM-5PM.

## Chittenden County

**Superior Court**, 175 Main St.(PO Box 187), Burlington, VT 05402. 802-863-3467 (EST) 8AM-4:30PM. Civil, Eviction.

**District Court**, Unit 2, PO Box 268, Burlington, VT 05402. 802-651-1800 (EST) 8AM-4:30PM. Felony, Misdemeanor, Small Claims.

**Probate Court**, PO Box 511, Burlington, VT 05402. 802-864-7481 (EST) 8AM-4:30PM M-Th, 8AM-4PM Fri. Probate.

## Chittenden Town

**Real Estate Recording**, Chittenden Town Clerk, Holden Road, Town Hall, Chittenden, VT 05737. 802-483-6647 10AM-2PM.

## Clarendon Town

**Real Estate Recording**, Clarendon Town Clerk, Middle Road, North Clarendon, VT 05759. 802-775-4274

## Colchester Town

**Real Estate Recording**, Colchester Town Clerk, 172 Blakely Road, Clochester, VT 05446. 802-655-0811 8AM-4PM.

## Concord Town

**Real Estate Recording**, Concord Town Clerk, City Hall, Concord, VT 05824. 802-695-2220 8AM-Noon,1-4PM (Closed Th).

## Corinth Town

**Real Estate Recording**, Corinth Town Clerk, Cookeville Road, Town Hall, Corinth, VT 05039. 802-439-5850 8:30AM-12, 1PM-4PM M,T,Th,F.

## Cornwall Town

**Real Estate Recording**, Cornwall Town Clerk, Town Hall, Jct. Rts 30 & 74, Town of Cornwall, Middlebury, VT 05753. 802-462-2775 12:30PM-4:30PM T,W,Th,F.

## Coventry Town

**Real Estate Recording**, Coventry Town Clerk, Coventry Community Center, Coventry, VT 05825. 802-754-2288 9:30AM-4PM M,Th.

## Craftsbury Town

**Real Estate Recording**, Craftsbury Town Clerk, Main Street, Town Hall, Craftsbury, VT 05826. 802-586-2823 8:30AM-4PM T-F.

## Danby Town

**Real Estate Recording**, Danby Town Clerk, Boro Hill, Danby, VT 05739. 802-293-5136 9AM-Noon, 1-4PM (Closed F).

## Danville Town

**Real Estate Recording**, Danville Town Clerk, Main Street, Town Hall, Danville, VT 05828. 802-684-3352 8AM-4:30PM.

## Derby Town

**Real Estate Recording**, Derby Town Clerk, Main Street, Town Hall, Derby, VT 05829. 802-766-4906 9AM-4PM.

## Dorset Town

**Real Estate Recording**, Dorset Town Clerk, Mad Tom Road, Town Hall, East Dorset, VT 05253. 802-362-1178 9AM-2PM.

## Dover Town

**Real Estate Recording**, Dover Town Clerk, Route 100 North, Town Clerk's Office, Dover, VT 05356. 802-464-5100 9AM-5PM.

## Dummerston Town

**Real Estate Recording**, Dummerston Town Clerk, Middle Road, Town Hall, Dummerston, VT 05346. 802-257-1496 9AM-3PM M,T,Th,F; 11AM-5PM Wed.

## Duxbury Town

**Real Estate Recording**, Duxbury Town Clerk, Route 100 Crossett Hill, Waterbury, VT 05676. 802-244-6660 8:30AM-1PM M,W,Th; 8:30AM-5PM T.

## East Haven Town

**Real Estate Recording**, East Haven Town Clerk, 19 Maple St., East Haven, VT 05837. 802-467-3772 4-7PM T; 8AM-Noon Th.

## East Montpelier Town

**Real Estate Recording**, East Montpelier Town Clerk, Kelton Road, Town Municipal Building, East Montpelier, VT 05651. 802-223-3313 9AM-5PM M-Th; 9AM-Noon F.

## Eden Town

**Real Estate Recording**, Eden Town Clerk, Route 100, Town Office Building, Eden Mills, VT 05653. 802-635-2528 8AM-4PM M-Th.

## Elmore Town

**Real Estate Recording**, Elmore Town Clerk, Town Hall, Towm Clerk's Office, Lake Elmore, VT 05657. 802-888-2637 9AM-3PM T,W,Th.

## Enosburg Town

**Real Estate Recording**, Enosburg Town Clerk, 95 Main Street, Enosburg Falls, VT 05450. 802-933-4421 9AM-Noon,1-4PM.

## Essex County

**District and Superior Court**, Box 75, Guildhall, VT 05905. 802-676-3910 (EST) 8AM-4:30PM. Felony, Misdemeanor, Civil, Eviction, Small Claims.

**Probate Court**, PO Box 426, Island Pond, VT 05846. 802-723-4770 (EST) 8:30AM-3:30PM. Probate.

## Essex Town

**Real Estate Recording**, Essex Town Clerk, 81 Main Street, Essex Junction, VT 05452. 802-879-0413 8AM-4:30PM.

## Fair Haven Town

**Real Estate Recording**, Fair Haven Town Clerk, 3 North Park Place, Fair Haven, VT 05743. 802-265-3610 8AM-Noon, 1PM-4PM.

## Fairfax Town
Real Estate Recording, Fairfax Town Clerk, Hunt Street, Town Office, Fairfax, VT 05454. 802-849-6111 9AM-4PM.

## Fairfield Town
Real Estate Recording, Fairfield Town Clerk, Town Hall, Fairfield, VT 05455. 802-827-3261 9AM-3PM.

## Fairlee Town
Real Estate Recording, Fairlee Town Clerk, Main Street, Fairlee, VT 05045. 802-333-4363 9AM-2PM M,T,Th,F; 1PM-6PM W.

## Fayston Town
Real Estate Recording, Fayston Town Clerk, North Fayston Road, Town Hall, Moretown, VT 05660. 802-496-2454 9AM-3PM M,T,Th,F.

## Ferrisburgh Town
Real Estate Recording, Ferrisburgh Town Clerk, Route 7, Town Hall, Ferrisburgh, VT 05456. 802-877-3429 8AM-4PM.

## Fletcher Town
Real Estate Recording, Fletcher Town Clerk, Town Hall, Fletcher, VT 05444. 802-849-6616

## Franklin County
Superior Court, Box 808 Church St, St Albans, VT 05478. 802-524-3863 (EST) 8AM-4:30PM. Civil, Eviction.

District Court, PO Box 314, St Albans, VT 05478. 802-524-7997 (EST) 8AM-4:30PM. Felony, Misdemeanor, Small Claims.

Probate Court, Church St, St Albans, VT 05478. 802-524-4112 (EST) 8AM-4:30PM. Probate.

## Franklin Town
Real Estate Recording, Franklin Town Clerk, Haston Library, Franklin, VT 05457. 802-285-2101 9AM-4PM M,T,Th,F; 9AM-Noon W & Sat.

## Georgia Town
Real Estate Recording, Georgia Town Clerk, Route 7, Town Hall, St. Albans, VT 05478. 802-524-3524 11AM-5PM, 7-9PM M; 8AM-4PM.

## Glover Town
Real Estate Recording, Glover Town Clerk, Municipal Building, Glover, VT 05839. 802-525-6227 9AM-5PM.

## Goshen Town
Real Estate Recording, Goshen Town Clerk, RR 3, Box 3384, Goshen, VT 05733. 802-247-6455 9AM-11AM T & W or by appointment.

## Grafton Town
Real Estate Recording, Grafton Town Clerk, Main Street, Grafton, VT 05146. 802-843-2419 9AM-12, 1PM-5PM M,T,Th,F.

## Granby Town
Real Estate Recording, Granby Town Clerk, Main Street, Granby, VT 05840. 802-328-3611

## Grand Isle County
District and Superior Court, PO Box 7, North Hero, VT 05474. 802-372-8350 (EST) 8AM-4:30PM. Felony, Misdemeanor, Civil, Eviction, Small Claims.

Probate Court, PO Box 7, North Hero, VT 05474. 802-372-8350 (EST) 8AM-4:30PM. Probate.

## Grand Isle Town
Real Estate Recording, Grand Isle Town Clerk, 9 Hyde Road, Grand Isle, VT 05458. 802-372-8830 8:30AM-4:30PM.

## Granville Town
Real Estate Recording, Granville Town Clerk, Route 100, Granville, VT 05747. 802-767-4403 9AM-3PM M-Th (Closed F).

## Greensboro Town
Real Estate Recording, Greensboro Town Clerk, Town Hall, Greensboro, VT 05841. 802-533-2911 8AM-Noon,1-4PM.

## Groton Town
Real Estate Recording, Groton Town Clerk, Route 302, Town Office, Groton, VT 05046. 802-584-3276 8AM-Noon, 12:30PM-3:30PM.

## Guildhall Town
Real Estate Recording, Guildhall Town Clerk, Route 102, Guildhall, VT 05905. 802-676-3797 1-3PM T,W,Th.

## Guilford Town
Real Estate Recording, Guilford Town Clerk, RR 3, Box 255, School Rd., Guilford, VT 05301. 802-254-6857 9AM-4PM M,T,Th,F; 9AM-Noon, 6:30PM-9PM Wed.

## Halifax Town
Real Estate Recording, Halifax Town Clerk, Branch Brook Rd., West Halifax, VT 05358. 802-368-7390 9AM-4PM M,T,F; 9AM-Noon Sat.

## Hancock Town
Real Estate Recording, Hancock Town Clerk, Rt 125, Hancock, VT 05748. 802-767-3660 9AM-3PM T-Th; 11AM-5PM F.

## Hardwick Town
Real Estate Recording, Hardwick Town Clerk, 2 Church Street, Hardwick, VT 05843. 802-472-5971 9AM-4PM T-F.

## Hartford Town
Real Estate Recording, Hartford Town Clerk, 15 Bridge Street, White River Junction, VT 05001. 802-295-2785 9AM-12, 1PM-4PM.

## Hartland Town
Real Estate Recording, Hartland Town Clerk, Damon Hall, Hartland, VT 05048. 802-436-2444 9AM-Noon,1-4PM.

## Highgate Town
Real Estate Recording, Highgate Town Clerk, Municipal Building, Route 78, Highgate Center, VT 05459. 802-868-4697 8:30AM-12, 1PM-4:30PM.

## Hinesburg Town
Real Estate Recording, Hinesburg Town Clerk, Main Street, Town Hall, Hinesburg, VT 05461. 802-482-2281

## Holland Town
Real Estate Recording, Holland Town Clerk, RFD 1, Box 37, Derby Line, Holland, VT 05830. 802-895-4440 10AM-Noon (and by appointment).

## Hubbardton Town
Real Estate Recording, Hubbardton Town Clerk, RR 1, Box 2828, Fair Haven, VT 05743. 802-273-2951

## Huntington Town
Real Estate Recording, Huntington Town Clerk, RD 1, Box 771, Huntington, VT 05462. 802-434-2032 9AM-4PM M,T,W,Th; 8:30AM-2PM F.

## Hyde Park Town
Real Estate Recording, Hyde Park Town Clerk, Route 15, Hyde Park Town Clerk's Office, Hyde Park, VT 05655. 802-888-2300 8AM-4PM.

## Ira Town
Real Estate Recording, Ira Town Clerk, RFD 1, West Rutland, VT 05777. 802-235-2745 By Appointment.

## Irasburg Town
Real Estate Recording, Irasburg Town Clerk, Route 58, Irasburg, VT 05845. 802-754-2242 9AM-4PM M,T,Th.

## Isle La Motte Town
Real Estate Recording, Isle La Motte Town Clerk, Rt 129, Town Hall, Isle La Motte, VT 05463. 802-928-3434 9AM-3PM T,Th; 9AM-Noon Sat.

## Jamaica Town
Real Estate Recording, Jamaica Town Clerk, White Building behind J.A.Muzzy, in center of Jamaica Village, Jamaica, VT 05343. 802-874-4681 9AM-Noon, 1-4PM T,W,Th,F.

## Jay Town
Real Estate Recording, Jay Town Clerk, RFD 2, Box 136, Jay, VT 05859. 802-988-2996 7AM-4PM (Closed M).

## Jericho Town
Real Estate Recording, Jericho Town Clerk, Route 15, Jericho, VT 05465. 802-899-4936

## Johnson Town
Real Estate Recording, Johnson Town Clerk, Pearl Street, Johnson, VT 05656. 802-635-2611 7:30AM-4PM.

## Kirby Town
Real Estate Recording, Kirby Town Clerk, RR 2, Lyndonville, VT 05851. 802-626-9386 8AM-3PM T,Th.

## Lamoille County

**Superior Court**, Box 490, Hyde Park, VT 05655. 802-888-2207 (EST) 8Am-4:30PM. Civil, Eviction

**District Court**, PO Box 489, Hyde Park, VT 05655-0489. 802-888-3887 (EST) 8AM-4:30PM. Felony, Misdemeanor, Small Claims.

**Probate Court**, PO Box 102, Hyde Park, VT 05655-0102. 802-888-3306 (EST) 8AM-4:30PM. Probate.

## Landgrove Town

**Real Estate Recording**, Landgrove Town Clerk, RR 1, Box 236 Landgrove, Londonderry, VT 05148. 802-824-3716 9AM-Noon Th.

## Leicester Town

**Real Estate Recording**, Leicester Town Clerk, RR 2, Box 2117-1, Brandon, VT 05733. 802-247-5961 1-4PM M,T,W; 9AM-1PM Th,F.

## Lemington Town

**Real Estate Recording**, Lemington Town Clerk, RR 1, Box 183, Canaan, VT 05903. 802-277-4814 Noon-3PM W.

## Lincoln Town

**Real Estate Recording**, Lincoln Town Clerk, RD 1, Bristol, VT 05443. 802-453-2980 9AM-4PM M,T,Th,F; 10AM-Noon Sat.

## Londonderry Town

**Real Estate Recording**, Londonderry Town Clerk, Old School St., South Londonderry, VT 05155. 802-824-3356 9AM-3PM T-F; 9AM-12 Sat.

## Lowell Town

**Real Estate Recording**, Lowell Town Clerk, 58 West, Lowell, VT 05847. 802-744-6559 9AM-2:30PM M & Th.

## Ludlow Town

**Real Estate Recording**, Ludlow Town Clerk, 37 Depot Street, Ludlow, VT 05149. 802-228-3232 8:30AM-Noon, 1-4:30PM.

## Lunenburg Town

**Real Estate Recording**, Lunenburg Town Clerk, 54 Main Street, Lunenburg, VT 05906. 802-892-5959 8:30AM-Noon, 1PM-4PM.

## Lyndon Town

**Real Estate Recording**, Lyndon Town Clerk, 20 Park Avenue, Lyndonville, VT 05851. 802-626-5785 7:30AM-4:30PM.

## Maidstone Town

**Real Estate Recording**, Maidstone Town Clerk, RR 1 Box 65, Susan Irwin, Guildhall, VT 05905. 802-676-3210 9AM-11AM M & Th.

## Manchester Town

**Real Estate Recording**, Manchester Town Clerk, Route 7A North, Manchester Center, VT 05255. 802-362-1315 8:30AM-4:30PM.

## Marlboro Town

**Real Estate Recording**, Marlboro Town Clerk, Town Office, Marlboro, VT 05344. 802-254-2181 9AM-2PM M,W,Th

## Marshfield Town

**Real Estate Recording**, Marshfield Town Clerk, Depot Street, Marshfield, VT 05658. 802-426-3305 8:30AM-4:30PM W-F; 8:30AM-5:30PM T.

## Mendon Town

**Real Estate Recording**, Mendon Town Clerk, RR 2, Box 8780, Rutland, VT 05701. 802-775-1662 9AM-3PM.

## Middlebury Town

**Real Estate Recording**, Middlebury Town Clerk, Municipal Building, 94 Main St., Middlebury, VT 05753. 802-388-4041 8:30AM-5PM.

## Middlesex Town

**Real Estate Recording**, Middlesex Town Clerk, RR 3, Box 4600, Montpelier, VT 05602. 802-223-5915 8:30AM-Noon, 1PM-4:30PM.

## Middletown Springs Town

**Real Estate Recording**, Middletown Springs Town Clerk, 20 Park Street, Middletown Springs, VT 05757. 802-235-2220 1-4PM M,T,F; 9AM-Noon Sat.

## Milton Town

**Real Estate Recording**, Milton Town Clerk, 6 Main Street, Milton, VT 05468. 802-893-4111 8AM-5PM.

## Monkton Town

**Real Estate Recording**, Monkton Town Clerk, RR 1, Box 2015, North Ferrisburg, VT 05473. 802-453-3800 8AM-2PM M,T,Th,F; 8:30AM-Noon Sat.

## Montgomery Town

**Real Estate Recording**, Montgomery Town Clerk, 3 Main Street, Montgomery Center, VT 05471. 802-326-4719 9AM-Noon, 1PM-4PM M,T,Th,F; 9AM-Noon Wed.

## Montpelier City

**Real Estate Recording**, Montpelier City Clerk, 39 Main Street, City Hall, Montpelier, VT 05602. 802-223-9500 8AM-4:30PM.

## Moretown Town

**Real Estate Recording**, Moretown Town Clerk, RD #1 P.O. Box 635, Moretown, VT 05660. 802-496-3645 9AM-4:30PM.

## Morgan Town

**Real Estate Recording**, Morgan Town Clerk, Town Clerk Rd., Morgan, VT 05853. 802-895-2927

## Morristown Town

**Real Estate Recording**, Morristown Town Clerk, 16 Main St., Morrisville, VT 05661. 802-888-6370 8:30AM-4:30PM M,T,Th,F; 8:30AM-12:30PM W.

## Mount Holly Town

**Real Estate Recording**, Mount Holly Town Clerk, School Street, Mount Holly, VT 05758. 802-259-2391 9:30AM-2PM M,T,Th,F.

## Mount Tabor Town

**Real Estate Recording**, Mount Tabor Town Clerk, Brooklyn Rd., Town Office, Mt. Tabor, VT 05739. 802-293-5282

## New Haven Town

**Real Estate Recording**, New Haven Town Clerk, RD 1, Box 4, North St., New Haven, VT 05472. 802-453-3516 9AM-3PM M,T,Th,F; Closed Wed.

## Newark Town

**Real Estate Recording**, Newark Town Clerk, RFD 1, Box 50C, West Burke, VT 05871. 802-467-3336 9AM-4PM M,W,Th.

## Newbury Town

**Real Estate Recording**, Newbury Town Clerk, Main St., Newbury, VT 05051. 802-866-5521

## Newfane Town

**Real Estate Recording**, Newfane Town Clerk, Rt 30, Main St., Newfane, VT 05345. 802-365-7772 9AM-1PM M; 9AM-3PM T-F; 9AM-Noon Sat.

## Newport City

**Real Estate Recording**, Newport City Clerk, 74 Main Street, Newport, VT 05855. 802-334-2112 8AM-4:30PM.

## Newport Town

**Real Estate Recording**, Newport Town Clerk, Vance Hill, Newport Center, VT 05857. 802-334-6442 9AM-5PM M,T,Th,F; 9AM-Noon Wed.

## North Hero Town

**Real Estate Recording**, North Hero Town Clerk, Route 2, Town Offices, North Hero, VT 05474. 802-372-6926 9AM-Noon, 1PM-4PM M,T,Th,F; Sat 9-Noon.

## Northfield Town

**Real Estate Recording**, Northfield Town Clerk, 26 South Main Street, Northfield, VT 05663. 802-485-5421 8AM-4:30PM.

## Norton Town

**Real Estate Recording**, Norton Town Clerk, Nelson Store, Norton, VT 05907. 802-822-5513 9AM-5PM M,T,Th; 9AM-Noon F,Sat.

## Norwich Town

**Real Estate Recording**, Norwich Town Clerk, Main St., Norwich, VT 05055. 802-649-1419 8:30AM-4:30PM.

## Orange County

**District and Superior Court**, RRI, Box 30, Chelsea, VT 05038-9746. 802-685-4870 (EST) 8AM-4:30PM. Felony, Misdemeanor, Civil, Eviction, Small Claims.

# Vermont

**Probate Court-Randolph District**, Clerk of Court, Chelsea, VT 05038. 802-685-4610 (EST) Probate.

**Probate Court-Bradford District**, PO Box 199, Fairlee, VT 05045. 802-333-9811 (EST) 8AM-4:30PM. Probate.

## Orange Town

Real Estate Recording, Orange Town Clerk, Rt 302, East Barre, VT 05649. 802-479-2673 8AM-Noon, 1PM-3PM M,W; 8AM-Noon F.

## Orleans County

**Superior Court**, 83 Main St, Newport, VT 05855. 802-334-3344 (EST) 8AM-4:30PM. Civil, Eviction.

**District Court**, 81 Main St, Newport, VT 05855. 802-334-3325 (EST) 8AM-4:30PM. Felony, Misdemeanor, Small Claims.

**Probate Court**, 83 Main St, Newport, VT 05855. 802-334-3366 (EST) Probate.

## Orwell Town

Real Estate Recording, Orwell Town Clerk, Main St., Orwell, VT 05760. 802-948-2032 9:30AM-Noon, 1-3:30PM.

## Panton Town

Real Estate Recording, Panton Town Clerk, RFD 3, Panton Corners, Vergennes, VT 05491. 802-475-2333 9AM-4:30PM M,T.

## Pawlet Town

Real Estate Recording, Pawlet Town Clerk, Town Hall, School Street, Pawlet, VT 05761. 802-325-3309 9AM-3PM T,W,Th; 9AM-Noon F.

## Peacham Town

Real Estate Recording, Peacham Town Clerk, Church St., Peacham, VT 05862. 802-592-3218 8AM-Noon M,T,Th,F; 1-4PM Th; 4PM-7PM W.

## Peru Town

Real Estate Recording, Peru Town Clerk, Main St., Peru, VT 05152. 802-824-3065 9AM-3PM T,W,Th.

## Pittsfield Town

Real Estate Recording, Pittsfield Town Clerk, Park Drive, Pittsfield, VT 05762. 802-746-8170 Noon-6PM T; 9AM-3PM W,Th.

## Pittsford Town

Real Estate Recording, Pittsford Town Clerk, Plains Road, Pittsford, VT 05763. 802-483-2931 8AM-4:30PM.

## Plainfield Town

Real Estate Recording, Plainfield Town Clerk, P.O. Box 217, Plainfield, VT 05667. 802-454-8461

## Plymouth Town

Real Estate Recording, Plymouth Town Clerk, Rt 100, Plymouth Union, Plymouth, VT 05056. 802-672-3655 8:30-11:30AM, 12:30-3:30PM.

## Pomfret Town

Real Estate Recording, Pomfret Town Clerk, Main St., Town Clerk, North Pomfret, VT 05053. 802-457-3861

## Poultney Town

Real Estate Recording, Poultney Town Clerk, 86-88 Main Street, Poultney, VT 05764. 802-287-5761 8:30AM-12:30, 1:30-4PM.

## Pownal Town

Real Estate Recording, Pownal Town Clerk, RD 1, Box 41, Pownal, VT 05261. 802-823-7757 9AM-2PM M,W,Th,F; 9AM-4PM T.

## Proctor Town

Real Estate Recording, Proctor Town Clerk, 45 Main Street, Proctor, VT 05765. 802-459-3333 8AM-4PM.

## Putney Town

Real Estate Recording, Putney Town Clerk, Town Hall, Main Street, Putney, VT 05346. 802-387-5862 9AM-2PM M, Th, F; 9AM-2PM, 7-9PM W; 9AM-12 Sat.

## Randolph Town

Real Estate Recording, Randolph Town Clerk, 7 Summer Street, Randolph, VT 05060. 802-728-5682 8AM-4:30PM.

## Reading Town

Real Estate Recording, Reading Town Clerk, Rt 106, Reading, VT 05062. 802-484-7250 9AM-Noon, 1PM-4PM, M,W,F.

## Readsboro Town

Real Estate Recording, Readsboro Town Clerk, School Rd., Readsboro, VT 05350. 802-423-5405 9AM-3PM.

## Richford Town

Real Estate Recording, Richford Town Clerk, Main St., Town Hall, Richford, VT 05476. 802-848-7751 8:30AM-4PM (F open until 5PM).

## Richmond Town

Real Estate Recording, Richmond Town Clerk, Bridge St., Richmond, VT 05477. 802-434-2221 8AM-4PM M-W; 8AM-5PM Th; 8AM-1PM F.

## Ripton Town

Real Estate Recording, Ripton Town Clerk, Rte 125, Ripton, VT 05766. 802-388-2266 2PM-6PM M; 9AM-1PM T,W,Th,F.

## Rochester Town

Real Estate Recording, Rochester Town Clerk, School St., Rochester, VT 05767. 802-767-3631 8AM-4PM.

## Rockingham Town

Real Estate Recording, Rockingham Town Clerk, Municipal in the Square, Bellows Falls, VT 05101. 802-463-4336 8:30AM-4:30PM.

## Roxbury Town

Real Estate Recording, Roxbury Town Clerk, Rt 12A, Roxbury, VT 05669. 802-485-7840 M,W-F 8AM-Noon.

## Royalton Town

Real Estate Recording, Royalton Town Clerk, Basement - Royalton Memorial Library, Safford Street, South Royalton, VT 05068. 802-763-7207

## Rupert Town

Real Estate Recording, Rupert Town Clerk, Route 153, Sherman's Store Complex, West Rupert, VT 05776. 802-394-7728 12:30PM-5PM M,T,Th.

## Rutland City

Real Estate Recording, Rutland City Clerk, 1 Strongs Avenue, City Hall, Rutland, VT 05701. 802-773-1801 9AM-Noon, 1-4:45PM.

## Rutland County

**Superior Court**, 83 Center St, Rutland, VT 05702. 802-388-7741 (EST) 8AM-4:30PM. Civil, Eviction.

**District Court**, 92 State St (PO Box 427), Rutland, VT 05702. 802-773-5880 (EST) 8AM-4:30PM. Felony, Misdemeanor, Small Claims.

**Probate Court-Fair Haven District**, North Park Place, Fair Haven, VT 05743. 802-265-3380 (EST) 8AM-4PM. Probate.

**Probate Court-Rutland District**, PO Box 339, Rutland, VT 05702. 802-775-0114 (EST) 8AM-4:30PM. Probate.

## Rutland Town

Real Estate Recording, Rutland Town Clerk, Route 4 West, Center Rutland, VT 05736. 802-773-2528 8AM-4:30PM.

## Ryegate Town

Real Estate Recording, Ryegate Town Clerk, Town Highway #1, Bayley-Hazen Road, Ryegate, VT 05042. 802-584-3880

## Salisbury Town

Real Estate Recording, Salisbury Town Clerk, Maple St., Salisbury, VT 05769. 802-352-4228 2PM-6PM M; 9AM-Noon T & F; 9AM-4PM W & Th.

## Sandgate Town

Real Estate Recording, Sandgate Town Clerk, RR 1,, Box 2466, Sandgate, VT 05250. 802-375-9075 10AM-3PM T, W; 7-9PM Wed; Th by appointment.

## Searsburg Town

Real Estate Recording, Searsburg Town Clerk, Route 9, Searsburg, VT 05363. 802-464-8081 8AM-Noon M,T,F.

## Shaftsbury Town

Real Estate Recording, Shaftsbury Town Clerk, East St., Shaftsbury, VT 05262. 802-442-4038 8AM-4PM M; 9AM-2PM T-F.

### Sharon Town

**Real Estate Recording**, Sharon Town Clerk, Rt 132, Sharon, VT 05065. 802-763-8268 7:30AM-12:30PM, 1:30-6PM T & Th; 7:30AM-12:30PM Wed.

### Sheffield Town

**Real Estate Recording**, Sheffield Town Clerk, Town Highway #32, Sheffield, VT 05866. 802-626-8862 9AM-2PM.

### Shelburne Town

**Real Estate Recording**, Shelburne Town Clerk, Route 7, Town Hall, Shelburne, VT 05482. 802-985-5116 8:30AM-4:30PM.

### Sheldon Town

**Real Estate Recording**, Sheldon Town Clerk, Main St., Sheldon, VT 05483. 802-933-2524

### Sherburne Town

**Real Estate Recording**, Sherburne Town Clerk, River Road, Killington, VT 05751. 802-422-3243 9AM-3PM.

### Shoreham Town

**Real Estate Recording**, Shoreham Town Clerk, Main Street, Shoreham, VT 05770. 802-897-5841 9AM-4PM.

### Shrewsbury Town

**Real Estate Recording**, Shrewsbury Town Clerk, RR 1, Box 658, Cuttingsville, VT 05738. 802-492-3511 12:30-4:30PM M,T,F; 12:30PM-4PM Th.

### South Burlington City

**Real Estate Recording**, South Burlington City Clerk, 575 Dorset Street, City Hall, South Burlington, VT 05403. 802-658-7952 8AM-4:30PM.

### South Hero Town

**Real Estate Recording**, South Hero Town Clerk, 333 Rt.2, South Hero, VT 05486. 802-372-5552 8:30AM-Noon, 1PM-4PM M-W; 8:30AM-Noon,1:30-6PM Th.

### Springfield Town

**Real Estate Recording**, Springfield Town Clerk, 96 Main Street, Springfield, VT 05156. 802-885-2104 8AM-4:30PM.

### St. Albans City

**Real Estate Recording**, St. Albans City Clerk, 100 N. Main, St. Albans, VT 05478. 802-524-1501 7:30AM-4PM.

### St. Albans Town

**Real Estate Recording**, St. Albans Town Clerk, Lake Road, St. Albans Bay, VT 05481. 802-524-9609 9AM-5PM M,T,Th,F; 9AM-Noon W.

### St. George Town

**Real Estate Recording**, St. George Town Clerk, RR 2, Box 455, Williston, VT 05495. 802-482-2522 4:30-8PM.

### St. Johnsbury Town

**Real Estate Recording**, St. Johnsbury Town Clerk, 34 Main Street, St. Johnsbury, VT 05819. 802-748-4331 8AM-5PM (May-September 7AM-4PM).

### Stamford Town

**Real Estate Recording**, Stamford Town Clerk, RR 1, Box 718, Stamford, VT 05352. 802-694-1361 11AM-4PM T & W; Noon-4PM, 7-9pm Th; Noon-4pm F.

### Stannard Town

**Real Estate Recording**, Stannard Town Clerk, Yolande Salo's House, Greensboro Bend, VT 05842. 802-533-2577 2PM-6PM M.

### Starksboro Town

**Real Estate Recording**, Starksboro Town Clerk, Rt 116, Starksboro, VT 05487. 802-453-2639

### Stockbridge Town

**Real Estate Recording**, Stockbridge Town Clerk, Blackmer Blvd., Stockbridge, VT 05772. 802-234-9371 9AM-3PM T,Th; 9AM-Noon W,F.

### Stowe Town

**Real Estate Recording**, Stowe Town Clerk, 67 Main St., Stowe, VT 05672. 802-253-6133 8AM-4:30PM.

### Strafford Town

**Real Estate Recording**, Strafford Town Clerk, Justin Morrill Highway, Strafford, VT 05072. 802-765-4411

### Stratton Town

**Real Estate Recording**, Stratton Town Clerk, West Jamaica Rd., West Wardsboro, VT 05360. 802-896-6184 9AM-Noon, 1-3PM M-Th.

### Sudbury Town

**Real Estate Recording**, Sudbury Town Clerk, RR 1, Box 1238, Sudbury, VT 05733. 802-623-7296 9AM-4PM M; 9AM-4PM W; 9AM-1PM Th.

### Sunderland Town

**Real Estate Recording**, Sunderland Town Clerk, South Rd., Sunderland, VT 05252. 802-375-6106 8AM-2PM M,T,Th,F; 8AM-Noon, 6-8PM W.

### Sutton Town

**Real Estate Recording**, Sutton Town Clerk, State Aid #1, Sutton, VT 05867. 802-467-3377

### Swanton Town

**Real Estate Recording**, Swanton Town Clerk, Academy Street, Swanton, VT 05488. 802-868-4421 9AM-5PM.

### Thetford Town

**Real Estate Recording**, Thetford Town Clerk, Rt. 113, Thetford Center, VT 05075. 802-785-2922 7PM-9PM M; 8AM-3PM T-F.

### Tinmouth Town

**Real Estate Recording**, Tinmouth Town Clerk, RR 1, Box 551, Wallingford, VT 05773. 802-446-2460 8AM-Noon, 1-4PM M & Th.

### Topsham Town

**Real Estate Recording**, Topsham Town Clerk, Town Hall, West Topsham, VT 05086. 802-439-5505 10AM-2PM M,T.

### Townshend Town

**Real Estate Recording**, Townshend Town Clerk, Rte 30, Town Hall, Townshend, VT 05353. 802-365-7300

### Troy Town

**Real Estate Recording**, Troy Town Clerk, Main Street, North Troy, VT 05859. 802-988-2663

### Tunbridge Town

**Real Estate Recording**, Tunbridge Town Clerk, Main St., Tunbridge, VT 05077. 802-889-5521 9:30AM-Noon, 1-4PM.

### Underhill Town

**Real Estate Recording**, Underhill Town Clerk, Main St., Town Hall, Underhill Center, VT 05490. 802-899-4434 8AM-4PM M,T,Th,F; 8AM-7PM W.

### Vergennes City

**Real Estate Recording**, Vergennes City Clerk, 120 Main St., Vergennes, VT 05491. 802-877-2841 8AM-4:30PM.

### Vernon Town

**Real Estate Recording**, Vernon Town Clerk, Rt.142, Vernon, VT 05354. 802-257-0292 8:30AM-4PM M-W; 8:30AM-6:30PM Th; 8:30AM-4PM F.

### Vershire Town

**Real Estate Recording**, Vershire Town Clerk, RR 1, Box 66C, Vershire, VT 05079. 802-685-2227 8AM-2:30PM T-Th.

### Victory Town

**Real Estate Recording**, Victory Town Clerk, E. Finkle - River Rd., North Concord, VT 05858. 802-328-2400 By Appointment.

### Waitsfield Town

**Real Estate Recording**, Waitsfield Town Clerk, RD, Box 390, Bridge Street, Waitsfield, VT 05673. 802-496-2218 9AM-Noon,1-4PM.

### Walden Town

**Real Estate Recording**, Walden Town Clerk, RR 1, Box 57, West Danville, VT 05873. 802-563-2220 9:30AM-4PM M,T,Th,F.

### Wallingford Town

**Real Estate Recording**, Wallingford Town Clerk, School St., Wallingford, VT 05773. 802-446-2336

## Waltham Town

**Real Estate Recording**, Waltham Town Clerk, Call for Directions, Vergennes, VT 05491. 802-877-3641 5PM-7PM Th; 9AM-1PM Sat.

## Wardsboro Town

**Real Estate Recording**, Wardsboro Town Clerk, Main St., Wardsboro, VT 05355. 802-896-6055 9AM-Noon, 1-4:30PM (Closed F).

## Warren Town

**Real Estate Recording**, Warren Town Clerk, Main St., Town Clerk, Warren, VT 05674. 802-496-2709 9AM-4:30PM.

## Washington County

**Superior Court**, Box 426, Montpelier, VT 05602. 802-828-2091 (EST) 8AM-4:30PM. Civil, Eviction.

**District Court**, 255 N Main, Barre, VT 05641. 802-479-4252 (EST) 8AM-4:30PM. Felony, Misdemeanor, Small Claims.

**Probate Court**, PO Box 15, Montpelier, VT 05601. 802-828-3405 (EST) 8AM-4:30PM M-Th, 8AM-4PM F. Probate.

## Washington Town

**Real Estate Recording**, Washington Town Clerk, Clerk's Office, Washington, VT 05675. 802-883-2218 8:30AM-2PM M,T.

## Waterbury Town

**Real Estate Recording**, Waterbury Town Clerk, 51 South Main Street, Waterbury, VT 05676. 802-244-8447 8AM-5PM.

## Waterford Town

**Real Estate Recording**, Waterford Town Clerk, State Aid #2, Lower Waterford, VT 05848. 802-748-2122 8:30AM-3:30PM M,Th,F; Noon-6PM T.

## Waterville Town

**Real Estate Recording**, Waterville Town Clerk, 102 Main St., Waterville, VT 05492. 802-644-5758

## Weathersfield Town

**Real Estate Recording**, Weathersfield Town Clerk, Rt. 5, Ascutney Village at Martin Memorial Hall, Ascutney, VT 05030. 802-674-2626 9AM-4PM M-Th.

## Wells Town

**Real Estate Recording**, Wells Town Clerk, Rt.30, Wells, VT 05774. 802-645-0486 9AM-1PM.

## West Fairlee Town

**Real Estate Recording**, West Fairlee Town Clerk, Rt 113, Town Clerk, West Fairlee, VT 05083. 802-333-9696 10AM-4PM M,W,F.

## West Haven Town

**Real Estate Recording**, West Haven Town Clerk, RFD, Box 3954, Fair Haven, VT 05743. 802-265-2080

## West Rutland Town

**Real Estate Recording**, West Rutland Town Clerk, Corner of Main and Marble, West Rutland, VT 05777. 802-438-2204 9AM-Noon, 1PM-3PM M-Th; Fri by appointment.

## West Windsor Town

**Real Estate Recording**, West Windsor Town Clerk, Rt. 44 & Hartland-Brownsville Rd., Brownsville, VT 05037. 802-484-7212 9AM-Noon, 1:30PM-4:30PM M,T,Th; 9AM-Noon, 1:30-4:30PM & 7-9PM W; 9AM-Noon Fri.

## Westfield Town

**Real Estate Recording**, Westfield Town Clerk, RR 1 Box 171, Westfield, VT 05874. 802-744-2484 8AM-Noon, 1PM-5PM M-Th.

## Westford Town

**Real Estate Recording**, Westford Town Clerk, RR 1, Box 30, Westford, VT 05494. 802-878-4587 8:30AM-4:30PM.

## Westminster Town

**Real Estate Recording**, Westminster Town Clerk, Rt. 5, Town Hall, Westminster, VT 05158. 802-722-4091 8:30AM-4PM M,W,F; 8:30AM-4PM, 5:30-9PM T.

## Westmore Town

**Real Estate Recording**, Westmore Town Clerk, RFD 2, Box 854, Orleans, VT 05860. 802-525-3007 9AM-Noon, 1PM-4PM M-Th.

## Weston Town

**Real Estate Recording**, Weston Town Clerk, On The Green, Town Clerk, Weston, VT 05161. 802-824-6645 9AM-1PM.

## Weybridge Town

**Real Estate Recording**, Weybridge Town Clerk, RD 1, Middlebury, VT 05753. 802-545-2450

## Wheelock Town

**Real Estate Recording**, Wheelock Town Clerk, Rt.122, Wheelock, VT 05851. 802-626-9094 9AM-3PM.

## Whiting Town

**Real Estate Recording**, Whiting Town Clerk, RR 1, Box 24, Whiting, VT 05778. 802-623-7813

## Whitingham Town

**Real Estate Recording**, Whitingham Town Clerk, Municipal Center, Jacksonville, VT 05342. 802-368-7887 9AM-2PM T-F; 9AM-2PM, 5:30-7:30PM W; 1st Sat of month 9AM-2pm.

## Williamstown Town

**Real Estate Recording**, Williamstown Town Clerk, Main Street, Williamstown, VT 05679. 802-433-5455 8AM-Noon, 1PM-4PM M,T,Th,F; 8AM-Noon, 1-5:30PM Wed.

## Williston Town

**Real Estate Recording**, Williston Town Clerk, 722 Williston Rd., Williston, VT 05495. 802-878-5121 8AM-4:30PM.

## Wilmington Town

**Real Estate Recording**, Wilmington Town Clerk, Main Street, Wilmington, VT 05363. 802-464-5836 8AM-Noon, 1PM-4PM.

## Windham County

**Superior Court**, Box 207, Newfane, VT 05345. 802-365-7979 (EST) 9AM-4PM. Civil, Eviction.

**District Court**, 6 Putney Rd, Brattleboro, VT 05301. 802-257-2800 (EST) 8AM-4:30PM. Felony, Misdemeanor, Small Claims.

**Probate Court-Westminster District**, PO Box 47, Bellows Falls, VT 05101. 802-463-3019 (EST) Probate.

**Probate Court-Marlboro District**, West River Rd(PO Box 523), Brattleboro, VT 05301. 802-257-2898 (EST) 8AM-4:30PM. Probate.

## Windham Town

**Real Estate Recording**, Windham Town Clerk, RR 1, Box 109, West Townshend, VT 05359. 802-874-4211 10AM-3PM T,Th,F.

## Windsor County

**Superior Court**, Box 458, Woodstock, VT 05091. 802-457-2121 (EST) 8AM-4:30PM. Civil, Eviction.

**District Court**, Windsor Circuit Unit 1, White River Junction, VT 05001. 802-295-8865 (EST) 8AM-4:30PM. Felony, Misdemeanor, Small Claims.

**Probate Court-Eindson District**, Cota & Cota Bldg Rte 106(PO Box 402), North Springfield, VT 05150. 802-886-2284 (EST) Probate.

**Probate Court-Hartford District**, Windsor Circuit Unit 1, White River Junction, VT 05001. 802-457-1503 (EST) 8AM-4:30PM. Probate.

## Windsor Town

**Real Estate Recording**, Windsor Town Clerk, 147 Main Street, Windsor, VT 05089. 802-674-5610 8AM-4PM (F open until 3:30PM).

## Winhall Town

**Real Estate Recording**, Winhall Town Clerk, River Rd., Bondville, VT 05340. 802-297-2122 9AM-Noon (Closed Th).

## Winooski City

**Real Estate Recording**, Winooski City Clerk, 27 West Allen Street, Winooski, VT 05404. 802-655-6419 8AM-5PM.

## Wolcott Town

**Real Estate Recording**, Wolcott Town Clerk, Main Street, Wolcott, VT 05680. 802-888-2746 8AM-3PM T-F; 6-8PM Tue.

## Woodbury Town

**Real Estate Recording**, Woodbury Town Clerk, Rt 14, Town Clerk, Woodbury, VT 05681. 802-456-7051 8:30AM-1PM T-Th; 6-8PM Th evening.

**County Records**

### Woodford Town

**Real Estate Recording**, Woodford Town Clerk, HRC 65 Box 600, Bennington, VT 05201. 802-442-4895 8:30AM-Noon M-Th.

### Woodstock Town

**Real Estate Recording**, Woodstock Town Clerk, 31 The Green, Woodstock, VT 05091. 802-457-3611 8:30AM-Noon, 1-3:30PM.

### Worcester Town

**Real Estate Recording**, Worcester Town Clerk, Vermont Rte. 12, Worcester, VT 05682. 802-223-6942 8AM-12, 1PM-3PM M,T,Th; 8AM-1PM F; 8AM-10AM Sat.

ic.

# Virginia

## Accomack County

**Real Estate Recording**, Accomack County Clerk of the Circuit Court, 23316 Courthouse Avenue, Accomac, VA 23301. 804-787-5776 (EST) 9AM-5PM.

**2nd Circuit Court**, PO Box 126, Accomac, VA 23301. 804-787-5776 (EST) Felony, Civil Actions Over $10,000, Probate.

**2A General District Court**, PO Box 276, Accomac, VA 23301. 804-787-5785 (EST) 9AM-5PM. Misdemeanor, Civil Actions Under $10,000, Small Claims.

## Albemarle County

**Real Estate Recording**, Albemarle County Clerk of the Circuit Court, 501 E. Jefferson St., Room 225, Charlottesville, VA 22902-5176. 804-972-4084 (EST) 8:30AM-4:30PM.

**16th Circuit and District Court**, 501 E Jefferson St, Charlottesville, VA 22902. 804-295-3182 (EST) 8:30AM-4:30PM. Felony, Misdemeanor, Civil, Eviction, Probate.

## Alexandria City

**Real Estate Recording**, Alexandria City Clerk of the Circuit Court, 520 King Street, Room 307, Alexandria, VA 22314. 703-838-4070 (EST) 9AM-5PM.

**10th Circuit Court**, 520 King St. #307, Alexandria, VA 22314. 703-838-4044 (EST) 9AM-5PM. Felony, Civil Actions Over $10,000, Probate.

**10th General District Court**, 520 King St #201, Alexandria, VA 22314. 703-838-4010 (EST) 8AM-4PM. Misdemeanor, Civil Actions Under $10,000, Small Claims.

## Alleghany County

**Real Estate Recording**, Alleghany County Clerk of the Circuit Court, 266 West Main Street, Covington, VA 24426. 703-965-1730 (EST) 9AM-5PM; 9AM-Noon Sat.

**25th Circuit Court**, PO Box 670, Covington, VA 24426. 703-965-1730 (EST) 9AM-5PM. Felony, Civil Actions Over $10,000, Probate.

**25th General District Court**, PO Box 139, Covington, VA 24426. 703-965-1720 (EST) 9AM-5PM. Misdemeanor, Civil Actions Under $10,000, Small Claims.

## Amelia County

**Real Estate Recording**, Amelia County Clerk of the Circuit Court, 16441 Court St., Courthouse, Amelia Court House, VA 23002. 804-561-2128 (EST) 8:30AM-4:30PM.

**11th Circuit Court**, PO Box 237, Amelia, VA 23002. 804-561-2128 (EST) 8:30AM-4:30PM. Felony, Civil Actions Over $10,000, Probate.

**11th General District Court**, PO Box 24, Amelia, VA 23002. 804-561-2456 (EST) 8:15AM-4:30PM. Misdemeanor, Civil Actions Under $10,000, Small Claims.

## Amherst County

**Real Estate Recording**, Amherst County Clerk of the Circuit Court, 100 East Court Street, Courthouse, Amherst, VA 24521. 804-946-9321 (EST)

**25th Circuit Court**, PO Box 462, Amherst, VA 24521. 804-929-9321 (EST) 8AM-5PM. Felony, Civil Actions Over $10,000, Probate.

**25th General District Court**, PO Box 513, Amherst, VA 24521. 804-956-9351 (EST) 8AM-5PM. Misdemeanor, Civil Actions Under $10,000, Small Claims.

## Appomattox County

**Real Estate Recording**, Appomattox County Clerk of the Circuit Court, Courthouse Square, Court Street, Appomattox, VA 24522. 804-352-5275 (EST) 8:30AM-4:30PM.

**10th Circuit Court**, PO Box 672, Appomattox, VA 24522. 804-352-5275 (EST) 8:30AM-4:30PM. Felony, Civil Actions Over $10,000, Probate.

**10th General District Court**, PO Box 187, Appomattox, VA 24522. 804-352-5540 (EST) 8:30AM-4:30PM. Misdemeanor, Civil Actions Under $10,000, Small Claims.

## Arlington County

**Real Estate Recording**, Arlington County Clerk of the Circuit Court, 1400 North Courthouse Road, Room 106, Arlington, VA 22201. 703-358-7242 (EST)

**17th Circuit Court**, 1435 N Courthouse, Arlington, VA 22201. 703-358-7010 (EST) 8AM-5PM. Felony, Civil Actions Over $10,000, Probate.

**17th General District Court**, 1435 N Courthouse Rd, Arlington, VA 22201. 703-358-4590 (EST) 8AM-4PM. Misdemeanor, Civil Actions Under $10,000, Small Claims.

## Augusta County

**Real Estate Recording**, Augusta County Clerk of the Circuit Court, 1 East Johnson Street, Courthouse, Staunton, VA 24401. 703-245-5321 (EST) 8AM-5PM.

**25th Circuit Court**, PO Box 689, Staunton, VA 24401. 703-245-5321 (EST) Felony, Civil Actions Over $10,000, Probate.

**25th General District Court**, 6 E Johnson St, 2nd Floor, Staunton, VA 24401. 703-245-5300 (EST) 8:30AM-4:30PM. Misdemeanor, Civil Actions Under $10,000, Small Claims.

## Bath County

**Real Estate Recording**, Bath County Clerk of the Circuit Court, Courthouse, Room 101, Warm Springs, VA 24484. 703-839-7226 (EST) 8:30AM-4:30PM.

**25th Circuit Court**, PO Box 180, Warm Springs, VA 24484. 703-839-7226 (EST) 8:30AM-4:30PM. Felony, Civil Actions Over $10,000, Probate.

**25th General District Court**, PO Box 96, Warm Springs, VA 24484. 703-839-7241 (EST) 8AM-4:30PM. Misdemeanor, Civil Actions Under $10,000, Small Claims.

## Bedford City

**Circuit and District Courts**, See Bedford County.

## Bedford County

**Real Estate Recording**, Bedford County Clerk of the Circuit Court, Main Street, Courthouse, Bedford, VA 24523. 703-586-7632 (EST) 8:30AM-5PM.

**24th Circuit Court**, PO Box 235, Bedford, VA 24523. 703-586-7632 (EST) 8:30AM-4:30PM. Felony, Civil Actions Over $10,000, Probate.

**24th General District Court**, Courthouse Building, Main St, Rm 204, Bedford, VA 24523. 703-586-7637 (EST) 8AM-4:30PM. Misdemeanor, Civil Actions Under $10,000, Small Claims.

## Bland County

**Real Estate Recording**, Bland County Clerk of the Circuit Court, Main Street, Courthouse, Bland, VA 24315. 703-688-4562 (EST) 8:30AM-5PM.

**27th Circuit Court**, PO Box 295, Bland, VA 24315. 703-688-4562 (EST) 8:30AM-5PM. Felony, Civil Actions Over $10,000, Probate.

**27th General District Court**, PO Box 157, Bland, VA 24315. 703-688-4433 (EST) 8AM-5PM. Misdemeanor, Civil Actions Under $10,000, Small Claims.

## Botetourt County

**Real Estate Recording**, Botetourt County Clerk of the Circuit Court, Main St. and Roanoke St., Courthouse, Fincastle, VA 24090. 703-473-8274 (EST) 8:30AM-4:30PM.

**25th Circuit Court**, PO Box 219, Fincastle, VA 24090. 703-473-8274 (EST) Felony, Civil Actions Over $10,000, Probate.

**25th General District Court**, PO Box 205, Fincastle, VA 24090. 703-992-8244 (EST) 8AM-4PM. Misdemeanor, Civil Actions Under $10,000, Small Claims.

## Bristol City

**Real Estate Recording**, Bristol City Clerk of the Circuit Court, 497 Cumberland Street, Room 210, Bristol, VA 24201. 703-645-7321 (EST) 9AM-5PM.

**28th Circuit Court**, 497 Cumberland St, Bristol, VA 24201. 703-466-2221 (EST) 9AM-5PM. Felony, Civil Actions Over $10,000, Probate.

**28th General District Court**, 497 Cumberland St, Bristol, VA 24201. 703-645-7341 (EST) 8:30AM-5PM. Misdemeanor, Civil Actions Under $10,000, Small Claims.

## Brunswick County

**Real Estate Recording**, Brunswick County Circuit Court, 216 N. Main St., Lawrenceville, VA 23868. 804-848-2215 (EST) 8:30AM-5PM.

**6th Circuit and District Court**, 216 N Main St, Lawrenceville, VA 23868. 804-848-2215 (EST) 8:30AM-5PM. Felony, Misdemeanor, Civil, Eviction, Probate.

## Buchanan County

**Real Estate Recording**, Buchanan County Clerk of the Circuit Court, Courthouse, 2nd Floor, Grundy, VA 24614. 703-935-6567 (EST) 8:30AM-5PM.

**29th Circuit and District Court**, PO Box 929, Grundy, VA 24614. 703-935-6575 (EST) 8:30AM-5PM. Felony, Misdemeanor, Civil, Eviction, Probate.

## Buckingham County

**Real Estate Recording**, Buckingham County Clerk of the Circuit Court, Highway 60, Courthouse, Buckingham, VA 23921. 804-969-4734 (EST) 8:30AM-4:30PM.

**10th Circuit Court**, PO Box 107, Buckingham, VA 23921. 804-969-4734 (EST) 8:30AM-4:30PM. Felony, Civil Actions Over $10,000, Probate.

**10th General District Court**, PO Box 127, Buckingham, VA 23921. 804-969-4755 (EST) 8:30AM-4:30PM. Misdemeanor, Civil Actions Under $10,000, Small Claims.

## Buena Vista City

**Real Estate Recording**, Clerk of Circuit Court, 2039 Sycamore Ave., Buena Visa, VA 24416. 703-261-6121 (EST) 8:30AM-5PM.

**25th Circuit and District Court**, 2039 Sycamore Ave, Buena Vista, VA 24416. 703-261-6121 (EST) 8:30AM-5PM. Felony, Misdemeanor, Civil, Eviction, Probate.

## Campbell County

**Real Estate Recording**, Campbell County Clerk of the Circuit Court, Main Street, New Courthouse, Rustburg, VA 24588-0007. 804-847-0961 (EST) X126 8:30AM-4:30PM.

**24th Circuit Court**, PO Box 7, Rustburg, VA 24588. 804-332-5161 (EST) 8:30AM-4:30PM. Felony, Civil Actions Over $10,000, Probate.

**24th General District Court**, Campbell County Courthouse, Rustburg, VA 24588. 804-332-5161 (EST) 8:30AM-4:30PM. Misdemeanor, Civil Actions Under $10,000, Small Claims.

## Caroline County

**Real Estate Recording**, Caroline County Clerk of the Circuit Court, Main St. & Courthouse Lane, Bowling Green, VA 22427. 804-633-5800 (EST) 8:30AM-5PM (Recording Hours 8:30AM-4:30PM).

**15th Circuit Court**, PO Box 309, Bowling Green, VA 22427. 804-633-5800 (EST) 8AM-4:30PM. Felony, Civil Actions Over $10,000, Probate.

**15th General District Court**, PO Box 511, Bowling Green, VA 22427. 804-633-5720 (EST) 8AM-4:30PM. Misdemeanor, Civil Actions Under $10,000, Small Claims.

## Carroll County

**Real Estate Recording**, Carroll County Clerk of the Circuit Court, 515 Main Street, Courthouse, Hillsville, VA 24343. 703-728-3117 (EST) 8AM-5PM.

**27th Circuit Court**, PO Box 218, Hillsville, VA 24343. 703-728-3117 (EST) 8AM-5PM. Felony, Civil Actions Over $10,000, Probate.

**27th General District Court**, PO Box 698, Hillsville, VA 24343. 703-728-7751 (EST) 8AM-4:30PM. Misdemeanor, Civil Actions Under $10,000, Small Claims.

## Charles City

**9th General District Court**, Charles City Courthouse, Charles City, VA 23030. 804-829-9211 (EST) 8:30AM-4:30PM. Misdemeanor, Civil Actions Under $10,000, Small Claims.

## Charles City County

**Real Estate Recording**, Charles City County Clerk of the Circuit Court, 10700 Courthouse Road, Intersection of Rts 5 and 155, Charles City, VA 23030. 804-829-9212 (EST) 8:30AM-4:30PM.

**9th Circuit Court**, PO Box 86, Charles City, VA 23030-0086. 804-829-2401 (EST) 8:30AM-4:30PM. Felony, Civil Actions Over $10,000, Probate.

## Charlotte County

**Real Estate Recording**, Charlotte County Clerk of the Circuit Court, Courthouse, Charlotte Court House, VA 23923. 804-542-5147 (EST) 8:30AM-4:30PM.

**10th Circuit Court**, PO Box 38, Charlotte Court, VA 23923. 804-542-5147 (EST) 8:30AM-4PM. Felony, Civil Actions Over $10,000, Probate.

**10th General District Court**, Charlotte County Courthouse and PO Box 1, Charlotte Court, VA 23923. 804-542-5600 (EST) 8:30AM-4:30PM. Misdemeanor, Civil Actions Under $10,000, Small Claims.

## Charlottesville City

**Real Estate Recording**, Charlottesville City Clerk of the Circuit Court, 315 East High Street, Charlottesville, VA 22901. 804-972-4084 (EST) 8:30AM-4:30PM.

**16th Circuit Court**, 315 E High St, Charlottesville, VA 22901. 804-295-3182 (EST) 8:30AM-4:30PM. Felony, Civil Actions Over $10,000, Probate.

**16th General District Court**, 606 E Market St, Charlottesville, VA 22902. 804-971-3385 (EST) Misdemeanor, Civil Actions Under $10,000, Small Claims.

## Chesapeake City

**Real Estate Recording**, Chesapeake Clerk of the Circuit Court, 300 Cedar Road, Chesapeake, VA 23320. 804-547-6111 (EST) 9AM-5PM.

**1st Circuit Court**, PO Box 15205, Chesapeake, VA 23320. 804-547-6111 (EST) 9AM-5PM. Felony, Civil Actions Over $10,000, Probate.

**1st General District Court**, PO Box 15205, Chesapeake, VA 23320. 804-547-6396 (EST) 9AM-5PM. Misdemeanor, Civil Actions Under $10,000, Small Claims.

## Chesterfield County

**Real Estate Recording**, Chesterfield County Clerk of the Circuit Court, 9500 Courthouse Road, Chesterfield, VA 23832. 804-748-1243 (EST) 8:30AM-5PM (Recording hours: 8:30AM-4PM M-Th; 8:30AM-3PM F).

**12th Circuit Court**, PO Box 125, Chesterfield, VA 23832. 804-748-1406 (EST) 8:30AM-5PM. Felony, Civil Actions Over $10,000, Probate.

**12th General District Court**, PO Box 144, Chesterfield, VA 23832. 804-748-1231 (EST) 8AM-4:30PM. Misdemeanor, Civil Actions Under $10,000, Small Claims.

## Clarke County

**Real Estate Recording**, Clarke County Clerk of the Circuit Court, 102 North Church Street, Courthouse, Berryville, VA 22611. 703-955-5116 (EST) 9AM-5PM.

**26th Circuit Court**, PO Box 189, Berryville, VA 22611. 703-955-5116 (EST) 9AM-5PM. Felony, Civil Actions Over $10,000, Probate.

**26th General District Court**, 1104 N Church St (PO Box 612), Berryville, VA 22611. 703-955-5128 (EST) 8:30AM-4:30PM. Misdemeanor, Civil Actions Under $10,000, Small Claims.

## Clifton Forge City

**Real Estate Recording**, Clifton Forge City Clerk of the Circuit Court, 547 Main St., Clifton Forge, VA 24422. 703-863-2508 (EST) 9AM-5PM.

**25th Circuit Court**, PO Box 27, Clifton Forge, VA 24422. 703-863-8536 (EST) 9AM-5PM. Felony, Civil Actions Over $10,000, Probate.

**25th General District Court**, 547 Main St, Clifton Forge, VA 24422. 703-863-2510 (EST) 9AM-5PM. Misdemeanor, Civil Actions Under $10,000, Small Claims.

## Colonial Heights City

**Real Estate Recording**, Clerk, Colonial Heights Circuit Court, 401 Temple Avenue, Courthouse, Colonial Heights, VA 23834. 804-520-9364 (EST) 8:30AM-5PM.

**12th Circuit Court**, 401 Temple Ave, Colonial Heights, VA 23834. 804-520-9364 (EST) 8:30AM-5PM. Felony, Civil Actions Over $10,000, Probate.

**12th General District Court**, 401 Temple Ave, Colonial Heights, VA 23834. 804-520-9346 (EST) 8:30AM-5PM. Misdemeanor, Civil Actions Under $10,000, Small Claims.

## Covington City

**Real Estate Recording**, Alleghany County Clerk of the Circuit Court, 266 West Main Street, Covington, VA 24426. 703-965-1730 (EST) 9AM-5PM; 9AM-Noon Sat.

**Circuit and District Courts**, See Alleghany County.

## Craig County

**Real Estate Recording**, Craig County Clerk of the Circuit Court, 303 Main Street, Courthouse, New Castle, VA 24127. 703-864-6141 (EST) 9AM-5PM.

**25th Circuit Court**, PO Box 185, New Castle, VA 24127. 703-864-6141 (EST) 9AM-5PM. Felony, Civil Actions Over $10,000, Probate.

**25th General District Court**, PO Box 232, New Castle, VA 24127. 703-864-5989 (EST) 8:15AM-4:45PM. Misdemeanor, Civil Actions Under $10,000, Small Claims.

## Culpeper County

**Real Estate Recording**, Culpeper County Clerk of the Circuit Court, 135 West Cameron Street, Culpeper, VA 22701. 703-825-8086 (EST) 8:30AM-4:30PM.

**16th Circuit Court**, 135 W Cameron St, Culpeper, VA 22701. 703-825-8086 (EST) 8:30AM-4:30PM. Felony, Civil Actions Over $10,000, Probate.

**16th General District Court**, 135 W Cameron St, Culpeper, VA 22701. 703-825-0065 (EST) 8:30AM-4:30PM. Misdemeanor, Civil Actions Under $10,000, Small Claims.

## Cumberland County

**Real Estate Recording**, Cumberland County Clerk of the Circuit Court, County Office Building, Cumberland, VA 23040. 804-492-4442 (EST) 9AM-4:30PM.

**10th Circuit Court**, PO Box 8, Cumberland, VA 23040. 804-492-4442 (EST) 9AM-4:30PM. Felony, Civil Actions Over $10,000, Probate.

**10th General District Court**, PO Box 24, Cumberland, VA 23040. 804-492-4848 (EST)

# Virginia

8:30AM-4:30PM. Misdemeanor, Civil Actions Under $10,000, Small Claims.

## Danville City

**Real Estate Recording**, Danville City Clerk of the Circuit Court, 212 Lynn Street, Danville, VA 24541. 804-799-5168 (EST) 8:30AM-5PM.

**22nd Circuit Court**, PO Box 3300, Danville, VA 24543. 804-799-5168 (EST) 8:30AM-5PM. Felony, Civil Actions Over $10,000, Probate.

**22nd General District Court**, PO Box 3300, Danville, VA 24543. 804-799-5179 (EST) Misdemeanor, Civil Actions Under $10,000, Small Claims.

## Dickenson County

**Real Estate Recording**, Dickenson County Clerk of the Circuit Court, Main Street, Courthouse, Clintwood, VA 24228. 703-926-1616 (EST) 8:30AM-4:30PM.

**29th Circuit Court**, PO Box 190, Clintwood, VA 24228. 703-926-1616 (EST) Felony, Civil Actions Over $10,000, Probate.

**29th General District Court**, PO Box 128, Clintwood, VA 24228. 703-926-1630 (EST) 8:30AM-4:30PM. Misdemeanor, Civil Actions Under $10,000, Small Claims.

## Dinwiddie County

**Real Estate Recording**, Dinwiddie County Clerk of the Circuit Court, Courthouse, Dinwiddie, VA 23841. 804-469-4540 (EST) 9AM-5PM.

**11th Circuit Court**, PO Box 63, Dinwiddie, VA 23841. 804-469-4540 (EST) Felony, Civil Actions Over $10,000, Probate.

**11th General District Court**, PO Box 280, Dinwiddie, VA 23841. 804-469-4533 (EST) 9AM-4:30PM. Misdemeanor, Civil Actions Under $10,000, Small Claims.

## Emporia City

**6th General District Court**, 201 S Main, Emporia, VA 23847. 804-634-5400 (EST) 8:30AM-4:30PM. Misdemeanor, Civil Actions Under $10,000, Small Claims.

## Essex County

**Real Estate Recording**, Essex County Clerk of the Circuit Court, 305 Prince Street, Tappahannock, VA 22560. 804-443-3541 (EST) 9AM-5PM.

**15th Circuit Court**, PO Box 445, Tappahannock, VA 22560. 804-443-3541 (EST) 9AM-5PM. Felony, Civil Actions Over $10,000, Probate.

**15th General District Court**, PO Box 66, Tappahannock, VA 22560. 804-443-3744 (EST) 8:30AM-4:30PM. Misdemeanor, Civil Actions Under $10,000, Small Claims.

## Fairfax City

**19th General District Court**, 10455 Armstrong, Fairfax, VA 22030. 703-385-7866 (EST) 8:30AM-4:30PM. Misdemeanor.

## Fairfax County

**Real Estate Recording**, Fairfax County Clerk of the Circuit Court, 4110 Chain Bridge Road, 3rd Floor, Fairfax, VA 22030. 703-246-4100 (EST) 8AM-4PM.

**19th Circuit Court**, 4110 Chain Bridge Rd, Fairfax, VA 22030. 703-246-2228 (EST) 8AM-4PM. Felony, Civil Actions Over $10,000, Probate.

**19th General District Court**, 4110 Chain Bridge Rd, Fairfax, VA 22030. 703-246-2153 (EST) 8AM-4PM. Misdemeanor, Civil Actions Under $10,000, Small Claims.

## Falls Church City

**17th General District Court**, 300 Park Ave, Falls Church, VA 22046. 703-241-5096 (EST) Misdemeanor, Civil Actions Under $10,000, Small Claims.

## Fauquier County

**Real Estate Recording**, Fauquier County Clerk of the Circuit Court, 40 Culpeper Street, Warrenton, VA 22186. 703-347-8608 (EST) 8AM-4:30PM.

**20th Circuit Court**, PO Box 985, Warrenton, VA 22186. 703-347-8610 (EST) 8:30AM-4:30PM. Felony, Civil Actions Over $10,000, Probate.

**20th General District Court**, 6 Court St, Warrenton, VA 22186. 703-347-8676 (EST) 8:30AM-4:30PM. Misdemeanor, Civil Actions Under $10,000, Small Claims.

## Floyd County

**Real Estate Recording**, Floyd County Clerk of the Circuit Court, 100 East Main Street, Room 200, Floyd, VA 24091. 703-745-9330 (EST) 8:30AM-4:30PM; 8:30AM-Noon Sat.

**27th Circuit Court**, 100 East Main St, #200, Floyd, VA 24091. 703-745-9330 (EST) 8:30AM-4:30PM M-F, 8:30AM-12:00PM. Felony, Civil Actions Over $10,000, Probate.

**27th General District Court**, 100 East Main St, Floyd, VA 24091. 703-745-9327 (EST) 8:30AM-4:30PM. Misdemeanor, Civil Actions Under $10,000, Small Claims.

## Fluvanna County

**Real Estate Recording**, Fluvanna County Clerk of the Circuit Court, Clerk's Office Bldg., Court Green & Rt. 15, Palmyra, VA 22963. 804-589-8011 (EST) 8AM-4:30PM.

**16th Circuit Court**, PO Box 299, Palmyra, VA 22963. 804-589-8011 (EST) 8:30AM-4:30PM. Felony, Civil Actions Over $10,000, Probate.

**16th General District Court**, Fluvanna County Courthouse, Palmyra, VA 22963. 804-589-8022 (EST) 8:30AM-4:40PM. Misdemeanor, Civil Actions Under $10,000, Small Claims.

## Franklin City

**22nd General District Court**, PO Box 569, Rocky Mount, VA 24151. 703-483-3060 (EST) 8:30AM-4:30PM. Misdemeanor, Civil Actions Under $10,000, Small Claims.

## Franklin County

**Real Estate Recording**, Franklin County Clerk of the Circuit Court, Courthouse Building, Rocky Mount, VA 24151. 703-483-3065 (EST) 8:30AM-5PM.

**22nd Circuit Court**, PO Box 126, Rocky Mount, VA 24151. 804-653-2200 (EST) Felony, Civil Actions Over $10,000, Probate.

## Frederick County

**Real Estate Recording**, Frederick County Clerk of the Circuit Court, 5 North Kent Street, Winchester, VA 22601. 703-667-5770 (EST) 9AM-5PM.

**26th Circuit and District Court**, 5 North Kent St, Winchester, VA 22601. 703-667-5770 (EST) 9AM-5PM. Felony, Misdemeanor, Civil, Eviction, Probate.

## Fredericksburg City

**Real Estate Recording**, Fredericksburg City Clerk of the Circuit Court, 815 Princess Anne Street, Fredericksburg, VA 22401. 703-372-1066 (EST) 8AM-4PM.

**15th Circuit Court**, PO Box 359, Fredericksburg, VA 22404-0359. 703-372-1066 (EST) 8:30AM-4PM. Felony, Civil Actions Over $10,000, Probate.

**15th General District Court**, PO Box 180, Fredericksburg, VA 22404. 703-372-1044 (EST) 8:30AM-4PM. Misdemeanor, Civil Actions Under $10,000, Small Claims.

## Galax City

**27th General District Court**, City of Galax Courthouse, PO Box 214, Galax, VA 24333. 703-236-8731 (EST) 8:30AM-5PM. Misdemeanor, Civil Actions Under $10,000, Small Claims.

## Giles County

**Real Estate Recording**, Giles County Clerk of the Circuit Court, 501 Wenonah Avenue, Pearisburg, VA 24134-0501. 703-921-1722 (EST) 9AM-5PM.

**27th Circuit Court**, PO Box 502, Pearisburg, VA 24134. 703-921-1722 (EST) 9AM-5PM. Felony, Civil Actions Over $10,000, Probate.

**27th General District Court**, Giles County Courthouse, Pearisburg, VA 24134. 703-921-3533 (EST) 8:30AM-4:30PM. Misdemeanor, Civil Actions Under $10,000, Small Claims.

## Gloucester County

**Real Estate Recording**, Gloucester County Clerk of the Circuit Court, Courts & Office Bldg, Room 207, 6489 Main Street, Gloucester, VA 23061. 804-693-2502 (EST) 8AM-4:30PM.

**9th Circuit Court**, Box N, Gloucester, VA 23061. 804-693-2502 (EST) 8AM-4:30PM. Felony, Civil Actions Over $10,000, Probate.

**9th General District Court**, PO Box 873, Gloucester, VA 23061. 804-693-4860 (EST) 8:30AM-4:30PM. Misdemeanor, Civil Actions Under $10,000, Small Claims.

## Goochland County

**Real Estate Recording**, Goochland County Clerk of the Circuit Court, 2938 River Road West, Goochland, VA 23063. 804-556-5353 (EST) 8:30AM-5PM.

**16th Circuit Court**, PO Box 196, Goochland, VA 23063. 804-556-5353 (EST) 8:30AM-5PM. Felony, Civil Actions Over $10,000, Probate.

**16th General District Court**, PO Box 47, Goochland, VA 23063. 804-556-5309 (EST) 8:30AM-5PM. Misdemeanor, Civil Actions Under $10,000, Small Claims.

## Grayson County

**Real Estate Recording**, Grayson County Clerk of the Circuit Court, 129 Davis Street, Independence, VA 24348. 703-773-2231 (EST) 8AM-5PM.

**27th Circuit Court**, PO Box 130, Independence, VA 24348. 703-773-2231 (EST) 8AM-5PM. Felony, Civil Actions Over $10,000, Probate.

**27th General District Court**, PO Box 280, Independence, VA 24348. 703-773-2011 (EST) 8AM-4:30PM. Misdemeanor, Civil Actions Under $10,000, Small Claims.

## Greene County

**Real Estate Recording**, Greene County Clerk of the Circuit Court, Courthouse, Court Square, Stanardsville, VA 22973. 804-985-5208 (EST) 8:15AM-4:30PM.

**16th Circuit Court**, PO Box 386, Stanardsville, VA 22973. 804-985-5208 (EST) 8:30AM-4:30PM. Felony, Civil Actions Over $10,000, Probate.

**16th General District Court**, Greene County Courthouse (PO Box 245), Stanardsville, VA 22973. 804-985-5225 (EST) 8AM-4:30PM. Misdemeanor, Civil Actions Under $10,000, Small Claims.

## Greensville County

**Real Estate Recording**, Greensville County Clerk of the Circuit Court, 337 South Main Street, Emporia, VA 23847. 804-348-4215 (EST) 9AM-5PM.

**6th Circuit Court**, PO Box 631, Emporia, VA 23847. 804-348-4215 (EST) 9AM-5PM. Felony, Civil Actions Over $10,000, Probate.

**6th General District Court**, Greensville County Courthouse, Emporia, VA 23847. 804-348-4226 (EST) 8:30AM-4:30PM. Misdemeanor, Civil Actions Under $10,000, Small Claims.

## Halifax County

**Real Estate Recording**, Halifax County Clerk of the Circuit Court, Courthouse Square, Halifax, VA 24558. 804-476-6211 (EST)

**10th Circuit Court**, PO Box 729, Halifax, VA 24558. 804-476-6211 (EST) 8:30AM-5PM. Felony, Civil Actions Over $10,000, Probate.

**10th General District Court**, Halifax County Courthouse, Halifax, VA 24558. 804-476-6217 (EST) 8:30AM-4:30PM. Misdemeanor, Civil Actions Under $10,000, Small Claims.

## Hampton City

**Real Estate Recording**, Hampton City Clerk of the Circuit Court, 101 Kingsway Mall, Hampton, VA 23669. 804-727-6896 (EST) 8:30AM-5PM.

**8th Circuit Court**, PO Box 40, Hampton, VA 23669. 804-727-6105 (EST) 8:30AM-4PM. Felony, Civil Actions Over $10,000, Probate.

**8th General District Court**, Courthouse, Hampton, VA 23669. 804-727-6480 (EST) 8:30AM-4PM. Misdemeanor, Civil Actions Under $10,000, Small Claims.

## Hanover County

**Real Estate Recording**, Hanover County Clerk of the Circuit Court, Highway (Rt.) 301 North, Courthouse, Hanover, VA 23069. 804-537-6150 (EST) 8:30AM-4:30PM.

**15th Circuit Court**, PO Box 39, Hanover, VA 23069. 804-537-6151 (EST) 8:30AM-4:30PM. Felony, Civil Actions Over $10,000, Probate.

**15th General District Court**, Hanover County Courthouse and PO Box 176, Hanover, VA 23069. 804-537-6000 (EST) 8AM-4PM. Misdemeanor, Civil Actions Under $10,000, Small Claims.

## Harrisonburg City

**Circuit and District Courts**, See Rockingham County.

## Henrico County

**Real Estate Recording**, Henrico Clerk of the Circuit Court, 4301 Parham Road, Richmond, VA 23228. 804-672-4979 (EST) 8AM-4:30PM; (Recording Hours 8AM-3:30PM).

**14th Circuit Court**, PO Box 27032, Richmond, VA 23273. 804-672-4764 (EST) 8AM-4:30PM. Felony, Civil Actions Over $10,000, Probate.

**14th General District Court**, PO Box 27032, Richmond, VA 23273. 804-672-4721 (EST) 804-672-4141. Misdemeanor, Civil Actions Under $10,000, Small Claims.

## Henry County

**Real Estate Recording**, Henry County Clerk of the Circuit Court, 1 East Main Street, Martinsville, VA 24112. 703-638-3961 (EST) 9AM-5PM.

**21st Circuit Court**, PO Box 1049, Martinsville, VA 24114. 703-638-3961 (EST) 9AM-5PM. Felony, Civil Actions Over $10,000, Probate.

**21st General District Court**, Henry County Courthouse, Martinsville, VA 24114. 703-638-7531 (EST) 9AM-5PM. Misdemeanor, Civil Actions Under $10,000, Small Claims.

## Highland County

**Real Estate Recording**, Highland County Clerk of the Circuit Court, Spruce Street, Courthouse, Monterey, VA 24465. 703-468-2447 (EST) 8:45AM-4:30PM.

**25th Circuit Court**, PO Box 190, Monterey, VA 24465. 703-468-2447 (EST) 8:45AM-4:30PM. Felony, Civil Actions Over $10,000, Probate.

**25th General District Court**, Highland County Courthouse, Monterey, VA 24465. 703-468-2445 (EST) 8:30AM-4:30PM. Misdemeanor, Civil Actions Under $10,000, Small Claims.

## Hopewell City

**Real Estate Recording**, Hopewell City Clerk of the Circuit Court, 100 E. Broadway, Room 251, Hopewell, VA 23860. 804-541-2239 (EST) 8:30AM-4:30PM.

**6th Circuit Court**, PO Box 354, Hopewell, VA 23860. 804-541-2239 (EST) Felony, Civil Actions Over $10,000, Probate.

**6th General District Court**, 100 E Broadway, Hopewell, VA 23860. 804-541-2257 (EST) 8:30AM-4:30PM. Misdemeanor, Civil Actions Under $10,000, Small Claims.

## Isle of Wight County

**Real Estate Recording**, Isle of Wight County Clerk of the Circuit Court, 17122 Monument Circle, Hwy 258, Courthouse, Isle of Wight, VA 23397. 804-357-3191 (EST) X233 9AM-5PM.

**5th Circuit Court**, Courthouse, Isle of Wight, VA 23397. 804-357-3191 (EST) 9AM-5PM. Felony, Civil Actions Over $10,000, Probate.

**5th General District Court**, Isle of Wight Courthouse, Isle of Wight, VA 23397. 804-357-3191 (EST) 8:30AM-5PM. Misdemeanor, Civil Actions Under $10,000, Small Claims.

## James City County

**9th General District Court**, James City County Courthouse, Williamsburg, VA 23187. 804-229-2228 (EST) 7:30AM-4PM. Misdemeanor, Civil Actions Under $10,000, Small Claims.

## James City County

**Real Estate Recording**, Williamsburg-James City County Clerk of the Circuit Court, 321-45 Court Street West, Williamsburg, VA 23185. 804-229-2552 (EST) 8:30AM-4:30PM.

**9th Circuit Court**, PO Box 385, Williamsburg, VA 23187. 804-229-2552 (EST) 8:30AM-4:30PM. Felony, Civil Actions Over $10,000, Probate.

## King George County

**Real Estate Recording**, King George County Clerk of the Circuit Court, 9483 Kings Highway, Courthouse, King George, VA 22485. 703-775-3322 (EST) 8:30AM-4:30PM.

**15th Circuit Court**, PO Box 105, King George, VA 22485. 703-775-3322 (EST) 8:30AM-4:30PM. Felony, Civil Actions Over $10,000, Probate.

**15th General District Court**, King George County Courthouse and PO Box, King George, VA 22485. 703-775-3573 (EST) 8AM-4:30PM. Misdemeanor, Civil Actions Under $10,000, Small Claims.

## King William County

**Real Estate Recording**, King William County Clerk of the Circuit Court, Route 619, King William, VA 23086. 804-769-2311 (EST) 8:30AM-4:30PM.

**9th Circuit Court**, PO Box 216, King William, VA 23086. 804-769-4938 (EST) 8:30AM-4:30PM. Felony, Civil Actions Over $10,000, Probate.

**9th General District Court**, PO Box 5, King William, VA 23086. 804-769-4947 (EST) 8:30AM-4:30PM. Misdemeanor, Civil Actions Under $10,000, Small Claims.

## King and Queen County

**Real Estate Recording**, King and Queen County Clerk of the Circuit Court, Route 681, Courthouse, King and Queen Court House, VA 23085. 804-785-2460 (EST) 9AM-5PM.

**9th Circuit Court**, PO Box 67, King & Queen Court House, VA 23085. 804-785-2460 (EST) 9AM-5PM. Felony, Civil Actions Over $10,000, Probate.

**9th General District Court**, King & Queen County Courthouse, King & Queen Court House, VA 23085. 804-769-4947 (EST) 8:30AM-4:30PM. Misdemeanor, Civil Actions Under $10,000, Small Claims.

## Lancaster County

**Real Estate Recording**, Lancaster County Clerk of the Circuit Court, Courthouse, Route 3, Lancaster, VA 22503. 804-462-5611 (EST)

**15th Circuit Court**, Courthouse Building, Lancaster, VA 22503. 804-462-5611 (EST) 9AM-5PM. Felony, Civil Actions Over $10,000, Probate.

**15th General District Court**, PO 129, Lancaster, VA 22503. 804-462-0012 (EST) 8:30AM-4:30PM. Misdemeanor, Civil Actions Under $10,000, Small Claims.

## Lee County

**Real Estate Recording**, Lee County Clerk of the Circuit Court, Main Street, Courthouse, Jonesville, VA 24263. 703-346-7763 (EST) 8:30AM-5PM; 9AM-Noon Sat.

**30th Circuit Court**, PO Box 326, Jonesville, VA 24263. 703-346-7763 (EST) 8:30AM-5PM M-F, 9AM-12PM Sat. Felony, Civil Actions Over $10,000, Probate.

**30th General District Court**, Lee County Courthouse, Jonesville, VA 24263. 703-346-7729 (EST) 8:30AM-4:30PM. Misdemeanor, Civil Actions Under $10,000, Small Claims.

## Lexington City

**Circuit and District Courts**, See Rockbridge County.

## Loudoun County

**Real Estate Recording**, Loudoun County Clerk of the Circuit Court, 18 North King Street, Leesburg, VA 22075. 703-777-0270 (EST) 9AM-4:30PM.

**20th Circuit Court**, 18 E Market St, PO Box 550, Leesburg, VA 22075. 703-777-0270 (EST) Felony, Civil Actions Over $10,000, Probate.

**20th General District Court**, 18 E Market St, Leesburg, VA 22075. 703-777-0312 (EST) 8:30AM-4:30PM. Misdemeanor, Civil Actions Under $10,000, Small Claims.

## Louisa County

**Real Estate Recording**, Louisa County Clerk of the Circuit Court, 102 Main Street, Courthouse, Louisa, VA 23093. 703-967-3444 (EST) 8:30AM-5PM (Stop Recording 4:15PM).

**16th Circuit Court**, Box 37, Louisa, VA 23093. 703-967-1212 (EST) 8:30AM-5PM. Felony, Civil Actions Over $10,000, Probate.

**16th General District Court**, PO Box 452, Louisa, VA 23093. 703-967-3443 (EST) 8:30AM-4:30PM. Misdemeanor, Civil Actions Under $10,000, Small Claims.

## Lunenburg County

**Real Estate Recording**, Lunenburg County Clerk of the Circuit Court, Courthouse, Lunenburg, VA 23952. 804-696-2230 (EST) 8:30AM-12, 1PM-5PM.

**10th Circuit Court**, Courthouse, Lunenburg, VA 23952. 804-696-2230 (EST) Felony, Civil Actions Over $10,000, Probate.

**10th General District Court**, Courthouse, Lunenburg, VA 23952. 804-696-5508 (EST) 8:30AM-5PM. Misdemeanor, Civil Actions Under $10,000, Small Claims.

## Lynchburg City

**Real Estate Recording**, Lynchburg City Clerk of the Circuit Court, 900 Court Street, Lynchburg, VA 24504. 804-847-1590 (EST) 8:30AM-4:45PM.

**24th Circuit Court**, PO Box 4, Lynchburg, VA 24505-0004. 804-847-1590 (EST) 8:30AM-4:45PM. Felony, Civil Actions Over $10,000, Probate.

**24th General District Court**, PO Box 60, Lynchburg, VA 24505. 804-847-1639 (EST) 8:30AM-4:30PM. Misdemeanor, Civil Actions Under $10,000, Small Claims.

## Madison County

**Real Estate Recording**, Madison County Clerk of the Circuit Court, Court Square, Madison, VA 22727. 703-948-6888 (EST) 8:30AM-4:30PM.

**16th Circuit Court**, PO Box 220, Madison, VA 22727. 703-948-6888 (EST) 8:30AM-4:30PM. Felony, Civil Actions Over $10,000, Probate.

**16th General District Court**, Madison County Courthouse, Madison, VA 22727. 703-948-4657 (EST) 8:30AM-4:30PM. Misdemeanor, Civil Actions Under $10,000, Small Claims.

## Manassas City

**Circuit and District Courts**, See Prince William County.

## Manassas Park City

**Circuit and District Courts**, See Prince William County.

## Martinsville City

**Real Estate Recording**, Martinsville City Clerk of the Circuit Court, 55 West Church Street, Martinsville, VA 24112. 703-656-5106 (EST) 9AM-5PM.

**21st Circuit Court**, PO Box 1206, Martinsville, VA 24114-1206. 703-638-3971 (EST) 8:30AM-4:30PM. Felony, Civil Actions Over $10,000, Probate.

**21st General District Court**, PO Box 1402, Martinsville, VA 24114. 703-656-5125 (EST) Misdemeanor, Civil Actions Under $10,000, Small Claims.

## Mathews County

**Real Estate Recording**, Mathews County Clerk of the Circuit Court, Courthouse Square, Mathews, VA 23109. 804-725-2550 (EST) 8AM-4PM.

**9th Circuit Court**, PO Box 463, Mathews, VA 23109. 804-725-2550 (EST) 8AM-4:30PM. Felony, Civil Actions Over $10,000, Probate.

**9th General District Court**, PO Box 169, Saluda, VA 23149. 804-758-4312 (EST) 8:30AM-4:30PM. Misdemeanor, Civil Actions Under $10,000, Small Claims.

## Mecklenburg County

**Real Estate Recording**, Mecklenburg County Clerk of the Circuit Court, Washington Street, Boydton, VA 23917. 804-738-6191 (EST) 8:30AM-5PM.

**10th Circuit Court**, PO Box 530, Boydton, VA 23917. 804-738-6191 (EST) 8:30AM-4:30PM. Felony, Civil Actions Over $10,000, Probate.

**10th General District Court**, Jefferson Street (PO Box 306), Boydton, VA 23917. 804-738-6191 (EST) 8:30AM-4:30PM. Misdemeanor, Civil Actions Under $10,000, Small Claims.

## Middlesex County

**Real Estate Recording**, Middlesex County Clerk of the Circuit Court, Route 17 Courthouse, Saluda, VA 23149. 804-758-5317 (EST) 8:30AM-4:30PM.

**9th Circuit Court**, PO Box 158, Saluda, VA 23149. 804-758-5317 (EST) 8:30AM-4:30PM. Felony, Civil Actions Over $10,000, Probate.

**9th General District Court**, PO Box 169, Saluda, VA 23149. 804-758-4312 (EST) 8:30AM-4:30PM. Misdemeanor, Civil Actions Under $10,000, Small Claims.

## Montgomery County

**Real Estate Recording**, Montgomery County Clerk of the Circuit Court, 1 East Main Street, Christiansburg, VA 24073. 703-382-5760 (EST) 8:30AM-4:30PM.

**27th Circuit Court**, PO Box 209, Christiansburg, VA 24073. 703-382-5760 (EST) 8:30AM-4:30PM. Felony, Civil Actions Over $10,000, Probate.

**27th General District Court**, Montgomery County Courthouse, Christiansburg, VA 24073. 703-382-5735 (EST) Misdemeanor, Civil Actions Under $10,000, Small Claims.

## Nelson County

**Real Estate Recording**, Nelson County Clerk of the Circuit Court, Court Street, Lovingston, VA 22949. 804-263-4069 (EST) 9AM-5PM.

**24th Circuit Court**, PO Box 10, Lovingston, VA 22949. 804-263-4069 (EST) 9AM-5PM. Felony, Civil Actions Over $10,000, Probate.

**24th General District Court**, Nelson County Courthouse, Lovingston, VA 22949. 804-263-4245 (EST) 8AM-4:30PM. Misdemeanor, Civil Actions Under $10,000, Small Claims.

## New Kent County

**Real Estate Recording**, New Kent County Clerk of the Circuit Court, 12001 Courthouse Circle, Courthouse, New Kent, VA 23124. 804-966-9520 (EST) 8:30AM-4:30PM.

**9th Circuit Court**, PO Box 98, New Kent, VA 23124. 804-966-9520 (EST) 8:30AM-4:30PM. Felony, Civil Actions Over $10,000, Probate.

**9th General District Court**, PO Box 159, Providence Forge, VA 23140. 804-966-9530 (EST) 8:30AM-4:30PM. Misdemeanor, Civil Actions Under $10,000, Small Claims.

## Newport News City

**Real Estate Recording**, Newport News Clerk of the Circuit Court, 2500 Washington Avenue, Courthouse, Newport News, VA 23607. 804-247-8561 (EST) 8AM-4:45PM.

**7th Circuit Court**, 2500 Washington Ave, Newport News, VA 23607. 804-247-8691 (EST) 8AM-4:45PM. Felony, Civil Actions Over $10,000, Probate.

**7th General District Court-Civil**, 2500 Washington Ave-Civil Div, Newport News, VA 23607. 804-247-2439 (EST) 7:30AM-4PM. Civil Actions Under $10,000, Small Claims.

**7th General District Court-Criminal**, 2500 Washington Ave-Criminal Div, Newport News, VA 23607. 804-247-8811 (EST) 7:30AM-4PM. Misdemeanor.

## Norfolk City

**Real Estate Recording**, Norfolk City Clerk of the Circuit Court, 100 St. Paul's Blvd., Norfolk, VA 23510-2773. 804-441-2461 (EST) 9AM-5PM.

**4th Circuit Court**, 100 St Paul's Blvd, Norfolk, VA 23510. 804-441-2461 (EST) 9AM-5PM. Felony, Civil Actions Over $10,000, Probate.

**4th General District Court**, 100 St. Paul's Blvd, Norfolk, VA 23510. 804-441-2368 (EST) 9AM-5PM. Misdemeanor, Civil Actions Under $10,000, Small Claims.

## Northampton County

**Real Estate Recording**, Northampton County Clerk of the Circuit Court, 16404 Courthouse Rd., Courthouse, Eastville, VA 23347. 804-678-0465 (EST) 9AM-5PM.

**2nd Circuit Court**, PO Box 36, Eastville, VA 23347. 804-678-0465 (EST) 9AM-5PM. Felony, Civil Actions Over $10,000, Probate.

**2nd General District Court**, PO Box 125, Eastville, VA 23347. 804-678-0466 (EST) 8AM-5PM. Misdemeanor, Civil Actions Under $10,000, Small Claims.

## Northumberland County

**Real Estate Recording**, Northumberland County Clerk of the Circuit Court, Highway 360, Courthouse, Heathsville, VA 22473. 804-580-3700 (EST) 9AM-5PM.

**15th Circuit Court**, PO Box 217, Heathsville, VA 22473. 804-580-3700 (EST) 9AM-5PM. Felony, Civil Actions Over $10,000, Probate.

**15th General District Court**, Northumberland Courthouse, PO Box 237, Heathsville, VA 22473. 804-580-4323 (EST) 8AM-4:30PM. Misdemeanor, Civil Actions Under $10,000, Small Claims.

## Norton City

**Circuit and District Courts**, See Wise County.

## Nottoway County

**Real Estate Recording**, Nottoway County Clerk of the Circuit Court, State Route 625, Courthouse, Nottoway, VA 23955. 804-645-9043 (EST) 8:30AM-4:30PM.

**11th Circuit Court**, Courthouse, Nottoway, VA 23955. 804-645-9043 (EST) 8:30AM-4:30PM. Felony, Civil Actions Over $10,000, Probate.

**11th General District Court**, Courthouse, Nottoway, VA 23955. 804-645-9312 (EST) 8AM-4:15PM. Misdemeanor, Civil Actions Under $10,000, Small Claims.

## Orange County

**Real Estate Recording**, Orange County Clerk of the Circuit Court, 109 West Main Street, Orange, VA 22960. 703-672-4030 (EST) 8:30AM-4:30PM.

**16th Circuit Court**, PO Box 230, Orange, VA 22960. 703-672-4030 (EST) 8:30AM-4:30PM. Felony, Civil Actions Over $10,000, Probate.

**16th General District Court**, Orange County Courthouse, Orange, VA 22960. 703-672-3150 (EST) 8:30AM-4:30PM. Misdemeanor, Civil Actions Under $10,000, Small Claims.

## Page County

**Real Estate Recording**, Page County Clerk of the Circuit Court, 116 South Court Street, Luray, VA 22835. 703-743-4064 (EST) 9AM-5PM.

**26th Circuit Court**, 118 S Court St, Luray, VA 22835. 703-743-4064 (EST) 9AM-5PM. Felony, Civil Actions Over $10,000, Probate.

**26th General District Court**, 101 S Court St, Luray, VA 22835. 703-743-5705 (EST) 8AM-4:30PM. Misdemeanor, Civil Actions Under $10,000, Small Claims.

## Patrick County

**Real Estate Recording**, Patrick County Clerk of the Circuit Court, Courthouse, Blue Ridge & Main Streets, Stuart, VA 24171. 703-694-7213 (EST) 9AM-5PM.

**21st Circuit Court**, PO Box 148, Stuart, VA 24171. 703-694-7213 (EST) 9AM-5PM. Felony, Civil Actions Over $10,000, Probate.

**21st General District Court**, PO Box 149, Stuart, VA 24171. 703-694-7258 (EST) 9AM-5PM. Misdemeanor, Civil Actions Under $10,000, Small Claims.

## Petersburg City

**Real Estate Recording**, Petersburg City Clerk of the Circuit Court, Courthouse Hill, Petersburg, VA 23803. 804-733-2367 (EST) 8AM-5PM.

**11th Circuit Court**, Courthouse Hill, Petersburg, VA 23803. 804-733-2367 (EST) 8AM-4:30PM. Felony, Civil Actions Over $10,000, Probate.

**11th General District Court**, 35 E Tabb St, Petersburg, VA 23803. 804-733-2374 (EST) 8AM-4:30PM. Misdemeanor, Civil Actions Under $10,000, Small Claims.

## Pittsylvania County

**Real Estate Recording**, Pittsylvania County Clerk of the Circuit Court, 1 North Main Street, Courthouse, Chatham, VA 24531. 804-432-2041 (EST) 8:30AM-5PM.

**22nd Circuit Court**, PO Drawer 31, Chatham, VA 24531. 804-432-2041 (EST) 8:30AM-5PM. Felony, Civil Actions Over $10,000, Probate.

**22nd General District Court**, Pittsylvania Courthouse, Chatham, VA 24531. 804-432-2041 (EST) 8:30AM-4:30PM. Misdemeanor, Civil Actions Under $10,000, Small Claims.

## Poquoson City

**Circuit and District Courts**, See York County.

## Portsmouth City

**Real Estate Recording**, Portsmouth City Clerk of the Circuit Court, 601 Crawford Street, Portsmouth, VA 23704. 804-393-8671 (EST) 9AM-5PM.

**3rd Circuit Court**, Drawer 1217, Portsmouth, VA 23705. 804-393-8671 (EST) 9AM-5PM. Felony, Civil Actions Over $10,000, Probate.

**3rd General District Court**, PO Box 129, Portsmouth, VA 23705. 804-393-8681 (EST) 8:30AM-4:30PM. Misdemeanor, Civil Actions Under $10,000, Small Claims.

## Powhatan County

**Real Estate Recording**, Powhatan County Clerk of the Circuit Court, 3880 Old Buckingham Road, Powhatan, VA 23139. 804-598-5660 (EST) 8:30AM-5PM (Recording until 4PM).

**11th Circuit Court**, PO Box 37, Powhatan, VA 23139. 804-598-5660 (EST) 8AM-5PM. Felony, Civil Actions Over $10,000, Probate.

**11th General District Court**, Courthouse, PO Box 113, Powhatan, VA 23139. 804-598-5665 (EST) Misdemeanor, Civil Actions Under $10,000, Small Claims.

## Prince Edward County

**Real Estate Recording**, Prince Edward County Clerk of the Circuit Court, 124 North Main Street, Courthouse, Farmville, VA 23901. 804-392-5145 (EST) 9AM-4:30PM.

**10th Circuit Court**, PO Box 304, Farmville, VA 23901. 804-392-5145 (EST) 9AM-4:30PM. Felony, Civil Actions Over $10,000, Probate.

**10th General District Court**, Courthouse, 3rd Floor, Farmville, VA 23901. 804-392-4024 (EST) 8:30AM-5PM. Misdemeanor, Civil Actions Under $10,000, Small Claims.

## Prince George County

**Real Estate Recording**, Prince George County Clerk of the Circuit Court, 6601 Courts Dr., Prince George, VA 23875. 804-733-2640 (EST) Recording Hours 8:30AM-4:30PM.

**6th Circuit Court**, PO Box 98, Prince George, VA 23875. 804-733-2640 (EST) 8:30AM-5:00PM. Felony, Civil Actions Over $10,000, Probate.

**6th General District Court**, P.C. Courthouse, Prince George, VA 23875. 804-733-2783 (EST) 8:30AM-4:30PM. Misdemeanor, Civil Actions Under $10,000, Small Claims.

## Prince William County

**Real Estate Recording**, Prince William County Clerk of the Circuit Court, 9311 Lee Avenue, Manassas, VA 22110. 703-792-6035 (EST) 8:30AM-4PM (Actual Recording); 8:30AM-5PM (General Information).

**31st Circuit Court**, PO Box 191, Manassas, VA 22110. 703-792-6042 (EST) 8:30AM-4:30PM. Felony, Civil Actions Over $10,000, Probate.

**31st General District Court**, 9311 Lee Ave, Manassas, VA 22110. 703-792-6149 (EST) 8:30AM-4:30PM. Misdemeanor, Civil Actions Under $10,000, Small Claims.

## Pulaski County

**Real Estate Recording**, Pulaski County Clerk of the Circuit Court, 1055 E. Main St., Pulaski, VA 24301. 703-980-7825 (EST) 8:30AM-4:30PM.

**27th Circuit Court**, PO Box 270, Pulaski, VA 24301. 703-980-7825 (EST) 8:30AM-4:30PM. Felony, Civil Actions Over $10,000, Probate.

**27th General District Court**, Pulaski County Courthouse, Pulaski, VA 24301. 703-980-7470 (EST) 8:30AM-4:30PM. Misdemeanor, Civil Actions Under $10,000, Small Claims.

## Radford City

**Real Estate Recording**, Radford City Clerk of the Circuit Court, 619 Second Street, Courthouse, Radford, VA 24141. 703-731-3610 (EST) 8:30AM-5PM.

**27th Circuit Court**, 619 2nd St, Radford, VA 24141. 703-731-3610 (EST) 8:30AM-5PM. Felony, Civil Actions Over $10,000, Probate.

**27th General District Court**, 619 2nd St, Radford, VA 24141. 703-731-3609 (EST) 8:30AM-4:30PM. Misdemeanor, Civil Actions Under $10,000, Small Claims.

## Rappahannock County

**Real Estate Recording**, Rappahannock County Clerk of the Circuit Court, Gay Street, Clerk's Office, Washington, VA 22747. 703-675-3621 (EST) 8:30AM-4:30PM.

**20th Circuit Court**, Gay Street (PO Box 517), Washington, VA 22747. 703-675-3621 (EST) 8:30AM-4:30PM. Felony, Civil Actions Over $10,000, Probate.

**20th General District Court**, Gay Street Courthouse (PO Box 206), Washington, VA 22747. 703-675-3518 (EST) 8:30AM-4:30PM. Misdemeanor, Civil Actions Under $10,000, Small Claims.

## Richmond City

**Real Estate Recording**, Richmond City Clerk of the Circuit Court, 800 East Marshall Street, Richmond, VA 23219. 804-780-6520 (EST) 9AM-3:30PM.

**13th Circuit Court, Division I**, Manchester Courthouse, 10th and Hull St, Richmond, VA 23224-0129. 804-780-6536 (EST) 9AM-4:45PM. Felony, Civil Actions Over $10,000, Probate.

**13th Circuit Court, Division II**, Manchester Courthouse, 10th and Hull St, Richmond, VA 23224-0129. 804-780-5370 (EST) 8:30AM-4:45PM. Felony, Civil Actions Over $10,000, Probate.

**13th General District Court, Division I**, 800 E Marshall St, Richmond, VA 23219. 804-780-6461 (EST) 8AM-4:15PM. Civil Actions Under $10,000, Small Claims.

**13th General District Court, Division II**, 905 Decatur St, Richmond, VA 23224. 804-780-5390 (EST) 8AM-4:30PM. Misdemeanor.

## Richmond County

**Real Estate Recording**, Richmond County Clerk of the Circuit Court, 10 Court Street, Warsaw, VA 22572. 804-333-3781 (EST) 9AM-5PM.

**15th Circuit Court**, PO Box 1000, Warsaw, VA 22572. 804-333-3781 (EST) 8:30AM-4:30PM. Felony, Civil Actions Over $10,000, Probate.

**15th General District Court**, Richmond County Courthouse, Warsaw, VA 22572. 804-333-4616 (EST) 8:30AM-4:30PM. Misdemeanor, Civil Actions Under $10,000, Small Claims.

## Roanoke City

**Real Estate Recording**, Roanoke City Clerk of the Circuit Court, 315 Church Ave S.W., Room 357, Roanoke, VA 24016. 703-981-2321 (EST) 8:30AM-4:30PM.

**23rd Circuit Court**, PO Box 2610, Roanoke, VA 24010. 703-981-2325 (EST) 8:30AM-4:30PM. Felony, Civil Actions Over $10,000, Probate.

**23rd General District Court**, 315 W Church Ave, Roanoke, VA 24016-5007. 703-981-2361 (EST) 8AM-4PM. Misdemeanor, Civil Actions Under $10,000, Small Claims.

## Roanoke County

**Real Estate Recording**, Roanoke County Clerk of the Circuit Court, 305 East Main Street, Salem, VA 24153. 703-387-6205 (EST) 8:30AM-4:30PM.

**23rd Circuit Court**, PO Box 1126, Salem, VA 24153, Attn. 703-387-6261 (EST) 8:30AM-4:30PM. Felony, Civil Actions Over $10,000, Probate.

**23rd General District Court**, PO Box 997, Salem, VA 24153. 703-387-6168 (EST) Misdemeanor, Civil Actions Under $10,000, Small Claims.

## Rockbridge County

**Real Estate Recording**, Rockbridge County Clerk of the Circuit Court, 2 South Main Street, Court House, Lexington, VA 24450-2599. 703-463-2232 (EST) 8:30AM-4:30PM.

**25th Circuit Court**, Courthouse Square, 2 S Main St, Lexington, VA 24450. 703-463-2232 (EST) 8:30AM-4:30PM. Felony, Civil Actions Over $10,000, Probate.

**25th General District Court**, 150 S Main St, Lexington, VA 24450. 703-463-3631 (EST) Misdemeanor, Civil Actions Under $10,000, Small Claims.

## Rockingham County

**Real Estate Recording**, Rockingham County Clerk of the Circuit Court, Courthouse, Harrisonburg, VA 22801. 703-564-3110 (EST) 9AM-5PM; Th-until 6PM.

**26th Circuit Court**, Courthouse, Harrisonburg, VA 22801. 703-564-3118 (EST) 9AM-5PM MTWF, 9AM-6PM Thr. Felony, Civil Actions Over $10,000, Probate.

**26th General District Court**, Courthouse, Harrisonburg, VA 22801. 703-564-3135 (EST) 8AM-4PM. Misdemeanor, Civil Actions Under $10,000, Small Claims.

## Russell County

**Real Estate Recording**, Russell County Clerk of the Circuit Court, Main Street, Courthouse, Lebanon, VA 24266. 703-889-8023 (EST) 8:30AM-4:30PM.

**29th Circuit Court**, PO Box 435, Lebanon, VA 24266. 703-889-8023 (EST) 8:30AM-4:30PM. Felony, Civil Actions Over $10,000, Probate.

**29th General District Court**, Russell County Courthouse, Lebanon, VA 24266. 703-899-8051 (EST) 8:30AM-4:30PM. Misdemeanor, Civil Actions Under $10,000, Small Claims.

## Salem City

**Real Estate Recording**, Salem City Clerk of the Circuit Court, 2 East Calhoun Street, Salem, VA 24153. 703-375-3067 (EST) 8:30AM-5PM.

**23rd Circuit Court**, 2 E Calhoun St, Salem, VA 24153. 703-375-3067 (EST) 8:30AM-5PM. Felony, Civil Actions Over $10,000, Probate.

**23rd General District Court**, 2 E Calhoun St, Salem, VA 24153. 703-375-3044 (EST) 8AM-4PM. Misdemeanor, Civil Actions Under $10,000, Small Claims.

## Scott County

**Real Estate Recording**, Scott County Clerk of the Circuit Court, 104 East Jackson Street, Courthouse, Suite 2, Gate City, VA 24251-3417. 703-386-3801 (EST) 8AM-Noon,1-5PM.

**30th Circuit Court**, 104 E Jackson St, Suite 2, Gate City, VA 24251. 703-386-3801 (EST) 8AM-5PM. Felony, Civil Actions Over $10,000, Probate.

**30th General District Court**, 104 E Jackson St, Suite 9, Gate City, VA 24251. 703-386-7341 (EST) 8AM-4PM. Misdemeanor, Civil Actions Under $10,000, Small Claims.

## Shenandoah County

**Real Estate Recording**, Shenandoah County Clerk of the Circuit Court, 112 South Main Street, Woodstock, VA 22664. 703-459-6150 (EST) 9AM-5PM.

**26th Circuit Court**, Main St, Woodstock, VA 22664. 703-459-3791 (EST) 9AM-4PM. Felony, Civil Actions Over $10,000, Probate.

**26th General District Court**, W Court St, PO Box 189, Woodstock, VA 22664. 703-459-4059 (EST) 8:30AM-4:30PM. Misdemeanor, Civil Actions Under $10,000, Small Claims.

## Smyth County

**Real Estate Recording**, Smyth County Clerk of the Circuit Court, Main Street, Courthouse, Marion, VA 24354. 703-783-7186 (EST) 9AM-5PM.

**28th Circuit Court**, PO Box 1025, Marion, VA 24354. 703-73-7186 (EST) 9AM-5PM. Felony, Civil Actions Over $10,000, Probate.

**28th General District Court**, Smythe County Courthouse, Rm 231, Marion, VA 24354. 703-783-5021 (EST) 8:30AM-4:30PM. Misdemeanor, Civil Actions Under $10,000, Small Claims.

## South Boston City

**Circuit and District Courts**, See Halifax County.

## Southampton County

**Real Estate Recording**, Southampton County Clerk of the Circuit Court, 22350 Main Street, Courthouse - Room 106, Courtland, VA 23837. 804-653-9245 (EST) 8:30AM-5PM.

**5th Circuit Court**, PO Box 190, Courtland, VA 23837. 804-653-2200 (EST) 8:30AM-5:30PM. Felony, Civil Actions Over $10,000, Probate.

**5th General District Court**, PO Box 347, Courtland, VA 23837. 804-653-2673 (EST) 8:30AM-5PM. Misdemeanor, Civil Actions Under $10,000, Small Claims.

## Spotsylvania County

**Real Estate Recording**, Spotsylvania County Clerk of the Circuit Court, 9101 Courthouse Road, Spotsylvania, VA 22553. 703-582-7090 (EST) 8AM-4:30PM (Recording Real Property 3:30PM).

**15th Circuit Court**, 9113 Coutrhouse Rd, PO Box 96, Spotsylvania, VA 22553. 703-582-7090 (EST) 8AM-4:30PM. Felony, Civil Actions Over $10,000, Probate.

**15th General District Court**, 9103 Courthouse Rd, PO Box 114, Spotsylvania, VA 22553. 703-582-7110 (EST) 8AM-4PM. Misdemeanor, Civil Actions Under $10,000, Small Claims.

## Stafford County

**Real Estate Recording**, Stafford County Clerk of the Circuit Court, 1300 Courthouse Rd., Stafford, VA 22554. 703-659-8750 (EST) 8:30AM-4:30PM.

**15th Circuit Court**, PO Box 69, Stafford, VA 22555. 703-659-8750 (EST) 8:30AM-4:30PM. Felony, Civil Actions Over $10,000, Probate.

**15th General District Court**, 1300 Courthouse Rd, Stafford, VA 22554. 703-659-8763 (EST) 8:AM-4PM. Misdemeanor, Civil Actions Under $10,000, Small Claims.

## Staunton City

**Real Estate Recording**, Staunton City Clerk of the Circuit Court, 113 East Beverly Street, Staunton, VA 24401. 703-332-3874 (EST) 8:30AM-5PM.

**25th Circuit Court**, PO Box 1286, Staunton, VA 24402-1286. 703-322-3874 (EST) Felony, Civil Actions Over $10,000, Probate.

**25th General District Court**, 113 E Beverly St, Staunton, VA 24401. 703-332-3878 (EST) 8:30AM-4:30PM. Misdemeanor, Civil Actions Under $10,000, Small Claims.

## Suffolk City

**Real Estate Recording**, Suffolk City Clerk of the Circuit Court, 441 Market Street, Municipal Building, Suffolk, VA 23434. 804-925-6450 (EST) 8:30AM-5PM.

**5th Circuit Court**, 441 Market St, Rm 112, Suffolk, VA 23434. 804-934-3111 (EST) 8AM-5PM. Felony, Civil Actions Over $10,000, Probate.

**5th General District Court**, 524 N Main St, Suffolk, VA 23434. 804-539-1531 (EST) 8AM-4PM. Misdemeanor, Civil Actions Under $10,000, Small Claims.

## Surry County

**Real Estate Recording**, Surry County Clerk of the Circuit Court, 28 Colonial Trail East, Courthouse, Surry, VA 23883. 804-294-3161 (EST) 9AM-5PM.

**6th Circuit Court**, Rt 10 and School St, Surry, VA 23883. 804-294-5201 (EST) 8:30AM-4:30PM. Felony, Civil Actions Over $10,000, Probate.

**6th General District Court**, Hwy 10 and School St, PO Box 322, Surry, VA 23883. 804-294-5201 (EST) 8:30AM-4:30PM. Misdemeanor, Civil Actions Under $10,000, Small Claims.

## Sussex County

**Real Estate Recording**, Sussex County Clerk of the Circuit Court, Route 735, 15088 Courthouse Road, Sussex, VA 23884. 804-246-5511 (EST) X274-6 9AM-5PM.

**6th Circuit Court**, PO Box 1337, Sussex, VA 23884. 804-246-5511 (EST) 9AM-5PM. Felony, Civil Actions Over $10,000, Probate.

**6th General District Court**, PO 1315, Sussex County Courthouse, Sussex, VA 23884. 804-246-5511 (EST) 8:30AM-4:30PM. Misdemeanor, Civil Actions Under $10,000, Small Claims.

## Tazewell County

**Real Estate Recording**, Tazewell County Clerk of the Circuit Court, 101 Main Street, Tazewell, VA 24651. 703-988-7541 (EST) 8AM-4:30PM.

**29th Circuit Court**, PO Box 968, Tazewell, VA 24651. 703-988-7541 (EST) 8AM-4:30PM. Felony, Civil Actions Over $10,000, Probate.

**29th General District Court**, PO Box 566, Tazewell, VA 24651. 703-988-9057 (EST) 8AM-4:30PM. Misdemeanor, Civil Actions Under $10,000, Small Claims.

## Virginia Beach City

**Real Estate Recording**, Virginia Beach City Clerk of the Circuit Court, Municipal Center, Virginia Beach, VA 23456-9017. 804-427-8818 (EST) 8:30AM-5PM.

**2nd Circuit Court**, Princess Ann Station, Judicial Center, Virginia Beach, VA 23456. 804-427-4181 (EST) 8:30AM-5PM. Felony, Civil Actions Over $10,000, Probate.

**2nd General District Court**, Judicial Center, Virginia Beach, VA 23456. 804-427-4277 (EST) 8:30AM-4:30PM. Misdemeanor, Civil Actions Under $10,000, Small Claims.

## Warren County

**Real Estate Recording**, Warren County Clerk of the Circuit Court, 1 East Main Street, Front Royal, VA 22630-3382. 703-635-2435 (EST) 9AM-5PM.

**26th Circuit Court**, 1 East Main St, Front Royal, VA 22630. 703-635-2435 (EST) 9AM-5PM. Felony, Civil Actions Over $10,000, Probate.

**26th District Court**, 1 East Main St, Front Royal, VA 22630. 703-635-2335 (EST) 8AM-4:30PM. Misdemeanor, Civil Actions Under $10,000, Small Claims.

## Washington County

**Real Estate Recording**, Washington County Clerk of the Circuit Court, 189 E. Main St., Abingdon, VA 24210. 703-676-6226 (EST) 8:30AM-5PM (Summer hours 7:30AM-5PM).

**28th Circuit Court**, Court St, Abingdon, VA 24210. 703-676-6224 (EST) 7:30AM-5PM. Felony, Civil Actions Over $10,000, Probate.

**28th District Court**, 191 E Main, Abingdon, VA 24210. 703-676-6279 (EST) 8:30AM-5PM. Misdemeanor, Civil Actions Under $10,000, Small Claims.

## Waynesboro City

**Real Estate Recording**, Waynesboro City Clerk of the Circuit Court, 250 South Wayne Avenue, Waynesboro, VA 22980. 703-942-6616 (EST) 8:30AM-5PM.

**25th Circuit Court**, 250 S Wayne Ave, Waynesboro, VA 22980. 703-942-6616 (EST) 8:30AM-5PM. Felony, Civil Actions Over $10,000, Probate.

**25th General District Court**, 250 S Wayne and PO Box 1028, Waynesboro, VA 22980. 703-942-6636 (EST) 8:30AM-4:30PM. Misdemeanor, Civil Actions Under $10,000, Small Claims.

## Westmoreland County

**Real Estate Recording**, Westmoreland County Clerk of the Circuit Court, Courthouse, Rte. 3 and Polk St., Montross, VA 22520. 804-493-0108 (EST) 9AM-5PM.

**15th Circuit Court**, PO Box 307, Montross, VA 22520. 804-493-0108 (EST) Felony, Civil Actions Over $10,000, Probate.

**15th General District Court**, PO Box 688, Montross, VA 22520. 804-493-0105 (EST) 8AM-4:30PM. Misdemeanor, Civil Actions Under $10,000, Small Claims.

## Williamsburg City

Circuit and District Courts, , VA. (EST).

## Winchester City

**Real Estate Recording**, Winchester City Clerk of the Circuit Court, 5 N. Kent Street, Winchester, VA 22601. 703-667-5770 (EST) 9AM-5PM.

**26th Circuit Court**, 5 N Kent St, Winchester, VA 22601. 703-667-5770 (EST) 9AM-5PM. Felony, Civil Actions Over $10,000, Probate.

**26th General District Court**, 5 N. Kent St., Winchester, VA 22601. 703-667-5770 (EST) 8AM-4PM. Misdemeanor, Civil Actions Under $10,000, Small Claims.

## Wise County

**Real Estate Recording**, Wise County Clerk of the Circuit Court, 125 Main Street, Courthouse, Wise, VA 24293. 703-328-6111 (EST) 8AM-5PM.

**30th Circuit Court**, PO Box 1248, Wise, VA 24293. 703-328-6111 (EST) 8AM-5PM. Felony, Civil Actions Over $10,000, Probate.

**30th General District Court**, Wise County Courthouse, PO Box 829, Wise, VA 24293. 703-328-3426 (EST) 8AM-4PM. Misdemeanor, Civil Actions Under $10,000, Small Claims.

## Wythe County

**Real Estate Recording**, Wythe County Clerk of the Circuit Court, 225 South Fourth Street, Wytheville, VA 24382. 703-228-6050 (EST) 8:30AM-5PM.

**27th Circuit Court**, 225 S Fourth St, Rm 105, Wytheville, VA 24382. 703-223-6050 (EST) 8AM-5PM. Felony, Civil Actions Over $10,000, Probate.

**27th General District Court**, 225 S. Fourth St., Rm 203, Wytheville, VA 24382. 703-223-6075 (EST) 8AM-4:30PM. Misdemeanor, Civil Actions Under $10,000, Small Claims.

## York County

**Real Estate Recording**, York County Clerk of the Circuit Court, 301 Main Street, Yorktown, VA 23690. 804-890-3350 (EST) 8:30AM-5PM.

**9th Circuit Court**, PO Box 371, Yorktown, VA 23690. 804-890-3350 (EST) 8:30AM-5PM. Felony, Civil Actions Over $10,000, Probate.

**9th General District Court**, PO Box 316, Yorktown, VA 23690. 804-890-3450 (EST) 8:30AM-4:30PM. Misdemeanor, Civil Actions Under $10,000, Small Claims.

# Washington

## Adams County

**Real Estate Recording**, Adams County Auditor, 210 West Broadway, Ritzville, WA 99169. 360-659-0090 (PST) 8:30AM-4:30PM.

**Superior Court**, 210 W Broadway (PO Box 187), Ritzville, WA 99169-0187. 360-659-0090 (PST) 8:30AM-4:30PM. Felony, Civil Actions Over $25,000, Eviction, Probate.

**Othello District Court**, 165 N 1st, Othello, WA 99344. 360-659-0090 (PST) 8:30AM-4:30PM. Misdemeanor, Civil Actions Under $25,000, Small Claims.

**Ritzville District Court**, 210 W Broadway, Ritzville, WA 99169. 360-659-1002 (PST) Misdemeanor, Civil Actions Under $25,000, Small Claims.

## Asotin County

**Real Estate Recording**, Asotin County Auditor, 135 2nd Street, Asotin, WA 99402. 509-243-2084 (PST) 9AM-5PM.

**Superior Court**, PO Box 159, Asotin, WA 99402-0159. 360-243-2081 (PST) 9AM-5PM. Felony, Civil Actions Over $25,000, Eviction, Probate.

**District Court**, PO Box 429, Asotin, WA 99402-0429. 360-243-4127 (PST) 8AM-5PM. Misdemeanor, Civil Actions Under $25,000, Small Claims.

## Benton County

**Real Estate Recording**, Benton County Auditor, 620 Market Street, Courthouse, Prosser, WA 99350. 509-786-5616 (PST) 8AM-5PM.

**Superior Court**, 7320 W Quinault, Kennewick, WA 99336-7690. 360-735-8388 (PST) 8AM-4PM. Felony, Civil Actions Over $25,000, Eviction, Probate.

**District Court**, 7320 W Quinault, Kennewick, WA 99336-7689. 360-735-8476 (PST) 7:30AM-4:30PM, Closed 12-1. Misdemeanor, Civil Actions Under $25,000, Small Claims.

## Chelan County

**Real Estate Recording**, Chelan County Auditor, 350 Orondo, Courthouse, Wenatchee, WA 98801. 509-664-5439 (PST) 8:30AM-5PM.

**Superior Court**, 401 Washington (PO Box 3025), Wenatchee, WA 98807-3025. 360-664-5380 (PST) 8:30AM-5PM. Felony, Civil Actions Over $25,000, Eviction, Probate.

**District Court**, Courthouse 4th Fl (PO Box 2182), Wenatchee, WA 98807. 360-664-5393 (PST) 8:30AM-5PM. Misdemeanor, Civil Actions Under $25,000, Small Claims.

## Clallam County

**Real Estate Recording**, Clallam County Auditor, 223 East Fourth Street, Port Angeles, WA 98362-3098. 360-417-2220 (PST) 8AM-4:30PM.

**Superior Court**, 223 E Fourth St, Port Angeles, WA 98362-3098. 360-417-2333 (PST) 8AM-5PM. Felony, Civil Actions Over $25,000, Eviction, Probate.

**District Court Two**, PO Box 1937, Forks, WA 98331. 360-374-6383 (PST) 8AM-5PM. Misdemeanor, Civil Actions Under $25,000, Small Claims.

**District Court One**, 223 E 4th St, Port Angeles, WA 98362. 360-417-2285 (PST) 8AM-5PM. Misdemeanor, Civil Actions Under $25,000, Small Claims.

## Clark County

**Real Estate Recording**, Clark County Auditor, 12th & Franklin, Vancouver, WA 98660. 360-699-2208 (PST) 8AM-5PM.

**Superior Court**, PO Box 5000, Vancouver, WA 98668. 360-699-2295 (PST) 8:30AM-4:30PM. Felony, Civil Actions Over $25,000, Eviction, Probate.

**District Court**, PO Box 5000, Vancouver, WA 98666-5000. 360-699-2411 (PST) 8:30AM-4:30PM. Misdemeanor, Civil Actions Under $25,000, Small Claims.

## Columbia County

**Real Estate Recording**, Columbia County Auditor, 341 East Main, Dayton, WA 99328-1361. 509-382-4541 (PST) 8:30AM-4:30PM.

**Superior Court**, 341 E Main St, Dayton, WA 99328. 360-382-4321 (PST) 8:30AM-4:30PM, Closed 12-1. Felony, Civil Actions Over $25,000, Eviction, Probate.

**District Court**, 341 E Main St, Dayton, WA 99328-1361. 360-382-4812 (PST) 8:30AM-4:30PM. Misdemeanor, Civil Actions Under $25,000, Small Claims.

## Cowlitz County

**Real Estate Recording**, Cowlitz County Auditor, 207 Fourth Avenue North, Kelso, WA 98626. 360-577-3006 (PST) 8AM-5PM.

**Superior Court**, 312 SW First Ave, Kelso, WA 98626-1724. 360-577-3016 (PST) 8:30AM-4:30PM. Felony, Civil Actions Over $25,000, Eviction, Probate.

**District Court**, 312 SW First Ave, Kelso, WA 98626-1724. 360-577-3073 (PST) 8:30AM-5PM. Misdemeanor, Civil Actions Under $25,000, Small Claims.

## Douglas County

**Real Estate Recording**, Douglas County Auditor, 213 South Rainier, Waterville, WA 98858. 509-884-9422 (PST) 8AM-5PM.

**Superior Court**, PO Box 516, Waterville, WA 98858-0516. 360-745-8529 (PST) 8AM-5PM. Felony, Civil Actions Over $25,000, Eviction, Probate.

**Bridgeport District Court**, 1206 Columbia Ave (PO Box 730), Bridgeport, WA 98813-0730. 360-686-2034 (PST) 8:30AM-4PM M,T,TH,F 9AM-1PM W. Misdemeanor, Civil Actions Under $25,000, Small Claims.

**East Wenatchee District Court**, 110 3rd St NE, East Wenatchee, WA 98802. 360-884-0708 (PST) 8:30AM-4:30PM. Misdemeanor, Civil Actions Under $25,000, Small Claims.

## Ferry County

**Real Estate Recording**, Ferry County Auditor, 350 East Delaware, Republic, WA 99166. 509-775-5200 (PST) 8AM-4PM.

**Superior Court**, 350 E Delaware, Republic, WA 99166. 360-775-5245 (PST) 8AM-4PM. Felony, Civil Actions Over $25,000, Eviction, Probate.

**District Court**, PO Box 214, Republic, WA 99166-0214. 360-775-5244 (PST) 8AM-4PM. Misdemeanor, Civil Actions Under $25,000, Small Claims.

## Franklin County

**Real Estate Recording**, Franklin County Auditor, 1016 North Fourth Street, Pasco, WA 99301. 509-545-3536 (PST) 8:30AM-5PM.

**Superior Court**, 1016 N 4th St, Pasco, WA 99301. 360-545-3525 (PST) 8:30AM-5PM. Felony, Civil Actions Over $25,000, Eviction, Probate.

**District Court**, 1016 N 4th St, Pasco, WA 99301. 360-545-3595 (PST) 8:30AM-5PM. Misdemeanor, Civil Actions Under $25,000, Small Claims.

## Garfield County

**Real Estate Recording**, Garfield County Auditor, Corner of 8th & Main, Pomeroy, WA 99347. 509-843-1411 (PST) 8:30AM-5PM.

**Superior Court**, PO Box 915, Pomeroy, WA 99347-0915. 360-843-3731 (PST) Felony, Civil Actions Over $25,000, Eviction, Probate.

**District Court**, PO Box 817, Pomeroy, WA 99347-0817. 360-843-1002 (PST) 8:30AM-5PM. Misdemeanor, Civil Actions Under $25,000, Small Claims.

## Grant County

**Real Estate Recording**, Grant County Auditor, 1st & C Street NW, Ephrata, WA 98823. 509-754-2011 (PST) 8AM-5PM.

**Superior Court**, PO Box 37, Ephrata, WA 98823-0037. 360-754-2011 (PST) 8AM-5PM, Closed 12-1. Felony, Civil Actions Over $25,000, Eviction, Probate.

**District Court**, PO Box 37, Ephrata, WA 98823-0037. 360-754-2011 (PST) 8AM-5PM. Misdemeanor, Civil Actions Under $25,000, Small Claims.

## Grays Harbor County

**Real Estate Recording**, Grays Harbor County Auditor, 101 Broadway, Montesano, WA 98563. 360-249-4232 (PST) 8AM-5PM.

**Superior Court**, 102 W Broadway, Montesano, WA 98563-0711. 360-249-3842 (PST) Felony, Civil Actions Over $25,000, Eviction, Probate.

**District Court No 2**, PO Box 142, Aberdeen, WA 98520-0035. 360-532-7061 (PST) 8AM-5PM. Misdemeanor, Civil Actions Under $25,000, Small Claims.

**District Court No 1**, 102 W Broadway, Rm 202, Montesano, WA 98563-0647. 360-249-3441 (PST) 8AM-5PM. Misdemeanor, Civil Actions Under $25,000, Small Claims.

## Island County

**Real Estate Recording**, Island County Auditor, 6th & Main, Coupeville, WA 98239. 360-678-5111 (PST) 8AM-4:30PM.

**Superior Court**, PO Box 5000, Coupeville, WA 98239-5000. 360-679-7359 (PST) 8AM-4:30PM. Felony, Civil Actions Over $25,000, Eviction, Probate.

# Washington

**District Court**, 4114 400th Ave W, Oak Harbor, WA 98277-2988. 360-675-5988 (PST) Misdemeanor, Civil Actions Under $25,000, Small Claims.

## Jefferson County

**Real Estate Recording**, Jefferson County Auditor, 1820 Jefferson Street, Port Townsend, WA 98368. 360-385-9116 (PST) 9AM-5PM.

**Superior Court**, PO BOX 1220, Port Townsend, WA 98368-0920. 360-385-9125 (PST) 9AM-5PM. Felony, Civil Actions Over $25,000, Eviction, Probate.

**District Court**, PO Box 1220, Port Townsend, WA 98368-0920. 360-385-9135 (PST) 9AM-5PM. Misdemeanor, Civil Actions Under $25,000, Small Claims.

## King County

**Real Estate Recording**, King County Records, 500 4th Avenue, Administration Building, Room 311, Seattle, WA 98104. 206-296-1570 (PST) 8:30AM-4:30PM: Recording Hours: 8:30AM-3:30PM.

**Superior Court**, 516 Third Ave, E-609 Courthouse, Seattle, WA 98104-2386. 206-296-9300 (PST) 8:30AM-4:30AM. Felony, Misdemeanor, Civil Actions Over $25,000, Eviction, Probate.

**District Court (Bellevue Div)**, 585 112th Ave SE, Bellevue, WA 98004. 206-296-7760 (PST) 8:30AM-4:30PM. Misdemeanor, Civil Actions Under $25,000, Small Claims.

**District Court (Federal Way Div)**, 33506 10th Pl South, Federal Way, WA 98003-6396. 206-296-7784 (PST) Misdemeanor, Civil Actions Under $25,000, Small Claims.

**District Court (Issaquah Div)**, 640 NW Gilman Blvd, Issaquah, WA 98027-2448. 206-296-7688 (PST) 8:30AM-4:30PM. Misdemeanor, Civil Actions Under $25,000, Small Claims.

**District Court (Aukeen Div)**, 1210 S Central, Kent, WA 98032-7426. 206-296-7740 (PST) 8:30AM-4:30PM. Misdemeanor, Civil Actions Under $25,000, Small Claims.

**District Court (Shoreline Div)**, 18050 Meridian Ave, N Seattle, WA 98133-4642. 206-296-3679 (PST) Misdemeanor, Civil Actions Under $25,000, Small Claims.

**District Court (Northeast Div)**, 15920 NE 85th (PO Box 425), Redmond, WA 98073-0425. 206-296-3667 (PST) 8:30AM-4:30PM. Misdemeanor, Civil Actions Under $25,000, Small Claims.

**District Court (Renton Div)**, 3407 NE 2nd St, Renton, WA 98056-4193. 206-296-3532 (PST) 8:30AM-4:30PM. Misdemeanor, Civil Actions Under $25,000, Small Claims.

**District Court (Seattle Div)**, 516 Third Ave E-327 Courthouse, Seattle, WA 98104-3273. 206-296-3565 (PST) 8:30AM-4:30PM. Misdemeanor, Civil Actions Under $25,000, Small Claims.

**District Court (Southwest Division-Seattle)**, 601 SW 149th St, Seattle, WA 98166. 206-296-0133 (PST) 8:30AM-4:30PM. Misdemeanor, Civil Actions Under $25,000, Small Claims.

**District Court (Southwest Div-Vashon)**, 19021 99th SW (PO Box 111), Vashon, WA 98070-0111. 206-296-3664 (PST) 8:30AM-4:30PM M,W,F. Misdemeanor, Civil Actions Under $25,000, Small Claims.

## Kitsap County

**Real Estate Recording**, Kitsap County Auditor, 614 Division Street, Room 106 /MS 31, Port Orchard, WA 98366. 360-876-7133 (PST) 8AM-4:30PM.

**Superior Court**, 614 Division St, Port Orchard, WA 98366-4699. 360-876-7164 (PST) 8AM-4:30PM. Felony, Civil Actions Over $25,000, Eviction, Probate.

**District Court South**, 614 Division St, Port Orchard, WA 98366. 360-876-7033 (PST) 8AM-4:30PM. Misdemeanor, Civil Actions Under $25,000, Small Claims.

**District Court North**, 19050 Jensen Way NE, Poulsbo, WA 98370-0910. 360-779-5600 (PST) 8AM-4:30PM. Misdemeanor, Civil Actions Under $25,000, Small Claims.

## Kittitas County

**Real Estate Recording**, Kittitas County Auditor, 205 West 5th, Room 105, Ellensburg, WA 98926-3129. 509-962-7504 (PST) 9AM-5PM.

**Superior Court**, 205 W 5th, Ellensburg, WA 98926. 360-962-7531 (PST) 9AM-5PM, Closed 12-1. Felony, Misdemeanor, Civil Actions Over $25,000, Eviction, Probate.

**District Court Upper Kittitas**, 618 E First, Cle Elum, WA 98922. 360-674-5533 (PST) 8AM-5PM. Misdemeanor, Civil Actions Under $25,000, Small Claims.

**District Court Lower Kittitas**, 5th and Main, Rm 180, Ellensburg, WA 98926. 360-962-7511 (PST) 9AM-5PM. Misdemeanor, Civil Actions Under $25,000, Small Claims.

## Klickitat County

**Real Estate Recording**, Klickitat County Auditor, 205 S. Columbus Avenue, Room 203, Goldendale, WA 98620. 509-773-4001 (PST) 9AM-5PM.

**Superior Court**, 205 S Columbus, Rm 204, Goldendale, WA 98620. 360-773-5744 (PST) 9AM-5PM. Felony, Civil Actions Over $25,000, Eviction, Probate.

**East District Court**, 205 S Columbus, Rm 107, Goldendale, WA 98620-9290. 360-773-4670 (PST) 8AM-5PM. Misdemeanor, Civil Actions Under $25,000, Small Claims.

**West District Court**, PO Box 435, White Salmon, WA 98672-0435. 360-493-1190 (PST) 9AM-5PM. Misdemeanor, Civil Actions Under $25,000, Small Claims.

## Lewis County

**Real Estate Recording**, Lewis County Auditor, 351 NW North Street, Chehalis, WA 98532. 360-740-1163 (PST) 8AM-5PM.

**Superior Court**, 360 NW North St, Chehalis, WA 98532-1900. 360-748-9121 (PST) 8AM-5PM. Felony, Misdemeanor, Civil Actions Over $25,000, Eviction, Probate.

**District Court**, PO Box 336, Chehalis, WA 98532-0336. 360-740-1203 (PST) 8AM-5PM. Misdemeanor, Civil Actions Under $25,000, Small Claims.

## Lincoln County

**Real Estate Recording**, Lincoln County Auditor, 450 Logan, Davenport, WA 99122. 509-725-4971 (PST) 9AM-4:30PM.

**Superior Court**, Box 369, Davenport, WA 99122-0396. 360-725-1401 (PST) 8AM-5PM. Felony, Misdemeanor, Civil Actions Over $25,000, Eviction, Probate.

**District Court**, PO Box 118, Davenport, WA 99122-0118. 360-725-2281 (PST) 8:30AM-5PM. Misdemeanor, Civil Actions Under $25,000, Small Claims.

## Mason County

**Real Estate Recording**, Mason County Auditor, 411 North 5th Street, Shelton, WA 98584. 360-427-9670 (PST) 8:30AM-5PM.

**Superior Court**, PO Box 340, Shelton, WA 98584. 360-427-9670 (PST) Felony, Misdemeanor, Civil Actions Over $25,000, Eviction, Probate.

**District Court**, PO Box "O", Shelton, WA 98584-0090. 360-427-9670 (PST) 8:30AM-5PM. Misdemeanor, Civil Actions Under $25,000, Small Claims.

## Okanogan County

**Real Estate Recording**, Okanogan County Auditor, Courthouse, 149 North 3rd, Okanogan, WA 98840. 509-422-7240 (PST) 8:30AM-5PM.

**Superior Court**, PO Box 72, Okanogan, WA 98840. 360-422-7275 (PST) 8AM-5PM. Felony, Misdemeanor, Civil Actions Over $25,000, Eviction, Probate.

**District Court**, PO Box 980, Okanogan, WA 98840-0980. 360-422-7170 (PST) 8AM-5PM. Misdemeanor, Civil Actions Under $25,000, Small Claims.

## Pacific County

**Real Estate Recording**, Pacific County Auditor, 300 Memorial Drive, South Bend, WA 98586. 360-875-9318 (PST) 8AM-5PM.

**Superior Court**, PO Box 67, South Bend, WA 98586. 360-875-9320 (PST) 8AM-5PM. Felony, Civil Actions Over $25,000, Eviction, Probate.

**District Court South**, PO Box 794, Ilwaco, WA 98624. 360-642-9417 (PST) 8:30AM-4PM. Misdemeanor, Civil Actions Under $25,000, Small Claims.

**District Court North**, Box 134, South Bend, WA 98586-0134. 360-875-9354 (PST) Misdemeanor, Civil Actions Under $25,000, Small Claims.

## Pend Oreille County

**Real Estate Recording**, Pend Oreille County Auditor, West 625 4th Street, Newport, WA 99156. 509-447-3185 (PST) 8AM-4:30PM.

**Superior Court**, 229 S Garden Ave (PO Box 5000), Newport, WA 99156-5020. 360-447-2435 (PST) 8AM-4:30PM. Felony, Civil Actions Over $25,000, Eviction, Probate.

**District Court**, PO Box 5030, Newport, WA 99156-5030. 360-447-4110 (PST) 8AM-4:30PM. Misdemeanor, Civil Actions Under $25,000, Small Claims.

## Pierce County

**Real Estate Recording**, Pierce County Auditor, 2401 South 35th Street, Room 200, Tacoma, WA 98409. 206-591-7440 (PST) 8:30AM-4:30PM.

**Superior Court**, 930 Tacoma Ave South, Rm 110, Tacoma, WA 98402. 206-591-7455 (PST)

8AM-4:30PM. Felony, Civil Actions Over $25,000, Eviction, Probate.

**District Court #4**, PO Box 110, Buckley, WA 98321-0110. 206-829-0411 (PST) Misdemeanor, Civil Actions Under $25,000, Small Claims.

**District Court #3**, PO Box 105, Eatonville, WA 98328-0105. 206-832-6000 (PST) 8AM-4:30PM. Misdemeanor, Civil Actions Under $25,000, Small Claims.

**District Court #2**, 6659 Kimball Dr NW, Bldg D, Gig Harbor, WA 98335-1229. 206-851-5131 (PST) 8:30AM-4:30PM. Misdemeanor, Civil Actions Under $25,000, Small Claims.

**District Court #1**, 930 Tacoma Ave S, Rm 601, Tacoma, WA 98402-2175. 206-592-7487 (PST) 8:30AM-4:30PM. Misdemeanor, Civil Actions Under $25,000, Small Claims.

## San Juan County

**Real Estate Recording**, San Juan County Auditor, 350 Court Street, Friday Harbor, WA 98250. 360-378-2161 (PST) 8AM-4:30PM.

**Superior Court**, 350 Court St, Rm 7, Friday Harbor, WA 98250. 360-378-2163 (PST) 8AM-4:30PM. Felony, Misdemeanor, Civil Actions Over $25,000, Eviction, Probate.

**District Court**, PO Box 127, Friday Harbor, WA 98250-0127. 360-378-4017 (PST) 8AM-5PM. Misdemeanor, Civil Actions Under $25,000, Small Claims.

## Skagit County

**Real Estate Recording**, Skagit County Auditor, 205 Kincaid Street, Mount Vernon, WA 98273. 360-336-9311 (PST) 8:30AM-4:30PM.

**Superior Court**, PO Box 837, Mount Vernon, WA 98273. 360-336-9440 (PST) 8:30AM-4:30PM. Felony, Misdemeanor, Civil Actions Over $25,000, Eviction, Probate.

**District Court**, 600 S 3rd, Mount Vernon, WA 98273. 360-336-9319 (PST) 8:30AM-4:30PM. Misdemeanor, Civil Actions Under $25,000, Small Claims.

## Skamania County

**Real Estate Recording**, Skamania County Auditor, 240 Vancouver Avenue, Stevenson, WA 98648. 509-427-9420 (PST) 8:30AM-5PM.

**Superior Court**, PO Box 790, Stevenson, WA 98648. 360-427-9431 (PST) 8:30AM-5PM. Felony, Misdemeanor, Civil Actions Over $25,000, Eviction, Probate.

**District Court**, PO Box 790, Stevenson, WA 98648. 360-427-5141 (PST) 8:30AM-5PM. Misdemeanor, Civil Actions Under $25,000, Small Claims.

## Snohomish County

**Real Estate Recording**, Snohomish County Auditor, Dept. R., M/S # 204, 3000 Rockefeller Avenue, Everett, WA 98201. 206-388-3483 (PST) 9AM-5PM.

**Superior Court**, Mission Bldg #246, 3000 Rockefeller, Everett, WA 98201. 206-388-3466 (PST) 9AM-5PM. Felony, Civil Actions Over $25,000, Eviction, Probate.

**Cascade District Court**, 415 E Burke, Arlington, WA 98223. 206-652-9552 (PST) 9AM-5PM. Misdemeanor, Civil Actions Under $25,000, Small Claims.

**Everett District Court**, 3000 Rockefeller MS 508, Everett, WA 98201. 206-388-3331 (PST) 8:15AM-5PM. Misdemeanor, Civil Actions Under $25,000, Small Claims.

**South District Court**, 20520 68th Ave W, Lynnwood, WA 98036-7457. 360-744-6805 (PST) 8:15AM-5PM. Misdemeanor, Civil Actions Under $25,000, Small Claims.

**Evergreen District Court**, 14414 179th Ave SE, Monroe, WA 98272-0625. 206-568-8572 (PST) 8AM-5PM. Misdemeanor, Civil Actions Under $25,000, Small Claims.

## Spokane County

**Real Estate Recording**, Spokane County Auditor, West 1116 Broadway, Spokane, WA 99260. 509-456-2270 (PST) 8:30AM-5PM.

**Superior Court**, W 1116 Broadway, Spokane, WA 99260. 360-456-2211 (PST) 8:30AM-5PM. Felony, Civil Actions Over $25,000, Eviction, Probate.

**District Court**, Public Safety Bldg, W 1100 Mallon, Spokane, WA 99260. 360-456-2230 (PST) 8:30AM-5PM. Misdemeanor, Civil Actions Under $25,000, Small Claims.

## Stevens County

**Real Estate Recording**, Stevens County Auditor, 215 South Oak, Colville, WA 99114. 509-684-7512 (PST) 8AM-4:30PM.

**Superior Court**, PO Box 350, Colville, WA 99114. 360-684-7575 (PST) 8AM-4:30PM, Closed 12-1. Felony, Civil Actions Over $25,000, Eviction, Probate.

**District Court**, PO Box 163, Colville, WA 99114-0163. 360-684-0524 (PST) 8AM-4:30PM, Closed 12-1. Misdemeanor, Civil Actions Under $25,000, Small Claims.

## Thurston County

**Real Estate Recording**, Thurston County Auditor, 2000 Lakeridge Drive SW, Olympia, WA 98502. 360-786-5405 (PST) 8AM-5PM.

**Superior Court**, 2000 Lakeridge Dr SW, Bldg 2, Olympia, WA 98502. 360-786-5434 (PST) 8AM-5PM. Felony, Misdemeanor, Civil Actions Over $25,000, Eviction, Probate.

**District Court**, 2000 Lakeridge Dr SW, Bldg 3 (PO Box 409, Olympia, WA 98502. 360-786-5450 (PST) 9AM-5PM. Misdemeanor, Civil Actions Under $25,000, Small Claims.

## Wahkiakum County

**Real Estate Recording**, Wahkiakum County Auditor, 64 Main Street, Cathlamet, WA 98612. 360-795-3219 (PST) 8AM-4PM.

**Superior Court**, PO Box 116, Cathlamet, WA 98612. 360-795-3558 (PST) 8AM-4PM. Felony, Misdemeanor, Civil Actions Over $25,000, Eviction, Probate.

**District Court**, PO Box 144, Cathlamet, WA 98612. 360-795-3461 (PST) 8AM-4PM. Misdemeanor, Civil Actions Under $25,000, Small Claims.

## Walla Walla County

**Real Estate Recording**, Walla Walla County Auditor, 315 West Main Street, Walla Walla, WA 99362. 509-527-3204 (PST) 9AM-5PM.

**Superior Court**, PO Box 836, Walla Walla, WA 99362. 360-527-3221 (PST) 9AM-5PM. Felony, Civil Actions Over $25,000, Eviction, Probate.

**District Court**, 328 W Poplar, Walla Walla, WA 99362. 360-527-3236 (PST) 9AM-4PM. Misdemeanor, Civil Actions Under $25,000, Small Claims.

## Whatcom County

**Real Estate Recording**, Whatcom County Auditor, 311 Grand Avenue, Bellingham, WA 98225. 360-676-6741 (PST) 8:30AM-4:30PM.

**Superior Court**, PO Box 1144, Bellingham, WA 98227. 360-676-6777 (PST) 8:30AM-4:30PM. Felony, Civil Actions Over $25,000, Eviction, Probate.

**District Court**, 311 Grand Ave, Bellingham, WA 98225. 360-676-6770 (PST) 8AM-4:30PM. Misdemeanor, Civil Actions Under $25,000, Small Claims.

## Whitman County

**Real Estate Recording**, Whitman County Auditor, North 404 Main, 2nd Floor, Colfax, WA 99111. 509-397-6270 (PST) 8AM-5PM (Recording Until 2:30PM).

**Superior Court**, Box 390, Colfax, WA 99111. 360-397-4622 (PST) 8AM-5PM. Felony, Civil Actions Over $25,000, Eviction, Probate.

**District Court**, N 404 Main St, Colfax, WA 99111. 360-397-6260 (PST) 8AM-5PM. Misdemeanor, Civil Actions Under $25,000, Small Claims.

**District Court**, PO Box 249, Pullman, WA 99163. 360-332-2065 (PST) 8AM-5PM. Misdemeanor, Civil Actions Under $25,000, Small Claims.

## Yakima County

**Real Estate Recording**, Yakima County Auditor, Second & B Street, Courthouse, Room 117, Yakima, WA 98901. 509-575-4048 (PST) 9AM-4:30PM.

**Superior Court**, 128 N 2nd St, Rm 323, Yakima, WA 98901. 360-575-4120 (PST) 8:30AM-4:30PM. Felony, Civil Actions Over $25,000, Eviction, Probate.

**District Court**, 505 S 7th St, Sunnyside, WA 98944. 360-837-3713 (PST) 8:30AM-4:30PM. Misdemeanor, Civil Actions Under $25,000, Small Claims.

**District Court**, PO Box 446, Toppenish, WA 98948. 360-865-5070 (PST) 8:30AM-5PM. Misdemeanor, Civil Actions Under $25,000, Small Claims.

**District Court**, 128 N 2nd St, Rm 225, Yakima, WA 98901-2631. 360-575-4013 (PST) 8:30AM-4:30PM. Misdemeanor, Civil Actions Under $25,000, Small Claims.

# West Virginia

## Barbour County

**Real Estate Recording**, Barbour County Clerk, 8 North Main Street, Courthouse, Philippi, WV 26416. 304-457-2232 (EST) 8:30AM-4:30PM.

**Circuit Court**, 8 N Main St, Philippi, WV 26416. 304-457-3454 (EST) 8AM-4:30PM. Felony, Civil Actions Over $5,000, Probate.

**Magistrate Court**, PO Box 541, Philippi, WV 26416. 304-457-3676 (EST) 8:30AM-4:30PM. Misdemeanor, Civil Actions Under $5,000, Eviction, Small Claims.

## Berkeley County

**Real Estate Recording**, Berkeley County Clerk, 100 West King Street, Martinsburg, WV 25401. 304-264-1927 (EST) 9AM-5PM.

**Circuit Court**, 100 W King St, Martinsburg, WV 25401. 304-267-3000 (EST) 9AM-5PM. Felony, Civil Actions Over $5,000, Probate.

**Magistrate Court**, 120 W John St, Martinsburg, WV 25401. 304-264-1956 (EST) 9AM-4PM. Misdemeanor, Civil Actions Under $5,000, Eviction, Small Claims.

## Boone County

**Real Estate Recording**, Boone County Clerk, 200 State Street, Madison, WV 25130. 304-369-7337 (EST) 8AM-4PM.

**Circuit Court**, 200 State St, Madison, WV 25130. 304-369-3925 (EST) Felony, Civil Actions Over $5,000, Probate.

**Magistrate Court**, 200 State St., Madison, WV 25130. 304-369-7300 (EST) 8AM-4PM. Misdemeanor, Civil Actions Under $5,000, Eviction, Small Claims.

## Braxton County

**Real Estate Recording**, Braxton County Clerk, 300 Main Street, Sutton, WV 26601. 304-765-2833 (EST) 8AM-4PM.

**Circuit Court**, 300 Main St, Sutton, WV 26601. 304-765-2837 (EST) Felony, Civil Actions Over $5,000, Probate.

**Magistrate Court**, 307 Main St, Sutton, WV 26601. 304-765-5678 (EST) Misdemeanor, Civil Actions Under $5,000, Eviction, Small Claims.

## Brooke County

**Real Estate Recording**, Brooke County Clerk, 632 Main Street, Courthouse, Wellsburg, WV 26070. 304-737-3661 (EST) 9AM-5PM; Sat 9AM-Noon.

**Circuit Court**, Brooke County Courthouse, Wellsburg, WV 26070. 304-737-3662 (EST) 9AM-5PM. Felony, Civil Actions Over $5,000, Probate.

**Magistrate Court**, 632 Main St, Wellsburg, WV 26070. 304-737-1321 (EST) 9AM-4PM. Misdemeanor, Civil Actions Under $5,000, Eviction, Small Claims.

## Cabell County

**Real Estate Recording**, Cabell County Clerk, Cabell County Courthouse, 750 Fifth Ave., Room 108, Huntington, WV 25701-2083. 304-526-8625 (EST) 8:30AM-4:30PM.

**Circuit Court**, PO Box 0545, Huntington, WV 25710-0545. 304-526-8622 (EST) 8:30AM-4:30PM. Felony, Civil Actions Over $5,000, Probate.

**Magistrate Court**, 750 5th Ave, Basement, Huntington, WV 25701. 304-526-8642 (EST) 8:30AM-4:30PM. Misdemeanor, Civil Actions Under $5,000, Eviction, Small Claims.

## Calhoun County

**Real Estate Recording**, Calhoun County Clerk, Main Street, Courthouse, Grantsville, WV 26147. 304-354-6725 (EST) 9AM-4:30PM.

**Circuit Court**, PO Box 266, Grantsville, WV 26147. 304-354-6910 (EST) 9AM-4:30PM, 9AM-Noon 1st Sat ea month. Felony, Civil Actions Over $5,000, Probate.

**Magistrate Court**, PO Box 186, Grantsville, WV 26147. 304-354-6698 (EST) 9AM-4:30PM. Misdemeanor, Civil Actions Under $5,000, Eviction, Small Claims.

## Clay County

**Real Estate Recording**, Clay County Clerk, Courthouse, 207 Main St., Clay, WV 25043. 304-587-4259 (EST) 8AM-4PM.

**Circuit Court**, PO Box 129, Clay, WV 25043. 304-587-4256 (EST) 8AM-4PM. Felony, Civil Actions Over $5,000, Probate.

**Magistrate Court**, PO Box 393, Clay, WV 25043. 304-587-2131 (EST) 8:30AM-4:30PM. Misdemeanor, Civil Actions Under $5,000, Eviction, Small Claims.

## Doddridge County

**Real Estate Recording**, Doddridge County Clerk, 118 East Court Street, Room 102, West Union, WV 26456-1297. 304-873-2631 (EST) 8:30AM-4PM.

**Circuit Court**, 118 E. Court St, West Union, WV 26456. 304-873-2331 (EST) 8:40AM-4PM. Felony, Civil Actions Over $5,000, Probate.

**Magistrate Court**, PO Box 207, West Union, WV 26456. 304-873-2694 (EST) 8AM-4PM. Misdemeanor, Civil Actions Under $5,000, Eviction, Small Claims.

## Fayette County

**Real Estate Recording**, Fayette County Clerk, Courthouse, Fayetteville, WV 25840. 304-574-1200 (EST) 8AM-4PM.

**Circuit Court**, 100 Court St, Fayetteville, WV 25840. 304-574-1200 (EST) 8AM-4PM. Felony, Civil Actions Over $5,000, Probate.

**Magistrate Court**, 100 Court St, Fayetteville, WV 25840. 304-574-1200 (EST) 9AM-9PM M-F, 9AM-12PM Sat. Misdemeanor, Civil Actions Under $5,000, Eviction, Small Claims.

## Gilmer County

**Real Estate Recording**, Gilmer County Clerk, 10 Howard Street, Courthouse, Glenville, WV 26351. 304-462-7641 (EST) 8AM-4PM.

**Circuit Court**, Gilmer County Courthouse, Glenville, WV 26351. 304-462-7241 (EST) 8AM-4PM. Felony, Civil Actions Over $5,000, Probate.

**Magistrate Court**, Courthouse Annex, Glenville, WV 26351. 304-462-7812 (EST) 8:30AM-4PM. Misdemeanor, Civil Actions Under $5,000, Eviction, Small Claims.

## Grant County

**Real Estate Recording**, Grant County Clerk, 5 Highland Avenue, Petersburg, WV 26847. 304-257-4550 (EST) 9AM-4PM.

**Circuit Court**, 5 Highland Ave, Petersburg, WV 26847. 304-257-4545 (EST) 9AM-4PM. Felony, Civil Actions Over $5,000, Probate.

**Magistrate Court**, 5 Highland Ave (PO Box 216), Petersburg, WV 26847. 304-257-4637 (EST) 9AM-4PM. Misdemeanor, Civil Actions Under $5,000, Eviction, Small Claims.

## Greenbrier County

**Real Estate Recording**, Greenbrier County Clerk, 200 North Court Street, Lewisburg, WV 24901. 304-647-6602 (EST) 8:30AM-4:30PM.

**Circuit Court**, PO Drawer 751, Philippi, WV 26416. 304-647-6626 (EST) 8:30AM-4:30PM. Felony, Civil Actions Over $5,000, Probate.

**Magistrate Court**, 200 North Court St, Lewisburg, WV 24901. 304-647-6632 (EST) 8:30AM-4PM. Misdemeanor, Civil Actions Under $5,000, Eviction, Small Claims.

## Hampshire County

**Real Estate Recording**, Hampshire County Clerk, Main Street, Courthouse, Romney, WV 26757. 304-822-5112 (EST) 9AM-4PM (F open until 8PM).

**Circuit Court**, PO Box 343, Romney, WV 26757. 304-822-5022 (EST) 9AM-4PM M-F 5PM-8PM Friday evening. Felony, Civil Actions Over $5,000, Probate.

**Magistrate Court**, 239 W Birch Ln, PO Box 881, Romney, WV 26757. 304-822-4311 (EST) 8:30AM-4PM. Misdemeanor, Civil Actions Under $5,000, Eviction, Small Claims.

## Hancock County

**Real Estate Recording**, Hancock County Clerk, 102 Court Street, New Cumberland, WV 26047. 304-564-3311 (EST) 8:30AM-4:30PM.

**Circuit Court**, PO Box 428, New Cumberland, WV 26047. 304-564-3311 (EST) 8:30AM-4:30PM. Felony, Civil Actions Over $5,000, Probate.

**Magistrate Court**, 106 Court St, New Cumberland, WV 26047. 304-564-3355 (EST) MTWF 8AM-4PM Th 8AM-9PM. Misdemeanor, Civil Actions Under $5,000, Eviction, Small Claims.

## Hardy County

**Real Estate Recording**, Hardy County Clerk, 204 Washington Street, Courthouse - Room 111, Moorefield, WV 26836. 304-538-2929 (EST) 9AM-4PM; Sat 9AM-Noon.

**Circuit Court**, 204 Washington St, RM 237, Moorefield, WV 26836. 304-538-7869 (EST) 9AM-4PM. Felony, Civil Actions Over $5,000, Probate.

**Magistrate Court**, 204 Washington St, Moorefield, WV 26836. 304-538-6836 (EST) 8AM-4PM. Misdemeanor, Civil Actions Under $5,000, Eviction, Small Claims.

## Harrison County

**Real Estate Recording**, Harrison County Clerk, 301 West Main Street, Courthouse, Clarksburg, WV 26301. 304-624-8612 (EST) 8:30AM-4PM.

**Circuit Court**, 301 W. Main, Suite 301, Clarksburg, WV 26301-2967. 304-624-8460 (EST) 8:30AM-4PM. Felony, Civil Actions Over $5,000, Probate.

**Magistrate Court**, 301 W. Main, Rm 203, Clarksburg, WV 26301. 304-624-8645 (EST) 8AM-4PM. Misdemeanor, Civil Actions Under $5,000, Eviction, Small Claims.

## Jackson County

**Real Estate Recording**, Jackson County Clerk, Court & Main Streets, P.O. Box 800, Ripley, WV 25271. 304-372-2011 (EST) 9AM-4PM; 9AM-Noon Sat.

**Circuit Court**, PO Box 427, Ripley, WV 25271. 304-372-2011 (EST) 9AM-4PM M-F, 9AM-12PM Sat. Felony, Civil Actions Over $5,000, Probate.

**Magistrate Court**, Court & Main St, Ripley, WV 25271. 304-372-2011 (EST) 9AM-4PM. Misdemeanor, Civil Actions Under $5,000, Eviction, Small Claims.

## Jefferson County

**Real Estate Recording**, Jefferson County Clerk, 100 East Washington Street, Courthouse, Charles Town, WV 25414. 304-728-3216 (EST) 9AM-5PM (F open until 7PM).

**Circuit Court**, PO Box 584, Charles Town, WV 25414. 304-725-9761 (EST) 9AM-5PM. Felony, Civil Actions Over $5,000, Probate.

**Magistrate Court**, PO Box 607, Charles Town, WV 25414. 304-725-0471 (EST) 8:30AM-4:30PM. Misdemeanor, Civil Actions Under $5,000, Eviction, Small Claims.

## Kanawha County

**Real Estate Recording**, Kanawha County Clerk, 409 Virginia Street East, Charleston, WV 25301. 304-357-0130 (EST) 8AM-4PM M,T,W,F; 8AM-7PM Th.

**Circuit Court**, PO Box 2351, Charleston, WV 25328. 304-357-0440 (EST) 8AM-5M MTWF, 8AM-7PM Th. Felony, Civil Actions Over $5,000, Probate.

**Magistrate Court**, 111 Court St, Charleston, WV 25333. 304-357-0400 (EST) 8:30AM-4:30PM. Misdemeanor, Civil Actions Under $5,000, Eviction, Small Claims.

## Lewis County

**Real Estate Recording**, Lewis County Clerk, 110 Center Avenue, Courthouse, Weston, WV 26452. 304-269-8215 (EST) 8:30AM-4:30PM.

**Circuit Court**, PO Box 69, Weston, WV 26452. 304-269-8210 (EST) 8:30AM-4:30PM. Felony, Civil Actions Over $5,000, Probate.

**Magistrate Court**, 111 Court St, Weston, WV 26452. 304-269-8230 (EST) Misdemeanor, Civil Actions Under $5,000, Eviction, Small Claims.

## Lincoln County

**Real Estate Recording**, Lincoln County Clerk, 8000 Court Avenue, Hamlin, WV 25523. 304-824-3336 (EST) 9AM-4:30PM.

**Circuit Court**, PO Box 338, Hamlin, WV 25523. 304-824-7887 (EST) 9AM-4:30PM. Felony, Civil Actions Over $5,000, Probate.

**Magistrate Court**, PO Box 573, Hamlin, WV 25523. 304-824-5001 (EST) 8AM-4:30PM. Misdemeanor, Civil Actions Under $5,000, Eviction, Small Claims.

## Logan County

**Real Estate Recording**, Logan County Clerk, Stratton & Main Street, Courthouse, Room 101, Logan, WV 25601. 304-792-8600 (EST) 8:30AM-4:30PM.

**Circuit Court**, Logan County Courthouse, Rm 311, Logan, WV 25601. 304-792-8550 (EST) 8:30AM-4:30PM. Felony, Civil Actions Over $5,000, Probate.

**Magistrate Court**, Logan County Courthouse, Logan, WV 25601. 304-792-8651 (EST) 8:30AM-4:30PM. Misdemeanor, Civil Actions Under $5,000, Eviction, Small Claims.

## Marion County

**Real Estate Recording**, Marion County Clerk, 211 Adams Street, Courthouse, Fairmont, WV 26554. 304-367-5440 (EST)

**Circuit Court**, PO Box 1269, Fairmont, WV 26554. 304-367-5360 (EST) 8:30AM-4:30PM. Felony, Civil Actions Over $5,000, Probate.

**Magistrate Court**, 200 Jackson St, Fairmont, WV 26554. 304-367-5330 (EST) 8:30AM-4:30PM MTWF, 8:30AM-9PM Th. Misdemeanor, Civil Actions Under $5,000, Eviction, Small Claims.

## Marshall County

**Real Estate Recording**, Marshall County Clerk, 7th Street & Tomlinson Avenue, Moundsville, WV 26041. 304-845-1220 (EST) 8:30AM-4:30PM (F open until 5:30PM).

**Circuit Court**, Marshall County Courthouse, 7th St, Moundsville, WV 26041. 304-845-2130 (EST) 8:30AM-4:30PM. Felony, Civil Actions Over $5,000, Probate.

## Mason County

**Real Estate Recording**, Mason County Clerk, 200 6th Street, Courthouse, Point Pleasant, WV 25550. 304-675-1997 (EST) 8:30AM-4:30PM.

**Circuit Court**, PO Box 402, Point Pleasant, WV 25550. 304-675-4400 (EST) 8:30AM-4:30PM. Felony, Civil Actions Over $5,000, Probate.

**Magistrate Court**, Cor. of 6th St and Viand, Point Pleasant, WV 25550. 304-675-6840 (EST) 8:30AM-4:30PM. Misdemeanor, Civil Actions Under $5,000, Eviction, Small Claims.

## McDowell County

**Real Estate Recording**, McDowell County Clerk, 90 Wyoming Street, Suite 109, Welch, WV 24801-2487. 304-436-8544 (EST) 9AM-5PM.

**Circuit Court**, PO Box 400, Welch, WV 24801. 304-436-8513 (EST) 8:30AM-4:30PM. Felony, Civil Actions Over $5,000, Probate.

**Magistrate Court**, PO Box 447, Welch, WV 24801. 304-436-8587 (EST) 9AM-5PM. Misdemeanor, Civil Actions Under $5,000, Eviction, Small Claims.

## Mercer County

**Real Estate Recording**, Mercer County Clerk, Courthouse Square, Princeton, WV 24740. 304-425-9571 (EST) 8:30AM-4PM.

**Circuit Court**, 1501 W. Main St, Princeton, WV 24740. 304-487-8369 (EST) Felony, Civil Actions Over $5,000, Probate.

**Magistrate Court**, 1428 Main St, Princeton, WV 24740. 304-425-7952 (EST) 8:30AM-4:30PM. Misdemeanor, Civil Actions Under $5,000, Eviction, Small Claims.

## Mineral County

**Real Estate Recording**, Mineral County Clerk, 150 Armstrong Street, Keyser, WV 26726. 304-788-3924 (EST) 8:30AM-5PM.

**Circuit Court**, 150 Armstrong St, Keyser, WV 26726. 304-788-1562 (EST) Felony, Civil Actions Over $5,000, Probate.

**Magistrate Court**, 105 West St, Keyser, WV 26726. 304-788-2625 (EST) 8:30AM-4:30PM. Misdemeanor, Civil Actions Under $5,000, Eviction, Small Claims.

## Mingo County

**Real Estate Recording**, Mingo County Clerk, 75 E. 2nd Ave., Williamson, WV 25661. 304-235-1638 (EST) 8:30AM-4:30PM.

**Circuit Court**, PO Box 435, Williamson, WV 25661. 304-235-4994 (EST) 8:30AM-4:30PM MTWF, 8:30AM-6:30PM Th. Felony, Civil Actions Over $5,000, Probate.

**Magistrate Court**, PO Box 986, Williamson, WV 25661. 304-235-2445 (EST) 8:30AM-4:30PM. Misdemeanor, Civil Actions Under $5,000, Eviction, Small Claims.

## Monongalia County

**Real Estate Recording**, Monongalia County Clerk, 243 High Street, Courthouse - Room 123, Morgantown, WV 26505-5491. 304-291-7230 (EST) 9AM-7PM M; 9AM-5PM T-F.

**Circuit Court**, County Courthouse, 263 High St, Morgantown, WV 26505. 304-291-7240 (EST) 9AM-5PM. Felony, Civil Actions Over $5,000, Probate.

**Magistrate Court**, 265 Spruce St, Morgantown, WV 26505. 304-291-7296 (EST) 8AM-7PM. Misdemeanor, Civil Actions Under $5,000, Eviction, Small Claims.

## Monroe County

**Real Estate Recording**, Monroe County Clerk, Main Street, Union, WV 24983. 304-772-3096 (EST) 8:30AM-4:30PM.

**Circuit Court**, PO Box 350, Union, WV 24983. 304-772-3017 (EST) 8AM-4PM. Felony, Civil Actions Over $5,000, Probate.

**Magistrate Court**, PO Box 4, Union, WV 24983. 304-772-3321 (EST) 8:30AM-4:30PM. Misdemeanor, Civil Actions Under $5,000, Eviction, Small Claims.

## Morgan County

**Real Estate Recording**, Morgan County Clerk of County Commission, 202 Fairfax Street, Suite 100, Berkeley Springs, WV 25411. 304-258-8547 (EST) 9AM-5PM M,T,Th; 9AM-1PM W; 9AM-7PM F.

# West Virginia

Circuit Court, 202 Fairfax St, Ste 101, Berkeley Springs, WV 25411-1501. 304-258-8554 (EST) 9AM-5PM MTTh, 9AM-1PM Wed, 9AM-7PM Fri. Felony, Civil Actions Over $5,000, Probate.

Magistrate Court, 202 Fairfax St, Ste 202, Berkeley Springs, WV 25411. 304-258-8631 (EST) 9AM-4:30PM. Misdemeanor, Civil Actions Under $5,000, Eviction, Small Claims.

## Nicholas County

Real Estate Recording, Nicholas County Clerk, 700 Main Street, Suite 2, Summersville, WV 26651. 304-872-3630 (EST) 8:30AM-4:30PM.

Circuit Court, 700 Main St, Summersville, WV 26651. 304-872-3630 (EST) 8:30AM-4:30PM. Felony, Civil Actions Over $5,000, Probate.

Magistrate Court, 511 Church St, Summersville, WV 26651. 304-872-3630 (EST) 8:30AM-4:30PM. Misdemeanor, Civil Actions Under $5,000, Eviction, Small Claims.

## Ohio County

Real Estate Recording, Ohio County Clerk, 205 City County Building, Wheeling, WV 26003-3589. 304-234-3656 (EST) 8:30AM-4PM.

Circuit Court, 1500 Chapline St, Wheeling, WV 26003. 304-234-3611 (EST) 8:30AM-5PM. Felony, Civil Actions Over $5,000, Probate.

Magistrate Court, Courthouse Annex, 46 15th St, Wheeling, WV 26003. 304-234-3709 (EST) 8AM-4:30PM. Misdemeanor, Civil Actions Under $5,000, Eviction, Small Claims.

## Pendleton County

Real Estate Recording, Pendleton County Clerk, Main Street, Courthouse, Franklin, WV 26807. 304-358-2505 (EST) 8:30AM-4PM; Sat 8:30AM-Noon.

Circuit Court, PO Box 846, Franklin, WV 26807. 304-358-7067 (EST) 8:30AM-4PM. Felony, Civil Actions Over $5,000, Probate.

Magistrate Court, PO Box 637, Franklin, WV 26807. 304-358-2343 (EST) 9AM-4PM. Misdemeanor, Civil Actions Under $5,000, Eviction, Small Claims.

## Pleasants County

Real Estate Recording, Pleasants County Clerk, Courthouse, 301 Court Lane, Room 101, St. Marys, WV 26170. 304-684-3542 (EST) 8:30AM-4:30PM.

Circuit Court, 301 Court Lane, Rm 201, St. Mary's, WV 26170. 304-684-3513 (EST) 8:30AM-4:30PM. Felony, Civil Actions Over $5,000, Probate.

Magistrate Court, 301 Court Lane, Rm B-6, St Mary's, WV 26170. 304-684-7197 (EST) 8:00AM-5:00PM. Misdemeanor, Civil Actions Under $5,000, Eviction, Small Claims.

## Pocahontas County

Real Estate Recording, Pocahontas County Clerk, 900C 10th Avenue, Marlinton, WV 24954. 304-799-4549 (EST) 9AM-4:30PM.

Circuit Court, 900-D 10th Ave, Marlinton, WV 24954. 304-799-4604 (EST) 9AM-4:30PM. Felony, Civil Actions Over $5,000, Probate.

Magistrate Court, 900 10th Ave, Marlinton, WV 24954. 304-799-6603 (EST) 9AM-4:30PM.

Misdemeanor, Civil Actions Under $5,000, Eviction, Small Claims.

## Preston County

Real Estate Recording, Preston County Clerk, 101 West Main Street, Room 201, Kingwood, WV 26537. 304-329-0070 (EST) 9AM-5PM (F open until 7PM).

Circuit Court, 101 W. Main St, Rm 101, Kingwood, WV 26537. 304-329-0047 (EST) 9AM-5PM M-Th, 9AM-7PM Fri. Felony, Civil Actions Over $5,000, Probate.

Magistrate Court, 328 Tunnelton, Kingwood, WV 26537. 304-329-2764 (EST) 8:30AM-4:30PM. Misdemeanor, Civil Actions Under $5,000, Eviction, Small Claims.

## Putnam County

Real Estate Recording, Putnam County Clerk, Route 35 Courthouse Drive, Winfield, WV 25213. 304-586-0202 (EST)

Circuit Court, PO Box 906, Winfield, WV 25213. 304-586-0203 (EST) 6AM-4PM MTWF, 8AM-7PM Th. Felony, Civil Actions Over $5,000, Probate.

Magistrate Court, PO Box 507, Winfield, WV 25213. 304-755-7234 (EST) 8:30AM-4:30PM. Misdemeanor, Civil Actions Under $5,000, Eviction, Small Claims.

## Raleigh County

Real Estate Recording, Raleigh County Clerk, 215 Main Street, Courthouse, Beckley, WV 25801. 304-255-9123 (EST) 8:30AM-4PM.

Circuit Court, 215 Main St, Beckley, WV 25801. 304-255-9135 (EST) 8:30AM-4:30PM. Felony, Civil Actions Over $5,000, Probate.

Magistrate Court, 116 N. Heber St, Beckley, WV 25801. 304-255-9197 (EST) 8AM-4PM. Misdemeanor, Civil Actions Under $5,000, Eviction, Small Claims.

## Randolph County

Real Estate Recording, Randolph County Clerk, 4 Randolph Avenue, Elkins, WV 26241. 304-636-0543 (EST)

Circuit Court, Courthouse, Elkins, WV 26241. 304-636-2765 (EST) 8AM-4:30PM. Felony, Civil Actions Over $5,000, Probate.

Magistrate Court, #2 Randolph Ave, Elkins, WV 26241. 304-636-5885 (EST) 8AM-4:30PM. Misdemeanor, Civil Actions Under $5,000, Eviction, Small Claims.

## Ritchie County

Real Estate Recording, Ritchie County Clerk, 115 East Main Street, Courthouse - Room 201, Harrisville, WV 26362. 304-643-2164 (EST) 8AM-4PM.

Circuit Court, 115 E. Main St, Harrisville, WV 26362. 304-643-2163 (EST) 8AM-4PM. Felony, Civil Actions Over $5,000, Probate.

Magistrate Court, 319 E. Main St, Harrisville, WV 26362. 304-643-4409 (EST) Misdemeanor, Civil Actions Under $5,000, Eviction, Small Claims.

## Roane County

Real Estate Recording, Roane County Clerk, 200 Main Street, Spencer, WV 25276. 304-927-2860 (EST) 9AM-4PM; 9AM-Noon 1st Sat of the month.

Circuit Court, PO Box 122, Spencer, WV 25276. 304-927-2750 (EST) 9AM-4PM M-F, Closed 12-1. Felony, Civil Actions Over $5,000, Probate.

Magistrate Court, PO Box 663, Spencer, WV 25276. 304-927-4750 (EST) 9AM-4PM. Misdemeanor, Civil Actions Under $5,000, Eviction, Small Claims.

## Summers County

Real Estate Recording, Summers County Clerk, Ballengee Street, Courthouse, Hinton, WV 25951. 304-466-7104 (EST) 8:30AM-4:30PM.

Circuit Court, PO Box 1058, Hinton, WV 25951. 304-466-7103 (EST) 8:30AM-4:30PM. Felony, Civil Actions Over $5,000, Probate.

Magistrate Court, PO Box 1059, Hinton, WV 25951. 304-466-7129 (EST) 8:30AM-4:20PM. Misdemeanor, Civil Actions Under $5,000, Eviction, Small Claims.

## Taylor County

Real Estate Recording, Taylor County Clerk, 214 West Main Street, Room 101, Courthouse, Grafton, WV 26354. 304-265-1401 (EST)

Circuit Court, 214 W. Main St, Rm 104, Grafton, WV 26354. 304-265-2480 (EST) 8:30AM-4:30PM, Closed 12-1. Felony, Civil Actions Over $5,000, Probate.

Magistrate Court, 214 W. Main St, Grafton, WV 26354. 304-265-1322 (EST) 8:30AM-4:30PM. Misdemeanor, Civil Actions Under $5,000, Eviction, Small Claims.

## Tucker County

Real Estate Recording, Tucker County Clerk, Courthouse, 215 First St., Parsons, WV 26287. 304-478-2414 (EST) 8AM-4PM.

Circuit Court, PO Box 267, Parsons, WV 26287. 304-478-2606 (EST) Felony, Civil Actions Over $5,000, Probate.

Magistrate Court, 203 Main St, Parsons, WV 26287. 304-478-2665 (EST) 8AM-4PM. Misdemeanor, Civil Actions Under $5,000, Eviction, Small Claims.

## Tyler County

Real Estate Recording, Tyler County Clerk, Corner of Main & Court Street, Middlebourne, WV 26149. 304-758-2102 (EST) 8AM-4PM.

Circuit Court, PO Box 8, Middlebourne, WV 26149. 304-758-4811 (EST) Felony, Civil Actions Over $5,000, Probate.

Magistrate Court, PO Box 127, 225 Main St, Middlebourne, WV 26149. 304-758-2137 (EST) Misdemeanor, Civil Actions Under $5,000, Eviction, Small Claims.

## Upshur County

Real Estate Recording, Upshur County Clerk, 40 W. Main Street, Courthouse - Room 101, Buckhannon, WV 26201. 304-472-1068 (EST) 8AM-4PM.

Circuit Court, 40 W. Main St, Rm 102, Buckhannon, WV 26201. 304-472-2370 (EST) 8AM-4PM. Felony, Civil Actions Over $5,000, Probate.

Magistrate Court, 69 W. Main St, Buckhannon, WV 26201. 304-472-2053 (EST) 8:30AM-

4:30PM. Misdemeanor, Civil Actions Under $5,000, Eviction, Small Claims.

## Wayne County

**Real Estate Recording**, Wayne County Clerk, 700 Hendricks Street, Courthouse, Wayne, WV 25570. 304-272-6372 (EST) 8AM-4PM; 9AM-12 Sat.

**Circuit Court**, PO Box 38, Wayne, WV 25570. 304-272-6359 (EST) 8AM-4PM. Felony, Civil Actions Over $5,000, Probate.

**Magistrate Court**, PO Box 667, Wayne, WV 25570. 304-272-5648 (EST) 8AM-4PM. Misdemeanor, Civil Actions Under $5,000, Eviction, Small Claims.

## Webster County

**Real Estate Recording**, Webster County Clerk, Courthouse - Room G-1, 2 Court Square, Webster Springs, WV 26288-1054. 304-847-2508 (EST) 8:30AM-4PM.

**Circuit Court**, 2 Court Square, Rm G-4, Webster Springs, WV 26288. 304-847-2421 (EST) 8:30AM-4PM. Felony, Civil Actions Over $5,000, Probate.

**Magistrate Court**, 2 Court Square, Rm B-1, Webster Springs, WV 26288. 304-847-2613 (EST) 8:30AM-4PM. Misdemeanor, Civil Actions Under $5,000, Eviction, Small Claims.

## Wetzel County

**Real Estate Recording**, Wetzel County Clerk, Main Street, Courthouse, New Martinsville, WV 26155. 304-455-8224 (EST) 9AM-4:30PM M,T,W,F; 9AM-4PM Th; 9AM-Noon Sat.

**Circuit Court**, PO Box 263, New Martinsville, WV 26155. 304-455-8219 (EST) 9AM-4:30PM. Felony, Civil Actions Over $5,000, Probate.

**Magistrate Court**, PO Box 147, 229 Main St, New Martinsville, WV 26155. 304-455-5040 (EST) 8:30AM-4:30PM. Misdemeanor, Civil Actions Under $5,000, Eviction, Small Claims.

## Wirt County

**Real Estate Recording**, Wirt County Clerk, Courthouse Square, Elizabeth, WV 26143. 304-275-4271 (EST) 8:30AM-4PM.

**Circuit Court**, PO Box 465, Elizabeth, WV 26143. 304-275-6597 (EST) 8:30AM-4PM. Felony, Civil Actions Over $5,000, Probate.

**Magistrate Court**, PO Box 249, Elizabeth, WV 26143. 304-275-3641 (EST) 8:30AM-4PM. Misdemeanor, Civil Actions Under $5,000, Eviction, Small Claims.

## Wood County

**Real Estate Recording**, Wood County Clerk, 3rd & Market Streets, Parkersburg, WV 26101. 304-424-1850 (EST) 8:30AM-4:30PM.

**Circuit Court**, Wood County Judicial, #2 Government Sq, Parkersburg, WV 26101-5353. 304-424-1700 (EST) 8:30AM-4:30PM. Felony, Civil Actions Over $5,000, Probate.

**Magistrate Court**, 208 Avery St, Parkersburg, WV 26101. 304-422-3444 (EST) 8:30AM-4:30PM. Misdemeanor, Civil Actions Under $5,000, Eviction, Small Claims.

## Wyoming County

**Real Estate Recording**, Wyoming County Clerk, Main Street, Courthouse, Pineville, WV 24874. 304-732-8000 (EST) 8AM-4PM.

**Circuit Court**, PO Box 190, Pineville, WV 24874. 304-732-8000 (EST) 9AM-4PM. Felony, Civil Actions Over $5,000, Probate.

**Magistrate Court**, PO Box 598, Pineville, WV 24874. 304-732-8000 (EST) 9AM-4PM M-Th, 9AM-6PM Fri. Misdemeanor, Civil Actions Under $5,000, Eviction, Small Claims.

# Wisconsin

## Adams County

**Real Estate Recording**, Adams County Register of Deeds, 402 Main Street, Friendship, WI 53934. 608-339-4206 (CST) 8AM-Noon, 1-4:30PM.

**Circuit Court**, PO Box 220, Friendship, WI 53934. 608-339-4208 (CST) 8AM-4:30PM. Felony, Misdemeanor, Civil, Eviction, Small Claims.

**Register in Probate**, PO Box 200, Friendship, WI 53934. 608-339-4213 (CST) 8AM-4:30PM. Probate.

## Ashland County

**Real Estate Recording**, Ashland County Register of Deeds, 201 West Main Street, Ashland, WI 54806. 715-682-7008 (CST) 8AM-Noon, 1PM-4PM.

**Circuit Court**, Courthouse Rm 307, Ashland, WI 54806. 715-682-7016 (CST) 8AM-4PM, Closed 12-1. Felony, Misdemeanor, Civil, Eviction, Small Claims.

**Register in Probate**, Courthouse Rm 203, Ashland, WI 54806. 715-682-7009 (CST) 8AM-4PM. Probate.

## Barron County

**Real Estate Recording**, Barron County Register of Deeds, 330 East LaSalle, Barron, WI 54812. 715-537-6210 (CST) 8AM-4PM.

**Circuit Court**, Barron County Courthouse, Barron, WI 54812. 715-537-6265 (CST) 8AM-4PM. Felony, Misdemeanor, Civil, Eviction, Small Claims.

**Register in Probate**, Courthouse Rm 218, Barron, WI 54812. 715-537-6261 (CST) 8AM-4PM. Probate.

## Bayfield County

**Real Estate Recording**, Bayfield County Register of Deeds, 117 East 5th, Washburn, WI 54891. 715-373-6119 (CST) 8AM-4PM.

**Circuit Court**, 117 E 5th, Washburn, WI 54891. 715-373-6108 (CST) 8AM-4PM. Felony, Misdemeanor, Civil, Eviction, Small Claims.

**Register in Probate**, 115 E 5th, Washburn, WI 54891. 715-373-6108 (CST) 8AM-4PM. Probate.

## Brown County

**Real Estate Recording**, Brown County Register of Deeds, 111 North Jefferson Street, Room 248, Green Bay, WI 54301. 414-448-4470 (CST) 8AM-4:30PM.

**Circuit Court**, PO Box 23600, Green Bay, WI 54305-3600. 414-448-4161 (CST) 8AM-4:30PM. Felony, Misdemeanor, Civil, Eviction, Small Claims.

**Register in Probate**, PO Box 23600, Green Bay, WI 54305-3600. 414-448-4275 (CST) 8AM-4:30PM. Probate.

## Buffalo County

**Real Estate Recording**, Buffalo County Register of Deeds, 407 Second Street, Alma, WI 54610. 608-685-6230 (CST) 8AM-4:30PM.

**Circuit Court**, 407 S 2nd, Alma, WI 54610. 608-685-6212 (CST) 8AM-4:30PM. Felony, Misdemeanor, Civil, Eviction, Small Claims.

**Register in Probate**, 407 S 2nd, Alma, WI 54610. 608-685-6212 (CST) 8AM-4:30PM. Probate.

## Burnett County

**Real Estate Recording**, Burnett County Register of Deeds, 7410 County Road K #103, Siren, WI 54872. 715-349-2183 (CST) 8:30AM-4:30PM.

**Circuit Court**, 7410 County Road K #115, Siren, WI 54872. 715-349-2147 (CST) 8:30AM-4:30PM. Felony, Misdemeanor, Civil, Eviction, Small Claims.

**Register in Probate**, 7410 County Road K #110, Siren, WI 54872. 715-349-2177 (CST) 8:30AM-4:30PM. Probate.

## Calumet County

**Real Estate Recording**, Calumet County Register of Deeds, 206 Court Street, Chilton, WI 53014. 414-849-2361 (CST) 8AM-12, 1PM-4:30PM.

**Circuit Court**, 206 Court St, Chilton, WI 53014. 414-849-1414 (CST) 8AM-4:30PM. Felony, Misdemeanor, Civil, Eviction, Small Claims.

**Register in Probate**, 206 Court St, Chilton, WI 53014. 414-849-1455 (CST) 8AM-4:30PM. Probate.

## Chippewa County

**Real Estate Recording**, Chippewa County Register of Deeds, 711 North Bridge Street, Chippewa Falls, WI 54729-1876. 715-726-7994 (CST) 8AM-4:30PM.

**Circuit Court**, 711 N Bridge St, Chippewa Falls, WI 54729-1879. 715-726-7758 (CST) 8AM-4:30PM. Felony, Misdemeanor, Civil, Eviction, Small Claims.

**Register in Probate**, 711 N Bridge St, Chippewa Falls, WI 54729. 715-726-7737 (CST) 8AM-4:30PM. Probate.

## Clark County

**Real Estate Recording**, Clark County Register of Deeds, 517 Court Street, Room 303, Neillsville, WI 54456. 715-743-5162 (CST) 8AM-Noon, 12:30-5PM.

**Circuit Court**, 517 Court St, Neillsville, WI 54456. 715-743-5181 (CST) 8AM-5PM. Felony, Misdemeanor, Civil, Eviction, Small Claims.

**Register in Probate**, 517 Court St, Rm 403, Neillsville, WI 54456. 715-743-5172 (CST) 8AM-5PM. Probate.

## Columbia County

**Real Estate Recording**, Columbia County Register of Deeds, 400 DeWitt Street, Portage, WI 53901. 608-742-2191 (CST) 8AM-4:30PM.

**Circuit Court**, PO Box 587, Portage, WI 53901. 608-742-2191 (CST) 8AM-4:30PM. Felony, Misdemeanor, Civil, Eviction, Small Claims.

**Register in Probate**, PO Box 221, Portage, WI 53901. 608-742-2191 (CST) 8AM-4:30PM. Probate.

## Crawford County

**Real Estate Recording**, Crawford County Register of Deeds, 220 North Beaumont Road, Prairie du Chien, WI 53821. 608-326-0219 (CST) 8AM-4:30PM.

**Circuit Court**, 220 N Beaumont Rd, Prairie Du Chien, WI 53821. 608-326-0211 (CST) 8AM-4:30PM. Felony, Misdemeanor, Civil, Eviction, Small Claims.

**Register in Probate**, 220 N Beaumont Rd, Prairie Du Chien, WI 53821. 608-326-0206 (CST) 8AM-4:30PM. Probate.

## Dane County

**Real Estate Recording**, Dane County Register of Deeds, 210 Martin Luther King Jr. Blvd., Room 110, Madison, WI 53709. 608-266-4143 (CST) 7:45AM-4PM.

**Circuit Court**, 210 Martin Luther King Jr Blvd, Rm 202, Madison, WI 53709. 608-266-4311 (CST) 7:45AM-4:30PM. Felony, Misdemeanor, Civil, Eviction, Small Claims.

**Register in Probate**, 210 Martin Luther King Jr Blvd, Rm 305, Madison, WI 53709. 608-266-4331 (CST) 7:45AM-4:30PM. Probate.

## Dodge County

**Real Estate Recording**, Dodge County Register of Deeds, 127 East Oak Street, Administration Building, Juneau, WI 53039-1391. 414-386-3720 (CST) 8AM-Noon, 12:30-4:30PM.

**Circuit Court**, 105 N Main, Juneau, WI 53039. 414-386-4411 (CST) 8AM-4:30PM. Felony, Misdemeanor, Civil, Eviction, Small Claims.

**Register in Probate**, 105 N Main St, Juneau, WI 53039-1056. 414-386-3550 (CST) 8AM-4:30PM. Probate.

## Door County

**Real Estate Recording**, Door County Register of Deeds, 421 Nebraska Street, Sturgeon Bay, WI 54235. 414-746-2270 (CST) 8AM-Noon, 12:30-4:30PM.

**Circuit Court**, PO Box 670, Sturgeon Bay, WI 54235. 414-746-2205 (CST) 8AM-4:30PM. Felony, Misdemeanor, Civil, Eviction, Small Claims.

**Register in Probate**, PO Box 670, Sturgeon Bay, WI 54235. 414-746-2280 (CST) 8AM-4:30PM. Probate.

## Douglas County

**Real Estate Recording**, Douglas County Register of Deeds, 1313 Belknap Street, Courthouse - Room 107, Superior, WI 54880. 715-394-0551 (CST) 8AM-4:30PM.

**Circuit Court**, 1313 Belknap, Superior, WI 54880. 715-394-0240 (CST) 8AM-4:30PM. Felony, Misdemeanor, Civil, Eviction, Small Claims.

**Register in Probate**, 1313 Belknap, Superior, WI 54880. 715-394-0229 (CST) 8AM-4:30PM. Probate.

## Dunn County

**Real Estate Recording**, Dunn County Register of Deeds, 800 Wilson Avenue, Menomonie, WI 54751. 715-232-1228 (CST) 8AM-4:30PM.

**Circuit Court**, 800 Wilson Ave, Menomonie, WI 54751. 715-232-2611 (CST) 8AM-4:30PM. Felony, Misdemeanor, Civil, Eviction, Small Claims.

**Register in Probate**, 800 Wilson Ave, Menomonie, WI 54751. 715-232-1449 (CST) 8AM-4:30PM. Probate.

## Eau Claire County

**Real Estate Recording**, Eau Claire County Register of Deeds, 721 Oxford Avenue, Courthouse, Room 1310, Eau Claire, WI 54703. 715-839-4745 (CST) 8AM-5PM.

**Circuit Court**, 721 Oxford Ave, Eau Claire, WI 54703. 715-839-4816 (CST) 8AM-5PM. Felony, Misdemeanor, Civil, Eviction, Small Claims.

**Register in Probate**, 721 Oxford Ave, Eau Claire, WI 54703. 715-839-4823 (CST) 8:30AM-4PM. Probate.

## Florence County

**Real Estate Recording**, Florence County Register of Deeds, 501 Lake Avenue, Florence, WI 54121. 715-528-4252 (CST) 8:30AM-Noon, 12:30-4PM.

**Circuit Court**, PO Box 410, Florence, WI 54121. 715-528-3205 (CST) 8:30AM-4PM. Felony, Misdemeanor, Civil, Eviction, Small Claims.

**Register in Probate**, PO Box 410, Florence, WI 54121. 715-528-3205 (CST) 8:30AM-4PM. Probate.

## Fond du Lac County

**Real Estate Recording**, Fond du Lac County Register of Deeds, 160 South Macy Street, Fond du Lac, WI 54935. 414-929-3018 (CST)

**Circuit Court**, PO Box 1355, Fond Du Lac, WI 54936-1355. 414-929-3041 (CST) 8AM-4:30PM. Felony, Misdemeanor, Civil, Eviction, Small Claims.

**Register in Probate**, PO Box 1355, Fond Du Lac, WI 54936-1355. 414-929-3084 (CST) 8AM-4:30PM. Probate.

## Forest County

**Real Estate Recording**, Forest County Register of Deeds, Madison Street, Crandon, WI 54520. 715-478-3823 (CST)

**Circuit Court**, 200 E Madison St, Crandon, WI 54520. 715-478-3323 (CST) 8:30AM-4:30PM. Felony, Misdemeanor, Civil, Eviction, Small Claims.

**Register in Probate**, 200 E Madison St, Crandon, WI 54520. 715-478-2418 (CST) Probate.

## Grant County

**Real Estate Recording**, Grant County Register of Deeds, 130 West Maple, Lancaster, WI 53813. 608-723-2727 (CST) 8AM-4:30PM.

**Circuit Court**, PO Box 46, Lancaster, WI 53813. 608-723-2752 (CST) 8AM-4:30PM. Felony, Misdemeanor, Civil, Eviction, Small Claims.

**Register in Probate**, 130 W Maple St, Lancaster, WI 53813. 608-723-2697 (CST) 8AM-4:30PM. Probate.

## Green County

**Real Estate Recording**, Green County Register of Deeds, 1016 16th Avenue, Courthouse, Monroe, WI 53566. 608-328-9439 (CST) 8AM-5PM.

**Circuit Court**, 1016 16th Ave, Monroe, WI 53566. 608-328-9433 (CST) Felony, Misdemeanor, Civil, Eviction, Small Claims.

**Register in Probate**, 1016 16th Ave, Monroe, WI 53566. 608-328-9430 (CST) 8AM-5PM. Probate.

## Green Lake County

**Real Estate Recording**, Green Lake County Register of Deeds, 492 Hill Street, Green Lake, WI 54941. 414-294-4021 (CST) 8:30AM-4:30PM.

**Circuit Court**, 492 Hill St, Green Lake, WI 54941. 414-294-4142 (CST) 8:30AM-4PM. Felony, Misdemeanor, Civil, Eviction, Small Claims.

**Register in Probate**, 492 Hill St, Green Lake, WI 54941. 414-294-4044 (CST) 8:30AM-4:30PM. Probate.

## Iowa County

**Real Estate Recording**, Iowa County Register of Deeds, 222 North Iowa Street, Dodgeville, WI 53533. 608-935-5628 (CST) 8:30AM-4:30PM.

**Circuit Court**, 222 N Iowa St, Dodgeville, WI 53533. 608-935-5052 (CST) 8:30AM-4:30PM. Felony, Misdemeanor, Civil, Eviction, Small Claims.

**Register in Probate**, 222 N Iowa St, Dodgeville, WI 53533. 608-935-5812 (CST) 8:30AM-4:30PM, Closed 12-1. Probate.

## Iron County

**Real Estate Recording**, Iron County Register of Deeds, 300 Taconite Street, Hurley, WI 54534. 715-561-2945 (CST) 8AM-4PM.

**Circuit Court**, 300 Taconite St, Hurley, WI 54534. 715-561-4084 (CST) 8AM-4PM. Felony, Misdemeanor, Civil, Eviction, Small Claims.

**Register in Probate**, 300 Taconite St, Hurley, WI 54534. 715-561-3434 (CST) 8AM-4PM. Probate.

## Jackson County

**Real Estate Recording**, Jackson County Register of Deeds, 307 Main, Black River Falls, WI 54615. 715-284-0204 (CST) 8AM-4:30PM.

**Circuit Court**, 307 Main St, Black River Falls, WI 54615. 715-284-0208 (CST) Felony, Misdemeanor, Civil, Eviction, Small Claims.

**Register in Probate**, 307 Main St, Black River Falls, WI 54615. 715-284-0213 (CST) 8AM-4:30PM. Probate.

## Jefferson County

**Real Estate Recording**, Jefferson County Register of Deeds, 320 South Main Street, Courthouse, Room 106, Jefferson, WI 53549. 414-674-7235 (CST) 8AM-4:30PM.

**Circuit Court**, 320 S Main St, Jefferson, WI 53549. 414-674-7150 (CST) 8AM-4:30PM. Felony, Misdemeanor, Civil, Eviction, Small Claims.

**Register in Probate**, 320 S Main St, Jefferson, WI 53549. 414-674-7245 (CST) 8AM-4:30PM. Probate.

## Juneau County

**Real Estate Recording**, Juneau County Register of Deeds, Courthouse, 220 E. State St., Mauston, WI 53948. 608-847-9325 (CST) 8AM-Noon, 12:30-4:30PM.

**Circuit Court**, 220 E State St, Mauston, WI 53948. 608-847-9356 (CST) 8AM-4:30PM, Closed 12-1. Felony, Misdemeanor, Civil, Eviction, Small Claims.

**Register in Probate**, 220 E State St, Mauston, WI 53948. 608-847-9346 (CST) 8AM-4:30PM. Probate.

## Kenosha County

**Real Estate Recording**, Kenosha County Register of Deeds, 912 56th Street, Courthouse, Kenosha, WI 53140. 414-653-6511 (CST) 8AM-5PM.

**Circuit Court**, 912 56th St, Kenosha, WI 53140. 414-653-6664 (CST) Felony, Misdemeanor, Civil, Eviction, Small Claims.

**Register in Probate**, 912 56th St, Kenosha, WI 53140. 414-653-6678 (CST) 8AM-5PM. Probate.

## Kewaunee County

**Real Estate Recording**, Kewaunee County Register of Deeds, 613 Dodge Street, Kewaunee, WI 54216-1398. 414-388-4410 (CST) X126 8AM-4:30PM.

**Circuit Court**, 613 Dodge St, Kewaunee, WI 54216. 414-388-4410 (CST) Felony, Misdemeanor, Civil, Eviction, Small Claims.

**Register in Probate**, 613 Dodge St, Kewaunee, WI 54216. 414-388-4410 (CST) 8AM-4:30PM. Probate.

## La Crosse County

**Real Estate Recording**, La Crosse County Register of Deeds, 400 North 4th Street, La Crosse, WI 54601. 608-785-9645 (CST) 8:30AM-5PM.

**Circuit Court**, 400 N 4th St, La Crosse, WI 54601. 608-785-9590 (CST) 8:30AM-5PM. Felony, Misdemeanor, Civil, Eviction, Small Claims.

**Register in Probate**, 400 N 4th St Rm 312, La Crosse, WI 54601. 608-785-9882 (CST) 8:30AM-5PM. Probate.

## Lafayette County

**Real Estate Recording**, Lafayette County Register of Deeds, 626 Main Street, Darlington, WI 53530. 608-776-4838 (CST) 8AM-4:30PM.

**Circuit Court**, 626 Main St, Darlington, WI 53530. 608-776-4832 (CST) 8AM-4:30PM. Felony, Misdemeanor, Civil, Eviction, Small Claims.

**Register in Probate**, 626 Main St, Darlington, WI 53530. 608-776-4811 (CST) 8AM-4:30PM. Probate.

## Langlade County

**Real Estate Recording**, Langlade County Register of Deeds, 800 Clermont Street, Antigo, WI 54409. 715-627-6209 (CST) 8:30AM-4:30PM.

**Circuit Court**, 800 Clairmont St, Antigo, WI 54409. 715-627-6215 (CST) Felony, Misdemeanor, Civil, Eviction, Small Claims.

**Register in Probate**, 800 Clermont St, Antigo, WI 54409. 715-627-6213 (CST) 8:30AM-4:30PM. Probate.

## Lincoln County

**Real Estate Recording**, Lincoln County Register of Deeds, 1110 East Main, Courthouse, Merrill, WI 54452. 715-536-0318 (CST) 8:15AM-4:30PM.

**Circuit Court**, 1110 E Main St, Merrill, WI 54452. 715-536-0320 (CST) Felony, Misdemeanor, Civil, Eviction, Small Claims.

**Register in Probate**, 1110 E Main St, Merrill, WI 54452. 715-536-0342 (CST) 8:15AM-4:30PM. Probate.

## Manitowoc County

**Real Estate Recording**, Manitowoc County Register of Deeds, 1010 South 8th Street, Courthouse, Manitowoc, WI 54220. 414-683-4010 (CST) 8:30AM-5PM M; 8:30AM-4:30PM T-F.

**Circuit Court**, PO Box 2000, Manitowoc, WI 54221-2000. 414-683-4030 (CST) 8:30AM-4:30PM. Felony, Misdemeanor, Civil, Eviction, Small Claims.

**Register in Probate**, 1010 S 8th St Rm 116, Manitowoc, WI 54220. 414-683-4015 (CST) 8:30AM-4:30PM. Probate.

## Marathon County

**Real Estate Recording**, Marathon County Register of Deeds, 500 Forest Street, Courthouse, Wausau, WI 54403-5568. 715-847-5214 (CST) 8AM-5PM.

**Circuit Court**, 500 Forest St, Wausau, WI 54403. 715-847-5495 (CST) 8AM-5PM (Summer hours 8AM-4:30PM Memorial-Labor Day). Felony, Misdemeanor, Civil, Eviction, Small Claims.

**Register in Probate**, 500 Forest St, Wausau, WI 54403. 715-847-5218 (CST) 8AM-5PM. Probate.

## Marinette County

**Real Estate Recording**, Marinette County Register of Deeds, 1926 Hall Avenue, Courthouse, Marinette, WI 54143. 715-732-7550 (CST) 8:30AM-4:30PM.

**Circuit Court**, PO Box 320, Marinette, WI 54143-0320. 715-732-7454 (CST) Felony, Misdemeanor, Civil, Eviction, Small Claims.

**Register in Probate**, PO Box 320, Marinette, WI 54143-0320. 715-732-7475 (CST) 8:30AM-4:30PM. Probate.

## Marquette County

**Real Estate Recording**, Marquette County Register of Deeds, 77 West Park, Montello, WI 53949. 608-297-9132 (CST) 8AM-Noon, 12:30-4:30PM.

**Circuit Court**, PO Box 187, Montello, WI 53949. 608-297-9102 (CST) 8AM-4:30PM, Closed 12-12:30. Felony, Misdemeanor, Civil, Eviction, Small Claims.

**Register in Probate**, 77 W Park St, Montello, WI 53949. 608-297-9105 (CST) 8AM-4:30PM. Probate.

## Menominee County

**Real Estate Recording**, Menominee County Register of Deeds, Courthouse Lane, Keshena, WI 54135. 715-799-3312 (CST) 8AM-Noon, 1PM-4:30PM.

**Circuit Court**, PO Box 428, Keshena, WI 54135. 715-799-3313 (CST) 8AM-4PM. Felony, Misdemeanor, Civil, Eviction, Small Claims.

**Register in Probate**, PO Box 428, Keshena, WI 54135. 715-526-9352 (CST) Probate.

## Milwaukee County

**Real Estate Recording**, Milwaukee County Register of Deeds, 901 North 9th Street, Milwaukee, WI 53233. 414-278-4005 (CST) 8AM-4:30PM.

**Circuit Court-Civil**, 901 9th St Rm G-9, Milwaukee, WI 53233. 414-278-4120 (CST) 8AM-4PM. Civil, Eviction, Small Claims.

**Circuit Court-Criminal**, 821 W State St Rm 136, Milwaukee, WI 53233. 414-278-4588 (CST) 8AM-4PM, Closed 12-1. Felony, Misdemeanor.

**Register in Probate**, 901 N 9th St Rm 207, Milwaukee, WI 53233. 414-278-4444 (CST) 8AM-5PM. Probate.

## Monroe County

**Real Estate Recording**, Monroe County Register of Deeds, 112 South Court Street, Courthouse, Sparta, WI 54656. 608-269-8716 (CST) 8AM-4:30PM.

**Circuit Court**, PO Box 186, Sparta, WI 54656. 608-269-8745 (CST) Felony, Misdemeanor, Civil, Eviction, Small Claims.

**Register in Probate**, PO Box 165, Sparta, WI 54656. 608-269-8701 (CST) 8AM-4:30PM. Probate.

## Oconto County

**Real Estate Recording**, Oconto County Register of Deeds, 300 Washington Street, Oconto, WI 54153-1621. 414-834-6807 (CST) 8AM-4PM.

**Circuit Court**, 300 Washington St, Oconto, WI 54153. 414-834-6855 (CST) 8AM-4PM. Felony, Misdemeanor, Civil, Eviction, Small Claims.

**Register in Probate**, 300 Washington St, Oconto, WI 54153. 414-834-6839 (CST) 8AM-4PM. Probate.

## Oneida County

**Real Estate Recording**, Oneida County Register of Deeds, Oneida Avenue, Courthouse, Rhinelander, WI 54501. 715-369-6150 (CST) 8AM-4:30PM.

**Circuit Court**, PO Box 400, Rhinelander, WI 54501. 715-369-6120 (CST) 8AM-4:30PM. Felony, Misdemeanor, Civil, Eviction, Small Claims.

**Register in Probate**, PO Box 400, Rhinelander, WI 54501. 715-369-6159 (CST) 8AM-4:30PM. Probate.

## Outagamie County

**Real Estate Recording**, Outagamie County Register of Deeds, 410 South Walnut Street, Appleton, WI 54911-5999. 414-832-5095 (CST) 8:30AM-5PM.

**Circuit Court**, 320 S Walnut St, Appleton, WI 54911. 414-832-5130 (CST) 8:30AM-5PM. Felony, Misdemeanor, Civil, Eviction, Small Claims.

**Register in Probate**, 320 S Walnut St, Appleton, WI 54911. 414-832-5601 (CST) 8:30AM-5PM, Closed 12-1. Probate.

## Ozaukee County

**Real Estate Recording**, Ozaukee County Register of Deeds, 121 West Main Street, Port Washington, WI 53074. 414-284-8260 (CST) 8:30AM-5PM.

**Circuit Court**, 1201 S Spring St, Port Washington, WI 53074. 414-284-8409 (CST) 8:30AM-5PM. Felony, Misdemeanor, Civil, Eviction, Small Claims.

**Register in Probate**, PO Box 994, Port Washington, WI 53074. 414-284-8370 (CST) 8:30AM-5PM. Probate.

## Pepin County

**Real Estate Recording**, Pepin County Register of Deeds, 740 7th Avenue West, County Government Center, Durand, WI 54736. 715-672-8856 (CST) 8:30AM-Noon, 12:30PM-4:30PM.

**Circuit Court**, PO Box 39, Durand, WI 54736. 715-672-8861 (CST) 8:30AM-4:30PM, Closed 12-12:30. Felony, Misdemeanor, Civil, Eviction, Small Claims.

**Register in Probate**, PO Box 39, Durand, WI 54736. 715-672-8859 (CST) 8:30AM-4:30PM, Closed 12-12:30. Probate.

## Pierce County

**Real Estate Recording**, Pierce County Register of Deeds, 414 West Main Street, Ellsworth, WI 54011. 715-273-3531 (CST) X213 8AM-5PM.

**Circuit Court**, PO Box 129, Ellsworth, WI 54011. 715-273-3531 (CST) 8:30AM-4:30PM. Felony, Misdemeanor, Civil, Eviction, Small Claims.

**Register in Probate**, PO Box 97, Ellsworth, WI 54011. 715-273-3531 (CST) 8AM-5PM. Probate.

## Polk County

**Real Estate Recording**, Polk County Register of Deeds, 100 Polk Plaza, Balsam Lake, WI 54810. 715-485-3161 (CST) 8:30AM-4:30PM.

**Circuit Court**, 100 Polk Plaza, Balsam Lake, WI 54810. 715-485-3161 (CST) 8:30AM-4:30PM. Felony, Misdemeanor, Civil, Eviction, Small Claims.

**Register in Probate**, 100 Polk Plaza, Balsam Lake, WI 54810. 715-485-3161 (CST) Probate.

## Portage County

**Real Estate Recording**, Portage County Register of Deeds, 1516 Church Street, County-City Building, Stevens Point, WI 54481. 715-346-1430 (CST) 7:30AM-4:30PM.

**Circuit Court (Branches 1, 2 & 3)**, 1516 Church St, Stevens Point, WI 54481. 715-346-

1351 (CST) 7:30AM-4:30PM. Felony, Misdemeanor, Civil, Eviction, Small Claims.

**Register in Probate**, 1516 Church St, Stevens Point, WI 54481. 715-346-1360 (CST) 7:30AM-4:30PM. Probate.

## Price County

**Real Estate Recording**, Price County Register of Deeds, 126 Cherry, Phillips, WI 54555. 715-339-2515 (CST) 8AM-Noon, 1-4:30PM.

**Circuit Court**, Courthouse, Phillips, WI 54555. 715-339-2353 (CST) 8AM-4:30PM, Closed 12-1. Felony, Misdemeanor, Civil, Eviction, Small Claims.

**Register in Probate**, Courthouse, Phillips, WI 54555. 715-339-3078 (CST) 8AM-4:30PM. Probate.

## Racine County

**Real Estate Recording**, Racine County Register of Deeds, 730 Wisconsin Avenue, Racine, WI 53403. 414-636-3208 (CST) 8AM-5PM.

**Circuit Court**, 730 Wisconsin Ave, Racine, WI 53403. 414-636-3333 (CST) Felony, Misdemeanor, Civil, Eviction, Small Claims.

**Register in Probate**, 730 Wisconsin Ave, Racine, WI 53403. 414-636-3137 (CST) 8AM-5PM. Probate.

## Richland County

**Real Estate Recording**, Richland County Register of Deeds, Seminary Street, Courthouse, Richland Center, WI 53581. 608-647-3011 (CST) 8:30AM-4:30PM.

**Circuit Court**, PO Box 655, Richland Center, WI 53581. 608-647-3956 (CST) 8:30AM-4:30PM. Felony, Misdemeanor, Civil, Eviction, Small Claims.

**Register in Probate**, PO Box 427, Richland Center, WI 53581. 608-647-2626 (CST) 8:30AM-4:30PM, Closed 12-1. Probate.

## Rock County

**Real Estate Recording**, Rock County Register of Deeds, 51 South Main Street, Janesville, WI 53545. 608-757-5657 (CST) 8AM-5PM.

**Circuit Court-South**, 250 Garden Ln, Beloit, WI 53511. 608-364-2010 (CST) 8AM-5PM. Felony, Misdemeanor, Civil, Eviction, Small Claims.

**Circuit Court-North**, 51 S Main, Janesville, WI 53545. 608-757-5556 (CST) 8AM-5PM. Felony, Misdemeanor, Civil, Eviction, Small Claims.

**Register in Probate**, 51 S Main, Janesville, WI 53545. 608-757-5635 (CST) Probate.

## Rusk County

**Real Estate Recording**, Rusk County Register of Deeds, 311 Miner Avenue, Ladysmith, WI 54848-0311. 715-532-2139 (CST) 8AM-4:30PM.

**Circuit Court**, 311 Miner Ave East, Ladysmith, WI 54848. 715-532-2108 (CST) 8AM-4:30PM. Felony, Misdemeanor, Civil, Eviction, Small Claims.

**Register in Probate**, 311 Miner East, Ladysmith, WI 54848. 715-532-2147 (CST) 8AM-4:30PM. Probate.

## Sauk County

**Real Estate Recording**, Sauk County Register of Deeds, 515 Oak Street, Courthouse, Baraboo, WI 53913. 608-355-3288 (CST) 8AM-4:30PM.

**Circuit Court**, PO Box 449, Baraboo, WI 53913. 603-356-5581 (CST) 8AM-4:30PM. Felony, Misdemeanor, Civil, Eviction, Small Claims.

**Register in Probate**, 515 Oak St, Baraboo, WI 53913. 608-355-3226 (CST) 8AM-4:30PM. Probate.

## Sawyer County

**Real Estate Recording**, Sawyer County Register of Deeds, 406 Main, Hayward, WI 54843. 715-634-4867 (CST) 8AM-4PM.

**Circuit Court**, PO Box 508, Hayward, WI 54843. 715-634-4887 (CST) 8AM-4PM. Felony, Misdemeanor, Civil, Eviction, Small Claims.

**Register in Probate**, PO Box 447, Hayward, WI 54843. 715-634-4887 (CST) 8AM-4PM. Probate.

## Shawano County

**Real Estate Recording**, Shawano County Register of Deeds, 311 North Main, Shawano, WI 54166. 715-524-2129 (CST) 8AM-4:30PM.

**Circuit Court**, 311 N Main Rm 206, Shawano, WI 54166. 715-526-9347 (CST) 8AM-4:30PM. Felony, Misdemeanor, Civil, Eviction, Small Claims.

**Register in Probate**, 311 N Main Rm 203, Shawano, WI 54166. 715-526-9352 (CST) 8AM-4:30PM. Probate.

## Sheboygan County

**Real Estate Recording**, Sheboygan County Register of Deeds, 615 North 6th Street, Courthouse - Room 106, Sheboygan, WI 53081. 414-459-3023 (CST) 8AM-5PM.

**Circuit Court**, 615 N 6th St, Sheboygan, WI 53081. 414-459-3068 (CST) 8AM-5PM. Felony, Misdemeanor, Civil, Eviction, Small Claims.

**Register in Probate**, 615 N 6th St, Sheboygan, WI 53081. 414-459-3068 (CST) 8AM-5PM. Probate.

## St. Croix County

**Real Estate Recording**, St. Croix County Register of Deeds, 1101 Carmichael Rd., Hudson, WI 54016. 715-386-4652 (CST) 8AM-5PM.

**Circuit Court**, 1101 Carmichael Rd, Hudson, WI 54016. 715-386-4629 (CST) 8AM-5PM. Felony, Misdemeanor, Civil, Eviction, Small Claims.

**Register in Probate**, 1101 Carmichael Rd, Rm 2242, Hudson, WI 54016. 715-386-4618 (CST) 8AM-5PM. Probate.

## Taylor County

**Real Estate Recording**, Taylor County Register of Deeds, 224 South 2nd Street, Medford, WI 54451. 715-748-1483 (CST) 8:30AM-4:30PM.

**Circuit Court**, PO Box 97, Medford, WI 54451. 715-748-1425 (CST) 8:30AM-4:30PM. Felony, Misdemeanor, Civil, Eviction, Small Claims.

**Register in Probate**, 224 S 2nd, Medford, WI 54451. 715-748-1435 (CST) 8:30AM-4:30PM. Probate.

## Trempealeau County

**Real Estate Recording**, Trempealeau County Register of Deeds, 1720 Main Street, Courthouse, Whitehall, WI 54773. 715-538-2311 (CST) 8AM-4:30PM.

**Circuit Court**, 1720 Main St, Whitehall, WI 54773. 715-538-2311 (CST) Felony, Misdemeanor, Civil, Eviction, Small Claims.

**Register in Probate**, 1720 Main St, Whitehall, WI 54773. 715-538-2311 (CST) 8AM-4:30PM. Probate.

## Vernon County

**Real Estate Recording**, Vernon County Register of Deeds, 400 Court House Square St., Court House Annex, Viroqua, WI 54665. 608-637-3568 (CST) 8:30AM-4:30PM.

**Circuit Court**, PO Box 426, Viroqua, WI 54665. 608-637-3220 (CST) Felony, Misdemeanor, Civil, Eviction, Small Claims.

**Register in Probate**, PO Box 448, Viroqua, WI 54665. 608-637-3872 (CST) 8:30AM-4:30PM. Probate.

## Vilas County

**Real Estate Recording**, Vilas County Register of Deeds, 330 Court St., Eagle River, WI 54521. 715-479-3660 (CST) 8AM-4PM.

**Circuit Court**, PO Box 369, Eagle River, WI 54521. 715-479-3632 (CST) Felony, Misdemeanor, Civil, Eviction, Small Claims.

**Register in Probate**, PO Box 369, Eagle River, WI 54521. 715-479-3642 (CST) 8AM-4PM. Probate.

## Walworth County

**Real Estate Recording**, Walworth County Register of Deeds, Courthouse - Room 102, Courthouse Square, Elkhorn, WI 53121. 414-741-4237 (CST) 8AM-5PM.

**Circuit Court**, PO Box 1001, Elkhorn, WI 53121. 414-741-4224 (CST) 8AM-5PM. Felony, Misdemeanor, Civil, Eviction, Small Claims.

**Register in Probate**, PO Box 1001, Elkhorn, WI 53121. 414-741-4256 (CST) 8AM-5PM. Probate.

## Washburn County

**Real Estate Recording**, Washburn County Register of Deeds, 110 West 4th Avenue, Shell Lake, WI 54871. 715-468-7421 (CST) 8AM-4:30PM.

**Circuit Court**, PO Box 339, Shell Lake, WI 54871. 715-468-7468 (CST) 8AM-4:30PM. Felony, Misdemeanor, Civil, Eviction, Small Claims.

**Register in Probate**, PO Box 316, Shell Lake, WI 54871. 715-468-2960 (CST) Probate.

## Washington County

**Real Estate Recording**, Washington County Register of Deeds, 432 East Washington Street, Room 2084, West Bend, WI 53095. 414-335-4318 (CST) 8AM-4:30PM.

**Circuit Court**, PO Box 1986, West Bend, WI 53095-7986. 414-335-4341 (CST) 8AM-4:30PM. Felony, Misdemeanor, Civil, Eviction, Small Claims.

**Register in Probate**, PO Box 1986, West Bend, WI 53095-7986. 414-335-4334 (CST) 8AM-4:30PM. Probate.

## Waukesha County

**Real Estate Recording**, Waukesha County Register of Deeds, 515 West Moreland Blvd., Courthouse, Room 109, Waukesha, WI 53188. 414-548-7590 (CST) 8AM-4:30PM.

**Circuit Court**, 515 W Moreland, Waukesha, WI 53188. 414-548-7524 (CST) 8AM-4:30PM. Felony, Misdemeanor, Civil, Eviction, Small Claims.

**Register in Probate**, 515 W Moreland, Waukesha, WI 53188. 414-548-7468 (CST) 8AM-4:30PM. Probate.

## Waupaca County

**Real Estate Recording**, Waupaca County Register of Deeds, 811 Harding Street, Waupaca, WI 54981. 715-258-6250 (CST) 8AM-4PM.

**Circuit Court**, PO Box 354, Waupaca, WI 54981. 715-258-6460 (CST) 8AM-4PM. Felony, Misdemeanor, Civil, Eviction, Small Claims.

**Register in Probate**, 811 Harding St, Waupaca, WI 54981. 715-258-6429 (CST) 8AM-4PM. Probate.

## Waushara County

**Real Estate Recording**, Waushara County Register of Deeds, 209 South St. Marie, Wautoma, WI 54982. 414-787-4631 (CST) 8AM-Noon, 1-4:30PM.

**Circuit Court**, PO Box 507, Wautoma, WI 54982. 414-787-4631 (CST) 8AM-4:30PM. Felony, Misdemeanor, Civil, Eviction, Small Claims.

**Register in Probate**, PO Box 508, Wautoma, WI 54982. 414-787-4631 (CST) 8AM-4:30PM. Probate.

## Winnebago County

**Real Estate Recording**, Winnebago County Register of Deeds, 415 Jackson Street, Courthouse, Oshkosh, WI 54901. 414-236-4883 (CST) 8AM-4:30PM.

**Circuit Court**, PO Box 2808, Oshkosh, WI 54903. 414-236-4848 (CST) 8AM-4:30PM. Felony, Misdemeanor, Civil, Eviction, Small Claims.

**Register in Probate**, PO Box 2808, Oshkosh, WI 54903. 414-236-4833 (CST) 8AM-4:30PM, Closed 12-1. Probate.

## Wood County

**Real Estate Recording**, Wood County Register of Deeds, 400 Market Street, Wisconsin Rapids, WI 54494. 715-421-8450 (CST) 8AM-Noon, 1-4:45PM.

**Circuit Court**, 400 Market St, Wisconsin Rapids, WI 54494. 715-421-8490 (CST) 8AM-4:45PM. Felony, Misdemeanor, Civil, Eviction, Small Claims.

**Register in Probate**, 400 Market St, Wisconsin Rapids, WI 54494. 715-421-8520 (CST) 8AM-4:45PM, Closed 12-1. Probate.

# Wyoming

## Albany County

**Real Estate Recording**, Albany County Clerk, Courthouse, Room 202, Laramie, WY 82070. 307-721-2541 (MST) 9AM-5PM.

**2nd Judicial District Court**, County Courthouse, 525 Grand, Rm 305, Laramie, WY 82070. 307-721-2508 (MST) 9AM-5PM. Felony, Civil Actions Over $3,000, Probate.

**County Court**, County Courthouse, 525 Grand, Rm 105, Laramie, WY 82070. 307-742-5747 (MST) 8AM-5PM. Misdemeanor, Civil Actions Under $7,000, Eviction, Small Claims.

## Big Horn County

**Real Estate Recording**, Big Horn County Clerk, 420 West C Street, Basin, WY 82410. 307-568-2357 (MST) 8AM-5PM.

**5th Judicial District Court**, PO Box 670, Basin, WY 82410. 307-568-2381 (MST) 8AM-5PM. Felony, Civil Actions Over $3,000, Probate.

**Justice Court**, PO Box 749, Basin, WY 82410. 307-568-2367 (MST) 8AM-5PM. Civil Actions Under $3,000, Small Claims.

## Campbell County

**Real Estate Recording**, Campbell County Clerk, 500 South Gillette Avenue, Suite 220, Gillette, WY 82716. 307-682-7285 (MST) 8AM-5PM.

**6th Judicial District Court**, 500 S Gillette Ave #348, Gillette, WY 82716. 307-682-3424 (MST) 8AM-5PM. Felony, Civil Actions Over $7,000, Probate.

**County Court**, 500 S Gillette Ave #301, Gillette, WY 82716. 307-682-2190 (MST) 8AM-5PM. Civil Actions Under $7,000, Eviction, Small Claims.

## Carbon County

**Real Estate Recording**, Carbon County Clerk, 415 West Pine, P.O. Box 6, Courthouse, Rawlins, WY 82301. 307-328-2630 (MST) 8AM-5PM.

**2nd Judicial District Court**, PO Box 67, Rawlins, WY 82301. 307-328-2628 (MST) 8AM-5PM. Felony, Civil Actions Over $3,000, Probate.

**County Court**, Attn: Chief Clerk, Courthouse, Rawlins, WY 82301. 307-324-6655 (MST) 8AM-5PM. Civil Actions Under $7,000, Eviction, Small Claims.

## Converse County

**Real Estate Recording**, Converse County Clerk, 107 North 5th Street, Douglas, WY 82633. 307-358-2244 (MST) 9AM-5PM.

**8th Judicial District Court**, Box 189, Douglas, WY 82633. 307-358-3165 (MST) 9AM-5PM. Felony, Civil Actions Over $7,000, Probate.

**County Court**, PO Box 45, Douglas, WY 82633. 307-358-2196 (MST) 8AM-5PM. Misdemeanor, Civil Actions Under $7,000, Eviction, Small Claims.

## Crook County

**Real Estate Recording**, Crook County Clerk, 309 Cleveland Street, P.O. Box 37, Sundance, WY 82729. 307-283-1323 (MST) 8AM-5PM.

**6th Judicial District Court**, Box 904, Sundance, WY 82729. 307-283-2523 (MST) 8AM-5PM. Felony, Civil Actions Over $7,000, Probate.

**Justice Court**, PO Box 117, Sundance, WY 82729. 307-283-2929 (MST) 8AM-5PM. Civil Actions Under $3,000, Small Claims.

## Fremont County

**Real Estate Recording**, Fremont County Clerk, 450 N. 2nd Street, Courthouse - Room 220, Lander, WY 82520. 307-332-2405 (MST) 8AM-5PM.

**9th Judicial District Court**, PO Box 370, Lander, WY 82520. 307-332-1134 (MST) 8AM-5PM, Closed 12-1. Felony, Civil Actions Over $7,000, Probate.

**Dubois County Court**, Box 952, Dubois, WY 82513. 307-455-2920 (MST) 8AM-Noon. Misdemeanor, Civil Actions Under $7,000, Eviction, Small Claims.

**Lander County Court**, 450 N. 2nd Rm 230, Lander, WY 82520. 307-332-3239 (MST) 8AM-5PM. Misdemeanor, Civil Actions Under $7,000, Eviction, Small Claims.

**Riverton County Court**, 818 S Federal Blvd, Riverton, WY 82501. 307-856-7259 (MST) 8AM-5PM. Misdemeanor, Civil Actions Under $7,000, Eviction, Small Claims.

## Goshen County

**Real Estate Recording**, Goshen County Clerk, 2125 East A Street, Torrington, WY 82240. 307-532-4051 (MST)

**8th Judicial District Court**, Clerk of District Court, PO Box 818, Torrington, WY 82240. 307-532-2155 (MST) 7:30AM-4PM. Felony, Civil Actions Over $3,000, Probate.

**County Court**, Drawer BB, Torrington, WY 82240. 307-532-2938 (MST) 7AM-4PM. Misdemeanor, Civil Actions Under $7,000, Eviction, Small Claims.

## Hot Springs County

**Real Estate Recording**, Hot Springs County Clerk, 415 Arapahoe Street, Courthouse, Thermopolis, WY 82443-2783. 307-864-3515 (MST) 8AM-5PM.

**5th Judicial District Court**, 415 Arapahoe St, Thermopolis, WY 82443. 307-864-3323 (MST) 8AM-5PM. Felony, Civil Actions Over $3,000, Probate.

**Justice Court**, 417 Arapahoe St, Thermopolis, WY 82443. 307-864-5161 (MST) 8AM-5PM. Misdemeanor, Civil Actions Under $3,000, Small Claims.

## Johnson County

**Real Estate Recording**, Johnson County Clerk, 76 North Main Street, Buffalo, WY 82834. 307-684-7272 (MST) 8AM-5PM.

**4th Judicial District Court**, 76 N Main, Buffalo, WY 82834. 307-684-7271 (MST) 8AM-5PM. Felony, Civil Actions Over $7,000, Probate.

**Justice Court**, 639 Fort St., Buffalo, WY 82834. 307-684-5720 (MST) 8AM-5PM. Misdemeanor, Civil Actions Under $3,000, Small Claims.

## Laramie County

**Real Estate Recording**, Laramie County Clerk, 1902 Carey, Room 202, Cheyenne, WY 82001. 307-638-4256 (MST) 8:30AM-5PM.

**1st Judicial District Court**, PO Box 787, Cheyenne, WY 82003. 307-638-4270 (MST) 8AM-5PM. Felony, Civil Actions Over $7,000, Probate.

**County Court**, 19th Carey Ave, Rm 108, Cheyenne, WY 82001. 307-638-4298 (MST) 8AM-5PM. Misdemeanor, Civil Actions Under $7,000, Eviction, Small Claims.

## Lincoln County

**Real Estate Recording**, Lincoln County Clerk, 925 Sage, Courthouse, Kemmerer, WY 83101. 307-877-9056 (MST) 8:30AM-5PM.

**3rd Judicial District Court**, PO Drawer 510, Kemmerer, WY 83101. 307-877-9056 (MST) Felony, Civil Actions Over $7,000, Probate.

**County Court**, PO Box 949, Kemmerer, WY 83101. 307-877-4431 (MST) 8AM-5PM. Misdemeanor, Civil Actions Under $7,000, Eviction, Small Claims.

## Natrona County

**Real Estate Recording**, Natrona County Clerk, 200 North Center, Casper, WY 82601. 307-235-9206 (MST) 8AM-5PM.

**7th Judicial District Court**, Clerk of District Court, PO Box 3120, Casper, WY 82602. 307-235-9243 (MST) Felony, Civil Actions Over $7,000, Probate.

**County Court**, PO Box 1339, Casper, WY 82602. 307-235-9266 (MST) 8AM-5PM. Misdemeanor, Civil Actions Under $7,000, Eviction, Small Claims.

## Niobrara County

**Real Estate Recording**, Niobrara County Clerk, 424 South Elm, Lusk, WY 82225. 307-334-2211 (MST) 8AM-4PM.

**8th Judicial District Court**, Clerk of District Court, PO Box 1318, Lusk, WY 82225. 307-334-2736 (MST) 8AM-4PM. Felony, Civil Actions Over $3,000, Probate.

**Justice Court**, PO Box 209, Lusk, WY 82225. 307-334-3845 (MST) 9AM-5PM. Misdemeanor, Civil Actions Under $3,000, Small Claims.

## Park County

**Real Estate Recording**, Park County Clerk, 1002 Sheridan, Cody, WY 82414. 307-587-5548 (MST) 8AM-5PM.

**5th Judicial District Court**, Clerk of District Court, PO Box 1960, Cody, WY 82414. 307-587-2204 (MST) 8AM-5PM. Felony, Civil Actions Over $7,000, Probate.

**County Court-Cody**, 1002 Sheridan Ave., Cody, WY 82414. 307-587-2204 (MST) 8AM-5PM. Misdemeanor, Civil Actions Under $7,000, Eviction, Small Claims.

**County Court-Powell**, 109 W. 14th, Powell, WY 82435. 307-754-5163 (MST) 8AM-5PM. Misdemeanor, Civil Actions Under $7,000, Eviction, Small Claims.

# Wyoming

## Platte County

**Real Estate Recording**, Platte County Clerk, 800 9th Street, Wheatland, WY 82201. 307-322-2315 (MST) 8AM-5PM.

**8th Judicial District Court**, PO Box 158, Wheatland, WY 82201. 307-322-3857 (MST) 8AM-5PM. Felony, Civil Actions Over $7,000, Probate.

**Justice Court**, PO Box 306, Wheatland, WY 82201. 307-322-3441 (MST) 8AM-5PM. Misdemeanor, Civil Actions Under $3,000, Small Claims.

## Sheridan County

**Real Estate Recording**, Sheridan County Clerk, 224 South Main Street, Suite B-2, Sheridan, WY 82801-9998. 307-674-6822 (MST) 8AM-5PM.

**4th Judicial District Court**, 224 S. Main, Suite B-11, Sheridan, WY 82801. 307-674-4821 (MST) Felony, Civil Actions Over $7,000, Probate.

**County Court**, 224 S. Main, Suite B-7, Sheridan, WY 82801. 307-672-9718 (MST) 8AM-5PM. Misdemeanor, Civil Actions Under $7,000, Eviction, Small Claims.

## Sublette County

**Real Estate Recording**, Sublette County Clerk, 21 South Tyler Avenue, Pinedale, WY 82941. 307-367-4372 (MST) 8AM-5PM.

**9th Judicial District Court**, PO Box 292, Pinedale, WY 82941. 307-367-4376 (MST) 8AM-5PM. Felony, Civil Actions Over $7,000, Probate.

**County Court**, PO Box 1796, Pinedale, WY 82941. 307-367-2556 (MST) 8AM-5PM. Misdemeanor, Civil Actions Under $7,000, Eviction, Small Claims.

## Sweetwater County

**Real Estate Recording**, Sweetwater County Clerk, 80 West Flaming Gorge Way, Green River, WY 82935. 307-872-6440 (MST)

**3rd Judicial District Court**, PO Box 430, Green River, WY 82935. 307-875-5343 (MST) Felony, Civil Actions Over $7,000, Probate.

**Green River County Court**, PO Drawer 1720, Green River, WY 82935. 307-872-6460 (MST) 8AM-5PM. Misdemeanor, Civil Actions Under $7,000, Eviction, Small Claims.

**Sweetwater County Court**, PO Box 2028, Rock Springs, WY 82902. 307-352-6817 (MST) 8AM-5PM. Misdemeanor, Civil Actions Under $7,000, Eviction, Small Claims.

## Teton County

**Real Estate Recording**, Teton County Clerk, 180 King Street, Jackson, WY 83001. 307-733-4430 (MST) 8AM-5PM.

**9th Judicial District Court**, PO Box 4460, Jackson, WY 83001. 307-733-2533 (MST) 8AM-5PM. Felony, Civil Actions Over $7,000, Probate.

**Justice Court**, PO Box 2906, Jackson, WY 83001. 307-733-7713 (MST) 8AM-5PM. Misdemeanor, Civil Actions Under $3,000, Small Claims.

## Uinta County

**Real Estate Recording**, Uinta County Clerk, 225 9th Street, Evanston, WY 82930. 307-789-1780 (MST) 8AM-5PM.

**3rd Judicial District Court**, PO Drawer 1906, Evanston, WY 82931. 307-789-1780 (MST) 8AM-5PM. Felony, Civil Actions Over $7,000, Probate.

**County Court**, 225 9th St, 2nd Fl, Evanston, WY 82931. 307-789-2471 (MST) 8AM-5PM. Misdemeanor, Civil Actions Under $7,000, Eviction, Small Claims.

## Washakie County

**Real Estate Recording**, Washakie County Clerk, 10th & Big Horn, Courthouse, Worland, WY 82401. 307-347-3131 (MST) 8AM-5PM.

**5th Judicial District Court**, PO Box 862, Worland, WY 82401. 307-347-4821 (MST) Felony, Civil Actions Over $7,000, Probate.

**Justice Court**, PO Box 927, Worland, WY 82401. 307-347-2702 (MST) 8AM-5PM. Misdemeanor, Civil Actions Under $3,000, Small Claims.

## Weston County

**Real Estate Recording**, Weston County Clerk, One West Main, Newcastle, WY 82701. 307-746-4744 (MST) 8AM-5PM.

**6th Judicial District Court**, 1 W Main, Newcastle, WY 82701. 307-746-4778 (MST) 8AM-5PM. Felony, Civil Actions Over $7,000, Probate.

**Justice Court**, 6 W Warwick, Newcastle, WY 82701. 307-746-3547 (MST) 8:30AM-4:30PM. Misdemeanor, Civil Actions Under $3,000, Small Claims.

**County Records**

**County Records**

# Section Two
# State Records

## What You Can Expect To Find In State Public Records*

*The following article is condensed from The Sourcebook Of State Public Records.*

What data will state government agencies' records tell you? How do you know if the records you are requesting will actually give you the information you seek? Are you legally permitted to access the record? Whether or not the information is available to the public, the degree of authority needed to obtain the record and the data to be found on the record are all subject to **individual state statutes**. Therefore, the answers to the questions above can, and do, vary significantly from state to state.

### I. Business Records

**Corporation**—You can check to see if a corporation is incorporated or qualified in a state with a "status check"— i.e. date of incorporation, status, type, registered agent and, sometimes, officers or directors. Some states permit status checks over the telephone. Also, articles of incorporation or amendments and copies of annual reports, when available, are a good place to start when seeking information about a business or business owner. Corporate records may not always be a good source of a business addresses because most states allow corporations to use a registered agent as the address for service of process.

**Partnership**—Many states have statutes that require registration of certain kinds of partnerships at the state level. Partner names and addresses may be available from the same office that handles corporation records. Some states have a department created specifically to administer limited partnerships and their records.

**Limited Liability Co**—A newer form of business entity, that looks like a corporation but has the favorable tax characteristics of a partnership, is known as the Limited Liability Company (LLC). LLC records are available in over 35 states.

**Trademark, Trade Name**—States will not let two entities use the same, or close to the same, name or trademark. A trademark may also be known as a "service mark". Trade names may be referred to as "fictitious names", assumed names, or "DBA's." The same state agency which oversees corporation records may maintain the files of trademarks and/or trade names. Most states will allow verbal status checks of names or worded marks. Some states will administer "fictitious names" while their respective counties administer "trade names", or vice versa.

### II. Lien and Security Interest Records

**Uniform Commercial Code (UCC)**—All 50 states and the District of Columbia have passed a version of the model Uniform Commercial Code (UCC). Article 9 of the Code covers security interests in personal property. UCC filings are used in financing transactions such as equipment loans, leases, inventory loans, and accounts receivable financing and to notify other possible lenders that certain assets of the debtor are being used to secure a loan or lease. Therefore, **UCC filings are a way to find bank accounts, security interests, financiers, and assets.**

Of the 7.5 million new UCC financing statements filed annually, 2.5 million are filed at the state level and 5 million are filed at the local level within the states. Although there are significant variations among state statutes, the state level is usually a good place to check for liens against an individual or business.

**Tax Liens**—The federal government and every state has some sort of taxes payable by individuals and businesses such as; sales, income, withholding, unemployment, personal property, etc. When these taxes go unpaid, the appropriate state agency can file a lien on the real or personal property of the subject. Normally, the same state agency administers both UCC records and tax liens. Tax lien documents are an excellent source of names, addresses, assets, and banking relationships. The lack of uniformity among the states in tax lien filing locations makes it essential for accurate searching that you be aware of the vast array of state idiosyncrasies.

Tax liens filed against individuals are generally maintained in separate files and even separate locations, from those liens filed against businesses. For example, a large number of states require liens filed against businesses to be filed at a central state location (i.e. Secretary of State's office) and liens against individuals to be filed at the county level (i.e. Recorder, Register of Deeds, Clerk of Court, etc.). Further, a federal tax lien will not necessarily be recorded at the same location/jurisdiction as a lien filed by the state on the same entity. This holds true for both individual liens and as well as business liens filed against personal property. Typically, state tax liens on personal property will be found where UCC's are filed. Tax liens on real property will be found where real property deeds are recorded, with few exceptions.

## III. Individual Records

**Criminal**—Every state has a central repository of major misdemeanor and felony arrest records and convictions. States submit criminal record activity to the National Crime Information Center (which is not open to public access). Of those states that will release records to the public, many require fingerprints or signed release forms. The information that *could be* disclosed on the report includes the arrest record, criminal charge, fine, sentencing and incarceration information.

Not all states open their records to the public. In this case, the best place to search for criminal record activity is at the city or county level with the county or district court clerk. Many of these searches can be done with a phone call. For further information regarding criminal record-keeping at the county level, please refer to BRB's *Sourcebook of County Court Records, 1995 Edition.*

**Vital Records**—Copies of vital record certificates are needed for a variety of reasons—social security, jobs, passports, family history, litigation, lost heir searching, proof of identity, etc. Most states understand the urgency of these requests and some offer an expedited service. A number of states will even take requests over the phone if you use a credit card. You must also be aware that in many instances certain vital records are not kept at the state level, so you must turn to city and county record repositories to find copies in these instances.

Older vital records may be found in the state archives, state historical societies, or state universities. Another source of historical vital record information is the Family History Library of the Mormon Church, located at 35 North West Temple, Salt Lake City 84150. They have millions of microfilmed records from church and civil registers from all over the world.

**Driver License and History**—The retrieval industry often refers to driving records as "MVRs." Typical information on an MVR might include full name, address, social security number, physical description and date of birth as well as the actual driving history. Also, license type and restrictions or endorsements can provide background data on an individual. The September 1994 passage of the Driver's Privacy Protection Act will cause significant debate and changes within state legislatures regarding the release of motor vehicle data to the public. Over the next 2 years, as states move towards making the data more readily available electronically, they are also closing the door to many users.

**Vehicle Ownership**—State repositories of vehicle registration and ownership records encompass a wide range of public accessible data. Generally, you submit a name to find vehicle(s) owned, or you submit vehicle information to find a name and address. The records may not be held by the same state agency that oversees driver records. Statutes from state to state regarding the release of these records for investigation purposes vary even more widely than those governing MVRs. State vehicle and owner databases can be an excellent source for asset and lien data, commercial mailing lists (when permissible) and vehicle recall uses.

# Alabama

**State Archives**, State of Alabama, Archives & History Department, Reference Room, 624 Washington Ave, Montgomery, AL 36130. 205-242-4435

**Attorney General**, Attorney General's Office, State House, Montgomery, AL 36130. 205-242-7300

**Corporate Records**, Secretary of State, Corporations Section, 11 S Union St, Ste 207, Montgomery, AL 36104. 205-242-5324 8:00 AM - 5:00 PM. Corporation Records, Limited Partnership Records, Trademarks/ Servicemarks, Fictitious Name, Limited Liability Company Records.

**State Court Administrator**, Director of Courts, 817 S. Court St, Montgomery, AL 36130. 205-242-0300

**Criminal Records**, Alabama Department of Public Safety, A.B.I., Identification Unit, 502 Washington St, Montgomery, AL 36102. 205-242-4244 8:00 AM - 5:00 PM.

**DMV-Accident Reports**, Alabama Department of Public Safety, Accident Records, 500 Dexter Ave, Montgomery, AL 36104. 205-242-4241 8:00 AM - 5:00 PM.

**DMV-Driver Records**, Department of Public Safety, Driver License Division, 500 Dexter Ave, Montgomery, AL 36104. 205-242-4400 8:00 AM - 5:00 PM M-TH 8:00 AM - 4:45 PM F.

**DMV-Vehicle Ownership, Vehicle Identification**, Motor Vehicle Division, Title and Registration Section, 50 North Ripley St, Montgomery, AL 36104. 205-242-9000 8:00 AM - 5:00 PM.

**Governor**, Governor's Office, State Capitol, Suite 101, Montgomery, AL 36130. 205-242-7100

**Legislation**, Alabama Legislature, State House, Room 709-Senate Bills, Room 512-House Bills, Montgomery, AL 36130. 205-242-7826 8:30 AM - 4:30 PM.

**Uniform Commercial Code**, UCC Division, Secretary of State, 11 South Union St, Suite 207, Montgomery, AL 36104. 205-242-5231 8:00 AM - 5:00 PM. Uniform Commercial Code, Federal Tax Liens, State Tax Liens.

**Vital Records-Birth Certificate**, Center for Health Statistics, Vital Records Division, State Office Bldg, 572 E Patton Ave, Montgomery, AL 36103. 205-242-5033 8:00 AM - 5:00 PM.

**Vital Records-Death Records**, Center for Health Statistics, Vital Records Division, State Office Bldg, 572 E Patton Ave, Montgomery, AL 36103. 205-242-5033 8:00 AM - 5:00 PM.

**Vital Records-Divorce Records**, Center for Health Statistics, Vital Records Division, State Office Bldg, 572 E Patton Ave, Montgomery, AL 36103. 205-242-5033 8:00 AM - 5:00 PM.

**Vital Records-Marriage Certificate**, Center for Health Statistics, Vital Records Division, State Office Bldg, 572 E Patton Ave, Montgomery, AL 36103. 205-242-5033 8:00 AM - 5:00 PM.

**Workers' Compensation**, Department of Industrial Relations, Workers' Compensation, 1789 Congress, Montgomery, AL 36131. 205-242-2868 8:00 AM - 4:30 PM.

# Alaska

**State Archives**, Department of Education, Archives Division, 141 Willoughby Ave, Juneau, AK 99801-1720. 907-465-2270

**Attorney General**, Attorney General's Office, Law Department, Capitol Bldg, Juneau, AK 99811. 907-465-3600

**Corporate Records**, Department of Commerce, Division of Banking, Securities & Corporations, 333 Willoughby Ave, 9th Floor of the State Office Bldg, Juneau, AK 99811. 907-465-2530 8:00 AM - 5:00 PM. Corporation Records, Trademarks/ Servicemarks, Fictitious Name, Assumed Name, Limited Partnership Records, Limited Liability Company Records.

**State Court Administrator**, Administrative Director of Courts, 303 K St, Anchorage, AK 99501. 907-264-0547

**Criminal Records**, Department of Public Safety, Records and Identification, 5700 E Tudor Rd, Anchorage, AK 99507. 907-269-5765 8:00 AM - 5:00 PM.

**DMV-Accident Reports**, Department of Public Safety, Driver Services, 450 Whittier, Room 450, Juneau, AK 99801. 907-465-4335 8:00 AM - 5:00 PM.

**DMV-Driver Records**, Division of Motor Vehicles, Driver's Records, 450 Whitter St, Room 105, Juneau, AK 99802. 907-465-4335 8:00 AM - 5:00 PM.

**DMV-Vehicle Ownership, Vehicle Identification**, Department of Motor Vehicles, Research, 2150 E Dowling Rd, Anchorage, AK 99507. 907-563-5589 X107 8:00 AM - 5:00 PM.

**Governor**, Office of the Governor, State Capitol, 3rd Floor, Juneau, AK 99811. 907-465-3500

**Legislation**, Alaska State Legislature, State Capitol, 130 Seward St, Suite 313, Juneau, AK 99801-1182. 907-465-4648 8:00 AM - 5:00 PM.

**Uniform Commercial Code**, UCC Central File Systems Office, Department of Natural Resources, 3601 C St, Suite 1140A, Anchorage, AK 99503-5925. 907-762-2104 8:30 AM - 4:00 PM. Uniform Commercial Code, Federal Tax Liens, State Tax Liens.

**Vital Records-Birth Certificate**, Department of Health & Social Services, Bureau of Vital Statistics, 350 Main, Room 114, Juneau, AK 99811. 907-465-3392 8:00 AM - 4:50 PM M-F (closed at noon hour M-W-F).

**Vital Records-Death Records**, Department of Health & Social Services, Bureau of Vital Statistics, 350 Main, Room 114, Juneau, AK 99811. 907-465-3392 8:00 AM - 5:00 PM M-F (Closed at noon hour M-W-F).

**Vital Records-Divorce Records**, Department of Health & Social Services, Bureau of Vital Statistics, 350 Main, Room 114, Juneau, AK 99811. 907-465-3392 8:00 AM - 5:00 PM M-F (closed noon hour M-W-F).

**Vital Records-Marriage Certificate**, Department of Health & Social Services, Bureau of Vital Statistics, 350 Main, Room 114, Juneau, AK 99811. 907-465-3392 8:00 AM - 5:00 PM M-F (closed noon hour M-W-F).

**Workers' Compensation**, Workers' Compensation, 1111 W Eighth St, Room 307, Juneau, AK 99802. 907-465-2790 8:00 AM - 4:30 PM.

## Arizona

**State Archives**, Library, Archives & Public Records Department, 1700 W Washington, Room 200, Phoenix, AZ 85007. 602-542-4035

**Attorney General**, Attorney General's Office, 1275 W Washington, Phoenix, AZ 85007. 602-542-5025

**Corporate Records**, Corporation Commission, 1300 W Washington, Phoenix, AZ 85007. 602-542-3026 8:00 AM - 5:00 PM. Corporation Records, Limited Liability Company Records, Limited Partnership Records.

**Corporate Records**, Secretary of State, Trademarks/Tradenames/Limited Partnership Division, 1700 W Washington, 7th Floor, Phoenix, AZ 85007. 602-542-6187 8:00 AM - 5:00 PM. Trademarks/ Servicemarks, Trade Names, Limited Partnership Records.

**State Court Administrator**, Office of the Courts, Arizona Supreme Court Building, 1501 W Jefferson, Phoenix, AZ 85007. 602-524-9301.

**Criminal Records**, Department of Public Safety, Criminal Records, 2102 W Encanto, Phoenix, AZ 85005. 602-223-2230 8:00 AM - 5:00 PM.

**DMV-Accident Reports**, Department of Public Safety, Accident Reports, 2102 W Encanto, 1st Floor, Phoenix, AZ 85005. 602-223-2000 8:00 AM - 5:00 PM.

**DMV-Driver Records**, Motor Vehicle Division, Record Services Section, Customer Records Services, 1801 W Jefferson, Lobby, Phoenix, AZ 85007. 602-255-7865 8:00 AM - 5:00 PM.

**DMV-Vehicle Ownership, Vehicle Identification**, Motor Vehicle Division, Record Services Section, Customer Records Services, 1801 W Jefferson, Lobby, Phoenix, AZ 85007. 602-255-7865 8:00 AM - 5:00 PM.

**Governor**, Governor's Office, State Capitol, W Wing, 1700 W Washington, Phoenix, AZ 85007. 602-542-4331

**Legislation**, Arizona Legislature, State Capitol - Room 203, Senate Wing, House Wing, Phoenix, AZ 85007. 602-542-3559 8:00 AM - 5:00 PM.

**Uniform Commercial Code**, UCC Division, Secretary of State, State Capitol, West Wing, 7th Floor, Phoenix, AZ 85007. 602-542-6178 Uniform Commercial Code, Federal Tax Liens, State Tax Liens.

**Vital Records-Birth Certificate**, Department of Health Services, Vital Records Section, 2727 W Glendale Ave, Phoenix, AZ 85030. 602-255-3260 8:00 AM - 5:00 PM M-F (counter closed at 4:30 PM).

**Vital Records-Death Records**, Department of Health Services, Vital Records Section, 2727 W Glendale Ave, Phoenix, AZ 85030. 602-255-3260 8:00 AM - 5:00 PM M-F (counter closes at 4:30 PM).

**Vital Records-Marriage Certificate, Divorce Records**, Records not available at state level.

**Workers' Compensation**, State Compensation Fund, 3031 N Second St, Phoenix, AZ 85012. 602-631-2050 8:00 AM - 5:00 PM.

## Arkansas

**State Archives**, Arkansas Historical Commission, One Capitol Hall, Little Rock, AR 72201. 501-682-6900

**Attorney General**, Attorney General's Office, 200 Tower Bldg, 323 Center St, Little Rock, AR 72201-2610. 501-682-2007

**Corporate Records**, Secretary of State, Corporation Department, State Capitol Bldg, Room 058, Little Rock, AR 72201-1094. 501-682-3409 8:00 AM - 4:30 PM. Corporation Records, Fictitious Name, Limited Liability Company Records, Limited Partnership Records.

**Corporate Records**, Secretary of State, Trademarks Section, State Capitol, Room 01, Little Rock, AR 72201. 501-682-3405 8:00 AM - 4:30 PM. Trademarks/ Servicemarks.

**State Court Administrator**, Administrative Office of Courts, 625 Marshall, Justice Bldg, Little Rock, AR 72201-1078. 501-376-6655

**Criminal Records**, Arkansas State Police, Identification Bureau, PO Box 5901, Little Rock, AR 72215. 501-221-8233 8:00 AM - 5:00 PM.

**DMV-Accident Reports**, Arkansas State Police, Accident Records Section, #3 National Resources Dr, Little Rock, AR 72215. 501-221-8236 8:00 AM - 5:00 PM.

**DMV-Driver Records**, Department of Driver Services, Driver Records Division, 7th & Wolfe Sts, Ledbetter Bldg, Room 127, Little Rock, AR 72202. 501-682-7207 8:00 AM - 4:30 PM.

**DMV-Vehicle Ownership, Vehicle Identification**, Office of Motor Vehicles, IRP Unit, 7th and Wolfe Sts, Ledbetter Bldg, Room 106, Little Rock, AR 72202. 501-682-3333 8:00 AM - 4:30 PM.

**Governor**, Governor's Office, State Capitol, Little Rock, AR 72201. 501-682-2345

**Legislation**, Arkansas Secretary of State, State Capitol, Room 256 (2nd Floor), Little Rock, AR 72201. 501-682-5070 8:00 AM - 4:30 PM.

**Uniform Commercial Code**, UCC Division, Secretary of State, State Capitol Bldg, Room 25, Little Rock, AR 72201-1094. 501-682-5078 Uniform Commercial Code, Federal Tax Liens, State Tax Liens.

**Vital Records-Birth Certificate**, Arkansas Department of Health, Division of Vital Records, 4815 W Markham St, Little Rock, AR 72205. 501-661-2134 8:00 AM - 4:30 PM.

**Vital Records-Death Records**, Arkansas Department of Health, Division of Vital Records, 4815 W Markham St, Little Rock, AR 72205. 501-661-2134 8:00 AM - 4:30 PM.

**Vital Records-Divorce Records**, Records not available at state level.

**Vital Records-Marriage Certificate**, Arkansas Department of Health, Division of Vital Records, 4815 W Markham St, Little Rock, AR 72205. 501-661-2134 8:00 AM - 4:30 PM.

**Workers' Compensation**, Workers Compensation Department, 25 Marshall St., Justice Bldg-Capitol Gr, Little Rock, AR 72201. 501-682-2533 8:00 AM - 4:30 PM.

**State Records**

## California

**State Archives**, Secretary of State, State Archives, 1020 "O" St, Sacramento, CA 95814. 916-653-7715

**Attorney General**, Attorney General's Office, Justice Department, 1515 K St, Suite 511, Sacramento, CA 94244. 916-445-9555

**Corporate Records**, Secretary of State, Certification Division, 1230 J St, Room 100, Sacramento, CA 95814. 916-445-0620 8:00 AM - 4:30 PM. Corporation Records, Limited Liability Company Records.

**Corporate Records**, Secretary of State, Limited Partnership Unit, 923 12th St, Room 301, Sacramento, CA 95814. 916-445-9872 8:00 AM - 4:30 PM. Limited Partnership Records.

**Corporate Records**, Secretary of State, Trademark Unit, 923 12th St, Room 301, Sacramento, CA 95814. 916-445-9872 8:00 AM - 4:30 PM. Trademarks/ Servicemarks.

**State Court Administrator**, Administration Office of Courts, 303 2nd St, S Tower, San Francisco, CA 94107. 415-396-9100

**Criminal Records**, State Repository, Reporting Evaluation & Analysis Section, PO Box 903417, Sacramento, CA 94203-3460. 916-227-3460 8:00 AM - 5:00 PM.

**DMV-Accident Reports**, Records not available at state level.

**DMV-Driver Records**, Department of Motor Vehicles, Information Request Counter, Bldg West-First Floor, 2570 24th St, Sacramento, CA 94244. 916-657-8098 8:00 AM - 5:00 PM.

**DMV-Vehicle Ownership, Vehicle Identification**, Department of Motor Vehicle, Consulting Room, Bldg East-First Floor, 2415 First Ave, Sacramento, CA 94244. 916-657-8098 8:00 AM - 5:00 PM.

**Governor**, Governor's Office, State Capitol, 1st Floor, Sacramento, CA 95814. 916-445-2841

**Legislation**, California State Legislature, State Capitol, Room B-32 (Legislative Bill Room), Sacramento, CA 95814. 916-445-4251 9:00 AM - 5:00 PM.

**Uniform Commercial Code**, UCC Division, Secretary of State, 1500 11th St, Sacramento, CA 95814. 916-445-8061 Uniform Commercial Code, Federal Tax Liens, State Tax Liens.

**Vital Records-Birth Certificate**, Office of the State Registrar, 304 S Street, Sacramento, CA 95814. 916-445-2684 8:00 AM - 4:30 PM.

**Vital Records-Death Records**, Office of the State Registrar, 304 S Street, Sacramento, CA 95814. 916-445-2684 8:00 AM - 4:30 PM.

**Vital Records-Divorce Records**, Records not available at state level.

**Vital Records-Marriage Certificate**, Office of the State Registrar, 304 S Street, Sacramento, CA 95814. 916-445-2684 8:00 AM - 4:30 PM.

**Workers' Compensation**, State Compensation Insurance Fund, 1275 Market St, San Francisco, CA 94103. 415-565-1234 8:00 AM - 5:00 PM.

## Colorado

**State Archives**, Administration Department, Archives & Public Records Division, 1313 Sherman St, Denver, CO 80203. 303-866-2055

**Attorney General**, Attorney General's Office, 1525 Sherman St, 5th Floor, Denver, CO 80203. 303-866-3617

**Corporate Records**, Secretary of State, Corporation Division, 1560 Broadway, Suite 200, Denver, CO 80202. 303-894-2251 X349 8:30 AM - 5:00 PM. Corporation Records, Trademarks/ Servicemarks, Fictitious Name, Limited Liability Company Records, Assumed Name.

**State Court Administrator**, State Court Administrator, 1301 Pennsylvania St, Suite 300, Denver, CO 80203. 303-861-1111

**Criminal Records**, Bureau of Investigation, State Repository, Identification Unit, 690 Kipling St, Suite 3000, Denver, CO 80215. 303-239-4208 8:00 AM - 4:00 PM.

**DMV-Accident Reports**, Department of Motor Vehicles, Traffic Records-Accident Reports, 140 W 6th Ave, Room 103, Denver, CO 80204. 303-623-9463 8:00 AM - 5:00 PM.

**DMV-Driver Records**, Motor Vehicle Division, Traffic Records, 140 W 6th Ave, Room 103, Denver, CO 80204. 303-623-9463 8:00 AM - 5:00 PM.

**DMV-Vehicle Ownership, Vehicle Identification**, Department of Motor Vehicles, Vehicle Records Section, 140 W 6th Ave, Denver, CO 80204. 303-623-9463 8:00 AM - 5:00 PM.

**Governor**, Governor's Office, 136 State Capitol Bldg, Denver, CO 80203-1792. 303-866-2471

**Legislation**, Colorado General Assembly, State Capitol, House-Room 271, Senate-Room 248, Denver, CO 80203. 303-866-2904 8:00 AM - 4:30 PM.

**Uniform Commercial Code**, UCC Division, Secretary of State, 1560 Broadway, Suite 200, Denver, CO 80202. 303-894-2200 8:30 AM - 5:00 PM. Uniform Commercial Code, Federal Tax Liens, State Tax Liens.

**Vital Records-Birth Certificate**, Colorado Department of Health, Vital Records Section HSVR-A1, 4300 Cherry Creek Dr S, Denver, CO 80222-1530. 303-756-4464 8:30 AM - 4:30 PM.

**Vital Records-Death Records**, Colorado Department of Health, Vital Records Section HSVR-A1, 4300 Cherry Creek Dr S, Denver, CO 80222-1530. 303-756-4464 8:30 AM - 4:30 PM.

**Vital Records-Marriage Certificate, Divorce Records**, Records not available at state level.

**Workers' Compensation**, Division of Workers Compensation, Customer Service, 1120 Lincoln St, 14th Floor, Denver, CO 80203-2295. 303-764-2929 8:00 AM - 5:00 PM.

## Connecticut

**State Archives**, Connecticut State Library, Archives Division, 231 Capitol Ave, Hartford, CT 06106. 203-566-5650

**Attorney General**, Attorney General's Office, 55 Elm St, Hartford, CT 06106. 203-566-2026

**Corporate Records**, Secretary of State, Corporation Records Division, 30 Trinity St, Hartford, CT 06106. 203-566-8570 8:45 AM - 3:00 PM. Corporation Records, Limited Partnership Records, Trademarks/Servicemarks, Limited Liability Company Records.

**State Court Administrator**, Chief Court Administrator, 231 Capitol Ave, Hartford, CT 06106. 203-566-4461

**Criminal Records**, Department of Public Safety, PO Box 2794, Middleton, CT 06759-9294. 203-238-6151 8:00 AM - 5:00 PM.

**DMV-Accident Reports**, Department of Public Safety, Reports and Records Section, PO Box 2794, Middletown, CT 06457. 203-238-6637

**DMV-Driver Records**, Department of Motor Vehicles, Copy Records Section, 60 State St, Room 305, Wethersfield, CT 06109-1896. 203-566-3197 8:30 AM-4:30 PM(T,W,F) 8:30 AM-7:30 PM (TH) 8:30 AM-12:30 (S).

**DMV-Vehicle Ownership, Vehicle Identification**, Department of Motor Vehicles, Copy Record Unit, 60 State St, Branch Operations, Wethersfield, CT 06109-1896. 203-566-3090 8:30 AM-4:30 PM (T,W,F) 8:30 AM -7:30 PM (TH) 8:30-12:30 (S).

**Governor**, Governor's Office, State Capitol, 210 Capitol Ave, Hartford, CT 06106. 203-566-4840

**Legislation**, Connecticut General Assembly, State Library, 231 Capitol Ave, Bill Room, Hartford, CT 06106. 203-566-5736 8:30 AM - 4:30 PM.

**Uniform Commercial Code**, UCC Division, Secretary of State, 30 Trinity St, Hartford, CT 06106. 203-566-4021 8:45 AM - 3:00 PM. Uniform Commercial Code, Federal Tax Liens, State Tax Liens.

**Vital Records-Birth Certificate**, Department of Public Health & Addiciton Services, Vital Records Section, 150 Washington St, Hartford, CT 06106. 203-566-1124 9:00 AM - 1:30 PM M-F (Genealogical searches 9:00-12:00 F).

**Vital Records-Death Records**, Department of Public Health & Addiction Services, Vital Records Section, 150 Washington St, Hartford, CT 06106. 203-566-1124 9:00 AM - 1:30 PM M-F (Genealogical searches 9:00-12:00 F).

**Vital Records-Divorce Records**, Records not available at state level.

**Vital Records-Marriage Certificate**, Department of Public Health & Addiction Services, Vital Records Section, 150 Washington St, Hartford, CT 06106. 203-566-1124 9:00 AM - 1:30 PM M-F (Genealogical searches 9:00-12:00 F).

**Workers' Compensation**, Workers Compensation Commission, 1890 Dixwell Ave, Hamden, CT 06514. 203-230-3400 8:30 AM - 4:30 PM.

## Delaware

**State Archives**, Department of State/Historical & Cultural Affairs, Hall of Records/Archives Division, PO Box 1401, Dover, DE 19903. 302-739-5313

**Attorney General**, Attorney General's Office, Carvel State Office Bldg, 820 N French S, Wilmington, DE 19801. 302-577-3047

**Corporate Records**, Secretary of State, Division of Corporations, John G Townsend Bldg, Dover, DE 19901. 302-739-4279 8:00 AM - 5:00 PM. Corporation Records, Limited Partnership Records, Trademarks/Servicemarks, Limited Liability Company Records, Assumed Name.

**State Court Administrator**, Administrative Office of the Courts, PO Box 1997, Wilmington, DE 19899. 302-577-3706

**Criminal Records**, Delaware State Police Headquarters, Criminal Records Section, 1407 N Dupont Highway, Dover, DE 19930. 302-739-5880 8:00 AM - 4:00 PM.

**DMV-Accident Reports**, Delaware State Police Traffic Section, Accident Records, 1441 N Dupont Hwy, Dover, DE 19903. 302-739-5931 8:00 AM - 4:00 PM.

**DMV-Driver Records**, Division of Motor Vehicles, Driver Services, Rt 113 Bay Rd, DPS Bldg, Dover, DE 19903. 302-739-4343 8:00 AM - 4:30 PM M-T-TH-F 12:00 PM - 8:00 PM W.

**DMV-Vehicle Ownership, Vehicle Identification**, Division of Motor Vehicles, Correspondence Section, US Rt 113 Bay Rd, Public Safety Bldg, Dover, DE 19903. 302-739-3147 8:30 AM - 4:30 PM M-T-TH-F 12:00 PM - 8:00 PM W.

**Governor**, Governor's Office, Legislative Hall, Dover, DE 19901. 302-577-3210

**Legislation**, Delaware General Assembly, Legislative Hall, Court Street, Room 29, Dover, DE 19903. 302-739-4114 8:00 AM - 4:30 PM.

**Uniform Commercial Code**, UCC Division, Secretary of State, Townsend Bldg, Federal & Duke of York Sts, Dover, DE 19901. 302-739-4279 8:30 AM - 4:30 PM. Uniform Commercial Code, Federal Tax Liens, State Tax Liens.

**Vital Records-Birth Certificate**, Department of Health, Office of Vital Statistics, William Penn & Federal Sts, Jesse Cooper Bldg, Dover, DE 19901. 302-739-4721 8:00 AM - 4:30 PM M-F (Counter closes at 4:20 PM).

**Vital Records-Death Records**, Department of Health, Office of Vital Statistics, William Penn & Federal Sts, Jesse Cooper Bldg, Dover, DE 19901. 302-739-4721 8:00 AM - 4:30 PM.

**Vital Records-Divorce Records**, Records not available at state level.

**Vital Records-Marriage Certificate**, Department of Health, Office of Vital Statistics, William Penn & Federal Sts, Jesse Cooper Bldg, Dover, DE 19901. 302-739-4721 8:00 AM - 4:30 PM.

**Workers' Compensation**, Labor Department, Industrial Accident Board, 820 N French St, 6th Floor, Wilmington, DE 19801. 302-577-2884 8:00 AM - 4:30 PM.

## District of Columbia

**District Archives**, Secretary of the District of Columbia Office, Archives/Public Records Office, 1300 Naylor Ct NW, Washington, DC 20001. 202-727-5082

**Corporate Records**, Department of Consumer & Regulatory Affairs, 614 H St, NW, Room 407, Washington, DC 20001. 202-727-7278 9:00 AM - 3:00 PM. Corporation Records, Limited Partnership Records, Limited Liability Company Records.

**District Court Administrator**, Executive Office, 500 Indiana Ave NW, Room 1500, Washington, DC 20001. 202-879-1700

**Criminal Records**, Superior Court, Criminal Division, 500 Indiana Ave NW, Washington, DC 20001. 202-879-1372 8:00 AM - 5:00 PM.

**DMV-Accident Reports**, Insurance Operations Branch, Accident Report Section, 65 "K" St, NE, Room 2100, 2nd Floor, Washington, DC 20002. 202-727-1159 7:00 AM - 3:00 PM.

**DMV-Driver Records**, Department of Motor Vehicles, Driver Records Division, 301 "C" St, NW - Rm 1157, Washington, DC 20001. 202-727-6761 8:15 AM - 4:00 PM M-T-TH-F 8:15 AM - 7:00 PM W.

**DMV-Vehicle Ownership, Vehicle Identification**, Department of Motor Vehicles, Vehicle Control Division, 301 "C" St, NW, Room 1063, Washington, DC 20001. 202-727-4768 8:15 AM - 4:00 PM M-T-TH-F 8:15 AM - 7:00 PM W.

**Mayor**, Office of the Mayor, One Judiciary Square, 441 4th St NW, Washington, DC 20001. 202-727-1000

**Legislation**, Council of the District of Columbia, 1350 Pennsylvania Ave, NW, Room 28, Washington, DC 20004. 202-724-8050 9:00 AM - 5:30 PM.

**Uniform Commercial Code**, UCC Recorder, District of Columbia Recorder of Deeds, 515 D Street NW, Room 310, Washington, DC 20001. 202-727-5190 Uniform Commercial Code, Federal Tax Liens, State Tax Liens.

**Vital Records-Birth Certificate**, Department of Health, Vital Records Branch, 613 G St, NW, 9th Floor, Washington, DC 20001. 202-727-5314 8:30 AM - 3:30 PM.

**Vital Records-Death Records**, Department of Health, Vital Records Branch, 613 G St, NW, 9th Floor, Washington, DC 20001. 202-727-5314 8:30 AM - 3:30 PM.

**Vital Records-Divorce Records**, Superior Court House, Divorce Records, 500 Indiana Ave, NW, Room 4230, Washington, DC 20001. 202-879-1410 9:00 AM - 4:00 PM.

**Vital Records-Marriage Certificate**, Superior Court House, Marriage Bureau, 500 Indiana Ave, NW, Room 4485, Washington, DC 20001. 202-879-4850 9:00 AM - 4:00 PM.

**Workers' Compensation**, Office of Workers Compensation, PO Box 56098 6th Floor, Washington, DC 20011. 202-576-6265 8:00 AM - 5:00 PM.

## Florida

**State Archives**, Library & Information Services Division, Archives & Records, R A Gray Bldg, Tallahassee, FL 32301. 904-487-2073

**Attorney General**, Attorney General's Office, Legal Affairs Department, The Capitol, Tallahassee, FL 32399-1050. 904-488-2526

**Corporate Records**, Division of Corporations, Secretary of State, 409 E Gaines St, Tallahassee, FL 32314. 904-488-9000 8:30 AM - 4:30 PM. Corporation Records, Limited Liability Company Records, Limited Partnership Records, Trademarks/ Servicemarks, Assumed Name.

**Corporate Records**, Secretary of State, Fictitious Names Division, 409 E Gaines St, Tallahassee, FL 32314. 904-487-6058 8:30 AM - 4:30 PM. Fictitious Names.

**State Court Administrator**, Court Administrator, Supreme Court Bldg, 500 S Duval, Tallahassee, FL 32399-1900. 904-922-5082

**Criminal Records**, Florida Department of Law Enforcement, Criminal Records Inquiry Section, 2331 Phillip Rd, Tallahassee, FL 32308. 904-488-6236 8:00 AM - 5:00 PM.

**DMV-Accident Reports**, Crash Records-rm A325, DHSMV, Neil Kirkman Bldg, 2900 Apalachee Prky, Tallahassee, FL 32399-0538. 904-488-5017 8:00 AM - 4:45 PM.

**DMV-Driver Records**, Department of Public Safety, Division of Drivers Licenses, 2900 Apalachee Pky, Rm B-239, Tallahassee, FL 32399-0575. 904-487-2369 8:00 AM - 4:30 PM.

**DMV-Vehicle Ownership, Vehicle Identification**, Division of Motor Vehicles, Information Research Section, Neil Kirkman Bldg, Room A126, Tallahassee, FL 32399. 904-488-5665 8:00 AM - 4:30 PM.

**Governor**, Governor's Office, The Capitol, Tallahassee, FL 32399-0001. 904-488-4441

**Legislation**, Joint Legislative Mgmt Committee, Legislative Information Division, 111 W Madison St, Pepper Bldg, Rm 704, Tallahassee, FL 32399. 904-488-4371 8:00 AM - 5:00 PM.

**Uniform Commercial Code**, UCC Division, Secretary of State, 409 E Gaines St, Tallahassee, FL 32314. 904-487-6055 8:00 AM - 4:30 PM. Uniform Commercial Code, Federal Tax Liens, State Tax Liens.

**Vital Records-Birth Certificate**, HRS, Office of Vital Statistics, 1217 Pearl St, Jacksonville, FL 32202. 904-359-6911 8:00 AM - 5:00 PM.

**Vital Records-Death Records**, HRS, Office of Vital Statistics, 1217 Pearl St, Jacksonville, FL 32202. 904-359-6911 8:00 AM - 5:00 PM.

**Vital Records-Divorce Records**, HRS, Office of Vital Statistics, 1217 Pearl St, Jacksonville, FL 32202. 904-359-6911 8:00 AM - 5:00 PM.

**Vital Records-Marriage Certificate**, HRS, Office of Vital Statistics, 1217 Pearl St, Jacksonville, FL 32202. 904-359-6911 8:00 AM - 5:00 PM.

**Workers' Compensation**, Workers Compensation Division, Information Management Unit, Forrest Bldg, 2728 Centerview Dr, Ste 20, Tallahassee, FL 32399. 904-488-3030 7:30 AM - 5:00 PM.

## Georgia

**State Archives**, Secretary of State, Archives & History Department, 330 Capitol Ave SE, Atlanta, GA 30334. 404-656-2392

**Attorney General**, Attorney General's Office, 40 Capitol Square SW, Atlanta, GA 30334-1300. 404-656-3300

**Corporate Records**, Secretary of State, Corporation Division, 2 M L King Dr, Suite 315, W Tower, Atlanta, GA 30334-1530. 404-656-2817 8:00 AM - 4:30 PM. Corporation Records, Limited Partnership Records, Limited Liability Company Records.

**Corporate Records**, Secretary of State, Trademark Division, 2 Martin Luther King, Room 315, W Tower, Atlanta, GA 30334. 404-656-2861 8:00 AM - 4:30 PM. Trademarks/ Servicemarks.

**State Court Administrator**, Court Administrator, 244 Washington St SW, Suite 550, Atlanta, GA 30334. 404-656-5171

**Criminal Records**, Georgia Crime Information Center, Identification Division, PO Box 370748, Decatur, GA 30037-0748. 404-244-2601 8:00 AM - 4:00 PM.

**DMV-Accident Reports**, Department of Public Safety, Accident Reporting Section, 959 E Confederate Ave, Atlanta, GA 30316. 404-624-7660 8:00 AM - 3:30 PM.

**DMV-Driver Records**, Department of Motor Vehicles, Driver's License Section, 959 E Confederate Ave, Atlanta, GA 30316. 404-624-7487 8:00 AM - 3:30 PM.

**DMV-Vehicle Ownership, Vehicle Identification**, Department of Revenue, Research, 270 Washington St, SW, Room 105, Atlanta, GA 30334. 404-656-4156 8:00 AM - 4:30 PM.

**Governor**, Governor's Office, 203 State Capitol, Atlanta, GA 30334. 404-656-1776

**Legislation**, General Assembly of Georgia, State Capitol, Room 351, Atlanta, GA 30334. 404-656-5040 8:30 AM - 4:30 PM.

**Uniform Commercial Code**, Uniform Commercial Code, Federal Tax Liens, State Tax Liens. Only some UCC records are available at state level. Call 404-988-8288 for more information.

**Vital Records-Birth Certificate**, Department of Human Resources, Vital Records Unit, 47 Trinity Ave, SW, Room 217-H, Atlanta, GA 30334. 404-656-7456 8:00 AM - 4:00 PM.

**Vital Records-Death Records**, Georgia Department of Human Resources, Vital Records Unit, 47 Trinity Ave, SW, Room 217-H, Atlanta, GA 30334. 404-656-7456 8:00 AM - 4:00 PM.

**Vital Records-Divorce Records**, Records not available at state level.

**Vital Records-Marriage Certificate**, Georgia Department of Human Resources, Vital Records Unit, 47 Trinity Ave, SW, Room 217-H, Atlanta, GA 30334. 404-656-7456 8:00 AM - 4:00 PM.

**Workers' Compensation**, Workers Compensation Department, One CNN Center, Suite 1000, S Tower, Atlanta, GA 30303-2788. 404-656-3818 8:00 AM - 4:30 PM.

## Hawaii

**State Archives**, General Services Department, Archives Division, Iolani Palace Grounds, Honolulu, HI 96813. 808-586-0329

**Attorney General**, Attorney General's Office, 425 Queen St, Honolulu, HI 96813. 808-586-1500

**Corporate Records**, Business Registration Division, 1010 Richard St, 1st Floor, Honolulu, HI 96810. 808-586-2727 8:00 AM - 4:00 PM. Corporation Records, Fictitious Name, Limited Partnership Records, Assumed Name, Trademarks/ Servicemarks.

**State Court Administrator**, Administrative Director of Courts, 417 S King St, Honolulu, HI 96813. 808-539-4900

**Criminal Records**, Hawaii Criminal Justice Data Center, Liane Moriyama, Administrator, 465 S King St, Room 101, Honolulu, HI 96813. 808-587-3106 9:00 AM - 3:00 PM.

**DMV-Accident Reports**, Traffic Violations Bureau, 1111 Alakea St, Honolulu, HI 96813.

**DMV-Driver Records**, Traffic Violations Bureau, Abstract Section, 1111 Alakea St, Honolulu, HI 96813. 808-548-5735 7:45 AM - 9:00 PM.

**DMV-Vehicle Ownership, Vehicle Identification**, Records not available at state level.

**Governor**, Office of the Governor, Leiopapa A Kamehameha Bldg, 235 S Beteta, Honolulu, HI 96813. 808-586-0034

**Legislation**, Hawaii Legislature, Leiopapa A Kamehameha Bldg, 235 S Beretania St, Honolulu, HI 96813. 808-587-0700 7:45 AM - 4:30 PM.

**Uniform Commercial Code**, UCC Division, Bureau of Conveyances, 1151 Punchbowl St, Dept. of Land & Natural Resources, Honolulu, HI 96813. 808-587-0154 7:45 AM - 4:30 PM. Uniform Commercial Code, Federal Tax Liens, State Tax Liens.

**Vital Records-Birth Certificate**, State Department of Health, Vital Records Section, 1250 Punchbowl St, Room 103, Honolulu, HI 96801. 808-586-4539 7:45 AM - 4:30 PM M-F (Counter closes at 4:00 PM).

**Vital Records-Death Records**, State Department of Health, Vital Records Section, 1250 Punchbowl St, Room 103, Honolulu, HI 96801. 808-586-4539 7:45 AM - 4:30 PM M-F (Counter closes at 4:00 PM).

**Vital Records-Divorce Records**, State Department of Health, Vital Records Section, 1250 Punchbowl St, Room 103, Honolulu, HI 96801. 808-586-4539 7:45 AM - 4:30 PM M-F (Counter closes at 4:00 PM).

**Vital Records-Marriage Certificate**, State Department of Health, Vital Records Section, 1250 Punchbowl St, Room 103, Honolulu, HI 96801. 808-586-4539 7:45 AM - 4:30 PM M-F (Counter closes at 4:00 PM).

**Workers' Compensation**, Labor & Industrial Relations, Disability Compensation Division, 830 Punchbowl St, Room 209, Honolulu, HI 96813. 808-586-9151 7:30 AM - 4:30 PM.

## Idaho

**State Archives**, Office of the State Board of Education, State Historical Society, 610 N Julia Davis Dr, Boise, ID 83702. 208-334-2120

**Attorney General**, Attorney General's Office, Capitol Bldg, 700 W Jefferson St, Boise, ID 83720. 208-334-2400

**Corporate Records**, Secretary of State, Corporation Division, Statehouse, Room 203, Boise, ID 83720. 208-334-2300 8:00 AM - 5:00 PM. Corporation Records, Limited Partnership Records, Trademarks/ Servicemarks, Limited Liability Company Records.

**State Court Administrator**, Administrative Director of the Courts, Supreme Court Building, 451 W State St, Boise, ID 83720. 208-334-2246

**Criminal Records**, State Repository, Criminal Indentification Bureau, 6064 Corporal Lane, Boise, ID 83704. 208-327-7130 8:00 AM - 5:00 PM.

**DMV-Accident Reports**, Idaho Transportation Department, Office of Highway Safety-Accident Records, 3311 W State St, Boise, ID 83707. 208-334-8101 8:00 AM-12:00 PM & 1:00 PM-5:00 PM.

**DMV-Driver Records**, Idaho Transportation Department, Driver's Services, 331 W State, Boise, ID 83701. 208-334-8736 8:30 AM - 5:00 PM.

**DMV-Vehicle Ownership, Vehicle Identification**, Idaho Transportation Department, Titles/Dealers Operations Section, 3311 W State St, Boise, ID 83707. 208-334-8663 8:00 AM - 5:00 PM.

**Governor**, Governor's Office, State Capitol Bldg, W Wing, 2nd Floor, Boise, ID 83720. 208-334-2100

**Legislation**, Idaho Legislature, State Capitol Bldg, State Capitol Bldg, Lower Level, East, Boise, ID 83720. 208-334-3175 8:00 AM - 5:00 PM.

**Uniform Commercial Code**, UCC Division, Secretary of State, 700 W Jerfferson, PO Box 83720, Boise, ID 83720. 208-334-3191 8:00 AM - 5:00 PM. Uniform Commercial Code, Federal Tax Liens, State Tax Liens.

**Vital Records-Birth Certificate**, State Department of Health, Center for Vital Statistics & Health Policy, 450 W State St, State House, Boise, ID 83720. 208-334-5988 8:00 AM - 5:00 PM.

**Vital Records-Death Records**, State Department of Health, Center for Vital Statistics & Health Policy, 450 W State St, State House, Boise, ID 83720. 208-334-5988 8:00 AM - 5:00 PM.

**Vital Records-Divorce Records**, Department of Health, Center for Vital Statistics & Health Policy, 450 W State St, State House, Boise, ID 83720. 208-334-5988 8:00 AM - 5:00 PM.

**Vital Records-Marriage Certificate**, Department of Health, Center for Vital Statistics & Health Policy, 450 W State St, State House, Boise, ID 83720. 208-334-5988 8:00 AM - 5:00 PM.

**Workers' Compensation**, Industrial Commission of Idaho, Workers Compensation Division, 317 Main St, Statehouse Mall, Boise, ID 83720. 208-334-6000 8:00 AM - 5:00 PM.

## Illinois

**State Archives**, Secretary of State, Archives Division, 213 State Capitol Bldg, 1st Floor E, Springfield, IL 62756. 217-782-4682

**Attorney General**, Attorney General's Office, 500 S 2nd St, Springfield, IL 62706. 217-782-1090

**Corporate Records**, Department of Business Services, Corporate Department, Corner of 2nd & Edwards Sts, Spingfield, IL 62756. 217-782-7880 8:00 AM - 4:30 PM. Corporation Records, Limited Partnership Records, Trade Names, Assumed Name.

**State Court Administrator**, Administrative Office of Courts, 118 W Edwards St, Springfield, IL 62704. 217-782-7770

**Criminal Records**, Illinois State Police, Bureau of Identification, 260 N Chicago St, Joliet, IL 60431. 815-740-2655 8:00 AM - 4:00 PM.

**DMV-Accident Reports**, Illinois State Police, Enforcement Records Bureau, 500 Iles Park Place, Ste 102, Springfield, IL 62718. 217-524-5994 8:00 AM - 5:00 PM.

**DMV-Driver Records**, Driver Analysis Section, Drivers Services Department, 2701 S Dirksen Prky, Springfield, IL 62723. 217-782-2720 8:00 AM - 4:30 PM.

**DMV-Vehicle Ownership, Vehicle Identification**, Vehicle Services Department, Record Inquiry, 408 Howlett Bldg, Springfield, IL 62756. 217-782-6992 8:00 AM - 4:30 PM.

**Governor**, Governor's Office, 207 State Capitol Bldg, Springfield, IL 62706. 217-782-6830

**Legislation**, Illinois General Assembly, State House, House Bills Division or Senate Bills Div, Springfield, IL 62706. 217-782-3944 8:00 AM - 4:30 PM.

**Uniform Commercial Code**, UCC Division, Secretary of State, Howlett Bldg, Room 30, Springfield, IL 62756. 217-782-7518 8:00 AM - 4:30 PM. Uniform Commercial Code, Federal Tax Liens, State Tax Liens.

**Vital Records-Birth Certificate**, State Department of Health, Division of Vital Records, 605 W Jefferson St, Springfield, IL 62702-5097. 217-782-6553 8:00 AM - 5:00 PM.

**Vital Records-Death Records**, State Department of Health, Division of Vital Records, 605 W Jefferson St, Springfield, IL 62702-5097. 217-782-6553 8:00 AM - 5:00 PM.

**Vital Records-Marriage Certificate, Divorce Records**, Records not available at state level.

**Workers' Compensation**, Industrial Commission, , IL. 312-814-6611 8:00 AM - 4:30 PM.

## Indiana

**State Archives**, Public Records Commission, Archive Division, 402 W Washington St, Room W472, Indianapolis, IN 46204. 317-232-3373

**Attorney General**, Attorney General's Office, 219 State House, Indianapolis, IN 46204. 317-232-6201

**Corporate Records**, Corporation Division, Secretary of State, 302 W Washington St, Room E018, Indianapolis, IN 46204. 317-232-6576 8:15 AM - 5:30 PM M-F / 9:00 AM - 12:00 PM SAT. Corporation Records, Limited Partnership Records, Fictitious Name, Assumed Name, Limited Liability Company Records.

**Corporate Records**, Secretary of State, Trademark Division, 302 W Washington St, IGC-East Rm E111, Indianapolis, IN 46204. 317-232-6540 8:45 AM - 4:45 PM. Trademarks/ Servicemarks.

**State Court Administrator**, State Court Administrator, 323 State House, Indianapolis, IN 46204. 317-232-2542

**Criminal Records**, Indiana State Police, Central Records, I.G.C.N, Room 302, 100 North Senate Avenue, Indianapolis, IN 46204. 317-232-8262 8:00 AM - 4:00 PM.

**DMV-Accident Reports**, State Police Department, Vehicle Crash Records Sections, Room N301, Indiana Government Center, Indianapolis, IN 46204. 317-232-8286 8:00 AM - 4:00 PM.

**DMV-Driver Records**, Bureau of Motor Vehicles, Driver Records, Room N405, Indiana Government Center, N, Indianapolis, IN 46204. 317-232-2894 8:15 AM - 4:30 PM.

**DMV-Vehicle Ownership, Vehicle Identification**, Bureau of Motor Vehicles, Vehicle Records, 100 N Senate Ave, Room N405, Indianapolis, IN 46204. 317-232-2795 8:15 AM - 4:45 PM.

**Governor**, Governor's Office, 206 State House, Indianapolis, IN 46204. 317-232-4567

**Legislation**, Legislative Services Agency, State House, 200 W Washington, Room 302, Indianapolis, IN 46204-2789. 317-232-9856 8:15 AM - 4:45 PM.

**Uniform Commercial Code**, UCC Division, Secretary of State, 302 West Washington St, Room E-018, Indianapolis, IN 46204. 317-232-6393 8:15 AM - 5:30 PM. Uniform Commercial Code, Federal Tax Liens, State Tax Liens.

**Vital Records-Birth Certificate**, State Department of Health, Division of Vital Records, 1330 W Michigan St, Room 111, Indianapolis, IN 46206. 317-633-0701 8:15 AM - 4:45 PM.

**Vital Records-Death Records**, State Department of Health, Division of Vital Records, 1330 W Michigan St, Room 111, Indianapolis, IN 46206. 317-633-0701 8:15 AM - 4:45 PM.

**Vital Records-Divorce Records**, Records not available at state level.

**Vital Records-Marriage Certificate**, State Department of Health, Division of Vital Records, 1330 W Michigan St, Room 111, Indianapolis, IN 46206. 317-633-0701 8:15 AM - 4:45 PM.

**Workers' Compensation**, Workers Compensation Board, 402 W Washington St, Room W196, Indianapolis, IN 46204-2753. 317-232-3808 8:00 AM - 4:30 PM.

## Iowa

**State Archives**, State Historical Society of Iowa, Library/Archives, 402 Iowa Ave, Iowa City, IA 52240. 319-335-3927

**Attorney General**, Attorney General's Office, Hoover Bldg, 2nd Floor, Des Moines, IA 50319. 515-281-5164

**Corporate Records**, Secretary of State, Corporation Division, 2nd Floor, Hoover Bldg, Des Moines, IA 50319. 515-281-5204 8:00 AM - 4:30 PM. Corporation Records, Limited Liability Company Records, Fictitious Name, Limited Partnership Records, Assumed Name, Trademarks/ Servicemarks.

**State Court Administrator**, State Court Administrator, State Capitol, Des Moines, IA 50319. 515-281-5241

**Criminal Records**, Division of Criminal Investigations, Bureau of Identification, Wallace State Office Bldg, Des Moines, IA 53019. 515-281-5138 8:00 AM - 5:00 PM.

**DMV-Accident Reports**, Department of Transportation, Office of Driver Services, Park Fair Mall, 100 Euclid, Des Moines, IA 50306-9204. 515-237-3070 8:00 AM - 4:30 PM.

**DMV-Driver Records**, Department of Transportation, Driver Service Records Section, Park Fair Mall, 100 Euclid, Des Moines, IA 50306. 515-237-3070 8:00 AM - 4:30 PM.

**DMV-Vehicle Ownership, Vehicle Identification**, Department of Transportation, Office of Vehicle Registration, Park Fair Mall, 100 Euclid, Des Moines, IA 50306. 515-237-3077 8:00 AM - 4:30 PM.

**Governor**, Office of the Governor, Statehouse, State Capitol Bldg, Des Moines, IA 50319. 515-281-5211

**Legislation**, Iowa General Assembly, Legislative Information Office, State Capitol, Des Moines, IA 50319. 515-281-5129 8:00 AM - 4:30 PM.

**Uniform Commercial Code**, UCC Division, Secretary of State, Hoover Bldg, East 14th & Walnut Sts., Des Moines, IA 50319. 515-281-5204 8:00 AM - 4:30 PM. Uniform Commercial Code, Federal Tax Liens, State Tax Liens.

**Vital Records-Birth Certificate**, Iowa Department of Public Health, Vital Records, 321 E 12th St, 4th Floor, Lucas Bldg, Des Moines, IA 50319. 515-281-4944 8:00 AM - 4:30 PM M-F (Application counter closes at 4:15).

**Vital Records-Death Records**, Iowa Department of Public Health, Vital Records, 321 E 12th St, 4th Floor, Lucas Bldg, Des Moines, IA 50319. 515-281-4944 8:00 AM - 4:30 PM M-F (Application counter closes at 4:15).

**Vital Records-Divorce Records**, Records not available at state level.

**Vital Records-Marriage Certificate**, Iowa Department of Public Health, Vital Records, 321 E 12th St, 4th Floor, Lucas Bldg, Des Moines, IA 50319. 515-281-4944 8:00 AM - 4:30 PM M-F (Application counter closes at 4:15).

**Workers' Compensation**, Workers Compensation Division, Industrial Services Section, 1000 E Grand Ave, Des Moines, IA 50319. 515-281-5934 8:00 AM - 4:30 PM.

**State Records**

## Kansas

**State Archives**, Historical Society, Archives Department, 120 W 10th St, Topeka, KS 66612. 913-296-4792

**Attorney General**, Attorney General's Office, Kansas Judicial Center, 2nd Floor, Topeka, KS 66612-1597. 913-296-2215

**Corporate Records**, Secretary of State, Corporation Division, 300 SW 10th St, Topeka, KS 66612-1594. 913-296-4564 8:00 AM - 5:00 PM. Corporation Records, Limited Partnership Records, Limited Liability Company Records.

**Corporate Records**, Secretary of State, Trademarks/ Servicemarks Division, 2nd Floor, State Capitol, Topeka, KS 66612. 913-296-2034 8:00 AM - 5:00 PM. Trademarks/ Servicemarks.

**State Court Administrator**, Judicial Administrator, Kansas Judicial Center, 301 W 10th St, Topeka, KS 66612-1507. 913-296-4873

**Criminal Records**, Kansas Bureau of Investigation, Criminal Justice Records Division, 1620 S W Tyler, Topeka, KS 66612-1837. 913-232-6000 8:00 AM - 5:00 PM.

**DMV-Driver Records, Accident Reports**, Department of Revenue, Driver Control Bureau, Docking State Office Building, 915 Harrison, 1st Floor, Topeka, KS 66612. 913-296-3671 8:00 AM - 4:45 PM.

**DMV-Vehicle Ownership, Vehicle Identification**, Division of Vehicles, Title and Registration Bureau, 915 Harrison, Topeka, KS 66612. 913-296-3621 7:30 AM - 4:45 PM.

**Governor**, Governor's Office, 2 State Capitol Bldg, Room 212S, Topeka, KS 66612-1590. 913-296-3232

**Legislation**, Kansas Legislature, Capitol Bldg, 3rd Floor, North Wing, Topeka, KS 66612. 913-296-3296 8:00 AM - 5:00 PM.

**Uniform Commercial Code**, UCC Division, Secretary of State, State Capitol, 300 W Tenth, 2nd Floor, Topeka, KS 66612-1594. 913-296-3650 8:00 AM - 5:00 PM. Uniform Commercial Code, Federal Tax Liens, State Tax Liens.

**Vital Records-Birth Certificate**, Kansas State Department of Health & Environment, Bureau of Vital Statistics, 900 SW Jackson, Landon State Office Bldg, Topeka, KS 66612-2221. 913-296-1400 8:30 AM - 4:30 PM.

**Vital Records-Death Records**, Kansas State Department of Health & Environment, Bureau of Vital Statistics, 900 SW Jackson, Landon State Office Bldg, Topeka, KS 66612-2221. 913-296-1400 8:30 AM - 4:30 PM.

**Vital Records-Divorce Records**, Kansas State Department of Health & Environment, Bureau of Vital Statistics, 900 SW Jackson, Landon State Office Bldg, Topeka, KS 66612-2221. 913-296-1400 8:30 AM - 4:30 PM.

**Vital Records-Marriage Certificate**, Kansas State Department of Health & Environment, Bureau of Vital Statistics, 900 SW Jackson, Landon State Office Bldg, Topeka, KS 66612-2221. 913-296-1400 8:30 AM - 4:30 PM.

**Workers' Compensation**, Human Resources Department, Workers Compensation Division, 800 SW Jackson, Suite 600, Topeka, KS 66612-1227. 913-296-3441 8:00 AM - 5:00 PM.

## Kentucky

**State Archives**, Libraries & Archives Department, 300 Coffee Tree Rd, Frankfort, KY 40602. 502-875-7000

**Attorney General**, Attorney General's Office, 116 State Capitol, Frankfort, KY 40601. 502-564-4002

**Corporate Records**, Secretary of State, Corporate Records, 700 Capitol Ave, Room 150, Frankfort, KY 40601. 502-564-7330 8:00 AM - 4:00 PM. Corporation Records, Limited Partnership Records, Assumed Name.

**Corporate Records**, Secretary of State, Legal Department, 700 Capitol Ave, Room 79, Frankfort, KY 40601. 502-564-7330 Trademarks/ Servicemarks.

**State Court Administrator**, Administrative Office of Courts, 100 Millcreek Park, Frankfort, KY 40601. 502-573-2350

**Criminal Records**, Kentucky State Police, Records Section, 1250 Louisville Rd, Frankfort, KY 40601. 502-227-8717 8:00 AM - 4:00 PM.

**DMV-Accident Reports**, Department of State Police, Records Section, 1250 Louisville Rd, Frankfort, KY 40601. 502-227-8700 7:30 AM - 4:30 PM.

**DMV-Driver Records**, Division of Driver's Licensing, MVRS-State Office Bldg, 501 High Street, 2nd Floor, Frankfort, KY 40622. 502-564-4711 8:00 AM - 4:30 PM.

**DMV-Vehicle Ownership, Vehicle Identification**, Department of Motor Vehicles, Division of Motor Vehicle Licensing, State Office Bldg, 3rd Floor, Frankfort, KY 40622. 502-564-2737 8:00 AM - 4:30 PM.

**Governor**, Governor's Office, 100 State Capitol, Frankfort, KY 40601. 502-564-2611

**Legislation**, Kentucky General Assembly, Legislative Research Commission, 700 Capitol Ave, Room 300, Frankfort, KY 40601. 502-564-8100 8:00 AM - 4:30 PM.

**Uniform Commercial Code**, UCC Division, Secretary of State, State Capitol Bldg, Rm 79, Frankfort, KY 40601. 502-564-2848 8:45 AM - 5:00 PM. Uniform Commercial Code, Federal Tax Liens, State Tax Liens.

**Vital Records-Birth Certificate**, Department for Human Resources, Vital Statistics, 275 E Main St, Frankfort, KY 40621. 502-564-4212 9:00 AM - 4:00 PM.

**Vital Records-Death Records**, Department for Human Resources, Vital Statistics, 275 E Main St, Frankfort, KY 40621. 502-564-4212 9:00 AM - 4:00 PM.

**Vital Records-Divorce Records**, Department for Human Resources, Vital Statistics, 275 E Main St, Frankfort, KY 40621. 502-564-4212 9:00 AM - 4:00 PM.

**Vital Records-Marriage Certificate**, Department for Human Resources, Vital Statistics, 275 E Main St, Frankfort, KY 40621. 502-564-4212 9:00 AM - 4:00 PM.

**Workers' Compensation**, Workers Claim Department, Perimitor Park West, 1270 Louisville Rd, Bldg C, Frankfort, KY 40601. 502-564-5550 8:00 AM - 5:00 PM.

## Louisiana

**State Archives**, Secretary of State, Archives & Records Division, 3851 Essen Lane, Baton Rouge, LA 70821. 504-922-1206

**Attorney General**, Attorney General's Office, Justice Department, PO Box 94005, Baton Rouge, LA 70804-9005. 504-342-7013

**Corporate Records**, Commercial Division, Corporation Department, 3851 Essen Lane, Baton Rouge, LA 70809. 504-925-4704 8:00 AM - 4:30 PM. Corporation Records, Limited Partnership Records, Limited Liability Company Records, Trademarks/ Servicemarks.

**State Court Administrator**, Judicial Administrator, Judicail Council of the Supreme Court, 301 Loyola Ave, New Orleans, LA 70112. 504-568-5747

**Criminal Records**, State Repository, Bureau of Criminal Indentification, PO Box 66614, Baton Rouge, LA 70896-6614. 504-925-6095 8:00 AM - 5:00 PM.

**DMV-Accident Reports**, Louisiana State Police, Accident Records, 265 S Foster Blvd, Baton Rouge, LA 70896. 504-925-6156 8:00 AM - 4:30 PM.

**DMV-Driver Records**, Dept of Public Safety and Corrections, Office of Motor Vehicles, 7701 Independence Blvd, Baton Bouge, LA 70896. 504-925-6009 8:00 AM - 4:00 PM T-S.

**DMV-Vehicle Ownership, Vehicle Identification**, Department of Public Safety & Corrections, Office of Motor Vehicles, 7701 Independence Blvd, Baton Rouge, LA 70896. 504-925-6146 8:00 AM - 4:00 PM T-S.

**Governor**, Office of the Governor, State Capitol, Baton Rouge, LA 70804. 504-342-7015

**Legislation**, Louisiana House (Senate) Representative, State Capitol, 2nd Floor, Room 207-House, Room 205-Senate, Baton Rouge, LA 70804. 504-342-6458 8:00 AM - 5:00 PM.

**Uniform Commercial Code**, Uniform Commercial Code, Federal Tax Liens, State Tax Liens. Records not available at state level.

**Vital Records-Birth Certificate**, Department of Vital Records, 325 Loyola Ave, New Orleans, LA 70112. 504-568-4980 8:00 AM - 4:00 PM.

**Vital Records-Death Records**, Department of Vital Records, 325 Loyola Ave, New Orleans, LA 70112. 504-568-4980 8:00 AM - 4:00 PM.

**Vital Records-Marriage Certificate, Divorce Records**, Records not available at state level.

**Workers' Compensation**, Labor Department, Office of Worker's Compensation, 1001 N 23rd, Baton Rouge, LA 70804. 504-342-7555 7:45 AM - 4:15 PM.

## Maine

**State Archives**, State Archives, Cultural Bldg, Station 84, Augusta, ME 04333-0084. 207-287-5790

**Attorney General**, Attorney General's Office, State House Station 6, Augusta, ME 04333. 207-626-8800

**Corporate Records**, Secretary of State, Reports & Information Division, Room 221, State Office Bldg, Corner Capitol & Seward Sts, Augusta, ME 04333. 207-287-4190 8:00 AM - 5:00 PM. Corporation Records, Limited Partnership Records, Trademarks/ Servicemarks, Assumed Name.

**State Court Administrator**, State Court Administrator, PO Box 368DTS, Portland, ME 04112. 207-822-0792

**Criminal Records**, Maine State Police, State Bureau of Identification, 36 Hospital St, Augusta, ME 04330. 207-624-7009 8:00 AM - 5:00 PM.

**DMV-Accident Reports**, Maine State Police, Traffic Section, 242 State St, Station 20, Augusta, ME 04330. 207-287-3397 8:00 AM - 5:00 PM M-T-TH-F 8:00 AM - 4:00 PM W.

**DMV-Driver Records**, Bureau of Motor Vehicles, Driver License & Control, State House Station 29, Augusta, ME 04333. 207-287-2576 8:00 AM-5:00 PM M-T,TH-F; 8:00 AM-4:00 PM W.

**DMV-Vehicle Ownership, Vehicle Identification**, Department of Motor Vehicles, Registration Section, State House Station 29, Augusta, ME 04333. 207-287-3556 8:00 AM-5:00 PM M-T,TH-F; 8:00 AM-4:00 PM W.

**Governor**, Governor's Office, State House Station 1, Augusta, ME 04333. 207-287-3531

**Legislation**, Maine Legislature, State House, Legislative Document Room, 3rd Floor, Augusta, ME 04333. 207-287-1692 8:00 AM - 5:00 PM.

**Uniform Commercial Code**, UCC Filing Section, Secretary of State, State Office Bldg, Capitol St, Rm 221, Augusta, ME 04333. 207-287-4177 8:00 AM - 5:00 PM. Uniform Commercial Code, Federal Tax Liens, State Tax Liens.

**Vital Records-Birth Certificate**, Maine Department of Human Services, Vital Records, 221 State St, Augusta, ME 04333. 207-287-3181 9:00 AM - 4:00 PM.

**Vital Records-Death Records**, Maine Department of Human Services, Vital Records, 221 State St, Augusta, ME 04333. 207-287-3181 9:00 AM - 4:00 PM.

**Vital Records-Divorce Records**, Maine Department of Human Services, Vital Records, 221 State St, Augusta, ME 04333. 207-287-3181 9:00 AM - 4:00 PM.

**Vital Records-Marriage Certificate**, Maine Department of Human Services, Vital Records, 221 State St, Augusta, ME 04333. 207-287-3181 9:00 AM - 4:00 PM.

**Workers' Compensation**, Workers Compensation Board, State House Station 27, Augusta, ME 04333-0027. 207-287-3751 7:30 AM - 5:00 PM.

## Maryland

**State Archives**, State Archives, Hall of Records, 350 Rowe Blvd, Annapolis, MD 21401. 410-974-3867

**Attorney General**, Attorney General's Office, 200 St Paul Place, Baltimore, MD 21202. 410-576-6300

**Corporate Records**, Department of Assessments and Taxation, Corporations Division, 301 W Preston St, Room 809, Baltimore, MD 21201. 410-225-1340 8:30 AM - 4:30 PM. Corporation Records, Limited Partnership Records, Trade Names, Limited Liability Company Records, Fictitious Name.

**Corporate Records**, Secretary of State, Trademarks Division, Annapolis, MD 21401. 410-974-5531 9:00 AM - 5:00 PM. Trademarks/ Servicemarks.

**State Court Administrator**, Court Administrator, Administrative Office of Courts, Court of Appeals Bldg, 3rd Floor, 361 Rowe Blvd, Annapolis, MD 21401. 410-974-2141

**Criminal Records**, Criminal Justice Information System, Central Repository, State Police Headquarters, 1201 Reisterstown Rd, Pikesville, MD 21208-3899. 410-764-4501 8:00 AM - 5:00 PM.

**DMV-Accident Reports**, Maryland State Police, Security Annex CRD, Baltimore, MD 21244. 410-768-7431 8:15 AM - 4:30 PM.

**DMV-Driver Records**, Department of Motor Vehicles, Motor Vehicle Adminstration, 6601 Ritchie Hwy, NE, Counter 212, Glen Burnie, MD 21062. 410-787-7705 8:15 AM - 4:30 PM.

**DMV-Vehicle Ownership, Vehicle Identification**, Department of Motor Vehicles, Vehicle Registration Division, Room 206, 6601 Ritchie Hwy, NE, Glen Burnie, MD 21062. 410-768-7250 8:15 AM - 4:30 PM.

**Governor**, Office of the Governor, State House, 100 State Circle, Annapolis, MD 21401. 410-974-3901

**Legislation**, Maryland General Assembly, State House, 90 State Circle, Rm G-17, Annapolis, MD 21401. 410-841-3810 8:00 AM - 5:00 PM.

**Uniform Commercial Code**, UCC Division, Department of Assessments & Taxation, 301 West Preston St, Baltimore, MD 21201. 410-225-1340 8:30 AM - 5:00 PM. Uniform Commercial Code, Federal Tax Liens, State Tax Liens.

**Vital Records-Birth Certificate**, Department of Health, Division of Vital Records, 4201 Patterson Ave, 1st Floor, Baltimore, MD 21215. 410-764-3038 8:00 AM - 4:30 PM M-F and 3rd Saturday of each month.

**Vital Records-Death Records**, Department of Health, Division of Vital Records, 4201 Patterson Ave, 1st Floor, Baltimore, MD 21215. 410-764-3038 8:00 AM - 4:30 PM M-F and 3rd Saturday of each month.

**Vital Records-Divorce Records**, Department of Health, Division of Vital Records, 4201 Patterson Ave, 1st Floor, Baltimore, MD 21215. 410-764-3038 8:00 AM - 4:45 PM M-F and 3rd Saturday of each month.

**Vital Records-Marriage Certificate**, Department of Health, Division of Vital Records, 4201 Patterson Ave, 1st Floor, Baltimore, MD 21215. 410-764-3038 8:00 AM - 4:45 PM M-F and 3rd Saturday of each month.

**Workers' Compensation**, Workers Compensation Commission, Six N Liberty St, Baltimore, MD 21201. 410-333-4700 8:30 AM - 4:30 PM.

## Massachusetts

**State Archives**, Massachusetts Archives at Columbia Point, Archives Division, 220 Morrissey Blvd, Boston, MA 02125. 617-727-2816

**Attorney General**, Attorney General's Office, One Ashburton Place, Room 2010, Boston, MA 02108. 617-727-2200

**Corporate Records**, Secretary of the Commonwealth, Corporation Division, One Ashburton Pl, 17th Floor, Boston, MA 02108. 617-727-9640 8:45 AM - 5:00 PM. Corporation Records, Trademarks/ Servicemarks.

**State Court Administrator**, Trial Court Administrator, 2 Center Plaza, Room 540, Boston, MA 02108. 617-742-8575

**Criminal Records**, Criminal History Systems Board, 1010 Commonwealth Ave, Boston, MA 02215. 617-727-0090 8:00 AM - 5:00 PM.

**DMV-Accident Reports**, Accident Records Section, Registry of Motor Vehicles, 1135 Tremont St, Boston, MA 02120. 617-351-9000 8:45 AM - 5:00 PM.

**DMV-Vehicle Ownership, Vehicle Identification**, Registry of Motor Vehicles, Customer Assistance-Mail List Dept., 1135 Tremont St, Boston, MA 02120. 617-351-4400 8:00 AM - 4:30 PM M-T-W-F 8:00 AM - 7:00 PM TH.

**Governor**, Governor's Office, State House, Room 360, Boston, MA 02133. 617-727-3600

**Legislation**, Massachusetts General Court, State House, Beacon St, Room 428 (Document Room), Boston, MA 02133. 617-722-2860 9:00 AM - 5:00 PM.

**Uniform Commercial Code**, UCC Division, Secretary of the Commonwealth, One Ashburton Pl, Room 1711, Boston, MA 02108. 617-727-2860 8:45 AM - 5:00 PM. Uniform Commercial Code, Federal Tax Liens, State Tax Liens.

**Vital Records-Birth Certificate**, Registry of Vital Records and Statistics, 470 Atlantic Ave, 2nd Floor, Boston, MA 02110-2224. 617-727-0110 8:45 AM - 4:45 PM M,TU,TH,F.

**Vital Records-Death Records**, Registry of Vital Records and Statistics, 470 Atlantic Ave, 2nd Floor, Boston, MA 02110-2224. 617-727-0110 8:45 AM - 4:45 PM M,TU,TH,F.

**Vital Records-Divorce Records**, Records not available at state level.

**Vital Records-Divorce Records-Insurance**, Merit Rating Board, 1135 Tremont St, 6th Floor, Boston, MA 02120-2103. 617-351-4400 8:00 AM - 4:30 PM M-T-W-F 8:00 AM - 7:00 PM TH.

**Vital Records-Divorce Records-Registry**, Registrar of Motor Vehicles, 1135 Tremont St, Boston, MA 02120. 617-351-9834 8:00 AM - 4:30 PM M-T-W-F 8:00 AM - 7:00 PM TH.

**Vital Records-Marriage Certificate**, Registry of Vital Records, 470 Atlantic Ave, 2nd Floor, Boston, MA 02110-2224. 617-727-0110 8:45 AM - 4:45 PM M,TU,TH,F.

**Workers' Compensation**, Keeper of Records, Industrial Accident Department, 600 Washington St, 7th Floor, Boston, MA 02111. 617-727-4900 9:00 AM - 5:00 PM.

## Michigan

**State Archives**, Bureau of History, Archives Section, Library & Historical Center, 717 W Alleg, Lansing, MI 48918-1800. 517-373-1408

**Attorney General**, Attorney General's Office, PO Box 30212, Law Bldg, Lansing, MI 48909. 517-373-1110

**Corporate Records**, Department of Commerce, Corporation Division, 6546 Mercantile Way, Lansing, MI 48909. 517-334-6302 8:00 AM - 5:00 PM. Corporation Records, Limited Liability Company Records, Fictitious Name, Limited Partnership Records, Assumed Name, Trademarks/ Servicemarks.

**State Court Administrator**, State Court Administrator, 611 W Ottawa, Lansing, MI 48909. 517-373-0130

**Criminal Records**, Michigan State Police, Applicant Ident. Team, Central Records Division, General Bldg, 7150 Harris Dr, Lansing, MI 48913. 517-322-1955 8:00 AM - 5:00 PM.

**DMV-Accident Reports**, Department of State Police, Central Records Division/Freedom of Information, 7150 Harris Dr, Lansing, MI 48913. 517-322-6092 8:00 AM - 5:00 PM.

**DMV-Driver Records**, Department of State Police, Commercial Look-up Unit, 7064 Crowner Dr, Lansing, MI 48918. 517-322-1624 8:00 AM - 4:45 PM.

**DMV-Vehicle Ownership, Vehicle Identification**, Department of State Police, Commercial Look-up Unit, 7064 Crowner Dr, Lansing, MI 48918. 517-322-1624 8:00 AM - 4:45 PM.

**Governor**, Governor's Office, Olds Plaza, Lansing, MI 48909. 517-373-3400

**Legislation**, Michigan Legislature Document Room, State Capitol, North Capitol Annex, Lansing, MI 48909. 517-373-0169 8:30 AM - 5:00 PM.

**Uniform Commercial Code**, UCC Section, Department of State, Secondary Complex, 7064 Crowner Dr, Dimondale, MI 48821. 517-322-1144 8:00 AM - 5:00 PM. Uniform Commercial Code, Federal Tax Liens, State Tax Liens.

**Vital Records-Birth Certificate**, Department of Health, Office of the State Registrar, 3423 N Logan, Martin Luther King, Jr Blvd, Lansing, MI 48909. 517-335-8656 8:00 AM - 5:00 PM.

**Vital Records-Death Records**, Department of Health, Office of the State Registrar, 3423 N Logan, Martin Luther King, Jr Blvd, Lansing, MI 48909. 517-335-8656 8:30 AM - 4:30 PM.

**Vital Records-Divorce Records**, Department of Health, Office of the State Registrar, 3423 N Logan, Martin Luther King, Jr Blvd, Lansing, MI 48909. 517-335-8656 8:30 AM - 4:30 PM.

**Vital Records-Marriage Certificate**, Department of Health, Office of the State Registrar, 3423 N Logan, Martin Luther King, Jr Blvd, Lansing, MI 48909. 517-335-8656 8:30 AM - 4:30 PM.

**Workers' Compensation**, Labor Department, Workers Disability Compensation Division, 7150 Harris Dr, Lansing, MI 48909. 517-322-1287 X2 8:00 AM - 5:00 PM.

## Minnesota

**State Archives**, Historical Society, Libraries & Archives, 345 Kellogg Blvd, W, St Paul, MN 55102-1906. 612-296-6126

**Attorney General**, Attorney General's Office, 102 State Capitol, St Paul, MN 55155. 612-296-6196

**Corporate Records**, Business Services Division, Secretary of State, 180 State Office Bldg, 100 Constitution, St Paul, MN 55155-1299. 612-296-2803 8:00 AM - 4:30 PM. Corporation Records, Limited Liability Company Records, Assumed Name, Trademarks/ Servicemarks, Limited Partnership Records.

**State Court Administrator**, State Court Administrator, 135 Minnesota Judicial Center, 25 Constitution Ave, St Paul, MN 55155. 612-296-2474

**Criminal Records**, Bureau of Criminal Apprehension, Records & Identification, 1246 University Ave, St Paul, MN 55104. 612-642-0673 8:15 AM - 4:00 PM.

**DMV-Accident Reports**, Department of Public Safety, Accident Records, 110 Transportation Bldg, 395 John Irelan, St Paul, MN 55155. 612-296-2045 8:00 AM - 4:30 PM.

**DMV-Driver Records**, Driver & Vehicle Services-Investigation Unit, Record Request, Room 108, 395 John Ireland Blvd, St Paul, MN 55155. 612-296-2023 8:00 AM - 4:30 PM.

**DMV-Vehicle Ownership, Vehicle Identification**, Driver & Vehicle Services, Records Department, Room 214, 395 John Ireland Blvd, St Paul, MN 55155. 612-296-6911 8:00 AM - 4:30 PM.

**Governor**, Governor's Office, 130 Capitol Bldg, 75 Constitution Ave, St Paul, MN 55155. 612-296-3391

**Legislation**, Minnesota Legislature, State Capitol, House-Room 231, Senate-Room 211, St Paul, MN 55155. 612-296-2887 7:30 AM - 5:30 PM.

**Uniform Commercial Code**, UCC Division, Secretary of State, 180 State Office Bldg, St Paul, MN 55155. 612-296-2434 Uniform Commercial Code, Federal Tax Liens, State Tax Liens.

**Vital Records-Birth Certificate**, Minnesota Department of Health, Section of Vital Records, 717 Delaware St, SE, Minneapolis, MN 55414. 612-623-5120 8:00 AM - 4:00 PM.

**Vital Records-Death Records**, Minnesota Department of Health, Section of Vital Records, 717 Delaware St, SE, Minneapolis, MN 55414. 612-623-5120 8:00 AM - 4:00 PM.

**Vital Records-Marriage Certificate, Divorce Records**, Records not available at state level.

**Workers' Compensation**, Labor & Industry Department, Workers Compensation Division - Records Section, 443 Lafayette Rd, St Paul, MN 55155. 612-296-2432 8:00 AM - 4:30 PM.

**State Records**

## Mississippi

**State Archives**, Archives & History Department, Archives & Library Division, PO Box 571, Jackson, MS 39205-0571. 601-359-6850

**Attorney General**, Attorney General's Office, PO Box 220, Jackson, MS 39205. 601-359-3680

**Corporate Records**, Corporation Commission, Secretary of State, 202 N Congress, Suite 601, Jackson, MS 39201. 601-359-1627 8:00 AM - 5:00 PM. Corporation Records, Limited Partnership Records, Limited Liability Company Records, Trademarks/ Servicemarks.

**State Court Administrator**, Court Administrator, 450 High St, Box 117, Jackson, MS 39205. 601-359-3697

**Criminal Records**. Records not available at state level.

**DMV-Accident Reports**, Safety Responsibility, Accident Records, 1900 E Woodrow Wilson, Jackson, MS 39216. 601-987-1260 8:00 AM - 5:00 PM.

**DMV-Driver Records**, Department of Public Safety, Driver Records, 1900 E Woodrow Wilson, Jackson, MS 39216. 601-987-1274 8:00 AM - 5:00 PM.

**DMV-Vehicle Ownership, Vehicle Identification**, Mississippi State Tax Commission, Registration Department, Titles-Room 601/Woolfolk Bldg, Registrations-Room 503/Woolfolk Bldg, Jackson, MS 39215. 601-359-1248 8:00 AM - 5:00 PM.

**Governor**, Governor's Office, 550 High St, 20th Floor, Sillers Bldg, Jackson, MS 39201. 601-359-3150

**Legislation**, Mississippi Legislature, New Capitol, Room 308, Room 308, 3rd Floor, Jackson, MS 39215. 601-359-3229 8:00 AM - 5:00 PM.

**Uniform Commercial Code**, UCC Division, Secretary of State, 202 N Congress St, Suite 601, Magnolia Federal Bank Bldg, Jackson, MS 39201. 601-359-1621 8:00 AM - 5:00 PM. Uniform Commercial Code, Federal Tax Liens, State Tax Liens.

**Vital Records-Birth Certificate**, State Department of Health, Vital Statistics & Records, 2423 N State St, Jackson, MS 39216. 601-960-7981 8:00 AM - 5:00 PM.

**Vital Records-Death Records**, State Department of Health, Vital Statistics, 2423 N State St, Jackson, MS 39216. 601-960-7981 8:00 AM - 5:00 PM.

**Vital Records-Divorce Records**, State Department of Health, Vital Statistics, 2423 N State St, Jackson, MS 39216. 601-960-7981 8:00 AM - 5:00 PM.

**Vital Records-Marriage Certificate**, State Department of Health, Vital Statistics, 2423 N State St, Jackson, MS 39216. 601-960-7981 8:00 AM - 5:00 PM.

**Workers' Compensation**, Workers Compensation Commission, 1428 Lakeland Dr, Jackson, MS 39216. 601-987-4200 8:00 AM - 5:00 PM.

## Missouri

**State Archives**, Secretary of State, Archives Division, 600 W Main St, Jefferson City, MO 65102. 314-751-3280

**Attorney General**, Attorney General's Office, Supreme Court Bldg, Jefferson City, MO 65102. 314-751-3321

**Corporate Records**, Secretary of State, Corporation Services, 600 W Main, Jefferson City, MO 65102. 314-751-4153 8:00 AM - 4:30 PM. Corporation Records, Fictitious Name, Limited Partnership Records, Assumed Name, Trademarks/ Servicemarks, Limited Liability Company Records.

**State Court Administrator**, State Court Administrator, 1105 Rear SW Blvd, Jefferson City, MO 65109. 314-751-4377

**Criminal Records**, Missouri State Highway Patrol, Criminal Record Division, 1510 E Elm St, Jefferson City, MO 65101. 314-751-3313 8:00 AM - 12:00 AM - 12:30 PM - 5:00 PM.

**DMV-Accident Reports**, Missouri Highway Patrol, Traffic Division, 1510 E Elm St, Jefferson City, MO 65102. 314-751-3313 8:00 AM - 5:00 PM.

**DMV-Driver Records**, Department of Revenue, Driver License Bureau, Truman Bldg, Room 470, Jefferson City, MO 65105. 314-751-4600 7:45 AM - 4:45 PM.

**DMV-Vehicle Ownership, Vehicle Identification**, Department of Motor Vehicles, Motor Vehicle Bureau, Truman Bldg, Room 370, Jefferson City, MO 65105. 314-751-4509 8:00 AM - 4:30 PM.

**Governor**, Office of the Governor, 216 State Capitol, Jefferson City, MO 65102. 314-751-3222

**Legislation**, Legislative Library, 117A State Capitol, Jefferson City, MO 65101. 314-751-4633 8:30 AM - 4:30 PM.

**Uniform Commercial Code**, UCC Division, Secretary of State, 600 W Main St, Jefferson City, MO 65101. 314-751-2360 8:00 AM - 5:00 PM. Uniform Commercial Code, Federal Tax Liens, State Tax Liens.

**Vital Records-Birth Certificate**, Department of Health, Bureau of Vital Records, PO Box 570, Jefferson City, MO 65102-0570. 314-751-6387 8:00 AM - 4:30 PM.

**Vital Records-Death Records**, Department of Health, Bureau of Vital Records, PO Box 570, Jefferson City, MO 65102-0570. 314-751-6370 8:00 AM - 4:30 PM.

**Vital Records-Marriage Certificate, Divorce Records**, Dept. of Health, Bureau of Vital Records, PO Box 570, Jefferson City, MO 65102-0570. 314-751-6370 8:00 AM - 5 PM.

**Workers' Compensation**, Labor & Industrial Relations Department, Workers Compensation Division, 3315 W Truman Blvd, Jefferson City, MO 65102. 314-751-4231 8:00 AM - 4:30 PM.

## Montana

**State Archives**, Historical Society, Archives Division, 225 N Roberts St, Helena, MT 59620. 406-444-2694

**Attorney General**, Attorney General's Office, Justice Bldg, 215 N Sanders, Helena, MT 59620. 406-444-2026

**Corporate Records**, Business Services Bureau, Secretary of State, State Capitol, Room 225, Helena, MT 59620. 406-444-3665 8:00 AM - 5:00 PM. Corporation Records, Limited Liability Company Records, Fictitious Name, Limited Partnership Records, Assumed Name, Trademarks/ Servicemarks.

**State Court Administrator**, Court Administrator, 215 N Sanders, Justice Bldg, Room 315, Helena, MT 59620-3002. 406-444-2621

**Criminal Records**, Department of Justice, Criminal History Records Program, 303 N Roberts, Room 374, Helena, MT 59620-1418. 406-444-3625 8:00 AM - 4:30 PM.

**DMV-Accident Reports**, Montana Highway Patrol, Accident Records, 303 N Roberts, Helena, MT 59620. 406-444-3278 8:00 AM - 5:00 PM.

**DMV-Driver Records**, Motor Vehicle Division, Drivers' Services, Records Unit, 303 N Roberts, Room 262, Helena, MT 59620. 406-444-4590 8:00 AM - 5:00 PM.

**DMV-Vehicle Ownership, Vehicle Identification**, Department of Justice, Title and Registration Bureau, 925 Main St, Deer Lodge, MT 59722. 406-846-1423 8:00 AM - 5:00 PM.

**Governor**, Governor's Office, State Capitol, Room 204, Helena, MT 59620. 406-444-3111

**Legislation**, State Legislature of Montana, State Capitol, Room 138, Helena, MT 59620. 406-444-3064 8:00 AM - 5:00 PM.

**Uniform Commercial Code**, Business Services Bureau, Secretary of State, State Capitol, Rm 225, Helena, MT 59620-2801. 406-444-3665 8:00 AM - 5:00 PM. Uniform Commercial Code, Federal Tax Liens, State Tax Liens.

**Vital Records-Birth Certificate**, Montana Department of Health, Vital Records, 1400 Broadway, Cogswell Bldg, Room C118, Helena, MT 59620. 406-444-4228 8:00 AM - 5:00 PM.

**Vital Records-Death Records**, Montana Department of Health, Vital Records, 1400 Broadway, Cogswell Bldg, Room C118, Helena, MT 59620. 406-444-4228 8:00 AM - 5:00 PM.

**Vital Records-Marriage Certificate, Divorce Records**, Records not available at state level.

**Workers' Compensation**, State Compensation Fund, PO Box 4759, Helena, MT 59604. 406-444-6485 8:00 AM - 5:00 PM.

## Nebraska

**State Archives**, Historical Society, Archives, 1500 R St, Lincoln, NE 68501. 402-471-3270

**Attorney General**, Attorney General's Office, 2115 State Capitol, Lincoln, NE 68509. 402-471-2682

**Corporate Records**, Secretary of State, Corporation Commission, 2300 State Capitol Bldg, Lincoln, NE 68509. 402-471-4079 8:30 AM - 5:00 PM. Corporation Records, Limited Liability Company Records, Limited Partnership Records, Trade Names, Trademarks/ Servicemarks.

**State Court Administrator**, Court Administrator, State Capitol #1220, Lincoln, NE 68509. 402-471-2643

**Criminal Records**, Nebraska Highway Patrol, CID, 1500 Nebraska Highway 2, Lincoln, NE 68502. 402-471-4545 8:00 AM - 4:00 PM.

**DMV-Accident Reports**, Department of Roads, Accident Records Bureau, 1500 Nebraska Highway 2, Lincoln, NE 68502. 402-479-4645 8:00 AM -5:00 PM.

**DMV-Driver Records**, Department of Motor Vehicles, Driver's Records, 301 Centennial Mall, S, Lincoln, NE 68509. 402-471-4343 8:00 AM - 5:00 PM.

**DMV-Vehicle Ownership, Vehicle Identification**, Department of Motor Vehicles, Titles and Registration Section, 301 Centennial Mall, S, Lincoln, NE 68509. 402-471-3910 8:00 AM - 5:00 PM.

**Governor**, Governor's Office, State Capitol, 2nd Floor NE, Lincoln, NE 68509. 402-471-2244

**Legislation**, Clerk of Legislature Office, State Capitol, Room 2018, Lincoln, NE 68509. 402-471-2271 8:00 AM - 5:00 PM.

**Uniform Commercial Code**, UCC Division, Secretary of State, 1305 State Capitol Bldg, Lincoln, NE 68509. 402-471-4080 7:30 AM - 5:00 PM. Uniform Commercial Code, Federal Tax Liens, State Tax Liens.

**Vital Records-Birth Certificate**, Department of Health, Bureau of Vital Statistics, 301 Centennial Mall S, Lincoln, NE 68508. 402-471-2871 8:00 AM - 5:00 PM.

**Vital Records-Death Records**, Department of Health, Bureau of Vital Statistics, 301 Centennial Mall S, Lincoln, NE 68508. 402-471-2871 8:00 AM - 5:00 PM.

**Vital Records-Divorce Records**, Department of Health, Bureau of Vital Statistics, 301 Centennial Mall S, Lincoln, NE 68508. 402-471-2871 8:00 AM - 5:00 PM.

**Vital Records-Marriage Certificate**, Department of Health, Bureau of Vital Statistics, 301 Centennial Mall S, Lincoln, NE 68508. 402-471-2871 8:00 AM - 5:00 PM.

**Workers' Compensation**, Workers' Compensation Court, State Capitol, 12th Floors, Lincoln, NE 68509. 402-471-9000 8:00 AM - 5:00 PM.

## Nevada

**State Archives**, State Library & Archives, Capitol Complex, Carson City, NV 89710. 702-687-5160

**Attorney General**, Attorney General's Office, Capitol Complex, Carson City, NV 89710. 702-687-3510

**Corporate Records**, Secretary of State, Status Division, Capitol Annex, Capitol Bldg, Carson City, NV 89710. 702-687-5203 8:00 AM - 5:00 PM. Corporation Records, Limited Partnership Records, Trademarks/ Servicemarks, Limited Liability Company Records.

**State Court Administrator**, Court Administrator, Capitol Complex, 201 S Carson St, Carson City, NV 89710. 702-687-5076

**Criminal Records**. Records not available at state level.

**DMV-Accident Reports**, Department of Motor Vehicles, Highway Patrol Division, 555 Wright Way, Carson City, NV 89711-0250. 702-687-5300 8:00 AM - 5:00 PM.

**DMV-Driver Records**, Department of Motor Vehicles and Public Safety, Records Section, 555 Wright Way, Carson City, NV 89711-0250. 702-687-5505 8:00 AM - 4:45 PM.

**DMV-Vehicle Ownership, Vehicle Identification**, Department of Motor Vehicles and Public Safety, Motor Vehicle Record Section, 555 Wright Way, Carson City, NV 89711-0250. 702-687-5505 8:00 AM - 4:45 PM.

**Governor**, Governor's Office, Executive Chambers, Capitol Complex, Carson City, NV 89710. 702-687-5670

**Legislation**, Nevada Legislature, 401 S Carson St, Carson City, NV 89701. 702-687-6825 8:00 AM - 5:00 PM.

**Uniform Commercial Code**, UCC Department, Secretary of State, Capitol Complex, Carson City, NV 89710. 702-687-5298 Uniform Commercial Code, Federal Tax Liens, State Tax Liens.

**Vital Records-Birth Certificate**, Nevada Department of Health, Office of Vital Statistics, 505 E King St, Carson City, NV 89710. 702-687-4481 8:00 AM - 4:00 PM.

**Vital Records-Death Records**, Nevada Department of Health, Office of Vital Statistics, 505 E King St, Carson City, NV 89710. 702-687-4481 8:00 AM - 4:00 PM.

**Vital Records-Marriage Certificate, Divorce Records**, Records not available at state level.

**Workers' Compensation**, State Industrial Insurance System, Workers Compensation Division, 515 E Musser St, Carson City, NV 89714. 702-687-5220 8:00 AM - 5:00 PM.

## New Hampshire

**State Archives**, Department of State, Records Management & Archives, 71 S Fruit St, Concord, NH 03301. 603-271-2236

**Attorney General**, Attorney General's Office, 33 Capitol St, Concord, NH 03301-6397. 603-271-3671

**Corporate Records**, Secretary of State, Corporation Division, State House, Room 204, Concord, NH 03301. 603-271-3244 8:00 AM - 4:30 PM. Corporation Records, Limited Partnership Records, Limited Partnership Records, Limited Liability Company Records, Trademarks/ Servicemarks, Trade Names.

**State Court Administrator**, Administrative Office of Courts, Supreme Court Bldg, Noble Dr, Concord, NH 03301. 603-271-2521

**Criminal Records**, State Police Headquarters, Criminal Records, James H. Hayes Bldg, 10 Hazen Dr, Concord, NH 03305. 603-271-2535 8:15 AM - 4:15 PM.

**DMV-Accident Reports**, Department of Safety, Reproduction Section, 10 Hazen Dr, Concord, NH 03305. 603-271-2128 8:15 AM - 4:15 PM.

**DMV-Driver Records**, Department of Motor Vehicles, Driving Records, 10 Hazen Dr, Concord, NH 03305. 603-271-2322 8:15 AM - 4:15 PM.

**DMV-Vehicle Ownership, Vehicle Identification**, Department of Public Safety, Bureau of Title, 10 Hazen Dr, Concord, NH 03305. 603-271-3111 8:15 AM - 4:15 PM.

**Governor**, Governor's Office, State House, 107 N Main St, Concord, NH 03301. 603-271-2121

**Legislation**, New Hampshire Legislature, State House, 20 Part St, Concord, NH 03301. 603-271-2239 8:00 AM - 4:30 PM.

**Uniform Commercial Code**, UCC Division, Secretary of State, State House Annex, 25 Capitol St, Concord, NH 03301. 603-271-3276 8:00 AM - 4:30 PM. Uniform Commercial Code, Federal Tax Liens, State Tax Liens.

**Vital Records-Birth Certificate**, Department of Health, Bureau of Vital Records, 6 Hazen Dr, Concord, NH 03301-6527. 603-271-4650 8:00 AM -4:30 PM.

**Vital Records-Death Records**, Department of Health, Bureau of Vital Records, 6 Hazen Dr, Concord, NH 03301-6527. 603-271-4650 8:00 AM - 4:30 PM.

**Vital Records-Divorce Records**, Department of Health, Bureau of Vital Records, 6 Hazen Dr, Concord, NH 03301-6527. 603-271-4650 8:00 AM - 4:30 PM.

**Vital Records-Marriage Certificate**, Department of Health, Bureau of Vital Records, 6 Hazen Dr, Concord, NH 03301-6527. 603-271-4650 8:00 AM - 4:30 PM.

**Workers' Compensation**, Labor Department, Workers Compensation Division, State Office Park S, 95 Pleasant St, Concord, NH 03301. 603-271-3174 8:00 AM - 4:30 PM.

## New Jersey

**State Archives**, Archives & Record Management, 2300 Stuyvesant Ave, CN-307, Trenton, NJ 08625. 609-530-3200

**Attorney General**, Attorney General's Office, Law & Public Safety Department, Justice Complex, CN-080, Trenton, NJ 08625. 609-984-1548

**Corporate Records**, Department of State, Division of Commercial Recording, 820 Bear Tavern Rd, West Trenton, NJ 08628. 609-530-6400 8:30 AM - 5:00 PM. Corporation Records, Limited Liability Company Records, Fictitious Name, Limited Partnership Records.

**Corporate Records**, Department of State, Trademark Division, 820 Bear Tavern Rd, 2nd Floor, West Trenton, NJ 08628. 609-530-6422 8:30 AM - 5:00 PM. Trademarks/ Servicemarks.

**State Court Administrator**, Administrative Office of Courts, RJH Justice Complex, Courts Building, Room CN-037, Trenton, NJ 08625. 609-984-0275

**Criminal Records**, Division of State Police, Records and Identification Section, PO Box 7068, West Trenton, NJ 08628. 609-882-2000 9:00 AM - 5:00 PM.

**DMV-Accident Reports**, New Jersey State Police, Criminal Justice Records Bureau, PO Box 7068, West Trenton, NJ 08628-0068. 609-882-2000 8:00 AM - 5:00 PM.

**DMV-Driver Records**, Motor Vehicle Services, Driver's Abstract Section, CN142, Trenton, NJ 08666. 609-633-8255 8:00 AM - 5:00 PM.

**DMV-Vehicle Ownership, Vehicle Identification**, Motor Vehicle Services, Certified Information Unit, CN146, Trenton, NJ 08666. 609-588-2424 8:00 AM - 5:00 PM.

**Governor**, Governor's Office, State House, Trenton, NJ 08625. 609-292-6000

**Legislation**, New Jersey State Legislature, State House, CN-068, Room B06, Trenton, NJ 08625. 609-292-4840 8:30 AM - 5:00 PM.

**Uniform Commercial Code**, UCC Division, Secretary of State, 820 Bear Tavern Rd, West Trenton, NJ 08628. 609-530-6426 8:30 AM - 5:00 PM. Uniform Commercial Code, Federal Tax Liens, State Tax Liens.

**Vital Records-Birth Certificate**, Department of Health, Vital Statistics, S Warren St, Room 504, Trenton, NJ 08625. 609-292-4087 8:45 AM - 4:45 PM.

**Vital Records-Death Records**, Department of Health, Vital Statistics, S Warren St, Room 504, Trenton, NJ 08625. 609-292-4087 8:45 AM - 4:45 PM.

**Vital Records-Divorce Records**, Public Information Center, CN-967, Trenton, NJ 08625. 609-777-0092 8:45 AM - 4:00 PM.

**Vital Records-Marriage Certificate**, Department of Health, Vital Statistics, S Warren St, Room 504, Trenton, NJ 08625. 609-292-4087 8:45 AM - 4:45 PM.

**Workers' Compensation**, Labor Department, Workers Compensation Division, John Fitch Plaza, CN381, Trenton, NJ 08625. 609-292-6026 8:00 AM - 4:30 PM.

## New Mexico

**State Archives**, State Records Center & Archives, 404 Montezuma, Santa Fe, NM 87503. 505-827-7332

**Attorney General**, Attorney General's Office, PO Drawer 1508, Santa Fe, NM 87504-1508. 505-827-6000

**Corporate Records**, State Corporation Commission, Corporate Department, PERA Bldg, 4th Floor, Room 418, Santa Fe, NM 87501. 505-827-4504 8:00 - 12:00 AM & 1:00 - 5:00 PM. Corporation Records, Limited Liability Company Records.

**Corporate Records**, Secretary of State, Tradename Division, State Capitol Bldg, Room 421, Santa Fe, NM 87503. 505-827-3609 8:00 AM - 5:00 PM. Trademarks/ Servicemarks, Trade Names.

**State Court Administrator**, State Administrative Office, Supreme Court Building, Room 25, Santa Fe, NM 87503. 505-827-4800

**Criminal Records**, Department of Public Safety, Records Bureau, 4491 Serrillos Rd, Santa Fe, NM 87504. 505-827-9181 8:00 AM - 5:00 PM.

**DMV-Accident Reports**, Department of Public Safety, Records, New Mexico State Police Complex, 4491 Cerrillos Rd, Santa Fe, NM 87504. 505-827-9300 8:00 AM - 5:00 PM.

**DMV-Driver Records**, Department of Motor Vehicles, Driver Services Bureau, Joseph M. Montoya Bldg, 1100 S St. Francis Dr, 2nd Floor, Santa Fe, NM 87504. 505-827-2241 8:00 AM - 5:00 PM.

**DMV-Vehicle Ownership, Vehicle Identification**, Department of Motor Vehicles, Vehicle Services Bureau, Joseph M. Montoya Bldg, 1100 S St. Francis Dr, 2nd Floor, Santa Fe, NM 87504. 505-827-2220 8:00 AM - 5:00 PM.

**Governor**, Governor's Office, State Capitol, Room 400, Santa Fe, NM 87503. 505-827-3000

**Legislation**, New Mexico State Legislature, State Capitol Bldg, Room 419, 4th Floor, Santa Fe, NM 87503. 505-986-4600 8:00 AM - 12:00 PM - 1:15 PM - 5:00 PM.

**Uniform Commercial Code**, UCC Division, Secretary of State, State Capitol Bldg, Room 420, Santa Fe, NM 87503. 505-827-3600 8:00 AM - 5:00 PM. Uniform Commercial Code, Federal Tax Liens, State Tax Liens.

**Vital Records-Birth Certificate**, Department of Health, Bureau of Vital Records & Health Statistics, 1190 St Francis Dr, Room 1050 N, Santa Fe, NM 87502. 505-827-2338 8:00 AM - 5:00 PM M-F (Counter Service: 9:00 AM - 4:00 PM).

**Vital Records-Death Records**, Department of Health, Bureau of Vital Records & Health Statistics, 1190 St Francis Dr, Room 1050 N, Santa Fe, NM 87502. 505-827-2338 8:00 AM - 5:00 PM M-F (Counter Service: 9:00 AM - 4:00 PM).

**Vital Records-Marriage Certificate, Divorce Records**, Records not available at state level.

**Workers' Compensation**, Workers Compensation Adminstration, 1820 Randolph Rd, SE, Albuquerque, NM 87125. 505-841-6000 8:00 AM - 5:00 PM.

# New York

**State Archives**, State Archives & Records Administrations, 11D40 Cultural Education Center, Albany, NY 12230. 518-474-8955

**Attorney General**, Attorney General's Office, Law Department, State Capitol, Albany, NY 12224. 518-474-7124

**Corporate Records**, Division of Corporations, Department of State, 162 Washington Ave, Albany, NY 12231. 518-473-2492 8:00 AM - 4:30 PM. Corporation Records, Limited Partnership Records, Fictitious Name.

**Corporate Records**, Department of State, Miscellaneous Records, 162 Washington Ave, Albany, NY 12231. 518-474-4770 8:30 AM - 4:30 PM. Trademarks/ Servicemarks.

**State Court Administrator**, (Upstate) NY State Office of Court Administrtion, Empire State Plaza, Agency Bldg #4, 20th Floor, Albany, NY 12223. 518-473-6087

**State Court Administrator**, NY State Office of Court Administration, 270 Broadway, Room 1400, New York, NY 10007. 212-417-2004

**Criminal Records**, Division of Criminal Justice Services, Executive Park Tower, Stuyvesant Plaza, Albany, NY 12203. 518-457-6043 8:00 AM - 5:00 PM.

**DMV-Accident Reports**, Public Services Bureau, Accident Report Section, Empire State Plaza, Swan St Bldg, Albany, NY 12228. 518-474-2381 8:00 AM - 4:30 PM.

**DMV-Driver Records**, Department of Motor Vehicles, Division of Data Preparation & Control, DMV Public Services, Empire State Plaza, Swan St Bldg, Albany, NY 12228. 518-474-2381 8:00 AM - 5:00 PM.

**DMV-Vehicle Ownership, Vehicle Identification**, Division of Data Preparation & Control, Empire State Plaza, Swan St Bldg, Room 430, Albany, NY 12228. 518-474-0642 8:00 AM - 5:00 PM.

**Governor**, Governor's Office, State Capitol, Albany, NY 12224. 518-474-8390

**Legislation**, New York State Legislation, Legislative Office Bldg, Room 317, State and Washington Sts, Albany, NY 12247. 518-455-7545 9:00 AM - 5:00 PM.

**Uniform Commercial Code**, UCC Division, Department of State, 162 Washington Ave, Albany, NY 12231. 518-474-4763 8:00 AM - 4:00 PM. Uniform Commercial Code, Federal Tax Liens, State Tax Liens.

**Vital Records-Birth Certificate**, State Department of Health, Vital Records Section, Empire State Plaza, Corning Tower, Albany, NY 12237-0023. 518-474-3038 8:30 AM - 4:30 PM.

**Vital Records-Birth Certificate-New York City, Death Records-New York City**, Department of Health, Bureau of Vital Statistics, 125 Worth St, Room 133, New York, NY 10013. 212-788-4506 9:00 AM - 4:00 PM.

**Vital Records-Death Records**, State Department of Health, Vital Records Section, Empire State Plaza, Corning Tower, Albany, NY 12237-0023. 518-474-3038 8:30 AM - 4:30 PM.

**Vital Records-Divorce Records**, State Department of Health, Vital Records Section, Empire State Plaza, Corning Tower, Albany, NY 12237-0023. 518-474-3038 8:30 AM - 4:30 PM.

**Vital Records-Marriage Certificate**, State Department of Health, Vital Records Section, Empire State Plaza, Corning Tower, Albany, NY 12237-0023. 518-474-3075 8:30 AM - 4:30 PM.

**Vital Records-Marriage Certificate-New York City, Divorce Records-New York City**, Municipal Archives, Department of Records & Information Sewrviccs, 31 Chambers St, New York, NY 10007-1288.

**Workers' Compensation**, NY Workers' Compensation Board, Director of Claims Office, 180 Livingston St, Room 416, Brooklyn, NY 11248. 718-802-6621 9:00 AM - 5:00 PM.

## North Carolina

**State Archives**, Cultural Resources Department, Archives & History Division, 109 E Jones St, Raleigh, NC 27601-2807. 919-733-5722

**Attorney General**, Attorney General's Office, Justice Department, PO Box 629, Raleigh, NC 27602. 919-733-3377

**Corporate Records**, Secretary of State, Corporations Section, 300 N Salisbury St, Raleigh, NC 27603-5909. 919-733-4201 8:00 AM - 5:00 PM. Corporation Records, Limited Partnership Records, Limited Liability Company Records, Trademarks/ Servicemarks.

**State Court Administrator**, Administrative Office of Courts, 2 E Morgan St, Justice Bldg, 4th Floor, Raleigh, NC 27602. 919-733-7107

**Criminal Records**, State Bureau of Investigation, Div of Criminal Information-Identification Section, 407 N Blount St, Raleigh, NC 27601-1009. 919-662-4500 X300 7:30 AM - 5:00 PM.

**DMV-Accident Reports**, Division of Motor Vehicles, Collision Reports Section, 1100 New Bern Ave, Room 101, Raleigh, NC 27697. 919-733-7250 8:00 AM - 5:00 PM.

**DMV-Driver Records**, Department of Motor Vehicles, Driver's License Section, 1100 New Bern Ave, Raleigh, NC 27697. 919-733-4241 8:00 AM - 5:00 PM.

**DMV-Vehicle Ownership, Vehicle Identification**, Department of Motor Vehicles, Vehicle Registration Section, 1100 New Bern Ave, Raleigh, NC 27697. 919-733-3025 8:00 AM - 5:00 PM.

**Governor**, Office of the Governor, State Capitol, Capitol Square, 116 W Jon, Raleigh, NC 27603-8001. 919-733-5612

**Legislation**, North Carolina General Assembly, State Legislative Bldg, 300 N Salisbury, 1st Floor, Raleigh, NC 27601. 919-733-7779 8:30 AM - 5:30 PM.

**Uniform Commercial Code**, UCC Division, Secretary of State, 300 North Salisbury St, Raleigh, NC 27603-5909. 919-733-4205 7:30 AM - 5:00 PM. Uniform Commercial Code, Federal Tax Liens, State Tax Liens.

**Vital Records-Birth Certificate**, Dept of Environment, Health & Natural Resources, Vital Records Section, 225 N McDowell St, Raleigh, NC 27602. 919-733-3526 8:00 AM - 4:00 PM.

**Vital Records-Death Records**, Dept of Environment, Health & Natural Resources, Vital Records Section, 225 N McDowell St, Raleigh, NC 27602. 919-733-3526 8:00 AM - 4:00 PM.

**Vital Records-Divorce Records**, Dept of Environment, Health & Natural Resources, Vital Records Section, 225 N McDowell St, Raleigh, NC 27602. 919-733-3526 8:00 AM - 4:00 PM.

**Vital Records-Marriage Certificate**, Dept of Environment, Health & Natural Resources, Vital Records Section, 225 N McDowell St, Raleigh, NC 27602. 919-733-3526 8:00 AM - 4:00 PM.

**Workers' Compensation**, Labor Department, Labor Bldg, 4 W Edenton St, Raleigh, NC 27601. 919-733-7166

## North Dakota

**State Archives**, Historical Society, State Archives & Historical Research Library, North Dakota Heritage Center, Bismarck, ND 58505-0830. 701-224-2666

**Attorney General**, Attorney General's Office, State Capitol, 1st Floor, 600 E Boulevard Ave, Bismarck, ND 58505. 701-224-2210

**Corporate Records**, Secretary of State, Corporation Division, 600 E Blvd Ave, 1st Floor, State Ca, Bismarck, ND 58505-0500. 701-224-4284 8:00 AM - 5:00 PM. Corporation Records, Limited Liability Company Records, Limited Partnership Records, Trademarks/ Servicemarks, Fictitious Name, Assumed Name.

**State Court Administrator**, Court Administrator, North Dakota Supreme Court, 1st Floor Judicial Wing, 600 E Boulevard Ave, Bismarck, ND 58505-0530. 701-224-4216

**Criminal Records**, Bureau of Criminal Justice, 4205 State St, Bismarck, ND 58501. 701-221-5500 8:00 AM - 5:00 PM.

**DMV-Accident Reports**, Driver License & Traffic Safety Division, Accident Report Section, 608 E Boulevard Ave, Bismarck, ND 58505-0700. 701-224-2603 8:00 AM - 5:00 PM.

**DMV-Driver Records**, Department of Transportation, Driver License & Traffic Safety Division, 608 E Boulevard Ave, Bismarck, ND 58505-0700. 701-224-2603 8:00 AM - 5:00 PM.

**DMV-Vehicle Ownership, Vehicle Identification**, Department of Transportation, Records Section/Motor Vehicle Div., 608 E Boulevard Ave, Bismarck, ND 58505-0700. 701-224-2725 8:00 AM - 4:50 PM.

**Governor**, Governor's Office, State Capitol, 600 E Boulevard Ave, 1st, Bismarck, ND 58505-0001. 701-224-2200

**Legislation**, North Dakota Legislative Council, State Capitol, 600 E Boulevard Ave, Bismarck, ND 58505. 701-224-2916 8:00 AM - 5:00 PM.

**Uniform Commercial Code**, UCC Division, Secretary of State, 600 E Boulevard Ave, Bismarck, ND 58505-0500. 701-224-3662 7:00 AM - 5:00 PM. Uniform Commercial Code, Federal Tax Liens, State Tax Liens.

**Vital Records-Birth Certificate**, State Department of Health, Vital Records/Statistical Services, 600 E Boulevard Ave., 1st Floor, Bismarck, ND 58505-0200. 701-224-2360 7:30 AM - 5:00 PM.

**Vital Records-Death Records**, State Department of Health, Division of Vital Records, 600 E Boulevard Ave, 1st Floor, Bismarck, ND 58505-0200. 701-224-2360 7:30 AM - 5:00 PM.

**Vital Records-Divorce Records**, Records not available at state level.

**Vital Records-Marriage Certificate**, State Department of Health, Division of Vital Records, 600 E Boulevard Ave, 1st Floor, Bismarck, ND 58505-0200. 701-224-2360 7:30 AM - 5:00 PM.

**Workers' Compensation**, Workers Compensation Bureau, 500 E Front Ave, Bismarck, ND 58504-5685. 701-224-3800 8:00 AM - 5:00 PM.

**State Records**

## Ohio

**State Archives**, Historical Society, Archives/Library, 1982 Velma Ave, Columbus, OH 43211-2497. 614-297-2300

**Attorney General**, Attorney General's Office, 30 E Broad St, 17th Floor, Columbus, OH 43266-0410. 614-466-4320

**Corporate Records**, Corporate Department, Secretary of State, 30 E Broad St, 14th Floor, Columbus, OH 43266-0418. 614-466-3910 8:00 AM - 5:00 PM. Corporation Records, Fictitious Name, Limited Partnership Records, Assumed Name, Trademarks/ Servicemarks.

**State Court Administrator**, Administrative Director, Supreme Court of Ohio, 39 E Broad St, 3rd Floor, Columbus, OH 43266-0419. 614-466-2653

**Criminal Records**, Ohio Bureau of Investigation, Identification Division, 1580 State Rte 56, London, OH 43140. 614-466-8204 8:00 AM - 5:45 PM.

**DMV-Accident Reports**, Department of Public Safety, Traffic Crash Records Section, 4795 Evanswood Drive, Columbus, OH 43229. 614-752-1575 7:00 AM - 4:15 PM.

**DMV-Driver Records**, Department of Motor Vehicles, Bureau of Motor Vehicles, 4300 Kimberly Pkwy, Columbia, OH 43232. 614-752-7600 8:00 AM - 5:30 PM M-T-W 8:00 AM - 4:30 PM TH-F.

**DMV-Vehicle Ownership, Vehicle Identification**, Bureau of Motor Vehicles, Motor Vehicle Records, 4300 Kimberly Pkwy, Columbus, OH 43232. 614-752-7634 8:00 AM - 5:30 PM M-T-W 8:00 AM - 4:30 PM TH-F.

**Governor**, Governor's Office, 77 S High St, 30th Floor, Riffe Center, Columbus, OH 43266-0601. 614-466-3555

**Legislation**, Ohio General Assembly, State House, , OH. 614-466-8842 8:30 AM - 5:00 PM.

**Uniform Commercial Code**, UCC Division, Secretary of State, 30 E Broad St, State Office Tower, Columbus, OH 43215. 614-466-3623 Uniform Commercial Code, Federal Tax Liens, State Tax Liens.

**Vital Records-Birth Certificate**, Ohio Department of Health, Bureau of Vital Statistics, 35 E Chestnut, 6th Floor, Columbus, OH 43215. 614-466-2531 7:45 AM - 4:30 PM.

**Vital Records-Death Records**, Ohio Department of Health, Bureau of Vital Statistics, 35 E Chestnut, 6th Floor, Columbus, OH 43215. 614-466-2531 7:45 AM - 4:30 PM.

**Vital Records-Marriage Certificate, Divorce Records**, Records not available at state level.

**Workers' Compensation**, Workers Compensation Bureau, Claims Information, 30 W Spring St, 10th Floor, Columbus, OH 43266-0581. 614-466-1000 7:30 AM - 4:30 PM.

## Oklahoma

**State Archives**, Libraries Department, Archives & Records Office, 200 NE 18th St, Oklahoma City, OK 73105-3298. 405-521-2502 X203

**Attorney General**, Attorney General's Office, 112 State Capitol, Oklahoma City, OK 73105. 405-521-3921

**Corporate Records**, Secretary of State, Corporate Records, 101 State Capitol, Oklahoma City, OK 73105. 405-521-3911 8:00 AM - 5:00 PM. Corporation Records, Limited Liability Company Records, Limited Partnership Records, Trademarks/ Servicemarks.

**State Court Administrator**, Administrative Director of Courts, 1915 N Stiles, #305, Oklahoma City, OK 73105. 405-521-2450

**Criminal Records**, State Bureau of Investigation, Criminal History Information, 6600 N Harvey, Bldg 6, Suite 140, Oklahoma City, OK 73116. 405-848-6724 8:30 AM - 4:30 PM.

**DMV-Accident Reports**, Department of Public Safety, Accident Reports Section, 3600 Martin Luther King Blvd, Oklahoma City, OK 73111. 405-425-2192 8:00 AM - 4:45 PM.

**DMV-Driver Records**, Department of Public Safety, Driver's Record Services, 3600 Martin Luther King Blvd, Oklahoma City, OK 73111. 405-425-2026 8:00 AM - 4:45 PM.

**DMV-Vehicle Ownership, Vehicle Identification**, Oklahoma Tax Commission, Motor Vehicle Division, Attn: Research, 2501 N Lincoln Blvd, Oklahoma City, OK 73194. 405-521-3221 8:00 AM - 5:00 PM.

**Governor**, Office of the Governor, State Capitol, Oklahoma City, OK 73105. 405-521-2342

**Legislation**, Oklahoma Legislature, State Capitol, Status Info-Room 309, Copies-Room 310, Oklahoma City, OK 73105. 405-521-5642 8:30 PM - 4:30 PM.

**Uniform Commercial Code**, UCC Recorder, Oklahoma County Clerk, 320 R.S. Kerr Ave, Rm 105, Oklahoma City, OK 73102. 405-278-1521 8:00 AM - 5:00 PM. Uniform Commercial Code, Federal Tax Liens, State Tax Liens.

**Vital Records-Birth Certificate**, State Department of Health, Vital Records Section, 1000 NE 10th St, Oklahoma City, OK 73117. 405-271-4040 8:30 AM - 4:00 PM.

**Vital Records-Death Records**, State Department of Health, Vital Records Section, 1000 NE 10th St, Oklahoma City, OK 73117. 405-271-4040 8:30 AM - 4:00 PM.

**Vital Records-Marriage Certificate, Divorce Records**, Records not available at state level.

**Workers' Compensation**, Workers Compensation, 1915 W Stiles, Oklahoma City, OK 73105. 405-557-7600 8:00 AM - 5:00 PM Computer available until 4:30..

## Oregon

**State Archives**, Secretary of State, Archives Division, 800 Summer St NE, Salem, OR 97310. 503-373-0701

**Attorney General**, Attorney General's Office, Justice Department, 1162 Court St NE, Salem, OR 97310. 503-378-4400

**Corporate Records**, Corporation Division, Commerce Bldg, 158 12th St NE, Salem, OR 97310-0210. 503-986-2200 8:00 AM - 5:00 PM. Corporation Records, Limited Partnership Records, Trademarks/ Servicemarks, Fictitious Name, Assumed Name, Limited Liability Company Records.

**State Court Administrator**, State Court Administrator, Supreme Court Bldg, 1163 State St, Salem, OR 97310. 503-378-6046

**Criminal Records**, Oregon State Police, Identification Services Section, 3772 Portland Rd NE, Salem, OR 97303. 503-378-3070 8:00 AM - 5:00 PM.

**DMV-Accident Reports**, Motor Vehicle Division, Records and Information, 1905 Lana Ave, NE, Salem, OR 97314. 503-945-5000 8:00 AM - 5:00 PM M-F (till 8:30 PM on W).

**DMV-Driver Records**, Department of Motor Vehicles, Customer Assistance Unit, 1905 Lana Ave, NE, Salem, OR 97314. 503-945-5000 8:00 AM - 5:00 PM M-T,TH-F (till 8:30 PM on W).

**DMV-Vehicle Ownership, Vehicle Identification**, Driver and Motor Vehicle Services, Customer Assistance, 1905 Lana Ave, NE, Salem, OR 97314. 503-945-5000 8:00 AM - 5:00 PM.

**Governor**, Office of the Governor, 254 State Capitol, Salem, OR 97310-0370. 503-378-3111

**Legislation**, Oregon Legislative Assembly, 5407 State Capitol-Information Services, State Capitol, Salem, OR 97310. 503-378-8551 8:00 AM - 5:00 PM.

**Uniform Commercial Code**, UCC Division, Secretary of State, 255 Capitol St, NE, Suite 151, Salem, OR 97310. 503-378-4146 8:00 Am - 5:00 PM. Uniform Commercial Code, Federal Tax Liens, State Tax Liens.

**Vital Records-Birth Certificate**, Oregon State Health Division, Vital Records Suite 205, 800 NE Oregon St, #23, Portland, OR 97232. 503-731-4095 8:00 AM - 4:30 PM.

**Vital Records-Death Records**, Oregon State Health Division, Vital Records, Suite 205, 800 NE Oregon St, #23, Portland, OR 97232. 503-731-4095 8:00 AM - 4:30 PM.

**Vital Records-Divorce Records**, Oregon State Health Division, Vital Records, Suite 205, 800 NE Oregon St, #23, Portland, OR 97232. 503-731-4095 8:00 AM - 4:30 PM.

**Vital Records-Marriage Certificate**, Oregon State Health Division, Vital Records, Suite 205, 800 NE Oregon St, #23, Portland, OR 97232. 503-731-4095 8:00 AM - 4:30 PM.

**Workers' Compensation**, Insurance and Finance Department, Workers Compensation Division, 21 Labor & Industries Bldg, Salem, OR 97310. 503-945-7585 8:00 AM - 5:00 PM.

## Pennsylvania

**State Archives**, Historical & Museum Commission, Archives & History Division, Box 1026, Harrisburg, PA 17108-1026. 717-787-3362

**Attorney General**, Attorney General's Office, Strawberry Square, 16th Floor, Harrisburg, PA 17120. 717-787-3391

**Corporate Records**, Corporation Bureau, Department of State, 302 N Office Bldg, Harrisburg, PA 17120. 717-787-1057 8:00 AM - 5:00 PM. Corporation Records, Limited Partnership Records, Trademarks/ Servicemarks, Fictitious Name, Assumed Name.

**State Court Administrator**, Court Administrator, 1515 Market St, Suite 1414, Philadelphia, PA 19102. 215-560-6300

**Criminal Records**, State Police Central Repository, 1800 Elmerton Ave, Harrisburg, PA 17110-9758. 717-783-5592 8:15 AM - 4:15 PM.

**DMV-Accident Reports**, State Police Headquarters, Accident Records Section, 1800 Elmerton Ave, Harrisburg, PA 17110. 717-783-5516 8:00 AM - 5:00 PM.

**DMV-Driver Records**, Department of Transportation, Information Sales Unit, Commonwealth & Forster Sts, North St Entrance, Harrisburg, PA 17123. 717-787-3130 7:30 AM - 4:30 PM.

**DMV-Vehicle Ownership, Vehicle Identification**, Department of Transportation, Information Sales Unit, Commonwealth & Forster Sts, North St Entrance, Harrisburg, PA 17123. 717-787-3130 7:30 AM - 4:30 PM.

**Governor**, Governor's Office, 225 Main Capitol Bldg, Harrisburg, PA 17120. 717-787-5962

**Legislation**, Pennsylvania General Assembly, Main Capitol Bldg, Room B35, Harrisburg, PA 17120. 717-787-2342 House-8:30 AM - 4:30 PM / Senate-8:30 AM - 5:00 PM.

**Uniform Commercial Code**, UCC Division, Department of State, North Office Bldg, Rm 308, Harrisburg, PA 17120. 717-787-8712 Uniform Commercial Code, Federal Tax Liens, State Tax Liens.

**Vital Records-Birth Certificate**, Department of Health, Division of Vital Records, 101 S Mercer St, New Castle, PA 16101. 412-656-3100 8:00 AM - 3:30 PM.

**Vital Records-Death Records**, Department of Health, Division of Vital Records, 101 S Mercer St, New Castle, PA 16101. 412-656-3100 8:00 AM - 3:30 PM.

**Vital Records-Marriage Certificate, Divorce Records**, Records not available at state level.

**Workers' Compensation**, Workmens Compensation Division, 1171 S Cameron St, Rm 103, Harrisburg, PA 17104-2501. 717-783-5421 7:30 AM - 5:00 PM.

# Rhode Island

**State Archives**, Secretary of State, Archives Division, 337 Westminster St, Providence, RI 02903. 401-277-2353

**Attorney General**, Attorney General's Office, 72 Pine St, Providence, RI 02903-2856. 401-274-4400

**Corporate Records**, Secretary of State, Corporations Division, 100 N Main St, Providence, RI 02903. 401-277-3040 8:00 AM - 5:00 PM. Corporation Records, Fictitious Name, Limited Partnership Records, Limited Liability Company Records.

**Corporate Records**, Secretary of State, Trademark Division, 100 N Main St, Providence, RI 02903. 401-277-2340 8:00 AM - 5:00 PM. Trademarks/ Servicemarks.

**State Court Administrator**, Court Administrator, 250 Benefit St, Room 705, Providence, RI 02903. 401-277-3263

**Criminal Records**, Department of Attorney General, Bureau of Criminal Identification, 72 Pine St, Providence, RI 02903. 401-274-2238 8:00 AM - 5:00 PM.

**DMV-Accident Reports**, Rhode Island State Police, Accident Record Division, 311 Danielson Pike, North Scituate, RI 02857. 401-444-1143 8:30 AM - 4:30 PM.

**DMV-Driver Records**, Driving Records Clerk, Operator Control, 345 Harris Ave, Providence, RI 02909. 401-277-2994 8:30 AM - 4:30 PM.

**DMV-Vehicle Ownership, Vehicle Identification**, Registry of Motor Vehicles, c/o Registration Files, Two Capitol Hill, Providence, RI 02903. 401-277-2064 8:30 AM - 3:30 PM.

**Governor**, Governor's Office, State House, Providence, RI 02903. 401-277-2080 X227

**Legislation**, Rhode Island General Assembly, State House, Document Room (Basement), Providence, RI 02903. 401-277-3580 8:30 AM - 4:30 PM.

**Uniform Commercial Code**, UCC Division, Secretary of State, 100 North Main St, Providence, RI 02903. 401-277-2249 Uniform Commercial Code, Federal Tax Liens, State Tax Liens.

**Vital Records-Birth Certificate**, State Department of Health, Division of Vital Statistics, Capitol Hill, Cannon Bldg, Room 101, Providence, RI 02908-2812. 401-277-2812 8:00 AM - 4:30 PM.

**Vital Records-Death Records**, State Department of Health, Division of Vital Statistics, Capitol Hill, Cannon Bldg, Room 101, Providence, RI 02908-2812. 401-277-2812 8:00 AM - 4:30 PM.

**Vital Records-Divorce Records**, Records not available at state level.

**Vital Records-Marriage Certificate**, State Department of Health, Division of Vital Statistics, Capitol Hill, Cannon Bldg, Room 101, Providence, RI 02908-2812. 401-277-2812 8:00 AM - 4:30 PM.

**Workers' Compensation**, Department of Labor, Division of Workers' Compensation, 610 Manton Ave, Providence, RI 02909. 401-272-0700 8:00 AM - 4:30 PM.

# South Carolina

**State Archives**, Archives & History Department, PO Box 11669, Columbia, SC 29211. 803-734-7914

**Attorney General**, Attorney General's Office, PO Box 11549, Columbia, SC 29211. 803-734-3970

**Corporate Records**, Department of Revenue, Annual Reports Division, 301 Gervias St, Columbia, SC 29201. 803-737-4866 8:30 AM - 4:30 PM. Annual Reports, Directors and Officers.

**Corporate Records**, Corporation Division, Capitol Complex, Wade Hampton Office Bldg, Room 109, Columbia, SC 29201. 803-734-2158 8:30 AM - 5:00 PM. Corporation Records, Trademarks/ Servicemarks, Limited Partnership Records.

**State Court Administrator**, Court Administration, 1015 Sumter, 2nd Floor, Columbia, SC 29201. 803-734-1800

**Criminal Records**, South Carolina Law Enforcement Division (SLED), Criminal Records Section, 440 Broad River Rd, Columbia, SC 29210. 803-737-9000 8:30 AM - 5:00 PM.

**DMV-Accident Reports**, Department of Public Safety, Accident Reports/Financial Responsibility, 955 Park St, Columbia, SC 29201. 803-251-2969 8:30 AM - 5:00 PM.

**DMV-Driver License Information, Driver Records**, Department of Public Safety, Driver Records Section, 955 Park St, Columbia, SC 29201. 803-251-2940 8:30 AM - 5:00 PM.

**DMV-Vehicle Ownership, Vehicle Identification**, Department of Motor Vehicles, Title and Registration Records Section, 955 Park St, Columbia, SC 29201. 803-251-2950 8:30 AM - 5:00 PM.

**Governor**, Governor's Office, PO Box 11369, State House, Columbia, SC 29211. 803-734-9818

**Legislation**, South Carolina Legislature, State House, 1st Floor, Current Bills Room, Columbia, SC 29211. 803-734-2060 9:00 AM - 5:00 PM.

**Uniform Commercial Code**, UCC Division, Secretary of State, Capital Complex, Rm 107, Wade Hampton Bldg, Columbia, SC 29201. 803-734-2175 8:30 AM - 5:00 PM. Uniform Commercial Code, Federal Tax Liens, State Tax Liens.

**Vital Records-Birth Certificate**, South Carolina DHEC, Vital Records & Public Health Statistics, 2600 Bull St, Columbia, SC 29201. 803-734-4830 8:30 AM - 4:30 PM.

**Vital Records-Death Records**, South Carolina DHEC, Vital Records & Public Health Statistics, 2600 Bull St, Columbia, SC 29201. 803-734-4830 8:30 AM - 4:30 PM.

**Vital Records-Divorce Records**, South Carolina DHEC, Vital Records & Public Health Statistics, 2600 Bull St, Columbia, SC 29201. 803-734-4830 8:30 AM - 4:30 PM.

**Vital Records-Marriage Certificate**, South Carolina DHEC, Vital Records & Public Health Statistics, 2600 Bull St, Columbia, SC 29201. 803-734-4830 8:30 AM - 4:30 PM.

**Workers' Compensation**, Workers Compensation Commission, 1612 Marion St, Columbia, SC 29202. 803-737-5700 8:30 AM - 5:00 PM.

## South Dakota

**State Archives**, State Historical Society, Cultural Heritage Center/State Archives, 900 Governors Dr, Pierre, SD 57501-2217. 605-773-3804

**Attorney General**, Attorney General's Office, State Capitol, 500 E Capitol Ave, Pierre, SD 57501-5070. 605-773-3215

**Corporate Records**, Corporation Division, Secretary of State, 500 E Capitol Ave, Suite B-05, Pierre, SD 57501-5070. 605-773-4845 8:00 AM - 5:00 PM. Corporation Records, Limited Partnership Records, Limited Liability Company Records, Trademarks/ Servicemarks.

**State Court Administrator**, State Court Administrator, State Capitol Bldg, 500 E Capitol Ave, Pierre, SD 57501. 605-773-3474

**Criminal Records**, Division of Criminal Investigation, Office of Attorney General, 500 E Capitol, Pierre, SD 57501-5070. 605-773-3331 8:00 AM - 5:00 PM.

**DMV-Accident Reports**, Department of Transportation, Accident Records, 118 W Capitol Ave, Pierre, SD 57501-9935. 605-773-3868 8:00 AM - 5:00 PM.

**DMV-Driver Records**, Division of Commerce & Regulation, Driver's License Program, 118 W Capitol, Pierre, SD 57501. 605-773-3191 8:00 AM - 5:00 PM.

**DMV-Vehicle Ownership, Vehicle Identification**, Division of Motor Vehicles, Information Section, 118 W Capitol Ave, Pierre, SD 57501-2080. 605-773-3541 8:00 AM - 5:00 PM.

**Governor**, Governor's Office, State Capitol, 500 E Capitol Ave, Pierre, SD 57501-5070. 605-773-3212

**Legislation**, South Dakota Legislature, Capitol Bldg - Legislative Documents, 500 E Capitol Ave, Pierre, SD 57501. 605-773-3835 8:00 AM - 5:00 PM.

**Uniform Commercial Code**, UCC Division, Secretary of State, 500 East Capitol, Pierre, SD 57501-5070. 605-773-4422 8:00 AM - 5:00 PM. Uniform Commercial Code, Federal Tax Liens, State Tax Liens.

**Vital Records-Birth Certificate**, South Dakota Department of Health, Vital Records, 445 E Capitol, Pierre, SD 57501-3185. 605-773-4961 8:00 AM - 5:00 PM.

**Vital Records-Death Records**, South Dakota Department of Health, Vital Records, 445 E Capitol, Pierre, SD 57501-3185. 605-773-4961 8:00 AM - 5:00 PM.

**Vital Records-Divorce Records**, South Dakota Department of Health, Vital Records, 445 E Capitol, Pierre, SD 57501-3185. 605-773-4961 8:00 AM - 5:00 PM.

**Vital Records-Marriage Certificate**, South Dakota Department of Health, Vital Records, 445 E Capitol, Pierre, SD 57501-3185. 605-773-4961 8:00 AM - 5:00 PM.

**Workers' Compensation**, Labor Department, Workers Compensation Division, 700 Governors Dr, Pierre, SD 57501. 605-773-3681 8:00 AM - 5:00 PM.

## Tennessee

**State Archives**, Secretary of State, State Library & Archives Division, 403 7th Ave N, Nashville, TN 37243-0312. 615-741-7996

**Attorney General**, Attorney General's Office, 500 Charlotte Ave, Nashville, TN 37243-0497. 615-741-3491

**Corporate Records**, Corporation Section, Secretary of State, James K Polk, Suite 1800, Nashville, TN 37243-0306. 615-741-0537 8:00 AM - 4:30 PM. Corporation Records, Limited Partnership Records, Fictitious Name, Assumed Name.

**Corporate Records**, Secretary of State, Trademarks/Tradenames Division, James K. Polk Bldg, Nashville, TN 37243-0306. 615-741-0531 8:00 AM - 4:30 PM. Trademarks/ Servicemarks, Trade Names.

**State Court Administrator**, Administrator of the Court, 1400 Nashville City Center, 511 Union St, Nashville, TN 37243-0607. 615-741-2687

**Criminal Records**, Tennessee Bureau of Investigation, Records and Identification Unit, 1144 Foster Ave, Menzler-Nix Bldg, Nashville, TN 37210. 615-741-0430 8:00 AM - 5:00 PM.

**DMV-Accident Reports**, Financial Responsibility Section, Accident Reports/Records Unit, 1150 Foster Avenue, Nashville, TN 37249. 615-741-3954 8:00 AM - 4:30 PM.

**DMV-Driver Records**, Dept. of Safety, Financial Responsibility Section, Driving License & Driving Records, 1150 Foster Ave, Nashville, TN 37249-4000. 615-741-3954 8:00 AM - 4:30 PM.

**DMV-Vehicle Ownership, Vehicle Identification**, Department of Motor Vehicles, Titling and Registration Division, Airways Plaza, Bldg 2, Suite 100, Nashville, TN 37243. 615-741-3101 8:00 AM - 4:30 PM.

**Governor**, Governor's Office, State Capitol, Nashville, TN 37243-0001. 615-741-2001

**Legislation**, Tennessee General Assembly, Office of Legislative Services, 620 War Memorial Blvd, Nashville, TN 37243. 615-741-3511 8:00 AM - 4:30 PM.

**Uniform Commercial Code**, UCC Division, Secretary of State, James K. Polk Bldg, Suite 1800, Nashville, TN 37243. 615-741-3276 Uniform Commercial Code, Federal Tax Liens, State Tax Liens.

**Vital Records-Birth Certificate**, Tennessee Department of Health, Office of Vital Records, Tennessee Tower, 3rd Floor, Nashville, TN 37247-0350. 615-741-1763 9:00 AM - 4:00 PM.

**Vital Records-Death Records**, Tennessee Department of Health, Office of Vital Records, Tennessee Tower, 3rd Floor, Nashville, TN 37247-0350. 615-741-1763 9:00 AM - 4:00 PM.

**Vital Records-Divorce Records**, Tennessee Department of Health, Office of Vital Records, Tennessee Tower, 3rd Floor, Nashville, TN 37247-0350. 615-741-1763 9:00 AM - 4:00 PM.

**Vital Records-Marriage Certificate**, Tennessee Department of Health, Office of Vital Records, Tennessee Tower, 3rd Floor, Nashville, TN 37247-0350. 615-741-1763 9:00 AM - 4:00 PM.

**Workers' Compensation**, Tennessee Department of Labor, Workers Compensation Division, 710 James Robertson Pwy, 2nd Floor, Nashville, TN 37243-0661. 615-741-2395 8:00 AM - 4:30 PM.

**State Records**

## Texas

**State Archives**, Library & Archives Commission, PO Box 12927, Austin, TX 78711. 512-463-5455

**Attorney General**, Attorney General's Office, Price Daniel, Sr Bldg, Austin, TX 78711. 512-463-2100

**Corporate Records**, Secretary of State, Corporation Section, Certification Unit, 1019 Brazos, Austin, TX 78701. 512-463-5555 8:00 AM - 5:00 PM. Corporation Records, Fictitious Name, Limited Partnership Records, Limited Liability Company Records, Assumed Name, Trademarks/ Servicemarks.

**State Court Administrator**, Office of Court Administration, 205 W 14th St, #600, Austin, TX 78701. 512-463-1625

**Criminal Records**, Crime Records Service, Correspondence Section, 5805 N Lamar, Austin, TX 78752. 512-465-2079 8:00 AM - 5:00 PM.

**DMV-Accident Reports**, Texas Department of Public Safety, Accident & Statistical Reports, 5805 N Lamar Blvd, Austin, TX 78752. 512-465-2296 8:00 AM - 5:00 PM.

**DMV-Driver Records**, License Issuance & Driver Records, Driver Records Section, 5805 N Lamar Blvd, Austin, TX 78752. 512-465-2032 8:00 AM - 5:00 PM.

**DMV-Vehicle Ownership, Vehicle Identification**, Department of Transportation, Production Data Control, 40th St and Jackson, Austin, TX 78779. 512-465-7611 8:00 AM - 5:00 PM.

**Governor**, Governor's Office, State Capitol, Austin, TX 78711. 512-463-2000

**Legislation**, Texas Legislature, State Capitol (Senate or House Copy Section), 1110 San Jacinto, Austin, TX 78701. 512-463-1252 8:00 AM - 5:00 PM.

**Uniform Commercial Code**, UCC Section, Secretary of State, 1019 Brazos St, Rm B-31, Austin, TX 78701. 512-475-2705 8:00 AM - 5:00 PM. Uniform Commercial Code, Federal Tax Liens, State Tax Liens.

**Vital Records-Birth Certificate**, Texas Department of Health, Bureau of Vital Statistics, 1100 W 49th St, Austin, TX 78756-3191. 512-458-7111 8:00 AM - 5:00 PM.

**Vital Records-Death Records**, Texas Department of Health, Bureau of Vital Statistics, 1100 W 49th St, Austin, TX 78756-3191. 512-458-7111 8:00 AM - 5:00 PM.

**Vital Records-Divorce Records**, Texas Department of Health, Bureau of Vital Statistics, 1100 W 49th St, Austin, TX 78756-3191. 512-458-7111 8:00 AM - 5:00 PM.

**Vital Records-Marriage Certificate**, Texas Department of Health, Bureau of Vital Statistics, 1100 W 49th St, Austin, TX 78756-3191. 512-458-7111 8:00 AM - 5:00 PM.

**Workers' Compensation**, Texas Workers' Compensation Commission, Southfield Bldg, 4000 S IH-35, MS-3, Austin, TX 78704-7491. 512-448-7900 8:00 AM - 5:00 PM.

## Utah

**State Archives**, Administratives Services Department, Archives Division, State Archives Bldg, Salt Lake City, UT 84114. 801-538-3010

**Attorney General**, Attorney General's Office, 236 State Capitol, Salt Lake City, UT 84114. 801-538-1015

**Corporate Records**, Commerce Department, Corporate Division, 160 E 300 S, Salt Lake City, UT 84145. 801-530-4849 8:00 AM - 5:00 PM. Corporation Records, Limited Liability Company Records, Fictitious Name, Limited Partnership Records, Assumed Name, Trademarks/ Servicemarks.

**State Court Administrator**, Court Administrator's Office, 230 S 500 E, #300, Salt Lake City, UT 84111. 801-578-3807

**Criminal Records**, Bureau of Criminal Identification, 4501 S 2700 W, Salt Lake City, UT 84119. 801-965-4561 8:00 AM - 5:00 PM.

**DMV-Accident Reports**, Driver's License Division, Accident Reports Section, 4501 S 2700, W, Salt Lake City, UT 84119. 801-965-4428 8:00 AM - 5:00 PM.

**DMV-Driver Records**, Department of Public Safety, Driver's License & Driving Records Section, 4501 S 2700, W, Salt Lake City, UT 84119. 801-965-4430 8:00 AM - 5:00 PM.

**DMV-Vehicle Ownership, Vehicle Identification**, State Tax Commission, Motor Vehicle Records Section, 1095 Motor Ave, Salt Lake City, UT 84116. 801-538-8300 8:00 AM - 5:00 PM.

**Governor**, Governor's Office, 210 State Capitol, Salt Lake City, UT 84114. 801-538-1000

**Legislation**, Utah Legislature, State Capitol, 319 State Capitol, Salt Lake City, UT 84114. 801-538-1035 8:00 AM - 5:00 PM.

**Uniform Commercial Code**, Division of Corporations and Commercial Code, State of Utah, 160 E 300 South, 2nd floor, Salt Lake City, UT 84110. 801-530-6025 8:00 AM - 5:00 PM. Uniform Commercial Code, Federal Tax Liens, State Tax Liens.

**Vital Records-Birth Certificate**, Department of Health, Bureau of Vital Records, 288 N 1460 W, Salt Lake City, UT 84116. 801-538-6380 8:00 AM - 5:00 PM.

**Vital Records-Death Records**, Department of Health, Bureau of Vital Records, 288 N 1460 W, Salt Lake City, UT 84116. 801-538-6380 8:00 AM - 5:00 PM.

**Vital Records-Divorce Records**, Department of Health, Bureau of Vital Records, 288 N 1460 W, Salt Lake City, UT 84116. 801-538-6380 8:00 AM - 5:00 PM.

**Vital Records-Marriage Certificate**, Department of Health, Bureau of Vital Records, 288 N 1460 W, Salt Lake City, UT 84116. 801-538-6380 8:00 AM - 5:00 PM.

**Workers' Compensation**, Industrial Commission, Workers Compensation Division, 160 E 300 S, Salt Lake City, UT 84114. 801-530-6880 8:00 AM - 4:30 PM.

## Vermont

**State Archives**, Secretary of State, State Papers Archives Division, 109 State St, Montpelier, VT 05609-1101. 802-828-2369

**Attorney General**, Attorney General's Office, 109 State St, Montpelier, VT 05609-1001. 802-828-3171

**Corporate Records**, Secretary of State, Corporation Division, River St, Heritage One, Montpelier, VT 05602. 802-828-2386 7:45 AM - 4:30 PM. Corporation Records.

**State Court Administrator**, Court Administrator, Administrative Office of the Courts, 109 State St, Montpelier, VT 05609-0701. 802-828-3278

**Criminal Records**, State Repository, Vermont Criminal Information Center, 103 S Main St, Waterbury, VT 05676. 802-244-8727 8:00 AM - 5:00 PM.

**DMV-Accident Reports**, Department of Motor Vehicles, Accident Report Section, 120 State St, Montpelier, VT 05603. 802-828-2050 7:45 AM - 4:30 PM.

**DMV-Driver Records**, Department of Motor Vehicles, Driver Improvement Information, 120 State St, Montpelier, VT 05603. 802-828-2050 7:45 AM - 4:30 PM.

**DMV-Vehicle Ownership, Vehicle Identification**, Department of Motor Vehicles, Registration & License Information/Records, 120 State St, Montpelier, VT 05603. 802-828-2000 7:45 AM - 4:30 PM.

**Governor**, Governor's Office, Pavilion Office Bldg, 5th Floor, 109 Sta, Montpelier, VT 05609. 802-828-3333

**Legislation**, Vermont General Assembly, State House-Legislative Council, 115 State St, Montpelier, VT 05633. 802-828-2231 8:00 AM - 4:30 PM.

**Uniform Commercial Code**, UCC Division, Secretary of State, 81 River St, Heritage One, Montpelier, VT 05602. 802-828-2388 7:45 AM - 4:30 PM. Uniform Commercial Code, Federal Tax Liens, State Tax Liens.

**Vital Records-Birth Certificate**, Vermont Department of Health, Vital Records Section, 108 Cherry St, Burlington, VT 05402. 802-863-7275 8:00 AM - 4:30 PM.

**Vital Records-Death Records**, Vermont Department of Health, Vital Records Section, 108 Cherry St, Burlington, VT 05402. 802-863-7275 8:00 AM - 4:30 PM.

**Vital Records-Divorce Records**, Vermont Department of Health, Vital Records Section, 108 Cherry St, Burlington, VT 05402. 802-863-7275 8:00 AM - 4:30 PM.

**Vital Records-Marriage Certificate**, Vermont Department of Health, Vital Records Section, 108 Cherry St, Burlington, VT 05402. 802-863-7275 8:00 AM - 4:30 PM.

**Workers' Compensation**, Labor and Industry, Workers Compensation Division, National Life Bldg, Montpelier, VT 05620. 802-828-2286 7:45 AM - 4:30 PM.

## Virginia

**State Archives**, State Library & Archives, Library Bldg, 11th St at Capitol Square, Richmond, VA 23219. 804-786-8929

**Attorney General**, Attorney General's Office, 900 E Main St, Richmond, VA 23219. 804-786-2071

**Corporate Records**, State Corporation Commission, Clerks Office, Tyler Bldg, 1st Floor, 1300 E Main St, Richmond, VA 23219. 804-371-9733 8:15 AM - 5:00 PM. Corporation Records, Limited Liability Company Records, Fictitious Name, Limited Partnership Records, Assumed Name, Trademarks/ Servicemarks.

**State Court Administrator**, Administrative Office of the Courts, Executive Secretary, Supreme Court Building, 100 N 9th St, 3rd Floor, Richmond, VA 23219. 804-786-6455

**Criminal Records**, Virginia State Police, CCRE, 7700 Midlothian Turnpike, Richmond, VA 23235. 804-674-2084 8:00 AM - 5:00 PM.

**DMV-Accident Reports**, Department of Motor Vehicles, Record Request, 2300 W Broad St, Richmond, VA 23269. 804-367-6600 9:00 AM - 6:00 PM M-F 9:00 AM - 1:00 PM S.

**DMV-Driver Records**, Department of Motor Vehicles, Motorist Information Administration, 2300 W Broad St, Richmond, VA 23269. 804-367-0538 9:00 AM - 6:00 PM M-F 9:00 AM - 1:00 PM S.

**DMV-Vehicle Ownership, Vehicle Identification**, Management Information Administration, Vehicle Research Section, 2300 W Broad St, Richmond, VA 23269. 804-367-6729 9:00 AM - 6:00 PM M-F 9:00 AM - 1:00 PM S.

**Governor**, Governor's Office, Capitol Bldg, 3rd Floor, Richmond, VA 23219. 804-786-2211

**Legislation**, Virginia General Assembly, State Capitol, 19th and Grace Sts, 1st Floor, Richmond, VA 23219. 804-786-6530 8:00 AM - 5:00 PM.

**Uniform Commercial Code**, UCC Division, State Corporation Commission, 1300 E Main St, Richmond, VA 23219. 804-371-9189 8:15 AM - 5:00PM. Uniform Commercial Code, Federal Tax Liens, State Tax Liens.

**Vital Records-Birth Certificate**, State Health Department, Division of Vital Records, 109 Governor St, 2nd Floor, Richmond, VA 23219. 804-371-7867 9:00 AM - 4:00 PM.

**Vital Records-Death Records**, State Health Department, Division of Vital Records, 109 Governor St, 2nd Floor, Richmond, VA 23219. 804-371-7867 9:00 AM - 4:00 PM.

**Vital Records-Divorce Records**, State Health Department, Division of Vital Records, 109 Governor St, 2nd Floor, Richmond, VA 23219. 801-538-6380 8:00 AM - 5:00 PM.

**Vital Records-Marriage Certificate**, State Health Department, Division of Vital Records, 109 Governor St, 2nd Floor, Richmond, VA 23219. 804-371-7867 9:00 AM - 4:00 PM.

**Workers' Compensation**, Workers Compensation Board, 1000 DMV Dr, Richmond, VA 23220. 804-367-8600 8:15 AM - 5:00 PM.

**State Records**

## Washington

**State Archives**, Secretary of State, State Archives, Legislative Bldg, 1120 Washington St SE Olympia, WA 98504. 206-753-5485

**Attorney General**, Attorney General's Office, 905 Plum St, Bldg #3, Olympia, WA 98504. 206-753-6200

**Corporate Records**, Secretary of State, Business & Licensing Services, 505 E Union, 2nd Floor, Olympia, WA 98504. 206-753-7115 8:00 AM - 4:00 PM. Corporation Records, Trademarks/ Servicemarks, Limited Partnership Records.

**Corporate Records**, Business & Licensing Services, 405 Blacklake Blvd, Bldg 2, Olympia, WA 98507. 206-586-4575 8:00 AM - 4:00 PM. Trade Names.

**State Court Administrator**, Court Administrator, Temple of Justice, PO Box 41174, Olympia, WA 98504-1174. 206-357-2121

**Criminal Records**, Washington State Patrol, Identification Section, 321 Cleveland Ave, #F, Tumwater, WA 98501. 206-705-5100 8:00 AM - 5:00 PM.

**DMV-Accident Reports**, Department of Licensing, Accident Reports, 210 11th St, SW, Olympia, WA 98507. 206-586-2638 8:00 AM - 4:30 PM.

**DMV-Driver Records**, Department of Licensing, Driver's Responsibility Division, 210 11th St, SW, Olympia, WA 98507. 206-753-6976 8:00 AM - 4:30 PM.

**DMV-Vehicle Ownership, Vehicle Identification**, Department of Licensing, Vehicles Services, 210 11th St, SW, Olympia, WA 98507. 206-753-6990 8:00 AM - 4:30 PM.

**Governor**, Office of the Governor, Legislative Bldg, Olympia, WA 98504. 206-753-6780

**Legislation**, Washington Legislature, State Capitol, Room 35, 1st Floor, Olympia, WA 98504. 206-753-5000 9:00 AM - 12:00 PM & 1:00 PM - 5:00 PM.

**Uniform Commercial Code**, UCC Division, Department of Licensing, 405 Black Lake Blvd, Building 2, Olympia, WA 98502. 206-753-2523 8:00 AM - 5:00 PM. Uniform Commercial Code, Federal Tax Liens, State Tax Liens.

**Vital Records-Birth Certificate**, Department of Health, Center for Health Statistics, 1112 S Quince St, Olympia, WA 98504. 206-753-5842 8:00 AM - 4:00 PM.

**Vital Records-Death Records**, Department of Health, Vital Records, 1112 S Quince St, Olympia, WA 98504. 206-753-5842 8:00 AM - 4:00 PM.

**Vital Records-Divorce Records**, Department of Health, Vital Records, 1112 S Quince St, Olympia, WA 98504. 206-753-5842 8:00 AM - 4:00 PM.

**Vital Records-Marriage Certificate**, Department of Health, Vital Records, 1112 S Quince St, Olympia, WA 98504. 206-753-5842 8:00 AM - 4:00 PM.

**Workers' Compensation**, Labor and Industries, Workers Compensation Division, 7273 Linderson Way SW, Tumwater, WA 98501. 206-956-5800 8:00 AM - 5:00 PM.

## West Virginia

**State Archives**, Culture & History Department, Archives & History Division, Cultural Center, State Capitol Complex, Charleston, WV 25305. 304-558-0220

**Attorney General**, Attorney General's Office, State Capitol, Room 26, E Wing, Charleston, WV 25305-0220. 304-558-2021

**Corporate Records**, Secretary of State, Corporation Division, State Capitol Bldg, Room W139, Charleston, WV 25305-0776. 304-558-8000 8:30 AM - 4:30 PM. Corporation Records, Limited Liability Company Records, Limited Partnership Records, Trademarks/ Servicemarks.

**State Court Administrator**, Administrative Director, Supreme Court of Appeals, Administration Office, E 400 State Capitol, 1900 Kanawhaa Blvd, Charleston, WV 25305-0830. 304-558-0145

**Criminal Records**, State Police, Criminal Identification Bureau, Records Section, 725 Jefferson Rd, South Charleston, WV 25309. 304-746-2277 8:00 AM - 5:00 PM.

**DMV-Accident Reports**, Division of Public Safety, Traffic Records Section, 725 Jefferson Rd, South Charleston, WV 25309-1698. 304-746-2128 8:30 AM - 4:30 PM.

**DMV-Driver License Information, Driver Records**, Division of Motor Vehicles, Safety and Enforcement, Bldg 3, State Capitol Complex, 1800 Kanawha Blvd, E, Charleston, WV 25317. 304-558-0238 8:30 AM - 4:30 PM.

**DMV-Vehicle Ownership, Vehicle Identification**, Division of Motor Vehicles, Titles and Registration Division, State Capitol Complex, Bldg 3, 1800 Kanawha Blvd, E, Charleston, WV 25317. 304-558-0282 8:30 AM - 4:30 PM.

**Governor**, Governor's Office, Office of the Governor, State Capitol Complex, 1900 Kanawha Blvd, Chalreston, WV 25305-0370. 304-558-2000

**Legislation**, West Virginia State Legislature, State Capitol, Passed-Rm MB27, Pending-Rm 217, Charleston, WV 25305. 304-558-8905 8:30 AM - 4:30 PM.

**Uniform Commercial Code**, UCC Division, Secretary of State, State Capitol Bldg, Rm W131, Charleston, WV 25305. 304-345-4000 8:30 AM - 4:30 PM. Uniform Commercial Code, Federal Tax Liens, State Tax Liens.

**Vital Records-Birth Certificate**, Bureau of Public Health, Vital Records, State Capitol Complex Bldg 3-Rm 516, Charleston, WV 25305. 304-558-2931 9:00 AM - 4:30 PM.

**Vital Records-Death Records**, Bureau of Public Health, Vital Records, State Capitol Complex Bldg 3-Rm 516, Charleston, WV 25305. 304-558-2931 9:00 AM - 4:30 PM.

**Vital Records-Divorce Records**, Bureau of Public Health, Vital Records, State Capitol Complex Bldg 3-Rm 516, Charleston, WV 25305. 304-558-2931 9:00 AM - 4:30 PM.

**Vital Records-Marriage Certificate**, Bureau of Public Health, Vital Records, State Capitol Complex Bldg 3-Rm 516, Charleston, WV 25305. 304-558-2931 9:00 AM - 4:30 PM.

**Workers' Compensation**, Bureau of Employment Programs, Workers Compensation Division, 601 Morris St, Charleston, WV 25301. 304-558-0653 8:00 AM - 5:00 PM.

## Wisconsin

**State Archives**, Historical Society, Archives Department, 816 State St, Madison, WI 53706. 608-264-6400

**Attorney General**, Attorney General's Office, Justice Department, PO Box 7857, Madison, WI 53707-7857. 608-266-1221

**Corporate Records**, Secretary of State, Corporations Division, 30 W Mifflin St, 9th Floor, Madison, WI 53703. 608-266-3590 7:45 AM - 4:30 PM. Corporation Records, Limited Partnership Records.

**Corporate Records**, Secretary of State, Tradenames/Trademarks Division, 30 W Mifflin St, 9th Floor, Madison, WI 53702. 608-266-5653 7:45 AM - 4:30 PM. Trademarks/ Servicemarks, Trade Names.

**State Court Administrator**, Director of State Courts, State Capitol, Room 213, NE, Madison, WI 53701. 608-266-6828

**Criminal Records**, Wisconsin Department of Justice, Crime Information Bureau, Record Check Unit, 123 W Washington Ave, Madison, WI 53701. 608-266-7314 8:00 AM - 4:30 PM.

**DMV-Accident Reports**, Wisconsin Department of Transportation, Traffic Accident Section, 4802 Sheboygan Ave, Room 804, Madison, WI 53707. 608-266-8753 7:30 AM - 4:30 PM.

**DMV-Driver Records**, Department of Motor Vehicles, License Record Section, 4802 Sheboygan Ave, Room 301, Madison, WI 53707. 608-264-7060 7:30 AM - 4:30 PM.

**DMV-Vehicle Ownership, Vehicle Identification**, Department of Transportation, Vehicle Records Section, 4802 Sheboygan Ave, Room 205, Madison, WI 53707. 608-266-3666 7:30 AM - 4:30 PM.

**Governor**, Governor's Office, State Capitol, Madison, WI 53707. 608-266-1212

**Legislation**, Wisconsin Legislature, Reference Bureau, PO Box 2037, Madison, WI 53701-2037. 608-266-0341 7:45 AM - 4:30 PM.

**Uniform Commercial Code**, UCC Division, Secretary of State, 30 West Mifflin, 10th Fl, Madison, WI 53703. 608-266-3087 7:45 AM - 4:30 PM. Uniform Commercial Code, Federal Tax Liens, State Tax Liens.

**Vital Records-Birth Certificate**, The Center of Health Statistics, Vital Records, One W Wilson St, Room 158, Madison, WI 53702. 608-266-1372 8:00 AM - 4:30 PM.

**Vital Records-Death Records**, The Center of Health Statistics, Vital Records, One W Wilson St, Room 158, Madison, WI 53702. 608-266-1372 8:00 AM - 4:30 PM.

**Vital Records-Divorce Records**, The Center of Health Statistics, Vital Records, One W Wilson St, Room 158, Madison, WI 53702. 608-266-1372 8:00 AM - 4:30 PM.

**Vital Records-Marriage Certificate**, The Center of Health Statistics, Vital Records, One W Wilson St, Room 158, Madison, WI 53702. 608-266-1372 8:00 AM - 4:30 PM.

**Workers' Compensation**, Dept of Industry, Labor and Human Relations, Workers Compensation Division, 201 E Washington Ave, Madison, WI 53707. 608-266-1340 7:45 AM - 4:30 PM.

## Wyoming

**State Archives**, Department of Commerce, Archives Division, 2nd Floor, 2301 Central, Barrett Bldg, Cheyenne, WY 82002. 307-777-7041

**Attorney General**, Attorney General's Office, 123 State Capitol, Cheyenne, WY 82002. 307-777-7841

**Corporate Records**, Corporations Division, Secretary of State, State Capitol, Cheyenne, WY 82002. 307-777-7311 8:00 AM - 5:00 PM. Corporation Records, Limited Liability Company Records, Limited Partnership Records, Fictitious Name, Trademarks/ Servicemarks.

**State Court Administrator**, Court Coordinator, Supreme Court Bldg, 2301 Capitol Ave, Cheyenne, WY 82002. 307-777-7581

**Criminal Records**, Division of Criminal Investigation, Criminal Record Section, 316 W 22nd St, Cheyenne, WY 82002. 307-777-7523 8:30 - 10:30 AM & 1:30 - 3:30 PM.

**DMV-Accident Reports**, Department of Transportation, Accident Records Section, 5300 Bishop Blvd, Cheyenne, WY 82002. 307-777-4450 8:00 AM - 5:00 PM.

**DMV-Driver License Information, Driver Records**, Wyoming Department of Transportation, Driver Services, 5300 Bishop Blvd, Cheyenne, WY 82002. 307-777-4802 8:00 AM - 5:00 PM.

**DMV-Vehicle Ownership, Vehicle Identification**, Department of Transportation, Motor Vehicle Licensing and Titles, 5300 Bishop Blvd, Cheyenne, WY 82002. 307-777-4717 8:00 AM - 5:00 PM.

**Governor**, Governor's Office, State Capitol, Cheyenne, WY 82002. 307-777-7434

**Legislation**, Wyoming Legislature, State Capitol, Room 213, Cheyenne, WY 82002. 307-777-6185 8:00 AM - 5:00 PM.

**Uniform Commercial Code**, UCC Division, Secretary of State, The Capitol, Cheyenne, WY 82002. 307-777-5372 Uniform Commercial Code, Federal Tax Liens, State Tax Liens.

**Vital Records-Birth Certificate**, Wyoming Department of Health, Vital Records Service, Hathaway Bldg, Cheyenne, WY 82002. 307-777-7591 9:00 AM - 4:00 PM.

**Vital Records-Death Records**, Wyoming Department of Health, Vital Records Services, Hathaway Bldg, Cheyenne, WY 82002. 307-777-7591 9:00 AM - 4:00 PM.

**Vital Records-Divorce Records**, Wyoming Department of Health, Vital Records Services, Hathaway Bldg, Cheyenne, WY 82002. 307-777-7591 9:00 AM - 4:00 PM.

**Vital Records-Marriage Certificate**, Wyoming Department of Health, Vital Records Services, Hathaway Bldg, Cheyenne, WY 82002. 307-777-7591 9:00 AM - 4:00 PM.

**Workers' Compensation**, Employment Department, Workers Compensation Division, Herschler Bldg, 2nd Floor E, 122 W 25th St, Cheyenne, WY 82002. 307-777-7159 8:00 AM - 4:30 PM.

# What You Can Expect To Find In State Public Records*

> \* *The following article and Chart are condensed from The Sourcebook Of State Public Records and reprinted with the permission of BRB Publications, Inc. For more information about this or any book in The Public Record Research Library, call BRB at 800-929-3811.*

What data will state government agencies' records tell you? How do you know if the records you are requesting will actually give you the information you seek? Are you legally permitted to access the record? Whether or not the information is available to the public, the degree of authority needed to obtain the record and the data to be found on the record are all subject to **individual state statutes**. Therefore, the answers to the questions above can, and do, vary significantly from state to state.

## I. Business Records

**Corporation**—You can check to see if a corporation is incorporated or qualified in a state with a "status check"— i.e. date of incorporation, status, type, registered agent and, sometimes, officers or directors. Some states permit status checks over the telephone. Also, articles of incorporation or amendments and copies of annual reports, when available, are a good place to start when seeking information about a business or business owner. Corporate records may not always be a good source of a business addresses because most states allow corporations to use a registered agent as the address for service of process.

**Partnership**—Many states have statutes that require registration of certain kinds of partnerships at the state level. Partner names and addresses may be available from the same office that handles corporation records. Some states have a department created specifically to administer limited partnerships and their records.

**Limited Liability Co**—A newer form of business entity, that looks like a corporation but has the favorable tax characteristics of a partnership, is known as the Limited Liability Company (LLC). LLC records are available in over 35 states.

**Trademark, Trade Name**—States will not let two entities use the same, or close to the same, name or trademark. A trademark may also be known as a "service mark". Trade names may be referred to as "fictitious names", assumed names, or "DBA's." The same state agency which oversees corporation records may maintain the files of trademarks and/or trade names. Most states will allow verbal status checks of names or worded marks. Some states will administer "fictitious names" while their respective counties administer "trade names", or vice versa.

## II. Lien and Security Interest Records

**Uniform Commercial Code (UCC)**—All 50 states and the District of Columbia have passed a version of the model Uniform Commercial Code (UCC). Article 9 of the Code covers security interests in personal property. UCC filings are used in financing transactions such as equipment loans, leases, inventory loans, and accounts receivable financing and to notify other possible lenders that certain assets of the debtor are being used to secure a loan or lease. Therefore, **UCC filings are a way to find bank accounts, security interests, financiers, and assets**.

Of the 7.5 million new UCC financing statements filed annually, 2.5 million are filed at the state level and 5 million are filed at the local level within the states. Although there are significant variations among state statutes, the state level is usually a good place to check for liens against an individual or business.

**Tax Liens**—The federal government and every state has some sort of taxes payable by individuals and businesses such as; sales, income, withholding, unemployment, personal property, etc. When these taxes go unpaid, the appropriate state agency can file a lien on the real or personal property of the subject. Normally, the same state agency administers both UCC records and tax liens. Tax lien documents are an excellent source of names, addresses, assets, and banking relationships. The lack of uniformity among the states in tax lien filing locations makes it essential for accurate searching that you be aware of the vast array of state idiosyncrasies.

Tax liens filed against individuals are generally maintained in separate files and even separate locations from those liens filed against businesses. For example, a large number of states require liens filed against businesses to be filed at a central state location (i.e. Secretary of State's office) and liens against individuals to be filed at the county level (i.e. Recorder, Register of Deeds, Clerk of Court, etc.). Further, a federal tax lien will not necessarily be recorded at the same location/jurisdiction as a lien filed by the state on the same entity. This holds true for both individual liens and as well as business liens filed against personal property. Typically, state tax liens on personal property will be found where UCC's are filed. Tax liens on real property will be found where real property deeds are recorded, with few exceptions.

## III. Individual Records

**Criminal**—Every state has a central repository of major misdemeanor and felony arrest records and convictions. States submit criminal record activity to the National Crime Information Center (which is not open to the public). Of those states that will release records to the public, many require fingerprints or signed release forms. The information that *could be* disclosed on the report includes the arrest record, criminal charge, fine, sentencing and incarceration information.

Not all states open their records to the public. In this case, the best place to search for criminal record activity is at the city or county level with the county or district court clerk. Many of these searches can be done with a phone call. For further information regarding criminal record-keeping at the county level, please refer to BRB's *Sourcebook of County Court Records, 1995 Edition.*

**Vital Records**—Copies of vital record certificates are needed for a variety of reasons—social security, jobs, passports, family history, litigation, lost heir searching, proof of identity, etc. Most states understand the urgency of these requests and some offer an expedited service. A number of states will even take requests over the phone if you use a credit card. You must also be aware that in many instances certain vital records are not kept at the state level, so you must turn to city and county record repositories to find copies in these instances.

Older vital records may be found in the state archives. Another source of historical vital record information is the Family History Library of the Mormon Church, located at 35 North West Temple, Salt Lake City 84150. They have millions of microfilmed records from church and civil registers from all over the world.

**Driver License and History**—The retrieval industry often refers to driving records as "MVRs." Typical information on an MVR might include full name, address, social security number, physical description and date of birth as well as the actual driving history. Also, license type and restrictions or endorsements can provide background data on an individual. The September 1994 passage of the Driver's Privacy Protection Act will cause significant debate and changes within state legislatures regarding the release of motor vehicle data to the public. Over the next 2 years, as states move towards making the data more readily available electronically, they are also closing the door to many users.

**Vehicle Ownership**—State repositories of vehicle registration and ownership records encompass a wide range of public accessible data. Generally, you submit a name to find vehicle(s) owned, or you submit vehicle information to find a name and address. The records may not be held by the same state agency that oversee driver records. Even more so than with MVRs, statutes vary widely from state to state regarding the release of these records for investigation purposes. State vehicle and owner databases can be an excellent source for asset and lien data, commercial mailing lists (when permissible) and vehicle recall uses.

**Occupational Licenses and Business Registrations**—Professional licensing boards and regulated permits represent a plethora of records that are readily available from various state agencies. A standard reason to call these agencies is to corroborate professional or industry credentials. In many instances, a telephone call to the agency may secure an address and telephone number. State hunting and fishing license information can be an information tool to locate an individual. Currently 31 states maintain a central repository of fishing and/or hunting license records which may be accessed in some manner by the public. Although some of these record repositories are "in boxes in the basement," more and more are becoming computerized.

# STATE PUBLIC RECORD RESTRICTIONS CHART

Codes: O = Open to Public  R = Some Access Restrictions Apply (Requesters Screened)  N/A = Not Available to the Public
F = Special Form Needed  S = Severe Access Restrictions Apply (Signed Authorization, etc.)  L = Available only at Local Level

| State | Criminal Records | UCC Records | Vital Records Birth | Vital Records Death | Vital Records Marriage | Divorce | Worker's Comp | Driver History* | Vehicle Records* | Accident Reports |
|---|---|---|---|---|---|---|---|---|---|---|
| Alabama | S | F | O | O | O | L | S | O | O | O |
| Alaska | N/A | F | R | S | R | R | O | S | O | S |
| Arizona | S | F | S | S | L | L | S | S | S | R |
| Arkansas | S | F | S | S | S | L | O | S | O | O |
| California | N/A | F | O | O | O | L | S | R,F | O | L |
| Colorado | R | F | R | R | L | L | S | O | F | O |
| Connecticut | S | F | S | O | O | L | O | F | R | L |
| Delaware | S | F | S | S | S | L | S | O | O | O |
| District of Columbia | S | F | R | R | O | O | R | O | O | O |
| Florida | O | F | O | O | O | O | S | O | O | O |
| Georgia | S | L | S | S | S | L | S | S | S | O |
| Hawaii | CALL | F | S | S | S | S | S | R | N/A | S |
| Idaho | S | F | S | S | S | S | S | O | O | O |
| Illinois | F | F | S | R | R,L | L | O | O | R | O |
| Indiana | R,F | F | S | S | L | L | S | O | O | O |
| Iowa | N/A,L | F | S | S | S | L | O | O | O | R |
| Kansas | S | F | S | S | S | S | O | O | O | O |
| Kentucky | S | R | O | O | O | O | R | O | O | O |
| Louisiana | N/A,L | L | S | S | L | L | R | O | O | O |
| Maine | O | F | R | R | R | R | O | O | O | O |
| Maryland | R | O | S | S | S | S | O | O | O | O |
| Massachusetts | R | F | R | R | O | L | S | R | O | O |
| Michigan | R | F | O | O | O | O | S | O | R | O |
| Minnesota | S | F | R | O | L | L | R | O | O | S |
| Mississippi | N/A,L | F | R | R | R | L | S | O | O | S |
| Missouri | S | F | S | S | L | L | N/A | O | O | R |

| State | Criminal Records | UCC Records | Vital Records - Birth | Vital Records - Death | Vital Records - Marriage | Divorce | Worker's Comp | Driver History* | Vehicle Records* | Accident Reports |
|---|---|---|---|---|---|---|---|---|---|---|
| Montana | O | F | R | R | L | L | S | R | O | S |
| Nebraska | O | F | S | S | R | R | R | O | O | O |
| Nevada | N/A,L | F | R | R | L | L | S | R | R | O |
| New Hampshire | S | F | S | S | S | S | S | O | O | O |
| New Jersey | N/A | F | O | O | O | O | O,F | O | O | O |
| New Mexico | S | R | R | S | L | L | S | R | R | O |
| New York | N/A | F | R | R | R | R | S | O | O | F |
| North Carolina | N/A,L | F | O | O | O | O | S | R | R,F | O |
| North Dakota | S | F | S | O | O | L | S | O | O | R |
| Ohio | S | F | O | O | L | L | S | O | O | O |
| Oklahoma | O | F | S | O | L | L | O | O | O | O |
| Oregon | O | F | S | R | R | R | S | O | O | O |
| Pennsylvania | F | F | S | S | L | L | N/A | S | S | S |
| Rhode Island | S | F | S | S | S | L | S | R | R | R |
| South Carolina | O | F | R | R | R | R | S | O | O | O |
| South Dakota | S | F | O | O | O | O | S | O | R | O |
| Tennessee | N/A | F | S | S | S | S | N/A | O | O | O |
| Texas | S | F | S | S | S | S | N/A | O | R | O |
| Utah | N/A | F | S | S | S | S | R | O | O | O |
| Vermont | N/A,L | F | O | O | O | O | S | O | O | O |
| Virginia | S | F | S | S | S | O | S | R | O | O |
| Washington | S | F | O | S | O | O | S | R | R | S |
| West Virginia | S | F | O | O | O | O | S | O | O | O |
| Wisconsin | O | F | S | S | R | R | S | O | O | O |
| Wyoming | S | F | R | S | S | S | S | O | O | O |

Codes: O = Open to Public  R = Some Access Restrictions Apply (Requesters Screened)  N/A = Not Available to the Public
F = Special Form Needed  S = Severe Access Restrictions Apply (Signed Authorization, etc.)  L = Available only at Local Level

**Source:** *The Sourcebook Of State Public Records* • With the Permission of BRB Publications, Inc. • (800) 929-3811

*Editor's Note: With the recent passage of the Driver's Privacy Protection Act by the federal government, we expect significant changes in the states' policies regarding the release of driver and vehicle information.

# Section Three
# Federal Records

**Federal Court Structure**

The Federal Court System includes three level of courts plus some special courts. You will find listings for the Courts of Appeals, the US District Court (USDC) and US Bankruptcy Court (USBC) which are courts of record, a few Special Courts, and the Federal Record Centers. (The US Supreme Court is the court of last resort and is not reviewed here.) The Courts are listed by state, alphabetized in city order where the courts reside with USBC's listed first.

**US Bankruptcy Courts**

There is a Bankruptcy Court for each state. Within a state there may be one or more judicial districts and within a judicial district there may be more than one location (division) where the courts hear cases. **ALL** bankruptcy actions are filed with the USBC.

**US District Courts**

US District courts are courts of general jurisdiction, or trial courts, for federal matters, excluding bankruptcy. Both civil and criminal cases come before these courts. You will find the US District Courts generally follow the **same geographic boundaries** as the US Bankruptcy Courts.

**Access and Record Keeping**

A *case number* is assigned when a case is first filed with a Federal Court and is therefore the primary indexing method. Courts store all case records by case number. Information from cover sheets and from documents filed as a case goes forward is recorded on the *docket sheet*. This document contains the case history from initial filing to the current status. **Most courts are computerized**, which means the docket sheet data is entered into a computer system.

There are **five ways** you can **access** information from Federal Courts: telephone; mail; in person, on-line; and by using a provider or retriever firm. It is significant to note the that most all courts are moving towards some type of electronic access. Two significant systems are PACER and ELF. Other systems are ACES, the Appellate Court Electronic Services and VCIS, the automated voice information system which serves the majority of the US Bankruptcy Courts.

**Federal Record Centers**

After a case is closed, the documents are held by Federal Courts themselves for a number of years (or months, in some cases) and then are stored at a Designated Federal Record Center (FRC). (See the Chart on the next page.) After 20 to 30 years, the records are transferred from the FRC to the Regional Archives Office of the National Archives and Records Administration.

Editor's Note: For more information regarding county courts and recording offices, we suggest you refer to two PRRL Sourcebooks—*Federal Courts (US District & Bankruptcy)* and the *Federal Court Locator*.

# US Appeals Courts and Federal Records Centers
## State Cross Reference Chart

| State | Circuit | Appeals Court | Federal Records Center |
|---|---|---|---|
| AK | 9 | San Francisco, CA | Anchorage (Some temporary storage in Seattle) |
| AL | 11 | Atlanta, GA | Atlanta |
| AR | 8 | St. Louis, MO | Fort Worth |
| AZ | 9 | San Francisco, CA | Los Angeles |
| CA | 9 | San Francisco, CA | Los Angeles (Central & Southern) San Francisco (Eastern & Northern) |
| CO | 10 | Denver, CO | Denver |
| CT | 2 | New York, NY | Boston |
| DC |  | Washington, DC | Washington, DC |
| DE | 3 | Philadelphia, PA | Philadelphia |
| FL | 11 | Atlanta, GA | Atlanta |
| GA | 11 | Atlanta, GA | Atlanta |
| GU | 9 | San Francisco, CA | San Francisco |
| HI | 9 | San Francisco, CA | San Francisco |
| IA | 8 | St. Louis, MO | Kansas City, MO |
| ID | 9 | San Francisco, CA | Seattle |
| IL | 7 | Chicago, IL | Chicago |
| IN | 7 | Chicago, IL | Chicago |
| KS | 10 | Denver, CO | Kansas City, MO |
| KY | 6 | Cincinnati, OH | Atlanta |
| LA | 5 | New Orleans, LA | Fort Worth |
| MA | 1 | Boston, MA | Boston |
| MD | 4 | Richmond, VA | Philadelphia |
| ME | 1 | Boston, MA | Boston |
| MI | 6 | Cincinnati, OH | Chicago |
| MN | 8 | St. Louis, MO | Chicago |
| MO | 8 | St. Louis, MO | Kansas City, MO |
| MS | 5 | New Orleans, LA | Atlanta |
| MT | 9 | San Francisco, CA | Denver |
| NC | 4 | Richmond, VA | Atlanta |
| ND | 8 | St. Louis, MO | Denver |
| NE | 8 | St. Louis, MO | Kansas City, MO |
| NH | 1 | Boston, MA | Boston |
| NJ | 3 | Philadelphia, PA | New York |
| NM | 10 | Denver, CO | Denver |
| NV | 9 | San Francisco, CA | Los Angeles (Clark County) San Francisco (Other counties) |
| NY | 2 | New York, NY | New York |
| OH | 6 | Cincinnati, OH | Chicago |
| OK | 10 | Denver, CO | Fort Worth |
| OR | 9 | San Francisco, CA | Seattle |
| PA | 3 | Philadelphia, PA | Philadelphia |
| PR | 1 | Boston, MA | New York |
| RI | 1 | Boston, MA | Boston |
| SC | 4 | Richmond, VA | Atlanta |
| SD | 8 | St. Louis, MO | Denver |
| TN | 6 | Cincinnati, OH | Atlanta |
| TX | 5 | New Orleans, LA | Fort Worth |
| UT | 10 | Denver, CO | Denver |
| VA | 4 | Richmond, VA | Philadelphia |
| VI | 3 | Philadelphia, PA | New York |
| VT | 2 | New York, NY | Boston |
| WA | 9 | San Francisco, CA | Seattle |
| WI | 7 | Chicago, IL | Chicago |
| WV | 4 | Richmond, VA | Philadelphia |
| WY | 10 | Denver, CO | Denver |

The following Federal Records Centers are located outside the city by which they are known:
  Atlanta—East Point, GA
  Boston—Waltham, MA
  Los Angeles—Laguna Miguel, CA
  New York—Bayonne, NJ
  San Francisco—San Bruno, CA

## US Courts of Appeals

**District of Columbia Circuit, US Court of Appeals**, United States Courthouse, 333 Constitution Ave, NW, Washington, DC, DC 20001-2866. 202-273-0310

**First Circuit, US Court of Appeals**, 1606 John W. McCormack PO and Courthouse, Boston, MA 02109. 617-223-0957

**Second Circuit, US Court of Appeals**, US Courthouse, Foley Square, New York, NY 10007. 212-791-0103

**Third Circuit, US Court of Appeals**, 21400 US Courthouse, 601 Market St, Philadelphia, PA 19106. 215-597-2995

**Fourth Circuit, US Court of Appeals**, 1100 E. Main St., Rm 501, Richmond, VA 23219. 804-771-2213

**Fifth Circuit, US Court of Appeals**, 100 US Courthouse, 600 Camp St, New Orleans, LA 70130. 504-589-6514

**Sixth Circuit, US Court of Appeals**, 538 US Courthouse Building, Fifth & Walnut Sts., Cincinnati, OH 45202. 513-684-2953

**Seventh Circuit, US Court of Appeals**, 219 Dearborn St, Chicago, IL 60604. 312-435-5850

**Eighth Circuit, US Court of Appeals**, 511 US Court and Custom House, 1114 Market St, St Louis, MO 63101. 314-539-3609

**Ninth Circuit, US Court of Appeals**, 121 Spear St., Sixth Floor, San Francisco, CA 94105. 415-744-9800

**Tenth Circuit, US Court of Appeals**, Byron White US Courthouse, 1823 Stout St, Denver, CO 80257. 303-844-3157

**Eleventh Circuit, US Court of Appeals**, 56 Forsyth St., NW, Atlanta, GA 30303. 404-331-6187

**Federal Circuit, US Court of Appeals**, 717 Madison Place, NW, Washington, DC, DC 20439. 202-633-6550

**US Court of Military Appeals**, 450 E St., NW, Washington, DC, DC 20442. 202-272-1488

**US Court of Federal Claims**, 717 Madison Place, NW, Washington, DC, DC 20005. 202-219-9657

**US Court of International Trade**, One Federal Plaza, New York, NY 10007. 212-264-2814

**US Tax Court**, 400 Second St., NW, Washington, DC, DC 20217. 202-606-8754

## Federal Records Centers

**Alaska**, Federal Records Center - Anchorage, 654 W 3rd Ave, Anchorage, AK 99501. 907-271-2441

**California**, Federal Records Center - Los Angeles, 24000 Avila Rd., Laguna Niguel, CA 92656. 714-643-4220

**California** Federal Records Center - San Francisco, 1000 Commodore Drive, San Bruno, CA 94066. 415-876-9001

**Colorado**, Federal Records Center - Denver, PO Box 25307, Denver Federal Center, Denver, CO 80225-0307. 303-236-0804

**District of Columbia**, Washington National Records Center, Federal Records Center - Washington, DC, 4205 Suitland Road, Suitland, MD, DC 20746. 301-763-7430

**Georgia**, Federal Records Center - Atlanta, 1557 St Joseph Avenue, East Point, GA 30344. 404-763-7474

**Illinois**, Federal Records Center - Chicago, 7358 South Pulaski Road, Chicago, IL 60629. 312-353-0162

**Massachusetts**, Federal Records Center - Boston, 380 Trapelo Rd., Waltham, MA 02154. 617-647-8104

**Missouri**, Federal Records Center - Kansas City, 2312 East Bannister Rd., Kansas City, MO 64131. 816-926-7272

**New Jersey**, Federal Records Center - New York, Building 22, Military Ocean Terminal, Bayonne, NJ 07002-5388. 201-823-7242

**Pennsylvania**, Federal Records Center - Philadelphia, 5000 Wissahickon Ave., Philadelphia, PA 19144. 215-951-5588

**Texas**, Federal Records Center - Fort Worth, 501 West Felix St., Fort Worth, TX 76115. 817-334-5515

**Washington**, Federal Records Center - Seattle, 6125 Sand Point Way NE, Seattle, WA 98115. 206-526-6504

# Alabama

**Anniston Division**, US Bankruptcy Court, Northern District, Room 103, 12th & Noble Sts, Anniston, AL 36201. 205-237-5631

**Birmingham Division**, US Bankruptcy Court, Northern District, Room 120, 1800 5th Ave N, Birmingham, AL 35203. 205-731-1614

**Birmingham Division**, US District Court, Northern District, Room 140, US Courthouse, 1729 5th Ave N, Birmingham, AL 35203. 205-731-1700

**Decatur Division**, US Bankruptcy Court, Northern District, Room 222, 400 Wells St, Decatur, AL 35601. 205-353-2817

**Decatur Division**, US District Court, Northern District, Clerk's Office, US Postoffice & Courthouse, 101 Holmes Ave NE, Huntsville, AL 35801. 205-534-6495

**Dothan Division**, US District Court, Middle District, c/o Montgomery Division, 15 Lee St, Montgomery, AL 36104. 334-223-7308

**Florence Division**, US District Court, Northern District, 101 Holmes NE, Huntsville, AL 35801. 205-534-6495

**Gadsden Division**, US District Court, Northern District, c/o Birmingham Division, Room 140, US Courthouse, 1729 5th Ave N, Birmingham, AL 35203. 205-731-1701

**Jasper Division**, US District Court, Northern District, c/o Birmingham Division, Room 140, US Courthouse, 1729 5th Ave N, Birmingham, AL 35203. 205-731-1701

**Mobile Division**, US Bankruptcy Court, Southern District, Clerk, 201 St. Louis St, Mobile, AL 36602. 334-441-5391

**Mobile Division**, US District Court, Southern District, Clerk, 113 St Joseph St, Mobile, AL 36602. 334-690-2371

**Montgomery Division**, US District Court, Middle District, Records Search, 15 Lee St, Montgomery, AL 36104. 334-223-7308

**Montgomery Division**, US Bankruptcy Court, Middle District, Suite 127, 1 Court Square, Montgomery, AL 36104. 334-223-7250

**Opelika Division**, US District Court, Middle District, c/o Montgomery Division, 15 Lee St, Montgomery, AL 36104. 205-223-7308

**Selma Division**, US District Court, Southern District, c/o Mobile Division, 113 St Joseph St, Mobile, AL 36602. 205-690-2371

**Tuscaloosa Division**, US Bankruptcy Court, Northern District, 1118 Greensboro Ave, Tuscaloosa, AL 35401. 205-752-0426

# Alaska

**Anchorage Division**, US Bankruptcy Court, Historic Courthouse, Suite 138, 605 W 4th Ave, Anchorage, AK 99501-2296. 907-271-2655

**Anchorage Division**, US District Court, Box 4, 222 W 7th Ave, Anchorage, AK 99513-7564. 907-271-5568

**Fairbanks Division**, US District Court, 604 Barnett St., Fairbanks, AK 99701. 907-452-9278

**Juneau Division**, US District Court, Room 979, Federal Bldg-US Courthouse, 709 W 9th, Juneau, AK 99802. 907-586-7458

**Nome Division**, US District Court, 2nd Floor, Federal Bldg, Front St, Nome, AK 99762. 907-443-5216

# Arizona

**Globe Division**, US District Court, c/o Tucson Division, Room 202, 44 E Broadway Blvd, Tucson, AZ 85701-1711. 520-670-6559

**Phoenix Division**, US Bankruptcy Court, Room 5000, 230 N 1st Ave, Phoenix, AZ 85025. 602-514-7321

**Phoenix Division**, US District Court, Room 1400, 230 N 1st Ave, Phoenix, AZ 85025-0093. 602-514-7101

**Prescott Division**, US District Court, c/o Phoenix Division, Room 1400, 230 N 1st Ave, Phoenix, AZ 85025-0093. 520-514-7101

**Tucson Division**, US Bankruptcy Court, Suite 8112, 110 S Church Ave, Tucson, AZ 85701-1608. 520-620-7500

**Tucson Division**, US District Court, Room 202, 44 E Broadway Blvd, Tucson, AZ 85701-1711. 520-620-7200

**Yuma Division**, US Bankruptcy Court, Suite D, 325 W 19th St, Yuma, AZ 85364. 520-783-2288

# Arkansas

**Batesville Division**, US District Court, Eastern District, c/o Little Rock Division, 600 W Capital, Room 402, Little Rock, AR 72201. 501-324-5351

**El Dorado Division**, US District Court, Western District, Room 205, 101 S Jackson, El Dorado, AR 71731. 501-862-1202

**Fayetteville Division**, US District Court, Western District, Room 523, 35 E Mountain, Fayetteville, AR 72701. 501-521-6980

**Fayetteville Division**, US Bankruptcy Court, Western District, 35 E Mountain, Fayetteville, AR 72701. 501-582-9825

**Fort Smith Division**, US District Court, Western District, Federal Courthouse, #307, 6th & Rogers Ave, Fort Smith, AR 72901. 501-783-6833

**Harrison Division**, US District Court, Western District, c/o Fayetteville Division, Room 523, 35 E Mountain, Fayetteville, AR 72701. 501-521-6980

**Helena Division**, US District Court, Eastern District, c/o Little Rock Division, 600 W Capital, Room 402, Little Rock, AR 72201. 501-324-5351

**Hot Springs Division**, US District Court, Western District, Room 347, Reserve & Broadway, Hot Springs, AR 71901. 501-623-6411

**Jonesboro Division**, US District Court, Eastern District, Federal Office Bldg, Room 312, 615 S Main St, Jonesboro, AR 72401. 501-972-4610

**Little Rock Division**, US Bankruptcy Court, Eastern District, Room 101, 600 W Capitol, Little Rock, AR 72201. 501-324-6357

**Little Rock Division**, US District Court, Eastern District, Room 402, 600 W Capitol, Little Rock, AR 72201. 501-324-5351

**Pine Bluff Division**, US District Court, Eastern District, US Post Office & Courthouse, 100 E 8th St, Rm 3103, Pine Bluff, AR 71601. 501-536-1190

**Texarkana Division**, US District Court, Western District, 500 State Line Ave, Texarkana, AR 75501. 501-773-3381

# California

**Fresno Division**, US Bankruptcy Court, Eastern District, Room 2656, 1130 O Street, Fresno, CA 93721. 209-487-5217

**Fresno Division**, US District Court, Eastern District, US Courthouse, Room 5000, 1130 "O" St, Fresno, CA 93721-2201. 209-487-5083

**Los Angeles Division**, US Bankruptcy Court, Central District, Room 906, 312 N Spring St, Los Angeles, CA 90012. 213-894-4696

**Los Angeles Division**, US District Court, Central District, US Courthouse Records Dept, 312 N Spring St, Los Angeles, CA 90012. 213-894-5261

**Modesto Division**, US Bankruptcy Court, Eastern District, Suite C, 1130 12th St, Modesto, CA 95354. 209-521-5160

**Oakland Division**, US Bankruptcy Court, Northern District, Suite 300, 1300 Clay St, Oakland, CA 94612. 510-273-7212

**Sacramento Division**, US Bankruptcy Court, Eastern District, 8308 US Courthouse, 650 Capitol Mall, Sacramento, CA 95814. 916-498-5525

**Sacramento Division**, US District Court, Eastern District, 2546 United States Courthouse, 650 Capitol Mall, Sacramento, CA 95814-4797. 916-551-2615

**San Bernardino Division**, US Bankruptcy Court, Central District, 699 N Arrowhead Ave, San Bernardino, CA 92401. 909-383-5717

**San Diego Division**, US District Court, Southern District, Room #4280, 880 Front St, San Diego, CA 92101-8900. 619-557-5600

**San Diego Division**, US Bankruptcy Court, Southern District, Office of the Clerk, US Courthouse, Room 5-N-26, 940 Front St, San Diego, CA 92189-0020. 619-557-5620

**San Francisco Division**, US Bankruptcy Court, Northern District, 235 Pine St, San Francisco, CA 94120. 415-705-3200

**San Jose Division**, US District Court, Northern District, Room 2112, 280 S 1st St, San Jose, CA 95113. 408-291-7783

**San Jose Division**, US Bankruptcy Court, Northern District, Room 3035, 280 S 1st St, San Jose, CA 95121. 408-291-7286

**Santa Ana Division**, US Bankruptcy Court, Central District, Room 506, 34 Civic Center Plaza, Santa Ana, CA 92701. 714-836-2993

**Santa Barbara Division**, US Bankruptcy Court, Central District, Room 101, 222 Carrillo St, Santa Barbara, CA 93101. 805-897-3870

**Santa Rosa Division**, US Bankruptcy Court, Northern District, 99 South E St, Santa Rosa, CA 95404. 707-525-8539

## Colorado

**Denver Division**, US Bankruptcy Court, US Custom House, Room 114, 721 19th St, Denver, CO 80202-2508. 303-844-4045

**Denver Division**, US District Court, US Courthouse, Room C-161, 1929 Stout St, Denver, CO 80294-3589. 303-844-3433

## Connecticut

**Bridgeport Division**, US Bankruptcy Court, 915 Lafayette Blvd, Bridgeport, CT 06604. 203-579-5808

**Bridgeport Division**, US District Court, Office of the Clerk, Room 400, 915 Lafayette Blvd, Bridgeport, CT 06604. 203-579-5861

**Hartford Division**, US Bankruptcy Court, 450 Main St, Hartford, CT 06103. 203-240-3677

**Hartford Division**, US District Court, 450 Main St, Hartford, CT 06103. 203-240-3200

**New Haven Division**, US District Court, 141 Church St, New Haven, CT 06510. 203-773-2140

## Delaware

**Wilmington Division**, US Bankruptcy Court, 824 Market St, 5th Floor, Wilmington, DE 19801. 302-573-6174

**Wilmington Division**, US District Court, US Courthouse, Lock Box 18, 844 N King St, Wilmington, DE 19801. 302-573-6170

## District of Columbia

**Washington Division**, US Bankruptcy Court, Court Clerk, Room 4400, 333 Constitution Ave NW, Washington, DC 20001. 202-273-0042

**Washington Division**, US District Court, US Courthouse, Clerk's Office, 333 Constitution Ave NW, Washington, DC 20001. 202-273-0555

## Florida

**Fort Lauderdale Division**, US District Court, Southern District, 299 E Broward Blvd, Fort Lauderdale, FL 33301. 305-356-7076

**Fort Lauderdale Division**, US Bankruptcy Court, Southern District, c/o Miami Division, Room 141, 51 SW 1st Ave, Miami, FL 33130. 305-536-5216

**Fort Myers Division**, US District Court, Middle District, 2301 First St, Fort Myers, FL 33901. 813-332-3937

**Fort Pierce Division**, US District Court, Southern District, c/o West Palm Beach Division, Room 402, 701 Clematis St, West Palm Beach, FL 33401. 407-659-7720

**Gainesville Division**, US District Court, Northern District, c/o Tallahassee Division, Suite 122, 110 E Park Ave, Tallahassee, FL 32301. 904-942-8826

**Jacksonville Division**, US Bankruptcy Court, Middle District, 311 W Monroe, Jacksonville, FL 32202. 904-232-2827

**Jacksonville Division**, US District Court, Middle District, Suite 110, 311 W Monroe St, Jacksonville, FL 32202. 904-232-2854

**Key West Division**, US District Court, Southern District, c/o Miami Division, Room 150, 301 N Miami Ave, Miami, FL 33128-4131. 305-296-4947

**Miami Division**, US District Court, Southern District, Room 150, 301 N Miami Ave, Miami, FL 33128-7788. 305-536-4131

**Miami Division**, US Bankruptcy Court, Southern District, Room 1517, 51 SW 1st Ave, Miami, FL 33130. 305-536-5216

**Ocala Division**, US District Court, Middle District, c/o Jacksonville Division, 1311 W Monroe St, Suite 110, Jacksonville, FL 32202. 904-232-2854

**Orlando Division**, US Bankruptcy Court, Middle District, 135 W Central Blvd, #950, Orlando, FL 32801. 407-648-6364

**Orlando Division**, US District Court, Middle District, Room 218, 80 North Hughey Ave, Orlando, FL 32801. 407-648-6366

**Panama City Division**, US District Court, Northern District, c/o Pensacola Division, Room 129, 100 N Palafox St, Pensacola, FL 32501. 904-433-2107

**Pensacola Division**, US Bankruptcy Court, Northern District, Suite 700, 220 W Garden St, Pensacola, FL 32501. 904-435-8475

**Pensacola Division**, US District Court, Northern District, US Courthouse, Room 129, 100 N Palafox St, Pensacola, FL 32501. 904-435-8440

**Tallahassee Division**, US District Court, Northern District, Suite 122, 110 E Park Ave, Tallahassee, FL 32301. 904-942-8826

**Tallahassee Division**, US Bankruptcy Court, Northern District, Room 3120, 227 N Bronough St, Tallahassee, FL 32301-1378. 904-942-8933

**Tampa Division**, US District Court, Middle District, Office of the Clerk, US Courthouse, 611 N Florida Ave, Tampa, FL 33602. 813-228-2105

**Tampa Division**, US Bankruptcy Court, Middle District, Suite 205, 4921 Memorial Hwy, Tampa, FL 33624. 813-225-7073

**West Palm Beach Division**, US District Court, Southern District, Room 402, 701 Clematis St, West Palm Beach, FL 33401. 407-659-7720

## Georgia

**Albany/Americus Division**, US District Court, Middle District, Room 106, 345 Broad Ave, Albany, GA 31701. 912-430-8432

**Athens Division**, US District Court, Middle District, c/o Macon Division, 475 Mulberry St, Room 216, Macon, GA 31202. 912-752-3497

**Atlanta Division**, US Bankruptcy Court, Northern District, 1340 US Courthouse, 75 Spring St SW, Atlanta, GA 30303-3361. 404-331-6886

**Atlanta Division**, US District Court, Northern District, 2211 US Courthouse, 75 Spring St SW, Atlanta, GA 30303-3361. 404-331-6496

**Augusta Division**, US Bankruptcy Court, Southern District, Room 150, 827 Telfair St, Augusta, GA 30901. 706-724-2421

**Augusta Division**, US District Court, Southern District, Room 143, 985 Broad St, Augusta, GA 30901. 706-722-2074

**Brunswick Division**, US District Court, Southern District, Room 229, 801 Glouchester, Brunswick, GA 31520. 912-265-1758

**Columbus Division**, US Bankruptcy Court, Middle District, 901 Front Ave, 1 Arsenal Pl, Columbus, GA 31902. 404-649-7837

**Columbus Division**, US District Court, Middle District, Room 216, 120 12th St, Columbus, GA 31901. 706-649-7816

**Dublin Division**, US District Court, Southern District, c/o Augusta Division, Room 143, 985 Broad St, Augusta, GA 30901. 706-722-2074

**Gainesville Division**, US District Court, Northern District, Room 201, Federal Bldg, 126 Washington SE, Gainesville, GA 30501. 770-534-5954

**Gainesville Division**, US Bankruptcy Court, Northern District, 126 Washington St, Room 203-C, Gainesville, GA 30501. 770-536-0556

**Macon Division**, US Bankruptcy Court, Middle District, 126 US Courthouse, 475 Mulberry St, Macon, GA 31202. 912-752-3506

**Macon Division**, US District Court, Middle District, 475 Mulberry, Macon, GA 31201. 912-752-3497

**Newnan Division**, US Bankruptcy Court, Northern District, Clerk, Room 220, 18 Greenville St, Newnan, GA 30263. 404-251-5583

**Newnan Division**, US District Court, Northern District, Greenville St, #352, Newnan, GA 30264. 404-253-8847

**Rome Division**, US Bankruptcy Court, Northern District, Clerk, 600 E 1st St, Rome, GA 30161. 706-291-5639

**Rome Division**, US District Court, Northern District, 600 E 1st St, Room 304, Rome, GA 30161. 706-291-5629

**Savannah Division**, US Bankruptcy Court, Southern District, Room 212, 125 Bull St, Savannah, GA 31412. 912-652-4100

**Savannah Division**, US District Court, Southern District, Room 306, 125 Bull St, Savannah, GA 31401. 912-652-4281

**Statesboro Division**, US District Court, Southern District, c/o Savannah Division, Room 306, 125 Bull St, Savannah, GA 31401. 912-652-4281

**Thomasville Division**, US District Court, Middle District, c/o Valdosta Division, Room 212, 401 N Patterson, Valdosta, GA 31603. 912-242-3616

**Valdosta Division**, US District Court, Middle District, Room 212, 401 N Patterson, Valdosta, GA 31603. 912-242-3616

**Waycross Division**, US District Court, Southern District, c/o Savannah Division, Room 306, 125 Bull St, Savannah, GA 31401. 912-652-4281

## Hawaii

**Honolulu Division**, US Bankruptcy Court, 1132 Bishop St, #250-L, Honolulu, HI 96813. 808-522-8100

**Honolulu Division**, US District Court, 1132 Bishop St, Honolulu, HI 96813. 808-541-1300

## Idaho

**Boise Division**, US Bankruptcy Court, US Courthouse, US Courthouse, 550 W Fort St, Room 493, Boise, ID 83724. 208-334-1074

**Boise Division**, US District Court, MSC 039, Federal Bldg, 550 W Fort St, Room 612, Boise, ID 83724. 208-334-9215

**Coeur d' Alene Division**, US Bankruptcy Court, c/o Boise Division, US Courthouse, 205 N 4th St, Coeur d'Alene, ID. 208-334-1074

**Coeur d' Alene Division**, US District Court, c/o Boise Division, Box 039, Federal Bldg, 550 W Fort St, Boise, ID 83724. 208-334-1361

**Moscow Division**, US Bankruptcy Court, c/o Boise Division, US Courthouse, 220 E 5th, Moscow, ID. 208-882-7612

**Moscow Division**, US District Court, c/o Boise Division, Box 039, Federal Bldg, 550 W Fort St, Boise, ID 83724. 208-334-1361

**Pocatello Division**, US Bankruptcy Court, c/o Boise Division, US Courthouse, 250 S 4th Ave, Pocatello, ID. 208-236-6911

**Pocatello Division**, US District Court, c/o Boise Division, Box 039, Federal Bldg, 550 W Fort St, Boise, ID 83724. 208-334-1361

## Illinois

**Benton Division**, US Bankruptcy Court, Southern District, 301 W Main, Benton, IL 62812. 618-435-2200

**Benton Division**, US District Court, Southern District, 301 W Main St, Benton, IL 62812. 618-438-0671

**Chicago Division**, US District Court, Northern District, Room 2050, 219 S Dearborn St, Chicago, IL 60604. 312-435-5670

**Chicago Division**, US Bankruptcy Court, Northern District, 219 S Dearborn St, Chicago, IL 60604-1802. 312-435-5694

**Danville Division**, US District Court, Central District, Federal Bldg, Room 106, 201 N Vermilion, Danville, IL 61832. 217-431-4805

**Danville Division**, US Bankruptcy Court, Central District, 201 N Vermilion, Danville, IL 61834. 217-431-4820

**East St Louis Division**, US District Court, Southern District, 750 Missouri Ave, East St Louis, IL 62201. 618-482-9371

**East St Louis Division**, US Bankruptcy Court, Southern District, 750 Missouri Ave, East St Louis, IL 62201. 618-482-9400

**Peoria Division**, US Bankruptcy Court, Central District, 131 Federal Bldg, 100 NE Monroe, Peoria, IL 61602. 309-671-7035

**Peoria Division**, US District Court, Central District, US District Clerk's Office, 135 Federal Bldg, 100 NE Monroe St, Peoria, IL 61602. 309-671-7117

**Rock Island Division**, US District Court, Central District, US District Clerk's Office, Room 40, Post Office Bldg, 211 19th St, Rock Island, IL 61201. 309-793-5778

**Rockford Division**, US Bankruptcy Court, Northern District, Room 110, 211 S Court St, Rockford, IL 61101. 815-987-4350

**Rockford Division**, US District Court, Northern District, Room 211, 211 Court St, Rockford, IL 61101. 815-987-4355

**Springfield Division**, US District Court, Central District, Clerk, Room 221, 600 E Monroe, Springfield, IL 62701. 217-492-4020

**Springfield Division**, US Bankruptcy Court, Central District, 226 US Courthouse, 600 E Monroe St, Springfield, IL 62705. 217-492-4559

## Indiana

**Evansville Division**, US Bankruptcy Court, Southern District, 352 Federal Building, 101 NW Martin Luther King Blvd, Evansville, IN 47702. 812-465-6440

**Evansville Division**, US District Court, Southern District, 304 Federal Bldg, 101 NW Martin Luther King Blvd, Evansville, IN 47708. 812-465-6426

**Fort Wayne Division**, US Bankruptcy Court, Northern District, 1188 Federal Bldg, 1300 S Harrison St, Fort Wayne, IN 46802. 219-420-5100

**Fort Wayne Division**, US District Court, Northern District, Room 1108, Federal Bldg, 1300 S Harrison St, Fort Wayne, IN 46802. 219-424-7360

**Hammond Division**, US District Court, Northern District, Room 101, 507 State St, Hammond, IN 46320. 219-937-5235

**Hammond at Gary Division**, US Bankruptcy Court, Northern District, 221 Federal Bldg, 610 Connecticut St, Gary, IN 46402-2595. 219-881-3335

**Hammond at Lafayette Division**, US Bankruptcy Court, Northern District, c/o Fort Wayne Division, 1300 S Harrison St, Fort Wayne, IN 46802. 219-420-5100

**Indianapolis Division**, US Bankruptcy Court, Southern District, 123 US Courthouse, 46 E Ohio St, Indianapolis, IN 46204. 317-226-6710

**Indianapolis Division**, US District Court, Southern District, Clerk, Room 105, 46 E Ohio St, Indianapolis, IN 46204. 317-226-7902

**Lafayette Division**, US District Court, Northern District, 232 N 4th St, Lafayette, IN 47902. 317-742-0512

**New Albany Division**, US Bankruptcy Court, Southern District, 102 Federal Bldg, 121 W Spring St, New Albany, IN 47150. 812-948-5254

**New Albany Division**, US District Court, Southern District, Room 210, 121 W Spring St, New Albany, IN 47150. 812-948-5238

**South Bend Division**, US District Court, Northern District, Room 102, 204 S Main, South Bend, IN 46601. 219-236-8260

**South Bend Division**, US Bankruptcy Court, Northern District, Room 224, US Courthouse, 204 S Main St, South Bend, IN 46601-2196. 219-236-8247

**Terre Haute Division**, US Bankruptcy Court, Southern District, 207 Federal Bldg, 30 N Central St, Terre Haute, IN 47808. 812-238-1550

**Terre Haute Division**, US District Court, Southern District, 207 Federal Bldg, Terre Haute, IN 47808. 812-234-9484

## Iowa

**Cedar Rapids Division**, US District Court, Northern District, Court Clerk, Federal Bldg, US Courthouse, 101 1st St SE, Room 313, Cedar Rapids, IA 52401. 319-364-2447

**Cedar Rapids Division**, US Bankruptcy Court, Northern District, Room 800, 425 2nd St SE, Cedar Rapids, IA 52401. 319-362-9696

**Council Bluffs Division**, US District Court, Southern District, Room 313, 8 S 6th St, Council Bluffs, IA 51501. 712-328-0283

**Davenport Division**, US District Court, Southern District, Room 215, 131 E 4th St, Davenport, IA 52801. 319-322-3223

**Des Moines Division**, US Bankruptcy Court, Southern District, 310 US Courthouse, E 1st and Walnuts Sts, Des Moines, IA 50309. 515-284-6230

**Des Moines Division**, US District Court, Southern District, Room 200, 123 E Walnut St, Des Moines, IA 50309. 515-284-6248

**Dubuque Division**, US District Court, Northern District, c/o Cedar Rapids Division, Federal Bldg, US Courthouse, 101 1st St SE, Room 313, Cedar Rapids, IA 52401. 319-364-2447

**Ft Dodge Division**, US District Court, Northern District, c/o Sioux City, Room 301, Federal Bldg, 320 6th St, Sioux City, IA 51101. 712-252-3336

**Sioux City Division**, US District Court, Northern District, Room 301, Federal Bldg, 320 6th St, Sioux City, IA 51101. 712-252-3336

## Kansas

**Kansas City Division**, US Bankruptcy Court, 500 State Ave, Kansas City, KS 66101. 913-551-6732

**Kansas City Division**, US District Court, Clerk, 500 State Ave, Kansas City, KS 66101. 913-551-6719

**Topeka Division**, US Bankruptcy Court, 240 Federal Bldg, 444 SE Quincy, Topeka, KS 66683. 913-295-2750

**Topeka Division**, US District Court, Clerk, US District Court, Room 490, 444 SE Quincy, Topeka, KS 66683. 913-295-2610

**Wichita Division**, US Bankruptcy Court, 167 US Courthouse, 401 N Market, Wichita, KS 67202. 316-269-6486

**Wichita Division**, US District Court, Court Clerk, Room 204, 401 N Market, Wichita, KS 67202-2096. 316-269-6491

## Kentucky

**Ashland Division**, US District Court, Eastern District, Suite 336, 1405 Greenup Ave, Ashland, KY 41101. 606-329-2465

**Bowling Green Division**, US District Court, Western District, 220 Federal Bldg, 240 E Main St, Bowling Green, KY 42101. 502-781-1110

**Covington Division**, US District Court, Eastern District, Clerk, US Courthouse, Room 201, 7th & Scott St, Covington, KY 41011. 606-655-3810

**Frankfort Division**, US District Court, Eastern District, Room 313, 330 W Broadway, Frankfort, KY 40601. 502-223-5225

**Lexington Division**, US Bankruptcy Court, Eastern District, 2nd Floor, Merrill Lynch Plaza, 100 E Vine St, Lexington, KY 40507. 606-233-2608

**Lexington Division**, US District Court, Eastern District, Room 206, 101 Barr St, Lexington, KY 40507. 606-233-2503

**London Division**, US District Court, Eastern District, 124 US Courthouse, 300 S Main St, London, KY 40741. 606-864-5137

**Louisville Division**, US Bankruptcy Court, Western District, 546 US Courthouse, 601 W Broadway, Louisville, KY 40202. 502-582-5145

**Louisville Division**, US District Court, Western District, Clerk, US District Court, 450 US Courthouse, 601 W Broadway, Louisville, KY 40202. 502-582-5156

**Owensboro Division**, US District Court, Western District, Federal Bldg, 423 Frederica St, Owensboro, KY 42301. 502-443-1337

**Paducah Division**, US District Court, Western District, Room 322, 501 Broadway, Paducah, KY 42001. 502-442-1919

**Pikeville Division**, US District Court, Eastern District, Office of the Clerk, 203 Federal Bldg, 102 Main St, Pikeville, KY 41501-1144. 606-437-6160

## Louisiana

**Alexandria Division**, US District Court, Western District, 515 Murray, Alexandria, LA 71309. 318-473-7415

**Alexandria Division**, US Bankruptcy Court, Western District, US Courthouse, US Courthouse, 300 Jackson, Alexandria, LA 71301. 318-473-7387

**Baton Rouge Division**, US Bankruptcy Court, Middle District, Room 301, 412 N 4th St, Baton Rouge, LA 70802. 504-389-0211

**Baton Rouge Division**, US District Court, Middle District, 777 Florida St, Baton Rouge, LA 70801. 504-389-0321

**Lafayette Division**, US District Court, Western District, Room 113, Federal Bldg, 705 Jefferson St, Lafayette, LA 70501. 318-262-6613

**Lafayette-Opelousas Division**, US Bankruptcy Court, Western District, Room 205, 250 S Union, Opelousas, LA 70570. 318-948-3451

**Lake Charles Division**, US District Court, Western District, 611 Broad St, Lake Charles, LA 70601. 318-437-7246

**Lake Charles Division**, US Bankruptcy Court, Western District, 205 Federal Bldg, Union and Vine Sts, Opelousas, LA 70570. 318-948-3451

**Monroe Division**, US District Court, Western District, Room 215, 201 Jackson St, Monroe, LA 71201. 318-322-6740

**Monroe Division**, US Bankruptcy Court, Western District, c/o Shreveport Division, 4B18 Federal Bldg, 500 Fannin St, Shreveport, LA 71101. 318-676-4267

**New Orleans Division**, US Bankruptcy Court, Eastern District, Room C-104, 501 Magazine St, New Orleans, LA 70130. 504-589-6506

**New Orleans Division**, US District Court, Eastern District, Clerk, Room 151, 500 Camp St, New Orleans, LA 70130. 504-589-4471

**Shreveport Division**, US District Court, Western District, Joe D. Waggonner Federal Bldg, Suite 1167, 300 Fannin St, Shreveport, LA 71101. 318-676-4273

**Shreveport Division**, US Bankruptcy Court, Western District, Suite 2201, 300 Fannin St, Shreveport, LA 71101-3089. 318-676-4267

## Maine

**Bangor Division**, US Bankruptcy Court, 202 Harlow St, Bangor, ME 04401. 207-945-0348

**Bangor Division**, US District Court, Court Clerk, Room 357, 202 Harlow St, Bangor, ME 04401. 207-945-0575

**Portland Division**, US Bankruptcy Court, 537 Congress St, Portland, ME 04101. 207-780-3482

**Portland Division**, US District Court, Court Clerk, 1 City Center, Portland, ME 04101. 207-780-3356

## Maryland

**Baltimore Division**, US Bankruptcy Court, 802 US Courthouse, 101 W Lombard St, Baltimore, MD 21201. 410-962-2688

**Baltimore Division**, US District Court, Clerk, Room 404, 101 W Lambard, Baltimore, MD 21201. 410-962-2600

**Rockville Division**, US Bankruptcy Court, 300 US Courthouse, 6500 Cherrywood Ln, Greenbelt, MD 20770. 301-344-8018

## Massachusetts

**Boston Division**, US District Court, Post Office & Courthouse Bldg, Room 707, Boston, MA 02109. 617-223-9152

**Boston Division**, US Bankruptcy Court, Room 1101, 10 Causeway, Boston, MA 02222-1074. 617-565-6051

**Springfield Division**, US District Court, 1550 Main St, Springfield, MA 01103. 413-785-0214

**Worcester Division**, US District Court, Room 506, 595 Main St, Worcester, MA 01601. 508-793-0552

**Worcester Division**, US Bankruptcy Court, 10 Mechanic St, Worcester, MA 01608. 508-793-0519

## Michigan

**Ann Arbor Division**, US District Court, Eastern District, PO Box 8199, 200 E Liberty, Ann Arbor, MI 48104. 313-741-2380

**Bay City Division**, US Bankruptcy Court, Eastern District, 1000 Washington Ave, Bay City, MI 48707. 517-894-8840

**Bay City Division**, US District Court, Eastern District, Room 220, 1000 Washington Ave, Bay City, MI 48708. 517-894-8800

**Detroit Division**, US Bankruptcy Court, Eastern District, Clerk, Room 1002, 231 W Lafayette, Detroit, MI 48226. 313-226-7064

**Detroit Division**, US District Court, Eastern District, 231 W Lafayette Blvd, Detroit, MI 48226. 313-226-7455

**Flint Division**, US Bankruptcy Court, Eastern District, Room 102 A, 600 Church St, Flint, MI 48502. 313-766-5050

**Flint Division**, US District Court, Eastern District, Clerk, Federal Bldg, Room 140, 600 Church St, Flint, MI 48502. 810-766-5020

**Grand Rapids Division**, US Bankruptcy Court, Western District, 110 Michigan NW, Grand Rapids, MI 49503. 616-456-2693

**Grand Rapids/Southern Division**, US District Court, Western District, 452 Federal Bldg, 110 Michigan Ave NW, Grand Rapids, MI 49503. 616-456-2381

**Kalamazoo Division**, US District Court, Western District, B-35 Federal Bldg, 410 W Michigan Ave, Kalamazoo, MI 49007. 616-349-2922

**Lansing Division**, US District Court, Western District, 113 Federal Bldg, 315 W Allegan, Lansing, MI 48933. 517-377-1559

**Marquette Division**, US Bankruptcy Court, Western District, 202 W Washington, Marquette, MI 49855. 906-226-8010

**Marquette/Northern Division**, US District Court, Western District, 229 Federal Bldg, Marquette, MI 49855. 906-226-2021

**Port Huron Division**, US District Court, Eastern District, c/o Detroit Division, 133 Federal Bldg, Detroit, MI 48226. 313-226-7455

## Minnesota

**Duluth Division**, US Bankruptcy Court, 416 US Courthouse, 515 W 1st St, Duluth, MN 55802. 218-720-5253

**Duluth Division**, US District Court, Court Clerk, 417 Federal Bldg, Duluth, MN 55802. 218-720-5250

**Fergus Falls Division**, US Bankruptcy Court, 204 US Courthouse, 118 S Mill St, Fergus Falls, MN 56537. 218-739-4671

**Minneapolis Division**, US Bankruptcy Court, 600 Towle Bldg, 330 2nd Ave S, Minneapolis, MN 55401. 612-348-1855

# Mississippi

**Minneapolis Division**, US District Court, Court Clerk, Room 514, 110 S 4th St, Minneapolis, MN 55401. 612-348-1821

**St Paul Division**, US Bankruptcy Court, 200 Federal Bldg, 316 N Robert St, St Paul, MN 55101. 612-290-3184

**St Paul Division**, US District Court, 708 Federal Bldg, 316 N Robert, St Paul, MN 55101. 612-290-3212

## Mississippi

**Aberdeen-Eastern Division**, US District Court, Northern District, 301 W Commerce, Room 310, Aberdeen, MS 39730. 601-369-4952

**Aberdeen-Eastern Division**, US Bankruptcy Court, Northern District, 205 Federal Bldg, Aberdeen, MS 39730. 601-369-2596

**Biloxi Division**, US District Court, Southern District, 725 Washington Loop, Room 243, Biloxi, MS 39530. 601-432-8623

**Delta/Clarksville Division**, US District Court, Northern District, c/o Oxford-Northern Division, Suite 369, 911 Jackson Ave, Oxford, MS 38655. 601-234-1971

**Greenville Division**, US District Court, Northern District, US Post Office & Federal Bldg, 305 Main, Greenville, MS 38702. 601-335-1651

**Hattiesburg Division**, US District Court, Southern District, Suite 200, 701 Main St, Hattiesburg, MS 39403. 601-234-1971

**Jackson Division**, US District Court, Southern District, Suite 316, 245 E Capitol St, Jackson, MS 39201. 601-965-4439

**Jackson Division**, US Bankruptcy Court, Southern District, 100 E Capitol St, Jackson, MS 39201. 601-965-5301

**Meridian Division**, US District Court, Southern District, c/o Jackson Division, Suite 416, 245 E Capiton St, Jackson, MS 39201. 601-695-4439

**Oxford-Northern Division**, US District Court, Northern District, Suite 369, 911 Jackson Ave, Oxford, MS 38655. 601-234-1971

**Vicksburg Division**, US District Court, Southern District, c/o Jackson Division, Suite 416, 245 E Capitol St, Jackson, MS 39201. 601-965-4439

## Missouri

**Cape Girardeau Division**, US District Court, Eastern District, 339 Broadway, Cape Girardeau, MO 63701. 314-335-8538

**Hannibal Division**, US District Court, Eastern District, c/o St Louis Division, Room 260, 1114 Market St, St Louis, MO 63101. 314-539-2315

**Jefferson City-Central Division**, US District Court, Western District, 131 W High St, Jefferson City, MO 65101. 314-636-4015

**Joplin-Southwestern Division**, US District Court, Western District, c/o Kansas City Division, 201 US Courthouse, 811 Grand Ave, Kansas City, MO 64106. 816-426-2811

**Kansas City-Western Division**, US Bankruptcy Court, Western District, Room 913, 811 Grand Ave, Kansas City, MO 64106. 816-426-3321

**Kansas City-Western Division**, US District Court, Western District, Clerk of Court, 201 US Courthouse, 811 Grand Ave, Kansas City, MO 64106. 816-426-2811 X27

**Springfield-Southern Division**, US District Court, Western District, 222 N John Q Hammons Pkwy, Suite 1400, Springfield, MO 65806. 417-865-3869

**St Joseph Division**, US District Court, Western District, 201 S 8th St, St Joseph, MO 64501. 816-279-2428

**St Louis Division**, US Bankruptcy Court, Eastern District, Room 702, 1114 Market St, St Louis, MO 63101. 314-539-2222

**St Louis Division**, US District Court, Eastern District, Room 260, 1114 Market St, St Louis, MO 63101. 314-539-2315

## Montana

**Billings Division**, US District Court, Clerk, Room 5405, Federal Bldg, 316 N 26th St, Billings, MT 59101. 406-657-6366

**Butte Division**, US District Court, Room 273, Federal Bldg, Butte, MT 59701. 406-782-0432

**Butte Division**, US Bankruptcy Court, 273 Federal Bldg, 400 N Main St, Butte, MT 59701. 406-782-3354

**Great Falls Division**, US District Court, Clerk, 215 1st Ave N, Great Falls, MT 59401. 406-727-1922

**Helena Division**, US District Court, Room 542, 301 S Park Ave, Helena, MT 59626. 406-449-5355

**Missoula Division**, US District Court, Room 251, 200 E Broadway, Missoula, MT 59802. 406-329-3598

## Nebraska

**Lincoln Division**, US District Court, 593 Federal Bldg, 100 Centennial Mall N, Lincoln, NE 68508. 402-437-5225

**Lincoln Division**, US Bankruptcy Court, 100 Centennial Mall N, 460 Federal Bldg, Lincoln, NE 68508. 402-437-5100

**North Platte Division**, US Bankruptcy Court, c/o Omaha Division, Room 9000, 215 N 17th St, Omaha, NE 68102. 402-221-4687

**North Platte Division**, US District Court, c/o Omaha Division, 215 N 17th St, Omaha, NE 68101. 402-221-4761

**Omaha Division**, US District Court, 215 N 17th St, Room 9000, Omaha, NE 68102. 402-221-4761

**Omaha Division**, US Bankruptcy Court, Room 8419, 215 N 17th St, Omaha, NE 68102. 402-221-4687

## Nevada

**Las Vegas Division**, US Bankruptcy Court, 300 Las Vegas Blvd S, #2130, Las Vegas, NV 89101. 702-388-6257

**Las Vegas Division**, US District Court, 300 Las Vegas Boulevard S, #4426, Las Vegas, NV 89101. 702-388-6351

**Reno Division**, US District Court, Room 1109, 300 Booth St, Reno, NV 89509-1385. 702-784-5515

**Reno-Northern Division**, US Bankruptcy Court, Room 4005, 300 Booth St, Reno, NV 89509. 702-784-5559

## New Hampshire

**Concord Division**, US District Court, 55 Pleasant St, Concord, NH 03302. 603-225-1423

**Manchester Division**, US Bankruptcy Court, Room 404, 275 Chestnut St, Manchester, NH 03101. 603-666-7532

## New Jersey

**Camden Division**, US District Court, Clerk, 401 Market St, Camden, NJ 08101. 609-757-5021

**Camden Division**, US Bankruptcy Court, 15 N 7th St, Camden, NJ 08104. 609-757-5422

**Newark Division**, US Bankruptcy Court, Martin Luther King Jr Fed Bldg, 50 Walnut St, Newark, NJ 07102. 201-645-2630

**Newark Division**, US District Court, 50 Walnut St, Newark, NJ 07102. 201-645-3730

**Trenton Division**, US Bankruptcy Court, Clerk of Court, 402 E State St, Trenton, NJ 08608. 609-989-2129

**Trenton Division**, US District Court, Clerk, US District Court, Room 301, 402 E State St, Trenton, NJ 08608. 609-989-2065

## New Mexico

**Albuquerque Division**, US Bankruptcy Court, 3rd Floor, 421 Gold Ave SW, Albuquerque, NM 87102. 505-248-6500

**Albuquerque Division**, US District Court, Room 10000, 500 Gold Ave SW, Albuquerque, NM 87102. 505-766-2851

**Las Cruces Division**, US District Court, c/o Albuquerque Division, Room 10000, 500 Gold Ave SW, Albuquerque, NM 87102. 505-766-2851

**Santa Fe Division**, US District Court, US Courthouse, Room 224, S Federal Pl, Santa Fe, NM 87501. 505-988-6481

## New York

**Albany Division**, US District Court, Northern District, 445 Broadway, Albany, NY 12207. 518-431-0179

**Albany Division**, US Bankruptcy Court, Northern District, James T Foley Courthouse, 445 Broadway, Albany, NY 12201. 518-472-4226

**Binghamton Division**, US District Court, Northern District, 15 Henry St, Binghamton, NY 13901. 607-773-2893

**Brooklyn Division**, US Bankruptcy Court, Eastern District, 75 Clinton St, Brooklyn, NY 11201. 718-330-2188

**Brooklyn Division**, US District Court, Eastern District, 225 Cadman Plaza E, Brooklyn, NY 11201. 718-330-7671

**Buffalo Division**, US Bankruptcy Court, Western District, 310 US Courthouse, 68 Court St, Buffalo, NY 14202. 716-551-4130

**Buffalo Division**, US District Court, Western District, Room 304, 68 Court St, Buffalo, NY 14202. 716-551-4211

**Hauppauge Division**, US District Court, Eastern District, c/o Brooklyn Division, 225 Cadman Plaza E, Brooklyn, NY 11201. 718-330-7671

**Hauppauge Division**, US Bankruptcy Court, Eastern District, 601 Veterans Memorial Hwy, Hauppauge, NY 11788. 516-361-8601

**New York City Division**, US District Court, Southern District, 40 Foley Square, New York, NY 10007. 212-791-0108

**New York Division**, US Bankruptcy Court, Southern District, 6th Floor, 1 Bowling Green, New York, NY 10004-1408. 212-791-2292

**Poughkeepsie Division**, US Bankruptcy Court, Southern District, 176 Church St, Poughkeepsie, NY 12601. 914-452-4200

**Rochester Division**, US Bankruptcy Court, Western District, Room 1220, 100 State St, Rochester, NY 14614. 716-263-3148

**Rochester Division**, US District Court, Western District, Room 282, 100 State St, Rochester, NY 14614. 716-263-6263

**Syracuse Division**, US District Court, Northern District, 100 S Clinton St, #7367, Syracuse, NY 13261. 315-448-0507

**Uniondale Division**, US District Court, Eastern District, c/o Brooklyn Division, 225 Cadman Plaza E, Brooklyn, NY 11201. 718-330-7671

**Utica Division**, US Bankruptcy Court, Northern District, Room 230, 10 Broad St, Utica, NY 13501. 315-793-8101

**Utica Division**, US District Court, Northern District, Alexander Pirnie Bldg, 10 Broad St, Utica, NY 13501. 315-793-8151

**Westbury Division**, US Bankruptcy Court, Eastern District, 1635 Privado Rd, Westbury, NY 11590. 516-832-8801

**White Plains Division**, US Bankruptcy Court, Southern District, 101 E Post Rd, White Plains, NY 10601. 914-682-6117

**White Plains Division**, US District Court, Southern District, 300 Quarropas St, White Plains, NY 10601. 914-390-4000

## North Carolina

**Asheville Division**, US District Court, Western District, Clerk of the Court, Room 309, US Courthouse, 100 Otis St, Asheville, NC 28801-2611. 704-271-4648

**Bryson City Division**, US District Court, Western District, c/o Ashville Division, Clerk of the Court, Room 309, US Courthouse, 100 Otis St, Ashville, NC 28801-2611. 704-271-4648

**Charlotte Division**, US Bankruptcy Court, Western District, 401 W Trade St, Charlotte, NC 28202. 704-344-6103

**Charlotte Division**, US District Court, Western District, Clerk, Room 210, 401 W Trade St, Charlotte, NC 28202. 704-344-6200

**Durham Division**, US District Court, Middle District, c/o Greensboro Division, Room 311, 324 W Market St, Greensboro, NC 27401. 919-333-5347

**Elizabeth City Division**, US District Court, Eastern District, c/o Raleigh Division, Room 578, 310 New Bern Ave, Raleigh, NC 27601. 919-856-4370

**Fayetteville Division**, US District Court, Eastern District, c/o Raleigh Division, Room 578, 310 Newbern Ave, Raleigh, NC 27601. 919-856-4370

**Greensboro Division**, US District Court, Middle District, Clerk's Office, Room 311, 324 W Market St, Greensboro, NC 27401. 910-332-6000

**Greensboro Division**, US Bankruptcy Court, Middle District, 202 S Elm St, Greensboro, NC 27401. 919-333-5647

**New Bern Division**, US District Court, Eastern District, Room 209, 413-415 Middle St, New Bern, NC 28560. 919-638-8534

**Raleigh Division**, US Bankruptcy Court, Eastern District, Room 206, Century Station Bldg, 300 Fayetteville St Mall, Raleigh, NC 27602. 919-856-4752

**Raleigh Division**, US District Court, Eastern District, Clerk's Office, Room 574, 310 New Bern Ave, Raleigh, NC 27601. 919-856-4370

**Rockingham Division**, US District Court, Middle District, c/o Greensboro Division, Room 311, 324 W Market St, Greensboro, NC 27401. 919-333-5347

**Salisbury Division**, US District Court, Middle District, c/o Greensboro Division, Room 311, 324 W Market St, Greensboro, NC 27401. 919-333-5347

**Shelby Division**, US District Court, Western District, c/o Ashville Division, Clerk of the Court, Room, 309, US Courthouse, 100 Otis St, Ashville, NC 28801-2611. 704-271-4648

**Statesville Division**, US District Court, Western District, Room 205, 200 W Broad St, Statesville, NC 28687. 704-873-7112

**Wilmington Division**, US District Court, Eastern District, Room 239, 2 Princess St, Wilmington, NC 28401. 910-343-4663

**Wilson Division**, US Bankruptcy Court, Eastern District, The Thomas Melton Moore Bldg, 1760 Parkwood Blvd, Wilson, NC 27893. 919-237-0248

**Winston-Salem Division**, US District Court, Middle District, c/o Greensboro Division, Room 311, 325 W Market St, Greensboro, NC 27401. 919-333-5347

## North Dakota

**Bismarck-Southwestern Division**, US District Court, 220 E Rosser Ave, Bismarck, ND 58501. 701-250-4295

**Fargo Division**, US Bankruptcy Court, Room 236, Federal Bldg & US Courthouse, Fargo, ND 58102. 701-239-5129

**Fargo-Southeastern Division**, US District Court, 655 1st Ave N, Fargo, ND 58107. 701-239-5377

**Grand Forks-Northeastern Division**, US District Court, c/o Southeastern (Fargo) Division, 655 1st Ave N, Fargo, ND 58107. 701-239-5377

**Minot-Northwestern Division**, US District Court, c/o Bismarck Division, 220 E Rosser Ave, Bismarck, ND 58501. 701-250-4295

## Ohio

**Akron Division**, US Bankruptcy Court, Northern District, 455 Federal Bldg, 2 S Main, Akron, OH 44308. 216-375-5840

**Akron Division**, US District Court, Northern District, 568 Federal Bldg, 2 S Main St, Akron, OH 44308. 216-375-5705

**Canton Division**, US Bankruptcy Court, Northern District, Frank T Bow Federal Bldg, 201 Cleveland Ave SW, Canton, OH 44702. 216-489-4426

**Cincinnati Division**, US Bankruptcy Court, Southern District, Atrium 2, 221 E. 4th St, Cincinnati, OH 45202. 513-684-2572

**Cincinnati Division**, US District Court, Southern District, Clerk, US District Court, 100 E 5th St, 324 Courthouse Bldg, Cincinnati, OH 45202. 513-684-2777

**Cleveland Division**, US Bankruptcy Court, Northern District, 201 Superior, Cleveland, OH 44114. 216-522-4373

**Cleveland Division**, US District Court, Northern District, 201 Superior Ave NE, Cleveland, OH 44114. 216-522-2140

**Columbus Division**, US Bankruptcy Court, Southern District, US Courthouse, 170 N. High St, Columbus, OH 43215. 614-469-6638

**Columbus Division**, US District Court, Southern District, Office of the Clerk, Room 260, 85 Marconi Blvd, Columbus, OH 43215. 614-469-5442

**Dayton Division**, US Bankruptcy Court, Southern District, Federal Bldg & US Courthouse 120 W 3rd St, Dayton, OH 45402. 513-225-2516

**Dayton Division**, US District Court, Southern District, Federal Bldg, PO Box 970, 200 W 2nd, Dayton, OH 45402. 513-225-2896

**Toledo Division**, US Bankruptcy Court, Northern District, Room 411, 1716 Spielbusch Ave, Toledo, OH 43624. 419-259-6440

**Toledo Division**, US District Court, Northern District, 114 US Courthouse, 1716 Spielbusch, Toledo, OH 43624. 419-259-6412

**Youngstown Division**, US District Court, Northern District, 337 Federal Bldg, 125 Front St, Youngstown, OH 44503. 216-746-1726

**Youngstown Division**, US Bankruptcy Court, Northern District, 9 W Front St, City Hall Annex, Youngstown, OH 44501. 216-746-7027

## Oklahoma

**Muskogee Division**, US District Court, Eastern District, Clerk, 101 N 5th, Muskogee, OK 74401. 918-687-2471

**Federal Court Records**

**Oklahoma City Division**, US Bankruptcy Court, Western District, 1st Floor, Old Post Office Bldg, 215 Dean A McGee Ave, Oklahoma City, OK 73102. 405-231-5141

**Oklahoma City Division**, US District Court, Western District, Clerk, Room 1210, 200 NW 4th St, Oklahoma City, OK 73102. 405-231-4792

**Okmulgee Division**, US Bankruptcy Court, Eastern District, PO & Federal Bldg, 4th & Grand, Okmulgee, OK 74447. 918-758-0126

**Tulsa Division**, US Bankruptcy Court, Northern District, Suite 320, 111 W 5th St, Tulsa, OK 74103. 918-581-7181

**Tulsa Division**, US District Court, Northern District, 411 US Courthouse, 333 W 4th St, Tulsa, OK 74103. 918-581-7796

## Oregon

**Eugene Division**, US District Court, 102 E 7th St, Eugene, OR 97401. 503-465-6423

**Eugene Division**, US Bankruptcy Court, 4th Floor, Room 404, 211 E 7th St, Eugene, OR 97401. 503-465-6448

**Portland Division**, US Bankruptcy Court, Suite 700, 1001 SW 5th Ave, Portland, OR 97204. 503-326-2231

**Portland Division**, US District Court, Clerk, 503 US Courthouse, 620 SW Main, Portland, OR 97205. 503-326-2202

## Pennsylvania

**Allentown Division**, US District Court, Eastern District, c/o Philadelphia Division, 601 Market St, Room 2609, US Courthouse, Philadelphia, PA 19106-1797. 215-597-7704

**Erie Division**, US Bankruptcy Court, Western District, 617 State St, Erie, PA 16501. 814-453-7580

**Erie Division**, US District Court, Western District, 227 US Courthouse, 617 State St, Erie, PA 16507. 814-453-4829

**Harrisburg Division**, US Bankruptcy Court, Middle District, 228 Walnut St, 3rd Floor, Harrisburg, PA 17101. 717-782-2260

**Harrisburg Division**, US District Court, Middle District, US Courthouse & Federal Bldg, 228 Walnut St, Harrisburg, PA 17108. 717-782-4445

**Johnstown Division**, US District Court, Western District, Penn Traffic Bldg, Room 208, 319 Washington St, Johnstown, PA 15901. 814-533-4504

**Philadelphia Division**, US Bankruptcy Court, Eastern District, Room 3726, 601 Market St, 3rd Floor, Philadelphia, PA 19106. 215-597-1644

**Philadelphia Division**, US District Court, Eastern District, Room 2609, US Courthouse, 601 Market St, Philadelphia, PA 19106-1797. 215-597-7704

**Pittsburgh Division**, US Bankruptcy Court, Western District, 1602 Federal Bldg, 1000 Liberty Ave, Pittsburgh, PA 15219. 412-644-2700

**Pittsburgh Division**, US District Court, Western District, US Post Office & Courthouse, Room 829, 7th Ave & Grant St, Pittsburgh, PA 15219. 412-644-3527

**Reading Division**, US Bankruptcy Court, Eastern District, Suite 300, The Madison, 400 Washington St, Reading, PA 19601. 215-320-5255

**Scranton Division**, US District Court, Middle District, Clerk's Office, 235 N Washington Ave, Scranton, PA 18503. 717-347-0205

**Wilkes-Barre Division**, US Bankruptcy Court, Middle District, Room 217, 197 S Main St, Wilkes-Barre, PA 18701. 717-826-6450

**Williamsport Division**, US District Court, Middle District, Federal Bldg, 240 W 3rd St, Williamsport, PA 17701. 717-323-6380

## Rhode Island

**Providence Division**, US Bankruptcy Court, 6th Floor, 380 Westminster Mall, Providence, RI 02903. 401-528-4477

**Providence Division**, US District Court, Clerk's Office, Room 119, Federal Bldg, Providence, RI 02903. 401-528-5100

## South Carolina

**Anderson Division**, US District Court, c/o Greenville Division, 300 E Washington St, Greenville, SC 29603. 803-233-2781

**Beaufort Division**, US District Court, c/o Charleston Division, Meeting St & Broad St, Charleston, SC 29401. 803-727-4688

**Charleston Division**, US District Court, 83 Broad St, Charleston, SC 29401. 803-727-4688

**Columbia Division**, US District Court, 1845 Assembly St, Columbia, SC 29201. 803-765-5816

**Columbia Division**, US Bankruptcy Court, 1100 Laurel St, Columbia, SC 29201. 803-765-5436 X0

**Florence Division**, US District Court, 401 W Evans St, Florence, SC 29501. 803-662-1223

**Greenville Division**, US District Court, 300 E Washington St, Greenville, SC 29601. 803-233-2781

**Greenwood Division**, US District Court, c/o Greenville Division, 300 E Washington St, Greenville, SC 29603. 803-233-2781

**Spartanburg Division**, US District Court, c/o Greenville Division, 300 E Washington St, Greenville, SC 29603. 803-233-2781

## South Dakota

**Aberdeen Division**, US District Court, c/o Western (Rapid City) Division, Room 302, 515 9th St, Rapid City, SD 57701. 605-342-3066

**Pierre Division**, US Bankruptcy Court, Clerk, Room 203, Federal Bldg, 225 S Pierre St, Pierre, SD 57501. 605-224-6013

**Pierre-Central Division**, US District Court, Federal Bldg & Courthouse, Room 405, 225 S Pierre St, Pierre, SD 57501. 605-224-5849

**Rapid City Division**, US District Court, Clerk's Office, Room 302, 515 9th St, Rapid City, SD 57701. 605-342-3066

**Sioux Falls Division**, US District Court, Room 220, Federal Bldg, 400 S Phillips Ave, Sioux Falls, SD 57102. 605-330-4447

**Sioux Falls Division**, US Bankruptcy Court, Room 104, 400 S Phillips Ave, Sioux Falls, SD 57102. 605-330-4541

## Tennessee

**Chattanooga Division**, US District Court, Eastern District, Clerk's Office, Room 309, 900 Georgia Ave, Chattanooga, TN 37402. 615-752-5200

**Chattanooga Division**, US Bankruptcy Court, Eastern District, Historic US Courthouse, 31 E 11th St, Chattanooga, TN 37402. 615-752-5163

**Columbia Division**, US District Court, Middle District, c/o Nashville Division, US Courthouse Room 800, 801 Broadway, Nashville, TN 37203. 615-736-7763

**Cookeville Division**, US District Court, Middle District, 1st Floor, 9 E Broad St, Cookeville, TN 38503. 615-526-3269

**Greeneville Division**, US District Court, Eastern District, 101 Summer St W, Greenville, TN 37743. 615-639-3105

**Jackson Division**, US Bankruptcy Court, Western District, Room 308, 109 S Highland Ave, Jackson, TN 38301. 901-424-9751

**Jackson Division**, US District Court, Western District, Federal Bldg, Room 101, 109 S Highland St, Jackson, TN 38301. 901-427-6586

**Knoxville Division**, US District Court, Eastern District, Clerk's Office, 501 Main, Knoxville, TN 37902. 615-545-4228

**Knoxville Division**, US Bankruptcy Court, Eastern District, Suite 1501, Plaza Tower, Knoxville, TN 37929. 615-545-4279

**Memphis Division**, US Bankruptcy Court, Western District, Suite 413, 200 Jefferson Ave, Memphis, TN 38103. 901-544-3202

**Memphis Division**, US District Court, Western District, Federal Bldg, Room 242, 167 N Main, Memphis, TN 38103. 901-544-3315

**Nashville Division**, US Bankruptcy Court, Middle District, Room 207 Customs House, 701 Broadway, Nashville, TN 37203. 615-736-5584

**Nashville Division**, US District Court, Middle District, US Courthouse Room 800, 801 Broadway, Nashville, TN 37203. 615-736-5498

**Winchester Division**, US District Court, Eastern District, c/o Chattanooga Division, PO Box 591, Chattanooga, TN 37401, 615-752-5200

## Texas

**Abilene Division**, US District Court, Northern District, Room 2008, 341 Pine St, Abilene, TX 79601. 915-677-6311

**Amarillo Division**, US District Court, Northern District, 205 E 5th St, Amarillo, TX 79101. 806-376-2352

**Amarillo Division**, US Bankruptcy Court, Northern District, Suite 100, 624 S Polk St, Amarillo, TX 79101-2389. 806-376-2302

**Austin Division**, US District Court, Western District, Room 308, 200 W 8th St, Austin, TX 78701. 512-482-5896

**Austin Division**, US Bankruptcy Court, Western District, First City Centre, Suite 1420, 816 Congress Ave, Austin, TX 78750. 512-482-5238

**Beaumont Division**, US Bankruptcy Court, Eastern District, Suite 110, 300 Willow, Beaumont, TX 77701. 409-839-2617

**Beaumont Division**, US District Court, Eastern District, Room 327, 300 Willow, Beaumont, TX 77701. 409-654-7000

**Brownsville Division**, US District Court, Southern District, Room 105, 500 E 10th, Brownsville, TX 78520. 210-548-2500

**Corpus Christi Division**, US District Court, Southern District, Clerk's Office, 521 Starr St, Corpus Christi, TX 78401. 512-888-3142

**Corpus Christi Division**, US Bankruptcy Court, Southern District, Room 113, 615 Leopard St, Corpus Christi, TX 78476. 512-888-3484

**Dallas Division**, US Bankruptcy Court, Northern District, Suite 12A24, 1100 Commerce St, Dallas, TX 75242. 214-767-0814

**Dallas Division**, US District Court, Northern District, Room 14A20, 1100 Commerce St, Dallas, TX 75242. 214-767-0787

**Del Rio Division**, US District Court, Western District, Room L100, 111 E Broadway, Del Rio, TX 78840. 210-775-2021

**Del Rio Division**, US Bankruptcy Court, Western District, Suite L-100, 111 E Broadway, Del Rio, TX 78840. 210-775-2021

**El Paso Division**, US Bankruptcy Court, Western District, 8515 Lockheed, El Paso, TX 79901. 915-779-7362

**El Paso Division**, US District Court, Western District, US District Clerk's Office, Room 108, 511 E San Antonio, El Paso, TX 79901. 915-534-6725

**Fort Worth Division**, US Bankruptcy Court, Northern District, 501 W 10th, Fort Worth, TX 76102. 817-334-3802

**Fort Worth Division**, US District Court, Northern District, Clerk's Office, 202 US Courthouse, 10th & Lamar, Fort Worth, TX 76102. 817-334-3132

**Galveston Division**, US District Court, Southern District, Clerk's Office, Room 411, 601 Rosenberg, Galveston, TX 77550. 409-766-3530

**Houston Division**, US Bankruptcy Court, Southern District, Room 4603, 515 Rusk Ave, Houston, TX 77002. 713-250-5500

**Houston Division**, US District Court, Southern District, Room 5300, 515 Rusk, Houston, TX 77002. 713-250-9500

**Laredo Division**, US District Court, Southern District, Room 319, 1300 Matamoros, Laredo, TX 78042. 210-723-3542

**Lubbock Division**, US Bankruptcy Court, Northern District, 102 Federal Bldg, 1205 Texas Ave, Lubbock, TX 79401. 806-743-7336

**Lubbock Division**, US District Court, Northern District, Clerk, Room C-221, 1205 Texas Ave, Lubbock, TX 79401. 806-743-7624

**Marshall Division**, US Bankruptcy Court, Eastern District, c/o Beaumont Division, Suite 117, 350 Magnolia, Beaumont, TX 77701. 409-839-2617

**Marshall Division**, US District Court, Eastern District, 100 E Houston, Marshall, TX 75670. 903-935-2912

**McAllen Division**, US District Court, Southern District, Suite 911, 1701 W Business Hwy 83, McAllen, TX 78501. 210-631-2205

**Midland Division**, US District Court, Western District, Clerk, US District Court, 200 E Wall St, Midland, TX 79701. 915-683-2001

**Midland/Odessa Division**, US Bankruptcy Court, Western District, Clerk, US District Court, Room 316, 200 E Wall St, Midland, TX 79701. 915-683-2001

**Pecos Division**, US Bankruptcy Court, Western District, 106 W 4th St, Pecos, TX 79772. 915-445-4228

**Pecos Division**, US District Court, Western District, US Courthouse, 106 W 4th St, Pecos, TX 79772. 915-445-4228

**Plano Division**, US Bankruptcy Court, Eastern District, Suite 3000B, 660 N Central Expressway, Plano, TX 75074. 214-423-6605

**San Angelo Division**, US District Court, Northern District, Clerk's Office, Room 202, 33 E Twohig, San Angelo, TX 76903. 915-655-4506

**San Antonio Division**, US District Court, Western District, US Clerk's Office, 655 E Durango, San Antonio, TX 78206. 210-229-6550

**San Antonio Division**, US Bankruptcy Court, Western District, 615 E Houston St, San Antonio, TX 78205. 210-229-6720

**Sherman Division**, US District Court, Eastern District, 216 Federal Bldg, 101 E Pecan St, Sherman, TX 75090. 409-892-2921

**Texarkana Division**, US Bankruptcy Court, Eastern District, c/o Beaumont Division, Suite 117, 350 Magnolia, Beaumont, TX 77701. 409-839-2617

**Texarkana Division**, US District Court, Eastern District, Clerk's Office, Room 301, 500 State Line Ave, Texarkana, TX 75501. 409-794-8561

**Tyler Division**, US District Court, Eastern District, 4th Floor, 211 W Ferguson, Tyler, TX 75702. 903-592-1212

**Tyler Division**, US District Court, Eastern District, Clerk, Room 106, 211 W Ferguson, Tyler, TX 75702. 903-592-8195

**Victoria Division**, US District Court, Southern District, Clerk US District Court, Room 406, 312 S Main, Victoria, TX 77902. 512-788-5000

**Waco Division**, US Bankruptcy Court, Western District, Room 303, 800 Franklin Ave, Waco, TX 76701. 817-754-1481

**Waco Division**, US District Court, Western District, Clerk, Room 303, 800 Franklin, Waco, TX 76701. 817-750-1501

**Wichita Falls Division**, US Bankruptcy Court, Northern District, c/o Dallas Division, 12th Floor, 1100 Commerce St, Dallas, TX 75242. 214-767-0814

**Wichita Falls Division**, US District Court, Northern District, Room 203, 1000 Lamar, Wichita Falls, TX 76301. 817-767-1902

# Utah

**Slat Lake Division**, US Bankruptcy Court, Court Clerk, Room 361, 350 S Main St, Salt Lake City, UT 84101. 801-524-5157

**Salt Lake Division**, US District Court, Clerk's Office, Room 150, 350 S Main St, Salt Lake City, UT 84101. 801-524-5160

# Vermont

**Burlington Division**, US District Court, Clerk's Office, Room 507, 11 Elmwood Ave, Burlington, VT 05401. 802-951-6301

**Rutland Division**, US Bankruptcy Court, 67 Merchants Row, Rutland, VT 05701. 802-747-7625

**Rutland Division**, US District Court, 151 West St, Rutland, VT 05701. 802-773-0245

# Virginia

**Abingdon Division**, US District Court, Western District, Clerk's Office, 180 W Main St, Abingdon, VA 24210. 703-628-5116

**Alexandria Division**, US District Court, Eastern District, Room 100, 200 S Washington St, Alexandria, VA 22314. 703-557-5128

**Alexandria Division**, US Bankruptcy Court, Eastern District, Suite 401, 206 N Washington St, Alexandria, VA 22314. 703-557-1716

**Big Stone Gap Division**, US District Court, Western District, 322 Wood Ave E, Big Stone Gap, VA 24219. 703-523-3557

**Charlottesville Division**, US District Court, Western District, Clerk, Room 304, 255 W Main St, Charlottesville, VA 22902. 804-296-9284

**Danville Division**, US District Court, Western District, Dan Daniel Post Office Bldg, Room 202, 700 Main St, Danville, VA 24541. 804-793-7147

**Harrisonburg Division**, US Bankruptcy Court, Western District, 116 N Main St, Harrisonburg, VA 22801. 540-434-8327

**Harrisonburg Division**, US District Court, Western District, Clerk, PO Bldg, Room 314, 116 N Main St, Harrisonburg, VA 22801. 540-434-3181

**Lynchburg Division**, US Bankruptcy Court, Western District, Room 226, 1100 Main St, Lynchburg, VA 24504. 804-845-0317

**Lynchburg Division**, US District Court, Western District, Clerk, Room 212, 1100 Main St, Lynchburg, VA 24504. 804-847-5722

**Newport News Division**, US District Court, Eastern District, Clerk's Office, 101 25th St, Newport News, VA 23607. 804-244-0539

**Newport News Division**, US Bankruptcy Court, Eastern District, Suite 201, 825 Diligence Dr, Newport News, VA 23606. 804-595-9805

**Norfolk Division**, US District Court, Eastern District, US Courthouse, Room 193, 600 Granby St, Norfolk, VA 23501. 804-441-3250

**Norfolk Division**, US Bankruptcy Court, Eastern District, US Courthouse, Room 400, 600 Granby St, Norfolk, VA 23501. 804-441-6651

**Richmond Division**, US District Court, Eastern District, 3rd Floor, Courthouse, 10th & Main, Richmond, VA 23219. 804-771-2612

**Richmond Division**, US Bankruptcy Court, Eastern District, Court Clerk, 1100 E Main St, Richmond, VA 23219. 804-771-2878

**Roanoke Division**, US District Court, Western District, Clerk, 210 Franklin Rd SW, Roanoke, VA 24011. 540-857-2224

**Roanoke Division**, US Bankruptcy Court, Western District, Commonwealth Bldg, 210 Church Ave, Roanoke, VA 24011. 540-857-2391

## Washington

**Seattle Division**, US Bankruptcy Court, Western District, Clerk of Court, 315 Park Place Bldg, 1200 6th Ave, Seattle, WA 98101. 206-553-7545

**Seattle Division**, US District Court, Western District, Clerk of Court, 215 US Courthouse, 1010 5th Ave, Seattle, WA 98104. 206-553-5598

**Spokane Division**, US Bankruptcy Court, Eastern District, Clerk of Court, W 904 Riverside, Spokane, WA 99201. 509-353-2404

**Spokane Division**, US District Court, Eastern District, Room 840, W 920 Riverside, Spokane, WA 99210. 509-353-2150

**Tacoma Division**, US District Court, Western District, Clerk's Office, Room 3100, 1717 Pacific Ave, Tacoma, WA 98402. 206-593-6313

**Tacoma Division**, US Bankruptcy Court, Western District, Suite 2100, 1717 Pacific Ave, Tacoma, WA 98402-3233. 206-593-6310

**Yakima Division**, US District Court, Eastern District, c/o Spokane Division, Room 215, 25 S 3rd St, Yakima, WA 98901. 509-353-2150

## West Virginia

**Beckley Division**, US District Court, Southern District, 400 Neville St, Beckley, WV 25801. 304-253-7481

**Bluefield Division**, US District Court, Southern District, Clerk's Office, 601 Federal St, Bluefield, WV 24701. 304-327-9798

**Charleston Division**, US District Court, Southern District, Room 5303, 500 Quarrier St, Charleston, WV 25301. 304-342-5154

**Charleston Division**, US Bankruptcy Court, Southern District, 500 Quarrier St, Charleston, WV 25301. 304-347-5114

**Clarksburg Division**, US District Court, Northern District, 2nd Floor, 500 W Pike St, Clarksburg, WV 26301. 304-622-8513

**Elkins Division**, US District Court, Northern District, 2nd Floor, 300 3rd St, Elkins, WV 26241. 304-636-1445

**Huntington Division**, US District Court, Southern District, Clerk of Court, Room 101, 845 5th Ave, Huntington, WV 25701. 304-529-5588

**Martinsburg Division**, US District Court, Northern District, c/o Elkins Division, 2nd Floor, 300 3rd St, Elkins, WV 26241. 304-636-1445

**Parkersburg Division**, US District Court, Southern District, Clerk of Court, Room 5102, 425 Julianna St, Parkersburg, WV 26101. 304-420-6490

**Wheeling Division**, US Bankruptcy Court, Northern District, 12th & Chapline St, Wheeling, WV 26003. 304-233-1655

**Wheeling Division**, US District Court, Northern District, Clerk, 12th & Chapline Sts, Wheeling, WV 26003. 304-232-0011

## Wisconsin

**Eau Claire** Division, US Bankruptcy Court, Western District, 500 S Barstow Commons, Eau Claire, WI 54701. 715-839-2980

**Madison Division**, US Bankruptcy Court, Western District, Room 340, 120 N Henry St, Madison, WI 53703. 608-264-5178

**Madison Division**, US District Court, Western District, 120 Henry St, Madison, WI 53703. 608-264-5156

**Milwaukee Division**, US Bankruptcy Court, Eastern District, Room 216, 517 E Wisconsin Ave, Milwaukee, WI 53202. 414-297-4070

**Milwaukee Division**, US District Court, Eastern District, Clerk's Office, Room 362, 517 E Wisconsin Ave, Milwaukee, WI 53202. 414-297-3372

## Wyoming

**Casper Division**, US District Court, c/o Cheyenne Division, Room 101, 111 S Walcott, Cheyenne, WY 82001. 307-772-2145

**Cheyenne Division**, US Bankruptcy Court, 6th Floor, 2120 Captiol Ave, Cheyenne, WY 82001. 307-772-2191

**Cheyenne Division**, US District Court, Room 2131, 2120 Capitol, Cheyenne, WY 82001. 307-772-2145

# PUBLIC RECORD RESEARCH LIBRARY

# Most People Don't See Our Covers

## (Because our Books are Always Open!)

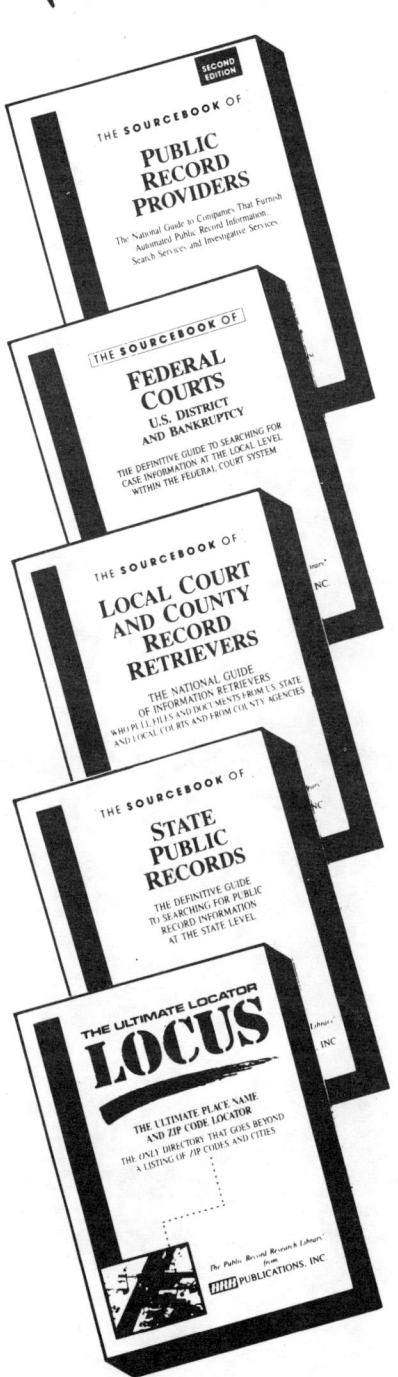

**PUBLIC RECORD PROVIDERS** — New Second Edition

A compendium profiling over 500 private public record information sources and professional information providers. Special attention is given to national and regional public record search firms, providers of proprietary database and CD-ROM products, distributors of national and regional record information, background screening firms, and firms utilizing on-line methodologies. Indexed by topic, content and locations.

ISBN #1-879792-13-3   Published 1994   Pages 288   Price $29.00

**FEDERAL COURTS** — Includes PACER/VCIS Updates

The ONLY Federal Court in-depth search guide to 500+ U.S. court locations and 13 Federal Records Centers. A full page of information on every individual court location maintaining civil, criminal or bankruptcy records provides extensive details and instructions.

**Additional research tools include:** County Court cross-reference lists, maps for every multiple U.S. District and Bankruptcy division, and an 18 page search guide giving search strategies and explanation of how to use the on-line retrieval and voice information systems.

ISBN #1-879792-10-9   Published 1993   Pages 672   Price $33.00

**LOCAL COURT AND COUNTY RECORD RETRIEVERS**

Now you can have at your fingertips a directory of more than 2100 firms that regularly retrieve public records from courthouses and county offices. Shown on a county by county basis, "hands-on" document retrievers are highlighted by their search expertise in these categories: local court civil and criminal cases, US District Court cases, US Bankruptcy Court cases, federal records centers, UCC liens and recordings, real property liens, recordings, taxes, and vital records

ISBN #1-879792-16-8   Published 1995   Pages 440   Price $45.00

**STATE PUBLIC RECORDS** — Second Printing July 1994

Presents the reader all the information needed for accurate, comprehensive searching at the state level. 19 subject matters with over 5,000 record center locations are referenced. Each major topic is covered in detail — address, telephone, office hours, search requirements, modes of access, costs, access and usage restrictions, indexing, when records are available, and more.

**Added Research Tools:** Each state chapter contains a broad list of agencies involved in occupational licensing and business registration.

ISBN #1-879792-12-5   Published 1995   Pages 360   Price $33.00

**THE COUNTY LOCATOR (LOCUS)**

The ONLY PUBLISHED DIRECTORY of place names and ZIP Codes that accurately indicates what counties a 5-digit ZIP Code covers. Three cross reference indices indicate: 95,000+ place names; 10,000+ ZIP Codes that cross one to four county lines; and 10,000+ ZIP Codes which are not for geographic addresses. A must for filers and searchers.

ISBN #1-879792-11-7   Published 1993   Pages 928   Price $25.00

### THE MVR BOOK

For Professionals Using Driver History Records and Motor Vehicle Records.

Individual state characteristics include: latest privacy laws and regulations, convictions that do not appear on driver history records, commercial access of vehicle ownership records, driver license format and classification facts.

Additional research tools: glossary of professional agencies and institutions, glossary of federal programs and national networks, reciprocity of conviction information between the states.

ISBN #1-879792-19-2          Published 1995          Pages 256          Price $18.00

### THE MVR DECODER DIGEST

For translating the codes and abbreviations used on state driver history records.

Individual state characteristics include: violations and codes, corresponding points, license classifications, endorsements and restrictions ...for both CDL and non-CDL drivers.

Additional research tools: compact and IRP membership table, reciprocity table of conviction information between states, the AAMVA Conviction/Withdrawal Code Dictionary (ACD) as mandated for 1995.

ISBN #1-879792-20-6          Published 1995          Pages 272          Price $18.00

# New Products Announcement

### COUNTY ASSET/LIEN RECORDS                                   New First Edition

This sourcebook, a companion to *County Court Records*, details how to obtain real estate, Uniform Commercial Code and tax lien records from 4,200+ city and county filing offices. UCC records, federal and state tax lien records, real estate records (transfers, current ownership, unpaid taxes, mortgages and deeds of trust) are examined in detail for search availability, how indexed, acceptable access methods (phone, mail, fax, etc.), required request forms, fees, copy costs, and more.

An extensive introductory section explains how to use thes records effectively in searching for background information about businesses and individuals. The Sourcebook also includes a city to county cross reference index to locate the correct jurisdiction to contact.

ISBN #1-879792-17-6          Published October, 1994          Pages 440+          Price $29.00

### COUNTY COURT RECORDS                           New Completely Revised Second Edition

The award winning national guide to the over 5,600 Main and Secondary Repositories of US County Court House Records. Entries for felony, misdemeanor, civil actions, and probate records are distinguished by specific search criteria such as mode of access, costs, restrictions, indexing methods, turnaround time and on-line capabilities. The structure of each state court system is summarized in detail including an extensive city to county cross reference index. Over 40,000 municipalitites are included.

ISBN #1-879792-16-8          Published October, 1994          Pages 560+          Price $33.00

### THE FEDERAL COURT LOCATOR                                   New First Edition

This new, handy loose-leaf binder is designed for our readers who need to find the answer "Which District or Bankruptcy Court Location has the records for this county?"

On one line you see at a glance the essential information about each county in the US —

- The Court Locator Section — the Federal Court District; Division Names for both US District and US Bankruptcy Court; cities and phone number where case records are kept; and the Automated Voice Case Information (VCIS) telephone number.

- Additional Sections include Pacer Access (On-line retrieval), Tax Liens, UCC, and Appeals/Federal Record Centers.

Best of all, the low price includes one free update in 1995!!!

ISBN #1-879792-18-4          Published August, 1994          Pages 144+          Price $29.00

### MAILER'S LOOK UP (County Locator) CD ROM

MAILER'S LookUp can provide the County Name and the ZIP+4 Code, City and State for every lookup. After retrieving the information you need you can place it by hitting a pre-programmed function key combination. You can use the program to look up and place information while in your favorite text-based word processor, data entry program or any of you other favorite applications. MAILER'S LookUp is versatile. It can look up information by full or partial address to find the correct ZIP+4, use City/State information to find the correct 5-digit ZIP or use ZIP/Area Code+Prefix to find the correct City and State. MAILER's LookUp, the programming answer to printed AIP Code directories!                              1995 Edition                    Price $65.00

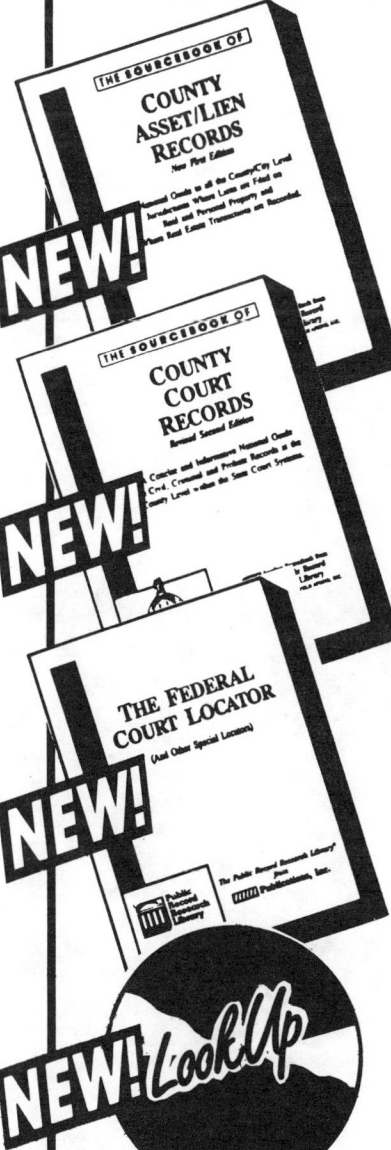

# Public Record Research Library

## FREE $25 VALUE

YOU WILL RECEIVE A FREE 1 YEAR SUBSCRIPTION TO OUR QUARTERLY NEWSLETTER *ON THE RECORD* WITH YOUR FIRST ORDER.

## order form

**ORDER:**

- FAX—800-929-4981
- TELEPHONE—800-929-3764

OR

- MAIL TO—
  BRB Publications, Inc.
  4653 S. Lakeshore #3
  Tempe, AZ 85282

*MONEY BACK GUARANTEE*

**PLEASE MAKE CHECK PAYABLE TO BRB**

CHECK MUST BE ENCLOSED OR PAY BY CREDIT CARD, PLEASE

| QTY | TITLE | Price | TOTAL |
|---|---|---|---|
| | The County Locator — LOCUS | 25.00 | |
| | State Public Records | 33.00 | |
| | Federal Courts — US District & Bankruptcy | 33.00 | |
| | Local Court & County Record Retrievers | 45.00 | |
| | County Court Records ★ New Second Edition ★ | 33.00 | |
| | Public Record Providers | 29.00 | |
| | The 1995 MVR Book | 18.00 | |
| | The 1995 Decoder Digest | 18.00 | |
| | County Asset/Lien Records ★ NEW ★ | 29.00 | |
| | Federal Court Locator ★ NEW ★ | 29.00 | |
| | Mailer's LookUp CD ROM ★ NEW ★ | 65.00 | |
| | Information Brokers Handbook | 34.95 | |
| | Armed Forces Locator Directory | 18.00 | |
| | **BOOK TOTAL** | | |
| | **DISCOUNT** | | |
| | **SUBTOTAL** | | |
| | *AZ TAX | | |
| | **S&H | | |
| | **TOTAL** | | |

**BOOK DISCOUNT SCHEDULE**
(MIX OR MATCH TITLES)

- 2 Books 5%
- 3-5 Books 10%
- 6-10 Books 15%
- 11-15 Books 20%
- 16+ Books 25%
- Call for 100+ discount

*Arizona Sales — Please add 5% sales tax.

**Shipping & Handling = $3 for first book, $1.50 each additional book

Name _____
Title _____ Telephone _____
Company _____
Street Address _____
City _____ State _____ Zip _____
☐ MasterCard ☐ VISA # _____
Expires _____ Signature: _____

☐ Check Enclosed ☐ Credit Card ☐ Please Invoice ☐ P.O. # _____ We will invoice established accounts.